Exploring Public Relations and Management Communication

Pearson

At Pearson, we have a simple mission: to help people make more of their lives through learning.

We combine innovative learning technology with trusted content and educational expertise to provide engaging and effective learning experiences that serve people wherever and whenever they are learning.

From classroom to boardroom, our curriculum materials, digital learning tools and testing programmes help to educate millions of people worldwide – more than any other private enterprise.

Every day our work helps learning flourish, and wherever learning flourishes, so do people.

To learn more, please visit us at **www.pearson.com/uk**

Exploring Public Relations and Management Communication

Fifth edition

Ralph Tench
Professor of Communication and Director of Research for Leeds Business School, Leeds Beckett University

Stephen Waddington
Managing Partner, Wadds Inc. and Visiting Professor, Newcastle University

Harlow, England • London • New York • Boston • San Francisco • Toronto • Sydney • Dubai • Singapore • Hong Kong
Tokyo • Seoul • Taipei • New Delhi • Cape Town • São Paulo • Mexico City • Madrid • Amsterdam • Munich • Paris • Milan

PEARSON EDUCATION LIMITED
KAO Two
KAO Park
Harlow CM17 9SR
United Kingdom
Tel: +44 (0)1279 623623
Web: www.pearson.com/uk

Previously published 2006, 2009 (print), 2014, 2017 (print and electronic)
Fifth edition published 2021 (print and electronic)

© Pearson Education Limited 2006, 2009 (print)
© Pearson Education Limited 2017, 2021 (print and electronic)

The rights of Ralph Tench and Stephen Waddington to be identified as authors of this work have been asserted by them in accordance with the Copyright, Designs and Patents Act 1988.

The print publication is protected by copyright. Prior to any prohibited reproduction, storage in a retrieval system, distribution or transmission in any form or by any means, electronic, mechanical, recording or otherwise, permission should be obtained from the publisher or, where applicable, a licence permitting restricted copying in the United Kingdom should be obtained from the Copyright Licensing Agency Ltd, Barnard's Inn, 86 Fetter Lane, London EC4A 1EN.

The ePublication is protected by copyright and must not be copied, reproduced, transferred, distributed, leased, licensed or publicly performed or used in any way except as specifically permitted in writing by the publishers, as allowed under the terms and conditions under which it was purchased, or as strictly permitted by applicable copyright law. Any unauthorised distribution or use of this text may be a direct infringement of the authors' and the publisher's rights and those responsible may be liable in law accordingly.

All trademarks used herein are the property of their respective owners. The use of any trademark in this text does not vest in the author or publisher any trademark ownership rights in such trademarks, nor does the use of such trademarks imply any affiliation with or endorsement of this book by such owners.

Pearson Education is not responsible for the content of third-party internet sites.

ISBN: 978-1-292-32174-5 (print)
   978-1-292-32176-9 (PDF)
   978-1-292-32178-3 (ePub)

British Library Cataloguing-in-Publication Data
A catalogue record for the print edition is available from the British Library

Library of Congress Cataloging-in-Publication Data
A catalog record for the print edition is available from the Library of Congress.
Names: Tench, Ralph, author. | Waddington, Stephen, author.
Title: Exploring public relations and management communication / Ralph
   Tench, Stephen Waddington.
Other titles: Exploring public relations
Identifiers: LCCN 2020032033 (print) | LCCN 2020032034 (ebook) | ISBN
   9781292321745 (hardcover) | ISBN 9781292321769 (ebook) | ISBN
   9781292321783 (epub)
Subjects: LCSH: Public relations.
Classification: LCC HM1221 .T46 2021 (print) | LCC HM1221 (ebook) | DDC
   659.2—dc23
LC record available at https://lccn.loc.gov/2020032033
LC ebook record available at https://lccn.loc.gov/2020032034

10 9 8 7 6 5 4 3 2 1
24 23 22 21 20

Cover design by Two Associates
Cover image © Walker and Walker/Stone/Getty Images

Print edition typeset in 9.5/12 pt Sabon LT Pro by SPi Global

NOTE THAT ANY PAGE CROSS REFERENCES REFER TO THE PRINT EDITION

Brief contents

About the authors — xvii
Foreword — xxiii
Preface — xxv

Part 1 The context of public relations — 1

1. Public relations origins: definitions and history — 3
2. Working with the media — 21
3. Social media for public relations — 37
4. Public relations, politics and democracy — 51
5. Community and society: corporate social responsibility (CSR) — 66
6. Intercultural and multicultural context of public relations — 94
7. Role of the public relations practitioner — 108

Part 2 Public relations theories and concepts — 145

8. Public relations theories: communication, relationships and persuasion — 147
9. Strategic public relations planning and management — 175
10. Measurement and evaluation for effectiveness and impact — 211
11. Disinformation, fake news and social reality — 233
12. Corporate image, reputation and identity — 244
13. Public relations' professionalism and ethics — 259

Part 3 Public relations specialisms — 281

14. Media relations — 283
15. Internal communication — 306
16. Issues management — 329
17. Crisis public relations management — 344
18. Public relations and the consumer — 365

19	Business-to-business public relations	381
20	Public affairs	395
21	Integrated marketing communications	417
22	Sponsorship	437
23	Corporate communication	459

Part 4 Sectoral considerations — 473

24	Strategic non-profit communication	475
25	Celebrities and influencers	490
26	Health communication	506
27	Sports public relations	528
28	Fashion public relations	547
29	Public relations and finance	570

Part 5 What next? — 589

30	Future issues for PR and strategic communication	591

Glossary	611
Index	617
Publisher's acknowledgements	630

Contents

About the authors — xvii
Foreword — xxiii
Preface — xxv

Part 1 The context of public relations — 1

1 Public relations origins: definitions and history — 3
Natalia Rodríguez-Salcedo and Tom Watson

Introduction — 4
Proto-public relations: the antecedents of modern public relations — 5
The expansion of public relations in the twentieth century — 9
The worldwide development of public relations since the mid-twentieth century: the springboards and restraints that shaped it — 15
How public relations grew — 16
Summary — 17
Bibliography — 18

2 Working with the media — 21
Scott Davidson

Introduction — 22
Media environments — 22
Exchange theories: the information subsidy — 24
Agenda setting and framing — 27
Power shift towards public relations practitioners — 30
Mediatisation — 31
Summary — 35
Bibliography — 35

3 Social media for public relations — 37
Karen Freberg

Introduction — 38
Defining social media — 39
Core theories that are utilised in social media and PR — 39
Emerging theories and perspectives — 40
Traditional viewpoints on PR for social media — 44
Opportunities for public relations professionals — 45
Challenges for public relations professionals to note — 47
Best practices and future considerations — 48
Summary — 49
Bibliography — 49

4 Public relations, politics and democracy
Øyvind Ihlen and Neil Washbourne
51

Introduction	52
Politics, democracy and communication	52
Communication strategies in the political realm	54
The contribution of public relations to democracy	55
Democratic concerns	56
Reflexivity and social change	59
Consensus and conflict	60
Summary	61
Recommended reading	62
Bibliography	62
Websites	65

5 Community and society: corporate social responsibility (CSR)
Ralph Tench
66

Introduction	67
Businesses are integral to our society(ies)	67
Social and economic change	68
Sustainable business: corporate social responsibility (CSR)	69
Business case for corporate social responsibility: why be socially responsible?	73
Organisational responsibilities to stakeholders	75
Organisational responsibilities to society	77
Regulatory frameworks	80
Ethics and business practice	84
Summary	87
Bibliography	90
Websites	93

6 Intercultural and multicultural context of public relations
Dejan Verčič
94

Introduction	95
The context of culture	95
Public relations and culture	96
Between universalism and relativism	97
Global principles and specific applications	99
Social media and activists in the global village	100
How to prepare for international and global public relations	101
Key principles in intercultural and multicultural public relations	102
Public diplomacy	103
Summary	104
Bibliography	104
Websites	107

7 Role of the public relations practitioner
Ralph Tench and Stephen Waddington
108

Introduction	109
Who are the public relations practitioners?	109
Who does what: the bigger picture?	110

Role of the communicator	117
Trust in communications	118
Trust in organisational advocates: external experts and leaders are top	118
Artificial Intelligence: high impact expected, but challenges and risks identified	119
Content creation and distribution: shared media and internal sources preferred	119
The PR practitioner as communicator	120
What public relations people do: individual practitioners	122
Skills for the ideal practitioner	124
Role of theory in practice	132
Professionalism	135
Education and research	138
Summary	139
Bibliography	139

Part 2 Public relations theories and concepts — 145

8 Public relations theories: communication, relationships and persuasion — 147
Martina Topić

Introduction	148
Communication theories in public relations	148
Relationships theories of public relations	149
Elaboration Likelihood Model	155
Theory of Planned Behaviour	158
Stages of Change Model	160
Nudge Theory	162
Inoculation theory	163
Cognitive Dissonance Theory	164
Summary	166
Bibliography	169

9 Strategic public relations planning and management — 175
Anne Gregory

Introduction	176
The importance of context	176
External environment	177
Internal environment	184
Implications of context	185
Strategic public relations programmes and campaigns	187
Why planning is important	187
Systems and alternative approaches to planning	188
Summary	203
Bibliography	208

10 Measurement and evaluation for effectiveness and impact — 211
Jim Macnamara

Why measure and evaluate?	212
Getting started with some definitions	213
Three types of evaluation: when and why?	215
Foundational theories of measurement and evaluation	216

	Applying measurement and evaluation in communication	218
	Reporting measurement and evaluation	228
	Summary	230
	Bibliography	230

11 Disinformation, fake news and social reality — 233
Jon White

Introduction	234
The role of public relations practitioners in the social construction of reality	235
Contributors to the social construction of reality	236
Disinformation and 'fake news' – their consequences	236
Countering disinformation and fake news	238
Public relations: obligations in countering disinformation and fake news	239
Staying ahead of developments in use of disinformation	241
Relevance of the growth of interest in fake news and extensive use of disinformation to public relations practice	241
Summary	242
Bibliography	242
Websites	243

12 Corporate image, reputation and identity — 244
Finn Frandsen and Winni Johansen

Introduction	245
The controversy of image in public relations	245
Understanding relationships	246
Reputation management and corporate branding	250
Measuring corporate image and reputation	254
A critical point of view	255
Summary	256
Bibliography	256
Websites	258

13 Public relations' professionalism and ethics — 259
Johanna Fawkes

Introduction	260
Defining professions – public relations and professionalism	261
Is public relations a profession?	262
Reframing the profession through a capabilities approach	263
Professional ethics and public relations	266
Summary	275
Bibliography	275

Part 3 Public relations specialisms — 281

14 Media relations — 283
Ramona Slusarczyk and Jonathan Ward

Introduction	284
Origins and development of media relations	284

Media relations as a strategic management function	285
The purpose of media relations	286
The media as gatekeeper	286
Media fragmentation	286
The rise of the influencer	287
Fake news: do audiences love being fooled?	291
Hacks versus flacks? An ongoing battle or an opportunity for excellence?	294
Shared spaces	294
Practical media relations	296
The techniques of media relations	297
Summary	302
Bibliography	303
Websites	305

15 Internal communication — 306
Ezri Carlebach

Introduction	307
What is internal communication? Perspectives and definitions	307
What does an internal communication function do?	310
What matters to employees: motivation in the workplace	312
Planning internal communication	313
Outcomes rather than outputs: choosing effective channels	320
The importance of evidence in internal communication planning and evaluation	321
Approaches to information gathering	322
Professionalisation: attributes, competencies and skills in internal communication	325
Summary	326
Bibliography	326

16 Issues management — 329
Tim Coombs

Introduction	330
Origins and essence	330
Models of issues management	331
Expanding issues management beyond public policy	336
The big picture for issues management	340
Summary	341
Bibliography	342

17 Crisis public relations management — 344
Tim Coombs

Introduction	345
Crisis public relations management: the context	345
The value of strategic communication	348
Where do crises come from?	349
How to prepare for a crisis	350
Communicating during a crisis	352
The internet and crisis public relations management	359
Summary	362
Bibliography	362

18 Public relations and the consumer — 365
Paul Willis

Introduction	366
Public relations and marketing	366
Targeting and tailoring	369
PR style over substance	369
Core activities	370
The media landscape: continuity and change	372
A shift to owned media	373
Branded content	374
Virtual influence	375
It's going to be a bumpy ride	377
Land-grab and reinvention	377
New activities and practices	378
Summary	379
Bibliography	379

19 Business-to-business public relations — 381
Helen Gill

Introduction	382
Core principles of business-to-business public relations	383
B2B PR as part of the wider marketing mix	384
B2B media relations	387
B2B social media	391
Summary	393
Bibliography	393
Websites	394

20 Public affairs — 395
Danny Moss

Introduction: the what and why of public affairs?	396
Locating the role of public affairs within the organisation	398
Defining public affairs: a confused professional identity	399
The scope of public affairs	399
Lobbying	403
International perspectives on public affairs and lobbying	407
Public affairs management	408
Summary	415
Bibliography	415
Websites	416

21 Integrated marketing communications — 417
Neil Kelley

Introduction	418
Defining integrated marketing communications	419
The planning process	422
Audiences	426
Marketing communications tactics	429
Touch points	431
Summary	434
Bibliography	435

22 Sponsorship 437
Ryan Sosna-Bowd, Ioannis Kostopoulos and Ralph Tench

Introduction 438
Definitions of sponsorship 441
Effective sponsorship and its impact for contemporary organisations 444
Strategic planning and management of sponsorship 447
Sponsorship in our digital reality 451
The future of sponsorship 455
Bibliography 455
Websites 457

23 Corporate communication 459
Stefania Romenti and Grazia Murtarelli

Introduction 460
Defining corporate communication in theory and practice 460
The role of corporate communication in society 462
The role of corporate communication in organisations 463
Corporate communication and intangible assets 465
Coordinating all forms of communication 467
Summary 468
Bibliography 468

Part 4 Sectoral considerations 473

24 Strategic non-profit communication 475
Markus Wiesenberg

Introduction 476
The third sector and non-profit organisations 476
Strategic non-profit communication in general 478
Non-profit communication management as a multi-level approach 485
Marketisation of third sector organisations and its consequences for strategic
non-profit communication 487
Summary 488
Bibliography 488

25 Celebrities and influencers 490
Kate Fitch

Introduction 491
What is celebrity? 492
Celebrity and society 493
Celebrity, the internet and influencers 495
Celebrity and influencers in public relations practice 499
Summary 502
Bibliography 502
Websites 505

26 Health communication
Audra Diers-Lawson and Noumaan Qureshi — 506

Introduction	507
The high stakes of health communication require a stakeholder relationship approach	507
Using persuasion theory to better understand factors affecting the 'healthcare stakeholder'	510
The crossover between mass campaigns and interpersonal health communication	515
Two-way symmetrical communication in healthcare	519
Summary	523
Bibliography	523

27 Sports public relations
Sian Rees and Iwan Williams — 528

Introduction	529
The business of sport	529
Sports as brands	532
Sports PR practitioners and the media	533
Digital sports PR	535
Promoting participation and fandom	537
PR and athlete transgressions	538
Sport social responsibility and ethics	540
Sport as culture	541
Summary	543
Bibliography	544

28 Fashion public relations
Martina Topić and Mirela Polić — 547

Introduction	548
The fashion industry: management and challenges for working in the fashion industry	548
Fashion public relations	551
The role of celebrities in fashion public relations	557
The role of social media influencers in fashion public relations	560
The role of bloggers and vloggers in fashion public relations	561
Summary	566
Bibliography	567

29 Public relations and finance
Clea Bourne — 570

Introduction	571
PR for global financial centres: changing contexts	572
Public relations for wholesale financial markets	575
Public relations for retail financial markets	577
Media in financial centres	579
Financial communication and social media	581
Public relations and the future of finance	583
Summary	585
Bibliography	586

Part 5 What next? — 589

30 Future issues for PR and strategic communication — 591
Ralph Tench and Stephen Waddington

Introduction	592
Macro issues facing PR	592
Challenges facing the work of practitioners	593
The future of PR practice	595
Management, automation and AI	600
Media in pain	604
Bibliography	609

Glossary	611
Index	617
Publisher's acknowledgements	630

Lecturer Resources

For password-protected online resources tailored to support the use of this textbook in teaching, please visit **go.pearson.com/uk/he/resources**

About the authors

Professor Ralph Tench is Director of Research at Leeds Business School, Leeds Beckett University, with responsibility for the research strategy for over 150 academics representing accounting and finance, strategy and economics, marketing, communications, public relations, journalism, leadership and human resource management. Ralph has led the Business School's recent Research Excellence Framework (REF) submission to Research England.

Ralph is the former subject head for public relations and communication at Leeds Beckett University, where for 10 years he oversaw the expansion of the undergraduate, postgraduate and professional course portfolio. As professor he teaches on undergraduate and postgraduate programmes, as well as supervising MA and PhD research students. His current focus is on developing and delivering major research projects in public relations and strategic communication in the UK and worldwide. He was the principal investigator for the first and largest EU public relations funded programme, the ECOPSI (European Communications Practitioners Skills and Innovation) programme. This project explored the education, skills and competency needs of European communication practitioners (www.ecopsi.org.uk). The three-year project contributed to competency frameworks for communications and the production of self-diagnostic tools (www.p4ace.org). This research builds on another international longitudinal research project (that celebrated its tenth year in 2016) funded by European bodies and private sector business, the European Communication Monitor (ECM) survey. The ECM (www.communicationmonitor.eu) is the largest transnational survey of public relations and strategic communication worldwide. It is a qualitative and quantitative trend survey of European communications directors using a sample of over 3000 practitioners from 46 countries each year. In 2020 the project expanded to a Global Communication Monitor Series with studies now in North America, Latin America and Asia Pacific regions. Reflecting the breadth of his research experience and application, Ralph directed another European-funded project exploring deliberative engagement and working in the SME sector (sme-engagement.eu) as well as supporting research projects such as the Public Health England Whole Systems Obesity multi-disciplinary project.

Ralph is a past external examiner for many UK and European universities, as well as a visiting professor. His doctoral students are engaged in research on issues of strategic communication related to trust, responsibility, reputation and branding, health communication and relationship management. He also supervises students on issues of professionalisation and the development of the public relations discipline. He has chaired over 30 PhD examinations and sat on panels for candidates in the UK, South Africa, Hungary, Ireland, Australia, Slovenia and Denmark.

Ralph is the past President (2017–2020) of the European Public Relations Research and Education Association (EUPRERA) and has been a member of the Board of Directors for the association since 2013. He is also past head of the Scientific Committee for the Annual Congress (2009–2015). He is a member of the International Communication Association (ICA) and sits on the editorial board for the *Journal of Communication Management*, the *Journal of Further and Higher Education*, *Corporate Communications: An International Journal*, *Public Relations Review*, *Journal of Public Affairs* and the *International Journal of Strategic Communication*.

Ralph is a regular guest and keynote speaker at academic and practitioner conferences and his research has been published and disseminated in over 200 books and journals worldwide. Previous editions of *Exploring Public Relations* have been translated into several European languages. Ralph has edited two volumes on his research interests in corporate social responsibility with Emerald – *Corporate Social Irresponsibility: A challenging concept* (2013), *Communicating Corporate Social Responsibility* (2014) and *The Critical State of Corporate Social Responsibility in Europe* (2018). In 2017 he published *Communication Excellence: How to develop, manage and lead an exceptional communication department*, a book based on an empirical evaluation of 10 years of ECM data.

Stephen Waddington is a business adviser and troubleshooter who helps organisations with planning, strategic decision making and execution. He is the Founder and Managing Partner of Wadds Inc., a professional advisory firm.

Stephen was previously managing director at Metia Group (2019 and 2020), an international digital marketing agency. It creates high-performance campaigns using research, content, demand and earned media. His clients included Amazon, BMW, Capita, Salesforce and Microsoft.

He was Chief Engagement Officer at Ketchum (2012 to 2018), an Omnicom-owned agency, responsible for driving the integration of digital and social capabilities in client engagements across the agency's international network. He provided lead senior counsel on integrated global accounts including IBM, IKEA and Phillips.

His role at Ketchum included change agent, ambassador and thought leader for the agency on modern forms of engagement and public relations practice. This included leveraging tools, resources and best practice from across the global network for all client engagements.

Stephen has held the role of Visiting Professor in Practice at Newcastle University since 2015, supporting the university and students through teaching and mentoring. He is also an external examiner for CIPR, the UK professional body for PR practitioners.

He is co-author of *#BrandVandals* (Bloomsbury, November 2013) and *Brand Anarchy* (Bloomsbury, February 2012), plus editor and contributor to *Platinum* (CIPR, September 2018), *Share This* (Wiley, July 2012) and *Share This Too* (Wiley, September 2013); in addition to editor of *Chartered Public Relations: Lessons from Expert Practitioners* (Kogan Page, February 2015).

Stephen wrote the foreword for the first two editions of #FuturePRoof, a community founded by Sarah Waddington aimed at reasserting the value of public relations. This follows the crowdsourced model that he established through #PRstack.

He was President of the CIPR in 2014, during which time he helped return the organisation to its roots of professionalism as set out in its Royal Charter. He is the former chairman of its Artificial Intelligence panel and Social Media panel. The two groups have led the characterisation of machines and social media on marketing and PR practice, the media and conversation in the public sphere.

Stephen originally trained as a journalist before following a career in public relations. He co-founded, managed and sold two award-winning public relations agencies, Rainier PR in 1998 and Speed in 2009.

At Speed, Stephen led the merger of three public relations agencies to develop a modern proposition, service model and workflow. Clients included The Associated Press, Optical Express, The Economist, Symantec, uSwitch for Business and Virgin Media Business.

Rainier PR was a technology PR agency founded in 1998 focused on technology expertise and a senior client service model. Clients included ARM, ntl (now Virgin Media Business), Toshiba and Wind River (now Intel). In 2017 Stephen received the PRCA's outstanding contribution to digital public relations.

Stephen has been named a top 10 UK public relations blogger by Vuelio for the last three years. He is a Chartered PR Practitioner, a CIPR Fellow (Hon), and a Fellow of the PRCA.

The contributors

Dr Clea Bourne is a Senior Lecturer in the Department of Media, Communications and Cultural Studies at Goldsmiths, University of London. Her research explores how twenty-first century economies are mediatised through various actors, practices and discourses. Clea is author of *Trust, Power and Public Relations in Financial Markets* (Routledge, 2017). She has also published widely in a range of journals and edited collections, and is currently writing her second monograph, entitled *Public Relations' Professional Discourses* (Palgrave-Macmillan). Clea co-convenes the 'Financial Capital and the Ghosts of Empire' network; and convenes the Heretical Finance Reading Group, a public outreach project hosted at Goldsmiths.

Ryan Sosna-Bowd is an award-winning strategic sport management, events, marketing and PR practitioner, who mixes a professional life of practice and academic teaching and learning. Recent work includes advisory to Qatar Foundation, Qatar National Tourism Council, Columbia Sportswear, International Sporting Events and Athletes Europe and GCC region. Prior to this he worked for the Josoor Institute in Doha, Qatar and IMG in London, United Kingdom. He has also lectured at Leeds Beckett University, Manchester Metropolitan University and Leeds University at under/postgraduate levels. He also worked at Weber Shandwick Public Relations and owned 1090 communications, the latter of which he sold in 2004 to Connectpoint PR.

Ezri Carlebach is a writer and consultant with virtual comms agency The PR Network and creative studio GW & Co. Drawing on more than 20 years' experience of leading in-house comms teams in non-profit, government and FTSE 100 organisations, Ezri delivers public relations, brand strategy and stakeholder engagement consultancy, runs training sessions and workshops, and writes speeches, articles, blogs, reports and reviews. He is a speaker and facilitator at international conferences on business communication, anthropology, education, and arts and culture, and was a Visiting Lecturer in Public Relations and Corporate Communications at the University of Greenwich from 2013 to 2019.

Professor Tim Coombs (PhD Purdue University in Public Affairs and Issues Management) is the George T and Glady H Abell Professor in Liberal Arts in Department of Communication at Texas A&M University. His primary areas of research are crisis communication and CSR including the award-winning book *Ongoing Crisis Communication*. He is the current editor for *Corporation Communication: An International Journal*. His research has appeared in *Management Communication Quarterly*, *Public Relations Review*, *Corporate Reputation Review*, *Journal of Public Relations Research*, *Journal of Communication Management*, *Business Horizons* and the *Journal of Business Communication*.

Dr Scott Davidson is a lecturer at the University of Leicester in the School of Media, Communication and Sociology. Before becoming an academic he worked for over a decade in public affairs and campaigns management for organisations such as AGE UK. He is the current director of the EUPRERA Network on Public Affairs and Lobbying in Europe. He was awarded his PhD by Loughborough University in 2008. His research includes publications on framing and other rhetorical strategies in PR, and on the problems of reforming PR so it becomes a better servant of democratic societies.

Dr Audra Diers-Lawson (PhD, University of Texas at Austin) is a Senior Lecturer at Leeds Beckett University, United Kingdom. She serves as chair of the Crisis Communication Division of the European Communication Research and Education Association (ECREA) and is the editor for the *International Journal of Crisis and Risk Communication Research*, and also sits on several journal editorial boards with recent publications on topics like consumer trust, intercultural crisis communication, crisis atonement, whistleblowing, and stakeholder anger at organisations in crisis.

Dr Johanna Fawkes PhD is Visiting Research Fellow at the University of Huddersfield and Visiting Fellow at Leeds Beckett University. She was Principal Research Fellow at Huddersfield (2016–18), leading an international team to produce a Global Capability Framework for Public Relations and Communications Management in conjunction with the Global Alliance. From 1990, Johanna developed undergraduate, postgraduate and doctoral degrees in public relations in three UK Universities and in Australia (2011–16), following a career in public sector communication. She has delivered keynote speeches and published articles and chapters on public relations and ethics. Her book, *Public Relations Ethics and Professionalism; The Shadow of Excellence*, was published by Routledge in 2015 (paperback 2017). She is working on a sequel.

Dr Kate Fitch is a Senior Lecturer in the School of Media, Film and Journalism at Monash University in Melbourne, Australia, where she coordinates the public relations specialisation. She previously worked at Murdoch University. Her book, *Professionalizing Public Relations: History, Gender and Education*, offered the first sociological history of Australian public relations in the twentieth century. Her book with Judy Motion, *Popular culture and Social Change: The Hidden Work of Public Relations* investigated the impact of public relations on contemporary culture. Kate is the Asia-Pacific regional editor for *Public Relations Inquiry* and served on the editorial board of *Public Relations Review* until 2018.

Professor Finn Frandsen is Professor of Corporate Communication, Department of Management, Aarhus University, Denmark. His primary research interests include organisational crises, crisis management and crisis communication, environmental communication and climate communication, stakeholder and intermediary theory, and the institutionalisation of strategic communication in private and public organisations. He has published articles in *CCIJ*, *International Journal of Business Communication*, *International Journal of Strategic Communication*, *Management Communication Quarterly*, *Public Relations Inquiry*, *Public Relations Review*, *Rhetorica Scandinavica*, and *Scandinavian Journal of Public Administration*. He is the co-editor of *Organizational Crisis Communication: A Multivocal, Approach* (Sage, 2017) and *Crisis Communication – Handbooks of Communication Science* (Mouton de Gruyter, 2020).

Dr Karen Freberg is an Associate Professor in Strategic Communications at the University of Louisville, where she teaches, researches and consults in social media strategy, public relations and crisis communication. Freberg has written several books including *The Roadmap in Teaching Social Media* (Amazon, self-published), *Digital Media Writing for Strategic Communication* (TopHat with Emily Kinsky and Amber Hutchins) and *Social Media for Strategic Communications: Creative strategies and research-based* applications (with SAGE).

Helen Gill is Founding Director of award-winning B2B marketing agency Engage Comms. Established in 2012, Engage Comms delivers integrated communications strategies and campaigns for ambitious clients in niche sectors including manufacturing and financial services, to enable them to fulfil their long-term potential. Helen has a Masters in PR and experience working in-house and in consultancy comms roles for regional and global organisations. She is an experienced speaker and lecturer and was named CIPR Outstanding Young Communicator Yorkshire & Lincolnshire 2010. In 2019, she founded the 'Internal Comms Network North' to help SMEs in Northern England harness the power of internal communications.

Professor Anne Gregory is Chair in Corporate Communication at the University of Huddersfield, heading specialist educational and research programmes for clients such as the UK Government and the European Commission. Professor Gregory is a recent Chair of the Global Alliance, has been awarded the Sir Stephen Tallents Medal by the Chartered Institute of Public Relations (CIPR) for her outstanding contribution to the profession and the Pathfinder Award for outstanding research by the US-based Institute of Public Relations. She has authored over 80 books, book chapters and academic and popular journal articles and is an acknowledged world-expert on strategic communication.

Dr Øyvind Ihlen is professor at the Department of Media and Communication, University of Oslo and co-director of POLKOM – Centre for the Study of Political Communication. He has over 130 publications, including *Public Relations and Social Theory: Key Figures and Concepts* (2009, 2nd expanded edition 2018, with Magnus Fredriksson), the award-winning edited *Handbook of Communication and Corporate Social Responsibility* (2011, with Jennifer Bartlett and Steve May), and *Handbook of Organizational Rhetoric* (2018, with Robert L. Heath). Ihlen was President of the European Public Relations Education and Research Association (EUPRERA) 2016–2017.

Professor Winni Johansen is Professor of Corporate Communication, Department of Management, Aarhus University, Denmark. Her primary research interests include crisis management and crisis communication, social media, communication consulting, environmental communication and the institutionalisation of strategic communication in private and public organisations. She is the co-editor of *Organizational Crisis Communication: A Multivocal, Approach* (Sage, 2017), *International Encyclopedia of Strategic Communication* (Wiley-Blackwell, 2018), *Crisis Communication – Handbooks of Communication Science* (Mouton de Gruyter, 2020). She has published articles in *Management Communication Quarterly, CCIJ, International Journal of Strategic Communication, Journal of Communication Management, Public Relations Review, Public Relations Inquiry, Rhetorica Scandinavica* and *Scandinavian Journal of Public Administration*.

Neil Kelley is a Senior Lecturer and Course Director for the Marketing Subject Group at Leeds Business School. Neil is responsible for all undergraduate marketing degrees; Marketing Management, Marketing with Retail Management and Marketing with Advertising Management. In addition to this he is a Chartered Marketer and a Lead Examiner with the Chartered Institute of Marketing for two modules, Digital Marketing and Marketing and Digital Strategy. Neil has co-authored a number of marketing texts, book chapters and published research into marketing education.

Dr Ioannis Kostopoulos is a Reader in Digital Marketing at Liverpool Business School, Liverpool John Moores University. Prior to his current position he has taught Marketing and PR at several universities in the UK, Greece and Italy and has participated in many consulting and research projects. Awarded his PhD in 2012 from Athens University of Economics and Business, he has more than 50 publications, including articles in peer-reviewed journals such as *European Management Review, Journal of Strategic Marketing, Information Technology and People* and *International Journal of Innovation Management*. In 2017 he published his first book on *Marketing Communications*.

Professor Jim Macnamarra is Distinguished Professor of Public Communication at the University of Technology Sydney (UTS). He is also a Visiting Professor at London School of Economics and Political Science, Media and Communications Department, and a Visiting Professor at the London College of Communication. He is internationally recognised for his research into evaluation of public communication and organisational listening, and is the author of more than 70 academic journal articles and book chapters and 16 books including *Organizational Listening: The*

Missing Essential in Public Communication and *Evaluating Public Communication: Exploring New Models, Standards, and Best Practice.*

Professor Danny Moss Professor of Corporate and Public Affairs at the University of Chester Business School and co-director of the University's International Centre for Corporate & Public Affairs Research. He led the development of Master's programmes in Public Relations at the University of Stirling and then at Manchester Metropolitan University and co-founded the annual Global Public Relations Research Symposium. Danny is the co-editor of the *Journal of Public Affairs* and has published papers in range of journals and has authored a number of books, and book chapters including *Public relations: A managerial perspective and International Public relation cases.*

Dr Grazia Murtarelli, PhD, is Assistant Professor of Corporate Communication at Università IULM in Milan (Italy), where she teaches Digital Communication Management and Web Analytics. Her research focuses on the analysis of online scenarios and, more specifically, on the following issues: social media-based relationship management, online dialogue strategies, digital visual engagement processes and social media measurement and evaluation. She is the Public Relations Student & Early Career Representative at International Communication Association. She is also a faculty affiliate of the Center of Research for Strategic Communication at Università IULM.

Mirela Polic is a consultant in a public relations agency IMC, Zagreb, Croatia. Mirela is also a PhD candidate at the Faculty of Humanities and Social Sciences, University of Zagreb. After she had obtained a Master's degree in public relations and political communication at the Faculty of Political Science (University of Zagreb), Mirela began her career in public relations in one of the largest Croatian public relations agencies, IMC, where she currently works as a public relations consultant. Mirela is a researcher on the European Public Relations Education and Research Association (EUPRERA) project, *Women in Public Relations.*

Noumaan Qureshi is currently pursuing his doctoral research from University of Mumbai, India, focusing on cultural context of communications for risks and crisis. He has done research work in understanding reputation risks for healthcare organisations. Healthcare is his area of specialisation, with two decades of work experience, including public relations consulting.

Dr Sian Rees is Associate Professor in public relations, marketing and branding and is the current Head of the Department of Media & Communications at Swansea University. During her industry career, Sian worked as Publishing Director for the Stuff and What Hi-Fi? Group of magazines and was managing director of her own marketing and PR consultancy. Industry experience has included developing and implementing strategic PR and marketing campaigns for FMCG, retail, entertainment, medical, education and technology sectors. Sian writes academically on authentic communications, PR and branding in the digital media age.

Dr Natalia Rodríguez Salcedo PhD earned a double degree in Journalism and in Advertising and Public Relations. She is deputy director of the Marketing and Media Management department, and deputy director of the Master's Degree in Corporate Reputation at the School of Communication of Universidad de Navarra, Spain, where she has been teaching since 2001. She has co-authored two books and published several chapters and articles on the history of public relations in Europe and Spain.

Professor Stefania Romenti PhD is Professor in Strategic Communication and PR at Università IULM (Milan, Italy) and Chair of the Master of Science in Strategic Communication. She is Director of the Executive Master in Corporate Public Relations (IULM) and Adjunct Professor at IE Business School (Madrid). She is Rector's Delegate for Sustainability and CSR. She is Founder and Director of the Research Center in Strategic Communication (CECOMS) and Member of the Board of the European Association of Public Relations Education and Research Association (EUPRERA). Her research focuses on strategic communication, corporate reputation, stakeholder management and engagement, dialogue, measurement and evaluation.

Ramona Slusarczyk is a lecturer in public relations at Newcastle University. A Chartered CIPR Practitioner she has taught public relations and media courses at RMIT International University, Vietnam, The Higher Colleges of Technology, UAE, and worked as a PR professional at a Dubai-based consultancy before returning to her former alma mater in Newcastle in 2017. Ramona has since introduced a new module, Global PR, to the University's curriculum and co-authored a couple of chapters dedicated to social media influencers, food mediatisation, and cultural identity issues within the EU. Her main research interests focus on international PR, CSR and nation branding.

Dr Martina Topić is a Senior Lecturer in Public Relations in Leeds Business School. Martina currently leads three projects, a British Academy funded project on women in the advertising industry, a EUPRERA project on women in public relations and a HEFCE funded project on Women Journalists. She is a member of the editorial board of several academic journals including *Sociology* (British Sociological Association) and she is an editor of the section 'Culture, Media and Film' of *Cogent Arts and Humanities Open Access journal* (Taylor and Francis). More information on her projects and publications can be found at https://www.martinatopic.com

Professor Dejan Verčič is Professor, Head of Department of Communication and Head of Centre for Marketing and Public Relations at the University of Ljubljana, and Partner in strategic consulting and communication company Herman & partnerji d.o.o., Slovenia. He received his PhD from the London School of Economics and Political Science, UK. He has recently received the Pathfinder Award, the highest academic honour bestowed by the Institute for Public Relations (IPR) in New York, and he was named a Distinguished Public Relations Scholar by the European Public Relations Education and Research Association (EUPRERA). Since 1994 he has organised an annual International Public Relations Research Symposium – BledCom.

Jonathan Ward is a lecturer in public relations at Newcastle University and course director for the MA in Media and Public Relations. He leads modules on PR theory, financial communications and postgraduate research. Prior to teaching, Jonathan worked as an award-winning regional journalist specialising in local government and then as a PR practitioner in the charity sector. He founded his own PR agency in 2006 and continues to provide consultancy for businesses and community groups. Jonathan's interests focus on community engagement, media relations and sports PR. He is a member of the CIPR and Fellow of the HEA.

Professor Tom Watson is emeritus professor of public relations in the Faculty of Media and Communication at Bournemouth University. He ran a successful PR consultancy for 18 years and was chairman of the UK's Public Relations Consultants Association from 2000 to 2002. Awarded his PhD in 1995 from Nottingham Trent University, Tom has written books, book chapters and a wide range of peer-reviewed academic papers in international academic journals. He established the annual International History of Public Relations Conference in 2010 and has edited the seven-volume *National Perspectives on the Development of Public Relations: Other Voices* series for Palgrave Macmillan.

Dr Jon White is a visiting professor at Henley Business School, University of Reading and honorary professor, Cardiff University School of Journalism, Media and Culture, began his career in communication roles with the Government of Alberta, Canada, progressing through university positions in Canada and the UK to independent consultancy for organisations including large corporations and international governmental organisations. Author of books and journal articles on public relations, he is an Honorary Fellow of the UK's Chartered Institute of Public Relations and holds a doctorate in psychology from the London School of Economics and Political Science.

Iwan Williams is a Public Relations lecturer at Swansea University. Prior to his entry into academia in 2013, he spent five years as Head of Media, Brand and e-democracy in the National Assembly for Wales. With over 20 years' experience as a strategic communications practitioner, he managed multimedia PR, marketing and advertising communications campaigns for organisations such as the Royal Navy, Microsoft and the government's Central Office of Information. As well as extensive experience of working in the private and public sectors in the UK, he has many years' experience of international communications in the USA, Australia and New Zealand.

Dr Markus Wiesenberg is a postdoctoral researcher at the Department of Communication Management at Leipzig University and freelance PR Consultant with Wiesenberg Communications. In his PhD project he examined the strategic communication of the German mainline churches and studied the non-profit area from diverse angels. During this time, he was a doctoral fellow of the European Public Relations Education and Research Association (EUPRERA) and managed the European Communication Monitor (ECM). His focal points in practice and research are non-profit and start-up communication as well as new trends in strategic communication (e.g. Big Data, Automated and Algorithmic PR).

Professor Paul Willis is Chair of Corporate Communication at the University of Huddersfield. He was previously Director of the Centre for Public Relations Studies at Leeds Business School. Before joining academia Paul was a board director in the PR consultancy sector advising organisations including BMW, BT, Proctor & Gamble, Walmart, UK Sport and The Football Association. In 2016, he was appointed a member of the Government's Future Communication Council by the UK Cabinet Office and Prime Minister's Office. Paul is the co-author of *Strategic Public Relations Leadership* and his other published research can be found in the field's leading journals and textbooks.

Foreword

What public relations is and could be, how to manage it for an organisation, what it does in and for society – these are the themes of this book. In the first edition, the editors promised a lively and comprehensive discussion regarding fundamental concepts and best practices of public relations. A student-centred book, a meeting place for students and teachers with well-known authors, taking the student by the hand to explore what public relations is. The book is grown-up now. Very well established as one of the best introductory texts in our field, mainly oriented at Europe but very international in its context, fundamental but also very practical. With this 5th edition the editors and authors succeeded once more in presenting meaningful updates of their contributions following the latest national and international developments and insights in the fast-changing world of public relations. After so many years, it is still one of a kind.

I have studied numerous books on public relations, and on corporate communication, communication management or strategic communication, as the field is often called in other countries. Most books are very technical 'how to' books, promising that you will be able to do the job as long as you follow the tips of the author. Some books are very theoretical, analysing merely one single theoretical focus, with the promise that you will become a good practitioner as long as you follow this approach. *Exploring Public Relations and Management Communication* is none of these, or to put it differently: it is all of these books in one. It is theoretical and practical at the same time, it provides an insight in almost all theoretical approaches and different ideas on how to look at and do public relations, and it raises unsettled questions about the definition, the tasks of the professional, the debate about professional ethics, and the issue of its impact. This is the most open-minded book I know.

Look at the prudent way in which the editors have challenged almost everything that is commonly left un-discussed in the educational and practical fields of public relations. That public relations has to do with persuasion and also with propaganda, that the public relations field has a problem with its legitimacy, that there is no consensus whatsoever about what public relations is and what its value is for organisations of all kinds. The authors try to avoid taking a stand, leading us through all the discussions, rumours and evidence about these issues. What a book! It is fresh and good, it covers all current topics and simultaneously opens up a lot of perspectives. And all this in a very user-friendly manner. The book is built on the premise that a textbook should put the student at the centre of the learning experience. And that is exactly what it does.

It is an excellent book for undergraduates who want to know more about the field. But at the same time it is also enlightening and very practical for professionals who want to open their windows and learn more about the field they are working in. It not only shows a variety of different approaches and models within the discipline of PR but also interdisciplinary connections with communication studies and the wider context of social sciences. This makes the book also relevant and important for master's programmes in public relations and communication studies. Public relations is an evolving discipline and its growth requires continual questioning to challenge its boundaries and establish its terrain. The authors have brilliantly succeeded in doing that.

The first edition of *Exploring Public Relations* was a milestone. It was both very British and very international. *Exploring Public Relations* not only provided helpful guidelines to practical action, but raised unsettling questions about impact and implications as well. It was diverse, different and consistently thoughtful in departing from the US norm. Instead of simple platitudes about equal exchanges, *Exploring Public Relations* looked at how to actually perform public relations in an ethical manner across very diverse cultures. It was also theoretically inclusive, with a light touch that challenged students to make up their own minds at the same time as they learned how to become competent practitioners. It was not uncritical of a field where technical mastery can override moral behaviour.

Subsequent editions were updated in an enviable way, including all kinds of new issues, for example about the media context of contemporary public relations and journalism, about the intercultural and multicultural context of public relations, about corporate image, reputation and identity, and last but not least about research and evaluation. This fifth edition has a further update, for example on communication theories (Chapter 8). The book includes reference to almost everything that has been written in the last couple of years. It is updated with the newest insights from European as well as American and Asian perspectives. What an effort!

The first part of the book provides you with the background knowledge you will require to understand the role and purpose of public relations set against the broader business and societal contexts in which it plays an active role. Part two demonstrates that public relations is multifaceted and can be interpreted through a number of theoretical perspectives. In part three the focus is laid on the practice of public relations and, finally, in part four all kinds of considerations are explored, on health communication, on corporate communication, on positioning celebrities and countries, and on the future of public relations.

This is a book every public relations author wished (s)he had written. It will help to provide students with an introduction into the field, and will also help teachers to discuss important topics with their students. You will not be disappointed.

Betteke van Ruler
Professor Emerita Corporate Communication
and Communication Management Department of
Communication Science University of Amsterdam
The Netherlands

Preface

A thank you first

Exploring Public Relations began in Leeds in the early 2000s with a collaboration between myself and Dr Liz Yeomans. Through four editions of the book, and working with exceptional friends and fellow academic colleagues, this book has innovated and led the way in the field of public relations and strategic communication textbooks. A path that – as a clear complement to the project – many other writers around the world have emulated and copied. We still think *Exploring Public Relations* is the leading book to guide students, lecturers and observers of the practice, and we get regular feedback to reinforce this point.

Since the 4th edition my good friend Liz has retired from full-time academic life. I must therefore convey my thanks to Liz for her friendship and collegial collaboration over the many years that we worked together and particularly on the four enjoyable versions of this book. Thank you, Liz.

Since Liz has ended her collaboration with me on the book I have of course thought long and hard about who to work alongside to take the book to the next stage of its journey. My editorial partner, Stephen Waddington, is someone I have known for many years – as have many of my international academic and practice colleagues – because he is a rare breed, what I like to call a thinking practitioner.

Stephen is a professor of practice at the University of Newcastle in the UK but also a well-known and respected senior communicator, author and commentator on the practice. As such he brings an understanding of education and research but also a clear and insightful appreciation that much of what we discuss in the classroom and in our academic reflections plays out in business and society. This is an invaluable asset and positive contribution for the book.

I have enjoyed working more closely with Stephen over the past couple of years as we looked to build on the strengths of the past editions of the book and make it even more relevant to students, lecturers and tutors as well as practitioners with an eye on deeper understanding of the practice.

Professor Ralph Tench

Welcome to a refreshed 5th edition

This has been an extraordinary edition of *Exploring* to write. Whilst the manuscript has been written and passed through the production phase, the whole world has experienced transformational change owing to COVID-19. The pandemic has and will affect all aspects of society and the economy. It is most definitely going to affect the communications industry. In this version of the book, as we went through the final edits, we capture some of those issues (see Crisis and the final chapter on the Future as well as others). Whilst we are not able to address the breadth of impact that these economic and social changes will have as the book goes to press, we can carry forward to readers the knowledge that things have and will continue to change in the world of organisational communication. Watch this space.

We first conceived of this book in the early 2000s and it started with the idea that a textbook should put the student at the centre of the learning experience. While it is true that textbooks in general are more student-centred for subjects as varied as biology, law, media and psychology, this was not and has not been the case in public relations.

Exploring Public Relations very much led the way in this approach for our discipline and the feedback and compliments the book regularly receives are testimony to this. With this approach we wanted students to have an improved learning experience by involving them in a personal journey that brought the subject to life on the page and spurred them on to find out more. And this is what we have tasked ourselves to do with this exciting fifth edition, *Exploring Public Relations and Management Communication*.

With our new editorial partnership, we have endeavoured to reflect on *Exploring Public Relations*, to take on board the many positive reviews, comments and feedback from students, tutors and members of the practice community. This encouraged us to build on the solid and successful foundations of the book and to critically evaluate each chapter and theme to ensure its contemporary relevance, a textbook for the discipline for the 2020s.

We've done this for the new edition. You'll notice the change to the title. It's a subtle but important shift that recognises the strategic importance of public relations to organisations and growing conversation about professionalism in practice.

Our earlier editions brought challenges and so has this version of the book. But we have benefited from the ability to listen to students and academic colleagues in how they read, study with and educate using the first four editions of the book and its supplements. And through this listening we have attempted to answer any questions or gaps in the earlier versions to ensure it is fit for purpose in a challenging, changing world of communication.

Some of the key areas we have addressed are the most obvious ones in contemporary life of how the techniques used in public relations and communication have been influenced by rapid technological change and its integration, a phenomenon that appears to speed up month by month. To reflect this we have introduced new and revised chapters on digital and social media, democracy and political discourse, disinformation and fake news, research and evaluation methods and techniques, the new world of media relations, how we interact with employees inside organisations (internal communications), how corporate communication operates, the importance of NGOs and charities in modern life, celebrities and influencers, health and well-being, the increased interest in leisure and therefore issues like sport and sports public relations and finally a little discussed but popular area of practice, fashion PR.

On top of this we have ensured that all chapters consider the implications of technology and change on the theory and practice of the discipline. Clearly, some chapters have integrated these influences more than others. One of the key features of the book is that it is an edited textbook and all chapters are written and reviewed within a consistent framework. This means that the book has a particular style and consistency that we have been keen to preserve. This is partly achieved by only working with senior and experienced academics and practitioners who share a mission to understand and explain the discipline. We are therefore pleased to be able to include contributors from around the world who are closely associated with us individually and collectively and have the same aspirations to improve the subject knowledge and application of public relations in society. Again we feel this was and continues to be a unique feature and strength of the book as it has evolved.

So who to write such a comprehensive text? For this we looked to our colleagues at Leeds Beckett University who teach on our well-established undergraduate, postgraduate and research programmes. We also engaged with our wider network – senior academics and practitioners worldwide who have contributed to our subject area.

Target audience

Feedback suggests there is a diverse range of readers for *Exploring Public Relations and Management Communication* from senior practitioners to undergraduate students. It is the preferred textbook for universities around the world as well as for professional bodies and professional courses which adopt it as their core text. Its content is comprehensive, which perhaps explains this broad appeal. That said, the book is written in a way that it can be used and read by someone who is totally new to the discipline as well as a student or practitioner with significantly more depth of understanding. The contents pages of the book demonstrate how it can be used to support more practical and theoretical aspects of the discipline and at different levels. Therefore it is a perfect accompaniment for undergraduates and postgraduates who are studying public relations as a single subject (i.e. a bachelor's or master's in public relations), jointly with another subject, or as a single module or unit within a wider programme.

Book style and structure

The book is divided into four parts. Part 1 provides important background knowledge to help students understand the broad business and societal context in which public relations plays a role. Included here, for example, are chapters on democracy and on the intercultural and multicultural context of public relations and digital and social media. In Part 2 there is a chapter on disinformation, fake news and social reality as well as a chapter on professional ethics – a topic of ever increasing importance; while Part 3 includes emerging specialisms such as issues management, sponsorship, corporate communication and public affairs. Part 4 comprises chapters that are not conventionally included within a public relations textbook; for example, the chapter on pressure groups and NGOS, health communication, celebrity and the importance of influencers as well as working in financial public relations and indeed fashion. The final chapter looks to the future and provides some themes and questions that we hope student readers will take up as topics for investigation and research. Public relations is an evolving discipline and its growth requires continual questioning to challenge its boundaries and establish its terrain. As students, teachers, researchers and practitioners we are all responsible for achieving this aim.

Pedagogy and its place

This is an educational textbook for public relations and therefore includes a number of devices that we hope will help both students and tutors to get the most out of the material. First, each chapter begins with a list of the **Learning outcomes** which students should achieve after engaging with the material. We have structured the book to have a range of consistent pedagogy which support the reader in understanding the chapter subject. For example, there are regular **Explore** features which give instructions on where to look for further information or how to engage further with topics. **Think abouts** are included to encourage reflection and for the reader to pause and think a little more deeply about the issues and ideas that are being presented and discussed. We have attempted to define terms or phrases that may not be universally understood or which form part of the specialist language related to that topic or area of study which are included in a glossary at the back of the book. Finally we have included many cases studies (**Case studies** and **Mini case studies**) which aim to exemplify and apply the principles under discussion.

Over to you, the reader

The warm response to the first four editions of the book has been both rewarding and motivating. These have been read and used for teaching literally all over the world and with gratifying endorsements of the original pedagogic strategy of making clear links between theory and practice. However, there are many questions about public relations and its practice which remain under explored. These we aim to highlight in this book, inspiring readers to investigate further, possibly through detailed research for undergraduate and postgraduate projects, dissertations and theses. We hope this revised fifth edition continues to bridge the divide between theory and practice and, above all, is a thought-provoking and enjoyable read for students, practitioners and tutors alike.

Acknowledgements

In addition to the invaluable contributors already mentioned, we would like to thank all those at Pearson Education for making this fifth edition possible.

Finally, but not least, we would like to thank our families. For Ralph, this dedication goes to my father John who passed away during the drafting of the manuscript for this edition. He was a man who loved to read anything, including a book on public relations.

For Stephen, my dedication is to my wife Sarah Waddington. She's a vocal advocate of the drive towards public relations as a management discipline. As President of the CIPR in 2018 she had a significant influence on the book's title and its scope. Her emotional and intellectual support is at the heart of all my projects.

Ralph Tench and Stephen Waddington, 2020

PART 1

The context of public relations

This first part of the book provides you with the background knowledge you will require to understand the role and purpose of public relations (PR) set against the broader business and societal contexts in which it plays an active role. Chapter 1 discusses how public relations is defined, its early origins, including proto-public relations practices, and how it evolved across the globe as the contemporary practice we recognise today. Chapter 2 discusses frameworks for analysing and understanding the relationship between public relations and the media/journalism, while recognising how both practices are changing in response to technological and economic developments. Chapter 3 examines technological developments in further depth, specifically digital and social media which continue to drive public relations and have become central to the practice function. Arguably, public relations is essential to modern democratic societies. In Chapter 4 the relationship between democracy and public relations is examined and critiqued drawing examples from recent uses of public relations in political discourse. Chapter 5 examines the societal context of public relations from the organisation's perspective, highlighting the theme of corporate social responsibility and how communicators help organisations to respond to the environments around them as increasingly the sustainability of some businesses is drawn into question. In Chapter 6, the international and multi-cultural context of public relations is introduced and debated. Finally, we turn to the role of the public relations practitioner in Chapter 7 to focus on what public relations practitioners do, how they deliver their role and function and how they should continue to learn and develop for the future.

CHAPTER 1

Natalia Rodríguez-Salcedo and Tom Watson

Public relations origins: definitions and history

Source: Rafal Cichawa/Shutterstock

Learning outcomes

By the end of this chapter you should be able to:

- identify, understand and discuss the main aspects of public relations development over time
- review and critique different interpretations of public relations history
- analyse and discuss different national and cultural interpretations of public relations and its history
- examine your understanding of historical research and identify sources, such as articles, books and archives, for future research.

Structure

- Proto-public relations: the antecedents of modern public relations
- The expansion of public relations in the twentieth century
- The worldwide development of public relations since the mid-twentieth century: the springboards and restraints that shaped it
- How public relations grew.

Introduction

In this chapter, the formation of public relations as a practice will be traced from its earliest indications in the ancient world through two millennia and up to the end of the twentieth century. There are many antecedents of public relations, mainly methods of promotion and disseminating information. It was not until the nineteenth century that the term 'public relations' was first used although public relations-like practices (also called proto-public relations) were already evident.

Organised communication practices, recognisable as public relations, were introduced in Germany and the United States in the latter part of the nineteenth century. In the United Kingdom, public relations was noticeable from the mid-1920s onward, primarily in government. Professionalisation in the form of university-level education and practitioner associations appeared after the Second World War. From the 1950s onwards, the practices of public relations as promotion (or marketing PR) and public relations as communication management continued to expand across countries in the Western world, although it was suppressed in the Soviet bloc of Eastern Europe and in China until the early 1990s. By the 1980s, public relations theory and practice were evolving in more sophisticated forms that focused on the formation of mutually beneficial relationships and as a support for organisational reputation. In this and following decades, it expanded internationally and, notably, attracted an increasingly feminised workforce that was educated at university level.

This chapter will consider the definitions of public relations as well as the antecedent, the springboard (impetuses for expansion) and the restraints that held it back in some regions of the world. Methods of interpreting the history of public relations will also be considered.

Box 1.1

What is public relations?

At the outset of a chapter on the history and origins of public relations, a definition of the topic is needed. How does it differ from advertising, publicity, propaganda and other forms of persuasional or promotional communication? There have been innumerable attempts to define public relations. Harwood Childs offered one early but still insightful attempt: 'Public relations is not the presentation of a point of view, not the art of tempering mental attitudes, nor the development of cordial and profitable relations. [. . .] The basic problem of public relations is to reconcile or adjust in the public interest those aspects of our personal and corporate behaviour which have a social significance' (Childs 1940: 3 and 13).

In the mid-1970s, the social scientist Rex Harlow (1977) identified more than 400 versions or variations. Since then, more have been proposed, discussed and, in some instances, dismissed. Watson and Noble (2014) comment that 'some commentators see the surfeit of definitions as a weakness of public relations; others appreciate the debate that surrounds them as an indication of vigour in the field' (p. 6). This chapter won't propose a single definition, but it will show there have been a wide range of cultural, managerial and political and religious influences upon the formation of public relations theories and practices. There are, however, some characteristics that shape the wide variety of forms of public relations:

- It is a planned communication and/or relationship-building activity with strategic or deliberate intent (Lamme and Russell 2015). Some definitions emphasise the management of communications (Grunig and Hunt 1984; Broom and Sha 2013), the management of relationships (Coombs and Holladay 2006) and the creation and maintenance of reputation (CIPR 2012).

- It seeks to create awareness among specific groups, often referred to as 'publics' or 'stakeholders', and engage their interest. The interest of the public should result in a mutually beneficial relationship or response, possibly as dialogue (Gutiérrez-García et al. 2015). Thus, it is different from publicity which only seeks to disseminate messages.

- In its most common form, public relations has been enacted through the media, which has been the gatekeeper of communication. This is an important difference from advertising which places messages through the purchase of advertisement space and airtime (radio, television and online). With the rise of social media, public relations activity has increasingly become a form of direct communication, bypassing media scrutiny.

- Although the US public relations pioneer Edward L. Bernays proposed that 'public relations attempts to engineer public support' (Bernays 1955: 4–5), the term 'to engineer' is rejected by many as implying manipulation rather than truth-telling. Many scholars and practitioners contend that ethical communication is the bedrock of professional public relations.

This chapter will thus consider how public relations gradually became identified as a planned, strategic practice whose purposes were to communicate and build relationships in a mutually beneficial and ethical manner. As it evolved, public relations developed from personal and organisational promotion, benefited from technologies such as print and, later, mass media, became an important element in empire- and nation-building, and has formed worldwide practices with increasing employment and economic importance (see Explore 1.1).

Explore 1.1

Defining public relations

As a group exercise, each member is going to write a definition of public relations. But how?

First, let us spark some reflection. Start creating two columns on your computer, tablet or sheet of paper. The left side should be labelled 'in' and the right side 'out'. Use the 'in' column to write words or expressions related to what you consider public relations is about, and the 'out' column to write words or expressions which you think are definitely NOT related to public relations activities. Compare and discuss your columns with the rest of the members of your group.

Now, try to incorporate the 'in' column ideas to write your own definition of public relations (PR). Think about how you arrived at that definition:

- Is it based on your observation of PR practitioners at work or personal experience of PR work?
- Is it influenced by representation of PR work and practitioners in popular culture such as TV, movies and books? Is it based on reporting of PR activity in the media (for example, 'a PR disaster')?
- Is it based on what lecturers have told you about PR?

Now compare the definitions each member wrote:

- How different are they?
- What do they have in common?
- What are the differences and why do they exist?

As a group exercise, work together on the preparation of a common set of ideas. Then share them with other groups and see how you agree or disagree.

Proto-public relations: the antecedents of modern public relations

When did public relations (or similar practices) start? Karl Nessman (2000: 211), in a tongue-in-cheek comment, suggests that it 'would date back to Adam and Eve, to the point when people had to win over the confidence of others'. See Explore 1.2. Other suggestions include Sumerian wall-markings from 2000 BC (in modern Iraq), the persuasive rhetors of Ancient Greece (400 BC) and Roman emperors. Al-Badr (2004) claims that a 4000-year-old cuneiform tablet found in Iraq was similar to a 'bulletin telling farmers how to grow better crops' and thus a form of promotional information. A precedent of election campaigns handbooks can be found in Roman orator Cicero's brother *Commentariolum Petitionis* (Comments on elections), in which he advised how to win over public opinion if he wanted to become Consul of the Roman Consulate (64 BC). Julius Caesar, when he was Roman Consul in 59BC, arranged a daily news tablet or sheet called *Acta Diurna* (Daily Gazette) that offered information to the Roman populus and showed him as an active leader. In the Christian era, Robert Brown (2015) presents the Apostle Paul as a first-century example of a public relations practitioner because of his influence on others, his campaigns to build relationships with faith communities and his writing and publication of 'letters' (books) of the Bible.

Other examples are the formation and promotion of saintly cults (Watson 2008). These are not specimens of public relations, because they were not 'seen as strategically planned activity in medieval times and . . . did not use the framing of language and accumulated best practice that are applied now' (Watson 2008: 20). 'They were PR-like but were not PR' but are 'proto-public relations' (ibid.), a term which is based on 'proto' meaning 'first in time', 'begining' or 'giving rise to' (Merriam Webster) (OED 2005) and draws to mind the term 'prototype' (Watson 2013: 12).

Asia

Around the world there were other antecedents to public relations. In China, PR-like activities can be traced for thousands of years, occurring mainly at state level 'with the intention of the ruler or the emperor to establish a credible reputation among his people, or to maintain a harmonious relationship with different sectors of society' (Hung-Baesecke and Chen 2014: 24). These occurred in three forms: collections of folklore and culture such as folk songs, lobbying between rival states in order to avoid war and prevent attacks, and diplomacy to open trade links such as the Silk Road across Asia. Chinese, Taiwanese and Vietnamese researchers also point to the tenets of Confucianism as both ancient and enduring influences on proto-public relations and modern practices. Keeping promises and valuing reputation, an emphasis on interpersonal relationships and 'relational harmony', being firm on principles and ethics yet flexible on strategy and the importance of propriety ('respect, benevolence, fairness, friendship, and harmony and being knowledgeable') (Hung-Baesecke and Chen 2014: 23) led to the formation of proto-public relations that was based on *guanxi* (personal connections). It is also found in Vietnam as *quan hệ* (personal network) (Van 2014: 148). Confucianism emphasises 'the importance of public opinion' (Wu and Lai 2014: 115) and thus has given a strong cultural base to modern public relations in East Asia in a manner not seen in other parts of the world. Proto-public relations in Thailand, which was never colonised, evolved through royal institutions from the thirteenth century onwards and was expressed in Buddhist religious beliefs and supported the unity of the nation (Tantivejakul and Manmin 2011). King Rama IV in the late nineteenth century 'used royal gazettes, printed materials, royal photographs and the release of information to the press' to provide clear evidence 'of PR type activity to support national governance and imperialism avoidance' (Tantivejakul 2014: 130). Although the western forms of public relations are practised in Japan, a culturally different form, *kouhou* (widely notify), was developed (Yamamura, Ikari and Kenmochi 2014: 64). The term first appeared in a leading newspaper and denoted an advertisement or announcement. In the Meiji restoration starting in 1867, many older social and political structures were broken down as part of modernisation although a more democratic society did not evolve. The government formed news agencies to supply information to the rapidly expanding newspaper sector and 'press agencies were the first organizations to systematically engage in the publicity business' (ibid.). Unlike China, Taiwan, Vietnam and Thailand, Japanese press agencies did not continue cultural and religious traditions.

India, which was a British colony from the eighteenth century to 1947, has a proto-public relations history that can be traced to the reign of King Ashoka (272 BC–232 BC) whose edicts and inscriptions on rocks and pillars 'were imperial communications to the subjects of his vast empire' (Vil'Anilam 2014: 35). During subsequent eras of Maurya, Gupta and Mogul rulers, rulers communicated with society through formal meetings (*Darbar*) at the emperor's court at which representations were made and decisions given. Vil'Anilam (2014: 35) argues that 'early practices of maintaining relations with the public cannot, however, be compared with modern public relations'. In this first phase of India's communication history until 1858, a 'propaganda' era (Reddi 1999), there was communication from the East India Company and the formation of India's first but short-lived newspaper in Calcutta in 1780. It was followed by the 'publicity and information' era until independence in 1947. Notably, this period included the formation of governmental Central Publicity Board during the First World War which was India's first organisational communication operation (Bardhan and Patwardhan 2004) and the development of public relations activities undertaken by Indian Railways. Some authors consider that Mahatma Gandhi, the leader of the Indian movement for independence from the British and a former newspaper editor, was the 'spiritual founder of Indian public relations' (Reddi 1999) because of his use of mass media in campaigns against the coloniser and to address poverty.

> ### Explore 1.2
>
> #### When did PR start?
>
> Although the term, public relations, has been widely used for a little more than a century, when do you consider that 'public relations' started as a practice? Was it at the beginning of the twentieth century or did it exist as an unnamed practice before then? You may want to consider the characteristics that define those activities as public relations and thus different from other promotional or persuasive means of communication.

Middle East and Africa

In the Arab world, before technology accelerated the speed of communication, traditional gathering points, such as the mosque and the *majlis* or *diwaniyya* (a public gathering place for men), were both formal and informal channels for dissemination and discussion of news (Badran 2014). Some scholars have traced antecedents back 1400 years to the era of the Prophet Mohammed when the new religion of Islam began to be disseminated among the tribes of the Arabian peninsula (Abdelhay-Altamimi 2014: 84). Poetry was important in this culture and the poet 'was considered to be the press secretary of the tribe, attacking the tribe's enemies, praising its accomplishments and strengthening the fighter's morale' (Fakhri et al. 1980: 34). It is a tradition that is still 'alive and well' in the modern Arabian Gulf region (Badran 2014: 8). The practice of public relations, prior to the arrival of Western corporate communication departments and agencies, was limited to a protocol role of organising events and taking care of visitors (Abdelhay-Altamimi 2014; Badran 2014). In colonial Africa during the nineteenth and early twentieth century, proto-public relations was in a governmental information form, often supporting the formation of newspapers in British colonies in Eastern and Southern Africa (Kiambi 2014; Natifu 2014) and Nigeria in West Africa (Ibraheem 2014). Kiambi has found evidence of a British Colonial Office information methodology that may have been applied in African, Asian and Caribbean colonies in the early to mid-twentieth century.

Australia and New Zealand

Australia and New Zealand, both British colonies until the start of the twentieth century, also saw government communication as the preparatory stage for public relations. In Australia, 'Government attempts to inform, convince and persuade the widely spread population relied on and exploited PR strategies more than any single entity private enterprise could hope to achieve' (Sheehan 2014: 11). Promotional activities undertaken by the province-type colonies that made up nineteenth-century Australia attracted immigrants to new settlements and miners to the mid-century Gold Rush, as well as lobbying the colonial master in London about independence and trade issues. Promoters of the New Zealand colony sought immigrants and investors and to position the country for a future separate from Australia as an independent dominion of the British Empire. Galloway (2014: 14) comments that nineteenth-century New Zealand 'began to develop some skill in the press agentry then beginning to emerge in the United States'. Strategic publicity for the colony took place in the London Great Exhibition of 1851 and the Vienna International Exposition of 1873.

Latin America

In Latin America, public relations is mostly seen as a recent phenomenon, dating from mid-twentieth century onwards. Only in Argentina, a Spanish colony until 1810, is there clear evidence of publicity-type activities in support of the nascent colony and its ambitions to attract investment from Europe. These included newspapers promoting political groups and the national interest, and a diplomatic lobbying campaign (Carbone and Montaner 2014). The start of public relations in Brazil is set at 1914 when a Canadian-owned tramway company in Sao Paolo set up the Public Relations Department, but progress was very slow until the 1950s. In Central America, corporate public relations activity supported the Panama Canal in 1914 but, like Brazil, this was a false dawn.

Europe

European antecedents vary and are subject to considerable debate. In Eastern Europe and Russia, some scholars (Boshnakova 2014; Ławniczak 2005; 2014) consider that public relations arose only after the fall of the Berlin Wall in 1989 and the subsequent collapse of the Soviet bloc. It was an outcome of the new democratic politics and governments. Others, however, have mapped out proto-public relations activity in preceding decades and centuries, including among former Soviet bloc nations such as the Czech Republic, former East Germany, Hungary, Romania and Slovenia. In Western Europe, it is Germany whose public relations sector was best developed with evidence of organised strategic communication in the eighteenth century.

Early proto-public relations activity can be traced to leading writers being employed 'as publicists and as state employees in the 1790s' and a Karl Varnhagen van Ense was hired as a 'full time "press officer"' by the Prussian Chancellor von Hardenberg during the Vienna Congress (1814–1815)' which sought to solve boundary issues arising from the French Revolution and the

Picture 1.1 The fall of the Berlin Wall in 1989 led to rapid expansion of public relations and political communication in Eastern Europe. However, the German Democratic Republic, which is now part of the Federal Republic of Germany, had 'socialist public relations' which employed more than 3000 people in the 1980s. (*source*: Luis Veiga/Stockbyte Unreleased/Getty Images)

Napoleonic Wars (Bentele 2015: 48–49). In 1841, a press bureau was started in Prussia 'to correct wrong press reports', with a succeeding Literarisches Cabinet or Buro (Literary Cabinet or Bureau) continuing until 1920. Official newspapers were established and government-friendly newspapers given financial support. Outside of political changes, 'economic and technical progress also shaped PR's development' (Bentele 2015: 50). Coal mining and steel manufacturing were the basis of German heavy industry; electronics and chemicals were innovative sectors. From companies like Krupp (steel), Siemens and AEG (electronics) and BASF, Bayer, Hoechst and Agfa (chemicals), which were seeking national and international markets, the beginnings of systematic, planned corporate and marketing public relations were established. Alfred Krupp was a leader and along with Werner Rathenau and Werner von Siemens 'simultaneously became leading businessmen as well as architects of PR in the nineteenth century' (ibid.). Krupp had a publicity coup of a 2.5-ton block of cast steel at the 1851 Great Exhibition at Crystal Palace, London. The reason that led Krupp to become the best 'public relations' for his company might be found in a phrase he wrote in 1866 and was found in his personal correspondence of the company's archives: 'I think the time has come for people, who are true to truth, to write reports about factories and companies for newspapers which are read throughout the world and can spread the knowledge of these companies' (Binder 1983: 170). In 1867, a full-time '*Literat*' (man of letters) was appointed as the manager of Krupp's corporate communications, followed in 1870 by a corporate press department whose role was to monitor coverage of the company in newspapers and prepare articles and brochures to promote Krupp and its products (Wolbring 2000). Other German companies also developed press relations operations. By the beginning of the twentieth century AEG was evaluating its press coverage in an organised manner and the sociologist Max Weber began research in 1910 into the sources of newspaper coverage. These actions demonstrate how well the media economy and promotional communication sectors were established.

In much of the rest of Western Europe, there is little evidence about proto-public relations or planned publicity and press relations that can be compared with the German experience. Although the United Kingdom appears to have had well-organised practices for informational communications in its colonies, these were not evident in the four home nations until after the First World War. There are exceptions such as the Marconi Company issuing news releases in 1910 about new trans-Atlantic telegraph services. In the Netherlands, there was a long tradition of *voorlichting* (a literal translation of 'Enlightenment'), giving people information in order that they could participate

> **Box 1.2**
>
> **The patron saints of public relations**
>
> Saint Bernadine of Siena is the patron saint of public relations, commemorated on 20 May each year. Bernardine (also known as Bernardino) was a Franciscan preacher born in 1380. He was a successful evangelist who travelled throughout Italy for 30 years. Following his death at L'Aquila, near Rome, in 1444, a basilica was built in the town and his relics are on display there.
>
> He was chosen in 1956 when a petition was brought by Cardinal Lecaro of Bologna for his nomination as patron saint of public relations practitioners in Italy. In 1960, Cardinal Feltin, Archbishop of Paris, obtained a similar designation of Bernardino as patron saint of French public relations professionals. Since then, the Italian preacher-writer has become the universal patron saint of public relations.
>
> Saint Paul (also known as the Apostle Paul) lived during the first century in ancient Cilicia (which is now part of Turkey), Syria, Israel, Greece and Italy. He is also considered as a patron saint of public relations workers as well as for journalists, authors and many others. Saint Paul travelled widely as a promoter of the new Christian faith and wrote many letters (books) of the Bible's New Testament.

in discussions about their society. *Voorlichters* travelled around giving information about health, farming, education, politics, etc. (van Ruler and Cotton 2015: 91–2). *Voorlichting*, however, can be interpreted as a communication mechanism 'to show people how to conduct themselves as good citizens and to control them'. The history of PR in the Netherlands can therefore be seen as a history of the battle for information and emancipation on the one hand and education and persuasion on the other but always under the ('Dutch uncle') dogma of 'knowing what is best' (van Ruler and Cotton 2015: 91). In Norway, socially radical policies were promoted by *potetprest* (potato priests of the Lutheran church) in public information campaigns in the mid-late eighteenth century aimed at alleviating poverty through the planting of potatoes. The priests used lectures, handbooks and their enthusiasm in these planned activities (Bang 2015).

The expansion of public relations in the twentieth century

As previous sections demonstrated, public relations has many, time-varied beginnings. In some countries and regions, it has been influenced by religion and culture; in others, it has been linked to political, governmental and economic developments such as industrialisation and the development of parliamentary democracies. In general, public relations is a phenomenon of the twentieth century. During the first half of the last century, its expansion was primarily in the United States with some disrupted progress in Germany. The United Kingdom's engagement with public relations commenced after the First World War, but expanded more rapidly from 1945 onwards, as did much of Western Europe and other regions of the world outside of Eastern Europe. In Asia, Thailand established governmental communications in the 1930s but other nations in that continent and in Africa developed public relations structures after independence, which mainly came in the 1960s. The People's Republic of China was closed by its Communist government from 1949 until 1979 after which public relations practice were gradually introduced as the economy re-opened. The advance of public relations in Latin America was varied as many countries were under forms of military government, often until the mid-1980s.

United States

Public relations practices were developed in the United States from the final decades of the nineteenth century onwards. These have been well recorded and taught around the world through popular textbooks and the example of US education. Although most countries have national approaches to public relations, there are 'International PR' models of practice in general and specialist areas that are used by multinational corporations and international organisations that have derived from US practice.

Railways companies, religious organisations and travelling entertainments (notably circuses) were all engaged in public relations activity in the final two or three decades of the nineteenth century (Lamme and

Mini case study 1.1
Ivy Lee's Declaration of Principles

This iconic statement was sent to newspaper editors by Ivy Lee in the spring of 1905 as a declaration of principles for its publicity agency, Parker and Lee. The journalist Sherman Morse made it public when he wrote to contrast the years of silence, 'abuse and inaccuracies' (1906: 457) of big corporations and trusts and the new manners of what he called 'the beginning of wisdom' (1906: 458). In the words of Morse (1906: 460):

> These principles reveal the position that will have to be taken by all publicity agents of corporations if they are to make a 'go' of their business. 'This is not a secret press bureau,' said Lee. 'All our work is done in the open. We aim to supply news. This is not an advertising agency; if you think any of our matter ought properly to go to your business office, do not use it. Our matter is accurate. Further details on any subject treated will be supplied promptly, and any editor will be assisted most cheerfully in verifying directly any statement of fact. Upon inquiry, full information will be given to any editor concerning those on whose behalf an article is sent out. In brief, our plan is, frankly and openly, on behalf of business concerns and public institutions, to supply to the press and public of the United States prompt and accurate information concerning subjects which it is of value and interest to the public to know about. Corporations and public institutions give out much information in which the news point is lost to view. Nevertheless, it is quite as important to the public to have this news as it is to the establishments themselves to give it currency. I send out only matter every detail of which I am willing to assist any editor in verifying for himself. I am always at your service for the purpose of enabling you to obtain more complete information concerning any of the subjects brought forward in my copy.'

(Morse 1906)

This declaration has become a reference point for the history of public relations in the US. While some consider it as the beginning of modern public relations, others offer a more sceptical view of what they call a 'new experiment of corporate press agentry' (Miller and Bishop 2009) at the beginning of the twentieth century.

What is your opinion? How does this 'declaration of principles' relate to its historical context? What was the reasoning behind it? Why could it be considered by many as the beginning of public relations? On the other hand, why could it have raised suspicion in others?

Russell 2010; Lamme 2015). The term 'public relations' appeared around that time but it did not gain strong recognition for three or four decades. The most common practices, as shown in the examples of circuses, were press agentry and publicity. Press agents earned their living by selling stories about their clients into newspapers (Russell and Myers, 2019). Publicists also sought media coverage for clients who paid them.

One US innovation which has been widely imitated is the external, advisory agency for communication activities. The Publicity Bureau of Boston, started by three former newspaper reporters as a 'general press agent business' in 1900, was the first of this type (Cutlip 1994). It lasted for only 12 years but represented some leading universities and American Telephone & Telegraph (AT&T). It was followed in 1902 by a New York agency set up by another newspaperman, William Wolf Smith, whose agency was a 'publicity business' aimed at assisting corporations in countering press attacks and regulatory legislation. The third agency, Parker & Lee in 1904, is especially notable as its co-owner was the former newspaperman Ivy L. Lee who became the first high-profile public relations adviser and a major influence on US practice until his early death in 1934 (see Mini case study 1.1). Lee's partner was George Parker, who had served as President Grover Cleveland's press agent in his three presidential campaigns for the Presidency. Apart from Parker, all founders of the pioneer US agencies came from newspapers. This set the style of practice as media relations for publicity purposes. Ivy Lee, however, would become a highly controversial policy adviser to clients such as the Pennsylvania Railroad and the magnate John D. Rockefeller (see Explore 1.3). Lee put forward the case for companies to make their cases to the public: 'If you go direct to the people and get the people to agree with you, you can be sure that ultimately legislatures, commissions and everybody else must give way in your favor' (Lee 1925: 60). Although Lee is portrayed as a public relations pioneer, he used the term 'publicity' as evidenced in his 1925 book, *Publicity: Some of the Things It Is and Is Not* and did not promote a clear, organised vision of public relations.

The agency business grew gradually and it was not until after the First World War in 1919 that the earliest active promoter of 'public relations' as a term and a

Explore 1.3

PR and activism

Public relations has often been presented as a tool of powerful organisations, such as governments and corporation, but it has activist roots especially in US labour movements. In 2014, a three-month advocacy campaign (July–October) through social media and public demonstrations by the environmental group Greenpeace against toy manufacturer Lego and energy corporation Shell led to the end of their partnership. Can you identify other campaigns by advocacy groups and charities that have successfully influenced public opinion and led to changes on government policy and laws?

---

communications practice set up in business. This was Edward L. Bernays (1891–1995), who with his soon-to-be wife Doris Fleischman started their agency in New York. Bernays's importance is more related to his books, *Crystallizing Public Opinion* (1923), *Propaganda* (1928) and *The Engineering of Consent* (1955), and less for his leadership in public relations in the 1920s and 1930s, when he was seen by peers as a relentless self-promoter. On starting his business, Bernays titled it as 'Edward L. Bernays, Counsel on Public Relations', thus presenting the concept of 'public relations counsel' as a higher professional skill and calling than those of 'publicist' or 'press agent'. He engaged with developments in psychology and sociology, as well as the study of public opinion. His importance, which came later among US practitioners from the 1950s until his death at 103 in 1995, was promoting public relations as being much more than the negotiation of coverage in the media; as a persuasive communication professional activity on behalf of clients. Lee and Bernays were not alone in writing about publicity and public relations activity in the 1920s. Often overlooked are Robert Wilder and Katharine Buell who ran a public relations firm in New York from 1919 to 1925 and published *Publicity: A Manual for the Use of Business, Civic, or Social Service Organisations* and Irving Squire and Kirtland Wilson's *Informing Your Public* (1924), which Ivy Lee recommended to Edward Bernays (Lamme 2015). By 1930, the work of publicists and public relations people was of such importance that they were being mentioned in major US novels such as John Dos Passos's *USA Trilogy* which had the publicist, J. Ward Morehouse as an important if morally crossed character in its first and third volumes. Public relations and publicity work grew through the 1920s until slowed by the Great Depression. It was a contested area. Media owners loathed press agents and publicists and called them 'space grabbers' because they obtained coverage in newspapers for clients without the need to buy advertisements (Tedlow 1979). They were also recruiting journalists to do their work, a practice that still continues.

After the First World War

In Europe, public relations and publicity activity expanded in Germany and the United Kingdom after the First World War. In Germany, it was well developed in industry, national government and, especially, local and regional government. This halted in 1933 when the Nazis came to power (Bentele 2015). The most important development in the United Kingdom was the formation of the 'first public relations agency', Editorial Services Ltd, by Basil Clarke in 1924 (Evans 2013). Clarke used the term 'industrial propaganda', especially in relation to communication with employees. Propaganda, prior to its blackening in the Nazi era, was widely used in government and industry as a synonym for informational communication and awareness-creating publicity. Stephen Tallents, another British pioneer in the establishment of public relations, led the work of the British government's promotional agency, the Empire Marketing Board (see Picture 1.2), to develop trade and business amongst nations, dominions and colonies of the British Empire. Tallents, who later went on to advise the BBC and government departments, was the foundation president of the Institute of Public Relations in 1948 (Anthony 2012). Other countries that were introducing public relations

Picture 1.2 The Empire Marketing Board campaigns run by Stephen Tallents in the 1920s and 1930s used rich visual images in posters and films to promote British Empire trade. (*source:* Granger Historical Picture Archive/Alamy Stock Photo)

included Australia, whose first self-styled public relations adviser was George Fitzpatrick in 1929 (Gleeson 2012; Crawford and Macnamara 2014). Many state governments had information and publicity departments by 1930. In Thailand, the government set up a Publicity Division, modelled on German practices, in 1933 to provide information to the public. It has since evolved into the Government Public Relations Department (GPRD) and plays a major role in managing government communication and relations with media industries (Tantivejakul 2014).

The Second World War

During the Second World War, all combatants established propaganda and information operations. In the United Kingdom, the Ministry of Information ran internal propaganda and public information campaigns. It continued as the Central Office of Information for decades until its closure in 2011. L'Etang (2004: 59) notes that 'by the end of the Second World War, the British State had invested heavily in a variety of propaganda activities to support political, economic, and diplomatic objectives'. In the United States, the armed forces had public relations staff who were trained to accompany units into war zones, as well as keep domestic audiences informed. An example was Daniel J. Edelman, who later formed the international agency of the same name. Edelman joined the US Army in late 1942 and underwent the Army Specialized Training Program as a public relations specialist before going to Europe in the final year of the Second World War (Wisner 2012). He, and other veterans, would drive the expansion of public relations in the US and internationally in decades to follow. The main propaganda organisations in the United States were the Office of War Information (OWI), which focused on disseminating information worldwide, and the War Advertising Council, which produced public service announcements. Both provided platforms for public relations and publicity employment, although as Lee (2015) found, employment in government departments dropped rapidly as the war ended. In Germany, a previously diverse media sector was forced to follow National Socialist doctrines after 1933 with information centralised under the Reich Ministry of Public Information and Propaganda headed by Propaganda Minister Goebbels. 'Needless to say, the entire system of public communication gained a propagandist character' (Bentele 2015: 52). By the beginning of the war in the Pacific in 1941, Japan had an established information division in its Cabinet office and the 'propaganda machine was in place' (Yamamura et al. 2014: 65).

1945 onwards

After the end of the Second World War in 1945, public relations' expansion gathered pace, especially in North America and Western Europe. Eastern Europe, which was under Soviet control, and China, which would come under Communist Party rule in 1949, were extensive, highly populated exceptions. Asia, Africa and Latin America would follow later.

In Western European, American influence was at its height in the nations that had been affected by the wartime conflict. US funding of the 'Marshall Plan' (the European Recovery Program) encouraged democratisation of politics, open economies and infrastructure reconstruction. In some countries, communicators travelled to the United States and were briefed on public relations and promotional activity. Belgium, which had pre-war experience of propaganda and promotional activity in its colonial industries, sent economic missions to the United States 'which led to the propagation of PR in different parts of Belgium' (van Ruler and Cotton 2015: 92). These visits found that successful companies nurtured relationships with publics through communication that had human dimensions. Germany, Greece, the Netherlands and Italy also benefited from the Marshall Plan. German public relations historian Günter Bentele calls the period from 1945 to 1958 a 'New beginning and upswing':

> *Postwar upswing and orientation towards American models in the early 1950s; emergence of a new professional identity in the context of democratic structures of the public sphere (PR defined as distinct from propaganda and publicity); rapid development of the professional field, particularly in the economic sphere.* (Bentele 2015: 47)

Thanks to the 'missions de productivité', sponsored by the Marshall Plan, French businessmen travelled to the United States where they discovered public relations, which was applied on their return. French subsidiaries of North American companies, especially the oil industry which was fearful of nationalisation, were the first to promote their adoption. Hence, some authors point to the oil companies as responsible for the introduction of public relations in French territory. Esso-Standard became the first to open a public relations department in France, under the direction of Jean Choppin de Janvry. The British Shell Petroleum and the American Caltex, whose public relations efforts were managed by Lucien Matrat, followed (Rodríguez-Salcedo 2012: 349).

In Greece, the exposure to American advertising agencies and public relations practices in the tourism market in the early 1950s was the springboard for the formation of early agencies (Theofilou 2015). In Italy, the United States Information Service (USIS) was very active in recruiting Italians, producing films and documents, offering exchange visits, and assisting the Christian Democracy (DC) party combat the influence of Communist Party (Muzi Falconi and Venturozzo 2015). However, Portugal and Spain, which were non-combatants in the Second World War and ruled by military dictatorships since the 1930s, were not part of the Marshall Plan funding and programmes. Development of their national public relations sectors would be delayed until the mid-1970s when both dictatorships broke down. Spain started its public relations sector during the final 15 years of the Franco regime (see Mini case study 1.2) but it was not until democracy returned in the mid-1970s that it gained momentum (Rodríguez-Salcedo and Xifra 2015). Portugal shrugged off the Salazar regime at the same time but took a decade longer than its Iberian neighbour to start developing a national public relations sector (Santos 2016).

Professionalisation

Other aspects of the post-war expansion of public relations were the formation of professional associations and the introduction of university-level education.

Professional associations

Although the Public Relations Society of America (PRSA) was formed in 1947, it had antecedent organisations that dated to 1936 (National Association of Accredited Publicity Directors). In the United Kingdom, the Institute of Public Relations (IPR) was launched in 1948 with the assistance of a trade union, the National Association of Local Government Officers. Other national bodies were formed at a similar time: Australia (1949), Belgium (1953), Denmark (1950), Finland (1947), France (1949), Germany (1958), Greece (1960), Netherlands (1946), New Zealand (1954), Norway (1949), Spain (1961) and Sweden (1950). Italy had three associations in the late 1950s, which merged into a single organisation in 1970. In 1955, after several years of talks, the International Public Relations Association (IPRA) was launched in London and, for around 15 years, became the cross-roads for international public relations. Although an organisation composed of individual senior practitioners, it played a leadership role in defining aspects of public relations practice such as codes of conduct and of ethics, early planning of public relations education and training, and seeking recognition for public relations as a profession. IPRA was important from 1955 to 1970 in promoting public relations through its Congresses, publications and by bringing practitioners together. From some of these connections, networks of agencies were built, some being acquired by the US agencies as they extended their offices and resources around the world. Also in Europe, the Confédération Européenne des Relations Publique (CERP) was formed on the initiative of Lucien Matrat of France in 1959. Matrat was its first President and also a prominent IPRA member. CERP's Research and Education wing later became the European Public Relations Education and Research Association (EUPRERA) in 2000. IPRA continues as an organisation although its role of international coordination and leadership has been taken over by the Global Alliance for Public Relations and Communication Management (see Think about 1.1).

Mini case study 1.2
Joaquin Maestre – founding influence of Spanish PR

Despite working under the censorship and political control of the Franco regime in 1960s Spain, Joaquin Maestre identified the opportunity to develop public relations services from a base in Barcelona and established the first Spanish successful agency business in 1960. Influenced by the French pioneer Lucien Matrat, he also helped form the first public relations association in his country and the first school of public relations. He was also the external face of Spanish public relations during the Franco era and beyond. After the dictator Franco died in 1975, Spanish public relations expanded quickly as a result of Maestre's and others leadership.

Source: Rodríguez-Salcedo 2015

Maestre who sent an invitation to IPRA to hold its Council Meeting and General Assembly of 1966 in Barcelona. He believed that by doing so IPRA would be providing support to a country did not have a national association, whilst helping to establish better comprehension of true public relations work in a setting where many people were offering their services and calling themselves PR consultants when, in reality, they were not legitimate colleagues'.

Source: Archivo General de la Universidad de Navarra (AGUN) / Fondo Joaquín Maestre 144 / Box 494

> **Think about 1.1**
>
> ## Academics versus practitioners
>
> Why does there appear to be a gap between academics and practitioners? The history of their relationship is illustrated by different approaches to definitions of PR and the development of education and training.
>
> - How do the definitions differ between those proposed by academics and practitioners?
> - Why do the differences exist?
>
> To explore this relationship, find examples of academic definitions and compare them with those from the professional association in your country. Consider the interests of the people who prepared the definitions and who the audiences they were prepared for.

Education

The education and training of practitioners was seen as a vital element in building the skills base of public relations and defining it as a professional activity. Although the first public relations course was offered at the University of Illinois in 1920, it was not until the late 1940s that the new professional associations started to actively discuss education. In the United States, Boston University established the first degree programme in 1947, although around 10 courses were offered at other universities. The first Canadian university PR course was taught at McGill University in 1948, but the first university degree was offered by Mount Saint Vincent University in 1977 (Wright 2011; Wright and Flynn 2017). For at least two decades, the United States was the leading provider of university-level studies, mainly in second- and third-tier establishments.

The professional associations had education and training as a priority. Sir Stephen Tallents said in his 1949 IPR presidential address that members' 'first function . . . was to educate themselves' (L'Etang 2004: 188). IPR drew up its first draft syllabus in 1954, although many senior members were dubious about the value of education. Sam Black, later to be an honorary professor of public relations and an internationally recognised educator, dismissed education as a requirement for practice: 'It is not necessary to have had any specialised training to have a good public relations outlook. So much depends on commonsense and good taste' (L'Etang 2004: 190). He was to change his stance and became one of the most widely travelled public relations educators and trainers, the author of several books and leader of some of IPRA's policy-making on university-level education.

IPRA took the lead in shaping international approaches to education. Its Gold Paper No. 2, *Public Relations Education Worldwide,* published in 1976, was primarily researched and written by the German public relations leader, Albert Oeckl. Unlike later Gold Papers, it proposed that public relations topics should be part of a general humanities degree. It was followed by three other Gold Papers in the succeeding 20 years (1982, 1990 and 1997), all of them used by universities and national associations to prepare degree programmes and accreditation processes. The Gold Papers increasingly focused education and training on skills for public relations practice, rather than a rounded syllabus. This created a tension that has long existed between practitioner organisations and universities around the world.

The adoption of public relations degree studies did not follow a continental or regional pattern. Early introductions, after the United States, were Japan (1951), Belgium (1957), Taiwan (1963), Thailand (1965), Turkey (1965), Egypt (early 1970s), Mexico (1976), Australia (mid-1970s) and Saudi Arabia (1976). Much of Europe, both Eastern and Western, launched courses in the 1980s and 1990s. In many countries, public relations courses were taught within other degree programmes or at Diploma level for one or two decades. The introduction in Eastern Europe came from 1991 onwards, after the collapse of the Soviet bloc.

The United Kingdom, which had started discussing education and training in 1948, waited 40 years before the first degrees commenced, firstly a Master's programme at the University of Stirling which started in 1988; followed by bachelor programmes in 1989 at Dorset Institute of Higher Education (now Bournemouth University); Leeds Polytechnic (now Leeds Beckett University) and the College of St Mark & St John, Plymouth.

International public relations

Western Europe became the target for American corporations as economies revived in the 1950s and 1960s. This impetus gave the platform for the establishment of the international arms of major public relations agencies and multinational corporations' corporate communication departments. The first agencies to expand from the United States were Hill & Knowlton, Burson-Marsteller and Barnet & Reef. Hill & Knowlton was established before the Second World War in Cleveland and then New York. Burson-Marsteller was set up in 1953 and Barnet & Reef, which no longer exists, started in 1959. The agencies started by linking with partners or associates in the new markets and later acquiring either the partner agency or another business. This enabled them to support American clients as they expanded into new territories and grow the agencies' businesses. This development and that of the corporate communication expansion also led to the use of common public relations and publicity approaches that could be planned and monitored from a central position. The outcome was that American models of public relations became known as 'International PR' with ubiquitous practices attempted in many countries of greatly varying culture, politics and societies. They have been very successful, as shown by their decades of operation, but not in all countries. In Thailand, for example, international agencies have come and gone. Often they tried to impose an international model of PR to satisfy clients but failed to gain desired results because they did not appreciate Thailand's Buddhist values and relationship culture (Tantivejakul 2014).

The worldwide development of public relations since the mid-twentieth century: the springboards and restraints that shaped it

During the 1970s, the momentum built for the worldwide expansion of public relations practices. Already, the early international agency networks were in place, corporate public relations departments were growing as governments and multinational corporations sought to expand their influence and the technology for faster communications, such as telephone, satellite communication and television, was evolving. News media was also expanding. In many Western countries, newspapers could be printed in several cities; television news was less reliant on film and able to access satellite-distributed material. All these developments sped up the news gathering and dissemination processes (Gorman and McLean 2009) and increased pressure on organisations to respond quickly. It was also the decade in the United States and Germany in which theoretical research began to flourish. James Grunig, a noted academic theorist, led the way in the United States by positioning public relations as a management function. His definition of public relations as 'the management of communication between an organisation and its publics' (Grunig and Hunt 1984: 4) is the most commonly cited. Other academics began to undertake research and the first academic journal, *Public Relations,* was established by Rex F. Harlow in 1945. For much of the next 20 years, American research and theorisation would dominate public relations, until the academic base became much more international.

Through the 1960s and 1970s, public relations was mainly focused on media relations. This was a reflection of the journalistic background of many entrants and the expectation of employers in companies and governments that media coverage was beneficial. Media relations remains a major part of practice today. This emphasis would change as graduates who had studied public relations and related communication topics increasingly entered agencies and organisations from the 1990s onwards. Now, around the world, public relations is a field in which the vast majority of practitioners have a bachelor degree or similar academic award. Although the most common form of public relations activity is in the tactical, publicity-orientated form often called 'marketing PR', the increased educational input led to the introduction of strategy-led campaigns and the understanding that publics and stakeholders could be contacted by methods other than through media gateways. This became known as the 'relationship management' model (Ledingham and Bruning 1998).

1990s

After the fall of the Berlin Wall in 1989 and the collapse of the former Eastern Bloc, public relations began to flourish in these countries. For some this development was wholly new, as it arose from the introduction of democratic governments while others interpreted public relations' rapid growth as the continuation of practices from the former socialist countries. They argued that many former governmental communications and propaganda people left their old jobs and became PR entrepreneurs using many of the same techniques and contacts.

In the 1990s, Europe led the PR world in two areas. The first was the formation of the International Communications Consultants Organisation (ICCO) which brought the world's PR trade bodies together and the second was the interpretation of the Quality Assurance (QA) movement into the public relations field. One factor that supported growth of employment and budgets had been the formation of national public relations professional and trade bodies. In addition to ICCO, the professional bodies formed the Global Alliance for Public Relations and Communication Management later in the same decade. IPRA was behind the formation of the International Quality in Public Relations organisation which promoted QA approaches to public relations. This was adopted in the UK as the Consultancy Management Standard created by the-then Public Relations Consultants Association and adopted by several countries.

In this decade, there was rapid expansion of public relations in consultancies, government and corporations. An important springboard was the privatisation of governmental organisations in many countries. This fuelled further internationalisation of agencies and corporate communication operations as companies moved rapidly into new markets through acquisition. Another sector to emerge strongly was public relations for non-profit organisations, such as charities and social organisations.

A second springboard was technology public relations from the mid-1990s onwards. This brought new types of expertise and communication methods such as email and the early internet that were used by practitioners and organisations as communication and promotional tools. The period was called Web 1.0 and was the beginning of the biggest transformation of public relations practices and strategies since the end of the Second World War. Until then, technology change was relatively slow with facsimile (fax) machines only recently replacing telex and post. With Web 1.0, the pace of change accelerated.

In Latin America, the ending of several military governments and controlled economies led to greater democracy in politics and open markets, which in turn fostered communication such as public relations, political communication and advertising. Watson (2015: 14) notes that after restraints were eased 'PR grew in all forms, as did education and training'. In the Middle East and Africa, a relatively liberal period allowed the expansion of public relations especially as the media environment became much more open and international. In Israel, the period since 1995 has been a 'golden age' for public relations (Magen 2014: 53).

Although the bursting of the dotcom bubble around 2001 slowed the growth of public relations, it was only temporary as employment continued to expand. For example, in 2004, it was estimated that 45,000 people worked in PR in the UK (CEBR 2005). By 2011, it had risen to about 60,000 and in 2016 to 83,000 (PRCA 2011; 2016). Similar growth has been experienced in many countries. For example, the annual *European Communication Monitor* survey is sent to 40,000 mid-to-senior level corporate communicators in 50 countries every year and is the longest running trend survey of the profession worldwide (see www.communicationmonitor.eu).

Mini case study 1.3
Women in public relations

Since the mid-1990s women have become the majority gender in public relations in most countries.

But in the field's history, women are under-represented. Of the US pioneers, only Doris Fleischman, business partner and wife of Edward L. Bernays, has been accorded the standing which she deserved. After the Second World War, it was not until 1973 that the Public Relations Society of America elected its first female president, Betsy Ann Plank. She was followed by Margaret Nally, elected by the Institute of Public Relations in the UK in 1975–76. Other national professional associations were also slow to elect women to leadership posts, although this has changed in the past two decades. In the UK, for example, six out of 12 past presidents of the Chartered Institute of Public Relations (since 2007) were women.

How public relations grew

In a study of the public relations histories of more than 70 countries, Watson (2015) analysed the antecedents of modern public relations, the factors that aided the expansion of these practices (springboards) and the restraints that slowed growth.

Antecedents

There were three common forms:

- early corporate communications (e.g. Krupp in Germany; railways in the United States);
- governmental information and propaganda methods, especially in British colonies;
- cultural influences linked to dominant religions (Buddhism, Confucianism and Islam) in North Africa, the Middle East and Asia.

Springboards

There was a frequently observed sequence of influences that enabled the expansion of public relations:

Governmental PR → Corporate communication → Formation of a professional association → Education at universities and colleges → Establishment of agencies

There were exceptions, especially in the focus on nation-building and politicised communication in post-colonial societies in Asia and Africa, but this sequence is seen in many more countries. In post-Second World War Western Europe and in Eastern Europe after 1989, there was strong influence from American models of practice, but these have been modified into national forms of public relations.

Restraints

Since the middle of the twentieth century public relations has not expanded at a uniform rate, even in adjacent countries, for economic and political reasons. Among the historic reasons were:

- closed or statist economies, one-party and military governments that stifled free expression, the media and the emergence of public relations;
- propaganda was dominant in some countries (notably Eastern Europe) until democratic politics was allowed;
- public relations was practised as a protocol activity to support rulers and not to foster dialogue (Middle East).

Box 1.3

Studying the history of public relations

Study of the history of a profession or organisation is valuable as it can shape understanding as to why and how current practices and theories emerged and it let us learn from the past. It indicates the influences, opportunities and pressures that have affected development (or decline) and shows that professions haven't always developed with a constant upward progression.

Historical research into public relations is a relatively new scholarly activity which, until recently, was strongest in the United States. One of the first biographies was about the pioneer Ivy L. Lee (Hiebert, 1966) but there were few books and articles until the 1990s when Scott Cutlip produced two histories of US public relations in mid-decade. Soon after, there were biographies of Edward L. Bernays (Tye 1998), John Hill and the Hill & Knowlton agency (Miller 1999) and Arthur W. Page (Griese 2001). In the UK, Jacquie L'Etang published a history of UK public relations (L'Etang 2004) and there were papers, books and a conference in Germany in the mid and late 1990s. However, the launch of the International History of Public Relations Conference in 2010 resulted in an explosion of research and publication in article and book form from around the world.

Researchers have used all the methods of historical research – the creation and investigation of archives based on documents and visual material from individual organisations; interviews with practitioners have been recorded and transcribed; biographical methodologies explored; documents such as industry journals and 'how-to' books have been read and analysed. The minutes of meetings and correspondence have, for example, proved valuable in establishing accurate accounts of important initiatives that had become mythologised over time.

To research PR's history further, you can access online resources such as websites (www.bournemouth.ac.uk) and a growing selection of texts from leading academic publishers. Leading public relations research journals, such as *Public Relations Review*, *Journal of Public Relations Research* and *Journal of Communication Management* have special issues devoted to the history of public relations.

Summary

Overall, public relations has expanded as a practice mostly in democratic environments in which there is an open economy. There are exceptions but these are mainly, as in 1960s Spain, when the controlling regime was beginning to ease controls on the media and politics. By the second decade of the twenty-first century, public relations has become a major communication practice around the world. The very small beginnings, such as Krupp in Germany and the first US PR agency business in 1900 led to widespread employment, extensive use of practices and increasing research and education. It is a long way from circuses, regional steam railways and telephone companies publicising their activities to a very limited range of print media.

Bibliography

Abdelhay-Altamimi, N. (2014). Kingdom of Saudi Arabia. In: T. Watson, ed., *Middle Eastern and African Perspectives on the Development of Public Relations: Other Voices*. Basingstoke: Palgrave Macmillan, pp. 83–96.

Al-Badr, H. (2004). *The Basics of Public Relations and Its Practices*. Riyadh: Dar Aloloom.

Anthony, S. (2012). *Public Relations and the Making of Modern Britain*. Manchester: Manchester University Press.

Badran, B.A. (2014). The Arab States of the Gulf. In: T. Watson, ed., *Middle Eastern and African Perspectives on the Development of Public Relations: Other Voices*. Basingstoke: Palgrave Macmillan, pp. 5–21.

Bang, T. (2015). Norway. In: T. Watson, ed., *Western European Perspectives on the Development of Public Relations: Other Voices*. Basingstoke: Palgrave Macmillan.

Bardhan, N. and P. Patwardhan (2004). Multinational Corporations and Public Relations in a Historically Resistant Host Culture. *Journal of Communication Management* 8(3), pp. 246–63.

Bentele, G. (2015). Germany. In: T. Watson, ed., *Western European Perspectives in the Development of Public Relations: Other Voices*. Basingstoke: Palgrave Macmillan, pp. 44–59.

Bernays, E.L. (ed.). (1955). *The Engineering of Consent*. Norman, OH: University of Oklahoma Press.

Binder, E. (1983). *Die Entstehung unternehmerischer Public Relations in der Bundes-republik Deutschland*. Munster: Lit Verlag.

Boshnakova, D. (2014). Bulgaria. In: T. Watson, ed., *Eastern European Perspectives on the Development of Public Relations: Other Voices*. Basingstoke: Palgrave Macmillan, pp. 5–13.

Broom G.M. and B. Sha (2013). *Cutlip and Center's Effective Public Relations*, 11th edn. Englewood Cliffs, NJ: Prentice Hall.

Brown, R. (2015). *The Public Relations of Everything – The ancient, modern and postmodern dramatic history of an idea*. Abingdon: Routledge.

Carbone, C. and M. Montaner (2014). Argentina. In: T. Watson, ed., *Latin American Perspectives on the Development of Public Relations: Other Voices*. Basingstoke: Palgrave Macmillan, pp. 5–16.

CEBR (Centre for Economic and Business Research) (2005). *PR Today: 48,000 Professionals; £6.5 Billion Turnover. Summary Document: The Economic Significance of Public Relations*. Report for Chartered Institute of Public Relations. [pdf] London: CEBR. Available at: https://www.cipr.co.uk/sites/default/files/CIPR%20full%20report%20-%20November%204%202005.pdf, accessed 26 April 2019.

Childs, H.L. (1940). *An Introduction to Public Opinion*. New York: John Wiley & Sons, Inc.

CIPR (2012). *About PR*, https://cipr.co.uk/CIPR/About_Us/About_PR.aspx, accessed 8 April 2020.

Coombs W.T. and S. Holladay (2006). *It's Not Just PR: Public Relations in Society*. Chichester: Wiley-Blackwell.

Crawford, R. and J. Macnamara (2014). An agent of change: public relations in early twentieth-century Australia. In: B. St. John III, M. O. Lamme and J. L'Etang, eds., *Pathways to Public Relations: Histories of Practice and Profession*. Abingdon: Routledge, pp. 273–89.

Cutlip, S. (1994). *The Unseen Power: Public Relations, a history*. Hillsdale, NJ: Lawrence Erlbaum.

Evans, R. (2013). *From the Front Line: The Extraordinary Life of Sir Basil Clarke*. Stroud: Spellmount.

Fakhri, S., A. Alsheekley and F. Zalzala (1980). *Public Relations*. Baghdad: Ministry of Higher Education and Research.

Galloway, C. (2014). New Zealand. In: T. Watson, ed., *Asian Perspectives on the Development of Public Relations: Other Voices*. Basingstoke: Palgrave Macmillan, pp. 14–19.

Gleeson, D.J. (2012). George William Sydney Fitzpatrick (1884–1948): An Australian Public Relations 'Pioneer'. *Asia Pacific Public Relations Journal* 13(2), pp. 2–12.

Gorman, L. and D. McLean (2009). *Media and Society into the 21st Century: A historical introduction*, 2nd edn. Chichester: Wiley-Blackwell.

Griese, N.L. (2001). *Arthur W. Page: Publisher, public relations pioneer, patriot*. Atlanta: Anvil Publishers.

Grunig, J.E. and T. Hunt (1984). *Managing Public Relations*. New York: Holt, Rinehart & Winston.

Gutiérrez-García, E., M. Recalde and A. Piñera-Camacho (2015). Reinventing the wheel? A comparative view of the concept of dialogue. *Public Relations Review* 41(5), pp. 744–53.

Harlow, R.F. (1977). Public Relations Definitions Through the Years. *Public Relations Review* 3(1), pp. 49–63.

Hiebert, R.E. (1966). *Courtier to the crowd: The story of Ivy Lee and the development of public relations*. Ames, IA: Iowa State University Press.

Hung-Baesecke, C-J.F. and Y-R.R. Chen (2014). China. In: T. Watson, ed., *Asian Perspectives on the Development of Public Relations: Other Voices*. Basingstoke: Palgrave Macmillan, pp. 20–33.

Ibraheem, I.A. (2014). Nigeria. In: T. Watson, ed., *Middle Eastern and African Perspectives on the Development of Public Relations: Other Voices*. Basingstoke: Palgrave Macmillan, pp. 97–108.

Kiambi, D. (2014). Kenya. In: T. Watson, ed., *Middle Eastern and African Perspectives on the Development of Public Relations: Other Voices*. Basingstoke: Palgrave Macmillan, pp. 67–82.

Lamme, M.O. (2015). *Public Relations and Religion in American History: Evangelism, Temperance, and Business*. New York: Routledge.

Lamme M.O. and K.M. Russell (2010). Removing the spin: Towards a new theory of public relations history. *Journalism Communication Monographs* 11(4), pp. 280–362.

Lamme, M.O. and K.M. Russell (2015). Theorizing Public Relations History: Strategic Intent as a Defining Characteristic. In: International History of Public Relations Conference. [online]. Bournemouth: Bournemouth University, pp. 199–206. Available at: https://microsites.bournemouth.ac.uk/historyofpr/files/2010/11/IHPRC-2015-Proceedings.pdf, accessed 23 April 2019.

Ławniczak, R. (2005). *Introducing Market Economy Institutions and Instruments: The Role of Public Relations in Transition Economies*. Poznan: Piar.pl.

Ławniczak, R. (2014). Poland. In: T. Watson, ed., *Eastern European Perspectives on the Development of Public Relations: Other Voices*. Basingstoke: Palgrave Macmillan, pp. 54–66.

Ledingham, J.A. and S.D. Bruning (1998). Relationship management in public relations: dimensions of an organization-public relationship. *Public Relations Review* 24(1), pp. 55–65.

Lee, M. (2015). Government is Different: A History of Public Relations in American Public Administration. In: B. St. John III, M. O. Lamme, and J. L'Etang, eds., *Pathways to Public Relations: Histories of Practice and Profession*. Abingdon: Routledge, pp. 108–127.

Lee, M., F. Likely and J. Valin (2017). Government public relations in Canada and the United States. In: T. Watson, ed., *North American Perspectives on the Development of Public Relations: Other Voices*. Basingstoke: Palgrave Macmillan, pp. 65–80.

Lee, I.L. (1925). *Publicity. Some of the Things It is and Is Not*. New York: Industries Publishing Company.

L'Etang, J. (2004). *Public Relations in Britain – A History of Professional Practice in the 20th Century*. Mahwah, NJ: Lawrence Erlbaum.

Magen, C. (2014). Israel. In: T. Watson, ed., *Middle Eastern and African Perspectives on the Development of Public Relations: Other Voices*. Basingstoke: Palgrave Macmillan, pp. 51–66.

Miller, K.S. (1999). *The Voice of Business, Hill & Knowlton and Postwar Public Relations*. Chapel Hill, NC: The University of North Carolina Press.

Miller, K.S. and C.O. Bishop (2009). Understanding Ivy Lee's declaration of principles: U.S. newspaper and magazine coverage of publicity and press agentry, 1865–1904. *Public Relations Review* 35(2), pp. 91–101.

Morse, S. (1906). An Awakening in Wall Street. How the Trusts, after Years of Silence, now speak through authorized and acknowledged Press Agents. *American Magazine* 62(5), pp. 457–63.

Muzi Falconi, T. and Venturozzo, F. (2015). Italy. In: T. Watson, ed., *Western European Perspectives in the Development of Public Relations: Other Voices*. Basingstoke: Palgrave Macmillan, pp. 75–88.

Myers, C. (2017). United States – Antecedents and Proto-PR. In: T. Watson, ed., *North American Perspectives on the Development of Public Relations: Other Voices*. Basingstoke: Palgrave Macmillan, pp. 5–19.

Natifu, B. (2014). Uganda. In: T. Watson, ed., *Middle Eastern and African Perspectives on the Development of Public Relations: Other Voices*. Basingstoke: Palgrave Macmillan, pp. 138–52.

Nessman, K. (2000). The origins and development of public relations in Germany and Austria. In: D. Moss, D., Verčič, D. and Warnaby, G., eds., *Perspectives on Public Relations Research*. London: Routledge, pp. 211–25.

OED (2005). *Oxford English Dictionary*. Oxford: Oxford University Press.

PRCA (Public Relations & Communications Association) (2011). *PR Census 2011*. London: PRCA.

PRCA (Public Relations & Communications Association) (2016). *PR Census 2016*. London: PRCA. Available at: http://prmeasured.com/wp-content/uploads/2016/06/PRCA-PR-Census-2016.pdf, accessed 26 April 2019.

Rodríguez-Salcedo, N. (2012). Mapping Public Relations in Europe: Writing National Histories against the US Paradigm. *Communication & Society* 25(2), p. 331–74.

Rodríguez-Salcedo, N. (2015). Contributions to the History of Public Relations in the Midst of a Dictatorship: First Steps in the Professionalization of Public Relations in Spain (1960–1975). *Journal of Public Relations Research* 27(3), pp. 212–28.

Rodríguez-Salcedo, N. and T. Watson (2017). The development of public relations in dictatorships – Southern and Eastern European perspectives. *Public Relations Review* 43(2), pp. 375–81.

Rodríguez-Salcedo, N. and J. Xifra (2015). Spain. In: T. Watson, ed., *Western European Perspectives in the Development of Public Relations: Other Voices*. Basingstoke: Palgrave Macmillan, pp. 123–38.

Reddi, C.V.N. (1999). Notes on PR Practice in India: Emerging New Human Environment – A Challenge. *Asia Pacific Public Relations Journal* 1, pp. 147–60.

Russell, K. and Myers, C. (2019). The misunderstood nineteenth century U.S. press agent. *Public Relations Review* 45(2): 246–57.

Santos, J.M. (2016). Roots of public relations in Portugal: Changing an old paradigm. *Public Relations Review* 42(5), pp. 792–800.

Sheehan, M. (2014). Australia. In: T. Watson, ed., *Asian Perspectives on the Development of Public Relations: Other Voices*. Basingstoke: Palgrave Macmillan, pp. 5–13.

Tantivejakul, N. (2014). Thailand. In: T. Watson, ed., *Asian Perspectives on the Development of Public Relations: Other Voices*. Basingstoke: Palgrave Macmillan, pp. 128–43.

Tantivejakul, N. and P. Manmin (2011). The practice of public relations in building national unity: A historical view of the kingdom of Thailand. In: International History of Public Relations Conference [online]. Bournemouth: Bournemouth University, pp. 276–97. Available at: http://microsites.bournemouth.ac.uk/historyofpr/files/2010/11/IHPRC-2011-Proceedings.pdf, accessed 23 April 2019.

Tedlow, R.S. (1979). *Keeping the Corporate Image: Public Relations and Business 1900-1950*. Greenwich, CT: JAI Press.

Theofilou, A. (2015). Greece. In: T. Watson, ed., *Western European Perspectives in the Development of Public Relations: Other Voices*. Basingstoke: Palgrave Macmillan, pp. 60–74.

Tye, L. (1998). *The father of spin: Edward L. Bernays and the birth of public relations*. New York: Crown Publishers.

Van, L.T.H. (2014). Vietnam. In: T. Watson, ed., *Asian Perspectives on the Development of Public Relations: Other Voices*. Basingstoke: Palgrave Macmillan, pp. 144–57.

van Ruler, B. and A-M. Cotton (2015). Netherlands and Belgium. In: T. Watson, ed., *Western European Perspectives in the Development of Public Relations: Other Voices*. Basingstoke: Palgrave Macmillan, pp. 89–106.

Vil'Anilam, J.V. (2014). India. In: T. Watson, ed., *Asian Perspectives on the Development of Public Relations: Other Voices*. Basingstoke: Palgrave Macmillan, pp. 34–47.

Watson, T. (2008). Creating the cult of a saint: Communication strategies in 10th century England. *Public Relations Review* 34(1), pp. 19–24.

Watson, T. (2013). *Keynote Address*. Presentation to the International History of Public Relations Conference, 24 June 2013, Bournemouth University, Bournemouth. England.

Watson, T. (2015). What in the World is Public Relations? In: T. Watson, ed., *Perspectives on Public Relations Historiography and Historical Theorization*. Basingstoke: Palgrave Macmillan, pp. 4–19.

Watson, T. and P. Noble (2014). *Evaluating Public Relations: A guide to planning, research and measurement*, 3rd edn. London: Kogan Page.

Wisner, F. (2012). *Edelman and the Rise of Public Relations*. New York: Eight Communications.

Wolbring, B. (2000). *Krupp und die Öffentlichkeit im 19. Jahrhundert: Selbstdarstellung, öffentliche Wahrnehmung und gesellschaftliche Kommunikation* [Krupp and the public sphere in the 19th Century. Self-presentation, public perception and societal communication]. Munich: C.H. Beck.

Wright, D. (2011). History and development of public relations education in North America: a critical analysis. *Journal of Communication Management* 15(3), pp. 236–55.

Wright, D. and T. Flynn (2017). Public Relations Education in Canada and the United States. In: T. Watson, ed., *North American Perspectives on the Development of Public Relations: Other Voices*. Basingstoke: Palgrave Macmillan, pp. 51–64.

Wu, Y-C. and Y-J. Lai (2014). Taiwan. In: T. Watson, ed., *Asian Perspectives on the Development of Public Relations: Other Voices*. Basingstoke: Palgrave Macmillan, pp. 114–27.

Yamamura, K., S. Ikari and T. Kenmochi (2014). Japan. In: T. Watson, ed., *Asian Perspectives on the Development of Public Relations: Other Voices*. Basingstoke: Palgrave Macmillan, pp. 63–77.

CHAPTER 2

Scott Davidson

Working with the media

Source: Martin Mecnarowski/Shutterstock

Learning outcomes

By the end of this chapter you should be able to:
- recognise some of the key theoretical approaches to understanding PR's relationship with the media
- explore how different theories attempt to evaluate PR's power and influence over media content
- explore how agenda setting and framing theory can be used to research mediatory power
- identify how theory can explain the day-to-day relationship between PR practitioners and journalists
- understand how the media influences PR practice and the long-term growth of the profession.

Structure

- Media environments
- Exchange theories: the information subsidy
- Agenda setting and framing
- Power shift towards public relations practitioners
- Mediatisation

Introduction

This chapter presents several different theories or frameworks for researching and understanding the close relationship between public relations, journalism and the media more widely. The production of news requires access to information. In the language of journalism studies 'sources' hold that information. Sources are often private individuals who may have been eyewitnesses or participants in an event, but the focus for this chapter is on how organisations and institutions are integral sources in the process of gathering information by journalists. Governments, business, NGOs, charities, trade unions, professional associations and activist groups all attempt to coordinate and strategically pursue their interactions with the media. As sources they allocate staff and resources to cultivate and manage their relationship with journalists. These employees can have varied job titles such as press officer or media relations manager, but regardless of job titles practitioners are normally closely integrated into the PR strategies of their employer. The media is a space where the role in society for organisations and corporations are debated, but also where products, services and political viewpoints are promoted (Ihlen and Pallas 2014). The chapter will look at the media systems that influence PR and then turn to the main form of 'exchange theory' that has been used to explore and explain the PR–Media relationship – the concept of the information subsidy. It will then move on to agenda setting, framing and mediatisation as key concepts for thinking more deeply about PR's relationship with the media.

Media environments

The social and technological trends that forge the shape of the media are a constant factor in understanding the growth and practices of PR. The initial growth of PR as a profession was closely linked to the growth of literacy and the mass media. For example, in the first part of the twentieth century in the UK and Europe populations became increasingly literate and were winning the right to vote in elections. At the same time there was an associated rise of mass-circulation newspapers, followed by new broadcast technologies: first radio, and then television. In both business and politics mass public opinion mattered and the media were central to the flow of information and public debate. Concurrently, demand for professionals who help organisations participate and influence the new mediated democracies grew.

The structural relationships between the PR and media industries are constantly evolving in the context of rapidly shifting media landscapes. Not least by the way in which digital technology and social media are transforming the production of media content (see Box 2.3 Rise of the robots, page 34). Newspapers and the wider print media peaked in sales in the 1950s and have been in steady decline ever since. However, they remain significant, with close to half of UK adults reading a daily newspaper at least three times a week (DCMS 2015). In many countries newspapers have lost sales as readers stop buying printed editions in favour of reading web versions of the same title, while at the same time income from advertising has been lost to the tech giants such as Google and Facebook who promise advertisers they can locate their target audience with much more precision. Some newspapers have stopped printing and shifted to online only; many others have closed altogether, no longer considered economically viable by their parent company. But there is evidence to suggest that some mainstream media institutions have adapted to the new digital world, will do more than just survive and will continue to exert considerable influence over public information seeking or the process of **agenda setting**. The UK's *Guardian* newspaper has continually declined in physical sales since the 2000s, now selling well below 200,000 copies per day, but has found new success online with over 12 million unique browsers visiting its site every day. Likewise, the *Daily Mail* enjoys over 13 million unique browsers per week (*source:* newsworks.org.uk).

Radio remains a popular form of media that is distinctive for the way in which it is consumed when travelling to work in the car or in the workplace itself. The additional ability to broadcast digitally and through internet streams, alongside the availability to listeners of time-shifting listening through podcasts, have meant radio has been less vulnerable to losing its markets because of new technology. Likewise, television remains a mass medium, although patterns of viewing are shifting. There has been a decline in the time people spend watching TV on TV sets in recent years, alongside an increase in the use of the on-demand services that most broadcasters now provide. Nonetheless, there has begun to be a decline in the overall minutes per day people spend watching live or time-shifted TV,

Box 2.1

Newsprint in pain as the COVID-19 virus bites

The COVID-19 crisis hastened the structural changes already underway in newsprint media.

Newspaper circulation in the UK during the COVID-19 crisis was hit by as much as a third by newsagents closing and a reduction in footfall on the high street, across travel hubs and in supermarkets.

Commuter newspapers such as *City AM*, *The Evening Standard* and *The Metro* all lost their means of distribution. *City AM* temporarily stopped publishing and *The Evening Standard* has switched its central London distributors to door-to-door deliveries albeit with a much-reduced circulation.

Further financial pain was inflicted by advertisers who pulled campaigns, either because businesses themselves were impacted by the crisis, or they simply didn't want their brand appearing alongside COVID-19 news.

Local and national newsprint impacted

The crisis was indiscriminate in its impact on local and national media. According to the Reuters Institute for the Study of Journalism, the income for local media fell by 50 per cent and national media by 30 per cent.

Reach, one of the largest newspaper publishers, announced a pay cut of 20 per cent for directors, senior management and editorial staff, and 10 per cent for all other staff. A fifth of the staff were furloughed. Reach publishes *The Daily Mirror*, *The Daily Express* and the *Daily Star*, and regional titles including *The Manchester Evening News*, *Liverpool Echo*, *Birmingham Mail* and *Bristol Post*. Similar stories unfolded at local newspaper companies JPI Media and Newsquest.

Traffic to news websites surged during the crisis as people at home consumed news online but advertising revenues, where brands were prepared to invest during the crisis, were a fraction of print. This is the challenge that the news industry has faced since the advent of the internet. The COVID-19 crisis is hastening the digitisation of news from print to internet services. Few news organisations have been able to make the shift at the same time as maintaining revenue and profit. There are notable winner-takes-all exceptions such as *The Financial Times* and *The New York Times* that have successfully built value around the knowledge and expertise of their journalists. Long form, reflective and specialist news journalism also appear to be robust. *The Economist*, *Private Eye*, *The Spectator* and *The Week* are all holding ground.

The numbers no longer add up

The Reuters Institute suggests that newspapers account for about two-thirds of investment in news provision in the UK. Print accounts for 80 per cent of UK newspaper revenues and digital 20 per cent. The split in advertising is roughly equal.

The inescapable fact is that the news business will be a lot smaller and leaner than it has been in the past. The media think tank Nieman Lab goes further. It described the crisis as a potential extinction event for US print media.

(Nielsen 2020)

---

with UK viewers watching an average of 202 minutes per day (OFCOM 2018). Within this trend a steady decline in viewing figures for news programmes on television has been detected over the last five years, with a pronounced decline in viewing by younger people: 'while major television channels are still pulling in large audiences, these audiences are eroding and ageing while a range of new entrants seem to pick up younger audiences' (Nielsen and Sambrook 2016: 5). An important qualification of the trend towards online news sources is that social media is most often used for celebrity, music and fashion news, but TV is most often used for more serious current affairs news, and that also held true for children aged 12–15 (OFCOM 2019: 107).

In this new media environment, the traditional media institutions which survive increasingly find themselves in a much more complex network of producers of what can be considered as news and media content. This new media world includes citizen journalists, expert bloggers and organisations themselves as significant producers of content. PR practitioners are increasingly employing or commissioning journalists to produce that content. This trend sometimes is described as **brand journalism,** as organisations draw on journalistic skills of creating stories, distributed through their own communication channels that attract the attention of target publics. Some brands such as Red Bull have become prolific producers of TV, short movies, mobile video and game content (Verčič and Verčič 2015).

Exchange theories: the information subsidy

Exchange theories typically draw on the ideas and concepts used in economics, but they have been frequently applied to other academic fields. Exchange theories assume individuals or groups interact with each other by one side giving something and the other receiving it. In sociology, people can be rational pursuers of their goals who regularly exchange valuable resources with others if the transaction is believed to help move towards attaining those goals. For these social exchanges to become a regular interaction they need to constitute a mutually rewarding process for both sides (Blau 1964).

In the exchange between PR and journalism, PR provides an information subsidy. Gandy provides a general definition of this subsidy as reducing 'the prices faced by others for certain information in order to increase its consumption' (Gandy 1982: 12). The significance is that the information subsidy provides a framework for exploring how PR can reduce the amount of time it takes for journalists to identify topics and research stories; in exchange the journalist's media outlet supplies public attention to the information and messages that the PR practitioner would wish them to see (Fengler and Ruß-Mohl 2008). As Turk (1985) neatly summarises: 'Public relations practitioners use information subsidies to systematize their attempts, on behalf of the organisations and institutions for which they work, to influence media content and the opinions of those who rely upon the media for information' (Turk 1985: 12). To understand how information subsidies operate, see Box 2.2 on how PR helps journalists do their work.

The information subsidy can be seen as a mechanism to explain how elites dominate media spaces. Organisations that can dominate, or even flood, media spaces with their information and their interpretations of current affairs will be able to influence public life. PR-subsidised information and news reporting becomes an indirect subsidy for influential political or policy-making elites as they frequently rely on information provided by the media in their decision-making (Gandy 1992). But the information subsidy also helps us understand how relatively resource-poor charities, NGOs and community groups can influence public agendas. PR practitioners working for these organisations have found that providing an effective information subsidy on the issues and causes on which they campaign has influenced or even changed the language and assumptions used in media reports. Information subsidies as a PR strategy are open to both elites and 'outsiders' (Davis 2002). A constant information subsidy can also build legitimacy. Being regularly quoted or associated on stories about a topic builds the organisation's reputation for holding expertise on the issue or being accepted as holding an interest in helping find solutions to help communities perhaps negatively impacted upon by the issue.

Explore 2.1

Fracturing television audiences

On Christmas Day 1977 27 million people in the UK watched the television specials of both the Mike Yarwood and Morecambe and Wise Shows (Washbourne 2010). This was not only before the ability to digitally download and watch programmes later, but also before most households owned a VHS or Betamax video recorder. The viewing figures for these shows approached nearly half of the whole population. It was the zenith of popular TV programmes as events that made an impression on the whole nation and its cultural reference points. Today, TV audiences are dispersed over an increasing array of **terrestrial**, digital, satellite, cable, internet and other viewing options. Understanding changes in audience consumption habits is an important task for PR practitioners devising their media relations strategies. The most recent trends can be explored by reading the latest reports produced by OFCOM – the regulator of UK communications industries – at http://stakeholders.ofcom.org.uk/

Picture 2.1 TV shows such as Morecambe and Wise used to attract simultaneous audiences of more than 27 million (*source:* Moviestore Collection Ltd/Alamy Stock Photo)

Think about 2.1

Media systems

When thinking about PR's relationship with the **media**, it is always important not to assume the 'media' work in identical ways across time periods, geographies and cultures. The media clearly plays differing roles, depending on the country being considered. Hallin and Mancini (2004) famously tried to develop an academic framework for understanding, for any country, why the media are as they are. They did this by comparing the media systems of different countries and put forward four dimensions for analysing media systems. Brüggemann et al. (2014) amended and developed these further.

- *Inclusiveness of the press market* – the importance of differences in terms of how far the press is only read by local elites, or if they reach a broad audience with an emphasis on reaching working class and female readers.

- *Political parallelism* – this is an indicator to compare to what extent journalists see themselves as being close to and supportive of political parties. In turn, how far do they allow this support to influence their reporting? This dimension includes the extent of political bias in news reporting and the degree to which audiences choose to consume media that fit with their own political preferences.

- *Journalistic professionalism* – this dimension includes indicators of professionalism. For example, the degree to which journalists are autonomous – able to report independent of forces inside or outside of their news organisation, i.e. politicians, advertisers, media owners – as well as the degree of common ethical standards and orientation to serving the public interest.

- *Role of the state* – this more complex dimension centres on the extent and ways in different countries that the state attempts to intervene and influence the media. The state can intervene by supporting public service broadcasters such as the BBC, or it can attempt to help newspapers by providing subsidies. The state might censor and prevent critical reporting of leaders or their political parties. Many states have rules to prevent rich individuals or corporations owning too many newspapers or TV stations.

Using these four dimensions, how would you categorise and then compare the media in the UK, USA and Russia? (Of course, you can choose to compare other countries.) Are there differences in the *political parallelism* of journalists working on newspapers compared to broadcast journalists on radio and TV? How would a stronger understanding of the media systems in these countries influence the strategies pursued by PR campaigns?

Box 2.2

How PR can make news reporting faster and cheaper

PR practitioners help journalists in several ways:

- **The provision of information, statistics and fact checking for journalists:** When researching a story, journalists need to find out or reassure themselves about the latest facts and research about the issue at hand. Often through inter-personal communications they receive advice and data from PR practitioners. The relationship works if the journalist believes the PR practitioner will provide reliable information and is a legitimate source of expertise on the topic.

- **Picture and events:** All forms of media, including traditional printed newspapers, place a high value on securing striking visual images. Strong visuals help tell the story but can also help increase newsstand sales or lengthen the time an online visitor spends on their website. Hiring professional photographers or bringing lots of people together for a public event are costly in terms of both time and money. PR practitioners know any event that produces quality, perhaps quirky, picture opportunities will have a good chance of securing coverage in target media.

- **Real-life case studies:** One highly time-consuming task for journalists is to find real people who have been affected by the issue in their story. Not only that, they need to find real people who will agree to be quoted or be filmed talking about this issue. The task becomes harder as people will be naturally reluctant

→

> **box 2.1 (continued)**
>
> to talk publicly about some issues such as personal, financial or health problems. This explains why PR practitioners, in advance of issuing a news release or organising a publicity event, will work hard on identifying people who are prepared to talk to the media.
>
> - **Ideas for stories:** PR can also subsidise the creative process of forward planning future media content. In her 1999 study, Curtin found that, even if they didn't use any of their text, journalists were heavily reliant on looking at news releases sent to them by PR practitioners for ideas for new stories or features (Curtin 1999). This process also takes place in the interpersonal communications between practitioners and certain journalists who speak on a regular basis. These form opportunities to float or pitch story ideas to the journalist. This process widens involvement in the forward planning process, and would be a significant cost to the media organisation if they had to pay for this creative advice coming from PR.
>
> - **Interviews and quotes:** A typically structured news story will include quotes from relevant people, including senior leaders in organisations involved in the event. PR speeds up the process of asking for a quote in response to an issue or story by supplying and distributing these quotes. Many organisational news releases consist just of a quote from a senior figure responding to a news event. Longer form interviews are also a regular media format and the process of finding and organising these interviews can be simplified and accelerated by PR practitioners.

Some PR departments, such as government departments (ministries) or global corporations, publish huge amounts of information, with new exchanges taking place with journalists on an hourly basis. This presents government communicators with the opportunity to use their position to develop news management strategies. Looking at the communications of the British government, Gaber (2000) was usefully able to break down news management strategies into their constituent parts. To begin with, PR departments who handle the publication of a large amount of information will, as much as possible, time announcements to maximum effect. Sometimes this will be to ensure maximum media coverage for an important or positive event; on other occasions practitioners might release stories as a 'firebreak' to divert attention away from other perhaps embarrassing stories. Equally, they will also sometimes pre-empt Sunday newspaper exclusives by releasing the story themselves on the Friday or Saturday. The story is still a negative one for the department, but an element of control has been reasserted by choosing when and how the information is released. Alternatively, disappointing statistics or reports can be released and buried while journalists are concentrating on another bigger event. Message coordination is another strategy: sometimes in the fear that different employees or representatives will provide journalists with conflicting viewpoints, the PR team will use internal communications to ensure anyone who speaks to the media is emphasising the desired message or narrative. These strategies can annoy and frustrate journalists, but a bigger source of tension in the relationship can come when PR practitioners attempt to reward or punish journalists for the content of their previous stories. For example, refusing to reward a journalist with an exclusive story because of unhappiness with their previous writing. The more a journalist is dependent on the information subsidy provided by PR, then in theory the more there is scope for PR departments to implement proactive, or what some might consider aggressive, news management strategies.

It is worth noting that the information subsidy is equally useful as a concept for exploring the relationship between PR practitioners working in public affairs and lobbying and their relationships with policy-makers and politicians. In this context, PR provides a constant supply of research that decision-makers rely on to make sense of current or future policy options (Gandy 1992). In media relations, PR seeks to provide information to journalists which fit with their concepts of what makes something newsworthy; in public affairs, PR will translate information to show how it helps policy-makers understand and solve problems facing society, with the prospect of PR departments gaining a competitive advantage over their rivals if successful (Davidson and Rowe 2015).

Finally, to conclude this section, as ever, it is important to consider social, economic, political and cultural contexts before assuming any concept might be universally applied to all relationships between PR and the media. Consider that, although most journalists and PR practitioners across the globe do not believe it is professional for the media to accept payments from PR sources in return for publishing a story, international surveys have found the practice to be widespread. This practice includes PR news releases being published in exchange for paid advertisements in the same media outlet or direct payments to a journalist by a news source (Tsetsura 2008). For example, in Russia, payments, either directly or through patronage, are accepted as routine by some journalists (Pasti 2005) and there is a documented history in southern Europe of payments of cash to journalists from grateful connections (Hallin and Papathanassopoulos 2002).

These differences can be an important difficulty for PR practitioners working across intercultural locations. As Fitch (2012) discovered, attitudes and expectations in relation to PR departments paying for journalists to write a story which clashes with the ethical norms of other PR practitioners, and the determination of some organisations to refuse to make such payments – even if they are non-controversial in a localised context. Where cash payments to journalists are widespread, there needs to be caution in assuming that an exchange took place primarily because PR practitioners were able to produce and subsidise genuinely newsworthy content.

Agenda setting and framing

Agenda setting

While exchange theories such as the information subsidy help explore and understand why PR practitioners have such a close working relationship with journalists, this section will look at what theories might help assess further how this might translate into influencing the way in which successful media relations strategies could be a significant factor in shifting or entrenching public opinion on various issues. The first of these will be the concept of *agenda setting*.

As communication studies moved away from making simplistic assumptions that media content would directly mould public opinion, there was a shift to theories that accepted that **media effects** were highly contingent on several factors. Agenda setting attracted interest and became credible because there appeared to be a strong link between issues that were prominent in news media and how audiences ranked the importance of issues that faced society (McCombs and Shaw 1972). For example, influential studies of TV news in the USA found that news programmes affect which social problems viewers believe to be the most important, and suggested problems that were the subject of prominent coverage on evening news bulletins were accorded more weight in how audiences evaluated the performance of the president (Iyengar et al. 1982). As Cohen (1963) so neatly summarised the concept: media content does not successfully tell audiences *what to think,* but can be stunningly successful in telling audiences *what to think about.* But, as we will see, the power to influence what audiences think about, in the right circumstances, will also impact on what they believe should happen about that issue.

The logical assumption behind agenda setting is that the process of the media frequently reporting and discussing certain issues will mean that large segments of the public will come to perceive these issues as being more important than others. It should also be noted that there is not a singular agenda – different

---

Think about 2.2

PR paying journalists' 'expenses'

1. Press releases are still a common feature of media relations in China; however, the host of a press event is expected to pay a travel allowance to journalists. This is typically around £50 to £200 depending on the seniority of the journalist.
2. (In China) Newspaper and magazine advertising departments continue to openly discuss their rates – even when a researcher making inquiries identifies herself as working for The New York Times . . . an account manager at Yashi Media, a Beijing agency that helps companies obtain coverage in print and broadcast media . . . said . . . 'If your boss wants to comment on something brief and we shoot him in a news program for 15 seconds, it would be $9,000. And if your boss wants an exclusive interview for 10 minutes, the rate is much higher.' (Source: Barboza, D. (2012). In China Press, best coverage cash can buy. *New York Times*, 3 April 2012. Available at: http://www.nytimes.com/2012/04/04/business/media/flattering-news-coverage-has-a-price-in-china.html?)

Can handing over envelopes full of cash to journalists to write stories be justified if other companies are also doing it? Or if it helps boost the income of reporters on low pay? What ethical responsibility do PR practitioners working for international brands have regarding the reliability of the media in countries such as China? Does the existence of this practice mean information subsidy theories need updating?

communities and sectors of society will each hold a variation in the configuration of issues they perceive to be important. So, for example, as well as the general public agenda, there will be a policy agenda for people involved in government and public affairs (Coleman et al. 2009). Put another way, this is a process where real-world issues are drawn to the attention of the media by organisations through their use of media relations strategies: the media increases its coverage of the issue; in turn, the media coverage amplifies the public's interaction with the issue in its real-world context; finally, an opinion leader, such as a large organisation or government, reacts to the rising public interest/concern (Johnson et al. 1996).

Fake news and agenda setting

Ethical PR relies on the integrity and trust of mainstream media in order to convey information to publics and to attempt to influence agendas in a manner that enables citizens to make informed decisions.

Historical processes for inhibiting the flow of misinformation to the public have been weakened and the problem of 'fake news' has become a prominent feature of current events. Fake news is a widely used phrase which has been open to abuse. To identify the problem of fake news and find ways of fighting back against misinformation we need to share a proper definition and understanding of the phenomenon.

Explore 2.2 The public versus other agendas

There is no one public agenda that accurately describes the priority concerns of all citizens. Differing sections of society will have variations in the issues they believe to be the most important, as well as differing views on what should be done about those issues.

There are several freely available resources to help us research the issues, concerns and attitudes of the public, the media and of those in politics and policy-making. Here are some suggestions.

Public attitudes

- British Social Attitudes – an annual survey looking at a wide range of social and political attitudes in the UK: http://www.natcen.ac.uk/
- Pew Research Center – conducts regular surveys of public opinion and attitudes in the USA: http://www.pewresearch.org/
- The polling and research company YouGov publish regular updates on the results of their work.
- YouGov findings on social attitudes: https://yougov.co.uk/
- YouGov data on public responses to issues affecting brands in the news: https://yougov.co.uk/topics/consumer/all
- Every month for decades the research company Ipsos MORI have been asking people what they believe are the most important issues facing Britain. Their results from 1974 until the current day are available on their website: https://www.ipsos-mori.com/researchpublications/

Media and policy agendas

There are several high-quality email newsletters that can be subscribed to that offer daily summaries of what issues are high on the media agenda and how politicians are responding. Two good examples are the daily email from Paul Waugh on the *Huffington Post* and the alerts from the policy and politics news organisation Politico.

- Paul Waugh of the *Huffington Post* daily briefing: sign up by visiting: huff.to/1CKGj5Y
- Politico have several email briefings you can subscribe to, including the daily London Playbook on what is happening in politics and media in the UK: https://www.politico.eu/

To complement the briefings from journalists, daily summaries from authoritative websites attached to the major political parties are also a good information resource:

- Sign up for the daily email from LabourList via: http://labourlist.org/
- Sign up for the daily email from ConservativeHome via: http://www.conservativehome.com/
- The Secretary General of the United Nations produces a daily briefing which gives insights into what is on the international agenda: http://www.un.org/press/en/content/noon-briefings

In addition to searching for stories and topics on newspaper websites, for students most university libraries subscribe to databases that allow you to search newspaper and magazine archives.

What is immediately obvious is that fake news can't be simply defined as information that you don't agree with. The core feature of fake news is that it is information that imitates the forms of traditional news media content – it is very easy to set up websites to look like they might be a mainstream magazine or news organisation – but does not have journalism's norms for ensuring the accuracy of the information (Lazer et al. 2018).

News fabrication is the main category of fake news that causes concern. Articles that are often deliberately deceptive, published in the style of news articles to create legitimacy. The producer of this kind of fake news has the intention of misinforming, in contrast to, according to Tandoc et al. (2018), categorisations of fake news such as news satire and parody content that is popular on social media. Producers of satire and parody content primarily promote themselves as a form of entertainment that uses humour or exaggeration to provide critiques of current affairs and politicians. TV satire such as the *Mash Report* in the UK or the *Daily Show* in the USA mimic news formats but sketches are usually backed up by research. Parody media such as *Private Eye* or *The Onion* might use non-factual information to generate their humour. But neither satire nor parody content typically seeks to pass itself as real news content (Tandoc et al. 2018).

Part of the problem of fake news is how successfully it gets amplified and spread around the internet. False information generates more retweets than true information and bots – automated social media accounts that impersonate humans – are estimated to be more than 10 per cent of Twitter accounts and as many as 60 million have been found on Facebook (Lazer et al. 2018). Fake news sites can be influential through their relationship with partisan media, that is blogs, social media accounts and websites who frame stories to advance an ideological or some other belief standpoint. Partisan media inspire fake news sites and conversely popular fake news memes impact on the content of partisan media, who in turn then influence the agendas and talking points of mainstream media (Thurman and Fletcher 2019). These circuits are further amplified as research is finding that 'people prefer information that confirms their pre-existing attitudes. . . view information consistent with their pre-existing beliefs as more persuasive. . . and are inclined to accept information that pleases them' (Lazer et al. 2018: 1095). The quality of decision making, and the trust in both PR and journalism is undermined by the prevalence of misinformation circulating online. Fake news should also be understood as unethical attempts at agenda setting.

Framing

PR practitioners are not simply supplying an information subsidy for an issue to gain media attention; they also pay great attention to assessing how this coverage could best advance their objectives on any given issue of the day. For any PR campaign, the objective will be to do more than merely set the agenda: framing theory provides a framework for exploring how issues are framed in order to build consensus on what needs to be done. **Framing** assumes that differences in how information is presented to us will influence the decisions we make. Research evidence suggesting variations in how information is presented on essentially identical decision-making scenarios will influence audience choices (Scheufele and Tewksbury 2006).

Framing involves a process of strategically highlighting a few elements of perceived reality and assembling a narrative that highlights connections among them to promote an interpretation, a decision to select some aspects of a perceived reality and make them more salient in a communicating text (Entman 1993). Entman suggested that fully developed frames typically perform four functions: *problem definition,* usually succinctly summarising a problem and the negative costs of its impact; *causal analysis* that suggests who or what is creating the problem; *moral judgments* are intimated regarding the people or values being associated with the cause of the problem; and *remedy promotion* where the frame suggests actions that would solve or at least alleviate the problem. But also, we can understand the mechanics of how framing influences public opinion through *priming*: 'frames *introduce or raise the salience or apparent importance of certain ideas, activating schemas that encourage target audiences to think, feel, and decide in a particularly way*' (Entman 2007: 164). So, in that way we can understand that the objective of media relations components of PR campaigns is to frame and prime and this makes it patently clear why PR practitioners typically take great care when selecting the words, visuals and message medium.

One essential element to framing theory is that PR campaigns, and their attempts to frame issues, take place in highly competitive environments. For any significant social or economic issue there will be differences of opinion with some groups likely to benefit, but equally some likely to lose out, depending on what policies are adopted. So, it will frequently be the case that the public will see and hear competing frames that make contradictory claims and recommendations for action. Chong and Druckman (2007) explored this aspect of framing by considering the issue of a hate group wanting to march through a town centre. This could be framed

> ### Think about 2.3
>
> ### Framing
>
> Entman's model of framing suggests frames typically perform four functions:
>
> - problem definition
> - causal analysis
> - moral judgement
> - remedy promotion.
>
> Consider the following three alternative descriptions of the same incident. Each accounts highlights or omits relevant information. For each account, how might an audience be expected to respond using Entman's four functions of framing?
>
> **Description 1:** An infant left sleeping in his cot was bitten repeatedly by rats while his 16-year-old mother went to a local post office to pick up a welfare payment. A neighbour had to respond to the cries of the abandoned child and took him to the local hospital.
>
> **Description 2:** An eight-month-old boy was treated in hospital yesterday after being bitten by rats while sleeping in his cot. Other tenants living in neighbouring flats said that repeated requests for the landlord to organise a visit from pest control had been ignored. Meanwhile, the landlord claimed that the tenants had ignored her reminders to properly dispose of their rubbish.
>
> **Description 3:** Rats bit eight-month old Michael Burns five times yesterday as he napped in his cot. Burns is the latest victim of a rat epidemic plaguing inner-city neighbourhoods. A spokesperson for the city council explained that central government cut backs had led to short-staffing at pest control and environmental health departments. A spokesperson for the local hospital confirmed admissions due to rodent bites had doubled over the last two years.
>
> *Source:* Adapted from Ryan (1991)

to them in order to ensure the media use their framing of an issue. For example, some PR practitioners will have access to greater resources to research the frames that appeal the most to the public or recruit important personalities or celebrities to help generate media interest (Chong and Wolinsky-Nahmias 2003).

Power shift towards public relations practitioners

Research and debates around concepts such as the information subsidy, agenda-setting and framing have recently been contextualised by what some believe is a power shift away from journalism and towards public relations. The speculation on the changing power relationships is grounded in how changes in economics and technology have impacted upon the news media as an industry.

Academics have long been interested in understanding how much news content is the result of proactive journalistic inquiry, and what proportion originates from the activities of public relations practitioners. This question is seen as important by some as it might indicate who is setting public agendas and the balance between 'pure' news values driving the agenda versus the possibility that outside interest groups are successfully moulding news agendas. Some believe PR's power over the media is a modern reality with a 'PR-saturated media environment' (Davis 2002) where 'Journalists . . . have generally become mere passive processors of unchecked, second-hand material, much of it contrived by PR to serve some political or commercial interest' (Davies 2008).

There is some longstanding evidence for the ability of PR to influence media content. In the 1970s it was estimated 45 per cent of newspaper stories originated in PR materials (Cutlip 1976), which were also highly influential on the content of TV news (Golding and Elliot 1979). One study tracked press releases and found that more than 98 per cent were successful in generating media interest, with up to 70 per cent of the content of some small trade, specialist and suburban media being sourced from PR activity (Macnamara 1993). Changes in the economic models of the media may have increased PR's influence. One more recent, and influential, study (Lewis et al. 2008) found that national newspapers in the UK on average included 24.4 pages of content, not including adverts; the number of pages had increased 30 years later to 41.0. However, the number of journalists employed by the newspapers has not increased in the same way and

as an issue of the right to free speech, or one of a threat to public safety. Some members of the public could potentially agree that both free speech and public safety are important to them. With such a conflict of reasonable arguments, individuals will tend to assess which frame is closest to their own personal values.

However, this is not to say that all organisations will have the same opportunity or resources available

journalists are expected to fill more pages. If we consider that it is also normal practice now for national newspaper journalists to write additional stories that are only published on the web version of the paper and also contribute to the production of video and podcast content, we can see how they might lack the space and time to do extensive research for new stories, and so accordingly may become more reliant on the information subsidy produced by PR. As with other debates about the extent of PR's ability to exert communicative power, in regard to the power to influence media content, PR's influence is highly contingent – it depends on a number of factors. PR practitioners are sometimes portrayed as being in some form of ascendency where they can manipulate and exploit beleaguered journalists desperate for news content. However, after conducting a set of interviews, Jackson and Moloney (2015) found that practitioners were telling them that they believed journalists working on national newspapers were still powerful and independent figures and, furthermore, the growth of the use of PR by all kinds of organisations meant that journalists were in a position to select from a large number of well-pitched story ideas. Although journalists working for national newspapers may retain much of their power, in other types of media the journalists could be said to hold much more subservient roles. For example, in the entertainment industry where it was revealed during the proceedings of the Leveson Inquiry into the culture, practices and ethics of the press, the high proportion of stories that appear in celebrity-focused magazines that are pre-agreed – that is to say a process of copy approval took place where the PR representative would have the right to see the story before it was printed and be able to suggest changes they wanted to see, or withdraw the magazine's right to print the interview. The editors of *Hello!* and *OK!* magazines told the inquiry that between 70 and 80 per cent of celebrity stories or interviews were pre-agreed with PR representatives (Leveson Inquiry 2012). This strongly suggests that, in contrast to the independence of the national news media, PR practitioners can exert high degrees of control over journalists working for entertainment and celebrity-focused magazines (see also Chapter 27 'Celebrity public relations').

A combination of structural changes to the PR and media industries is leading many to believe that PR is increasingly able to exert high levels of influence over journalists. These changes are driven by continuing growth in the employment of PR practitioners by large organisations, but also by the realisation by smaller organisations that good media relations strategies might allow them to punch above their weight. At the same time there has been a decline in editorial resources. Some forms of media, such as local newspapers, have lost readers and advertising income to the internet and have reduced staffing levels. Finally, organisations can also create their own media content and distribute this to their publics via websites and social media platforms.

Mediatisation

The theories and concepts that have been the focus so far for this chapter are without doubt valid and useful for studying the way the PR and media industries have become so closely intertwined. However, there is a potential problem in the way that they could suggest that the relationship was a binary one, where if one side is gaining power, then automatically that must mean the other side is losing influence. Exchange theories, agenda setting and framing are clearly useful theories for understanding day-to-day PR–media interactions and for exploring the contests to influence the production of media content. But what if the relationship was less of an exchange or a power struggle, but was instead more of a free-flowing circuit of interaction and influence, with no visible joins or borders between the two industries? This final section will look at the process that arises out of the actions initiated by organisations who believe the media is powerful, and because of this power they place considerable effort in trying to influence the media, so much effort that they begin to mirror or internalise the media's logics, values and assumptions.

Mediatisation theory can broadly be separated into an institutional and a social-constructivist tradition (Hepp and Krotz 2014). The focus here is the institutional paradigm which assumes the media are

Picture 2.2 The fragmentation of media has led many to believe that PR practitioners have an assertive role (*source:* Thinglass/Shutterstock)

a network of independent social institutions that operate according to their own sets of rules and practices. Together these rules constitute media logic. Organisations will need to understand and make compromises with media logic if they want to be recognised and attain media coverage of their brand or issue. There is also the social-constructivist paradigm, which places the media as holding a ubiquitous presence in everyday life and as such the media have become central to the social construction of reality. As Hjarvard summarises, overall mediatisation can be defined as 'the process whereby culture and society to an increasing degree become dependent on the media and their logic in that the media have become integrated into the operations of other social institutions as a consequence [. . .] social interactions [. . .] increasingly take place via the media' (Hjarvard 2013: 17).

Institutional mediatisation and media logic

Institutional mediatisation is primarily concerned with understanding the rules and routines that underpin media practice and how organisations and social institutions adapt themselves in order to fit in with media logic. PR practitioners can be conceptualised as boundary spanners who attempt to harmonise and reconcile the logic and needs of their own organisations to the logic and the needs of the media. Because media coverage is frequently viewed as a vital component in any issue campaign or branding exercise, PR is at the forefront of accommodating the logic of news values, editorial routines and journalistic techniques for storytelling. Indeed, this is an important way of conceptualising the media's power over PR: the media are powerful exactly because people and organisations will adapt to their logic (Altheide and Snow 1979). In many modern societies the ability to secure media attention is a vital component of potential influence, so PR practitioners across various sectors, but particularly those who wish to influence public opinion on issues and policies, place a high value on publicity initiatives and building relationships with journalists. They do so in the understanding that their competitors are seeking to implement a similar strategy and that to be successful their events and news content need to conform to the logic of their target media (Blumler and Gurevitch 1996).

Some caution is required. There could never be a single unified media logic, one that applied equally to all media institutions in all situations. Also, it would be unwise to assume all PR practitioners work for organisations who will always automatically bend to media logic, not least because their organisation and the sector within which it is located, is likely to also hold their own needs and logic.

One important area for studying this issue has been in assessing how the logics of the media and of politics intermittently clash or harmonise with each other. In politics, the primary focus is on issues and problems that face society, with processes and motivations centred on potential solutions and the need to gain legitimacy for a chosen path of action (Patterson 1993). In any country, Strömbäck (2008) has argued that the degree to which politics has been mediatised depends on four factors: 1) how far the media are the most important source of information on political issues; 2) the level of media independence from political control; 3) the degree to which the media themselves accept political logic when reporting on issues; 4) conversely, the degree to which politicians believe they need to bend to media logic to be successful.

Mini case study 2.1
How mediatisation impacts on the work of civil servants in Norway

Research in Norway (Thorbjørnsrud et al. 2014) has found how media logic transfers, initially via the PR and communications department, and alters the daily practices, routines and priorities of civil servants. The study focused on the daily working practices of civil servants working in two organisations: the Norwegian Ministry of Justice and the Directorate of Immigration.

The researchers identified four characteristics of a process of intensifying mediatisation of the working lives of civil servants. The first characteristic was an *adaptation to the rhythm of news*. Interaction with journalists has become part of the normal daily routine of civil servants. In contrast to some of the long-term projects that civil servants are working on, journalists are typically working to tight deadlines and expect a quick response to their requests. Attending to these urgent deadlines meant that other important tasks would be delayed and, even though civil servants would initially ask the journalists to speak to the PR team, they would still be needed if the journalist required a detailed briefing on a policy or set of statistics. Because the needs of the media were being attended to daily, pressure was exerted on the civil servants to come up with ideas for positive news stories about the work of their organisation. The second characteristic was the *visible adaptation of the language and format of* news. News writing is typically short form and favours simplicity, use of everyday language and is centred on personalised stories and narratives. In contrast, following the logic of good governance, civil servants are orientated towards correctly following procedures and producing comprehensive documents full of information and often using technical or legalistic language in order to be compliant with legislative requirements. In order to improve the daily interactions with journalists, media training is organised for civil servants by their PR colleagues and this has started to impact on their style of writing, often adopting journalistic styles when communicating directly with the public. The third characteristic is a *belief in the significance of news*. In this instance civil servants, politicians and communications staff accept and invite the media to carry out its democratic function of being a **watchdog** scrutinising the work of government. But, also the politicians with power over civil servants see the media as vital in managing their own reputation or issue campaigns. Consequently, this belief in the legitimacy and significance of the news media leads to the fourth characteristic, the *reallocation of resources and responsibilities*. Most obviously this has resulted in increasing financial and time resources being devoted to media relations. But, this effect also manifests itself in changes to the personal skill sets seen as important for senior civil service jobs, such as the ability to work quickly in order to respond to fast-moving 24-hour news cycles. The research also tells us that if an issue is gaining a lot of media attention, this issue becomes a priority, not just for PR staff, but for non-communications civil servants who will prioritise the issue over others. For example, when the media take an interest in an individual immigration case involving a family, this would be brought to the front of the queue for attention, raising the prospect that the decision on immigration status might result in a different outcome than the one likely if there had been no media interest.

Source: Thorbjørnsrud, K., T. U. Figenschou and Ø. Ihlen, (2014). Operationalizing mediatization: A typology of mediatization in public bureaucracies. Communications: The European Journal of Communication Research, 39(1), 3-22

Mediatisation is an overarching theoretical concept which can be used to study any of the relationships and interactions between media and PR, as well as how these relate to cultural or technological change in society. As seen in this section, the continual process of mediated social change has prompted organisations to draw on PR expertise to understand how they might be able to *accommodate* media logic. The role the media play in social change also applies to: how it *extends* human communication capacity with increasing time and space; the manner in which the media *substitute* social activities such as online banking in place of high street banks, or apps for internet chat replacing face-to-face conversation; and the *amalgamation* or merger of media and non-media activities such as jogging and listening to the radio, or watching TV while simultaneously discussing TV on a social media platform (Schulz 2004).

Through the combination of the information subsidy and the relentless activism and creativity of PR practitioners, it could be argued that the mainstream media have become dependent on PR. Mediatisation suggests this comes at the cost to organisations of privileging media conceptions of what constitutes a news story (news values), and the best timing of an event (news routines). But, this process should not be in any way a neutral or objective process – power is a constant variable when attempting to understand PR's interaction with the social world. Some PR practitioners work for powerful organisations with a high profile; others work for smaller organisations who may need to engage, sometimes reluctantly, with powerful media institutions. As Bentele and Nothaft (2008: 36) summarise: 'While one organisation may be very powerful and able to impose its own rules on journalists, another organisation may find it necessary to make concessions in order to attract any journalistic attention at all.' This could lead to a belief that there exists in some form a mutually influential relationship between PR practitioners and journalists, although caution is required as there is no reason to believe this in any way translates into constituting a balanced or mutually beneficial relationship, or indeed, one that might meet normative expectations of producing media content that informs or empowers citizens in a democracy.

Finally, as mentioned earlier in this chapter, digital technology and social media are transforming journalism and public relations. A glimpse into the changing methods of media and PR content production, discussed in Box 2.3, suggests that a chapter on PR and the media may look very different in the future.

Box 2.3

Rise of the robots: how algorithms are influencing journalism and PR

Although still in its early stages, we can see the emergence of a wave of automation in the generation of media content, and in the way citizens encounter and discursively interact with PR content. By automation we mean how software and technology is used to support, and replace, the need for human workers. Part of this process is the role of algorithms.

These are rules which tell social media and other digital apps how to respond to data generated on the internet; for example, Google and Facebook use algorithms to determine what content is giving the most prominence on user accounts, often creating *filter bubbles* where the algorithm chooses to highlight content and viewpoints which it believes the user already agrees with or likes. Some examples of this trend are outlined below.

'Robot journalism'

The news wire service Associated Press (AP) have already begun to publish stories written by 'robots'. Working with a company called Automated Insights, AP now uses 'automation technology' to regularly convert financial data in news stories on subjects such as corporate results and estimates for future share earnings. In 2011 Statsheet began to use algorithms to automatically generate stories and baseball match reports based on game statistics and a set of stock phrases (van Dalen 2012). Significantly Clerwall (2014) found that readers were not able to tell apart automated content from content written by a human.

'Robot PR'

As algorithmic journalism evolves, so we see mirror trends in PR.

The PR industry is driven by a need to understand and interpret shifts in public attitudes and behaviours. Digital technology has opened huge flows of potentially useful data to practitioners, particularly in relation to sentiment expression on social media. Several companies seek to monetise this demand by offering, often rather rudimentary, analysis that assists sense-making of online content, which is then utilised to categorise citizens into segmented clusters. This has begun to enable the automation of the creation of media content that is targeted and transmitted to individuals. At the time of writing this chapter (2019), the cosmetic brand Dove tracked tweets that were possible utterances by females of negative self-esteem, which then automatically generated 'positive' advice tweets in response.

At the level of global geo-politics both the US and Russian governments have been documented as developing programmes of 'online persona management', or in more everyday language, armies of 'sock puppets': creating feasible online personas so that comments and opinions can be posted on newspaper websites that appear to be from real people.

Communicators are also using algorithms alongside 'nudge' theories to design online interactions with content to prompt publics into making 'better' decisions in areas such as health and personal finance.

Think about 2.4

Kaku (2014) argues that no one is going to accidentally build a robot, or an algorithm, that wants to rule the world; for that to happen, first someone would need to build a 'super-bad robot', before that someone must build a 'mildly bad robot' and before that a 'not-so-bad robot'. Think about the quote from Kaku: in what ways will the automation of news and information benefit society, but equally, what are the potential risks or unintended outcomes?

Summary

This chapter locates a large proportion of the PR industry and its practitioners as holding a close, rather symbiotic relationship with the media. Indeed, the line between 'real' journalism and the informational or promotional content produced by PR practitioners is increasingly blurred. It has examined several theoretical approaches for understanding the relationship between PR and the media, in the process providing conceptual tools for exploring the debates around if and how PR is able to influence media content, and in turn, public attitudes to issues or brands. When thinking critically about PR and the media this chapter provides tools to support discussions and debates as to whether their relationship is beneficial or harmful to modern, democratic societies. Finally, this chapter briefly considers how both journalism and PR are being shaped by developments in digital technology and social media.

Bibliography

Altheide, D. and R. Snow (1979). *Media Logic*. Beverly Hills, CA: Sage Publications.

Bentele, G. and H. Nothaft (2008). The intereffication model: Theoretical discussions and empirical research in Zerfass et al. (Eds.), Public relations research: European and international perspectives and innovations. VS: Wiesbaden (2008), pp. 33–47

Blau, P. (1964). *Exchange and Power in Social Life*. New York: Wiley

Blumler, J. and M. Gurevitch (1996) Media Change and Social Change: Linkages and Junctures. In: Curran, J. and M. Gurevitch (eds.) *Mass Media and Society*. London: Edward Arnold.

Brüggemann, M., S. Engesser, F., Büchel, E. Humprecht and L. Castro (2014). Hallin and Mancini revisited: Four empirical types of western media systems. *Journal of Communication* 64(6): 1037–65.

Chong, D. and J. Druckman (2007). Framing theory. *Annual Review of Political Science* 10 (2007): 103–26.

Chong, D. and Y. Wolinsky-Nahmias (2003). Framing the growth debate. Paper presented at the Annual Meeting of the American Political Science Association, Philadelphia, 28–31 August 2003.

Clerwall, C. (2014). Enter the Robot Journalist. *Journalism* 8(5).

Cohen, B. (1963). *The Press and Foreign Policy*. Princeton, Princeton University Press.

Coleman et al. (2009). Agenda setting. Chapter 11 in Wahl-Jorgensen, K. and T. Hanitzsch (Eds.) *The Handbook of Journalism Studies*. London: Routledge.

Curtin, P.A. (1999). Re-evaluating public relations information subsidies: Market-driven journalism and agenda-building theory and practice. *Journal of Public Relations Research* 11(1): 53–90.

Cutlip, S. (1976). Public relations in the government. *Public Relations Review* 2(2), 5–28.

Davidson, S. and O. Rowe (2015). 'Emerging from the shadows? Perceptions, problems and potential consensus on the functional and civic roles of public affairs practice'. Accepted for publication September 2015, *Public Relations Inquiry*.

Davies, N. (2008). 'Our Media have Become Mass Producers of Distortion'. *The Guardian*, 4 February 2008.

Davies, N. (2011). *Flat Earth News: An award-winning reporter exposes falsehood, distortion and propaganda in the global media*. Chicago: Random House.

Davis, A. (2002). *Public Relations Democracy: Public Relations, Politics and the Mass Media in Britain*. Manchester University Press.

DCMS. (2015). *Taking Part 2014/15, Focus on Newspaper Readership*. Department for Culture, Media and Sport. Statistical Release. November 2015.

Entman, R.M. (2007). Framing bias: Media in the distribution of power. *Journal of Communication* 57(1): 163–73.

Fengler, S. and S. Ruß-Mohl (2008). Journalists and the information-attention markets: Towards an economic theory of journalism. *Journalism* 9(6): 667–90.

Fitch, K. (2012). Industry perceptions of intercultural competence in Singapore and Perth. *Public Relations Review* 38(4): 609–18.

Gaber (2000). Government by spin: an analysis of the process. Media, *Culture & Society* 22(4): 507–18.

Gandy, O.H. (1982). *Beyond Agenda Setting: Information Subsidies and Public Policy*. Norwood, NJ: Ablex.

Gandy, O.H. (1992). Public relations and public policy: The structuration of dominance in the information age. In E.L. Toth and R.L. Heath (Eds.), *Rhetorical and Critical Approaches to Public Relations* (pp. 131–164). Hillsdale, NJ: Lawrence Erlbaum Associates, Inc.

Golding, P. and P. Elliott (1979). *Making the News*. London: Longman.

Hallin, D. and S. Papathanassopoulos (2002). Political clientelism and the media: Southern Europe and Latin America in comparative perspective. *Media, culture & society* 24(2), 175–95.

Hallin, D. and P. Mancini (2004). *Comparing Media Systems: Three Models of Media and Politics.* Cambridge: Cambridge University Press.

Hepp, A. and F. Krotz (2014) 'Mediatized worlds: Understanding everyday mediatization', in A. Hepp and F. Krotz (eds.) *Mediatized Worlds: Culture and society in a media age.* London: Palgrave, pp. 1–15.

Hjarvard, S. (2013) *The Mediatization of Culture and Society.* London: Routledge.

Ihlen, Ø. and J. Pallas (2014). Mediatization of corporations. In K. Lundby (Ed.), *Handbook on Mediatization of Communication.* Berlin: De Gruyter Mouton, pp. 423–41.

Iyengar, S., D.R. Kinder and M. Peters (1982). Experimental Demonstrations of the 'Not-So-Minimal' Consequences of Television News Programs. *The American Political Science Review* 76(4): 848–858.

Kaku, M. (2014). *The Future of the Mind.* New York: Doubleday.

Leveson Inquiry (2012). Leveson Inquiry: Culture, Practices and Ethics of the Press. November 2012. Transcript of Morning Hearing 18 January 2012.

Jackson, D. and Moloney, K. (2015). Inside Churnalism: PR, journalism and power relationships in flux. *Journalism Studies* (ahead-of-print), 1–18.

Johnson, T., W. Wanta, T. Boudreau, J. Blank-Libra, K. Schaffer and S. Turner (1996). Influence dealers. A path analysis model of agenda building during Richard Nixon's war on drugs. *Journalism and Mass Communication Quarterly* 73: 181–94.

Lazer, D.M., M. A. Baum, Y. Benkler, A.J. Berinsky, K.M. Greenhill, F. Menczer and M. Schudson (2018). The science of fake news. *Science*, 359(6380): 1094–96.

Lewis, J., A. Williams, B. Franklin, J. Thomas and M. Mosdel (2008). The Quality and Independence of British Journalism. Mediawise report. http://www.cardiff.ac.uk/jomec/resources/QualityIndependenceofBritishJournalism.pdf.

Macnamara, J. (1993). Public relations and the media: A new influence in agenda-setting and content. Unpublished master's thesis, Deakin University, Geelong, Australia.

McCombs, M. and D. Shaw (1972). The Agenda-Setting Function of the Mass Media. *Public Opinion Quarterly* 36(2): 176–817.

Nielsen, R. (2020). What will the coronavirus pandemic mean for the business of news? Reuters Institute for the Study of Journalism, 25 March 2020. https://reutersinstitute.politics.ox.ac.uk/risj-review/what-will-coronavirus-pandemic-mean-business-news [accessed 29 April 2020].

Nielsen, R.K. and R. Sambrook (2016). *What is happening to television news?* Reuters Institute for the Study of Journalism.

OFCOM (2018). *Media Nations: UK 2018.* OFCOM 2018. Available for download at: https://www.ofcom.org.uk/__data/assets/pdf_file/0014/116006/media-nations-2018-uk.pdf

OFCOM (2019) Children and parents: Media use and attitudes report 2019. https://www.ofcom.org.uk/research-and-data/media-literacy-research/childrens/children-and-parents-media-use-and-attitudes-report-2019

Pasti, S. (2005) Two Generations of Contemporary Russian Journalists, *European Journal of Communication* 80(1): 89–115.

Patterson, T. (1993). *Out of Order.* New York: Vintage.

Ryan, C. (1991). *Prime Time Activism: Media strategies for grassroots organizing.* Boston: South End Press.

Scheufele, D.A. and D. Tewksbury (2006). Framing, agenda setting, and priming: The evolution of three media effects models. *Journal of Communication* 57(1): 9–20.

Schulz, W. (2004). Reconstructing mediatization as an analytical concept. *European Journal of Communication* 19(1): 87–101.

Strömbäck, J. (2008) Four phases of mediatization: An analysis of the mediatization of politics. *International Journal of Press Politics* 13(3): 228–46.

Tandoc, C Jr., W.L. Zheng and R. Ling (2018) Defining 'Fake News', *Digital Journalism*, 6(2), 137–53.

Thorbjørnsrud, K., T.U. Figenschou and Ø. Ihlen, (2014). Operationalizing mediatization: A typology of mediatization in public bureaucracies. Communications: The European Journal of Communication Research, 39(1), 3–22.

Thurman, N. and R. Fletcher (2019). Had Digital Distribution Rejuvenated Readership? *Journalism Studies* 20(4), pp. 542–62.

Tsetsura, K. (2008). Media Transparency Initiative: An exploratory study of global media practices. Paper presented to the IPRA Summit, June 2008, London. Available at: http://www.instituteforpr.org/global-media-relations-practices-2008/

Turk, J.V. (1985). Information subsidies and influence. *Public Relations Review* 11(3): 10–25.

Van Dalen, A. (2012). The algorithms behind the headlines: How machine-written news redefines the core skills of human journalists. *Journalism Practice* 6(5–6): 648–58.

Verčič, D. and A.T. Verčič (2015). The new publicity: From reflexive to reflective mediatisation. *Public Relations Review* 14.

Washbourne, N. (2010). *Mediating Politics: Newspapers, radio, television and the internet.* New York: Open University Press.

CHAPTER 3

Karen Freberg

Social media for public relations

Source: Kletr/Shutterstock

Learning outcomes

By the end of this chapter you should be able to:

- identify current global trends, opportunities and challenges in social media within public relations
- review social media core principles, skills, and expectations for public relations professionals
- evaluate current areas of specialisation of social media within public relations
- analyse and apply social media theories and principles into practice
- explore future trends and best practices for public relations professionals working in social media.

Structure

- Defining social media
- Core theories that are utilised in social media and PR
- Emerging theories and perspectives
- Traditional viewpoints on PR for social media
- Opportunities for public relations professionals
- Challenges for public relations professionals to note
- Best practices and future considerations

Introduction

Social media has transformed public relations both in terms of research and in practice. The importance of social media to practice is reflected in the rise of social media research over the past decades (Duhé 2015). With each advance that occurs in the social media industry, public relations research adapts and explores these various changes and discusses the implications this has on the field, society and the practice. Social media has been at the forefront of bringing both pain and delight for brands, organisations and public relations professionals over the past decade. It is at the forefront and focus of some of the more recognisable campaigns as well as crises in the public relations profession.

Freberg (2016) described social media as providing the ultimate personalised online networked hub of information, dialogue and relationship management. Essentially, social media combines the use of innovative strategies with digital communication technology platforms, enabling the user to share knowledge, engage in digital storytelling through conversations and visual components, collaborate with others, engage in crowdsourcing tasks and contribute ideas to solve problems, conduct strategic monitoring and analytic analysis online, and build relationships within a community sharing common interests, investments and needs.

The overall purpose of this chapter is to outline the key conceptualisations emerging from the literature on social media, how it is integrated within public relations, main theoretical foundations for social media, and the best practices for public relations professionals to consider for the future in social media.

Mini case study 3.1

Nike is one of the leading global brands in the athletic market and has established itself as a brand that has integrated itself not only with its strong product lines, but also iconic campaigns and slogans.

Considering its recent and previous engaging campaigns with athletes like Serena Williams, Nike wanted to increase its market share and presence in the female market of athletic shoe and apparel market. The commercial, which was called 'Crazy' (Gallucci n.d.) was released during the Oscars and was voiced by Serena Williams and focused on identifying certain stereotypes of how female athletes are portrayed as well as providing words of empowerment and encouragement to being different, or in other words, 'crazy' as others have labelled these athletes who are different.

This commercial was indeed released during the Oscars, but it also came right after the crisis that sparked on the college basketball floor. Zion Williamson, the dominant freshman basketball player from Duke University, was injured during the Duke vs. UNC rivalry game when his Nike shoes fell apart at the seams (Nike dreams 'Crazier' in powerful new Oscars spot | CMO Strategy – Ad Age n.d.). This caught the attention for most marketing and public relations professionals as a hit towards Nike's overall brand image (Winchel 2019).

After the crisis, Nike issued a statement that said, 'The quality and performance of our products are of utmost importance. While this is an isolated occurrence, we are working to identify the issue.' (A Blown-Out Sneaker, An Injured Superstar And A Night To Forget For Nike n.d.)

With both campaigns, they are 'crazy' for different reasons, and both drew different feelings towards the brand. The timing of the 'Crazy' campaign was an element to consider, especially considering what happened to Zion during the basketball game. There were certainly some key strategies that took place here.

First, the overall message and launch of the 'Crazy' commercial was integrated. While the commercial was launched officially at the Oscars, the video was also uploaded on YouTube and shared across different social media platforms. Second, not only was this shared by Nike on their channels, but the company utilised their network of athletes (like Serena) to share the video on their own networks with their community, which made them influencers for this campaign. This is an example of how building relationships with key publics and influencers can help amplify the messages in a campaign such as this. In addition, this case resulted not just in a widespread viral sensation on social media, but it integrated the various social media components that did significant damage for Nike as a brand. When brands are in crisis, it is one thing to handle a small number of critics towards the situation which the brand is involved in. However, when the situation is live for the world to see and react to on social media, and having high-profile reactions (e.g. President Obama) displayed and created into gifs, that raises the situation to a whole other level for the brand (Zion Williamson's Ripped Sneaker Puts Nike in a Bad Spot – WSJ n.d.).

Lastly, this campaign showed how one brand can have both a hit, as well as a crisis, all at the same time. Yet, even though the brand took some damage during the shoe crisis with Zion, they were still able to sustain their overall brand perception with an empowering message. It is important to note that the key player in both cases is timing. Time is always a factor in a story, especially those that emerge on social media, which makes this an important element for public relations professionals to consider as they move forward in their careers.

Here are some questions to consider in both cases:

1. Creative thinking: evaluate the 'Crazy' campaign from a strategic point of view. Do you think this is a good brand move for Nike? What are three things the company could do to expand this message to more audiences?
2. Social strategy: with both cases involving Nike, the main content form that was used was video. How would these cases turn out if the 'Crazy' commercial was just photos and text? Would the Zion Williamson shoe crisis have been as big if it was just a picture? Explain and support your perspectives on this.
3. Critical thinking: what are the reputation and brand implications Nike has in both campaigns?

Defining social media

Social media has been at the forefront of bringing both pain and delight for brands, non-profit entities, academic institutions and organisations over the past decade across various areas of society and the communications industry (Allagui and Breslow 2016). It is at the forefront and focus of some of the more recognisable campaigns, as well as becoming a rising area of specialisation within the academic community. These new communication technology tools allow individual users and organisations to engage with, reach, persuade, and target key audiences more effectively across multiple platforms. As social media has evolved, it has given rise to new business practices, technologies and even new challenges and opportunities (boyd 2015).

Key definitions of social media. In the academic literature, there are many definitions focused on specific platforms (Mangold and Faulds 2009), construction of profiles to build digital connections (boyd and Ellison 2008), and a collection of tools and practices that emerged from the dot-com crash (boyd 2015). Felix et al. (2017: 123) defined social media as 'an interdisciplinary and cross-functional concept that uses social media (often in combination with other communications channels) to achieve organisational goals by creating value for stakeholders'. Freberg (2016) defined social media as:

Social media provide a personalised, online networked hub of information, dialogue, and relationship management. These new communication technology tools allow individual users and organisations to engage with, reach, persuade, and target key audiences more effectively across multiple platforms. Industry professionals, scholars, and social media users have contributed several different definitions and conceptualisations of the concept of social media. (Freberg 2016)

As presented, disciplines will evaluate and define social media in different capacities. Yet, each definition focuses on specific elements that are unified across the board. Social media is also not an area of focus that is housed in 'one discipline'. It is a hub area of focus where many different disciplines from the humanities to social sciences come together to explore, discuss and elaborate on the growing trends happening in these digital communities and platforms.

Core theories that are utilised in social media and PR

Theory needs to be focused on explaining behaviour as well as being able to predict behavioural actions by others. Social media theoretical research has been more along the lines of applying other theories from other disciplines rather than solidifying unique and specific theories that are applied and integrated within the platforms themselves.

As Taylor and Kent (2010) noted, public relations focuses on building relationships and understanding between organisations and their key publics. Public relations seeks to create meaning in conversations among different parties, which can take place in person or on social media. Most of the literature that focuses on social media has used established theories from public relations (Duhé 2015), but has borrowed approaches from other fields as well such as marketing (Alalwan et al. 2017; Khang et al. 2012), advertising (Knoll 2016), business communications, and even social psychology. In addition, social media research has extended past discipline and professional boundaries for research and practice, which has allowed more opportunities for transdisciplinary research and collaborative projects. Research examining challenges and opportunities of communication via social media channels has been on the rise (Rains and Brunner 2015; Stoycheff et al. 2017).

There are specific theories that are being utilised to focus on specific aspects of public relations and social media, such as dialogic theory (Sommerfeldt et al. 2012), which focuses on the exchange of ideas and perspectives through various channels, which in essence is what social media is all about. Relationship management has also been explored (Sweetser and Kelleher 2016), focusing on the online relationships that are formatted on these channels between an organisation and their key publics. In addition, there has been significant amount of research exploring the various crisis messages on social media using the situational crisis communication theory (Schultz et al. 2011) and the social-mediated crisis communication model (originally called the blog-centered crisis communication model; Jin and Liu 2010).

While there may not be a dominant theory or perspective being utilised in social media and public relations research yet, this does leave room for the field to grow. Social media and public relations theory needs to do more in explaining behaviour rather than focus on micro aspects of each of the platforms. In addition, most of the research and theory development in social media and public relations has been applying other theories to try and 'fit' in the social media context, rather than exploring new concepts and perspectives within the channels themselves.

Emerging theories and perspectives

Current state of social media. There are several key characteristics that make social media different from traditional media outlets like television, radio, newspapers and magazines. First, social media is open and dynamic in span and presence. While traditional media appears to be focused on one-way forms of communication, social media content is emerging in real-time with multiple parties involved. The barriers to entry for establishing one's presence on social media is much lower and easier to overcome than those involved with establishing a presence in traditional media. Social media users can bypass the traditional media gatekeepers, who attempt to set the narrative and frame the stories from their point of view. Social media presents widely diverse points of view and allows the individual users or consumers to make the ultimate decision about the information they want, how they want it, and whether the information fits their overall needs and expectations.

Myths and truths about social media. There are a lot of myths and preconceived notions of what social media is, and there are certain truths that are present and accounted for here for the industry as well as the individual platforms.

One of the biggest myths out there presently still to this day is that social media is a fad and will go away. With over a decade under some of the platforms' belts, social media is not going to go away any time soon. In fact, the industry is just getting started. More jobs, positions and opportunities are arising due to the increased demand and focus social media positions and jobs bring to the table.

In addition to this myth, a common misperception that is often faced with public relations students is the job market in this industry. Compared to other industries, social media jobs are not only prominent in the industry but are in high demand. Many brands, agencies and professions are adding more roles in this area than ever before.

One of the other myths that does happen a lot of times in the industry is that anyone can work in social media if you just have a profile. 'Gurus', 'experts' and 'change evangelists' are coming out of the woodwork and saying they are experts in social media for just having a platform profile and knowing how to tweet, update and share a story. Working in social media is much more than just creating content. Being a social media professional is about understanding how and why we are using these platforms to engage, cultivate relationships and spark dialogue with our content amongst our global audiences. Key specialised skills like listening and monitoring analytics, reporting data, community management, cultivating creative strategies, creating content, handling crises, and telling authentic and transparent stories are just some of the responsibilities social media professionals need to have today. These can be accomplished and gained through education (as most universities are offering social media courses in their curriculum), certifications (like

Facebook Blueprint, HubSpot and Hootsuite ones), and experience (internships, fellowships and client work).

Key platforms. With social media platforms, there are some that come around every day, and then there are some of the more dominant and established platforms. For public relations professionals, there are several that need to be noted as being the top ones to focus on, which are Facebook, Twitter, Instagram, LinkedIn, Snapchat and YouTube (see Table 3.1).

While all these platforms started at different times and for different audiences, all have become an integrated medium for public relations professionals to engage, enhance and cultivate relationships with their audiences, publics and other communities. Each platform has evolved tremendously over the years, some adding new features and elements, while others have risen to prominence and have since seen a reduction in their user base due to age cohort trends and crises.

Facebook is the biggest social networking site in the world now, but others emerging from other countries are rising in popularity among various age cohorts. Facebook has over 2 billion users on their site, and it continues to be the biggest social networking platform out there. However, with recent crises that have hit the company both as far as privacy goes and data collection related to the 2016 Presidential election, the level of trust towards the platform has

Platforms'	Features	Benefits	Challenges
Facebook	■ Updates ■ Live video ■ Stories ■ 360 video and photos ■ Notes + Long form content	■ Engaged networks ■ Group and community features ■ Insights and analytics ■ Integrate experience into VR (Oculus Rift)	■ Reputation challenges (e.g. Fake news) ■ Algorithm changes ■ 'Pay to play' model is key for Facebook posts for audiences
Twitter	■ Updates (280 characters) ■ Photos, GIFs, and videos can be shared ■ Live video ■ Twitter Moments	■ Engaged community through Twitter chats ■ Sharing real time news ■ Utilised by media, sports, and news industries in particular	■ Risk of fake news or rumours to be spread ■ Cyberbullying ■ Trolls and bots
Instagram	■ Updates in Feed ■ Stories ■ Live Video	■ Create a specific aesthetic for brand ■ Utilising visual storytelling ■ Creator focused platform	■ Fake bots, likes ■ Focus on fraud and fake influencers ■ Metrics and verification are challenging to achieve
Snapchat	■ Snaps and Stories ■ Lens ■ Filters	■ Creator focused ■ Opportunity to create filters and lenses ■ Augmented reality (AR) features are innovative	■ Focused on specific audiences ■ Many of the features from Snapchat are now on Instagram ■ Hard to determine ROI ■ Advertising is expensive
LinkedIn	■ Updates ■ LinkedIn Posts (e.g. Blog Posts) ■ LinkedIn Live	■ Business networking focused ■ Reach audiences outside of network ■ Recruitment and personal branding for opportunities	■ Limited interface and features without LinkedIn Premium ■ Analytics and insights are hard to get ■ Advertising is expensive
YouTube	■ Videos ■ YouTube Live	■ Great for creators and storytellers to share videos	■ Ads are expensive ■ Payment for ads and criteria for creators to have certain exclusive features seems to change

Table 3.1 Features and overview of social media platforms

declined each year, resulting in many audience members going to different platforms for their community engagement efforts. In addition, the 'pay to play' mentality involving the decline of organic reach on Facebook has caused many brands and media outlets to think differently about how much they will be spending promoting posts or creating ads on the platform without any return.

As shown in Figure 3.1, Facebook is one of the top platforms used by adults today along with YouTube (Pew Research Center 2019). Even with the challenges they have had with privacy issues, data breaches, accusations of passing along fake news, and hacks, Facebook continues to be one of the more dominant platforms in the social media space.

Twitter has had its own ups and downs over the years but is still the dominant microblogging platform used by journalists, media, brands and public relations professionals to share news, updates, event coverage, and even in times of crisis. Brands have also found success in utilising the platform to showcase their brand voice, and even occasionally sending some 'shade' over to other brands that sparks reactions from their community. Brands who have been successful in utilising Twitter to create this type of engagement have been brands like Wendy's, Moon Pies and Steak Umm.

However, other brands such as Southwest Airlines have utilised Twitter, like other brands, to be the digital front door for the brand as far as customer services goes. This is referred to as social care, or customer service that is conducted publicly or privately on social media channels. Audiences gravitate to social media first if they have a concern or issue, and the social media community manager and their team are usually the front line for the brand digitally.

In addition, Twitter is used to cultivate some communities virtually through the form of hosting Twitter chats, a scheduled time where audiences come together to discuss a brand-related topic at hand. Brands like Cinnabon (#SweetTalk), Edible Arrangements (#EdibleChat), Adobe Education (#CreateEDU) and Adobe (#AdobeChat) have created communities and a virtual conversation around certain topics each week with their community, which helps again foster ongoing relationships for each of these brands. The other benefit that Twitter has compared to some of the other platforms is their level of access to their API (application program interface) when it comes to measurement and evaluation. Facebook, LinkedIn

Facebook, YouTube continue to be the most widely used online platforms among U.S. adults

% of U.S. adults who say they ever use the following online platforms or messaging apps online or on their cellphone

- YouTube 73%
- Facebook 69
- Instagram 37
- Pinterest 28
- LinkedIn 27
- Snapchat 24
- Twitter 22
- WhatsApp 20
- Reddit 11

Note: Pre-2008 telephone poll data is not available for YouYube, Snapchat and WhatsApp. Comparable trend data is not available for Reddit.
Source: Survey conducted Jan. 8-Feb. 7, 2019.

PEW RESEARCH CENTER

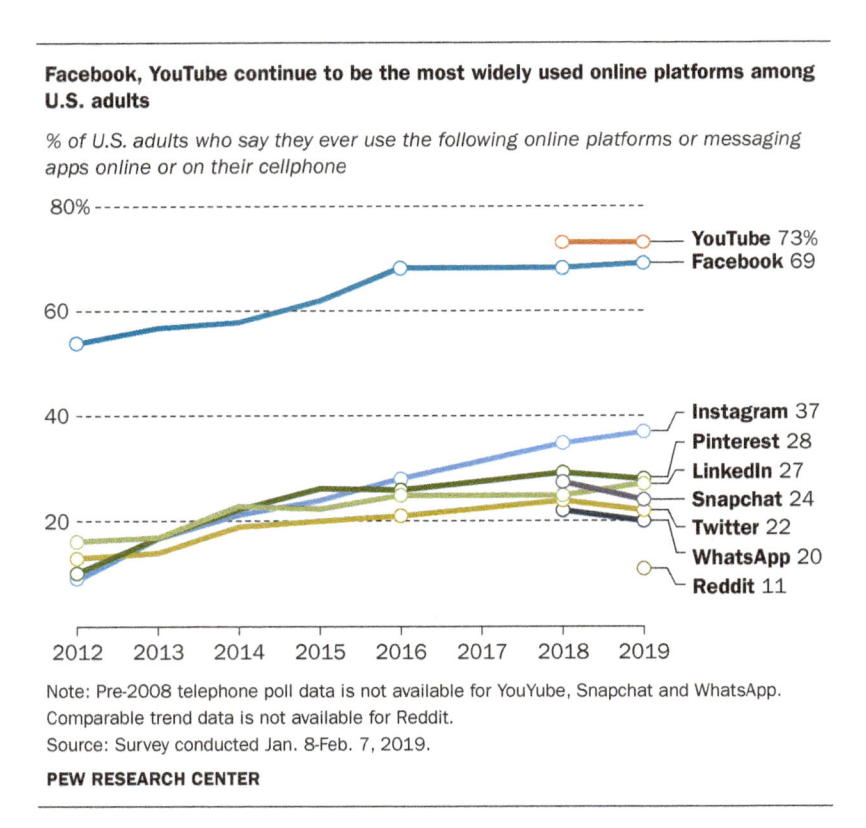

Figure 3.1 Pew Research Center report on social media usage in the United States in 2019 (*source*: Facebook, YouTube Continue to Be the Most Widely Used Online Platforms among U.S. Adults. Pew Research Center, 9 Apr. 2019)

and Instagram have their own analytics like Twitter does of course, but Twitter has been open to other third party tools like Zoomph, Talkwalker, Meltwater and Salesforce in evaluating data coming from the site to their own designated listening and monitoring platforms.

Visual and snackable content forms like Instagram and Snapchat are emerging as dominant platforms among users, particularly in the younger generations of audience members. Instagram has become the dominant social visual platform and has integrated their overall presence to include not just their visual feeds but has added stories (a feature taken from Snapchat) and live video as key features to grow as a dominant social media platform. Brands like Starbucks, National Geographic and GoPro have established their visual presence with clean aesthetics in their branding, graphics and overall presence on the social media platform. Snapchat has had its highs and lows – bringing the new perspective of consumable visual content that has a time limit to it. Celebrities such as Kylie Jenner and DJ Khalid gained huge fame on the platform for their partnerships and exclusive insights into their daily lives. Brands such as Disney and Taco Bell created unique filters and lenses for users and audiences to share with each other. Snapchat is also the one platform that really was the first to integrate augmented reality components (AR) into their platform with their lenses and filters. Users can create their own filters and have lenses for specific events and purposes with Lens Studio.

LinkedIn has been traditionally viewed as a business networking site, yet it has become a dynamic social media platform that integrates many features that are commonly seen on other specific social media platforms such as Facebook and Twitter. LinkedIn has utilised new features like LinkedIn Live, which allows users to broadcast live video to their community on the platform. Early adopters have gained access to utilise these features like virtual reality expert Cathy Harkel, content creator Goldie Chan and non-profit social media strategist Chris Strub.

YouTube is one of the dominant platforms and is the number 2 search engine behind Google. Many individuals have gravitated to YouTube due to the power it has in creating content visually and to be able to share these stories and perspectives through video for the world to see. YouTube content creators are some of the more influential and financially successful individuals in the social media space. YouTubers like Casey Neistat, Ryan and Amy Landino have all benefited tremendously in utilising YouTube for their brand and making a name for themselves in their respective industries.

Industry. The social media industry is constantly changing and evolving as new expectations, features, platforms and brands emerge in the digital marketplace. The future of work identifies some of the new opportunities that are out there and how students are going to be working in positions that are yet to be discovered or implemented. In social media, the same could be said here for what are the growing changes and expectations the field has on young professionals who are just starting their career. This brings forth many opportunities, but also raises some challenges on how to adapt to the evolving landscape and have the necessary skills that can be sustainable and relevant for the industry while competing with individuals from all age cohorts for these positions. The social media industry is extremely competitive – everyone wants to be part of the 'shiny new object' or profession that is generating the most engagement, buzz and financial support in the industry. Presently, this is where the social media industry is at.

In addition to figuring out where you would want to work in social media (e.g. start up, agency, brand, organisation, or for yourself as an entrepreneur or consultant), there are some must-haves to be successful in the industry. First, having a digital portfolio of work to show you not only know social media, but you have worked in the industry and have real-world experience is crucial. It is not only about knowing what social media is, but showing you have the experience and ability to adapt to the growing changes and evolution emerging from the field. Second, it's not only what you have done that is important, but who knows your work. Establishing networking opportunities and connections is as important as having the skills to be able to be successful in the social media space. This means being active in networking on the social media platforms, creating your own content on your own platforms (e.g. blogs, websites), and sharing your perspective to your community to build your online presence and voice of authority on topics in the industry.

Keep in mind, while social media is not a relatively 'new' field, it is indeed getting more established as time goes on. Social media positions are becoming more mainstream and established as a key part of the communication and business sector. However, with the changes happening on the individual platforms and new features being introduced, this means the skills, responsibilities and expectations for these roles will continue to change. Public relations students who wish to work in social media must be adaptable in learning new skills and approaches and be willing to invest in their learning beyond the classroom in this industry to be successful.

Traditional viewpoints on PR for social media

Public relations has a natural connection to social media, but there are other disciplines which want to take on and have a seat on the 'Social Media Throne' – to connect it back to the Game of Thrones. In fact, to describe the current social media landscape and competition on who 'owns' social media, Game of Thrones is probably the most appropriate analogy to use.

Depending on who you talk to, each discipline will note they are the ones that have a valid claim to 'own' or 'house' social media. Journalists state they are the original storytellers and main voices in social media, so they have a claim. Advertising points out it is a 'pay to play' situation now, so they should oversee social media responsibilities. Marketing says everything falls under their umbrella of responsibilities, including public relations and advertising with social media. Even English, where programmes are redefining their discipline as 'digital media storytelling' are putting their hat into the competitive landscape. However, with all these disciplines vying to be the leader and authority on social media, social media is not 'owned' by one discipline, but it is integrated and a hub collection of platforms that are integrated and complex to be used and applied in different ways. Instead of dividing disciplines based on ownership, barriers my need to be taken down and responsibilities should be shared. This is how collaborations are formed, which is what we are currently seeing in the industry. Public relations is a natural bridge to connect all these associated disciplines together based on the emphasis they place on relationship management and community building.

Most academic public relations programmes around the world are found within journalism programmes, and the relationship is somewhat 'complicated.' Public relations is sometimes viewed as 'the step-child' of journalism, and journalists claim they are the 'real storytellers' and writers for the profession. Now, we can play nice and work together, so this is not always the case. Yet, public relations and journalism do need to work together. We are seeing journalism programmes adapt and change along with public relations programmes. More media outlets are letting their reporters and journalists go, while the number of public relations professionals and jobs continues to grow. Many times, journalists come 'to the dark side' of public relations after their careers in journalism stall.

Advertising traditionally has focused a lot on the measurement and impact that their work and messaging has gotten through concrete metrics, whereas public relations has traditionally had a difficult time measuring and evaluating the impact they have made for their audiences. The differences have been on the measurement front, which will be discussed later in this book. However, as the lines have blurred, both disciplines must acknowledge these points and see how to work together to address these for their campaigns.

Marketing and public relations must work together and have done so for many decades. In most cases, the public relations department is part of the marketing department for major organisations, and it is a key part of the integrated marketing communication programme. Yet, public relations and marketing remain very different areas. Marketing, compared to public relations, focuses on the larger picture of how to persuade audiences through a range of different techniques and skills with the objective of encouraging the audience to make a purchase. Public relations focuses on the relationship and communication factors needed to build a bridge between the public and the organisation. Marketing and public relations professionals must work together in order to achieve these goals.

Even though some disciplines are aligned and the lines in social media are blurring together, this also raises the case for new specialised areas to emerge from the trends and evolving strategic applications social media brings to public relations. One of the rising areas of focus for public relations professionals is in influencer marketing. Influencer marketing is the specialisation that is involved in researching, listening, engaging and working with individuals who have an established presence and voice on either a platform or multiple platforms and can persuade and motivate audiences to take actions based on what they share on social media.

Within influencer marketing, there are of course different types of influencers like celebrity influencers (Reese Witherspoon and George Takei), macro influencers (Casey Neistat, Gary Vaynerchuk and Simon Sinek), micro influencers (individuals who have a following of 10k or less), and nano influencers. Influencers are used in social media campaigns by public relations professionals due to several factors. First, they are perceived as more relatable to the audience members compared to a paid spokesperson. Second, they have built their community based on their engagement with their audiences, so they are actively listening and creating content that is relevant and important to the group. This in part helps build stronger relationships and trust for the influencer and the audience member. However, as will be discussed in the next section of this chapter, influencers have of course raised new challenges for public relations professionals.

Opportunities for public relations professionals

There are of course both opportunities and challenges social media brings to the table for public relations professionals that need to be noted here.

Personal branding. First, let us go over some of the opportunities that social media brings to public relations overall. Social media first and foremost is social, which allows users and brands to be able to cultivate relationships and engage with their audiences in real time, breaking down the barriers in time and location. In addition, social media has allowed users to have unprecedented access to individuals who they may have never thought they would have the chance to connect with virtually like celebrities on social media. One strong example of a celebrity that has utilised social media for personal branding very successfully has been Dwayne Johnson, aka The Rock. The Rock has used his own channels to promote, engage and share exclusive news about his movies, shows and new product launches with the athletic company Under Armour. This has resulted in The Rock being named the number one celebrity on social media. In addition, some creators and influencers have made the jump from being just an influencer to a global celebrity. Lilly Singh, a prominent YouTuber, has made the transition from creating entertaining videos on YouTube to becoming the first Indian female late night television host. Social media in many ways has broken down the doors and barriers of entry for many individuals, bringing forth new opportunities professionally and personally to their users.

Storytelling. Social media brings forth the opportunity to be able to share stories and experiences with audiences to be able to make an emotional connection

---

Box 3.1

Impact of influencers

Influencers have become a growing entity in the public relations and social media sector. However, it is a specialised area that has been impacted by negative incidents with influencers, from the disaster concert and influencer-generated event Fyre Festival, to the rise of fake likes, followers and bots that are used to amplify a false view of influence. Platforms have taken an initiative to address these challenges, most notably Instagram. In July of 2019, Instagram, the popular photo and video-sharing platform that is owned by Facebook, began hiding likes on accounts as a trial in some countries.

Another platform has taken a different approach in their relationships with influencers. Snapchat, the popular video mobile app that gained popularity with celebrities such as DJ Khalid and Kylie Jenner, launched a campaign titled 'Real Friends' in August 2019 to bring the focus back on connections and relationships based on 'real' interactions. This is a shift in the field from self-promotion to authentic and transparent connections.

In looking towards the future, some influencers are moving from traditional platforms such as Instagram and YouTube for their content creation to emerging platforms among younger generation of audiences such as TikTok. TikTok, a video-sharing platform that is a combination of Vine and Musical.ly, has captured the younger audience with dynamic content that integrates music in short form videos. Brands, such as Vineyards Vines and universities like the University of Florida, have all embraced a presence on TikTok to engage with potential influencers and audiences who may be interested in their content and story.

Box 3.2

Use of Instagram, Snapchat and Facebook Stories

In order to create a strong personal brand on social media, an individual must not only have the expertise and experience that shows they are a thought leader in the industry, but they must also demonstrate strategic use of the social media platforms to tell their story. One way to do this effectively is through the Stories features on various platforms.

The main platforms that are using the Stories feature includes Snapchat, Instagram and Facebook. Stories are short videos or photos that are vertically presented and are usually only 10 seconds in length. However, there is a strategy that can be implemented to use these features to a public relations professional's advantage to help their personal brand:

- **Create a storyboard before shooting video.** Consider outlining what shots or videos you want to create before you create the story on each of the

→

box 3.2 (continued)

- **Think about how, where and why you are creating stories.** You do not want to create stories for the sake of creating stories. Consider how you want to use this content, and where. Testimonials, takeovers, behind the scenes exclusives, announcements and event coverage are all aspects to consider.

- **Focus on quality of stories, not quantity.** Attention is the most important currency, and the amount of time audiences are willing to spend looking at stories is low. Consider having stories that are focused and of quality, rather than taking a lot of shots.

- **Insights are your friend.** All three platforms have the capability to report analytics and insights on your story content. Story completion, story drop-off, view of profile, view of story, and other associated stories (example: if you are tagging a city or location, there may be other users who see your story because of it), are all good insights to determine what stories worked, what content was the cause of any drop-off, and what to consider next time.

- **Consider filters and additional features to enhance story content.** GIFs, stickers, location tags and even interactive features (e.g. polls) are a few ways to generate some interactive content to create engagement within your audience.

- **Have the right tools to create stories.** If you are not a graphic designer, do not worry. There are tools to help create professional content from your mobile device. Applications such as Adobe Spark, StoryArt, Unfold and Mojo are great tools to have on hand when creating stories.

---

that is real, relevant and unique. As shown in the first case study of this chapter, Nike has launched several campaigns that sparked a lot of emotional reaction for the brand by the community. One example of this was shown when the athletic brand signed Justin Gallegos, an athlete at Oregon who had cerebral palsy, and this was a first for the running community (Runner becomes first pro athlete with cerebral palsy to sign with Nike, October 2018). The video sparked a lot of emotional support and praise for the brand, but it also tied back to the overall brand mission for the company. By integrating strong content with authentic video telling a story, Nike was able to utilise social media to not only motivate audiences to view and consume their content but share it with their audience members. This metric, behavioural intentions, is crucial to be able to see the overall impact social media content has for the campaign and brand.

Another aspect of storytelling is allowing other audiences besides the brand to tell and create stories to be shared on social media. This is where influencers and advocates come to the table, but there is another area that is equally as powerful and effective for brands in their public relations and social media practices. This is referred to as employee advocacy, which is discussed in the box below.

Think about 3.1 — Employee advocacy as a form of storytelling

Employee advocacy embraces the individuals who work within a company, brand or organisation to be empowered to tell stories, share content and be accessible with audiences on various communication channels, including social media. Many brands over the years have utilised employee advocacy programmes to allow employees to share their insights, expertise and stories with outside audiences. Brands such as IBM, FedEx, General Motors, Humana and Target have all incorporated these principles together.

Adobe, the global technology and software company, has taken this approach and integrated this within their influencer marketing endeavours. Adobe has a program called Adobe Insiders, bringing together both employees and influencers to the table to collaborate, brainstorm and share ideas and stories on behalf of Adobe. These individuals represent diverse backgrounds and expertise which they can bring to the table. Like all aspects tied to transparency and accountability, Adobe Insiders must disclose they are either an employee at Adobe, or if they are being compensated for being part of the program (e.g. influencers) in their content creation.

Relationship building. Social media has also allowed brands to be part of pop culture and rejuvenate their brand in new ways. For example, Oreo, the American iconic cookie, has been around for over one hundred years, but is one of the most creative and engaged brands on social media. They came to fame in 2013 when they created the 'You can still dunk in the dark' viral tweet during the Super Bowl in New Orleans. Since then, they have integrated their brand as part of current and pop culture references, including the 2019 marketing campaign for the TV show Game of Thrones. By cultivating entertaining and timely integrations for a current topic, brands like Oreo can stay relevant but are able to build on the relationships they already have with their fan base.

Challenges for public relations professionals to note

Of course, while there are many opportunities social media brings to the table, there are some significant challenges and issues public relations professionals need to be aware of and address for their current practices.

Fake bots, influencers and news. The focus on identifying fake news, bots, news and professionals who are misrepresenting themselves has become somewhat of a global epidemic in the social media community. Identifying truthful information in a time of crisis is essential, and some of the platforms like Facebook have come under fire for their handling of some of these challenges. In addition, platforms like Twitter and Instagram have acted in identifying fake bots who follow/unfollow accounts to create the illusion they are real or share spam on their accounts. Not only have these platforms identified these accounts, they have also suspended many of them.

Fraud and impact of influencer marketing. The most iconic case that could be looked at for this challenge in social media is the 2018 Fyre Festival. The Fyre Festival case study will be the poster child case for what not to do when organising an event. This event was misleading across the board with promoting the event with established influencers like Kendall Jenner and Bella Hadid to create the illusion that it was a 'luxury' experience in the Bahamas. However, it was quite the opposite. Founders Billy McFarland and Ja Rule are facing numerous lawsuits from the festival, and McFarland is in jail. Two documentaries from Netflix and Hulu detail this case study, which should be a must watch for all public relations professionals in the significant risks this can bring towards a brand and community. This case also has raised the ethical and legal issue pertaining to influencer marketing as a key area of specialisation within public relations (The Fyre Effect: More questions are being asked of influencer marketing in wake of documentaries n.d.).

Privacy and data collection. Social media has brought forth many challenges for public relations professionals, and one of the biggest ones has been dealing with the concerns over privacy and data collection. The European General Data Protection Regulation (GDPR) is a regulation that protects data and privacy for everyone within the European Union. The issue of privacy became a big topic of conversation related to the breaches and access to data many opt the platforms collect on behalf of their users. Facebook has been prominent in this discussion for the most part, but others have been in the news as well for this. TikTok, the popular musical video app used by teenagers, was found to be collecting children's data on their app, and had to pay the Federal Trade Commission (FTC) a record fine of $5.7 million dollars (TikTok violates Federal Trade Commission rules, pays $5.7 million fine, n.d.)

Viral challenges tied to brands and individuals. One of the other challenges public relations professionals have to address here with the rise of social media is when your brand becomes the centre of a meme or even 'internet challenge'. There are several that integrated brands heavily, which they had to immediately respond and act. Tide was in the news for the Tide Pod Challenge, which teenagers and young adults would eat Tide Pods and film them doing it for the world to see (Tide pod challenge: What is it, and why is the viral video dare dangerous?, n.d.). Not only is this dangerous, but there were several deaths involved. Tide had to respond accordingly across all channels and made sure they provided warnings on all their products. Another brand that also was part of the viral challenge was Netflix and the Birdbox challenge. Users would do dangerous activities while being blindfolded, and as a result, caused some serious issues and accidents (Andriani 2019). Netflix also had to respond accordingly and make sure users were not doing this type of behaviour since it was dangerous.

Since these challenges emerged on YouTube, the company has acted to making sure these types of videos are banned from the site.

Mini case study 3.2
Rejuvenating a brand on social media: Mr. Peanut and The Super Bowl

One of the brands that has become a new social media powerhouse is a peanut. Mr. Peanut, part of the Planter Peanuts brand, came on to the social media scene in a big way in 2019. Mr Peanut, which is a client of Gary Vaynerchuk and VaynerMedia, got everyone's attention here with their social media presence with their GIFs, engagement with brands, and their giveaways they were sending out to people during the 2019 Super Bowl event. The brand launched their very first commercial at the event, but utilised social media as well to create engagement, interactions and buzz surrounding their giveaways. In addition, the brand was able to provide a new brand voice on social media for the iconic consumer product on social media, which received praise from media about this new integrated use of social media to introduce an iconic brand to a new audience.

Picture 3.1 Mr. Peanut, part of the Planter Peanuts brand, has become a social media powerhouse (*source:* James Kirkikis/Shutterstock)

Best practices and future considerations

There are many best practices and future considerations public relations professionals need to be aware of moving forward in the social media industry. Social media is a fast paced, constantly evolving, and dynamic profession with many opportunities and challenges. Here are a few things to consider and think about when entering the social media field.

Social media is a combination of both science and art. In order to be successful in social media, public relations professionals must embrace the science (research and theory) and art (creativity and practical application) of the field. Each perspective works together to create unique experiences and exceptional stories that engage audiences and enhance established relationships between an organisation and their key publics.

Authentic relationships on social are extremely valuable. More than ever, people want to have authentic and transparent relationships with their community online. With the challenges being raised by fraud, fake news and influencers misleading audiences while violating their trust, individuals on social media want to spend time with individuals and brands who are true and consistent on and offline.

Invest in your education every day. Social media is an industry that is constantly changing. New tools, trends, features and platforms are arising each day. Learning does not stop after the graduation or when a class is over. In fact, this is where the learning continues to grow and flourish. Investing in certification programs (Facebook Blueprint, Hootsuite, HubSpot, Stukent and Talkwalker) are just some of the ways to continue in this education in social media.

Key ethical and professional principles still matter. Being professional, ethical and following the legal expectations of a public relations professional are still important in the social media space. With the rise of cyberbullying, trolls and additional ethical challenges facing brands and professionals, the core ethical principles public relations professionals hold dear are as important as ever before.

Be your best PR professional online. As a public relations professional, it is important to be able to not only tell the story for your brand and client, but also recognise the power which social media can offer for personal branding. Organisations, agencies and other positions are looking for professionals who are not only skilled in the areas of social media, but also are able to have their own respective presence online with their established community and authoritative voice in the industry.

Summary

Social media is becoming a prominent component and specialisation within the public relations profession. This specialisation is not just here for the short term for public relations. It's a rising area of focus for agencies, corporations and entrepreneurs to master and integrate within their daily practices. However, social media practices will evolve along with the platforms. Each year, more expectations, duties and responsibilities will be added on for these social media roles for public relations professionals. It is the responsibility of the professional to invest in education, training and experience to be successful in social media. While the tools and platforms may change daily, some of the fundamental practices public relations has always embraced as a profession will be always be relevant. These practices in many ways are timeless even with these constant technological advancements happening in society.

Resources for social media professionals (certifications)

- HubSpot Academy Social Media Certification: https://academy.hubspot.com/courses/social-media
- Hootsuite Academy: https://education.hootsuite.com/
- Facebook Blueprint: https://www.facebookblueprint.com/student/catalog
- Stukent: https://www.stukent.com/

Bibliography

'A Blown-Out Sneaker, An Injured Superstar And A Night To Forget For Nike.' *NPR.org*. https://www.npr.org/2019/02/21/696565989/a-blown-out-sneaker-an-injured-superstar-and-a-night-to-forget-for-nike (2 April 2019).

Alalwan, A.A., N.P. Rana, Y.K. Dwivedi and R. Algharabat (2017). Social media in marketing: A review and analysis of the existing literature. *Telematics and Informatics* 34(7): 1177–90.

Allagui, I. and H. Breslow (2016). Social media for public relations: Lessons from four effective cases. *Public Relations Review* 42(1): 20–30. https://doi.org/10.1016/j.pubrev.2015.12.001

Andriani, R. (2019). 'Bird Box Challenge: Why Blindfolding Yourself and Walking into Walls Is Even More Stupid than It Sounds | Ria Andriani.' *The Guardian*. https://www.theguardian.com/media/2019/jan/08/bird-box-challenge-why-blindfolding-yourself-and-walking-into-walls-is-even-more-stupid-than-it-sounds (26 April 2019).

boyd, d. (2015). Social Media: A Phenomenon to be Analyzed. *Social Media + Society* 1(1), 205630511558014. https://doi.org/10.1177/2056305115580148

boyd, d.m. and N.B. Ellison (2008). Social network sites: Definition, history, and scholarship. *Journal of Computer-Mediated Communication* 13: 210–30.

Duhé, S. (2015). An overview of new media research in public relations journals from 1981 to 2014. *Public Relations Review* 41(2), 153–69. doi: http://dx.doi.org/10.1016/j.pubrev.2014.11.002

Felix, R., P.A. Rauschnabel and C. Hinsch (2017). Elements of strategic social media marketing: A holistic framework. *Journal of Business Research* 70: 118–26.

Freberg, K. (2016). Social Media. In C. Carroll (Ed.), *Encyclopaedia for Corporate Reputation*. Sage Publications. Thousand Oaks, CA.

Gallucci, N. 'Nike's 'Dream Crazier' Ad Is an Empowering Visual Love Letter to Women.' *Mashable*. https://mashable.com/video/nike-women-dream-crazier-ad/ (2 April 2019).

Kent, M.L. and M. Taylor (2016). From Homo Economicus to Homo dialogicus: Rethinking social media use in CSR communication. *Public Relations Review* 42(1): 60–67. doi: http://dx.doi.org/10.1016/j.pubrev.2015.11.003

Li, Z. (2016). Psychological empowerment on social media: Who are the empowered users? *Public Relations Review* 42(1): 49–59. doi: http://dx.doi.org/10.1016/j.pubrev.2015.09.001

Jin, Y. and B.F. Liu (2010). The blog-mediated crisis communication model: Recommendations for responding to influential external blogs. *Journal of Public Relations Research* 22, 429–55. https://doi.org/10.1080/10627261003801420

Knoll, J. (2016). Advertising in social media: a review of empirical evidence. *International Journal of Advertising* 35(2), 266–300. https://doi.org/10.1080/02650487.2015.1021898

Khang, H., E-J. Ki and L. Ye (2012). Social media research in advertising, communication, marketing, and public relations, 1997-2010. *Journalism & Mass Communication Quarterly* 89(2), 279–98. https://doi.org/10.1177/1077699012439853

Mangold, W.G. and D.J. Faulds (2009). Social media: The new hybrid element of the promotion mix. *Business Horizons* 52, 357–65.

'Nike Dreams 'Crazier' in Powerful New Oscars Spot | CMO Strategy – Ad Age.' https://adage.com/article/cmo-strategy/nike-s-oscars-spot/316734/ (2 April 2019).

NW, 1615 L. St, Suite 800 Washington, and DC 20036USA202-419-4300 | Main202-857-8562 | Fax202-419-4372 | Media Inquiries. 'Share of U.S. Adults Using Social Media, Including Facebook, Is Mostly Unchanged since 2018.' *Pew Research Center.* https://www.pewresearch.org/fact-tank/2019/04/10/share-of-u-s-adults-using-social-media-including-facebook-is-mostly-unchanged-since-2018/ (26 April 2019).

Rains, S.A. and S.R. Brunner (2015). What can we learn about social network sites by studying Facebook? A call and recommendations for research on social network sites. *New Media & Society* 17(1), 114–31. https://doi.org/10.1177/1461444814546481

'Runner Becomes First pro Athlete with Cerebral Palsy to Sign with Nike.' https://www.cbsnews.com/news/justin-gallegos-nike-oregon-cerebral-palsy/ (26 April 2019).

Schultz. F., S. Utz and A. Göritz (2011). Is the medium the message? Perceptions of and reactions to communication via twitter, blogs, and traditional media. *Public Relations Review* 37: 20–27.

Sommerfeldt, E.J., M.L. Kent and M. Taylor (2012). Activist practitioner perspectives of website public relations: Why aren't activist websites fulfilling the dialogic promise? *Public Relations Review* 38(2): 303–12. doi: http://dx.doi.org/10.1016/j.pubrev.2012.01.001

Stoycheff, E., J. Liu, K.A. Wibowo and D.P. Nanni (2017). What have we learned about social media by studying Facebook? A decade in review. *New Media & Society* 19(6): 968–80. https://doi.org/10.1177/1461444817695745

Sweetser, K.D. and T. Kelleher (2016). Communicated commitment and conversational voice: Abbreviated measures of communicative strategies for maintaining organization-public relationships. *Journal of Public Relations Research* 28(5–6): 217–31.

Taylor, M. and M.L. Kent (2010). Anticipatory socialization in the use of social media in public relations: A content analysis of PRSA's Public Relations Tactics. *Public Relations Review* 36(3): 207–14. doi: http://dx.doi.org/10.1016/j.pubrev.2010.04.012 'A Blown-Out Sneaker, An Injured Superstar And A Night To Forget For Nike.' *NPR.org.* https://www.npr.org/2019/02/21/696565989/a-blown-out-sneaker-an-injured-superstar-and-a-night-to-forget-for-nike (2 April 2019).

'The Fyre Effect: More Questions Are Being Asked of Influencer Marketing in Wake of Documentaries – Digiday.' https://digiday.com/marketing/fyre-effect-questions-asked-influencer-marketing-wake-documentaries/ (26 April 2019).

'Tide Pod Challenge: What Is It, and Why Is the Viral Video Dare Dangerous? The Washington Post.' https://www.washingtonpost.com/news/to-your-health/wp/2018/01/13/teens-are-daring-each-other-to-eat-tide-pods-we-dont-need-to-tell-you-thats-a-bad-idea/?noredirect=on&utm_term=.ffd4845eb736 (26 April 2019).

'TikTok Violates Federal Trade Commission Rules, Pays $5.7 Million Fine – Vox.' https://www.vox.com/the-goods/2019/2/28/18244996/tiktok-children-privacy-data-ftc-settlement (26 April 2019).

Winchel, B. (2019). 'Nike's Stock Price and Brand Image Falter after NCAA Star's Shoe Blowout.' *PR Daily.* https://www.prdaily.com/nikes-stock-price-and-brand-image-falter-after-ncaa-stars-shoe-blowout/ (2 April 2019).

'Zion Williamson's Ripped Sneaker Puts Nike in a Bad Spot – WSJ.' https://www.wsj.com/articles/zion-williamsons-ripped-sneaker-puts-nike-in-a-bad-spot-11550784831 (2 April 2019).

CHAPTER 4

Øyvind Ihlen and Neil Washbourne

Public relations, politics and democracy

Source: Tim Graham/Alamy Stock Photo

Learning outcomes

By the end of this chapter you should be able to:
- identify and discuss the relationship between public relations, politics and democracy
- understand different theories of democracy centred on the process whereby scarce resources and burdens are distributed
- discern different types of communication strategies in the political realm, such as political public relations and lobbying
- discuss the contributions of public relations and lobbying to democracy
- identify and problematise the negative consequences of public relations and lobbying
- discuss the potential for reflexivity and social change through public relations
- understand the role of conflict in society and how this might also have a positive function for democracy.

Structure

- Politics, democracy and communication
- Communication strategies in the political realm
- The contribution of public relations to democracy
- Democratic concerns
- Reflexivity and social change
- Consensus and conflict

Introduction

This chapter is a critical analysis of the role played in democracy by public relations, focusing on the role of political public relations and lobbying. This exploration is necessary, firstly, because of the neglect of discussion of democracy in recent and influential public relations texts. Secondly, it is necessary because of the ethical dilemmas that face contemporary public relations, which relate both to structural problems with its role in the world and well-founded perceptions of the negative consequences of public relations for democratic life. The perspective from which this chapter is written is a critical one that recognises problems in the great inequality existing in (the communication channels of) contemporary society. This critical approach argues that there are problems with the liberal pluralist assumption that we should be satisfied with the validity and diversity of information in the current 'marketplace of ideas', which does not take seriously the implications of such inequalities. The existence of such inequalities raises challenging questions about how to reform the institutions and practices of public relations to benefit democracy. Embracing reflexivity and recognising needs for social change is one step. Reconciling public relations with the role of conflict in democracies is another.

Politics, democracy and communication

Politics and democracy are key to how we organise society. Harold Lasswell (1936) argued that politics could be defined by asking the question *who gets what, when and how?* Politics concerns the distribution of scarce resources and burdens. Other definitions present politics as 'the authoritative allocation of values [in society]' (Bennett and Entman 2001: 2) or 'the constrained use of power' (Goodin 2009: 3). 'Constrained' here means that there are countervailing powers that can work for other interests and that power is curtailed by legal and social structures. The type of governance known as democracy is one such legal and social structure.

Democracy has its linguistic roots in Greek and means 'rule by the people' (Held 2006). In large-scale societies citizens cannot be involved in every decision and are both physically distant from where decisions are made and mentally distant from the array of expertise necessary to understand complex contemporary political life. Hence, representative democracy has become the most common form of democracy.

Representative democracy should ensure that even though citizens are not actually present at the making of political decisions, their interests, values and concerns *are* properly considered *in* those decisions. Voting institutionalises a degree of power vested in citizens to remove politicians and governments and elections as special events in which that power is expressed. However, representation means more than voting (Saward 2010). Representation by elected representatives also goes on between elections. Representation is evident in the content of politicians' speeches as they address 'the people'. It is also evident in the consultation of individuals and interest groups that occurs when proposed legislation and policy are discussed. Further, such representation is present in various forms of media content as well as in face-to-face meetings. Contemporary democracy involves a complex attempt at representation, of which the election itself is only an important and highly visible manifestation.

Different *normative* democracy models have also been debated among scholars, distinguishing between, for instance, competitive democracy where political parties have to win votes (Schumpeter 2003), participatory democracy where it is argued for active citizen engagement (Putnam 2000), and deliberative democracy striving for better decisions through dialogue

---

Box 4.1

Democracy definitions

* Direct democracy: citizens vote every time a decision has to be made

* Representative democracy: citizens vote for representatives that in turn make decisions

Also, normative models:

   Competitive: political parties have to win votes

   Participatory: citizens are active and engaged through, for instance, direct action

   Deliberative: procedures are created to achieve better political decisions through reasoned dialogue and broad political inclusion

(McLean and McMillan 2018; Held 2006)

(Habermas 1984). What is evident, is that communication plays an important part for the realisation of all these types of democracy. In a competitive democracy, citizens have to form opinions about who deserves their votes and the political elites and parties have to distinguish themselves from their competitors. In a participatory democracy, citizens are expected to communicate views actively and the political elites have to be responsive and encourage participation in the political processes. Finally, in a deliberative democracy, an even greater focus is put on the arenas for political discussions and rules for participation and engagement. The ideal here is that the better argument prevails over self-interested ones, that everyone is able to participate and that resources like capital do not matter.

Democratic values include political equality, encouragement and support for wide-spread participation (including space and time to enable deliberation) and the defence of rights, in particular for minorities. Furthermore, a democratic society relies on a free press and media where political debate can take place, and where representatives can be held to account (Washbourne 2010). As such, two normative goals can be formulated for 'mediated democracy'. Firstly, it should involve citizens in debates and contribute to their awareness both of a range of political knowledge and concerning policies, parties, pressure groups and problems. Secondly, it should link citizens' thoughts, perceptions and concerns captured in such debates to those with responsibility for political decisions – governments, ministers and MPs. The activities of public relations practitioners involve them in influencing both aspects of mediated democracy.

Democratic ideals are but imperfectly realised anywhere in the World. Ideals of the democratic involvement of citizens in debate and decision making appear to fall short even in those countries widely accepted as leading democracies (Washbourne 2010). This suggests that democracy is not so much an end point at which to aim, but rather, a process potentially without end whose progress is uncertain (see Think about 4.1).

A recent concern for democracy has been the development of communication technology and social media issuing fake news (see Box 4.2). Russia has for instance been accused of interfering with the US elections and the Brexit election in the UK in this way (see e.g., Persily 2017, Cadwalladr 2017). Distress has also been expressed over the status of truth and lack of concern for facts. The term *bullshit* has been applied by the philosopher Harry G. Frankfurt (2005) to describe how discourse is used to serve certain goals without paying attention to whether the presented facts are true or false. A politician might sway the electorate despite using such discourse, since he or she might be going in a direction the electorate approves, or appeal to certain values and confirm certain beliefs. In the book *Post-Truth: How Bullshit Conquered the World*, journalist James Ball (2017) deconstructs the bullshit strategy this way: 'make a claim, have it echoed in print, on TV and online, and then get further coverage as the rival campaign challenges its truth . . . if challenged, it provokes a story about the row that repeats the claim for days at a time; if unchallenged, the claim seems unanswerable' (p. 5). Given the sliding news media readership, sinking numbers of journalists, and dwindling advertising revenues of legacy media, this tendency might be strengthened. One researcher put it this way: 'What is different now is the difficulty, if not impossibility, of sustaining rational, fact-based, scientific claims about reality as categorically true and dominant at a time when any assertion about truth and reality can become public, reach wide audiences, and get broad attention in the Internet' (Waisbord 2018: 20) (see Think about 4.2).

Think about 4.1

Does thinking about democracy as 'representation' rather than as voting make a difference to how public relations practitioners might influence it?

What difference might serving or engaging democracy as 'democratic representation' – rather than democracy as merely elections and voting – make to the professional lives and activities of public relations practitioners? Is voting in elections really the only role for citizens? Can public relations practitioners facilitate debate or is their role likely to impede debate? What roles in democracy do public relations practitioners have (or should they have)? Can you find (or imagine) contexts when these roles *might* come into conflict with the ideal of political equality of all citizens?

Box 4.2

Fake news definition

Fake news is text that is intentionally misleading and false, while mimicking how news produced by journalists looks (Tandoc Jr et al. 2018).

> **Think about 4.2**
>
> Can you come up with examples of politicians or public relations practitioners that fit the description of a bullshitter? In what way do they qualify to this label? In what way does social media contribute to such practice?

Communication strategies in the political realm

All forms of governance, including authoritarian ones, are reliant on communication in one way or another. The practice of *propaganda* has been perfected by regimes of different political valour and calibre ever since popular opinion was recognised as a political factor. While the word propaganda has negative connotations of deceit and lies, some definitions point in other directions. Jowett and O'Donnell (2018) define propaganda as 'the deliberate, systematic attempt to shape perceptions, manipulate cognitions and direct behaviour to achieve a response that furthers the desired intent of the propagandist' (p. 7). Taylor (2003) similarly sees propaganda as 'the *deliberate* attempt to persuade people to think and behave *in a desired way*' (original emphasis) (p. 6). Ellul (1965/1973) argued that 'in propaganda we find techniques of psychological influence combined with techniques of organisation and the envelopment of people with the intention of sparking action' (p. xiii). In other words, there are some aspects of these definitions that are somewhat familiar with the practice of public relations and the definitions of public relations found elsewhere in this book (see Chapter 11). Indeed, the first people that used the term public relations were also concerned with opinion formation and the successful use of propaganda during the First World War (Bernays 1923/1934; Bernays 1928/2005).

Importantly, however, Jowett and O'Donnell differentiate between *white* and *black* propaganda (2018). While white propaganda identifies its source and builds messages on facts, black propaganda contains lies and deceptions, and might hide its origin. Some public relations scholars urge that 'whether propaganda is ethical or not has to be assessed in relation to the context in which it is practiced, the ends to which it is used, the quality of transparency in terms of the persuader's openness about the "ends" they are seeking to achieve, and, as far as one is able to judge, the consequences of those ends' (Weaver et al. 2006: 13). According to these scholars, public relations is a form of weak propaganda.

What is certain is that the use of communication strategically in the political realm is a tradition that goes far back in time in many regions (Chen and Culbertson 2009; St. John III et al. 2014). The argument has also been made that public relations actually was born in the political sphere (Lamme and Russell 2009; L'Etang 2004). In the US setting, for instance, the so-called Boston Tea Party in 1773 is singled out as an important example of how to achieve publicity for a political purpose, that of protesting the British taxation of the American colonies (Cutlip 1995). Other early examples include how German authorities in 1841 established a department to curtail negative media coverage (Bentele and Wehmeier 2009; Nessmann 2000/2003). In other words, the relationship between public relations and politics is a long one.

Public relations has grown in funding and importance since the 1980s in the UK and Western Europe. It has further expanded and intensified its activities in the US, and been spread around the world, by adopting US practices or establishing and developing local ones. These developments have put public relations into a relationship of deep significance to democracy everywhere (Davis 2002; Moloney 2006).

The first book to explicitly use the term *political public relations* was published in 1956. Here, it is argued that governments have to rely on public opinion and that politicians need to get closer to the people and vice versa. Public relations can assist in this regard (Kelley 1956). Still, the term has not been put to much use in scholarship (Martinelli 2011; Strömbäck and Kiousis 2011; Strömbäck and Kiousis 2019). Furthermore, when it actually has been used, it is primarily to denote media relations or publicity (e.g. McNair 2011; Froehlich and Rüdiger 2006). Looking beyond such rather limited and media-centric understandings, Strömbäck and Kiousis (2019) present the following definition:

> *Political public relations is the management process by which an actor for political purposes, through communication and action, seeks to influence and to establish, build, and maintain beneficial relationships and reputations with key publics and stakeholders to help support its mission and achieve its goals.*

These authors maintain that political public relations is concentrated around relations that are formed through communication. Their edited volume *Political*

Public Relations, now in its second edition, focuses on a range of different actors. Interestingly enough, they also remove the normative focus on mutually beneficial relationships that many public relations scholars have and state explicitly that this is an empirical question. The definition bears close resemblances with definitions presented elsewhere in this book.

A more widespread term than political public relations is *public affairs,* at least in the UK setting. This term is used to describe 'communication activities in relation to government, pressure groups and sometimes financial affairs at a corporate level, i.e. excluding customers/prospects and probably employees' (Harris and Fleisher 2017: 3).

A perhaps even more frequently used term is *lobbying*. Lobbying is understood as any attempt to influence political decision makers as well as bureaucrats regarding a particular policy issue (Baumgartner et al. 2009). It is 'essentially a form of persuasive communication in the political arena' (McGrath 2007: 269). Lobbying is typically preformed directly, in face-to-face meetings with politicians and bureaucrats. It can also have an indirect form, working through news media coverage or grassroots initiatives in which organisations aim at reaching the general public and in turn influence decision makers. The goal of such indirect public lobbying campaigns is to present a particular take on an issue and/or to put pressure on politicians. Social media also provides easy opportunities for lobbyists to engage with politicians, and here the line between indirect and indirect lobbying can be blurred. A Twitter message might for instance be directed at a politician but is obviously also a public utterance since it is visible for other Twitter users and followers.

Some prefer to label indirect lobbying as a type of outsider strategy. It is something that is used by organisations lacking the access that insiders have to decision makers (Dür and Mateo 2016). In other words, it is what resource-poor groups have to rely on in order to gain influence. Recent research, however, indicates that professional actors are relying on integrated campaigns, using both social media and legacy media, as well as traditional lobbying through direct meetings (Trapp and Laursen 2017; Figenschou and Fredheim 2019).

As indicated above, many of the same strategies and tools are used by organisations for political purpose no matter whether the activity is called political public relations, public affairs or lobbying. A big question, however, is what contribution is made to democracy of this type of activity. The jury is split to say the least. First, the positive voices and perspectives.

The contribution of public relations to democracy

Starting with the more specific practice of lobbying, a positive contribution to democracy can be claimed by pointing out that politicians and decision makers need input from voters and those that are affected by political decisions and policies. Hence, in many countries, politicians view lobbying favourably (Ihlen et al. 2020). According to the voices in this camp, it would simply be absurd if politicians did not listen to concerns from individual members of the public or affected organisations and businesses. In countries where the democratic systems have relied on corporatism, lobbying represents a break from this and potentially widens the possibility for input in the political system. In corporatist societies, certain interest groups or organisations have privileged access to decision makers through institutionalised arrangements like formalised, regular meetings (Rommetvedt 2017).

Moving to the public relations literature, some scholars do hold public relations up as a democratic paragon. Public relations is seen as being 'dedicated to truth and understanding' since 'dialogue represents a model with much closer correspondence to the lived reality of public relations' (Taylor and Kent 2014: 389) rather than practices of monologue or propaganda. In the literature, there are also several suggestions for ethical principles that would spur public relations practice in such a direction (e.g. Parsons 2016; Fitzpatrick and Bronstein 2006; Bowen 2010). Thus, it is argued that public relations in general is a valuable social activity (Holtzhausen 2012; Taylor 2010; Coombs and Holladay 2013). In terms of the recent COVID-19 crisis, for instance, it was imperative that the authorities used public relations to reach the public, both in terms of disseminating advice about behaviour, but also to create legitimacy for the strict measures used to combat the pandemic. While it is certainly possible for the lawmakers to introduce bans on concerts, traveling, shopping and so forth, it is necessary to create an understanding and acceptance for such measures. Here the public relations activities of the health authorities become key.

Recognition is also given to how practitioners could help to increase communicative equality and secure voice to the less privileged (Moloney 2000; Moloney 2006). A somewhat similar vision has called upon practitioners to see themselves as activists within their organisations. Practitioners should 'always question the nature of their own institutions and strive to improve them and make them more just' (Holtzhausen 2012: 234). The goal is that organisations and their stakeholders should share power (Berger 2005). Robert L. Heath (2011) argues that public relations should look to rhetoric for this endeavour as this discipline helps in focusing on how organisations and their stakeholders can have different interpretations of issues. For him meaning is necessarily co-defined and co-created. Through the fostering of mutually beneficial relationships, he thinks public relations and rhetoric can bridge managerial and sociopolitical discourse (Heath 2011). Public relations is really a means by which discourse is brought to bear on matters of fact, value, policy and identification.

According to Heath (2001, 2007) rhetoric helps people to take part in society's debates, thus it is ethically grounded but also ethically challenged. As a normative ideal it is not necessarily descriptive and 'emergent' is probably a better description. However, in a paper written with Damion M. Waymer and Michael J. Palenchar (2013), he pointed to a positive role for public relations to help organisations become 'stewards for democracy' (p. 271). Public relations can, for instance, create platforms and other infrastructure for collaborative, engaged decision-making to take place. A premise here is that relationships advance collective interests, not merely private ones. This also means that public relations can help democracy by creating 'discourse space[s]' in which public and private interests collide and become public interests' (p. 278). Summed up: democracy needs public relations, as public relations needs democracy.

Proponents of public relations also claim that public relations aids democracy by taking it out of the arena of old-style politics which was deeply unresponsive to citizens and voters. We often forget that contemporary democracies were very undemocratic even in the recent past. In the UK and the US between the 1920s and 1960s national (prime ministers or presidents) or local (municipal council leaders, US city mayors and state governors) 'bosses' often took the most important decisions in backrooms away from democratic debate. Such 'bosses' thought about their supporters as 'clients' requiring services *not* citizens to be involved in debate. Though 'bossism' might well have served some of the important material interests of citizen clients, such as finding them a job or a home, it also produced a highhanded attitude towards voters and citizens as potential political *discussants* (Kelley 1956; Bloom 1973; Lees-Marshment 2014; Lees-Marshment 2008). Such 'bossism' did not usually acknowledge that it was undemocratic, yet the democratic credentials of such 'bossism' were very much 'a sham' (Kelley 1956: 217). The activity of public relations practitioners may be an improvement on this. In its criticism of 'bossism', public relations authors have argued that public relations' use of surveys and focus groups to capture the thoughts, values and concerns of ordinary citizens means they can be *listened to* and that political leaders are thus able to know and address their concerns (Leach 2009; Washbourne 2010). Thus, the idea is that the use of public relations can lead to something significantly closer to democratic ideals than bossism did. Public relations claims to aid two-way communication between actors – citizens/publics/stakeholders/politicians – where they may otherwise mutually misunderstand each other (Pimlott 1951; Kelley 1956). Public relations practitioners are here credited with uncommon expertise in communicational skills and specialist knowledge of media which may benefit others. These claims are also underpinned by the notion that public relations *can* both involve ethical acts and function as a neutral mediator and, thereby, play a positive public role for democracy (Leach 2009).

Democratic concerns

A large part of the claims concerning public relations and democracy, however, relates to the idea that public relations may be harming the fulfilment of democratic ideals. The mainstream literature has had a tendency to describe public relations as having evolved from more or less unethical publicity activities to today's ethical practice of communication management (Duffy 2000; Moloney 2006). Some of the literature seems to conflate the normative ideals of public relations with its observed day-to-day practice, or at least express unwarranted optimism. As for the post truth-condition described earlier in the chapter, public relations, or at least the publicity seeking part of the industry, is accused of being a 'significant player in the economics of bullshit' (Ball 2017: 208). Looking at the history of public relations, it also becomes evident that public relations for the most part has been looking out for the interests of powerful organisations, commercial as well as non-commercial.

We do not have to be hyperbolic about public relations' influence on public discussion and democracy in the contemporary world but rather track its dominant modes and major attempts to influence such debate. In spite of the importance of public relations to democracy, however, public relations texts have often neglected consideration of democracy. Davis (2002) has negatively labelled contemporary political regimes 'Public Relations Democracy', which is dominated by 'promotional culture' rather than open argument. He argues that public relations practitioners have a significant and negative influence on democratic politics. According to him, this influence has led to the illicit side-lining of public and political institutions as public relations offers to 'listen to' the thoughts and feelings of citizens through polls and surveys on behalf of parties and governments. This privatises the thinking of citizens rather than allowing it to emerge in, and contribute to, debate. Davis also asserts that the impact of this 'privatisation' of discussion is exacerbated by public relations practitioners' likely support for political policy 'solutions' based on the so-called 'free market' and the denigration of forms of public provision. The negative effects of side-lining of specifically political institutions can be seen in public relations' contributions to the deficit of political, regulatory, oversight of financial institutions before and during the last financial crisis (Davis 2013; Davis 2002). Public relations practitioners acted to limit relevant institutional reform of finance in promoting the interests of corporations and fund managers rather than citizens (Boomgaarden et al. 2011).

Public relations can cause harm to democracy by not making debates public, by silencing or making issues invisible. This is seen in concerns over public relations practitioners' relations with journalists ('fake' news) and politicians ('secret' lobbying). As such, long-standing issues in critical analyses of public relations (i.e. Pimlott 1951; Davis 2002). These silences concern not so much the question of manufacturing mass consent but, in a key feature of 'Public Relations Democracy', that of 'excluding both the general public and non-corporate elites' from debate or being made aware of significant developments (Davis 2002: 82). Research has shown how organisations indeed often are interested in steering issues away from the public eye to the domain of 'quiet politics' (Culpepper 2011) to avoid politicisation of issues and to get proposals across.

In general, it can be said that while lobbying has increased in importance and professionalisation, this development has not been accompanied by more transparency regarding strategies and methods. If this also means that those with the most resources are better at adapting to the social changes and achieving their goals, this poses a challenge for democracy. Take for instance the usual lobbying strategy of making appeals to the public interest (Ihlen et al. 2018a). This latter concept is seldom defined. Instead, users invoke it and define it strategically for their own purpose. It has been characterised as 'an empty vessel, waiting to be filled with whatever values the user wishes. This lack of definition renders the concept vulnerable to capture by interest groups' (Feintuck 2004: 2). The problem then is whether the pursuit of private interests is really taking place under the pretence of pursuing the public interest. Hence, there is a need to understand how political actors frame their own interest and what they claim to be a public interest, what function this has in lobbying campaigns and what results are produced.

Important questions include: What are the democratic implications when 'all' actors have become adept at arguing that 'everyone' benefits from their proposal? Are the lobbyists primarily taking care of special interests or contributing to well-informed decision-making processes (Uhre and Rommetvedt 2019)?

Lobbying poses a problem for democracy if access to politicians is reserved for those with resources. Lobbying also raises broader concerns about side-lining the open debate that is central to democracy (Dinan and Miller 2007; Davis 2002). The problem is that powerful interests will both influence governments to create policy or legislation that serves their interests – but not the public interest – all the while conducting their activity in secret thereby ensuring that their influence cannot be challenged. Those concerns have led to the creation of organisations to bring to light and criticise the activity of lobbyists in and across countries (Spinwatch, Alliance for Lobbying Transparency – see Think about 4.3). In general, it can be said that it is necessary to bring 'conflicts out into the open where their special claims can be seen as appraised, where they can be discussed and judged in the light of more inclusive interests that are represented by either of them separately' (Dewey 1935/2000: 81). Similarly, many countries have taken steps to regulate lobbying (Crepaz et al. 2019; Greenwood and Dreger 2013; Chari et al. 2010/2012). Opponents argue that regulations are ineffective, introduce unnecessary bureaucracy, and demonstrate little trust in politicians and those voting them in. Proponents, however, argue that while lobbying regulation might be imperfect, it is a step in the right direction.

Think about 4.3

Watchdogs of lobbying: Do they serve democratic purposes?

Are lobby watch style organisations (Spinwatch and the Alliance for Lobbying Transparency) necessary to hold public relations practitioners to account? Are they of benefit for ethical public relations activities and only a problem for unethical ones? What defence, if any, of 'secret' lobbying do you find convincing? Why? What role should it have, if any, in a democracy? Fawkes (2014) argues that these transparency bodies may be important in revealing public relations' manipulation of media and the inadequate use of disciplinary procedures by public relations professional bodies with regards to errant individuals and firms. See also Chapter 13, Public relations' professionalism and ethics.

Case study 4.1
ExxonMobil, climate change and the European Union Parliament

On 21 March 2019, a public hearing was held by the European Parliament Committees on Petitions and Environment, Public Health and Food Safety. The topic of the hearing was 'Climate Change Denial', and the stated goal was 'to explore the topic of climate change denial under different perspectives and to examine the communication techniques used in politics or by private companies and other actors in society to mislead the public on the negative impact of certain industrial activities or policies on the climate' (www.europarl.eu).

The EU committees invited several researchers to give presentations. Among these were Geoffrey Supran, who two years earlier had co-published a journal article attacking the fossil fuel corporation ExxonMobil for misleading the public (Supran and Oreskes 2017). The researchers compared leaked internal documents with paid, editorial-style advertisements in *The New York Times*. A conclusion was that the corporation expressed doubt about climate change and its implications in the latter texts, while the internal documents acknowledged that climate change is both real and human-caused.

ExxonMobil declined to participate in the hearing, citing concern for ongoing climate litigation in the United States and that 'public commentary, such as would be elicited at the hearing, could prejudice those pending proceedings' (letter from Nikolaas Baeckelmans, ExxonMobil Vice President European Union Affairs; 20 March 2019; Foodwater Europe).

A letter to the committee chairs had attached an evaluation report from 22 February 2018 commissioned by ExxonMobil. In the report, Kimberly A. Neuendorf stated that the content analysis by Supran and Oreskes 'lacks reliability, validity, objectivity, generalisability, and replicability' (Exxon Mobil).

Neuendorf accused the authors of biases against ExxonMobil and for using 'highly involved, heavily interrelated, non-blind coders'. The letter from ExxonMobil also pointed out that 'As you may be aware, ExxonMobil has operated in Europe for more than a century and we continue to contribute substantially to the European economy. We have approximately 14,000 European employees across 16 EU member states, and invested more than [EURO]10 billion in Europe between 2012 and 2017' (Foodwater Europe).

Some questions to ponder: What strategy did ExxonMobil use in the face of criticism in this case? To what extent is this a permissible action? What is the status of the commissioned expert? How does ExxonMobil strengthen her credibility? The expert states that the journal paper lacks objectivity because of the author's prior activist stance. Do you agree? The letter ExxonMobil sent to the committee chairs was not public. Hence, the corporation was accused of operating in the shadows, rather than speaking publicly. Is this a fair criticism?

Sources: Supran, G. and Oreskes, N. (2017) 'Assessing ExxonMobil's climate change communications (1977–2014)', *Environmental Research Letters*, 12(8), pp. 084019 https://iopscience.iop.org/article/10.1088/1748-9326/aa815f/meta

Accompanying video: https://cdn.iopscience.com/content/1748-9326/12/8/084019/Mmedia/abstract-video-cf74dcb5327d002a57119cb942e893de.converted.mp4

ExxonMobil's original response: https://energyfactor.exxonmobil.com/perspectives/flawed-study-claiming-exxonmobil-misled-public-disappointing/

Link to the Neuendorf report: http://cdn.exxonmobil.com/~/media/global/files/energy-and-environment/Neuendorf-Report.pdf

Response from Supran: https://www.euractiv.com/section/climate-environment/opinion/exxonmobil-misled-the-public-now-theyre-trying-to-mislead-the-european-parliament/

Information on the EU hearing: http://www.europarl.europa.eu/committees/en/envi/events-hearings.html?id=20190313CHE06141

Response letter from ExxonMobil: https://twitter.com/FoodWaterEurope/status/1108672260020285440

Twitter-video from Geoffrey Supran after his testimony: https://twitter.com/geoffreysupran/status/1109083684957810688?lang=en

Reflexivity and social change

There is a need for reflexivity concerning ethics and the contribution to society of public relations. That is, there is a need to question how public relations work, and also what it does '*in, to, and for organizations, publics, or the public arena, in other words, society as a whole*' (Ihlen et al. 2018b: 428).

Professional bodies in public relations have made different attempts to regulate the ethics of their members and to install codes of ethics. Walle (2003) has argued that the public relations codes in a range of countries – the US (PRSA), Canada (CPRS), Australia (PRIA), New Zealand (PRINZ) and South Africa (RISA) – have in common neglect of broader responsibilities such as 'practitioners' duties towards the public and to society in general' (Walle 2003: 2–3). Moreover, she also found that ethical commitments are often in tension with these broader duties by being orientated to ease relations with clients. For example, she found that none of the codes imposed obligations to 'truthfulness' of public relations practice. The codes may often disavow lying but do not require full and truthful disclosure therefore making it easy to support clients' requirements but routine to contribute to misleading others. She also noted the absence in codes of directives 'that might help practitioners navigate the complex relations between truthfulness and public interest' (Walle 2003: 3). She also found that the codes did not require public relations practitioners' responsibility for client behaviour even where it might conflict with 'the social good'. None mentioned assessment of social interest in client selection. Walle (2003) expresses concern over the lack of encouragement of moral reflection. Such moral reflection might be beneficial to public relations practitioners in negotiating real-world dilemmas.

Much criticism has been directed at public relations, not least through scholarly as well as journalistic exposes of work conducted for big business, and interests such as tobacco, asbestos and oil (Miller and Dinan 2008; Rampton and Stauber 2001). Frequently, public relations is condemned more or less wholesale, thus choosing to ignore that organisations of today are dependent on the practice of public relations. It is really not possible for organisations to not conduct some kind of public relations. At the same time as the mentioned research can be faulted for a rather narrow perspective on public relations, it is arguably very valuable in calling out unethical public relations and its implications. Furthermore, moving the *systemic* criticism brings in a needed political perspective.

As pointed out in the section of the positive contributions to society, a number of alternative visions have been introduced for what public relations can be in a democracy. Some scholars have called for 'reconfiguring' public relations and developing 'the field away from insularity and in the direction of environmental improvement, inclusive egalitarianism and sustainable enterprise' (McKie and Munshi 2007: 145). Principles of sustainability should be taken on board and the practice should be put to work for the good of the whole of society. In this quest, it has been declared that there is a need to reclaim participative democracy (Motion and Leitch 2015). A success criteria in this regard would be

Picture 4.1 Over the years, the United Arab Emirates (UAE) has hired different public relations agencies to improve its image in the US and Western Europe (*source:* Yin Bogu/Xinhua/Alamy Stock Photo)

whether public relations has contributed to 'the democratic, deliberative and decision-making roles of civil society' (Motion and Leitch 2015: 148). An opposite function would be when public relations attempts to block alternative viewpoints from being presented publicly, for instance by threatening legal action.

The democratic ideal that has been held up by some scholars sees public relations as safeguarding 'a radical democracy that ensures equality for all, respect for cultural plurality and requires confrontational intolerance of injustice' (Holtzhausen 2012: 239). In a similar vein, the need for social change is emphasised (Demetrious 2013) and it is called for a public relations practice that truly engages with the public interest (Johnston 2016). This would also include challenging 'the hegemonic assumptions in public relations around gender' and race (Daymon and Demetrious 2013: 3; Waymer and Heath 2015). Public relations should call out manipulative and oppressive practice (Trujillo and Toth 1987) and deconstruct or reveal configurations of knowledge within the field with the goal of enhancing human freedom (Pieczka 2015; Moloney and McKie 2015). Emancipation can be had through reflexivity is the line of thinking in much of this literature, at least when public relations embrace and promote social change of some sort or the other (Ihlen 2017).

Consensus and conflict

As should be evident from other chapters in this book, public relations is often portrayed as a way of dissolving conflict. Communication is used as a tool to ease out wrinkles in relationships and reach consensus that is beneficial to organisations and stakeholders alike. An alternative perspective is that public relations assists organisations in furthering particular interests (Ihlen 2007; Ihlen 2017). In political conflicts relationship building and dialogue will obviously be important. These cannot, however, be the only tools when political values are at stake. In some instances, it can be necessary to position the organisation *against* others or the values of others (see Mini case study 4.1). In general, public relations theory favour consensus, but politics thrive on an antagonistic dimension, on conflict. Here, an *agonistic* approach (Mouffe 2005; Mouffe 2000/2005) is of interest for public relations, as suggested by several scholars (Ramsey 2015; Davidson 2016). An agonistic approach suggests ethical ways of approaching, and indeed, embracing conflict while also handling the destructive dimension that conflict also can entail.

In the political philosophy of Mouffe, society is seen as 'the product of a series of practices whose aim is to

Mini case study 4.1
Lobbying and influence

Over the years, the United Arab Emirates (UAE) has hired different public relations agencies to improve its image in the US and Western Europe. In a detailed report from Spinwatch, the influence on British democracy is analysed. The report traces several attempts to influence both the news media and MPs. It argues that pro-UAE pieces were the result of meetings with journalists, and 'we can also reveal that Quiller consultants, a lobbying company in London employed by the UAE until 2015, was asked to draw up names of Emirati dissidents in London who had claimed asylum and research BBC journalists who were deemed unsympathetic to the UAE for their alleged links to the Muslim Brotherhood' (Delmar-Morgan and Miller 2018: 6). The report also provides details about donations to think tanks and also about sums paid to the former Prime Minister Tony Blair.

The report states that while 'lobbying is a legal activity and is an important element of democracy – everyone has the right to make their voice heard. But there have to be limits. Promising billions in return for influence in the US, infiltrating the British media to smear rivals, threatening to interfere in British parliamentary select committee reports, buying politicians' loyalty with lavish trips, donating to think tanks and trying to influence them, targeting political opponents, trying to influence media coverage and protesting against press freedom – something that the UAE does not itself recognise – some would see as a step too far' (Delmar-Morgan and Miller 2018: 42).

establish order in a context of contingency' (Mouffe 2013: 2). Politics is made up of institutions, practices and discourses of democracy that seek to establish hegemonic order. It is different from *the political* which refers to the antagonistic dimension that society cannot escape. Mouffe does not agree with views of democratic theory that argue that a rational debate will help to reach an inclusive and universal consensus between different interests. The agreement or order that is the result of such debates will always be an expression of power relations and some viewpoints are necessarily excluded. When 'the inescapable moment of decision' arrives, the limit of any rational consensus is demonstrated by remaining antagonism (Mouffe 2013: 3). Nonetheless, conflict, difference, social division and emotions are constitutive for society. Indeed, identity necessitates difference. The challenge for democracy is that such dimensions of us versus them can potentially develop into a friend/enemy dimension.

Since it is not a viable route to attempt to ignore, suppress or condemn conflict, it should be harnessed to work for democratic values and relationships that are agonistic rather than antagonistic. The difference being expressed as conflict between adversaries, rather than enemies. Struggles and emotions are part and parcel of a vibrant democracy (Mouffe 2013). Certain core values lie at the basis of this perspective, including 'liberty' and 'equality'. Democratic designs should be constructed to uphold such values, while at the same time letting people argue for their particular interpretation of the values and how they should be implemented. The ability to forward dissent or the legitimacy of the right to fight for a particular interpretation should not be questioned (Mouffe 2005; Ramsey 2015; Davidson 2016). Unlike many other political philosophies, Mouffe also reserves a positive role of passion. Passion and emotions create engagement and identification, and could be mobilised for good democratic purposes 'towards democratic designs, by creating collective forms of identification around democratic objectives' (Mouffe 2013: 9).

Building on an agonist approach, Davidson (2016) urges public relations to:

'. . . elevate contest above neutral deliberation, instil a regard for opponents, an even stronger regard for disadvantaged publics who lack communication resources, and abhorrence of permanent winners and openness to new issues and challenges. It would also entail fostering of public space that welcome emotional, passionate engagement, a commitment to make power transparent and an end to the illusory assumption that policy issues are somehow neutral or technical matters awaiting communicative solution, but are always choice between conflicting alternatives.' p. 160

This presents public relations practitioners with concrete suggestions for how to handle conflict ethically and how to change from an antagonistic mindset to an agonistic one. Still, like many of the other normative suggestions for a new practice, it does place high hopes on practitioners and their autonomy (Moloney and McKie 2015). Being an activist practitioner working for power sharing with stakeholders and eradicating social problems is obviously laudable. Still, the ideals might not always fare well in practice. At the end of the day, some organisations are bound by more short-sighted goals of profit, growth, power or the like, rather than betterment of democracy. Then again, some insist that the win–win scenario is possible, that responsibility begets profit (see Think about 4.4).

Think about 4.4

What causes and social values have public relations been put to use for? What causes and social values *can* public relations been put to use for? A commercial by Gillette targeted 'toxic masculinity' (YouTube) and urged 'men to do the right thing, to act the right way' (http://www.thebestmencanbe.org). This caused a storm of criticism on social media. What considerations do you think Gillette made before launching this campaign? Did they expect criticism? Did they expect to lose customers? Do they stand to gain others? Do we welcome corporations taking active stances on broader social issues?

Summary

This chapter has pointed to how communication is crucial in politics and democracy. It has highlighted some of the ways that communication is used strategically in the political realm and also pointed to how the practice can strengthen democracy. The flipside is that public relations and lobbying also can work to the detriment of democracy. Questions of resources and dubious ethical practice are mentioned, alongside the lack of transparency concerning strategies and tactics. While codes of conduct for practitioners have been launched, many scholars call for reform of the practice based in principles of sustainability or social change. There is a need for reflexivity concerning the practice and its relationship to democratic principles of, for instance, equality.

Mainstream public relations theories often seem to suggest that they have the ability to dissolve conflicts. Implicit or explicit in these theories is the perspective that conflicts are costly and should be avoided. To avoid conflict, organisations need to conduct proper 'communicative groundwork' through listening and, if needed, adjusting to stakeholders' perspective and needs. In this chapter, however, it is advocated that public relations also must embrace conflict. Such a perspective, however, should not be read as an invitation to pursue own interests at all costs since 'conflict is good'. Thinking along with Mouffe (2005, 2013) and scholars who have applied her work (Ramsey 2015; Davidson 2016), public relations should be urged to support certain democratic values. Simultaneously, conflict over interpretation and implementation of these values are not only seen as legitimate, but as fundamental to democracy. If, on the other hand, public relations practice frames a certain political alternative as the only legitimate one, this is a contribution to antagonistic conflict and something that does not serve the democracy.

Recommended reading

Godwin, R.K., Ainsworth, S.H. and Godwin, E.K. (2013). *Lobbying and Policymaking: The public pursuit of private interests.* London: CQ Press.

Ihlen, Ø. and Fredriksson, M. (eds.) (2018). *Public Relations and Social Theory: Key figures, concepts and developments,* 2nd edn. New York: Routledge.

Strömbäck, J. and Kiousis, S. (eds.) (2019). *Political Public Relations: Principles and applications,* 2nd edn. New York: Routledge.

Bibliography

Ball, J. (2017). *Post-truth: How bullshit conquered the world.* London: Biteback Publishing.

Baumgartner, F.R., Berry, J.M., Hojnacki, M., Kimball, D.C. and Leech, B.L. (2009). *Lobbying and Policy Change: Who wins, who loses, and why.* Chicago, IL: University of Chicago Press.

Bennett, W.L. and Entman, R.M. (2001). 'Mediated politics: An introduction', in Bennett, W.L. and Entman, R.M. (eds.) *Mediated Politics: Communication in the future of democracy.* Cambridge, England: Cambridge University Press, pp. 1–30.

Bentele, G. and Wehmeier, S. (2009). 'Commentary: Linking Sociology with Public Relations – Some Critical Reflections in Reflexive Times', in Ihlen, Ø., van Ruler, B. and Fredriksson, M. (eds.) *Public relations and social theory: Key figures and concepts.* New York: Routledge, pp. 341–61.

Berger, B.K. (2005). 'Power over, power with, and power to relations: Critical reflections on public relations, the dominant coalition, and activism', *Journal of Public Relations Research* 17(1), pp. 5–28.

Bernays, E.L. (1923/1934). *Crystallizing Public Opinion.* New York: Boni and Liveright.

Bernays, E.L. (1928/2005). *Propaganda.* New York: Ig Publishing.

Bloom, M.H. (1973). *Public Relations and Presidential Campaigns: A crisis in democracy.* New York: Crowell.

Boomgaarden, H.G., Van Spanje, J., Vliegenthart, R. and De Vreese, C.H. (2011). 'Covering the crisis: Media coverage of the economic crisis and citizens' economic expectations', *Acta Politica* 46(4), pp. 353–79.

Bowen, S.A. (2010). 'The nature of good in public relations: What should be its normative ethic?', in Heath, R.L. (ed.) *The SAGE handbook of public relations.* Thousands Oaks, CA: Sage, pp. 569–84.

Cadwalladr, C. (2017). 'The great British Brexit robbery: How our democracy was hijacked', *The Guardian,* 7.

Chari, R., Hogan, J. and Murphy, G. (2010/2012). *Regulating Lobbying: A global comparison.* Manchester, England: Manchester University Press.

Chen, N. and Culbertson, H.M. (2009). 'Public relations in mainland China: An adolescent with growing pains', in Sriramesh, K. and Vercic, D. (eds.) *The global public relations handbook*: na, pp. 23–45.

Coombs, W.T. and Holladay, S.J. (2013). *It's not just PR: Public relations in society,* 2nd edn. Malden, MA: Blackwell.

Crepaz, M., Chari, R., Hogan, J. and Murphy, G. (2019). 'International Dynamics in Lobbying Regulation', in Dialer, D. and Richter, M. (eds.) *Lobbying in the European Union*: Springer, pp. 49–63.

Culpepper, P.D. (2011). *Quiet Politics and Business Power: Corporate control in Europe and Japan.* New York: Cambridge University Press.

Cutlip, S.M. (1995). *Public Relations History: From the 17th to the 20th century.* Hillsdale, NJ: Lawrence Erlbaum.

Dan, V., Ihlen, Ø. and Raknes, K. (2019). Political public relations and strategic framing: Underlying mechanisms, success factors, and impact. In J. Strömbäck and S. Kiousis (Eds.), *Political public relations: Principles and applications* (2 edn., pp. 146–14). London: Routledge.

Davidson, S. (2016). 'Public relations theory: An agonistic critique of the turns to dialogue and symmetry', *Public Relations Inquiry* 5(2), pp. 145–67.

Davis, A. (2002). *Public Relations Democracy: Public relations, politics and the mass media in Britain.* Manchester, UK: Manchester University Press.

Davis, A. (2013). *Promotional Cultures: The rise and spread of advertising, public relations, marketing and branding.* London: Polity.

Daymon, C. and Demetrious, K. (eds.) (2013). *Gender and Public Relations: Critical perspectives on voice, image and identity.* London: Routledge.

Delmar-Morgan, A. and Miller, D. (2018). *The UAE lobby: Subverting British democracy?* : Spinwatch/Public Interest Investigations.

Demetrious, K. (2013). *Public Relations, Activism, and Social Change: Speaking up.* Routledge.

Dewey, J. (1935/2000). *Liberalism and Social Action.* Amherst, NY: Prometheus Books.

Dinan, W. and Miller, D. (eds.) (2007). *Thinker, Faker, Spinner, Spy: Corporate PR and the assault on democracy.* London: Pluto.

Duffy, M.E. (2000). 'There's no two-way symmetrical about it: A postmodern examination of public relations textbooks', *Critical Studies in Mass Communication* 17(3), pp. 294–315.

Dür, A. and Mateo, G. (2016). *Insiders Versus Outsiders: Interest group politics in multilevel Europe.* Oxford, UK: Oxford University Press.

Ellul, J. (1965/1973). *Propaganda: The formation of men's attitudes.* Translated by: Kellen, K. and Lerner, J. New York: Vintage Books. Reprint, 1973.

Exxon Mobil (see http://cdn.exxonmobil.com/~/media/global/files/energy-and-environment/Neuendorf-Report.pdf, accessed 5 February 2020.

Fawkes, J. (2014). *Public Relations Ethics and Professionalism: The shadow of excellence.* London: Routledge.

Feintuck, M. (2004). *'The Public Interest' in Regulation.* New York: Oxford University Press.

Figenschou, T.U. and Fredheim, N. (2019). 'Social media lobbying: Interest groups' use of a networked media logic for organisational and political aims ', *Journal of Public Affairs.*

Fitzpatrick, K.R. and Bronstein, C.B. (2006). *Ethics in Public Relations: Responsible advocacy.* Thousand Oaks, CA: Sage.

Foodwater Europe (1) see https://twitter.com/FoodWaterEurope/status/1108672260020285440), accessed 4 February 2020.

Frankfurt, H.G. (2005). *On bullshit.* Princeton, NJ: Princeton University Press.

Froehlich, R. and Rüdiger, B. (2006). 'Framing political public relations: Measuring success of political communication strategies in Germany', *Public Relations Review* 32(1), pp. 18–25.

Goodin, R.E. (2009). 'The state of the discipline, the discipline of the state', in Goodin, R.E. (ed.) *The Oxford Handbook of Political Science.* Oxford: Oxford University Press.

Greenwood, J. and Dreger, J. (2013). 'The Transparency Register: A European vanguard of strong lobby regulation?', *Interest Groups & Advocacy* 2(2), pp. 139–62.

Habermas, J. (1984). *The Theory of Communicative Action.* Cambridge, UK: Polity Press.

Harris, P. and Fleisher, C.S. (2017). 'Introduction: The continuing development of international corporate and public affairs', in Harris, P. and Fleisher, C.S. (eds.) *The SAGE Handbook of International Corporate and Public Affairs.* London: Sage, pp. 1–15.

Heath, R.L. (2001). 'A rhetorical enactment rationale for public relations: The good organisation communicating well', in Heath, R.L. (ed.) *Handbook of Public Relations.* Thousand Oaks, CA: Sage, pp. 31–50.

Heath, R.L. (2007). 'Management through advocacy: Reflection rather than domination', in Toth, E.L. (ed.) *The future of excellence in public relations and communication management: Challenges for the next generation.* Mahwah, NJ: Lawrence Erlbaum, pp. 41–65.

Heath, R.L. (2011). 'External organisational rhetoric: Bridging management and sociopolitical discourse', *Management Communication Quarterly* 25(3), pp. 415—35.

Heath, R.L., Waymer, D. and Palenchar, M.J. (2013). 'Is the universe of democracy, rhetoric, and public relations whole cloth or three separate galaxies?', *Public Relations Review* 39(4), pp. 271–79.

Held, D. (2006). *Models of Democracy.* Stanford University Press.

Holtzhausen, D.R. (2012). *Public Relations as Activism: Postmodern approaches to theory & practice.* New York: Routledge.

Ihlen, Ø. (2007). 'Building on Bourdieu: A sociological grasp of public relations', *Public Relations Review* 33(3), pp. 269–74.

Ihlen, Ø. (2017). 'Fanning the flames of discontent: Public relations as a radical activity', in Bridgen, E. and Vercic, D. (eds.) *Experiencing public relations: International perspectives.* London: Routledge, pp. 165–73.

Ihlen, Ø., Binderkrantz, A. and Öberg, P. (2020). 'Lobbying in Scandinavia', in Skogerbø, E., Ihlen, Ø., Kristensen, N.N. and Nord, L.W. (eds.) *Nordic Political Communication.* Gothenburg: NORDICOM.

Ihlen, Ø., Raknes, K., Somerville, I., Valentini, C., Stachel, C., Lock, I., Davidson, S. and Seele, P. (2018a) 'Framing "the Public Interest": Comparing public lobbying campaigns in four European states', *Journal of Public Interest Communications* 2(1).

Ihlen, Ø., Verhoeven, P. and Fredriksson, M. (2018b). 'Conclusions on the compass, context, concepts, concerns and empirical avenues for public relations', in Ihlen, Ø. and Fredriksson, M. (eds.) *Public relations* and social theory: Key figures, concepts and developments, 2nd edn. New York: Routledge, pp. 414–31.

Johnston, J. (2016). *Public Relations and the Public Interest*. New York: Routledge.

Jowett, G.S. and O'Donnell, V. (2018). *Propaganda and Persuasion*, 7th edn. London: Sage.

Kelley, S.J. (1956). *Professional Public Relations and Political Power*. Boston, MA: Johns Hopkins University Press.

L'Etang, J. (2004). *Public Relations in Britain: A history of professional practice in the Twentieth Century*. Mahwah, NJ: Lawrence Erlbaum.

Lamme, M.O. and Russell, K.M. (2009). 'Removing the spin: Toward a new theory of public relations history', *Journalism & Communication Monographs* 11(4), pp. 280–362.

Lasswell, H.D. (1936). *Politics: Who gets what, when, how*. New York: Peter Smith.

Leach, R. (2009). 'Public relations and democracy', in Tench, R. and Yeomans, L. (eds.) *Exploring Public Relations*, 2nd edn. Harlow, England: FT Prentice Hall.

Lees-Marshment, J. (2008). *Political Marketing and British Political Parties*, 2nd edn. Manchester: Manchester University Press.

Lees-Marshment, J. (2014). *Political Marketing: Principles and applications*, 2nd edn. London: Routledge.

Martinelli, D.K. (2011). 'Political public relations: Remembering its roots and classics', in Strömbâck, J. and Kiousis, S. (eds.) *Political public relations*. London: Routledge, pp. 33–53.

McGrath, C. (2007). 'Framing lobbying messages: Defining and communicating political issues persuasively', *Journal of Public Affairs* 7(3), pp. 269–80.

McKie, D. and Munshi, D. (2007). *Reconfiguring Public Relations: Ecology, equity and enterprise*. New York: Routledge.

McLean, I. and McMillan, A. (2018). *The Concise Oxford Dictionary of Politics*, 4th edn. Oxford: OUP Oxford.

McNair, B. (2011). *An Introduction to Political Communication*, 5th edn. London: Routledge.

Miller, D. and Dinan, W. (2008). *A Century of Spin: How public relations became the cutting edge of corporate power*. London: Pluto Press.

Moloney, K. (2000). *Rethinking Public Relations: The spin and the substance*. London: Routledge.

Moloney, K. (2006). *Rethinking Public Relations: PR propaganda and democracy*, 2nd edn. London: Routledge.

Moloney, K. and McKie, D. (2015). 'Changes to be encouraged: Radical turns in PR theorisation and small-step evolutions in PR practice', in L'Etang, J., McKie, D., Snow, N. and Xifra, J. (eds.) *Routledge Handbook of Critical Public Relations*. London: Routledge, pp. 151–61.

Motion, J. and Leitch, S. (2015). 'Critical discourse analysis: a search for meaning and power', in L'Etang, J., McKie, D., Snow, N. and Xifra, J. (eds.) *Routledge handbook of critical public relations*. London: Routledge, pp. 142–50.

Mouffe, C. (2000/2005). *The Democratic Paradox*. London: Verso.

Mouffe, C. (2005). *On the Political*. London: Routledge.

Mouffe, C. (2013). *Agonistics: Thinking the world politically*. London: Verso Books.

Nessmann, K. (2000/2003). 'The origins and development of public relations in Germany and Austria', in Moss, D., Verčič, D. and Warnaby, G. (eds.) *Perspectives on public relations research*. London: Routledge, pp. 211–25.

Parsons, P.J. (2016). *Ethics in Public Relations*, 3rd edn. London: Kogan Page.

Persily, N. (2017). 'The 2016 US election: Can democracy survive the internet?', *Journal of democracy* 28(2), pp. 63–76.

Pieczka, M. (2015). 'Dialogue and critical public relations', in L'Etang, J., McKie, D., Snow, N. and Xifra, J. (eds.) *Routledge handbook of critical public relations*. London: Routledge, pp. 76–89.

Pimlott, J.A.R. (1951). *Public relations and American democracy*. Princeton, NJ: Princeton University Press.

Putnam, R. (2000). *Bowling Alone: The collapse and revival of American community*. New York: Touchstone.

Rampton, S. and Stauber, J. (2001). *Trust Us, We're Experts! How industry manipulates science and gambles with your future*. New York: Jeremy P. Tarcher/Putnam.

Ramsey, P. (2015). 'The public sphere and PR: Deliberative democracy and agonistic pluralism', in L'Etang, J., McKie, D., Snow, N. and Xifra, J. (eds.) *Routledge handbook of critical public relations*. London: Routledge, pp. 65–75.

Rommetvedt, H. (2017). 'Scandinavian corporatism in decline', in Knutsen, O. (ed.) *The Nordic Models in Political Science*. Stavanger, Norway, pp. 171–92.

Saward, M. (2010). *The Representative Claim*. London: Oxford University Press.

Schumpeter, J.A. (2003). *Capitalism, Socialism and Democracy*. London: Routledge.

St. John III, B., Lamme, M.O. and L'Etang, J. (eds.) (2014). *Pathways to Public Relations: Histories of practice and profession*. London: Routledge.

Strömbäck, J. and Kiousis, S. (2011). 'Political public relations: Defining and mapping an emergent field', in Strömbäck, J. and Kiousis, S. (eds.) *Political Public Relations: Principles and applications*. London: Routledge, pp. 1–32.

Strömbäck, J. and Kiousis, S. (2019). 'Defining and mapping the field of theory and research on political public relations ', in Strömbäck, J. and Kiousis, S. (eds.) *Political Public Relations: Principles and applications*, 2nd edn. New York: Routledge.

Supran, G. and Oreskes, N. (2017). 'Assessing ExxonMobil's climate change communications (1977–2014)', *Environmental Research Letters* 12(8), pp. 084019.

Tandoc Jr, E.C., Lim, Z.W. and Ling, R. (2018). 'Defining "fake news" A typology of scholarly definitions', *Digital Journalism* 6(2), pp. 137–53.

Taylor, M. (2010). 'Public relations in the enactment of civil society', in Heath, R.L. (ed.) *The SAGE handbook of public relations*. Thousand Oaks, CA: Sage, pp. 5–16.

Taylor, M. and Kent, M.L. (2014). Dialogic engagement: Clarifying foundational concepts. *Journal of Public Relations Research* 26(5), 384–98.

Taylor, P.M. (2003). *Munitions of the mind: A history of propaganda from the ancient world to the present day*, 3rd edn. Manchester, UK: Manchester University Press.

Trapp, N.L. and Laursen, B. (2017). 'Inside out: interest groups' 'outside' media work as a means to manage 'inside' lobbying efforts and relationships with politicians', *Interest Groups & Advocacy* 6(2), pp. 143–60.

Trujillo, N. and Toth, E.L. (1987). 'Organizational perspectives for public relations research and practice', *Management Communication Quarterly* 1(2), pp. 199–231.

Uhre, A.N. and Rommetvedt, H. (2019). 'Civil associations and interst groups in the polocy-making priocesss: Pluralisation and generalisation of interests', *Interest Groups & Advocacy*.

Waisbord, S. (2018). 'The elective affinity between post-truth communication and populist politics', *Communication Research and Practice* 4(1), pp. 17–34.

Walle, M. (2003). 'Commentary: What happened to public responsibility? The lack of society in public relations codes of ethics', *PRism* 1(1).

Washbourne, N. (2010). *Mediating politics: Newspapers, radio, television and the Internet*. New York: McGraw-Hill Education (UK).

Waymer, D. and Heath, R.L. (2015). 'Critical race and public relations: The case of environmental racism and risk bearer agency', in L'Etang, J., McKie, D., Snow, N. and Xifra, J. (eds.) *Routledge handbook of critical public relations*. London: Routledge, pp. 289–302.

Weaver, K., Motion, J. and Roper, J. (2006). 'From propaganda to discourse (and back again): Truth, power, the public interest and public relations', in L'Etang, J. and Pieczka, M. (eds.) *Public relations: Critical debates and contemporary practice*. Mahwah, NJ: Lawrence Erlbaum, pp. 7–21.

YouTube (see https://www.youtube.com/watch?v=koPmuEyP3a0&t=1s). Accessed 5 February 2020.

Websites

https://www.europarl.eu (see http://www.europarl.europa.eu/committees/en/envi/events-hearings.html?id=20190313CHE06141).
https://www.globalalliancepr.org/code-of-ethics
https://www.cipr.co.uk/ethics
https://www.prsa.org/ethics/code-of-ethics/
https://www.alter-eu.org/
https://corporateeurope.org/en
http://spinwatch.org/
https://www.prwatch.org/

CHAPTER 5

Ralph Tench

Community and society
Corporate social responsibility (CSR)

Source: Volodymyr Burdiak/Shutterstock

Learning outcomes

By the end of this chapter you should be able to:
- critically evaluate the role of organisations in their society(ies)
- define the concept of corporate social responsibility in the context of relevant regulatory frameworks
- define and critically evaluate the role of ethics in business policy and practice
- diagnose ethical problems and identify strategies for making ethical decisions in organisational/cultural contexts
- appreciate the environmental complexities that influence organisational communication and public relations strategies.

Structure

- Businesses are integral to our society(ies)
- Social and economic change
- Sustainable business: corporate social responsibility (CSR)
- Business case for corporate social responsibility: why be socially responsible?
- Organisational responsibilities to stakeholders
- Organisational responsibilities to society
- Regulatory frameworks
- Ethics and business practice

Introduction

If you saw a child helping an elderly citizen cross the road or giving up a seat for them on the train, you would probably think it was a mature and generous act by someone with a considered view of their place in society. If the child then went home and wrote about it in their private diary it may still be viewed as a positive action being considered and reflected on to inform the child's future behaviour in similar situations. The child could then share the experience over dinner with family members to elicit praise, credit or a reward of a coveted sweet or drink. What if they then went to their school headteacher (principal) soliciting further praise, even a headteacher's award, which may attract interest from outside the school through a parental contact with the local paper? And the accolades pour in.

A little far-fetched perhaps, but is this analogous with organisations and their involvement in society through corporate social responsibility? It may be for some. Certainly criticisms have been levelled at some companies for over-promoting their acts of corporate giving, particularly around major incidents such as September 11 in the US and the Asian tsunami in December 2004. We have also been forced to reflect on major corporations' responsibilities and responsible behaviour in the aftermath of the 2008 economic crises. Significantly, companies' involvement with communities has transformed over the years. What are organisations' motivations and interests in their communities? How much are they interested in doing something 'good' and how much in being acknowledged, recognised and rewarded for this act? Earlier in the text we discussed the role of organisations in their communities and in this chapter we will explore the different ways in which organisations apply their individual interpretations of community involvement and how this can have various outcomes, outputs, benefits and rewards for them and the communities they are involved with.

The chapter will therefore build understanding of an organisation's role in society and importantly how they manage their responsibilities and, crucially, the communication of those commitments.

Businesses are integral to our society(ies)

Google, Facebook, Amazon, eBay and Apple are some of our favourite and most used brands day to day. But they also top the hit list of corporate pariahs for many. In April 2019, of the Fortune 500 companies that had already filed their 2018 taxes, 60 were profitable and yet avoided all US federal income tax, according to an Institute on Taxation and Economic Policy (ITEP) (Sherman 2019). The total US income of the 60 (which includes companies such as Amazon, Chevron, General Motors, Delta, Halliburton and IBM) was more than $79 billion and the effective tax rate was -5 per cent. On average, the report claims, they got tax refunds. On a similar vein in 2016 a similar list of high-profile companies were accused of avoiding £1 billion of UK tax (*Huffington Post*, 3 February 2016) and this behaviour repeats with subsequent years seeing repeated exposure and critique of big corporates and their tax avoidance. So, it seems corporate behaviour continues to be questioned and more worryingly serious wrongdoing is not going away. You might have thought that financial crises and corporate scandals would put executives off steering their companies down a path that will clearly raise the hackles of consumer groups and key stakeholders. In the past 20 years we have seen corporate goliaths like Volkswagen, Unilever, WorldCom, Enron, Shell UK, Union Carbide, BP, Wal-Mart, Lehman Brothers and Exxon Corporation fall under the worldwide media spotlight for their corporate actions and activities. Executives from these companies have at varying times over the past two decades been vilified by the media, attacked by shareholders and customers and in some instances imprisoned. Why? Because the organisations they represent have had a major impact on the social and physical environments in which they operate (e.g. oil and chemical leaks and more recently financial mismanagement). This chapter will explore the role of organisations in society and how, irrespective of the profit or not-for-profit imperatives, many are taking a critical view of their roles and responsibilities. In many instances (including some of the companies above), this has involved a radical repositioning of the organisation's *vision and values* that are impacting on the operational as well as the public relations (communication) strategies they employ.

Concern for the environment in which a business operates is not a new phenomenon but its prevalence in business policy across the globe is growing and, due to the internationalisation of markets and business practice, this is influencing corporate strategy for large PLCs and small- to medium-sized enterprises (SMEs) throughout the world. These corporate policy changes are encouraging organisations to increase their awareness and concern for the society(ies) in which they operate. An additional development is in the more sophisticated business use of the societal relationship as part of the corporate strategy and as a marketing tool. This has been demonstrated through the expansion of sponsorship programmes (see Chapter 22) as well as through the development of cause-related marketing (CRM) – associating companies or brands with charitable causes. This chapter will describe in detail the relationships between an organisation and the community within which it operates. It will explore the complex issue of business ethics with guidelines on how to promote ethical decision making in practice. There are links from this chapter to Chapter 16, which explores how public relations is responding to an increasingly CSR-conscious business environment through the development of communications programmes (see Case study 5.1).

Social and economic change

All our societies are continually changing and evolving. Factors such as economic and financial performance have a significant influence on our standards of living and manifest themselves in day-to-day measures such as inflation, taxation, fuel and food prices. These issues are increasingly being highlighted and recognised as the world comes to terms with the significant changes in economic power as North America and Europe move in and out of more regular economic downturns. It is relevant to note the impact worldwide of the US originated 'credit crunch' in 2008/9 where the ability for banks to lend money to businesses and individuals had a major rippling effect on established economies and even brought down some major companies such as Lehman Brothers in September 2008. The effect from this credit crunch reverberated for many years, impacting significantly other economic regions with the Eurozone suffering severe financial crises in 2012 and leading to an ongoing lack of confidence across Europe raising questions about its viability and sustainability, not least with the UK's threatened withdrawal from the EU in 2016. This led to the divisive Brexit debates in the UK which split opinions almost 50–50 in leave and remain camps after a much criticised referendum on the topic and culminated in an eventual withdrawal decision in 2019/20. As some national economies have experienced recession or a slow down in growth others, such as India, China and parts of South America, expanded rapidly but then also faced economic slow down and instability. Brazil saw this in sharp focus during 2016 when it should have been celebrating the arrival of the international caravan that is the Rio Olympics, the country was in financial and economic turmoil with a health crisis on top. The role of business is therefore put into the spotlight as we witness patterns of change in the climate and the environment more generally. Issues such as health

Case study 5.1
British Airways – supporting humanitarian efforts

The UK flagship airline British Airways (BA) supports humanitarian relief partners including Oxfam, UNICEF and Save the Children to transport emergency aid and supplies to countries devastated by disaster. Along with relief flights, BA assists with donations and fundraising events for victims. Since 2005 it has made available more than 1,000 disaster response specialists who ensure that the right aid is given to those in need. During the Asian Tsunami, BA supported UNICEF's emergency response by transporting 190 tonnes of vital supplies. Similarly, it dispatched vehicles and other equipment for the Red Cross during the Haiti earthquake. Other significant contributions include the donation of 40 relief aircrafts to Oxfam personnel during the Kenyan food crisis.

Impact

BA's emergency response is claimed to have:

- supported experts and charities to provide both physical and psychological aid to several disaster-ravaged countries;
- deployed BA flights to even countries the airline doesn't serve, thereby providing immediate response to victims.

Source: www.britishairways.com

scares (AIDS or the Zeka virus, 2016) and the ongoing issue of global warming are as a consequence brought into sharp focus by a range of campaign and interest groups as well as by senior public and political figures (Kofi Anan with the United Nations, Bill Gates and former US presidential candidate Al Gore). Al Gore's book (2007) and film (2006) *An Inconvenient Truth* (www.climatecrisis.net) focused on and highlighted the environmental damage being caused by modern, consumptive societies/businesses. Although a debated concept, Gore's work did raise the level at which such discussions were being held in nation states. It is not directly as a consequence but in line with this increased awareness there are now many more and powerful organisations asking questions about the role and responsibilities of business in a global society (see the Global Responsible Leadership Initiative (www.grli.org) and the UN Global Compact established in 2000 (www.unglobalcompact.org)).

More recently challenges are being made on the foundations of business principles and how they are 'governed'. Particularly this has relevance following the lack of governance in the finance sector which was blamed in large part for the 2008 financial crisis (Sun et al. 2011; Clarke 2009). It has been argued this system permitted and even encouraged corporations to manipulate share price and abuse corporate accounting principles in the name of shareholder value (see Enron, WorldCom, Lehman Brothers and others and captured in the hit film *The Big Short* in 2015). In this context we have seen a lot of new governance codes in the UK and USA since 2008 but we are still experiencing accusations of excessive bonuses for CEOs and senior managers as well as banks perceived as 'too big to fail'. From this perspective Sir Mervyn King, Governor of the Bank of England, claimed Britain was at risk of another financial crisis without reforms to the banks (*The Telegraph*, 5 March 2011) and Nobel prize-winning economist Robert Shiller (2015, 2016) also warned of repeats of the economic collapse worldwide.

B Corporations

A more recent business structure is the B Corporation. Certified B Corporations are businesses that meet the highest standards of verified social and environmental performance, public transparency and legal accountability to balance profit and purpose. They are prevalent in the US but spreading worldwide as a different way of structuring and managing a business. Their aim is to generate a global culture shift to redefine success in business and build a more inclusive and sustainable economy. B Corps aim to use their profits and growth as a means to improve performance and the experience of their employees and wider communities. The B Corporation community works towards reduced inequality, lower levels of poverty, a healthier environment, stronger communities and the creation of more high-quality jobs. Certified B Corporations achieve a minimum verified score on the B Impact Assessment – a rigorous assessment of a company's impact on its workers, customers, community and environment. They also make their B Impact Reports available on bcorporation.net. Certified B Corporations also amend their legal governing documents to require their board of directors to balance profit and purpose. To date, more than 3,000 companies globally have become B Corps after completing a certification process. High-profile B Corporations include The North Face, The Body Shop, Danone and Procter & Gamble.

Sustainable business: corporate social responsibility (CSR)

There is no agreement on the extent companies should engage with societies in which they operate (Topic and Tench 2016; Tench et al. 2014; Dahlsrud 2008; Carroll 1979).

Individual members and groups in the community in which an organisation operates are increasingly being recognised as important *stakeholders* in the long-term security and success of large and small enterprises. Building relationships with these community groups is, therefore, an important issue in corporate and communications strategy. In order to understand how this can be achieved it is essential to understand in more detail the complexities of the relationships between a business and its community(ies). It is also important to define some of the business terminology that is frequently used when analysing businesses in their societal contexts.

Corporate social responsibility

A well-used business and management term, corporate social responsibility (CSR), is often associated with the phrase 'enlightened self-interest' – how organisations plan and manage their relationships with key stakeholders. CSR is, therefore, an organisation's defined responsibility to its society(ies) and stakeholders. Although

70 Part 1 THE CONTEXT OF PUBLIC RELATIONS

organisations are not a state, country or region, they are part of the infrastructure of society and as such they must consider their impact on it. A simple analogy for the impact organisations have on their community has been presented by Peach (1987; see Figure 5.1), which shows the ripples from a stone thrown into a pond to represent the impact of a business on its environment. There are three levels of impact ranging from the *basic*, in which a company adheres to society's rules and regulations, to the *societal*, where a company makes significant contributions towards improving the society in which it operates. In the middle level, companies are perceived to manage their activities so they adhere to the level and go beyond it. For example, this might be a company obeying legal requirements on employment rights as a foundation and then providing more generous interpretations of these legal rulings. Also the company may seek to reduce the negative impact of the organisation on its society without necessarily taking positive action to make improvements that would take it to level three (see also Box 5.1).

Companies operating at the highest level, *societal*, do exist: companies are increasingly obtaining public recognition and visibility for their positive corporate actions. For example, in the UK, Business in the Community (BITC) has a CommunityMark (launched in 2007 and formerly the Percent Standard/Club, started in 1986 which was awarded as a voluntary benchmark to companies donating at least 1 per cent of pre-tax profits to community/social benefits). The CommunityMark was launched with an initial 21 member companies which met the five principles (see CommunityMark discussed at www.bitc.org.uk). See also Box 5.2 and Figure 5.2.

> **Box 5.1**
> # Peach model in action
>
> Some clear examples at the *basic* level might be a company in the supermarket retail sector that is profitable, pays its taxes and maintains minimum terms and conditions for its employees. At the highest, *societal*, level you could describe a supermarket retailer that conforms to society's rules and laws but also contributes to its society by funding community initiatives (e.g. holidays for disadvantaged children, investments in school facilities, transport for elderly people, lobbying for improved treatment of waste by local companies in line with its initiatives, contributing to positive legislation change in support of society, surpassing national and international employment rights and conditions, innovation in childcare or part-time mothers' conditions of work, etc.).

Level three: **Societal**
- Responsibility for a healthy society
- Help remove/alleviate society's ills (problems)

Level two: **Organisational**
- Minimise negative effects
- Act in the spirit of the law

Level one: **Basic**
- Pay taxes
- Observe the law
- Deal fairly

Figure 5.1 Impact of business on its environment (*source:* after Peach 1987: 191–3)

Box 5.2

CommunityMark Pioneer Companies (UK)

The 21 initial businesses to achieve the CommunityMark at the launch in September 2008 were:

Axis, Barclays, Blackburn Rovers Football & Athletic Club, BT, Contract Scotland, Deloitte, Design Links, Elementus, Ernst & Young, GlaxoSmithKline, HBOS, Heart of Midlothian Football, KPMG, Marks and Spencer, PricewaterhouseCoopers, Rangers Football Club, RWE npower, Sainsbury's, Tesco, The Town House Collection, Zurich Financial Services (UK). A list of the latest CommunityMark holders is published at http://www.bitc.org.uk/services/awards-recognition/communitymark/current-holders-communitymark

In 2018 the Lloyds Banking Group was the UK Business in the Community (BITC) Responsible Business of the Year. For the case studies of winners from previous years see: https://www.bitc.org.uk

Source: Business in the Community (www.bitc.org.uk)

Explore 5.1

Business impact on society

Identify, name and describe a company or organisation that fits into each of the levels in the 'stone in the pond' analogy.

What would those organisations in levels one and two need to do to move towards the third, societal level?

Feedback

You need to consider what changes in ethical business policy or practice would make a difference to society. It is not enough just to make statements of intent.

When considering CSR it is important to make a distinction between corporate activities that are intended to contribute to the society and charitable acts or philanthropy (see Explore 5.1).

Philanthropy

One simple definition of *philanthropy* is that 'corporations perform charitable actions'. This is very different from CSR, with philanthropy being a charitable act

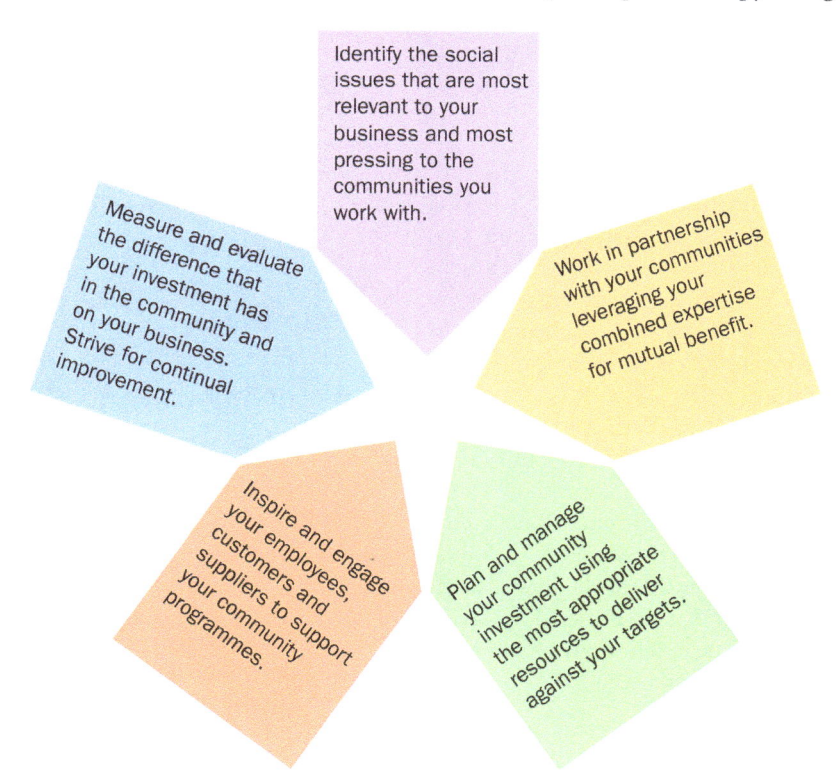

- Identify the social issues that are most relevant to your business and most pressing to the communities you work with.
- Work in partnership with your communities leveraging your combined expertise for mutual benefit.
- Plan and manage your community investment using the most appropriate resources to deliver against your targets.
- Inspire and engage your employees, customers and suppliers to support your community programmes.
- Measure and evaluate the difference that your investment has in the community and on your business. Strive for continual improvement.

Figure 5.2 BITC CommunityMark five principles (*source*: Training Course: Community Investment Strategy – London." Business in the Community, https://www.bitc.org.uk/event/training-course-community-investment-strategy/)

not necessarily linked to the expectations of society. Philanthropy did occur in large industrial firms in the UK during the nineteenth century (such as Joseph Rowntree, Titus Salt) through the donation of money and amenities such as schools, hospitals or housing for employees and their communities. *Corporate philanthropy* can be perceived as a short-term one-way relationship, which is unpredictable on behalf of the recipient and therefore more difficult to manage and strategically plan for. For example, during the dotcom boom (during the late 1990s when the financial performance and market impact of web-based businesses and technology companies in general were seriously exaggerated), technology company directors commonly gave large sums in charitable donations.

Corporate giving is reported by different bodies including the Giving Institute in the US reporting every June. For 2018/19 the Institute reported the total giving of over $400 billion for the first time. The breakdown for the figures for the preceding tax year were:

- **Giving by individuals** at an estimated $286.65 billion, rising 5.2 per cent in 2017 (an increase of 3.0 per cent, adjusted for inflation).
- **Giving by foundations** increased 6.0 per cent, to an estimated $66.90 billion in 2017 (an increase of 3.8 per cent, adjusted for inflation).
- **Giving by corporations** is estimated to have increased by 8.0 per cent in 2017, in total $20.77 billion (an increase of 5.7 per cent, adjusted for inflation).

(The Giving Institute 2018)

Depending on the general and sector-specific economic performance, individuals go on or off the giving lists, reinforcing the unpredictable nature of this type of activity. For example, Bill Gates (the world's richest man and Microsoft's founder) was on the list in 2001 with $2 billion in gifts. In 2005 Gates made the largest ever private donation of £400 million ($750 million) to the child health charity he set up with his wife, Melinda, the Bill and Melinda Gates Foundation (www.gatesfoundation.org). In 2008 Bill Gates relinquished his management of Microsoft to become non-executive chairman and his foundation to date has given grants and donations totalling $50.1 billion (audited financial accounts for 2018). He has also set up with fellow businessman Warren Buffet 'The Giving Pledge' to encourage the super rich to give away their wealth. Buffet is quoted (www.slate.com 2011):

'I've worked in an economy that rewards someone who saves the lives of others on a battlefield with a medal, rewards a great teacher with thank-you notes from parents, but rewards those who can detect the mispricing of securities with sums reaching into the billions,' Buffett wrote, reiterating his decision to give away 99 percent of his wealth. 'That reality sets an obvious course for me and my family: Keep all we can conceivably need and distribute the rest to society, for its needs.'

Although gifts can be turned on and off by the donor like a tap, there are some benefactors who donate through trusts, which enable the act to be sustained over longer periods of time (e.g. the Rowntree Foundation or the Wellcome Trust in the UK, the John D. Rockefeller Foundation or the Bill and Melinda Gates Foundation) (see Explore 5.2).

In recognition of the interest shown by various stakeholder groups – employees, customers and particularly the financial community and investors – it is now common business practice for large and small- to medium-sized enterprises (SMEs) to publish corporate literature and brochures giving details of their community activities and CSR. Non-financial reporting on corporate responsibility in annual reports became prevalent in the mid-1990s. In the UK, for example, BT's annual review and summary financial statement (1996/7) included a section called 'Why we are helping the community: we're all part of the same team'. Within the report BT stated that:

It is increasingly clear that businesses cannot regard themselves as in some way separate from the communities in which they operate. Besides, research has shown that the decision to purchase from one company rather than another is not a decision about price alone.

Explore 5.2

Identifying CSR and philanthropic actions

List examples of what you might consider to be CSR or philanthropic actions by an organisation/company.

Feedback

Can you make distinctions between the two? Think about each organisation's objectives for the action. What was the intended outcome? What did it hope to achieve? Was it long term? Was it pre-planned or in response to an individual(s) request?

Business case for corporate social responsibility: why be socially responsible?

Organisations in developed economies are today influenced by public opinion, shareholders, stakeholders (who can be shareholders, consumers and members of campaign groups) and the political process. Consequently, organisations that ignore their operational environment are susceptible to restrictive legislation and regulation. This is a particular issue in Europe with the increasing power and influence of the European Union, the single currency and the European parliamentary process. Representative bodies for business such as Business in the Community (BITC), CSR Europe, Institute of Business Ethics, Business for Social Responsibility, and the Prince of Wales International Business Leaders Forum (IBLF) have formed to help senior managers deal with the demands of varied stakeholder groups.

In 2004, the European Commission issued recommendations asking for 'raising awareness and improving knowledge on CSR, developing the capacities and competences to help mainstreaming CSR', and 'ensuring an enabling environment for CSR' (European Multistakeholder Forum on CSR Report and Recommendations, 2004). The EU's CSR policy from 2004 came as a result of European NGOs and trade unions that pressured companies for more responsible behaviour, especially in non-Western societies (Blowfield 2005). Other international organisations also defined CSR, e.g. the World Bank (2003), World Business Council for Sustainable Development (2015) and UNIDO (2015). What is common to all definitions is the emphasis on the crucial role of stakeholders even if they put more emphasis on different matters that constitute CSR (e.g. environment, worker's rights, etc.). Also outside the EU, influencers such as the United Nations (UN Global Compact) are making an impact on business and political decision making.

As noted earlier, another recent development are Certified B Corporations. Certified B Corporations are businesses that meet the highest standards of verified social and environmental performance, public transparency and legal accountability to balance profit and purpose. B Corps are said to be driving an acceleration towards a global culture shift that redefines success in business and builds a more inclusive and sustainable economy. B Corporations include outdoor clothing manufacturer Patagonia, smoothie drinks brand Innocent as well as Ben & Jerry's ice cream.

But a question still comes up for organisational leaders: Is CSR good business practice? On the one hand, many companies profited from unethical practices in the early part of the twentieth century, as demonstrated by the success of textile and mining industries and more recently with companies manufacturing chemical-based products such as asbestos. Furthermore, Milton Friedman has been championed as the consistent (if sometimes mis-quoted) business voice stating that the business of business is simply to increase profits and enhance shareholder value. Friedman (1970) wrote key articles arguing these views in the 1960s and 1970s. Although there are few contemporary academic papers supporting his views, they are frequently cited as the opposing arguments to CSR.

On the other hand, in contrast to Friedman's views, there are the examples of both old and new companies benefiting themselves, their stakeholders and employees through more ethically based practice. Worldwide examples include Cadbury, Lever's, IBM, Co-Operative Bank and Coca-Cola. Even before corporate responsibility became a boardroom agenda item around the turn of the millennium, there

---

Box 5.3

Four strategies of CSR response

Four strategies of response to stakeholder perspectives on CSR have been identified, as follows:

1. An *inactive* strategy: resisting societal expectations and sometimes government regulation.

2. A *reactive* strategy: responding to unanticipated change after the significant change has occurred.

3. A *proactive* strategy: attempting to 'get ahead' of a societal expectation or government regulation (often coupled with efforts to influence the outcome).

4. An *interactive* strategy: anticipating change and blending corporate goals with those of stakeholders and societal expectations. An organisation employing an interactive strategy consciously reduces the gap between its performance and society's expectations. An interactive strategy is often accomplished by management's commitment to a serious dialogue with stakeholders.

is evidence of its commercial value. For example, Johnson & Johnson's chief executive officer, James Burke, demonstrates that companies with a reputation for ethics and social responsibility grew at a rate of 11.3 per cent annually from 1959 to 1990 while the growth rate for similar companies without the same ethical approach was 6.2 per cent (Labich 1992). Furthermore, arguments and evidence are put forward to support CSR's contribution to the financial performance of organisations (Little and Little 2000; Moore 2003).

CSR can contribute to corporate image and reputation (Lewis 2003; Sagar and Singla 2004). The importance of a good reputation can include the following:

- Others are more willing to consider the organisation's point of view.
- It helps to strengthen the organisation's information structure with society and therefore improve resources in all areas.
- It makes it easier for the organisation to motivate and recruit employees – and to promote increased employee morale (Lines 2004).
- It will enhance and add value to the organisation's products and services.

A socially responsible reputation is also a way of differentiating organisations and providing competitive advantage. This is supported by announcements from companies such as McDonald's and BT in the UK that they would be investing more time and resources into socially responsible activities. BT was influenced by a MORI report, which stated that 80 per cent of respondents believed it was important to know about an organisation's socially responsible activities in order to form a positive opinion about them. CEOs worldwide are starting to recognise that CSR is an important agenda item. Research by the India Partnership Forum (2003) claimed that nearly 70 per cent of CEOs stated that CSR was 'vital' to profitability and that, irrespective of economic climate, it would remain a high priority for 60 per cent of CEOs across the globe.

A company with an acknowledged strategy change on corporate responsibility and environmental engagement is oil firm Royal Dutch/Shell. During 1998, Shell had its first meeting with institutional shareholders (major company investors, e.g. on behalf of pension funds) to explain the company's new policies on environmental and social responsibilities. This initiative came following criticism of the company's action in high-profile environmental issues (e.g. when Shell was challenged by campaign groups over its decision to dismantle the Brent Spar oil platform at sea rather than on land owing to the supposed environmental impact) and human rights cases (execution of human rights activist Ken Sara Wiwo, in Ogoniland, where Shell had a dominant interest).

At the meeting with shareholders, Mark Moody Stuart of Shell Transport and Trading (the company's UK arm) stated that he did not agree with arguments that institutional shareholders were not interested in issues such as social responsibility: 'I don't think there is a fundamental conflict between financial performance and "soft" issues. Many shareholders want outstanding financial returns in a way they can feel proud of or comfortable with.' (See Think abouts 5.1 and 5.2.)

The business case for CSR continues to be made and particularly by communications professionals. Zerfass et al. (2008) in a survey of over 1500 communications practitioners across Europe (European Communication Monitor) found that three out of four of them are involved directly with CSR activities as part of their job (profit and not for profit organisations). Furthermore they found that the main driver for CSR in the sample (70 per cent) was for reputation management. Again according to Zerfass et al.'s study the main focus of communication on CSR is for enhancing the corporate profile (values

Think about 5.1

Shell Europe

During both the Brent Spar and Ogoniland crises, Shell faced a Europe-wide consumer boycott of its fuel products as well as significant media criticism (see above, www.shelluk.co.uk, www.greenpeace.org.uk). Why do you think Shell took the potentially risky strategy of reopening debate about environmental and societal issues after such high-profile vilification by the two important stakeholder groups (consumers of their products and the media)?

Feedback

This initiative by Shell clearly demonstrates the company directors' desire to tackle key issues head on but also to make the company more accountable to its publics and specifically to the communities (and therefore stakeholder groups) in which it operates.

Chapter 5 Community and society: corporate social responsibility (CSR) 75

> **Think about 5.2**
>
> ### Business effects of CSR
>
> Does CSR stretch an organisation's relationship with, and activities of, its supply chains (companies that supply products and services)? Can you think of suppliers for a company that it should not be associated with?
>
> ### Feedback
>
> Some companies have developed supplier policies that define the requirements for supplier organisations. For example, it would not be socially responsible for a furniture retailer that operates a 'green' purchasing policy to buy its raw materials from suppliers who purchase their wood from unsustainable sources.

and strategies of the organisation). Interestingly though regional differences in Europe were identified with social action being a priority in Southern and Eastern Europe whereas corporate ethics plays a more important role for organisations in Northern and Western Europe. Also through monitoring predictions of the most important disciplines in communication management across Europe the ECM survey, now in its fourteenth year (Zerfass et al. 2007, 2008, 2009, 2010, 2011, 2012, 2013, 2014, 2015, 2016, 2017, 2018, 2019, 2020) has found that CSR is predicted to gain in importance for communication practitioners working in profit and not-for-profit organisations (Tench et al. 2017; see also www.communicationmonitor.eu).

Organisational responsibilities to stakeholders

Stakeholder analysis is a clear way of defining those groups and individuals who have a significant relationship with an organisation (see also Chapters 8 and 9). Stakeholders can be described as those with a vested interest in the organisation's operations. Figure 5.3 simply demonstrates the most common stakeholders in for-profit organisations.

These are simplified stakeholder groups which can be expanded and broken down into subgroups. In order for an organisation to act with social responsibility it is necessary to understand the fundamental elements of the organisation's operations and its

Picture 5.1 Ken Saro-Wiwa was a human right activist from Ogoniland where Shell had a dominant interest. (*source:* PIUS UTOMI EKPEI/AFP/Getty Images)

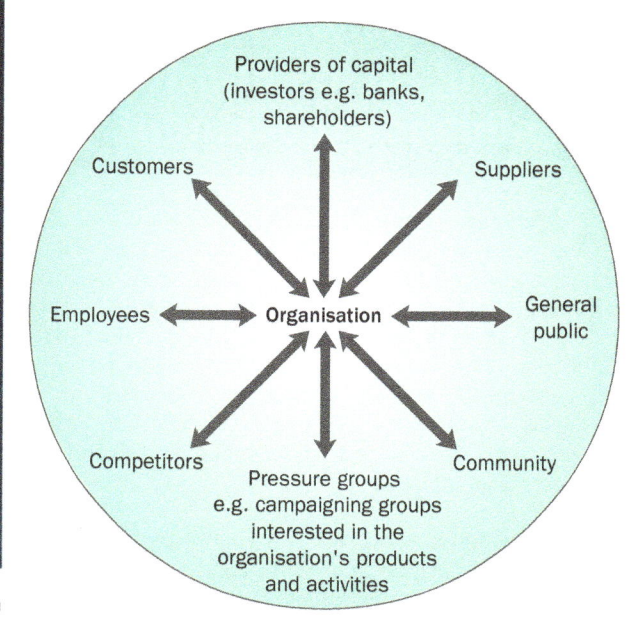

Figure 5.3 Typical for-profit organisational stakeholders

relationships with stakeholders. To achieve this it can be helpful to ask and analyse the following questions:

1. How is the organisation financed, e.g. shareholders, private ownership, loans, etc.?
2. Who are the customers for the products and services, e.g. agents, distributors, traders, operators, end users, etc.?
3. What are the employee conditions and terms, including status, contracts and hierarchical structures?
4. Are there community interactions at local, regional, national and international levels?
5. Are there governmental, environmental or legislative actions that impact on the organisation?
6. What are the competitor influences on the organisation, e.g. markets, agents, distributors, customers, suppliers?
7. What are the supplier influences on the organisation, e.g. other creditors, financial supporters, competitors?
8. Are there any issues or potential risks that may be affected by local, national or international pressure groups or interests?

CSR from a stakeholder perspective may bring the organisation closer to its stakeholders and importantly improve the two-way flow (Grunig and Hunt 1984) of information and subsequently understanding.

Once stakeholders are identified, you need to define the responsibilities you have towards them and then define and develop strategies to manage these relationships (see Explore 5.3).

> **Explore 5.3**
>
> **Defining organisational stakeholders**
>
> a. Choose an organisation and define its stakeholders.
> b. How would you prioritise these stakeholders in terms of their importance to financial performance for the organisation?
>
> **Feedback**
>
> Financial performance is important for all organisations but this prioritised list may look different if instead it were arranged according to CSR performance towards stakeholders.

> **Mini case study 5.1**
>
> **Always #LikeAGirl: Turning an insult into a confidence movement**
>
> Proctor and Gamble's (P&G) feminine care brand Always 'like a girl' campaign is a female empowerment initiative. A survey conducted by P&G for the campaign showed that over 70 per cent of girls – particularly those around puberty – lose self-confidence due to unfavourable social conditions. The research also found that the negative connotations associated with the expression 'like a girl' had an adverse effect on girls with just 19 per cent of them recognising the expression as a compliment.
>
> The long-term campaign aims to redefine perceptions about the phrase 'like a girl' which often depicts femininity as belittling. The campaign is supported by an empowering video which puts forward the rhetorical question, When did doing something 'like a girl' become an insult? In the video which was considered a social experiment, different groups of girls, men and young women are asked to throw, run and fight 'like a girl'. While prepubescent girls carried out the task in a much more confident manner with strong connections, the older women and men acted in a stereotypical way demonstrating how the expression is erroneously perceived by society. The campaign, therefore, is a prominent example of breaking up such gender stereotypes to empower females to improve their self-esteem.
>
> The 'like a girl' campaign went viral after its launch in June 2014, and even became more popular after its video was aired during the 2015 Super Bowl. It was adjudged the best cause-marketing campaign in 2015 at the PRWeek awards and also claimed the coveted Grand prix award at the Cannes Lions in the same year.
>
> Post campaign research showed that 76 per cent of women between the ages of 16 and 24 no longer perceive the phrase as negative. Two out of three men who also watched the video indicated they would be more careful about using 'like a girl' in a way that is demeaning.
>
> *Source:* Adapted from http://www.pg.com

Picture 5.2 Always #LikeAGirl aims to break stereotypes to empower girls everywhere (*source:* Erik McGregor/Pacific Press/Alamy Stock Photo)

Organisational responsibilities to society

Business ethics writer Carroll (1991) argues there are four kinds of social responsibility: economic; legal; ethical; and philanthropic, demonstrated through the CSR pyramid in Figure 5.4.

To aid managers in the evaluation of an organisation's social responsibilities and to help them plan how to fulfil the legal, ethical, economic and philanthropic obligations, Carroll designed a 'stakeholder responsibility matrix' (see Table 5.1). Carroll makes the clear distinction that social responsibility does not begin with good intentions but with stakeholder actions.

Carroll's matrix is proposed as an analytical tool or framework to help company managers make sense of their ideas about what the firm should be doing, economically, legally, ethically and philanthropically, with respect to its defined stakeholder groups. In practice, the matrix is effective as it encourages the manager to record both descriptive (qualitative) and statistical data to manage each stakeholder. This information is then useful when identifying priorities in long- and short-term business decision making that involves the multiple stakeholder groups that influence most organisations. It enables these decisions to be made in the context of the company's or organisation's value systems – what it stands for – as well as accommodating economic, social and environmental factors. To express this simply, the manager is able to make decisions in a more informed way with a clear map of the numerous factors that will impact on these decisions. It is a detailed approach to stakeholder management but is one way of providing informed foundations about stakeholders to enable strategies, actions or decisions

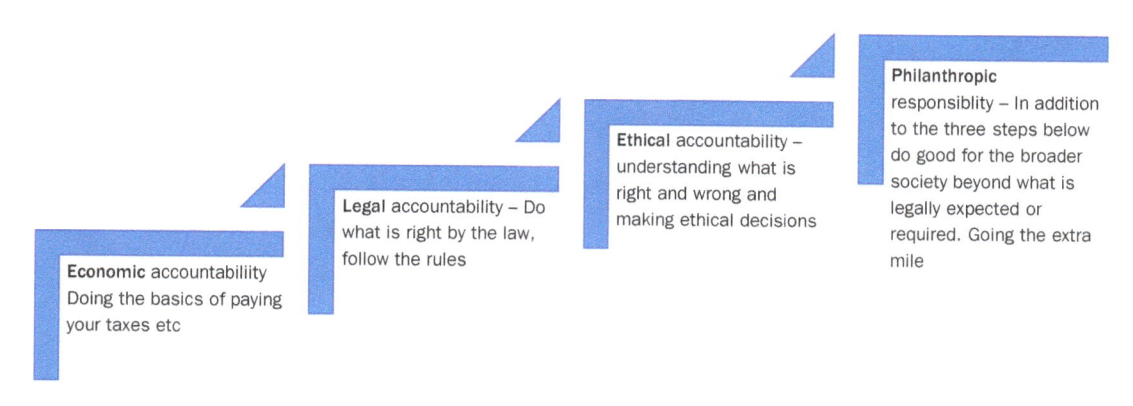

Economic accountability Doing the basics of paying your taxes etc

Legal accountability – Do what is right by the law, follow the rules

Ethical accountability – understanding what is right and wrong and making ethical decisions

Philanthropic responsiblity – In addition to the three steps below do good for the broader society beyond what is legally expected or required. Going the extra mile

Figure 5.4 Corporate social responsibility pyramid (*source:* Based on Carroll, A.B. (1991). 'The pyramid of corporate social responsibility: toward the moral management of organizational stakeholders.' Business Horizons 34(4): 39–48)

Stakeholders:	Economic	Legal	Ethical	Philanthropic
Investors (banks)/owners				
Consumers (or customers)				
Internal staff/employees				
The wider society and local community				
Market competition/competitors				
Suppliers				
NGOs and pressure groups				
General population				

Table 5.1 Stakeholder responsibility matrix

to be taken that reflect the complex environment in which most organisations operate (see also Figure 5.5).

Table 5.2 provides an example of the matrix applied to one stakeholder group and the types of recorded data required. The organisation is a small clothing manufacturing business. The stakeholder group used for the analysis is customers. Each social responsibility cell has been considered in the context of this stakeholder group and data input currently available about the responsibility the firm acknowledges towards this group. Clearly the data included are not exhaustive and further records could be sought or gaps in information identified and subsequently commissioned by the public relations or communications team. This information

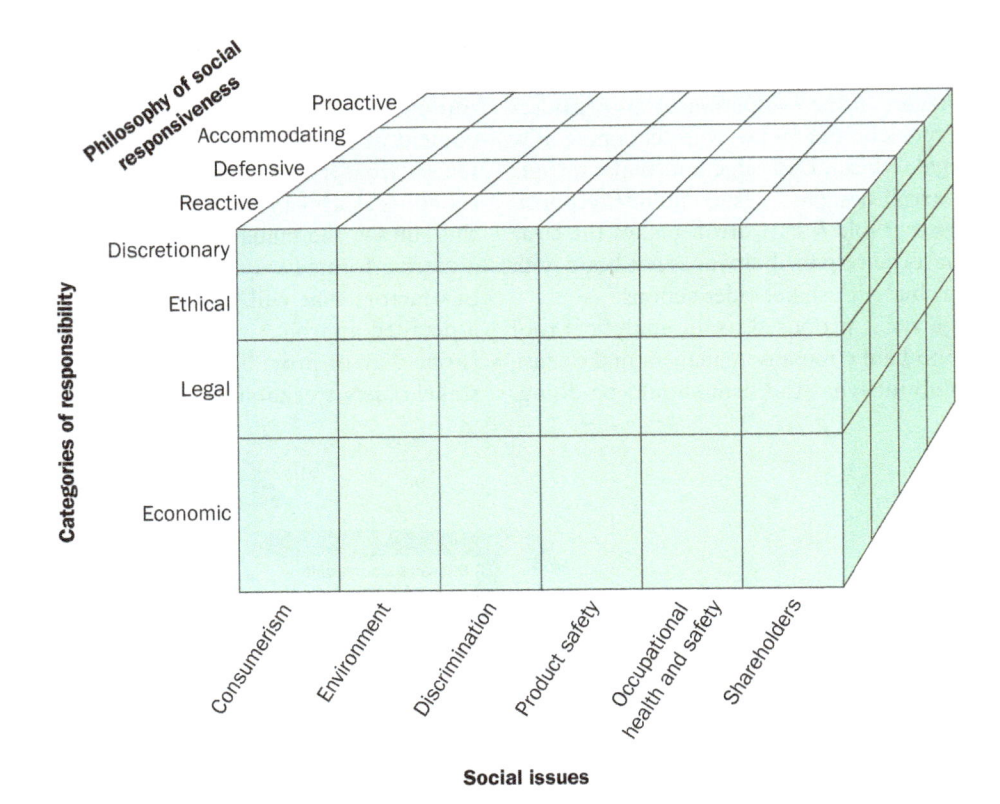

Figure 5.5 CSR responsibility matrix (*source:* Adapted Carroll, A.B. (1979). 'A Three-Dimensional Conceptual Model of Corporate Performance.' The Academy of Management Review Vol. 4, No. 4 (Oct., 1979), pp. 497–505)

Stakeholders	Economic	Legal	Ethical	Philanthropic
Customers	Financially well-managed company	Conform to consumer health and safety product guidelines (e.g. quality controls and standards for fire safety of garments, etc.)	Fairly priced products	Give waste products to needy organisations
	Clear financial reporting	Correct labelling	Highest quality	Give unsold products to customers' preferred charities or homeless groups
		National and transnational product labelling, e.g. European standards	Products are designed for and fit for purpose (e.g. if for specialist sector such as workwear)	Support other employee and customer initiatives
			Provide best products with the highest standards of care for employers and suppliers	Etc.
			Transparent sourcing of materials (no use of child labour or low-paid employees)	
			Do not abuse our suppliers or workers	

Table 5.2 An application of the stakeholder responsibility matrix to a small clothing manufacturer

will help managers when the organisation is defining corporate strategies for long- and short-term decisions to ensure they accommodate the multiple stakeholder interests.

Corporate responsibility and irresponsibility

Tench et al. (2007) and Jones et al. (2009) build on and critique some of Carroll's early work to discuss alternative interpretations. The main conclusions of this discussion are in the exploration of corporate social irresponsibility (CSI) as a concept in contrast to Corporate Social Responsibility and the consequences of this dichotomy for corporate communications. The CSI–CSR model is described, explained, analysed and used as a conceptual tool to make the theoretical move from a pyramid or level-based approach (Carroll) to a more dynamic corporate framework for communication.

Figure 5.6 serves to show that internal and external variables, as well as mixing with and affecting each other, also interact and impact on the CSI–CSR continuum. The model is a rotating sphere intersected by its axis, the continuum. The need of business to make profit can, and does at times, coincide as well as conflict with its stated ethical aims and objectives. Competing stakeholders with differing needs, rights and obligations have to be managed to ensure conflict is minimised, the business survives, grows and is able to meet its commitments to CSR.

The model moves away from a definition, explanation and analysis of CSR as a staged hierarchy; as espoused by Carroll (1991) in his pyramid of corporate social responsibility. Here, an alternative conceptualisation is suggested based on the notion that CSI should be separated out from CSR to facilitate greater understanding of the terms, their meaning, nature and purpose. Issues interspersed and feeding into the CSI–CSR continuum are affected by internal and external environmental factors. Such factors give shape, form and context to corporate governance and CSR. Placing Carroll's (1991) pyramid of corporate social responsibility metaphorically in the sphere recognises that the levels of responsibility are intrinsic to the way in which

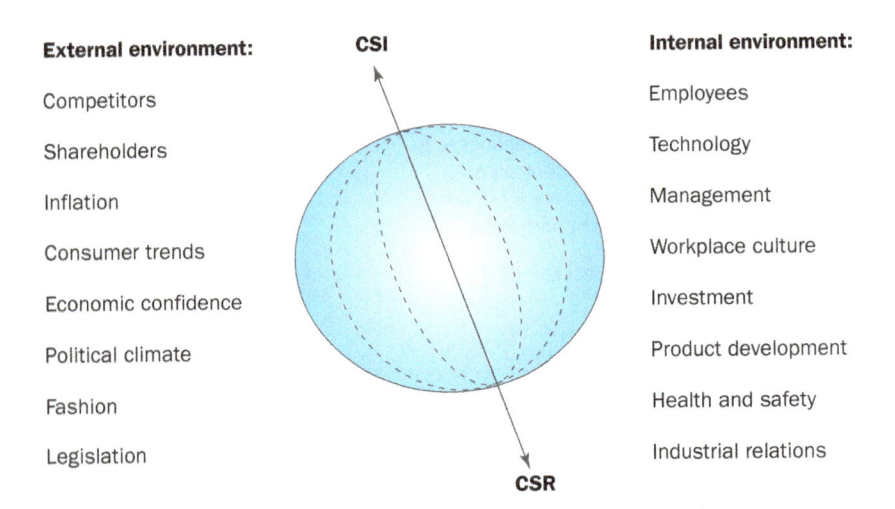

External environment:
- Competitors
- Shareholders
- Inflation
- Consumer trends
- Economic confidence
- Political climate
- Fashion
- Legislation

Internal environment:
- Employees
- Technology
- Management
- Workplace culture
- Investment
- Product development
- Health and safety
- Industrial relations

Figure 5.6 CSI–CSR Environmental Dynamic model (*source:* Jones, B.; Tench, R. and Bowd, R. (2009). 'Corporate irresponsibility and corporate social responsibility: competing realities'. Social Responsibility Journal, Emerald Volume 5, No. 3 2009)

CSR is conceived. However, in suggesting that the pyramid, and by implication the levels, can be rotated the inference is that the levels are neither hierarchical or static but fluid and necessary to each other. By introducing the concept of CSI it counteracts the tendency to treat the concept of CSR as a one-dimensional single entity and unpacks the terms to reveal multi-faceted layers of complexity that are shaped by context.

The majority of companies are keen to embrace CSR issues and of their own volition go beyond legal minimum requirements. Not only do companies want to do well by doing good, but also some want to do good because they believe it to be the right and proper thing to do. Not all businesses are communicating what it is they do in regards to CSR to best effect. Regarding their social responsibility practices a CSI–CSR audit can help businesses identify areas of strength and areas for improvement. In itself such an exercise can act as a useful vehicle of and for communication.

This view actually effectively explains what has happened to companies such as Starbucks that do treat their employees well but fail to do well in other aspects so they have faced boycotts from critical NGOs. For example, Starbucks faced a boycott in 2012 for avoiding paying taxes in the UK even though the company offers generous packages for employees. However, employment packages did not spare them criticism when avoiding paying taxes.

Adding to and supporting this debate in their empirical analysis based on an extensive 15-year panel dataset that covers nearly 3,000 publicly traded companies in the USA, Kotchen and Moon (2011) find that companies actually engaged in CSR in order to offset their CSI. CSI is a rich and challenging alternative concept to CSR and as a conceptual field of enquiry is discussed in detail in an edited volume of essays on the topic by Tench et al. (2014). As discussed, it is increasingly recognised that adopting a CSR approach can be both an ethical and profitable way to manage a business. Ethics and profit are not mutually exclusive terms but have a symbiotic relationship in the form of CSR. Though nevertheless, at the end of the day and as Friedman (1962) rightly noted, the purpose of business is to make profit.

Regulatory frameworks

Whilst present public attention is on business and the economy it is being recognised increasingly that a greater understanding of the role and societal impact of business is essential (see Table 5.3). This is reflected in a range of transnational initiatives such as the EU's new sustainability and responsibility policy for business and the launch in 2010 of the ISO CSR standards which were updated in 2011 to focus explicitly on SMEs (European Commission Enterprise and Industry 2016; ISO 26000 CSR Guidance 2010). The OECD Guidelines for Multinational Enterprises also provides a regular forum for debating these issues with participants from governments, businesses, trade unions and civil society (OECD Conference June 2016). The UK CBI (2011) – a business lobby organisation representing UK business and commerce – in its current priorities has recognised this need to focus on the role of business in society and the important role that business plays in creating and sustaining communities. This 'higher ambition' (Beer et al. 2011) of a responsibility of businesses

Human rights	Principle 1: Businesses should support and respect the protection of internationally proclaimed human rights; and
	Principle 2: make sure that they are not complicit in human rights abuses.
Labour standards	Principle 3: Businesses should uphold the freedom of association and the effective recognition of the right to collective bargaining;
	Principle 4: the elimination of all forms of forced and compulsory labour;
	Principle 5: the effective abolition of child labour; and
	Principle 6: the elimination of discrimination in respect of employment and occupation.
Environment	Principle 7: Businesses should support a precautionary approach to environmental challenges;
	Principle 8: undertake initiatives to promote greater environmental responsibility; and
	Principle 9: encourage the development and diffusion of environmentally friendly technologies.
Anti-corruption	Principle 10: Businesses should work against corruption in all its forms, including extortion and bribery. employee development increased staff morale enhanced relations with local decision makers motivated, high-quality recruits improved corporate image.

Table 5.3 The Global Compact's ten principles (*source:* The Ten Principles: UN Global Compact. Retrieved from https://www.unglobalcompact.org/what-is-gc/mission/principles)

for creating and balancing both economic and social value is becoming more widely accepted, increasing in parallel with the negative impact of recessionary economic trends on consumer and society confidence as well as trust in business and wider institutions.

The business case is reinforced in 'higher ambition' (Beer et al. 2011) with research showing the positive relationship of these business values with business performance. The success and longevity of brand names such as Cadbury and Kellogg, illustrate the way in which both economic and social values can be balanced to deliver strong business performance over generations (Hopper and Hopper 2007; Cadbury D 2010).

As consumers we have product choice – do we go for brand, price or even ethical or corporate responsibility performance? Companies such as Shell, Nike and Nestlé have experienced the threat and financial effects of global boycotts and are realising that greater mobility of stakeholders and globalisation of communication mean that reputation management is increasingly important. One manifestation of this is the speed of communication and in particular news distribution globally via new technology, satellite and the emergence of 24-hour news channels. The process of news gathering has been speeded up as has the news production cycle – all of which is crucial for public relations when managing reputation and communication for organisations. Research by the World Economic Forum back in 2003 revealed that 48 per cent of people express 'little or no trust' in global companies. These figures are repeated annually through the Edelman Trust Barometer. Consequently, even large and powerful corporations must adopt more ethical working practices in order to reduce risk and maintain favourable reputation. The growth of organisations such as Business in the Community in the UK, the B Corp Community and CSR Europe are helping to place CSR in the mainstream of business thinking and encourage more organisations to leverage the opportunities of CSR. This has a number of implications, including the increased need for guidance for companies. Subsequently the past few years have seen the emergence of an increasing number of standards and guidelines in the areas of CSR and sustainable development. These include:

- Dow Jones Sustainability Index
- FTSE 4 Good Index
- Business in the Community's Corporate Responsibility Index

- Global Reporting Initiative's (GRI) Reporting Guidelines
- B Corp Directory

Public and business attitudes have changed over recent years and in 1999 a global poll of 25,000 citizens (MORI 1999) showed that perceptions of companies was more strongly aligned with corporate citizenship (56 per cent) than either brand quality (40 per cent) or the perception of the business management (34 per cent). Further evidence of the public attitude change was reported in the *Financial Times* (2003), which claimed that in the late 1970s the British agreed by two to one that the profits of large companies benefited their customers. In 2003 the public disagreed by two to one. This attitude change is reiterated by Fombrum and Shanley (1990), who found in earlier studies that a business that demonstrates responsiveness to social concerns and gives proportionately more to charity than other firms receives higher reputation ratings by its publics.

More worryingly and mirroring the questions raised by Sir Mervyn King earlier in the chapter, the US Chicago Booth/Kellogg School Financial Trust Index highlights fluctuating trust of financial institutions (see Figure 5.7).

As Sapienza and Zingales, the joint authors from the Chicago Booth/Kellogg Schools, suggested when they reported in December 2015:

'Shares of European and American banks tumbled and lost more than one quarter of their value this year. Markets are scared by the eurozone economy, exposure to the energy sector and China, and problems in banks' balance sheets,' said Sapienza. *'But these fears are not currently reflected in the public's trust in banks.'*

'The Financial Trust Index peaked in December 2015,' said Zingales. *'As in previous surveys, we see that the public's trust is highest in credit unions and in their local banks, and significantly lower in the national banks.'*

The Edelman Trust Barometer (2016, 2019) reported an interesting dichotomy of responses with what the report called a 'yawning trust gap is emerging between elite and mass populations'. The global survey asks respondents how much they trust the four institutions of government, business, nongovernmental organisations and media to do what is 'right'. The Edelman survey shows that trust is rising in the elite or 'informed public' group – who are defined in the survey as those with at least a college/university education, and who are very engaged in media, and have an income in the top 25 per cent. However, in the 'mass population' (the remaining 85 per cent of the sample), trust levels have barely moved since the 2008/9 financial crisis.

There is a range of research that demonstrates consumers' willingness to reward socially responsible companies, with far-reaching effects. One such effect is the changing focus of investment decisions. This has resulted in the emergence of *'triple bottom-line'* reporting whereby social and environmental performance hold equal importance to financial performance. It can therefore be argued that, in the eyes of consumers, the media, legislators and investors, social and environmental responsibilities are increasingly powerful drivers of reputation.

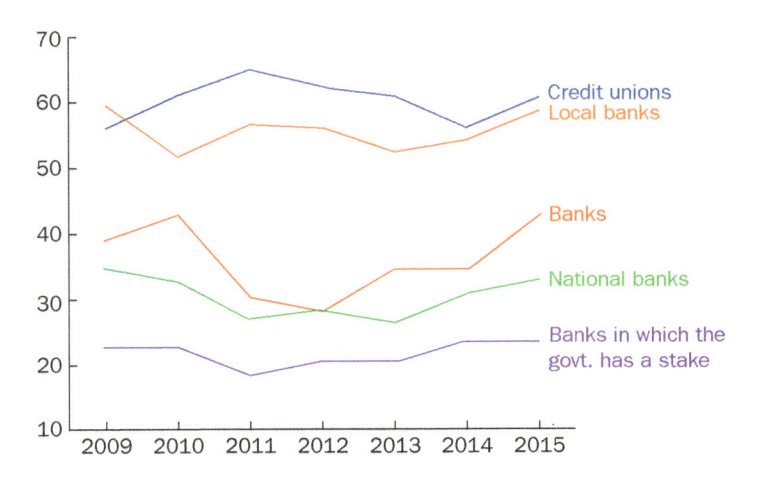

Figure 5.7 Percentage of people trusting various components that comprise the Financial Trust Index (*source:* Chicago Booth/Kellogg School Financial Trust Index Reveals Heightened Public Trust in Local Banks, Credit Unions. Retrieved from http://www.financialtrustindex.org/resultswave24.htm)

Case study 5.2
The M&S and Oxfam Clothes Exchange

The UK clothes retailer Marks and Spencer (M&S) and Oxfam Clothes Exchange aim to encourage customers to recycle more and to help to reduce the amount of clothing going to landfill. The campaign attracted a lot of interest and comment and was supported with national television adverts in April and May 2012. The campaign used the actress Joanna Lumley, with the aim of changing clothes shopping habits towards greater recycling. During the campaign, M&S completely covered a street – including trees and a dog – with clothes in East London's Brick Lane fashion district to highlight the amount thrown into UK landfill every five minutes. In the initiative customers are encouraged to return their used M&S clothes to Oxfam and receive a £5 voucher, which can be redeemed when they spend £35 or more in an M&S store.

In 2013, 'Shwop at work' was introduced in partnership with BITC to extend the clothes exchange campaign to UK businesses. Clothes recycling boxes or 'shwop drop' boxes are placed within offices and employees similarly receive vouchers for clothing gifted.

Reported in the *Huffington Post* in April 2012, M&S chief executive Marc Bolland said: 'We're leading a change in the way we all shop for clothing, forever. This is the right, responsible move for the UK's biggest clothing retailer and the ultimate goal is simple – to put a complete stop to clothes ending up in landfill. We want to get back one garment for every one we sell. For us that's 350 million a year. It is a big number, but with our customers' help, we will do it.'

Impact
The campaign is claimed to have:

- Received more than 4.6 million clothes since its launch in 2012.
- Raised over £9.5 million for Oxfam projects through reselling the clothes that customers return.
- Saved millions of pounds for M&S customers through the redemption of the £5 vouchers.
- Destroyed only 1 per cent of donated garments.

Picture 5.3 The UK clothes retailer Marks and Spencer (M&S) and Oxfam Clothes Exchange aim to encourage customers to recycle more and to help to reduce the amount of clothing going to landfill. The 'Plan A' campaign attracted a lot of interest and comment and was supported with national television adverts (*source:* Dhiraj Singh/Bloomberg/Getty Images)

Ethics and business practice

Before looking in detail at the techniques for operating a business in society we need to consider the important issue of *ethics* and ethical business practice. *Business ethics* is a substantial issue and an important part of understanding what is called corporate governance. It ranges from high-profile issues about equal opportunities, 'glass ceilings' for women in work, whistleblowing (employees reporting on unethical or illegal activities by their employers), whether large PLCs pay their SME suppliers or contractor on time down to whether it is all right for a director or senior manager to take a ream of paper home for a computer printer, when this is a sackable offence for an office junior!

Business ethics is therefore about us as individual members of society, as part of the community or as part of organisations (whether these are work or leisure/interest organisations). For example, we may be an employee of a national supermarket chain and a trustee for a local school or scout group. We make decisions within these environments that have ethical implications and societal impact (see Peach 1987: Figure 5.1). Ethics is an important part of business reality, as managers make decisions that affect a large range of stakeholder groups and communities from the employees of the organisation to the residents who live close to its business sites (see Think abouts 5.3, 5.4 and 5.5; see also Box 5.3).

> ### Think about 5.3
> #### Ethical dilemmas
> Ethical dilemmas occur when we are faced with decisions that cause dissonance (conflict) in our loyalty (taken from Festinger's theory of cognitive dissonance, see Chapter 12). Take the example of a cheating colleague who is extracting small amounts of money from the organisation through false expenses claims. If we know about their actions, should we show loyalty to them or to our organisation? We are left with an 'ethical decision'. What do you think you would say or do if it were a director or management colleague in this case? How would you manage the ethical dilemma?
>
> #### Feedback
> 'Ethical problems are not caused entirely by "bad apples". They're also the product of organisational systems that either encourage unethical behaviour or, at least, allow it to occur' Trevino and Nelson (1995: 13).
>
> You need to gather all the facts and also consider the impact of your decisions/actions on the organisation as a whole. See the section on ethical decision making.

> ### Think about 5.4
> #### Good apples and bad apples
> The 'good' and 'bad apple' analogy is frequently used in the context of ethics. Apply this analogy to your own experience and think of an example of unethical conduct. Was it the responsibility of the individual (apple) or the organisation (barrel) or was it a combination of the two?
>
> #### Feedback
> Arguably, we are born amoral, not moral or immoral. Psychologists have argued that ethics, as such, are not innate. They are culturally bound and influenced by the social environment we grow up in. We develop and change our personalities throughout our lives – including during our adult life – and research (Rest and Thoma 1986) has found that adults in their 30s who are in moral development programmes develop more than young people.

> ### Think about 5.5
> #### Individual and corporate ethics
> Dissonance or conflict is what causes individual problems with corporate ethics and there are stark examples such as a religious person working for a pharmaceutical company that decides to market an abortion product, or an environmentally conscious employee working for a high-polluting company. What should these individuals do to manage the conflict? What should their management do?

Ethical decision making: theory and practice

Business ethics author Snell (1997) argues that there are two approaches to the teaching and understanding of business ethics by practitioners. One of these is termed 'systematic modernism', which is the more explanatory, conservative voice of business leaders and political leaders on societal issues. The explanations are more functional and seek resolutions in the short to medium term, i.e. through legislation, the use of law and order and reliance on individual's social responsibility. In contrast, 'critical modernism' is the current 'underdog' yet this has been influenced more by theoretical ethical debates. It is argued therefore that the critical approach takes

Box 5.4

Example of ethical guidelines

Unilever has published its ethical guidelines – or ethical principles – as follows: 'Unilever believe that economic growth must go hand in hand with sound environmental management, equal opportunities world-wide and the highest standards of health and safety in factories and offices.'

Its code of business principles covers sensitive issues such as bribery: 'Unilever does not give or receive bribes in order to retain business or financial advantages. Unilever employees are directed that any demand or offer of such a bribe must be immediately rejected.'

Source: www.unilever.com

Explore 5.4

Ethics in everyday life

Think about how you act in different situations. How would you react if a college friend started telling jokes about people with physical disabilities? Would you smile in an embarrassed way, laugh and hope they wouldn't carry on, confront the speaker and ask them to stop, or what?

Feedback

It is often useful to reflect on our codes of ethics, what we see as right and wrong, and on whether we act on our beliefs or are more interested in how others perceive or see us.

---

business ethics a stage further than just face-value explanations of why something is right or wrong.

Table 5.4 (below) highlights how the two schools of thought operate and interpret different ethical issues (see Explore 5.4).

Philosophers have studied ethical decision making for centuries and tend to focus on decision-making tools that describe what should be done in particular situations (see also Chapter 13). The most well-known philosophical theories are categorised as consequentialist, regarding the consequences of actions, with utilitarianism being the best known and associated with the 'greatest happiness' principle (i.e. the greatest happiness for the greatest number of people). Trevino and Nelson (1995: 67) state that a utilitarian approach to ethical decision making should 'maximise benefits to society and minimise harms. What matters is the net balance of good consequences over bad.'

Generally, utilitarian ethical decision making is therefore focused on what we do and what are the consequences of our actions, i.e. who will be harmed or affected. In a business context, this means which stakeholders will be affected. One method of testing this

Issue	Typical systematic modern narrative	Typical critical modern narrative
Corruption: bribery and extortion	Bad because it dents local or national pride, deters inward investment and is a sign of backwardness	Bad because it is inherently unfair, disadvantaging the politically and economically weak
Protection of the environment	Our sons and daughters will suffer or perish unless we adopt proper controls	Indigenous (native) peoples, rare animal species and future citizens are entitled to a habitable environment
Inflated executive salaries	One should set up systems of corporate governance overseen by non-executive directors to safeguard minority shareholders' interests	One should campaign for wider social justice, including action to help the poor and reduce unemployment
Function of codes of ethics	They are tools for inspiring the confidence of customers and investors, and a means of controlling staff	They are a starting point only. People should be encouraged to develop their own personal moral code
Preferred Kohlberg stages	Conventional reasoning: preserving stability, the rule of law and order and social respectability	Post-conventional reasoning: concern for social welfare, justice and universal ethical principles

Table 5.4 Competing modern narratives on business ethics (*source:* Snell, R. (1997). 'Management learning perspectives on business ethics' in Management Learning. J. Burgoyne and M. Reynolds. (Eds). London: SAGE Publications)

approach is to ask if everyone acted in the same way, what sort of environment would be created? Just imagine what the impact would be if each of us dropped our lunch wrappers and leftovers onto the floor every day! Extend this out to all businesses draining their waste water/fluids into the nearest river/ocean outlet. This theory does underlie a lot of business writing and thinking and people's approaches to ethical decision making.

A second strand of philosophical thinking is categorised under deontological theories which focus on motives and intentions through duties or the action itself rather than the outcome or results. German philosopher Emmanuel Kant wrote about the 'categorical imperative', which asks whether your ethical choice is sound enough to become universally accepted as a law of action that everyone should follow (see Kant 1964). The obvious example is whether telling lies is ever acceptable. Imagine a company context where it was perceived that telling a lie for the good of the company was to its benefit. Kant would argue against this case unless the company is prepared to accept that from that point forward all employees were permitted to lie – a 'categorical imperative'. You need only consider the case of Enron in the USA to appreciate where such an ethical management system will lead with regard to telling mistruths and lies to a range of stakeholders.

Another ethical approach that is popular with business ethics academics and fits into the business context is virtue ethics, which is also founded in traditional philosophical theory. It focuses on the integrity of the actor or individual more than on the act itself. Within this approach it is important to consider the relative importance of communities or stakeholder groups. For example, in a professional context you may be bound by community standards or practical codes of conduct. This can help the individual make ethical decisions because it gives them boundaries to work within.

Changing the culture and changing organisational ethics

Any attempt to change ethical practice within an organisation must be based on a simple assumption that all human beings are essentially good and capable of development and change. Changing ethical practice through changing the culture of an organisation is not a quick fix; it takes time as you have to address the formal and informal organisational subcultures. The culture of an organisation clearly affects what is appropriate or inappropriate behaviour. To understand the culture an audit is necessary and can be carried out through surveys, interviews and observations.

Having completed an audit, the next stage is to write a culture change intervention plan that includes targeting the formal and informal systems.

The formal systems are more transparent and easier to change, as follows:

- draw up new codes of conduct;
- change structure to encourage individuals to take responsibility for their behaviour;
- design reward systems to punish unethical behaviour;
- encourage *whistleblowers* and provide them with appropriate communications channels and confidentiality;
- change decision-making processes to incorporate attention to ethical issues.

For the informal system, the following may be important:

- re-mythologise the organisation – revive old myths and stories about foundations, etc. that guide organisational behaviour (revived myths must, however, fit with reality).

See Explore 5.5 and Case study 5.3.

Explore 5.5

Ethics in practice

To conclude this chapter on business and its role in communities and society, think about the following.

Managers are the key to ethical business practice as they are the potential role models for all employees, customers, suppliers, etc. and also the endorsers of ethical policies. Due to changes in management practice, business process reengineering and the downsizing of Western companies, many modern businesses have fewer managers today – yet each manager has more staff to control:

1. How should organisations be ethical? Identify three or four reasons. Divide these reasons into those that are linked to financial gain and those that are societally sympathetic.

2. Are employees attracted to ethical employers? Give reasons why you believe they may or may not be.

3. List those companies you would be proud to work for and those that you would be ashamed to be employed by or represent. What are the key features of each? What are the similarities and differences?

Case study 5.3
Lidl in the UK and Croatia

Topic and Tench (2016) conducted an analysis of the leading supermarket company, Lidl, in two countries, the UK and Croatia. This case specifically looks at how the company uses communication campaigns to disseminate and possibly promote its CSR activities. From the analysis it's clear they are following a standard European stakeholder orientation in their business. This is particularly visible in the fact they report on their relations with employees, customers and suppliers in their statements on CSR on their website. On the other hand, this policy is then transformed into corporate advertising but in different ways.

When it comes to Croatia, Lidl's communication strategy showed superior understanding of the social context and, therefore, Lidl promotes employment opportunities in a social context where bullying at work and low employee rights are a social reality. However, to accomplish this Lidl turned to CSR Advertising and imposed CSR policies as a measurement of what it means to be European. Lidl is clearly *selling* CSR as a measurement of what it means to be a good company in a context where this is not normally important by promoting itself as a good employer and as a generous philanthropist, and as such the company is also *selling* CSR.

On the other hand, CSR is not implemented in the UK almost at all, while in Croatia Lidl donates large amounts to philanthropic activities even though this is not required. This is in the context that Lidl has developed a new strategy in the UK to appeal to higher demographic groups (e.g. the middle classes) and it is perhaps unusual that they did not develop a CSR policy in the UK. However, research from the UK Government (2014) has shown there is a decrease in ethical purchase, which may have encouraged Lidl to estimate that introducing CSR is not necessary to achieve their business goals, and this then had an effect on their communication strategy.

Arguably in the UK a lot of attention to CSR has come from loud and critical NGOs such as the *Ethical Consumer* that often launches campaigns against various companies, while new research shows that ethical purchasing is in decline (UK Government 2014; Ethical Consumer 2013). It seems, therefore, that Lidl has clearly recognised this trend and decided to push its CSR strategy aside and focus on a change of image while in the Croatian case, the company has clearly focused on addressing social issues to achieve better positioning and has, consequentially, used CSR in their advertising and communication campaigns. On the other hand, given the lack of CSR initiatives in the UK it is difficult to speak of genuine CSR in Croatia when the available research shows that consumers in the West also do not like exposing CSR policies as a means of promoting the business (Morsing et al. 2008; Nielsen and Thompen 2007; Mohr et al. 1998; O'Sullivan 1997), which might be another reason for refraining from using CSR for positioning in the UK market.

Nevertheless, in the Croatian case, CSR is seems to be driven by the EU with programmes for (re)awarding companies that enforce CSR while in the UK CSR seems to be driven by the Government and again not so much by the market. In other words, CSR is driven from the above as a top-down measure. In this particular case, Lidl is apparently trying to cope with that by exploiting CSR in one context and by downplaying the CSR in the other. Future research emerging from this case could look at demographics more closely, i.e. to examine who are the drivers of CSR in the EU, who are the people who care for CSR and ethical purchasing, and how many people in general genuinely care about ethical purchasing. In addition, future work should look at the role of the EU and national Governments in driving CSR given the fact the British government considered stricter CSR measures even though ethical purchase does not show any increase but rather stagnation or downfall, while in Croatia the EU is funding an award programme for companies that enforce social responsibility policies even though the public does not express an interest in CSR.

Source: Topić, M. and R. Tench (2016). 'The corporate social responsibility in Lidl's communication campaigns in Croatia and the UK.' The Qualitative Report 21(2): 352

Summary

Milton Friedman's perception that the business of business is simply to increase profits and enhance shareholder value has less credibility in the twenty-first century. Also the public is increasingly sophisticated on health, environmental and ethical issues such as: global warming; worldwide natural disasters such as the Asian tsunami 2004, Hurricane Katrina in 2005, earthquakes during 2011 in Turkey and New Zealand and the Zica virus in 2016, with the related business responses; animal testing; hunting with dogs in the UK; or whale hunting.

summary (continued)

There is rising power for the consumer in national and international contexts as demonstrated by Shell (fuel filling station protests), Nestle (palm oil and deforestation, 2010) and Fruit of the Loom (union rights of workers, 2010). The influence of corporate image and reputation on an organisation's business success (Lehmann Brothers; Andersen; McDonald's/ McLibel) is increasingly recognised, as is the use of business ethics to create competitive advantage (Co-Operative Bank; Fairtrade, the Body Shop). Enhanced communication (social media and the internet) for and with stakeholders and interest groups, media expansion and global influence (24-hour news) and the mobilisation of national and international issue and pressure groups (such as Greenpeace; the 'occupy movement in 2011 or the anti war lobbies; UN Global Compact; or influential and high-profile figures such as Greta Thunberg, Al Gore and Leonardo DiCaprio) can all separately and together affect any business today.

This chapter has focused on the role organisations play in their society(ies) and how the understanding of business ethics and CSR may improve business performance and enhance reputation through more effective use of public relations and communication to build understanding and awareness.

Discussion in this chapter has focused on:

- responsible and irresponsible business behaviour
- stakeholder influences
- ethical decision making
- changing cultural and organisational ethics.

Case study 5.4
Everyone's a Winner – Airbus

When a cost-cutting task force in Airbus' Broughton site in North Wales set out to stop a trend of increasing spend on consumable items, it applied an innovative approach to encourage employees to bin bad behaviours. Having already tried shock tactics such as live waste sorts which involves bins being emptied and sorted in front of employees to highlight the amount of items which should not be discarded and information campaigns to raise awareness of the cost of the equipment and tools being recovered from waste containers, team members took things to a new level with a campaign called 'Waste Less, Give More'.

The idea was simple – help the site meet its target for consumables (i.e. don't overspend!) and a large cash donation would be given to local charities. Mark Hibbert, an integration manager who was working in Step Change in Broughton at the time of the campaign, said: 'It was a very good campaign. It made a difference in Step Change hitting its targets for consumables in 2017. It made the operators aware of detailed costs and how they support in savings. We also had ideas being raised on how to make savings.'

Leading by example

Developed in the first half of 2017, 'Waste Less, Give More' launched in August 2017 and relied heavily on support from managers and support teams working in operational areas. It was the manager and support teams' role to engage their colleagues with the campaign materials and make full use of items such as new branded display areas designed to help them showcase the consumable spend in their area, along with the site's overall consumable spend. This comparison helped teams see how they were performing. The campaign ran until December 2017 and had three main objectives:

- slow down the rate of spend on consumable items in production areas so the site's annual target of €32.7 million was not overspent;
- capture and implement ideas from production teams on how to make savings on consumable spend;
- give local charities a cash injection of £10,000.

Production areas were targeted for the campaign as data from Broughton's recycling centre showed it was the area with the greatest opportunity. In addition, financial reporting processes offered a measurement tool to help track the effectiveness of 'Waste Less, Give More' with a decline in consumable spend indicating a positive impact. Chris Arthur, an integration manager working in Plant Service Centre at the time of the campaign, said: 'I feel the campaign worked well to create awareness of consumables. Even if a small number consciously think about what is being used and how they are using it, then the campaign was well worth running.'

The Result

The site's consumable target spend for consumable items across all production areas was €32.7 million. This was a significant achievement, particularly given the fact that in the first half of 2017, consumable spend in many areas was over target month on month. In addition, more than 15 ideas from across the business were submitted by operators and were shared so they could be adopted elsewhere. Donna Lloyd, head of communication in the UK, who was part of the task force and also helped create and deliver the campaign said: 'In all the communication linked to the campaign we highlighted the point that even if the target was beaten by just one Euro then the £10,000 donation would be unlocked. For the teams to make savings not far off one million Euro is amazing.'

Next steps

Airbus in the UK operates a scheme called Community Awards which is an annual initiative which results in local charities and organisations receiving cash donations from Airbus. In April 2018, the Broughton scheme gave double the amount it usually gives thanks to the £10,000 boost generated by the 'Waste Less, Give More' activity. On the shop-floor, operators are continuing their efforts to improve recycling and a range of steps such as increased use of vending machines to issue consumables is helping to control spend on materials such as paint brushes and gloves.

Campaign materials

- Stickers for bins
- Stickers on mirrors in toilets
- Manager information and instruction pack
- Team display area
- Hanging and pop-up banners in production areas
- Bin stunt – wheelie bin made to look like it is falling through the floor due to the weight of its contents
- Postcard and post-boxes for ideas about savings to be posted
- Internal TV network video content

What worked well?

- Agency support – Airbus appointed Salford-based Carbon Creative to help it develop its ideas and bring its ideas for visuals to life. This approach bolstered the Airbus resources and helped guerrilla tactics make it off the page.
- Before the campaign was devised, a team of graduates from different business areas in Airbus were recruited to do some research into the problem – increasing spend on consumables – and to generate some ideas about how the problem could be tackled through communication. This was a valuable exercise as it provided an opportunity to put some fresh ideas on the table and to engage some of the production teams on the topic. It also helped rule out ideas which may not be suitable for the environment in which the campaign was being delivered.
- Identified network of support throughout the business – each business area had a person responsible for being a campaign representative. This helped ensure campaign tactics were being delivered in line with the schedule and provided a two-way communication flow between internal communication and the business.
- The charitable link – this was a completely new dimension and the results showed it worked well. Previously, campaigns had focused on how much waste cost; however, from the research undertaken it was apparent, when the money being wasted is coming from the company's purse and not an individual's, the care factor is not always there. By making a direct link between a person's actions and helping local good causes, the behaviour change was far more prominent.

Areas for improvement

- More time to brief employees – the campaign relied heavily on managers briefing their teams on what the campaign was all about and why. Managers have limited time to do such briefings in fast-paced industrial environments. If the campaign was to run again, techniques to reach employees direct should be considered to ensure a 'belt and braces' approach. This may help enhance the 'connection' employees feel with the campaign.
- The green angle – any future campaign would benefit from highlighting the environmental benefits of the waste reduction in addition to the opportunity to give cash to local good causes.

Picture 5.4 The 'Waste Less, Give More' campaign for Airbus (*source*: Reprinted with permission of Airbus)

Think about 5.6 — Why companies get involved in community relations

Company stock valuation is one reason for being involved in community relations. What others can you think of that might benefit the organisation?

Feedback

Some businesses are increasingly concerned with educational development of the community, in what is termed 'cradle to grave'. Community relations can influence this process by education-based sponsorship. This creates awareness in local schools and establishes the company as a desirable employer. This may, in turn, influence future recruitment or create a positive image around products/services/outputs. Also, the community initiatives can provide employees with opportunities to develop further skills by working with local schools and organisations. The benefits of such education are a properly trained and developed workforce, which is crucial to the company's future success.

Explore 5.6 — Finding examples of community relations

Think about an organisation you know well or are interested in and research its website and external activities. Make a list of those activities you believe might be regarded as community relations. Note down what you believe the organisation and the recipient got out of the relationship.

Feedback

Community relations are diverse and the involvement need not be significant. Typically, community relations programmes involve one or more of the following techniques or tactics:

1. sponsorships
2. targeted donations
3. awards
4. hospitality
5. employee volunteering
6. use of facilities (loan of equipment)
7. training/seminars
8. secondments (staff)
9. partnerships

Links between organisations and community groups are normally made with organisations in areas such as sports, arts, education, the environment, occupational health and safety, charities, youth/young people's groups, senior citizens, the disadvantaged, disability, heritage and many other groupings.

Bibliography

Beer, M., Eisenstat, R.A., Foote, N., Fredberg, T. and Norrgren, F. (2011). *Higher Ambition: How Great Leaders Create Economic and Social Value*, Boston, MA: Harvard Business Press Books.

Blowfield, M. (2005). 'Corporate Social Responsibility: reinventing the meaning of development?' *International Affairs* 81(3): 515–24.

Cadbury, D. (2010). *Chocolate Wars: From Cadbury to Kraft: 200 Years of Sweet Success and Bitter Rivalry*. London: Harper Collins.

Cadbury Report. (1992). Report on the Committee of The Financial Aspects of Corporate Governance, 1 December 1992. The Committee on the Financial Aspects of Corporate Governance and Gee and Co. Ltd.

Carroll, A.B. (1991). 'The pyramid of corporate social responsibility: toward the moral management of organizational stakeholders.' *Business Horizons* 34(4): 39–48.

CBI (2011). CBI website: CBI priorities at http://www.cbi.org.uk/campaigns/the-role-of-business-in-society, accessed 5 November 2011).

Chicago Booth /Kellogg School Financial Trust Index. (2011). 19 October 2011 http://www.financialtrustindex.org/resultswave12.htm, accessed 5 November 2011.

Clarke, T. (2009). 'A Critique of the Anglo-American Model of Corporate Governance.' CLPE Research Paper 15/2009, 5(3), available at: http://ssrn.com/abstract=1440853.

Concise Oxford English Dictionary, 8th edition (1995). Oxford: Clarendon Press.

Cutlip, S.M., Center, A.H. and Broom, G.M. (2000). *Effective Public Relations*, 8th edn. Upper Saddle River, NJ: Prentice Hall.

Dahlsrud, A. (2008). 'How corporate social responsibility is defined: an analysis of 37 definitions.' *Corporate social responsibility and environmental management* 15(1), 1–13.

Edelman Trust Barometer Findings. (2016). http://www.edelman.com/insights/intellectual-property/2016-edelman-trust-barometer/, accessed 16 June 2016.

European Commission Enterprise and Industry (2011). Published October 2011. http://ec.europa.eu/enterprise/policies/sustainable-business/corporate-social-responsibility/index_en.htm, accessed 7 November 2011.

European Multistakeholder Forum on CSR Report and Recommendations (2004). *European Multistakeholder Forum on CSR: Final results & recommendations*. Available at: http://www.corporatejustice.org/IMG/pdf/CSR_20Forum_20final_20report.pdf, accessed 5 March 2015.

Fombrum, C. and Shanley, M. (1990). 'What's in a name? Reputation building and corporate strategy.' *Academy of Management Journal* 33: 233–58.

Friedman, M. (1970). 'The social responsibility of business is to increase its profits.' *New York Times Magazine* 13 September: 32.

Gore, A. (2006) 'An Inconvenient Truth'. Paramount, director, David Guggenheim.

Gore, A. (2007) *An Inconvenient Truth*. Viking Juvenile (10 April 2007).

Grunig, J. and T. Hunt (1984). *Managing Public Relations*. New York: Holt, Rinehart & Winston.

Hopper, K. and Hopper, W. (2007) and (2009). *The Puritan Gift: Reclaiming the American dream amidst global financial crisis*. London: I. B. Taurus.

Huffington Post (2016) http://www.huffingtonpost.co.uk/ryan-curran/google-tax_b_9125406.html, accessed 8 June 2016.

India Partnership Forum (2003). www.ipfndia.org/home, accessed 30 September 2008.

ISO 26000 CSR Guidance (2010). http://www.iso.org/iso/home/standards/iso26000.htm, accessed 8 June 2016.

Jones, B., Tench, R. and Bowd, R. (2009). 'Corporate irresponsibility and corporate social responsibility: competing realities.' *Social Responsibility Journal* 5(3).

Kant, I. (1964). *Groundwork of the Metaphysic of Morals*. London: Harper & Row.

Kotchen, M.J. and Moon, J.J. (2011). 'Corporate Social Responsibility for Irresponsibility', National Bureau of Economic Research Working Paper 17254, available at http://www.nber.org/papers/w17254.

King, M. (2011). Sir Mervyn King, Governor of the Bank of England in Speech To the Institute of Directors, St George's Hall, Liverpool, 18 October 2011, Bank of England.

Labich, K. (1992). 'The new crisis in business ethics.' *Fortune* 20 April: 167–176.

Lewis, S. (2003). 'Reputation and corporate social responsibility.' *Journal of Communication Management* 7(4): 356–64.

Lines, V.L. (2004). 'Corporate reputation in Asia: Looking beyond the bottom line performance.' *Journal of Communication Management* 8(3): 233–45.

Little, P.L. and Little, B.L. (2000). 'Do perceptions of corporate social responsibility contribute to explaining differences in corporate price-earnings ratios? A research note.' *Corporate Reputation Review* 3(2): 137–42.

Luigi Zingales (2011) citation in Marketwatch, 19 October 2011.

Mohr, L.A., Eroğlu, D. and Ellen, S.P. (1998). 'The development and testing of a measure of skepticism toward environmental claims in marketers' communications.' *Journal of Consumer Affairs* 32(1): 30–55.

Moore, G. (2003). 'Hives and horseshoes, Mintzberg or MacIntyre: What future for corporate social responsibility?' *Business Ethics: A European Review* 12(1): 41–53.

MORI (1999). 'Winning with integrity.' London: MORI.

Morsing, M., Schultz, M. and Nielsen, K.U. (2008). 'The "catch 22" of communicating CSR: Findings from a Danish study.' *Journal of Marketing Communications* 14(22): 97–111.

Nielsen, A.E. and C. Thomsen (2007). 'What they say and how they say it.' *Corporate Communications: An International Journal* 12(1): 25–40.

OECD (2016) Guidelines for Multinational Enterprises, conference 8–9 June 2016, http://mneguidelines.oecd.org/globalforumonresponsiblebusinessconduct/#d.en.230714, accessed 14 June 2016.

Occupy London (2011). http://occupylondon.org.uk/, accessed 5 November 2011.

Occupy Wall Street (2011). http://occupywallst.org/, accessed 6 November 2011.

O'Sullivan, T. (1997). 'Why charity schemes need a delicate touch.' *Marketing Week* 20: 20–24.

Peach, L. (1987). In *Effective Corporate Relations*. N. Hart (ed.). Maidenhead: McGraw-Hill.

Rest, J.R. and Thoma, S.J. (1986). 'Educational programs and interventions' in *Moral Development: Advances in research and theory*. J. Rest (ed.). New York: Praeger.

Sagar, P. and Singla, A. (2004). 'Trust and corporate social responsibility: Lessons from India.' *Journal of Communication Management* 8(3): 282–90.

Sherman, E. (2019) Fortune, 11 April 2019, accessed http://fortune.com/2019/04/11/amazon-starbucks-corporate-tax-avoidance/?utm_source=emailshare&utm_medium=email&utm_campaign=email-share-article&utm_content=20190416

Shiller, R.J. (2015). *Irrational exuberance.* Princeton, Princeton University Press.

Shiller, R.J. (2016). 'Fighting the Next Global Financial Crisis.' *Project Syndicate,* 18 May 2016, https://www.project-syndicate.org/commentary/financial-regulation-public-narratives-by-robert-j--shiller-2016-05

Sir Adrian Cadbury (1998). 'The Future for Governance', Gresham Special Lecture, Gresham College delivered at Mansion House, Tuesday 12 May 1998.

Snell, R. (1997). 'Management learning perspectives on business ethics' in *Management Learning*. J. Burgoyne and M. Reynolds. (Eds). London.

Sun, W., Stewart, J. and Pollard, D. (Eds). (2011). *Corporate Governance and the Global Financial Crisis: International Perspectives.* Cambridge: Cambridge University Press.

Tench, R., Zerfass, A., Moreno, A., Verčič, D. and Verhoeven, P. (2017) *Communication Excellence: How to Develop, Manage and Lead Exceptional Communication Departments.* London: Palgrave Macmillan.

Tench, R., Sun, W. and Jones, B. (Eds.). (2014). *Communicating Corporate Social Responsibility: Perspectives and Practice* (Vol. 6). Emerald Group Publishing.

Tench, R., Bowd, R. and Jones, B (2007). 'Perceptions and perspectives: corporate social responsibility and the media.' *Journal of Communication Management* 11(4): 348–70.

Tench, R., Verčič, D., Zerfass, A., Moreno, A. and Verhoeven, P. (2017). *Communication Excellence – How to Develop, Manage and Lead Exceptional Communications.* London: Palgrave Macmillan.

The Giving Institute (2018). 'Billion to Charity in 2017, Crossing the $400 Billion Mark for the First Time', The Giving Institute.

Think Big (2011). http://www.o2sustainability.co.uk/2010, accessed 17 November 2011.

Topic, M. and Tench, R. (2016). 'The Corporate Social Responsibility in Lidl's Communication Campaigns in Croatia and the UK.' *The Qualitative Report* 21(2): 352.

Trevino, L.K. and Nelson, K.A. (1995). *Managing Business Ethics: Straight talk about how to do it right.* New York: Wiley & Sons.

UN (2011). United Nations Millennium Development Goals 2015, www.un.org/millenniumgoals/, accessed 17 November 2011.

World Bank (2003). *Public Policy for Corporate Social Responsibility.* Available at: http://info.worldbank.org/etools/docs/library/57434/publicpolicy_econference.pdf, accessed 5 March 2015.

World Business Council for Sustainable Development (2015). *Definition of CSR.* Available at: http://www.wbcsd.org/work-program/business-role/previous-work/corporate-social-responsibility.aspx, accessed 5 March 2015.

World Economic Forum (2003). www.weforum.com, accessed 26 March 2005.

Zerfass, A., Tench, R., Verhoeven, P., Verčič, D. and Moreno, A. (2018). *European Communication Monitor 2018. Strategic communication and the challenges of fake news, trust, leadership, work stress and job satisfaction. Results of a survey in 48 Countries.* Brussels: EACD/EUPRERA, Quadriga Media Berlin.

Zerfass, A., Moreno, A., Tench, R., Verčič, D. and Verhoeven, P. (2017). *European Communication Monitor 2017. How strategic communication deals with the challenges of visualisation, social bots and hypermodernity. Results of a survey in 50 Countries.* Brussels: EACD/EUPRERA, Quadriga Media Berlin. (Booklet and Chart Version.)

Zerfass, A., Verhoeven, P., Moreno, A., Tench, R. and Verčič, D. (2016). *European Communication Monitor 2016. Exploring trends in big data, stakeholder engagement and strategic communication. Results of a Survey in 43 Countries.* Brussels: EACD/EUPRERA, Quadriga Media Berlin. (Booklet and Chart Version).

Zerfass, A., Verčič, D., Verhoeven, P., Moreno, A. and Tench, R. (2015). *European Communication Monitor 2015. Creating communication value through listening, messaging and measurement. Results of a Survey in 41 Countries.* Brussels: EACD/EUPRERA, Helios Media. (Booklet and Chart Version.)

Zerfass, A., Tench, R., Verčič, D., Verhoeven, P. and Moreno, A. (2014). *European Communication Monitor 2014. Excellence in Strategic Communication – Key Issues, Leadership, Gender and Mobile Media. Results of a Survey in 42 Countries.* Brussels: EACD/EUPRERA, Helios Media. (Booklet and Chart Version.)

Zerfass, A., Moreno, A., Tench, R., Verčič, D. and Verhoeven, P. (2013). *European Communication Monitor 2013. A Changing Landscape – Managing Crises, Digital Communication and CEO Positioning in Europe. Results of a Survey in 43 Countries*. Brussels: EACD/EUPRERA, Helios Media. (Booklet and Chart Version.)

Zerfass, A., Verčič, D., Verhoeven, P., Moreno, A. and Tench, R. (2012). *European Communication Monitor 2012. Challenges and Competencies for Strategic Communication. Results of an Empirical Survey in 42 Countries*. Brussels: EACD/EUPRERA. (Booklet and Chart Version.)

Zerfass, A., Verhoeven, P., Tench, R., Moreno, A. and Verčič, D. (2011). *European Communication Monitor 2011. Empirical Insights into Strategic Communication in Europe. Results of a Survey in 43 Countries*. Brussels: EACD/EUPRERA. (Booklet and Chart Version.)

Zerfass, A., Tench, R., Verhoeven, P., Verčič, D. and Moreno, A. (2010). *European Communication Monitor 2010. Status Quo and Challenges for Public Relations in Europe. Results of an Empirical Survey in 46 Countries*. Brussels: EACD/EUPRERA. (Booklet and Chart Version.)

Zerfass, A., Moreno, A., Tench, R., Verčič, D. and Verhoeven, P. (2009). *European Communication Monitor 2009. Trends in Communication Management and Public Relations. Results of a Survey in 34 Countries*. Brussels: EACD/EUPRERA. (Booklet and Chart Version.)

Zerfass, A., Moreno, A., Tench, R., Verčič, D. and Verhoeven, P. (2008). European Communication Monitor 2008. Trends in Communication Management and Public Relations – Results and Implications. Brussels, Leipzig: EUPRERA, University of Leipzig. Available at: www.communicationmonitor.eu

Zerfass, A., Van Ruler, B., Rogojinaru, A., Verčič, D. and Hamrefors, S. (2007). European Communication Monitor 2007. Trends in Communication Management and Public Relations – Results and Implications. Leipzig, Brussels: University of Leipzig, EUPRERA. Available at: www.communicationmonitor.eu

Websites

BBC: www.bbc.co.uk
Bill and Melinda Gates Foundation: www.gatesfoundation.org
British Society of Rheology: www.bsr.org.uk
Business in the Community: www.bitc.org.uk
CadburySchweppes: www.CadburySchweppes.com
Chartered Institute of Public Relations: www.cipr.co.uk
Co-operative Bank: www.co-operativebank.co.uk
CSR Europe: www.csreurope.org
European Communication Monitor www.communicationmonitor.eu
The Gap: www.gap.com

GlaxoSmithKline: www.gsk.com
Global Responsible Leadership Initiative (GRLI): www.grli.org
Greenpeace: www.greenpeace.org.uk
Institute of Business Ethics: www.ibe.org.uk
Nike: www.nike.com
02: www.mm02.co.uk
The Shell Group: www.shell.com
Slate 60 www.slate.com
United Nations Global Compact: www.unglobalcompact.org
Unilever: www.unilver.co.uk

For glossary definitions relevant to this chapter, visit the **selected glossary** feature on the website at: www.pearsoned.co.uk/tench

CHAPTER 6

Dejan Verčič

Intercultural and multicultural context of public relations

Source: Johnny Adolphson/Shutterstock

Learning outcomes

By the end of this chapter you should be able to:

- identify and discuss relevant key theories, principles and their development up to the present day in relation to the intercultural and multicultural context of public relations
- review and critique relevant key theories and principles in relation to the intercultural and multicultural context of public relations
- analyse and apply an intercultural and multicultural context of public relations theories/principles to practice
- evaluate your learning about intercultural and multicultural context of public relations and pursue further sources for investigation.

Structure

- The context of culture
- Public relations and culture
- Between universalism and relativism
- Global principles and specific applications
- Social media and activists in the global village
- How to prepare for international and global public relations
- Key principles in intercultural and multicultural public relations
- Public diplomacy

Introduction

Culture is a noun with many meanings. Each of us carries her or his own individual combination of cultural traits that we have acquired as members of several collectives – class, ethnic, gender, national, professional, racial, voluntary and other organisations and communities. All these can be described as having certain qualities we recognise as cultures. They exist in larger collective systems denoted as societies, having their own societal cultures. Because we are born into our cultures, they exist as our 'true' nature and we are rarely aware of them. It is when we geographically or socially move and meet (or even collide with) cultures different from ours that we become conscious of others and/or our differentness. In recognition of us being different from others we develop our sameness, i.e. identity (Sha et al. 2012). Public relations as management of communication and relationships between an organisation (with its culture) and its stakeholders (with their cultures) is always an intercultural practice (Ni et al. 2018) and public relations practitioners are intercultural interpreters (Banks 1995).

> ### Explore 6.1
>
> #### The nature/nurture debate
>
> Everybody has an opinion about how much of what we are is given to us biologically (in genes) and how much culturally (through learning). It is a centuries-old debate. Western scientists and philosophers prefer culture over nature (or anything else larger than us) as an explanatory variable of our behaviour. A book on the topic summarising arguments is Prinz's (2012) book, *Beyond Human Nature: How culture and experience shape our lives*.
>
> #### Feedback
>
> Where do you stand on the nature/nurture debate? How much of what you are is in your genes (or anything else permanent and directly passed on from your parents) and how much in how you were brought up?
>
> Can we transcend our nature?

The context of culture

Culture entered the language of management to alert leaders that social organisations (like companies) are not as easily engineered as machines. The latter follow rules of Newtonian causality: providing resources, you can make or break them at your will and if designed and produced properly, they will automatically follow an author's instructions. Companies and other human organisations behave more like plants than machines: you must nurture (cultivate) them, for certain processes they take their own time, and they behave as if following their own will which is different from the will of their constructors and/or members. In this sense managers talk of corporate cultures they would like to manage. Dominant cultures can be further broken into sub-cultures and often contra-cultures that defy the ruling interpretation of the right order of a system (organisation or a society). In that sense, culture is also about power and dominance (Dutta 2012).

Throughout history, travellers have encountered a different sense of culture: that of other countries and peoples. With the emergence first of empires and then of multinational companies, national cultures gained prominence in helping people understand why others behave differently than us. Today, international and global operations of all kinds of organisations – companies, non-governmental organisations, governments, international governmental and non-governmental organisations – depend on intercultural and multicultural knowledge. Public relations – as it is presented throughout this book – is an occupation that is continuing to gain in importance as an essential carrier of that knowledge.

You don't have to travel to be exposed to other cultures. Some major towns are themselves multicultural – London has 8 million inhabitants who speak more than 300 languages. You may live in Sub-Saharan Africa and be influenced by foreign interests searching for minerals. In Asia you may be employed by a multinational company from the West, or by an Asian company expanding its operations worldwide. Or you may live in Europe and experience effects of the Chinese Dream and One Belt, One Road initiative (Hung-Baesecke and Xu 2018). There is no place to hide from other cultures and there is no alternative but to learn how to live with and in them. All of us share several cultures – not only ethnic/national, but also professional, racial, gender, class or caste, organisational, associational or gang. Humans are multicultural beings.

> **Think about 6.1**
>
> **Cultures, nations, countries and states**
>
> What is in English language commonly referred to as a country or a nation, international law defines as sovereign state. Although there seems to be a correspondence between ethnic cultures and sovereign states – sometimes referred to as nation-states (i.e. France is a sovereign state of French, China of Chinese and Nigeria of Nigerians), the real world is far more complicated (even when discounted for international migrations). Even in France as a highly centralised state, there are different populations that are French by citizenship but not ethically – Basques on the border with Spain or Corsicans on the island of Corsica in the Mediterranean sea. In Switzerland they speak three major languages – French, German and Italian, and one minor – Retroroman. England is a country in the United Kingdom (Scotland, Wales and Northern Ireland being other constitutive entities of the monarchy). Although over 90 per cent of Chinese citizens belong to the largest ethnic group – Han, the government recognises 55 other distinct ethnic groups. In India, currently the second largest country in the world and projected by 2025 to surpass China and become the most populated country in the world, where four of the world's major religions originated – Hinduism, Buddhism, Jainism and Sikhism, there are 30 languages spoken by more than a million and 122 languages spoken by more than 10,000 speakers. In Indonesia there are around 300 different ethnicities living in that country and speaking 742 different languages and dialects. Nigeria, the most populous country in Africa and with one of the fastest growing populations in the world, has more than 250 ethnic groups. South Africa has eleven languages recognised in its constitution. In the United States of America, some federal States (Arizona, New Mexico and Texas) have Spanish next to English as their *de jure* or/and *de facto* official language.
>
> At the beginning of 2020, there were 195 member states of the United Nations, and there are at least a dozen more states that are not included in the UN system and whose sovereignty is disputed.
>
> **Feedback**
>
> Try to list as many countries per continent as you can.
>
> For selected countries, try to see how many ethnic cultures and major religions you can identify.

Picture 6.1 Public relations has a critical role as part of society and government (*source:* PlusONE/Shutterstock)

Public relations and culture

If we think of public relations as purposeful, persuasive communication, then it is as old as the human race. But as a contemporary practice of strategic communication responsible for the management of mutually beneficial relations between organisations and their publics, it is of a much more recent origin (Sriramesh 2008). We can think of public relations as a social technology that exploits developments in social sciences to influence human behaviour. To flourish, it needs educational and institutional infrastructure to enable training and funding for practitioners and their activities (Edwards 2012). It emerged in the second half of the nineteenth century in Europe and in the United States and its birth was closely related to developments in information and communication technology, specifically the mass media.

Investments in the practice of public relations are unequally distributed around the world (Sriramesh and Verčič 2007). Societies provide resources that are needed for public relations to work: practitioners, equipment, funding... Societies also provide institutional environments that are hospitable to public relations practices: generally, public relations requires open democratic social environments with free speech and rights to communication and association; dictatorships and autocratic regimes don't use communication and relationships to rule – they rely on physical force. (They use public relations in other countries to try to polish their image abroad, or, in the words of *The Guardian,* for 'reputation laundering'; Sweney 2017.) Social, political and media cultures of a country in that respect determine ways in which public relations can be practiced in a country and in that context we can say that culture operates as an antecedent to public relations (Sriramesh 2012).

But as on one side social (and political) cultures determine ways in which public relations can be practised in a country, so does public relations co-create these very societal (and political) cultures (Bridgen and Verčič 2018; Heath 2012; Ławniczak 2005; McKie and Munshi 2007; Mickey 2003). The ways in which we see ourselves, objects around us, other people and nations is today presented to us with the help and support of public relations work. Public relations is a great force today in creating meaningful social environments for us. In that context we can say that culture not only operates as an antecedent to public relations, but it is also a consequence of these very public relations practices.

Not only that, we can extend the metaphor of culture further, also to organisations practicing public relations and to the very occupation of public relations. We can describe organisations as having different cultures, open or closed, more mechanical, machine-like, or organic, like biological organisms. Organisational or corporate (similarly as societal) cultures are environments promoting or hindering the use of public relations (Sriramesh and Verčič 2012). Therefore, the usefulness of public relations is dependent not only on the skills of practitioners, but also on expectations and support of their clients (see also Chapter 23, Corporate communication).

Even public relations as an occupation can be observed as having a culture of its own (Edwards 2012) and it is different from cultures of e.g. managers (Verčič and White 2012): while managers are usually focused, goal- and numbers-oriented, public relations practitioners are often seen to be much 'softer', creative and communication and not so results-oriented. Verčič (2012) also analysed public relations firms using differences in their cultures as a criterion. He found out that there are public relations agencies that are specialised in producing publicity and that sell mainly journalistic skills of practitioners who are often ex-journalists. Then there are public relations services operating as outsourcing posts for communication departments of corporate clients – their rationale is often critiqued as buy cheap (young, mainly female workers or interns) and sell expensive. And there are public relations consultancies some of which are really in the business of providing research-based advice, with the best being founded on public relations theoretical knowledge.

It is not only products, services and organisations as whole corporate bodies, but countries also use public relations tools to build (Taylor and Kent 2006) and to present themselves (Taylor 2001; Kunczik 1997).

The notion of culture has become so important for contemporary life that an anthropologist Grant McCracken wrote a book proposing for each company to employ its own *Chief Culture Officer* (2009).

Think about 6.2

Public relations around the world

It is easy to forget that both management and public relations are concepts of a Western origin, and therefore culturally loaded. Furthermore, in their current dominant interpretation they are very North-American. It is impossible to translate the term 'public relations' in many languages, and there are differences in popular understanding of the term even between British and American English. While public relations in American English commonly stands for 'management of relationships with publics', in British English it often means 'relations with the media' (with 'public affairs' in British English standing for American English 'public relations' – while 'public affairs' in American English stands for 'government relations'). The term 'public relations' was translated in German as Öffentlichkeitsarbeit (literally meaning 'public work' and in German often described as work in public for the public), referring to work in general public or public sphere. Similar problems exist in other Germanic and Slavonic languages (generally translating 'public relations' into 'relations' or 'contacts with the public' in the singular. Other language groups and cultures have even more approximate and vague translations.

Feedback

How many different meanings of the term 'public relations' do you know in your language?

How many similar terms used as synonyms for 'public relations' do you know?

Discuss denotations and connotations of these different terms. ('Denotation' stands for 'literal', 'vocabulary', or explicit and primary meaning of a term and 'connotation' for 'subjective', 'emotional', implicit or secondary meaning of the term, usually implying valuation, related positive and negative associations.)

Between universalism and relativism

The current public relations theory and practice are founded in the West, predominantly Western Europe and the US. Only recently have researchers addressed the issue of differences in thinking and doing public relations around the world. In the past 25 years, several key books have been published on the subject: Culbertson and Chen (1996) – *International Public Relations: A comparative analysis*; Curtin and Gaither (2007) – *International Public Relations: Negotiating culture, identity, and power*; Ruler and Verčič (2004) – *Public Relations and Communication Management in Europe: A nation-by-nation introduction to public relations theory and practice*; Sriramesh (2004) – *Public Relations in Asia: An anthology*; Sriramesh and Verčič (2009) – *The Global Public Relations Handbook: Theory, research, and practice*; Sriramesh and Verčič (2012) – *Culture and Public Relations – Links and implications*; and Tilson and Alozie (2004) – *Toward the Common Good: Perspectives in international public relations*.

Research shows that public relations practitioners are more numerous in the most developed parts of the world, although their services might be more needed elsewhere (Verčič and Sriramesh 2007). Observations of large multinationals headquartered in the UK have found that their offices in different parts of the world vary significantly, from one to ten practitioners, without any consistency in size or the scope of their work in relation to their responsibilities. Moss et al. (2012) found that the UK headquarters and their closest offices in Europe had numerically more and more qualified staff than more distant offices, even if these were covering much larger territories.

Mini case study 6.1
Others are different: the bribery scandal at Siemens AG

Siemens AG is the largest Europe-based electronics and electrical engineering company, operating in the industry, energy and healthcare sectors. Headquartered in Munich, Germany, it is 160 years old and together with its subsidiaries it employs over 400,000 people in practically all countries in the world. Its global revenue in 2010 was €76 billion and net income €4.1 billion. 'For decades, Munich-based Siemens paid kickbacks and bribes to win contracts in places including Russia, Bangladesh, Venezuela and Nigeria, according to investigations in more than a dozen countries' (www.bloomberg.com/news/2011-01-27/siemens-bribery-scandal-leaves-von-pierer-unbowed-in-his-ceo-memoir-books.html). After being investigated in several countries, including the US and Germany, in 2008 Siemens agreed to settle cases of bribery, corruption and trying to falsify corporate books. The total fine for Siemens was more than US$2.6 billion to clear its name: US$1.6 billion in fines and fees in Germany and the United States and more than US$1 billion for internal investigations and reforms. Top management has been replaced. The new management has put compliance with new rules, values and principles at the centre of its business (Pohlmann 2008). Siemens is today one of the promoters of the United Nations Global Compact, which 'is a strategic policy initiative for businesses that are committed to aligning their operations and strategies with ten universally accepted principles in the areas of human rights, labour, environment and anti-corruption. By doing so, business, as a primary driver of globalisation, can help ensure that markets, commerce, technology and finance advance in ways that benefit economies and societies everywhere' (http://www.unglobalcompact.org/).

The UN Global Compact's Ten Principles
Human Rights
Principle 1: Businesses should support and respect the protection of internationally proclaimed human rights; and

Principle 2: make sure that they are not complicit in human rights abuses.

Labour
Principle 3: Businesses should uphold the freedom of association and the effective recognition of the right to collective bargaining;

Principle 4: the elimination of all forms of forced and compulsory labour;

Principle 5: the effective abolition of child labour; and

Principle 6: the elimination of discrimination in respect of employment and occupation.

Environment
Principle 7: Businesses should support a precautionary approach to environmental challenges;

Principle 8: undertake initiatives to promote greater environmental responsibility; and

Principle 9: encourage the development and diffusion of environmentally friendly technologies.

Anti-corruption
Principle 10: Businesses should work against corruption in all its forms, including extortion and bribery.

> Companies such as Siemens before 2008 are victims of cultural myopia (short-sightedness): rules in other countries seem to them different than those at home and so they believe that they can do things abroad they wouldn't dare do at home.
>
> Transparency International is the global civil society organisation leading the fight against corruption (http://www.transparency.org/). In its reports on corruption around the world, Finland always comes out as one of the least corrupt countries. Yet Patria, a defence company which is majority owned by Finish government, is suspected of exporting corruption by paying bribery in places like Egypt, Slovenia and Croatia (Helsingin Sanomat 2008; Roselfeld 2011).
>
> **Feedback**
>
> Do you think that corruption is a cultural phenomenon, being more acceptable in some rather than in other countries?
>
> Do you think that international initiatives like the Global Compact to promote human rights, fair labour practices, respect for the natural environment and to fight corruption make a difference to the world in which we live?

Certain principles, like those inscribed in the Ten Principles of the Global Compact seem to be universal and need to be followed worldwide. Respect for local cultures, localisation of organisational practices and communications is responsible only if it adheres to the highest ethical standards. But somehow many people believe that when abroad, they can lower their moral guard and do things they would never do at home. This is a problem of double standards that many multinational companies (MNCs) are accused of: Jahansoozi et al. (2012) provided a thorough and vivid description of the double standards that Shell and other MNC oil companies use in Nigeria as compared to their behaviour in, for example, Canada.

It seems that humans have evolutionarily developed a tendency to categorise other humans between 'us' and 'them'. 'We' belong to the same culture, while 'they' think, decide and behave differently. This goes symmetrically in all directions: 'they' are always different from 'us', and 'we' are different from 'them'. And it is 'we' who know what is right, and if they do it differently, it is 'wrong'. Every civilisation in history wanted to 'civilise' others. The very term 'barbarian' which nowadays stands for describing uncivilised behaviour or individuals, originated in Old Greek and it was originally describing anybody who was not Greek.

Global principles and specific applications

A general explanation of how public relations adds value to organisations is proposed in the *Excellence Theory* (Grunig et al. 2002). It is a result of a decade-long research project aimed at the development of a general theory of public relations and it is generally credited to be the mainstream theory in public relations in American academia and around the world (see also Chapter 7 for a discussion and critique). This theory proposes nine general principles or characteristics public relations needs to contribute to organisational effectiveness: (1) involvement of public relations in strategic management; (2) empowerment of public relations in the dominant coalition or a direct reporting relationship to senior management; (3) integrated public relations function; (4) public relations as a management function separate from other functions; (5) the role of the public relations practitioner; (6) two-way symmetrical model of public relations; (7) a symmetrical system of internal communication; (8) knowledge potential for managerial role and symmetrical public relations; and (9) diversity embodied in all roles (Grunig 1992; Dozier et al. 1995; Grunig et al. 2002).

In 1989, Anderson proposed to distinguish between international public relations and global public relations. International public relations denotes practices when organisations develop distinctive programmes for different markets in different locations. Global public relations, however, denotes an overall perspective, an approach to work in two or more countries, recognising similarities while adapting to differences (Anderson 1989).

Verčič et al. (1996) adopted the nine excellence principles of public relations as global principles and adjusted their use around the world using specific (localised) applications determined by five environmental variables:

1. political ideology;
2. economic system (including the level of development of the country's economy);

Explore 6.2 Worldviews

At the beginning of the new Millennium, Western scholars were full of optimism in seeing their way of life and their worldview as a model for the whole world. Francis Fukuyama, an American political scientist, even declared *The End of History* (1992). In the three decades since the publication of his book (which is an expanded version of the argument first presented three years earlier in a journal article) everything changed, and not only did history not stop, it seems to be accelerating. Cultural presuppositions implicit in the mainstream public relations theories (individual human rights, political liberalism and market economy) have recently not only been challenged from Asia, but also Africa. Huang (2012) presents her arguments from a Chinese perspective: 'The difference between Chinese and Western worldviews, respectively, can be succinctly summarised: (1) emphasis on wholeness versus parts, (2) complex interpersonal relationships versus individuals, (3) emphasis on emotional/spiritual versus cognitive outcomes, and (4) nature of communication being intuitively and directly experienced versus language-centered' (p. 96). She notes two reasons for a shortage of cultural sensitivity in research: deliberate avoidance that favours context-free research to contextualised knowledge and careless oversight due to ethnocentric insensitivity.

Twenty-six years after declaring *The End of History*, Fukuyama published a new book on *Identity: The demand for dignity and the politics of resentment* (2018).

Feedback

Can you explain differences in worldviews from a Western, a Confucian, a Buddhist and a Taoist perspective? Use the internet to learn more about them, adding also other non-Western worldviews you can find.

---

3. degree of activism (the extent of pressure organisations face from activists);
4. culture;
5. media system (the nature of the media environment in a country).

Sriramesh and Verčič (2009) collapsed these five variables into three factors:

1. a country's infrastructure (composed of political system, economic system and level of development, legal system and social activism);
2. media environment (with media control, media diffusion and media access being critical);
3. societal culture.

The notion of culture and public relations has been taken further by Sriramesh and Verčič (2012).

Social media and activists in the global village

When Marshal McLuhan in his book *The Guttenberg Galaxy: The making of Typographic Man* (1962) put forward an idea that the world has been contracted into a village by electronic technology and the instantaneous movement of information from one continent to another, social media were not yet invented. Fifty years later we really live on a contracted planet where we live in what Manuel Castells calls *The Rise of the Network Society* (2010).

The emergence of social media and mobile technologies in the first decade enabled a mushrooming of activism, demonstrations and social movements at the beginning of the second decade of the twenty-first century. TIME's Person of the Year 2011 was *The Protester* – from 26-year-old street vendor Mohamed Bouazizi who set himself on fire in the Tunisian town of Sidi Bouzid, to millions protesting in Greece, Egypt, Myanmar, Nigeria, Russia, Spain, USA – all around the globe.

Picture 6.2 The emergence of social media and mobile technologies in the first decade enabled a mushrooming of activism, demonstrations and social movements (*source:* MOHAMMED ABED/AFP/Getty Images)

Box 6.1

Eight out of ten PR professionals work internationally

International and global public relations is a part of daily business for eight out of ten public relations professionals in Europe. This is the result of the largest longitudinal study in practice: The European Communication Monitor.

Of those 80 per cent of practitioners who operate internationally, the majority is working in or with more than five countries and nearly a quarter with over 20 countries.

When asked about the most challenging issues in international public relations, they mentioned 'developing communication strategies with social, cultural and politic sensitivity', 'monitoring public opinion and understanding stakeholders', and 'understanding structures of media systems and public sphere'.

The study also revealed that globalisation of public relations practice is led by corporations, while non-profit and government sectors are lagging behind.

See: Verčič et al. 2015; Zerfass et al. 2013

How to prepare for international and global public relations

In a book summarising a decade-long project studying public relations practice in Europe, *Communication Excellence: How to develop, manage and lead exceptional communications,* Tench et al. (2017: xxcii) proposed nine commandments of excellence. The first among them is to be globalised: 'Excellent organisations are connected to their environments and stakeholders, which requires them to be globalised, mediatised and reflective.'

Technology has enabled globalisation, and together they have changed our lives forever. We travel for education, business or fun to other countries, we meet people coming to our towns and villages from around the world. We can try (in vain) to stop the world going round, or we can prepare for living in a multicultural global society. If planning to work internationally, one should consider enlisting on an *intercultural training programme.* Browsing on the internet produces long lists of public and commercial providers of seminars and other educational formats for acquiring intercultural competence for different parts of the world. (In general, most of these programmes are for Westerners moving to other parts of the world.) Such programmes have four goals. First, they are preparing people to '*enjoy and benefit* from their experiences with people from other cultures'. Second, they try to make 'these positive feelings *reciprocated by host nationals* with whom sojourners work'. Third, 'sojourners should be able to *manage the stress* that is inherent in overseas assignments.' And finally, fourth, sojourners should be able to '*accomplish the tasks* called for in their work assignments' (Brislin 2008: 2331–2332).

Intercultural public relations is more than just practicing public relations geographically away from home – it doesn't even need to be a question of physical distance. Intercultural public relations is interesting because it is a matter of social distance that is invisible to the eye and often can be experienced only in one's heart.

Explore 6.3

Understanding 'the other'

In a chapter proposing a framework for indigenous engagement based on examples related to New Zealand Maori, Motion et al. (2012) concluded that we need to develop a culturally contextualised public relations practice that is open, adaptable and flexible in relations with groups which are different from us in one or another respect.

Feedback

How often do you engage in communication with people that you perceive as different from you, because they belong to another ethnicity, have a different legal status (illegal or temporary immigrants), or maybe simply belong to another class, caste or any other group characteristic that is meaningful to you? What are your experiences from such encounters?

Mini case study 6.2
When operating procedures and cultures collide

With 3.2 million employees, the US Department of Defence is the largest employer in the world. It is also one of the most multicultural organisations in the world. Its personnel are of different races, ethnic origin, gender, occupational and military specialities, and deployed all around the globe. The US Department of Defence is investing in research, education and training of its public relations function, which they call 'public affairs'.

Allen and Dozier (2012) present a case study on relations between the US military public affairs officers (PAOs) and Arab journalists in the Middle East. The US military are Western trained professionals favouring personal responsibility and exchange relations enabling expediency, while Arab journalists belong to a culture founded on family, community and giving importance to honour. The PAOs have relatively short deployments in a foreign country, so they can't develop long-term, communal relations with the Arab media. This experience is shared by expatriates working in multinational companies or international organisations: they are responsible for 'establishing and maintaining symbiotic relationships with relevant publics', but they are limited in their opportunities to do so, because they are called back home or moved to another position somewhere else. While in host cultures it could take years to develop trusted relationships and become an accepted member of a community, operating procedures of many organisations prevent their employees 'going local' by moving them before they can 'localise'.

Key principles in intercultural and multicultural public relations

Intercultural and multicultural public relations is the management of diverse public relations practices: there is a multitude of people and worldviews around us and we must learn to embrace the rainbow. This, however, is far from easy and there are no quick recipes for the management of successful multicultural programmes. Instead of searching for short-cuts, it is better to face the practical challenges and attempt to resolve what may appear to be paradoxes in the delivery of public relations programmes.

- *Increase the complexity and focus on simplicity.* If an organisation operates in a culturally rich environment (and it is practically impossible to operate differently), it must work towards increasing its own cultural richness internally. Only that way it can understand and communicate with various publics. But cultural multitude is not the same as chaos. Common values should provide guiding principles that bring simplicity to the multitude. Communication is instrumental in coproduction of common foundations.

- *Communication belongs to the top and can only work at the bottom.* Public relations is more than a set of tools to broadcast messages from the top of an organisation downwards and outwards. Public relations can best serve organisations by performing a role of ears and eyes of management through which it is tuned to the larger society. To be influential at the top, public relations needs to have its top person positioned at the top of an organisation. But it is impossible to communicate to everybody everywhere from there, so local teams are needed to have local experiences and relationships needed to perform well.

- *Good external communication is founded in good internal communication.* Organisations can be trusted only if they communicate what they mean and in that respect internal communication provides a foundation for authenticity of expressions for organisational members when they engage with others. Even before social media penetrated organisational borders, they were anything but firm. In today's information environments, all organisations leak all the time. Engaging insiders is a prerequisite for successful engagement with anybody else.

- *The science of communication is universal, but the art of communication is always cultural = local.* Modern science based on empirical research is a powerful force that has transformed humanity in the past three to four hundred years. Social sciences are with us a half of that period, and public relations as an applied communication and management science have only been extensively studied since the 1980s. But scientific research in public relations offers powerful technological solutions that easily travel around the globe. However, human communication can never be only scientifically programmed and there is always an artistic, creative side to human intercourse closely linked to cultures as small universes of meanings.

Public diplomacy

When watching international news on television, one can see that we live in a violent world. But '[v]iolence has declined by dramatic degrees all over the world in many spheres of behaviour: genocide, war, human sacrifice, torture, slavery, and the treatment of racial minorities, women, children, and animals' (Pinkler 2012; see also Pinkler 2011). And notwithstanding the current depressive economic and political climate in the Western world, there is a good chance that our lives will continue to get better (Diamandis and Kotler 2012) – but progress is not an automatic ride, it is a human made condition. And at the centre of that condition is communication.

International relations, relations between states or countries, can be conducted by war, trade or diplomacy, i.e. force, money or communication. Traditional diplomacy covers communication between representatives of governments. It is possible to talk about cultural diplomacy that has been practiced for centuries between traders and scholars travelling to other countries in search of profit, knowledge or simple adventure. 'Public diplomacy' meant only civility when it first emerged in English language in the mid-nineteenth century. In the mid-twentieth century it stepped into political language to replace the term 'international propaganda' that

---

Think about 6.3   Can('t) buy me love

In 1953, the US President Dwight Eisenhower established the United States Information Agency 'to understand, inform, and influence foreign publics in the promotion of the US national interest, and to broaden the dialogue between Americans and U.S. institutions, and their counterparts abroad' (USIA 1998). In 1961, John F. Kennedy appointed Edward R. Murrow the director of the USIA. Murrow was previously a prominent US broadcast journalist who had made his name first during his wartime reporting from Europe from 1938 to 1945, and then by producing a series of TV news reports that were instrumental in censuring Senator Joseph McCarthy, an infamous fighter against Red Scare (communism) in 1950s USA. Murrow resigned as the director of the USIA due to illness in 1964 and died in 1965 due to lung cancer he developed as a chain-smoker. In 1965, the Edward R. Murrow Centre of Public Diplomacy was established at the Fletcher School of Law and Diplomacy at Tufts University – its Dean, Edmund Gullion, is credited with inventing the term 'public diplomacy' in its present usage. The same activities were previously known, and are still referred to by critics, as 'international propaganda'. The USIA is known for being effective in influencing public opinion behind the Iron Curtin during the Cold War, but was in mid 1990s downsized as part of budget-cutting 'peace dividend'. In 1999, the Clinton administration merged the USIA into the State Department. Before being abolished, the USIA had a budget of US$ 1.109 billion and was employing 6,352 employees.

Inside the US State Department, public diplomacy is now run by the Under Secretary for Public Diplomacy and Public Affairs which defines its mission as follows:

> The mission of American public diplomacy is to support the achievement of U.S. foreign policy goals and objectives, advance national interests, and enhance national security by informing and influencing foreign publics and by expanding and strengthening the relationship between the people and government of the United States and citizens of the rest of the world.
>
> The Under Secretary for Public Diplomacy and Public Affairs leads America's public diplomacy outreach, which includes communications with international audiences, cultural programming, academic grants, educational exchanges, international visitor programs, and U.S. Government efforts to confront ideological support for terrorism. The Under Secretary oversees the bureaus of Educational and Cultural Affairs, Public Affairs, and International Information Programs, and participates in foreign policy development.

(US Department of State 2012)

In fiscal year 2006, the US budget for public diplomacy was US$ 2.03 billion, which constitutes 3.7 per cent of $55.3 billion budget of the US international affairs spending (US Department of State 2017). Comparing sizes and international responsibilities, one could say that the US government is seriously underinvesting in public diplomacy. Many still believe that dismantling of the USIA was a strategic mistake. However, US$ 2.3 billion per year is still a respectable sum of money. It is interesting to see how it reflected in public opinion in Western Europe, the closest ally of the US in the world.

Feedback

What are the similarities and differences between propaganda, public relations and public diplomacy?

How would you answer a question posed by a US diplomat Richard Holbroke: 'How can a man in a cave outcommunicate the world's leading communications society?' (Where 'a man in a cave' denotes Osama bin Laden and 'the world's leading communication society' the USA.)

was largely discredited during the Second World War. Defined simply, public diplomacy means communication of governments with peoples of other countries. McClellan (2004) defines it as 'the strategic planning and execution of informational, cultural and educational programming by an advocate country to create a public opinion environment in a target country or countries that will enable target country political leaders to make decisions that are supportive of advocate country's foreign policy objectives.'

Related to public diplomacy is the notion of soft power:

The basic concept of power is the ability to influence others to get them to want what you want. There are three major ways to that: one is to threaten them with sticks; the second is to pay them with carrots; the third is to attract them or co-opt them, so that they want what you want. If you can get others to be attracted, to want what you want, it costs you much less in carrots and sticks. (Nye 2004)

For Nye (2004), soft power is founded in a nation's 'culture (in places where it is attractive to others), its political values (when it lives up to them at home and abroad), and its foreign policies (when they are seen as legitimate and having moral authority)' (p.11). Soft power, therefore, comes from a nation's behaviour and not from symbols it uses to present itself to others. In 2018, three European countries topped *The Soft Power 30: A Global Ranking of Soft Power* index – the United Kingdom, France and Germany (McClory 2018).

Today, practically all countries use public diplomacy with varying degrees of success.

Summary

We live in a multicultural world and public relations practitioners are in the business of intercultural mediation. Wherever we live, we are exposed to other cultures. Cultures as mental programming of our minds are not reflecting only our ethnic or national background, but also class, professional, racial, gender and other differences. We trust our cultural views to be 'natural' because we are born in them – but so are others in theirs. Public relations as management of communication and relationships is directly concerned with the management of cultural differences. To provide an alternative image and comparison we can also say that public relations practitioners are required to perform like intercultural interpreters.

Bibliography

Allen, M.R. and D.M. Dozier (2012). When cultures collide: Theoretical issues in global public relations. In K. Sriramesh and D. Verčič (Eds.), *Culture and public relations: Links and implications.* New York/London: Routledge.

Andersen, K. (2011). The protester. *The Time*, 14 December. Retrieved from: http://www.time.com/time/specials/packages/article/0,28804,2101745_2102132,00.html

Anderson, G. (1989). A local look at public relations. In B. Cantor (Ed.), *Experts in action: Inside public relations* (2nd edn, pp. 412–22). New York: Longman.

Banks, S.P. (1995). *Multicultural Public Relations: A Social-Interpretive Approach.* Thousand Oaks, CA: Sage.

Bridgen, E. and D. Verčič (2018). *Experiencing public relations: International perspectives.* London and New York: Routledge.

Brislin, R.W. (2008). Intercultural communication training. In W. Donsbach (Ed.), *International Encyclopedia of Communication*, Vol. VI (pp. 2331–33). Malden, MA: Blackwell.

Castells, M. (2007). Communication, power and counter-power in the network society. *International Journal of Communication* 1: 238–66.

Castells, M. (2009). *Communication Power.* Oxford/New York: Oxford University Press.

Castells, M. (2010). *The Rise of the Network Society*, 2nd edn. Chichester, UK: Willey-Blackwell.

Center for Strategic and International Studies (2008). Appendix to Armitage-Nye Joint Testimony before U.S. Senate Foreign Relations Committee, 24 April. Retrieved on 26 June 2012 from http://csis.org/files/media/csis/congress/ts0804024Armitage-Nye_Appendix.pdf

Culbertson, H.M. and N. Chen (Eds.) (1996). *International Public Relations: A Comparative Analysis.* Mahwah, NJ: Lawrence Erlbaum.

Curtin, P.A. and T. Gaither (2007). *International Public Relations: Negotiating Culture, Identity, and Power.* Thousand Oaks, CA: Sage.

Debeljak, A. (2012). In praise of hybridity: Globalization and the modern Western paradigm. In K. Sriramesh and D. Verčič (Eds.), *Culture and Public Relations: Links and implications* (pp. 42–53). New York: Routledge.

Diamandis, P.H. and S. Kotler (2012). *Abundance: The future is better than you think.* New York: Free Press.

Dozier, D.M., L.A, Grunig and J.E. Grunig (1995). *Manager's Guide to Excellence in Public Relations and Communication Management.* Mahwah, NJ: Lawrence Erlbaum Associates.

Dutta, M.J. (2012). Critical interrogations of global public relations. In K. Sriramesh and D. Verčič (Eds.), *Culture and public relations: Links and implications* (pp. 202–17). New York/London: Routledge.

Edwards, L. (2012). Public relations' occupational culture: Habitus, exclusion and resistance in the UK context. In K. Sriramesh and D. Verčič (Eds.), *Culture and public relations: Links and implications* (pp. 142–62). New York/London: Routledge.

Fukuyama, F. (1992). *The End of History and the Last Man.* New York: The Free Press.

Fukuyama, F. (2018). *Identity: The demand for dignity and the politics of resentment.* New York: Farrar, Straus and Giroux.

Grunig, J.E. (Ed.) (1992a) *Excellence in Public Relations and Communication Management.* Hillsdale, NJ: Lawrence Erlbaum Associates.

Grunig, L.A., J.E. Grunig and D.M. Dozier (2002). *Excellent Public Relations and Effective Organizations: A study of communication management in three countries.* Mahwah, NJ: Lawrence Erlbaum Associates.

Heath, R.L. (2012). Western classical rhetorical tradition and modern public relations: Culture of citizenship. In K. Sriramesh and D. Verčič (Eds.), *Culture and public relations: Links and implications* (pp. 25–41). New York/London: Routledge.

Helsingin Sanomat (2008). Finland's central criminal police to investigate Patria deals in Slovenia and Egypt. *Helsingin Sanomat: International Edition*, 15.5.2008. Retrieved on 19 June 2012 from http://www.hs.fi/english/article/1135236367677

Huang, Y.-H. C. (2012). Culture and Chinese public relations research. In K. Sriramesh and D. Verčič (Eds.), *Culture and public relations: Links and implications* (pp. 91–104). New York/London: Routledge.

Hung-Baesecke, C.-J. F. and M. Xu (2018). From propaganda to public diplomacy: the Chinese context. In E. Bridgen and D. Verčič (Eds.), *Experiencing public relations: International voices* (pp. 137–51). London and New York: Routledge.

Jahansoozi, J., K. Eyita and N. Izidor (2012). Mago Mago: Nigeria, petroleum and a history of mismanaged community relations. In K. Sriramesh and D. Verčič (Eds.), *Culture and public relations: Links and implications* (pp. 105–23). New York/London: Routledge.

Kunczik, M. (1997). *Images of Nations and International Public Relations.* Mahwah, NJ: Lawrence Erlbaum.

Ławniczak, R. (2005). *Introducing market economy institutions and instruments: The role of public relations in transition economies.* Poznań: Piar.pl.

McClellan, M. (2004). Public diplomacy in the context of traditional diplomacy. Presented to Vienna Diplomatic Academy on 14 October 2004. Retrieved on 13 June 2012 from http://www.publicdiplomacy.org/45.htm

McClory, J. (2018). *The soft power 30: A global ranking of soft power 2018.* London: Portland, Facebook and USC Center on Public Diplomacy. www.softpower30.com

McCracken, G. (2009). *Chief Culture Officer: How to Create a Living, Breathing Corporation.* New York: Basic Books.

McKie, D. and D. Munshi (2007). *Reconfiguring Public Relations: Ecology, equity, and enterprise.* London/New York: Routledge.

McLuhan, M. (1962). *The Guttenberg Galaxy: The Making of Typographic Man.* Toronto: University of Toronto Press.

Mickey, T.J. (2003). *Deconstructing Public Relations: Public Relations Criticism.* Mahwah, NJ: Lawrence Erlbaum Associates.

Moss, D., C. McGrath, J. Tonge and P. Harris (2012) Exploring the management of the corporate public affairs function in a dynamic global environment. *Journal of Public Affairs* 12: 47–60.

Motion, J., J. Haar and S. Leitch (2012). A public relations framework for indigenous engagement. In K. Sriramesh and D. Verčič (Eds.), *Culture and public relations: Links and implications* (pp. 54–66). New York/London: Routledge.

Ni, L., Q. Wang and B-L. Sha (2018). *Intercultural public relations: Theories for managing relationships and conflicts with strategic publics.* New York and London: Routledge.

Nye, J. (2004). *Soft Power: The means to success in world politics.* New York: Public Affairs.

Pinkler, S. (2011a). A history of violence: *Edge* Master class 2011. Retrieved on 13 June 2012 from http://edge.org/conversation/mc2011-history-violence-pinker

Pinkler, S. (2011b). *The Better Angels of Our Nature: The decline of violence in history and its causes.* London: Penguin.

Pinkler, S. (2012) *The Better Angels of Our Nature: Why Violence Has Declined*, Steven Viking Books.

Prinz, J.J. (2012). *Beyond Human Nature: How culture and experience shape our lives.* London: Allen Lane.

Pohlmann, A. (2008). A new direction for Siemens: Improving preventive systems. *Compact Quarterly.* Retrieved on 18 June 2012 from http://www.enewsbuilder.net/globalcompact/e_article001149152.cfm?x=bd2Hd2m

Rubenfeld, S. (2011). Finland expands Patria bribery investigation into Croatia sales. *The Wall Street Journal Europe,* 4 January 2011. Retrieved on 19 June 2012 from http://blogs.wsj.com/corruption-currents/2011/01/04/finland-expands-patria-bribery-investigation-into-croatia-sales/

Ruler, B. van and D. Verčič (Eds.) (2004). *Public Relations and Communication Management in Europe: A Nation-by-Nation Introduction to Public Relations Theory and Practice.* Berlin/New York: Mouton de Gruyter.

Sha, B.-L., N.T.J. Tindall and T.-L. Sha. (2012). Identity and culture: Implications for public relations. In K. Sriramesh and D. Verčič (Eds.), *Culture and public relations: Links and implications* (pp. 67–90). New York/London: Routledge.

Signitzer, B. and C. Wamser (2006). Public Diplomacy: A Specific Governmental Public Relations Function. In C. H. Botan and V. Hazleton (Eds.), *Public Relations Theory II* (pp. 435–64). Mahwah, NJ: Lawrence Erlbaum.

Sriramesh, K. (Ed.) (2004). *Public Relations in Asia: An Anthology.* Singapore: Thomson Learning.

Sriramesh, K. (2008). Public Relations, Intercultural. In W. Donsbach (Ed.), *International Encyclopedia of Communication, Vol. IX* (pp. 4016–4020). Malden, MA: Blackwell.

Sriramesh, K. (2012). Culture and public relations: Formulating the relationship and its relevance to the practice. In K. Sriramesh and D. Verčič (Eds.), *Culture and public relations: Links and implications* (pp. 9–24). New York/London: Routledge.

Sriramesh, K. and D. Verčič (2007). Introduction to this special section: The impact of globalization on public relations. *Public Relations Review* 33: 355–59.

Sriramesh, K. and D. Verčič (Eds.) (2019). *The Global Public Relations Handbook: Theory, Research, and Practice,* 3rd edn. New York: Routledge.

Sriramesh, K. and D. Verčič (Eds.) (2012) *Culture and Public Relations: Links and implications.* New York: Routledge.

Shweder, R.A., J.J. Goodnow, G. Hatano, R.A. LeVine, H.R. Markus and P.J. Miller (1998) The Cultural Psychology of Development: One Mind, Many Mentalities. In W. Damon (Series Ed.) and R.M. Lerner (Vol. Ed.), *Handbook of Child Psychology: Vil. 1. Theoretical models of human development* (5th edn, pp. 865–937). New York: Wiley.

Sweney, M. (2017). 'Reputation laundering' is lucrative business for London PR firms. *The Guardian,* 5 September 2017. Retrieved on 30 April from https://www.theguardian.com/media/2017/sep/05/reputation-laundering-is-lucrative-business-for-london-pr-firms

Taylor, M. (2001). International Public Relations: Opportunities and Challenges for the 21st Century. In R.L. Heath (Ed.), *Handbook of Public Relations* (pp. 629–37). Thousand Oaks, CA: Sage.

Taylor, M. and M.L. Kent (2006). Public Relations Theory and Practice in Nation Building. In C.H. Botan and V. Hazleton (Eds.), *Public Relations Theory II* (pp. 341–59). Mahwah, NJ: Lawrence Erlbaum.

Tench, R., D. Verčič, A. Zerfass, A. Moreno and P. Verhoeven (2017). *Communication Excellence: How to develop, manage and lead exceptional communications.* London: Palgrave Macmillan.

Tilson, D.J. and E.C. Alozie (Eds.) (2004). *Toward the Common Good: Perspectives in International Public Relations.* Boston: Pearson.

U.S. Department of State (2012). Under Secretary for Public Diplomacy and Public Affairs. Retrieved on 17 June 2012 from http://www.state.gov/r/

U.S. Department of State (2017). 2017 comprehensive annual report on public diplomacy and international broadcasting. Retrieved on 1 May 2019 from https://www.state.gov/pdcommission/reports/274698.htm

USIA (1998). *United States Information Agency.* Washington, DC: USIA. Retrieved on 13 June 2012 from http://dosfan.lib.uic.edu/usia/usiahome/overview.pdf

Verčič, D. (2012). Public relations firms and their three occupational cultures. In K. Sriramesh and D. Verčič (Eds.), *Culture and public relations: Links and implications* (pp. 243–57). New York/London: Routledge.

Verčič, D., L.A. Grunig and J.E. Grunig (1996). Global and specific principles of public relations: Evidence from Slovenia. In H. M. Culbertson and N. Chen (Eds.), *International Public Relations: A Comparative Analysis* (pp. 31–65). Mahwah, NJ: Lawrence Erlbaum Associates.

Verčič, D., A. Zerfass and M. Wiesenberg (2015). Global public relations and communication management: A European perspective. *Public Relations Review* 41(5): 785–93.

Verčič, D. and J. White (2012). Corporate public relations as a professional culture: between management and journalism. In K. Sriramesh and D. Verčič (Eds.), *Culture and public relations: Links and implications* (pp. 237–42). New York/London: Routledge.

Zerfass, A., Á. Moreno, R. Tench, D. Verčič, and P. Verhoeven (2013). *European Communication Monitor 2013. A changing landscape – Managing crises, digital communication and CEO positioning in Europe. Results of a survey in 43 countries.* Brussels: EACD/EUPRERA, Helios Media.

Websites

The European Public Relations Education and Research Association: www.euprera.org
The Global Alliance for Public Relations and Communication Management: www.globalalliancepr.org
The International Association of Business Communicators: www.iabc.com
The International Public Relations Association: www.ipra.org
Human development index – http://hdr.undp.org/en/statistics/hdi/ Transparency international – http://www.transparency.org/

CHAPTER 7

Ralph Tench and Stephen Waddington

Role of the public relations practitioner

Source: Mathisa/Shutterstock

Learning outcomes

By the end of this chapter you should be able to:
- describe issues and debates surrounding the role of the public relations practitioner
- consider the role of public relations in society
- recognise the range of activities undertaken by practitioners
- evaluate the skills needed by individual practitioners
- recognise the issues around the education and training of the public relations practitioner
- apply the above to real-life contexts.

Structure

- Who are the public relations practitioners?
- Who does what: the bigger picture?
- Role of the communicator
- Trust in communications
- Trust in organisational advocates: external experts and leaders are top
- Artificial Intelligence: high impact expected, but challenges and risks identified
- Content creation and distribution: shared media and internal sources preferred
- The PR practitioner as communicator
- What public relations people do: individual practitioners
- Skills for the ideal practitioner
- Role of theory in practice
- Professionalism
- Education and research

Introduction

It's impossible to explain exactly what a public relations (PR) practitioner does as the job is varied depending on your employer or the type of agency you work for and even the country you are working in. However, this chapter will explore what PR practitioners do on a day-to-day basis and highlight the huge variety in the types of work that a PR practitioner does. It is an exciting and often challenging environment and the reality is often a long way from the traditional views of what public relations people do.

If you've already read other chapters in this book you will see that each chapter addresses an area of public relations theory or practice, which shows that PR is used by a wide variety of organisations, governments and individuals for a whole range of purposes and in its delivery is well thought through and actioned by professional individuals and teams.

This chapter aims to show where people work in public relations and what they do in their jobs. It explores the problems caused by difficulties in defining the field, but also the opportunities for individual and professional development. Public relations practice is linked to public relations theory and the need for individuals to undertake lifelong learning is stressed. The role of education and the question of professionalism are also discussed, along with the role of professional and trade bodies.

This chapter aims to bridge the divide between detailed academic books and 'how to' textbooks by setting practice clearly in a theoretical context and including examples of practice from different countries. It also reflects a range of experiences, through case studies and diaries, of being a practitioner in the twenty-first century. Throughout the chapter you will be able to read mini case histories and diaries of public relations practitioners who are working in different types of settings to help you appreciate the diversity of the practice and gain an insight into what people do.

Explore 7.1   What is public relations all about?

If you've ever asked your friends and family what they think PR is and/or which PR practitioners they have heard of you will get a variety of answers.

Feedback

Many will describe activities or individuals with a significant media interest in areas such as sport, music or politics, and may not all be positive. Yet the bona fide public relations practitioner will not be seeking exposure for themselves, but for the client or the organisation they work for.

You may also find that media relations, rather than public relations, is the function or activity most closely associated with these high-profile individuals or sectors. However, the breadth and range of subject matter covered in this book will dispel the misunderstanding that most people will have of the practice.

Who are the public relations practitioners?

Because of the huge variety of industries to work in and public relations roles within different environments there remains a lot of confusion about who does what in public relations – see Explore 7.1. It may be helpful to look at some facts about the industry in Britain (see Box 7.1). You can explore the many PR associations' websites as most countries worldwide have a PR association that represent practitioners. Many are busy lobbying on behalf of the industry and engaging in research into the state of the profession in their country. Most of these professional bodies are members of the Global Alliance for Public Relations and Communication Management (www.globalalliancepr.org), which formally started operating in July 2002 with 25 members including all major PR member associations. Its vision is to enhance the role and value of public relations and communication management to organisations, and to global society. It aims to define universal principles of public relations whilst embracing diversity. See Box 7.2 for a review of the origins of PR in some of its key members' countries.

> **Box 7.1**
>
> # Key facts about public relations in the UK
>
> The CIPR and PRCA track the public relations sector in the UK via an annual State of the Profession and bi-annual PR Census, respectively. The data below is from the 2019 reports.
>
> ### Size
>
> In 2019, the public relations and communications industry was worth £14.9 billion. The industry grew by 7.9 per cent since 2018 when the industry was worth £13.8 billion. The PR and communications industry grew to 95,000 employees. This shows significant growth since 2018 when there was a total of 86,000 employees.
>
> ### Diversity
>
> Public relations is failing to make progress on diversity. More than nine in ten (92 per cent) now classify themselves as white – compared to 88 per cent in 2018 and 90 per cent in 2017. This is despite the widely held belief that public relations is more effective when practiced by teams that are diverse and represent the communities that they seek to engage.
>
> ### Social mobility
>
> More than a quarter (28 per cent) of respondents to the State of the Profession Survey said they had attended a fee-paying school. This is four times higher than the national UK average of 7 per cent and a significant rise on the 16 per cent figure reported in the 2015/16 State of the Profession report.
>
> ### Gender pay gap
>
> The average difference between full-time income for males and females, before regression analysis, is £9,991 – £579 less than 2018 and £2,325 than 2017. When a multiple linear regression analysis of full-time income is conducted, which takes into consideration all factors that influence pay such as seniority and length of service, the true gender pay gap is £5,202.
>
> ### Mental health
>
> More than one fifth (21 per cent) of respondents live with, or have previously lived with, a diagnosed mental health condition. Based on the Office of National Statistics UK PR population data, this percentage equates to more than 16,000 PR professionals. More than half (53 per cent) of respondents said their work contributes highly to their diagnosis.
>
> ### Strategic role
>
> Despite calls for public relations professionals to shift away from tactics towards strategic influence, practitioners are still overwhelmingly engaged in tactical delivery. In both senior and junior roles, copywriting and editing and media relations are the two most commonly undertaken activities.
>
> ### Average salaries
>
> Average salaries amongst full-time employees grew by almost £1,500 to £53,044 per year. The average salary for all practitioners is £51,804 (median figure is £30,000). Chartered Practitioners earn an average of £18,000 more per year than the average respondent, while those with a professional qualification earn an average £3,800 more. Full-time CIPR members earn £2,963 more than non-members.
>
> *Sources:* CIPR State of the Profession 2019: https://www.cipr.co.uk/sites/default/files/11812%20State%20of%20Profession_v12.pdf; PRCA PR and Communication Census 2019: https://www.prca.org.uk/sites/default/files/PRCA_PR_Census_2019_v9-8-pdf%20%285%29.pdf

Who does what: the bigger picture?

Definitions of field

Chapter 1 has already explored the historical evolution of PR and discussed the various definitions that are provided from a range of sources including academics, practitioners, national and international professional bodies.

This lack of an agreed definition is, however, still a problem for the practice. Deciding what it is and what people do has evidently caused much distraction and expenditure of individual and collective energies. Some of the long-winded definitions still do not easily convey what the discipline stands for and what people do. Fawkes (2008) argues that the synthesised UK CIPR definition of PR below is one that at least simplifies the discussion and helps students and practitioners understand what it is they do or should be doing: 'Public relations is about reputation – the result of what you

Box 7.2

Country profiles from the Global Alliance – a sample

The following is a sample from different continents to indicate the range and variety of PR education, with a brief history of the development of the field or the professional organisation to indicate the relationship between the two. For further, more current, details on the status of PR in a range of countries, see the Global Alliance website: www.globalalliancepr.org.

Europe

United Kingdom
According to L'Etang (1996, 2002) the origins of British PR lie in the public rather than private sector: during and after the Second World War, the number of PR consultants appointed in government departments increased greatly to enable the handling of information and intelligence, propaganda and psychological warfare and persuasion and public relations. The UK professional body, the Chartered Institute of Public Relations (CIPR) has been involved in education since its inception in 1948, though originally these were closer to training than academic courses. PR education in Britain in the past 20 years has seen an expansion in public relations courses, often influenced by the location of the course in either a business or media school. Tench and Fawkes (2005) suggest there are two types of courses: a business school curriculum and a media school curriculum. Most PR education has moved from technical training in skills required by public relations practitioners, embodied in the Public Relations Education Trust (PRET) Matrix to a broader, more academic approach. While most PR educators have practitioner backgrounds, many have more than a decade of teaching and research experience. However, according to Tench and Fawkes (2005) 'the pressure on the post-1992 sector to manage large cohorts and prioritise teaching over research', has left a gap in UK research into PR.

The Netherlands
Van Ruler and Verčič (2004) argue that the rebuilding of the Dutch society after the Second World War involved the promotion business and social goods, although society had a new, powerful repugnance towards propaganda. In 1945, the first professional association to ease the exchange of knowledge between journalists and PR officers representing government, businesses and agencies was established, leading to the Association for Public Contact, later renamed the Association for Public Relations in the Netherlands, and now the Dutch Association of Communication.

The first course in PR in the Netherlands was in 1940 and this was offered as optional in Universities under 'mass communication' and 'journalism'. Current PR education in the Netherlands is well developed, with about 30 full Bachelor of Arts (BA) programmes in organisational communication or communication management. They further state that all 13 research universities offer BA streams in the area of organisational communication or communication management. The Netherlands School of Communication Research (NESCoR) offers a Doctorate in Philosophy (PhD) programme in communication science.

France
The communicational paradigm in France that emerged during the early 1980s was the Communicational Director model due to the emergence of the concept of corporate image, management requirements, institutional advertising and that of consultancy agencies in 'overall communications'. The term PR is rarely used even though it is popular in consultancies. In the PR educational field, van Ruler and Verčič (2004) state that 'the number of professional University training courses is extremely high', as a result of which, the private sector plays a minor role in education. France has undergraduate BA programmes as well as postgraduate education and Doctoral programmes, with some doctorates in information and communication science.

Germany
Public relations development in Germany has been related to political, economic and social conditions (Van Ruler and Verčič 2004). Six periods of German public relations history, including Nazi era propaganda have been defined. After 1945, PR did redefine its tenets of practice under a democratic government, but PR and research in PR are in their initial stages, with purpose-free research undertaken in universities, and applied research, which aims to solve concrete practical problems, privately financed.

In the 1980s PR entered the universities and polytechnics and in the 1990s, several universities established PR courses within their communication programmes. Most universities in Germany today offer BA, Masters and Doctorate in Philosophy (PhD) programmes. In some polytechnics PR Diploma courses are offered.

Bulgaria
The term 'public relations' was first mentioned in Bulgaria in 1972 in an article by Svetozar Krastev as a component

box 7.2 (continued)

of marketing. Bulgaria discovered the real PR profession after the changes to democracy in 1989. In 1996 the first Bulgarian professional association – the Bulgarian Public Relations Society – was founded. It constitutes practitioners and teachers in the sphere of PR, marketing, communication and advertising.

Attempts to teach PR as an academic subject were made by the first private university in Bulgaria – New Bulgarian University Sofia. In March 1991, the Department of Mass Communication of the new private University opened its first three-year experimental course in PR as a separate speciality. Bulgarian Universities now offer a three-year degree, and postgraduate education and PhD courses, in PR.

Romania
In Romania multinational companies were the first to introduce public relations at the beginning of the 1990s. Today there are PR agencies, PR departments within companies and advertising agencies, officers and specialists within government institutions. Non-Governmental Organisations (NGOs) also employ public relations specialists. There have been several institutions trying to represent PR practitioners and promote PR in Romania, including the Romanian Public Relations Association (ARRP); the Club of the Romanian Public Relations Agencies; and the Forum for International Communications.

The first recognised college-level course in public relations was not taught in Romania until 1993 at the University of Bucharest. This PR course was added to undergraduate programmes for The Faculty of Journalism and Communication Studies and, according to the Global Alliance, was a milestone in the development of PR practice in the country which was followed by a couple of other state and private universities.

Italy
The Federazione Relazione Pubbliche Italiana and Associazione Comunicazione Pubblica (FERPI) since the mid-1950s have helped in the development of PR in Italy. The history of PR has gone through many phases from the late 1940s through to the 1990s. FERPI has currently about 70,000 practitioners who operate professional PR in the private, public and not-for-profit organisations, according to Global Alliance (2006).

In the last ten years, with a focus on the University reorganisation, the Italian academy has seen an expansion in degree programmes in Communication Science in PR, with postgraduate specialisation in the fields of communication, public relations and organisation. According to Van Ruler and Verčič (2004) many in Italian universities question the scope of PR and its roots in sociological, psychological, historic-geographic, legal and economic disciplines.

The Americas
Canada
The professional body Canadian Public Relations Society (CPRS) was founded in 1948 in two original groups, first in Montreal and second in Toronto. The CPRS has about 2000 members – it is estimated that 10 per cent of practitioners become members. Owing to the dual culture of the country national public relations includes special considerations for communication with the Francophone market. Public relations education in Canada is a vital area, with many students graduating with majors and minors in public relations; in addition to the formal education, colleges and other adult education courses offer certificates in public relations.

The United States of America (USA)
The subject of public relations has been taught in universities for more than 70 years IPRA (1990) and there are now reported to be over 3000 degrees in the discipline. The US public relations education is associated with schools and departments of journalism or mass communications; with the first practitioners being trained journalists, priority was given to the ability to write well.

In 1975 the first commission for public relations education recommended that public relations programmes should consist of a minimum of 12 hours per semester, which was upgraded in 1978. A model curriculum consisting of a minimum of five courses in public relations was later introduced (Grunig and Grunig 2002). It has been argued that while several practitioners emphasised the increase in international public relations, the fact that public relations education in the USA focused on technical skills rather than on theory and research resulted in this area being overlooked to a large degree in public relations programmes.

The Port of Entry (1999) and The Professional Bond (2006), research-based reports by the Public Relations Society of America (PRSA), demonstrated a congruity between what practitioners and scholars believe is vital to the public relations curriculum. The Port of Entry recommended undergraduate and graduate education in which curricular models are grounded in the liberal arts, theory-based across the curriculum and with the emphasis on courses rather than departments where these courses are undertaken.

It has been suggested that in the US PR education is technical training, in contrast to Europe where strategic communication is the focus of public relations education. This has led some to question whether the public relations profession will be able to handle the challenges to be faced in the twenty-first century. However, an area of strength that American public relations has is the issue of ethics. Verwey (2000) suggests the practice of ethical public relations may become a force to reckon with in the twenty-first century for public relations professionals. This will invariably demarcate the lines that the postmodern public relations practitioner will need to serve as the agent for change to an organisation and being the conscience of the organisation.

Argentina
The growth of public relations was affected by Argentine's military rule, but when the country emerged as an independent and democratic nation, PR played a more prominent part in society. Argentina has two professional councils of public relations, the first founded in 1997 to represent public relations professionals with university and other tertiary education degrees in public relations or related communication fields. There are two professional associations active in the province of Buenos Aires: the Professional Council of Public Relations of the Buenos Aires Province and the Professional Council of Public Relations.

According to GAPR&CM (2006), public relations education is still developing; there are also specialised educational courses offered by universities and institutions, including three- to five-year programmes in PR.

Puerto Rico
Public relations in Puerto Rico follow US practice closely but adapted to the cultural implications of the Puerto Rican society. The driving force of PR in Puerto Rico is the Asociación de Relacionistas Profesionales de Puerto Rico (ARPPR). The ARPPR was founded in 1970 and now has more than 200 members.

Communication programmes can now be found in various educational institutions in Puerto Rico, offering Bachelor's degree in communications or journalism, or related curriculum as part of social science programmes.

Africa
It has been suggested that the concept of PR was practiced in Africa long before colonialism, if one sees the similarity between the task of a PR practitioner and that of a chief's spokesperson in traditional African villages.

The move towards democracy on a broad front has promoted the development of public relations in Africa. As regards education, courses in public relations in Africa are varied and range from in-service training by employers and within government ministries (Ferreira 2003) to formal tertiary diploma, degree and post-degree courses. A variety of short courses are offered in different countries by development agencies, professional institutes and private colleges and at tertiary level, many public relations programmes are taught as part of a Bachelor's degree in communication, mass communication or journalism (Ferreira 2003). Some universities also teach public relations to complement other disciplines such as marketing and business management. Several distance learning programmes in public relations are also available in Africa.

However, Ferreira (2003) states that one cannot pin down or make a generalisation of the state of public relations education in Africa. He is of the view that some public relations officers have entered the career through journalism, as in the UK and the US – indeed some of these officers have been trained abroad. In some countries the training is informal and is undertaken by other external bodies such as banks and private institutions, private companies and sometimes by the public relations institute or societies in that country.

Asia and the Middle East
India
Public relations began to increase in India in the early 1990s when the government opened the economy and multinational corporations began to enter the country. Public relations companies emerged offering strategic advice and integrated communication solutions. Specialisation has become increasingly important and firms are demanding higher qualifications and skill sets from workers (GAPR&CM 2006).

The Public Relations Consultants Association of India (PRCAI) was established in 2001 to develop standards, ethics, expertise and knowledge in the public relations industry in India. In each of these areas, the primary objective is to align the public relations industry in India with international practices.

Sriramesh (1996) argues that almost all of India's big companies have separate public relations departments, either working in marketing, social welfare or consumer affairs.

> **box 7.2 (continued)**
>
> **China**
> According to Culbertson and Chen (1996b) the development of public relations in China began 20 years ago with much emphasis on interpersonal communication. About 150 public relations societies exist throughout China at the local and provincial as well as national levels. The China International Public Relations Association (CIPRA) seeks to enhance professionalism, according to Culbertson and Chen (1996b). The CIPRA sets standards for PR education, not the national Ministry of Education. CIPRA and Shanghai Public Relations Association (SPRA) both encourage and support academic research and theory development. According to CIPRA, there are only two PR Master's degree programmes in China.
>
> Culbertson and Chen (1996b) suggest that Chinese public relations education has undergone many challenges, that public relations in China is diverse, and is offered in interdisciplinary programmes, mass communication or in departments of journalism, and units that offer speech and interpersonal communication. Public relations education is offered in four-year baccalaureate degree programmes, in two-year technical colleges, and through television and distance learning targeted at older and non-traditional PR students. In 2001, the CIPRA introduced the first accreditation examination for public relations practitioners.
>
> Culbertson and Chen (1996b) describe public relations professors in China treating theory and practice equally, using Confucius and other classic Chinese philosophers, in addition to Western ideas.
>
> **Australasia**
> Although there are historical, cultural and economic differences between Australia and New Zealand, public relations has evolved in similarly ways. The development of public relations in New Zealand has been described as following a meeting in the Auckland Star Hotel in 1954, which led to the creation of the Public Relations Institute of New Zealand (PRINZ). Singh and Smyth (2000) state that, public relations practitioners in New South Wales formed a professional body in Australia, five years ahead of practitioners in New Zealand, which led to the national Public Relations Institute of Australia (PRIA) which has divisions in all states. The PRIA currently has more than 3,000 members.
>
> Australia has developed an approach to public relations education, which bridges and co-operates between educators and practitioners. Formal education in public relations began in New Zealand in the latter part of the 1960s.
>
> **Summary**
>
> The pattern which emerges from this brief survey of the development of professional organisations and PR education in a range of countries is that most of the former were founded in the post-war period with exceptions where democracy (or, in the case of China, capitalism) was not established until later.
>
> Most early practitioners in the countries covered were originally journalists, a fact which influenced the content of early PR education. This largely consisted of technical training for many years, with a growth of theoretical and reflective approaches at undergraduate and postgraduate levels in the 1990s. Some countries are still in the technical stage, with PR officers envisaged as little more than errand boys (Deflagbe 2004). Most have found a correlation between the development of under and postgraduate courses and the status of the profession.

do, what you say and what others say about you.' The CIPR goes on to explain that public relations is the discipline which looks after reputation, with the aim of earning understanding and support and influencing opinion and behaviour. 'It is the planned and sustained effort to establish and maintain goodwill and mutual understanding between an organisation and its publics' (CIPR 2015). It also defines organisation, publics and understanding with organisation being any corporation, government or voluntary body or service, publics as audiences that are important to the organisation and that understanding is a two-way process of engagement.

Tench and Deflagbe (2008) noted that PR education was responding to the challenges of the globalisation of communication and economies – but slowly and unevenly. They identified that problems defining the field are multiplied when the different cultural perspectives on public relations itself come into play. Even within Europe the term has varying connotations reflecting cultural associations with the public sphere. Several scholars express concern that the lack of a central concept for PR is weakening its hold in the marketplace. These debates in the literature reflect tensions between academics and between academics and practitioners and illustrate some of the problems facing the project of a global curriculum (see also Chapter 6 for a discussion on intercultural and multicultural issues for public relations).

Professional bodies, academics and most practitioners are keen to ensure that education continues to play its crucial role in improving the professional standards of public relations, producing reflective and engaged practitioners and enhancing, rather than limiting, public relations' important role in the changing global environment.

Despite the CIPR's definition of PR, detailed above, modern ideas about PR are moving away from reputation management as the key concept, to relationship building, so the CIPR definition may be revised or fade from use. The Public Relations Society of America adopted a new definition of public relations in March 2012 following a global crowdsourcing campaign and public vote. It reads: 'Public relations is a strategic communication process that builds mutually beneficial relationships between organisations and their publics.'

Note also the rather different description by the Spanish public relations association (www.adecec.com) and the varied country profiles of public relations in Box 7.2. In fact, it is worth pointing out that the problem with definitions extends to problems with language. As Verčič et al. (2001) point out, the term public relations is founded wholly on US references and does not translate across the Atlantic. Their own three-year research programme on public relations in Europe (European Body of Knowledge (EBOK)) showed that all except English speakers had problems with the term 'public relations'. For example, the German Offentlich keitsarbeit carries associations with the public sphere and public opinion, perhaps rooted in the origins of European public relations through public bodies, such as central and local government, rather than the corporate work of early public relations in the United States.

So, shall we abandon the search for a decent description? It could be said that they encourage ring-fencing and competition and work against integrated communication approaches to problem solving. Other disciplines, such as marketing, share these challenges.

However, Hutton (2001) says that public relations has lost the battle for supremacy with marketing and is terminally threatened by its failure to define itself and to develop sophisticated and progressive theory or develop its central tenet or core concept. He comments that there remains a critical need for public relations to define its intellectual and practical domain ... to regain control of its own destiny (2001: 205). See Explore 7.2. More recent texts on public relations includes *Trust Me, PR is Dead*, by Robert Phillips (2015) who charts the demise of traditional industries, disciplines, hierarchy and command and control and the rise of individual empowerment and the need for radical transparency at the heart of business. Critics, however, argue that he is correct in arguing that businesses should be accountable and transparent, leading and responding to key social and environmental challenges, but that good communication is still at the heart of engaging with stakeholders. They also argue that this crowdfunded e-book may not have had the rigorous editing process that a traditional book publisher would provide. The debate continues to unfold in journals and textbooks and at conferences and will do so for years to come. In the meantime, students and practitioners still need to be able to describe their jobs in terms meaningful to their friends and family. This chapter aims to provide information and insight to assist in that goal.

Of course, the answers to many of the questions raised by Explore 7.2 will depend on the type of role, its level and whether it is in-house or consultancy. The next section looks at how organisations see the role of the PR practitioner, before going on to look at what individuals do daily.

> **Explore 7.2**
>
> ### Job descriptions
>
> One way of gathering information about what PR practitioners do is to look at the job ads. Look online at *PR Week,* and *The Guardian* for PR jobs (see websites for these outlets, e.g. www.prweekjobs.co.uk or www.theguardian.com or www.linkedin.com (LinkedIn). Read the adverts and make a note of what the employers are looking for. What job titles are advertised? What skills do they mention? How many ask for relevant qualifications? What specific knowledge (e.g. social media)? What personal qualities?
>
> ### Feedback
>
> Some of the job titles will vary, even for similar positions. The duties described may not vary so much. The differences and similarities in these ads offer real insight into what people do in PR.

Case study 7.1
Public relations role and the communication management field in Brazil

Since 1914, Public Relations Day has been celebrated on 2 December by the biggest country in South America, Brazil. Brazil is one of the emerging democratic nations and the seventh largest economy in the world. For over a century the country has celebrated public relations, in which professionals dynamically work across this vast multi-ethnic and diverse country, from north to south and east to west, in a wide variety of sectors, in both in-house and agencies.

The date 30 January 1914 represents a cornerstone in the history of PR in Brazil when the first Department of Public Relations was created at the São Paulo Tramway Light & Power Company Limited, currently AES Eletropaulo (ABRP 2020). Eduardo Pinheiro Lobo founded the in-house office in order to enhance the firm's media relations with the public and the public's services. This date also signifies the institutionalisation of PR activity, a philosophy of communication and relationship management, which cuts across enterprises that value dialogue, transparency, quality and ethics, and has developed as Brazil's business environment has also flourished, grown and diversified. Subsequently, the Public Relations Brazilian Association (ABRP) was founded in São Paulo, on 21 July 1954, and focused on uniting professionals for vocational and corporate purposes. According to Professor Cleuza Gimenes Cesca (2020), a former and retired professor at the Faculty of Public Relations of the Pontifical Catholic University of Campinas, in São Paulo, Brazil, the public relations activity in Brazil was developed by self-taught people until higher education courses in public relations were developed in 1967 at the University of São Paulo. A few years before, Getulio Vargas Foundation, in São Paulo, included a PR discipline at the Business Programme in 1955.

However, public relations undertook a period of stagnation in the period of the military dictatorship that was imposed on the country from 1964 to 1985. In 1967, the profession was accredited as an academic discipline and the first bachelor's degree programme was founded by Candido Teobaldo de Souza Andrade, at the University of São Paulo (Universidade de São Paulo, known as USP in Brazil). He launched the first Dicionário Profissional de Relações Públicas e Comunicação (Dictionary of PR and COMM), in Brazilian Portuguese, 1978.

Currently, there are 56 PR programmes at universities (e.g. public and private) in the country (SINPRORP 2020). São Paulo city has the highest number of universities with over 10 faculties across the capital city of the State of São Paulo. Each year, over 1,900 students graduate after a four-year part time course (Guia da Carreira 2020; MEC 2020).

A significant change in the education of PR happened in 2015: the public relations programmes must fit the curriculum guidelines approved in September 2013 by the government's Ministry of Education. These major changes are: the professional placement is now mandatory; the class duration increases from 50 to 60 minutes for each lecture; hours went up from 2,700 to 3,200 in four years and the dissertation, which previously could be done in a group, became an individual piece of work (Guia do Estudante 2020; MEC 2020). According to the ABRP São Paulo (2020), there are 800 corporate communications agencies in Brazil, 17 per cent are PR and other professionals as well; the most demanded PR activities are media relations (35 per cent of profits), communication training (8 per cent), internal communication (7 per cent), and communication in social networks (7 per cent). Currently, the Public Relations Brazilian Association's São Paulo unit proposes to increase research on the market of public relations, with two main streams: (i) Focus on sectors of the economy that have not been reached by other organisations, such as communications institutions like ABRACOM, ABERJE and CONFERP, and work in partnership with the organisations representing these sectors (such as APADI, UBRAFE, ABEOC, ABIH, FIESP, CIESP, Sebrae, Fecomercio), as well as the public sector, expanding perspectives on and the recognition of PR activity; (ii) Engage students of PR courses in processes for the production and processing of such data, combining research and practices under faculty supervision as well as community involvement. Furthermore, according to the Public Relations Brazilian Association, SP (ABRP 2020), their professional values are as follows: quality, dialogue, entrepreneurship, engagement, respect, memory and collaboration. Besides the Public Relations Brazilian Association, in some states there are several Regional Councils of Public Relations Professionals (CONRERPs) delivering training, conferences, events, research and management of professionals' memberships. The Federal Council of Public Relations, CONFERP, is located in Brasilia, D.F., the Capital of Brazil, and is in charge of enhancement of the PR profession with regards to the laws, elections, ethics, trends, conferences, awards and international institutions links.

It is known that PR market grew by 5 per cent in 2018, according to The Holmes Report study, and the 250 largest agencies in the segment totalled US$ 12.3 billion in revenue last year, five of which are Brazilian companies. The presence of these Brazilian companies reflects the maturity of the public relations industry in Brazil (Meio and Mensagem 2020).

According to the Federal Council of Public Relations (CONRERP 2019), around 20,000 professionals are officially registered with the institution. However, it is known that there are more graduate professionals who are not associates or who do not work in PR positions. Moreover, the European and Latin American Communication Monitor (www.communicationmonitor.eu) are the largest and longest running longitudinal studies of international trends in strategic communication and public relations and are listed on the Council's webpage. Furthermore, the Communication Monitor has joint research with USP since 2018.

Professor Cleuza Gimenes Cesca (2020) concludes that, after following the teaching and the market of PR in Brazil for 40 years, it is possible to say that many transformations occurred during that period as the curricula have undergone many adaptations in order to meet the demands of the labour market. But the big change came with the arrival of the internet. Public relations professionals needed to adapt to these new tools that changed the way of communicating and made it faster and more efficient. Due to the digital era, some authors say that we do have a 'new public relations'. Although public relations has, at times, had part of its space invaded by marketing, publicity and advertising, public relations professionals as well as academics are very clear about what each activity does. Undoubtedly, in certain moments, one area can be an instrument of the other. However, in daily life, this does not always happen, but there has been a lot of effort, mainly by external consultants.

In times of change, reinventions are needed. In this complex-oriented, reputational-based, and business-related context, PR professionals and researchers have certainly tracked communications management inquiries, at the institutional or organisational firms, at the marketplace or marketspace.

References

ABRP – Public Relations Brazilian Association (2020). Available at http://abrpsp.org.br/institucional-2/

Cleuza Gimenes Cesca, Dr. (2020) Interviewed by email.

CONFERP – Federal Council of Public Relations (2019). Available at http://www.conferp.org.br/

Source: Fabiana Gondim Mariutti

Role of the communicator

In Chapter 9 we discuss the division between managers and technicians in PR practice. However, the dichotomy is not always clear-cut. Most PR practitioners are involved in both manager and technician work, but it is generally accepted that one role may dominate. On entry into the practice and at the start of their career, most recruits are given technical tasks. Through experience and after time this generally means they move on to fulfilling the more managerial role (see mini case studies on practitioner roles and responsibilities and Figure 7.1).

The emphasis on these roles of the communicator has also influenced the advancement of women in PR, as is explored more fully in Chapter 8. Another issue about the roles of communicators is that so many of the texts have traditionally been US based, but this is changing with many more books emerging from Europe and Australasia as well as long-term macro studies of the roles of communicators such as Tench et al.'s 2011–13 study of competences (Tench and Moreno 2015).

In many ways, the struggle to define the role of the communicator has an edge to it: this is not just an academic debate. PR practitioners need to demonstrate their value to the employing organisations – whether it is reputation management or relationship building that they are offering.

These debates are supported by European research (Zerfass et al. 2007–20) in annual surveys of communication practice across Europe. This research has been conducted every year since 2007 as a longitudinal study to enable annual comparisons of trends in public relations across Europe. For 2019, the thirteenth edition of the survey, the number of countries expanded to 46 with 2689 senior communicators responding to an in-depth, online survey (see www.communictionmonitor.eu). From the 2019 data there were some interesting findings on the evolving complexity of communication, which affects the role of the modern practitioner.

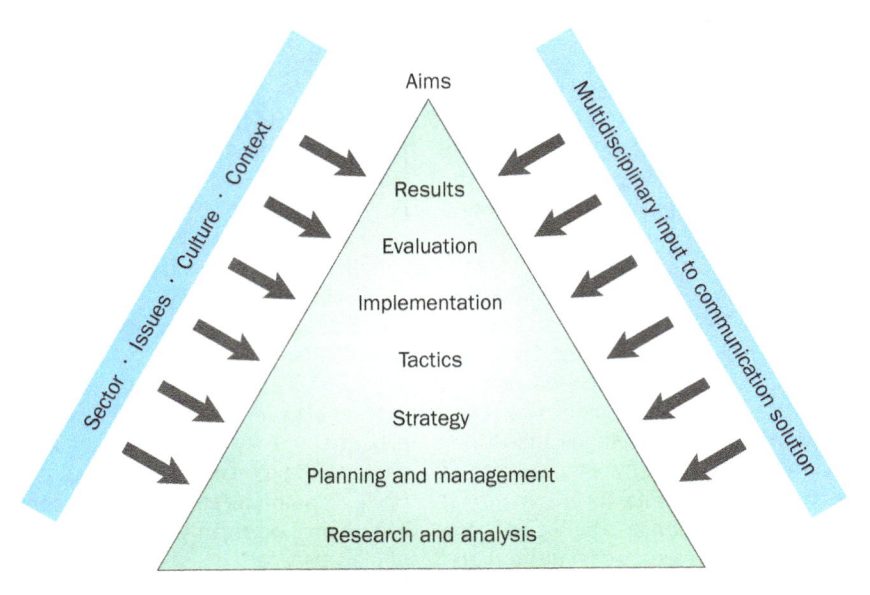

Figure 7.1 The public relations practitioner as 'communicator'

ECM 2019 highlights

- Communication practitioners experience a low level of trust in their profession, but feel confident on a personal level with their colleagues, bosses, clients and audiences.
- External experts and top management are rated as the most trusted organisational advocates with marketing/sales and communications lagging behind.
- Artificial Intelligence is expected to impact the profession, but communication practitioners lack competencies and experience.
- Sponsored content is frequently used by every second organisation in Europe.
- There are significant differences between countries, as well as companies and non-profits across Europe.

Trust in communications

In many countries, trust in the mass media and journalism is declining. This loss of trust might also be true for other communicators, especially those who communicate on behalf of companies and organisations. This is a key challenge for the profession, as communicators need to be trusted by the people they work for, such as senior executives and internal clients. Additionally, they are also dependent on the trust of journalists, bloggers, influencers and the general public.

Results show that communication professionals experience low levels of trust in their line of work. The profession is only trusted by two thirds of top executives (67 per cent), and by a minority of influencers and bloggers (47 per cent), journalists (39 per cent) and ordinary people (27 per cent). But respondents are more positive about the perceived trust in their departments or agencies. 85 per cent of the respondents reported a positive attitude by executives or by clients, followed by 73 per cent perceived trust from journalists, 70 per cent from the general public and 68 per cent from influencers and bloggers. Professionals are the most positive about the perceived trust they enjoy personally. A vast majority feel trusted by their colleagues, bosses and internal clients, as well as by external stakeholders and audiences.

Trust in organisational advocates: external experts and leaders are top

Communication and PR professionals are not the only people speaking on behalf of organisations. Formal representatives like CEOs, board members or marketing and sales people, as well as other employees or members of the organisation play a role, whether they are coached by practitioners or not. External experts in the field, customers, supporters and even activists with overlapping interests can also be spokespeople. Knowing about different advocates and choosing or supporting them carefully is an important part of strategic communication.

Interestingly, practitioners think that most of these advocates are more trustworthy than themselves. They perceive external experts in the field as the most trusted (70 per cent), followed by leaders of the organisation (CEOs, board members and top executives; 66 per cent) and external supporters such as customers or clients (63 per cent). Other employees or members of the organisation are reported to achieve a similar level of trust to communication professionals (61 per cent). Marketing and sales representatives are rated lower (43 per cent). Public trust in external organisations, such as activists, acting as advocates for organisations is perceived surprisingly low (31 per cent).

Artificial Intelligence: high impact expected, but challenges and risks identified

Strategic communication is entering a new phase with the introduction of Artificial Intelligence (AI). This has major implications for the professional communication of organisations, as people might be replaced or supported by software agents and devices. Three quarters of the respondents (77 per cent) think that AI will change the communication profession, but only 15 per cent of the practitioners have proven to be AI experts already.

A total of 56 per cent state that it is difficult to secure competencies of communication practitioners, followed by 54 per cent who believe that information technology, budgets or organisational structure are important hurdles. Professionals among various types of organisations have different views on this: not-for-profits rate organisational challenges for implementing AI higher, while motivation of practitioners is a strong concern in agencies. Organisational struggles with varied staff competencies are identified as the major risk of bringing AI to communications.

Content creation and distribution: shared media and internal sources preferred

Companies, not-for-profits and governmental organisations are no longer just providers of information for journalists and mass media, but they have become content producers and distributors on their own. The concept of Paid – Earned – Shared – Owned Media (PESO) analyses this trend by distinguishing complementary approaches to distribute content and influence stakeholders. 57 per cent of the practitioners confirm the rising importance of earned media during the last three years. 54 per cent of respondents have experienced the same for owned media and 77 per cent for content published on social media platforms by supporters of any kind (shared media). There are differing views about paid media: 38 per cent of the practitioners think this approach has gained in importance, while 36 per cent believe its value has reduced and 26 per cent see no changes. Sponsored social media content is used by every second communication department and agency (53 per cent). The major sources for regularly creating content in European communication departments and agencies are internal: products and services, input from members of the organisation or clients and organisational strategies. Eight out of ten respondents confirm these as content inspiration. External input from users of owned media or products/services as well as topics discussed in mass or social media are considered less often.

Picture 7.1 The European Communication Monitor (ECM) is a longitudinal research project looking into communication trends. The ECM has been running since 2007 and is the largest transnational research project in public relations (www.communicationmonitor.eu) (*source:* Ralph Tench)

The PR practitioner as communicator

Despite calls for public relations professionals to shift away from tactics towards strategic influence, practitioners are still overwhelmingly engaged in tactical delivery.

The under-representation of public relations practitioners at board level was identified as the second biggest challenge facing the profession after media change (down from first place in the previous two years) by the CIPR Census 2019. Less than 1 in 10 (9 per cent) of respondents in senior roles are executive members of a Board (compared to 11 per cent in 2018) and 5 per cent are non-executive members (up slightly from 2018). Amongst senior practitioners just under 40 per cent are directly answerable to one or more Board of Directors.

However, a majority of senior in-house practitioners (59 per cent), consultancy and agency practitioners (57 per cent) and independent practitioners (68 per cent) influence their organisation's or clients' overall business strategy. When asked if they are directly responsible for business strategy these figures drop significantly – 4 per cent for senior in-house practitioners, 23 per cent for consultancy and agency practitioners and 16 per cent for independent practitioners.

Other evidence suggests a flourishing time ahead for PR. For example, PR was considered the best return on investment by entrepreneurs in a survey for the *Financial Times* in 2004, and in 2014 Forbes.com reported that 'In today's socially connected world, public relations is more important than ever before'.

Mini case study 7.1 illustrates the kind of career available in PR and the richness (and challenge) of the PR role at a senior level. The communicator is often expected to play a wide range of roles.

The PR practitioner must be adaptable, energetic, versatile, diplomatic and resilient to get along with a mixed group of clients and stakeholder groups. Pieczka refers to the existence of 'an expertise which is distinctive yet flexible enough to be applicable across a wide field' and suggests that public relations expertise is a complex interactive structure organised through experience and current exigencies (demands), which modifies itself through action (Pieczka 2002: 321–322).

This perspective would suggest that there is no one paradigm or template for the role but that it is a dynamic process created through the interface of our past and our interactions with the present. Figure 7.2 presents a model that uses systems theory as the basis for the concept of this role as a dynamic, interactive and open system.

Mini case study 7.1
Katherine Bennett CBE – Senior Vice President, Airbus

Role at Airbus

Katherine joined Airbus in August 2004 and became UK Director of Communications and Government Affairs in 2007. She was Vice President, Head of Political Affairs for Airbus SAS from October 2010 to July 2017 and since then has held the role of Senior Vice President for Airbus where she is the lead external-facing UK executive.

Her previous government affairs role encompassed managing relationships between Airbus and national, regional and local government. She takes the lead on all public policy issues affecting the company and ensures that key government and interested stakeholders are kept informed and aware of company developments. Her time is split between Bristol, where Airbus SAS UK's HQ is based and an office in Westminster, London. The Government Affairs Department has a direct reporting function to the managing director in the UK.

In the public affairs industry, the managing director's direct involvement is a prerequisite for the function. Government affairs needs to be integral in company strategy and direction. This integration can take several forms, whether in considerations over avoidance of risk, ensuring there is a supportive legislative background for the company's forward plans and product development or indeed issues surrounding sustainability and CSR.

Airbus's Communications Team is a sister department to Government Affairs and the two functions are closely aligned, which allows joint allocation of resources when required and the necessary coordination of messages to Airbus's key audiences.

Issue management

Airbus is the market leader in aircraft manufacturing and sales, employing over 50,000 people worldwide, of which 13,000 are in the UK and represent highly skilled research and development (R&D) and manufacturing jobs. The UK business is the Airbus Centre of Excellence for wing design and manufacture and heads up the integration of landing gear and fuel systems for Airbus aircraft.

One of Katherine's first challenges was to ensure the UK business was fully represented and involved in the

Source: WENN Rights Ltd/Alamy Stock Photo

unveiling of the new A380 aircraft. With the capacity of seating 555 passengers, this is the largest civil airliner ever launched and brought a completely new dimension to the aircraft market in terms of customer offering and innovative systems technology.

The unveiling ceremony took place in Toulouse, France, in front of over 5,000 assembled media, government representatives and customer representatives. Katherine undertook the coordination of the logistics, media activity and protocol surrounding the participation of UK Prime Minister Tony Blair. The key part of this activity was to ensure the smooth running of a two-way satellite link between Blair and Airbus employees back in the UK.

The event was probably one of the largest product unveilings ever seen and the media coverage reflected this. Over 500 media representatives with 60 film crews attended the ceremony. In the UK, the event attracted 650 separate items of media coverage, including BBC/ITV main TV news slots of more than two minutes. The Airbus website had live coverage and received 3,419,398 hits that day.

Background

Katherine is a member of the CIPR and graduated in history and politics from Leicester University. She has a postgraduate diploma in marketing from the Chartered Institute of Marketing. Katherine's previous employment was with Vauxhall/GM UK where for nearly nine years she also headed up their government affairs function. Her time at Vauxhall involved managing numerous public policy lobbying campaigns and issues management such as major industrial restructuring programmes and CSR. Her time with GM included several months based in the USA. Before joining Vauxhall, Katherine was an account manager in the Public Affairs Department of Hill and Knowlton (an international PR company) working on behalf of energy, charity and automotive clients. While at Hill and Knowlton she undertook several in-house training courses. Katherine was awarded the Commander of the British Empire in January 2019 for services to the aerospace industry having previously (2004) been awarded an OBE (Order of the British Empire) for services to the motor industry and charity.

Source: based on interview with author and information supplied by Katherine Bennett

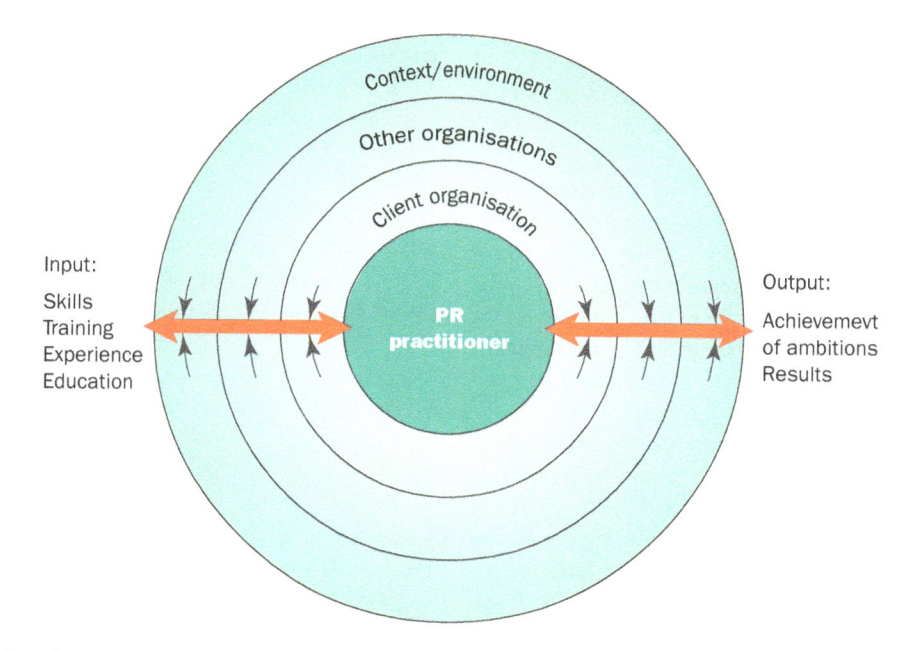

Figure 7.2 Public relations practitioner role within systems theory

Systems theory works on the basis that everything in the social world is part of a system that interacts with other systems in that the whole equals more than the sum of its parts (von Bertalanffy 1969). Building on the work of Katz and Kahn (1978), PR scholars (e.g. Cutlip et al. 2000, 2008) use systems theory to explain the interactions between organisations and their environments, interactions between organisations and interactions within organisations. (Systems theory is fully explained in Chapter 8.)

This model assumes that the PR practitioner is part of an open system interacting with other systems, and therefore the nature of the role will not be fixed but depend on the influences both in and out of the system, from early experiences and education through to ongoing continuing professional development (CPD). Key to this model is that the system does not exist in isolation, but only exists insofar as it relates to other systems. This model also reaffirms that the PR practitioner as counsel must be aware of the context of their own role, and the context of the organisation or client they are representing and acting as the boundary spanner. That requires an interest in, and understanding of, the wider community, whether it is political, economic, sociological, and any number of other ways to frame the narrative of the twenty-first century.

> *Definition: CPD (continuing professional development) acknowledges in all professions (law, medicine, accountancy, PR, etc.) the role of continued learning and updating throughout the career*

There is an increasing body of research, with enormous potential for further development, looking at the role of the practitioner and using several methodologies to explain and measure the role. Moss et al. (2004) have identified several common themes in both the UK and USA among senior practitioners, such as their part in the dominant coalition and their contribution to strategic decision making.

Wilkin (2001) provides an interesting and controversial perspective on the implications of global communication; Allan (2000) on the social divisions and hierarchies reproduced by the news media. Research among employers' needs in graduates tends to highlight the requirement for employees who can manage change and understand the context the organisation is functioning in and can evidence the more abstract cognitive powers.

The argument supports the notion that the role of the public relations practitioner is a very wide-ranging one, far wider than many public relations exponents might feel happy with, but worth considering if we want to move public relations onto a higher plane. Those with a background in corporate communications will already recognise the role. It is often with the introduction of a corporate communicator and the playing out of territorial and functional wars that the true potential of a role, which both oversees and connects, is appreciated, not only by senior management but also by the organisation and significantly by other functions within the organisation (such as marketing). This is a role which, with the right training and development, can become synonymous with the public relations role (see Figure 7.3). (See also Chapter 9 on the management and planning of public relations activities.) See Think about 7.1.

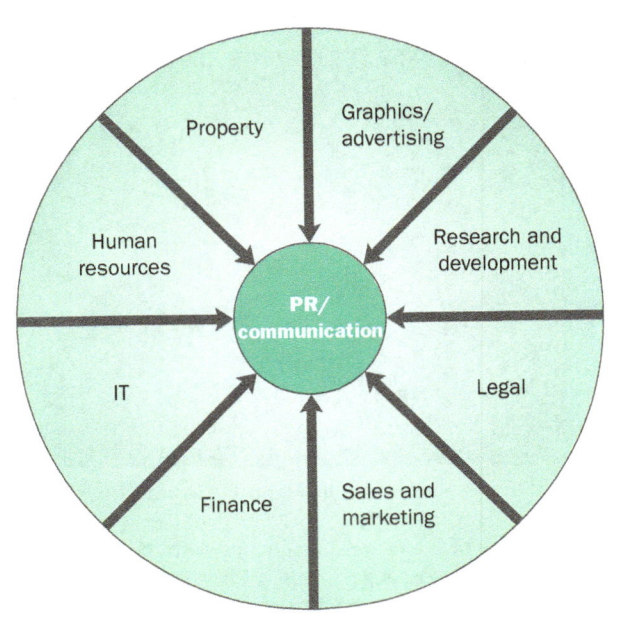

Figure 7.3 Public relations/communication role within an organisation

Think about 7.1

Public relations and its influence within organisations

Is there anywhere in the organisation where public relations does not have a role to play?

Consider the role that PR plays in communicating with employees as well as external stakeholders.

What public relations people do: individual practitioners

Lots of people work in PR and in a range of roles. As Explore 7.2 showed, there is a huge variety of job titles in job adverts for PR practitioners, including public relations/corporate communications consultant, executive, manager, director, officer, advisor, counsellor, etc.

To help us understand in more detail what these individuals are doing it is necessary to simplify and classify the locations in which they are working. So, there are three simple categories of where people work in public relations:

1. In-house (employed by an organisation, whether a public or private company or a public body, charity or non-governmental organisation, NGO).
2. Consultancy (agency where practitioners work for one or more different clients for a fee).
3. Freelance practitioner (where an individual works for himself and is employed by in-house departments or consultancies on a short-term contract basis either for a specific project or to fill in during peaks in demand or because staff absence requires additional resource).

While much of the work is the same across these categories, there are key differences:

- In-house: get to know one organisation in depth, work across wide range of public relations activities, from writing/editing house journals, blogs, websites to arranging visits by or to MPs/opinion formers, etc. In-house people also know their sector and industry very well, be it music, motoring, education, engineering, high street fashion or even farming and travel.
- Consultancy: work across many accounts, with a variety of clients, and may work in specialist areas such as technology, finance or public affairs. Consultants tend to be specialists in either business to business PR or business to consumer PR, with both areas providing vibrant and varied careers.

Fawkes (2008) argues that understanding the practice is helped by analysing how people engage in different activities. She does this by describing the common PR areas with examples of what practitioners will do in each area (see Table 7.1, Box 7.3 and Explore 7.3).

Type of public relations	Stakeholders	Example tactics
Business to business	Customers, trade analysts and trade journalists	Exhibitions, events, media relations
Community	Head teachers, doctors and councillors	Letters, events, social media, media relations
Consumer	Public, and consumer and national journalists	Media relations and social media
Corporate	Trade organisations and business media	Conferences, events and web sites
Internal communications	Employees	Events, posters and social networks
Investor relations	Financial markets, analysts and business media	Media relations and web sites
Public affairs	Local and national government, government organisations and politicians	Events, conferences, reports

Table 7.1 Roles and responsibilities of public relations practitioners. Adapted from Fawkes, J. (2008). 'What is public relations?' in *Handbook of Public Relations*, 3rd edn. A. Theaker (ed.). London: Routledge.

Box 7.3

Public relations competency debate – some definitions

Knowledge: can be defined as what practitioners are required to know in order to do their job/role effectively (see PRSA Professional Bond/Port of Entry, 1999, 2006 and Gregory 2008).

Skills: these are the things practitioners are able to do to perform their job/role effectively (Katz 1974; Goodman 2006; PRSA 1999, 2006; and Gregory 2008). Identifying skill will be a complex process, but a useful definition by Proctor and Duttan (1995: 18) will help us: 'goal-directed, well-organised behaviour that is acquired through practice and performed with economy of effort'.

Personal attributes: are defined in the literature as separate from competencies, the distinction being that personal attributes can determine how well a competency is performed and secondly competencies can be taught while personal attributes are modelled or fostered (Jeffrey and Brunton 2011: 69).

Competencies: are the sets of behaviours the person can perform. These behaviours are based on the application, combination and potential integration of knowledge and skills (see Boyzatis 1982; Bartram 2004; Gregory 2008; Jeffrey and Brunton 2011).

> **Explore 7.3**
>
> **In-house and consultancy jobs**
>
> Look at the job ads you gathered in Explore 7.2. How many of them are for in-house, how many for consultancy jobs? What differences are there in the skills, qualifications and interests they require?
>
> **Feedback**
>
> It may be easier to find in-house jobs, especially for public sector jobs, as they are more likely to advertise in national newspapers. Consultancies often advertise in *PR Week* in the UK or recruit informally through word of mouth and headhunting (asking an individual to change agencies). You can find out about some of these jobs by looking at the PR agency's website.

Skills for the ideal practitioner

So what skills are needed to work in PR? It would probably be quicker to identify those which are not required, although that is not easy either. Because there are so many kinds of work and so many kinds of employer, there is room in PR for everyone from the extrovert to the researcher glued to their tablet or PC.

However, some indication of what employers are looking for can be gleaned by their responses to questions posed by Fawkes and Tench (2004b) (see Table 7.2). This research shows that there was agreement from employers that literacy was the primary skill required by PR graduates. This is supported by the UK's CIPR whose annual State of the Profession report, 2015, found that competencies remain focused on traditional PR skills like written communication and interpersonal skills (64 per cent). There is an increasing demand for digital and technical skills, such as SEO, HTML and coding when hiring junior and senior PR practitioners (20 per cent). Both in-house and consultancy employers also ranked teamwork as the next most important attribute, followed by problem solving, analytical thinking, research skills, IT skills and numeracy. There were some variations between the employer groups, with in-house employers giving greater weighting to IT skills over research skills – the opposite of consultants' priorities.

Furthermore, research suggests that some practitioners may exaggerate their contribution, particularly consultants. Zerfass et al. (2008) for example showed that 83 per cent of respondents working in agencies (consultancies) thought that they were used for strategic and/or market insight/experience. However only 42 per cent of their clients agreed (see Figure 7.4). Further to the 2008 survey the 2012 European Monitor research found that both advisory and executive influence were down in Europe. Advisory is the perception of how seriously senior managers take the recommendations of communication professionals, and executive influence is the perception of how likely it is that communication representatives will be invited to senior-level meetings dealing with organisational strategic planning. The perception of advisory influence went down from nearly 78 per cent in 2011 to less than 70 per cent in 2012. Executive influence went down from almost 77 per cent to 72 per cent (Zerfass et al. 2011, 2012). 2012 was the first year since the monitor started that these figures have dropped. A comparison shows that communication functions in the United States are better in these dimensions on

Employers – combined evaluation of skills	Not important	%	Fairly important	%	Very important	%
Numeracy	7	7	65	63	28	27
Literacy	0	0	0	0	101	98
IT skills	2	2	49	47.5	49	47.5
Problem solving	1	1	21	20	77	75
Analytical thinking	0	0	26	25	73	70
Teamwork	0	0	11	10	87	84
Research skills	0	0	56	54	45	44

Table 7.2 Key graduate skills (*source:* Based on Fawkes, J. and R. Tench (2004b). 'Public relations education in the UK'. A research report for the Chartered Institute of Public Relations)

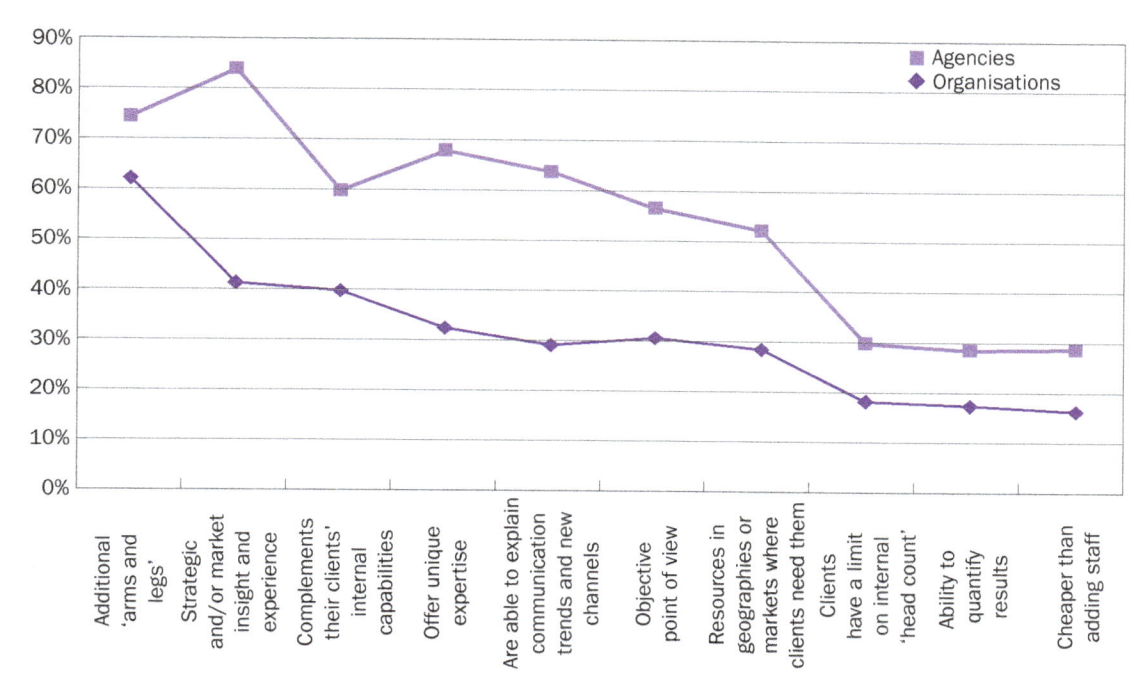

Figure 7.4 Reasons for cooperation: different perceptions between PR agencies and their clients (*source:* Zerfass, A., A. Moreno, R. Tench, D. Verčič and P. Verhoeven (2008) European Communication Monitor 2008. Trends in Communication Management and Public Relations – Results and Implications Brussels, Leipzig: Euprera/University of Leipzig, November 2008)

average – however all Scandinavian states as well as Germany, the United Kingdom and the Netherlands report a stronger and partially much stronger executive influence (see Figure 7.5).

From the 2008 European ECM study, when results were compared with data from a US study it was apparent that clients in Europe are less dependent on agencies than their counterparts in the US (see Figure 7.6).

Before turning to the academic debates about skills, it is worth looking at Mini case study 7.2, which lists the kind of skills required by one sector, financial and investor relations (IR). (See also Chapter 29.)

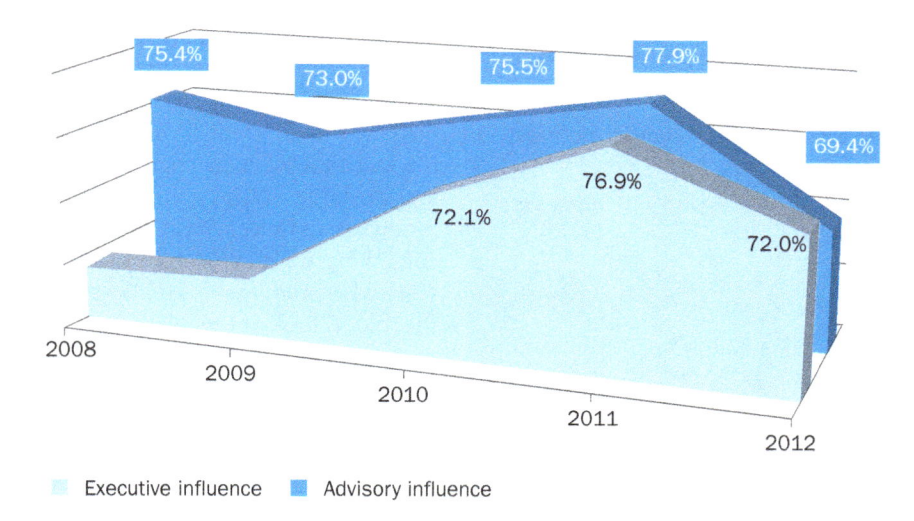

Figure 7.5 Decline in influence across Europe? (*source:* Zerfass, A., D. Verčič, P. Verhoeven, A. Moreno and R. Tench (2012). European Communication Monitor 2012. Challenges and Competencies for Strategic Communication. Results of an Empirical Survey in 42 Countries. Brussels: EACD/EUPRERA, Helios Media)

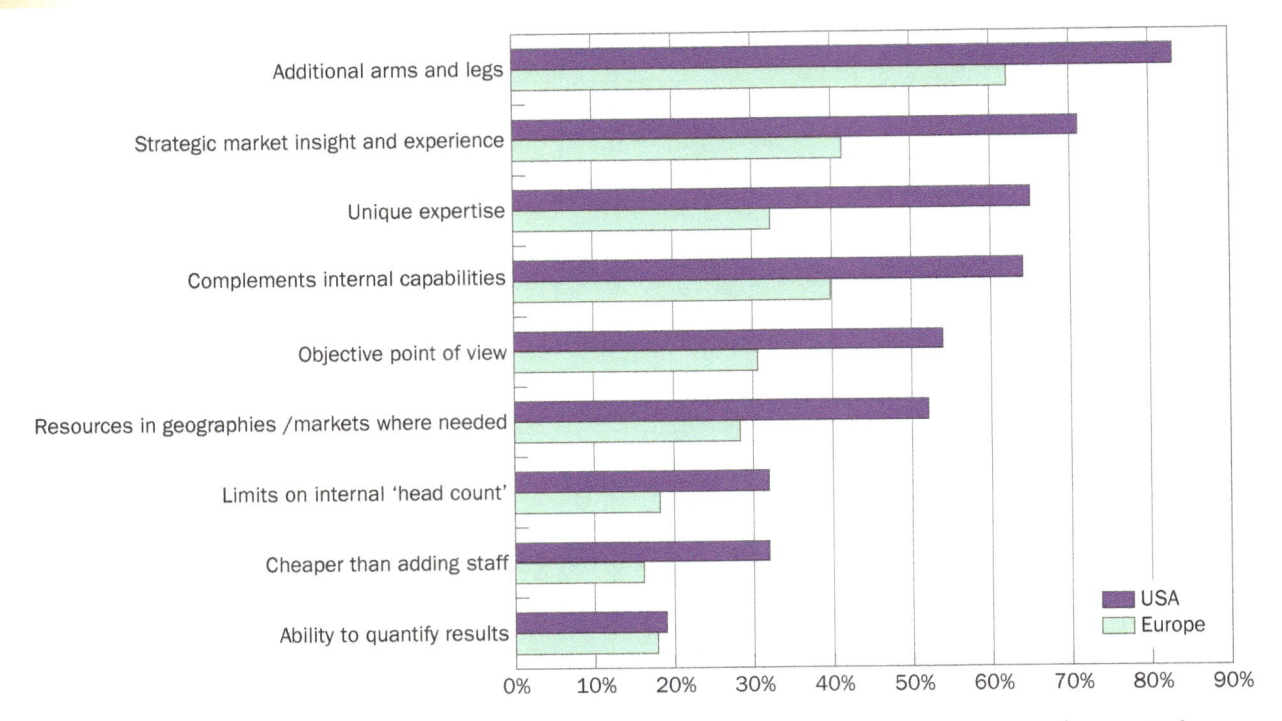

Figure 7.6 Clients in Europe are less dependent on agencies and consultancies than those is the US (*source:* Zerfass, A., A. Moreno, R. Tench, D. Verčič and P. Verhoeven (2008) European Communication Monitor 2008. Trends in Communication Management and Public Relations – Results and Implications Brussels, Leipzig: Euprera/University of Leipzig, November 2008)

Mini case study 7.2
Financial investor relations skills

- Understand in-depth how the markets work
- Count top opinion formers among contacts
- Able to talk to top broadsheet financial journalists and key bloggers
- Have the ear of the board members, if not on the board
- Understand the financial calendar and rules/regulations of the Stock Exchange
- Overview of all online and offline communication activity related to financial and investor relations
- Oversee production of annual report, etc.
- Effective proof-reading skills/on-press checking
- Manage media events
- Train senior management in media interviews
- Produce media and other stakeholder information

The skills debate

What skills do PR practitioners need in order effectively to deliver results and how do they acquire these skills? The wider UK contextual framework for education and training puts skills centre stage. In some ways this has worked in favour of PR education and training. No one will argue with the need for skills in one form or another. In many areas the creative industries (which include public relations consultancies) are a growth sector. The debate over skills has been muddied by the different terminologies employed and by the fact that whereas some skills may be transferable and portable, others are very subject specific. Undergraduates may lack basic literacy skills, for example, something we might (and practitioners do, according to Fawkes and Tench 2004a) see as essential for the PR role. A look at the job specs for PR positions today reveal an increasing trend for digital and online media skills especially at executive level (see Chapter 3).

Skills have become an integral component of benchmarking (setting achievement and quality levels) and are therefore now part of the curriculum. There has been a trend in the last decade towards generic skills and towards the involvement of employers and educationalists in defining those skills. This has led to new concepts such as employability and externality. These have translated in the UK into the requirement for all students to have a personal progress file, which records and reflects on their individual achievements, and which follows on from school-based records of achievement. This sits well with the portfolio-based work of many public relations-related HE courses. As discussed earlier skills is also an important agenda item for practitioners in the training, development and continuing evolution of the practice (see Tench et al. 2012; Tench and Moreno 2015).

This at least provides us with a potential paradigm for the PR practitioner where they become a lifelong learner and can reflect on their own learning and development throughout their career (and beyond). Education and training does not end with the last day of term or the last exam. From school, through education and training where learning logs or portfolios are used to evidence and assess certain skills, including reflection, through to CPD responsibility for our own learning, we never stop learning (see Case study 7.3).

Hargie (2000) suggests that competence in a profession involves three sets of skills:

1. cognitive (the knowledge base)
2. technical or manipulative skills inherent in a profession
3. social or communication skills.

He points out that education and training have usually focused on the first at the expense of interpersonal skills. For the PR practitioner, interpersonal skills must surely be as important as any other and perhaps even a given.

This is a confusing situation, but the graduate in disciplines related to PR has the advantage that the sector already encompasses skills and employability as a key component, even intrinsic to the subject matter. Therefore, a portfolio that may evidence skills the student has mastered, illustrated in outcomes such as strategic campaign planning, online social media and activities, press release writing or event management, may also be valuable for taking around to interviews to show employers what the student can do and has done.

The Hargie approach to the skills debate, outlined above, mirrors the earlier suggestion that PR practitioners must have a wide range of skills to move up the continuum. The UK-based perspective is supported by evidence from the United States. The PRSA studies (1999, 2006) and the Commission on Public Relations Education (2017) provide a wide perspective on addressing the next PR crisis, which is ensuring appropriate education and training (see Table 7.3). The

Necessary knowledge includes	Necessary skills include
Communication and public relations theories	Research methods and analysis
Societal trends	Management of information
Legal requirements and issues	Problem solving and negotiation
Public relations history	Management of communication
Multicultural and global issues	Strategic planning
Participation in the professional PR community	Issues management
Working with a current issue	Audience segmentation
Applying cross-cultural and cross-gender sensitivity	Informative and persuasive writing
Communication and persuasion concepts and strategies	Community relations, consumer relations,
Strategies	employee relations, other practice areas
Relationships and relationship building	Technological and visual literacy
Ethical issues	Managing people, programmes and resources
Marketing and finance	Sensitive interpersonal communication
Use of research and forecasting	Fluency in a foreign language
Organisational change and development	Ethical decision making
Message production	
Public speaking and presentation	

Table 7.3 Port of Entry and Professional Bond recommendations on knowledge and skills (*source*: PRSA 1999 and 2006)

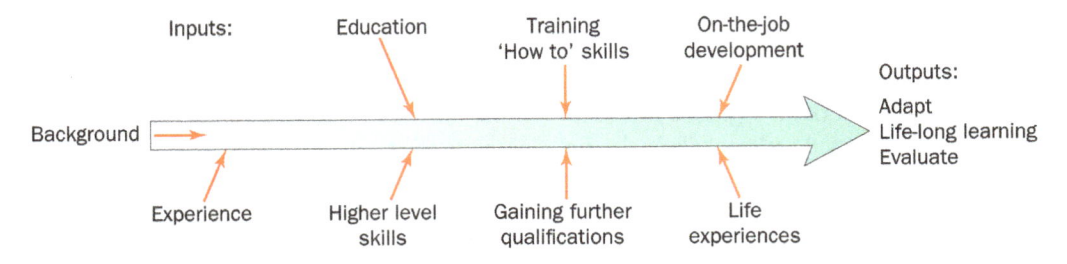

Figure 7.7 Public relations practitioner lifecycle

emphasis here is on the complementary approach of knowledge that graduates are expected to have and skills specific to the profession (see Figure 7.7).

This debate continues and the Commission on Public Relations Education published a follow-up research report in 2017 on the state of undergraduate education. This report was based upon research conducted with practitioners as well as bringing together a panel of international education ad practice experts. Tench was part of the panel. The commission held an Educator Summit on public relations education in 2015 in New York where approximately 50 international public relations industry leaders and educators debated topics related to undergraduate public relations education, with a heavy focus on how best to prepare students for a career in the public relations industry (see www.commissionPRed.org). The 2017 report is the summation of the two-year project.

Case study 7.2

A week in the life of a PR agency account director: Kyla Flynn, Account Director, MCG, London and Leeds

A typical Monday involves a lot of planning and creativity. It's when I sit down with the team to discuss the week. But before I even get to the office, I check Facebook, Twitter and Instagram for our clients.

I always have my phone attached to me, it's part and parcel of having a job where you're on the go all the time. So much communication now takes place across social media; most of our communication strategies we offer to clients are integrated. Social media is such a big talking point throughout the day from the minute I wake up to when I go to bed. For example, all our clients would love to be involved with TV programmes like the BBC's Great British Bake Off, so I'm permanently attached to my phone so I can check for opportunities. We do have a dedicated social media person in the office, and she keeps an eye on all our clients' channels and conversations on social. She also keeps her eyes peeled for new business opportunities. However, those opportunities often spring from conversations we have. We direct Alice to keep an eye on certain brands we'd like to work with, to see what they're doing, so a lot of our work is research. We also use social media to keep a check on what our client's competitors are doing, what creative and campaign content they are pushing. We really want to take our clients into a different sphere be it lifestyle, fitness, fashion, beauty etc. so it can lead to a lot of conversations. Bloggers are also a key target area for us. Many have made strong business models out of their blogs, the reach and influence they have can be phenomenal. Look at vloggers like Zoella, she's baking, she's bought a house, so she now includes cooking and interiors as well as fashion and make-up in her blog posts. We really must keep an eye on what and who's trending. I use Tweetdeck and Facebook apps to manage all my pages in one place. For Instagram I use my personal account for all my clients, as it still has a bit of a way to go to become as sophisticated as other popular social media channels, but they now do sponsored links which is progress. Pinterest is a growing platform which I also check throughout the week.

We work with different clients in different ways; some must approve every comment and interaction, whereas others have agreed a tone of voice with us so we can respond immediately and use our own discretion.

I also check my phone for calls. Then I go for a run, which I do every day, a run on Hampstead Heath, and then I check my phone and the apps again after this. I don't know what I'd do without Hampstead Heath, it's my escape. Once I'm in the office we have Monday morning catch-up meetings. I have colleagues based in different offices so I usually FaceTime colleagues. We refer regularly to our planner because it details what has been approved by the client and it means we know exactly what's coming up, and what to look out for. For example, it was national curry week last week. We know about it well in advance and therefore work hard to get coverage for our food clients through strategically planned approaches.

We always know that a few months in advance we need to be speaking to the long leads like the monthly magazines, and a month in advance for the short leads, like the dailies and the bloggers, to see what they are doing and what we might be able to do together. The planner gets printed onto A3 and I'll ask the account executives what they're doing to address the planner, and any feedback from the previous week's conversations with journalists and bloggers. For instance, my colleague might say she's spoken to *Country Living* magazine and they've finished putting together their December edition. Therefore, we need to start thinking about Valentine's Day and get some creative ideas agreed upon. If we're working towards a regular calendar of events we must make sure the communications integrates for both traditional and social media. They're both so key to help us achieve little and big goals. I also check this against our targets for the client to make sure we're working well.

We speak to people in the team constantly, so we all know what we're doing. We're not afraid to keep asking what everyone's doing to make sure nothing is missed. If we've got an event coming up that tends to take priority, but we also review things that slip to the bottom of the pile from the week before.

Each Friday we print off an update for each client and if there are any discussion points from that we roll it over to the Monday morning discussion.

On a Monday the directors and I will sit down and discuss budgets. We also review our strategies to make sure we're on target for the next quarter campaigns. I also keep my hand in with journalists and I struggle to balance my time between being strategic, working with the client and making sure I still have that daily contact with journalists. I've worked so hard to build these contacts over the last seven years. You've got to work hard at these relationships; talking to an editorial assistant is so powerful as they may become lifestyle editor one day for example. My relationships are my currency!

Now I'm working on between six retained and a few project-based clients. For example, I've got three or four clients who all want to be on BBC's Great British Bake Off. Most clients are realistic and know that we're not going to get branded goods onto such a popular BBC programme. They understand that it's more about the discussion around the programme, although we did get Mary Berry wearing one of our client's blazers, which was brilliant. An apple-producing client won't be featured but we'll be tweeting about our client and their products during and after the programme each week.

We speak to clients as and when they want to speak to us; we can go a couple of weeks without speaking to them, and we can get on with the work. But we also have hourly conversations with others, especially if they have a problem or a great opportunity comes up. That's the nature of agency work. We are there to support our clients, we're at their beck and call. Fortunately, I've never had an overly demanding client.

I've got a restaurant opening in a couple of weeks and I'm speaking to the client regularly. It's often about reassurance and telling them what's going on every step of the way. You can't be afraid to pick up the phone and speak to people, clients much prefer that to worrying about what's going on.

I'm in a planning meeting with a client on Tuesday to strategically plan next year's key activities. We're meeting in a central London hotel, away from the offices. It's important to be in a nice surrounding with the client. We have a journalist's breakfast on Wednesday morning, then back in the office till the afternoon when I've got a meeting with a magazine to discuss some issues a client has had with them and how we can resolve those issues.

We've found that sending a press release and product to a journalist must have a standout factor. We often send products and press releases by bike or post, and of course by email. The journalists get so many releases every day, so you need to work on what's going to give you that. We know the product on its own isn't going to give you the standout so you must work hard to make it standout. Last week we launched a new Indian food range for a client, so we took hot meals to all of our relevant journalist contacts. We delivered a whole Curry Club Bag to them. We usually do that in person as I want to be in front of the journalist to see what they think. We always ring in advance, make an appointment or say we're popping round, can you come to reception to meet us.

When we did a delivery drop recently another agency had dropped off a cheese product with reception, the journalist came down and the receptionist just gave it to him. He didn't know anything about it, and he gave it to us, he wasn't eating cheese and didn't know who it had come from. Some agencies just use couriers to do the drops.

The fashion journalist we're meeting for breakfast will be telling us what her priorities are for the next few

case study 7.2 (continued)

months. Even though it's October we'll be discussing when she will be featuring spring shoes for example. We need to know what themes they might be thinking of, we'll also make suggestions, and build on the relationship. I enjoy getting to know the journalists well. I often find I get calls from them asking for advice on careers as well as helping them out with a story idea because they've got to know us. Everybody is helping each other but you have to work hard to build trust and be able to respond quickly to their requests. Our office is full of fridge freezers and clothes racks galore to store our clients' products so we can fulfil journalists' requests quickly and plan our drops.

I usually have lunch on the go, but often I'm at nice restaurants with clients or journalists. You really have to offer journalists a good experience, you have to know the best cafes, bars and new places to go that a journalist will want to experience. If I don't have a lunch appointment I like to get out of the office, even if it's for 20 minutes.

We monitor our clients' coverage through a cuttings service, and many of our clients also have a cuttings service. We use Scout to keep an eye on online platforms. We've got good contacts who will tell us what's going on in the media. Usually we get a quick call from the journalist to let us know if our client is going to be featured. We also buy the papers and magazines every day too.

I share a flat with a PR person who works in health, so we share knowledge, and I have a lot of in-house PR contacts too. It's always really useful to get their perspective on PR agencies. I also go to client evening events, and breakfast briefings which can be really useful to network at, get your agency name around, and listen to guest speakers such as editors from the big publications.

We tend to finish work at 5:30pm, but I know of other PRs who work much longer hours. Our directors recognise we have to turn off at some point. We always check there are no issues that have been left undone towards the end of the day.

If a crisis hits that will take priority, the senior members of the team will get together and often stay late; it's a different ball game when that happens. We make sure journalists have our mobiles so we can keep the lines of communication going, even if it's to say, 'we'll have to get back to you on that' or 'comment'.

The things I would never want to be without are my mobile and my laptop; having access to the cloud means I can access information wherever I am. I can work anywhere in London with them, I'm always nipping into coffee shops and hotels where I know I can log into the cloud. It's a fun job, but it's demanding, I can't think of anything else I'd rather be doing.

Picture 7.2 Kyla Flynn, pictured centre, with colleagues at MCG (*source:* Reprinted with permission of Kyla Flynn)

The model of the PR practitioner is now someone who encompasses both higher level and how to skills and is still (and always will be) learning. This provides a continuum with, at one end, someone ready to learn and, at the other, no end point as there is always room to learn more. What point they are at on that continuum will depend on background and experiences and the context in which they function. The school leaver who joins an agency on a trial period or an apprenticeship programme will be at one end of the continuum. If the employer provides in-house training, supports them through further education and training and the student wants to learn and develop, then they are as likely to get to the boardroom position in due course as someone who has come up a different route. They will be moving up the continuum. Their ability to succeed will be a combination of their own abilities and experiences and the expectations and input of others around them. This links well with the model of the practitioner as a system.

Competencies of public relations practitioners

What is clear from studies of skills, knowledge and personal attributes is that they overlap in terminology and that there is a pattern forming about how skills, knowledge and personal attributes lead to broader competencies. Gregory (2008: 216) uses the following definition of competencies in a study of senior communication managers in the UK: 'behavioural sets or sets of behaviours that support the attainment of organisational objectives. How knowledge and skills are used in performance.' This distinguishes competencies from skills, knowledge and personal attributes (see Table 7.4).

Jeffrey and Brunton (2011: 60) highlight the advantage of studying competencies over roles 'as . . . roles outline tasks and responsibilities in the job description, in today's dynamic workplace these same roles are likely to change frequently. In contrast, competencies

Skills	Knowledge	Personal attributes
Writing and oral communication	Business knowledge/literacy	Handling pressure
Project planning and management	Current awareness	Leadership
Critical thinking	Theoretical knowledge	Integrity/honesty/ethical
Problem solving	Knowledge of PR history	Objectivity
Media skills	Knowledge of other cultures	Listening
Persuasion	Knowledge of communication models	Confidence/ambition
Strategic thinking	Knowledge of how to apply PR theory	Team player
Mentoring and coaching		Energy/motivation
Advanced communication skills		Discipline
IT skills (including new media channels)		Intelligence
Crisis management		Ability to get on with others/interpersonal skills
Research		Wide interests
Reading comprehension		Intellectual curiosity
Community relations		Creativity
Consumer relations		Flexibility
Employee relations		Judgement and decision making
Professional service skills		Time management
Social responsibility		Respect for hierarchy
PR ethics		Follows organisational rules
		Honesty
		Adaptability
		Integrity
		Ambition
		Reliable attendance
		Willingness to accept assignments
		Completes work on time

Table 7.4 Range of skills, knowledge and personal attributes identified in public relations literature

are the underlying foundational abilities that are integral to successfully carrying out the tasks and responsibilities, and thus remain a stable blueprint for practice over time'.

The difficulty in establishing a workable definition of competencies has been discussed in work for the European Centre for the Development of Vocational training (CEDEFOP) which aimed to clarify the concepts of knowledge, skills and competences (Winterton et al. 2005: 15). This highlights the usefulness of competencies as providing a link between education (and skills) and job requirements (roles). For example, there is:

1. conceptual competence which refers to knowledge about an entire domain;
2. procedural competence which refers to the application of conceptual competence in a particular situation; and
3. performance competence which is required to assess problems and select a suitable strategy for solving them.

In the context of public relations, Oughton (2004) suggests that there is a difficulty with defining competency because it can refer either to the ability to perform a task or how people should behave in order to carry out the role. Szyszka (1995) sub-divides two categories of competencies of PR practitioners:

1. specific qualifications – those qualifications which are directly connected to the topic public relations; and
2. unspecific qualifications – those qualifications, like leadership, which can be seen as a core competence for PR practitioners.

Although some studies have focused on the skills, knowledge and personal attributes of practitioners, there was no definitive research that brought these elements together in a single study until the EU-funded ECOPSI project (Tench et al. 2012; Tench and Moreno 2015). Given the focus of roles and labelling practitioners according to the tasks they undertake, or where they are in the organisational hierarchy, specialisms are difficult to define. There is also a lack of research on social media practice within the PR sector, and the skills, knowledge and personal attributes needed to fulfil this role efficiently.

The ECOPSI programme has taken the broad labels provided by prior research and used them to examine four roles: internal communications, social media,

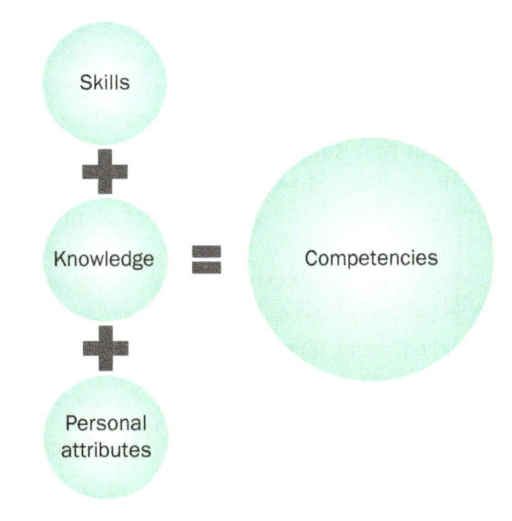

Figure 7.8 Skills, knowledge and personal attributes contributing to competencies. (*source:* Tench et al. 2012; Tench and Moreno 2015)

crisis communication and communication director. This research fills a gap in knowledge about how these roles are enacted across Europe, and the skills, knowledge and personal attributes required, which subsequently contribute to the competencies needed by practitioners to fulfil these roles efficiently. Figure 7.8 illustrates how ECOPSI views skills, knowledge and personal attributes.

Role of theory in practice

The value of theory as underpinning practice is up for discussion. Some practitioners will have managed very well for many years without theory, or rather they will have relied on their own version of common sense theory. Others have taken postgraduate courses, like a Master's degree or professional postgraduate qualifications (such as those from the CIPR) and been exposed to theory through education. Increasingly, public relations graduates who have studied theoretical modules in their degree courses are joining the profession and shaping the expectations of the next generation. The theory that practitioners have been exposed to will inform the role they play.

Relevant to this discussion is research conducted by Tench and Fawkes (2005) into PR education in Britain. Research was conducted with employers of PR students who were asked about different aspects of the curriculum and its value. In relation to theory

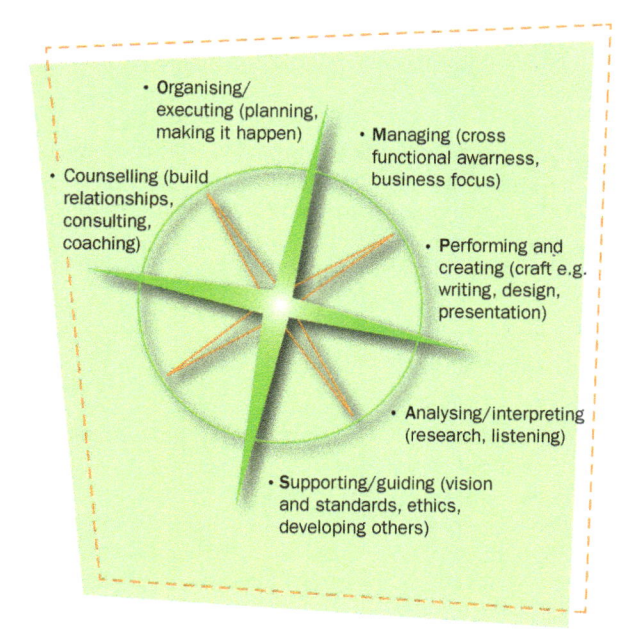

Figure 7.9 COMPAS (Tench et al. 2012, 2013c). This acronym defines the competencies in the Communication Roles Matrix developed from the largest EU-funded research project into communication in Europe, www.p4ace.org.uk

- Organising/executing (planning, making it happen)
- Managing (cross functional awarness, business focus)
- Counselling (build relationships, consulting, coaching)
- Performing and creating (craft e.g. writing, design, presentation)
- Analysing/interpreting (research, listening)
- Supporting/guiding (vision and standards, ethics, developing others)

the practitioners were asked about the dissertation and how important it was as a core part of a public relations curriculum. The research found there was more enthusiasm for dissertations among in-house employers than consultancies, with over three-quarters (78 per cent) of the former supporting dissertations, as against 56 per cent of consultancies. Qualitative comments help explain these responses. Support for the dissertation was expressed as: '[proves] the student's understanding and application of theory and practice, assuming that the topic of the dissertation is relevant'; 'closest thing to thinking through a situation from start to finish which is what is required to handle PR campaigns for clients'; 'a dissertation shows an ability to think and analyse, takes planning and writing skills and hopefully places demands on a student'. It should be noted that a minority of employers were extremely dismissive of all theory, and dissertations in particular: 'PR is concise; dissertations are long', said one.

Tench and Fawkes argue that the supporters seem to appreciate what a dissertation involves, unlike the detractors who clearly place no value at all on abstract thought. They argue that there are serious implications 'for the intellectual health of the industry. There is also evidence of a "shopping list" approach to education, with [a number of] employers mentioning the lack of benefit to them of a dissertation.'

The range of theory relevant to public relations is explored in Chapter 8, but it is worth pointing out here that the majority of employers do value the role of theory in educating practitioners, albeit not so much as they value actual practical experience. Moreover, it is not only the views of employers that count in this debate. See Think about 7.2, as Cheney and Christensen (2001: 167) point out:

Still, it is important that a discipline's theoretical agenda not simply be beholden to trends already present or incipient in the larger society. Otherwise, a discipline can fail to exercise its own capacity for leadership on both practical and moral grounds.

Think about 7.2 — Disciplines that inform public relations

Which subject disciplines could inform the PR role (apart from PR)?

Feedback

There are lots of disciplines that are relevant to the education and training of the PR practitioner:

- business and management/human resource management
- communication subject areas: marketing/marketing communication/advertising
- psychology
- cultural studies
- politics/sociology/social psychology
- media
- human geography.

The list is, in fact, endless. Are there any that are not in some way relevant?

Case study 7.3
Lisa Potter, Communications Team Leader, Perth & Kinross Council

Lisa started working life as a journalist and moved into PR almost 15 years ago, completing a post graduate CIPR Professional PR Diploma along the way.

Her career as an in-house practitioner has been spent in the public sector in generalist roles combining media relations, internal communication, stakeholder engagement, digital channels, newsletter editing, photography and videography.

This diary describes a recent role as communications team leader for Perth & Kinross Council. It combines communications with line management responsibilities, with the goal of delivering the strategic communications objectives for the organisation.

Traditional communications vs. new channels

There's still a significant commitment in my weekly work for traditional communications – writing news releases, answering media enquiries, publishing internal bulletins. These are still the things non-communications colleagues are looking for from my team when they ask for communications support.

Even where the requests are for different channels, the request is often framed as a request to publish – Tweet it so I can share; email it to the distribution group; post it on Facebook.

Avoiding being the team who sends out stuff is a daily task. It involves asking why a lot.

Asking why the childcare team wanted me to promote training sessions aimed at men entering the childcare profession resulted in a 50 per cent increase in the number of men signing up for the course. By asking why, I was able to find out that not only are men underrepresented in the career, but also that the increase in funded nursery hours being introduced by the Scottish Government meant there were more jobs available in childcare for people with the right experience and qualifications.

Using targeted Facebook advertising I was able to work with the childcare team to try out different types of content to attract more men to apply for the dedicated training course. The next step is looking at what happens to those participants, and whether they end up in a childcare job.

Planning ahead

To try and reduce the last-minute requests we have an annual communications plan which is agreed each April. These are the priority projects for the year. The ones with clear objectives which proactive communications can help to deliver. Creating this annual plan and getting sign-off from senior managers helps to manage these activities and ensure they aren't forgotten, but it doesn't stop the everyday demands.

An average week

My normal week starts out by preparing a round-up of the previous week for senior managers and councillors. This includes the biggest media stories about us in the past week, as well as engagement statistics for our social media channels, showing what content resonated with people, and what actions they took as a result. Tying this in more closely with our Google Analytics to follow through what happens for referrals to our website from social media is the next stage of development.

Tuesdays are team meeting days. This is always a good chance to make sure the whole team is up to speed on priorities for the week. Out of six people in the corporate communications team (including me) only three of us work full-time, so it's important to take this time together.

Most Wednesdays will have a Council committee. Someone from the team will attend the meeting so that we know what was discussed. We also manage the cameras for recording. Depending on how the meeting goes that could take up most of the day. If it's a contentious report – closure of a school or change to a bin collections policy – the fallout on social media and from traditional media will last into the weekend, and beyond. While some of this will be pre-prepared, there's always the chance something will be said or decided in committee that we had no chance of foreseeing.

> The first Thursday of the month is team learning time. As a local authority we don't have a big budget to spend on all the training opportunities I'd love to give the team access to. So, instead once a month we dedicate a couple of hours to sharing learning between us. Each member of the team takes a turn to lead the session. It can be anything from feeding back on a conference or one of the rare paid-for training courses, to looking into the value of recording audio as part of a proactive communications campaign and then letting the team know what they need to do to start doing that.
>
> Friday is the look ahead to the coming week and get ready for it all to start again on Monday.
>
> ### Keep learning
>
> Comms people are busy, at work and in our lives, and making time to learn can be a challenge if you don't know where to start.
>
> My approach is a combination of podcasts, blogs, e-newsletters, formal CPD, Facebook groups, Twitter, books, in-work learning opportunities, and anything else which comes my way.
>
> I listen to podcasts every day on the commute to and from work, and while walking the dog, and use blog follows, email newsletters and Twitter lists to learn from communicators who work out loud and share their practice. All these combined with reading short-form case studies, full-length books and webinars, are recorded as CPD annually through my membership of the CIPR.
>
> For me learning isn't just something that should be left to external training courses or formal qualifications. Look around and you'll find great sources of learning from people across communications, all of which will help you improve as a practitioner and prepare you for the next challenge in your career.

Professionalism

The issue of defining public relations to protect its jurisdiction, discussed at the beginning of the chapter, has an impact not only on practice, as described earlier, but also on issues concerning the professionalisation of public relations (L'Etang and Pieczka 2006).

There are several different approaches (called trait and process) to what defines a profession and some controversy over whether public relations qualifies for the term. For example, practitioners are not licensed, as doctors or lawyers are – indeed, even the UK CIPR's 10,000 plus members represent relatively few of its estimated 70,000 practitioners.

In 2000 the Global Alliance of public relations associations, however, declared its guiding principles of professionalism to be characterised by:

- mastery of a particular intellectual skill through education and training;
- acceptance of duties to a broader society than merely one's clients or employers;
- objectivity and high standards of conduct and performance.

The problematic nature of some of these concepts, such as defining or measuring objectivity or the difficulties in controlling members' standards of behaviour, is not examined.

Merkelson (2011) suggests that being or feeling part of a profession adds value to career development and that building a profession is a way of ensuring legitimacy. Meanwhile Gilmore and Williams (2007) identify a profession as having tightly defined professional standards that drive its educational syllabus, has principle texts, commissions its own research and has highly technical processes of quality assurance that govern its education programmes. L'Etang (2002) called education the 'crucial plank in PR's quest for professional status' and this view is shared by the PRSA Port of Entry (1999), which quotes Kerr (1995) as saying 'a profession gains its identity by making the university the port of entry'.

Research on the legitimacy of PRs to operate in 2008 identified that a revolution of the sector had been enhanced by developments in the digital generation, global integration and stakeholder empowerment (Johansson and Ottestig 2011: 146). However, despite the consequential communications needs generated by the internet for business and organisations, the opportunity for PR to gain 'internal status and legitimacy appear to be dependent on the attitudes of other executives' (ibid.).

For PR the route to professionalisation seems to be linked to boardroom acceptance, 'empowerment legitimacy is dependent on attitudes of senior executives' (Johansson and Ottestig 2011: 164). This view appears to be embedded in PR theory: 'degrees of influence are

> **Think about 7.3**
>
> ## Professions
>
> Is PR a profession? Throughout this book we do use the term profession and associate it clearly with PR. However, it is important to acknowledge that, according to sociological definitions of professions, there is debate about whether PR meets the criteria. This is a useful topic for future discussion, research and student dissertations.

also leading factors in CEO's decision to grant a role within dominant coalition' (Berger 2005 quoted in Valentini 2010: 158).

Merkelson (2011) argues that 'theoretical development is a precondition to professionalisation'. It would seem that PR's role is less to do with legislation and established practice and more to do with social capital of the individual. 'Having extended personalised networks of influence is an asset for a career conscious PR practitioner' (Valentini 2010: 160).

The 2012 ECM survey (Zerfass et al. 2012) focused on the issue of professionalism and ethics in practice. A large majority of the respondents stated that a lack of understanding of communication practice within the top management (84 per cent) and difficulties of the profession itself to prove the impact of communication activities on organisational goals (75 per cent) are the main barriers for further professionalisation of the practice. The key challenges for European communication professionals were reported as the need to explain the communication function to top management and to prove the value of communication for organisations. Other barriers are, in decreasing order, a shortage of up-to-date communication training (54 per cent), a poor reputation of professional communication and public relations in society (52 per cent), the phenomenon that experience is valued more highly than formal qualifications in communication or public relations (52 per cent), the status of PR and communication associations and professional bodies (40 per cent).

Although a lack of formal accreditation systems for the profession is only seen as a barrier by every fourth respondent, most practitioners did see advantages of such systems, which are already in place in the United Kingdom, Brazil and other countries. 70 per cent of the respondents responded that national or international accreditation could help to improve the recognition and the reputation of the field. But only 58 per cent thought that a global accreditation system will help to standardise the practice of public relations and 54 per cent agreed that accreditation ensures that practitioners will have proper knowledge of recent communication tools and trends.

The skills and attributes that Chief Executive Officers (CEOs) are looking for in their top communications executives have expanded. Experience in communications is taken for granted, and not considered enough anymore. 'CEOs want communications executives who are business savvy, with a deep understanding of their companies from top to bottom. CEOs also want communications chiefs to be proficient in three key modes of operation – reactive, proactive and interactive. CEOs see their communications chief as a critical part of their team, and across the board. There are categories of decision making in which CEOs would consider it grossly negligent not to have that individual at the table' (Arthur Page Society, Authentic Enterprise White Paper, 2008). The European Communications Monitor (ECM) 2011 reports that 59.9 per cent of senior communicators in Europe report to the CEO and 17.8 per cent have a seat on the board, compared to 45 per cent of communications practitioners reporting to the CEO in the US (Arthur Page Society 2008) and close to 80 per cent of practitioners being a member of the senior management group in Sweden in 2009 (Johansson et al. 2011: 143).

From these four different research projects, spanning nearly ten years, it is clear that European PR practitioners are better represented in the boardroom than their US colleagues and more of them report directly to the CEO. The ECM 2011 also shows a better representation at board level by PR practitioners in northern Europe than their colleagues working in southern Europe. 'Often the degree of influence and power held by PR practitioners are leading factors in determining CEOs' decisions of granting a role within the dominant coalition' (Berger 2005 cited in Valentini 2010: 158). It could therefore be argued that the legitimacy of the PR industry has been granted by this influential group of publics.

Research into CEOs' view on PR in the UK indicated that a valued practitioner understands the organisational context, stakeholder requirements, the business model and organisational drivers and has the confidence to challenge. However CEOs recognise they 'under-invest in PR and that if there were the right measures to evaluate its contribution, they would spend more' (Gregory 2011: 99). While the profession has come a long way in ten years it is still considered a soft discipline, rather than a core discipline for many organisations.

Representative bodies

Another requirement for a profession is the existence of a body that represents and, in some cases – although not for PR – licenses its members to practise. The UK's professional body is the CIPR. The industry also has a trade body called the PRCA.

Key facts about the UK's CIPR:

- The CIPR was founded in 1948 and awarded charter status in 2005.
- The Institute has over 10,000 members, with a turnover of £3 million.
- The CIPR is the largest professional body for PR practitioners in Europe.
- The CIPR is a founding member of the Global Alliance for Public Relations and Communication Management.
- CIPR membership has more than doubled in the last 10 years.
- Approximately 60 per cent of its members are female – this has grown from only 20 per cent in 1987.
- 45 per cent of its members work in public relations consultancy and 55 per cent work in-house.
- Two-thirds of CIPR members are based outside London.
- The CIPR has a strict code of conduct that all members must abide by.

The purpose of the CIPR is outlined in its Royal Charter:

a. to promote for the public benefit high levels of skill, knowledge, competence, and standards of practice and professional conduct on the part of public relations practitioners;

b. to promote the study, research and development of the practice of public relations and publish or otherwise make available the useful results of such study and research;

c. to promote public understanding of the contribution of effective public relations in encouraging ethical communication and in enhancing the efficiency and performance of all sectors of the economy;

d. to act as an authoritative body for the purpose of consultation in matters of public and professional interest concerning public relations;

e. to represent the interests of members in all public fora; and

f. to advance the interests of members and to provide facilities and services for members.

Source: www.cipr.co.uk (CIPR)

The following statements and comments are from the press release (February 2005) from the Chartered Institute of Public Relations.

The CIPR announced its Royal Charter status approval for the Institute in 2005. The CIPR's Royal Charter includes the power to grant Chartered Public Relations Practitioner status to individuals who meet the required standard of professional distinction.

Just as chartered status is the norm in other professions, the CIPR see it as their mission to build a chartered public relations profession. The membership includes hundreds of Chartered PR Practitioners and each year more are awarded chartered status.

According to the CIPR, Chartered status represents the highest standard of professional excellence and integrity. As well as reflecting an individual's breadth of experience and achievements, it also reflects whether members are keeping pace in a fast-moving profession and updating knowledge and skills through continuing professional development (CPD).

The benefits of chartered status are described by the CIPR as:

- Demonstrate to your peers that you have met the rigorous criteria set out for chartered status.
- Enjoy greater influence within your organisation and in the profession.
- Gain a professional competitive edge and enhance your career prospects.
- Reassure prospective employers and clients that you practise to the highest standards.
- Chartered Public Relations Practitioners are entitled to use the designation Chart.PR and a supporting logo.

Source: www.cipr.co.uk (CIPR)

Box 7.4 details other European associations. All their websites contain much relevant information for further investigation (see Explore 7.4).

Box 7.4

European public relations associations

- PRVA – Public Relations Verband (Austria)
- BPRCA – Belgian Public Relations Consultants Association
- APRA – Czech Association of Public Relations Agencies
- DKF – Dansk Kommunikationsfrening (Denmark)
- STiL – Finnish Association of Communicators
- Information, Presse & Communication (France)
- DPRG – Deutsche Public Relations Gesellschaft EV (Germany)
- HPRCA – Hellenic Public Relations Consultancies Association (Greece)
- PRII – Public Relations Institute of Ireland
- FERPI – Federazione Relazioni Pubbliche Italiana
- Beroepsvereniging voor Communicatie (Netherlands)
- Kommunikasjonsfreningen (Norway)
- NIR – Norwegian Public Relations Consultants Association
- APECOM – Association of Public Relations Consultancies in Portugal
- PACO – Russian Public Relations Association
- APRSR – Public Relations Association of the Slovak Republic
- PRSS – Public Relations Society of Slovenia
- ADECEC – Assoc de Empresas Consultoras en Relaciones Publicas (Spain)
- SPRA – Swedish Public Relations Association
- BPRA – Bund der Public Relations Agenturen der Schweiz (Switzerland)
- PRCI – Public Relations Consultancies Inc. of Turkey
- PRCA – Public Relations Communications Association (UK)

Source: Tench and Waddington

Explore 7.4

Join an institute

Find the web address of the national institute where you are studying or working. Search the website for details about the national association. How many people are members? What benefits does membership bring? Could you be an associate or student member? Talk to a friend or colleague about the benefits of membership. If it is possible for you to be a member, why not think about joining?

Education and research

The first UK undergraduate degree in PR was launched at Bournemouth in 1989, followed by Leeds Beckett (Metropolitan) University and the College of St Mark and St John, Plymouth in 1990 (See also Chapter 1). The pioneer postgraduate courses were launched at Stirling University in 1989 and Manchester Metropolitan University shortly after. Research conducted in 2003 found 22 PR or similar undergraduate degrees in Britain, of which 13 were then approved by the CIPR. With the addition of non- or recently approved CIPR courses, it is estimated that approximately 500 PR undergraduates enrolled on UK PR courses in 2004 (Tench and Fawkes 2005).

PR education continues to evolve (Fawkes and Tench 2004a) and while most PR educators have practitioner backgrounds, many in Britain now have over two decades of teaching and research experience. Teaching academics in the UK institutions are also increasingly acquiring doctorates and other research qualifications. New ideas, drawing on critical theory and other cultural and political approaches (see below) are being developed and taught as academics seek to expand the theoretical frameworks with which to critique PR and its role in society.

There has been a worldwide growth in courses at higher education (HE) level that aim to feed the profession, including general degrees covering PR as one part of a wider remit and the specialist CIPR approved PR degrees that focus on PR and its related context, with a commensurate growth in academics and academic publishing. According to Fawkes and Tench (2004b) even here the emphasis in the programmes differ, from PR as a management discipline with an emphasis on strategy (in the business schools) to PR as an aspect of media activity with an emphasis on communication (media schools) and PR as a social science.

For many years the United States was the main repository of PR research; now Britain and Europe have developed an impressive research base. The term public relations may not be familiar in other European countries, but the roles are similar. Van Ruler and Verčič (2004) highlight both the common underlying themes, such as professionalisation and the influence of communication technologies, set against the 'similar yet idiosyncratic' national backdrops, where differences are more obvious, from a study of PR within national contexts.

In addition, there are many other academic and functional disciplines, such as the social sciences, business and management, cultural studies, linguistics, media studies and psychology that also input into the research underpinning for the sector. This interdisciplinary approach is a strength; it provides a wide range of methodological options, such as a cultural studies approach to deconstruct PR case studies (Mickey 2003) rather than sticking to the traditional PR methodologies. This is known as theoretical pluralism (Cobley 1996). A number of academics discount the term interdisciplinary now, preferring post-disciplinary, and the implication that out-dated structures have given way to more fluid fields of study.

Drawing on a wide range of references such as those outlined in Chapter 8 should increase the credibility in terms of knowledge and expertise of the practitioner who is pursuing a PR qualification.

Another backdrop to the role are the national apprenticeship initiatives within Britain at secondary and HE levels to encourage more vocational and skills-based programmes as a complement to the traditional academic route. This trend, which also attracts funding, means that a discipline such as PR, which successfully links academic, skills and employability, is well positioned for growth. PR can be taught as a new-style foundation degree in the way that other subjects might not, given the inherent employer input prerequisite. Again, this may prove to be both a strength and a weakness: a strength because this offers a way forward where funding in more traditional programmes has been curtailed; a weakness because PR may lose academic credibility and become just another vocational training ground.

Summary

This chapter has demonstrated the range of skills demanded of public relations practitioners and, it is hoped, dispelled the false images of celebrity or spin presented in the introduction. It has shown the different ways in which public relations is organised and delivered in various countries and examined the issue of professionalism, as well as highlighting information about professional bodies in Britain and elsewhere. Finally, it addressed the evolving role of education in shaping the future of public relations by providing the public relations practitioner of the future.

This ideal practitioner will be able to manage the complex, dynamic context and functions of their organisation as they will possess the cognitive, technical, social and communication skills to gain the confidence of colleagues from other sectors and functions. They will facilitate communication within their organisation, as well as with external publics; they will be able to advise senior management using their higher level skills as well as oversee more detailed hands-on activity (not least because they will have a clear understanding of relevant theories and their value to practice); they will be committed to lifelong learning and continual professional development, as well as being active in the professional body; and they will also educate others about the value of public relations and in this way help reinforce the position of public relations as a profession.

Is this too much to ask? Perhaps, but it is not impossible that practitioners of the future, who will achieve these kinds of standard are, even now, reading this chapter.

Bibliography

Ahles, C.B. (2004). 'PR skills vs. personal skills: what matters most to the boss?' *PR Tactics,* April 2004: 12–13.

Allan, S. (2000). *News Culture*. Milton Keynes: Open University Press.

Bernstein, D. (1986). *Company Image and Reality*. London: Cassell.

Bartram, D. (2005). 'The great eight competencies: A criterion-centric approach to validation.' *Journal of Applied Psychology* 90(6): 1185–203.

Boyatzis, R.E. and Royatzis, R. (1982). *The Competent Manager: A model for effective performance.* New York, USA: Wiley.

Brody, E.W. (1992). 'We must act now to redeem PR's reputation'. *Public Relations Quarterly* 37(3) in F. Cropp and J.D. Pincus (2001). 'The mystery of public relations' in *Handbook of Public Relations.* R.L. Heath (ed.). Thousand Oaks, CA: Sage.

Brown, A. and L.T. Fall (2005). 'Using the port of entry report as a benchmark: survey results of on-the-job training among public relations internship site managers', *Public Relations Review* 31(2): 301–04.

BVC, Dutch Professional Association for Communication (2002). *Job profile Descriptions in Communication Management.* Third revised edition. The Hague: BVC & VVO.

Chan, G. (2000). 'Priorities old and new, for the research of public relations practice in the UK and their implications for academic debate'. Internal paper cited in 'How far do professional associations influence the direction of public relations education?'. A. Rawel. *Journal of Communication Management* 7(1): 71–78.

Chartered Institute of Public Relations. www.cipr.co.uk. Charter status: https://www.cipr.co.uk/CIPR/Learn_and_develop/Chartership/CIPR/Learn_Develop/Chartership_.aspx?hkey=e483a868-f6d7-43be-97c7-2120d5a88575, accessed 6 February 2020.

Cheney, G. and L.T. Christensen (2001). 'Public relations as contested terrain' in *Handbook of Public Relations.* R.L. Heath (ed.). Thousand Oaks, CA: Sage.

Cobley, P. (ed.) (1996). *The Communication Theory Reader.* London: Routledge.

Commission on Public Relations Education (2017). Fast Forward: Commission on Public Relations 2017 Report, Commission on Public Relations Education, New York www.CommisionPRed.org

Culbertson, H.M. and N. Chen (1996). *International Public Relations: A comparative analysis.* Lawrence Erlbaum Associates, Mahwah, NJ.

Cutlip, S.M., A.H. Center and G.M. Broom (2000). *Effective Public Relations,* 8th edn. Upper Saddle River, NJ: Prentice Hall.

Cutlip, S.M., A.H. Center and G.M. Broom (2008). *Effective Public Relations,* 9th edition. Upper Saddle River, NJ: Prentice Hall.

Daflagbe, D. (2004). How the Internet is Modifying the Day-To-Day Practice of Public Relations (PR) in Ghana, (unpublished MA dissertation).

Dearing Report (1997). Higher education in the learning society: Report of the National Committee. The National Committee of Inquiry into Higher Education. London: HMSO.

DeSanto, B. and D. Moss (2004). Defining and refining the core elements in public relations/corporate communications context: What do communication managers do? Paper presented at the 11th International Public Relations Symposium, Lake Bled, Slovenia.

DiStaso, M.W., D.W. Stacks and C.H. Botan (2009). 'State of public relations education in the United States: 2006 report on a national survey of executives and academics', *Public Relations Review* 35(3): 254–69.

Dowling, G. (2001). *Creating Corporate Reputations.* Oxford: Oxford University Press.

Dozier, D.M. and G.M. Broom (2006). 'The centrality of practitioner roles to public relations theory', in C.H. Botan and V. Hazleton (eds) *Public Relations Theory II.* London: Lawrence Erlbaum, pp.137–70.

Fawkes, J. (2008). 'What is public relations?' in *Handbook of Public Relations,* 3rd edn. A. Theaker (ed.). London: Routledge.

Fawkes, J. and R. Tench (2004a). Does practitioner resistance to theory jeopardise the future of public relations in the UK? Paper presented at the 11th International Public Relations Research Symposium, Lake Bled, Slovenia.

Fawkes, J. and R. Tench (2004b). Public relations education in the UK. A research report for the Chartered Institute of Public Relations. Published by Leeds Metropolitan University.

Ferreira, E.M. (2003). Vocationally-oriented public relations education in globalised contexts: an analysis of technikon-level public relations education. Johannesburg: RAU. (Dissertation – D.Litt. et Phil.)

Garnham, N. (2000). 'Information society as theory or ideology'. *Information, Communication and Society* 3: 139–52.

Gilmore, S. and S. Williams (2007). Conceptualising the Personnel Profession, *Personnel Review* 36(3): 398–414.

Goodman, M.B. (2006). 'Corporate communication practice and pedagogy at the dawn of the new millennium', *Corporate Communications: An International Journal,* 11(3): 196–213.

Green, L. (2002). *Communication Technology and Society.* Thousand Oaks, CA: Sage.

Gregory, A. (2005). Research into competency characteristics of senior communicators for the UK Communications Directors' Forum. Research seminar presented at Leeds Metropolitan University, February.

Gregory, A. (2008). 'Competencies of senior communication practitioners in the UK: an initial study', *Public Relations Review* 34(3): 215–23.

Gregory, A. (2011). 'The state of the public relations profession in the UK: A review of the first decade of the twenty-first century'. *Corporate Communications: An International Journal* 16(2): 89–104.

Grunig, J.E. and L.A. Grunig (2002). Implications of the IABC Excellence Study for PR Education. *Journal of Communication Management* 7(1): 34–42.

Grunig, J.E. and L.A. Grunig (2000). 'Implications of the IABC excellence study for PR education'. *Journal of Communication Management* 7(1): 34–42.

Hague, P. (1998). *Questionnaire Design,* 3rd edn. London: Kogan Page.

Hardin, M.C. and D. Pompper (2004). 'Writing in the public relations curriculum: practitioner perception versus pedagogy'. *Public Relations Review* 30(3): 357–64.

Hargie, O. (2000). *The Handbook of Communication Skills,* 2nd edn. London: Routledge.

Heath, R.L. (2001). 'Shifting foundations: Public relations as relationship building' in *Handbook of Public Relations*. R.L. Heath (ed.). Thousand Oaks, CA: Sage.

Holtzhausen, D. (2002). 'Towards a post-modern research agenda for public relations'. *Public Relations Review* 28(3): 251–64.

Hutton, J.G. (1999). 'The definition, dimensions and domain of public relations'. *Public Relations Review* 25(2): 199–214.

Hutton, J.G. (2001). 'Defining the relationship between public relations and marketing' in *Handbook of Public Relations*. R.L. Heath (ed.). Thousand Oaks, CA: Sage.

Hutton, J.G., M.B. Goodman, J.B. Alexander and C.M. Genest (2001). 'Reputation management: the new face of corporate public relations?' *Public Relations Review* 27(3): 247–61.

Institute of Public Relations (2004). Profile 42, April: 7.

IPA Bellwether Report (2012). see http://www.ipa.co.uk/page/IPA-Bellwether-Report?menu=open, accessed 14 June 2012.

Jeffrey, L.M. and M.A. Brunton (2011). 'Developing a framework for communication management competencies', *Journal of Vocational Education and Training* 63(1): 57–75.

Johansson, C. and A. Ottestig (2011). Communication executives legitimacy to operate, *Journal of Communications Management* 15(2), 2011, pp. 144–64.

Katz, D. and R.L. Kahn (1978). *The Social Psychology of Organizations,* 2nd edition. New York: John Wiley & Sons.

Kerr, C. (1995). *The Use of the University,* 4th edn. Cambridge, MA and London: Harvard University Press.

Kim, E. and T.L. Johnson (2009). 'Sailing through the port: does PR education prepare students for the profession?' 12th Annual International Public Relations Research Conference.

Katz, R.L. (1974). 'Skills of an effective administrator'. *Harvard Business Review* 52(5): 90–102.

L'Etang, J. (1999). 'Public relations education in Britain: An historical review in the context of professionalisation'. *Public Relations Review* 25(3): 261–89.

L'Etang, J. (2002). 'Public relations education in Britain: A review at the outset of the millennium and thoughts for a different research agenda'. *Journal of Communication Management* 7(1): 43–53.

L'Etang, J. and M. Pieczka (eds) (1996). *Critical Perspectives in Public Relations*. London: ITBP.

L'Etang, J. and M. Pieczka (eds) (2006). *Public Relations: Critical Debates and Contemporary Problems*. NJ: Lawrence Erlbaum Associates

Liu, B.F., S. Horsley and A.B. Levenshus (2010). 'Government and corporate communication practices: do the differences matter?' *Journal of Applied Communication Research* 38(2), pp.189–213.

Logeion (2012, 17 February). Beroepsniveauprofielen [Job level profiles]. Retrieved from http://www.logeion.nl/beroepsniveauprofielen.

McCleneghan, J.S. (2006). 'PR executives rank 11 communication skills', *Public Relations Quarterly* 51(4): 42–46.

McQuail, D. (2002). *Mass Communication Theory*. London: Sage.

Merkelson, H. (2011). 'The double-edged sword of legitimacy in Public Relations'. *Journal of Communications Management* 15(2): 125–43.

Mickey, T. (2003). *Deconstructing Public Relations*. Hillsdale, NJ: Lawrence Erlbaum Associates.

Miles, S. (2001). *Social Theory in the Real World*. London: Sage.

Molleda, J.C. and A. Moreno (2006). 'The transitional socioeconomic and political environments of public relations in Mexico'. *Public Relations Review* 32, 104–09.

Moreno, A., Navarro, A. Zerfass and R. Tench. (2015). 'Does social media usage matter? An analysis of online practices and digital media perceptions of communication practitioners in Europe'. *Public Relations Review* 41(2): 242–53.

Moreno, A., P. Verhoeven, R. Tench and A. Zerfass (2014). 'Increasing power and taking a lead – What are practitioners really doing? Empirical evidence from European communications managers'. *International Public Relations Journal* 4(7): 73–94.

Moss, D., A. Newman and B. DeSanto (2004). Defining and redefining the core elements of management in public relations/corporate communications context: What do communication managers do? Paper presented at the 11th International Public Relations Research Symposium, Lake Bled, Slovenia.

Neff, B.D., G. Walker, M.F. Smith and P.J. Creedon (1999). 'Outcomes desired by practitioners and academics'. *Public Relations Review* 25(1): 29–44.

Oughton, L. (2004). 'Do we need core competences for local government communications?' in *Local Government Communication Leaders Development Programme, Ideas in Communication Leadership*. London: Improvement and Development Agency, pp.65–72.

Pieczka, M. (2002). 'Public relations expertise deconstructed'. *Media, Culture and Society* 24(3): 301–23.

Pieczka, M. (2002). 'Public relations expertise deconstructed'. *Media Culture and Society* 24(3): 301–23.

Pieczka, M. and J. L'Etang (2001). 'Public relations and the question of professionalism' in *Handbook of Public Relations*. R.L. Heath (ed.). Thousand Oaks, CA: Sage.

Proctor, R.W. and A. Duttan (1995) Skill Acquisition and Human Performance. London: Sage.

PRSA (Public Relations Society of America) (1999). (National Commission on Public Relations Education) A Port of Entry – public relations education for the 21st century. New York: PRSA.

PRSA (Public Relations Society of America) (2006) Education for the 21st Century. The Professional Bond. Public Relation Education and the Practice, PRSA (2006) www.compred.org/report/2006. Report of the Commission edited by J. VanSlyke Turk, November 2006.

Rawel, A. (2002). 'How far do professional associations influence the direction of public relations education?' *Journal of Communication Management* 7(1): 71–78.

Riedel, J. (2011). Was sind die Kompetenzen für Social Media? [which competencies are required in Social Media?] URL: http://social-media-experten.de/2011/03/16/was-sind-die-kompetenzen-fur-social-media/

Ruler, B. van, D. Verčič, G. Bütschi and B. Flodin (2000). The European Body of Knowledge on Public Relations / Communication Management: The Report of the Delphi Research Project 2000. Ghent/Ljubljana: European Association for Public Relations Education and Research.

Schick, E. and T. Mickeleit (2010). Ein Plädoyer für das PR-Volontariat. In: Bundesverband deutscher Pressesprecher (BdP) & Deutsche Public Relations Gesellschaft (DPRG) (Hrsg.): Das PR-Volontariat – PR-Qualifizierung in deutschen Agenturen und Unternehmen. Berlin, Germany: Helios Media.

Schirato, T. and S. Yell (2000). *Communication and Culture*. London: Sage.

Sha, B-L. (2011a). '2010 practice analysis: professional competencies and work categories in public relations today'. *Public Relations Review* 37(3):187–96.

Sha, B-L. (2011b). 'Does accreditation really matter in public relations practice? How age and experience compare to accreditation'. *Public Relations Review* 37(1): 1–11.

Sha, B-L. (2011c). 'Accredited vs. non-accredited: the polarization of practitioners in the public relations profession'. *Public Relations Review* 37(2): 121–28.

Singh, R. and R. Smyth (2001). 'Australian public relations: Status at the turn of the 21st century'. *Public Relations Review* 26(4): 387–401.

Sriramesh, K. (1996). 'Power distance and public relations: an ethnographic study of Southern Indian organizations' in *International Public Relations: A comparative analysis* (pp. 171–90). H.M. Culberton and N. Chen (eds). Mahwah, NJ: Lawrence Erlbaum Associates.

Szyszka, P. (1995). Öffentlichkeitsarbeit und Kompetenz: Probleme und Perspektiven künftiger Bildungsarbeit. In *PR-Ausbildung in Deutschland* (pp. 317–42). VS Verlag für Sozialwissenschaften.

Tench, R. (2003). 'Stakeholder influences on the writing skills debate: A reflective evaluation in the context of vocational business education'. *Journal of Further and Higher Education* 27(4), November.

Tench, R. and J. Fawkes (2005). Mind the gap – exploring attitudes to PR education between academics and employers. Paper presented at the Alan Rawel CIPR Academic Conference, University of Lincoln, March.

Tench, R. and D. Deflagbe. (2008). 'Towards a Global Curriculum: A summary of literature concerning public relations education, professionalism and globalisation'. Report for the Global Alliance of Public Relations and Communication Management, Leeds Metropolitan University, UK.

Tench, R., A. Zerfass, A. Moreno, D. Vercic, P. Verhoeven and A. Okay (2012). European Public Relations Skills and Innovation Programme, see www.leedsmet.ac.uk/ecopsi

Tench, R., P. Verhoeven and H. Juma (2015). 'Turn Around When Possible: Mapping European Communication Competences'. *Studies in Media and Communication* 3(2): December 2015.

Tench, R. and M. Konczos (2015). 'Mapping European communication practitioners' competencies – A review of the European Communication Professional Skills and Innovation Programme: ECOPSI'. *Pannon Management Review* 4(2–3): September 2015.

Tench, R. and A. Moreno (2015) 'Mapping communication management competencies for European practitioners: ECOPSI an EU study'. *Journal of Communication Management* 19(1): 39–61.

Tench, R., Verčič, A., Tkalac and H. Juma (2013) 'Contemporary Issues Impacting European Communication Competencies'. *Media Studies* 4(7): 111–23.

Theaker, A. (2004). 'Professionalism and regulation' in *Handbook of Public Relations*. A. Theaker (ed.). London: Routledge.

Turk, J.V., C. Botan and S.P. Morreale (1999). 'Meeting education challenges in the information age'. *Public Relations Review* 25(1): 1–4.

Valentini, C. (2010). 'Personalised networks of influence in public relations'. *Journal Of Communications Management* 14(2): 153–66.

van Ruler, B. and D. Verčič (eds) (2004). *Public Relations and Communication Management in Europe.* Berlin: de Gruter.

Valentini, C. (2010). 'Personalised networks of influence in public relations'. *Journal of Communications Management* 14(2): 153–66.

van Ruler, B. and D. Verčič (eds) (2004). *Public Relations and Communication Management in Europe.* Berlin: de Gruter.

Varey, R. (1997). 'Public relations in a new context: a corporate community of co-operation'. Paper presented at the 3rd Annual Conference of the Public Relations Educators' Forum.

Verčič, D., B. van Ruler, G. Butzchi and B. Flodin (2001). 'On the definition of public relations: A European view'. Public Relations Review 27(4): 373–87.

Verwey, S. (2000). 'Public relations: a new professionalism for a new millennium?' *Communicare* 19(2): 51–68, December.

von Bertalanffy, L. (1969). *General Systems Theory: Foundations, development, applications,* 2nd edn. New York: Braziller.

Wilcox, D.L., P.H. Ault and W.K. Agee (2003). *Public Relations: Strategies and Tactics,* 5th edn. New York: Addison–Wesley.

Wilkin, P. (2001). *The Political Economy of Global Communication: An introduction.* London: Pluto Press.

Windahl, S., B. Signitzer and J. Olson (1992). *Using Communication Theory.* London: Sage.

Winterton, J., F. Delamare-Le Deist and E. Stringfellow (2005) *Typology of Knowledge, Skills and Competences: Clarification of the Concept and Prototype.* Thessaloniki: CEDEFOP.

Zerfass, A. (1998). Management-Knowhow für Public Relations [Management Know How in Public Relations]. In: *Medien Journal* 3/1998 – Public Relations: Qualifikation & Kompetenzen, pp. 3–15.

Zerfass, A., A. Moreno, R. Tench, D. Verčič and P. Verhoeven (2008) European Communication Monitor 2008. Trends in Communication Management and Public Relations – Results and Implications Brussels, Leipzig: Euprera / University of Leipzig, November 2008 Available as a free PDF document at www.communicationmonitor.eu

Zerfass, A., A. Moreno, R. Tench, D. Verčič and P. Verhoeven (2010). European Communication Monitor 2010. Status Quo and Challenges for Communication Management in Europe. Results of an empirical study in 46 countries. Brussels, Leipzig: Euprera/University of Leipzig Available at: www.communicationmonitor.eu.

Zerfass, A., A. Moreno, R. Tench, D. Verčič and P. Verhoeven (2009). European Communication Monitor 2009. Trends in Communication Management and Public Relations— Results of a survey in 34 countries. Brussels, Leipzig: Euprera/University of Leipzig Available at: www.communicationmonitor.eu.

Zerfass, A., P. Verhoeven, R. Tench, A. Moreno and D. Verčič (2011). European Communication Monitor 2011. Empirical Insights into Strategic Communication in Europe. Results of an Empirical Survey in 43 Countries. Brussels: EACD, EUPRERA.

Zerfass, A., D. Verčič, D., P. Verhoeven, A. Moreno and R. Tench (2015). European Communication Monitor 2015. Creating communication value through listening, messaging and measurement. Results of a Survey in 41 Countries. Brussels: EACD/EUPRERA, Helios Media.

Zerfass, A., R. Tench, D. Verčič, P. Verhoeven and A. Moreno (2014). European Communication Monitor 2014. Excellence in Strategic Communication – Key Issues, Ledership, Gender and Mobile Media. Results of a Survey in 42 Countries. Brussels: EACD/EUPRERA, Helios Media.

Zerfass, A., A. Moreno, R. Tench, D. Verčič and P. Verhoeven (2013). European Communication Monitor 2013. A Changing Landscape – Managing Crises, Digital Communication and CEO Positioning in Europe. Results of a Survey in 43 Countries. Brussels: EACD/EUPRERA, Helios Media.

Zerfass, A., D. Verčič, P. Verhoeven, A. Moreno and R. Tench (2012). European Communication Monitor 2012. Challenges and Competencies for Strategic Communication. Results of an Empirical Survey in 42 Countries. Brussels: EACD/EUPRERA, Helios Media.

www.awpagesociety.com 'The Authentic Enterprise' White Paper 2008.

PART 2

Public relations theories and concepts

There is no one unifying 'public relations theory'. This section will demonstrate that public relations is multifaceted and can be interpreted through a number of relevant theoretical perspectives. The key theoretical discussions in Chapter 8 take us from theories that describe how a profession ought to behave (normative theories) through to alternative theoretical approaches drawn from rhetorical and feminist perspectives, and postmodern and socio-cultural theories. Chapter 9 introduces our first 'concept': public relations as planned communication, in which public relations is presented as a strategic management process for achieving organisational objectives. Continuing the planning theme, Chapter 10 discusses the role of programme research and evaluation in the public relations process. Chapter 11 delves more deeply into the challenges technology and media change is creating as it explores disinformation, fake news and the management of social realities. There is sometimes confusion around the concepts of image, reputation and identity. Chapter 12 attempts to unpack this confusion as well as firmly identify these concepts as important to understanding public relations within a corporate context. Finally, the ethical issues raised by public relations and its role in society inevitably leads to a discussion of public relations' professionalism and ethics, which is found in Chapter 13.

CHAPTER 8

Martina Topić

Public relations theories
Communication, relationships and persuasion

Source: Reinhard Dirscherl/Alamy Stock Photo

Learning outcomes

By the end of this chapter you should be able to:
- understand the role of communication and its link with public relations
- understand how people communicate, and why communication theories are relevant to PR practitioners
- understand the importance of public relations theories for PR practitioners
- be able to apply public relations theories to practical cases
- understand how communication theories and social psychology theories can be useful to PR practitioners.

Structure

- Communication theories and public relations
- Relationship theories of public relations
- Elaboration likelihood model
- Theory of planned behaviour
- Stages of change model
- Nudge theory
- Inoculation theory
- Cognitive dissonance theory

Introduction

This chapter offers an overview of theories that can be of use for public relations (PR) practitioners. Since PR is ultimately about communicating with publics, we will firstly start with *communication theories* in PR, which describe how the communication process works. We will then continue with a group of theories also considered to form part of communication theories in PR, i.e. *relationships theories* that discuss what are the relations are between PR practitioners and the public. After that, we will discuss persuasion theories and models, namely theory of planned behaviour, elaboration likelihood model, stages of change model, inoculation theory, nudge theory and cognitive dissonance.

This chapter introduces communication and relationship theories and builds on these to link communication to persuasion theories and models. While persuasion theories and models were developed in the field of social psychology they still have relevance for PR practice (Pfau and Wan 2006), and therefore they are the subject of analysis in this chapter.

Excellence scholars have tried to distance themselves from persuasion, and thus the Excellence theory came as a result of that process. For that reason, refreshing knowledge of this theory is essential so that readers can fully engage with persuasion theory, as well as criticism of the Excellence theory from the persuasion theorists and advocates. The communication approach is however central to an understanding of PR in this chapter and communication approach is inextricably linked with persuasion theories. Therefore, a shorter version of communication theories that can be used in PR opens this chapter to refresh the memory of our readers, and thus enables them to fully engage with new theories presented in subsequent sections of the chapter.

Communication theories in public relations

Debating communication theories in public relations means seeing PR as a form of communication. Nevertheless, PR practitioners are seen as part of the communications industry, because they plan communication campaigns. While the field of communication is rich and well researched, this does not mean that all PR practitioners turn to theories when embarking on campaign design, even though they should because, to paraphrase Lewin (1943), there is nothing so practical as a good theory. However, concepts from communication theories can be found in PR campaigns, but there is evidence that PR practitioners tend to use technical approach to PR campaigning rather than the research one (Windahl et al. 1992; Butterick 2011; van Ruler 2005).

However, since the success of PR campaigning largely relies on understanding people's behaviour, attitudes and communication, being able to conduct research and analyse potential publics can help in designing better communication messages and thus create more successful PR campaigns.

There is no single theory that can claim to provide all knowledge about the communication process and its effects; however, there are many different communication theories and approaches that help in explaining how communication works. Nevertheless, it will be up to each PR practitioner to put these theories into practice and decide on the spot which one to apply when designing communication campaigns.

Communication is the most important aspect of human life because we communicate both verbally and non-verbally. Both aspects of communication are important for PR practitioners because we have to make sense not only of *what people say* but also what *they do not* say (Littlejohn 2002). For example, according to psychological research, 96 per cent of face-to-face communication falls to non-verbal communication such as body language (Stainton Rogers 2011).

The ground-breaking development in the communication field was the development of the mass media communication and the growth of communications technology, and these developments were followed with developments in marketing communications and advertising (Butterick 2011; Littlejohn 2002), and then also PR.

Harold Laswell analysed communication from the point of behavioural psychological theory and with the case study from Nazi Germany, famous for its propagandistic techniques in mass communication that ensured large support from the German population towards Hitler's notorious regime. Laswell's well-known communication model centred on asking the following questions, 'Who? Says what? In which channel? To whom? With what effect?' (Laswell 1948: 37). This way of analysing the communication message enables understanding of the effects of communication (Figure 8.1).

Who → Says what → In which → To whom → With what
Communicator   Message   Medium   Receiver   Effect

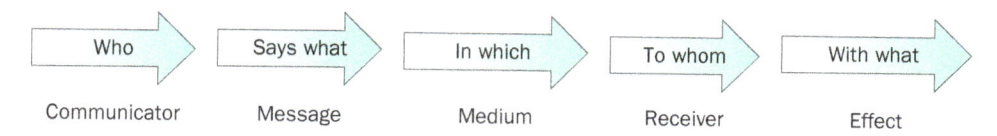

Figure 8.1 Laswell's model of Communication (*source:* 'Lasswell, H. D. (1948). The structure and function of communication in society. In L. Bryson (Ed.), The communication of ideas (pp. 37-51). New York: Harper and Row.')

Laswell's research was largely influenced by the growth of mass media and the influence of the media on the population. However, Laswell's core questions remain fundamental for the analysis of every communication process regardless of the method we are using for analysis.

Shannon and Weaver (1949) added to Laswell's theory and developed the so-called Linear Model of Communication based on the Information Theory that also takes into consideration effects of the communication process and not just its description. In other words, Shannon and Weaver (1949) thought of communication as a process that involves a source that selects the message, which is then transmitted via the transmitter to the receiver over a certain channel. However, both of these models are based on a one-way communication model, while there are scholars who are calling for two-way communication as a way of achieving excellence in PR.

The two-way communication model is based on Lazarsfeld's and Katz's (1955) research on media effects during election campaigns. They developed a Two-step Communication Model to explain how the mass media communicate with publics by emphasising the role of influencers that spread the information from the mass media to the audience (Katz and Lazarsfeld 1955).

What is fundamental to PR is the *necessity to understand who we are communicating with* and to understand communicating with groups, i.e. when we develop PR campaigns we are always targeting one specific group of people. Groups in public relations are usually called 'publics' while in mass communication and media studies the term used for groups is 'audience'. The audience thus presents a group of people who will receive the communication that might have an *effect*, while publics represent a group that will receive the communication as well as be *affected* by that communication.

Think about 8.1

Think whether you ever heard anyone using the expression crazy when talking about a girl who is showing some characteristics of a leader or anger. What did you think about it then? How did it make you feel about yourself and/or about girls in your life? What do you think about the issue after you became aware of the campaign? Do you think that PR can change the perception of girls as not being suitable for certain roles, and empower them? Do you think it is the role of PR to entice social change? Do you think that brands should be ambassadors and champions of social change?

Now, look at the series of films in Always' Like a girl' campaign. Analyse differences and similarities between the Always campaigns and the Nike campaign. Then analyse mission statements from both companies that launched campaigns and see how this form of social campaigning fits into the organisational mission.

Which of the two campaigns did you like more? Why?

Explore 8.1

Analyse the American brand Nike and its PR campaigns entitled 'Dream Crazier' (https://www.youtube.com/watch?v=whpJ19RJ4JY).

Think what were the central messages of the campaigns? What model of communication did Nike use in their campaign? Which PR theory best describes this model of communicating in these PR campaigns? Was there an impact on publics, and which one? Was there a media coverage and reputation issue because of this campaign (positive or negative)?

Relationships theories of public relations

Views on how PR practitioners should communicate with the public differ. In that, a very influential theory in public relations scholarship is relationship theory (which encompasses also systems theory and situational theory). This theory is relevant also because it is developed by PR scholars and thus contributes towards establishing of PR as a recognised academic discipline. In the following two sections, we will explain the basic focus of these theories, and in the subsequent section, these theories will be discussed against persuasion theories.

Systems theory of public relations

Systems theory of PR emerged in the second half of the twentieth century, and this theory starts from the view of PR practitioners working for an organisation that has PR activities, which are meant to achieve/increase benefits for the organisation (Edwards 2014). The first advocates of this approach were James E. Grunig and Todd Hunt (1984) who developed a typology of PR.

Systems theory, if looking from the point of view of the organisation, is about communicating in a way to create relationships in order to achieve organisational goals (Lattimore et al. 2009). According to Grunig et al. (2002) organisations are interdependent with their environment that includes customers, potential employees, and suppliers. In this, there are two types of organisation, open systems organisations and closed systems organisations. In the first case, PR brings the information collected among publics and based on the feedback they are looking at how to enhance this relationship. On the other hand, closed system organisations do not seek feedback from publics but operate based on previous experiences and personal preferences (Lattimore et al. 2009).

Grunig and Hunt (1984) also developed a typology of publics by explaining that the publics are a group of people sharing the same view on an issue regardless of their origin. The four types of publics are:

- **non-public** (where there is no impact between the organisation and the public over each other);
- **latent** (where a group is endangered by the organisation, however, there is no awareness or collective action against it);
- **aware** (where a certain group recognises there is a problem); and
- **active** (where a certain group recognises the problem and then organises collective action to solve the problem).

Grunig and Hunt (1984) believed that common mistake PR practitioners make is by starting the communication with groups only when an action is organised, instead of developing the communication earlier and during the decision-making process. Instead, they proposed a typology of four models of PR, arguing there are four types of practices in the industry, and emphasising that not all four models give equal importance to publics. Clearly, Grunig and Hunt considered publics as the core of everything that public relations do. In terms of the four models of PR, they proposed the:

- **press agentry/publicity** model;
- **public information** model;
- **two-way asymmetric** model; and
- **two-way symmetric** model (Grunig and Hunt 1984).

In the first case, the foundation for identifying the model is based on the history of PR and as such, it derives from the analysis of nineteenth-century PR practitioners such as press agents and publicists who are considered as some sort of precursor to present-day public relations. The goal of these practitioners was to get as much publicity as possible, and they used selective information to persuade people to act in certain ways and to get as much as possible media coverage. Grunig and Hunt (1984: 21) linked this type of activity directly to propaganda by saying 'Public Relations serves a propaganda function in the press agentry/publicity model. Practitioners spread the faith of the organisation involved, often through incomplete, distorted or half-true information'.

On the other hand, the second model is also based on the historical example of PR practice in the US such as the work of big companies that dominated the US economy, particularly in the last century. These companies were involved in sending information to the public and following the rule that the public must be informed. The focus on the necessity of informing the public is founded in the work of Ivy Lee often considered as the first PR practitioner (IPR 2012), and even though the public is informed about activities of the organisation this model is considered as unsatisfactory because it is a one-way communication with an intention to persuade. The only difference between the first and the second model is there is no attempt to deceive the public because the information is not selected in a way that can cause misinterpretation since the model is based on honesty in communication. Grunig and Hunt proposed this model in 1984 when this approach to PR was the most commonly used model and the internet and communication via websites and social media were not available as they are now.

The third model is the two-way asymmetric model associated with the work of Edward Bernays (1923; 1927; 1945), who approached communication by trying to build its foundation in an approach. This model is similar to the first model of press agentry just that this model is not making an attempt to solely persuade the publics by manipulating them as press agents did in the past. Instead, this model uses persuasion in a different way, and it does not rely on manipulation and deceiving but on behavioural change supposed to be achieved for the purpose of the client. The only intention is to improve the message to achieve either sale of a product or to foster behavioural change, and the persuasive element is found in feedback the company gets from the public. This feedback is then used to persuade the public to support the organisation or to buy the product. In this sense, this is a two-way communication because publics are communicating with companies, and this model is the most commonly used model among PR practitioners who work for a client.

Finally, the two-way symmetric model is an ideal model where PR listens to the public and changes according to the public's needs and desires. This is then considered as a real dialogue with the stakeholders, and this model is clearly linked with corporate social responsibility (CSR) where the stakeholder theory has taken over in public debates on the expectations of businesses (Tench et al. 2014). However, because it is the PR department that engages in dialogue with the publics and launches social initiatives, there is a lot of scepticism about CSR as part of PR and the promotional mix to promote products and services. Speaking of the two-way symmetric model, the communication process is considered as symmetric in a sense both parties are equal in the communication and there is no attempt to persuade the publics from the side of corporations. This approach is mostly found in campaigns from charities in their communication with publics although other models of communication can be found in charity campaigns as well.

Following this initial research, Grunig and Hunt (1984) then conducted extensive research on the PR practice in the US and developed an Excellence approach in PR arguing that excellent PR encompasses four different levels in the organisation. However, excellence in PR was still seen through meeting the organisation's goals, and thus the excellence approach still forms part of the systems theory. This is visible in Grunig's (1992) definition of the effectiveness of PR, which is clearly linked to excellence, i.e.:

Public relations contributes to organisational effectiveness when it helps to reconcile the organisation's goals with the expectations of its strategic constituencies. This contribution has monetary value to the organisation. Public relations contributes to effectiveness by building quality, long-term relationships with strategic constituencies. Public Relations is most likely to contribute to effectiveness of when the senior PR manager is a member of the dominant coalition (that is the ruling group who actually run a company) where he or she is able to shape the organisation's goals and help determine which external publics are most strategic.

(Grunig, 1992: 156)

This approach clearly takes into consideration expectations of what later, with the rise of influence of CSR, became known as stakeholders or stakeholder orientation (Freeman 1984; 2010; Freeman et al. 2010; Tench et al. 2014). However, the difference between CSR orientation and this orientation is in the view of stakeholders as strategic constituencies where stakeholders are seen to have strategic importance for the benefit of the organisation, and not in itself. The crucial aspect of this strategic relationship is on communication that can be one-way and two-way, as well as symmetric and asymmetric.

In Grunig's (1992) view, two-way symmetric communication is of crucial importance for excellent PR. Nowadays, symmetric communication is linked with ethical communication and understood as good for PR as a profession (Brown 2010; Cutlip et al. 2000; Edwards 2014). However, the theory has faced criticism because of the idealistic nature of symmetric communication whereas PR is seen as a profession primarily dictated by the self-interest and not a genuine will to do good for the wider society (L'Etang and Piezcka 1996). The criticism of symmetric communication as an unachieved ideal can be linked to the general criticism of PR as an industry based on spin and deceiving the publics to achieve the client's goals. This criticism and the fact many attempts to do good by companies are labelled as 'just PR', prompted some scholars to defend PR as a discipline and to emphasise its good sides (Coombs and Holladay 2007).

In addition, the theory has been challenged from the cultural side because it only focuses on American organisational culture, which does not apply to all other cultures for this theory presents one general theory of PR and excellence in PR. The main criticism of PR scholars advocating the cultural approach is that PR practice will be shaped by cultural and social expectations of each country, political system, economic system, political economy, the media system and the forms of activism (Sriramesh and Vercic 1995; Sriramesh 2010).

Finally, the approach has been criticised from the side of persuasion authors who stated that the Excellence theory's main attempt is to create a public relations theory and to distance public relations from persuasion, and by doing so, scholars who promote the Excellence theory are confusing means and ends of public relations as a profession (Pfau and Wan 2006). This criticism is explored in detail in the section on persuasion in this chapter.

Situational theory in public relations

Grunig and Repper (1992) argued that organisations should communicate with their stakeholders, however, they also recognised this is not always possible because not all stakeholders are interested in having a dialogue with the organisation. On the other hand, it is not even possible to communicate with absolutely all stakeholders and, therefore, a new approach was needed if the dialogue was to become a part of the organisational goals.

Therefore, Grunig and Repper (1992) identified publics as members of sub-groups that need to be monitored purposely. For example, when it comes to elections only active voters among all voters who registered should be given attention (Lattimore et al. 2009). Grunig and Hunt (1984) then called this approach a situational theory arguing that organisations need to assess publics' communication needs by dividing publics to those who actively seek information and to those who only passively receive the information.

According to Grunig and Hunt (1984) three variables will predict when publics seek information, i.e. problem recognition (publics must be aware of an issue at stake), constraint recognition (perceived obstacles towards resolving the issue among publics), and level of involvement (how much individual members of publics care for the issue) (Lattimore et al. 2009).

The theory is clearly related to segmentation as PR practitioners must learn how to identify the appropriate stakeholders and then develop an approach to reach them and achieve effective support (McKeever et al. 2015; Kim 2011; Grunig 1989; Grunig and Hunt 1984; Grunig and Repper 1992). According to the situational theory, segmentation of publics must be done before and after public relations action in order to ensure that the population is broken down into strategic subgroups such as 'active/activist public, aware public, latent public, and non-public' (Kim 2011: 2), and an often used method is summation that categorises the population in an additional way by taking the population categories discussed above and then categorising them to groups based on the issue at stake (Kim 2011). In order to ensure that the categorisation processes do not fail, PR practitioners must monitor issues and organisational responses as well as activism to be able to segment the publics in an efficient way.

This theory is particularly useful for campaigns tackling sensitive issues, and where there is a threat of activism of critical NGOs. NGOs are often able to initiate protests and consumer boycotts, and being able to assess to what extent publics are aware of the problem as well as doing research to find out to what extent people care about the problem, can help organisations in communicating their policies to the public. For example, if we know there are many people in the local community who care about a certain issue and who find organisational involvement in the local community negative, it is necessary to approach the public and communicate the position of the organisation straight away.

A good example can be found in changes to the diet in schools in the UK, which initiated protests in Rotherham where parents were seen passing burgers to their children through the school fence, arguing the schools were not giving them what they needed (Wainwright 2006). Jamie Oliver's Ministry of Food opened in Rotherham and he, as a celebrity chef went there to use his popularity to argue for changes and acceptance among members of the public. However, he faced opposition from parents led by Julie Critchlow, who he eventually hired to cook with him first to gain support among the local population (Renton 2008). This example shows why the Government failed in communicating health changes and why they needed help from Jamie Oliver, i.e. by not identifying the problem and assuming that people will immediately accept a new policy, they ended up with protests and even worse dietary habits. Appropriate segmentation of the British public would have helped in prevention had there been a segmented communication of the reasons why diet has changed.

Nevertheless, research conducted in the United States showed that the situational theory can also explain fundraising and charity campaigning, as well as help charities in increasing donations if adopting an appropriate approach. For example, McKeever et al. (2015) explored fundraising events and found that charities need to develop messages aimed at creating positive attitudes amongst the members of the public in fundraising events to initiate situational support, i.e. a donation on the event will occur if people will perceive the aim positively and if the aim is communicated in a way that enables changing attitudes and behaviours.

In other words, the situational theory of publics has the ability to explain when and why people seek information and the decision-making process following communication (Grunig 2003; 1989; Kim and Grunig 2011). The theory uses three variables to explain and predict communication behaviour, i.e. problem recognition, level of involvement, and constraint recognition.

Or, 'a person who perceives a problem, a connection to it, and few obstacles to doing something about it are likely to seek and attend to information about the problem' (Kim and Grunig 2011: 121). On the other hand, when it comes to problem-solving, the publics will go through three processes, i.e. information selection, information transmission, and information acquisition (ibid.). The extent to which each element will be explored depends on personal involvement with the issue. This personal involvement is explained in the mini picture in the chart on the situational theory of publics where the problem solving also depends on the level of involvement that influences ways and the extent to which the person will seek information about an issue, i.e. the extent the person cares and feels personally involved.

Persuasion theories

Persuasion presents an interesting and well-researched field in PR and other similar disciplines, such as media studies and social psychology. However, there has been an attempt to distance from persuasion amongst PR scholars (Pfau and Wan 2006). The reason for this is that most commonly cited work in PR related to persuasion comes from one of the alleged fathers of PR, Edward Bernays. Critics like to quote his theory and definition of persuasion to portray that the whole history of PR is a history of spin. Bernays (1955) argued that persuasion is inherent to PR practice and in that he stated that PR practitioners use 'information, persuasion, and adjustment to engineer public support for an activity, cause, movement, or institution' (Bernays 1955: 3–4). Bernays also argued that PR professionals achieve engineered consent through the creation of 'symbols which the public will respond to, analysing the responses of the public, finding strategies that resonate with receivers, and adapting communication to receivers' (Bernays 1923: 173).

The persuasion theory is somewhat in conflict with the Excellence theory explained earlier in this chapter. As already mentioned, Excellence theory is the only PR theory developed specifically for the PR field and by PR scholars with which the theory helps in professionalising PR as a profession. However, some scholars argued that distancing too much from persuasion is flawed because persuasion is inherent to PR, and the fact publics are being persuaded by PR practitioners does not necessarily mean that persuasion is unethical, as some scholars stipulate.

For example, Pfau and Wan (2006) emphasised that James Grunig and his associates led the way in distancing PR from persuasion to develop a two-way symmetrical approach, which emphasises the need for mutual understanding and shared interests as opposed to what they perceived as the two-way asymmetrical model proposed by Bernays. As opposed to this, Pfau and Wan (2006) see PR as strategic communication in which persuasion forms an inherent part. Pfau and Wan (2006) therefore define persuasion in PR as 'the use of communication in an attempt to shape, change, and/or reinforce perception, affect (feelings), cognition (thinking), and/or behaviour' (Pfau and Wan 2006: 102). In this way, Pfau and Wan (2006) argue that persuasion is inherent to PR practice because many of the core practices of PR profession require persuasion to succeed (e.g. media relations, community relations, crisis communication) (ibid.).

The support for persuasion in PR can be found in the work of other PR scholars too. For example, Miller (1989) argued that persuasion and PR are two Ps of PR practice and this is the case because PR is essentially advocacy (Jones 1955), whether for a social cause or the organisation. In other words, PR practitioners are always engaged with advocacy either to maintain or improve organisational reputation or to persuade publics to back a certain cause. The fact advocacy is pivotal to PR practice is recognised by several scholars in the field, including Grunig who developed the Excellence theory that seeks to distance PR from persuasion (Grunig and Grunig 1992; Barney and Black 1994). Grunig also argued that 'many, if not most, practitioners consider themselves to be advocates for or defenders of their organisations and cite the advocacy system in law as an analogy' (Grunig and Grunig 1990: 32).

However, PR scholars who embrace the Excellence theory agree with Grunig that two-way symmetrical model is more ethical than persuasive models because it is based on shared interest and mutual understanding between an organisation and its publics (Grunig and Grunig 1992). Thus, understanding is more important than persuading, however, some scholars disagree with this view and argue that the Excellence theory is an attempt to erase the roots of PR in communication and social psychology of communication (Pfau and Wan 2006) and the reason for this also lies in bad reputation of both persuasion and public relations' link with this practice because of which some PR practitioners become defensive when challenged about the morality of their profession. Thus, the name of the PR job role is getting changed to corporate communications and other titles (Barney and Black 1994; Seitel 1998; Pfau and Wan 2006). Authors therefore suggest that Excellence theory neglects different goals that evidently exist between organisation and the publics (Vasquez 1996), in which case Grunig's statement that organisations can find a solution through conversation is tautological because 'incompatible goals are, by their very nature, often intractable and defy magical transformation into compatible goals by virtue of the use of public relations process' (Pfau and Wan 2006, p. 104). In other words, interests of organisations and publics are rarely aligned (Murphy 1991) and thus persuasive advocacy is often needed.

A good example to explain how there may be a conflict between publics and the organisation is Bernays' campaign from the 1929 entitled 'Torches of Freedom' where he hired influential suffragettes to publicly smoke during the Easter Day parade to encourage more women to smoke and become product users, as desired by his client, a tobacco company. In that, he portrayed smoking as women's liberation which was against societal views of the time where women who smoked were frowned upon and where women were facing all sorts of barriers in social and political life. In other words, women were encouraged to light up 'torches of freedom' and smoking has been portrayed as coming a long way towards women liberation.

Critics often say that this campaign is an example of persuasive communication with an intention to deceive and that Bernays' use of propaganda and persuasive communication did not win the PR industry friends. Nevertheless, 'in a letter to President Franklin Roosevelt, Supreme Court Justice Felix Frankfurter described Bernays and Lee as "professional poisoners of the public mind, exploiters of foolishness, fanaticism and self-interest"' (Stauber and Rampton 1995: 24). However, at the time when cigarettes were promoted, it was not known that tobacco was harmful to health (see an interview with Bernays at Spector PR, 2010). According to staunch critiques of the PR industry Stauber and Rampton (1995), it was only in the early 1950s that scientific studies started to show that smoking tobacco can cause cancer, and it wasn't until 1952 that *Reader's Digest* ran an article entitled 'Cancer by the Carton' whereas a 1953 report by Dr Ernst L. Wynder provided more evidence that smoking can cause cancer. The tobacco industry then again turned to PR for help, but this time it wasn't Bernays who ran the campaign. It was John Hill from PR firm Hill and Knowlton (ibid.).

Therefore, with 'Torches of Freedom' campaign, Bernays made an impact on suffragette's campaign for women liberation while also serving interests of the client, which can be seen through utilitarian theory as acceptable. Nevertheless, in his book 'Propaganda' he recommended the use of propaganda to women to achieve equality and he also emphasised that women can organise and 'use their newly acquired freedom in a great many ways to mold the world into a better place to live' (Bernays 2005 [1928]: 134), with which he expressed feminist views. But, in terms of symmetrical and asymmetrical model, in this particular case, it would not be possible to deploy a two-way symmetrical model because there was no consensus amongst publics and thus advocacy and persuasion were necessary since 'prior to World War I, smoking cigarettes was considered unrefined for women and effeminate for men (. . .) The war brought cigarettes into vogue for men, and during the Roaring Twenties, the American Tobacco Company turned to PR to develop a vast new market – American women – for sales of its Lucky Strike brand' (Stauber and Rampton 1995: 25).

This also leads to the question of means and ends in PR practice. In other words, persuasion is often seen as unethical, and this particularly applies to Bernays' practice because Bernays emphasised persuasion (and propaganda) as inherent to PR practice, which some scholars then saw as manipulation of the public in favour of clients (Grunig 1989b; Grunig and White 1992). Pfau and Wan (2006) add to this that while persuasion is inherently manipulative this does not mean it is always unethical. In other words, 'there is nothing inherently unethical about means or ends. Rather, both means and ends require scrutiny for their ethical appropriateness' (Pfau and Wan 2006: 107). Miller (1989: 48) correctly argued that ethical issues are 'relevant to *particular* political, policy, or product ends and to the *specific* persuasive means used to pursue these ends' (emphasis in the original). Therefore, Pfau and Wan (2006: 107) correctly argue that 'it is ethically proper to employ legitimate tools of persuasion in the pursuit of legitimate ends'. Naturally, making up information and deceiving would be seen as unethical regardless of the end (Pfau and Wan 2006).

If going back to Bernays' 'Torches of Freedom' campaign this would mean that he did not act in an unethical way because women were indeed not allowed to smoke and thus giving them the same right did eventually encourage liberation of women due the attention of the press the campaign received. In addition, the campaign

Picture 8.1 Influential suffragettes were encouraged to light up 'torches of freedom' in Bernays' campaign (*source:* Popperfoto/Getty Images)

stands on utilitarianism, due to the fact the campaign provided the greatest benefit for a great number of people while those members of the public who were frowning upon women who smoked and sought liberation could not be seen as losers in this persuasive communication effect. In other words, John Stuart Mill (1859) argued that utilitarianism (or happiness theory, as he also called it) is, 'the creed which accepts as the foundation of morals, Utility, or the Greatest Happiness Principle, holds that actions are right in proportion as they tend to promote happiness, wrong as they tend to produce the reverse of happiness. By happiness is intended pleasure, and the absence of pain; by unhappiness, pain, and the privation of pleasure' (Mill 2015 [1859]: 121).

To be more specific, Mill did not mean that one who promotes something should be happy but quite the contrary, 'for that standard is not the agent's own greatest happiness, but the greatest amount of happiness altogether; and if it may possibly be doubted whether a noble character is always the happier for its nobleness, there can be no doubt that it makes other people happier, and that the world, in general, is immensely a gainer by it (. . .) According to the Greatest Happiness Principle (. . .) the ultimate end, with reference to and for the sake of which all other things are desirable (whether we are considering our own good or that of other people), is an existence exempt as far as possible from pain, and as rich as possible in enjoyments. . . ' (Mill 2015 [1859]: 125).

We know today that smoking is harmful to health, but as already emphasised, this was not the case back in the 1920s when Bernays launched the campaign. Many research studies have shown that equal societies 'are better to live in (. . .) and better for (Djerf-Pierre 2011: 43), and thus Bernays' PR practice has contributed towards women's liberation. In addition, universalism in ethics argues that 'morality should be judged on intentions and motives rather than consequences' (Weeks 2011: 264) and since Bernays's primary motive was to satisfy the client we could question his morality even though he did personally express feminist beliefs. However, this does not say anything about the use of persuasive communication as a legitimate means in campaigning. In other words, the Excellence theory and its distancing from persuasion by calling it manipulation are 'placing the ethical onus on means as opposed to ends' (Pfau and Wan 2006: 107).

Now have explained what persuasion is and how persuasion can be seen as ethical and inherent to PR practice, we will explain theories and models that are associated with persuasion and analysing human behaviour, i.e. elaboration likelihood model, the theory of planned behaviour, stages of change model, inoculation theory, nudge theory and cognitive dissonance theory.

Think about 8.2

Watch the campaign 'Unsung Hero' at this link: https://youtu.be/uaWA2GbcnJU

Now discuss this campaign in line with persuasive communication framework, and debate whether it was ethical for an insurance company to use emotional advertising. Use frameworks of persuasive communication and ethics to decide whether emotional advertising is ethical or not.

After that, watch the documentary film 'Starsuckers' and reflect on your initial ideas on emotional advertising based on criticism of the advertising industry in the film. You can watch the film free of charge using this link: https://topdocumentaryfilms.com/starsuckers/

Elaboration Likelihood Model

The Elaboration Likelihood Model (ELM) has been introduced by Cacioppo and Petty (1984) and it has been one of the most used models to analyse consumer behaviour so far (See Figure 8.2). However, the fact the model originally derives from the field of psychology and that it has been used to analyse consumer behaviour and reception to advertising does not mean this model cannot be of use in PR.

The ELM is a persuasive model, which proposes that people have central and peripheral routes in persuasive communication. Unlike cognitive response approach, the ELM sees recipients of messages indifferent towards persuasive appeals; however, recipients are then prone to persuasive influences due to a certain factor or a number of factors. Therefore, 'when conditions foster people's motivation and ability to engage in issue-relevant thinking, the elaboration likelihood is said to be high. This means that people are likely to (a) attend to the appeal; (b) attempt to access relevant associations, images, and experiences from memory; (c) scrutinise and elaborate upon the externally provided message arguments in light of the associations available from memory; (d) draw inferences about the merits of the arguments for a recommendation based upon their analyses of the data extracted from the appeal and accessed from memory; and (e) consequently derive an overall evaluation of, or attitude towards, the recommendation'. (Cacioppo and Petty 1984, n.p.).

This furthermore means that the central route to persuasion represents 'the processes involved when elaboration likelihood is high and the 'peripheral

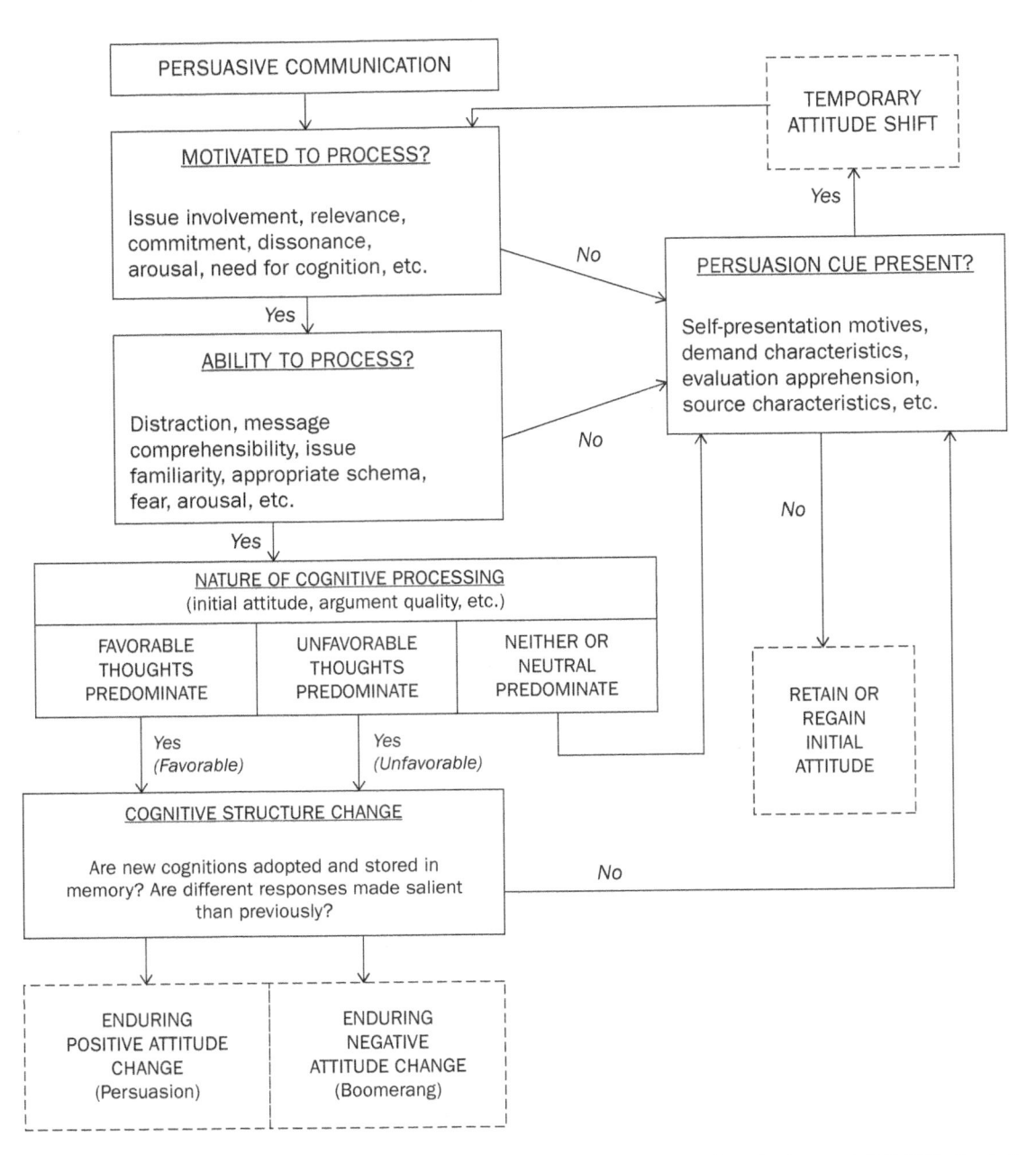

Figure 8.2 The Elaboration Likelihood Model (*source:* Adapted from Petty, R. E. and J.T. Cacioppo, J. T. (1983). Central and peripheral routes to persuasion: Application to advertising. Advertising and Consumer Psychology, 1, 3-23. Lexington, MA: D.C. Heath and Company (pp. 3-23))

route' typifying the processes operative when elaboration likelihood is low' (ibid). The idea of the ELM is that when elaboration likelihood is low recipients will focus on other tasks and processes and thus the message may not be persuasive whereas when the elaboration likelihood is high it is more likely that recipients will be persuaded by the message (ibid.).

The ELM is concentrated on analysing two routes of cognitive reception among consumers (or publics). Or, 'when we are motivated and able to pay attention, we take a logical, conscious thinking, central route to decision-making. This can lead to a permanent change in our attitude as we adopt and elaborate upon the speaker's arguments. In other cases, we take the peripheral route. Here we do not pay attention to persuasive arguments but are swayed instead by surface characteristics such as whether we like the speaker. In this case, although we do change, it is only temporary (although it is to a state where we may be susceptible to further change)' (Changing Minds 2019).

The theory thus works with an assumption that there are four groups of people, 'Gullible people who are easily influenced; Skeptic, opinionated and argumentative people who cannot be easily influenced; People with firm beliefs but with bad communication skills; People who are leaders, who trust others as well as make others follow their thinking and ideas' (Maharjan 2018, n.p.).

Recently, the ELM has been used in environmental campaigning. Manca and associates (2019) looked at designing persuasive messages to change people's behaviour when it comes to choosing transport. They looked at past behaviour, attitude and emotions as variables that can predict behaviour. The results have shown that feelings of fear and guilt had the most impact on behaviour, i.e.' feelings concerning the negative consequences of a potential unsustainable behaviour prove to be the main predictor of both the rational-intentional proenvironmental choice and the automatic unaware proenvironmental preference' (Manca et al. 2019: 22). In addition, the feeling of fear or risk has also shown success. Therefore, the authors concluded that the ELM can be of good use for environmental campaigning, especially if past behaviour is taken into consideration.

In summary, the ELM has been used for decades and it has almost like a celebrity status in marketing and advertising literature. As such, the model can be used in public relations due to its explanatory power. However, this does not mean that the model has been without criticism. Questions have been raised as to whether the ELM is still applicable in digital time when consumers are more empowered and when we are processing multiple channels every day. In other words, Kitchen and associates (2014) argued that the model was developed in the 1980s during the time of the mass media proliferation and this means that those who are planning campaigns using this model may be using planning from the 1980s when message processing was different.

Nevertheless, Kitchen and associates (2014) questioned the descriptiveness of the model and the lack of replicability when conducting research using the ELM. In addition, some authors questioned whether persuasion 'will be elaborated on under central route conditions is confounded because attitude change can potentially occur under other means. That is, a lack of evidence of attitude change does not mean an absence of persuasion, but rather that one particular form of persuasion failed under those particular circumstances' (ibid.: 2038–2039; see also Cook et al. 2004).

Nevertheless, whether one accepts criticism of the ELM or not, this model can still be used at least in analysing consumer demographics and predicting which route to use for persuasive communication.

Mini case study 8.1
PETA's Go Veg Campaign (International)

PETA launched the 'Go Veg' campaign to encourage veganism, which further contributes towards their campaigning for animal rights. In that, PETA provided detailed guidance on what to buy, what to make and where to eat.

PETA also included some facts and figures about veganism and thus alerted its readers that each person who stops eating meat saves more than 100 animals a year (PETA 2019). The campaign website also provided a video encouraging readers to view the video to see what kind of cruelty they will be stopping if they go vegan (https://www.peta.org/issues/animals-used-for-food/factory-farming/).

The campaign website also offers a free guide (vegan starter kit) which anyone can order.

In addition, the website guides readers to PETA's other websites such as learning how to wear vegan (PETA, 2019b) and this website again gives guidance on what to wear, where to shop and what materials should be avoided, which is similar to the go vegan website.

This campaign is a good example of the use of Elaboration Likelihood model due to the fact that messages are communicated persuasively and are trying to provide a variety of information that will appeal to people's central route.

Picture 8.2 PETA launched the 'Go Veg' campaign to encourage veganism, which further contributes towards their campaigning for animal rights (*source:* marlee/Shutterstock)

Explore 8.2

Explore PETA's website 'Go Veg' and design a PR campaign to re-enforce the brand message. Consider communication models discussed earlier in the chapter, as well as persuasive communication. In particular, consider the elaboration likelihood model and how this model was applied in the campaign.

After you write up your campaign proposal, justify it from an ethical point of view as discussed at the beginning of the persuasive communication section. For example, comment on whether your campaign proposal meets utilitarian argument, whether your message is persuasive, and if so, whether it is truthful and aims towards a greater good.

After that, watch the following video on ELM: https://youtu.be/EC7VLjIw8hY

After you have watched the video, find other advertising examples of food campaigning and discuss them against PETA's videos and your own ideas.

Think about 8.3

Visit the campaign website 'Tips for former smokers' launched by the US Center for Disease Control and Prevention to tackle smoking. The campaign website is available at this link: https://www.cdc.gov/tobacco/campaign/tips/index.html

Analyse all campaign materials using the Elaboration Likelihood Model. Consider the feelings associated with the campaign after you read the materials. Did reading made you want to know more? If you are a smoker, how did you feel when you read the campaign materials? Identify the route through which you processed the information from the campaign. Following personal reflection, look for other health campaigning examples and compare the messages.

Theory of Planned Behaviour

The Theory of Planned Behaviour was originally proposed by Ajzen (1988; 1991) and this theory up to today presents a very influential framework for studying human behaviour. This theory could be of particular use to PR practitioners as the theory tends to explain how humans behave and act, which can be beneficial when attempting to build relationships with them.

According to this theory, 'human behaviour is guided by three kinds of considerations: beliefs about likely consequences or other attributes of the behaviour (behavioural beliefs), beliefs about the normative expectations of other people (normative beliefs), and beliefs about the presence of factors that may further or hinder performance of the behaviour (control beliefs)' (Ajzen 2002: 665).

This furthermore means that each of these beliefs has a consequence or 'behavioural beliefs produce a favourable or unfavourable *attitude toward the behaviour*; normative beliefs result in perceived social pressure or *subjective norm*; and control beliefs give rise to *perceived behavioural control,* the perceived ease or difficulty of performing the behaviour. In combination, attitude toward the behaviour, subjective norm, and perception of behavioural control lead to the formation of a behavioural intention' (ibid., emphasis in the original).

This theory came as a result of social psychology research, which was consistently showing that attitudes do not necessarily influence behaviour (Terry et al. 1999). For example, studies assessing attitudes towards organisations and institutions, minority groups as well as individuals have failed to predict the actual behaviour, and thus some scholars called for abandoning the attitude research concept (Wicker 1969). This then gave rise to the theory of planned behaviour, which then postulated that 'by aggregating different behaviours, observed on different occasions and in different situations, these other sources or influence tend to cancel each other, with the result that the aggregate represents a more valid measure of the underlying behavioural disposition than any single behaviour' (Ajzen 1991: 180). This does not mean that aggregate analysis of behaviour is the only solution to understanding human behaviour. The aggregate analysis is meant to demonstrate 'that general attitudes and personality traits *are* implicated in human behaviour, but that their influence can be discerned only by looking at broad, aggregated, valid samples of behaviour' (ibid.: 181, emphasis in the original).

The theory of planned behaviour is a continuation of the theory of reasoned action (Ajzen and Fishbein 1980; Fishbein and Ajzen 1975). The reason theory of reasoned action was extended to the theory of planned behaviour is that the theory of reasoned action could not explain human responses to involuntary situations. A central factor 'in the theory of planned behaviour is the individual's *intention* to perform a given behaviour (. . .) As a general rule, the stronger the intention to engage in behaviour, the more likely should be its performance' (Ajzen 1991: 181, emphasis in the original). However, all of this is conditional to a person having control over their behaviour.

In practice, this means that we can analyse human behaviour accurately if three conditions are met. Firstly, 'the measures of intention and of perceived behavioural control must correspond to (. . .) or be compatible with (. . .) the behaviour that is to be predicted' (ibid., p. 185). Secondly, 'intentions and perceived behavioural control must remain stable in the interval between their assessment and observation of the behaviour' (ibid.). Finally, 'prediction of behaviour from perceived behavioural control should improve to the extent that perceptions of behavioural control realistically reflect actual control' (ibid.). However, while the theory has been well received, some scholars also criticised it. For example, Ogden (2003) argued that the theory cannot be disapproved, that the models leave too much variance in intentions and behaviour, and that behaviour is measured through self-reporting rather than objective measuring. However, Ajzen and Fishbein (2004) responded to this criticism by arguing that studies conducted using this model have shown that self-reporting is quite accurate. For example, in a study by Jaccard et al. (2002) participants accurately reported condom use. In other words, Ogden (2003) assumed that people may not be accurate or truthful when reporting behaviour; however, this depends on the individual behaviour.

For example, in a study by Topić et al. (2018) participants reported high reliance on the mass media in forming an opinion on sustainability even though some researchers have expressed concerns that people would not admit they are influenced by the media because of which agenda-setting research on mass media influence often involves conducting research in a setting where participants do not always know what is being researched.

However, Ajzen and Fishbein (2004) also noted that participants do not always report accurate results on sensitive issues such as drug use, drunk driving and medical adherence, which means that there are situations where participants cannot be trusted, but 'often, the bias is due to a tendency for some respondents to overstate performance of socially desirable behaviors' (Ajzen and Fishbein 2004: 432). This means that this type of bias can contaminate some results in regards to the correlation between cognition and behaviour but that does not automatically invalidate the theory as a whole (ibid.).

To put this theory in perspective, we will use an example from sports research. Hausenblas and associates (2011) analysed likely behaviour towards exercise. Since the intention is seen as the strongest predictor of behaviour along with behavioural control, this means that our intention to perform a certain behaviour will be influenced partially by our attitude and then partially by the perceived control of the situation. The elements that would need to be considered in intention towards exercising would then be attitude to whether exercising is perceived as useful, intention to exercise regularly, perceived opinion of others (subjective norm) and very importantly the control over the behaviour as perceived by the participant, e.g. whether the person perceives they can make sufficient changes in their daily routines to find time to exercise (see Figure 8.3).

Theory of Planned Behavior Sample Items

For me to exercise regularly during the winter will be: [Attitude]	useless	useful
	1 2 3 4	5 6 7
I intend to exercise regularly during the winter. [Intention]	strongly disagree	strongly agree
	1 2 3 4	5 6 7
Most people who are important to me would like me to exercise regularly during the winter. [Subjective Norm]	strongly disagree	strongly agree
	1 2 3 4	5 6 7
How much control do you have over exercising during the winter? [Perceived Behavioral Control]	very little control	complete control
	1 2 3 4	5 6 7

Figure 8.3 Theory of Planned Behaviour and Exercise (*source:* Hausenblaus et al, 2011. Retrieved from https://psychology.iresearchnet.com/sports-psychology/sport-motivation/the-theory-of-planned-behavior/ (24 April 2019)

Stages of Change Model

The Stages of Change Model (also called the Transtheoretical Model) was developed during the 1970s by Prochaska and DiClemente (1983) and it is a model that was developed through studying smokers and addicts in general, which is clearly a common case study in persuasion theory and behavioural research.

This model focuses on the decision-making process of individuals and discusses the intentional change, which is a similarity with the previously discussed Theory of Planned Behaviour that also states the importance of intention in changing behaviour (Ajzen 1991). However, this theory argues that the behavioural change happens as a cyclical process and thus individuals move through six stages of change: precontemplation, contemplation, preparation, action, maintenance, and termination. The model is well illustrated in Figure 8.4.

In the precontemplation stage, 'there is no intention to change behavior in the foreseeable future' (Prochaska et al. 1992: 1103). This means that individuals who are in this stage do not recognise that they have a problem (e.g. a certain addiction) and it is usually external factors that are trying to push them to reach this recognition. These factors can be parents, family, family courts or anyone with the power to put an individual in a situation when they have to act; however, once the individual feels they are in control they can quickly revert to their old ways.

The second stage is then a contemplation stage when individuals start thinking about the change but this does not mean this period is short. In studies where individuals were observed, in some cases, it took two years before individuals moved towards the next stage. In other words, individuals know what they want to achieve but they are not ready to do so yet (DiClemente and Prochaska 1985; Prochaska and DiClemente 1984; Prochaska et al. 1992).

The next stage is the preparation stage where individuals are intending to change their behaviour and they plan to take action in the next month or so after having been taken action in the previous year. These individuals, according to DiClemente and associates (1991), demonstrate small changes in behaviour such as, for example, smoking five cigarettes less a day.

Action stage follows next, and in this stage, individuals are actively modifying their behaviour and this requires energy and commitment, which in this stage individuals are willing to commit to. This stage is still not a change even though the environment of the individual may think so after the action stage has commenced; however, the action is seen as leading to a change if individuals are able to demonstrate action for a period of time, such as, for example, six months. A good example is smoking where an individual in action stage would be cutting down cigarette consumption by 50 per cent (Prochaska et al. 1995).

Maintenance stage follows next, and in this stage individuals work towards relapse prevention and this stage is often seen as very static. This stage in

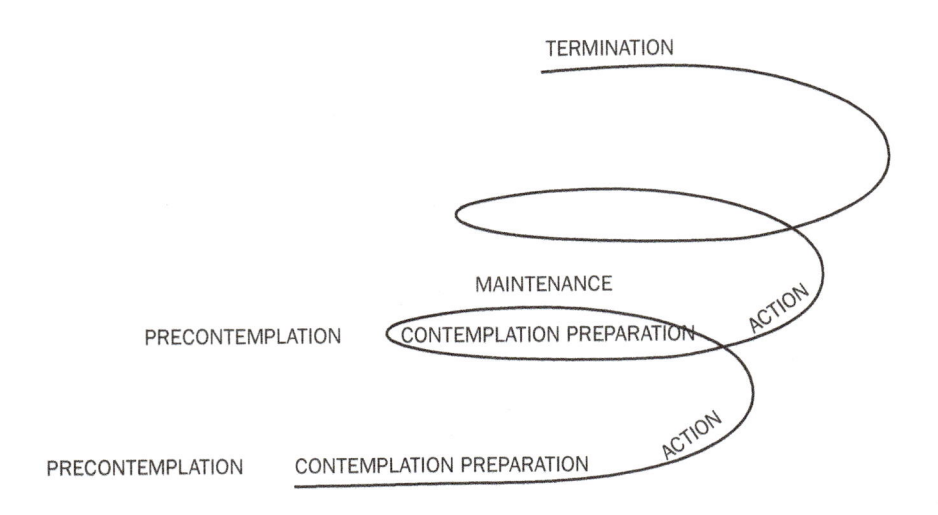

Figure 8.4 The Stages of Change Model (*source:* Prochaska, J. O., DiClemente, C. C., & Norcross, J. C. (1992). In search of how people change: Applications to addictive behaviors. American Psychologist, 47(9), 1102–1114)

addiction research can be, for example, from six months onwards (ibid.).

Prochaska et al. (1992) also argued that psychoanalysis systematically shows that people do change with professional treatment but it fails to describe how people change. The latter is the subject of interest of the Stages of Change model where authors investigated how people change and what stages they go through when they are determined to change their behaviour without having to attend psychotherapy. Therefore, when it comes to addiction, for example, studies found several reasons such as, 'Inadequate motivation, resistance to therapy, defensiveness, and inability to relate are client variables frequently invoked to account for the imperfect outcomes of the change enterprise. Inadequate techniques, theory, and relationship skills on the part of the therapist are intervention variables frequently blamed for lack of therapeutic success have observed that many addicts relapse and thus fail to change' (Prochaska et al. 1992: 1102; see also Krstić 2014). Thus, this model asks when and how people change (DiClemente and Prochaska 1982; Prochaska and DiClemente 1983).

However, the model is not without criticism. For example, Davidson (1992) argued that the models suffers from several flaws. Some of the objections are that 'behaviour change can occur because its personal

Explore 8.3

Look for similar domestic campaigns in your country (if based in Australia, look for other similar campaigns). Discuss in groups what were the campaign messages, who was the target of campaigning (e.g. victims, victim's family members, the general public, etc.) and discuss whether targeting was done right in your opinion.

After that, look at the media coverage and social media debates to establish the effect of campaigning (Laswell).

Finally, propose a campaign of your own using a charity of your choice.

Mini case study 8.2
Bursting the Bubble Campaign (Australia)

Bursting the Bubble is an Australian campaign against domestic violence. The organisation behind the campaign is the Domestic Violence Resource Centre Victoria and on their website the organisation states that they 'make websites, videos, apps, brochures, posters and lots more to help people understand what family violence is, why it happens, how to recognise it and how to help others who are experiencing it. We also run training classes for people who work with family violence victim/survivors and professionals who work to prevent more violence from happening' (WOAH, 2019, n.p.).

The website provides information on childhood stories of domestic violence from real people, tips on creating safety plans and keeping the victims safe, support advice on dealing with feelings and taking care of oneself, tips meant to help recognising what domestic violence and abuse are, information on available help and knowing how to ask for help and who to talk to (ibid.).

The campaign originally started in 2003 but it continues until the present day, and the only difference is that the website is now dedicated to domestic violence and support in general rather than one campaign only.

The website also features three sections, blue, gold and indigo and each colour is dedicated to a separate age group. For example, the blue site is for 14–17 years olds, gold is for 10–13 years old and indigo is for 'adult allies' who suspect that child is in danger (ibid.).

The campaigners also provided useful booklets for victims of domestic violence, such as for example a booklet called 'Something not right at home?' (https://www.dvrcv.org.au/sites/default/files/Bursting%20the%20bubble%20%28booklet%29.pdf)

The campaign was embraced by the Australian Government, which recommended the Domestic Violence Centre on its website (https://apps.aifs.gov.au/cfcaregister/projects/814).

> **Think about 8.4**
>
> Think about domestic violence as a form of deviant behaviour and analyse it using the Stages of Change model. Then think how a PR campaign could influence behavioural change. What message would you send?
>
> Next, discuss colours used in Australian Bursting the Bubble campaign. How this fits into the general rule that people react to colours as per the video in the previous exercise (Explore 8.2)? How could the ELM model help in analysing this campaign?

construction or functional significance alters. Some successful individuals are not aware of contemplating, actioning or maintaining change (...) Has there really been good evidence that specific treatment interventions can be optimally matched with each stage to improve outcome?' (p. 821).

Nudge Theory

Thaler and Sunstein (2009) identified the nudge theory as necessary for understanding behaviour. In the view of nudge advocates, humans are too lazy or too busy to process all information available on a daily basis, which means that we have some sort of cognitive bias and policymakers should help us make the right choices to help ourselves by nudging us to act in a certain way. This is necessary according to these authors because humans tend to make quick and simple decisions, which is due to the fact human action is more driven with emotion than with rationality, and as such, humans are prone to nudging. In addition, nudge advocates also identified choice architects, who are the people responsible for organising 'the context in which people make decisions' (ibid.: 3). In other words, anyone who works in any industry can be a choice architect so long as they are organising products and services and presenting them to others, thus nudging individuals to use them.

A key feature of behavioural strategies is that they aim to change 'people's behavior in a predictable way without forbidding any options or significantly changing their economic incentives. To count as a mere nudge, [an] intervention must be easy and cheap to avoid. Nudges are not mandates' (Thaler and Sunstein 2009: 6, cited from Benartzi et al. 2017: 1041).

A good example of the nudge theory is the hotel's policy of nudging guests to re-use the towels by emphasising how many guests have chosen to do so. If the number is high, people are more likely to re-use towels without feeling they are being forced to do so, and thus this brings both ecological and economic benefits (Oullier et al. 2010). Another example comes from the health sector where people are nudged to become organ donors. For example, from spring 2020 all patients of NHS England will be considered organ donors if they have made no statement specifically stating they do not wish to donate their organs after they die. This system is called 'opt out' (NHS 2019). As stated by Oullier and associates (2010), opting out from these options often involves administrative procedure but, most importantly, going against social norms and thus potentially being seen as selfish. Another example also includes subscriptions and free trials. For example, people are often nudged to take a free trial, which can be cancelled at any time, e.g. Netflix's one-month free trial, which then continues into a monthly subscription if not cancelled (Netflix 2019). Very often, people continue buying the service because they have been nudged to try it for free.

The popularity of the nudge behavioural theory is visible in the fact many governments have implemented nudge units in their policy departments. These departments are staffed by behavioural professionals who are designing behavioural interventions to encourage desirable behaviour, and this process is seen as beneficial to the economy as it improves performance while giving Governments the possibility not to be seen as too restrictive (Benartzi et al. 2017).

PR practitioner Simon Maule (2015) emphasised in *PR Week* that the PR industry also needs to turn to the nudge theory because awareness campaigns, at the core of PR work for decades, do not always work. In his words, 'for campaigns attempting to stop bad behaviour, heightened awareness can even be counter-productive and encourage the very behaviour it is intended to stop. Instead, we need to recognise the cognitive biases we all suffer from and the thinking shortcuts we use when making decisions – be that a preference for immediate gratification, a tendency to follow our peers or difficulties understanding probabilities – and apply the growing body of behavioural science insight to communications campaigns' (n.p.). In addition, some other agencies used this theory in campaigning. For example, Rowena Spinks (2015)

> **Explore 8.4**
>
> A nudge in PR campaigns can take several strategies, such as framing, mindlessness, positioning and mood (Spinks, 2015), which means that PR practitioners can use multiple techniques to design campaigns. Many of these techniques are already used in PR, for example, framing is a well-known media theory used in PR. Whilst in the media framing is used to make certain issues more important than others and thus push them onto the media and public agenda, in PR framing is used to frame messages positively such as, for example, using positive statistics, running your own research, etc. Nudging these messages is then done through mindlessness, or simplifying messages to nudge publics to act in a certain way. Positioning is then done in the context of the message and it has an environmental implication because the environment impacts people's decision-making processes whereas mood is linked to people's feelings. The latter is common, for example, in emotional advertising when some campaigners created campaigns that appeal to people's emotions.

wrote on the company's blog page that her team used nudge theory for the *Project Pictogram* campaign, which was a road safety campaign designed to influence driver behaviour using five new industry standard pictograms.

Critics of nudge theory express concerns about too much power of the Government in eliciting behavioural change. In addition, some critics stated that 'the new behavioural economics still offers a thin conception of human agency, and an underdeveloped sense of social structure (. . .)' (Leggett 2014: p. 17). Nevertheless, some authors also raised an issue of the private sector and their use of nudging stating that Governments in the US and the UK that first started to use nudging in public policy are being ethical about it, however, the private sector is still shady because there is no effective control as with Governments, which can be voted out of the office in a democratic society (Thaler 2015, n.p.).

Inoculation theory

Inoculation theory presents a different approach to human behaviour, in a sense that it debates how to defend from influence, even though this process is challenging (Pfau and Wan 2006). The purpose of inoculation theory is therefore to 'explain resistance to influence' (Eagly and Chaiken 1993: 560). In other words, the inoculation theory investigates firm beliefs among individuals about various issues and argues that once individuals form their opinion, it becomes very difficult to change it. This is particularly the case if the opposing argument is perceived as weak or unconvincing.

The inoculation theory, therefore, presents an analysis of the resistance strategy to resist change by strengthening existing opinion (Pfau and Wan 2006). In other words, 'the theory posits that refutational treatments, which introduce challenges to existing attitudes while simultaneously offering preemptive refutation to those challenges, threaten the individual, which triggers the person's motivation to bolster attitudes against change and, as a result, confers resistance to counterarguments which a person might be exposed to' (Pfau and Wan 2006: 123).

The inoculation has been found in resistance to advertising, social marketing messages, political campaigns and social campaigns such as stopping smoking (Pfau 1992; Pfau 1990; Burgoon et al. 1995).

In PR, this theory can be very useful because if a person has formed a positive opinion and it is relevant for PR professionals that this opinion remains the same, which is likely to happen if the opposing arguments against an organisation are not strong. However, to avoid forming strong counter-opinion it is important for organisations to avoid crises as well as to keep re-enforcing positive messages to keep the reputation and relationship positive.

Inoculation thus serves as a vaccination that prevents individuals from accepting opposing messages and the theory, when put in practice, creates an immunity that can go in favour of PR professionals. The term inoculation nevertheless comes from a medical term vaccination and it was coined by a psychologist William McGuire (1964) who believed that people can defend themselves from both viruses and persuasive attempts to instigate attitudinal change.

Early research on inoculation theory was applied to rarely contested areas, such as brushing teeth where the attitude was rarely if ever, counter-argued. Thus, people's opinion was not likely to change (Banas and Rains 2010). In advertising, this theory has been applied through campaigning directed towards existing users, thus strengthening their views and brand loyalty while also informing them there is a competitor in the market. Another good example of inoculation theory in practice is 'Get a Mac' campaign where Apple was emphasising what their strengths are as opposed to PC and this campaign was named as the best campaign of the new millennium (Nudd 2011).

However, the theory has also been accused of being manipulative because of its popularity among some large corporations. For example, in the middle of the lawsuit about too much acetaminophen and small print on bottles of Tylenol (over-the-counter medicine) which killed a child, Johnson and Johnson launched a campaign on responsible dosing. The campaign was a success, and in line with the inoculation theory served the company as a protection from future attacks (Veil and Kent 2008).

Cognitive Dissonance Theory

The theory of cognitive dissonance first became known through its creator, Leon Festinger (1957) who centred his research on the way individuals react to inconsistent mental states, with particular emphasis on the feeling of discomfort and the intention to decrease discomfort to reestablish the mental balance. Festinger believed that individuals actively avoid information that could cause them dissonance.

Festinger (1964) also developed his theory based on attitude research; however, his research has found a correlation between attitudes and behaviour and thus his research is not essentially an attempt to undermine attitude research entirely. However, his did emphasise that his study has shown that 'the fact that existing attitudes relate to overt behavior does not tell us whether or not an attitude *change* brought about by exposure to a persuasive communication will be reflected in a *change* in subsequent behavior. To answer this question we need studies in which, after people have been exposed to persuasive communication, a measure of attitude or opinion is obtained on the basis of which attitude change can be assessed' (Festinger 1964: 406–407). For example, in his study of white students and their willingness to sit with a black student in classroom and have a photo taken has proven a link between attitude on blacks and willingness to sit together and take a photo where people with prejudicial attitudes were less likely to sign a statement accepting to take a photo as opposed to people with more favourable views (ibid.).

However, this finding alone does not explain how could change happen and the role of persuasive communication. Festinger (1964) therefore suggested that 'when opinions or attitudes are changed through the momentary impact of a persuasive communication, this change, all by itself, is inherently unstable and will disappear or remain isolated unless an environmental or behavioral change can be brought about to support and maintain it' (Festinger 1964: 415).

In practice, this means that 'in order to produce a stable behavior change following opinion change, an environmental change must also be produced which, representing reality, will support the new opinion and the new behavior. Otherwise, the same factors that produced the initial opinion and the behavior will continue to operate to nullify the effect of the opinion change' (Festinger 1964: 416).

Akerlof and Dickens (1982) nicely summarised what cognitive dissonance represents, i.e. any situation in which an individual's belief is challenged. For example, 'in practice most cognitive dissonance reactions stem from peoples' view of themselves as 'smart, nice people.' Information that conflicts with this image tends to be ignored, rejected, or accommodated by changes in other beliefs' (Akerlof and Dickens 1982: 308). In addition, individuals asked to do something they normally do not agree with or something they would not normally do, tend to amend their beliefs to be able to perform the task. For example, in a study by Glass (1964) students who were asked to perform electroshock first lowered their opinion of victims, and with this they avoided the feeling of cognitive dissonance.

Studies that tested this framework concluded that Festinger was right in assuming that individuals would seek to reduce the intake of information that could cause dissonance but they do not always avoid that type of information (Brehm and Cohen 1962). However, Bolin (1988) found that any natural disaster has an impact on both individuals affected by the disaster as well as those who read about it in the news. Therefore, many organisations who work in crisis response specifically design communication plans to reach out to individuals who may avoid the news on natural disasters (Eisenman et al. 2007).

While cognitive dissonance theory is a social psychology theory, its application has extended to other fields as well. As it is typical for all behavioural research, this theoretical framework is often used in studying smokers (Gibbons et al. 1997; Telci et al. 2011).

Some offered revisions of the theory; however, the revision did not undermine the original concept but merely offered further explanations of what can influence the feeling of dissonance, for example, the self-concept (which is the result of people's perceived image of themselves and the actions they actually do), unwanted consequences, which make people questioning their ways of doing things and this causes dissonance, and moral integrity problem, or when a person behaves in a way that they themselves do not perceive as moral (Steele 1988; Cooper and Carlsmith 2001; Telcia et al. 2011).

Cognitive dissonance has also been used in management, and this is where the theory gets closer to PR practice. For example, scholars have studied cognitive dissonance in managing change process within organisations, which is usually stressful for employees. However, studies showed that if staff feels they have no influence over the process of change they are more likely to experience a dissonance. Therefore, it becomes important to manage the process of change in an inclusive way and in a way that gives staff a sense they are the ones who can participate in making the change too (Burnes and Hakeem 1995; Harmon-Jones and Mills 1999). This internal communication of the organisational change is often the role of PR professionals, and thus understanding what can cause cognitive dissonance can be of invaluable use to PR practitioners.

Mini case study 8.3
Iceland's Rang-Tan Christmas Campaign (UK)

Iceland is a UK supermarket specialising predominantly in frozen food. The UK supermarket industry is generally a very lucrative industry with fierce competition amongst supermarket companies. Part of that competition is extensive Christmas campaigning, in which companies compete on who will have the most creative Christmas campaign.

While some campaigns are product oriented, many campaigns are PR masterpieces that instigate major interest from UK's media organisations and public debate.

For example, Sainsbury's 'Christmas Truce' campaign from 2014 instigated a public debate and more than 800 requests to the Advertising Standards Agency (ASA) to ban the ad. The request was not upheld and the ASA did not ban the advert. The reason why the advert was complained about is that it centres on a historical event from WWI when English and German troops took a break from war to play football on Christmas day. Supporters of the campaign argued that the campaign promotes peace and the unnecessity of the war while critics said it romanticised the war (see ASA 2015; Fogg 2014; Critchlow 2014; Hooton 2014; Adams and Topić 2016). Media outlets even ran polls to establish how the British public felt about the advert. This campaign was part of Sainsbury's rich Corporate Social Responsibility (CSR) policy and proceedings from the campaign (it promoted chocolate as well as a partnership with a charity) were going to the British Legion, a UK-based charity that looks after families of war veterans.

In 2018, Iceland ran an advert called Rang-Tan. The advert narrated destruction of rainforests and the extermination of orangutans. The advert was also created as a cartoon and the narration was developed as a child's poem. At the end of the film, letters appear stating it was dedicated to the orangutans we lose every day and that Iceland does not use palm oil.

This campaign was labelled as the most powerful Christmas campaign of 2018. The campaign drew from a similar campaign by Greenpeace and it was banned from broadcasting on TV so Iceland's communication team posted it on social media. The film was blocked from TV by broadcast approval body Clearcast for breaking a rule in the advertising code against content from political organisations (*The Grocer* 2018) and a petition was launched soon afterwards to run the campaign on TV. Research conducted after the film was released on social media found the film to be very effective and Iceland was ranked on top ahead of other retailers including M&S, Sainsbury's and John Lewis. In a survey of 1,184 consumers, covering 22 brands, Iceland's film was rated top for 10 out of 12 factors including 'persuasion', 'enjoyment' and 'brand love'. Researchers for Kantar Millward Brown's annual study also analysed facial expression to gauge emotional response and found Iceland's ad elicited the broadest range.

Sainsbury's campaign Christmas Truce can be found on this link:

https://www.youtube.com/watch?v=NWF2JBb1bvM&t=3s

Iceland's Rang-Tan campaign can be found on this link: https://www.youtube.com/watch?v=JdpspIIWI2o

Picture 8.3 Supermarket company Iceland ran a Christmas advert called Rang-Tan that highlighted the destruction of rainforests and the extermination of orangutans. (*source:* Jklingebiel/Shutterstock)

Explore 8.5

Look at Christmas campaigns from the UK's main retailers (Tesco, Sainsbury's, Marks and Spencer, John Lewis and Waitrose) released in a period between 2011 and 2018.

Discuss which one is your favourite and reflect on how each campaign made you feel. Analyse your emotions towards each campaign using emotions in public relations, persuasive communication and ELM. Think what kind of member of the public you are and how each campaign managed or failed to get you interested.

If you were assigned to design a Christmas campaign what would you do and why? If your campaign theme is potentially controversial, how would you address cognitive dissonance?

Summary

This chapter gives an overview of theories that can be useful to PR practitioners. In this context, the chapter explains initial communication theories such as Laswell's communication model, as well as relationship theories. In addition, the chapter explores persuasion theories due to the inherently persuasive character of PR as a profession. Through the wealth of contemporary exploring boxes and case studies aligned with theories discussed in the chapter, you can investigate and build an understanding of what public relations is as a profession and how we can use communication and persuasion theories to plan PR campaigns. While PR practitioners and practical PR literature do not always explicitly reference communication and social theories in their work, it is apparent that these theories do have a value for campaign design. As such, this chapter helps to engage with PR theories and increases your ability to apply theory to practice.

Mini case study 8.4
Ban Bossy (USA)

It has been well known from feminist research that when girls assert themselves, they are called bossy whereas when boys assert themselves, they are called leaders. Therefore, Sheryl Sandberg, Facebook's COO has started a foundation called LeanIn.Org which then launched a campaign called 'Ban Bossy'. In the explanation of the rationale for the campaign, the campaigners said the following: 'Words like bossy send a message: don't raise your hand or speak up. By middle school, girls are less interested in leading than boys - a trend that continues into adulthood. Together we can encourage girls to lead. Pledge to Ban Bossy' (Ban Bossy 2019, n. p.).

The campaign attracted lots of celebrities including Beyoncé who is still the face of the campaign, and in the campaign film, Beyoncé states: 'I am not bossy, I am the boss' (https://youtu.be/6dynbzMlCcw).

The campaign has not centred only on campaign films and ads, but the authors and promoters also went forward and developed materials to encourage girls to lead. For example, the campaign website features leadership tips for girls, parents, teachers and managers. These materials include pdf documents available for free downloads, such as a document with 10 tips to help girls lead, must know facts and figures on girls' leadership and activities for girls to step outside of their comfort zone (http://banbossy.com/girls-tips/).

The website also features stories from successful women and this section includes further tips on encouraging girls to lead (http://banbossy.com/things-we-love/).

The campaign has received wide media attention and started a debate on women and leadership. The campaign thus provided a link with research that shows how girls are systematically discouraged from leading, and this campaign also goes in line with Always' campaign 'Like a Girl' which also presented a series of campaign films showing how girls get discouraged in meeting their full potential by society (Topić 2015).

Chapter 8 Public relations theories: communication, relationships and persuasion

Explore 8.6

Review the website of the Ban Bossy campaign, and discuss the campaign. What was the central message of the campaign? What is the campaign trying to communicate and why? Use Laswell's model of communication to think what was communicated, to whom and what was the effect of the communication.

Next, the take a look at the media coverage and discuss media framing of the issue. What was the framing of the US media? What was the framing of international media? What were the central arguments in the media coverage in the US and abroad?

Consider the stage of change model to analyse how could the PR profession contribute towards a wider societal change of behaviour towards girls and women.

Mini case study 8.5
Nike's Women Campaigning (USA)

Nike has a long tradition of campaigning for women's rights.

Their first campaign for women's rights was launched in the 1990s, however, the focus on women in business started much earlier. Many scholars interpret these campaigns as greenwash and as a cover up for other bad business decisions (Cole and Hribar 1995; Goldman and Papson 1998; Helstein 2003; Lafrance 1998; Lucas 2000), however, some scholars argue that Nike has a long tradition of campaigning for women and that Nike's campaigning as well as 'the advertising produced, for the women's brand, during the 1990s, played a significant role in shifting the way females were represented in mediated images in the United States' (Grow 2006: 2).

In 1978, the business focus of the company captured 'Nike Women' and the company started to turn towards women as customers, and not just men. The new business was featured in the Lady Waffle Trainer, which was a line specifically designed for women. Then in 1981 when the Olympic Committee voted to include women in its marathons, Nike launched two ads, 'The Olympics Will Never Be the Same' and 'Finally!' (Nike 2019).

In 1984, Joan Benoit Samuelson won the first women's marathon in LA and this was featured in Nike's ads and the 1980s were generally the years when Nike intensified women advertising. This led to the 1990s, a decade recognised in scholarship as the start of Nike's extensive women campaigning (Grow 2006). In 1991, 'Nike released an eight-page print magazine insert that started with the words, "You Were Born a Daughter," and took the reader through the growth and development of a woman's life' (Nike 2019) and this led to Nike's iconic women advocacy campaign 'If You Let Me Play'. This campaign was released as a film and 'the film introduced a new approach to inspire female athletes, emphasising how sports benefit the lives of girls. The campaign was chosen as one of the best ads of 1995 by readers of USA Today' (ibid.). Janet Champ, chief copywriter of Nike's women advertising during the 1990s stated 'It wasn't advertising. It was the truth (. . .) We weren't selling a damn thing. Just the truth. And behind the truth, of course, the message was brought to you by Nike.' Champ was describing the creative process behind the award-winning ad, 'If You Let Me Play,' part of the powerful Participation campaign that featured teenage girls on a playground talking about the meaning of sports in their lives). Her remark illuminates the defiance that typified that creative process but also shows the personal meaning she derived from having created the ad (Grow and Wolburg 2006: n.p.).

In 1999, the American women's national team won a world's soccer championship, which was featured in Nike's campaign 'Girl In America'. In the ad spot, Mia Hamm stated, 'There is a girl being born in America. Someone will give her a doll. Someone will give her a ball. And someone will give her a chance' (ibid.). In the 2000s, Nike continued with women campaigning but this time with a focus on empowerment of women. 'My Body Parts' campaign discussed the size and strength of a female athlete's butt and thighs, whereas the 2004

→

mini case study 8.5 (continued)

campaign 'Mi heroe es una chava,' (My hero is a girl) celebrated 400-meter sprinter Ana Guevera who 'became the first Mexican female track athlete to win a gold medal in a major international competition in 2003, and won silver in Athens' (ibid.).

In 2006, Maria Sharapova featured in Nike's campaign titled 'I Feel Pretty,' and the message was 'that beneath Maria's beautiful, feminine exterior lives the intense competitive appetite of one of the top athletes in the world' (ibid.).

On 4 April 2007, 'during Women's March Madness, the Rutgers women's basketball team was the focus of a string of offensive remarks. It sparked conversations that led to the Athlete campaign. The video component involved a bevy of athletes and coaches, including Mia Hamm, Picabo Street, Serena Williams and Gabrielle Reece, voicing their opinions and challenging gender stereotypes. Nike also ran a full-page ad in The New York Times that read, 'Thank You Ignorance. Thank you for starting the conversation. Thank you for unintentionally moving women's sport forward' (ibid.).

In 2008 however, Nike continued the dialogue with 'Here I Am,' a multi-media campaign that 'showed how girls in sport are stronger in body and mind by highlighting the mental strength of young world-class athletes like Sofia Boutella and Maria Sharapova' (ibid.). In 2004, Serena Williams became Nike's face of women campaigning and this collaboration is continuing up to the present day, due to the fact Williams is still an active athlete despite multiple injuries and giving birth to a baby. However, the women campaigning continues concurrently in other areas, and this started in the 2010s with a campaign entitled 'Make Yourself' which encouraged women 'to think about who they want to be and how sport can help them find the confidence they need to become their best' (ibid.). In 2012, Nike released a film 'Voices' to celebrate women in sport on the 40th anniversary of Title IX. 'The film features Joan Benoit Samuelson, Lisa Leslie, Marlen Esparza and Diana Taurasi' (ibid.).

Nike also launched the campaign 'Dare to aim higher than the sky' to celebrate the success of Li Na, the first Asian woman to win Grand Slam tournament in tennis and when she announced her retirement Nike launched a campaign 'Be the Bird that Sticks Out' (ibid.).

One of the most known women campaigns is the 2015 #betterforit campaign, which captured the history of Nike's campaigning for women whereas in 2016 Nike campaigned to remove the word female from athlete and put just athlete (Bureau Borsche 2019).

In 2017, Nike launched women campaigns in Russia, the Middle East and Turkey. The campaigns challenged women stereotypes and were launched on International Women's Day (Jardine 2017). In 2018, Nike also joined the plight for women diversity and thus launched a campaign and a new product featuring Nike's hijab and thus sending the message that Muslim women who wear traditional gowns can also be athletes (Ahmed 2017). Finally, in 2019, Nike launched a new campaign called 'Dream Crazier' with a message inviting women to dream crazy and just do it (Binlot 2019), which challenges also prejudices long recognised in feminist research of women being seen as problematic when they aspire to do something good or when they get angry, etc.

Explore 8.7

Explore the media coverage of the Nike's #betterforit campaign. Make a distinction between news media and specialist magazines (marketing and advertising). What has news media reported about? What was the central message of media articles?

Next, select two articles from different media outlets with lots of user comments. How did the society responded to the campaign, and the media article about it? What are the main arguments on the campaign among members of the general public?

What type of public relations is this? Has Nike achieved excellence in PR with this campaign?

Bibliography

Adams, S. and Topić, M. (2015). Towards an Ethical PR? An Exploration into Student's Ethical Perceptions towards the Sainsbury's WWI Campaign. *International Journal of Ethics* 3(1), 1–29.

Ahmed, S. (2017). Nike's Pro Hijab: a great leap into modest sportswear, but they're not the first. *The Guardian,* 8 March. Retrieved from https://www.theguardian.com/sport/blog/2017/mar/08/Nike-performance-hijab-female-muslim-athletes (23 April 2019).

Ajzen, I. and Fishbein, M. (2004). Editorial comment – Questions Raised by a Reasoned Action Approach: Comment on Ogden (2003). *Health Psychology* 23(4), 431–434.

Ajzen, I. (2002). Perceived Behavioral Control, Self-Efficacy, Locus of Control, and the Theory of Planned Behaviour. *Journal of Applied Social Psychology* 32(4), 665–683.

Ajzen, I. (1991). The theory of planned behavior. *Organizational Behavior and Human Decision Process* 50, 179–211.

Ajzen, I. (1988). *Attitudes, personality, and behavior.* Chicago, IL: Dorsey.

Ajzen, I. and Fishbein, M. (1980). *Understanding attitudes and predicting social behavior.* Englewood Cliffs, NJ: Prentice-Hall.

Akerlof, G. A. and Dickens, W. T. (1982).The Economic Consequences of Cognitive Dissonance. *The American Economic Review* 72(3), 307–319.

ASA (2015). *2014's most complained about ads.* Retrieved from https://www.asa.org.uk/News-resources/Media-Centre/2015/2014-most-complained-about-ads.aspx#.Vhe3c6NwaHs (9 October 2015).

Austin, E.W. and Pinkleton, B.E. (2006). *Strategic Public Relations Management: Planning and managing effective communication programs,* 2nd edn. London: Taylor & Francis.

Banas, J.A. and Rains, S.A. (2010). A meta-analysis of research on inoculation theory. *Communication Monographs* 77(3), 281–311. doi:10.1080/03637751003758193

Ban Bossy (2019). *Campaign website.* Retrieved from http://banbossy.com/ (23 April 2019)

Barney, R. and Black, J. (1994). Ethics and professional persuasive communications. *Public Relations Review* 20, 233–248.

Benartzi, S., Beshears, J., Milkman, K.L., Sunstein, C.R., Thaler, R.H., Shankar, M., Tucker-Ray, W., Congdon, W.J. and Galing, S. (2017). Should Governments Invest More in Nudging? *Psychological Science* 28(8), 1041–1055.

Bernays, E.L. (2005[1928]). *Propaganda.* N. Y. Ig Publishing.

Bernays, E.L. (1955). The theory and practice of public relations: a resume. In - Bernays, E. L. (ed.) *The engineering of consent* (pp. 3–25). Norman: University of Oklahoma Press.

Bernays, E. (1945). *Public Relations.* Boston: Bellman Publishing Company.

Bernays, E. (1927). *An Outline of Careers: A Practical Guide to Achievement by Thirty-Eight Eminent Americans.* New York: George H. Doran Company.

Bernays, E. (1923). *Crystallizing Public Opinion.* New York: Boni and Liveright.

Binlot, A. (2019). Nike And Serena Williams Inspire Women To 'Dream Crazier' With New Campaign. *The Forbes,* 28 February. Retrieved from https://www.forbes.com/sites/abinlot/2019/02/28/Nike-and-serena-williams-inspire-women-to-dream-crazier-with-new-campaign/ (23 April 2019)

Bolin, R. (1988). Response to natural disasters. In - Lystad, M. (ed.). *Mental health responses to mass emergencies* (pp. 22–51). New York: Bruner Mazel.

Brehm, J. and Cohen, A. (1962). *Explorations in cognitive dissonance.* NewYork: Wiley.

Brown, R. (2010). Symmetry and its critics: antecedents, prospects and implications for symmetry in a postsymmetry era. In - Heath, R. L. (ed.) *The SAGE Handbook of Public Relations.* Thousand Oaks: SAGE.

Burnes, B. and Hakeem, J. (1995). Culture, cognitive dissonance and the management of change. *International Journal of Operations and Production* 15, 14–33.

Bureau Borsche (2019). Retrieved from https://bureauborsche.com/projects/Nike-campaigns-2016 (23 April 2019)

Burgoon, M., Pfau, M. and Birk, T. (1995). An inoculation theory explanation for the effects of corporate issue/advocacy advertising campaigns. *Communication Research* 22, 485–505.

Butterick, K. (2011). *Introducing Public Relations: Theory and Practice.* London: SAGE.

Cacioppo, J.T. and Petty, R.E. (1984). The elaboration likelihood model of persuasion. *Advances in Consumer Research* 11, 673–675. Retrieved from http://

acrwebsite.org/volumes/6329/volumes/v11/NA-11 (22 April 2019)

Changing Minds (2019). *The Elaboration Likelihood Model*. Retrieved from http://changingminds.org/explanations/theories/elaboration_likelihood.htm (23 April 2019)

Cole, C.L. and Hribar, A. (1995). Celebrity Feminism: Nike Style Post-Fordism, Transcendence, and Consumer Power. *Sociology of Sport Journal* 12(4), 347–369.

Cook, A., Moore, K. and Steel, G. (2004). The taking of a position: a reinterpretation of the elaboration likelihood model. *Journal for the Theory of Social Behaviour* 34(4), 315–331.

Coombs, W.T. and Holladay, S.J. (2007). *It's Not Just PR: Public Relations in Society*. Malden: Blackwell Publishing.

Cooper J. and Carlsmith, K.M. (2001). Cognitive dissonance. In- Smelzer, N.J., and Baltes, P.B. (eds.) *International encyclopedia of the social and behavioral sciences* (pp. 2112–2114). New York: Elsevier.

Critchlow, A. (2014). Sainsbury's 1914 Christmas truce ad exploits memory of Great War. *The Telegraph Online*. Retrieved from: http://www.telegraph.co.uk/comment/personal-view/11228839/Has-Sainsburys-1914-Christmas-truce-ad-exploited-memory-of-war.html (31 March 2015).

Cutlip, S.M., Center, A.H. and Broom, G.M. (2000). *Effective Public Relations*, 8th edition. Upper Saddle River: Prentice Hall.

Davidson, R. (1992). Prochaska and DiClemente's model of change: a case study? *British Journal of Addiction* 87, 821–822.

DiClemente, C.C., Prochaska, J.O., Fairhurst, S.K., Velicer, W.F., Velasquez, M.M. and Rossi, J.S. (1991). The process of smoking cessation: An analysis of precontemplation, contemplation, and preparation stages of change. *Journal of Consulting and Clinical Psychology* 59, 295–304.

DiClemente, C.C., Prochaska, J.O. and Gibertini, M. (1985). Self-efficacy and the stages of self-change of smoking. *Cognitive therapy and Research*, 9(2), 181–200.

DiClemente, C.C. and Prochaska, J.O. (1985). Processes and stages of change: Coping and competence in smoking behavior change. In - Shiffman, S., and Wills, T. A. (eds.) *Coping and substance abuse* (pp. 319–343). San Diego, CA: Academic Press.

DiClemente, C.C. and Prochaska, J.O. (1982). Self-change and therapy change of smoking behavior: A comparison of processes of change in cessation and maintenance. *Addictive Behaviors* 7, 133–142.

Djerf-Pierre, M. (2011). The Difference Engine. *Feminist Media Studies* 11(1), 43-51.

Eagly, A.H. and Chaicken, S. (1993). *The psychology of attitudes*. Fort Worth, TX: Harcourt, Brace, and Janovich.

Edwards, L. (2014). Public Relations Theories: An Overview. In - Tench, R., and Yeomans, L. (eds.) (2014) *Exploring Public Relations*, 3rd edition. Longman: Pearson.

Eisenman, D.P., Cordasco, K.M., Asch, S., Golden, J.F. and Glik, D. (2007). Disaster planning and risk communication with vulnerable communities. *American Journal of Public Health* 97(1), 109–115.

Festinger, L. (1964). Behavioral Support for Opinion Change. *The Public Opinion Quarterly* 28(3), 404–417.

Festinger, L. (1957). *A theory of cognitive dissonance*. Evanston, IL: Row, Peterson and Company.

Freeman, R.E. (2010). *Strategic Management: A Stakeholder Approach*. Cambridge, Cambridge University Press.

Freeman, R.E., Harrison, J.S., Wicks, A.C., Parmar, B.L. and De Colle, S. (2010). *Stakeholder Theory: The State of Art*. Cambridge: Cambridge University Press.

Fishbein, M. and Ajzen, I. (1975). *Belief, attitude, intention, and behaviour: An introduction to theory and research*. Reading, MA: Addison-Wesley.

Fogg, A. (2014). Sainsbury's Christmas Ad is a Dangerous and Disrespectful Masterpiece. *The Guardian Online*. Retrieved from: http://www.theguardian.com/commentisfree/2014/nov/13/sainsburys-christmas-ad-first-world-war (11 February 2015).

Gibbons, F.X., Eggleston, T.J. and Benthin, A.C. (1997). Cognitive reactions to smoking relapse: the reciprocal relation between dissonance and self-esteem. *Journal of Personality and Social Psychology* 72(1), 184–95.

Glass, D. (1964). Changes in Liking as a Means of Reducing Cognitive Discrepancies between Self-Esteem and Aggression. *Journal of Personality* 32, 531–49.

Goldman, R. and Papson, S. (1998). Nike Culture: The Sign Of the Swoosh. London: Sage.

Grow, J.M. (2006). Stories of Community: The First Ten Years of Nike Women's Advertising. Accepted version. American Journal of Semiotics 22(1–4), 165–194. Marquette University e-Publications@ Marquette Repository. Retrieved from https://

epublications.marquette.edu/cgi/viewcontent.cgi?article=1022&context=comm_fac (23 April 2019)

Grow, J.M. and Wolburg, J.M. (2006). Selling Truth: How Nike's Advertising to Women Claimed a Contested Reality Philosophy Documentation Center. *Advertising and Society Review* 7(2). Retrieved from: https://muse-jhu-edu.ezproxy.leedsbeckett.ac.uk/article/202976 (22 April 2019).

Grunig, J.E. (2003). Constructing public relations theory and practice. In Dervin, B. and Chaffee, S. (eds.) *Communication: another kind of horse race: Essays honouring Richard F. Carter* (pp. 85–115). Cresskill, NJ: Hampton Press.

Grunig, L.A., Grunig, J.E. and Dozier, D.M. (2002). *Excellent Public Relations and Effective Organizations*. Mahwah: Lawrence Erlbaum Associates.

Grunig, L.A., Toth, E.L. and Hon, L.C. (2001). *Women in Public Relations: How gender influences practice*. New York: The Guilford Press.

Grunig, L.A., Toth, E.L. and Hon, L.C. (2000). Feminist values in public relations. *Journal of Public Relations Research* 12(1), 49–68.

Grunig, J.E. (1992). *Excellence in Public Relations and Communication Management*. Hillsdale: Lawrence Erlbaum Associates.

Grunig, J.E. and White, J. (1992). The effect of worldviews on public relations theory and practice. In - Grunig, J.E., Dozier, D.M., Ehling, W.P., Grunig, L.A., Repper, F.C. and White, J. (eds) *Excellence in public relations and communication management* (pp. 31–64). Hillsdale, NJ: Lawrence Erlbaum Associates.

Grunig, J.E. and Repper, F. (1992). Strategic Management, Publics, and Issues. In – Grunig, J. E. (ed.) (1992). *Excellence in Public Relations and Communication Management* (pp. 117–158). Hillsdale, NJ: Erlbaum.

Grunig, J.E. and Grunig, L.A. (1992). Models of public relations and communication. In - Grunig, J.E., Dozier, D.M., Ehling, W.P., Grunig, L.A., Repper, F.C. and White, J. (eds) *Excellence in public relations and communication management* (pp. 285–326). Hillsdale, NJ: Lawrence Erlbaum Associates.

Grunig, J.E. (1989). Publics, audiences and market segments: Models of receivers of campaign messages. In – Salmon, C. T. (ed.) *Information campaigns: Managing the process of social change* (pp. 197–226). Newbury Park, CA: SAGE.

Grunig, J.E. (1989b). Symmetrical presuppositions as a framework for public relations theory. In – Botan, C.H. and Hazleton, V. (eds) *Public relations theory* (pp. 17–44). Hillsdale, NJ: Lawrence Erlbaum Associates.

Grunig, J.E. and Hunt, T. (1984). *Managing Public Relations*. New York: Holt, Rinehart and Winston.

Harmon-Jones E. and Mills, J. (1999). *Cognitive dissonance: Progress on a pivotal theory in social psychology*. Washington, DC: American Psychological Association.

Hausenblas, H.A., Giacobbi, P., Cook, B., Rhodes, R.E. and Cruz, A. (2011). A prospective examination of pregnant and nonpregnant women's physical activity beliefs and behaviours. *Journal of Infant and Reproductive Psychology* 29, 308–319.

Helstein, M.T. (2003). That's who I Want to be: The Politics and Production of Desire within Nike Advertising to Women. *Journal of Sport and Social Issues* 27(3), 276–292.

Hooton, C. (2014). 'Sainsbury's Christmas Advert Is Like A 4-Minute 'F*** You' To John Lewis And Monty The Penguin'. *The Independent Online*. Retrieved from: http://www.independent.co.uk/arts-entertainment/tv/news/sainsburys-trenchesbased-christmas-advert-is-like-a-4minute-f-you-to-john-lewis-9857588.html (11 February 2015)

IPR (2012). *IPR.org.uk – Public Relations – Public Relations through Time*. Retrieved from http://www.ipr.org.uk/public-relations-through-time.html (21 January 2016)

Jaccard, J., McDonald, R., Wan, C.K., Dittus, P.J. and Quinlan, S. (2002). The accuracy of self-reports of condom use and sexual behaviour. *Journal of Applied Social Psychology* 32, 1863–1905.

Jardine, A. (2017). *These powerful NIKE ads challenge female stereotypes in Russia, Turkey and the Middle East*. Retrieved from https://adage.com/creativity/work/what-are-girls-made/51186 (23 April 2019).

Jones, J.P. (1955). Organization for public relations. In Bernays, E. L. (ed) *The engineering of consent* (pp. 156–184). Norman: University of Oklahoma Press.

Katz, R. and Lazarsfeld, P.F. (1955). *Personal Influence*. New York: Free Press.

Kim, J-N. (2011). Public segmentation using situational theory of problem solving: Illustrating summation method and testing segmented public profiles. *PRism* 8(2). Retrieved from http://www.prismjournal.org/homepage.html (9 December 2015)

Kim, J-N, and Grunig, J.E. (2011). Problem Solving and Communicative Action: A Situational Theory of Problem Solving. *Journal of Communication* 61, 120–149.

Kitchen, P.J., Kerr, G., Schultz, D.E., McColl, R. and Pals, H. (2014). The elaboration likelihood model: review, critique and research agenda. *European Journal of Marketing* 48(11/12), 2033–2050.

Krstić, M. (2014). Rational choice theory and addiction behaviour. *Tržište* 26 (2), 163–177.

Lafrance, M.R. (1998). Colonizing the Feminine: Nike's Intersections of Postfeminism and Hyperconsumption. In – Rail, G. (ed) *Sport and Postmodern Times* (pp. 117–139). Albany: State University of New York Press.

Lattimore, D., Baskin, O., Heiman, S.T. and Toth, E.L. (2009). *Public Relations: The Profession and the Practice*, 3rd edition. New York: McGraw-Hill.

L'Etang, J. and Pieczka, M. (1996). Critical Perspectives in Public Relations. In - L'Etang, J., and Pieczka, M. (eds.) *Critical Perspectives in Public Relations*. London: International Thompson Business Press.

Lucas, S. (2000). Nike's Commercial Solution: Girls, Sneakers, and Salvation. *International Review for the Sociology of Sport* 35(3), 149–164. Retrieved from https://www.youtube.com/watch?v=VhB3l1gCz2E (21 January 2016)

Leggett, W. (2014). The politics of behaviour change: nudge, neoliberalism and the state. *Policy and Politics* 42(1), 3–19.

Lewin, K. (1943). Psychology and the process of group living. *Journal of Social Psychology*, 17, 113–131. Reprinted in – Martin, E. (eds) (1999, pp. 333–345).*The complete social scientist: A Kurt Lewin reader Gold.*

Littlejohn, S.W. (2002). *Theories of Mass Communication*. Balmont, CA: Wadsworth Publishing (pp. 128–130).

Maharjan, P. (2018). Elaboration Likelihood Model. *Businesstopia*, January 8. Retrieved from https://www.businesstopia.net/communication/elaboration-likelihood-model (24 April 2019)

Manca, S., Altoe, G., Wesley Schultz, P. and Fornara, F. (2019). The Persuasive Route to Sustainable Mobility: Elaboration Likelihood Model and Emotions Implicit Attitudes. *Environment and Behavior.* Online first. Retrieved from https://journals.sagepub.com/doi/abs/10.1177/0013916518820898 (28 April 2019)

Maule, S. (2015). A nudge and a think – applying behavioural science in PR. *PR Week,* September 10. Retrieved from https://www.prweek.com/article/1363503/nudge-think-applying-behavioural-science-pr (27 April 2019).

McGuire, W.J. (1964). Inducing resistance to persuasion: some contemporary approaches. In Berkowitz L. (ed.) *Advances in Experimental Social Psychology,* Vol. 1 (pp. 191–229). New York, NY: Academic Press.

McKeever, B.W., Pressgrove, G., McKeever, R. and Zheng, Y. (2015). Toward a theory of situational support: A model for exploring fundraising, advocacy and organizational support. *Public Relations Review.* Online first. doi: 10.1016/j.pubrev.2015.09.009

Mill, J.S. (20152015[1859]). *On Liberty, Utilitarianism and Other Essays.* Oxford: Oxford University Press.

Miller, G.R. (1989). Persuasion and public relations: Two 'ps' in a pod. In – Botan, C. H., and Hazleton, V. (eds) *Public relations theory* (pp. 45–66). Hillsdale, NJ: Lawrence Erlbaum Associates.

Murphy, P. (1991). The limits of symmetry: A game theory approach to symmetric and asymmetric public relations. In – Grunig, J., and Grunig, L. (eds) *Public relations research annual* (Vol. 1, pp. 87–96). Hillsdale, NJ: Lawrence Erlbaum Associates.

Netflix (2019). *Subscription information.* Retrieved from https://www.netflix.com/signup (27 April 2019).

NHS (2019). *Organ donation law in England is changing.* Retrieved from https://www.organdonation.nhs.uk/uk-laws/organ-donation-law-in-england/ (27 April 2019).

Nike (2019). Retrieved from https://news.Nike.com/news/Nike-tech-pack-fall-2018 (23 April 2019).

Nudd, T. (2011). Apple's 'Get a Mac,' the Complete Campaign. *The Ad Week,* April 13. Retrieved from https://www.adweek.com/creativity/apples-get-mac-complete-campaign-130552/ (29 April 2019).

Ogden, J. (2003). Some problems with social cognition models: A pragmatic and conceptual analysis. *Health Psychology* 22, 424–428.

Oullier, O., Cialdini, R., Thaler, R.H. and Mullainathan, S. (2010). Improving public health prevention with a nudge. Chapter 3. In Oullier, O. and Sauneron, S. (eds) *Improving public health prevention with behavioural, cognitive and neuroscience.* Paris: Centre for Strategic Analysis, The French Government, Office of the Prime Minister. Retrieved from http://oullier.free.fr/files/2010_Oullier-Cialdini-Thaler-Mullainathan_Neuroscience-Prevention-Public-Health_Nudge-Behavioral-Economics.pdf (27 April 2019).

PETA (2019). *Go veg campaign website.* Retrieved from http://features.peta.org/how-to-go-vegan/ (23 April 2019).

PETA (2019b). *How to wear vegan campaign website.* Retrieved from http://features.peta.org/how-to-wear-vegan/ (23 April 2019).

Petty, R.E. and Cacioppo, J.T. (1983). Central and peripheral routes to persuasion: Application to advertising. *Advertising and Consumer Psychology,* 1, 3–23. Lexington, MA: D.C. Heath and Company (pp. 3–23).

Pfau, M. and Wan, H.H. (2006). Persuasion: An Intrinsic Function of Public Relations. In Botan, C.H. and Hazleton, V. (eds) *Public Relations Theories II.* N. Y.: Lawrence Erlbaum Associates.

Pfau, M. (1992). The potential of inoculation in promoting resistance to the effectiveness of comparative advertising messages. *Communication Quarterly* 40, 26–44.

Pfau, M. (1990). A channel approach to television influence. *Journal of Broadcasting and Electronic Media* 34, 195–214.

Pfau, M. and Burgoon, M. (1988). Inoculation in political campaign communication. *Health Communication Research* 15, 91–111.

Prochaska, J.O., DiClemente, C.C. and Norcross, J.C. (1992). In Search of How People Change Applications to Addictive Behaviors. *American Psychologist* 47(9), 1102–1114.

Prochaska, J.Q. and DiClemente, C.C. (1984). *The transtheoretical approach: Crossing traditional boundaries of change.* Homewood, IL: Dorsey Press.

Prochaska, J. and DiClemente, C. (1983). Stages and processes of self-change of smoking: towards an integrated model of change. *Journal of Consulting Clinical Psychology* 51, 390–395.

Renton, A. (2008). Jamie Oliver's Ministry of Food goes to Rotherham. *The Guardian,* 1 October. Retrieved from http://www.theguardian.com/lifeandstyle/wordofmouth/2008/oct/01/jamie.oliver.ministry.food (8 December 2015).

Seitel, F.P. (1998). *The practice of public relations* (7th edition). Upper Saddle River, NJ: Prentice Hall.

SpectorPR (2010). *Interview with Edward Bernays.* Retrieved from https://www.youtube.com/watch?v=6pyyP2chM8k (24 April 2019).

Spinks, R. (2015). How Nudge Theory techniques can benefit PR professionals. *360 Integrated PR blog website.* Retrieved from https://www.360integrated.com/blog/how-nudge-theory-techniques-can-benefit-marketers/ (27 April 2019).

Sriramesh, K. and Verčič, D. (1995). International public relations: a framework for future research. *Journal of Communication Management* 6(2), 103–117.

Sriramesh, K. (2010). Globalization and public relations: opportunities for growth and reformulation. In Heath, R.L. (ed.) *The SAGE Handbook of Public Relations.* Thousand Oaks: SAGE.

Stainton Rogers, W. (2011). *Social Psychology,* 2nd edition. New York: Open University Press and McGraw-Hill Education.

Stauber, J. and Rampton, S. (1995). *Toxic sludge is good for you: Lies, damn lies and the public relations industry.* Monroe, Maine: Common Courage Press.

Steele, C. (1988). The psychology of self-affirmation: Sustaining the integrity of the self. *Advances in Experimental Social Psychology* 21, 261–346.

Strong, E.K., Jr. (1925). Theories of Selling. *Journal of Applied Psychology,* 9, 75–86.

Thaler, R.H. (2015). The Power of Nudges, for Good and Bad. *The New York Times,* 31 October. Retrieved from https://www.nytimes.com/2015/11/01/upshot/the-power-of-nudges-for-good-and-bad.html (27 April 2019).

Thaler, R. and Sunstein C. (2009 [2008]). *Nudge: Improving decisions about health, wealth and happiness.* London: Penguin.

The Grocer (2018). *Iceland's palm oil ad ranked 'most powerful' ad of Christmas 2018.* Retrieved from https://www.thegrocer.co.uk/marketing/icelands-palm-oil-ad-ranked-most-powerful-xmas-2018-ad/574500.article (24 April 2019).

Telcia, E.E., Madenb, C. and Kanturc, D. (2011).The theory of cognitive dissonance: A marketing and management perspective. *Procedia Social and Behavioral Sciences* 24, 378–386.

Tench, R., Sun. W. and Jones, B. (2014). Introduction: CSR Communication as an emerging field of study (pp. 3–25). In Tench, R., Sun, W. and Jones, B. (Eds.) *Communicating Corporate Social Responsibility: Perspectives and Practice.* Howard House: Emerald.

Terry, D.J., Hogg, M.A. and White, K.M. (1999). The theory of planned behaviour: Self-identity, social identity and group norms. *British Journal of Social Psychology* 38, 225–244.

Topić, M., Mitchell, B. and Munroe, O. (2018). *Product and Packaging Innovation: Attitudes, Behaviours, and Strategies for Sustainable Packaging.* Leeds: The Retail Institute, Leeds Beckett University.

Topič, M. (2015). Public relations theories: an overview. In Tench, R. and Yeomans, L. (eds) *Exploring Public Relations* (4th edition). Longman: Pearson.

Van Ruler, B. (2005). Commentary: Professionals are from Venus, scholars are from Mars. *Public Relations Review* 31, 159–173.

Vasquez, G.M. (1996). Public relations as negotiation: An issue development perspective. *Journal of Public Relations Research* 8, 57–77.

Veil, S. and Kent, M. (2008). Issues management and inoculation: Tylenol's responsible dosing advertising. *Public Relations Review* 34, 399–4.2.

Wainwright, M. (2006). The battle of Rawmarsh. *The Guardian,* 20 September. Retrieved from http://www.theguardian.com/education/2006/sep/20/schoolmeals.schools (8 December 2015).

Weeks, M. (2011). *Philosophy in Minutes*. London: Quercus.

Wicker, A.W. (1969). Attitudes versus actions: The relationship of verbal and overt behavioural responses to attitude objects. *Journal of Social Issues* 25, 41–78.

Windahl, S., Signitzer, B. and Olson, J.T. (1992). Using Communication Theory: An introduction to planned communication. London: Sage.

WOAH (2019). *The Campaign website.* Retrieved from https://woah.org.au/indigo/ (23 April 2019).

CHAPTER 9

Anne Gregory

Strategic public relations planning and management

Source: Nature Picture Library/Alamy Stock Photo

Learning outcomes

By the end of this chapter you should be able to:

- describe and assess the approaches to planning and managing campaigns and choose an appropriate one
- explain and use strategic tools to analyse the principal external and organisational context in which planning and management takes place
- plan a research-based strategic campaign or programme
- effectively manage and evaluate the impact of campaigns and programmes
- critique and apply relevant underlying theories.

Structure

- The importance of overall context
- External environment
- Internal environment
- Implications of context
- Strategic public relations programmes and campaigns
- Why planning is important
- Systems and alternative approaches to planning

Introduction

Every organisation has its own approach to the way it plans and manages its public relations campaigns and programmes. That is because there are significant differences in the types of organisations there are, the context in which they operate, and their specific public relations needs. A single-issue pressure group will have a very focused purpose and its publics and stakeholders may be very specific. A large government department – for example, a Department of Health – will touch the lives of every citizen in a variety of ways, from prenatal care to childhood and adult illnesses through to end-of-life care. Some business enterprises operate in tiny niche markets in one country, while others such as Virgin operate in several markets on a global scale. Airbnb as an organisation exists purely online, but many supermarkets have a large physical presence. However, because of the ubiquity of online, every organisation has the potential to be seen and known globally, and potentially anyone who takes an interest can take a stake in it, that is, exert influence that might affect it in some way.

The first part of this chapter examines a range of factors that influence the way public relations campaigns and programmes are planned within organisations. It will be seen that understanding and analysing organisational context is vitally important. Public relations campaigns and programmes do not stand in isolation: they are both 'buffers' and 'bridges' (Meznar and Nigh 1995: 976) to the world and therefore a profound understanding of this outside environment is imperative. Public relations campaigns and programmes are often directed at or involve staff within the organisation, and they too have lives outside work, thus any formal communication with them must make sense within the broader context of their lives.

Importantly, the pace of change is increasing, and the external environment is becoming ever more complex. As Borge Brende, President of the World Economic Forum (WEF) says in the Global Risks Report for 2019 (WEF 2019: 5):

The world is facing a growing number of complex and interconnected challenges—from slowing global growth and persistent economic inequality to climate change, geopolitical tensions and the accelerating pace of the Fourth Industrial Revolution.

However, as he goes on to say:

There has never been a more pressing need for a collaborative and multi-stakeholder approach to shared global problems.

This is both the opportunity and challenge facing public relations professionals today who advise leaders on and put into effect these collaborations and it calls for a systematic yet flexible response. That is at the heart of strategic planning and management.

The second part of the chapter examines in detail the planning and management of campaigns using a framework designed to ensure all the essential steps are covered.

The importance of context

Business history is littered with companies that have not been able to adapt to changing global and industry trends or have struggled to do so. High street retailers and banks have had to adapt to online shopping and radically change their business model – some failed to do so – such as Borders, the book retailer. Polaroid struggled with the advent of digital cameras but has adjusted to a reduced market and extreme competition from mobile phone and tablet manufacturers.

Although it is true that everyone in an organisation communicates both between themselves and with external groups too, public relations is the formal management function that organisations use to handle the relationships they have with numerous publics and stakeholder groups, both internally and externally. Of course, they are not the only ones with this formal responsibility; for example, marketing and legal departments are also tasked with developing relationships with key groups of stakeholders (see Box 9.1) and HR usually has a major role in employee communications. However, even where it does not have direct formal responsibility for key relationships, public relations often has a role in assisting these other departments with their communication tasks.

These stakeholder groups comprise people who are, in turn, affected by developments, trends and issues in society. The environment in which modern organisations operate is dynamic, rapidly changing and complex. The forces at play are difficult to understand and their consequences hard to predict and new issues and trends arise, some of them very rapidly. For example, the issues created by Brexit, the UK's exit from the European Union, has far-reaching effects not only on organisations in the UK and Europe, but on all organisations that trade with Europe. Investors are anxious too. The rise of insurgent groups, and political and economic instabilities in Iraq, Syria and parts of Africa and Asia, have created a huge flow of refugees and immigrants into

Box 9.1
Stakeholders and publics

The words stakeholder and publics are often used interchangeably. In this chapter stakeholders are those groups that have a 'stake' in an organisation i.e. those who are affected by or can affect it (Freeman, 1984).

Stakeholders can have very loose or intermittent relationships with an organisation and can be passive. Publics on the other hand are active: they have an issue, a problem or see opportunities and are supportive of the organisation. They have much closer engagement with it (Grunig and Hunt 1984). Any stakeholder has the potential to become a public. See more on this in Chapter 10. For ease of reference the word 'stakeholder' is used in this chapter to denote any individual or group who has a significant relationship in the organisation.

---

adjoining countries such as Jordan and wider afield to Europe, Australasia and the USA. The impact of this in the longer term is still playing out, but issues around social, economic and cultural integration and the implications for political leaders are considerable.

Organisations themselves are changing. For example, there are more women and part-time workers and, in many countries, more migrant employees. Furthermore, attitudes are changing. Because, certainly in the Western world, people feel empowered in their lives outside work and have more choices about where they live, their lifestyles and what they will spend their income on, they are no longer willing to be disempowered at work and this can bring challenges to employers (Myers 2016). In addition, organisations now find themselves much more accountable to external groups who want to know what they stand for and how they conduct themselves.

This endlessly dynamic, more complex and ever-changing context has an impact on planning. The traditional strategic planning models were developed in the twentieth century when business life could be said to be more predictable and slower, and where the dominant business philosophy was that an organisation could, given the right analysis and plan, impose itself on the market (see academics such as Igor Ansoff (1988) and Michael Porter (1980)). Therefore, although planning is important, plans themselves must be agile and flexible in order to be able to react to – and at times lead – the ongoing and changing conversations that organisations have with their stakeholders (van Ruler 2015). Context is of course different for each organisation and depends critically on, for example, what sector the organisation operates in, where it is based geographically, its size, areas of operation and culture.

External environment

The external context is vitally important for organisations because they have limited influence over it. Smart organisations constantly scan the external environment to identify emerging trends and issues. Having spotted these issues early, precious time is bought for the organisation to adjust itself to them, to engage with them and, sometimes, to influence their development. The public relations function is a natural organisational 'boundary spanner' (White and Dozier 1992), because building relationships requires it to build links from inside the organisation to the outside world and vice versa, and within the organisation itself. Therefore, public relations is perfectly placed to do this environmental scanning.

The external environment can be divided into two categories: the 'macro' and the 'task' environment (Grant 2016).

Macro environment

The macro environment can be described as the 'big picture' over which the organisation has no control but could well impact on it. These are the issues that emerge from the actions of governments, economic and social trends and from scientific and technological developments. Sometimes called the 'remote' or 'societal' environment, the macro environment develops beyond and independent of any organisation's operating situation (de Wit 2017).

To make sense of the macro environment, analysts use frameworks which help them systematically examine environmental influences. The most well-known analytical tool is PEST, which divides the overall environment into four categories – Political, Economic,

> ### Think about 9.1
>
> #### Macro trends
>
> What macro or global trends do you think are important? What are their possible implications for public relations professionals? Suppose you are in change of a children's immunisation campaign: how might you communicate with rural communities in emerging countries that do not have online access or very limited mobile technology?
>
> #### Feedback
>
> For further information about global trends look at https://www.pwc.co.uk/issues/megatrends.html and watch https://www.youtube.com/watch?v=hqthrSDHqZw

Political	Economic
Change of Government	Fluctuation in currency values
New political alliances within and between nations	International trade agreements
Employment legislation	Interest rates
Industry regulation	Skills level in workforce
Environmental legislation	Levels of employment
	Inflation
Social	**Technological**
Social attitudes	Impact of technology on work practices
Demographic changes	Developments in IT
Lifestyle developments	Access to technology
Purchasing habits	Cost of research and development
Levels of education	Speed of change

Figure 9.1 Example of a PEST analysis

Social and Technological. Figure 9.1 provides some examples of topics that fall under each of these headings. What is important is the impact they may have on an existing relationship or what they reveal about the need to develop a relationship. For example, a potential change in industry regulation may indicate the need to deepen relationships with the trade organisation and develop contacts with government departments for lobbying purposes. In addition, the identification of certain topics could present potential issues for the organisation (see Chapter 20 'Public affairs' for further discussion).

Given the increasing complexity of the macro environment, PEST is beginning to be regarded as a rather limited tool. A development of PEST is EPISTLE, which includes the four elements of PEST, but also forces consideration of Information, Legal and the green Environment. The 'information' heading invites special consideration of the fact that empowerment comes to groups and individuals through new technologies, although it must be remembered that people who are deprived of relevant technology will become increasingly disenfranchised and unable to engage in debate effectively. The legal environment is becoming more complex. Organisations not only have to be aware of national regulations, but also of transnational legislation such as trading laws and other legal agreements such as those reached at the climate summit held in Paris, December 2015 and affirmed in by 184 nations and the European Union in 2018. There are also non-binding, but moral undertakings agreed to by nations such as the Sustainable Development Goals adopted by the United Nations where all member states have committed to their achievement by 2030 (see Box 9.2).

Clearly, different organisations will be affected in different ways by these macro issues. A car manufacturer will be very susceptible to political, technological, environmental and social pressures to design engines that are carbon efficient, or to offer electric alternatives. A fashion manufacturer needs to be acutely aware of social trends and how consumer preferences and changing lifestyles will impact on their business, but also of the issues created by them around body image and throwaway fashion. A careful eye needs to be kept on all these macro trends because issues arising from them are often interrelated – technological developments can drive social change and vice versa. Also, some issues could be placed in more than one category, for example, educational achievement not only has social consequences, but economic and political relevance too. While there are dozens of issues and trends in the wider environment is worth picking out a few for special mention because of their direct impact on public relations work.

Box 9.2
Sustainable development goals

According to the United Nations, the Sustainable Development Goals are a blueprint to achieve a better and more sustainable future for all. They address global challenges including poverty, inequality, climate, environmental degradation, prosperity, and peace and justice. There are 17 goals in total and they are targeted to be achieved by 2030. The 17 goals are:

For more details on this initiative and on each goal, go to https://www.un.org/sustainabledevelopment/sustainable-development-goals/

1. End poverty in all its forms	2. Zero Hunger	3. Health
4. Education	5. Gender equality & women's empowerment	6. Water & sanitation
7. Energy	8. Economic growth	9. Infrastructure & industrialization
10. Inequality	11. Cities	12. Sustainable consumption and production
13. Climate change	14. Oceans	15. Biodiversity, forests, desertification
16. Peace, justice & strong institutions	17. Partnerships	

Picture 9.1 The United Nations Sustainable Development Goals are a blueprint to achieve a better and more sustainable future (*source:* White House Photo/Alamy Stock Photo)

Globalisation

Public relations people working for global organisations will understand the need to communicate across time zones, cultures, languages and different communication delivery systems. But, even if the organisation is local, what it does may have global implications and attract global attention. A local delicatessen may buy products from an intermediary who is supplied by a global grower who damages the environment in developing countries. Organisations also need to be sensitive about what they put on their websites and social media platforms for local audiences as these may be accessed by people from other cultures who

> **Explore 9.1**
>
> **Awareness of facts in the media**
>
> Fake news is a big topic of discussion, but even the reputable press have their news agendas and 'frame' stories without wanting to tell untruths. We are all susceptible to the prevailing narrative in the media. Go to Gapminder.org and take the Gapminder test.
>
> **Feedback**
>
> If you scored less than 6, what practical steps can you take to broaden your worldview and knowledge of current affairs? Do you always go to news and information sources that reinforce your own point of view? How might you access other sources that will give you an alternative? How often do you ask yourself the question 'how can I find out if this is true'?

may take exception. For example, encouragement to drink alcohol may be offensive in cultures where alcohol is frowned on.

Shifts in power

Jim O'Neill of Goldman Sachs came up with the term BRICs in 2001 to describe what was believed then to be the new powerhouse economic nations: Brazil, Russia, India and China. South Africa was later incorporated into the group. While all may not have turned out as predicted, the traditional Western economic powers are being overtaken by China in particular, with India making rapid strides. This means that the old comfortable alliances are being reshaped and new ways of doing business and new cultures are coming into the organisational world. For public relations practitioners this means that business stakeholder groups are likely to expand beyond traditional boundaries. They will have to become adept at operating in a variety of cultures and alert to the context in which public relations operates, such as the differing media, political and social norms which can be tricky to navigate and where language proficiency can be an issue. Alternatively, there is a rich opportunity for the public relations practitioner to become the guardian of these crucial relationship because their knowledge of context will be broad and deep.

Information technology

When linked to the theme of globalisation this is a very powerful force. The fact that information can be sent and accessed immediately across time and geographical boundaries brings great opportunities but can also introduce threats for the public relations professional. Activists can organise quickly and globally and spread news of malpractice or disseminate misinformation and fake news worldwide instantly. Contrariwise, organisations can connect and converse with stakeholders in new, enriching and innovative ways. This capability brings opportunities and pressures for organisations and public relations practitioners who needed to be geared for action 24 hours a day, seven days a week, 365 days a year.

Immigration, migration and pluralism

In an era of mass migration, easy travel and accessible information, society is becoming more plural. The merging of values and ideals, together with an understanding and acceptance of different cultures and alternative views are taken as a sign of advancing civilisation. But at the same time, it increases uncertainty and insecurity and Ritzer (2019) says that in order to replace the old certainties people in developed societies are seeking out like-minded others who share their tastes and values: the number of pressure groups, non-governmental organisations (NGOs) and special interest groups is burgeoning. Furthermore, in order to introduce meaning and simplicity to complex lives with few certainties, there has been a rise in nationalism, fundamentalism and activism whose proponents appear to provide straightforward answers. Stepping around the tensions involved is a great challenge for public relations professionals. They find themselves having to assert or defend a position while knowing they will offend someone.

News media

The traditional news media comprising newspapers and broadcast channels have been revolutionised over the last few years (see also Chapter 14). Global news businesses owned by powerful groups and individuals, often with their own political agendas, were, up until the mid-2000s, setting and leading public opinion. However, they then found themselves threatened

Explore 9.2

Stakeholders

Who are the stakeholders of a University? How would you describe the relationship linkages between the University and its:

- students (home and overseas);
- lecturers;
- governors;
- local residents;
- central government education departments;
- other universities?

Feedback

Using de Wit's web of relational actors (see Figure 9.2), where would you place each of these stakeholders in this web?

---

be free of bias, for example that provided by public relations professionals. While this provides openings and opportunities to public relations, there are dangers in the 'PRisation of the media' (Moloney 2006). A free press requires resources to operate independently and challenge vested interests. There should be a distance between public relations practitioners and journalists because they have very different jobs to do (see Chapter 2).

Knowledge of global issues is not just important because of its impact on public relations work, but increasingly all organisations, including those in the private sector, are seen to be accountable for contributing to some of these problems, such as environmental damage, and for solving some of them. They are seen not to be isolated economic units, but, partly because of the huge size of these corporations, big social actors. Look at Mini case study 9.1 about the Bill and Melinda

as online sources of information become more ubiquitous. Since then many newspapers have closed or changed their mode of operating with online coming to the fore. According to the American Pew Research Centre's *State of the News Media 2017* (Pew Center 2019), the audience for every major sector of the US news media, including digital-native news sites' audiences, fell in 2017, with the only exception being radio. Newspaper circulation declined by 11 per cent from 2016 to 2017 and the number of newsroom jobs, also according to Pew fell by 45 per cent from 2008 to 2017. Interestingly, digital advertising across all digital channels, not just news, jumped by 25 per cent from 2016 to 2017 and 68 per cent of US adults obtain at least some of their news via social media platforms.

In distinction to this, the 2019 Edelman Trust Barometer (Edelman 2019) identified a significant rise in engagement with the news agenda, which they noted was 22 points up from 2018. This was accompanied by a desire to look to reliable sources such as the traditional media, rather than relying on social media which respondents saw as being more prone to fake news.

The impact of job losses in news is concerning, since rather than researching their own stories, hard-pressed journalists are becoming increasingly dependent on other sources including citizen-generated material and content which cannot be guaranteed to

---

Mini case study 9.1
The Bill and Melinda Gates Foundation

Bill Gates, the former CEO of Microsoft and his wife Melinda, now dedicate their time to solving some of the big societal issues such as health and poverty alleviation in developing countries. This is not new though. Throughout their lives they have been committed to giving back to local communities and volunteering.

It was in 1997 that they were prompted to act. They read an article about children in developing countries who were dying from diseases that had long disappeared in the US and determined to do something about it. Since then the Foundation has given grants worth $46 billion, much of this to developing world projects. According to the Gates Foundation Annual Letter of 2018 projects in the developing world receive received funding of $4 billion per year.

The Gates also give to projects in the USA. Building on their background in the computing industry and believing that personal computing can be an activity for public and social good, in 1997 they launched the Gates Library Foundation giving £200 million to allow all public libraries to offer free online access.

For more information on the Gates Foundation see https://www.gatesfoundation.org

Political	Economic
Devolution	Currency
Government	Employment rates
International alliances	Financial market performance
Legislation	Inflation
Local government	Interest rates
	International trade agreements
Social	**Technological**
Buying behaviour	Artificial intelligence
Demographics	Cloud services
Educational attainment	Mobile technologies
Family make-up	R&D
Social mindset	Workflow change

Figure 9.2 de Wit's Web of Relational Actors (*source:* Adapted from De Wit, R. and R. Meyer (2010). Strategy: process, content, context. London: Thomson)

Gates Foundation to see how one of the great entrepreneurs of the current century considers his social responsibility.

Task environment

The task environment consists of those forces and organisations that the organisation interacts with regularly and which can affect its performance. The task environment is normally categorised into groups of influential stakeholders with identifiable characteristics such as customers, suppliers, regulators, competitors and pressure groups.

A useful categorisation of stakeholders is that provided by de Wit (2017), who identifies the web of relational actors that an organisation interacts with (see Figure 9.2).

- *Upstream vertical (supplier) relations are relatively self-explanatory.* Suppliers include providers of raw materials and business services but also include labour and information that is external to the organisation and upon which it draws.
- *Downstream vertical (buyer) relations.* These can be clients, customers or intermediaries who sell the products of the organisation.
- *Direct horizontal (industry insider) relations.* This includes relationships between the organisation and others in their industry – they are at the same level.
- *Indirect (industry outsider) relations.* This is where an organisation has relationships with others outside its industry, for example those who will provide complementary goods or services such as a bedroom furniture manufacturer working with an interior design organisation.
- *Sociocultural actors.* Those individuals or organisations that have an impact on societal values, beliefs and behaviours. These may include community groups, the media, religious organisations, NGOs and opinion leaders.
- *Economic actors.* Those organisations who influence the general economic context such as central banks, stock exchanges, taxation authorities, trade organisations.
- *Political/legal actors.* These are organisations which set or influence the regulatory regime and include government, regulatory bodies, international institutions and special interest groups.
- *Technological actors.* Given the importance of technology to modern life, those who influence the pace and direction of technological developments and the development of new knowledge are critical. Organisations such as universities, research bodies, government agencies and patent offices play a role here.

Of course, one of the issues in categorising stakeholders like this is that it does not give a realistic picture of how stakeholders interact with each other, or the position of the organisation in their lives. The reality is that organisations are part of a network and are pulled towards different stakeholders at different times and with different intensity depending on context. This stakeholder network acts as an eco-system and there are different forces in play at any one time which generate re-configurations. For example, after the

Box 9.3
Circuits of communication

Boundary-less organisations such as Uber and Airbnb are defined by stakeholder transactions and conversations with and about them. Stakeholders gather around the feature of the organisation they are interested in, for example reviews, anti-social behaviour, price and location. The totality of the conversations defines the organisation. The diagram below shows the organisation's stakeholders clustered around issues-based interactions and conversations (Gregory and Halff 2017).

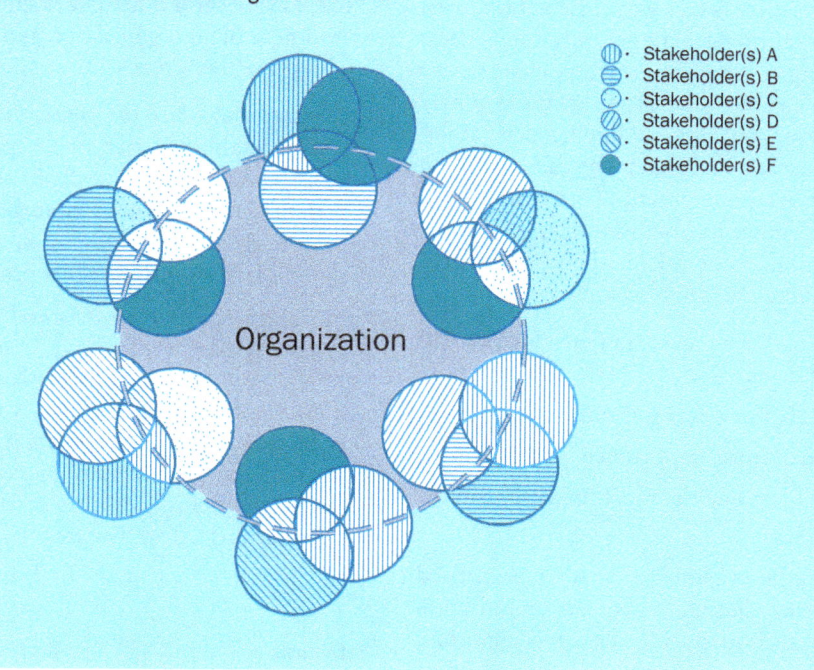

- Stakeholder(s) A
- Stakeholder(s) B
- Stakeholder(s) C
- Stakeholder(s) D
- Stakeholder(s) E
- Stakeholder(s) F

---

global financial crisis banks were pulled closer to regulatory and governmental stakeholders as they sought to control them. The stakeholder network has a tension, rather like a spider's web, with the organisation seeking equilibrium between the competing demands of a range of interconnected stakeholders. This is an important understanding for public relations practitioners, particularly as organisations are changing their form and structure because of technology. Indeed, many organisations in the sharing economy such as Uber, Booking.com and Airbnb do not have traditional structures at all, and Gregory and Halff (2017) claim they can only be described as organisations because they have 'circuits of communication' which define them (see Box 9.3).

Even this explanation is only partial. Organisations themselves and their clusters of stakeholders are a part of wider networks which are all interacting and within which there are ebbs and flows. All this means a complex mix of moving parts which the practitioner needs to be aware of because the wider macro environment also surrounds all these moving parts and exerts pressure at different points within it. For example, the change in the public mood over plastics has had a negative economic effect on producers of single-use plastics, but a positive one on producers of sustainable packaging and a resurgence of interest in local food as people become increasingly aware of the impact of food-buying habits on the environment. The ripples of the plastics controversy have spread much wider than the plastics industry. Chapter 10 provides more detail on the nature of stakeholders and publics, but it is worth making the point here that the notion of organisations as stakeholding communities is important because it is stakeholder groups who ultimately give an organisation 'permission' to exist (or not) by supporting its 'licence to operate' or by removing that support.

Analysis of the macro and task environment may seem more appropriate to the identification of strategic business issues rather than public relations. However, practitioners need to be alert to the wider contextual issues because they will affect stakeholders and force some sort of action from their organisation: action always has communication dimensions. Early warning of issues allows organisations to manage future and potential risks and this is a strategic input that public relations can make at senior management level. Given the speed at which activists can galvanise action, even the most astute practitioner may get only the briefest or even no warning of an issue which could develop into a crisis. However, most issues gestate more slowly and forward-thinking and diligent intelligence gathering can help predict many of them. The early-warning system that public relations practitioners can provide is of strategic importance to organisations.

The main questions to be asked when undertaking this kind of environmental analysis are:

- what are the long-term macro and task factors that are developing now?
- which ones affect this organisation?
- which ones are of most importance now?
- which ones will become the most important in the next five years?

From this it will be possible to derive a prioritised list of the main issues that will affect the organisation over a reasonable time horizon. However, it is important not to totally dismiss those which appear not to affect the organisation because there are often subtle linkages between issues which mean that those apparently unconnected to the organisation at one stage will become more relevant at another. For example, the mass migration into Europe in 2015 and 2016 appeared to be a political and social issue remote from many organisations, but those refugees and migrants are now employees. Some still suffer badly from the trauma of their experience and have recurring mental health issues which need sensitive and long-term handling. This is a complex workforce challenge and may have impacts on others in the workforce which need careful consideration.

Internal environment

Having identified the broader external issues that affect the organisation, it is now appropriate to look at the organisation itself and those things over which it has greater control.

A classic way to undertake this internal analysis is to use a technique called SWOT. The first two elements, **s**trengths and **w**eaknesses, are particular to the organisation and are usually within the organisation's power to address. The third and fourth, **o**pportunities and **t**hreats, are generally external to the organisation and can be determined from the wider analysis of the macro and task environment and the selection of those issues most relevant to it. An example of SWOT analysis is given in Figure 9.3.

There are several other issues that affect the internal environment of an organisation and its public relations activities. For example:

- *The sector in which the organisation is located.* If this is well established and stable such as the civil construction industry, this will allow for significant pre-planning. Fast-growing and turbulent sectors such as those in the sharing economy will require quick, reactive public relations as well as proactive programmes.

- *Size and stage of organisational development.* Small organisations usually have small, multifunctional public relations departments or are serviced by a consultancy. Large ones may well have substantial public relations departments with several specialisms, also complemented by consultancy support. When the organisation is at start-up stage, public relations effort is often focused on 'growing

Strengths	*Weaknesses*
Financially strong	Risk averse investment
Leading edge products	Limited product line
Innovative	Lack of investment in R&D
Good leadership	Traditional and hierarchical
Loyal workforce	Limited skills base
Opportunities	*Threats*
Cheap supplies from Asia	Reputational issues re labour exploitation
New market opportunities in China	Slowdown in Chinese economy
Potential to acquire competitors	Danger of being taken over by larger conglomerate
Favourable tax breaks if offices relocated	Loss of loyal workforce

Figure 9.3 Example of SWOT analysis.

the business', that is, marketing public relations. Because of size, internal communication is often face to face and relatively informal. When companies reach maturity, it is probable that they will undertake the full range of public relations activity including investor relations, public affairs and sophisticated internal communication programmes.

- *Culture*. This topic is covered in Chapter 6, but briefly culture can define the way people think and behave within an organisation, and the tone of the organisation set by its leaders. A hierarchical, non-involving culture will often see public relations as a way of enforcing the management will. More open and involving cultures will see public relations and communication as integral to the fabric of the organisation, both being shaped by and shaping the way 'things' are done.

Chapter 15 covers internal communication in detail, but it is important to say here that understanding the potential of internal communication talent is crucially important in a planning context. Many employees also have direct contact with and knowledge of the stakeholders that public relations professionals engage with and it makes sense to capture their knowledge so that a rounder picture can be formed. Furthermore, they have the potential to be outstanding ambassadors for the organisation. Their day-to-day interactions with others are the organisational narrative and often much more important to stakeholders than 'official' communication. They are also 'naturally' communicating. They have discussions, are engaged on social media and so on. Harnessing their talent by engaging with them and training them to listen and to be conscious of their communication capability provides not only a myriad of opportunities to gain more information about the external world but empowers them to be the organisational voice. Through such means, the organisation can become contextually intelligent, constantly sensing what is going on and being equipped to respond to and lead the conversations that define it.

An analysis of external and internal influences is critical to understanding the context in which public relations programmes will be undertaken. However, equally important is the fact that strategic public relations programmes address the issues that organisations face – the most impactful programmes are issues-based. They can be seen to contribute directly to solving organisational problems. Furthermore, the ability to undertake that vital systematic internal and external environmental monitoring (Lerbinger 1972) and analysis, again positions public relations as a strategic management function.

> **Think about 9.2**
>
> ### Employee experience
>
> Go to the McKinsey article on Employee Experience. You can access it by searching Employee Experience via https://www.mckinsey.com. It's also listed in the bibliography.
>
> How do you think empowering employees to undertake organisational communication on an 'official' basis might add to their experience?
>
> ### Feedback
>
> Would what you are suggesting make employees feel they had 'yet another job to do', or do you think it would enrich their working life? In both cases, why?

Implications of context

Monitoring and reporting of the external and internal environment on their own are, however, not enough. The question must be answered 'why is this important?' A simple answer to this is because an organisation has choices in the way it makes decisions, what decisions it makes and how it behaves as a result. Stakeholders hold organisations to account for those choices, especially if they impact on their lives. Thus organisations, in a world of increased accountability, must constantly renew and maintain their mandate, or 'licence to operate', which is given to them by stakeholders because this is always fragile and at risk.

To realise this opportunity, understanding the way organisations work and are structured and the contribution that public relations can make is vital. The work of South African public relations scholar Dr Benita Steyn (Steyn 2007) is important here. She points out that there are different strategic levels within organisations and understanding these helps to define a matching role for public relations. Building on her work, Gregory and Willis (2013) argue that the different levels of strategy can also help to define the different types of stakeholders by which an organisation is held to account. They outline four levels: societal, corporate, value chain and functional.

Societal level

At the societal level, organisations seek a 'licence to operate' from society. An organisation's place, perceived purpose and actions determine whether it is supported by public opinion and hence by society. At this level, the organisation's fundamental values, mission and ways of operating are examined, and judgements passed on them. For example, an organisation whose purpose is to purely to maximise profits without any regard to how it treats its workforce or suppliers, or the environment will most likely find its license to operate threatened unless it changes its ways of working.

Public relations plays a role in assisting the organisation to clarify its purpose and intended actions by helping to frame and test these internally and externally. It does this via the boundary-spanning work mentioned earlier; being in constant dialogue with stakeholders and constantly monitoring the external environment and public opinion. It also promotes the organisation by clear and honest communication with stakeholders.

Corporate level

Managerial decisions at corporate level are usually about marshalling resources to deliver the organisation's mission. The temptation here is to allow financial considerations to dominate in order to provide a good return to shareholders in the private sector and value for money in public sector and NGO organisations. The public relations function can make a vital contribution by helping managers take decisions which have proper regard for the legitimate interests of all stakeholders, including non-human ones such as the environment, in order to ensure that public support will be maintained.

It is also the task of the public relations professional to predict how the organisation's potential decisions are likely to be perceived by stakeholders in order keep the organisation alert to any reputational or relational risks. It is also their job to involve stakeholders in, and inform them of, management-level decisions in a way that is appropriate to them. For example, an organisation may wish to move location in order to reduce costs. However, finance is just one part of that decision. Other considerations, such as the impact on suppliers and the local community and the overall impact on reputation, need to be taken into account and those potentially affected involved where possible.

Value chain

At the value-chain level, the focus will be on those stakeholders and publics directly involved with the organisation on a regular basis. Their closeness distinguishes them from societal-level stakeholders, often called the 'general public', who may have no direct link. Typically, value chain stakeholders include customers, service users, delivery partners, suppliers, distributors, regulators, employees and the like. The public relations function will be engaged with these 'close' stakeholders and publics and understand the 'accountabilities' they may exert. They do this by listening and involving them, although the evidence that this happens is thin. Research done by Jim Macnamara (2016) provides ample evidence that organisations build architectures of telling not of listening. Furthermore, the public relations function can help in identifying what may be the conflicting demands of stakeholder groups and navigating the complex relationships between those groups, as well as those relationships between stakeholder groups and the organisation.

Functional level

At this level, the role of public relations is to work with the other areas of the organisation on communication tasks. They will also coach and mentor colleagues throughout the organisation to be 'communicatively competent' so that they can undertake public relations tasks themselves or be alert to when they need to enlist the help of the specialists. For public relations this may mean planning specific programmes and campaigns or providing ongoing advice. For example, they may work with the human resources department on communicating changes in employee contracts.

As a specialist function, public relations will make its own unique contribution too in developing public relations programmes and campaigns. For example, lobbying activities aimed at local politicians, financial relations initiatives aimed at key investors or community relations campaigns.

Each plan will be different depending on its purpose, who is involved and their communication needs. However, the processes behind the campaigns are the same and conform to recognised business planning norms as the second part of this chapter will show.

Identifying these strategic levels helps to clarify the types of input that public relations can make to the organisation. It also shows that public relations planning must be seen within a broader organisational context and identifies, in a systematic way, which stakeholder groups will hold it to account.

Against this backdrop, strategic public relations programmes and campaigns are planned. The second half of this chapter provides an overview of the planning process.

Strategic public relations programmes and campaigns

According to Thompson et al. (2017: 5), 'strategy is about how organisations cope with the world, which is dynamic and emergent' and in their glossary of terms they define it as 'the means by which organisations achieve (and seek to achieve) their objectives and purpose' (ibid.: 607). Strategic management is 'the process by which an organisation establishes its objectives, formulates actions (strategies) designed to meet these objectives in the desired timescale, implements the actions, and assesses progress and results' (ibid.: 607). Strategic public relations programmes and campaigns are those therefore that are designed to help their organisation cope with the world: they are proactive, planned and have a purpose. They have an impact and contribute to meeting organisational objectives; they are not just activities for the sake of it. Those objectives may change. Certainly, the way the organisation moves towards them will vary from the plan because as Donald Rumsfeld famously said, 'stuff happens' and increasingly plans, as discussed earlier in this chapter, sensibly embrace context and the input of those they are designed for whether that be employees, customers or the local community. Co-creation is not just for content, but for planning programmes themselves. Planning will not make a poorly conceived programme successful, but planning means that a programme is likely to be well conceived in the first place even if, as is inevitable, adjustments will need to be made along the way.

Box 9.4 explains the difference between programmes and campaigns, but in the rest of this chapter the word programme is used to embrace both types of activity.

Why planning is important

There are several practical reasons for planning public relations programmes. It:

- improves effectiveness by focusing on achieving agreed objectives;
- ensures efficiency and value for money by setting milestones, thinking through resource implications and agreeing budgets from the outset;
- encourages forward-thinking by requiring the planner to look to the organisation's future needs, preparing it for change and helping it manage future risks. It also helps to identify any potential difficulties and conflicts which can then be thought through at an early stage;
- minimises mishaps; thinking through potential scenarios means that most eventualities can be covered, and contingency plans put in place.

Most importantly, planning is about a mindset, one that constantly asks a series of important, structured questions instead of working in a random fashion and/or to a set of unchallenged assumptions. As indicated earlier, while strategic planning takes the practitioner through a systematic process, they must be mindful that a level of flexibility and pragmatic adjustment will be required along the way. Indeed, unseen events, such as a takeover, a major natural disaster or a change in stakeholder priorities may require a radical departure from the best-laid plans. Counter-intuitively, the more turbulent and unpredictable the context becomes, the greater the need to plan and consider carefully what the options are and the possible scenarios that might unfold. This must be combined with a willingness to constantly re-group and adapt. A good analogy for this way of working is jazz, as espoused by Falkheimer and

---

Box 9.4
Campaigns and programmes

A campaign: a planned set of public relations activities, normally over a limited period and with specific objectives addressing an issue and involving an identified group. For example, a local pharmacy may wish to inform customers in its neighbourhood of extended opening hours, or the tax authorities may run a campaign to increase the number of tax returns from self-employed people over 60.

A programme: ongoing, planned activities over an extended period that call for continuing relationships with groups of stakeholders, often including complex and inter-linked objectives. For example, community engagement programmes and relationships with regulatory authorities.

Heide (2010), building on the work of Weick (1998). There needs to be a basic structure and form which keeps the whole 'piece' together, but the ability to extemporise is vital. This means an absolute commitment to vary plans according to circumstances as they change and indeed, a welcoming of contributions from stakeholders as plans are initiated and progress. This extemporisation is not only to adjust plans for instrumental reasons, i.e. to make them more effective so that the organisation can meet its objectives, but so that genuine listening can take place and the concerns, aspirations and good ideas of stakeholders are properly accommodated for mutual benefit. Thus, joint ownership of plans is secured, and ongoing fruitful relationships and future success made more likely.

Systems and alternative approaches to planning

Public relations planning is traditionally located within the positivist framework and maps across well to the systems view of organisations (see Chapter 8 for more discussion of systems theory). The 'open system' is an important concept for public relations planning because it assumes that an organisation is an organism or 'living entity with boundaries, inputs, outputs, "throughputs", and enough feedback from both the internal and external environments so that it can make appropriate adjustments in time to keep on living' (McElreath 1997: 13).

Broom and Sha (2012) provide an open systems model of public relations that identifies how these systems characteristics map onto the planning process (see Figure 9.4).

So, for example, 'input' refers to actions taken by, or information about, publics (called stakeholders in this chapter). These inputs in turn are transformed into goals (aims) and objectives which underpin the desired relationships with publics. By contrast, a 'closed' approach might neglect to consider information about publics and thus the planner might formulate aims and objectives in isolation.

Apart from the systems approach to planning there are others that have come largely from the management literature. More recently, management scholars have developed thinking on stakeholding and the importance of cooperation to the point where they envisage stakeholders being involved in strategy formulation and implementation. Scharmer and Kaeufer (2010), in *U Theory*, state that managers can deal with complexity and envisage new futures by working with others to divest themselves of past thinking, observing with them what is going on in the present and connecting to best possible futures by quickly developing protype ideas, receiving feedback from those who have an interest and, through an iterative process with them, achieving desired results. They see this as a thoroughly

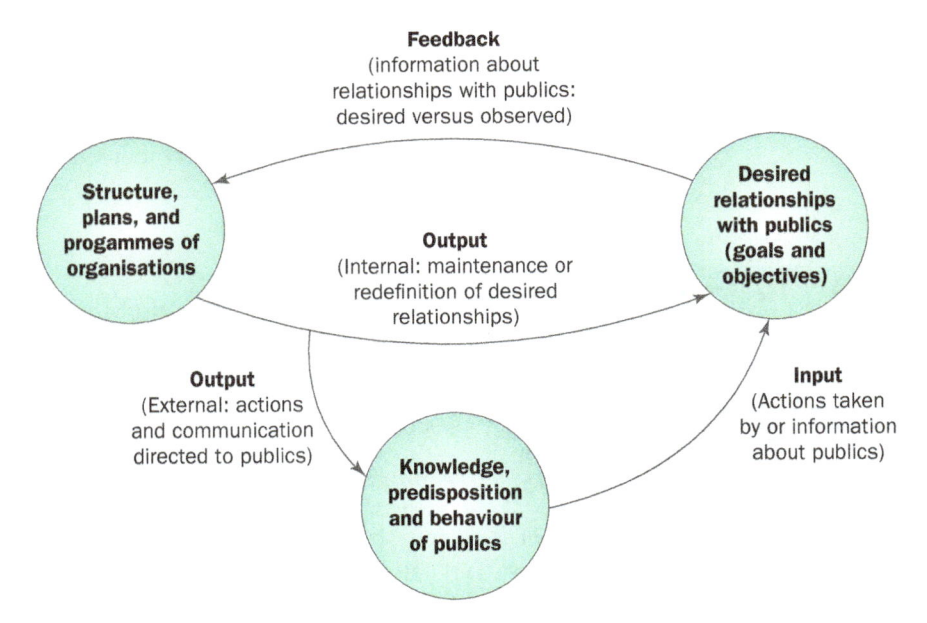

Figure 9.4 Open systems model of public relations (*source: Cutlip and Center's Effective Public Relations*, 11th edition. Upper Saddle River, NJ: Prentice-Hall, Inc. (Broom & Sha, 2012))

collaborative process, using the terms co-sensing, co-presencing and co-creating.

Matzler et al. (2014) advocate participatory strategy which promotes wide stakeholder engagement to develop and operationalise strategy. They refer to open and open-source strategy-making, arguing that social media is a mechanism that can be used to enable this.

The concept of organisational agility and agile planning (Sutherland 2014; Denning 2016a, b; Rigby et al. (see Box 9.5) 2016) has emerged in the twenty-first century as a reaction against the systematised, rigid approach to project planning and management prevalent in earlier years.

An advocate of agile planning is the Dutch academic Betteke van Ruler, who in her article 'Agile planning in public relations' (van Ruler 2015) combined the basic logic that underpins the systematic method with Agile. In simple terms she advocates that at all stages of planning and implementing a programme, the team involved should re-group, examine what is going on, reassess whether changes need to be made and move forward based on new knowledge that has been acquired through ongoing dialogue with those involved (see Figure 9.5).

Thus, in the academic literature, in management thinking as well as in public relations practice there is a dawning realisation that organisations are part of ecosystems: dependent on others, prone to rapidly changing contexts and driven by a pace of change that is ever quickening. They also suggest that when planning public relations campaigns, the principles of cooperation, collaboration and coproduction should be included.

All this is good news because communication is at the heart of all these approaches.

Scope of public relations planning

Planning can be applied to long-term activity such as the ongoing work by governments to prevent drivers from drinking or taking drugs. It can also be applied to short-term campaigns such as the launch of a new product or even to a single event such as fund-raising for a local charity.

Approaches to planning

The planning process takes the practitioner through several key steps. It is helpful to see it as answering six basic questions:

1. What is the problem? (Researching the issue.)
2. What does the plan seek to achieve? (What are the aims and objectives?)
3. Who should be communicated with? (With whom should a relationship be developed?)
4. What should be said? (What is the content?)
5. How should the content be communicated? (What tactics should be used?)
6. How can success be measured? (How will the work be evaluated against the objectives?)

Box 9.5
Agile planning

Agile is an umbrella term for a range of management practices that promote adaptive planning, continuous improvement and rapid innovation. It originated in the IT industry where rapid innovation is a requirement and is based on the idea of self-organising teams, often including collaborators from other parts and outside the organisation who work together on a problem (or new product), come up with what they think is a working solution quickly, test it out, adjust and improve it.

Professional accountability	Decisional and social accountability				Performative accountability
Vision	Inputs	Sprint planning	Sprint and scrum	Validation	Results
■ On the profession ■ On priorities	■ Assignment ■ Ambition ■ Team ■ Project backlog	■ Goal and strategy ■ Sprint backlog ■ Alliances ■ To do list	■ Actions ■ Regulation reflections	■ Review of results ■ Evaluation of process (retrospective)	■ Mutually agreed outcomes

Figure 9.5 Van Ruler's Agile public relations planning model (*source:* Used with permission from Betteke van Ruler)

All planning processes follow a basic sequence whether they are for the strategic management of the organisation or for public relations, and this is provided in Figure 9.6.

Gregory's planning model in Figure 9.7 provides a sequence of activities and captures the essence of all the public relations planning approaches. It will be used to examine the steps of the planning process in detail. Although apparently linear, Gregory views planning as iterative and circular with a constant process of review and preview being undertaken. Thus, for example, as context and stakeholders are researched and detailed information discovered, objectives may need to be revised and proposed resources adjusted. The model shows stakeholders as one stage of the planning process, but stakeholders are seen to be outside the model too, because they are ever present and must be listened to, engaged with and brought into the process as appropriate. The two sets of spirals at each side of the main twelve-stage planning model also indicates that there is a constant iterative process going on: with planners constantly thinking forwards and thinking back, reassessing and adjusting their plans depending on feedback. Two further points need to be made at this stage. First, although the planning template is not meant to be applied rigidly because practitioners must move rapidly in response to unpredictable events, even in these circumstances, it can be used as a mental checklist to ensure that all the essential elements are being borne in mind. Second, the degree to which any element of planning process is applied will vary according to the task in hand. For example, a detailed analysis of the organisation's external macro environment will not be required to run an effective fun day for families.

It is important to understand the structure of the first part of the diagram. Ideally, the public relations practitioner would undertake analysis of the situation before determining aims and objectives. In practice, they are often given aims and objectives by their managers. In these circumstances it is still vital that the objectives themselves are scrutinised to see if they are appropriate. For example, an organisation may wish to resist the introduction of a piece of legislation because it will be expensive to implement. However, on investigation the public relations practitioner may discover that a lobbying campaign against it is futile because stakeholders are very much in favour and there is no realistic chance that lobbying will prevail.

The 'aim' element can on occasion be omitted because sometimes a project or campaign has a single, simple objective that does not need an overarching aim. If the programme is particularly large, it may be necessary to break down the whole into a series of sub-projects that follow the same basic steps. Each project will have its own specific objectives, stakeholders and content. This then needs to be incorporated into a larger plan which provides a coordinating framework with overall aims, objectives and consistent content guidance which ensure that the individual projects do not conflict (see Figure 9.8).

Analysis

Analysis is the first step in the process, and this will identify the issues or specific problems on which to base the programme.

Analysis can include a thorough investigation of both the external and internal environments already mentioned earlier in this chapter. However, a key component of analysis entails a careful examination of stakeholders to discover what their attitudes are towards the organisation itself, to the wider issue identified by the EPISTLE and SWOT processes or to the issue that management have asked the public relations department to address.

Chapter 10 goes into detail about how to conduct research with stakeholders, including the range of social scientific methods that can be employed and the latest online tools that can be used. It is important to mention here that the analysis stage makes use of all available information and intelligence in order to ensure the programme is well founded. This

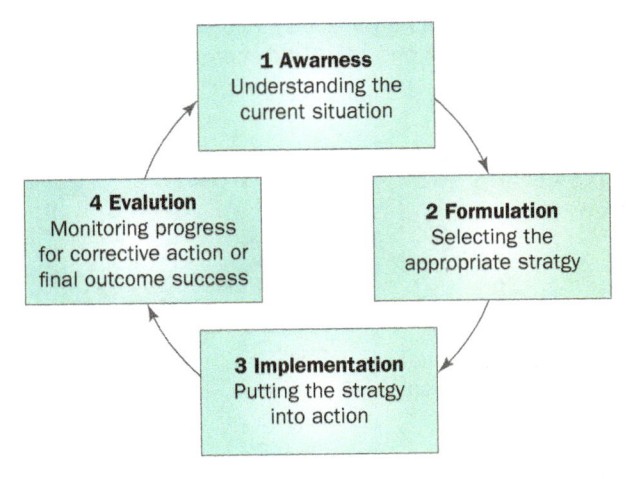

Figure 9.6 Basic business planning model

Chapter 9 Strategic public relations planning and management

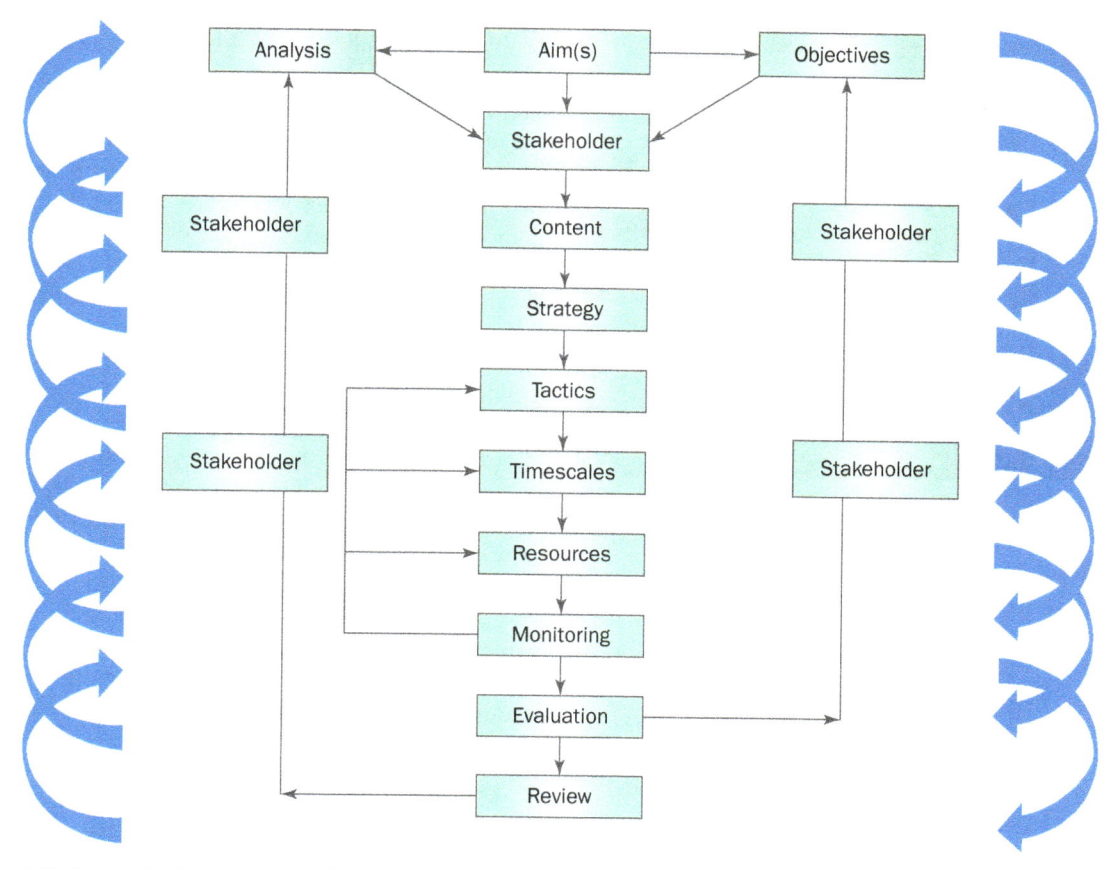

Figure 9.7 Gregory's planning model (*source:* Gregory, A. (2015). Planning and Managing Public Relations Campaigns, 4th edition. London: Kogan Page)

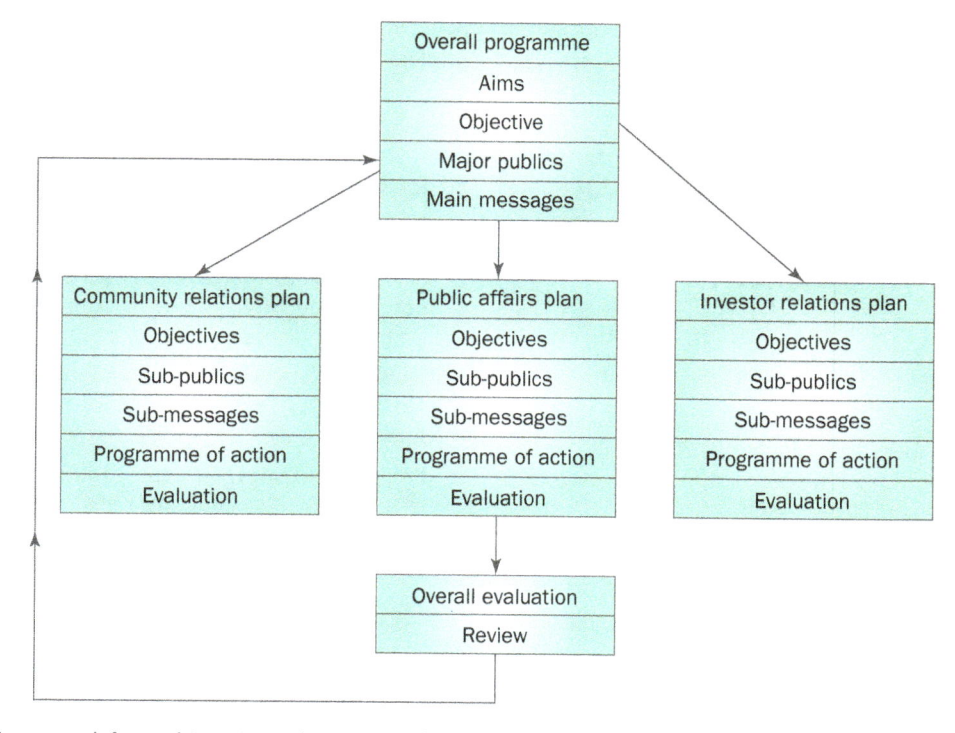

Figure 9.8 Framework for multi-project relations plan (*source:* Adapted from Gregory, A. (2015). Planning and Managing Public Relations Campaigns, 4th edition. London: Kogan Page)

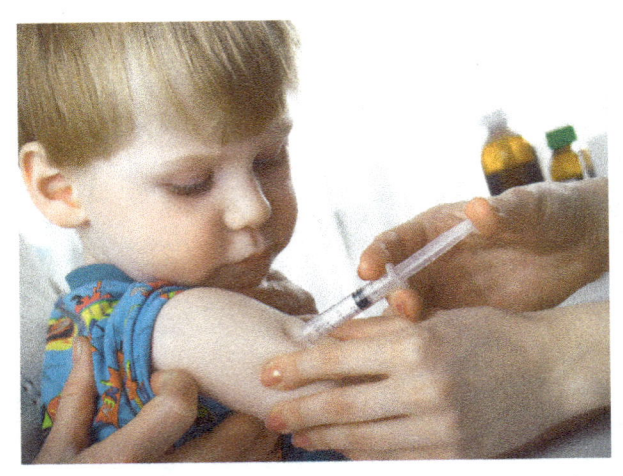

Picture 9.2 Vaccine take-up may be low because of lack of information or the wrong sort of information (*source: sergei telegin/Shutterstock*)

preparation work is critical to answering the first basic question, 'What is the problem?'

Having identified the issue or problem, the planner then must decide whether it can be remedied purely through communication. Windahl et al. (2009) define a communication-based problem in two ways: first, a problem may arise from the *lack of* or *wrong* sort of communication. For example, a new child vaccination is not being requested by parents because it has only been publicised to doctors (lack of information) and because it has been described by its technical name, not its popular name (wrong sort of information) – this problem can easily be solved by communication. Second, the problem is a communication problem if it can be solved by communication alone. For example, if the uptake of child vaccinations has also been affected by suspicions about side effects, or if there are a limited number of clinics where it is available, then this is more than a communication problem. Some other measures such as independent opinion to confirm the vaccine is safe or wider distribution may be needed to stimulate use. In this case the public relations professional needs to bring these problems to management attention and once they are addressed, communication can step in. Thus, analysis not only identifies the issues, but also what needs to be done and the precise contribution that public relations can make. Part of this analysis stage will also identify exactly what purpose or impact the communication activity is meant to achieve and the nature of the intervention required. Box 9.6 shows the types of assistance communication can provide when Governments and public sector organisations are attempting to engage populations with policy initiatives.

Setting aims and objectives

Setting realistic aims and objectives is complicated, but through analysis public relations planners can scope the size and nature of the communication task. The aim or aims will state what the programme seeks to achieve in overall terms. Aims must be agreed before implementation and must be linked to organisational

---

Box 9.6

European Commission's types of aims

According to guidance provided by the European Commission (European Commission 2015) for Government and public sector organisations, there are five types of aims for communication:

- **Persuade** – get someone or a group to do something that they otherwise would not have done.
- **Inform** – give basic information about a new policy, stance, service, regulation or requirement, without necessarily prompting action.
- **Normalise** – give people the sense that everyone else is doing the same as the activity you suggest (such as taking 'flu precautions), that there is a societal expectation for people to do a certain thing – or not do something (such as smoking near children). Or, that by not doing it, they are missing out.
- **Inspire** – motivate someone to want to do something new, to continue doing something or to stop doing something. It tends to prompt an emotional response.
- **Engage** – to engage people around an issue and encourage participation in a debate or activity (e.g. encourage contribution to a consultation); a two-way dialogue.

Source: TOOLKIT for the evaluation of the communication activities. (2017) Retrieved from https://ec.europa.eu/info/sites/info/files/communication-evaluation-toolkit_en.pdf

Box 9.7

The GREAT Britain campaign

The aim of the campaign is to increase the levels of trade, investment and tourism, and high-quality students coming to the UK, leading to a measurable economic impact of at least £1 billion over three to five years and the creation of over 10,000 direct jobs for the UK economy.

aims. If the corporate aim is to become the employer of choice for skilled games technology graduates, then public relations activity must be focused on that. A good aim should be able to be evaluated at the end of the programme by turning it into a question. Thus, the aim 'to become the employer of choice for skilled games technology graduates within five years' becomes the evaluative question 'are we the employer of choice for skilled games technology graduates within our set timescale?'

Box 9.7 shows the aim of the UK Government's GREAT campaign whose purpose is to grow the UK economy.

Objectives are the specific, measurable steps that break the aims into what are effectively key milestones for the programme. Research on stakeholders will have uncovered their position on any topic which provides a starting point, or benchmark. The planner then needs to decide what movement if any is required: a legitimate objective may be to confirm existing attitudes or actions. Objectives can be set at three levels:

- *Awareness objectives* deal with information and knowledge. This focuses on providing the *cognitive* or thinking element of the content and on what information publics should be exposed to, know, understand and remember.
- *Feeling objectives* deal with how people react to information. This focuses on the *affective* or feeling elements of the content and on what emotional response is generated. This affect interests and attitudes.
- *Action objectives* deal with the hoped-for response. This focuses on the *conative* or behavioural outcomes that might be generated when people are exposed to the content of the programme.

Table 9.1 shows how objectives can be set at these levels.

It is much more difficult to get someone to *behave* in a certain way than it is to prompt them to *think* about something, the notable exception being over hot issues (see Chapter 30, 'Future issues for public relations and strategic communication'). According to Grunig and Hunt (1984) three things should be borne in mind that will make the achievement of objectives easier:

1. The level of effect (or outcome) should be chosen with care. If the public relations planner wants to induce radical change, it will be sensible to set cognitive objectives first, rather than hoping for conative effects from the start.
2. Choose stakeholders with advocacy in mind. Research should have identified those who already support the position of the organisation; they can then act as advocates on its behalf.

Cognitive (means related to thoughts, reflection, awareness)	Encouraging the target public to *think* about something or to create awareness. For example, local government might want the local community to be aware that it is holding a housing information day. The whole community will not need the service, but part of local government's reason for making them aware is so that they know what a proactive and interested local council they have
Affective (means related to feelings, emotional reaction)	Encouraging the target public to form a particular attitude, opinion or feeling about a subject. For example, a pressure group may want moral support for or against gun ownership
Conative (means related to behaviour, actions or change)	Encouraging the target public to *behave* in a certain way. For example, the local hospital may use social media to ask for emergency blood donors following a major incident

Table 9.1 Objectives set at one of three levels

3. Organisations can change too. Sometimes minor adjustments in the organisation's stance can elicit a major, positive response from stakeholders.

A key point in setting aims and objectives is to focus on what outcome or impact is wanted from the communication activity. In the author's experience of judging award entries, public relations programme objectives all too often describe the tactic, that is, what the planner will do, instead of the desired outcome. In the 'employee' public example below, a tactical objective would be to issue the corporate plan to every employee. However, the objective that focuses on the desired outcome for employees is 'to ensure every employee is aware of the four key objectives in the new corporate plan'.

All objectives should be SMART: specific, measurable, achievable (within the planner's ability to deliver), resourced and time bound. Examples of SMART objectives are given below, with the desired outcome highlighted in italics.

- Employees: *Ensure every employee is aware* of the four key objectives in the new corporate plan by 10 November.
- Community: Use sponsorship of 20 local junior football teams to generate *more positive opinion* about the company among parents.
- Corporate: Change legislation on taxation of charity giving within two years by *influencing voting behaviour of government ministers* via a lobbying campaign.
- Trade: Double amount of coverage in online trade media in one year to *overcome lack of awareness* among key suppliers.
- Consumer: Increase social media interactions with consumers by 20 per cent in 18 months to *counter perception of company being remote*.

To show how issues flow through to the framing of aims and one exemplar objective, Table 9.2 provides several examples. Note how the objectives do not go into the detail of the tactics.

Setting sound aims and objectives is fundamental to public relations planning. They define what the outcomes of the programme will be, they provide the rationale for the strategy, set the agenda for tactical actions and are the benchmark against which the programme will be evaluated. Their importance cannot be overstated. This section on objectives answered the second basic question in planning programmes, 'What does the plan seek to achieve?'

Issue	Aim	Objective
Company viewed as environmentally irresponsible	Demonstrate environmental credentials	Increase community awareness of company recycling scheme by 40% in two years
After-sales service perceived as slow and unresponsive by purchasers	Change customer perceptions of service by alerting them to improvements	Ensure 100% of all new product purchasers are aware of aftersales service and track perceptions of aftersales users from the benchmark position over a three-year period.
Proposed new housing development will damage environmentally sensitive area	Ensure environmentally sensitive areas are preserved while supporting housing development in principle	Persuade decision-makers on planning authority of case for environmental planning restrictions

Table 9.2 Examples of the link between issues, aim and objective

Identifying stakeholders

This next section answers the third question, 'Who should we talk to?' Chapter 10 is devoted to audiences, publics and stakeholders so this part will be relatively brief.

Research for the proposed programme will have identified the significant stakeholders. Sometimes they are apparent. If the programme is to support a product launch, then existing and potential customers will be a priority. However, groups that can be easily defined often are not homogenous. It is incorrect to assume that all-embracing categorisations such as the 'local community' comprise individuals who are similar or who will act in the same way. They will have very different interests and concerns. It is likely that many individuals will belong to more than one stakeholding group. Employees of an organisation may well be volunteers in an organisation who are partners in a community relations campaign or consume their organisation's products or services; they may be shareholders.

There are many ways in which stakeholders and publics can be segmented (placed into groups with a defined range of characteristics) and the type of campaign will determine the best way to do that. For example, if a government wants to introduce a new benefit targeted at lower-income families, it makes sense to segment stakeholders by income and where they live. A charity wanting to start up a counselling service for refugees may wish to segment by ethnicity and political affiliation; a leisure company wanting to set up Saturday morning clubs for children will segment by age and locality. (See Box 9.8 for popular ways of segmenting publics.)

The practitioner must decide the most appropriate ways to undertake the segmentation of stakeholders. This could be done based on selecting the two most important variables for the situation being addressed and then making a matrix out of them.

The power/attention matrix (see Figure 9.9) is a popular combination used in strategic planning (Johnson et al. 2017) and can be readily transferred to the communication context. It categorises stakeholders depending on the amount of power they must influence others and the level of attention they give to an issue. Clearly the more power and attention they have, the more likely their actions are to impact on the organisation, so the support of this group is crucial.

	Level of interest	
Power	Low	High
Low	A Minimal effort	B Keep informed
High	C Keep satisfied	D Key players

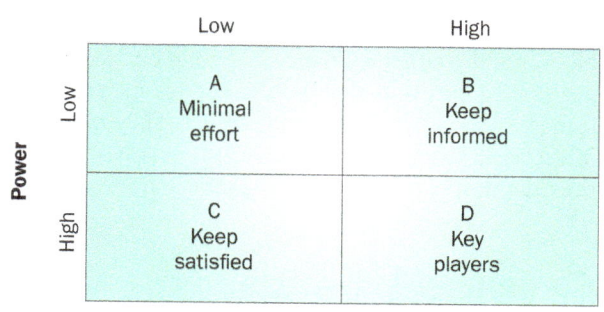

Figure 9.9 Power/interest matrix (*source*: adapted from Mendelow 1991, cited in Johnson et al. 2013: 124)

It is possible, even desirable at times, that stakeholders in one segment should move to another. For example, powerful, institutional investors often reside in segment C. It may be in times of crisis that the communicator will want to move them to segment D by stimulating their attention so that they can use their power and influence with others to support the organisation.

Similarly, just because a stakeholding group appears not to have much attention or power does not mean that it is not important. For public sector organisations these groups often contain the neediest and are very important for them to reach.

It is informative to map stakeholders in several ways. For example, not only can current position and desired position be mapped, but a useful exercise is to map how stakeholders might move in relation to a developing issue and whether this is desirable, preventable or inevitable. Communication strategies can then be devised that accommodate these movements.

The segmentation method outlined above is based on the organisation itself determining which characteristics are important. However, there are other powerful techniques that are especially suitable for issues-based publics. Using online search, it is perfectly possible to discover where communities of interest congregate. For example, those interested in cars will visit influential websites, blogs and engage in social media around the topic. It is relatively easy for those planning campaigns to identify the relevant 'hot spots' for information and discussion and engage with the target audience directly. In this way audiences segment themselves by clustering around the topic of cars. By the same process further segmentation is also possible around topics such as the make of car, performance, and customisation and sales.

Once categorised according to a suitable method, the groups need to be prioritised and the amount of communication effort devoted to them apportioned.

Box 9.8
Ways to segment publics

- geographic – where they live, work
- demographics – age, gender, income
- psychographics – attitudes, opinions
- group membership – e.g. clubs, societies, parents
- media consumption – e.g. newspapers, TV, websites, bloggers
- overt and covert power – e.g. religious leader, information gatekeeper, level of connectedness
- role in decision process – e.g. financial manager, CEO, parent

The number of stakeholders that are communicated with and the depth of that communication are likely to be limited by either a financial or time budget. However, it is important that all the key 'gatekeepers' or leaders of active groups are identified. They may well interpret information for others, act as advocates on the organisation's behalf and catalyse action.

Content

The fourth basic question is, 'What should be said?' Traditionally, public relations people have focused on messages. There are many kinds of campaigns where messages are critically important, especially in public information campaigns. Road safety messages are encapsulated in easy to remember and often repeated slogans such as 'Don't drink and drive'.

Messages are important for four main reasons. They:

1. Assist the awareness and attitude-forming process. Publics who can repeat a message are demonstrating that it has been received.
2. Demonstrate that the communication channels have been appropriate: the message reached the recipient.
3. Are essential in the evaluation process. Messages received and then recalled show that the communication has been, at least in part, effective. Message recall is a classic 'outtake' evaluation measure. If it can be demonstrated that the message has not only been received but acted on, then this is an example of an 'outcome' measure. (See more on this in Chapter 10.)
4. Help focus management minds: summarising an argument down to its essentials encapsulated in a message imposes discipline on woolly thinking.

However, messages have limitations. They indicate one-way communication: the originator simply checks to see if their communication has been received. If an organisation genuinely wants to enter a dialogue with publics where the result will be mutually determined, messaging is not appropriate apart from as a mechanism to begin a conversation. For example, if a new organisation wants to discuss with its employees what its values and goals should be, dialogue is required. (For more on the different models of communication and their purpose, see Chapter 8.)

As indicated earlier, organisations are now seen more as communities of stakeholders and there is growing acceptance that collaboration with stakeholders to solve problems and to gain their input and support is a better way of working (Agerwal and Helfat 2009; de Wit 2017). Collaboration and co-operation requires consultation and involvement; in other words, dialogue. Furthermore, the developments in social media and mobile technologies are forcing even the most reluctant organisations into having conversations. As a result, the most forward looking are transforming their communication processes away from an emphasis on telling and messaging to designing architectures of listening too (Macnamara 2016). In the public sector there is a growing move towards co-production of solutions to problems and consensus-building where conflict is avoided and the public 'own' the solutions that are arrived at because they have contributed to them directly through dialogue-based activities. Techniques such as deliberative engagement (see Box 9.9), which requires time, effort and resources, are becoming increasingly prevalent. There is also evidence that the private sector is doing similar things with their supply chain partners (De Wit 2017; Johnson et al. 2017; Thompson et al. 2017). An example of this dialogic way of working is given in Mini case study 9.2. Here it is clear that face-to-face communication enabled the company to develop co-created content that is helping fight the anti-vaccine movement in Indonesia.

How then can programmes that involve dialogue be evaluated if messages are one of the ways to measure communication effectiveness? The answer is: by examining whether there have been improvements in the quality of the relationships that result from the

Explore 9.3

Message design

Devise an overarching message or slogan for a 'grass roots' or community-led campaign aimed at stopping children dropping litter outside the school premises. The local community have been complaining about litter being thrown in their gardens. What would be a suitable sub-message for children? For parents? For teachers? For the local community?

Feedback

Make sure your sub-messages have a clear link to the overarching message or you will either dilute your communication or run the risk of the community thinking there is more than one campaign running.

Box 9.9
Deliberative engagement

Deliberative engagement brings together a representative cross-section of the stakeholding group to deliberate on an issue. The process provides the time for participants to truly understand the issues.

By being involved, participants take part in the decision-making process. They are given access to information and experts, can ask questions, seek clarification, learn about and consider complex issues, make compromises and gradually move towards a consensus.

Mini case study 9.2
Bio Farma-Indonesia's face-to-face work to counter anti-vaccine movements

Indonesia, with a population of 261 million, is the largest Muslim-majority country in the world. It is seeking to increase its national health index and achieve maximum immunisation coverage. Previously, the government has had no significant obstacles with vaccination; however, with the ubiquity of the internet and social media, the dissemination of fake news and false information has become more significant: 106 million people from the population are social media users. This issue is difficult to resolve since it intersects with religion.

Bio Farma-Indonesia, a vaccine producing pharmaceutical company, found that health issues accounted for 27 per cent of the 1,000 news samples researched between February 2016 and February 2017 with the three predominant topics being counterfeit vaccines, diphtheria outbreaks and the refusal of immunisation urged by anti-vaccine groups.

Most Muslims in Indonesia, around 225 million people, believe that the Indonesian Ulama Council (MUI), a national religious body, has authority regarding religious affairs and fatwas. In 2018 MUI issued a fatwa that the measles-rubella vaccine was haram or prohibited and this decision made people concerned even though the MUI issued a revision stating that the vaccination was allowed in an emergency. Data from the Indonesian Basic Health Research (Riskesdas) 2018 showed that immunisation coverage in several regions is still relatively low and vaccines are being positively rejected in religious areas such as Aceh Province. This is a cause for serious concern given the public health implications and something that neither the Government nor those working in health could leave unaddressed.

Working with the Ministry of Health and the Indonesian Pediatrician Association, Bio Farma-Indonesia undertook a series of face-to-face interactions with key influencers in the discussion about vaccinations, Islamic students and Ulama (Islamic leaders) being the main groups, but also health practitioners and mothers with children under five years old. The primary purpose of the campaign was to educate Islamic students and Ulama about the truth and importance of vaccines and to turn them into advocates for vaccination by demonstrating their own willingness to be vaccinated. Speakers at these events included speakers from Bio Farma, medical experts, government, Islamic leaders and the media.

The principal methods of communication were roadshows to Islamic schools and boarding schools, one-to-one meetings with Ulama, talk shows, workshops and seminars with health practitioners and mothers. These face-to-face interactions uncovered the level of false information about vaccines, including out-dated research, misinformation about side effects, inaccuracies about religious aspects including concerns about what was halal and what was haram and doubts about the content and production process of vaccines. Bio Farma-Indonesia found that the combination of speakers and the face-to-face nature of the interactions enabled questions about medical facts, religious concerns, fake media coverage and vaccine production to be discussed and addressed in detail. These conversations identified the main issues and the arguments that needed to be formulated to address them.

Alongside these face-to-face methods, a range of amplifiers were also used in parallel which including printed

→

Mini case study 9.2 (continued)

media, social media, internal magazines in the Islamic schools. The students, religious leaders and women with children in turn used their own favoured channels to promote the message of vaccination and to show their own willingness to be vaccinated.

This is an ongoing campaign and the pre- and post-evaluation of the work in Islamic schools show that their lack of understanding about vaccinations is being addressed, but about half are still afraid. Nevertheless, the efficacy of the face-to-face work is being realised and the conclusion is that as the education work continues, a solid advocacy movement from within the student and religious leaders will gain increasing influence.

Note: (Halal means permissible under Islamic law); while Haram means not allowed under Islamic law).

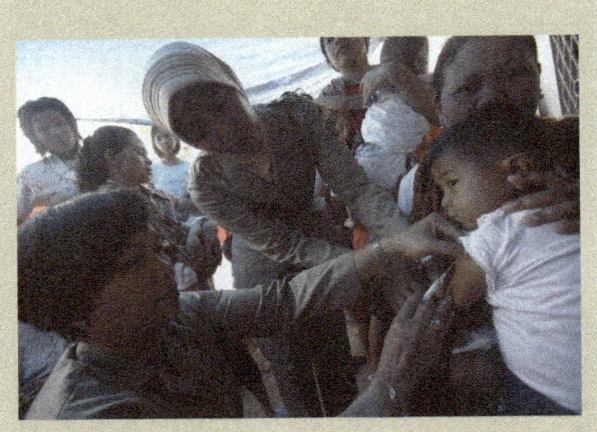

Picture 9.3 Students at an Islamic School being vaccinated (*source:* Dimas Ardian/Getty Images News/Getty Images)

dialogue and the level of mutual co-operation, support and advocacy (see Chapter 10).

An important concept and growing area of scholarship in the area of content is 'framing'. Framing has been imported from the fields of anthropology and linguistics and essentially proposes that interactions between human beings are 'framed' by the cultural context and heritage that individuals have experienced. Furthermore, academics Kahneman and Tversky (1979) found that the choice of words and visual context are critical to the response that is evoked. Cornelissen (2017) states that models of framing propose that messages consist of three elements:

- activation of an overall frame by use of certain key words or formulations of forms;
- manifest or latent reasoning or arguments as part of the frame;
- connections with deeper and culturally shared categories of understanding that supports and legitimises the framing as a whole.

He uses climate change as an example of how that debate has been framed differently by various groups. So, for example, some politicians and corporate leaders have stated that the science is still uncertain, therefore immediate policy action and draconian legislation is not required. Other groups have framed action on climate change as conflicting with economic growth and progress. Environmental groups and activists have placed discussion in a moral frame – there is a moral obligation, even if there are uncertainties about the science, to ensure that the world is not left in a worse condition for future generations. These different framing approaches will generate quite different reactions depending on the background, belief systems and life experiences of the people to whom they are directed.

Framing is used by the media with great skill. Looking at world news on different news channels from different countries makes the point very forcefully. The point here is that *how* the message or content is presented is just as important as *what* the message contains.

The importance of content cannot be over-emphasised. It is the point of contact, providing the meaning between an organisation and its stakeholders. It is 'given' by the organisation, and 'received' by its publics and vice versa. Once mutually understood and internalised it can be said that the meaning is mutually 'owned'. If content is poorly conceived and the way it is conveyed poorly executed, it can be the end of the communication process.

Strategy

The fifth basic question, 'How should the content be communicated?' falls into two parts: strategy and tactics. The temptation for the public relations planner is to move immediately to tactics because in many ways it is easier and more exciting to think of a raft of ideas that will deliver the objectives than to think about the rationale behind them. An underpinning strategy provides coherence, focus and is a driving force. Strategy is the guiding principle (sometime called the 'big idea') that determines the overall approach and hence the menu of activities and gives purpose. Strategy is the 'how' of the programme, not the detailed 'what'. Strategy is the bridge between the aim(s) of the programme (what is to be achieved) and the tactics (what is going to be done). Tactics are the methods used to deliver the strategy. In the three examples in Figure 9.10 the first shows how strategy can describe the nature of, and summarise the tactical campaign for, a simple, single objective campaign. The second example is for a conceptual proposition, the third for a slogan-driven campaign encapsulating a key theme. All are equally valid. Figure 9.11 also shows how the strategy emerging from the stakeholder analysis, using the power/attention matrix, points the way to the most relevant tactics.

Tactics

It is obvious that tactics should be linked to, and flow from, strategy. Strategy should guide brainstorming and be used to reject activities that do not support the strategic thrust or the programme objectives. There should be a clear link between aim, objectives, strategy and tactics.

A level of caution is required when planning the tactics of a programme. The aim is to build a programme that reaches the right people in enough numbers and that has the right level of impact to do the job required, all within acceptable costs and timescales. Sometimes that can be focused around a single activity – for example, as part of the Apple Watch and iPhone 6 launch, Apple gave a free download of the latest U2 album *Songs of Innocence,* gaining unprecedented publicity for themselves and U2, not all of which was favourable.

More usually a raft of complementary tactics over a period is required. These will vary depending on the nature of the programme, so the practitioner will need to draw from a palette of tactics as appropriate. For example, if a company wants to launch new and highly visual products such as a range of expensive household accessories, it is important that tactics are selected that will show how these products look and feel. In this case tactics might include displays at exhibitions and in-store, product samples, YouTube clips showing the products in use, a Twitter campaign led by satisfied customers and high-quality billboard posters.

In a different situation, for example, if the campaign involves lobbying over some aspect of financial legislation, quite different tactics, such as research reports, seminars, opinion-former briefings and one-to-one meetings with politicians would be more appropriate.

When designing the tactical elements of a campaign, two questions should be asked:

1. Is the tactic *appropriate*? Will it reach the target publics? Will it have the right impact? Is it credible and influential? Does it suit the content in terms of creative treatment and compatibility with other techniques used?

2. Is the tactic *deliverable*? Can it be implemented successfully? Is there enough budget? Are the timescales correct? Are there the right people with the right level of expertise to implement it?

It is always useful to undertake a check of the main requirements of a campaign against the tactics chosen to ensure that there is a close match. Figure 9.12 shows a matrix showing the essential criteria of a campaign on the vertical axis with the type of tactics across the horizontal plane. From this example there is an issue with Reach with this range of tactics, but more positively, that tactic 3 is particularly effective.

	Example 1	Example 2	Example 3
Aim	Publicise new product	Establish organisation as thought-leader	Encourage people to eat healthily
Strategy	Mount trade media campaign	Position as industry think-tank	Drive health awareness through memorable message
Tactic	Exclusive interviews, photos, videos, competition, special offers	Research reports, speaker platforms, online information resource, sponsorship of university research etc.	Traditional and social media campaign, apps, games, website, school curriculum initiative, etc.

Figure 9.10 Aim, strategy, tactic linkage

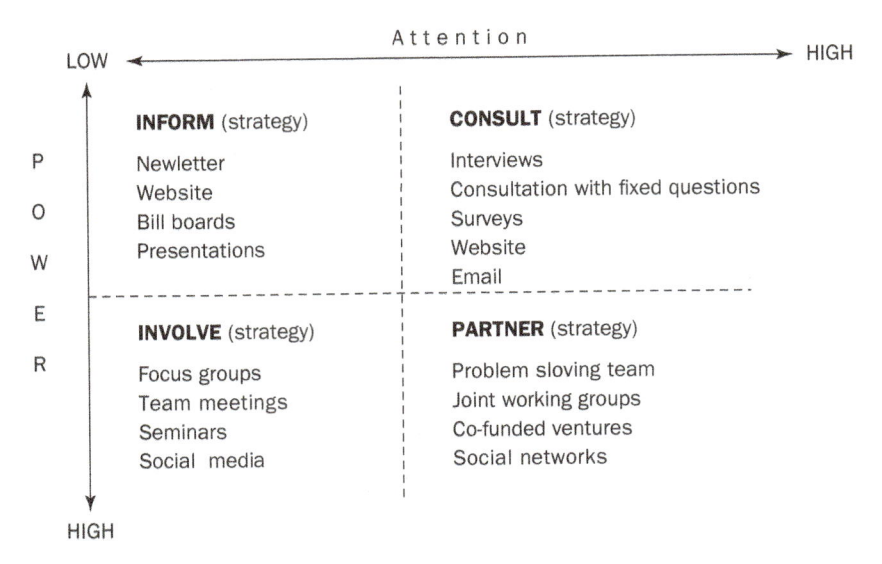

```
                      Attention
LOW  ◄─────────────────────────────────────► HIGH

P        INFORM (strategy)      │  CONSULT (strategy)
O        Newletter              │  Interviews
W        Website                │  Consultation with fixed questions
         Bill boards            │  Surveys
E        Presentations          │  Website
R                               │  Email
         ─────────────────── ── ┼ ─────────────────────
         INVOLVE (strategy)     │  PARTNER (strategy)
         Focus groups           │  Problem sloving team
         Team meetings          │  Joint working groups
         Seminars               │  Co-funded ventures
         Social media           │  Social networks

HIGH
```

Figure 9.11 Strategic approach depending on stakeholder segmentation, based on the COI's strategic approach (*source:* Gregory, A. (2015). Planning and Managing Public Relations Campaigns, 4th edition. London: Kogan Page)

Key Factors	Tactic 1	Tactic 2	Tactic 3	Tactic 4
Reach?	x		x	
Suitability for content?	x	x	x	
Credibility?			x	
Emotional impact?	x	x	x	x
Cost?		x	x	x
Contribution to objective?	x	x	x	x

Figure 9.12 The tactics effectiveness matrix

Time

Time is a finite commodity and the life of a public relations practitioner is notoriously busy. Furthermore, public relations often involves the cooperation of others, and getting them to observe deadlines requires firmness and tact.

Deadlines can be externally imposed or internally driven by the organisation. Internal events may include the announcement of annual results, launching a new service or the appointment of a senior executive. External events may be major calendar dates, such as the Olympic Games, Chinese New Year or Thanksgiving.

To ensure deadlines are met, all the key elements of a project must be broken down into their individual parts and a timeline put against them. Box 9.10 contains a list of the main elements of a VIP facility visit.

Each of these elements will need its own action plan and timescale. Thus, preparing the visit areas may include commissioning display boards with photographs and text and a video. That in turn will mean briefing photographers, and printers, video producers, getting content approved by senior management and so on. It may also involve liaising with security, organising cleaners and arranging for porters to move furniture and erect the displays.

> **Box 9.10**
>
> **Checklist for main elements of a VIP facility visit**
>
> 1. Draw up invitation list
> 2. Alert relevant departments
> 3. Select visit hosts
> 4. Book catering
> 5. Book photography
> 6. Issue invitations
> 7. Choose gifts for VIP
> 8. Prepare display materials
> 9. Write speeches
> 10. Prepare information packs
> 11. Brief visit hosts
> 12. Follow up invitations
> 13. Prepare visit areas
> 14. Collate final attendance list
> 15. Rehearse with visit hosts
> 16. Facilitate visit
> 17. Follow up

Having split the project down into its individual tasks, it is then useful to use techniques such as critical path analysis (CPA) and other project management tools to ensure the project is managed and delivered on time. If tasks must be done to a short timescale, time-saving measures will have to be implemented, such as employing a specialist agency to help or using existing display material.

An annual activity plan which collates everything into one accessible and visible place allows the peaks and troughs of activity to be identified so that they can be resourced accordingly. The times when activity is less intense can be used for reviewing or implementing other proactive plans.

Resources

There are three areas of resourcing that underpin public relations work: human resources, implementation costs and equipment (Gregory 2020). Having the right staff skills and competencies as well as an adequate budget are critical to success. Skilled investor relations personnel, for example, are rarer and more expensive than public relations generalists. Usually, a single practitioner with a few years' experience can handle a broad-ranging programme of limited depth or a focused in-depth specialism, such as internal communication.

Ideally, the organisation decides its optimum communication programme and resources it accordingly. The reality is usually a compromise between the ideal and the actual budget allocated. However, it must be borne in mind that public relations is relationship-driven and therefore people are more valuable than materials. Investor relations work may survive without expensive information packs, but it cannot survive without people.

When considering the implementation costs of a programme, public relations practitioners have a duty to be effective and efficient. So, for example, for an investor relations campaign it may be decided that a regular monthly update is appropriate. Should that be online or hard copy? If hard copy is best, choices must be made on the number of colours, quality of paper, frequency of publication, and so on. If budgets are restricted, it is important to think creatively about how a similar result can be obtained at a fraction of the cost. Joint ventures with complementary organisations, sponsorship and piggyback mailings (i.e. when one mailing such as an annual statement is used to include other information) should be considered. Online may be seen to be a cheap option and often is longer term, but set-up and maintenance costs and the cost of the human support needed to make it a success have to be done realistically.

Sometimes it can be more effective and efficient to spend slightly more money. Holding an employee conference off-site may cost more but may guarantee their attention. Sending an analyst's briefing to other key stakeholders may cost a little extra, but it may retain their support.

While not requiring excessive amounts of equipment, it is important that practitioners have the right technology to ensure quick and easy access to key stakeholders in a manner that is appropriate. Up-to-date mobile technology is a must these days.

Time and resource planning are essential elements of good management and judgements will be made about the efficient and effective running of campaigns. There are numerous online tools available which help with project planning and an online search will quickly reveal several. Some are tailored for use in communication.

Evaluation

Chapter 10 goes into detail about evaluation, but it is important to cover some basic principles here. Monitoring and evaluation answers the sixth key question: 'How can success be measured?' Public relations is like any other business function. It is vital to know whether the planned programme has done what it set out to do and, if not, why not.

All the planning approaches emphasise the importance of ongoing monitoring. Throughout its duration, practitioners will be regularly checking to see if the programme is on track. So, for example, media coverage will be monitored regularly to see if the selected media are using the material and to judge how they are using it.

Sometimes evaluation is relatively easy; for example, if the aim was to achieve a change in legislation and that has happened, then clearly it was successful. Often the situation is rather more complicated. If the plan is to change societal attitudes towards people who have mental health problems, it will take a long time. Different publics will require different amounts and types of communicative effort and as a result the evaluation programme will need to be much more sophisticated and longer term, and will need to employ formal social scientific research methods.

Building in evaluation focuses effort, demonstrates effectiveness and efficiency, and encourages good management and accountability. However, research shows that there is still a limited amount of evaluation done in the public relations industry and it is fraught with debate and difference.

There are several principles that can help to make evaluation easier:

- Building in evaluation from the start: if aims and objectives are set with evaluation in mind, the task is simpler.
- Setting smart objectives: if objectives are clear and measurable, then judging whether they have been achieved is relatively easy.
- Agreeing measurement criteria with whoever will be judging success.
- Monitoring as the programme progresses: using ongoing monitoring as a management information tool.
- Taking an objective and a scientific approach: the requirement to provide facts and figures about the programme means that the planner may need training in research methods or to employ trained specialists.
- Evaluating processes: the planner needs to make sure they are managing the programme well, within budget and to timescales.
- Establishing open and transparent monitoring processes, through for example, monthly review reports.

Evaluation is a contentious issue among public relations practitioners. Few believe that public relations should not be evaluated, but there is significant debate about how and what metrics should be used. The Barcelona Principles launched in 2010 and updated as Barcelona Principle 3.0 (AMEC 2020) have helped to set an international base point for evaluation. The UK Government Communication Service (GCS) has made evaluation of government campaigns compulsory and in 2018 produced an updated set of evaluation standards (GCS 2018). The GCS model for evaluation clearly links communication objectives to organisational and policy objectives and shows how they can be evaluated at various stages.

Review

While monitoring and evaluation are both an ongoing and end-of-programme process, a thorough review of all public relations activity should be undertaken regularly, but on a less frequent basis, every 12 months or so. As part of this, the external and internal environment should be surveyed systematically to ensure that all issues have been captured and any new ones accommodated. Campaign strategies should be tested to see if they are still entirely appropriate. Tactics should be reviewed to see if they need refreshing with any new creative input and to ensure that they are addressing the needs of the target publics.

Where a major review is required, it is important to take a holistic approach. Programmes always need to be dynamic and flexible enough to embrace stakeholder input, opportunities and challenges, but sometimes a fundamental reappraisal must take place. If that is the case, all the steps in the planning process outlined in this chapter need to be taken again.

Explore 9.4

Planning online

To consolidate your learning, go to the AMEC website at amecorg.com and look at the tutorial. It will take you through the planning process step by step and help you produce a strategic campaign plan.

Feedback

What did you learn from thinking through the whole process at one go? Can you detect a 'golden thread'; that is, how one step leads and links to the next to produce a coherent approach that provides a compelling narrative?

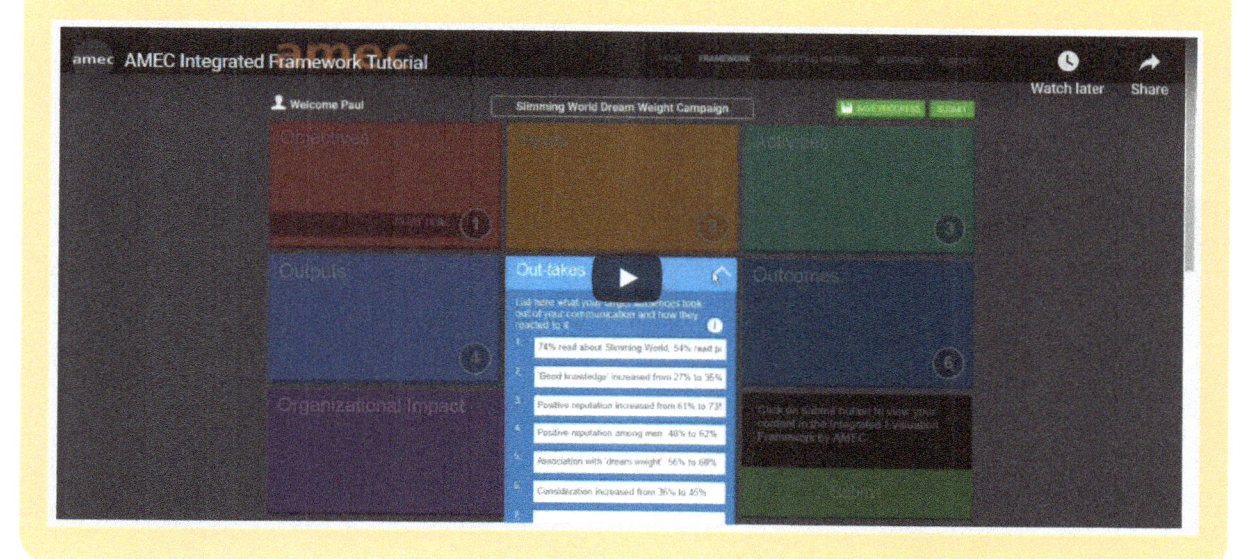

source: AMEC Integrated Framework Tutorial

Summary

This chapter has sought to show that strategic public relations is critical to organisational success. Public relations has a crucial role in organisations, not only in implementing impactful programmes, but in understanding the external and internal context. Without this wider understanding the full contribution of public relations at all levels within the organisation will not be understood or realised. Successful public relations programmes do not just happen: professionals plan. They plan to take a wide view of the organisation in context and within a framework that recognises a much broader contribution. While it is not the only contribution to organisational success that public relations professionals can make, delivering programmes that make a difference is a most tangible one. Seeing a planned public relations programme come to life is exciting and rewarding. It also clearly demonstrates to organisational peers and employers that public relations can make a real, measurable difference.

To bring together all the principles given in the second half of this chapter, a longer case study is now presented.

Glossary of terms for case study 9.1

To understand the case, this glossary of terms will assist.

Hapū (sub-tribe, or, most comparable with local community. These people will have a close family connection, or, be several families with close shared ancestor)

Hui (meeting)

Iwi (tribal group – all connect through a shared ancestor)

Kahui (cluster of hapū / sub-tribes – groups brought together to negotiate as part of collective)

Glossary of terms for case study 9.1 (continued)

Kaupapa (topic of focus/matter for discussion/can also be used for aspiration, e.g. we are aligned in our thinking)

Kaumatua (older man/respected leader of tribe or sub-tribe)

Korero (to talk)

Kuia (grandmother, or older lady)

Mokopuna (grandchild)

Tamariki (children)

Te Puni Kokiri (Ministry of Maori Economic Development)

Whakapapa (genealogy – this is not just your family tree but also how you connect to the land where your family base is, the local river, sea and mountain, which are all anchors that we connect to)

Whanau (family – immediate and extended family. Term is used for your mum, dad, siblings, aunty, uncle, grandparents)

Case study 9.1
The Te Wairoa Treaty Settlement

Picture 9.4 Prime Minister James Bolger and 'Maori Queen' Arikinui Dame Te Atairangikaahu after the signing of the historic treaty (*source:* Torsten Blackwood/AFP/Getty Images)

This case study illustrates best practice in planning and managing public relations for a very sensitive issue, but it also demonstrates agility in implementation. It combines the best of planned and responsive action and has transformed the communities for which it was designed.

The Te Wairoa Treaty Settlement

In 1840 the Treaty of Waitangi was signed between the British Crown and Maori Chiefs of the North Island of New Zealand. Although the precise interpretation is disputed, in essence the purpose of the Treaty was to enable British settlers ('pakeha') and the Māori people to live together under a common set of laws or agreements. It involved Maori ceding sovereignty to the Crown, while protecting their rights to keep their land, forests, fisheries and treasures. Since its signing, the Treaty and the agreement between Maori and the Crown have had a tumultuous history including wars and land confiscation. Historic violations of the Treaty have been the source of long-standing grievances for Maori, and the Treaty Settlement process was established in 1975 to resolve outstanding claims and to pave a way forward for the future.

To settle a claim, groups of Maori in localities are formed into Trusts approved by the Government. These Trusts then negotiate a Settlement with the Crown – the New Zealand Government's traditional name because of its historic connections to the UK. The Treaty Settlements do two things: provide reparation for past injustices and agree a partnership for the future. Eligible members of the Trust then vote to accept or reject the settlement.

Background

By late 2015, the iwi and hapū of Te Wairoa had worked to progress their historic Treaty of Waitangi claims for more than 30 years, trying to achieve a settlement for the people of Wairoa – a poor, disadvantaged region on the East Coast. The negotiating Trust, Te Tira Whakaemi o Te Wairoa (Te Tira) needed help to get through the final stages to achieve settlement. At the heart of the problem was ensuring enough eligible Maori would register and vote to support ratification of the settlement. They approached Campbell Squared Communications for that assistance.

Analysis

Preliminary research revealed that Te Tira had fewer than 100 registered members, did not have their up-to-date contact details, there was no website, social media profile or database, and many were elderly and/or without internet or smartphone access. There was deep distrust of the Government and widespread lack of understanding about the proposed terms of the settlement.

To exacerbate matters the seven groups of Maori that had been put together as a collective in the Trust to negotiate and agree terms for the whole area, had fought with each other in the New Zealand Land Wars of the 1860s. Maori culture is deep-rooted in family and history, and these Wars are still very raw to the iwi and hapū. In addition, some had become disillusioned with the lack of agreement and progress and were thinking of leaving the collective.

In a 2.5 hour 'fact finding' first meeting, one of the leading Trustees spent an hour berating the agency, thinking they were representatives of the Crown and wanting to trick them into settling.

Campbell Squared's preparedness to change their plans during the meeting and simply listen, turned out to be the first important step in building trust – a commodity in very short supply. The insight they gained into the levels of distrust allowed them to develop their strategy for the ratification campaign. They also captured initial key thoughts about the importance of the settlement from six elders 'in their words' and these later became a series of videos, which were crucial as the campaign unfolded.

Aim

To gain enough support in the ratification vote to convince the Crown to approve the Deed of Settlement for the iwi and hapū of Wairoa.

Objectives

- To engage iwi and hapū members and encourage them to support the kaupapa (approach).
- To shift mindsets from grievance mode or apathetic, to future-focused and invested.
- To encourage iwi and hapū members to register with Te Tira, vote in the ratification process, and vote 'yes' to the Settlement. Specifically, to register 900 people, to achieve 35 per cent voter return and to achieve 'yes' from 75 per cent of all those voting.

Target audiences and status

Iwi and hapū members including:	
■ trustees/elected reps ■ Kuia and kaumātua (elders) ■ young people (18–24 years) ■ parents ■ Whānau	
Already registered	■ Less than 100 – and no contact details/database.
Not yet registered	■ Estimated up to 34,000 people across the world could be eligible to register, but no database.
Engaged with their hapū or iwi (generally living in Wairoa)	■ Very few. ■ Many elderly. ■ A lot of poverty. ■ Limited/no internet access. ■ High level of mistrust (in the process, and sometimes each other).
Disengaged from their hapū or iwi (generally living elsewhere in New Zealand, Australia or further overseas)	■ Most in this category. ■ Apathetic/no reason to engage. ■ Generally living in bigger cities – Auckland, Wellington, Gold Coast, Perth. ■ Medium level of mistrust (in the process).
Government	
Minister for Treaty Negotiations, and his advisors	■ Need confidence that process is robust and majority of iwi and hapū support the Settlement. ■ Evidence based. ■ High level of public scrutiny.

Case study 9.1 (continued)

Office of Treaty Settlements (OTS) officials	■ Report to Minister. ■ Formal, rigid, legal based. ■ Challenging relationship for Te Tira.
Te Puni Kōkiri officials	■ Report to Minister. ■ Less formal than OTS but much more hands-off. ■ Watching/facilitating role.
Other iwi	
Pre-Settlement, neighbouring	■ Keeping a close eye on progress ■ Informal kōrero (talking among whānau)
Media	
Māori	■ Interested in key players, any criticism/protest, what this means for the people, who is getting what.
Mainstream	■ Want to know why this settlement is newsworthy. Government spending $100 million. Any significant criticism.
Regional	■ Focus on how this will impact on the wider community.

Content

There were several key messages that permeated the campaign:

- E tū te Wairoa! (Stand up for our people).
- Now is our time. Let's build a better future for our whānau.
- Our settlement, and the future of our whānau, depends on your vote.
- This is your whakapapa and your kids' future.
- Show your support for our people at home.
- This is a once-in-a-lifetime opportunity.
- We need as many votes as possible to make this happen.

These were rolled out across five phases in the campaign, Registration, Voting soon, Voting open, Voting closing, Results/Signing ceremony, with each phase also having specific content.

Strategy

The problem Campbell Squared had identified, as evidenced in their research, was a total lack of understanding of what the settlement was. All people knew was that it was worth $100 million. Iwi and hapū members on the ground had no idea what it could do for them, what impact it would have for the future, or how the Settlement would work in practical terms. Before the campaign, it was simply a legal/accounting/government process. It needed to be made relevant and meaningful. To address the problem a three-pronged strategy was developed:

- Hearts and minds: take the focus of the communication away from being about the *process* and move towards 'hearts and minds' – outlining the meaningful long-term benefits for the people and generations to come.

- By the people, for the people: secure buy-in from Te Tira trustees and elected representatives so *they* 'owned' the process. They were the ones to be talking to their people directly, not Campbell Squared. Key influencers and spokespeople delivered content in person through a series of meetings, so all could see 'the whites of their eyes'.

- Bring Wairoa closer: show disengaged iwi and hapū members living outside Wairoa, of which there were many eligible to vote, who/what Te Tira is and what is happening and re-engage them with their community.

Tactics

Video: 'In their words' featured Te Wairoa Kuia and Kaumātua (not trustees) – talking about what the settlement meant to them. These videos were shared on social media and housed on the Te Tira website. A video 'plug and play' presentation was created for the Ratification hui and all hui and events were livestreamed.

Web: a website (www.tetirawhakaemi.iwi.nz), ensured important information was easy to find, read and understand for all key audiences. This included an online voter registration form and a downloadable PDF, to ensure there were no barriers to registration.

Facebook: a Facebook page for Te Tira (www.facebook.com/tetirawhakaemi) was a crucial engagement tool.

Content targeted iwi and hapū members so they saw relevant messaging. As Te Tira grew its database (as people registered), lookalike audiences were targeted on Facebook to encourage new registrations. Voting messages were focused on those already registered to vote. Event pages were set up for all nine-ratification hui around the country and the ceremony, with targeted boosted posts to registered members in each region.

Email: engaged with iwi and hapū members throughout the campaign. Email informed new members that their registration was successful and was used to inform the entire database with ratification hui dates linking through to Facebook events.

Integrated communications: integration across platforms, with emails linking to Facebook events, which then linked to the website for more information.

Although online platforms were a major channel to grow the audience, traditional tactics were still integral for engaging elderly audiences and those without internet access.

Media: five media releases, coinciding with each phase of the campaign and active engagement with key reporters and media outlets.

Print: an information booklet for Te Tira, and an official Ratification booklet.

Hui and elected representatives: Chairperson Tāmati Olsen and Trustee John Whaanga featured at every hui around the country. They answered questions, as the 'face' of Te Tira, ensuring a consistent voice for whānau concerns. The elected representatives of the seven kahui (clusters) were 'foot-soldiers' for the kaupapa and were supplied with key messages, interviewed and filmed. All were given a challenge: to register at least 100 people each.

Most iwi and hapū members live outside Wairoa and had never engaged with Te Tira before. To solve the disconnect, Wairoa was brought to them through livestreaming. Every major event in the campaign was livestreamed, starting from the initialling of the Deed of Settlement at Parliament. The journey of those coming from Wairoa for the ceremony and the ceremony itself was livestreamed and filmed. This footage was valuable for making short videos later to share on social media and inspire and engage viewers and potential voters.

Each Ratification hui was also live-streamed and the official Settlement signing ceremony. This allowed whānau from around the world to tune in to watch hui and the signing celebration. Facebook chat was used to engage with those watching, so they could ask questions and discuss key aspects. Comments from iwi and hapū members watching expressed their gratitude to 'experience' the historic occasion and excitement to see their whānau online back home.

Efficient hui were another challenge for Te Tira to overcome. Previously they struggled to complete presentations (written by lawyers), as attendees would interrupt with many questions. The 'plug and play' video presentation developed by Campbell Squared, was used for the first 20 minutes of each hui, then the Chairman and trustees would answer questions – but there was usually no need, as these had been answered through the 'plug and play'. When people did speak, most expressed their support and encouraged others to get on board.

Results and follow-up

Te Tira gained overwhelming support in the voting results, quickly gaining the Crown's approval on the Settlement for the Iwi and Hapū of Wairoa.

Communications objectives were fully met.

1. Iwi and hapū members were engaged to support the kaupapa:

   - Over 30,000 Facebook engagements (including likes, shares, comments and click throughs) occurred during the campaign period. This exceeded the goal by 900 per cent.
   - Each Ratification hui was attended by an average of 49 people (ranging from 89 at one, to 24 at another), with a combined total of 489 attendees. Previous hui had between four and ten people attend.
   - Te Tira videos were viewed 21,058 times (watched for three seconds or more). This exceeded the goal by over 4,000 per cent.
   - All livestreamed Ratification hui and the Settlement signing ceremony had an online audience, averaging 444 views per livestream.
   - Facebook was a crucial channel for sharing messaging and engaging iwi and hapū members. Regular posts were made over a six-month period, with a 408 per cent increase in page likes (from 198 likes in February to 1,006 likes in August). More than 100,000 people were reached through Facebook.

Case study 9.1 (continued)

Iwi and hapū members became 'champions' for the online campaign; they wanted to get involved and spread the word. They tagged their whānau and friends in Facebook posts and uploaded their own videos of support, encouraging whānau to register and vote for the Settlement.

2. Mindsets were shifted from grievance mode or apathetic, to future focused and invested:

    - 99 per cent positive/supportive comments on Facebook and at Ratification hui.
    - 90 per cent positive media coverage, with Te Tira key messages, including ten stories from Māori media outlets, ten from mainstream media outlets, six stories from regional media outlets.

3. Iwi and hapū members register to vote with Te Tira, vote in the ratification process, and vote 'yes' to the Settlement:

    - Nearly 6,500 iwi and hapū members (3,602 eligible voters) registered before voting closed (exceeding the goal by 300 per cent).
    - 56.39 per cent voter return (exceeding the goal by 61 per cent).
    - 96.88 per cent of voters voted 'yes' to the Settlement (exceeding the goal by 29 per cent).

In his report to the Minister, the Chairman, Tāmati Olsen, attributed the success to the communications: 'We employed all modern communication mediums in achieving not only a national, but global reach well beyond our expectations. Much of which has given us valuable insights and hints on how we can keep our young, mobile, global beneficiary base informed and participating into the future in a post-settlement environment.'

He went on, 'the success of our ratification strategy has also thrown up some challenges. In creating the high levels of participation, we have also rightly created high levels of expectation from our beneficiaries – especially in relation to our next steps and the impending establishment of our post settlement governance entity, Tātau o Te Wairoa Trust.'

Tatau Tatau o Te Wairoa Trust, now has a large, engaged audience to move forward with. They have also learned about new ways to connect the whole community and have committed to use contemporary communication channels such as livestreaming and Facebook, alongside the traditional Maori methods of communication such as the hui.

Lessons from the case

Several key lessons come from this case:

- Planning is vitally important, but within the plan must be flexibility to adjust and adapt given the realities that are encountered.
- Honouring the culture, traditions and deeply held beliefs of those being engaged is vital: in this case listening and recognising the history of the iwi and hapū was the point at which trust began to develop.
- It was only when trust had been established that the Maori communities were open to trying the non-traditional methods of communication recommended by the agency.
- Once confidence had grown, the Maori communities were able to reach out and engage with their wider, global family and with third parties rather than being consumed with their own differences and concerns.
- The agency saw their role as one of facilitation and service to the community, helping them find their voice. The principles of co-production, co-delivery and partnership was characteristic of the campaign.
- Both the agency and the Maori communities learned life-lessons from each other, have developed their understanding of each other and will use this to enrich their own work in building 'one New Zealand'.

Bibliography

Agerwal, R. and C. Helfat (2009). Strategic renewal of organizations. *Organization Science* 20(2): 281–293.

Ansoff, I. (1988). *Corporate Strategy*. Revised Edition. London: Penguin Books.

Broom, G.M. and B.L. Sha (2012). *Cutlip and Center's Effective Public Relations*, 10th edn. Upper Saddle River, NJ: Prentice-Hall, Inc.

Cornelissen, J. (2017). *Corporate Communication*. London: Sage.

De Wit. R. (2017). *Strategy: An International Perspective,* 6th edition. Andover, UK: Cengage Learning EMEA.

Denning, S. (2016a). How to make the whole organization 'Agile'. *Strategy & Leadership* 44(4): 10–17.

Denning, S. (2016b). *HBR's embrace of Agile.* Forbes. com, 21 April 2016. www.forbes.com/sites/stevedenning/2016/04/21/hbrs-embrace-of-agile/

European Commission (2015). *Toolkit for the evaluation of the communication activities.* Brussels, Directorate General for Communication. Available at http://ec.europa.eu/dgs/communication/about/evaluation/documents/communication-evaluation-toolkit_en.pdf

Edelman. (2019). 2019 Edelman Trust Barometer. Available at https://www.edelman.com/sites/g/files/aatuss191/files/2019-03/2019_Edelman_Trust_Barometer_Global_Report.pdf?utm_source=website&utm_medium=global_report&utm_campaign=downloads

Falkheimer, J. and M. Heide (2010). On Dropping the Tools: From Planning to Improvisation. In W.T. Coombs, Ed. *Handbook of Crisis Communication.* Malden, MA: Wiley-Blackwell, pp. 511–526

Freeman, R.E. (1984). *Strategic Management: A Stakeholder Approach.* Boston, MA: Pitman.

Gates Foundation (2018), Annual letter: 10 tough questions we get asked, https://www.gatesnotes.com/2018-Annual-Letter

GCS (2018). GCS Evaluation Framework 2.0. Available at https://gcs.civilservice.gov.uk/wp-content/uploads/2018/06/6.4565_CO_Evaluation-Framework-2.0-v11-WEB.pdf

Grant, R.M. (2016). *Contemporary Strategy Analysis,* 9th edn. Chichester: John Wiley & Sons ltd.

Gregory, A. (2020). *Planning and Managing Public Relations Campaigns,* 5th edn. London: Kogan Page.

Gregory, A. and G. Halff (2017). Understanding public relations in the 'sharing economy'. *Public Relations Review* 43(1): 4–13.

Gregory, A. and P. Willis (2013). *Strategic Public Relations Leadership.* London: Routledge.

Grunig, J.E. and Hunt, T. (1984). *Managing Public Relations.* New York: Holt, Rinehart & Winston.

Johnson, G., R. Whittington, K. Scholes, D. Angwin and P. Regner (2017). *Exploring Corporate Strategy,* 11th edn. London: Pearson Education.

Kahneman, D. and A. Tversky (1979). Prospect theory: an analysis of decision under risk. *Econometrica* 47, pp. 263–291.

Lerbinger, O. (1972). *Designs for Persuasive Communication.* Englewood Cliffs, NJ: Prentice Hall.

Macnamara, J. (2016). *Organizational Listening.* New York: Peter Lang.

Marston, J.E. (1997). *Modern Public Relations.* New York: McGraw Hill

Matzler, K., J. Füller, K. Hutter, J. Hautz and D. Stieger (2014). *Open strategy: Towards a research agenda.* Social Science Research Network. Retrieved from https://ssrn.com/abstract=2416937 or http://dx.doi.org/10.2139/ssrn.2416937

McElreath, M.P. (1997). *Managing Systematic and Ethical Public Relations Campaigns,* 2nd edn. Madison, WI: Brown and Benchmark.

Meznar, M.B. and D. Nigh (1995). Buffer or Bridge: Environmental Determinants of Public Affairs Activities in American Firms. *Academy of Management Journal* 38(4): 975–96.

Moloney, K. (2006). *Rethinking Public Relations.* Abingdon: Routledge.

Myers, C. (2016). *Common sense: the key to an empowered workforce.* Available at https://www.forbes.com/sites/chrismyers/2016/09/05/common-sense-the-key-to-an-empowered-workplace/#662cb86c7ff3

Pew Center (2019). *The State of the Media 2017.* Available at https://www.pewresearch.org/fact-tank/2018/08/21/5-facts-about-the-state-of-the-news-media-in-2017/

Porter, M.E. (1980). *Competitive Strategy.* New York: Free Press.

Rigby, D.K., J. Sutherland and H. Takeuchi (2016). Embracing Agile. *Harvard Business Review,* April 2016.

Ritzer, G.F. (2019). *The McDonalisation of Society: into the digital age,* 9th edn. Thousand Oaks, Cal: Sage Publications, Inc.

Scharmer, C.O. and K. Kaeufer (2010). In front of the blank canvas: sensing emerging future. *Journal of Business Strategy* 31(4): 21–29.

Steyn, B. (2007). Contribution of public relations to organisational strategy formulation. In E.L. Toth (ed.). *The Future of Excellence in Public Relations and Communication Management.* Mahwah, NJ. Lawrence Erlbaum Associates.

Sutherland, J. (2014). *Scrum: The Art of Doing Twice The Work In Half The Time,* Crown Business.

Thompson, J., J.M. Scott and F. Martin (2017). *Strategic Management: Awareness and Change,* 8th edn. Andover: Cengage Learning EMEA.

van Ruler, B. (2015). Agile Public Relations Planning: the reflective communication scrum. *Public Relations Review* 41(2):187–194.

WEF (World Economic Forum) (2019). *The Global Risks Report*. Edition 14. Geneva: World Economic Forum.

Weick, K.E. (1998). Improvisation as a mindset for organizational analysis. *Organization Science: A Journal of the Institute of Management Sciences*, 9(5), 543–556.

White, J. and D.M. Dozier (1992). Public Relations and Management Decision Making. In J.E. Grunig (Ed.). *Excellence in Public Relations and Communication Management*. Hillsdown, NJ: Lawrence Erlbaum Associates.

Windahl, S. and B. Signitzer (with J.E. Olson) (2009). *Using Communication Theory*. London: Sage.

CHAPTER 10

Jim Macnamara

Measurement and evaluation for effectiveness and impact

Source: Johan Swanepoel/Shutterstock

Learning outcomes

By the end of this chapter you should be able to:
- understand the uses and benefits of measurement and evaluation in communication
- identify the relevant stages and steps to implement measurement and evaluation
- plan appropriate methods of measurement and evaluation
- know how to apply measurement and evaluation in public relations and communication management.

Structure

- Why measure and evaluate?
- Getting started with some definitions
- Three types of evaluation: when and why?
- Foundational theories of measurement and evaluation
- Applying measurement and evaluation in communication
- Reporting measurement and evaluation

Why measure and evaluate?

The development of *mass communication* media and technologies in the twentieth century led to a belief that public communication practices such as advertising and public relations could have direct and strong effects on people. For example, it was long believed that TV and movies caused violence and that propaganda through media campaigns could cause attitudinal and behavioural changes such as a desire to fight or surrender during war. On the positive side, it was thought that communication campaigns could readily solve health problems by promoting healthy lifestyles and ensure compliance with the law. These theories and practices were based on what is variously termed the *injection model*, the *hypodermic needle* concept of communication, and *bullet theory* (Schramm 1971; Severin and Tankard 2001). Such beliefs are represented in the Shannon and Weaver (1949) model of communication and other early so-called communication models developed by Schramm (1954), Berlo (1960), and others. These models conceptualise communication as a one-way transmission of information and messages via various channels with the assumption that the messages will be received and have the desired effect.

Advertising and public relations do have effects – if they did not, they would not be used as extensively as they are. However, recent research has shown that the effects of communication are contingent and contextual. In simple terms, the effects of communication depend on several factors, such as how audiences understand and interpret information, the presence of other influences, and the context such as the economic social, cultural, political circumstances at the time (Bryant and Oliver 2009; Sparks 2006).

The internet has brought increased opportunities for communication and increased expectations of communication at a local, national and even on a global scale. However, today it is clear that much of the content of mass media and the internet does not have the effects that the creators desire. Political campaigns often fail, or produce divided results such as *Brexit*, or lead to unanticipated results such as the election of Donald Trump. Massive investments in road safety campaigns have not stopped road accidents or even reduced them in many countries. Despite a plethora of health communication campaigns, many people continue to smoke or become obese. While some corporate communication and public relations programmes are very successful, others have limited or no impact. This may not be the fault of the communicators. As stated above, communication is contingent and contextual. Factors such as corporate behaviour, political instability, or product quality can affect outcomes. Also, competing voices and messages may be present and be more persuasive or cause confusion. Furthermore, many studies in linguistics, language studies and psychology have shown that receivers of information can interpret it to gain a different meaning than that intended by the sender, as revealed in *encoding/decoding* theory (Hall 1973). Audiences also can resist messages that conflict with their existing attitudes and behaviour, referred to as *cognitive dissonance* (Festinger 1957), and sometimes people completely reject messages or do the opposite, referred to as *reactance* (Dillard and Shen 2005). Humans have *agency* – that is, a level of independence and autonomy to make decisions based on their individual personality, circumstances and interests, as well being influenced by their peers, media and other sources of information. Professional communicators must recognise that despite all the knowledge, skills and effort that they apply,

Picture 10.1 Planning and management are as important to practice as flight planning in the aviation industry (*source:* Steve Collender/123RF)

communication sometimes does not achieve the objectives set because of the reasons stated above.

Therefore, measurement and evaluation are essential. Professional communicators cannot assume that public relations and communication management will always be successful in achieving objectives.

To plan and undertake public relations and communication management without measurement and evaluation is like a pilot taking off in an aircraft without a flight plan and then 'flying blind' (i.e. with no instrument data or map). If you did that, you wouldn't know the best way to get to where you wanted to go, and you wouldn't know when you had got there. In fact, there is a good chance that you would never get there at all.

There is a second important reason to undertake measurement and evaluation. Studies by pioneering public relations scholars Glen Broom and David Dozier identified four types of public relations and communication practitioners (Broom 1982; Broom and Dozier 1986), which Dozier later summarised into two main types. He described practitioners as being communication *technicians* or communication *managers* (Dozier 1992). As the term suggests, communication technicians are primarily involved in the technical aspects of public relations and communication management such as writing (e.g. media releases), producing publications and website content, arranging events, calling journalists to arrange interviews or news conferences, and so on. Communication *managers* focus on planning to address problems or take advantage of opportunities, developing strategy, overseeing programmes, and presenting and reporting to senior management. While technician work is an important part of day-to-day public relations and communication, it can be directionless and ineffective without a clear and well-formed strategy. As we will see in the following sections of this chapter, early and progressive measurement and evaluation are essential for developing effective evidence-based strategy. Also, measurement and evaluation at the end of projects and campaigns are fundamental for reporting to management, which increasingly demands evidence of outcomes and impact rather than a pile of media clippings or anecdotal information.

This points to a third reason to be able to undertake measurement and evaluation. Senior management today in both the private and public sectors expect and often demand accountability in all functions of an organisation. It is common today for corporations, government departments and agencies, non-government organisations (NGOs) and non-profits to employ performance measurement and use methods such as key performance indicators (KPIs); balanced score cards, which were developed by Kaplan and Norton (1992) for business and subsequently applied to public relations and communication management (Fleisher and Mahaffy 1997);

> **Think about 10.1**
>
> ### Why evaluation is important
>
> Why do you think evidence is important in relation to the reporting?
>
> When is communication effective – when you put information out, or when audiences respond in a desired way?

as well as dashboards, return on investment (ROI), and other methods of reporting effectiveness. To align with the policies of an organisation and to meet management requirements, public relations and communication management professionals need to be able to understand and apply measurement and evaluation.

Getting started with some definitions

To have a common language to discuss practices and avoid confusion, it is useful to begin with definitions of several key terms. At the most basic level, we need to address the two key terms: 'measurement' and 'evaluation'. These are often used interchangeably, and measurement is quite often used as an umbrella term for the range of activities involved in these practices. For example, the International Association for Measurement and Evaluation of Communication (AMEC) uses both terms in its name. However, its peak annual event is called the AMEC 'Summit on Measurement'. In management literature there is considerable focus on *performance measurement*, although ultimately this is seen as part of the wider field of business performance management (BPM). So, what is the difference in these practices?

Measurement

Measurement literally means 'taking measures'. It involves the collection and analysis of data in relation to objects, processes, conditions or people. For example, parents measure the height and weight of their children as they grow and develop. We measure our own weight for both health and aesthetic reasons. Our doctor measures our blood pressure and other variables such as cholesterol levels. When we are driving a vehicle, we refer to instruments that measure our speed and how much fuel we have. Measurement is important in many aspects of life. Without various measurements we are like a pilot 'flying blind'.

However, simple statistics and what many call *metrics* tell us little or nothing without interpretation and contextualisation. For instance, is driving at 60 miles per hour (100 kilometres per hour) fast or slow; safe or dangerous? If a person weighs 220 pounds (100 kilograms), is that appropriate, overweight or even obese? The answers to these questions are gained through evaluation.

Evaluation

Evaluation is defined in both the Oxford and Merriam-Webster dictionaries as 'to judge' or the act of 'making a judgement' about the significance or value of something (Evaluation 2016a, 2016b). Evaluation involves interpretation of information and data to determine what it means in the circumstances. Interpretation involves and can be based largely or wholly on human subjectivity – we all make judgements about situations and people every day based on intuition or what is colloquially called gut feel. However, in a professional environment, evaluation based on one's personal subjectivity (i.e. opinion) is not enough. Three important elements inform evaluation and provide rigour and relevance.

First, evaluation requires criteria against which judgements can be made. These are usually established by setting objectives and targets, a process that will be examined in detail later in this chapter.

Second, evaluation is aided by various analysis methods and techniques, which will also be explained and explored.

In addition, and very importantly, interpretation is informed by context. In the preceding examples, a body weight of 220 pounds (100 kilograms) might be considered excessive for a young woman or an adolescent male, but it could be quite appropriate – even necessary – for a Rugby or football player. Driving at 60 miles per hour (100 kilometres an hour) would be considered acceptable on a highway and even slow on a motorway or autobahn, but it would be dangerous and irresponsible in a narrow urban street.

From this can we see that measurement and evaluation go together – like 'two peas in a pod', as the saying goes. Evaluation is subjective and potentially biased without data collected through various measures. But measurement is of limited or no use on its own – it produces numbers that can be meaningless or even misleading without context. Because they go together, and because the ultimate purpose of measurement is usually evaluation, many use the single term 'evaluation' in a professional context to incorporate measurement or abbreviate the terms to M&E for simplicity. In this chapter whenever the single term 'evaluation' is used, it is meant as incorporating measurement that informs the evaluation.

The online Research Methods Knowledge Base says, 'evaluation is the systematic acquisition and assessment of information to provide useful feedback about some object' (Trochim 2006, para, 3). In educational literature, evaluation is defined as 'the process of gathering information about the merit or worth of a program for the purpose of making decisions about its effectiveness or for program improvement' (Owston 2007: 606). Note the important phrase 'for the purpose of making decisions' referring to effectiveness and programme improvement. Evaluation involves *data plus decisions* or, put another way, evaluation can be described as data informed judgements. Even more specific definitions of evaluation describe the process as 'the systematic application of research procedures to understand the conceptualisation, design, implementation, and utility of interventions' (Valente 2001: 106). Noteworthy in this definition is that, in addition to emphasising a systematic approach, it stipulates that research procedures should be used to inform evaluation – not casual observation, anecdotal information, or even 'black box' automated systems based on secret algorithms. Valente goes on to spell out that a comprehensive evaluation framework should include:

- assessing needs;
- conducting formative research to design messages;
- designing activities (referred to as treatments or interventions in health communication) and monitoring methods;
- conducting process research;

Think about 10.2

What do you value and how?

Think about objects or processes that are important in your life – such as your mobile device or computer, car, home, or visiting the library (physically or online)? How do you determine the value of these? You are likely to expect your mobile device or computer to have fast processing and download speeds. You can measure your car in terms of its year of manufacture and how many miles or kilometres it has done. You can obtain a quotation on the price of your home if it was to be sold. But is the *value* of these for you determined solely in terms of megabytes or gigabytes per second; dates; metrics such as miles or kilometres; how many pounds, dollars or euro your home is worth on the market; or even the number of books and articles in your library? Think about how you identify their value, as distinct from the various measurements that can be applied.

- conducting summative research; and
- sharing results with stakeholders and other researchers (cited in Rice and Atkin 2002: 428).

This above list of key elements in an *evaluation framework* includes steps and terms that lead us to recognising that there are several different types of evaluation research. One study identified up to 22 types of evaluation (Stufflebeam 2001). However, most research in the field breaks evaluation down into three main types. These were identified by Rice and Atkin in their leading text *Public Communication Campaigns* as (1) *formative* evaluation; (2) *process* evaluation; and (3) *summative* evaluation, although they noted that summative evaluation is sometimes referred to as *outcome* evaluation (Rice and Atkin 2013: 13). In a chapter in the same book specifically discussing evaluation, Valente and Kwan (2013: 83) also identified three main phases of evaluation as formative, process and summative. Some collapse these three types into two: formative evaluation (also referred to as (*ex-ante*)) and *summative* evaluation (also referred to as *ex-post*) (Trochim 2006; Scriven 1972). In Trochim's view, process evaluation is part of formative evaluation. However, there are benefits in examining the three types because they occur at different times during a communication project or campaign and they involve different metrics and methods.

Three types of evaluation: when and why?

Formative evaluation

Formative evaluation, also referred to as formative research because it usually involves research, is undertaken before (*ex-ante*) a public relations or communication project or campaign is developed. It should be part of planning, because the findings will inform the design of public relations and communication. Some suggest that formative evaluation should even precede the setting of objectives, as the discussion of 'SMART objectives' and some of the models examined later in this chapter will explain. There are several key reasons why formative evaluation is important – even essential.

First, formative evaluation establishes baseline data, which provide benchmarks for later comparison. For example, if you are planning a campaign to increase the rate of cervical cancer screening among women aged 50 + you need to know the current rate of cervical cancer screening in that group. Otherwise, you will have no basis on which to show your campaign was

Picture 10.2 Gathering data from relevant publics is critical to good public relations planning and measurement (*source:* Emily Brain/Alamy Stock Photo)

successful. Similarly, if you are planning a campaign to improve the reputation of a company, you will need formative research to identify its current reputation.

Second, you need to understand the stakeholders and/or publics with whom you wish to communicate. If current cervical cancer screening rates are low, why? What do women aged 50 + think about cervical cancer screening? What is holding them back from having screens – is it fear, apathy, lack of information, lack of access to screening facilities, or something else? Understanding one's audience is essential to ensure communication addresses the most relevant issues, that it contains the most relevant messages, and that it uses an appropriate voice and tone.

A third reason for undertaking formative evaluation is identifying the media or other channels of communication that are most used and relevant for the audience, often referred to as *channel preference*. This involves gaining insights into both the volume and frequency of use of media and other channels, as well as identifying those with the highest credibility and influence. Simple audience statistics and circulation data are not enough. For instance, when planning a health communication aimed at women aged 54–70 from minority ethnic groups, particularly recent immigrants, researchers found that women in these groups watched TV programmes extensively, but they placed little credibility on TV in terms of health information. What sources and channels did they rely on and trust for information about women's health issues? Formative research involving focus groups found that, along with their local doctor, these women relied on their daughters for information about women's health issues. Hence, a campaign was developed to engage daughters of mature-aged women in these communities, as well as local GPs in areas with high target audience populations. (See Case study 10.2 later in this chapter.)

Many campaigns fail because of a lack of audience understanding, also referred to as audience insights. Formative evaluation identifies existing awareness, attitudes and behaviours; challenges to address such as lack of trust, misinformation or fear; the media and other sources of information that the audience uses and finds most credible; and even potential partners, such as local doctors in the case mentioned above.

Process evaluation

Process evaluation refers to the tracking of communication activities as they are implemented. The best-known forms of process evaluation are media monitoring and media analysis (officially known as *media content analysis*). It needs to be recognised that metrics such as 'clip counts', follows and video views do not provide evidence that the target audience is changing their attitudes or behaviour in line with the objectives of a project or campaign. Similarly, process evaluation such as counting the number of attendees at events does not indicate that they will take away the messages that the event was designed to convey. However, process evaluation does indicate whether public relations and communication management are on track. For example, positive feedback and data such as high numbers of web page and video views, likes, shares, retweets and registrations for more information provide data to show that a campaign is at least engaging the intended audience. Conversely, if process evaluation shows that audiences are not responding to communication such as web pages, videos and not registering for planned events, strategy can be adapted, and new approaches tried.

Summative evaluation

Summative evaluation is the type that most communication management professionals refer to when they use the term evaluation. It is evaluation done after (*ex-post*) a project or campaign to identify the extent to which the objectives were achieved. Clearly, summative evaluation is important. But it is essential to recognise that formative and process evaluation substantially improve the chances that objectives will be achieved. Too many practitioners skip formative evaluation, only to find later that important insights could have been gained at the beginning that would have substantially increased the chances of success.

During summative evaluation, data collected after a communication project or campaign are compared with baseline data, which indicates the degree of change. For

Box 10.1
Proving causality?

There are three rules to demonstrate causality – sometimes referred to as causation. To plausibly claim that effects were caused by certain activities, you must show:

1. *Temporal precedence* – the alleged cause must precede the alleged effect (e.g. sometimes practitioners claim that positive media publicity caused a share price increase, but time/date checking reveals that the positive publicity followed the share price lift).

2. *Covariation of cause and effect* – or, in simpler terms, there must be a clear link between cause and effect. In communication, this requires evidence that the audience accessed and engaged with the information provided.

3. *No plausible alternative* – as far as possible, you must show that there was no other likely cause of the effect reported.

example, if the cervical cancer screening rate among women aged 50 + was 30 per cent before a communication campaign and *ex-post* data showed a 45 per cent screening rate in the same group, then there is clear evidence of success – albeit note that *causality* needs to be shown – that is, did the communication cause the increase, or could it have been caused by something else?

In a summary of 10 years of research among 20,000 communication professionals in Europe conducted as part of the European Communication Monitor, Tench et al. (2017) concluded that evaluation is the *Alpha* and the *Omega* of strategy. That is, it is the first thing that practitioners should do and the last thing that they should do if they wish to implement effective strategic and communication management.

Foundational theories of measurement and evaluation

Evaluation, incorporating measurement, has been developed in several fields and, while our purpose in this chapter is to focus on communication management, it is useful to note the key theories, concepts and models that have been applied in other fields. These inform many of the latest frameworks and models and communication evaluation and give insights into future directions.

Evaluation theory and models originated in the late 1960s in public administration (Suchman 1967) and aid programmes such as the early logical framework approach, referred to as *log frames,* of the US Agency for International Development (USAID) (Practical Concepts 1979). During the 1970s and 1980s several evaluation theories, models and methods were produced in international development, public administration, education and health services. More recently they have been applied extensively to neighbouring fields of communication practice such as health communication.

Programme theory and theory of change

Evaluation theory is grounded in and derived from *programme theory* and *theory of change.*

Programme theory was pioneered by Joseph Wholey (1979, 1983, 1987), a professor of public administration at the University of Southern California for more than 30 years, followed by Peter Rossi and Huey Chen, who championed the notion of theory-driven evaluation (Chen and Rossi 1983; Rossi et al. 2004). Other influential figures in developing programme theory for evaluation included Carol Weiss (1972) and, later, Leonard Bickman (1990).

Wholey summarises programme theory as that which 'identifies program resources, program activities, and intended outcomes, and specifies a chain of causal assumptions linking program resources, activities, intermediate outcomes, and ultimate program goals' (1987: 78).

Theory of change emerged from programme theory in the mid-1990s as a way of analysing initiatives that seek to create change and explain how change is achieved. Development was led by programme evaluation researchers and initiatives such as the Aspen Institute Roundtable on Community Change (Anderson 2005), and continues today through groups such as the Center for Theory of Change in New York (www.theoryofchange.org). In simple terms, theory of change focuses on identifying the short-term and mid-term changes that need to be achieved in order to produce longer-term outcomes and impacts (see Clark 2004; Clark and Taplin 2012).

While programme theory, which incorporates *program theory evaluation* (PTE), and theory of change initially were applied to evaluating the delivery of human and social services such as aid, health services and education, this knowledge has been progressively taken up in several other fields ranging from agricultural programmes to large construction projects and contemporary management. Rossi et al. say that programme evaluation based on programme theory and theory of change is 'useful in virtually all spheres of activity in which issues are raised about the effectiveness of organised social action' and they specifically note its relevance for advertising, marketing and other communication activities (2004: 6).

Programme logic models

The stages and elements of programme theory are commonly illustrated in what are called *programme logic models,* which are graphic illustrations of the processes in a programme from setting objectives and pre-programme planning to measurement of its outcomes and impact (Wholey 1979). The Kellogg Foundation (2004) and the University of Wisconsin Extension programme (UWEX) have developed programme logic models that are used by many organisations today across many sectors and industries. The Kellogg Foundation model breaks programmes into five key stages referred to as *inputs, activities, outputs, outcomes* and *impact* (see Figure 10.1).

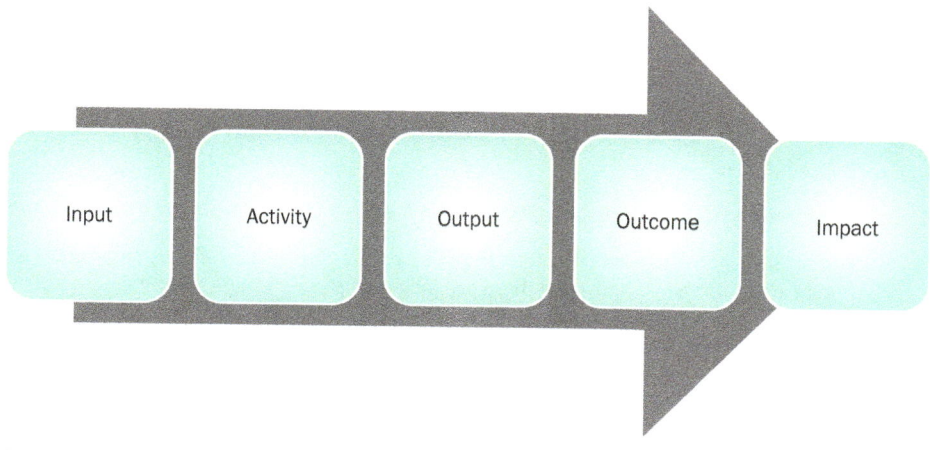

Input → Activity → Output → Outcome → Impact

Figure 10.1 A basic programme logic model (*source:* Kellogg Foundation. (2004). Logic model development guide. Battle Creek, MI. [online] Available at: https://www.wkkf.org/resource-directory/resource/2006/02/wk-kellogg-foundation-logic-model-development-guide [Accessed 28 Mar. 2019]. (Original work published 1998))

Resources → Activities → Outputs → Short-term Outcomes → Intermediate term Outcomes → Long-term Outcomes → Impact

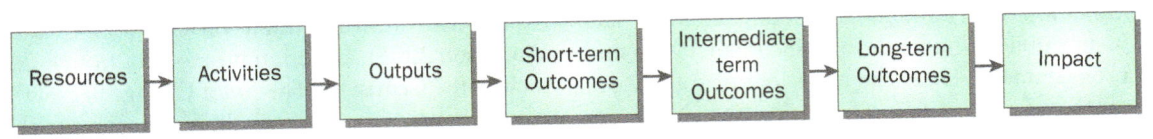

Figure 10.2 Programme logic model proposed by Knowlton and Phillips (2013: 37) in their *Logic Models Guidebook*

Some models identify up to seven stages in programmes by breaking outcomes into short, medium and long term (see Figure 10.2). The UWEX *Developing a Logic Model: Teaching and Training Guide* notes that 'many variations and types of logic models exist' (Taylor-Power and Henert 2008: 2). The Kellogg Foundation similarly says that 'there is no one best logic model' (2004: 13). However, there are several common concepts and principles in programme logic models for evaluation.

The two most common and important principles of programme logic model approaches are (1) they identify that communication occurs in stages in which the focus and what is measured in each is quite different, and (2) that communication occurs over time – sometimes considerable time. These two key principles clearly show that a single method or metric for evaluation or and communication management is impossible.

In their guidelines for evaluation design for communication campaigns, Atkin and Freimuth point out: 'As a means to attaining the bottom-line behavioural objectives, campaign messages must first have an impact on preliminary or intermediate variables along the response chain' (2013: 58). This notion of a *response chain* is important because it helps identify the response from audiences that communicators need to achieve at each stage. To further explain this concept of a response chain and how it applies at various stages, Table 10.1 provides examples of responses that can demonstrate progress at each stage.

Other approaches

Another approach to evaluation, termed *realist* evaluation, adds two further key considerations in evaluation. Realist evaluation (RE) places emphasis on the context of programmes and the interests of all 'actors' – the organisation, stakeholders and society. A common methodology for realist evaluation is *context-mechanism-outcome* (CMO) analysis which, as the name suggests, starts with context, tracks mechanisms used in a project or campaign, and then assesses the outcomes for all parties involved or affected (Salter and Kothari 2014). The principle of considering all affected parties in evaluation will be further discussed in the following sections that examine frameworks and models of evaluation for communication management.

Applying measurement and evaluation in communication

'SMART' objectives

An essential step for applying evaluation is to ensure that you have what are called SMART objectives. This acronym denotes objectives that are:

- Specific – objectives should not be broad and general such as 'increase awareness' or 'support sales'. Specific objectives mean that they will contain numbers in most instances, such as 'increase awareness

Stage	Example responses
Inputs/resources	Feedback from audiences on their existing awareness, attitudes, interests, needs, communication channel preferences, etc.
Activities	Attendance at events
Outputs	Volume and quality of publicity appearing in media, social media likes and follows, views of videos, etc.
Outcomes	Short term, these can include recall, inquiries, expressions of interest (e.g. subscriptions for more information), while longer term these can include high satisfaction rates; increased trust levels, reputation improvements, and compliance actions such as increased membership or sales, reduced incidents of speeding by motorists, and so on
Impact	Downstream results of communication such as customer retention leading to profits, improved employee retention leading to reduced costs and higher productivity, improved public health, and other organisation or societal benefits

Table 10.1 Examples of responses that can be tracked at various stages of communication.

of . . . by 30 per cent'; 'generate at least 15,000 inquiries about . . . '; 'reduce speeding offences by 15 per cent'; etc.

- Measurable – as noted previously, evaluation starts in the planning stage of any project or campaign. Part of planning is to identify baseline data, against which post-campaign data can be compared. Also, the methods required and available to collect data necessary to inform progressive evaluation need to be identified in advance. If they are not built into a project or campaign, the necessary data may not be collected and, therefore, process and summative evaluation will be difficult or impossible.

- Achievable – make sure that your objectives are achievable. Sometimes management and practitioners have unrealistic expectations. Case studies and literature review (review of published research papers) can identify whether similar projects or campaigns have been effective.

- Relevant – communication objectives must align with and support the organisation's objectives (Volk and Zerfass 2018). In addition, objectives should align with the interests of stakeholders, local communities and the environment, as will be discussed further in examining some widely used evaluation models and frameworks in the next section. If an organisation's PR and communication management objectives conflict with stakeholders, success is unlikely, and activities can lead to tensions and even crises.

- Timely (also referred to as time-bound) – specific timeframes should be set, such as 'within 12 months' or 'by 30 June'.

Models

One of the first widely used models of evaluation for communication was presented by Cutlip et al. (1985) in the sixth edition of their widely used textbook, *Effective Public Relations*. This identified three stages, which they called preparation, implementation and impact, leading to this being referred to as the PII model. This model arranged the stages and responses that could be measured as a series of steps, which is a useful illustration. But the PII model did not incorporate all the stages common to programme logic models, instead it included stages named *preparation* and *implementation* (see Figure 10.3).

Other models proposed for communication management during the 1990s and early 2000s included:

- The 'three measures' (output, *outtake*, outcome) developed by UK consultant Michael Fairchild (1997).

- The PR Effectiveness Yardstick developed by Walter Lindenmann (1993) in the USA, which proposed evaluation in three stages, which he called outputs, *outgrowths* and outcomes.

- The five-stage Unified Evaluation Model for Public Relations developed by UK evaluation specialists Paul Noble and Tom Watson (1999) focused on input, output, impact, *effect* and *result* (see also Watson and Noble 2007: 93).

- A model developed jointly by the German Public Relations Association Communication, the German Association of Public Relations Agencies, and the *International Controller Verein*, a European association of business process controllers (DPRG/ICV 2009; Huhn et al. 2011: 13). This model, which is

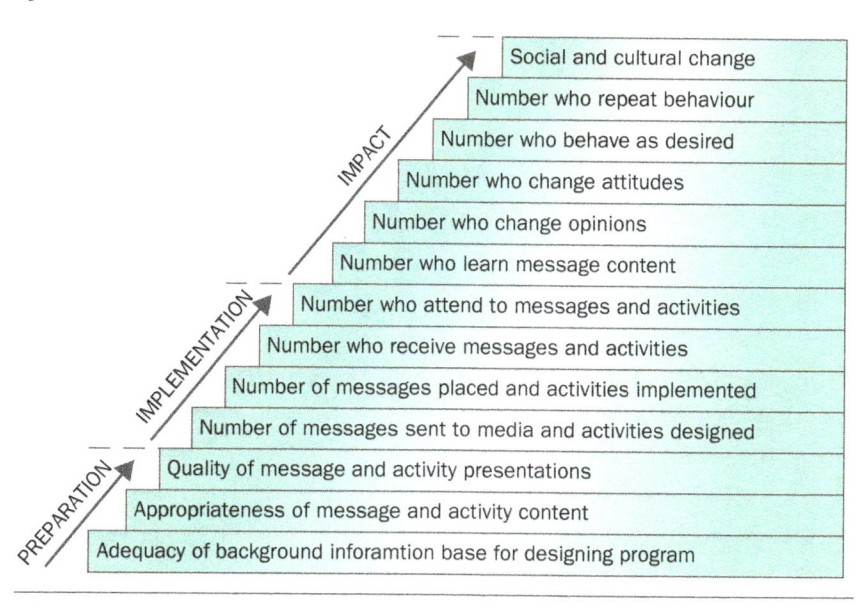

Figure 10.3 The planning, implementation and impact (PII) model (*source:* Cutlip, M., A. Center, A and G. Broom (1985). Effective public relations (6th ed.). Englewood Cliffs, NJ: Prentice-Hall)

often referred to as a communication controlling model, named four stages as input, output, outcome and *outflow*.

The italicised terms for stages in the above descriptions of various models show that many evaluation models for communication management have not followed commonly used programme logic models, as advocated by Knowlton and Phillips (2013) and many other evaluation researchers. While customisation for industries can be important, the range of terms including outtakes, outflows and outgrowths has caused confusion among practitioners and has prevented the establishment of standards.

However, more recently, several significant developments in evaluation for communication management have occurred, which provide guidelines for students and practitioners today and into the future. Several of these are explained in the following.

The AMEC Integrated Evaluation Framework

In 2016 AMEC launched what it called its Integrated Evaluation Framework (IEF) and, after a period of international consultation, this was upgraded to the AMEC Integrated Evaluation Framework 2.0 in 2017 (AMEC 2017). The AMEC IEF represents a significant breakthrough in evaluation of communication management in several respects. The first noteworthy feature is that the IEF is an online application, not a static model that simply illustrates processes. Users can enter data such as their communication objectives and then progressively add data on audience response at each stage of a communication or campaign. Data entry is aided by 'pop-up' information tabs at each stage, which provide users with tips of what types of data are relevant to that stage. Multiple evaluation reports can be created, saved and produced as PDF files and printed if required.

The framework (application) is also supported by a taxonomy of evaluation that provides a table with definitions of each stage, examples of what can be expected to occur at each stage, and a list of relevant metrics and appropriate methods for generating those metrics. This is available from the AMEC website at https://amecorg.com/. The main interface screen of the AMEC IEF is shown in Figure 10.4.

As shown in Figure 10.4, the AMEC IEF is also slightly different to classic programme logic models in that, apart from its visual presentation as a 'tiled' online interface, it incorporates six stages of evaluation after setting objectives by retaining *outtakes* as a stage

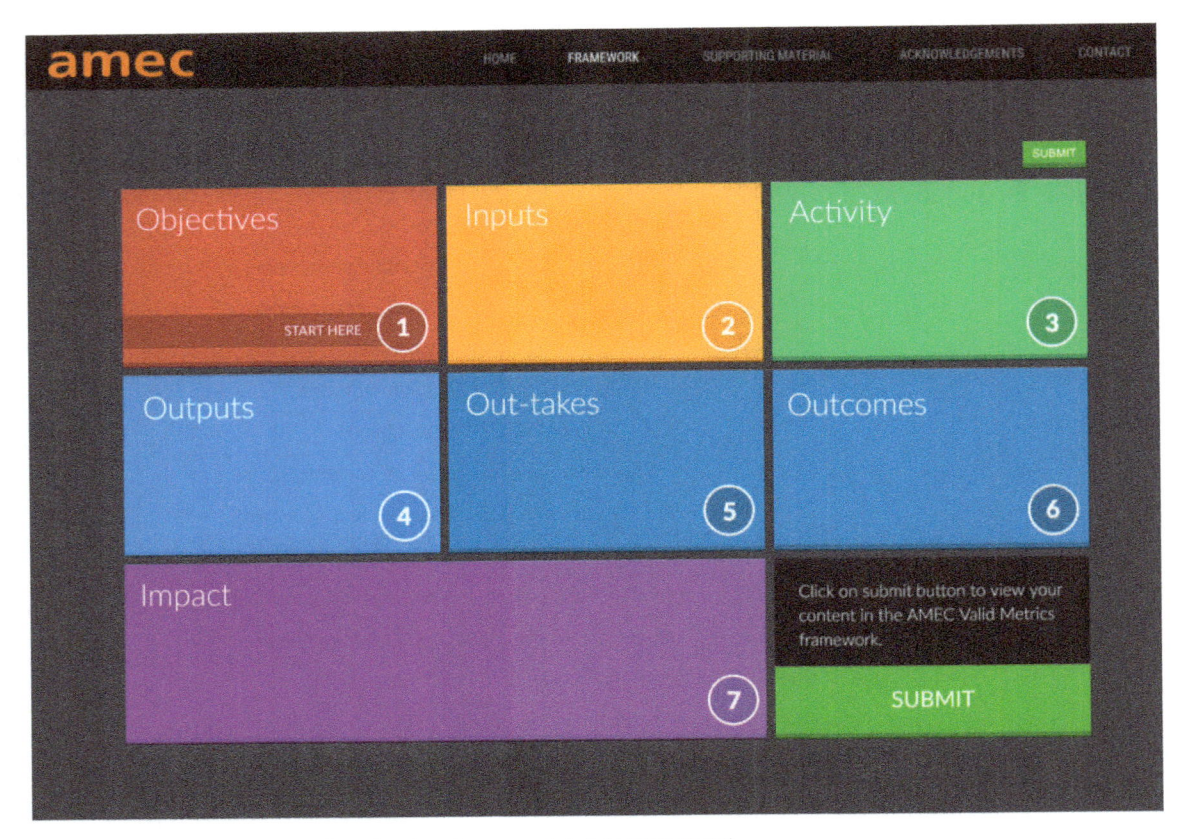

Figure 10.4 The AMEC Integrated Evaluation Framework 2.0 (AMEC 2017)

from early PR evaluation literature, as well as inputs, activities, outputs and outcomes. Furthermore, it names the final stage 'organisational impact' – a more specific and narrow term than that used in traditional programme logic models (see Figure 10.4).

The inclusion of outtakes as a stage amounts to a minor difference, as it equates to short-term outcomes in other programme logic models such as that presented by Knowlton and Phillips (2013: 37). However, the narrowing of impact to 'organisational impact' is challenged by several evaluation researchers and is contrary to corporate communication theory. Excellence theory called for evaluation to be conducted from the perspective of: (a) the specific programme (such as did it achieve its objectives); (b) the function (i.e. the effectiveness of the department or unit); (c) from an organisational perspective; and (d) from a broader societal perspective, which includes stakeholders and communities (Grunig et al. 2002: 91–2). More recently, an evaluation model developed by Buhmann et al. (2018), despite its inconsistent arrangement of stages of evaluation, also proposed that evaluation should include product, programme, campaign, organisation and society as units of analysis.

While many evaluation models emphasise the importance of and communication management evaluation aligning with the objectives and goals of the organisation (Huhn et al. 2011; Volk and Zerfass 2018), such a focus is *organisation-centric* – that is, it privileges the interests of the organisation and does not consider impact on stakeholders and society other than in terms of impact desired by the organisation (Macnamara and Gregory 2018). This is important because positive impact on an organisation, such as increased profits or approval to conduct mining or oil drilling, may have negative impacts on local communities and the environment. Also, there can be unintended as well as intended impact. For example, increasing the price of pharmaceutical products may boost a company's profits, but result in many people being unable to afford important treatments.

The UK Government Communication Service (GCS) evaluation framework

The UK Government Communication Service (GCS) evaluation framework, introduced in 2016 and updated in 2018, closely follows the AMEC IEF by including 'outtakes' and defining the final stage as 'organisational impact' (GCS 2018). Thus, despite a commendable commitment to evaluation and an investment in training to provide accountability for taxpayers' money spent on communication, the GCS framework also focuses on the government's objectives in its evaluation framework (see Figure 10.5).

Bringing evaluation theory, concepts and principles together

A broader, more holistic approach to evaluation was piloted by the Public Relations Institute of Australia and subsequently adopted (PRIA 2017) and was published in a further updated form in *Evaluation Public Communication: Exploring New Models, Standards and Best Practice* (Macnamara 2018). See Figure 10.6.

As well as following widely used programme theory and programme logic models, this expanded model illustrates five factors that are not adequately explained in other models and which are important.

1. Stakeholders, publics and society are explicitly represented in the model, whereas they are not in other evaluation models of communication management. The visual arrangement of the model with the organisation shown at the top is not meant as hierarchal; rather the model seeks to

Explore 10.1

The AMEC Evaluation Framework

Go online to explore the AMEC Evaluation Framework. You can access it via the Resource centre available on the AMEC website at https://amecorg.com/. First, read the Introduction that explains the rationale of the framework and how it was developed and why (see https://amecorg.com/amecframework/home/framework/introduction).

Then, spend some time reading and reviewing the 'taxonomy' of evaluation terms, metrics and methods to obtain these metrics (see https://amecorg.com/amecframework/home/supporting-material/taxonomy). This provides an extensive list of definitions and the metrics that are appropriate at each stage of evaluation, as well as the methods of data collection and research to gain those metrics.

Finally, go into the interactive online evaluation tool itself, which is freely available for use by anyone (see https://amecorg.com/amecframework/framework/interactive-framework). You can enter sample objectives and then plan how evaluation can be conducted at each stage. As you roll your mouse over the stages, 'pop-up' information boxes will give you hints and suggestions for metrics and methods that can apply.

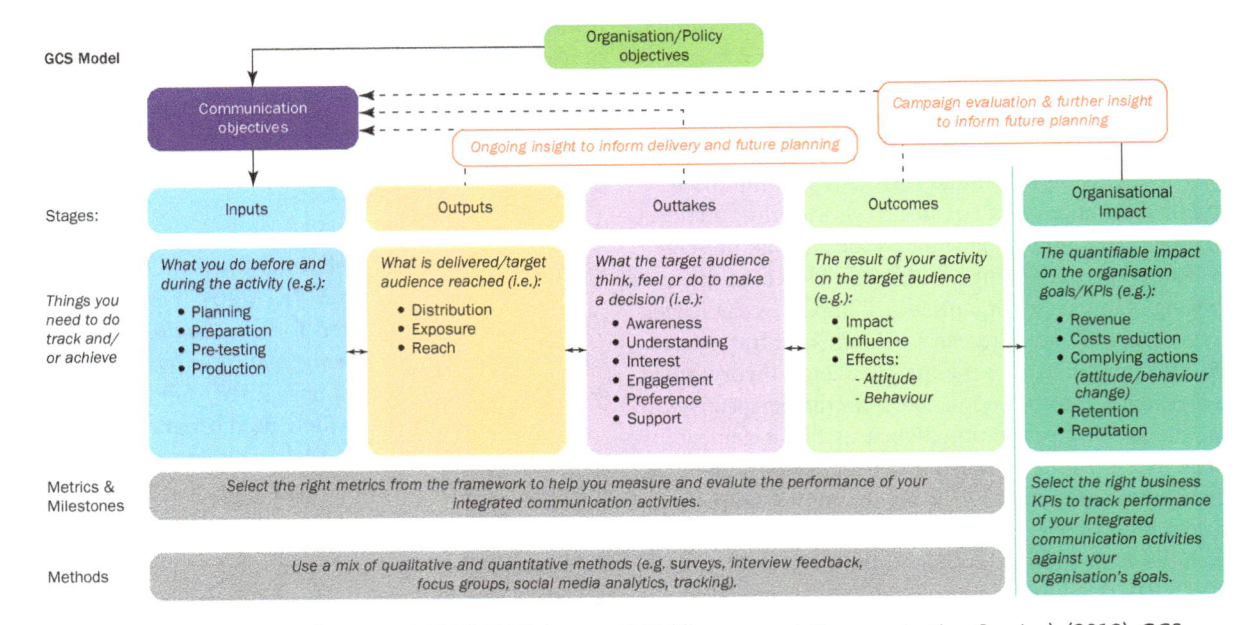

Figure 10.5 GCS evaluation framework (GCS 2018) (*source:* GCS (Government Communication Service). (2018). GCS evaluation framework 2.0. [online] Available at: https://gcs.civilservice.gov.uk/wp-content/uploads/2018/06/6.4565_CO_Evaluation-Framework-2.0-v11-WEB.pdf [Accessed 28 Mar. 2019])

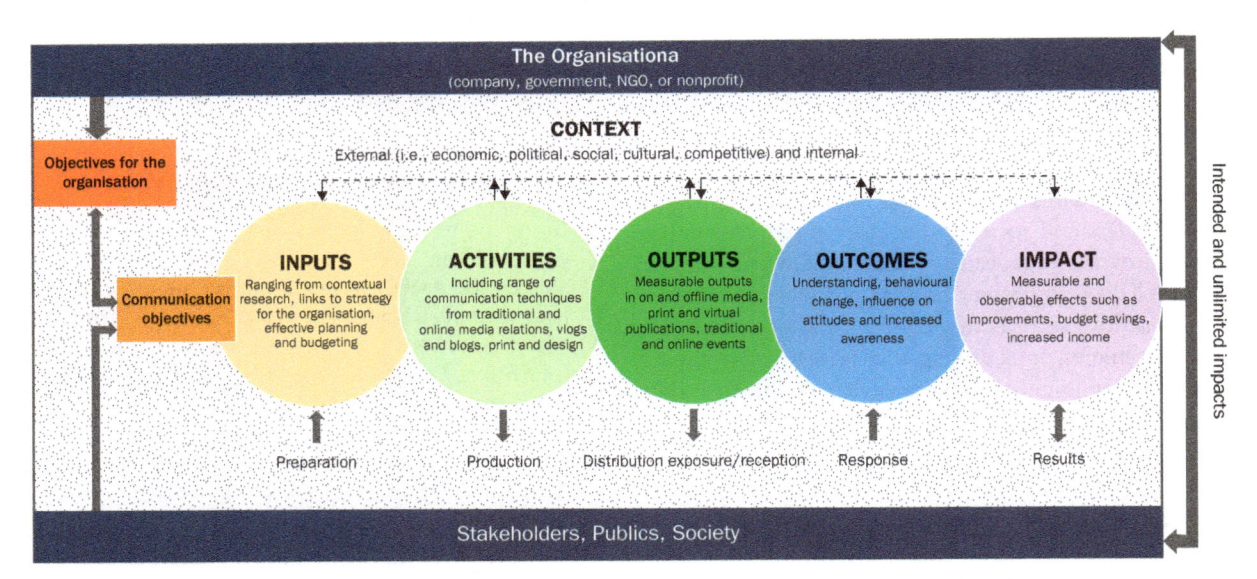

Figure 10.6 Integrated model of evaluation of public communication (*source:* Macnamara, J. (2018). Evaluating public communication: Exploring new models, standards and best practice. Abingdon, UK: Routledge)

show an organisation and its stakeholders, publics and society collectively as 'actors' in various stages of interaction.

2. Context is also represented in the model as the background that influences interactions and relationships. This includes economic, political, social, cultural, competitive and internal context. It must be recognised that contexts change over time, which may necessitate adjustments in strategy. In terms of evaluation, this means that the context in which the organisation and its stakeholders, publics and society interact needs to be continuously evaluated (e.g. through environmental scanning, consultation and ongoing stakeholder engagement).

3. While communication objectives must necessarily be designed to support organisational objectives, communication objectives also should consider the needs, expectations and interests of stakeholders, publics and society. This two-way flow of information and insight is illustrated by the arrows shown in Figure 10.6. Formative research, stakeholder engagement and public consultation

are ways in which an understanding of the expectations, needs and interests of stakeholders, publics and society can be identified and considered in setting communication objectives.

4. While activities and outputs primarily flow from the organisation to stakeholders, publics and society during the processes of production, distribution and exposure, inputs to planning should flow from stakeholders, publics and society, not only top-down from organisation management. Inputs can come from informal feedback, stakeholder engagement, social and market research, public consultation, complaints analysis, and other interactions. Evaluation should ensure that these formative research and response mechanisms are in place and effective so that the organisation is 'listening' and able to adapt its strategy if required. Also, outcomes are identified by response and information flowing from stakeholders and publics to the organisation – again emphasising the two-way flow of information and interaction as shown by the arrows in Figure 10.6.

5. Finally, and very importantly, impact must be recognised as bidirectional and as potentially including negative as well as positive impacts, whether intended or unintended. Organisations legitimately seek to change awareness, attitudes and behaviour among stakeholders and publics in many instances. In addition, however, organisations should be open to change their awareness, attitudes and behaviour at times. Evaluation helps create a learning organisation that adapts to its environment and changing contexts.

Methods

Once the stages of a communication project or campaign are understood and once formative, process and summative evaluation are planned as part of a project or campaign, there are several methods available to implement evaluation. An extensive list of both formal and informal methods for evaluation is provided in the AMEC taxonomy available at https://amecorg.com/. Some of the most widely used and highly regarded methods are also described in the following sections, tables and case studies.

Informal evaluation

Informal methods can be used in evaluation, particularly for measurement to collect basic data that informs evaluation. Many involve little or no cost, which is an advantage. However, informal methods do not provide statistically reliable data in most instances and only rarely can they support high-level evaluation of outcomes and impact. Informal refers to methods that do not involve primary social science research. For example, informal methods include feedback that is obtained spontaneously or by request, but not systematically from a statistically reliable or valid purposive sample. Feedback is typically provided by those who feel motivated to provide comments and is not necessarily representative of all people in a group or category.

One of the most widely used methods of measurement in communication management is media monitoring to obtain counts and copies of press clippings and transcripts or recordings of broadcast media content. In the digital age, this has been expanded to social media monitoring, which records online posts and related data. Monitoring predominantly provides measurement of quantity at an output stage, as discussed earlier in this chapter, but it does not identify the outcomes or impact of the media content and, thus, it does not show its value.

It should be noted that attempts to describe the volume of media coverage gained as a 'value', such as *advertising value equivalents* (AVEs) are invalid for several reasons identified by academic researchers (Watson and Noble 2007: 230–232) and AMEC (https://amecorg.com/2017/06/the-definitive-guide-why-aves-are-invalid). One obvious reason that AVEs are not the value of media coverage is that the calculations are an estimated *cost* of equivalent paid media advertising. The value of advertising is not measured by how much it cost, but rather by its reach and impact on audiences. So, it does not make sense to purport to evaluate editorial media coverage in such terms. Also, paid media advertising and other forms of media content are not equivalent – in fact, they are substantially different in presentation, level of content and placement control, and audience perception.

Qualitative analysis of media content – both traditional and social media – is undertaken using *content analysis*, a formal research method, which is explained in Tables 10.2 and 10.3.

Other informal methods of evaluation include automatically generated data produced by websites and social media platforms including web statistics such as page views, video views and downloads and social media metrics such as likes, follows, shares and retweets. It is important to recognise that, while these are useful and relatively easy to obtain, they indicate only short-term, low-level forms of outcomes such as engagement with content. They do not and cannot indicate awareness, attitude or behaviour change.

Research method	Brief description	Advantages/disadvantages
Random controlled trials (RCTs)	Highly structured experiments that compare a randomly selected treatment group and a 'control group' before and after an intervention of some kind, usually in a laboratory or clinical setting	■ Statistically reliable if all protocols and procedures are followed ■ Time-consuming and expensive ■ Findings may not apply in daily life
Other experiments (e.g. observational trials)	Structured experiments that are often in the 'field' involving observation of people exposed to some experience or intervention	■ Can be reliable, although there is usually no control group for comparison ■ Time-consuming and relatively expensive
Physiological testing (e.g. eye movement tracking; galvanic skin response)	Tests carried out on participants exposed to information in a studio setting with equipment to measure eye movement, heart rate, perspiration, etc. Commonly used in evaluating advertising	■ Scientifically accurate in measuring human physical response to exposure to information ■ Despite physical reaction, people may not retain or act beyond the initial response
Surveys	Structured questionnaires that are administered as printed forms or online, mostly using closed-end questions such as multiple choice or scales	■ Statistically reliable when probability samples are used and enough levels of response received (e.g. =400) ■ Relatively low cost, particularly online ■ Data collected is self-reporting. Respondents may exaggerate or lie ■ Surveys are often filled out by people outside the sample (e.g. children fill out many household surveys and online participation often cannot be controlled)
Structured interviews	Structured questionnaires administered face to face or, most commonly, by telephone (CATI)	As above
Content analysis	A method of identifying the issues or topics discussed, themes, messages, and voices in content such as media reports, publications or transcripts by coding the text into categories based on keywords. Quantitative content analysis uses an *a priori* coding list and relies primarily on counts of how many times key words are mentioned to identify key messages, etc.	■ Widely used for analysing media content ■ Automated and semi-automated software applications are available for fast, low-cost analysis ■ Automated systems can produce statistics about messages, placement and reach ■ While content analysis identifies messages, themes, etc. in content, this is not necessarily what humans interpret from the content, and it gives no indication of whether humans believed, retained or acted in relation to the content
Net Promoter Score (NPS)	A simple survey administered online or by phone post any interaction which asks people how likely they are to recommend the organisation, product or service to a friend or colleague based on their experience	■ Gains fast feedback ■ The score is a simple 0–10 number ■ Needs to include open-end questions to understand reasons for the score to be of significant value
Social network analysis	Identifiers 'nodes' (participants), connections between various internet users in relation to an issue, and 'hubs' (the centre of clusters of connections), usually done using specialist SNA software applications	■ Relatively low-cost using SNA software ■ Identifies individuals and organisations active and dominant in online discussion ■ Informs influencer mapping and engagement
Customer journey mapping (also called customer decision journey)	A synthesising form of evaluation that examines customers' (or others') experience at multiple touchpoints with an organisation (e.g. pre-sale, at sale, post-sale, online and face to face)	■ Provides a holistic view of customers' or others' experience ■ Requires integration of multiple data sets (e.g. satisfaction surveys, call centre records, complaints, etc.) ■ Requires considerable manual work

Table 10.2 Major quantitative methods used for formative and evaluative research

Research method	Brief description	Advantages/disadvantages
Depth interviews	One-to-one interviews conducted face-to-face or by telephone seeking open-ended responses on issues or topics, usually lasting up to one hour or more	■ Provide deep insights into perceptions, concerns, needs, etc. ■ Findings cannot be generalised; they are context-bound ■ However, patterns emerge ■ Time consuming
Focus groups	Applies an open-ended interviewing technique to small groups, usually conducted by an independent moderator. Groups need to be drawn from a similar sample to gain useful findings (e.g. culture, generation, socioeconomic status, etc.)	■ As above ■ Relatively cost-efficient ■ Can lead to 'group think' ■ Need sensitive moderation to avoid dominant individuals and be inclusive
Content analysis/ textual analysis	Content analysis can be conducted qualitatively as well as quantitatively by applying techniques from textual analysis and related methods such as narrative, thematic, rhetorical and semiotic analysis. Beyond counting key words, qualitative content analysis closely examines the tone and symbolic features in texts, such as adjectives, metaphors, similes, images, emoticons, etc.	■ Widely used due to the large amount of textual data available such as media reports, social media comments, correspondence, complaints, transcripts of interviews and focus groups, submissions to consultations, etc. ■ Some fully automated commercial software applications measure tone and sentiment. However, these are not reliable in interpreting text as humans do ■ A range of computer aided applications are available (e.g. SAS Analytics, NVivo, MaxQDA, etc.)
Ethnography	Direct observation of people in their natural setting, such as at work or home, over a period (e.g. several months), derived from anthropology. Ethnography can include interviews and participation in a group or activity to gain deep understanding. Evidence is recorded in notes (journaling), interview transcripts, collection of artefacts (e.g. photos or samples), and video ethnography is increasingly used	■ Provides direct first-hand evidence ■ Is naturalistic – i.e. observes 'real world' behaviour, rather than laboratory or reported behaviour as in surveys ■ Very time-consuming ■ Requires high levels of reflexivity by the observer to avoid influencing the participants or injecting her/his subjectivity
Netnography	Observation of online activity, such as in social media or online communities	■ Low cost ■ Reaches participants not observable physically ■ Online claims and behaviour often do not reflect reality and can even be false
Action research	A method of research in which one or more researchers investigate and test solutions to a problem or improvements to a process *in situ* (i.e. through observation of and participation in the activity)	■ Highly applicable to professional practice and practical problems (i.e. applied research) ■ Time consuming
Participatory action research (PAR)	Action research in which one or more researchers and those responsible for an activity collaboratively investigate and test solutions to a problem or improvements to a process	■ As above ■ Very in-depth and grounded as it draws on the experience of those involved ■ Requires careful management to avoid internal 'politics' or conflicts of interest

Table 10.3 Major qualitative methods used for formative and evaluative research

Case study 10.1
The Communication Monitor

For more than a decade a major study of the work practices and views, perceptions and priorities of PR and communication practitioners has been conducted in Europe (The European Communication Monitor), and since 2015 it has been extended to Asia-Pacific, South America and now North America.

The Communication Monitor is funded and supported by major communication industry organisations such as the European Public Relations Education and Research Association (EUPRERA) and the European Association of Communication Directors (EACD) in Europe, as well as sponsors, whose objective is to identify the issues of main concern to and communication management practitioners, trends and challenges identified for the future. For example, the study examines practices, views and attitudes towards issues such as uses of social media, ethics, the rise of 'fake news', and trust in organisations (e.g. Zerfass et al. 2018).

So how can the practices, views and attitudes of practitioners be evaluated? And how can they be evaluated in a way that is evidence-based and reliable?

The team of researchers who undertake this study in Europe and elsewhere developed and implement an annual survey (bi-annual in some smaller markets). To gain representative and statistically reliable data across the diverse economies, cultures and types of communication management practice in Europe, the 2018 European Communication Monitor gained completed survey questionnaires from more than 3,000 practitioners in 48 European countries (Zerfass et al. 2018). In Asia-Pacific, the 2017/18 Communication Monitor gained responses from more than 1,300 practitioners in 22 countries (Macnamara et al. 2017).

The survey questionnaire has 25 or more questions using quantitative social science survey question formats such as multiple choice and Likert scales (e.g. 5-point 'Very Important' to 'Not Important' and 'Strongly Agree' to 'Totally Disagree'), as well as some open-ended qualitative questions.

This approach ensures that:

- the research is representative of practices, attitudes and perceptions of practitioners on each continent and in each country in which a large sample of participants is obtained;
- a wide range of issues is explored so that the most important issues and concerns are identified;
- the evaluation does not take up too much time of participants. If evaluation is time intensive for participants, this increases the drop-out rates and reduces the sample size, which in turn reduces the reliability of the research.

See http://www.communicationmonitor.eu and http://www.zerfass.de/APCM-WEBSITE

Case study 10.2
'Pink Sari' health campaign – results and awards

As occurs in many countries including the UK, Australian health authorities found that women from BAME backgrounds, particularly recent immigrants, in the age group for which breast screenings (mammograms) are recommended (54–70) had very low rates of breast screening. In Australia, women from Indian and Sri Lankan backgrounds were identified as a key group in which increased breast screening could improve public health through early detection and treatment of breast cancer. The New South Wales (NSW) Multicultural Health Communication Service (MHCS) was given funding to develop a campaign to increase awareness, change attitudes towards breast screening, and increase screening rates within this group by at least 5 per cent over a 12-month period. This was the SMART objective (specific, measurable, achievable, relevant and timely).

In line with what has been discussed in this chapter, the MHCS in partnership with university researchers started with formative research to identify awareness levels and attitudes towards breast screening. In simple terms, the planners wanted and needed to know why these women were not having breast screens; what were the barriers to having breast screens; and what media or other channels did they use and trust for information about personal health issues. Statistical data available from the Cancer Institute NSW showed the numbers of breast screenings performed each year by clinics across the state and the age, country of birth, and main language spoken (i.e. ethnicity) of those who had breast screens. All data used was de-identified to protect privacy – an important

Picture 10.3 Marketing communication collateral from the Pink Sari health campign (*source:* AboliC/Shutterstock)

ethical consideration in undertaking research. As well as obtaining statistical data on screenings for prior years, formative research involved:

- a global literature review to gain insights from previous studies in relation to promotion of cancer screening among BAME/CALD communities (i.e. what others had learned);
- a survey of Indian and Sri Lankan women aged 54–70 (n=300);
- focus groups (4) with Indian and Sri Lankan women aged 54–70 to gain more in-depth information; and
- meetings and consultation with key community organisations including the Indian and Sri Lankan Welfare Association, the Indian Doctors' Association and the NSW Refugee Health Service.

Formative evaluation fundamentally informed the design and implementation of the campaign. The surveys and focus groups revealed that women in this group harboured concerns about modesty (undressing); beliefs that there was no cure for breast cancer; and even superstitions that acknowledging the possibility of cancer in a family could reduce the marriage prospects of daughters. Furthermore, and importantly, formative evaluation revealed that, while women in this group watched TV extensively and read ethnic newspapers (e.g. Tamil, Hindi and Sinhalese language press), they did not use or trust either paid or unpaid content in these media for health information. Where did they go for information and advice on health? Unsurprisingly, the first 'port of call' was their local doctor (GP). But, unexpected by the MHCS, daughters of women aged 54–70 were their second most trusted sources of information and advice about personal health issues. Formative research also revealed the key role that community groups play in the lives of women in this group and their deep understanding of these communities.

Based on formative evaluation, a steering committee was formed involving all the organisations that regularly interacted with women in this group, as well as 'community champions' – community leaders who supported the objectives, such as Indian and Sri Lankan women doctors and heads of community organisations.

The design and implementation of the campaign was then put in the hands of the steering committee and community champions and all elements and activities were developed through collaboration and coproduction. The social marketing and communication staff of the MHCS and various professional agencies required for photography, video shooting and graphic design served as professional support. Even the name of the campaign, The Pink Sari Project, was decided by the steering committee and community champions.

As well as traditional and communication tactics such as a special website and social media sites, the Pink Sari Project that rolled out in 2015 and 2016 involved:

- Information sheets and posters in multiple languages written by local community leaders such as doctors that were not literal translations of English language materials, which were found to be confusing or even offensive (e.g. literal translations of some words had sexual rather than clinical connotations).
- Community forums and information evenings organised and chaired by local doctors and community leaders. In the first 12 months 55 Pink Sari events were organised and attended by 10,462 women.
- A Pink Sari pledge to have a breast screen that daughters asked their mothers to sign, based on a finding that 'giving one's word' is strongly correlated to behaviour in these cultures.
- A Pink Sari fashion show that attracted a large crowd and media publicity.
- A Pink Sari calendar featuring photos of 12 Indian and Sri Lankan women who had survived breast cancer through early detection and treatment with their stories briefly told underneath.
- A 'nag your mother' initiative among young Indian and Sri Lankan women implemented directly through

case study 10.2 (continued)

- word of mouth (WOM) and through recorded videos that were shown in forums and posted online.
- 100 Tamil speaking doctors voluntary engaged in 'outreach' to their patients and Indian and Sri Lankan women generally through talk at forums and information evenings.
- Around 100 Indian and Sri Lankan women marched in pink saris in the *Parramasala* parade, a major Indian and Sri Lankan cultural event held annually in Parramatta, a major area of western Sydney.

Several of the above events gained media publicity and all publicity was highly favourable. However, media publicity was not a key part of the campaign based on the audience research conducted. And paid advertising was not used at all. Many of the above activities are not part of typical and communication campaigns, which are often designed top-down based on the expertise and experience of communication professionals and which had been unsuccessful in the past. In this case, the campaign was designed and largely implemented bottom-up by the community through collaboration and coproduction.

As well as tracking progress through process evaluation, summative evaluation found that the number of breast screens undertaken by Indian and Sri Lankan women in the target age group living in NSW increased overall by 8 per cent during the period of the campaign – 62.5 per cent above the target objective. In the following year, total breast screens undertaken increased by a further 6 per cent and the number of Indian and Sri Lankan women having a breast screen for the first time increased by 21 per cent (Macnamara and Camit 2017). Further major indications of outcomes and impact were:

- Tamil doctors sought approval to extend the campaign to bowel cancer screening.
- Other states sought approval to use the campaign.
- The approach of the campaign was extended to other BAME/CALD communities in Australia in 2018, such as women from Italian backgrounds, who also have relatively low breast screening rates.
- Perhaps most significantly of all, after the Cancer Institute NSW funding ceased, the community groups involved took over the campaign and it continued as a self-funding cooperative, Pink Sari Incorporated (Cancer Institute NSW 2018).

The Pink Sari Project went on to win a number of awards including a Local Health District Excellence for Innovations Award and two international AMEC awards in 2016 – the Gold Award for evaluation in the category of 'Public and not-for profit sector' and the overall Grand Prix Platinum Award for 'evaluation research by a consultancy or in-house communication team' (AMEC 2016).

Formal quantitative and qualitative research methods

In the scope of this chapter it is not possible to review all the formal quantitative and qualitative methods of research that are available to use as part of evaluation. However, Table 10.2 briefly describes and summarises the key advantages and disadvantages of the most widely used quantitative research methods. Table 10.3 briefly describes and summarises the key advantages and disadvantages of the most widely used qualitative research methods. The case studies in this chapter give examples of some of these methods being applied.

Reporting measurement and evaluation

As indicated earlier in this chapter, reporting to management is usually done progressively, not only at the end of projects and campaigns, based on formative, process and summative evaluation. As far as possible, reporting should be evidence-based, rather than anecdotal. Furthermore, as this chapter has emphasised, practitioners should endeavour to report outcomes and impact – not only activities and outputs. A simple way of thinking about the focus of evaluation is to recognise that when you are producing activities and outputs (such as arranging events, distributing media releases and producing web content), you are a *cost centre* in your organisation. It only when you can show that you are achieving or at least contributing to outcomes and impact that you can demonstrate that you are a *value-adding centre* or function. Senior management seeks to reduce cost centres and give priority to value-adding centres and functions.

The format of reporting is usually determined by the requirements of senior management. Often, rigorous evaluation requires reports of social and market research such as surveys, focus groups or interviews, which often need to be undertaken by specialist external firms because of the expertise required and the benefits of independence. However, because senior managers are usually very busy, brief forms of reporting are often preferred to long written reports. In addition to reports of research studies, common reporting formats and methods include:

- Key Performance indicators (KPIs) – reporting data against several key indicators agreed in advance with management, often arranged in a table. KPIs vary to suit each organisation – for example, they can include satisfaction rates of key stakeholders such as customers, employees, or members; numbers of registrations, subscriptions, cancer screenings, etc.; or a Net Promoter Score (NPS).

- Dashboards – a condensed set of charts or other visuals, statistics and summary comments that summarise key outputs, outcomes and impacts in a period, usually arranged on a single page or screen. Data is displayed on a dashboard should be agreed with management in advance, to ensure that it meets requirements. See an extract from a communication dashboard in Figure 10.7.

- Media content analysis – this typically reports not only the volume, but the quality of media coverage

Figure 10.7 A sample of a dashboard, reporting and communication management (Macnamara 2018: 279) (source: Department for Transport)

in terms of tone and messages. However, as noted in Tables 10.2 and 10.3, evaluating what appears in media does not necessarily indicate what is in people's minds.

- Social media analysis – this applies content analysis to social media content, as well as including automatically generated data such as page and video views, likes, follows, shares, and retweets.

- Return on investment (ROI) – this financial method of reporting is commonly used in many fields of evaluation, but it is often difficult to apply to and communication management because outcomes and impact are often not financial. For instance, government communication may seek to reduce the road accident rate or increase cancer screening rates as reported in Case study 10.2. Some campaigns are designed to influence government policy. A review of ROI use in public relations and communication management warned against attempting to calculate ROI in 'loose and fuzzy' ways and concluded that, in many cases, 'the complexity of communication processes and their role in business interactions means it is not possible to calculate return on investment in financial terms' (Watson and Zerfass 2012: 11). However, the models in this chapter and Tables 10.2 and 10.3 show many methods for conducting and reporting evaluation.

Summary

Measurement involves the collection of various measures that can provide data (sometimes referred to as metrics) to support evidence-based evaluation of communication management. Evaluation can and should be conducted before, during and after communication projects and campaigns – termed *formative*, *process* and *summative* evaluation. This recognises that projects and campaigns go through stages – commonly identified in programme logic models as *inputs*, *activities*, *outputs*, *outcomes* and *impact*, with some including *outtakes* as a stage of short-term outcomes. As well as conducting formative evaluation at the inputs stage as part of planning, and process evaluation for progress tracking, evaluation must extend to identifying outcomes and impact, such as awareness, attitude or behaviour change – not simply report outputs such as articles placed in media.

The effectiveness and value of PR and communication management are determined from an organisation's perspective by the extent to which outcomes and impact are achieved that contribute to achieving the objectives of the organisation. To achieve this, SMART objectives should be set for all PR and communication management – that is, communication objectives should be *specific*, *measurable*, *achievable*, *relevant* and *timely*. However, in addition to supporting organisational objectives, relevant means that public relations and communication management should also reflect and respect the interests and needs of stakeholders and society generally. Organisations that conduct public relations and communication management that serve the interests of the organisation, but not those of stakeholders and society, are unlikely to be sustainable. Conversely, organisations that can create and demonstrate positive outcomes and impact for themselves and for their stakeholders and society earn a good reputation, trust and sustainability.

Bibliography

AMEC (Association for Measurement and Evaluation of Communication). (2016). 2016 AMEC award winners. [online] Available at: https://amecorg.com/amec-awards-winners-2016 [Accessed 28 Mar. 2019].

AMEC (Association for Measurement and Evaluation of Communication). (2017). AMEC integrated evaluation framework. [online] Available at: https://amecorg.com/amecframework [Accessed 28 Mar. 2019].

AMEC (Association for Measurement and Evaluation of Communication). (2017), A taxonomy of evaluation towards standards, https://amecorg.com/amecframework/home/supporting-material/taxonomy/

Anderson, A. (2005). *The community builder's approach to theory of change: A practical guide to theory and development.* New York, NY: The Aspen Institute Roundtable on Community Change.

Atkin, C. and V. Freimuth (2013). Guidelines for formative evaluation research in campaign design. In: R. Rice and C. Atkin, eds, *Public communication campaigns.* 4th ed. Thousand Oaks, CA: Sage, pp. 53–68.

Berlo, D. (1960). *The process of communication: An introduction to theory and practice.* New York, NY: Harcourt/Holt, Rinehart & Winston.

Bickman, L. (1990). Using program theory to describe and measure program quality. *New Directions for Evaluation,* 47, pp. 61–72.

Broom, G. (1982). A comparison of sex roles in public relations. *Public Relations Review,* 8(3), pp. 17–22.

Broom, G. and D. Dozier (1986). Advancement for Public Relations Role Models. *Public Relations Review,* 7(1), pp. 37–56.

Bryant, J. and M. Oliver (eds) (2009). *Media effects: Advances in theory and research.* 3rd ed. New York, NY: Routledge.

Buhmann, A., F. Likely and D. Geddes (2018), Communication Evaluation and Measurement: Connecting Research to Practice. *Journal of Communication Management,* 22(1), pp. 113–119.

Cancer Institute NSW. (2018). Pink Sari. [online] Available at: https://www.cancer.nsw.gov.au/how-we-help/programs-we-support/pink-sari [Accessed 28 Mar. 2019].

Chen, H. and P. Rossi (1983). Evaluating with sense: the theory-driven approach. *Evaluation Review,* 7, pp. 283–302.

Clark, H. (2004). *Deciding the scope of a theory of change.* New York, NY: ActKnowledge.

Clark, H. and D. Taplin (2012). *Theory of change basics: A primer on theory of change.* New York, NY: Actknowledge.

Cutlip, M., A. Center, A and G. Broom (1985). *Effective public relations* (6th ed.). Englewood Cliffs, NJ: Prentice-Hall.

Dillard, J. and L. Shen (2005). On the Nature of Reactance and its Role in Persuasive Health Communication. *Communication Monographs,* 72(2), pp. 144–168.

Dozier, D. (1992). The organisational roles of communications and public relations practitioners. In J. Grunig. ed., *Excellence in public relations and communication management.* Hillsdale, NJ: Lawrence Erlbaum, pp. 327–356.

DPRG/ICV (Deutsche Public Relations Gesellschaft and International Controller Verein). (2009). DPRG/ICV framework for communication controlling. [online] Available at: http://www.communicationcontrolling.de/index.php?id=280&type=98&tx_ttnews[tt_news]=&L=3 [Accessed 28 Mar. 2019].

Evaluation. (2016a). Merriam-Webster dictionary. Available at: http://www.merriam-webster.com/dictionary/evaluate [Accessed 20 Feb. 2019].

Evaluation. (2016b). Oxford Dictionaries. Available at: http://www.oxforddictionaries.com/definition/english/evaluation [Accessed 20 Feb. 2019].

Fairchild, M. (1997). *How to get Real value from public relations.* London, UK: ICO.

Festinger, L. (1957). *A theory of cognitive dissonance.* Palo Alto, CA: Stanford University Press.

Fleisher, C. and D. Mahaffy (1997). A balanced scorecard approach to public relations management assessment. *Public Relations Review,* 23(2), pp. 117–123.

GCS (Government Communication Service) (2018). GCS evaluation framework 2.0. [online] Available at: https://gcs.civilservice.gov.uk/wp-content/uploads/2018/06/6.4565_CO_Evaluation-Framework-2.0-v11-WEB.pdf [Accessed 28 Mar. 2019].

Grunig, L., J. Grunig and D. Dozier (2002). *Excellent organizations and effective organizations: A study of communication management in three countries.* Mahwah, NJ: Lawrence Erlbaum.

Hall, S. (1973). Encoding/Decoding. In S. Hall, D. Hobson, A. Lowe and P. Willis, eds, *Culture, media, language.* London, UK: Hutchinson, pp. 26–27.

Huhn, J., J. Sass and C. Storck (2011). Communication Controlling: How to Maximize and Demonstrate the Value Creation through Communication. [online] Available at: http://www.communicationcontrolling.de/fileadmin/communicationcontrolling/sonst_files/Position_paper_DPRG_ICV_2011_english.pdf [Accessed 28 Mar. 2019].

Kaplan, R. and D. Norton (1992). The Balanced Scorecard: Measures that Drive Performance. *Harvard Business Review,* 70(1), pp. 71–79.

Kellogg Foundation. (2004). *Logic model development guide.* Battle Creek, MI. [online] Available at: https://www.wkkf.org/resource-directory/resource/2006/02/wk-kellogg-foundation-logic-model-development-guide [Accessed 28 Mar. 2019]. (Original work published 1998).

Knowlton, L. and C. Phillips (2013). *The logic models guidebook: Better strategies for great results.* 2nd ed. Thousand Oaks, CA: Sage.

Lindenman, W. (1993). An 'Effectiveness Yardstick' to Measure Public Relations Success. *Public Relations Quarterly,* 38(1), pp. 7–9.

Macnamara, J. (2018). *Evaluating public communication: Exploring new models, standards and best practice.* Abingdon, UK: Routledge.

Macnamara, J. and M. Camit (2016). Effective CALD Community Health Communication through Research and Collaboration: An Exemplar Case Study. *Communication Research & Practice,* 3(1), pp. 92–112.

Macnamara, J. and A. Gregory (2018). Expanding Evaluation to Enable True Strategic Communication: Beyond Message Tracking to Open Listening. *International Journal of Strategic Communication,* 12(4), pp. 469–486.

Macnamara, J., M. Lwin, A. Adi and A. Zerfass (2017). *Asia-Pacific Communication Monitor 2017/18: Strategic challenges, social media and professional competencies – Results of a survey in 22 countries.* [online]

Available at: http://www.zerfass.de/APCM-WEBSITE [Accessed 28 Mar. 2019].

Noble, P. and T. Watson (1999). Applying a unified public relations evaluation model in a European context. Paper presented to the Transnational Communication in Europe: Practice and Research Congress, Berlin, Germany.

Owston, R. (2007). Models and methods for evaluation. In: J. Spector, D. Merrill, J. van Merriënboer and M. Driscoll, eds, *Handbook of research on educational communications and technology*. 3rd ed. New York, NY: Routledge, pp. 605–617.

Practical Concepts. (1979). *The logical framework. A manager's guide to a scientific approach to design and evaluation*. [online] Available at: http://pdf.usaid.gov/pdf_docs/pnabn963.pdf [Accessed 20 Oct. 2018].

PRIA (Public Relations Institute of Australia). (2017). Measurement and evaluation framework. [online] Available at: https://www.pria.com.au/resources/measurement-evaluation [Accessed 28 Mar. 2019].

Rice, R. and C. Atkin (2002). Communication campaigns: Theory, design, implementation, and evaluation. In: J. Bryant & D. Zillman, eds, *Media effects: Advances in theory and research*. 2nd ed. Mahwah, NJ: Lawrence Erlbaum, pp. 427–451.

Rossi, P., M. Lipsey and H. Freeman (2004). *Evaluation: A systematic approach*. 7th ed. Thousand Oaks, CA: Sage.

Salter, K. and A. Kothari (2014). Using Realist Evaluation to Open the Black Box of Knowledge Translation: A State-of-the-art Review. *Implementation Science*, 9(115), pp. 1–14.

Schramm, W. (1954). How communication works. In: W. Schramm (ed.), *The process and effects of communication*. Urbana, IL: University of Illinois Press, pp. 3–26.

Scriven, M. (1972). Pros and Cons about Goal Free Evaluation. *Journal of Educational Evaluation*, 3(4), 1–7.

Severin, W. and J. Tankard (2001). *Communication theories: Origins, methods and uses in the mass media*. 5th ed. New York, NY: Addison Wesley Longman.

Shannon, C. and W. Weaver. (1949). *The mathematical theory of communication*. Urbana, IL: University of Illinois.

Sparks, G. (2006). *Media effects research: A basic overview*. 2nd ed. Belmont, CA: Thomsom Wadsworth.

Stufflebeam, D. (2001). Evaluation models. *New Directions for Evaluation*, 89, 7–98.

Suchman, E. (1967). *Evaluative research: Principles and practice in public service and social action programs*. New York, NY: Russell Sage Foundation.

Taylor-Power, E. and E. Henert (2008). *Developing a logic model: Teaching and training guide*. [online] Available at: https://fyi.uwex.edu/programdevelopment/files/2016/03/lmguidecomplete.pdf [Accessed 28 Mar. 2019].

Tench, R., D. Verčič, A. Zerfass, A. Moreno and P. Verhoeven (2017). *Communication excellence: How to develop, manage and lead exceptional communications*. London, UK: Palgrave Macmillan.

Trochim, W. (2006). Evaluation research. Research methods knowledge base. [online] Available at: http://www.socialresearchmethods.net/kb/evaluation.php [Accessed 20 Feb. 2019].

Valente, T. (2001). Evaluating communication campaigns. In: R. Rice & C. Atkin, eds, *Public communication campaigns*. 3rd ed. Thousand Oaks, CA: Sage, pp. 105–124.

Valente, T. and P. Kwan (2013). Evaluating communication campaigns. In: R. Rice & C. Atkin, *Public communication campaigns* (4th ed., pp. 83–97). Thousand Oaks, CA: Sage.

Volk, S. and A. Zerfass (2018). Explicating a Key Concept in Strategic Communication. *International Journal of Strategic Communication*, 12(3), pp. 433–451.

Watson, T. and P. Noble (2007). *Evaluating public relations: A best practice guide to public relations planning, research and evaluation*. 2nd ed. London, UK: Kogan Page.

Watson, T. and A. Zerfass (2012). ROI and PR evaluation: Avoiding 'smoke and mirrors'. International Public Relations Research Conference, Miami, FL. [online] Available at: https://www.instituteforpr.org/wp-content/uploads/Watson-Zerfass-ROI-IPRRC-Miami-2012.pdf [Accessed 20 Feb. 2019].

Weiss, C. (1972). *Evaluation research: Methods of assessing program effectiveness*. Englewood Cliffs, NJ: Prentice Hall.

Wholey, J. (1979). *Evaluation: Promise and performance*. Washington, DC: Urban Institute Press.

Wholey, J. (1983). *Evaluation and effective public management*. Boston, MA: Little Brown & Co.

Wholey, J. (1987). Evaluability Assessment: Developing Program Theory. *New Directions for Evaluation*, 33, pp. 77–92

Zerfass, A., R. Tench, P. Verhoeven, D. Verčič and A. Moreno (2018). European Communication Monitor 2018. Strategic communication and the challenges of fake news, trust, leadership, work stress and job satisfaction. Results of a survey in 48 countries. Brussels: EACD/EUPRERA, Quadriga Media Berlin.

CHAPTER 11

Jon White

Disinformation, fake news and social reality

Source: Bildagentur Zoonar GmbH. Shutterstock

Learning outcomes

By the end of this chapter you should be able to:
- have a fuller understanding of the role of public relations in the social construction of reality
- be able to suggest approaches to countering disinformation and the problems created by 'fake news'
- understand the obligations of public relations practitioners to work against disinformation, 'fake news' and their consequences
- take steps personally to maintain current and relevant knowledge of emerging techniques available for the transmission of disinformation and 'fake news' to be able to work against them as necessary.

Structure

- The role of public relations practitioners in the social construction of reality
- Contributors to the social construction of reality
- Disinformation and 'fake news' – their consequences
- Countering disinformation and 'fake news'
- Public relations: obligations in countering disinformation and fake news
- Staying ahead of developments in the use of disinformation
- Relevance of the emergence of 'fake news' and extensive use of disinformation to public relations practice

Introduction

Public relations' role in the creation of social reality has been touched on in academic discussions of public relations (White 1987) but not thoroughly investigated and appreciated by practitioners. Defining social reality has been left to philosophers and social scientists trying to understand society and how people understand their place in society. Berger and Luckmann (1966) argue that what people see as social reality is a construction, arising out of social interaction. In this, people select from available information – as it is presented through social interaction, exposure to many sources of information, such as the traditional media and now social media – to develop a picture of the world. What things mean is a matter of conversation, discussion, argument, dispute and negotiation. The possibilities for the presentation of information, conversation about what it means, have been greatly increased in recent years with the development of social media. The writers of the Cluetrain manifesto identified the creation of possibilities for conversation as one of the main outcomes of technological progress at the end of the last century (Cluetrain Manifesto 1999). What the public regard as social reality is a construction to which each member contributes by selecting from all available information to develop a picture of the world. To do so, people negotiate with other people regarding the meaning of the information provided. A logical extension of this theory is that public relations influences the meaning of reality. In organisations that deal with the public, complex social relationships, power, politics, and influence all affect the way problems are defined and small portions of reality constructed in order to make decisions and pursue solutions. Public relations practitioners construct the meaning of the environment for organisations (for example, by describing the consequences of their interaction with the public) and represent the organisations to the outside world (for example, through media), presenting constructions of reality to both sides which are then negotiated.

Recognising that public relations practitioners are involved in this process of the social construction of reality raises questions about practice and its relationship to the truth. Truth, in social settings, is to be arrived at, rather than a given. Public relations practice surfaces ethical questions relating to practitioners' responsibilities to be 'truthful' and practitioners need to be prepared for the responsibilities that they have in shaping social truth.

Mini case study 11.1
Brexit

Brexit means Brexit

In 2016, as an outcome from a commitment made by the United Kingdom's Conservative government, the people of the country voted – by a small majority – in a national referendum to leave the European Union. The process of leaving the Union was described earlier as Brexit, but such was the lack of preparation for a decision to leave that after the vote, government and others faced what Brexit might mean. Different groups presented different views of what it might mean. Unhelpfully, the government, under new leadership and headed by a Prime Minister who, ahead of the referendum had campaigned to remain in the Union, declared that Brexit means Brexit. But did this mean severing all ties, or remaining in market and customs arrangements, or developing new relationships? The process of negotiating the meaning of Brexit continued throughout the period of negotiating the UK's exit from the Union, and – at the time of writing – remains unresolved. The case illustrates the process by which meaning is negotiated. It also shows how different groups – for example committed leavers – presented information in ways that after the referendum decision were described as misleading and dishonest. The truth of claims made was questioned, challenged – in some cases through the courts – and discredited. The case also shows how groups made use of slogans and misrepresentation of facts to influence the result of the referendum – for example, Leave campaigners suggested that a decision to leave the Union would 'take back control' for the UK to govern its own affairs, whereas any discussion of future trade negotiations, outside the Union, quickly showed how little control the UK would actually have in those negotiations.

Picture 11.1 Vote Leave's false claim 'We send the EU £350 million a week – let's fund our NHS instead' was a feature of the Brexit campaign (*source:* Matt Cardy/Getty Images)

The role of public relations practitioners in the social construction of reality

Public relations practitioners make use of communication to achieve the objectives of practice. These have to do with influencing behaviour in relationships – winning support for the directions an organisation has chosen, or trying to minimise potential opposition, for example. Communication is a tool of public relations practice, but not all that the practice involves.

Communication requires selection of information and its presentation through channels chosen for their reach, their suitability against the interests and expectations of the groups, individuals to be reached and influenced.

The selection and presentation of information – the development of content for transmission through channels to important groups – means that a view of the world, the organisation's objectives in that world, are presented onwards for consideration. The groups and individuals receiving this information will also have other information to consider.

Public relations practitioners are recognisable as boundary-spanning individuals, working across organisational boundaries, to represent the organisation's environment and actors within it to organisational decision-makers and to represent the organisation, its interests and objectives, to groups and individuals outside the organisation (Tushman and Scanlan 1981).

In this role, they are presenting views of reality, within and outside the organisation, for consideration by relevant groups and individuals.

Explore 11.1

Facebook's view of the world

In October 2018, Facebook appointed Sir Nick Clegg as vice-president of global affairs and communications putting him into a position of speaking for the company, representing its interests to important groups affecting, and affected by, the company. In April 2019, the company, speaking through Sir Nick Clegg as its representative set out to begin to shape the global conversation about internet regulation.

1. Looking at the announcement made by the company consider how it presented its view of how the internet and Facebook's activities should be regulated.
2. Look at how the boundary-spanning individual – in this case Sir Nick Clegg – made the company's arguments and presented a view of the world in which the company operates.
3. Others, cited in the Bloomberg article, present different views of the world and the way regulation should be developed and applied to Facebook. How do these differ from Facebook's views, and how do you think these views and Facebook's can be reconciled? Can they be reconciled, and by what processes?

Contributors to the social construction of reality

Public relations practitioners share with many others the possibilities of making presentations contributing to the process of constructing social reality. In practice, groups in this position of interest include politicians and policy makers, leaders of business and industry, civil society organisations, the traditional media, educators and – more recently – those who would be defined as influencers. Influencers can exert influence through connections to large numbers of people, who may follow them through social media connections.

An additional use of stakeholder maps – visualisations of groups in a social network around an organisation or issue of interest — would enable analysis of the views of reality presented by different groups in the network. This would allow an assessment of the relative strength of the views represented in the picture.

Disinformation and 'fake news' – their consequences

There has been growing interest in, and concern about, the consequences of disinformation and 'fake news' over recent years. This has coincided with the realisation that groups such as terrorist organisations, hostile governments, and less scrupulous politicians are successfully using the potential of modern communication to mislead, confuse, weaken and otherwise disrupt social cohesion and stability for political or other ends.

Disinformation is false information spread deliberately to deceive. A UK House of Commons Committee set up to examine its use defined it as 'the deliberate creation and sharing of false and/or manipulated information that is intended to deceive and mislead audiences, either for the purposes of causing harm, or for political, personal or financial gain' (House of Commons DCMS Committee Report on Disinformation and Fake News 2019). It is distinguished from

Box 11.1

UK Government cracks down on spread of COVID-19 disinformation

The UK Government stepped up its fight against disinformation on the internet at the outset of the COVID-19 crisis with the creation of a Rapid Response Unit. Its targets ranged from individuals and organisations sharing disinformation to criminal fraudsters running phishing scams.

According to the Bruno Kessler Foundation (De Domenico and Sacco 2020) misinformation about the virus itself behaves like a virus, spreading exponentially via messaging applications and social media. The foundation reported that at the outset of the crisis in March 2020, 46,000 tweets were posted every day linking to unreliable information about the virus. These ranged from conspiracy theories that China had created COVID-19 in a lab to fake cures advising people to drink bleach, gargle water or eat garlic. It led the World Health Organization to suggest that the COVID-19 had given rise to both an epidemic and an infodemic.

The UK Rapid Response Unit sits at the heart of Government coordinating a response with appropriate departments. This includes direct rebuttal on social media, working with Google, Facebook and Twitter to remove harmful content and ensuring public health campaigns are promoted through reliable sources. The Government reported that up to 70 incidents a week, often false narratives containing multiple misleading claims, were being identified and resolved at the outset of the crisis. One such example is an alleged network of 128 fake National Health Service Twitter accounts that were claimed to be sharing Government propaganda. The claim was directly refuted by the Government and Twitter.

The Rapid Response Unit is one of the teams feeding into the wider Counter Disinformation Cell led by the Department for Digital, Culture, Media and Sport (DCMS), made up of experts from across Government and in the tech sector. The Counter Disinformation Cell is engaging with social media platforms and with disinformation specialists from civil society and academia, to establish a comprehensive overview of the extent, scope and impact of disinformation related to coronavirus.

Chapter 11 Disinformation, fake news and social reality 237

Picture 11.2 Disinformation and alleged Russian interference were featured in the US election (*source:* Mladen Antonov/AFP/Getty Images)

misinformation, which may be unintentional and involve the inadvertent sharing of false information. 'Fake news' has been given currency recently in American politics by political leaders suggesting that the news media are not to be trusted, that their methods result in the misuse and distortion of information. As a King's College and NATO Road Map to Fake News makes clear, fake news is not new (King's College and NATO 2018), but its transmission is now so much easier and faster.

Traditional media have always gathered information according to rules which will involve the selection of information, and its presentation in a way that will attract and sustain audience interest. They tell stories, which involve selection from available facts, interpretation of these and their presentation in a variety of required formats. These are partial representations of the world as seen and interpreted by journalists and others preparing content for the media. They are presentations of reality which can be called into question, but with a number and mix of media outlets the consumer of news has access to a variety of views of reality and can use these sources to develop their understanding of the world.

Disinformation is more pernicious and harder to identify and counter. Examples are to be found in international relations. The success of hostile groups in using disinformation in hybrid warfare or in support of the objectives of terrorist groups has led governments to set up agencies to work against these developments such as the US Government's Global Engagement Centre, and the British government's establishment of specialist intelligence and military groups to work against disinformation (for a discussion of military thinking, see the Wavell Room 2019).

Disinformation has become a feature of election campaigns in countries such as the United States and the members of the European Union. The Mueller Report (Mueller 2019), detailing an investigation into Russian interference in the 2016 US Presidential Election, found that there had been extensive and systematic interference. This came through social media interventions from front organisations exerting influence around politically sensitive questions, such as relations between disadvantaged groups and wider society.

These kinds of interventions are hard to counter and to trace back to their originators. Similar problems were identified in the campaigns around the UK's decision to leave the European Union.

Think about 11.1   The threat of disinformation

Comments from the Chair of the House of Commons Digital, Culture, Media and Sport Committee on Disinformation and Fake News (Final Report, April 2019)

Damian Collins MP, Chair of the DCMS Committee:

Our inquiry over the last year has identified three big threats to our society. The challenge for the year ahead is to start to fix them; we cannot delay any longer.

Democracy is at risk from the malicious and relentless targeting of citizens with disinformation and personalised 'dark adverts' from unidentifiable sources,

delivered through the major social media platforms we use every day. Much of this is directed from agencies working in foreign countries, including Russia.

The big tech companies are failing in the duty of care they owe to their users to act against harmful content, and to respect their data privacy rights.

Companies like Facebook exercise massive market power which enables them to make money by bullying the smaller technology companies and developers who rely on this platform to reach their customers.

→

think about 11.1 (continued)

These are issues that the major tech companies are aware of, yet continually fail to address. The guiding principle of the 'move fast and break things' culture often seems to be that it is better to apologise than ask permission.

We need a radical shift in the balance of power between the platforms and the people. The age of inadequate self-regulation must come to an end. The rights of the citizen need to be established in statute, by requiring the tech companies to adhere to a code of conduct written into law by Parliament and overseen by an independent regulator.

We also have to accept that our electoral regulations are hopelessly out of date for the internet age. We need reform so that the same principles of transparency of political communications apply online, just as they do in the real world. More needs to be done to require major donors to clearly establish the source of their funds.

Much of the evidence we have scrutinised during our inquiry has focused on the business practices of Facebook; before, during and after the Cambridge Analytica data breach scandal.

We believe that in its evidence to the Committee Facebook has often deliberately sought to frustrate our work, by giving incomplete, disingenuous and at times misleading answers to our questions.

Even if Mark Zuckerberg doesn't believe he is accountable to the UK Parliament, he is to the billions of Facebook users across the world. Evidence uncovered by my Committee shows he still has questions to answer yet he's continued to duck them, refusing to respond to our invitations directly or sending representatives who don't have the right information. Mark Zuckerberg continually fails to show the levels of leadership and personal responsibility that should be expected from someone who sits at the top of one of the world's biggest companies.

We also repeat our call to the Government to make a statement about how many investigations are currently being carried out into Russian interference in UK politics. We want to find out what was the impact of disinformation and voter manipulation on past elections including the UK Referendum in 2016 and are calling on the Government to launch an independent investigation.

Think about these comments

What are some of the implications of these comments for the quality and integrity of public communication?

If companies such as Facebook will not act to deal with malicious content, what additional demands does this make on others concerned with public communication and its reliability (trustworthiness, completeness and accuracy)?

Do public relations practitioners have a role in ensuring the quality and integrity of public communication?

Countering disinformation and fake news

Concern about the increasing prevalence of disinformation and fake news has led to responses from government agencies.

In the United Kingdom the Government Communication Service (GCS) has identified the problems associated with disinformation and produced a detailed guide to countering it (RESIST 2019).

The agency recognises that 'when the information environment is deliberately confused this can:

- threaten public safety;
- fracture community cohesion;
- reduce trust in institutions and the media;
- undermine public acceptance of science's role in informing policy development and implementation;
- damage our economic prosperity and our global influence; and
- undermine the integrity of government, the constitution and democratic processes'.

It also recognises that disinformation is the combination of a malign intention or goal with several unethical communicative principles into a communication technique. The principles are simple, labelled by the Government Communication Service as the 'FIRST' principles of disinformation:

- Fabrication manipulates content: for example, a forged document or manipulated image.
- Identity disguises or falsely ascribes a source: for example, a fake social media account or an imposter.
- Rhetoric makes use of malign or false arguments: for example, trolls agitating commenters on a chat forum.

- Symbolism exploits events for their communicative value: for example, terror attacks.
- Technology exploits a technological advantage: for example, bots automatically amplifying messages. These FIRST principles of disinformation are combined to create unethical communication techniques.

Public relations: obligations in countering disinformation and fake news

A defining and continuing challenge for public relations and its aspirations towards professional status is the fight for standards in public debate, in the public interest. National and international associations of practitioners have commitments to the integrity of channels of public communication. For example, the International Public Relations Association set out in the Code of Venice in 1961 the requirement that members should not engage in practice which tends to corrupt the integrity of channels of public communication. The Canadian Public Relations Society expects its members to practice the highest standards of honesty, accuracy, integrity and truth, and to not knowingly disseminate false or misleading information.

These standards imply an interest in, and obligation to protect the integrity of channels of communication, and to work to ensure accuracy in content conveyed through them. They push practitioners towards paying close attention to the preparation and presentation of content, and towards responsible use of available channels of communication. They should also encourage challenges to misuse, false and misleading information, and to those preparing misleading information, or misusing channels of communication.

Arguments against practitioners assuming these responsibilities will be that public relations practice has narrower interests – to serve clients, to achieve client or employing organisations' objectives. Another will be that the practice lacks the resources to take on these responsibilities, in terms of time and attention.

Think about 11.2

Ethical responsibility for information

From your own reading of international and national codes of conduct established to guide behaviour in practice, what obligations would you identify for practitioners to challenge and work to mitigate the effects of disinformation and fake news?

Who, in practice, should be responsible for challenging disinformation and fake news?

Where should the resources for doing this come from, and what alliances with other groups – such as associations of professional journalists – should be struck to counter disinformation and fake news?

How would you assess the effectiveness of efforts to do this?

Box 11.2

Disinformation techniques

Astroturfing: Falsely attributing a message or an organisation to an organic grassroots movement to create false credibility.

A source pays or plants information that appears to originate organically or as a grassroots movement.

Bandwagon effect: A cognitive effect where beliefs increase in strength because they are shared by others.

A person is more willing to share an article when seeing it is shared by many people.

Bot: Automated computer software that performs repetitive tasks along a set of algorithms.

Impersonator bots: Bots which mimic natural user characteristics to give the impression of a real person.

Spammer bots: Bots which post repeat content with high frequency to overload the information environment.

Bots can be used to amplify disinformation or to skew online discussion by producing posts and comments on

box 11.2 (continued)

social media forums and other similar tasks – sometimes they focus on quantity and speed (spammer bots); other times they attempt to mimic organic user behaviour (impersonator bots) – bots can also be used for hacking and to spread malware.

Botnet: A network of hijacked computers used to execute commands. Infests personal computers with malware, contribute to DDoS attacks, and distributing phishing attacks.

Cheerleading: The overwhelming promotion of positive messages. A dissenting opinion is crowded out by positive messages perpetuated by an abundance of commentators cheerleading the 'right' opinion.

Dark ads: Targeted advertisements based on an individual user's psychographic profile, 'dark' insofar as they are only visible to targeted users. An advertisement containing false information is targeted to social media users with personality traits deemed susceptible to this messaging, with the goal of shaping their opinions in a specific direction.

Deep fakes: Use of digital technology to fabricate facial movements and voice, sometimes in real time. A fabricated video of a politician shows them saying something outrageous or incriminating, with the goal of undermining confidence in government.

Echo chamber: A situation where certain ideas are reinforced by repetition within a social space online. Creation of internet sub-groups, often along ideological lines, where people engage with like-minded people, which reinforces pre-existing beliefs.

Fake news: Deliberate disinformation disguised as news. A non-journalist fabricates a news story to influence public opinion and to undermine the credibility of mainstream media, which is published on a private platform.

Fake platform: Identity of a web platform is disguised to promote fabricated content. A web platform is designed to appear like an official site, with the goal of creating the appearance of a credible source of information.

Filter bubble: Algorithms which personalise and customise a user's experience on social media platforms might entrap the user in a bubble of his or her own making. The social media flow of a user interested in Brexit gradually adapts to consumed content to eventually only show information in favour of Brexit.

Flooding: The overflowing of a target media system with high-volume, multi-channel disinformation. Multiple commentators, both in the form of bots and real users, make an overwhelming amount of posts with nonsense content to crowd out legitimate information.

Forgery: Product or content is wholly or partly fabricated to falsely ascribe the identity of the source. A false document with an official-looking government heading is produced to discredit the government.

Hijacking: Unlawful seizure of a computer or an account. A website, hashtag, meme, event or social movement is taken over by an adversary or someone else for a different purpose.

Laundering: The process of passing of disinformation as legitimate information by gradually distorting it and obscuring its true origin. A false quote is referenced through multiple fake media channels until the original source is obscured and the quote is accepted as real by legitimate actors.

Leaking: Disseminating unlawfully obtained information. Unlawfully obtained emails are leaked to compromise individual actors or to undermine public confidence.

Malign rhetoric: Ruses using language aimed at undermining reasonable and legitimate debate and silencing opinions.

Name calling: A propaganda technique based on abusive or insulting language directed against a person or a group.

Manipulation: Alteration of content to change its meaning. An image is cropped to only show some of the participating parties in an incident.

Misappropriation: Falsely ascribing an argument or a position to another's name. A public figure is incorrectly cited or falsely attributed as a source.

Phishing: A method to unlawfully obtain information online via malware distributed over emails or web platforms. Malicious links are distributed via email which lead to phishing sites.

Point and shriek: Exploitation of sensitivity to perceived injustices in society to create outrage. A commentator diverts from a real issue at hand by pointing out the audacity of a make-believe incident which play on pre-existing social grievances.

Raiding: Temporarily disrupting a platform, event, or conversation by a sudden show of force. Several automated accounts are coordinated to disrupt a conversation by temporarily spamming nonsense messages.

Satire and parody: Ridiculing and humouring of individuals, narratives or opinions to undermine their legitimacy. A public figure is ridiculed using memes where non-factual opinions are ascribed to the public figure.

Shilling: To give credibility to a person or a message without disclosing intentions or relationships. An actor endorses certain content while appearing to be neutral but is in fact a dedicated propagandist.

> **Sock puppets:** Use of digital technology to disguise identity, to play both sides of a debate. A user creates two or more social media accounts under opposing identities, i.e. one pro-fox hunting, one against, with the aim of playing the identities against one another.
>
> **Spiral of silence:** The decrease in audibility of deviant opinions due to non-conforming beliefs. A person with non-conforming minority beliefs is less willing to share his or her opinions.
>
> **Tainting:** Leaked contents are tainted with forgeries. Leaked documents are distributed together with carefully placed fakes.
>
> **Terrorism:** Imagery from real-world events is used to make political claims.
>
> Images of violence are used to support false narratives, with the aim of creating a climate of fear or justifying a political argument.
>
> **Trolling:** Deliberate commenting on internet forums to provoke and engage other users in argument. Social media users deliberately post provocative comments to create emotional outrage in other users.
>
> (*Source:* UK Government Communication Services RESIST guide 2019)

National associations are limited to relying on volunteer support, will not have the research capacity to identify examples of disinformation or the ability to criticise the originators of disinformation.

Staying ahead of developments in use of disinformation

Belated recognition of the skill with which hostile groups have been able to use modern techniques of communication for the purposes of spreading disinformation have forced government and other agencies to try to catch up. They have done this by setting up specialist units to study and deal with the threat. An example is the US Government's Global Engagement Center.

The UK Government Communication Services RESIST guide (2019) is an example of a resource created to help communications professionals keep up to date with aids to tracking disinformation.

Its glossary of disinformation techniques is a useful summary of currently recognised techniques.

The challenge in practice is to recognise current forms and sources of disinformation, while being alert to the emergence of new techniques. It's a challenge that calls for environmental scanning, and the use of aids to analysis, such as stakeholder mapping as a form of network analysis. The RESIST guide provides pointers to useful scanning techniques.

Traditional media organisations have also taken steps to counter fake news and disinformation. The *New York Times,* for example, recently prepared a video guide to Russian use of disinformation (*New York Times* 2018). CNN has a series of advertisements stressing the need to stay close to facts – Facts First – to counter fake news, arguing that lies may become truth, if allowed, and emphasising the role of the media in reporting the facts (CNN, reported in Ad Age, 5 November 2018).

Relevance of the growth of interest in fake news and extensive use of disinformation to public relations practice

There has been a long-running discussion of the distinctions that can be drawn between public relations and propaganda, with some suggesting that – in some countries – public relations practice emerged from government propaganda practice. Public relations associations have tried to distinguish public relations from propaganda (Traverse-Healy 1988).

The distinctions will continue to attract the attention of academics and researchers (for example, L'Etang 2007). However, in practice propagandists, public relations practitioners and now purveyors of disinformation and fake news share similar interests in trying to shape the way people, groups, wider publics see the world. Context, motives and objectives may differ, but the intention – to influence perceptions, views of reality and ultimately behaviour – is the same.

The DCMS Report on Disinformation and Fake News (2019) cited earlier gives an example of comments made by Vladislav Surkov, a senior advisor to President Putin, in an article published in the Russian daily *Nezavisimaya Gazeta,* on 11 February 2019. He said that 'Foreign politicians blame Russia for meddling in elections and referenda all over the planet. In fact, it's even more serious than that: Russia is meddling in their brains and they don't know what to do with their changed consciousness' (2019: 74). The suggestion is that Russian disinformation efforts are directed to changing the way people consciously see the world.

Public relations practitioners recognise that they too are working to change perceptions. Leaf (2014), a veteran practitioner, describes public relations as concerned with changing perceptions, through the art of perception management. If the way people see things can be changed, their behaviour will change accordingly. Perception becomes reality and – although this phrase is often used without attribution to the sociologists who set this out as a theorem (Thomas and Thomas 1928) – they are real in their consequences. The original theorem suggests: 'if a man defines situations to be real, they will be real in their consequences.' Leaf and the consultancy he worked for, Burson-Marsteller, used the idea of perception management to define public relations practice and the work of the consultancy for several years.

The relevance of increasing use of techniques of disinformation and fake news to public relations is that they are techniques with which practitioners need to be thoroughly familiar. There are, in practice, some who believe that their value to clients and employers will come through use of similar techniques on their behalf. Practitioners operating in this way do so in contradiction of some of the codes of conduct that practitioners are invited or required to subscribe to. When discovered, their use of these techniques can lead to censure against these codes and even removal from practice (see, for example, the reaction to the now disgraced and defunct Bell Pottinger's activities in Segal 2018).

Practitioners need familiarity with the techniques of disinformation so that they can be countered and so that they are able to advise clients and employing organisations against the use of these techniques. This advice is given on the grounds of ethical practice and for hard practical reasons. If used, and discovered, as in an age of quick transparency, easy discovery, the willingness of those with knowledge of their use to 'blow the whistle' or leak information, they will be, the damage to reputation and to legitimate activities will be serious, and in some cases terminal.

Summary

In this chapter, we have explored how public relations practice contributes to what sociologists have described as the social construction of reality. They do this by presenting information that is used by others as they develop their understanding of social reality. Many others contribute to this process, which now is modified by the possibilities for information gathering provided by social media. Others include politicians, policy makers, educators, the media.

Through the chapter, we have seen how this process may be corrupted, using disinformation, which is intended to mislead and confuse, for reasons that benefit the perpetrators of disinformation. The consequences are serious, leading to breakdown in social cohesion, to increases in social tensions and conflict. The consequences are particularly serious in their effects on political stability, national interests and international cooperation.

The arguments made in this chapter are that public relations practice has interests in the dissemination of accurate information and the use of traditional and social media in the public interest. Codes of conduct – weak though they may be in many ways – recognise these interests and set out expectations for professional practice.

Public relations practitioners need familiarity with the techniques now being used to disseminate and derive benefit from disinformation, to counter and advise against them. In the interests of practice development, these techniques need to be exposed and called out by practitioners. They represent a clear danger to social cohesion and an obstacle to progress on dealing with larger problems facing national and international communities.

Bibliography

Berger, P. and Luckmann, T. (1966) *The Social Construction of Reality: A Treatise in the Sociology of Knowledge*. London: Allen Lane.

De Domenico, M. and Sacco P. (2020). COVID-19 Infodemics, Bruno Kessler Foundation, 9 March 2020. https://www.fbk.eu/en/ [Accessed 29 April 2020].

Fake News, A Road Map, King's Centre for Strategic Communications and NATO Strategic Communications Centre of Excellence, Latvia 2018, https://www.stratcomcoe.org/fake-news-roadmap

House of Commons Digital, Culture, Media and Sport Committee, *Disinformation and 'fake news':* Final Report Eighth Report of Session 2017–19 Report, February 2019, https://www.parliament.uk/business/committees/committees-a-z/commons-select/digital-culture-media-and-sport-committee/news/fake-news-report-published-17-19/

Leaf, R. (2014) *The Art of Perception: Memoirs of a Life in PR,* London: Atlantic Books.

L'Etang, J. (2007) *Public Relations and Propaganda: Conceptual Issues, Methodological Problems, and Public Relations Discourse* in J. L'Etang and M. Pieczka (Eds.) Public Relations: Critical Debates and Contemporary Practice (pp. 23–40), Lawrence Erlbaum Associates, Mahwah, NJ.

Mueller, R.S. (2019) *Report on the Investigation into Russian Interference in the 2016 Presidential Election,* US Department of Justice, Washington DC.

RESIST: *Counter-Disinformation Toolkit,* UK Government Communication Service (2019) https://gcs.civilservice.gov.uk/wp-content/uploads/2019/03/RESIST_Toolkit.pdf

Segal, D. (2018) How Bell Pottinger, PR Firm for Despots and Rogues, Met its End in South Africa, 2 February 2018, *New York Times,* https://www.nytimes.com/2018/02/04/business/bell-pottinger-guptas-zuma-south-africa.html.

Thomas, W.I. and D.S. Thomas (1928) *The child in America: Behavior problems and programs.* New York: Knopf.

Traverse-Healy, T. (Ed.) (1988) *Public Relations and Propaganda – Values Compared,* London, International Foundation for Public Relations Studies, International Public Relations Association (IPRA).

Tushman, M.L. and Scanlan (1981) Boundary Spanning Individuals: Their Role in Information Transfer and Their Antecedents, *The Academy of Management Journal* 24(2) (June 1981), pp. 289–305.

White, J. (1987) *Public relations in the Social Construction of Reality: Theoretical and Practical implications of Berger and Luckmann's View of the Social Construction of Reality,* Paper, Association for Education in Journalism and Mass Communication Conference, San Antonio, Texas, August 1987 (https://eric.ed.gov/?id=ED285189).

Websites

CNN (reported in Ad Age, 5 November 2018) https://adage.com/creativity/work/cnn-facts-first-lies-can-become-truth-if-we-let-them/957036

Facebook Top Lobbyist calls for 'Good Regulation' of Global Web, Bloomberg, 1 April 2019, https://www.bloomberg.com/news/articles/2019-03-31/facebook-top-lobbyist-calls-for-good-regulation-of-global-web

The New York Times: Opinion Video Series Operation Infektion: Russian Disinformation from Cold War to Kanye: https://www.nytimes.com/2018/11/12/opinion/russia-meddling-disinformation-fake-news-elections.html

The Cluetrain Manifesto (1999): www.cluetrain.com

The Wavell Room, *Information, Disinformation and Misinformation,* April 2019, https://wavellroom.com/2019/04/11/information-disinformation-misinformation-new-character-of-conflict-twenty-first-century/

United States State Department, https://www.state.gov/bureaus-offices/under-secretary-for-public-diplomacy-and-public-affairs/global-engagement-center/

CHAPTER 12

Finn Frandsen and Winni Johansen

Corporate image, reputation and identity

Source: Cultura RM/Alamy Stock Photo

Learning outcomes

By the end of this chapter you should be able to:
- understand the importance and implications of living in a 'brand society'
- understand the complexity of relationships
- define the key concepts of corporate image, reputation and identity
- explain how new concepts, such as status, stigma and reputation commons, can contribute to our understanding of corporate reputation
- describe and understand the process of reputation management (corporate branding).

Structure

- The controversy of image in public relations
- Understanding relationships
- Reputation management and corporate branding
- Measuring corporate image and reputation
- A critical point of view

Introduction

According to many scholars, we are living in a 'brand society' where product brands as well as corporate brands transform the way we manage organisations and live our lives (Kornberger 2010). Since the early 1990s, the idea that persons and organisations operate in a 'symbolic marketplace', where they are forced to build up a symbolic capital, that is, to create a favourable image or reputation (Schultz et al. 2000), has spread to more and more areas of society.

Private companies not only brand their products and services (product branding), but also the organisation behind these products and services (corporate branding). The driving force behind is a search for strategic differentiation. As the 'corporatisation' of public organisations has become more evident, public authorities, regions and municipalities have also started branding themselves in front of their citizens. City branding and nation branding have established themselves as new disciplines and practices to attract more inhabitants, tourists and firms. Personal branding has also seen the light of day.

In all the cases mentioned above, three concepts are pivotal: image, reputation and identity. Persons and organisations must communicate who they are, and what they stand for, in order to create a favourable image or reputation among their stakeholders.

To possess a strong symbolic capital seems to be an advantage for organisations in many ways. A good product or corporate brand is instrumental to differentiating a company and its products from its competitors and their products. A good corporate brand makes it easier for the company to attract new investors (investor branding) and facilitates the process of attracting and maintaining valuable employees (employer branding). Finally, a good corporate brand also makes it easier for the company to recover from a severe organisational crisis.

The controversy of image in public relations

The concept of image has been subject to a major controversy within the field of public relations. At the beginning of the 1990s, James E. Grunig introduced a distinction between two types of relationships between an organisation and its publics: symbolic relationships and behavioural relationships; a distinction that Grunig at that moment considered part of 'perhaps the most important paradigm struggle in the field today' (Grunig 1993). Grunig defined the symbolic relationships as based on superficial and short-term activities (communication), whereas he saw the behavioural relationships as based on substantive and long-term activities (actions). However, he also admitted that the two types of relationships are closely related: 'Although I consider long-term behavioural relationships to be the essence of public relations, I do not dismiss symbolic relationships. Symbolic and behavioural relationships are intertwined like strands of a rope' (Grunig 1993: 123).

Grunig (2006) replaced this relationship distinction with an alternative demarcation between two paradigms of public relations approaches: a symbolic, interpretive paradigm and a behavioural, strategic management paradigm. According to the first paradigm, the role of public relations is to influence how publics interpret the organisation. The focus is on tactical activities, publicity, media relations and media effects. According to the second paradigm, the role of public relations executives is to participate in strategic decision-making to help manage the behaviour of the organisation.

> **Think about 12.1**
>
> ## Image, communication and behaviour
>
> Think of a private company that you know reasonably well. It may be a production company such as the Coca Cola Company, an airline such as Ryanair, a chain of supermarkets such as Carrefour or a retail bank such as Barclays. How has the actual image that you have created of the company and its products or services, come to existence? Is it because of the behaviour of the company (product, service encounter, etc.)? Is it because of the words and pictures used by the company in its external communication (advertising campaigns, corporate website, etc.)? Or is it because of a completely different source of information (family, friends, the media)?
>
> What is communication, and what is not communication? Is it only words and pictures (what we say) that communicate a message? Or can behaviour (what we do) also communicate? Is it possible to distinguish between communication and actions?

Today, more than 30 years later, Grundig's distinction between communication and behaviour appears a little too narrow, if not misleading. Instead of defining image as the production of organisationally controlled messages for the purpose of manipulating media images, academics and practitioners have started defining and working with image as the dynamic result of interactions or negotiations between an organisation and its publics. Words, pictures and actions form part of this process. Instead of viewing image as a sender-determined construct, academics and practitioners now understand image as a receiver-determined construct (Wan and Schell 2007).

During the last two or three decades, corporate communication and strategic communication, two disciplines that are closely related to public relations in many aspects, have been institutionalised as professional practices and academic disciplines.

They build on two basic assumptions, between which there is a certain tension, and which are summarised in the concepts of integration and relation (Frandsen and Johansen 2014).

Integration, because the proponents of the two subdisciplines assume that the communication activities of an organisation will be most effective and efficient, if both its external communication activities (public relations and marketing communication) and its internal communication activities (organisational communication) are coordinated to a certain extent. This mindset has given birth to the idea of integrated corporate branding focusing on coherence, not only between the external and internal dimensions of the communication activities, but also between what an organisation says (brand promise) and what it does (brand experience).

Relation, because the proponents of corporate communication and strategic communication assume that the complex and dynamic relationships between an organisation and its stakeholders is of vital importance, and that an organisation in many cases will benefit from differentiating its corporate branding depending on which stakeholder group(s) it is interacting with. Investors expect something different from the organisation than employees, although they can of course be the same individual wearing different hats. Both integration and relation are expected to contribute to the creation of a favourable image or reputation.

With the rise of corporate communication and strategic communication there is a new focus on the ideational dimensions of organisations, including the crucial role played by corporate image, reputation and identity (Alvesson 1990). In accordance with this mindset and practice, Cornelissen (2017) defines corporate communication in the following way:

Corporate communication is a management function that offers a framework for the effective coordination of all internal and external communication with the overall purpose of establishing and maintaining favourable reputations with stakeholder groups upon which the organization is dependent.

(Cornelissen 2017: 5)

Understanding relationships

Public relations researchers have been more preoccupied with understanding the relationship between an organisation and its key publics than with understanding reputation. We are often told that relationships are the building blocks of every organisation's reputation.

According to Grunig and the Excellence Theory, public relations first and foremost contributes to organisational effectiveness by building 'quality, long-term relationships with strategic constituencies' (Grunig et al. 2002: 97). According to John A. Ledingham, the originator of Relationship Management Theory, an OPR is 'the state which exists between an organisation and its publics in which the actions of either can impact the economic, social, cultural or political well-being of the other' (Ledingham 2003: 184).

Recently, Coombs and Holladay (2015) have claimed that the strong focus on relationships in public relations research has led to the development of a 'relationship identity'. It is a characteristic feature of this 'identity' that its conceptualisation of OPRs is based on a model of interpersonal communication. This may seem innocent. However, by pretending that the communication between an organisation and its customers or employees, is like 'a conversation' between two persons, we risk oversimplifying our understanding of relationship. We tend to see them as dyadic, direct, and linear and forget that they are always mediated by the small or large dynamic networks in which they are embedded.

One way to solve this problem would be to introduce the concept of intermediaries. Frandsen and Johansen (2015) define an intermediary as 'an individual, a group of individuals, an organisation, or a meta-organisation, who belongs to a specific area in society [. . .], and whose primary function or mission is to mediate, that is, to represent an organisation and/or a specific stakeholder group, and/or to intervene between them either by furthering or by impeding the interests and activities of the organisation in question and/or its stakeholders in a specific situation or over time' (p. 257).

Intermediaries represent a diverse category of actors: trade associations, trade unions, public relations agencies, think tanks, the media, government agencies, etc. Some of these intermediaries represent either the focal organisation (e.g. trade associations) or the stakeholder group in question (e.g. interest organisations fighting for the rights of the consumers). Other intermediaries such as the media cover both sides of the 'arrow of influence'.

Finally, the introduction of intermediaries also affect how we conceptualise reputation. From now on, we must distinguish between three different levels: (1) the level of the corporate reputation: (2) the level of the industry or sector reputation (the reputation commons): and (3) the level of the intermediary reputation.

Corporate image and reputation

The first key concept is the concept of image, that is, how a person or an organisation is perceived by people (stakeholders). Corporate image studies were conducted already in the 1950s, and it is not until the 1990s that the concept of corporate image is joined by its close relative, the concept of corporate reputation. Referring to Aaker and Meyers (1982), Australian professor of marketing, Grahame Dowling defines image as:

> *An image is the set of meanings by which an object is known and through which people describe, remember and relate to it. That is the result of the interaction of a person's beliefs, ideas, feelings and impressions about an object.*
>
> *(Dowling 1986: 110)*

Dowling adds that the word 'object' can be replaced with either 'brand', 'product' or 'company', etc. to gain a definition of the image one is interested in studying.

Organisations are concerned about how they are perceived by others, that is, the image that various types of key stakeholders produce of the organisations. An image is not something that belongs to the organisation – stakeholders hold an image of the organisation. Very often organisations mirror themselves in the global evaluation made by their stakeholders, creating a realistic self-image (Christensen and Cheney 2000).

However, an image is not a unitary, monolithic phenomenon. Each group of stakeholders perceives the company, its employees and/or its products depending on their stakes, the context and their relationship with the organisation over a shorter or longer period. If you are a consumer of products and services, you will most probably be interested in the quality and price of products and services, sustainability, animal welfare or the 'brand promise' made by the company. But even consumers form a very heterogeneous group of stakeholders producing many different images of the same company. If you are an investor, you will probably first be interested in the profitability and overall economic performance of the company, but also in its overall reputation and legitimacy. If you are a citizen, and let's say the neighbour of a large company, you are probably interested in how the organisation in question contributes to the local community. Does it create new jobs for the members of the local community? Are the products or the production processes harming the environment or the climate?

Another important question: where do the stakeholders get the information from? Are they in direct contact with a company – that is, they work for the company or they buy and consume its products? Or are they only indirectly in contact with the company – that is, they get the information from members of their social and professional networks (family, friends, colleagues), or they get the information from the press (stakeholder by proxy)?

But if corporate image is 'the global evaluation (comprised of a set of beliefs and feelings) a person has about an organization' (Dowling 2001: 19), what then is corporate reputation? In the early days of corporate communication, people did not highlight the difference. The two concepts were considered synonyms and accordingly used at random. Today, most researchers and practitioners make a clear distinction, based on a variety of dimensions, between the concept of image and the concept of reputation.

A first-dimension concerns time; that is, reputation as a time-based construct. A corporate image can be viewed as a momentary snapshot based on a short-term, emotional evaluation of the company, whereas a corporate reputation can be viewed as a kind of background set based on a long-term and more rational evaluation of the company. Schultz (2005) defines corporate reputation as 'the longitudinal judgement of who the company is and what it stands for among multiple stakeholders' (Schultz 2005: 43).

According to crisis communication researcher W. Timothy Coombs and his situational crisis communication theory, the reputation of an organisation builds upon the relationship between the organisation and its stakeholders, which has developed over time (Coombs 2015; see also Ledingham's (2005) relationship management theory). Thus, an organisational crisis can be defined as a 'relational damage'.

A second-dimension concerns reputation as a value-based construct. In his book entitled *Reputation – Realizing Value from the Corporate Image* (1996), Charles J. Fombrun from the Reputation Institute defines corporate reputation as 'the overall estimation in which a company is held by its constituents' (Fombrun 1996: 37). This estimation is based on the perceptions of a series of values such as reliability, credibility, social responsibility and trustworthiness. Dowling also sees corporate reputation as a value-based construct. He defines the notion in the following way: 'Corporate reputation: the attributed values (such as authenticity, honesty, responsibility, and integrity) evoked from the person's corporate image' (Dowling 2001: 19).

Values are about beliefs and ideals, used by human beings to give preference of something over something else. They reflect a person's sense of what is important, desirable, good, right, etc. Thus, whether an organisation has a good or bad reputation, is connected to the degree of accordance between the way an organisation acts and the values that a stakeholder or stakeholder group considers to be personally or socially preferable for an appropriate behaviour of an organisation. Basic assumptions of human beings are thought to be relatively stable, whereas values, whether societal or personal, develop faster and in a more dynamic way over time, influenced by internal as well as external circumstances. A good example of this is the debate about climate change and the possibilities of citizens and organisations to influence the evolution in the right way. This development of society has clearly influenced the attitude of consumers to sustainability and the use of climate and environmentally friendly products.

Today, organisations are very engaged in the creation of a strong and good reputation because this is a way to make them stand out from their competitors, whether it is about growth and turnover, attracting the best workforce or gaining political influence. For the very same reason, the symbolic capital plays a central role, on a par with financial capital, human capital and social capital.

New concepts

The past decade has seen a considerable growth in the literature on corporate reputation. New concepts have been introduced to improve our understanding of the symbolic capital of private and public organisations. Among these concepts, we find the concepts of status, stigma and reputation commons (Barnett and Pollock 2012).

Status is a concept that is related to but distinct from reputation. While reputation is economically determined, status is socially and culturally determined. It represents an organisation's position in a hierarchical order and is generated by relations and affiliations to other actors. 'What is important is not what you do, but who you do it with' (Barron and Rolfe 2012). Organisations that are viewed as high status will have an advantage over organisations that are viewed as low status. However, high-status organisations are also more conspicuous in the eyes of the stakeholders, and the stakeholders have higher expectations of these organisations. This often means that deviations from the core market identity will be punished more severely (cf. the Volkswagen Dieselgate scandal in 2015).

Stigma is another concept that is related to but distinct from (bad) reputation. While reputation will always be multi-dimensional (cf. the multiple stakeholders who try to make sense of the communication and behaviour of the organisation in which they have a stake), stigma is one-dimensional, as it reflects that an organisation possesses a 'fundamental, deep-seated flaw' (Devers et al. 2009: 157). The concept of stigma is derived from the sociology of deviance and can help us explain why certain companies and industries have difficulty creating a favourable reputation (cf. the tobacco industry).

The concept of reputation commons is an attempt to understand the interdependent dimension of corporate reputation (King et al. 2002). This can be a situation in which the reputation of several different companies, typically in an industry, is tarnished due to the actions of a single firm within the group. It therefore refers to the fact that a company's reputation is tied to the reputation of other companies and that reputation may be a common resource shared by all members of an industry. 'The company you keep affects the company you keep' (Barnett and Hoffman 2008). Like natural

---

Think about 12.2

Favourable and not so favourable reputations

Think of persons and organisations that have either a very good or a very bad reputation. It may be a private company or a public organisation. It may be a political party or an NGO. It may be a football player or a golfer. Try to explain why. What kind of factors have an impact on the reputation of persons and organisations?

Picture 12.1 Lance Armstrong racing Marco Pantani in the Tour de France (*source:* Pascal George/AFP/Getty Images)

resources, the reputation commons of an industry can be over-exploited

Many things make up a corporate identity, just like a personal identity. Think about famous people as well as brands and what makes up their identity: how they look, how they perform and how they behave.

Corporate identity

The third key concept is the concept of identity (from Latin idem, 'same') referring to what an organisation is, and what it stands for. It is a complex concept – a so-called macro-concept – covering different understandings and developments of what the identity of an organisation is.

According to Hatch and Schultz (2000), the concept of identity within management, organisation and communication studies has emerged simultaneously, but along different paths.

First, the concept of corporate identity was coined within a research tradition, which is rooted in marketing management (brand management). The concept refers to how an organisation expresses and differentiates itself in relation to its external stakeholders. Cees van Riel defines corporate identity in the following way:

Corporate identity is the self-presentation of an organisation; it consists in the cues which an organisation offers about itself via the behaviour, communication, and symbolism which are its forms of expression.

(van Riel 1995: 36)

Scholars often make a distinction between two different approaches to corporate identity (Balmer 1995).

The first approach is the visual school of identity, emphasising the visual or tangible manifestations of what an organisation is, and what it stands for (such as the name, logo, architecture or design of the organisation, e.g. Apple and Coca Cola). Today, many organisations also include, for example, sound (sound logo, jingle, brand music and brand theme, e.g. Nokia and Intel) as an integrated part of their corporate identity mix. The second approach is the strategic school of identity, focusing on the ideas behind the organisation including its mission and vision statements, philosophy and values. From this perspective, corporate identity is viewed as part of a planned process linking the strategy of the organisation with its image or reputation (see the 'Reputation management and corporate branding' section of this chapter).

Second, the concept of organisational identity was established within a research tradition, which is rooted in organisation studies. The concept refers to how the members of an organisation perceive and understand 'who we are' and 'what we stand for'. Many interpretations of organisational identity are based on a version of social identity theory examining how people identify themselves by referring to the social group to which they (do not) belong (Jenkins 2008). Contrary to the concept of corporate identity, which applies an organisation-external perspective, the concept of organisational identity applies an organisation-internal perspective (all the members of the organisation). In this sense, there is affinity to the concept of organisational culture. Albert and Whetten (1985) define organisational identity as a kind of question.

The question, 'What kind of organisation is this?' refers to the features that are arguably core, distinctive and enduring and reveal the identity of the organization.

(Albert and Whetten 1985: 292)

Also, here, scholars often make a distinction between two different approaches to organisational identity (Whetten 1997). The first approach highlights the employee's 'identification with' the organisation. To what extent do employees define themselves by the same attributes that they believe define the organisation? To what extent is there congruence between the goals and values of the employees and the goals and values of the organisation? To what extent do they demonstrate a sense of belonging? The second approach focuses on 'the identity of' the organisation. How do the employees of an organisation see themselves as an organisation? Where the first approach is interested in the personal level, the latter conducts analyses at the organisational level.

Some scholars, such as Hatch and Schultz (2000), have suggested that we combine the concepts of corporate identity and organisational identity turning them into a single concept of identity, whereas other scholars, such as Cornelissen (2017), insist on maintaining the difference between the two concepts. In the concept of corporate identity, the focus is on creating identity with the explicit purpose of differentiating the organisation in relation to its external stakeholders, whereas in the concept of organisational identity, the focus is on patterns of meaning and sense-making leading to common values, identification and belonging among members of an organisation.

The debate on postmodernity, which started in the 1980s and which took place across many academic disciplines, has also had an impact on research conducted within identity studies. In the modern society, some sociologists claim, the individual saw it as an important existential task to construct an identity and to maintain it as a stable 'core' throughout his or her life. However, in the postmodern society, nobody any longer believes that identity has such an essence. An identity is and will always remain a social construction, that is, a preliminary product of the social and cultural contexts in which we live and interact with other people over time. In such a society, the task of the individual is to avoid fixation and to keep the options open (Bauman 1996). This debate has recently been revitalised by the concept of the authentic company, that is, an organisation that is 'true to itself' (Gilmore and Pine 2007).

> *Corporations, places, and offerings have actual identities (the selves to which they must be true to be perceived as authentic), not just articulations of those identities (the representations that must accurately reflect those selves to be perceived as authentic). There's an old saw in advertising circles: nothing makes a bad product fail faster than good advertising. There should be a new one in branding circles: nothing makes a real branding effort fail faster than a phony product. Such phoniness results from representations detached from the reality of a company's actual identity.*
>
> *(Gilmore and Pine 2007: 129)*

Reputation management and corporate branding

To work strategically with reputation management involves several disciplines or fields of practice such as corporate strategy, stakeholder management, issues management and crisis management. However, corporate branding constitutes one of the cornerstones if an organisation wants to strengthen its reputation among its internal and/or external stakeholders.

Branding is a universal phenomenon. All human beings can create mental pictures of themselves and the phenomena that they meet in the outside world. What we call branding today is the strategic and goal-oriented exploitation of this human ability, in order to build up relationships between people and the products of a company or the company itself. Corporate branding can be defined as: 'The process of creating, nurturing, and sustaining a mutually rewarding relationship between a company, its employees and external stakeholders' (Schultz in Schultz et al. 2005: 48).

As it appears from Table 12.1, corporate branding has undergone a rapid development since its appearance in the 1990s. It has moved from the first wave, where the emphasis was on a short-term, marketing-oriented and campaign-driven approach with a focus on visual identity, to the second wave – and very recently even to a third wave. Today, corporate branding is viewed as a strategic asset of increasing importance for the entire organisation, and the brand is viewed as something that is constantly being co-created in dynamic interaction between stakeholders, their networks and the organisation.

According to Hatch and Schultz (2008), the second wave of corporate branding emerges in the first decade of 2000. At this moment corporate branding has developed into a discipline with a more strategic and long-term way of thinking about the corporate brand. It is no longer just anchored in the department of marketing or public relations but is embedded in a long series of functions and disciplines across the organisation with a focus on the interaction between the vision of management, the organisational culture and the images of the stakeholders.

However, in 2008 Hatch and Schultz start talking about the rise of a third wave of corporate branding. Even though there is a certain accordance between the understanding of the second and the third wave of corporate branding, they want to emphasise that a paradigm shift has occurred when it comes to the new stakeholder focus. There has been a shift from primarily thinking separately and with a few stakeholder

First wave (mid-1990s) Marketing mindset	Second wave (2005–present) Corporate mindset	Towards the third wave Enterprise mindset
Grounded in a marketing and campaign approach (uni-functional and myopic)	Grounded in a strategic cross-functional approach (multi-functional and fragmented)	Grounded in a strategic holistic approach (inter-functional and integrated)
Product-oriented, short-sighted, tactical and narrow focus on visual identity and aesthetics Internally anchored understanding of 'who we are' and 'what we stand for'	Branding as a part of the continuous adaptation and development of the company Long-term oriented development of culture, vision and image based on 'who we are' Integration across disciplines Involvement of employees and customers (employer brands)	The brand as the voice, not just of the company, but of the entire enterprise encompassing the interests and expectations of the full range of a company's stakeholders To gain the perspective of the whole enterprise and develop the awareness of the symbolism involved Stakeholder capitalism: thinking in terms of network relations
Communication: sender-oriented transmission	Communication: receiver-oriented, interaction, co-creation of brand meaning	Communication: many voices will participate in the shaping and informing of the corporate brand
The corporate brand as a sense giver	The corporate brand as a facilitator of relations between sense giving and sense making	The corporate brand as conversant (as initiator of conversations)
A linear process	A dynamic process Five principles: Know thyself Be facilitator Lead through interaction Embrace paradoxes Think dynamic	A co-creational process Five principles: Corporate branding is dynamic Anticipate the future by celebrating the past Listen and you will speak volumes Serve your customers by delighting your employees Think like an enterprise

Table 12.1 Corporate branding: towards the third wave (*sources:* Schultz et al. (2005) and Hatch and Schultz (2008))

groups, such as customers or employees, to having a broader stakeholder perspective and thinking in stakeholder networks. Local communities, NGOs and politicians all contribute to the co-creation and brand meaning of the corporate brand. For that reason, reputation management is not only the duty of one or two departments but must penetrate all functions of an organisation in an integrated, holistic way. Thus, reputation management is demonstrated in practice by the tension between an organisation and its promises and relations to its (networks of) stakeholders.

Corporate branding is a strategic management discipline with the scope to make the organisation attractive to current and potential stakeholders in order to strengthen its image and reputation and to make its vision come through.

Typically, a corporate branding process is initiated by doing a situational analysis to find out about the identity, beliefs, positions, core competencies and performances of an organisation. Thus, it is important to carry out analyses of possible gaps between what you are, what you want to be and the way you are perceived by your key stakeholders. If the gaps have grown too big, you often as an organisation want to strengthen or to change the image and reputation of the company in relation to various key stakeholders.

The next step is to make strategic decisions. It must be decided what should be the branding platform and how to live up to the new visions and goals. It includes questions about key values, common starting points (CSPs), and stories the organisation lives, that must be considered in an integrated, holistic communications perspective. It also deals with the choice of branding

Case study 12.1
Re-branding Carlsberg

Perched on Valby hill in Copenhagen, the Carlsberg brewery was founded in 1847 by J.C. Jacobsen, a young man interested in natural science, industrial innovation and high-quality yeast. In 1882, J.C. Jacobsen carved his now famous 'golden words' into the stonework of the original Carlsberg Brewery: 'In working the brewery it should be a constant purpose, regardless of immediate gain, to develop the art of making beer to the greatest possible degree of perfection so that this brewery as well as its products may ever stand out as a model, and through their example, assist in keeping beer brewing in this country at a high and honourable level.'

J.C. Jacobsen's 'golden words' were brought to live again 134 years later in 2016 when Carlsberg's new CEO started implementing an ambitious and aggressive growth strategy. In 1999, Carlsberg was still primarily a regional brewer in Scandinavia and the UK. However, only a few years later Carlsberg saw itself as the market leader in Northern Europe and parts of Eastern Europe and Asia. In 2008, Carlsberg acquired Scottish & Newcastle, the biggest acquisition ever made in Denmark.

Today, Carlsberg has become the Carlsberg Group – the fourth largest brewery in the world. The Group has more than 140.000 employees, it is present in more than 150 countries, and it represents more than 600 different product brands.

As the Carlsberg Group grew bigger new strategies were required to manage the group and its growth. Thus, in May 2016, Carlsberg's CEO announced a revised long-term strategy assigned the name, SAIL'22. As the name suggests, with this strategy the group is embarking on a rebranding journey that will see Carlsberg transform into a business that aims to deliver long-term, sustainable value creation.

During the second half of 2015, the top 60 leadership team of Carlsberg worked together and identified, evaluated and concluded on a range of strategic options. The engagement of the top leadership team in this process was very important to ensure tapping into the vast knowledge base in the company, as the new CEO did not have a brewery background.

To guide Carlsberg on the journey, Carlsberg's top 60 management team set a compelling new ambition and fundamentally changed how to prioritise and operate.

Picture 12.2 How Carlsberg, a major brewing company, is communicating its brand through sponsorship (*source:* stuart emmerson/Alamy Stock Photo)

Carlsberg is now focusing its efforts against a narrower and more precisely-defined set of priorities. More importantly, the Carlsberg Group aim to foster a greater sense of ownership; rigorously follow up on the delivery of results and drive a high-performance, team-based culture. To develop a winning team and performance-based culture, the group rolled out the triple A concept. This was designed to deliver cultural transformation and in 2016, 4,500 members of the company have been trained. The remaining 37,000 Group employees were to be trained during 2017/18.

While SAIL'22 strategy recognised the changes within the global market, one important element of SAIL'22 was that it clearly said that Carlsberg would continue to operate in its current three regions. Following the significant growth in Carlsberg Group's Asian business 2011–2016, the decline of the Russian beer market, and the stagnant Western Europe, its portfolio of markets is better balanced than earlier. The dependency of the Russian market is declining, and the Group has robust local businesses, with strong market positions and promising portfolios of local and international brands, in all three regions.

SAIL'22 says that the Group's current markets still offer many opportunities and that these can be realised by building on the strong assets that the Group already has. This means growing organically. It also recognises that the Group has a strong portfolio of more than 100 brands, consisting of both local and international brands, as well as specialty brands like Grimbergen, Jacobsen and Brooklyn and together this portfolio of brands meets a broad range of consumer needs.

SAIL'22 recognised not only Carlsberg's many strengths but coupled that with the rich heritage and highlighted Carlsberg's founders' mentality. Illustrating the Group's history and contribution to society, the launch of SAIL'22 coincided with the re-brew project, commemorating the Carlsberg Research Laboratory and Carlsberg Foundation's 140 Jubilee: www.rebrewproject.com/.

Sustainability is strongly embedded in the SAIL'22 rebranding strategy. Carlsberg wants to create a more resilient business and has elaborated on its strategy: Together towards ZERO (cf. Sustainability Report 2018) with four sustainability ambitions that the group wants to target for 2022 and 2030: zero carbon footprint, zero water waste, zero irresponsible drinking, and zero accident's culture. For instance, to reduce plastic waste and lower CO_2 impact, Carlsberg has introduced a new plastic free Snap Pack. It introduces an innovative glue technology to hold multipacks together, meaning 'you just snap the packs away'. Snap Pack is supposed to reduce the use of plastic by 50–76 per cent. See www.carlsberggroup.com and YouTube for further information.

Box 12.1

The corporate branding process

Situational analysis	Who are we? What are our main challenges? How are we perceived by our key stakeholders? Any gaps?	
	Stakeholder analysis, gap analysis, market analysis, etc.	
	⇒ adaptation or development of new position	
Strategic decisions	Who do we want to be, and how will we become what we want to be? What is the vision, the goals, and the new strategies? How do we differentiate ourselves from others?	
	Branding platform (brand-architecture, CSPs, organisational stories, behaviour, symbols, visual and verbal communication)	
	Organisational changes (structure, culture, etc.)	
Implementation	How to put the decisions into action? Execution of plans (how to communicate internally and to the outside world)	
	Planning and execution of communication strategies: goals, stakeholder groups, content, tactical organising of CSPs and key stories, choice of media, budget and resources	
Evaluation	What images and what reputation do we have now? What kind of dynamics? New gaps? How far have we come?	
	Alignment between vision/strategy, culture/identity and images/reputation Measuring our corporate/organisational identity, images and reputation as viewed by our key stakeholders	

THE CORPORATE BRAND

STAKEHOLDERS

> **Box 12.2**
>
> ## The corporate branding toolkit (Hatch and Schulz 2001)
>
> **Diagnostic questions for analysing gaps between:**
>
> **Vision and culture**
> - Does the organisation practise the values it promotes?
> - Does the organisation's vision inspire all its subcultures?
> - Are the organisation's vision and culture sufficiently differentiated from those of its competitors?
>
> **Culture and image**
> - What images do stakeholders associate with the organisation?
> - In what ways do its employees and stakeholders interact?
> - Do employees care what stakeholders think of the organisation?
>
> **Image and vision**
> - Who are the organisation's stakeholders?
> - What do the stakeholders want from the organisation?
> - Is the organisation effectively communicating its vision to its stakeholders?
>
> *Source:* Hatch, M.J. and M. Schultz (2001). 'Are the strategic stars aligned for your corporate brand? Harvard Business Review. February 2001'

architecture. Should you go for a monolithic structure (single all-embracing identity, e.g. Virgin and Heinz), an endorsed structure (identity badged with parent company name, e.g. Sony (Sony Electronics, Sony PlayStation, etc.) or a branded identity structure (each business, unit or product has its own name, e.g. Proctor and Gamble (Always, Ariel, Duracell, etc.), Inditex (Zara, Massimo Dutti, etc.), and Unilever (Becel, Lipton, etc.))?

The third step is to develop and implement the strategic decisions. The decisions must be put into action. Plans must be elaborated and implemented, for instance about the brand architecture, the role of communication and the communication tactics.

However, it is not just about implementing new strategies. It is also about a dynamic, ongoing process during which the corporate brand is constantly negotiated between an organisation and its stakeholders. This is the reason why it is important as the fourth step to continuously make evaluations of the development of the brand and of the achievements of the strategic goals.

According to Hatch and Schultz (2001) and Schultz et al. (2005), the ideal branding process takes its point of departure in the corporate brand identity. It constitutes the core aligning of the three strategic stars: (1) the strategic vision, i.e. the central idea that expresses top management's aspiration for the achievements of the company in the future; (2) the organisational culture, i.e. values, beliefs and basic assumptions that reflect the heritage of the company as well as the (emotional) relations of the employees to the company; and (3) stakeholder images, i.e. views of the organisation developed by its external stakeholders.

To be able to evaluate to what extent the three strategic stars are aligned, Hatch and Schultz have developed the corporate branding tool kit. By means of three sets of diagnostic questions the organisation can find out whether gaps have opened between the three interfaces of: (1) vision and culture (a gap opens when employees do not understand or support the strategy); (2) culture and image (a gap opens when the organisation does not live up to its promises); and (3) vision and image (a gap opens when there is a conflict between the vision and the views of the stakeholders).

Measuring corporate image and reputation

The image and reputation of private companies are measured and evaluated on a regular basis by various organisations. These evaluations are followed closely by the companies themselves and by many of their key stakeholders (competitors, investors, employees and the media). It is one of the characteristics of the new 'audit society' (Power 1997) or 'evaluation society' (Dahler-Larsen 2011).

Rankings in business magazines and newspapers such as *Fortune* magazine's Most Admired Companies survey or the *Financial Times'* World's Most Respected Companies are among the most well-known and

Chapter 12 Corporate image, reputation and identity

> ### Explore 12.1
>
> **The reputation of universities**
>
> Is your university or business school represented on one or more academic ranking lists such as Times Higher Education? If yes, on which list(s) is it represented? What are the criteria applied by the ranking list(s) in question? How good or bad are the selected criteria? Is it the university or business school that is ranked, or is it a specific faculty or department? What is the position of your university or business school?
>
> Who will be affected by such rankings (if anybody)? And how?
>
> What made you choose your university or business school? Geographical location, recommendations made by your parents or friends (including students who already studied at the university or business school), or an official university or business school ranking?
>
> Go to the Times Higher Education's website and see how this ranking list has been made.

respected rankings. *Fortune* magazine evaluates the image and reputation of a company based on criteria such as quality of management, quality of products and services, innovativeness, long-term investment value, financial soundness, ability to attract, development and retainment of talent, and community and environmental responsibility. The *Financial Times* also includes criteria such as successful change management, business leadership, and robust and human corporate culture.

An organisation of interest when it comes to measuring the images and reputations of companies, cities and nations, is the Reputation Institute in New York. It is a private consultancy and research firm with a global network of local offices, which has specialised in corporate reputation management. The work of the Reputation Institute is based on a reputation quotient model launched as the Global RepTrak™ Pulse in 2006. Not only the images and reputations of large companies are assessed. Also the symbolic capital of public authorities such as municipalities and taxation authorities, cities such as Tokyo, Sydney, Copenhagen and Vienna (the top four of the City RepTrak™ in 2018), and countries such as Sweden, Finland, Switzerland and Norway (the top four of the Country RepTrak™ in 2018) are being evaluated (see Explore 12.2).

> ### Explore 12.2
>
> **Reputation Institute and the Global RepTrak™ Pulse**
>
> The Reputation Institute (RI) was founded in 1997 by Charles J. Fombrun, Professor of Management at Stern School of Business, New York University, and Cees B.M. van Riel, Professor of Corporate Communication at the Business School at Erasmus University. The Reputation Institute first evaluates the reputation of large private companies based on a measuring tool formerly known as the Reputation Quotient model, and which was relaunched in 2006 as the Global RepTrak™ Pulse. The model assumes that the reputation of a company is based on the emotional attachment between a company and its stakeholders (admiration, trust, good feeling and general esteem). Seven key dimensions are the drivers behind the reputation of a company: products/services, innovation, workplace, governance, citizenship, leadership and performance. Each of these key dimensions comprises a series of attributes.
>
> The Reputation Institute also evaluates city and country reputations. Go to the website of the Reputation Institute and examine how both the Global RepTrak™ Pulse, the City RepTrak™ and the Country RepTrak™ are structured and how these measurement tools are applied.

A critical point of view

Brands are pervasive and ubiquitous. We take them for granted – from pop art to McDonald's, from Starbucks to Greenpeace, brands are the mechanism that connects organizations and people.

(Kornberger 2010: 263–264)

During the last two decades, the concepts of image, reputation and identity have conquered the mind and soul of many a communication executive or manager, not only in the business world, but also in many public organisations (see the introduction of this chapter). However, the popularity of corporate communication is counter-balanced by a growing number of critical voices coming from within the academic community. One of these voices belongs to two Danish communication researchers, Lars Thøger Christensen and Mette Morsing, joined by their American colleague, Georges Cheney.

Christensen et al. (2008) define corporate communication as 'a management ideal with wide-ranging organizational implications' (Christensen et al. 2008: 168). At the heart of their critique lies the concept of integration – that is, the idea that for an organisation to be effective and efficient there must be a high degree of coherence between the strategic vision of the organisation, its culture, its internal and external communication activities, and its image and reputation among external stakeholders.

One of the organisational implications of applying an integrated perspective in practice, according to the three scholars, is that this approach easily transforms the organisation into a tightly coupled system, that is, a system where input and output are closely connected, and where even the slightest change in principle will prompt a response (action) in all parts of the system. To put it differently, in such a system integrated corporate branding will be enforced as a global solution turning all the members of the organisation (top management, employees) into the same type of 'brand evangelists' (Ind 2001).

The idea may seem very promising, especially if you adopt a traditional leadership style based on control and predictability. However, Christensen et al. (2008) claim an integrated perspective will also make the organisation vulnerable. Today, both private and public organisations are faced with many expectations and demands from their stakeholders. At the same time, organisations are operating in socio-cultural contexts, which have become much more complex and dynamic due to globalisation and new information and communication technologies. They have to demonstrate 'strategic readiness', they have to prepare for change.

Flexibility is the solution to this new situation. But how flexible is an organisation whose communication activities are based on the idea of integration? If we return to the Carlsberg case: how, on the one hand, can the Carlsberg Group integrate the local (national) brand heritage of the Danish brewery with all the new brands and, on the other, be flexible enough to be able to meet the expectations and demands from both internal and external stakeholders working and living in more than 150 different markets, cultures and societies all over the world? See also Frandsen and Johansen (2014) for a 'criticism of the criticism'.

Summary

This chapter has sought to show how the field of corporate communication and the concepts of corporate image, reputation and identity have become important in a society obsessed by brands and the idea of a 'symbolic capital'. Image is the global evaluation (comprising a set of beliefs, ideas, feelings and impressions) that a person has about a product and/or an organisation. Compared to image, reputation is a time-based and value-based construct. It is built up over time and based on the relationship between the organisation and its multiple stakeholders. Identity refers to who an organisation is, and what it stands for. An organisation very often has multiple identities and images. In a complex, dynamic and ever-changing society, organisations must balance the need for both integration (global control) and flexibility (local responsiveness).

Bibliography

Aaker, D. and J.C. Meyers (1982). *Advertising Management*. New Dehli: Prentice Hall.

Albert, S. and D.A. Whetten (1985). 'Organizational identity', in L.L. Cummings and M.M. Staw (eds). *Research in Organizational Behavior* Vol. 7 (pp. 263–95). Greenwich, Conn.: JAI Press.

Alvesson, M. (1990). 'Organization: from substance to image?' *Organization Studies* 11(3): 373–94.

Balmer, J.M.T. (1995). 'Corporate branding and connoisseurship', *Journal of Grand Management* 21(1): 22–46.

Balmer, J.M.T. and S.A. Greyser (eds) (2003). *Revealing the Corporation: Perspectives on identity, image, reputation, corporate branding, and corporate-level marketing*. London: Routledge.

Barnett, M.L. and A. Hoffman (2008). 'Beyond corporate reputation: Managing reputational interdependence', *Corporate Reputation Review* 11(1): 1–9.

Barnett, M.L. and T.G. Pollock (eds) (2012). *The Oxford Handbook of Corporate Reputation*. Oxford: Oxford University Press.

Barron, D.N. and M. Rolfe (2012). 'It ain't what you do. It's who you do it with: Distinguishing reputation and status', in M.L. Barnett and T.G. Pollock (eds). *The Oxford Handbook of Corporate Reputation* (pp. 160–78). Oxford: Oxford University Press.

Bauman, Z. (1996). 'From pilgrim to tourist – or a short history of identity', in S. Hall and P. du Gay (eds). *Questions of Cultural Identity*. London: Sage.

Bernays, E.L. (1977). 'Down with image, up with reality', *Public Relations Quarterly* 22(1): 12–14.

Christensen, L.T. and G. Cheney (2000). 'Self-absorption and self-seduction in the corporate identity game', in M. Schultz, M.J. Hatch and M. Holten Larsen (eds). *The Expressive Organization: Linking Identity, Reputation, and the Corporate Brand*. Oxford: Oxford University Press.

Christensen, L.T., M. Morsing and G. Cheney (2008). *Corporate Communications: Convention, complexity, and critique*. Los Angeles: Sage.

Coombs, W.T. (2015). *Ongoing Crisis Communication: Planning, managing, and responding*, 4th edition. Los Angeles: Sage.

Coombs, W.T. and S.J. Holladay (2015). 'Public relations' 'relationship identity' in research: Enlightenment or illusion. *Public Relations Review* 41(5): 689–95.

Cornelissen, J. (2017). *Corporate Communication: A guide to theory and practice*, 5th edition. London: Sage.

Dahler-Larsen, P. (2011). *The Evaluation Society*. Stanford: Stanford University Press.

Devers, C.E., T. Dewett, Y. Mishina and C.A. Belsito (2009). 'A general theory of organizational stigma', *Organization Science* 20(1): 154–71.

Dowling, G. (1986). 'Managing your corporate image', *Industrial Marketing Management* 15: 109–15.

Dowling, G. (2001). *Creating Corporate Reputations: Identity, image and performance*. Oxford: Oxford University Press.

Fombrun, C.J. (1996). *Reputation: Realizing value from the corporate image*. Boston, MA: Harvard Business School Press.

Frandsen, F. and W. Johansen (2014). 'Corporate communication', in V. Bhatia and S. Bremmer (eds). *The Routledge Handbook of Language and Professional Communication*. London: Routledge.

Frandsen, F. and W. Johansen (2015). 'Organisations, stakeholders, and intermediaries: Towards a General Theory', *International Journal of Strategic Communication* 9(4): 253–71.

Gilmore, J.H. and B.J. Pine II (2007). *Authenticity: What consumers really want*. Boston: Harvard Business School Press.

Grunig, J.E. (1993). 'Image and substance: From symbolic to behavioral relationships', *Public Relations Review* 19(2): 121–39.

Grunig, J.E. (2006). 'After 50 years: The value and values of public relations'. The Institute for Public Relations 45th Annual Distinguished Lecture. The Yale Club, New York. 9 November 2006.

Grunig, L., J.E. Grunig, and D. Dozier (2002). *Excellent Public Relations and Effective Organizations: A Study of Communication Management in Three Countries*. Mahwah, NJ: Lawrence Erlbaum.

Hatch, M.J. and M. Schultz (2000). 'Scaling the Tower of Babel: Relational differences between identity, image, and culture in organizations', in M. Schultz, M.J. Hatch and M. Holten Larsen (eds). *The Expressive Organization: Linking Identity, Reputation, and the Corporate Brand*. Oxford: Oxford University Press.

Hatch, M.J. and M. Schultz (2001). 'Are the strategic stars aligned for your corporate brand? *Harvard Business Review*. February 2001.

Hatch, M.J. and M. Schultz (2008). *Taking Brand Initiative*. San Francisco: Jossey-Bass.

Ind, N. (2001). *Living the Brand: How to transform every member of your organization into a brand champion*. London: Kogan Page.

Jenkins, R. (2008). *Social Identity*. Oxon: Routledge.

King, A.A., M.J. Lenox and M.L. Barnet (2002). 'Strategic responses to the reputation commons problem', in A. Hoffman and M.J. Ventresca (eds). *Organizations, Policy, and the Natural Environment: Institutional and Strategic Perspectives* (pp. 393–406). Palo Alto: Stanford University Press.

Kornberger, M. (2010). *Brand Society: How brands transform management and lifestyle*. Cambridge: Cambridge University Press.

Larkin, J. (2003). *Strategic Reputation Risk Management*. New York: Palgrave Macmillan.

Ledingham, J.A. (2003). 'Explicating relationship management as a general theory of public relations', *Journal of Public Relations Research* 15(2): 181–98.

Ledingham, J.A. (2005). 'Relationship management theory', in R.L. Heath (ed.). *Encyclopedia of Public Relations Vol. 2*. Thousand Oaks, CA: Sage.

Power, M. (1997). *The Audit Society: Rituals of verification*. Oxford: Oxford University Press.

Schultz, M., M.J. Hatch and M. Holten Larsen (2000). 'Introduction: Why the expressive organization?' in M. Schultz, M.J. Hatch and M. Holten Larsen (eds). *The Expressive Organization: Linking identity, reputation, and the corporate brand*. Oxford: Oxford University Press.

Schultz, M. (2005). 'A cross-disciplinary perspective on corporate branding', in M. Schultz, Y.M. Antorini and F.F. Csaba (eds) *Corporate Branding: Purpose, people, process*. Copenhagen: Copenhagen Business School Press.

Schultz, M., Y.M. Antorini and F.F. Csaba (eds) (2005). *Corporate Branding: Purpose, people, process*. Copenhagen: Copenhagen Business School Press.

van Riel, C.B.M. (1995). *Principles of Corporate Communication*. London: Prentice Hall.

Wan, H.-H. and R. Schell (2007). 'Reassessing corporate image: An examination of how image bridges symbolic relationships with behavioral relationships', *Journal of Public Relations Research* 19(1): 25–45.

Whetten, D.A. (1997). 'Theory development and the study of corporate reputation', *Corporate Reputation Review* 1(1): 26–34.

Websites

Carlsberg Breweries: www.carlsberg.com
Financial Times: www.ft.com
Fortune: www.money.cnn.com/magazines/fortune
Reputation Institute: www.reputationinstitute.com
Times Higher Education: www.timeshighereducation.co.uk

CHAPTER 13

Johanna Fawkes

Public relations' professionalism and ethics

Source: ChameleonsEye/Shutterstock

Learning outcomes

By the end of this chapter you should be able to:
- discuss whether or not public relations is a profession
- apply capability approaches to public relations as a profession
- describe a variety of approaches to professional ethics
- compare and critique views of public relations ethics
- identify different ways of imagining public relations
- evaluate the effect of PR images on PR ethics
- reflect on the way you make ethical decisions.

Structure

- Defining professions – public relations and professionalism
- Is public relations a profession?
- Reframing the profession through a capabilities approach
- Professional ethics and public relations

Introduction

This chapter deals with two key concepts in public relations – professionalism and ethics. The first idea is usually taken for granted, as everyone assumes public relations is a profession, but the second is often avoided because it leads to serious confusion and discomfort. Most writers will try and solve this unease by giving you a box for decision making or a list of 'dos and don'ts'. This chapter takes a different approach and encourages the reader to understand – not avoid – their own confusion on ethical issues.

But first, it explores ideas about professions and professionalism, and whether or not they contribute to society. Different ways of understanding public relations, including a capability approach help explain the variety of functions that comprise the profession, worldwide. Given the importance of ethics to claiming professional status, the chapter then looks at different kinds of professional ethics, and discusses some of the philosophical issues behind codes and ethical policies. It also asks whether ethical claims are truer in theory than in practice. After each description of an ethical approach, examples are given where public relations scholarship has adopted that approach.

The main case study concerns a senior press officer who felt under pressure to 'spin' her employer's story and is given in depth to illustrate the complexities of trying to operate to ethical standards in real life.

Let's start with some examples of the kind of ethical conflict that can confront public relations practitioners and students (see Think about 13.1).

Think about 13.1 — Ethical communication dilemmas

- You work for a digital communications agency and become aware the data you are using to target potential customers is acquired by dubious methods. What do you do?
- An online retail client asks you to blame IT issues for poor customer ratings. You know there have been real problems with deliveries. How do you frame your response?
- You're on work placement and the public relations agency asks you to say you're doing student research for the university/college rather than for the agency.
- You're pitching for a new account that will save the agency. You see that the previous team left their pitch details in the waiting room. Do you use this information?
- A high street coffee chain that's been getting protests over its treatment of staff and suppliers asks you to do an ethical makeover – to its image, not its employment or trade activities. What should you do?
- You organise meetings between the local authority and community groups to explain new council policies. Do you make it clear that the authority is interested in their views but unlikely to make major changes?

Feedback

We'll come back to these examples at the end of the chapter, so you can compare how you think about them now and later.

Mini case study 13.1 — The Bell Pottinger scandal

The London-based global PR agency Bell Pottinger was established in 1985, enjoyed the support of prime ministers and boasted of its global success in working for regimes and dictatorships with dubious human rights records. But its ethical downfall came, not from its past client list, but from revelations in 2017 that it was running a secret campaign in South Africa to stir up racial tensions on behalf of the powerful Gupta family, which sought to influence upcoming elections (Conner 2017).

The UK trade association, the Public Relations and Communications Association (PRCA) called it the 'worst

Picture 13.1 Bell Pottinger went out of business after several ethical breaches of industry codes of conduct. Challenges to the company included their handling of communications about fracking in the UK (*source:* Andrew Cowie/AFP/Getty Images)

ethical breach in [our] history' and expelled the agency from its membership, a highly unusual step. The scandal surrounding this campaign led to the closure of the South African branch of the organisation, but this did not prevent the collapse of the whole agency in the following weeks. While its founder, Lord Tim Bell, distanced himself from the debacle, his attitude to ethics may explain the culture of the agency: 'Morality is a job for priests. Not PR men' (Segal 2018).

Defining professions – public relations and professionalism

The strongest defence against scandals such as the Bell Pottinger story is the claim to be a profession, which, as this section explains, involves a sense of duty to society as well as client.

The term professional is used very loosely in public relations literature, yet is the foundation of many claims to reputation, autonomy and social value. It is used as if its meaning is self-evident, though associations may vary from 'doing a decent job' or 'getting paid' through 'objectivity' to aspects of appearance, such as suits and briefcases or even masculinity and whiteness. The description offered by a major US report into public relations education illustrates this:

> If you work in public relations, or teach it, you probably have used the word 'profession' from time to time. Indeed, when we define public relations in its broadest sense—as an essential management function that helps an organization and its publics build relationships that enable them to understand and support one another—a case can certainly be made that public relations is a profession (PRSA: 11).

Gregory describes public relations professionalism as 'taking education and training as seriously as other professions. . . and [joining] the appropriate professional body' (Gregory 2009: 275). However, the case for the professional status of public relations proves to be somewhat elusive on closer inspection.

Professions are usually seen as originating in clergy, medical work and law (fifteenth century), with changes in the industrial revolution (nineteenth century) and the introduction of nationalised bureaucracies for managing society (twentieth century). Recent decades have seen the emergence of knowledge workers (twenty-first century), the broad grouping in which public relations resides. Similar developments can be found across European countries, with differences beyond the region. It is interesting to note that the older professions, particularly medicine and law, continue to earn respect and have not lost professional status, despite being joined by so many new occupations. Freidson (1994) distinguishes between the older professions that have legally protected licences to practice and those less prestigious occupations that are protected by professional bodies. The discussion in this chapter focuses on the latter group, to which public relations belongs.

The study of professions can be broadly grouped into what are sometimes called *trait* or *functionalist* approaches and those considered to be based in understanding of *power* or *revisionist* approaches. The first grouping has its roots in the work of founding sociologist Emile Durkheim (1858–1917), who stresses the positive rewards of social duty, including the creation of 'solidariness' within groups and societies. He theorises the role of groups and institutions as buffers between excessive state domination and individual alienation, including the family, religious institutions and 'occupational groups' or professions. This somewhat idealistic approach was adopted – and adapted – as part of the wider, functionalist approach spearheaded by US scholar Talcott Parsons (1951). Parsons endowed professions with moral purpose that was not always evident empirically (Sciulli 2005), while the detailed discussion focused on definitions and descriptions of professional work (its *traits*), rather than scrutiny of moral claims. This view dominates the field and underpins the role of professional bodies and codes of ethics in most Western professional or occupational groups.

From the mid-1960s, this concept of professionalism was critiqued and challenged by the power approach (or *revisionists,* to use Sciulli's 2005 term) drawing on the seminal work of Max Weber (1864–1920) following the English translation of his *Theory of social and economic organisation* in 1964. While both are concerned with the division of labour in society, Weber is more critical than Durkheim about the role of professions and their acquisition and maintenance of power over others. As Sciulli (2005: 917) puts it,

> *revisionists also consider the rise of expert occupations with monopolies in the services market to be, if anything, a malevolent force in civil society, not*

a salutary addition. They reject outright as apologetic and ideological Parsons' conjecture that professions contribute in any way, let alone intrinsically, to social integration as opposed to social control.

One of the leading scholars of professionalism, Magali Larson (1977) draws on Weberian analysis to critique what she terms the 'professional project', the means whereby a group of workers evolve through occupational status to form a profession, a movement which involves creating professional monopolies, guarding them in jurisdictional contests and mythologising their achievements. She deploys Weber's model of the ideal-typical profession, by which desired characteristics and domains are outlined, not as a descriptor of reality but as a benchmark or reference point, suggesting professions have proceeded as if the idealised version was descriptive rather than prescriptive. Larson emphasises professionalism as a dynamic process of securing and maintaining social status, 'the process by which producers of special services sought to constitute *and control* a market for their expertise . . . Professionalization appears also as a collective assertion of special social status and as a collective process of upward social mobility' (1977: *xvi*, emphasis in original). Revisionists, such as those cited above, consider the trait approach moribund and inflexible; yet professional bodies and practitioners still tend to conceive of professions according to their core tasks.

Despite these disputes, it is worth closing this brief overview of professionalism literature with Cooper's (2004: 61–63) definitions of a profession as comprising:

- esoteric knowledge – theoretical or technical – not available to the general population;
- commitment to social values, such as health or justice;
- national organisation to set standards, control membership, liaise with wider society;
- extra-strong moral commitment to support professional values.

Is public relations a profession?

Those scholars who have seriously asked whether public relations warrants professional status (Bivins 1993; Breit and Demetrious 2010; Pieczka and L'Etang 2001; Sriramesh and Hornaman 2006; van Ruler 2005) have tended to conclude in the negative as it meets some but not all of the criteria of a profession outlined above, given the open entry to this work and the difficulty of imposing ethical and other standards on the membership. L'Etang (2008: 26) goes further, suggesting that 'only when practitioners have a good facility to understand and carry out a variety of research can the occupation move forwards to professional status'. And of course, unlike medicine or law, anyone can practise PR; as Macnamara (2012) points out, only 3,000 practitioners belonged to the Australian professional body in 2009 out of an estimated 21,000 potential members, a point made earlier by van Ruler (2005) regarding European representation. However, undaunted by the difficulty of controlling practitioners, the field has strenuously sought professional status, because:

that would give credibility and reputation to the industry, increase the accountability and credibility of practitioners, enhance the quality of work produced by practitioners, and give practitioners greater opportunities to contribute to organizational decision making. (Sriramesh and Hornaman 2006: 156)

In other words, professional status is good for business. The last point is particularly poignant as it speaks to the longing to be taken seriously in the boardroom and looks to professionalism as offering a path to that table. This is also consistent with Larson's understanding of the professional project, the means by which an occupational group improves its social standing. This debate is contextualised by van Ruler (2005: 161), who summarises the literature of professions to produce four models of professions applicable to public relations:

a. *knowledge model,* in which professionalisation develops from expertise, with a commitment to both the client and society;

b. *status model,* whereby an organised elite secure power and autonomy;

c. *competition model,* which focuses on the client's demands and evaluation in competition with other professionals; and

d. *personality model,* which is suggested as the development of experts who build a reputation with clients by virtue of expertise and personal charisma.

Van Ruler finds that the knowledge model is strongly represented in US literature, with the competition model endorsed by others, though she points out that the first is over-reliant on the 'body of knowledge', while the second leads to confused identity – she argues that public relations needs a professional 'brand'.

Sriramesh and Hornaman's (2006: 157) survey of literature suggests that for public relations to be accepted as a profession (which the majority of their sources say has not yet happened), it must satisfy the following criteria:

1. Maintaining a code of ethics and professional values and norms
2. Commitment to serve in the public interest and be socially responsible
3. Having a body of esoteric, scholarly knowledge
4. Having specialised and standardised education, including graduate study
5. Having technical and research skills
6. Providing a unique service to an organisation and the community
7. Membership in professional organisations
8. Having autonomy in organisations to make communication-related decisions.

This summary is close to the definitions explored above, though it's not clear which of these hurdles PR fails to leap. Pieczka and L'Etang (2001) are critical scholars of public relations who challenge assertions made about public relations' professionalism. They believe open access to practice and unenforceable ethics provide obstacles to professional status, noting a tendency to describe what PR professionals *do* (the trait approach), rather than reflect on their wider role which, they say, is due to 'professionalisation efforts that necessarily rely on an idealistic understanding of the profession' (Pieczka and L'Etang 2001: 229). As they say, most approaches to professionalism in public relations rely on a very optimistic view of the profession in society, based on Durkheim and Talcott Parson's benign understanding of professionalism, concepts abandoned by the sociology of professionalism in the 1970s. Their view, that PR is not a profession, is shared by McKie and Munshi (2007: 102) who note that the concepts of public relations as a profession which are prevalent in core texts tend to reinforce idealised versions of the field.

Of course, PR is not alone in finding the concept elusive and this chapter will continue to use the term, because as Cheney (2010: 7) points out, 'occupation . . . is not as suggestive of lifestyle, social pressures and one's place in society'. I particularly like Brown and Duguid's (2001) phrase 'community of practice' because it includes academics and other commentators, not just practitioners, and this chapter uses the term profession in this encompassing spirit.

Many professions have been exposed in recent years as falling below their self-proclaimed standards, including banking, accounting, the clergy, the medical and caring professions, professional sports people and sports institutions – the list goes on. The Edelman public relations agency conducts an annual survey measuring the trust that the public holds in different institutions, such as government, media, educators, charities and so on. In recent years, trust among the general public of all these institutions has plummeted though it is regaining some ground among the well informed (Edelman 2019). They note trust has been transferred from institutions to employers, 'Globally, 75 percent of people trust "my employer" to do what is right, significantly more than NGOs (57 percent), business (56 percent) and media (47 percent)' (Edelman 2019). See the company website for past and present reports.

However, public relations does have a particular problem with the concept of professionalism, as the Bell Pottinger story (above) illustrates. Every day, websites such as spinwatch.com and corporatewatch.com provide examples of PR ethical lapses, from creating false grass-roots organisations (astroturfing) to PR people masquerading as journalists. Some scholars (see Sussman 2011) consider public relations as propaganda for corporations and industries, such as pharmaceuticals and fossil fuels, which have contributed to the degradation of human and planetary existence. In these debates there is often confusion about what public relations does, with the emphasis on media relations and lobbying rather than strategic communication. The next section tries to clarify the situation.

Reframing the profession through a capabilities approach

A major obstacle to establishing public relations as a profession lies in the confusion around the scope of the sector. Hutton (1999, 2001, 2010) considers that public relations' failure to identify its core concept threatens its very survival, especially as its closest rival, marketing, is much clearer about what it is as a discipline. This section summarises a two-year project undertaken by the University of Huddersfield for the Global Alliance (GA) to construct a framework that would help professional bodies worldwide more accurately describe the scope of the field (Gregory, A. and Fawkes, J. 2019). In response, a nine-country academic 2019 research partnership was created, representing institutions in seven continents (Asia, Scandinavia, Europe, Africa, Australasia, North America, South America) who agreed to work with their national and regional professional associations and employers on a country-based research project. The results from each country were synthesized to form a matrix comprising the core capabilities of public relations as a profession (i.e. applied across the field, not expected of each individual). The brief from the GA was that the research should: offer practical value to GA affiliated professional bodies and their members, worldwide; reflect cultural and regional variations in public relations as a global profession; be forward looking in its approach; and meet academic standards for rigour.

Unlike previous work on public relations' competencies (Gregory 2008; Manley and Valin 2017; Tench et al. 2013), which focus on the skills required of individual PR practitioners at different career stages, this research expanded concepts of capability in professions (Stan Lester 2014; 2016; Sen 1999). The core concepts of Sen's capability approach are summarised as: the centrality of a person's (or group's) well-being to human flourishing; distinctions between the capacity to flourish and the functioning or demonstration of valued achievements; and the freedom to choose what is valued. It is an approach that stresses potential and identifies obstacles to achieving potential (internal and external) rather than describing existing skill sets (Walker and Unterhalter 2007: 2–7).

This offered valuable insights for researching not only what practitioners considered to be the core capabilities of the public relations profession as a whole, but also what might prevent individuals – and the profession – from realising their potential. Using a mix of expert panels, surveys and focus groups in each participating country, the research team identified a set of 11 capability statements, which describe an aspect of public relations seen as core to the discipline, together with sets of sub-capabilities, which provide more detail and depth to the eleven statements. While individual country-based research showed some (often minor) differences in emphasis, there was strong agreement that the final set of statements reflected the views of practitioners and academics consulted across the continents (see Table 13.1).

Communication Capabilities

To align communication strategies with organisational purpose and values

To identify and address communication problems proactively

To conduct formative and evaluative research to underpin communication strategies and tactics

To communicate effectively across a full range of platforms and technologies

Organisational Capabilities

To facilitate relationships and build trust with internal and external stakeholders and communities

To build and enhance organisational reputation

To provide contextual intelligence

Professional Capabilities (those expected of any professional)

To provide valued counsel and be a trusted advisor

To offer organisational leadership

To work within an ethical framework on behalf of the organization, in line with professional and societal expectations

To develop self and others, including continuing professional learning

Capabilities	Sub Capabilities
To align communication strategies with organisational purpose and values	You set clear communication objectives that are aligned to organisational objectives and then see them through
	You act as an architect of communication plans, enacting the purpose, values and policies of the organisation
	You understand how communication can – and cannot – help an organisation realise its objectives
To identify and address communication problems proactively	You create short and long-term narratives to facilitate communication with multiple organisational stakeholders
	You identify opportunities to design organisational communication, and outline core content
	You develop integrated communication operations

Capabilities	Sub Capabilities
To conduct formative and evaluative research to underpin communication strategies and tactics	You use research to listen to and understand situations before, during and after communication and relationship-building activities
	You manage research design, data collection and analysis to improve communication outcomes
	You establish evaluation systems to demonstrate the impact of communication
To communicate effectively across a full range of platforms and technologies	You have command of communication specialties, such as investor relations, and understand the optimum channels for specific stakeholders
	You communicate effectively across paid, earned, shared and owned (PESO) channels
	You have or can source strong written and visual skills to create and tell stories that engage and connect with diverse publics
	You synthesise complex concepts and convert them to simple, clear and relevant content
To facilitate relationships and build trust with internal and external stakeholders and communities	You identify, analyse and listen to stakeholders and their communication needs
	You develop stakeholder engagement strategies and partnerships that are mutually beneficial
	You communicate sensitively with stakeholders and communities across a range of cultural and other values and beliefs
To build and enhance organisational reputation	You identify, analyse and strategically advise on key issues and risks for the organisation
	You help the organisation to define and enact its purpose and values
	You help shape organisational culture and its processes
	You understand and manage key intangible assets (e.g. brand, culture, sustainability)
To provide contextual intelligence	You see the bigger picture - socially, culturally, politically, technologically and economically
	You identify strategic opportunities and threats, issues and trends
	You operate in a connected world, demonstrating broad understanding of local and global diversity in culture, values and beliefs
To provide valued counsel and be a trusted advisor	You combine a long term perspective with the agility to manage crises
	You offer strategic counsel to executive management, particularly regarding the interests of multiple stakeholders
	You influence organizational decision-making and development
	You negotiate with empathy and respect for all parties
To offer organisational leadership	You are part of or have access to the executive management team and help build internal alliances within the organization
	You demonstrate communication leadership by encouraging management based on dialogue
	You demonstrate business and financial acumen through sound knowledge of the organisation's business and core processes
To work within an ethical framework on behalf of the organisation, in line with professional and society's expectations	You consider business objectives in the light of society's expectations
	You clarify the consequences of a proposed action on others, ensuring potential outcomes are understood by decision-makers
	You understand and apply ethical frameworks
	You recognise and observe the societal obligations of professionals
To develop self and others, including continuing professional learning	You take responsibility for your own continuous professional development, through a range of activities including training and education
	You participate in industry events, represent the industry in public, and educate others on the role and value of public relations to employers and clients
	You are able to offer professional guidance which involves, motivates and contributes to personal and team development

Table 13.1 Global capability framework for public relations and communication management (*source:* Gregory, A. and Fawkes, J. (2019). A Global capability framework: Reframing public relations for a changing world. Public Relations Review. Vol. 45, No. 3, Article 101781 https://doi.org/10.1016/j.pubrev.2019.05.002)

266 Part 2 PUBLIC RELATIONS THEORIES AND CONCEPTS

It is important to note that the framework is not a definitive statement and that it encompasses everything the profession is capable of, whether in an organisation or more generally. No individual will be expected to perform across all these indicators. It allows for specialisms within teams and within the occupational group as a whole. The table encourages individuals and managers to identify personal or team strengths and highlights other capabilities that may or may not be relevant to the particular workplace. This flexibility and practical application should help address issues of identity at the level of individual practitioner, group or department, and for the profession as a whole.

So far, this chapter has explored issues of professionalism and whether or not public relations qualifies for the term. It has established that the commitment to social value or ethics is a core element of claiming to be a profession. The next section explores professional ethics in more detail, providing examples of where scholars have applied each approach to public relations.

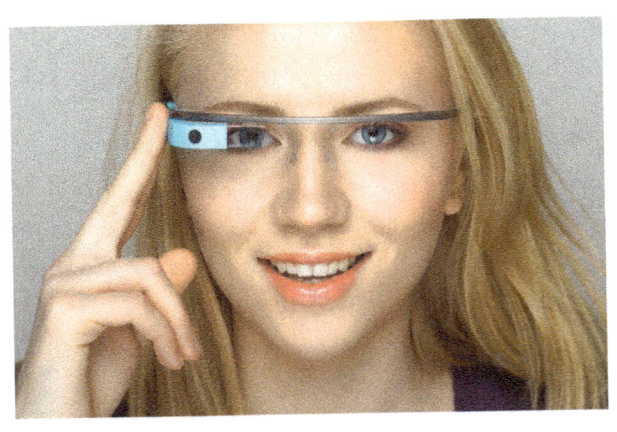

Picture 13.2 As suspicion about data usage rises, global tech companies are turning to ethics (*source:* Peppinuzzo/Shutterstock)

Professional ethics and public relations

For the first half of the twentieth century, professional ethics focused on the specific conflicts facing particular professions, such as patient confidentiality or accounting procedures – following the trait approach discussed

Box 13.1
Digital ethics

As suspicion about data usage rises, global tech companies are turning to ethics, according to analysts (Stackpoole 2019). Companies like Facebook and Google are under pressure from law makers in the USA and the European Union, as well as users. Some commentators suggest that the drive to deliver data ethics is driven by fear, 'Given that the tech giants . . . have been ethics-free zones from their foundations [and] owe their growth partly to the fact that they have, to date, been entirely untroubled by legal regulation' (Naughton 2019).

Indeed, failure to engage with the ethics around cyber hacking and data breaches has public relations implications: 'If you don't spend the time and money that might be necessary to get the ethics right, you could have a horrible public relations nightmare,' said Lucy C. Erickson, an American Association for the Advancement of Science & Technology Policy Fellow hosted by the National Science Foundation (quoted in Stackpoole 2019).

However, their efforts are not always successful: in 2019, Google abandoned its Ethics Advisory Council on Artificial Intelligence (AI) only days after announcing it, because of the public relations damage caused by the selection of Council members, including a leading Trump supporter with a history of discriminatory statements and a drone company with military interests. Luciano Floridi, head of ethics at Oxford University's Internet Institute, described Google's Council appointments as 'a grave error and sends the wrong message about the nature and goals' of the council. 'From an ethical perspective, Google has misjudged what it means to have representative views in a broader context,' he said (Water 2019). Moreover, Google's code of ethics has been criticised as consisting of empty promises to be 'accountable' with no clarity of process or regulation (Naughton 2019), echoing points about weak codes of ethics made elsewhere in this chapter.

Facebook was listed in the US PRDaily.com list of worst PR disasters of 2018 for repeated ethics violations that led to reputational damage and scrutiny from law makers in many countries. It was accused of using user data for competitive advantage and in political campaigns, including the Trump campaign and the Brexit referendum, without informing users. The journalist who exposed this, Carol Cadwalladr, explains the story in a very clear TED talk (2019). The range and depth of these breaches have raised serious concerns about the ethical culture in the global company (Working 2018).

> **Explore 13.1**
>
> The following links take you to a variety of posts written by practitioners about how they practice ethically and reflecting on the problems facing the profession regarding ethical standards. Several discuss the Bell Pottinger case outlined above and consider its implications for public relations as a whole.
>
> - Ella Minty, Talking about the State of PR (04/04/2019) (Ella Minty 2019).
> - Paul Seaman, Getting to Grips with Corporate and PR Ethics (21/05/2013) (Seaman 2013).
> - Flagship Consulting, The Importance of Ethics in OPR: How PR practitioners are upping their game (30/01/2018) (Flagship 2018).
> - Charlotte Dowd, MK Public Relations, The Importance of Ethics in PR (26/05/2017) (Dowd 2017).

> **Think about 13.2**
>
> How clear are the practitioners' statements about ethics? Are they convincing? Do they give examples or suggest ethical decisions can be hard?

> **Explore 13.2**
>
> Consequentialism concentrates on the effects or outcomes of ethical decisions – should you abandon a sick member of a group when escaping danger if that improves the survival chances for the rest? Should you immunise all babies against measles because the chances of a reaction to the jab are tiny compared to the health risks of measles to the whole population? These dilemmas are sometimes called 'The Trolley Problem' and the best explanation of this can be found in Professor Michel Sandel's Harvard University workshops on Justice (Sandel 2009) and a short discussion of the Trolley Problem (Sandel 2016).

earlier (Cooper 2004). Then wider reading of classical philosophy introduced ethics that focus on the consequences of actions or the duty of professionals to clients, patients or society generally or, more often, an ad-hoc combination of both. Most discussion of professional ethics concentrates on the relative merits of consequentialist and deontological approaches, as developed by Bentham and Kant respectively (Lefkowitz 2003), which are discussed below.

Utilitarianism/consequentialism

This approach was developed by Bentham and Mill in the nineteenth century and concerns making ethical choices that will maximise the 'good' for the majority. Bentham (1748–1832) stated that happiness was the highest human goal and that decisions that enhanced general, rather than individual, human happiness must be ethical. This approach underpins many modern business practices but can be used to justify deception ('if the truth were known, we'd go out of business and then everyone would be unhappy') or the victimisation of smaller or less powerful groups ('the customers prefer being served by men, so we don't employ women'). And, on an individual basis, how often have you told a friend he/she has a great figure/haircut/partner just to keep them happy?

Public relations applications of utilitarian ethics

This entails balancing duties to client and duties to society, something which many professionals find challenging, particularly where those clients may undertake lawful but harmful business, as in fossil fuels, tobacco, arms and so on. Challenges also arise when practitioners are asked to emphasise some aspects of a situation over others, for example stressing the good work a charity does to offset claims of abuse. Greenwashing is the term used to describe public relations campaigns which seek attention for an industry's environmental contributions, while downplaying environmental harms. So, in practice, it is important to examine such claims in detail before they can be said to be without harmful consequences.

Deontology

The eighteenth-century philosopher Immanuel Kant (1724–1804) argued that members of society have a range of duties (deontology) that we are all obliged to carry out, regardless of consequences. He also suggested we should behave as if our actions were subject to a universal law, and not make rules that apply only to us. He called this duty the *categorical imperative*, so that if it's OK for you to copy something from a friend's assignment, then it's OK for everyone to do so. He also says that we should treat others as 'ends in themselves' – that is, not as a means of getting something we want. This approach places a high value on honesty and respect and resembles the fundamental laws of many faiths, including the Golden Rule to 'Do Unto Others as You would be Done By' (Cooper 2004: 221). The difficulty with this approach is that it assumes high ideals beat in the breasts of all and offers no help when confronted with two conflicting duties. For example, a friend tells you, in absolute confidence, that she/he is cheating on their partner, who later asks you to tell him/her the truth. Do you break a promise or tell a lie?

Public relations applications of deontological ethics

Bowen (2007) declares that excellence ethics conform closely to Kant's imperatives, finding that 'ethics is a single excellent factor and the common underpinning of all factors that predict excellent public relations' (Bowen 2007: 275). Most writing from the excellence perspective on ethics draws on the systems theory (McElreath 1996) which underpins this approach. For example, Bowen (2008: 273) asserts that systems theory 'provides a normative theoretical framework to explain why public relations is the best suited function to advise senior management on matters of ethics'. Codes of ethics tend to follow the deontological approach and many PR codes stress that practitioners do not lie, withhold information, or behave unethically (Parkinson 2001). This is the discourse which generates the 'ethical guardian' image, which persists as an idea, despite L'Etang's (2003) challenge that public relations practitioners do not have the training to take on such an idealised role.

Discourse ethics

Discourse ethics is based on the idea of equal access to ethical debate and decision making, founded in Habermas' (1989) theory of dialogic communication. These principles have been summarised as:

- participants must have an equal chance to initiate and maintain discourse;
- participants must have an equal chance to make challenges, explanations or interpretations;
- interaction among participants must be free of manipulations, domination or control; and
- participants must be equal with respect to power. (Burleson and Kline 1979, cited in Day et al. 2001: 408)

Like the earlier descriptions, discourse ethics requires a process of reasoning and argument to ensure equality of access for all parties – a requirement not often found in contemporary professional practice (Curtin and Boynton 2001).

Public relations applications of dialogic ethics

An emerging theme in PR ethics is ethical dialogue (Kent and Taylor 2002), though Pieczka (2010: 117) suggests that while many public relations scholars have stressed the centrality of dialogue to the field, there has only been superficial engagement with dialogic theory and 'there is very little in public relations scholarship to help the discipline think about how dialogue can become an expert communication skill'. Curtin and Boynton (2001) explore how Habermas' discourse ethics has been applied to public relations by Pearson (1989) and Leeper (1996), particularly in attempts to construct procedures that will allow everyone taking part to communicate equally. However, as they point out, this rules out advocacy approaches and requires rational application of procedural rules, which are more likely to be observed in theory than practice. In a recent article (Bowen 2019) Shannon Bowen stresses the potential of good dialogue in building bridges, but also the high standards required to operate at this level:

In a world full of divisiveness, PR pros can enhance their own worth by being the reasonable voice, the facilitator of accord, and a leader respected by all who creates a zone of understanding. Being a conscientious facilitator requires us to be active and mindful, rather than simply convinced of the rightness of our causes. And we're required to be flexible, patient and resilient when forging a path through this difficult and divisive terrain.

Virtue ethics

In recent decades, virtue ethics, as described by MacIntyre (1984) and others, has had a considerable impact on the field of professional ethics. The virtue approach is particularly useful in its lack of reliance on external rules or codes to prescribe acceptable ethical behaviour, relying instead on character and reflection and making it an agent-based ethics. The main ideas are summarised as:

- an action is right if, and only if, it is what an agent with a virtuous character would do in the circumstances (this is sometimes turned into a game of 'what would [insert hero] do?');
- goodness is prior to rightness (trying to be good is a better moral guide than trying to do the right thing);
- the virtues are irreducibly plural intrinsic goods (there isn't a 'best' virtue);
- the virtues are objectively good (that is, honesty and justice are not subjective);
- some intrinsic goods are agent-relative (but some people will value some virtues more highly than others); and
- acting rightly does not require that we maximise the good (we aim to do the best possible in the circumstances, not to be perfect).

(Based on Oakley and Cocking 2001)

Aristotle uses the term *phronesis* to describe practical wisdom, which results not from being right but from finding a midpoint between extremes, so that courage lies somewhere between cowardice and recklessness, for example. The influence of virtue ethics on professional ethics has led to much examination of concepts such as integrity, transparency and authenticity in contemporary professional practice, with different authors championing particular virtues.

Public relations applications of virtue ethics

Rhetorical approaches to public relations ethics often deploy aspects of virtue ethics (Baker and Martinson 2002; Edgett 2002; Harrison and Galloway 2005; Pater and van Gils 2003). Ideas of advocacy are found here, as rhetoric is less hostile to persuasion and seeks to balance multiple demands rather than perform idealised acts. Heath (2007) explores the tension between the symmetry proposed as the basis of ethics in the excellence approach and the ethical aspects of advocacy, noting Grunig's (2001) acceptance that not all ethical dialogue can be symmetrical, or there would be no room for debate. Rather, argues Heath, ethical advocacy requires equal access to the structures and platforms of debate. Porter (2010: 128) goes further, suggesting that 'rhetoric provides a framework for ethical public relations'. Harrison and Galloway's (2005: 14) analysis of the public relations practitioner's roles found that 'virtue ethics can explain how "good" people can be led into acting badly because they care for the wrong person or organisation'. Edgett (2002) proposes ten principles for ethical advocacy, while Baker and Martinson (2002) suggest five principles, which they call the TARES test (Truthfulness, Authenticity, Respect, Equity and Social Responsibility), both drawing on virtue ethics (see Think about 13.1 and 13.2). As outlined earlier, this approach addresses the personality of the communicator and asks them to reflect on their own motives and behaviours, shifting the focus from action to agent.

Situationist/marketplace ethics

Situationist ethics combines consequentialist and deontological approaches by starting from the specifics of the ethical dilemma, before evaluating both principle and likely outcomes. This is sometimes called contingency ethics (Curtin and Boynton 2001), and a series of social psychological experiments have demonstrated the degree to which individual ethical behaviour is influenced by circumstances, such as a pleasant aroma (Appiah 2008). However, as Day et al. (2001) point out, it is often confused with *situational ethics*, which is a kind of 'anything goes' approach, suggesting a reluctance to engage with underlying ethical principles.

Marketplace theory (Fitzpatrick and Bronstein 2006), argues that all organisations are entitled to have a voice: 'Marketplace theory is predicated, first on the existence of an objective "truth" that will emerge from a cacophony of voices promoting various interests; second on a marketplace in which all citizens have the right – and perhaps the means – to be both heard and informed; and third, on the rational ability of people to discern "truth"' (Fitzpatrick 2006: 4). It is strongly US-based, citing the First Amendment as inspiration, as well as social responsibility theory. The problems with the 'objectivity' of truth (despite the inverted commas) are not explored.

Public relations applications of marketplace ethics

This approach recognises that public relations often plays a more asymmetrical or persuasive role than is encompassed by the boundary spanner, and, while it is uncritical of free market morality, it does acknowledge the need for awareness of factors such as access, process, truth and disclosure (Fitzpatrick 2006).

Critical and other ethical approaches

There are other approaches to professional ethics, drawing on Confucianism, social identity theory, post-modern and feminist approaches. Many of these seek to move away from Anglo-American approaches and find some universal, globally applicable approach. For example, Benhabib (1992) takes a post-modern approach and rejects universal claims to truth, arguing that concepts of reality are socially constructed. Feminist scholars particularly challenge the reliance on rationality as the ground for ethical decision making and the absence of emotional bases for moral judgement. Increasingly, new voices in professional ethics are challenging the traditional reliance on rational decision making and procedural systems for ethics, calling for greater reliance on internal values rather than external codes.

Public relations applications of critical ethics

Critical writers scrutinise the power dynamics of organisations and their publics and often reveal persistent involvement of PR practitioners in propaganda and deception, past and present. While the previously covered models share an optimistic view of public relations' contribution to democracy and tend to minimise the role of propaganda in the formation of the field, critical scholars are more sceptical (L'Etang 2006; Moloney 2006; Weaver et al. 2006).

Curry Jansen (2017) divides critics into two groups: insider and outsider. Outsider critics (Miller and Dinan 2008; Stauber and Rampton 2004) tend not to have experience in practice and view corporate and other forms of public relations in a somewhat crude and utterly malign monolith. They particularly highlight the distortions these cause to the democratic process, such as the creation by PR firms of 'artificial' grass roots campaigns, which they term 'astroturfing', or the planting of questions in press conferences by PR staff masquerading as journalists, as well as the systematic campaigns of distortion or suppression allegedly undertaken in the campaign to win the 'climate change' debate, or recent elections and referenda (UK and US).

There is also a group of internal critics, public relations scholars who take a critical perspective but continue to teach and sometimes practice within the field, such as Pieczka, L'Etang, Moloney, Weaver, Pfau, Holtzhausen and McKie, all cited above. They accept the role of propaganda in the formation of public relations, and reach outside the field to frame ethical debates in different ways. For example, Holtzhausen (2012: 33) takes a post-modern approach to ethics, whereby 'there can never be a justification for moral codes or sets of ethical rules because they are all socially constructed and therefore serve some hidden purpose in society'.

New writing on public relations and promotional culture includes a detailed analysis of the promotional industries and their influence from Davis (2013), a sociological overview (Cronin 2018) which considers public relations relationship with capitalism, and discussion of celebrity and PR (Fitch 2017). In particular, Edwards (2018) suggests a socio-cultural 'turn' encourages examination of language and discourse as a form through which ethical – and unethical – relationships between groups are constructed. Moreover, 'Paying attention to the promotional culture in which public relations thrives prompts ethical questions about the kind of world that we want to live in and public relations' role in constructing (or obstructing) it' (Edwards 2018: 211–212).

Table 13.2 summarises the above text, highlighting how a particular understanding of the public relations function gives rise to its own ideas about role and identity which in turn impact approaches to ethics. For example, if you think the PR person is the ethical guardian of the organisation, their behaviour would look different than if you think the PR purpose is to argue the employer's case in the media (see also Fawkes 2012). The Hayley Court case study (below) illustrates these tensions.

Picture 13.3 How far should public relations professionals go to defend clients and employers? (*source:* Wenn Rights Ltd/Alamy Stock Photo)

Term	Theoretical school of origin	Description	Research (examples)	Ethical identity
Boundary Spanner	Excellence/ systems theory	Represents the public to the organisation and vice versa	(Grunig et al. 1992) (White and Dozier 1992)	Diplomat Ethical guardian
Relationship Manager	Relationship Management	Responsible for building and maintaining internal and external relationships	(Ledingham and Bruning 2001); (Hon and Grunig 1999)	Carer Trust manager
Advocate (1)	Rhetoric/persuasion	Argues the case for the client/employer in democratic context	(Heath 2001); (Porter 2010)	Orator Ethical persuader
Advocate (2)	Marketplace theory Free Speech	Argues the case for the client/employer in marketplace	(Fitzpatrick and Bronstein 2006)	Lawyer
Propagandist	Critical Theory	Distorts the truth to protect client	(Miller and Dinan 2008); (Ewen 1996)	Con merchant Fake news
Cultural generator	Promotional theory	Shapes values and behaviours in society	(Edwards 2018; Cronin 2018; Davis 2013)	Influencer

Table 13.2 A taxonomy of ethical identities in public relations

Case study 13.1
Hayley Court and South Yorkshire Police

Introduction

The dispute about ethics between Senior Press Officer, Hayley Court, and her employer, the South Yorkshire Police (SYP), illustrates a grey area of ethics. It is presented here in broadly chronological order, so you can see how events evolved.

While you are reading this, ask yourself:

- Are employers entitled to ask PR people to present facts in a favourable light?
- Is it unethical to repeat slurs which have been proven false?
- How far do PR professionals have to go to defend employers/clients before they cease being professional?
- What is the difference between 'spin' and legitimate advocacy?

Background

On 15 April 1989, 96 Liverpool fans were killed at the Hillsborough Stadium in Sheffield, UK in the worst stadium-related disaster in English sports history. Some fans trying to carry the injured to waiting ambulances were prevented from doing so by the police cordon which had been placed across the pitch and while a total of 44 ambulances arrived at the ground officers prevented all but one from entering the stadium. In the end only 14 of the 96 who were fatally injured arrived at hospital.

South Yorkshire police officers would later accuse Liverpool fans of having caused the deaths themselves, claiming they were drunk, late, violent and uncooperative. The deaths were ruled accidental at the end of the original 1991 inquest. But those verdicts were quashed following the 2012 Hillsborough Independent Panel report, which concluded that a major cover-up had taken place in an effort by police and others to avoid the blame for what happened. The new jury concluded that blunders by the police and ambulance service on the day had 'caused or contributed' to the disaster and that the victims had been unlawfully killed.

Case study 13.1 (continued)

After the verdict, South Yorkshire Police Chief Constable David Crompton said his force 'unequivocally' accepted the verdict of unlawful killing and the wider findings reached by the jury (Sawer 2017).

Hayley Court's complaint

Hayley Court was employed as a Senior Press Officer by South Yorkshire Police (SYP) just after the above hearings began in 2014. She later claimed she was asked to encourage the media to report evidence favourable to the police case, including that fans were partly to blame. This was the basis of her formal complaint to the Independent Police Complaints Commission (IPCC).

Ms Court said when she took the job, she had hoped to illustrate that the SYP force of 2014, when the inquests began, was not the same as it had been in 1989 – the year of the disaster. But she said 'very quickly' she felt like she 'had been fed a line'. She felt she had been told her job would be one thing, but actually it was something very different. And if that meant perpetuating the comments about fans being drunk, if that meant perpetuating comments about fans forcing gates, then that is how they were going to do it and what she was expected to do.

She said she was surprised that the force was continuing with a defensive stance, despite issuing an apology for police failures in 2012, more than a year before the inquests began. Ms Court claimed she was repeatedly told to tell the media what line they should be reporting and that her job may be under threat if she didn't.

The force investigated some of Ms Court's complaints but a report did not rule in her favour. It listed areas of Ms Court's work that were said to need improvement. Among them, she was said to have failed to address some of the bias or imbalance in the media's reporting of the inquests. The impact being that evidence in support of the force was not being reported adequately or accurately. A 20-week appraisal, written after Ms Court raised her concerns, also included comments that she was asked to encourage the media to report on the positives, while acknowledging and accepting that they would also report the negatives aspects of the case.

SYP response

In a statement, the South Yorkshire Police said it was aware of the concerns and would be open to an opportunity to discuss them with Ms Court and to then enter a process of independent review and mediation.

The report discussed how some of the issues raised have been considered before through the force's grievance procedure. Specifically in relation to the concerns raised about suggested unethical practices, but these were not substantiated at the time. The report went on to acknowledge that the staff member remained concerned about her experiences and following the outcome of the Hillsborough inquests and that they would like to talk to her and give her concerns further consideration.

CIPR Response (May 2016)

The UK professional body, the Chartered Institute of Public Relations (CIPR), said in a statement that Court's allegations 'expose the pressure that PR advisers can be placed under in carrying out their duties'. The CIPR statement points to its Code of Conduct, which it says can be used by PRs and clients as a 'guide to professional ethics', and can be used by members and non-members alike. Court is not a CIPR member.

'It's entirely unacceptable for any organisation to expect their employees to deceive or misrepresent on their behalf. A public relations professional who feels they are being put under pressure to act in a way that could break our code of conduct is right to speak out about it and push back against unreasonable and unethical expectations,' said CIPR president Rob Brown, managing partner of Manchester agency Rule 5 (Burne Jones 2016).

Former boss (May 2016)

Dave King, Hayley Court's former editor at the *Swindon Advertiser*, posted:

> I'm not sure what all the fuss is about. Spinning is something all press officers and marketeers do from whatever section of industry they represent. It is part and parcel of their work they do to cast their employers or clients in a favourable light. . . , although it might be considered unseemly for a police force to provide briefings at an inquest, those sort of briefings have been going on for years (Sharman 2016).

The IPCC response (November 2016)

The Independent Police Complaints Commission (IPCC) found no case to answer for misconduct or unsatisfactory performance. Its report said:

> Four instances were examined where the superintendent allegedly told Miss Court to 'schmooze' the media. Investigators concluded that Miss Court was encouraged to build a working relationship with journalists,

however no corroborating evidence was found to support the allegations that this was a deliberate attempt to manipulate the media.

Miss Court's predecessor stated that the only brief she had when carrying out the role had been to ensure 'balanced and fair reporting' of the proceedings. If Miss Court was given the alleged instructions, it seems likely that similar instructions would have been given to anyone carrying out the communications specialist role.

Investigators concluded that Miss Court may have misunderstood some of her directions and highlighted a lack of clear unambiguous written guidance on how the force's staff should engage with the media during court proceedings. (Pidd 2016)

Hayley Court's response (November 2016)

The IPCC report was questioned by Ms Court, who said she was disappointed with the conclusion. She said:

The public of South Yorkshire, police officers and staff deserve high-quality leaders within their police force who act with integrity and support the reporting of unethical behaviour.

Sadly, this was not my experience when I first raised concerns in September 2014 – 19 months before the Hillsborough inquests concluded. . . . I'm disappointed by the IPCC's findings, as anyone who has made significant professional sacrifices to highlight concern of wrongdoing would be. Nevertheless, I am grateful to those who examined my claims and carried out as detailed an investigation as their narrow remit allowed.

Any suggestion that I simply misunderstood my instructions is manifestly wrong.

I am, as any experienced press officer should be, acutely aware of the value of strong working relationships with the media. My instructions went beyond that and, in my opinion, breached the code of ethics designed to make the police service more open, transparent and accountable.

I stand by my claims and feel it was in the public interest to speak out. I only hope that anyone who encounters unethical practices within the police or any public sector body is not dissuaded from whistleblowing after seeing the outcome of this particular investigation.

(Source: Thomas 2016)

Explore 13.3 Professional bodies and codes of ethics

In recent years, professional bodies in public relations and communication management have done considerable work in enhancing their ethical guidance to members. For example, Global Alliance for Public Relations and Communication Management (GA) has several helpful case studies worth investigating. The CIPR has a range of useful resources, including podcasts, videos and guidelines for ethical practice.

Compare the codes of ethics that you can find at the following locations:

- CIPR (www.cipr.co.uk)
- Global PR (www.globalalliancepr.org)
- PRIA (www.pria.com.au)
- PRSA (www.prsa.org)

Feedback

Now compare the codes under the following headings:

- *Language* – do the same terms keep cropping up?
- *Do's and don't's* – what differences are there between what they advise against? For example, do some codes mention refusing bribes?
- *Best practice* – do they describe 'ideal' behaviour?
- *Culture/nationality* – are there differences that stem from the culture of the code-writers? If so, how does that affect global codes?
- *Moral claims* – do the codes claim the profession makes a moral contribution to society?

Think about 13.3

The ethics of codes

The primary tool upholding and enhancing social mores for most professional bodies is their code of conduct – as Abbott (1983: 856) says, 'ethics codes are the most concrete cultural form in which professions acknowledge their societal obligations', but it is questionable whether they also play a part in determining the ethical behaviour of those they govern. Freidson (2001) suggests that professional codes fall into three types of obligation: (a) obey law/regulations; (b) practice competently; and (c) reflect values in behaviour, such as care and trust. Generally, codes involve seeking to do good, reducing harm, being fair to individuals, respecting their autonomy and behaving with integrity in line with the profession's aims and values (Rowson 2006). However, despite these laudable claims, some say that the main function of codes of practice is to improve the reputation of the professional organisation rather than change the behaviour of members. Kultgen (1988: 120) suggests that this may be because 'the *Urmythos* from which all of the myths in the professional mythology spring is that professions are oriented to the service of humanity'. Many codes reflect this sense of duty but, as Rowson (2006: 52) comments:

> *Portraying ethics in the professions as obedience to rules can have undesirable effects . . . As regulatory codes have proliferated in recent years, and as examples of unethical behaviour in professions have increasingly made the headlines, the cry has gone up that what is needed is fewer rules and a greater sense of individual moral responsibility among professionals.*

Explore 13.4

Philosophical approaches to ethical dilemmas

How do you think a consequentialist and a deontologist would respond to the following scenario?

You work for a large pharmaceutical company that has been developing a new male contraceptive. But the latest laboratory results suggest some cases of cancer in rats. Do you:

- deny the results, because the company's bound to get it right eventually;
- deny the results, because the company could go bust if word gets out;
- prepare to answer questions from the media, but only for use if word leaks out;
- prepare a press release announcing the setback;
- resign;
- leak the information to the media.

Feedback

How do you make ethical decisions? By thinking or feeling? Who do you discuss them with, if anyone? What influences your decisions?

Think about 13.4

Solving ethical dilemmas

To help the practitioner facing dilemmas such as those in Think about 13.1, Baker and Martinson (2002) have put together five principles to act as guiding principles for ethical persuasive public relations, which they call the TARES test:

1. **T**ruthfulness – the commitment to honesty in communication.
2. **A**uthenticity – relates to personal and professional integrity.
3. **R**espect – for the rights of your audience.
4. **E**quity – relates to fairness, not manipulation.
5. **S**ocial responsibility – awareness of the effects of communication on the wider society.

Feedback

Are these still rather idealistic ways of describing PR practice?

Mini case study 13.2

Iceland's ethics in action

The Iceland supermarket gathered much positive PR in 2018 from its decision to ban plastic from its stores within five years, a much stronger commitment than the UK government's plastic-free in 25 years target. It amplified this position by making a Christmas TV ad exposing the environmental damage done by palm-oil production This was too strong for mainstream TV and instead went viral on social media, where it was watched 65 million times (Griggs and McKinlay 2018).

> **Think about 13.5**
>
> ## Facing ethical challenges
>
> It is inevitable that we will all come across situations that make us uncomfortable or challenge our ethics in our workplaces. Whether you are a student or practitioner you can ask yourself some simple everyday questions when considering the ethics of a situation:
>
> - Am I comfortable with this decision? If not, why not? Is it because my pride/self-image/security is threatened or do I fear harm will come from it?
> - Am I prepared to raise this discomfort? If not, why not? Am I in a position of power or powerlessness? Am I abusing that position/abdicating responsibility?
> - Who do I blame for ethical failures? What does this say about me?
> - Is there a 'safe' forum for expressing doubts? If not why not?
>
> And if you don't have time to ask these questions, or if that is too hard, draw breath, check your own inner responses and have the courage to pause and ask those around you: Are we *sure* about this?

Summary

This chapter has explored some of the confusion surrounding professional ethics in general, and public relations ethics in particular. It suggests that the confusion is made worse because different ways of looking at PR imply different ethics, but that these differences are hidden rather than explored.

Ethical confusion is increased by confusion about the nature and scope of the profession: the capabilities approach was used to present research describing the range of PR functions as a profession, globally.

Most PR ethics is still reliant on procedural, structural and rational approaches, with little discussion of where an individual might look for internal guidance, rather than more rules. Virtue ethics does open this debate to a certain extent, but can still end up as a competition for best practice. Codes have been shown to be empty – not only in PR, but in professions generally. There is an argument in the field for encouraging greater reflection in individual professionals and in professional associations. Instead of looking for rules or accepting situations that 'feel' wrong but are legal, perhaps practitioners need to learn to trust their discomfort. Without reflection, it is hard to see how PR can earn back lost trust. It is new practitioners, graduates from educational and professional qualifications, who will shape this future.

Bibliography

Appiah, A. (2008). *Experiments in ethics*. Cambridge, Mass. ; London: Harvard University Press.

Baker, S. and D.L. Martinson (2002). Out of the Red-Light District: Five Principles for Ethically Proactive Public Relations. *Public Relations Quarterly*, 47(3), 15–19.

BBC. (2016). Hillsborough inquests: South Yorkshire police 'spin' evidence. Retrieved from https://www.bbc.com/news/uk-england-merseyside-36216684

Benhabib, S. (1992). *Situating the self: gender, community, and postmodernism in contemporary ethics*. New York, NY: Routledge.

Bivins, T.H. (1993). Public relations, professionalism and the public interest. *Journal of Business Ethics*, 12, 117–126.

Bowen, S.A. (2007). The extent of ethics. In E. L. Toth (Ed.), *The future of excellence in public relations and communication management* (pp. 275–297). Mahweh, NJ: Lawrence Erlbaum.

Bowen, S.A. (2008). A State of Neglect: Public Relations as 'Corporate Conscience' or Ethics Counsel. *Journal of Public Relations Research*, 20(3), 271–296. Retrieved from http://dx.doi.org/10.1080/10627260801962749.

Bowen, S.A. (2019, 05/04/2019). PR pros can help people unite – or we can help them divide. *PR Week*. Retrieved from https://www.prweek.com/article/1581262/pr-pros-help-people-unite-help-divide

Bowen, S. A., R.L. Heath, J. Lee, G. Painter, F.J. Agraz, D. McKie and M. Toledano (2006). *The business of truth: a guide to ethical communication*. San Francisco: International Association of *Business* Communicators.

Breit, R. and K. Demetrious (2010). Professionalisation and Public relations: An ethical mismatch. *Ethical Space,* 7(4), 20–29.

Brown, J.S. and P. Duguid (2001). Knowledge and Organization: a social-practice perspective. *Organization Science,* 12(2), 198–213.

Burleson and Kline 1979, cited in Day et al. 2001: 408). Day, K. D., Dong, Q., & Robins, C. (2001). Public Relations Ethics: An overview and Discussion of Issues for the 21st Century. In R.L. Heath (Ed.), *The handbook of public relations* (pp. 403–410). Thousand Oaks, CA: Sage.

Burne Jones, S. (2016). CIPR applauds police press officer for speaking out against Hillsborough 'spin'. *PR Week.* Retrieved from https://www.prweek.com/article/1394070/cipr-applauds-police-press-officer-speaking-against-hillsborough-spin

Cadwalladr, C. (2019) Facebook's role in Brexit – and the threat to democracy https://www.youtube.com/watch?v=OQSMr-3GGvQ

Cheney, G. (2010). *Just a job? Communication, ethics, and professional life.* Oxford; New York: Oxford University Press.

Conner, C. (2017). PR Infamy: UK's Bell Pottinger Nearing Closure After 'Worst Ethical Breach In History'. *Forbes Magazine.* Retrieved from https://www.forbes.com/sites/cherylsnappconner/2017/09/08/pr-infamy-uks-bell-pottinger-agency-nearing-closure-after-worst-ethical-breach-in-history/#29fb633d7c50

Cooper, D.E. (2004). *Ethics for professionals in a multicultural world.* Upper Saddle River, N.J.: Prentice Hall.

Cronin, A.M. (2018). *Public relations capitalism : promotional culture, publics and commercial democracy.* Basingstoke: Palgrave Macmillan.

Curtin, P.A. and L.A. Boynton (2001). Ethics in public relations: theory and practice. In R.L. Heath (Ed.), *Handbook of public relations* (pp. 411–422). Thousand Oaks, CA: Sage.

Davis, A. (2013). *Promotional cultures: the rise and spread of advertising, public relations, marketing and branding.* Cambridge; Malden: Polity.

Dowd, C. (2017). The Importance of Ethics in PR . Retrieved from https://mkpublicrelations.co.uk/importance-ethics-pr/. Accessed 7 February 2020.

Edelman. (2019). *2019 Edelman Trust Barometer.* Retrieved from https://www.edelman.com/sites/g/files/aatuss191/files/2019-02/2019_Edelman_Trust_Barometer_Executive_Summary.pdf

Edgett, R. (2002). Toward an ethical framework for advocacy. *Journal of Public Relations Research,* 14(1), 1–26.

Edwards, L. (2018). *Understanding public relations: theory, culture and society.* Thousand Oaks, CA: Sage.

Ella Minty (2019). Talking about the state of PR. See: http://ellaminty.com/uncategorized/talking-about-the-state-of-pr/. Accessed 7 February 2020.

Ewen, S. (1996). *PR!: a social history of spin.* New York: BasicBooks.

Fawkes, J. (2012). Saints and sinners: Competing identities in public relations ethics. *Public Relations Review,* 38(5), 865–872.

Fawkes, J. (2015). A Jungian conscience: Self-awareness for public relations practice. *Public Relations Review* (3).

Fitch, K. (2017). Seeing the unseen hand: Celebrity, promotion and public relations. *Public Relations Inquiry,* 6(2), 157–169.

Fitzpatrick, K. (2006). Baselines for Ethical Advocacy in the 'Marketplace of Ideas'. In K. Fitzpatrick & C. Bronstein (Eds.), *Ethical Public Relations: Responsible Advocacy* (pp. 1–17). Thousands Oaks, CA: Sage.

Fitzpatrick, K. and C. Bronstein (2006). *Ethics in public relations: responsible advocacy.* Thousand Oaks, CA; London: SAGE.

Flagship (2018). The importance of ethics in PR: how PR practitioners are upping their game. Retrieved from https://flagshipconsulting.co.uk/blog/2018/01/30/importance-ethics-pr-pr-practitioners-upping-game/. Accessed 7 February 2020.

Freidson, E. (1994). *Professionalism reborn: theory, prophecy, and policy.* Cambridge: Polity.

Gregory, A. (2008). Competencies of senior communication practitioners in the UK: An initial study. *Public Relations Review,* 34(3), 215.

Gregory, A. (2009). Ethics and professionalism in public relations. In R. Tench & L. Yeomans (Eds.), *Exploring Public Relations* (2nd ed., pp. 273–289). Harlow, Essex: Pearson Education.

Gregory, A. and J. Fawkes (2019). A Global Capability Framework: Reframing public relations for a changing world. *Public Relations Review,* 45(3), 101781. https://doi.org/10.1016/j.pubrev.2019.05.002.

Griggs, I. and R. McKinlay (2018). The Eight biggest PR stories of 2018, *PR Week,* London: Haymarket: https://www.prweek.com/article/1521459/eight-biggest-pr-stories-2018 (accessed May 2019).

Grunig, J.E. (2001). Two-Way Symmetrical Public Relations: Past, Present and Future. In R.L. Heath (Ed.), *The handbook of public relations* (pp. 11–30). Thousands Oaks, CA: Sage.

Grunig, J.E., D.M. Dozier, W.P. Ehling, L.A. Grunig, F.C. Repper and J. White (1992). *Excellence in public relations and communication management*. Hillsdale. N.J.: Lawrence Erlbaum.

Habermas, J. (1989). *The structural transformation of the public sphere: an inquiry into a category of bourgeois society*. Cambridge, Mass.: MIT Press.

Harrison, K. and C. Galloway (2005). Public relations ethics: a simpler (but not simplistic) approach to the complexities. *Prism, 3*. Retrieved from http://www.praxis.massey.ac.nz, accessed 14 March 2007.

Heath, R.L. (2001). A Rhetorical Enactment Rationale for Public Relations: The Good Organisation Communicating Well. In R. L. Heath & G. Vasquez (Eds.), *Handbook of Public Relations* (pp. 31–50). Thousand Oaks, CA: Sage.

Heath, R.L. (2007). Management through advocacy: reflection rather than domination. In J. E. Grunig, J.E., L.A. Toth and L.A. Grunig (Eds.), *The future of excellence in public relations and communications management*. Mahwah, NJ: Lawrence Erlbaum Associates.

Holtzhausen, D. (2012). *Public Relations as Activism: Postmodern approaches to theory and practice*. New York, NY: Routledge.

Hon, L.C. and J.E. Grunig (1999). Guidelines for measuring relationships in public relations (online), http://www.instituteforpr.com.

Hutton, J.G. (1999). The definition, dimensions and domain of public relations. *Public Relations Review, 25*(2), 199–214.

Hutton, J.G. (2001). Defining the relationship between public relations and marketing. In R.L. Heath (Ed.), *The Handbook of Public Relations* (pp. 205–214). Thousand Oaks, CA: Sage.

Hutton, J.G. (2010). Defining the relationship between public relations and marketing: public relations' most important challenge. In R. L. Heath (Ed.), *The SAGE handbook of public relations* (pp. 509–522). Los Angeles: SAGE Publications.

Jansen, S.C. (2017). *Stealth communications: the spectacular rise of public relations*. Cambridge: Polity Press.

Kent, M.L. and M. Taylor (2002). Toward a dialogic theory of public relations. *Public Relations Review, 14*(28), 21–37.

Kultgen, J. (1988). *Ethics and Professionalism*. Philadelphia, PA: University of Philadelphia Press.

L'Etang, J. (2003). The myth of the 'ethical guardian': an examination of its origins, potency and illusions. *Journal of Communication Management, 8*(1), 53–67.

L'Etang, J. (2006). Public relations and propaganda: conceptual issues, methodological problems and public relations discourse. In J. L'Etang & M. Pieczka (Eds.), *Public relations, critical debates and contemporary practice* (pp. 23–40). Mahweh NJ: Lawrence Erlbaum.

L'Etang, J. (2008). *Public relations: concepts, practice and critique*. Los Angeles: SAGE.

Larson, M.S. (1977). *The rise of professionalism : a sociological analysis*. Berkeley; London: University of California Press.

Ledingham, J.A. and S.D. Bruning (2001). *Public relations as relationship management: a relational approach to the study and practice of public relations* (2nd ed.). Mahwah, N.J.; London: L. Erlbaum.

Leeper, K.A. (1996). Public relations ethics and communitarianism, a preliminary investigation. *Public Relations Review, 22*, 163–179.

Lefkowitz. (2003). *Ethics and values in industrial-organisational psychology*. Mahwah, NJ: Lawrence Erlbaum Associates.

Lester, S. (2014). Professional standards, competence and capability. *HE, Skills & Work-Based Learning Higher Education, Skills and Work-Based Learning, 4*(1), 31–43.

Lester, S. (2016). *Communicating Professional Competence*. London: Erasmus+ programme of the EU. Stan Lester Developments.

MacIntyre, A. (1984). *After virtue: a study in moral theory* (2nd edn). Notre Dame, IN: University of Notre Dame Press.

Macnamara, J.R. (2012). *Public relations: theories, practices, critiques* (1st ed.). Frenchs Forest, N.S.W.: Pearson Australia.

Manley, D. and J. Valin (2017). A Global Body of Knowledge. *Public Relations Review*.

McElreath, M.P. (1996). *Managing Systematic and Ethical Public Relations* (2nd ed.). Madison, WI: Brown and Benchmark.

McKie, D. and D. Munshi (2007). *Reconfiguring Public Relations: ecology, equity, and enterprise*. London: Routledge.

Miller, D. and W. Dinan (2008). *A century of spin: how public relations became the cutting edge of corporate power*. London: Pluto.

Moloney, K. (2006). *Rethinking public relations: PR propaganda and democracy* (2nd ed.). London: Routledge.

Naughton, J. (2019). Are big tech's efforts to show it cares about data ethics simply another diversion? *The Observer*.

Oakley, J. and D. Cocking (2001). *Virtue Ethics and Professional Roles*. Cambridge, England: Cambridge University Press.

Parkinson, M. (2001). 'The PRSA Code of Professional Standards and Member Code of Ethics: why they are neither professional nor ethical'. *Public Relations Quarterly* 46(3): 27–31.

Parsons, T. (1951). *The Social System*. London: Routledge and Kegan Paul ltd.

Pater, A. and A. van Gils (2003). Stimulating Ethical Decision-making in a Business Context: Effects of Ethical and Professional Codes. *European Journal of Management*, 21(6), 762–772.

Pearce, C. (2012). A personal view on ethics in public relations. Retrieved from http://craigpearce.info/public-relations/personal-view-ethics-public-relations/

Pearson, R. (1989). Beyond Ethical Relativism in public relations: co orientation, rules and the ideal of communication symmetry. In J. E. Grunig & L. A. Grunig (Eds.), *Public Relations research annual, vol 1* (Vol. 1, pp. 67–87). Hillside, NJ: Lawrence Erlbaum Associates.

Pidd, H. (2016). Hillsborough: police media officer loses 'coercion to spin' case. *The Guardian*. Retrieved from https://www.theguardian.com/uk-news/2016/nov/29/hillsborough-police-media-officer-loses-coercion-to-spin-case

Pieczka, M. (2010). Public relations as dialogic expertise? *Journal of Communication Management, 15*(2), 108–124.

Pieczka, M. and J. L'Etang (2001). Public relations and the question of professionalism. In R. L. Heath (Ed.), *The Handbook of Public Relations* (pp. 223–235). Thousand Oaks, CA: Sage.

Porter, L. (2010). Communicating for the good of the state: A post-symmetrical polemic on persuasion in ethical public relations. *Public Relations Review*, 36, 127–133.

PRSA (2006). *The Professional Bond: public relations education in the 21st century*. Retrieved from New York: https://apps.prsa.org/SearchResults/view/6I-2006/0/The_Professional_Bond_Public_Relations_Education_i#.X09bV8hKg2w. Accessed 2 September 2009.

Rowson, R. (2006). *Working Ethics: How to be fair in a culturally complex world*. London: Jessica Kingsley Publishers.

Sandel, M. (2009). Justic. Retrieved from https://www.youtube.com/watch?v=kBdfcR-8hEY. Accessed 7 February 2020.

Sandel, M. (2016). Trolley cart dilemma. Retrieved from https://www.youtube.com/watch?v=TSH-m5GtrzE. Accessed 7 February 2020.

Sawer, P. (2017) What happened in Hillsborough in 1989? London: Telegraph Newspapers.

Sciulli, D. (2005). Continental Sociology of Professions Today: Conceptual Contributions. *Current Sociology*, 53(6), 915–942.

Seaman, P. (2011). A new moral agenda for PR. 21st Century PR Issues. Retrieved from http://paulseaman.eu/wp-content/uploads/2011/04/a-new-moral-agenda-for-PR1.pdf

Seaman, P. (2013) Getting to grips with corporate and PR ethics. Retrieved from http://paulseaman.eu/2013/05/getting-to-grips-with-corporate-and-pr-ethics/. Accessed 7 February 2020.

Segal, D. (2018). How Bell Pottinger, P.R. Firm for Despots and Rogues, Met Its End in South Africa. *New York Times*. Retrieved from https://www.nytimes.com/2018/02/04/business/bell-pottinger-guptas-zuma-south-africa.html

Sen, A. (1999). *Development as freedom*. New York: Knopf.

Sharman, D. (2016). Spin all part of the job says Hillsborough press officer's ex-editor. HoldtheFrontPage.co.uk. Retrieved from http://www.holdthefrontpage.co.uk/2016/news/spin-part-and-parcel-of-pr-says-hillsborough-press-officer-ex-editor/

Smith, C. (Writer). (2019). Fyre: The Greatest Party That Never Happened. In: Netflix.

Sriramesh, K. and L. Hornaman (2006). Public Relations as a Profession An Analysis of Curricular Content in the United States. *Journal of Creative Communications, 1*(2), 155–172. Retrieved from http://crc.sagepub.com/content/1/2/155.short.

Stackpoole, B. (2019). Data-rich organizations turn focus to ethical data mining. Retrieved from https://searchbusinessanalytics.techtarget.com/feature/Data-rich-organizations-turn-focus-to-ethical-data-mining

Stauber, J.C. and S. Rampton (2004). *Toxic sludge is good for you: lies, damn lies and the public relations industry*. London: Robinson.

Sussman, G. (2011). *The propaganda society: Promotional culture and politics in global context*. New York: Peter Lang.

Tench, R., A. Zerfass, P. Verhoeven, D. Verčič, A. Moreno and A. Okay (2013). *Competencies and Role Requirements of Communication Professionals in Europe. Insights from quantitative and qualitative studies*. Retrieved from Leeds, UK.

Thomas, J. (2016). Ex-SYP press officer stands by claims force tried to 'spin' Hillsborough inquests. *Liverpool Echo*. Retrieved from https://www.liverpoolecho.co.uk/news/liverpool-news/ex-syp-press-officer-stands-12249186

van Ruler, B. (2005). Professionals are from Venus, scholars are from Mars. *Public Relations Review, 31*, 159–173.

Walker, M. and Unterhalter, E. (2007). Amartya Sen's capability approach and social justice in education. New York, NY: Palgrave Macmillan.

Water, R. (2019, 05/04/2019). Google scraps ethics council for artificial intelligence. *Financial Times*. Retrieved from https://www.ft.com/content/6e2912f8-573e-11e9-91f9-b6515a54c5b1

Weaver, C.K., J. Motion and J. Reaper (2006). From propaganda to discourse (and back again): truth, power the public interest and public relations. In J. L'Etang & M. Pieczka (Eds.), *Public relations, critical debates and contemporary practice* (pp. 7–21). Mahwah NJ: Lawrence Erlbaum.

White, J. and D.M. Dozier (1992). Public relations and management decision making. In J.E. Grunig (Ed.), *Excellence in public relations and communication management* (pp. 91–108). Hillsdale, NJ: Lawrence Erlbaum Associates.

Working, R. (2018). 9 PR Blunders of 2018. *Ragan's PR Daily*. Retrieved from https://www.prdaily.com/9-pr-blunders-of-2018/

PART 3

Public relations specialisms

This part of the book focuses on the practice of public relations. We have divided it into 10 distinct chapters in recognition of the increasingly specialist knowledge, experience and skills required to achieve an effective programme or campaign on behalf of an organisation or client. Each chapter therefore: examines the broad context of the specialism; discusses the main theories and principles of building effective relationships with key publics; and identifies some of the methods of achieving successful results. Each chapter integrates mini case studies and long case studies to illustrate the theories, principles and methods described. The chapters cover the following themes and areas: media relations, internal communication, issues management, crisis communication, consumers and brand, business to business communication, integrated marketing communication, sponsorship and public relations and finally corporate communication.

CHAPTER 14

Ramona Slusarczyk and Jonathan Ward

Media relations

Source: Ruimin Wang/Shutterstock

Learning outcomes

By the end of this chapter you should be able to:

- discuss media relations from historical and professional perspectives
- understand the role and purpose of media relations as part of a strategic management function, including its application in different cultural contexts
- understand the impact that digital media has had on media relations, such as the emergence of influencer relations and the impact of fake news
- understand some of the tools and techniques of practical media relations
- evaluate your learning about media relations and pursue further sources for investigation.

Structure

- Origins and development of media relations
- Media relations as a strategic management function
- The purpose of media relations
- The media as gatekeeper
- Media fragmentation
- The rise of the influencer
- Fake news: do audiences love being fooled?
- Hacks versus flacks? An ongoing battle or an opportunity for excellence?
- Shared spaces
- Practical media relations
- The techniques of media relations

Introduction

It is widely understood that the first example of a press release was created in 1906 by Ivy Lee to inform journalists about the Pennsylvania Rails train crash. Soon after, media relations became part of the overall strategy of organisations, leading to the development of modern public relations (Supa 2014). Journalists are an important stakeholder for any organisation due to their ability to control news agendas and reach mass audiences which can make or break reputation. Therefore, an understanding of media relations and an ability to apply its tools and techniques is essential for any practitioner.

The emergence of a fragmented digital media landscape has somewhat diminished journalists' and editors' role as gatekeepers. Mainstream news channels may remain more trusted, but influencer relations are now on par with traditional media as a key to reputation management.

This chapter will analyse how digital channels have transformed understanding of media relations while acknowledging that neither traditional nor online media relations are an end in themselves and can only partly contribute towards organisational objectives. Issues around trust, credibility and objectivity mean that PR practitioners need to broaden their understanding and skills when engaging with the media, journalists and influencers.

Origins and development of media relations

Media relations is considered the most visible aspect of PR with UK-based practitioners ranking it as the most commonly undertaken activity after copywriting, campaign management and strategic planning (CIPR 2020). In many other countries, such as the UAE or Japan, it is still seen as the paramount function of the profession (PRWeek 2019; Kimball 2017) and various political, social and cultural factors have a profound impact on media relations practice internationally. Before reading further, see Think about 14.1.

As is the case with many characteristics of the public relations profession, scholars have failed to establish a unified theory of media relations that might assist practitioners. This is understandable, as the dynamic nature of PR and media relations makes the development of a prescriptive theory a challenging task (Supa 2014), but most often the term 'media relations' refers to relationships of PR practitioners with journalists working in mass media outlets (Supa and Zoch 2009) and it is considered to have emerged in the age of mass media.

The birth of modern media relations, therefore, is associated with the creation of a press release by Ivy Lee, which was intended to inform journalists first-hand about the Pennsylvania Rails train crash in 1906. In this particular case of crisis management, accuracy of facts and remaining in control of the information flow was crucial and hence it is considered an example of the public information model (Grunig and Hunt 1984). Since it is often noted that the modern era of public relations began with Ivy Lee's Declaration of Principles, which led to media relations becoming part of the big strategies of large corporations, PR can be seen as having originated from media relations (Supa 2014). The Declaration of Principles itself set the foundations for contemporary ethical approaches that practitioners should maintain while carrying out media relations activities. Based on Lee's belief that honesty and transparency would earn the public's trust, the Declaration stated:

> *Our matter is accurate. Further details on any subject treated will be supplied promptly, and any editor will be assisted most cheerfully in verifying directly any statement of fact (. . .). Our plan is, frankly and openly, on behalf of business concerns and public institutions, to supply to the press and public of the United States prompt and accurate information concerning subjects which it is of value and interest to the public to know about.* (Cited in Russell and Bishop 2009)

Lee clearly intended to veer the profession away from spin and stunts to factual information, but his media contemporaries saw it merely as a 'new experiment of corporate press agentry' (ibid.), and thus voicing scepticism that has permeated the relationship between journalists and PR practitioners ever since as exemplified in the term 'hacks versus flacks'.

While the emergence of mass communication triggered the blossoming of commercial PR into an entire industry, the twentieth century also saw the rise of press agentry with governments employing the media to influence public opinion and broadcast their messages with little regard to accuracy. In Europe, a flagship example of propaganda being used as a chief communication tool is linked to the rise of Nazi Germany, but press agentry was deployed by other governments, particularly those involved in military conflicts. For example, during the war in Vietnam, the American military held daily press briefings aimed at making the international press dependent on official information and downplaying the growing US role in

> ### Think about 14.1
> ## Impact of culture on media relations
>
> In collectivist societies, interpersonal communication skills are often more valued than 'technical' skills and media relations is often driven by personal connections (Freitag and Stokes 2009). Since communication is a fundamental component of culture, country-specific elements can affect media relations practice to a great extent.
>
> In South East Asia, for example, a practice called *guanxi*, refers to a network of business and personal connections. Maintaining such connections often involves the exchange of gifts and favours, helping a company to get positive coverage in the media (Chen and Culbertson 2009). Although some international companies try to implement a degree of transparency and forbid their practitioners from giving money, they still allow the practice of rewarding journalists with gifts and often send presents to media professionals on personal occasions, such as birthdays, weddings or funerals (Slusarczyk 2012). Similarly, in the Middle East, close relationships with journalists and opinion leaders is called *wasta* and can be translated as 'personal connections' (Almahraj 2017).
>
> What are the positive and negative impacts of personal connections leveraged within the context of media relations? Which Grunig and Hunt communication model does it represent?
>
> #### Feedback
>
> Using personal connections can be useful in media relations and help an organisation gain positive coverage regardless of its content being of value to the public. It undermines, however, the transparency of the PR profession, blurring boundaries between earned and paid content. It also leads to the situation where journalists publish press releases in their original form, without facts being verified, and thus contributing to the decreasing trust in traditional media.
>
> This communication model doesn't fit within Grunig and Hunt's original theoretical paradigms. In 1995, Grunig et al. identified the Personal Influence Model, which encapsulates the complexity of the relationships between PR practitioners and key individuals in media, legislators or activist groups. Those relationships are fostered to achieve organisations' goals and in that sense leverage personal influence based on social hierarchy and power. From a Western-centric perspective, this facilitates an interdependent relationship, inducing gift-giving in return for favours, and thus often leading to unethical behaviour and bribery (Valentini 2009). However, various studies (Huang 2000; Chen and Culbertson 2009; Slusarczyk 2012) show this may not be culturally considered as merely bribing for preference, but a means of cultivating relationships through recognition and reciprocity.

Vietnam. Unsurprisingly, the journalists dubbed them 'Five O'Clock Follies' due to a credibility gap between presented official reports and the reality (McKinney 2000) with the Associated Press Saigon bureau chief stating they were 'the longest-playing tragicomedy in Southeast Asia's theatre of the absurd' (Martin 2011).

Despite the emergence of digital media platforms encouraging two-way communication due to their intrinsically interactive and shareable nature, the press agentry model is still faring well. Flagship cases of such practice include Red Bull Stratos jump or Tesla's Space X launch, with these organisations using an exceptionally appealing concept of space travel to create buzz on social media platforms and secure mainstream media coverage as part of wider brand marketing campaigns.

While a press agentry approach seems still effective, the advent of digital media triggered a fundamental change in what can be perceived as media relations. Traditionally, it focused on the relationship between organisations and stakeholders with the mainstream media acting as a gatekeeper; however, this seems no longer the case as influencers have taken the space of journalists.

Media relations as a strategic management function

There is little doubt that the media remains one of the 'big three' publics of PR. Together with employees and customers, these are stakeholders who can tangibly make or break the reputation of an organisation. A restaurant critic's favourable review can bring customers to an establishment for months ahead, just as a negative report may mean cancelled bookings and loss of revenue. But whereas the restaurant critic's main channel may once have been the pages of a weekend supplement or television show, the fragmented media landscape now means that opportunities to promote and protect reputation exist far beyond the traditional media to bloggers, online influencers and citizen journalists. This section will focus on media relations as a stakeholder management function supporting an approach of relationship building rather than viewing the media as a vessel through which to secure quick wins.

The purpose of media relations

While media relations – communication with those who provide content for online and traditional editorial space – contributes towards organisational outcomes, the process should not be viewed as an end but as a means to meeting those goals.

Media relations is often described as a symbiotic association with the PR practitioner promoting clients via media channels which invariably seek to report news, disseminate information or entertain. The balance works because carefully researched and packaged content can have news value for the myriad of channels that exist.

To take a more theoretical view, Jefkins' Transfer model (1988) is useful in helping to explain how media relations works. Jefkins suggests public relations is a process, whereby negative states – the attitudes and perceptions held about an organisation – are improved by way of carefully managed communication often via earned and owned media channels. The process starts with awareness and ends with support and understanding. In essence, media relations becomes a transaction between the PR practitioner and the journalist, an exchange of content for reputation. This process helped position media relations as synonymous with PR practice in the mass media era of the twentieth century where a relatively small number of media gatekeepers held the key to organisational reputation. It could be levelled that the initial awareness-raising stage of the transfer process is a predominantly one-way communication flow which replicates Grunig and Hunt's publicity and public information models. Here, the relationship is as much about outputs and opportunities, as it is about meaningful balanced engagement with all stakeholders.

The media as gatekeeper

In this one-dimensional communication flow, the media can be viewed as an agenda-setting gatekeeper. Its role is to inform, entertain and educate, acting as a watchdog but with the capability to mould the views, opinions and attitudes of the publics that organisations want to reach. For decades this model was the norm, with media relations operating efficiently to target publics and swiftly reach audiences of millions.

What's more, the media has credibility. Audiences tend to trust editorial produced by daily newspapers and flagship current affairs programmes because it's viewed as independent and objective. Think of that restaurant review again. When you consider that an independently written endorsement is going to carry far more weight with potential customers than a syrupy statement on the restaurant's own website, you can understand why editorial content is the credible, cost-effective option.

Edelman's annual Trust Barometer reveals that in 2019 traditional media was still the most trusted news source in the UK, with owned media and social media lagging some way behind. That's a picture repeated globally too, with Edelman reporting 65 per cent of its 33,000 respondents across 27 countries trusting traditional media compared to 43 per cent for social media.

Media fragmentation

Despite significant trust for traditional media, we are now in an era when anyone can be a content producer, commenting and engaging on issues, brands and campaigns in which they share a common interest. A digitised media does not mean there is a distinction between traditional copywriting journalists and online bloggers and influencers; essentially all media is digital today. Instead, we need to look beyond the tools, technologies and channels and understand the role journalists – whether hardened hack or millennial influencer – play in shaping organisational reputation.

Fragmentation means that traditional media's role as a gatekeeper has diminished. Editors, journalists, broadcasters, commentators and producers have had this responsibility diluted and even surpassed by the new generation of bloggers, opinion leaders and citizen journalists. These are today's gatekeepers who, although they may lack the experience, ethical values and qualifications of professional journalists, hold the key to unlocking engagement with much broader and harder to reach stakeholders.

At the same time as stripping down the cosy but fractious symbiosis between organisation and journalist, digital media has provided influencers with the ways and means of targeting specific publics more with more pace, efficiency and often, more relevance. Stephen Waddington's essay 'Your audience with the public' (2019) describes this fragmentation as enabling anyone to become a content publisher – and thereby a channel to reach publics – where communities form around organisations and issues.

Philip Sheldrake's Business of Influence model (2011) goes further to suggest that everyone now influences everyone else, with fluid communication between all stakeholders including the organisation, the media and competitors.

But if everyone is influencing everyone else, does that not create concern around trust, credibility, truth and the ethical practice of influencers? The next sections in

> **Explore 14.1** **Global media outlets**
>
> Despite the continuing fragmentation of the international media landscape, prominent global media outlets still have the ability to reach vast audiences around the world. A single news story reported by one of those media mammoths can earn you coverage across the continents, but the competition is fierce.
>
> ### Know them, know their international audiences
>
> For global social issues, including climate change, human trafficking or refugee crises, you may choose to target *Al Jazeera*, *BBC World News* or *BBC World Service*. Before you contact them, however, make sure you do your homework: research the outlet, make sure your story matches its agenda, and find out which editor or presenter it is best to approach.
>
> In the Middle East, *Al Jazeera* is considered the most prominent media outlet reaching audiences across the Arab world. Similarly, to target Chinese citizens globally, consider pitching your story to *CCTV News* and *China Xinhua News Network Corporation*, but bear in mind that your particular public may place little trust in those outlets due to their political affiliations with the government.
>
> Also, consider targeting newspapers with international scope, including *The Guardian* (UK, US and Australia), *The Financial Times* (US, UK, Europe, Asia, Middle East and China), or *The Wall Street Journal* (US, Asia, India, Europe and Latin America; alongside its digital versions in Chinese, Japanese, Korean, Bahasa Indonesia and Portuguese).
>
> Similarly, you can reach massive international audiences by targeting mainstream wire services which issue their content to subscriber media outlets. A single article press release published by *Agence France-Presse (AFP)*, *Associated Press (AP)*, or *Reuters* can gain you coverage across a vast number of media outlets in different countries.
>
> ### Mind the time
>
> If you issue your campaign announcement at 9am in London, it will be 11am in Doha, Qatar and 8pm in Sydney, Australia – too late to get your story across. One way to tackle this is to disseminate your story 'under embargo' – this gives journalists time to prepare the story in advance while preventing them from publishing or airing it before the time specified in the embargo.
>
> *Source:* adapted from Alaimo 2017

this chapter will explore the rise of the influencer and the impact fake news has had on trust, credibility and reputation.

The rise of the influencer

With audiences having the means to engage in conversations directly with brands, media relations has shifted from pitching stories to traditional media, to collaborating with a broad scope of individuals across a variety of digital media platforms (Waddington 2018), triggering the rise of influencer marketing. Since every company has the capacity to disseminate messages through engagement with influential bloggers and other online content producers in a strategic manner, the term 'influencer relations' seems more appropriate within the context of public relations (Parker 2012).

The inclusion of influencer relations in PR strategies, however, is not necessarily new. A 1948 study on political communication by Lazarsfeld et al. claimed that the majority of people are influenced by information coming from opinion leaders. These included influential speakers, community leaders or prominent media figures holding the power to influence public opinion though their authority and expertise (Charlesworth 2014). With the exponential growth of the social media landscape, the opinion leader role has transformed into one of an influencer using blogs, tweets and other online channels. But the scope of that role has remained essentially the same: acting as an independent third party endorser with the power to shape audience attitudes (Freiberg et al. 2011).

While traditionally media relations was focused on the news media (Coombs and Holladay 2010), influencers create opportunities for engagement with broader and harder to reach publics. Those include wide-interest driven communities which are not defined or held back by geographical or demographic boundaries, and particularly those who opt to stay out of the mainstream media and traditional marketing reach. A study carried out by Forbes revealed that while only 1 per cent of millennials would find a compelling advertisement to increase their trust in a brand, 62 per cent admit they are more likely to become a loyal customer if a brand engages with them on social networks (Schawbel 2015). They expect brands to not only be present on social networks, but to engage in conversation. This means that influencer relations require PR practitioners to identify relevant and engaging individuals, capable of creating conversations with a brand's audiences who seek interaction with individuals to whom they can relate (Hickman 2018). Therefore, a tangible synergy between brand and influencer value is key to reaching audiences more directly and promoting brands through shared personal experience as 'there is no real influence from fake influencers' (Perse 2018). This is seconded by the findings of 'The Age of Social Influence' report (Celebrity Intelligence 2017), highlighting the desire for authentic interactions particularly among the younger generation, 'who are placing their trust in individuals who are more like themselves' (p. 9).

While audiences may value a personalised element in their digitised day-to-day lives, PR practitioners need to deploy a strategic approach to developing relationships with social media influencers to ensure excellent fit with a brand. Therefore, and similarly to traditional media relations, influencers should be approached as equal partners of a brand rather than simply as media platforms used to amplify organisations' messages. Organisations should aim for long-term relationships, authentic engagement and testimonials as part of their communication programmes instead of focusing on one-off, short-lived collaborations. It is therefore of paramount importance to differentiate between influencers who value and protect their own reputation by only engaging in mutually beneficial relationships with organisations and so-called 'entertainment or star celebrities' who often make a living out of promoting brands and have a more business-like approach to collaboration (see Box 14.1).

The leverage and the potential of influencer relations lies within a unique relationship between the influencer and their publics, stemming from the two-way communication nature of social media platforms.

Box 14.1

Hierarchy of influencers

The following description of different classes of influencers is based on the experience of key executives from Ketchum (Waddington 2018). Note how different types of influencers determine their place within the PESO model.

Executives and employees – earned

These individuals are typically leaders of an organisation. They are generally employees helping develop relationships by humanising the organisation, having a clear point of view, and promoting it through thought leadership. Employees can also be engaged more broadly via blogs and social networks.

Industry experts – earned

Fact and fiction travel at equal speed on the internet but topic experts still have authority. Informed opinion from an expert carries weight particularly in a business-to-business community. Health professionals can be influential on issues related to health and wellbeing and a specialist journalist can change the conversation around current affairs and political issues.

Bloggers – earned and paid

Bloggers are writers who share their own experiences and stories on their own websites and third party sites such as LinkedIn and Medium. They are one of the original forms of internet influencer and cover a wide range of consumer topics including food, style, DIY and parenting. Professional blogs are also popular in the business-to-business sector.

Short form influencers – earned and paid

As new social media platforms have launched, influencers have created content and built audiences. Instagram has amassed huge followings skewed towards a younger audience. Short form influencers create content around topics including humour, fashion, music and food.

Celebrities – paid

Brands sought out celebrities as ambassadors long before the internet. Today celebrities use their own media to engage with fans frequently rivalling the reach of traditional media. Their profile often limits their ability to engage in conversations. The value of celebrities lies in endorsement and starting conversations.

Video stars – paid

YouTube's launch in 2005 provided the means for anyone to create and publish video content to a global audience via the internet. Video influencers produce high-quality content around a specialised topic such as beauty, comedy, gaming or music. They have large and loyal following and are able to demand a premium for brand partnership.

Source: Stephen Waddington, How to do influencer marketing, March 14. Retrieved from https://wadds.co.uk/blog/2018/3/14/how-to-do-influencer-marketing

Case study 14.1
Lion Lager – iLobola Nge Bhubesi

Relaunching a legacy large in South Africa

Lion Lager is an iconic South African beer manufactured by brewer AB inBev. The brand once held the largest market share of the beer market back in the 1980s and 1990s before being shelved due to strong competition from cooler and more relevant competitors in the market.

When Johannesburg-based agency DNA Brand Architects was asked to relaunch the brand our start point was a recognition that South Africa has high levels of inequality and alcohol brands often exclude low-income consumers in their communication. DNA Brand Architects had an opportunity to change this through a ground-breaking iLobola Nge Bhubesi campaign centred around iLobola, the South African tradition whereby the man pays the family of his fiancée for her hand in marriage.

Strategy: repositioning a beer brand as a champion in South Africa

In recent years, Lion Lager lost relevance to cooler and more aspirational competitors in beer and there was a lack of awareness of what the brand stood for in the market. The brand had little to no activity in previous years. DNA Brand Architects had a huge opportunity to reposition the brand as more than just a beer brand, but a brand that was a champion of authentic South African stories that celebrated the resilient spirit of South Africans.

More than any other brand Lion Lager still triggered that nostalgic feeling amongst South Africans; however, to understand the beer drinker, DNA Brand Architects worked with AB inBev to research the market.

Research: understanding Lion Lager's modern consumer

DNA Brand Architects wanted Lion Lager to appeal to younger audience of predominately black men aged between 25 to 45 years old who are active on social media. Through an internal study conducted by the AB inBev Consumer Insights team DNA Brand Architects determined the following:

- Its consumers are blue-collar workers. It's a predominantly black male market who live in urban to peri-urban areas.
- They are part of society that is largely 'left behind' and often feel invisible at times.
- They may not be in the world of green bottles (the aspirational set of the market) but that does not necessarily mean doom and gloom for them. There is a level of pride in the lives they lead.

Audience research also showed that this audience focuses on culture and custom. This informed our PR strategy and social media channels selection.

Insights: local pride

- Family and traditional values give our audience a sense of belonging, dignity and pride.
- The best way to engage with the audience is digital media.
- Language is important to the target audience who value their home language.

The campaign: iLobola Nge Bhubesi

It was clear from the research that Lion Larger needed to build a relationship with consumers. DNA Brand Architects decided to do this through culture by telling the story of Lobola, which is a tradition in South African custom whereby the man pays the family of his fiancée for her hand in marriage. It told the story of lobola through a series iLobola Nge Bhubesi, that was born out of the desire to bring pride back to black culture and reintroduce Lion Lager through an authentic South African story.

Campaign execution

To bring the campaign to life Lion Lager partnered with likeminded individuals and suppliers who understood the cultural nuances of the story using a phased approach.

- Content Shoot – partnership with black female-owned production company OSU who developed the treatment and shot the series over two days in Soweto.
- Digital Roll Out – Lion Lager had no social media presence so we built it from the ground up. Five episodes were shared across multiple platforms every Monday and Thursday over the course of four weeks. This also included memes and Gifs from series which were shared on Facebook, Twitter and YouTube to drive engagement.
- Influencers – lead character Bafana Mthembu was the campaign anchor influencer supported by micro influencers who helped to get the masses engaging with the content.

case study 14.1 (continued)

- Media relations – having rolled out the content on digital it was key that we land the story on tier 1 media platforms. Our strategy was to curate reviews on entertainment media, features for the film's breakout talent which landed us on broadcast and print media in our consumers' native tongue and online.
- Collaboration – we partnered with the country's biggest newspaper *Daily Sun* to help us drive engagement on social media platforms and gain critical mass.

Picture 14.1 Behind the scenes shooting of iLobola Nge Bhubesi digital video assets (*source:* Monare Matema)

Effectiveness and results

Objective	Results
Storytelling – Relaunch the brand through an innovative digital series that would expose the brand to new audiences	We delivered five episodes, a 10-minute short film, memes, gifs, and behind the scenes content, that entertained and drove engagement
Community – Build an active Lion Lager Community on social media and reach more than a million people on Facebook, twitter and YouTube	Before the campaign broke Lion Lager didn't have an existing online community, however once the campaign broke the amount of engagement with its pages grew rapidly. More than 14 million people were exposed to the campaign
Business outcomes – Contribute meaningfully to business results by increasing units sold by 10000 during the campaign period	During the period the campaign sales increased 170% to 27,135 units

Thanks to AB inBev, DNA Brand Architects and ICCO. The campaign won the Media Relations category in the ICCO Global Awards 2019.

In the words of Philip Trippenbach, Head Influencer at Edelman UK: 'if you have an influencer with a million followers, that's not like a TV channel with a million viewers – it's a person with a million one-to-one relationships' (cited in: Hickman 2018). This view is seconded by a survey carried out among senior industry figures in *PRWeek*, which revealed that 'many of them see influencer engagement as more important than traditional celebrity endorsements and, in some respects, even media relations' (Harrington 2018).

Although influencer relations undoubtedly creates new possibilities, it poses several challenges related to cost, evaluation and transparency. According to Waddington (2019), one of the chief challenges leading to his assessment of influencer relations being in its infancy, stems from the progressively blurred boundaries between PR and marketing. The CIPR's Skills Guide, 'The Ethics of Paid and Earned Media', classifies influencers' engagement as Earned media within the PESO model (Dietrich 2018), stipulating that generating content from bloggers and social media influencers who do not reveal when they are paid to promote a product, service or brand, is against its Code of Conduct.

Complete transparency is the only ethical approach for all social media posts, and therefore the CIPR recommends the use of the #ad hashtag introduced by the Advertising Standards Authority in 2014 as a way for influencers to identify paid-for posts. While it is widely understood that the failure to declare paid-for endorsements is against both the law and the ethical duty to ensure brands and influencers commit to transparency, hundreds of astroturfing and misleading cases (Oakes 2019) prove that this is not the case. For example, the influencers who endorsed 2017's ill-fated Fyre Festival were paid up to $250,000 without using #ad, and while the event turned out to be a complete fiasco, the influencers in question faced no punishment (Tait 2019).

There are also controversies surrounding the evaluation of influencer relations. In the past, the success of the publicity model was measured in column inches or airtime; nowadays practitioners count the number of likes, shares and mentions. While media coverage may lead to raising awareness of an organisation, there's no proof it will instil attitudinal or behavioural changes and for that reason output measures shouldn't be used to evaluate a campaign outcomes. Similarly, Trippenbach (cited in Hickman 2018) claims he has 'never seen evidence' of influencer relations bringing substantial ROI when used to promote specific products on Instagram. This view is also reflected by The 'Age of Social Influence' report (Celebrity Intelligence 2017) stating that marketing specialists see measuring ROI or the effectiveness of an influencer campaign as a challenge with 60 per cent of consultancies still using press coverage as a means to measure success. This means influencer relations is viewed as the end purpose rather than an element serving as a means to a strategically developed end.

Undoubtedly, influencer relations helps to serve new public engagement possibilities, but the practice itself seems to lag behind the ever-changing landscape of the social media world. Therefore, the fundamentals of good media relations practice spelled out by Ivy Lee in 1906, with the emphasis on relevance, authority, engagement and relationship (Parker 2012), seem to still be of a paramount importance to maintain ethical standards of the PR profession as a whole.

Fake news: do audiences love being fooled?

While 'fake news' has proliferated political debate since the beginning of Donald Trump's presidency in 2017, there is no consensus to what the expression actually means. Some scholars identify fake news as a 'news articles that are intentionally and verifiably false and could mislead readers' (Alcott and Gentzkov 2017), but the British government, for example, rejected the term, arguing that it has taken on a variety of meanings, including statements simply not liked or agreed with by the reader and therefore, clarifying the term 'fake news' ultimately misleading. 'Fake news' has been removed from official documents and legislation and instead an agreed definition of the words 'misinformation' and 'disinformation' has been put forward (Digital, Culture, Media and Sports Committee 2018).

At the same time, an Ogilvy Global Media Influence survey among media practitioners reported that journalism across the board has suffered a drop in trust due to reports of 'fake news', leading to the decrease in the credibility of traditional media outlets (Ogilvy 2018). Still, traditional media leads as the most trusted news sources (50 per cent globally), followed by company websites and press releases (34 per cent in Europe, with 24 per cent in Asia Pacific, an overall increase from 2017). With Facebook acting as the primary gatekeeper for news, most journalists believe that both the news industry and social media platforms should collaborate to combat the 'echo chambers' of self-selected media.

One of the biggest issues surrounding fake news stems from the fact that even organisations who own social media do not seem to recognise the full extent of their potential in influencing publics. By definition, Facebook is not and never was launched as a media company, but it serves as one – its founder and CEO Mark Zuckerberg argued time and time again that it's a networking platform, but during the US election campaign fake news stories generated more engagement on Facebook than the top election stories from 19 major news outlets with a staggering 66 per cent of American voters using it as a news source (Chang et al. 2016). Following allegations that the proliferation of fake news on Facebook influenced the result of the 2016 Presidential election in the US, Zuckerberg defended his company, arguing that the platform wasn't a news source. But he backtracked 10 months later promising to implement strict measures to stop fake news. Seeing the unfolding crisis of data breaches and privacy issues plaguing Facebook, it seems improbable for the platform to achieve the levels of transparency and journalistic diligence reputable traditional media brands still uphold.

Another example illustrating the pitfalls of fake news and the challenges it poses for traditional media is the aftermath of the 2016 terrorist attack in Manchester with social media users posting different kinds of false information, such as reporting there was a gunman outside the hospital, or pictures of assumed victims. The problem was that mainstream media, such as the *Daily Express* and *Daily Mail UK,* reposted these stories and thus widened their reach.

This begs two interrelated questions: why do people read and share fake news and do publics enjoy being fooled? To answer that, Reuters Institute for Journalism published a report on the perceptions of fake news by audiences in Europe, revealing that 39 per cent of publics trust news media because 'they just do' as they trust in reporters 'trying their best' and still see the media as a watchdog (2017). Essentially, mainstream news media still seems more credible and serves as a default source of news verification based on the audiences' belief in journalistic process during which reporters distinguish facts from fiction. However, the same report showed that a similar percentage of respondents (33 per cent) see social media as a credible source of information since digital platforms offer a broader range of sources, wider access to unbiased content and ensure pluralism.

In addition, audiences perceive fake news in numerous ways, ranging from innocuous satire – and thus not seen as 'real news stories' – through sensationalist journalism, political spin or fabrication, to sponsored content (Newman et al. 2017). With credibility of organisational messages being a key feature of PR, this means that any sponsored content should be appropriately labelled, including advertorials.

Regardless of fake news proliferating the tech industry, there is no doubt that traditional media outlets – and thus earned content – remain resilient, which means that PR practitioners should develop and maintain close relationships with reporters and editors to enable credibility of sources, fact and accreditation of the right people. In addition, and to compete in a fake-news environment, for organisations to build trust with publics, Edelman has proposed leveraging stories through its Cloverleaf Framework which utilises two spheres of influence: one focusing on social media networks, including messaging services, search engines and personalised news curators; and one on publishers, including media outlets, influencers and organisations' own digital platforms (Rubel 2016).

Case study 14.2
An all-Russian initiative: 'Vote for your skating rink!'

Promoting active lifestyle and supporting public sports matches, the philosophy of NIVEA, one of the world's leading cosmetic brands. Its core value is care, and the brand shows it not only via its high-quality skincare products, but also by means of improving their customers' lives and well-being.

In 2013, NIVEA launched a nationwide campaign aimed at restoring abandoned outdoor neighbourhood skating rinks – something that no company has ever done in Russia before. The winter of 2018/2019 saw the fifth season of the project.

Audience: Russian citizens

- Russian citizens – people living mainly in the countryside (outside the capital). Primarily, families with children aged five+ with average and low income. Hockey, soccer and figure skating are the top-three sports most popular with Russians: 32–34 per cent watch them. However, not so many actually do them: hockey, with 3 per cent, being one of the last choices (source: MAGRAM Market Research, 11/2019). Experts connect the popularity of certain sports with the available infrastructure (which is especially important for team games, such as hockey).
- Journalists – working for nationwide and local media outlets (news, general interest and lifestyle). In many areas of Russia, the media market is ill-developed: local outlets often write about everything, without clear specialisation. Not much is happening in small towns, so journalists are 'hungry' for interesting news. For nationwide media, however, local newsbreaks are usually too small (this had to be considered when planning the campaign).
- Bloggers – nationwide and local influencers writing about family life and lifestyle. Bloggers with 100+ followers were given a priority.
- Local authorities – while they can be passive and not easy to cooperate with, local governments are eventually interested in projects that benefit the citizens of their area. They welcome external investment as it helps to save the city budget.

Objective: encouraging participation in ice skating

The campaign's strategic goal is contributing to popularisation of active lifestyle among Russian families and facilitating the development of public sports.

Objectives for the 2018/2019 season:

- Reach >110M people (+100 per cent vs. previous season).
- Earn 300+ pieces of media coverage mentioning the initiative and the NIVEA brand (100+ per cent vs. previous season), of them at least 50 in nationwide and 250 in local outlets.
- Gather 150+ applications for ice rink restoration from across the country (based on previous years' average).
- Ensure 40.000 votes for applications, which was an important indicator of the audience's engagement (based on previous years' average).
- Ensure 300+ attendees at each skating rink opening event on average (based on previous years).

Campaign idea: using skating rinks to connect with Russian citizens

Restoring outdoor skating rinks was a simple way to give a boost to the local sports infrastructure and help revive the culture of active lifestyle and mass sports. It worked for both winter and summer outdoor activities. The campaign focused on neighbourhood skating rinks as they were accessible and free. Such objects can become the heart of the district bringing people together and brightening up the life of the whole community.

To ensure that skating rinks are given to those who really need them, engage people and motivate them to use these facilities, a nationwide competition was announced: citizens were offered to decide themselves which facility needed to be restored, vote for their location, and get their friends and neighbours' support. In other words, people needed to show they cared, and care would be rewarded by NIVEA.

The campaign was named 'Vote for your skating rink!'

Campaign execution

In February 2018, a call for entries was announced via nationwide and local media, as well as via social media and bloggers. The news releases inspired citizens to use this chance to give their neighbourhood a new, modern skating rink; they talked about the 12 rinks already restored within the campaign and how they changed people's lives in those areas.

Participants submitted applications via the NIVEA website: they needed to upload photographs and explain why their skating rink deserved a new life. NIVEA encouraged entrants to be as active and creative as possible to earn more votes. People responded by sharing their stories and appeals in social networks, engaging friends and even summoning the local media!

By summer, three winning towns were selected: Nelidovo, Samara and Khabarovsk, and restoration work began.

By winter, the rinks were ready and opening events were organised in each city. But how to attract the citizens and encourage the media to cover a corporate initiative? NIVEA invited Olympic figure-skating champion Alexey Yagudin to perform at the opening events and give skating workshops to local children. Highlighting the campaign's connection with the trend for a healthy lifestyle and showing the benefits of the new facilities for the city also helped win the journalists' loyalty.

Given the differences between the nationwide and local media, the communication support of the openings was planned separately at the federal and regional level.

Locally, the campaign included four stages:

1. Announcing that a renovated ice rink will soon open in town and telling a story and philosophy of NIVEA's initiative.
2. Inviting the citizens to the opening event, with the date and programme.
3. Revealing the name of a guest star.
4. A post release following the opening event.

At a nationwide level, the campaign featured only one stage: distributing a post release with the results of the 2018 to 2019 season of NIVEA's campaign.

In social media, the initiative was supported via citywide communities and popular family and lifestyle bloggers. The bloggers were asked to share their personal stories about outdoor activities they enjoy and ways to actively spend leisure time with their family, their childhood memories etc. In their own authentic manner, they encouraged the followers to go out to a skating rink and informed them about NIVEA's initiative.

The opening ceremonies took place in December in both Samara and Nelidovo, and in January in Khabarovsk. Each event was a real feast for the whole town, with lots of entertainment activities for the whole family and, of course, an unforgettable meeting with the Olympic champion.

The events featured press conferences where NIVEA top managers told local journalists in person about the achievements of the campaign and its connection with NIVEA's philosophy of care. The speakers advocated active family lifestyle and highlighted the importance of developing local sports facilities.

Effectiveness and results

- 540 pieces of media coverage mentioning the initiative and the NIVEA brand (3.5 times more than in 2017/2018 and exceeding the KPI two-fold), of them 106 stories in nationwide and 434 in local outlets.
- 338 applications for skating rink restoration (twice over the KPI) scoring 45,895 votes.
- 1,500+ attendees at opening events – 500+ on average (67 per cent over the KPI).

Most importantly, three more communities got places where families can spend their leisure time enjoying sports and outdoor games. And who knows, perhaps these skating rinks will see the rise of new sport stars?

Thanks to ICCO, NIVEA and Pro-Vision Communications. The campaign won the Lifestyle Award category in the ICCO Global Awards 2019.

Hacks versus flacks? An ongoing battle or an opportunity for excellence?

The relationship between journalists and PR practitioners is often fractious. At best, the symbiotic approach of PR providing stories for content-hungry news and entertainment channels, has served both disciplines well. At worst, the hacks versus flacks debate has muddied the waters creating an atmosphere of frustration and distrust.

A panel at the 2019 Oxford Media Convention hosted by the *Institute for Public Policy Research* think tank, described journalism as being in an existential crisis threatened by a fragmented media landscape which has become the playground of influencers, fake news and unsustainable channels. Certainly, journalists are becoming increasingly uncertain of their role and function within a democratic system. For more than a century in the age of mass media, the BBC's Reithian ideals of informing, educating and entertaining, have helped cement journalists' position as watchdogs, acting as the eyes and ears of the population at large.

Collectively, the Oxford panellists – who included senior editors of some of the leading online news platforms – agreed that journalism helps audiences to understand how the world works and how we can help it to change. But in a media landscape awash with content and often steered by the hand of paid media, it is becoming more difficult for journalists to permeate those filters to activate audiences to make them notice, care or change their actions.

Shared spaces

More than ever, journalists and PR practitioners are operating in shared spaces where news values can meet and support organisational agendas. By adopting Grunig's excellence approach to media relations, both sides can begin to forge more meaningful relationships which not only meet organisational objectives but help publics to understand better how the world works and how they can make meaningful change.

Certainly, journalists feel that in the public interest, investigative journalism which holds those in power to account is essential to a flourishing democracy (Foster-Gilbert 2018). PR can help those important processes to thrive by maintaining open and transparent relationships between organisations, politicians, corporations and charities, and the journalists who are driven by the need to act as the public's eyes and ears.

If we break down journalistic tasks and those within PR's media relations toolbox, there are similarities. A journalist may start with research, fact-checking, conducting interviews and collating information, while a PR practitioner adopts the same behaviours when writing a news release. The output may be a long-form magazine feature or a click-bait listicle on an online platform, but the processes in reaching audiences are largely the same.

What has become more abstract is the channels through which content – news, information, entertainment, gossip – reach audiences. While technology guarantees that consumption of media is higher than at any point in history and that currently, the branded channels through which content is consumed is less obvious or distinct. Just a decade or so ago, the mainstream news production giants could be pretty certain that their output was the one that was reaching mass audiences and therefore in some way helped mainstream media to control the agenda.

Today, however, technology allows audiences to consume more news through many more indistinct and transient channels. For PR, this is an opportunity to bypass traditional media gatekeepers which comes at the cost of blurring the boundaries between independent editorial and content marketing and branding.

For journalism, this creates a problem where its desire to ensure output of quality, balanced content is threatened by channels driven more by financial than public interest. Some commentators – including those at the Oxford Media Convention – have even suggested that the fragmented media landscape has polarised news output and consumption around ideological frameworks with journalism becoming increasingly faith-based rather than fact-based.

But look at that idea of public interest again. Journalism has its own reputational issues and an urgency to clearly explain its function and role of collating, checking and verifying news while holding power to account. Public relations can help with that if it stays true to its goal of open, balanced communication. In an age of increasing distrust and misinformation, there is a duty for both disciplines to move beyond symbiosis and towards genuine engagement, finding common ground to help explain the world better.

Box 14.2

Perspectives on media relations

Jez Davison and Andy Richardson are seasoned communicators who have worked as both journalists and PR practitioners. Andy was a music journalist who later moved into PR, before returning to regional newspapers eventually becoming the editor of The Northern Echo, one of the UK's oldest regional papers, in 2016. He now runs his own media consultancy. Jez was editor of a national business lifestyle magazine before joining a large regional newspaper as a business reporter. He is now a freelance PR practitioner.

How has the Relationship Changed Between PR and Journalism?

Andy: The essence of the relationship is the same as ever. Newsrooms that still care about public interest journalism regard PR-generated content with suspicion. As a newspaper editor, I instinctively mistrusted any PR content and encouraged my reporters to do the same. That's not to say that PR companies cannot produce good stories – the better ones do – but the vast majority of content fails to pass the public interest test.

Jez: It's a relationship that has changed massively. When I started on a magazine, we were sent pictures by post, but things started to digitise pretty quickly around 2003. In those days, it was all about cultivating relationships, usually by phone but often meeting up to build up a rapport. A lunch or a coffee, when things were off the record, was a great way to build up trust on both sides. Now, it's difficult to build rapport with journalists because they are so over-stretched, there simply isn't the time. Emails and phone calls just don't seem to get the response.

What can the Two Disciplines Learn From Each Other?

Andy: As the internet became the dominant platform for breaking news, journalism was forced to acknowledge something that PR companies have known forever – content is a commodity which has a monetary value.

Analytics mean that a financial value can be placed on every piece of content and that the commercial value of every journalist is measurable. Editors can learn from PR how to convert advertising budgets into content. PR firms can learn how to produce compelling content which generates audience.

Jez: There is an opportunity for PR to help journalists understand why specific stories are important for their readers. That starts with PR understanding what kind of content journalists want and helping to create specific unique content – but that's hindered by fewer opportunities to have those useful engagements with journalists.

What are the Frustrations with Working with PR?

Andy: PR companies have been slow to react to the changing demands of newsrooms. Given the choice, news editors would reject 90 per cent of the content they receive from PR sources as it fails to have a significant commercial or news value. PR companies need to realise that analytics are being used by newsrooms to measure the impact of their content. As an editor, I always suspected that stories, such as a piece about a company's charity fundraising event, was of little interest to the general reader. Digital analytics can now tell me that is the case.

What has Been the Impact of a Digital Media Landscape?

Jez: Shared media is becoming the primary channel for getting out messages as opposed to traditional media and that is a shame. Stories are driven by getting as much traffic as possible to the website and, more often than not, that reduces the quality of the information. Regional business pages used to be dominated by stories about the economic impact of big contract wins, but that seems to have been superseded by quick look content which drives online views.

Andy: The voracious demand for content and myriad digital platforms means that publishers need large quantities of free, user-generated stories, pictures and videos. This gives PR companies more opportunities than ever to get their content published. The value of that content to their clients is questionable – the stories may be published but is anyone reading them?

How do you see Things Changing in the Future?

Andy: Things are moving at a rapid pace. Savvy PR firms are working with journalism to create platforms which generate audience and revenue for both parties. These take the form of niche publications such as business supplements, visitor guides, sport specials and the like. PRs should spend less time trying to produce 'news' stories and concentrate on building partnerships with publishers to deliver specialist publications and sponsored content.

Jez: PR has to work a lot harder and a lot smarter. But there is a golden opportunity for PR to help journalists explain their stories and why they are important and meaningful to people's lives – perhaps even an opportunity for the PR industry to help restore and protect the reputation of journalism. The dialogue has got to improve and to increase the value for both to gain reputation, trust and credibility.

Practical media relations

The practical tools and techniques of media relations should be equally familiar to both PR practitioners and communications students. The press release, news conference or briefing have been used since the days of Ivy Lee as a way of reaching publics via a targeted set of journalists. This section will analyse some of the tools of media relations making a distinction between these and the techniques which can be used to create news, such as launches, stunts, events and surveys. We will also learn how technology has both enhanced and transformed these practices creating a more two-way, transparent participatory experience, which – while contributing towards greater engagement with publics – carries threats to credibility and trust due to the open border landscape of digital media.

The six-step approach

The fourth edition of *Exploring Public Relations* identified a useful six-step workflow for PR practitioners proactively seeking media coverage. This starts with research – understanding target media, their interests and audiences before then researching potential issues, stories and spokespeople within the organisation. Next comes developing relationships with key journalists based around a shared news agenda, and then offering specific news packages to priority media using the tools and techniques outlined below. The fifth stage is to follow up with journalists to facilitate publication or to understand why the package was not used. Finally, media coverage should be monitored and evaluated.

This approach remains both relevant and practicable in today's digital and social media landscape where opportunities to publish content are more fragmented. The research stages in particular are essential, identifying not just the key journalists, bloggers, vloggers and influencers, but also the issues that trigger them, their habits, opinions and usefulness.

The tools of media relations

The news release

Much has been written about the inverted pyramid structure of a news release with numerous books and online sources advising on writing the perfect news hook, eye-catching intro and quote.

Simply, the news release is a written document which communicates information, key messages and human interest quotes from credible sources. The purpose is to encourage the journalist to create a story based upon those facts and, if appropriate, to delve a little deeper. A news release often affords an opportunity for independent endorsement from a high credibility editorial channel if the output is supportive. But the opposite can also be true with the risk of the release being edited, re-written or ignored altogether, leading to reputational damage and ultimately a counter-productive exercise.

For decades, the standard format was a single-sided, double-spaced written document sent directly to a journalist by post or later by fax. Today, releases are inserted directly into the body of an email, but this carries the risk of spamming journalists and therefore a more targeted approach which clearly identifies the news value of the information is essential.

The digital news release

Technology has had a significant impact on the news release, re-purposing its format with a greater emphasis on links, images, bullet-pointed facts alongside traditional messages and quotes.

This appealing multi-media content greatly increases the chances of the information being shared quickly and widely. That impacts on how a digital news release is written, often more as an informal article than a structured 'news report'.

The digital release also has the potential for a much wider audience and can be used as a reputational tool to be efficiently shared with many more publics – be they customers, employees, influencers or even competitors. Many switched-on brands are now using the news release format as a motivational tool within internal communications.

News conferences

While news conferences were once a commonly practiced tool for organisations to communicate, aside from crisis management situations, their practice has dwindled. Social media has made it much easier to reach publics directly without having to get past journalists and their tricky questions. But digitisation and specifically live streaming has triggered a curious phenomenon – the news conference as a staged event. Global tech giants, movie and music superstars and even politicians are now hosting 'news conferences' as a way of reaching a largely supportive public. A Premiership football pre-match conference may now be viewed live by thousands of fans, many commenting and sharing in real time and therefore contributing to reputational capital. In a sense, the traditional media relations role of these spectacles becomes subsidiary as a guide rather than gatekeeper.

Picture 14.2 Interviews with a journalist are an import aspect of media relations, enabling a journalist to scrutinise a story or issue in detail (*source:* LightField Studios/Shutterstock)

Media interviews

Providing relevant people for journalists to interview is a significant part of practical media relations. The practitioner's role here is to not only identify interview opportunities and relevant spokespeople, but to prepare them so that they stay on message to promote and protect the reputation of the organisation.

When preparing clients for media interview, it is essential that the practitioner understands the needs of different media. If it's a magazine interview, it's likely the journalist will delve deeper and need more time with your client; or the visual impact of a TV interview means your client needs to be comfortable in front of the cameras. Likewise, how will the interview be conducted? Will it be on the telephone or in a studio or on location; will it be broadcast live or pre-recorded?

Getting the message right

The options, opportunities and challenges of media interviews are many and therefore, being prepared is key. Spokespeople need to be confident, competent and comfortable if they are to be interviewed on live TV or radio. Above all, they need to be familiar with the key messages and prepared for any difficult or unexpected questions.

Your interview subject needs stay on message – be clear what that is, make it memorable and express it in understandable terms and language. Key messages should be identified before the interview and framed as what the client wants to get across in a way which will appeal to the journalist and hence their audiences.

The techniques of media relations

While the news release or conference, may be the vessel containing the message, the trigger to spark interest and inquiry is often subtler. Likewise, technology has enhanced the tools and techniques in ways which would have been unimaginable 20 years ago. Ultimately, it all comes back to storytelling – the simple ability to prepare a narrative that will resonate with publics across a range of platforms.

The exclusive

Offering a media outlet 'an exclusive' – in essence, excluding other outlets access to a story – is an established and often effective media relations technique. The exclusive is normally associated with the tabloid newspaper industry, where getting news ahead of competitors is an indicator of success but is also common within local and regional journalism as a way of differentiating from rival titles.

The embargo

The embargo is a media relations technique which helps journalists prepare content ahead of time, on the understanding it is not to be published until an official launch date or announcement. This technique can be useful for building trust between a PR practitioner and journalist, particularly if some degree of exclusivity can be guaranteed as part of the embargo. But equally, there is a risk if the journalist breaks the embargo, which would inevitably damage future media relations.

Noon

Softer news – often described as News Out Of Nothing – is a another commonly practiced media relations technique. Using research and surveys or creating event days and celebrations – for example, National Fish and Chip Week – can prove effective in creating stories for both traditional and online platforms. The risk here, however, is that such opportunities can be perceived as facile by under-pressure journalists who view them as little more than vain and trivial attempts to wrap client messages in questionable news values. In *Flat Earth News*, the former journalist and PR adversary Nick Davies (2009) describes these as fabricated 'pseudo-events' which 'fill the news vacuum'.

Explore 14.2   Pitching the story

You are an account manager providing PR support for a sportswear brand which has developed a new high-performance training shoe. The product has been endorsed by a globally recognised Olympic athlete and will bring 150 new jobs to the brand's manufacturing facility in the north of England.

Research similar product launches and think about the media relations techniques that may be adopted. Which media channels would you approach for the launch? What kind of journalists would you contact and what would the angle be?

For the regional media the angle is likely to be the economic boost the investment will bring to the local area. Business journalists may want to interview the directors of the business while gaining endorsement from politicians will bring a wider regional affairs interest. An initial pitch to the news editor for print media or desk editor for broadcast will help to direct your story to the most relevant contact.

The national media will be attracted by the endorsement of the Olympic athlete. Will there be a launch event with opportunities for pictures, video and interviews? Can exclusivity be offered or even an embargo? A live-streamed news conference featuring your endorser and technical experts from the brand will reach an audience far beyond the traditional media.

Specialists such as sports or technology journalists will also be interested, particularly on the features that make the new product different or how it has enhanced the performance of the athlete. As with all media relations, using your networks will help when making initial contacts with specialist journalists or outlets.

And don't forget the online influencers. There are likely to be bloggers and vloggers who have huge audiences attracted to the fashion, performance and sports aspects of the product launch.

Practitioner's Diary: Anne-Marie Lacey

Fire&Ice InDurham

Filament PR works with the Durham Business Improvement District (BID) to promote a season of events to increase footfall to the city and boost the local economy. Fire&Ice InDurham is a trail of ice sculptures placed around the City lit by flaming beacons. This is supported by live ice-carving demonstrations and the chance for visitors to have a go themselves. A huge selling point in terms of media relations is that each sculpture is designed and carved by the team who worked on the set of *Game of Thrones*.

Targeting family audiences, which mainly consumes news online, our strategy is online-first, followed by print and broadcast. This is supported by earned media coverage and amplified through paid activity, by working with a well-known family blogger in the region. Here's how we managed media and influencer relations in the run-up to and the weekend of Fire&Ice InDurham 2019.

Tuesday 22 February

Over the last few weeks, we've been drip-feeding content to the media about Fire&Ice InDurham to keep the event fresh. We have confirmed the theme, announced

Picture 14.3 Master carver, Matt Choloner from Glacial Arts, wows crowds with a live ice carving demonstration at Fire&Ice InDurham (*source:* Durham, Durham BID and Fire&Ice InDurham!)

the programme and today we're announcing the line-up of specific ice sculptures, including a trail map.

Our press release has been approved, along with images of last year's event, to give a taste of what people can expect, and artwork for the trail map. We issue the press release to regional print, online and broadcast media.

The sell in is straightforward, as we had already told our journalist contacts that the ice sculpture line-up press release would be coming today. We also included a media call, inviting journalists to an exclusive preview of the day before the event opens across the City.

We're also working with a blogger – *My Boys Club*. Before engaging, we did our checks to make sure content was appropriate and could access an engaged target audience. We need to ensure that the blogger is fully disclosing her content as being an ad, so we check the content once it's gone live, to ensure it is following the relevant rules and regulations – it's something we must do with influencers but isn't necessary for traditional media.

Wednesday 23 February

We have a media partnership agreement with BBC Newcastle and today they're interviewing the Manager of Durham BID about Fire&Ice InDurham. We've provided media training, so the key spokesperson is very comfortable talking to journalists. Before he goes on air, we give him a full briefing, including what questions the journalist is likely to ask, suggested responses and key messages to weave into his answers.

The interview is live via phone and all goes well. Looking at Google Analytics, we can certainly see a spike in traffic to the BID website. It's likely due to the interview and the fact the coverage from the press release went live today.

Thursday 24 February

It's media call day. The ice sculptors are at Durham Cathedral for a live demo of a brand new sculpture. The Cathedral is stunning – plus, it's a beautiful sunny day – so it should make for some great visuals for print and broadcast, as well as radio's online content.

All of the media we've invited turn up. We manage interviews and photo opportunities with our key spokesperson from Durham BID and the ice sculptor, so that each journalist has the content that they need. Again, ahead of the media call, we briefed the different interviewees and listened in on all interviews to make sure outputs were on message and communicating the facts. Following the media call, we drop the journalists and blogger a note thanking them for their time and reiterating some key facts and top tips. Simple things like coming into the City as early as possible as the ice sculptures do melt as the day goes on, but you'd be surprised by how many questions we get like this on social media. As we've learned from previous experiences, we've taken these questions and turned them into an infographic. We have signposted our media contacts to it on the BID's website as part of our follow-up calls.

Friday 25 February

Day one of the event. It's a busy day of managing the media. *ITV Tyne Tees* and *BBC Look North* turn up and we facilitate those interviews, so that they can get footage of the ice sculptures, live demos and vox pops from people attending.

The piece is due to go out on the evening news, so there isn't time to include footage of the grand finale in the Market Place. However, the BBC does come back into the City that night to get some footage for a round-up piece tomorrow.

Saturday 26 February

We're seeing lots of coverage appear from the event yesterday. One of the outlets was News North, a newswire agency, which sent along a photojournalist. One of the hero pictures has been picked up in *The Daily Telegraph* as its image of the day.

Sunday 27 February

Official footfall figures from Fire&Ice InDurham won't be available until tomorrow, although we have a good feeling it's been a record-breaking year. A number of businesses in the City have told us that they had unprecedented takings during the festival.

In anticipation, we prepare a post-event press release recounting the weekend's events, while leaving space to drop in the footfall figures as soon as we have them. We also use this to announce that Fire&Ice InDurham has been commissioned again for next year – it's a case of 'strike while the iron is hot'. We pick out the best photographic images from the event and bundle them up into a package ready to issue to the media in the morning along with the post-event press release.

Monday 28 February

The results are in and our gut feeling was right! Fire&Ice InDurham 2019 was the busiest February weekend on record for the City. We include this info in the press release, have it approved by the client and send it out.

Then, we start collating all media coverage, pulling reports from social and Google Analytics, and begin our measurement and evaluation. We also check in with the blogger to access her stats to include in our report, as in the next couple of weeks we'll be back at Durham BID's offices to present the outputs, outcomes and outtakes, as well as sharing learnings and advising on how we can improve Fire&Ice Durham further.

Think about 14.2 — What do journalists want?

The skillset of journalists has changed significantly in the digital world. At one time, good writing skills, a nose for a story, and 100 words per minute shorthand were the entry-level skills to get a first job on a local paper. But journalists now need to think far beyond words, to pictures, video footage and recorded sound. In the early 2000s, digital newsrooms broadened traditional news gathering and writing skills to photography, shooting video and recording sound. Later, the ability to edit copy for online platforms and share quickly and efficiently via social media became the norm.

That has undoubtedly put pressure on journalists to become more multi-media content managers than public watchdogs and newshounds. So, what is it that journalists want from PR and how can practitioners help?

Feedback

Ultimately, journalists are looking for a good story, something that has news value and will appeal to target readers, viewers and listeners. It's about supply and demand, with the PR practitioner supplying information, facts, angles, interviews and feature ideas which match the profile of the target media.

Ellen Gunning's sound advice in *Public Relations a Practical Approach*, suggests: 'Your relationship with the media should be consistent: honest, factual and accurate. You should always check the content of media releases before issuing – for sense, accuracy, grammar and spelling – and you should always be clearly identified as the source of the information.'

Case study 14.3
The Northern Spire Bridge opening

The **Northern Spire Bridge,** over the River Wear in Sunderland, opened in August 2018. The project cost £117 million involving 2,000 people working over three years with two-thirds paid from central government and the remainder from Sunderland City Council.

Sunderland City Council recognised the importance of effective communications throughout a project of this scale and therefore appointed PR agency DTW to work with them to manage the communications, putting community engagement and media relations at the heart of the strategy.

The vision

There had been calls for an additional River Wear crossing for at least 40 years, but the project was initially beset by a sense of cynicism fed by publics having a poor understanding of the benefits and how it would serve the community.

Sunderland City Council's vision was to connect communities and create opportunities for major new development, making it an economic driver for future investment in the city.

From an early stage, the Council invested in communications as one of the key work-streams. DTW was embedded on site to gain the trust and buy-in of the construction and planning teams.

Picture 14.4 The community walk over day for the Northern Spire Bridge over the River Wear in Sunderland, Tyne & Wear, before it opened to traffic (*source:* Reprinted with permission of DTW)

The approach

DTW realised quickly that media support would help to drive positive attitudes and community engagement. As a significant construction project, Northern Spire presented the opportunity for some huge set piece events, which would maximise media impact.

Target media were categorised into the local and regional newspapers and broadcasters; national TV; and the trade and professional press, which were essential for positioning Sunderland as a great place for investment.

Strategies for media relations:

- Open and honest communications to build trust and rapport, adding value wherever possible to journalist's requests.
- Attack as the best form of defence, proactively identifying the developments that people would want to know about.
- Maximising media opportunities and communicating these alongside key messages, providing journalists with the information they needed to create compelling stories.
- Identifying key partners and planning consistent messages to eliminate contradictory information.
- Being firm but flexible with the media, finding solutions to requests which would not compromise project objectives.

Key messages

Getting the message right was essential when engaging with the media and wider publics.

- **Northern Spire is just one part of a much wider regeneration project for Sunderland.** This helped communicate the bigger picture that wider investment would lead to long-term regeneration, prosperity and jobs.
- **Quality is at the heart of everything and the project will not be rushed.** This made clear that the new bridge was a huge investment for the city and that would play a pivotal role in Sunderland's future. It also helped to manage expectations, particularly towards the end when poor weather held up progress and the opening date had to be put back.
- Headline figures were consistently used in messaging. **Northern Spire costs £117 million, two thirds of which is funded from central government. The project involves 2,000 people over three years.**
- Softer key messages were developed around the city's sense of pride and community ownership, as well as the opportunity to ease traffic congestion.

Tactics

- Regular media training for a wide range of partners, many from the construction industry for whom the media was a new world.
- The DTW team embedded itself on site establishing a communications cabin and media mound to understand issues and identify media opportunities.
- Developed very clear media-friendly set pieces that hit time frames. These were explained in a way that would make interesting stories, while emphasising their importance to the project.

Successes

With Northern Spire being such a visual project, identifying and managing set piece events played a significant role in ensuring the project remained in the spotlight.

The raising of the pylon

One of the most striking opportunities was the arrival and raising of the 100-metre centre pylon, which was transported across the North Sea from Belgium. Tidal and weather conditions had to be just right for transporting the pylon from Belgium and for piloting along the River Wear, so some flexibility in the programme was essential. Dates of set pieces were often approximate, being confirmed sometimes just a day or two in advance. In these circumstances, it was important for DTW to communicate clearly and honestly and to liaise frequently with journalists. The communications team viewed this as a crucial aspect of their media relations strategy, with journalists being supportive, rather than critical, which helped to galvanise wider public support.

Royal opening

The flagship event for Northern Spire was the visit of Prince William and Princess Catherine in February 2018. There was an enormous amount of unseen work to manage the protocols of a royal visit, while also accommodating the demands of 45 journalists representing the likes of *Hello*, *Vanity Fair* and international picture agencies.

With all on-site required to wear protective clothing, images were transmitted across the world of the royal couple wearing branded Sunderland City Council hard hats and high-vis.

The One Show

Perseverance with one of BBC's most popular TV shows paid off when the One Show produced a film focusing on the installation of the 28 cable stays that supported the bridge.

Strictly Come Dancing

The most surprising media opportunity came in the form of the hit BBC show Strictly Come Dancing when contestant Faye Tozer danced over the bridge.

Knowing Faye lived locally, the communications team called the BBC to ask if they could get her involved. The BBC agreed, but suggested the bridge be closed to traffic

case study 14.3 (continued)

with a strict embargo until after the segment had been broadcast. Moments after the show went out to approximately 11 million viewers, images and a news release were sent out creating significant additional media coverage, including 16,000 Wikipedia searches for Northern Spire.

The opening weekend

The official opening came during the August Bank Holiday weekend, with a refresher training session for media partners, followed by a community walk over before the bridge was finally opened to road traffic. The communications team wanted to create compelling media stories while thanking the local community who had provided so much support.

By opening Northern Spire exclusively for walkers, cyclists and families the day before the bridge opened to traffic, 20,000 people were drawn to the bridge including cycling and running clubs, musicians, artists and photographers and picnicking families. In the evening, the bridge's lights were switched on for the first time providing a celebratory atmosphere.

The successful launch created a distinct sense of community celebration with publics supporting and understanding the role the bridge would play in the future prosperity of Sunderland. Social media chat about Northern Spire enthused traditional media to feed off the genuine sense of pride that was being felt for the project.

Evaluation and lessons learned

Incredibly, media coverage of Northern Spire reached an estimated 302 million people across print and broadcast alone. But media relations was just one part of continuing success for Northern Spire.

Chris Taylor, managing director of DTW, said: 'We had to think like so many different publics – the man on the street, the lorry driver, the shop keeper, the construction worker, and the near neighbours. The media are just one of the cogs in the wheel, but they are the ones who set the agenda and ultimately who will help to determine perception. You have to be proactive and relentlessly positive to build momentum. It became about thinking like a journalist, being receptive to their needs and as far as possible, providing what they wanted.'

Summary

In researching this chapter, one theme that repeatedly emerged was the desire for a more balanced and mutual relationship between journalists and PR practitioners. If traditional journalism feels threatened by the onslaught of influencers, then perhaps public relations can help restore trust in the journalistic role of holding organisations to scrutiny.

This creates a challenge for a PR industry which is often focused on outcomes rather than engagement and relationships. Whatever the shape of the media landscape, stakeholder relationships must be at the heart of it. Stephen Waddington (2019) reflects on this:

> 'Much public relations remains focused on the organisation rather than the intended public. It's frequently broadcast with no effort to listen or engage. The result is pointless at best and a reputational issue at worst.'

In the digital media world, there is therefore an opportunity for PR to practice symmetrical relationships, maintained in real time with more efficiency and connectivity.

All relations, whether with traditional journalists or online influencers, should be maintained as opportunities to nurture and learn from.

But does that mean that the role of traditional media and journalists will eventually become insignificant? Certainly not. The CIPR's annual state of the profession survey continues to remind practitioners of the prominence and importance of media relations, while Edelman's Trust Barometer firmly places traditional media as by far the most compelling source of news and information.

In the era of fake news, the desire for credible information has never been more important. PR practitioners have to work harder to engage with journalists and not view them as gatekeepers but strive for a mutually beneficial relationship dedicated to providing audiences with factual and newsworthy information which adheres to codes of ethical conduct. Transparent communication should be maintained across all media platforms with strict attention paid to truth, otherwise PR practitioners will be contributing to the erosion of trust in news media and undermine the credibility of both disciplines.

Bibliography

Alaimo K. (2017). *Pitch, Tweet, or Engage on the Street. How to Practice Global Public Relations and Strategic Communication.* New York: Routledge.

Alcott H. and M. Gentzkov (2017). Social Media and Fake News in the 2016 Election. *Journal of Economic Perspectives,* [online] Volume 31(2), pp.211–236. Available at: https://web.stanford.edu/~gentzkow/research/fakenews.pdf [Accessed 12 April 2019].

Almahraj, Y. (2017). *The profession of public relations in Saudi Arabia: a socio-cultural perspective.* PhD. Queen Margaret University.

Bradley, D. (2017). Study: threat of fake news is elevating trust in traditional media. *PRWeek,* [online]. Available at: https://www.prweek.com/article/1443764/study-threat-fake-news-elevating-trust-traditional-media [Accessed 12 April 2019].

Brittain Richardson, K. and M. Hinton (2015) *Applied Public Relations: Cases in stakeholder management.* 3rd ed. New York: Routledge.

Brown, R. and S. Waddington (2013) *Share This Too: More social media solutions for PR professionals.* Chichester: CIPR and John Wiley & Sons Ltd.

Celebrity Intelligence (2017) *Report: The Age of Social Influence.* [online]. London: Centaur Communications Limited, p.9, 31. Available at: https://www.slideshare.net/AlmudenaPastor/celebrity-intelligenceageofsocialinfluenceukoriginal?from_action=save [Accessed 12 April 2019].

Chang, J., J. Lefferman, C. Pedersen and G. Martz (2016). *When Fake News Stories Make Real News Headlines.* ABC News [online]. Available at: https://abcnews.go.com/Technology/fake-news-stories-make-real-news-headlines/story?id=43845383 [Accessed 12 April 2019].

Charlesworth, A. (2014). *Digital marketing: a practical approach.* 2nd ed. London: Routledge.

Coombs, W.T. and S. Holladay. (2010). *PR: Strategy and application.* Oxford: Wiley-Blackwell.

Chen, N. and H.M. Culbertson (2009). Public relations in Mainland China: An adolescent with growing pains. In: K. Sriramesh and D. Vercic, eds. *The Global Public Relations Handbook, Revised and Expanded Edition: Theory, Research, and Practice,* 2nd ed. New York: Routledge, pp. 175–198.

Chartered Institute of Public Relations (CIPR). (2020). *CIPR – The State of PR 2019/20 [online].* Available at: https://cipr.co.uk/CIPR/Our_work/Policy/CIPR_State_of_the_Profession_2019_20.aspx [Accessed 20 March 2019].

Davies, N. (2009) *Flat Earth News* London: Vintage Books.

Dietrich, G. (2018). *PR Pros Must Embrace the PESO model* [online]. Available at: https://spinsucks.com/communication/pr-pros-must-embrace-the-peso-model/ [Accessed 12 March 2019].

Digital, Culture, Media and Sport Committee, (2018). *Disinformation and 'fake news': Interim Report* [online]. London: House of Commons, p. 8. Available at: https://publications.parliament.uk/pa/cm201719/cmselect/cmcumeds/363/363.pdf [Accessed 12 April 2019].

Edeleman, (2019). *Edelman Trust Barometer – Global Report [online].* Available at: https://www.edelman.com/trust-barometer [Accessed 4 March 2019].

Foster-Gilbert, C. (ed.) (2018) *The Power of Journalists* London: Haus Publishing.

Freiberg, K., K. Graham, K. McGaughey and L. Freberg (2011). Who are the social media influencers? A study of public perceptions of personality. *Public Relations Review,* [online], Volume 37(1), pp. 90–92. Available at: https://www.sciencedirect.com/science/article/pii/S0363811110001207 [Accessed 12 April 2019].

Freitag, A.R. and A.Q. Stokes (2009). *Global Public Relations. Spanning borders, spanning cultures.* London: Routledge.

Grunig, J., L. Grunig, K. Sriramesh, Y. Huang and A. Lyra (1995). Models of public relations in an international setting. *Journal of Public Relations Research* Volume 7(3), pp. 163–186.

Grunig, J.E. and T. Hunt (1984). *Managing Public Relations.* New York: Holt, Rinehart and Winston.

Gunning, E. (2019). *Public Relations – A practical approach.* 3rd ed. London: Red Globe Press.

Harrington, J. (2018). Exclusive survey: what PR and marketing chiefs really think about influencer marketing. *PRWeek,* [online]. Available at: https://www.prweek.com/article/1491798/exclusive-survey-pr-marketing-chiefs-really-think-influencer-marketing [Accessed 12 April 2019].

Hickman, A. (2018). 'Influencers aren't effective for product marketing' – Edelman's head of influencer. *PRWeek,* [online]. Available at: https://www.prweek.com/article/1494047/influencers-arent-effective-product-marketing-edelmans-head-influencer [Accessed 12 April 2019].

Huang, Y.H. (2000). The personal influence model and gao guanxi in Taiwan Chinese public relations. *Public Relation Review,* Vol. 26(2), pp. 219–236.

Institute of Public Policy Research (2019). IPPR Oxford Media Convention – Remaking the UK media system.

https://oxfordmediaconvention.com/ [Convention attended 18 March 2019].

Jefkins, F. (1988). *Public Relations Techniques*. Oxford: Heinemann Publishing Limited.

Keen, A. (2008). *The Cult of the Amateur*. London: Nicholas Brealey Publishing.

Kimball, D. (2017). *The Importance of Media Relations in Japan*. [Blog] KyodoPR. Available at: http://kyodo-pr.co.jp/en/blog/ [Accessed 12 April 2019].

Lazarsfeld, P.F., B. Berelson and H. Gaudet (1948). *The people's choice; how the voter makes up his mind in a presidential campaign*. 2nd ed. New York: Columbia University Press.

Martin, T. (2011). Barry Zorthian, U.S. Diplomat in Vietnam, Dies at 90. *The New York Times*, [online]. Available at: https://www.nytimes.com/2011/01/06/world/asia/06zorthian.html [Accessed 12 April 2019].

McKinney, B. (2000) Public Relations in the Land of Ascending Dragon: Implications in Light of the US/Vietnam Bilateral trade Agreement. *Public Relations Quarterly*, 45 (4), pp. 23–26.

Newman, N, R. Fletcher, A. Kalogeropoulos, D. A.L. Levy and R.K. Nielsen (2017). Reuters Institute Digital News Report 2017 [online]. Available at: https://reutersinstitute.politics.ox.ac.uk/sites/default/files/Digital%20News%20Report%202017%20web_0.pdf [Accessed 12 April 2019].

Oakes, O. (2019). Hundreds of Influencers Warned by ASA. *PRWeek*. [online]. Available at: https://www.prweek.com/article/1522834/hundreds-influencers-warned-asa [Accessed 12 April 2019].

Ogilvy (2018). Fake News: Not Just a Social Media Problem. *PRNewswire*, [online]. Available at: https://www.prnewswire.com/news-releases/fake-news-not-just-a-social-media-problem-300667334.html [Accessed 12 April 2019].

Parker, A. (2012). Media Relations Modernised. In: Chartered Institute of Public Relations and Waddington, S. *Share This*. Chichester: John Wiley & Sons Ltd., pp. 129–137.

Perse, K. (2018). Why Brands Need to Prioritize Real Influencers Over the Fake Ones. *AdWeek*, [online]. Available at: https://www.adweek.com/brand-marketing/why-brands-need-to-prioritize-real-influencers-over-the-fake-ones/ [Accessed 12 April 2019].

Rubel, S. (2016). *The Edelman Cloverleaf Forecast. Strategies That Extend the Lifecycle of a Narrative*. [Blog] Insights. Available at: https://www.edelman.com/post/edelman-cloverleaf-forecast [Accessed 12 April 2019].

Russell, K.M. and C.O. Bishop (2009). Understanding Ivy Lee's declaration of principles: U.S. newspaper and magazine coverage of publicity and press agentry, 1865–1904. *Public Relations Review* [online] 35(2), pp. 91–101. Available at: https://doi.org/10.1016/j.pubrev.2009.01.004 [Accessed 12 April 2019].

Schawbel, D. (2015). 10 New Findings About The Millennial Consumer. *Forbes*, [online]. Available at: https://www.forbes.com/sites/danschawbel/2015/01/20/10-new-findings-about-the-millennial-consumer/#5bf8c1996c8f [Accessed 12 April 2019].

Sheldrake, P. (2011). *The Business of Influence: Reframing Marketing and PR for the Digital Age*. Chichester: John Wiley & Sons Ltd.

Slusarczyk, R. (2012). *Public Relations in Vietnam. A study of the perception of Public Relations industry among Vietnamese Public Relations practitioners*. MA thesis. Newcastle University.

Supa, D.W. and L.M. Zoch (2009). Maximizing Media Relations Through a Better Understanding of the Public Relations-Journalist Relationship: A Quantitative Analysis of Changes Over the Past 23 years. *Public Relations Journal* [online] Vol. 3(4). Available at: http://apps.prsa.org/searchresults/view/6D-030402/0/Maximizing_Media_Relations_Through_a_Better_Unders#.XLXkm-hKiUk [Accessed 12 April 2019].

Supa, D.W. (2014). The Academic Inquiry of Media Relations as both a Tactical and Strategic Function of Public Relations [online]. Available at: https://instituteforpr.org/wp-content/uploads/OrgSupa1stIssue1.pdf [Accessed 12 April 2019].

Tait, A. (2019). Forcing social-media influencers to be clear about #ads? Good luck with that. *The Guardian*, [online]. Available at: https://www.theguardian.com/commentisfree/2019/jan/25/social-media-influencers-clear-ads-celebrities-authorities [Accessed 12 April 2019].

Tench, R. and L. Yeomans (2017). *Exploring Public Relations – Global strategic communication*, 4th ed. London: Pearson.

Theaker, A. and H. Yaxley (2013). *The Public Relations Strategic Toolkit*. Abingdon: Routledge.

Valentini, C. (2009). The struggle for recognition. Personal Influence Model, Cultural Premises and Corruption – Understanding Societal Orientations towards Informal Relations. In: *EUPRERA 2009 Congress 'Corporate citizens of the third millennium. Towards a Shared European Perspective.'* [online]. Bucharest: Tritonic, pp. 365–84. Available at: https://www.

researchgate.net/publication/228418267_Personal_Influence_Model_of_Public_Relations_A_Case_Study_in_Indonesiaas_Mining_Industry [Accessed 12 April 2019].

Waddington, S. (2018). *How to do influencer marketing*. [Blog] wadds.co.uk. Available at: https://wadds.co.uk/blog/2018/3/14/how-to-do-influencer-marketing [Accessed 12 April 2019].

Waddington, S. (2019). *Your audience with the public*. [Blog] wadds.co.uk. Available at: https://wadds.co.uk/blog/2019/2/12/your-audience-with-the-public [Accessed 14 March 2019].

Websites

Chartered Institute of Public Relations (CIPR): www.cipr.co.uk
Edelman Trust Barometer: www.edelman.com/trust-barometer
PRStack: www.prstack.co.uk
Spin Sucks: www.spinsucks.com
Stephen Waddington Blog: www.wadds.co.uk

CHAPTER 15

Ezri Carlebach

Internal communication

Source: Black-legged kittiwakes (Rissa tridactyla) colony on the cliffs of Alkerfjellet, Svalbard, Arctic

Learning outcomes

By the end of this chapter you should be able to:
- define internal communication and recognise its development as a discipline
- identify the roles of the professional practitioner
- identify the communication options available to the internal communication practitioner in helping an organisation achieve its objectives
- segment internal publics within an organisation using more than one research method
- assess and evaluate the channels that are available to internal communicators
- explain how data gathering and research insights help practitioners to develop and evaluate internal communication strategies.

Structure

- What is internal communication? Perspectives and definitions
- What does an internal communication function do?
- What matters to employees: motivation in the workplace
- Planning internal communication
- Outcomes rather than outputs: choosing effective channels
- The importance of evidence in IC planning and evaluation
- Approaches to information gathering
- Professionalisation: attributes, competencies and skills in internal communication

Introduction

Communication is the defining factor in whether a group of humans cooperating towards some common purpose are 'an organisation' or not. It is the means through which people express a common purpose, agree on objectives and work together. An organisation's culture, which can be crucial in determining its success or ensuring its failure, is created and expressed primarily through communication.

Moreover, communication happens inside all organisations, whether it is managed or not, and it can occur in formal, semi-formal and informal modes. Informal daily interaction between colleagues is a necessary part of getting your job done, and of getting along with your fellow workers. Meanwhile, the principals in any organisation (i.e. the owners, or representatives of the owners, who direct the actions of others) also need to ensure that employees understand the organisation's goals, know how their role contributes to achieving those goals, and are told how well they are doing. This will partly be contained in semi-formal internal communications such as job descriptions, quality standards and other policy documents. But it mainly requires a combination of effective formal organisational communication and an appropriately enabling culture. These latter two elements comprise the core concerns of internal communication as a strategic management function.

However, as organisations grow larger and more complex, so does the challenge of engaging employees in the 'bigger picture' – the many challenges, threats and opportunities faced by the organisation as a whole, along with the job benefits, sense of personal fulfilment, and career aspirations which lie at the heart of individual human motivation. Internal communication (often abbreviated to 'internal comms') has developed into a strategic function within organisations over the past 30–40 years. Its practitioners come to it through many different routes, including from inside the broader fields of strategic public relations, corporate communication, project management and human resources. Just as the concerns of public relations have developed beyond one-way broadcasting of messages, so internal comms has developed beyond the top-down cascade of instructions to the creation and management of internal 'conversations' (Macaulay 2014). In the same way that public relations is not just about media relations, internal comms is about much more than company newsletters or holiday-season parties.

Nor is internal comms just a concern for multinational or other large organisations that need to communicate with thousands of employees. While it is essential for an international company such as Sony or BT to have a sophisticated communication system in order to engage with their employees worldwide, a small, family-owned business also benefits from information sharing and feedback to help the business perform better. Indeed, effective internal communication is found to be one of the main contributors to improved productivity in the UK's small- and medium-sized businesses (CBI 2019).

Further, internal comms is also vital when an organisation of any size or sector is undergoing some form of change or transformation. Internal publics need a clear understanding of what is expected from them in such situations. Businesses must explain customer needs, public sector organisations must promote understanding of service priorities, and every organisation must have people who are committed to, and enthused about the task at hand.

This chapter, which combines academic and practitioner perspectives, discusses the role that internal communication plays in contemporary workplaces. It discusses, in particular, the importance of the concept of employee engagement, how internal comms is managed, planned and measured, and some of the tools and approaches used. We also examine the role that communication professionals play in supporting an organisation's leadership, and consider the potential impact on internal comms of the rapidly growing use of artificial intelligence (AI) in organisations.

What is internal communication? Perspectives and definitions

Internal communication is the term used to describe an organisation's managed communication system, where employees are regarded as an internal public or stakeholder group (Verčič et al. 2012). Other terms used are 'employee communication', 'organisational communication' and 'internal marketing'. An organisation's managed communication system may include a variety of channels and activities, including printed and electronic newsletters, environmental channels (noticeboards, graphic displays, etc.), staff briefings and intranets.

Until relatively recently, internal communication received little attention from public relations theorists since their focus was on external communication. However, internal communication is widely regarded as a strategic imperative (Lee 2002; Dolphin 2005) and theorists are re-examining it in the light of developments such as employee engagement and employee voice (Welch 2011; Karanges et al. 2014; Zerfass et al. 2015; Soares and Del Gáudio 2018).

Among early public relations theorists advocating the 'excellence theory', James Grunig asserted that if a system of two-way symmetrical communication is adopted, then 'open, trusting, and credible relationships with strategic employee constituencies [groups] will follow' (Grunig 1992: 559). Kennan and Hazleton (2006) take a relational perspective that places emphasis on trust between management and employees, and identification or connectedness among employees as the key features of internal relationship building. The corporate communication school of thought, on the other hand, regards employees as important stakeholders whose behaviour and communication contribute to corporate identity and project it to external stakeholders, thereby exerting a significant influence on corporate reputation (Welch and Jackson 2007; Gillis 2008).

The development of a 'strategic communication' perspective in public relations over the past decade (Hallahan et al. 2007) has led some theorists to consider internal communication differently, placing greater emphasis on helping employees to make sense of organisational change and complexity. Furthermore, all employees, not just managers and communication specialists, are understood to have a communication role within organisations and to contribute to sense-making (Yeomans 2008; Heide and Simonsson 2011; Mazzei 2014).

Box 15.1
A brief history of internal communication

Little has been documented on the history of internal communication within public relations scholarship, although it has been written about extensively by practitioners. Its history seems to be closely intertwined with changing attitudes to management practice and the need to motivate employees (FitzPatrick 2008).

A recent account of the history of internal communication from a UK perspective by Yaxley and Ruck (2015) draws on archival, academic, practitioner and anecdotal sources to trace its development. The authors note that the roots of formal internal communication lie in the production of the 'employee publication', which emerged from nineteenth- and twentieth-century industrialisation in Europe and the United States. As companies grew larger, so grew the need for a means of communication between employers and employees.

From these early days, a tension existed between giving the employees control of their own publication and producing a 'house organ' under the company's editorial control. For example, Lever Brothers, the British soap manufacturer, established an employee-run publication *Port Sunlight Monthly Journal* in 1895, but this was superseded by a company run journal, *Progress*, in 1899, which 'was a "means of intercommunication" between the company's head office and its Port Sunlight works, branch offices in the UK, offices and other concerns overseas, as well as "customers and friends" (Yaxley and Ruck 2015: 5).

This tension between giving employees a voice, and an internal communication system controlled by managers, continues to the present day in terms of debates on who has ownership of internal social media. Yaxley and Ruck (2015) present four historic strategies in internal communication, reflecting a 'telling and selling' approach through to an 'engage and consult' approach as follows:

1. **Paternalism. Nineteenth century** – the establishment of the employee publication. Companies at the forefront of this practice were concerned with the welfare of their employees. Such welfarism can also be seen as a strategy to combat organised labour and industrial unrest (see also Yates 1985).

2. **Presentation. 1940s** – the era of the 'in-house journalist' or industrial editor who was paid to write stories that employees would find interesting. The struggle for a credible, professional editorial role, independent of management interference, characterised the role of the industrial editor. Both the Institute of Internal Communication in the UK, and the US-based International Association of Business Communicators can trace their origins to this 'industrial editor' model.

3. **Persuasion. 1980s** – emphasis on internal communication presenting 'a case for change' to employees during a period of economic upheaval. A 'what's in it for you' message reflected a period of persuading employees. Internal communication as a system of planned communication became more closely aligned with management.

4. **Participation. Early twenty-first century** – a period which reflects an interest in the concepts of 'engagement' and 'consultation' with employees against the backdrop of factors including a lack of trust in management and an 'engagement deficit', changing labour practices and transformational communication technologies.

Yaxley and Ruck (2015) argue that while these four strategies are linked to four historical periods, they do not

| 19th century | 1940s | 1980s | 21st century |
| Paternalism | Presentation | Persuasion | Participation |

←——— **Propaganda** ———→

| House organs — written by employees for employees | **Employee voice** | Social media — facilitating employee engagement |

| Industrial editors seek management endorsement | **Professionalism** | Internal communication qualifications underpin strategic practice |

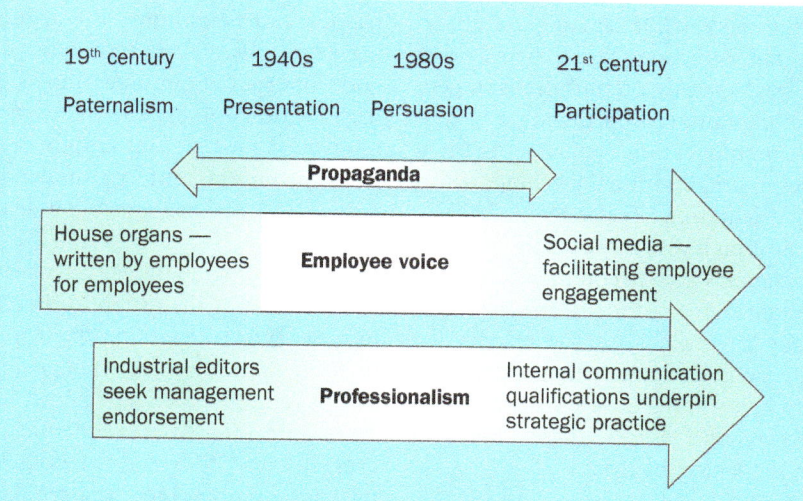

Figure 15.1 Propaganda, voice and professionalism (*source*: Yaxley, H. and K. Ruck (2013). Tracking the rise and rise of internal communication from the 1980s)

belong exclusively to these periods. They shift back and forth and overlap, thus, '[r]ather than seeing the history of internal communications simply as one of progression, a model is proposed that sees trends or themes continuing or replicating over time' (Yaxley and Ruck 2015: 11. See Figure 15.1). The three recurring trends or themes are:

1. **Propaganda:** within the context of internal communication, 'management propaganda' refers to one-way information giving, which prioritises management-controlled messages over other content and presents the organisation in a favourable light at the expense of more credible content and two-way exchange of ideas. This is a continuing theme for internal communication.
2. **Employee voice:** refers to the opportunity for employees to have their voice heard. While 'voice' was evident in the very early days of internal communication practice when employees were found to run their own publications, the voice of the employee has been subject to ebbs and flows in perceived importance in organisations. While staff surveys are one way of capturing the employee voice, social media potentially empowers employees to write their own blogs and tweet ideas – within the framework of company policy on using these tools.
3. **Professionalism:** refers to the increasing professionalism of internal communication – from industrial editors in the 1980s seeking management support, through to internal communication as a strategic practice underpinned by a qualification. The 'downside' of seeking strategic management status, however, is a potential move away from considering the 'employee voice'.

Definitions of internal communication vary. Early in the twentieth century, internal communication was taken to mean the combination of accumulated documents in an organisation, from an archival or records management perspective (Yates 1985). However, even at that point, the dissemination of fit-for-purpose information to employees – and its potential for unintended consequences – featured in satirical expressions of employees' views. More recently, records management has become knowledge management, a separate although related discipline, and the focus of internal comms is now on an organisation's ability to tell its employees what is happening, and what is expected of them.

For example, a Europe-wide study of practitioners found that internal communication is commonly defined as a tactical, one-way function that is responsible for producing and disseminating internal media (Verčič et al. 2012). This contradicts definitions of internal communication as a function that enables two-way communication, including the definition that has been presented in earlier editions of this book. Nevertheless, the management concept of employee engagement, which we discuss later, suggests that 'building two-way, trusting relationships with internal publics, with the goal of improving organisational effectiveness', is a strategic concern for leaders (Yeomans and Carthew 2014) and practitioners (FitzPatrick and

Valskov 2014). Furthermore, while listening to employees and other stakeholders through research and other techniques is often neglected by organisations in general, and in internal communication planning in particular, 'excellent' communication departments use a variety of techniques in organisational listening, which suggests a two-way orientation (Zerfass et al. 2015).

Internal communication is also inextricably linked to supporting an organisation's need to communicate information about important change – for example, a merger with another company, a re-branding or the introduction of a new CEO. In theory, at least, internal publics should be among the first to know about these changes, so that they are shown to be included in the change process and can see their part in the 'bigger picture'.

What does an internal communication function do?

Internal communication teams are involved in a range of activities. Priorities will, of course, vary from organisation to organisation and will depend on the needs and opportunities in each organisational context. Senior leaders also hold varying levels of expectation in terms of how internal comms contributes to achieving organisational objectives. Broadly speaking, most of the communication activities fall under six general headings that relate to organisations and their employee-related objectives (FitzPatrick 2016):

- ensuring the organisation meets its legal obligations to communicate with employees;
- ensuring employees know what is expected of them, and how to achieve it;
- supporting major change;
- promoting collaboration and a sense of community in the workplace;
- promoting external advocacy – getting employees to tell a positive story to the outside world about their organisation; and
- encouraging good employees to stay.

An internal comms team operating to a strategic plan will focus on activities that support organisational objectives, and can be measured accordingly. For example, in some industries, such as oil and gas, shortages of highly skilled technicians make it a business imperative to retain staff. A hospital might need to explain hygiene and hand-washing policies to staff; or an airport might encourage workers to explain to friends and neighbours the arguments for developing new runways and terminals. In all of these cases, good internal communication will contribute to the organisation's ability to achieve its objectives – retaining valued staff, getting employees to follow essential rules, promoting external understanding of a major issue – and will use sensible indicators to confirm its impact.

Encouraging employee advocacy, persuading them to stay, winning their support for change programmes – in other words, enabling them to 'go the extra mile' in doing their job – are often grouped under the heading of 'employee engagement'. This is a subject of increasing interest to academics, practitioners and, crucially, to CEOs and the boards they report to, as well as to shareholders and regulators (Fawkes 2007; MacLeod and Clarke 2009; Welch 2011; Schaufeli 2014; Johansson 2015; Scarlett 2016; Soares and Del Gáudio 2018).

Employee engagement: Helping people stay, work harder and speak up

Employee engagement can be defined in a number of ways, but there are consistent themes that focus on 'an attitude, a psychological or motivational state, or a personality trait' (Welch 2011: 335). Writers talk about outcomes such as engaged employees saying positive things about their organisation internally and externally, staying or committing to being a member of the team, even though there are other opportunities elsewhere, and working harder by putting in extra time, energy and effort (Schaufeli 2014).

Organisations are interested in high levels of employee engagement because there is evidence that links engagement with profitability, customer service, productivity and innovation in the workplace. Engagement is also specifically linked with low levels of voluntary resignations (or 'employee turnover'), lower absence or sickness levels and lower accident rates (Bridger 2015).

Communicators are interested in this area because engagement is a mix of attitudes (feeling positive or proud), behaviours (recommending the company as a place to work or working harder) and outcomes (better organisational performance), which can all be strongly influenced by communication (Bridger 2015; Soares and Del Gáudio 2018). Internal comms can specifically influence factors such as employees' perceptions of fairness at work, and of the recognition (or otherwise) of their efforts.

Box 15.2

Meet the practitioner: Anne-Sophie Duchene

Anne-Sophie is Head of Internal and Change Communication at Brussels-based Euroclear. Her role is to lead a communications function to communicate to the 4,000 or so staff who provide the financial infrastructure to allow banks and stock exchanges to buy and sell securities and bonds. 'I don't really have a typical day,' she explains, 'because my role can include anything from keeping the internal news portal updated to advising the CEO on her messages, and from helping manage communications around a major internal project to supporting simple tactics to get colleagues to take more exercise!' At the time of writing, Anne-Sophie and her team of seven have been auditing the channels they use to get information to Euroclear's staff and long-term contractors. Through a series of focus groups and interviews they have been looking at whether they have the right mix of channels and content to connect staff with the corporate strategy and plans.

'Building an understanding of our corporate direction is a priority of our leadership,' she stresses. 'I spend time with our CEO helping her find ways to explain where we're going and keeping her briefed on how well messages are landing.' She adds that she is spending a lot of time planning an annual leadership conference. 'We have historically had regular meetings of our 100 most senior leaders and now we need to help them tell our story to their people. Bringing senior managers together is a big investment for any organisation and we have to make it pay off in terms of better staff understanding and engagement.'

In her normal work, she will expect to spend time with several of the directors. 'As well as one-to-one time with the CEO, I also find myself talking a lot with the HR business partners, as much of their work will need explaining to staff and I'm currently collaborating closely with the Chief Operations Officer on an important office relocation.' Moving staff between offices requires careful communication, and Anne-Sophie's team is involved in the strategic planning and the detailed messaging that will be needed when the moves take place. 'We have to make sure that people don't just know the practicalities of when and how the move is happening but also we have to show them that they are valued.'

The team is therefore planning a lot of face-to-face briefing for colleagues who may be moving, and supporting line mangers with tool kits and materials they can use in discussions with their teams. Because people's employment terms might be potentially impacted, care is needed to ensure that content is consistent and compliant with HR rules. As well as investing a lot of time in planning line manager communication, Anne-Sophie and her team also produce a range of content that staff can see online. This might include news of colleagues in Poland hosting an open day for students, or sharing updates of new joiners as well as a video briefing from the public affairs team about European elections. 'The work I do is varied and I need to be a senior advisor, a creative thinker and an organised manager' concludes Anne-Sophie 'and because I lead a team and am responsible for budgets, I have to make time to ensure that things actually happen and run smoothly.'

Think about 15.1 Learning about the organisation

Think about an organisation you have worked for – perhaps as a part-time, casual or seasonal employee. How were you made aware of the organisation's products or services and other activities? Was it through your line manager, colleagues or other methods? List the methods of communication that helped you to understand your employer's business and your role in it.

Now list the methods of communication that you have used to communicate with a line manager and colleagues. Why did you choose these methods? Consider which methods were likely to be the most effective.

Feedback

It is likely that you will have learned about the organisation from your line manager, more formally, and from your colleagues on an informal basis. Other methods, such as e-newsletters, provide the 'bigger picture' on what the business is about. However, you may prefer to communicate with people, including your line manager, face to face.

People will decide if there are opportunities for personal growth, based on the stories they hear about their colleagues or information about the availability of training (often called 'learning and development', particularly in larger organisations). And, as discussed below, the material rewards and benefits of a job are frequently not as motivating as the psychological, emotional and social elements.

What matters to employees: motivation in the workplace

Most of the time, we get to choose where we work and are entitled to be treated well and with respect at work. Even if we feel trapped in a job, because of high unemployment or limited opportunities elsewhere, we make a choice about how much effort to make at work. For some time, commentators on employee engagement have talked about 'discretionary effort', arguing that money only makes us show up for work; doing a good job once we get there depends on our motivation (Yankelovich and Immerwahr 1983; Schaufeli 2014).

Historically, communicators were influenced by the work of Abraham Maslow and his theory of the hierarchy of human needs (Maslow 1943). Maslow argued that people need to satisfy basic physiological needs, such as finding security, food and shelter before turning to more psychologically fulfilling factors such as personal achievement (Mullins 2013). In the workplace, Maslow's ideas suggest that people fearful of losing their job, or struggling to survive on their wages, are less likely to be receptive to messages about the latest product innovation or the CEO's vision for the future. However, the concept might be less useful for explaining positive motivations; i.e. what makes people choose to work harder or more effectively?

Later work by Herzberg et al. (1959) suggested there are two types of motivational factors at work (see Mullins 2013). Herzberg described these as Hygiene (or Maintenance) factors and Motivator (or Growth) factors. Hygiene factors – such as being properly paid, treated fairly and provided with a safe environment – only matter when they are absent. They are a source of discontent, rather than a basis for positive satisfaction. By contrast, extrinsic factors (which originate externally to the individual) such as the opportunity for advancement or recognition, add to the desire to work harder and better.

> **Think about 15.2**
>
> ### What motivates you in your job?
>
> If you have a job, what motivates you in your work? Is it the chance to earn money? Perhaps you like the people you work with, think the work is enjoyable, or feel you are helping people somehow?
>
> #### Feedback
>
> What makes people feel engaged will vary from person to person, and organisation to organisation. People working in a bank might base their engagement on the size of their bonus, whereas a doctor's commitment might be shaped by their desire to help patients. An engineer might want to work within a professional community sharing a fascination with solving technical problems. Smythe (2007) contends that organisations should identify the drivers of engagement that are peculiar to them, and shape the employee experience around those drivers.

The main contribution of Herzberg's two-factor theory is that it enables jobs to be designed with 'quality of work life' in mind (Mullins 2013: 258). A communicator will understand that talking endlessly about pay and fairness will not necessarily excite people. Rather, celebrating achievements, acknowledging individuals' contributions and highlighting personal development opportunities make for more compelling messages when trying to create positive expectations and engagement.

Popular narratives draw on the theory of intrinsic motivation to highlight three components that help to get workers enthused about their jobs (Pink 2009). These motivations come from our universal desire to be self-determining individuals:

- Autonomy: the urge to be in charge of our own lives.
- Mastery: the desire to keep improving the way we do something we care about.
- Purpose: the drive to have a greater reason for doing what we do.

Essentially, if people are to stay, work more effectively, speak positively about their employer and be supportive of change, they need to have some control over their working day, a chance to develop themselves and something to believe in (Isles 2010). Understanding human motivation and how it manifests itself in different organisations is therefore an important part of the internal communicator's role. At a *tactical* level, internal comms teams have to create and share content that people will want to engage with. However, given the opportunity to provide *strategic counsel* to leaders on how to interest and enthuse employees, internal comms practitioners have a much better chance of influencing overall levels of employee engagement.

Employer brands and employee value propositions

When we begin to talk about motivation, it quickly becomes clear that large parts of the 'deal' between employer and employee are rarely formally defined. An employment contract may cover issues such as pay, bonuses and expected behaviour, but says nothing about fundamental concerns such as how to get promoted, navigate the working culture, or find out what really matters to the organisation's leaders. This unwritten, or 'psychological' contract is often addressed through the conventions of marketing or brand management, and internal communicators can be called on to help define and implement an *employer brand* (Ambler and Barrow 1996; Parry 2018) or *employee value proposition* (Mascarenhas 2019); tasks that would not be possible without a firm grasp of workplace motivation. Importantly, they hinge on the idea of trust; employees have to trust employers to keep their end of the unwritten bargain (Middlemiss 2011). When trust breaks down, people are less willing to be flexible or change ways of working, which can lead to a toxic workplace culture with all the associated reputational, financial and even existential threats.

Communicators have an important role in maintaining trust in the workplace. Trust includes *cognitive* elements – delivery of practical components such as pay or promotions – and *affective* components, which support emotional attachment (Atkinson 2007). It seems that until the practical or cognitive elements are satisfied, the emotional attachment cannot develop. But it is precisely this emotional factor that is linked to employees enhancing their contribution (Atkinson 2007).

Organisations now devote considerable time to defining their employee value proposition, thinking through the elements which are tangible (e.g. pay and benefits) and intangible (e.g. workplace culture, corporate values or impact on employees' future employability). And they call on communicators to help articulate all of these components in a way that makes current and potential employees feel able to speak positively, work harder and remain loyal.

Planning internal communication

Internal comms practitioners are increasingly concerned with demonstrating the impact of what they do. Just as an advertising campaign is intended to influence consumers to buy a product and a public health public relations campaign aims to encourage the adoption of healthier lifestyles, internal communication campaigns are intended to promote specific employee actions or behaviours. However, the relationship between advertising and public relations campaign originators and their intended audiences is qualitatively different to the relationship between employers and employees. Therefore, approaches that might be fit-for-purpose in the former relationship may not be in the latter.

In the past, internal communicators may have been valued primarily for producing good internal news stories and having project management skills. Increasingly, however, organisations expect to see demonstrable results from internal communication linked to business objectives, so communicators need to focus more on the impact of their activities – i.e. the *outcomes* – and less on the content they produce, i.e. the *outputs*. (See Case study 15.1. See also Chapters 9 and 10.)

Picture 15.1 Working on internal communications for big brands worldwide – IBM Russia (*source:* Kapustin Igor/Shutterstock)

Case study 15.1
Matching channels to maximise messages: Internal and external comms working together at IBM Russia

Valery Levchenko's main role at IBM Russia and the CIS countries is to manage media relations, building networks with journalists and pitching story ideas about the wealth of research and development and business activities that go on within the IT and business consultancy giant's offices in Russia and elsewhere. Levchenko does not see a big division between IBM's internal and external communication activities, since all communication managers cooperate very closely within the company's matrix operating structure. 'The corporate comms structure is like an inverted pyramid,' says Levchenko, 'with few people on the ground, supporting a wide range of local and visiting experts in different disciplines with great stories to tell in public.' These subject matter experts – or SMEs as they are known internally – are somewhat like a university's academic community, because they are focused on their respective research and/or business application areas and keen to share knowledge with colleagues, customers and the general public.

IBM's communication managers are organised in pairs in a country-by-country or region-by-region structure and handle internal or external communication, with the focus of their activities being framed by the priorities in each country. 'This structure is quite different to most local and many foreign companies,' Levchenko points out, 'because, locally, we don't have large public relations departments and often each of us serves a number of country offices. For example, in 2018 I had advised dozens of experts in the Russian Federation, Azerbaijan, Kazakhstan, Ukraine and Uzbekistan creating and wanting to share stories about what they're doing.'

Levchenko describes his main task in relation to leadership communications, for example about change projects or company strategy, as one of aligning external speaking and media opportunities for senior leaders with internal talking points for leaders to discuss with their teams. 'In the case of a big news story,' he adds, 'such as the 2019 $34 billion acquisition of enterprise Linux vendor Red Hat, I will adapt a global information pack, prepare talking points and include the relevant Q&A documents.'

The main distinction between internal and external communication responsibilities in the IBM's Russia and the CIS office lies in the different channels used. Internally, the usual core of corporate email and intranet is supplemented by blogs, vlogs and wikis. With the sheer volume of stories generated by the SMEs and shared through these channels, Levchenko finds that internal communication often leads external communication as internal stories are picked up, processed within the External Relations vertical and shared with other audiences. Matching the desire of colleagues to contribute with the amount of bandwidth available, both in terms of channels and attention, can be a tricky balance to strike. Levchenko is keen to avoid what he calls 'information pollution', so that there is clear space for important business communication, from major deals and global quarterly results announcements to the local leadership changes.

Business processes in the communications organisation are handled via collaboration tools, both created by IBM, such as Connections, and third-party offerings, such as Airtable, Box, etc. Many of these tools are widely used, where appropriate, for the enterprise social network too. 'I am especially excited about the recently introduced news and engagement platform that allows my internal communications colleagues to share IBM's news with employees and get their feedback,' says Levchenko. 'And, by the way, all the internal collaborative and social tools are available both as desktop and mobile applications.'

Like most internal comms practitioners, Levchenko and colleagues use face-to-face opportunities to share messages internally. In addition to electronic internal communications, all-managers meetings are held on a quarterly basis by the local country manager, after which all-hands meetings take part across the main departments. There are also regular lectures by the technical leaders and by the subject matter experts. Each IBMer commits at least 40 hours a year to attending courses, classes and online studies, so demand for face-to-face lectures, conveniently provided in the local language, is quite high. And, unsurprisingly given IBM's business, artificial intelligence is being used internally as well. 'AI is a kind of umbrella definition,' Levchenko points out, 'which includes functionality like chatbots, individual targeting of messages, intelligent search, and so on. The way I see it is that AI tools are incorporated here and there across IBM's social enterprise network.'

Setting objectives

An opening question in any communication planning process is, therefore, 'what steps do we want people to take as a result of our communication?' As noted above, business objectives in internal comms might be keeping employees loyal to an organisation, persuading them to follow specific instructions, encouraging them to be external advocates, or embracing change (FitzPatrick 2016).

As a shorthand, many practitioners approach objective-setting by laying out three essential outcomes. This is illustrated in Table 15.1 – three planning questions reflecting the practitioner's interest in messages that elicit conative (doing), affective (emotional) and cognitive (thinking/knowing) responses (Gregory 2014). The approach suggests that we *do* things because we *feel* that they are a good idea, because of what we *know*. Although human actions can have more subtle and complex drivers, many communicators find this a useful starting point for planning (FitzPatrick and Valskov 2014: 46).

Two-way communication and impact

As globalisation has spread, and awareness has grown of both the value and complexities of diverse workforces, so it has become crucial for organisations to demonstrate that they understand how particular communication styles impact on different groups. In English-speaking Western cultures, it is commonly held that individuals prefer a literal, explicit communication style, but are less likely to adopt desired behaviours if they are seen to be imposed via one-way broadcast (Meyer 2014).

Researchers and practitioners in leadership communication stress the value of meaningful 'conversations' and dialogue, rather than the delivery of monologues or speeches with no scope for feedback (Men 2014; Murray 2014; Illes and Mathews 2015; Macaulay 2014). There are two main reasons why this is likely to be true. First, even if communication were a simple process of transmitter and receiver, few pieces of information are fully understood at first hearing. Many complex factors affect message comprehension, including a good deal of filtering according to effort, motivation and interest (Früh 1980, cited in Windahl and Signitzer 2008: 181). Commonly, as participants in social networks, we need to check that we have understood something, and if others have received and understood the same thing (Rogers and Kincaid 1981). Impactful internal communication processes therefore allow people to ask questions, discuss internal news and access channels for meaningful feedback. When a message is only sent by email, there may be no opportunity to ask questions. A team meeting would, by contrast, be a good place to test if a message is understood.

A second reason to promote 'conversations' is that people are more likely to do something if they are part of a genuine dialogue from the outset and have a hand in deciding what actions are necessary (Quirke 1995; Smythe 2007). If employees have been consulted and their views taken into account, there is a powerful emotional motivation to execute the plan (Kotter 2014; Dewhurst and FitzPatrick 2019).

Securing one party's understanding is a necessary but not sufficient condition for effective communication. Both parties to that communication – in this case employers (leaders, managers, supervisors, etc.) and employees – must also be *listened to*. As it is a basic

What should people do as a result of our communication?	What should people feel or believe as a result of our communication?	What should people know as a result of our communication?
Conative	**Affective**	**Cognitive**
Are there specific behaviours that our organisation needs to promote, such as good customer service, safe working or selling new products?	What do people need to believe in order to prompt the desired behaviours, e.g. that good customer service matters, that safety is a personal responsibility or that selling a new product will generate better commission?	What information do people need in order to shape their beliefs? This could be data about customer satisfaction, case studies about safety incidents or details of a new sales commission structure.

Table 15.1 Three planning questions

human capability, individual leaders and managers should be good listeners, but how can organisations 'listen'? It is possible to create structures and processes for organisational listening, but they will only work well in an organisation that actively promotes a culture of listening (Macnamara 2016). See also Box 15.3.

In practice, few organisations have the resources, capacity or patience to involve all employees in planning or strategy development. However, there is often scope for teams to decide how a plan or strategy will be implemented locally. Considerable effort is invested in communications that support managers to hold such conversations.

Picture 15.2 How to develop a listening culture inside organisations (*source:* Andriy Popov/123RF)

Box 15.3

We're all ears: What is a 'listening' organisation?

In a much-quoted quip, digital culture expert Euan Semple entitled his 2012 guide to the 'social web' *Organizations Don't Tweet . . . People Do*. It highlights the paradox of ascribing individual human actions to an abstract concept – in this case, an organisation. The same thing could be said of listening – people listen, organisations don't, so how do you create a 'listening organisation'? Macnamara acknowledges this challenge, describing organisational listening as a 'wicked problem', a term applied to problems that are 'complex and usually require multifaceted approaches' (2016: 245). He is also quick to point out that new technologies – however useful – do not provide the whole answer. The critical factor is organisational culture, and the behaviour of the CEO is a leading indicator of a listening culture within an organisation. Nevertheless, clearly defined, mandated and monitored processes and behaviours are required to realise the potential benefits of a workplace where people feel 'heard', particularly the well-documented bottom line impact of enhanced trust and engagement. As Macnamara points out, one of the challenges for internal comms teams is ensuring that processes set up for 'listening' – such as town hall-style meetings, awaydays, enterprise social networks, and so on – do not become vehicles for employees' voices 'only when they echo the messages of the organization' (2016: 209).

Social media inside organisations

There is much interest in exploring the role that social media inside organisations can play in collecting ideas and promoting conversation and involvement. Recent years have seen the appearance inside organisations of many tools designed to mimic popular social media tools that exist outside (Lombardi 2015: 156). Lombardi highlights that internal (or 'enterprise') social networks are typically considered as vehicles for:

- co-creation – bringing together people to solve a particular problem or challenge;
- collaboration – enabling people with a similar problem or as members of a work or project group to support each other with advice and information; and
- community – helping people with work or recreational interests to connect with each other for predominantly social purposes.

Lombardi also points out that managing these enterprise social networks requires specific skills and clarity of roles. Without care, organisations can invest considerable sums in internal social media platforms, only to find limited usage or involvement and little relevance to overall organisational objectives (see also Case study 15.2).

Understanding the diversity of internal publics

Internal communication practitioners need to have a good understanding of the stakeholders or publics with whom they are working (Verčič et al. 2012). Internal

Case study 15.2
A sense of belonging

Dina Vekaria started at Pearson 12 years ago, and has worked in various customer-facing roles. She describes herself as 'a self-taught digital maven' who takes every opportunity to learn about digital technology. Her main goal is to apply that technology in a way that makes the work environment more human.

'For me, digital competency is key to succeeding in anything that you do. Also, being able to up-skill constantly, to be always learning,' she says, adding that 'always learning' is the Pearson corporate tagline. She started vlogging (video blogging) for Pearson in 2017, seeing it as something 'cool' that could help the business understand its people's capabilities. With support and encouragement from her manager, she taught herself video lighting, editing, sound and related software tools. 'Being given permission to go and learn something was wonderful. After all, we're an education company, if we don't let employees learn it would go against everything we believe in.'

Her current role as Global Community Manager has moved around a lot. 'We've moved from HR to Global Corporate Affairs and Marketing, and this has allowed us to flex our skills across a variety of teams including the media and employee communication teams, and now we're in the digital channels and experience team. DC&E feels like home, as we put our internal customer at the heart of everything we do. We're looking forward to expanding this to our external customers too through external communities.'

Pearson's Employee Communications function also sits in Global Corporate Affairs & Marketing. That team manages strategic internal communication, and Vekaria works closely with them. 'I'm a community manager,' she says, 'and my community is where the internal communication goes. When we have CEO comms coming out, an email goes directly to everyone's inbox. I guide and coach leaders on blogging, and help them post the same messages on Neo, our community site, because that's where people will actually engage with it.'

Neo was created in 2010 from a merger of 127 different company intranets, requiring a huge content migration project. At that point, Vekaria was the 'owner' of one of the intranets being merged. This can be a frustrating experience, but in her case she immediately saw the potential of Neo, and soon made the move to join the team that had built the new community platform. Before Neo, Vekaria says she knew little about other Pearson staff, particularly those in different countries. 'When I was in customer services, I searched for "customer services" on Neo and found 10 other people with that job title or area of expertise, and contacted them all. Of the 10, seven came back to me. So migrating the intranet to Neo opened up a whole new world of opportunity, getting to know other Pearson people. Launching Neo was

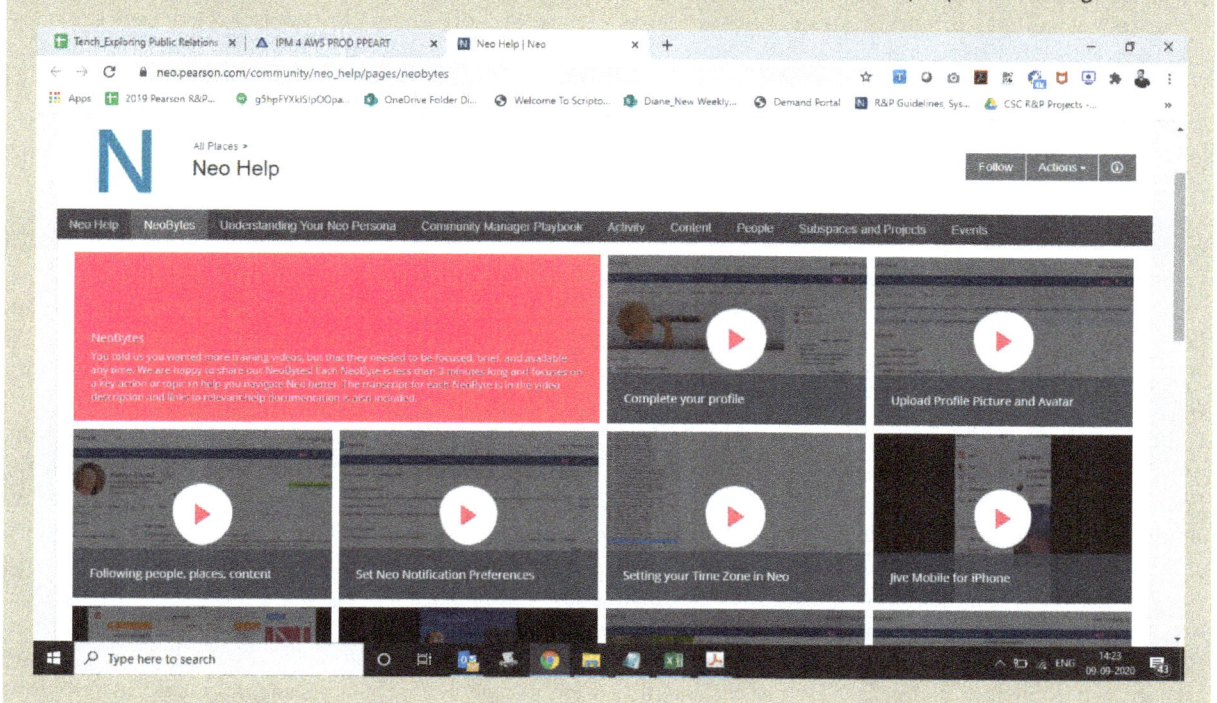

Picture 15.3 Video blogging as one form of internal communication at Pearson through Neo (*source:* Pearson Education Ltd.)

> **case study 15.2 (continued)**
>
> the best decision this company has made. And, after nine years, Neo is the longest-running collaboration tool that everyone in Pearson has access to.'
>
> Apart from the technical success of Neo, Vekaria says the best part of her job is seeing the sense of belonging that people gain from joining the Neo community. In that context, she explores some of the most difficult challenges in the modern working environment.
>
> 'When somebody joins our community they feel like they belong, and that they can talk to someone and make a connection with them. I did a panel event on Neo last year on mental health and spoke about my own mental health. From that event, three people reached out with their own stories. They told me that if they hadn't seen the panel on Neo, they wouldn't know other people in Pearson were willing to talk about these things. Neo is so much more than just a platform where people are collaborating and working. That's great, of course, but for me it's about people being inspired and empowered by each other.'
>
> Having that kind of conversation in a business setting is a relatively new thing, but it's clear, as Vekaria says, that 'allowing people to tell their story means they connect more with others, because storytelling is at the heart of human relations. When you tell a story, it resonates more than just using facts and figures.' With the growing role of AI in organisations (see Box 15.4) workplaces that understand and support people in this way will surely enjoy a competitive advantage.

communication has to cope with a number of special dimensions. It may be argued, for instance, that employees are naturally a more knowledgeable stakeholder group than most others. They know what works and what does not work in the organisation, and they may know its history. As a result, they are often more demanding consumers of information, and potentially more critical or sceptical of messages perceived as corporate 'spin' (Theofilou and Watson 2014).

Moreover, official communication is not the only reliable source of information within the organisation. People may like to receive information from trade unions or communities of professional practice. Less helpfully, gossip and rumours from (and about) colleagues and events usually travel faster than official versions. Sociological studies of organisational culture provide interesting insights into the dark side of employee behaviour. For example, negative or hostile chat among frontline workers can damage company performance and reputation (Harris and Ogbonna 2012). Employees also draw inferences from what they see and experience. An organisation might claim to value diversity, for example, but staff will reach their own conclusions if the bullying of a gay colleague is ignored, or if senior roles are dominated by people of similar backgrounds and characteristics.

Although they may work for the same organisation, employees won't perceive things in a uniform way. Marketeers may view the world differently from finance people; factory workers may not share interests with maintenance engineers. This is because different occupational groups develop their own norms and values, possibly due to their specific professional training, or simply because they are located in a part of the organisation that is remote from central services (Hofstede and Hofstede 2010).

A communicator needs to understand the diversity that exists within their organisation, and be ready to help leaders tailor messages to reflect the needs of diverse internal publics (Edmondson et al. 2009). As discussed earlier in this chapter, internal communicators need to be aware of what motivates their colleagues. When communicators know why their colleagues come to work and what enthuses them, they can create appealing communications and encourage actions that support a positive organisational culture (see Box 15.4).

Leadership communication

It is not difficult to find examples of poor leadership communication undermining trust inside an organisation. Disastrous comments by senior executives, and the impact on employees, are frequently reported in business news. Equally, leaders who excel at communication are often mentioned and celebrated.

Internal comms practitioners can help avoid disasters by helping senior leaders to lead. Usually, this means ensuring that senior managers' visions and plans are clear and engaging. However, as we have argued earlier in this chapter, effective communication involves more than top-down communication, albeit with follow-up processes to ensure that messages are received and understood. Therefore, it's worth examining two key concepts of leadership which are relevant to internal communication.

The first, and perhaps most popular concept is 'transformational' leadership, whereby leaders provide

Box 15.4
Organisations and cultures

Organisations and their cultures have been defined and interpreted in many different ways, and continue to fascinate researchers. It is essential for internal communicators to understand the implications. Among the most widely cited analyses is the work of Edgar Schein, who argued that, while first encounters of an organisation might reveal some aspects of culture – for example, open plan offices, informal dress and enthusiastic staff, it is the underlying 'cultural assumptions' that should be understood to explain an organisation's culture and possible source of conflict or misunderstanding (Schein 2010).

Underlying assumptions, or norms, are learned and tacitly understood between groups of workers and may be based on past experience or the ideas of a group leader. For example, Schein (2010: 12) found that engineers at Amoco held the assumption that they did not have to 'go out and sell themselves' because 'good work should speak for itself'. The engineers' assumptions may have run parallel to very different assumptions held by Amoco's senior executives.

Researchers note that while organisations espouse a common corporate culture through values statements, it is groups of people, known as subcultures, who hold a 'shared interpretation of their organisation' which 'differentiates them from other groups of employees' (Conrad and Poole 1998: 117). Organisational subcultures might include professional, administrative and customer interface groups (Hofstede and Hofstede 2010).

The challenge for communicators arises when there are 'cultural rifts', large gaps which open up when a group of workers (e.g. doctors) has significantly different perspectives and concerns about an issue from another group (e.g. senior executives). Organisational cultures and subcultures are also likely to be influenced by a range of intercultural norms or assumptions arising from national cultures, gender, religion, class and generational differences (Hofstede and Hofstede 2010). In an increasingly globalised business environment, it is therefore vital for communicators to be sensitive to cultural diversity and dissimilarity (Banks 2000; Kent and Taylor 2011).

---

compelling visions and clear plans and ensure that dialogue with employees on their plans takes place in order to achieve their objectives. However, transformational leadership has been criticised for placing too much emphasis on leaders, and not enough on involving employees in decision making (Tourish 2013). A second concept is 'communicative' leadership. Here, a leader consciously places emphasis on communication and empowerment. This type of leader engages 'employees in dialogue, actively shares and seeks feedback, practices participative decision making, and is perceived as open and involved' (Johansson et al. 2014: 155).

The key difference between the two concepts lies in the distribution of power. Empowerment occurs when there is greater opportunity for workers to influence decision making. For cultural and political reasons, examples of empowerment and 'communicative leadership' are often found in Scandinavian countries.

The challenge for the internal communicator is to know when and how to support senior leaders. Naturally, there are times when it is appropriate for the CEO or other senior executives to lead communications; and other times, such as when the subject is trivial or needs detailed local or team-level explanation, where it would be unnecessary. Any communication programme should include careful analysis of the CEO's role and the channels through which they normally communicate. For example, a major organisational change programme requires leaders to be 'visible', making themselves available for honest discussion about the likely impact on employees. In this scenario, a communicator's role is to advise on the importance of face-to-face communication, manage accessible feedback channels, and facilitate constructive responses to employees' input. A good leader will recognise the value of this activity.

The importance of local managers

As mentioned earlier in this chapter, the role of line managers or supervisors in effective employee communication processes has been a preoccupation of practitioners and researchers for some time. Writers on management processes have long advocated making clear and effective communication a specific responsibility of those holding leadership roles (Buckingham and Coffman 1999). Processes based on military models of hierarchical information and order-giving were widely recommended (McGeough 1995). This has been referred to as treating managers like animated noticeboards (FitzPatrick and Valskov 2014: 122).

Thinking has evolved over the years, and managers are now more commonly expected to be flexible in how they manage conversations with their teams. This is accompanied by an increasing emphasis on problem solving and discussion, rather than the delivery of instructions (D'Aprix 2011; Illes and Mathews 2015). Managers matter in the communication process because of their ability to explain things in terms that are relevant to their immediate teams. A corporate announcement about a new strategy, for example, will need to be translated into practical terms for the people tasked with its implementation. A local manager is able to explain how the announcement might change people's day-to-day priorities, and can provide clarification in relatable terms.

However, managers are not always the best channel of internal communication. A manager might be the ideal person to talk about changing shift patterns, but ill-equipped to explain the technicalities of a pension scheme or the sensitivities around mental health issues. Sinickas (2004) suggests that no one expects a manager to be an expert in every single topic that might come up, and that employees generally prefer to hear from the person who is the most knowledgeable on a particular subject. In many, but – crucially – not all cases, that could be their local manager or supervisor. An internal comms team will therefore be involved in helping managers and supervisors communicate across a wide range of topics, and refer appropriately when they don't have the relevant answers. FitzPatrick (2008) argues that line manager communication works best when effort has been invested in:

- explaining to managers that communication is one of their responsibilities;
- briefing or educating managers about the issues;
- providing training in communication skills;
- providing materials that managers can use in team meetings; and
- gathering feedback and making sure senior leaders understand and respond to line managers' concerns.

Outcomes rather than outputs: choosing effective channels

Every organisation needs mechanisms to deliver messages. A communications manager will commonly want several different channels at their disposal to ensure that information and feedback touch every corner of the workforce in ways that are appropriate, accessible and measurable. For example, an online forum may be popular with office workers but have little uptake in a factory where access to computers is limited. A poster series may be an exciting and powerful way to remind people about workplace safety, but is ineffective at explaining detailed changes to company rules and procedures. Additionally, channels themselves may have several different purposes. The in-house magazine may not be much use for sharing urgent news, but could be ideal for building a sense of community or providing background on current issues. Broadly speaking, an organisation will want channels to:

- **push** out information such as news, company results or changes to policies and procedure;
- allow staff to **pull** out information as they need it;
- aid **understanding,** because we often want to check what we think we heard, or get help to see the personal implications of an important announcement;
- promote **community** by helping people feel that they are part of something and can support or ideas from their colleagues (see Case study 15.2); and
- generate **debate,** giving employees a place to ask questions and share their views (see Table 15.2).

A communication manager might also be responsible for promoting collaboration across the organisation. Not every internal comms team has this role but, if they do, it is likely that specific channels will be dedicated to helping people share work problems and ideas for solutions.

Previously, we mentioned that employees are more likely to support change if they are also involved in its planning and development. But it is not always practical to involve everyone, so an organisation will want to identify those groups who need to be more deeply

Think about 15.3

Why are line managers trusted more than organisations?

In a workplace, who would you expect to be trusted more by regular employees? The chief executive officer (CEO) or a local supervisor/team leader?

Feedback

On the one hand the CEO will know about the direction of an organisation, how well it is performing overall and what plans exist for the future. Yet a local manager will have a personal relationship with the team. They will know about their likes and their concerns. There will be a shared history; team members will know when a manager can be depended upon to keep their promises and they will know how to 'read' them. The CEO can seem remote; perhaps being based far away. A local manager is present and – theoretically – accessible.

Purpose	Common channels or media
Push	Staff emails News pages on intranet Newsletters or magazines Internal TV Noticeboards or digital displays Memos left on desks SMS or text messaging
Pull	Intranet Video content on intranet 'Change Champions' – well-briefed colleagues with a deep understanding of issues or events
Understanding	Team meetings Training Face-to-face events (e.g. lunch with the CEO, internal roadshows)
Community building	Intranet news Events Collective activity with social/philanthropic purpose Instagram Enterprise social network
Debate	Enterprise social network Online forums including webinars Face-to-face events (conferences or focus groups)

Table 15.2 Common internal communication channels and their uses

involved than others perhaps because of their skills, expertise or location. Accordingly, different groups will need different approaches to communication. For colleagues who only need to be kept informed, a rapid digital channel such as an intranet or group WhatsApp message could be enough.

The importance of evidence in internal communication planning and evaluation

Evidence matters when planning and evaluating internal communication (see Chapter 10 'Measurement and evaluation'). Although personal judgement and experience help the communication manager to develop good instincts about messages, facts and figures are needed for securing budgets, defining the best approaches and understanding of what is working (and what is not).

Internal comms managers approach the tasks involved in developing understanding and gathering evidence in a number of ways. These include using a range of informal and formal research methods, such as those listed in Table 15.3. Some of the most common methods for evidence-gathering in internal communication are discussed below.

Many organisations conduct an annual survey of their employees (Bridger 2015). These surveys will commonly address issues such as overall morale and commitment. They routinely ask a few questions about communication, and offer at least some insight into whether employees are receiving the information they need to do their jobs. However, many surveys

Think about 15.4
Communicating good and bad news: is the medium the message?

In internal communication, as with other communication disciplines, how you say something is just as important as what you say.

Imagine you work for an organisation that announces job losses to the media before telling employees, or that you hear you've been sacked via a text message. How would you feel, and how might that influence how you feel about your employer?

Or perhaps you work for a big company, but the chief executive comes and finds you in person to thank you for a recent project. What impact might that have on your commitment?

Feedback
From an internal comms perspective, there are practical constraints which have to be observed. You might want to ensure everyone hears important news at the same time, but you might have to observe financial regulations about telling the local stock exchange first. Putting yourself in the shoes of the employee will help you to think through possible emotional reactions to the same message using different channels.

Purpose	Common approaches
Understanding internal demographics	Reviewing HR data about employee numbers, grades and locations
	Tracking HR information such as sickness rates or resignations
Understanding employee attitudes and knowledge	Participant-observer studies, from the most basic level of 'getting out and about' to advanced ethnographic approaches
	Job shadowing
	'Temperature' or 'pulse' checks (brief surveys run at specific points in the year)
	Focus groups
	Monitoring internal forums for comments
	Annual staff surveys
	Reviewing feedback from line managers
	Deep statistical analysis of other surveys
Communications processes	Comms audits
	Monitoring channel usage (e.g. intranet page visits, email opening rates, attendance at employee meetings)
	Surveying users of individual channels
	User focus groups
	Qualitative content analysis of employee feedback

Table 15.3 General approaches to information gathering

are limited in their usefulness for internal communicators, because they only touch on a few aspects of the internal communication mix or because the study only happens once a year (Walker 2012). Furthermore, many of these studies are disconnected from the actual effectiveness of the organisation (Coco et al. 2011). Just because the survey results are positive, it does not mean that everything is running smoothly. Additionally, measuring an issue through a survey does not mean that action has been taken to improve it (Bridger 2015).

Communicators therefore tend to look for a mix of evidence that tells them what people are thinking, which channels are working and what messages people are taking away from internal comms activities. Since communication is just one thing that influences attitudes and behaviours, it is helpful to understand what else matters to employees.

Approaches to information gathering

Building informal knowledge of the workforce

Communicators are routinely advised to spend time away from their desks talking to colleagues (FitzPatrick and Valskov 2014). If the value of a specialist advisor lies in knowing stakeholders better than anyone else, meeting and listening to colleagues has to be a priority for internal comms practitioners. From this experience, the practitioner becomes more aware of the size and shape of the workforce. It's equally essential to do desk research into employee numbers, locations, ages, gender, languages spoken and other demographic, professional and cultural data. It is also possible to get a feel for morale and commitment from data on sickness rates, customer complaints or labour disputes (Walker 2012).

Monitoring channel usage

A communicator will be interested in knowing what tools or channels are working, and how to maximise their usefulness to the organisation and its internal publics. There is much to be learnt from information acquired through desk research, such as monitoring the number of people who are accessing particular types of information on an intranet. Widely-used email programmes can be used to determine how many people open the latest message from the CEO, and how many times links in emails are clicked on (i.e. *quantitative* information). As well as tracking usage statistics, the communicator can learn a lot from reactions shared by employees to the content of messages (i.e. *qualitative* information). What comments are they leaving in online forums, or through enterprise social network platforms? What questions do they ask at 'town halls' or similar open employee meetings? Leaders will often ask for immediate feedback on specific communication activity, and the internal comms team is best placed to explain what's working, where more effort is needed, and whether emerging channels might be worth trying.

Managing formal internal communication research

Using informal research methods, such as job shadowing, can be valuable for building an awareness of colleagues' perspectives. Additionally, a communicator will want to formalise continuing information gathering. Broadly speaking, as suggested above, communicators can choose qualitative research, such as focus groups and interviews; or quantitative tools, such as surveys (Walker 2009); or, in some cases, a mix of the two. The practices are similar to those used in external communication research. (See also Chapter 10 'Measurement and evaluation'.)

One of the fastest-growing methodologies for internal communication research is known as 'in-house ethnography'. Ethnography is the 'participant-observer' approach to gathering detailed knowledge of particular groups of people and cultural practices. It originates in the work of anthropologists, who conduct scientific studies of human beings and their beliefs, relationships and cultures. Anthropological studies of organisations have been carried out over the last century, but since the late 1970s there has been a growing presence of anthropologists working in and for organisations such as businesses (Cefkin 2009). In internal comms, ethnography can provide a rich understanding of how employees function in a particular setting, or what behaviours might be acting as barriers to desired change. Developing an ethnographic research capability within an organisation does not necessarily mean hiring an anthropologist (although many companies – particularly in the technology sector – are doing just that). Ethnographic practice can be learned and applied relatively easily with appropriate training, support from leadership and commitment from internal comms practitioners.

Designing research also requires specific skills, to ensure that the findings are credible. Commissioning research from an external agency is an option if in-house research skills are limited. There are many suppliers who offer support with the research process, and they bring the benefit of experience and objectivity. If budgets are tight, however, utilising (and, where possible, upgrading) in-house research skills may be the only option. Whether the work is done internally or is outsourced, a communication manager must define the purpose of the intended study and prepare a proper brief to ensure that the results are of value (Walker 2012).

Preparing a research brief

Clearly defining the purpose and related aims of the research study is essential. For example, is it to gain insight into employees' opinions of a new intranet? Or is the research more comprehensive, intending to cover all channels? It is important to consider ethical and cultural issues, to avoid bias in the results.

Confidentiality and anonymity

Employees are often asked to express opinions which they fear might damage their workplace relationships or prospects. Even when such fear is unfounded, researchers should be aware that responses could be unreliable. Therefore, proper steps should be taken to assure participants' anonymity. This might include employing an external contractor, limiting the detail with which groups are reported on, or simply by not asking questions which could allow individuals to be identified.

Action

Employees expect something to happen as a result of their feedback. Declining response rates in employee surveys are often due to a perception that the whole exercise is a waste of time, because nothing was done after the previous survey. This means it is vital to report back openly on what has happened, or is happening, as a result of their comments. If nothing could be done about a particular issue for valid reasons, that can be explained honestly too.

Culture

Whilst every organisation attempts to develop its own internal culture (usually through a mix of intentional and unintentional means), they may also be shaped by the social and cultural norms of employee groups, occupational or professional cultures, and national cultures locally and, in a multinational, wherever the head office is located (Hofstede and Hofstede 2010). For example, workers in China may approach a questionnaire differently to their Dutch colleagues; engineers in a focus group might behave differently to HR professionals; and older employees may have a different view of digital media to younger team members. A researcher has to recognise the potential for cultural bias inside the workplace and adjust the design and evaluation of research accordingly. This is an area where ethnographic thinking can be particularly valuable (Hasbrouck 2018).

Explore 15.1

Outsourcing research

Go online and search for firms that conduct internal communication research. What do these firms offer to the internal comms specialist? What information do they require from their clients in order to undertake a research project?

Telling the story: reporting on data-gathering

Employees are often cynical about data gathering, because they believe nothing ever happens to the feedback they share (Walker 2012). When people doubt the value of answering questions or taking part in discussion, participation rates suffer. This in turn reduces the reliability of the findings. Organisations therefore need to act constructively on the basis of data gathered, or provide an explanation of why action was not possible, and empower internal communicators to share those messages accordingly. By doing so, a virtuous cycle is established, in which employees are more likely to respond to surveys and in other research methodologies. It is therefore vital for internal comms teams to know how to present employee feedback effectively to leadership. This involves producing a summary of the results in a format that enables senior leaders to take decisions. A report might cover a list of actions from the research undertaken, detailing the products, materials or events produced, and for what ends (FitzPatrick and Valskov 2014). Additionally, it would be helpful to report on upcoming issues and potential risks, drawing on the internal comms team's knowledge of employee groups. When decisions have been taken and actions implemented, the virtuous cycle is continued by telling study participants what happened and how their feedback has helped to shape policy. This might involve technical information about the introduction of new processes or policies, or it may be no more complicated than a reference in an intranet article or a thank-you message from a senior manager.

Gathering and analysing data on a large scale is one of the primary drivers for the introduction of artificial intelligence (AI) in organisations. This increasingly includes employee data, raising questions about the application and management of AI and its implications for internal comms. It may sound 'futuristic', but it is already happening in all kinds of organisations around the world (Box 15.5).

Picture 15.4 AI is being regularly used in employee engagement (*source:* Metamorworks/Shutterstock)

Box 15.5

Don't fear the robots, learn to tell their story

Artificial intelligence (AI) has been around since the 1950s, but has come to the forefront recently due to three related developments: Big data, cloud computing and mobile devices. Together, these provide the volume and the velocity of data needed to power computer systems that can learn.

'AI applications are based on natural language processing and machine learning. With natural language processing, the system understands human speech,' says AI expert, author and former business journalist Silvia Cambié. 'If I say "once in a blue moon", a human will know from the context that I'm not talking about the moon or the colour blue. AI systems also know how to use context when processing unstructured data. Some 80% of the world's data is unstructured, because it's in tweets, emails, videos, or sounds, or is collected from sensors via the Internet of Things. Thanks to natural language processing, AI systems can process it.'

Machine learning occurs when a system, programmed with an algorithm, makes a correlation between a pattern and an outcome, formulates a hypothesis, and integrates human feedback into its next hypothesis. 'For example,' Cambié notes, 'a wine grower in California uses an app powered by AI to promote their wines. I'm looking for a wine that goes well with fish, so the app recommends one, and I try it. I think it's great with sea bass but not with lobster, so I give the app my feedback. That gets integrated into the next recommendation, which is how the machine learns.'

AI applications are already in use in PR and journalism, as well as internal communication and related areas such as HR and employee engagement. Cambié has been working on Watson, IBM's AI system. 'IBM has developed a bot called MyCa, short for My Career, which learns from data points like your preferences, the training you have been doing and your career path and interests, and recommends next steps for your career.

You can ask MyCa questions that you might not want to ask your human line manager.'

Cambié has identified three areas where internal communicators have a crucial role in the deployment of AI: explainability, value alignment and fairness. Explainability means that the purpose and processes of an algorithm are clear to end users. 'For instance, why is MyCa recommending a job for me in another country? But explainability in an internal comms context also means that the function has a role in telling the story behind any AI project. Why is the company going down that road? It may be to improve customer experience, or to help employees be safer at work.'

The second area is value alignment. Ethical organisations will want AI applications to reflect their values, not contradict them. Cambié points to the use of AI to support workers on oil rigs. 'Riggers are equipped with sensors in their safety helmets which not only measure blood pressure and other vital signs, but also listen for what we call in AI a "wake" word, like when they say, "I can't figure this out" or "what am I going to do now?" The bot can help them, but it's important to respect their privacy as well, so the recording self-deletes every five seconds. That way, the company is not eavesdropping on employees, but can still help them to stay safe.'

Finally, there's fairness, which is closely linked to notions of bias. 'I'm particularly concerned about gender bias,' Cambié adds, 'but there are all sorts of biases. If you use data sets produced by humans to train a system, the algorithm will be biased and the outcomes will be biased. So you have to use bias-detection mechanisms. There is tech to do that, but we must all be aware of the nature of any data sets being used, and the importance of input from humans who recognise – and act against – bias in the system. There is definitely scope for internal comms practitioners to lead in this area.'

Silvia Cambié is an AI influencer, Wiproite and former IBMer

Professionalisation: attributes, competencies and skills in internal communication

Over the years, internal communication has developed as a body of specialist professional practitioners who enjoy a growing status among their peers in corporate communication, HR, marketing and other branches of public relations. The Institute of Internal Communication, having recently celebrated its seventieth anniversary, continues to represent practitioners at national level in the UK, develop academic and practical training courses, and provide networking events and awards programmes where practitioners can compare their work with the best in the industry. At a global scale, the International Association of Business Communicators (IABC) also has a long history of professional development covering, as the name suggests, the range of communication disciplines, but with a focus on employee communication.

Moreover, CIPR Inside, the internal communication section of the UK Chartered Institute of Public Relations, is one of the largest and most popular of its groups. This reflects in part the value placed on internal comms by directors of communication. Research across Europe routinely identifies internal communication as a priority for communication managers (Zerfass et al. 2010, 2019; Tench et al. 2017).

As a strategic management function, internal communication demands a variety of skills, ranging from technical abilities in writing, channel development and project management through to high-level skills in counselling the most senior leaders in organisations and providing sensitive advice to boards and other decision-making bodies. Therefore a practitioner's attributes, competencies and skills can be very varied. A practitioner-led research study found an emphasis on the importance of advisory and managerial skills (Dewhurst and FitzPatrick 2007). Although being able to produce high-quality materials and write well were deemed valuable, these represented only one set of competencies from a list of 12 core areas that also includes the ability to develop relationships, understand the overall business, conduct research and manage projects. Recent studies highlight the central importance for internal comms managers of 'social and empathic antenna', i.e. the ability to develop relationships, understand different groups, and step into another individual's shoes (Jin 2010; Tench and Moreno 2015; Tench et al. 2017). An aspiring internal communicator can expect their professional development to involve recognising the significance of personal attributes alongside professional competencies and management skills, such as data-gathering and analysis, that are applicable in other disciplines outside the world of PR and corporate communication.

Summary

This chapter has examined the strategic management function known as internal communication. Some regard it as a specialism within public relations, although it is increasingly seen as a stand-alone communication discipline. In the chapter we discussed the key considerations and skills that internal communicators need to help organisations achieve better relationships with employees and therefore better results. We argue that a sound, evidence-based understanding of the diversity of internal publics and their motivations and concerns is the starting point for strategic, impactful and measurable communication. We also argue that good communication involves listening as well as talking, and looked at the role of the internal comms professional in helping managers and leaders to create a work culture that enables employees to have a voice. Finally, we introduced the rapidly growing use of ethnography and artificial intelligence within organisations, both of which have major implications for internal communication practice.

Bibliography

Ambler, T. and S. Barrow (1996). The employer brand. *Journal of Brand Management*, 4(3): 185–206.

Atkinson, C. (2007). Trust and the psychological contract. *Employee Relations*, 29(3): 227–46.

Banks, S.P. (2000). *Multicultural Public Relations: A social-interpretive approach*, 2nd edition. Ames, IA: Iowa State University Press.

Bridger, E. (2015). *Employee Engagement*. London: Kogan Page.

Buckingham, M. and C. Coffman (1999). *First, Break all the Rules: What the world's greatest managers do differently*. NY: Simon and Schuster.

CBI (2019) *Great Job: Solving the productivity puzzle through the power of people.* London: Confederation of British Industry.

Cefkin, M. (ed.) (2009). *Ethnography and the Corporate Encounter*. Oxford: Berghahn Books.

Coco, C.T., F. Jamison and H. Black (2011). Connecting people investments and business outcomes at Lowe's: Using value linkage analytics to link employee engagement to business performance. *People & Strategy*, 34(2): 28–33.

Conrad, C. and M.S. Poole (1998). *Strategic Organizational Communication: Into the twenty-first century*, 4th edition. Fort Worth, TX: Harcourt Brace.

D'Aprix, R. (2011). The challenges of employee engagement: Throwing rocks at the corporate rhinoceros. In Gillis, T. (ed.) *The IABC Handbook of Organizational Communication: A Guide to Internal Communication, Public Relations, Marketing, and Leadership*, 2nd edition. NY: Jossey Bass.

Dewhurst, S. and L. FitzPatrick (2007). *How to Develop Internal Communicators*. London: Melcrum Publishing.

Dewhurst, S. and L. FitzPatrick (2019). *Successful Employee Communications: A Practitioner's Guide to Tools, Models and Best Practices for Internal Communication*. New York, NY: Kogan Page.

Dolphin, R. (2005). Internal Communications: Today's Strategic Imperative. *Journal of Marketing Communications*, 11:3, 171–90.

Edmondson, V.C., G. Gupte, R.H. Draman and N. Oliver (2009). Focusing on communication strategy to enhance diversity climates. *Journal of Communication Management*, 13(1): 6–20.

Fawkes, J. (2007). Employee engagement: A review of the literature. In Smythe, J. *The CEO: Chief Engagement Officer*. Aldershot: Gower.

FitzPatrick, L. (2008). Internal communication. In Theaker, A. (ed.) *The Public Relations Handbook*. London: Routledge.

FitzPatrick, L. (2016). Internal communication. In Theaker, A. (ed.) *The Public Relations Handbook*. 5th edition. Abingdon, Oxon: Routledge.

FitzPatrick, L. and K. Valskov (2014). *Internal Communication: A manual for practitioners*. London: Kogan Page.

Gillis, T. (2008) *The Human Element: Employee Communication in Small to Medium-sized Businesses*. San Francisco, CA: International Association of Business Communicators.

Gregory, A. (2014). Strategic public relations planning and management. In Tench, R. and L. Yeomans (eds). *Exploring Public Relations*, 3rd edition. Harlow: Pearson Education.

Grunig, J.E. (1992). Symmetrical systems of internal communication. In J.E. Grunig (ed.) *Excellence in Public Relations and Communication Management*. Hillsdale, NJ: Lawrence Erlbaum Associates.

Hallahan, K., D. Holtzhausen, B. van Ruler, D. Verčič and K. Sriramesh (2007). Defining strategic communication. *International Journal of Strategic Communication*, 1(1): 3–35.

Harris, L. and S. Ogbonna (2012). Forms of employee negative word-of-mouth: a study of frontline workers. *Employee Relations*, 35(1): 39–60.

Hasbrouck, J. (2018). *Ethnographic Thinking*. New York, NY: Routledge.

Heide, M. and C. Simonsson (2011). Putting coworkers in the limelight: New challenges for communication professionals. *International Journal of Strategic Communication*, 5(4): 201–20.

Herzberg, F., B. Mausner and B.B. Snyderman (1959). *Motivation to Work*. New York, NY: John Wiley and Sons, Inc.

Hofstede, G.H. and G.J. Hofstede (2010). *Cultures and Organizations: Software of the Mind*, 3rd edition. New York, NY: McGraw-Hill.

Illes, K. and M. Mathews (2015). *Leadership, Trust and Communication: Building trust in companies through effective leadership communication*. London: University of Westminster/Top Banana Ltd.

Isles, N. (2010). *The Good Work Guide: How to make organizations fairer and more effective*. London: Earthscan.

Jin, Y. (2010). Emotional leadership as a key dimension of public relations leadership: a national survey of public relations leaders. *Journal of Public Relations Research*, 22(2): 159–81.

Johansson, C., V.D. Miller and S. Hamrin (2014). Conceptualizing communicative leadership – a framework for analysing and developing leaders' communication competence. *Corporate Communication: An International Journal*, 19(2): 147–65.

Johansson, C. (2015). Empowering employees through communicative leadership. In Melo, A.D., I. Somerville and G. Goncalves (eds), *Organisational and Strategic Communication Research: European Perspectives II*. Braga, Portugal: CECS.

Karanges, E., A. Beatson, K. Johnston and I. Lings (2014). Optimizing employee engagement with internal communication: A social exchange perspective. *Journal of Business Marketing Management*, 7(2): 329–53.

Kennan, W.R. and V. Hazleton (2006). Internal public relations, social capital, and the role of effective organizational communication. In *Public Relations Theory II*. Botan, C. H. and V. Hazleton (eds). Mahwah, NJ: Lawrence Erlbaum Associates.

Kent, M. and M. Taylor (2011). How intercultural communication theory informs public relations practice in global settings. In Bardhan, N. and C.K. Weaver (eds) *Public Relations in Global Cultural Contexts*. New York and Abingdon, Oxon: Routledge.

Kotter, J. (2014). *Accelerate*. Boston: Harvard Business Review Press.

Lee, T. (2002) Twelve Dimensions of Strategic Internal Communication. *Strategic Communication Management*. January 2002.

Lombardi, G. (2015). Social media inside a large organisation. In Ruck, K. (ed.) *Exploring Internal Communication: Towards informed employee voice*, 3rd edition. London: Gower.

Macaulay, K. (2014). *From Cascade to Conversation: Unlocking the collective wisdom of your workforce*. London: AB Publishing.

McGeough, P. (1995). *Team Briefing: A practical handbook*. London: The Industrial Society.

MacLeod, D. and N. Clarke (2009). *Engaging for Success: Enhancing performance through employee engagement*. London: Department for Business, Innovation and Skills.

Macnamara, J. (2016). *Organizational Listening: The Missing Essential in Public Communication*. New York, NY: Peter Lang.

Mascarenhas, B.G. (2019) Employer Branding, Employee Value Proposition, and Employee Experience: New Approaches for People Management in Organizations. In Thornton G., V. Mansi, B. Carramenha & T. Cappellano (eds) *Strategic Employee Communication*. Cham: Palgrave Macmillan.

Maslow, A.H. (1943). A theory of human motivation. *Psychological Review*, 50(4): 370–396.

Mazzei, A. (2014). Internal communication for employee enablement. *Corporate Communications: An International Journal*, 19(1): 82–95.

Men, L.R. (2014). Why leadership matters to internal communication: Linking transformational leadership, symmetrical communication, and employee outcomes. *Journal of Public Relations Research*, 26(3): 256–79.

Meyer, E. (2014). *The Culture Map: Breaking Through the Invisible Boundaries of Global Business*. New York, NY: PublicAffairs.

Middlemiss, S. (2011). The psychological contract and implied contractual terms: synchronous or asynchronous models? *International Journal of Law and Management*, 53(1): 32–50.

Mullins, L.J. (2013). *Management and Organisational Behaviour*, 10th edition. London: FT Publishing International.

Murray, K. (2014). *Communicate to Inspire*. London: Kogan Page.

Parry, S. (2018). *Take Pride: How to build organisational success through people*. London: Unbound.

Pink. D. (2009). *Drive: The surprising truth about what motivates us*. Edinburgh: Canongate Books.

Quirke, B. (1995). *Communicating Change*. Maidenhead: McGraw-Hill Companies.

Rogers, E.M. and D.L. Kincaid (1981). *Communication Networks: Toward a paradigm for research*. New York, NY: Free Press.

Scarlett, H. (2016). *Neuroscience for Organizational Change: An evidence-based practical guide to managing change*. London: Kogan Page.

Schaufeli, W. (2014). What is engagement? In *Employee Engagement in Theory and Practice*. C. Truss, A. Kerstin, R. Delbridge, A. Shantz and E. Soane (eds). Abingdon, Oxon: Routledge.

Schein, E. (2010). *Organizational Culture and Leadership*, 4th edition. San Francisco, CA: Jossey-Bass.

Semple, E. (2012). *Organizations Don't Tweet... People Do: A Manager's Guide to the Social Web*. Chichester: John Wiley & Sons.

Sinickas, A. (2004). *Making Managers Better Communicators*. Melcrum Publishing.

Smythe, J. (2007). *The CEO: Chief Engagement Officer*. Aldershot: Gower Publishing Ltd.

Soares, P.H.L. and R. Del Gáudio (2018). *Megaphones Out, Smartphones In: Practices, challenges, and dilemmas of communication with employees*. São Paulo: Aberje Editorial.

Tench, R. and A. Moreno (2015). Mapping communication management competencies for European practitioners. *Journal of Communication Management*, 19 (1): 39–61.

Tench, R., D. Verčič, A. Zerfass, A. Moreno and P. Verhoeven (2017) *Communication Excellence: How to Develop, Manage, and Lead Exceptional Communicators*. Cham: Palgrave Macmillan.

Theofilou, A. and T. Watson (2014). Sceptical employees as CSR ambassadors in times of financial uncertainty. In Tench, R., W. Sun and B. Jones (eds) *Communicating Corporate Social Responsibility: Perspectives and practice*. Bingley: Emerald Group Publishing.

Tourish, D. (2013). *The Dark Side of Transformational Leadership: A critical perspective*. Hove: Routledge.

Verčič, A., D. Verčič and K. Sriramesh (2012). Internal communication: Definition, parameters and the future. *Public Relations Review*, 38(2): 223–30.

Walker, S. (2009). Measurement. In Wright, M. (ed.) *The Gower Handbook of Internal Communication*, 2nd edition. London: Gower Publishing Ltd.

Walker, S. (2012). *Employee Engagement and Communication Research*. London: Kogan Page.

Welch, M. (2011). The evolution of the employee engagement concept: Communication implications. *Corporate Communications: An International Journal*, 16(4): 328–46.

Welch, M. and P.R. Jackson (2007). Rethinking internal communication: A stakeholder approach. *Corporate Communications: An International Journal*, 12(2): 177–98.

Windahl, S. and B. Signitzer (2008). *Using Communication Theory: An introduction to planned communication*, 2nd edition. London: Sage.

Yankelovich, D. and J. Immerwahr (1983). Putting the work ethic to work. *Society*, 21(2): 58–76.

Yates, J. (1985). Internal Communication Systems in American Business Structures: A Framework to Aid Appraisal. *American Archivist*, 48(2): 141–58.

Yaxley, H. and K. Ruck (2015). Tracking the rise and rise of internal communication. In Ruck, K. (ed.) *Exploring Internal Communication: Towards informed employee voice*, 3rd edition. London: Gower.

Yeomans, L. (2008). '. . . It's a general meeting, it's not for us . . . '. Internal communication and organizational learning – an interpretive approach. *Corporate Communications: An International Journal*, 13(3): 271–86.

Yeomans, L. and W. Carthew (2014). Internal communication. In Tench, R. and L. Yeomans (eds). *Exploring Public Relations*, 3rd edition. Harlow: Pearson Education.

Zerfass, A., R. Tench, P. Verhoeven, D. Verčič and A. Moreno (2010). *European Communication Monitor 2010. Status quo and challenges for public relations in Europe: Results of an Empirical Survey in 46 Countries* (chart version). Brussels: EACD, EUPRERA. www.communicationmonitor.eu

Zerfass, A., D. Verčič, P. Verhoeven, A. Moreno and R. Tench (2015). *European Communication Monitor 2015. Creating communication value through listening, messaging and measurement. Results of a Survey in 41 Countries*. Brussels: EACD/EUPRERA, Helios Media.

Zerfass, A., D. Verčič, P. Verhoeven, A. Moreno, and R. Tench (2019). *European Communication Monitor 2019. Exploring trust in the profession, transparency, artificial intelligence and new content strategies. Results of a survey in 46 countries*. Brussels: EACD/EUPRERA, Quadriga Media Berlin.

CHAPTER 16

Tim Coombs

Issues management

Source: Makieni/Shutterstock

Learning outcomes

By the end of this chapter you should be able to:
- define and describe the concept and models of issues management
- recognise the value of communication to issues management
- understand why there has been a shift in issues management from public to social issues
- apply the models of issues management to actual issues management cases
- understand the effects of digital channels and reputation management on issues management.

Structure

- Origins and essence of issues management
- Models of issues management
- Expanding issues management beyond public policy
- The big picture for issues management

Introduction

Many people have heard of blood or conflict diamonds but far fewer people know about conflict minerals. Just as diamonds can be mined through forced labour or profits used to fund violent armed conflict, the same can hold true for tin, tungsten, tantalum and gold. Taken together, these are conflict minerals. Various non-governmental groups (NGOs), have been trying to raise awareness of these types of activities and to get corporations and government to take action on various conflict minerals for over a decade (Coombs and Holladay 2010). In January 2021, the new EU Conflict Minerals Regulations will go into effect. Imports of the four minerals along with smelters and refiners must document the supply chain of these minerals to demonstrate they have been sourced responsibly. This will include creating annual reports to document due diligence in the supply chain and to provide third-party audits of supply chain due diligence (European Commission 2017). The goal is to force suppliers of the minerals to be responsible if those organisations want to conduct business with firms in the EU. The process is similar to the way blood diamonds have been pushed from the marketplace through the certification of the Kimberly process.

The conflict mineral regulation in the EU is an example of issues management. Attention was drawn to the problem and action was taken intended to reduce the negative effects of the issue on society. Issues management is primarily a strategic communication function. This chapter explains the origins of issues management, the two dominant models of issues management, and the evolution of issues management to move beyond policy decisions.

Origins and essence

The 1950s was a great time to be in the corporate world because back then people loved businesses. From this golden age there has been a steady decline in how people perceive corporations – corporate reputations have fallen precipitously. The Edelman Trust Barometer (2019) has documented more recent concerns about corporate reputations but the slide in stakeholder perceptions was very noticeable even in the 1960s and 1970s. The 1960s and 1970s were interesting times for corporations. It was during this time period that environmentalists got their voices heard and realised significant gains in advancing policy changes related to corporate pollution. Activists effectively argued that corporations were the source of pollution. The vilification of corporations as polluters allowed activists to win a number of regulatory and legislative efforts designed to reduce pollution. These policy changes proved very expensive for the corporations (Conley 2006). Though no name was attached to it at the time, the environmental activists were creating issues management. In 2019, the global study of trust in corporations in the Edelman Trust Barometer found trust in business had increased in 21 of the 26 countries they surveyed. The average level of trust in business was now 56 per cent. In 2019, trust in the UK has rose to 47 per cent while it had risen to 47 per cent in Germany, 48 per cent in Argentina, 44 per cent in Japan, and 56 per cent in Canada (Edelman 2019). While rising, trust in corporations is relatively low globally.

Howard Chase is the name most closely associated with the emergence of issues management. Chase was a corporate public relations person who coined the term 'issue management' in 1976 and developed the first issue management model in 1977. (Though it began life as 'issue management' the concept is more commonly referred to as 'issues management', hence, this chapter adopts the latter terminology.) Chase (1984) conceptualised issues management as a reaction to the corporate failures to prevent environmental and other regulatory changes in the 1960s and 1970s – it was a response to activist success. What Chase does not acknowledge is that issues management co-opted many of the strategies and tactics the environmental activists used to win those regulatory battles (Conley 2006; Coombs and Holladay 2010).

The origins of issues management are inextricably linked to policy making. For Chase, the essence of issues management was participation in the policy-making process (Chase 1984). By participating in the public policy-making process, corporations could influence the outcomes of policy decisions such as the creation of regulations that could affect corporate practices and profitability. Chase (1984) viewed issues management as an important shift away from the 'defensive skill' of portraying a 'company in the best possible light' to a more proactive stance through involvement in policy making (p. 8).

There is a similar emphasis on issues management and policy making from the academic side as well. Robert Heath (1988), an academic pioneer in issues management, observed, 'As a countermeasure to unwarranted regulation, the growth of issues management is recognition that the private sector does not have to be held hostage by dramatic public policy changes that can harm the bottom line' (p. 3). Heath's comments reflect what he felt was a need for corporations to adapt to their new and more demanding policy environment. In short, issues management arises because corporations are repeatedly losing policy-making battles with activists. Issues management provides a framework to allow corporations to become more proactively and hopefully more successfully engaged in policy decisions such as environmental regulatory decisions. Heath (1997) defined issues management as 'the management of organizational and community resources through the public policy process to advance organizational interest and rights by striking a mutual balance with those of stakeholders' (p. 9). Originally, issues management can be conceptualised as communicative efforts intended to influence policy decisions. Issues management was intended to be a communicative means of trying to create a more favourable operating environment for an organisation by anticipating and attempting to systematically influence policy decisions.

It is important to realise that there were forces in business and academia that resisted the idea of issues management. A key point was whether or not issues management was unique or simply old public relations ideas given a new label. Much of the early published articles about issues management involved justifications for its practice. Researchers argued that issues management was not a fad and that it did constitute a unique perspective for strategic communication. These arguments were successful in helping to establish issues management as a unique sub-field within public relations and strategic communication (Botan and Taylor 2004).

As this chapter will demonstrate, issues management has shifted away from its narrow focus on policy making. However, it retains its proactive nature and influence on decisions that shape corporate behaviour. The shift away from just the policy-making arena reflects a larger society shift in how activists seek to influence corporate behaviour. Activists are increasingly seeking to have a direct influence on corporate decisions rather than an indirect influence through policy decisions.

Models of issues management

It is very abstract to say issues management is about employing communication to systematically influence public policy decisions. Lobbying and advocacy advertising could all fall under this rubric. We can clarify the conceptualisation of issues management by examining the two dominant models in the field: (1) Chase and Jones and (2) issue catalyst. Exploring each model will give a greater sense of what issues management is and how it is practiced.

Definition: 'Issue or issues?' 'Issue management' is sometimes referred to as 'issues management'. Asked about this question, Howard Chase, the 'father' of the discipline, is reported to have said it should always be 'issue management', not 'issues management', for the same reason that it is 'brain surgery', not 'brains surgery'.

Think about 16.1

Communicating risk and science

Many high-profile issues revolve around risk, science and technology. Competing parties involved in the issue may interpret risk in very different ways and may disagree completely about what is presented as an indisputable 'fact'. A good example would be whether mobile phone towers affect the health of the nearby community. Think about the factors that make science-based issues more difficult to manage. Why do scientists and experts sometimes find it hard to communicate and persuade? Why do experts and non-experts often reach different conclusions about risk?

Feedback

Scientists and other experts are usually trained to focus on facts and data that can be proven. Their training encourages them to find the 'right answer'. But many issues also involve emotions and opinions, and many risks are judged by concepts such as degree of control, trust, dread, fairness, familiarity and whether it is voluntary or enforced. Organisations should never ignore or misrepresent the facts, but they must recognise that many issues cannot be resolved by facts alone.

Think about 16.2

Confrontation or negotiation?

Think about the issues or situations where a confrontational strategy might be appropriate. How do those issues or situations differ from when negotiation may be best?

Imagine yourself as a senior executive of a 'target' organisation facing a significant issue. Would you prefer to face a high-profile assault, which you might be able to dismiss as a one-off stunt, or would you rather commit time and resources to prolonged negotiation that might require you to compromise your position on the issue?

Feedback

In dealing with an issue, choosing confrontation or negotiation is not necessarily right or wrong, but just different. Activists who prefer confrontation sometimes claim that negotiators are 'getting into bed with the enemy', while groups who prefer to negotiate may say the direct action people are only interested in headlines, and that stunts 'trivialise' the issue. These are two very different roles, and they enable big corporates and big government to divide and conquer, or pick and choose who they deal with. Either course of action could lead to a quick or easy resolution to the issue but it may not always be the best outcome.

Box 16.1

Chase and Jones model: five steps

1. Issue identification: scan for potential issues.
2. Issue analysis: analyse relevant issues.
3. Issue change strategy options: select your strategy for addressing the issue.
4. Issue action: create and implement your communication effort.
5. Evaluation of results: assess the effectiveness of the issues management effort.

The Chase and Jones model

When Howard Chase created the field of issues management, he offered a model for its practice. That model has been a significant influence on the field ever since its articulation. Though a focal piece in his book *Issue Management: Origins of the Future,* the model was first published as Chase and Jones in a 1979 journal article in *Public Relations Review* co-authored by Jones and Chase. The journal article became the seminal work for public relations scholars; hence, the model is predominantly known as the Chase and Jones model. Chase (1984) refers to it as a process model of issue management. The Chase and Jones model unfolds in five steps: (1) issue identification; (2) issue analysis; (3) issue change strategy options; (4) issue action programming; and (5) evaluation of results. You will note that the model reflects the general strategic communication model of research, action, communication and evaluation. Any process model of strategic communication will contain those elements. The Chase and Jones model adapts the ideas of strategic communication to policy making.

For Chase (1984), an issue is 'an unsettled matter which is ready for decision' (p. 38). Issue identification is about finding issues before they emerge. Qualitative and quantitative research methods are used to identify trends, the visible changes that emerge prior to the arrival of an issue. Chase refers to these at futurists methodologies – ways of trying to predict or project the future. The goal of the issue identification stage is to locate emerging issues and create an initial prioritisation of those issues. Managers do not have the time or resources to manage every issue. Therefore, emerging issues must be prioritised. The most promising issues are moved to the issue analysis step.

The issue analysis stage involves thoroughly researching the emerging issues. Existing data about the issue is collected and evaluated. This past information provides important contextual information about the issue by locating the origins of the issue. By tracking the issue since its origin, managers can understand how it has developed and how it might progress in the future. For instance, it is helpful to know who is involved with the issue and why they are interested in the issue. Next, the managers assess the current situation for the emerging issue. Two important resources are the views of opinion leaders and media coverage of the issue. Both of these data sources can indicate if an issue is rising or falling in importance. For example, if opinion leaders and the media are 'talking about' the issue, it is rising in importance. The goal of the issue analysis phase is thorough research of the issue that allows managers to create a final prioritisation of the issues. Based upon that research, managers decide how to respond to the issues.

The issue change strategy option stage is when managers decide what course of action to take on each issue. Managers determine if the issue is a threat or an opportunity and how much time and effort to devote to the issue. Chase identifies three change strategies:

(1) reactive; (2) adaptive; and (3) dynamic. The change strategies are not mutually exclusive and which is the best option will vary by the nature of the issue. In other words, no one change strategy is always superior or preferable to the others. It is during this step that the term policy option becomes relevant. A policy option is one potential solution or means of resolving an issue.

The reactive change strategy is the choice to do nothing. Managers decide not to make any changes or attempt to influence the issue. While passive, the reactive change strategy recognises the importance of the issue and that the issue might affect the organisation in the future. Chase refers to this as stonewalling an issue and he warns that the reactive change strategy can make an organisation a victim of the change. Still, there may be times when the organisation either lacks the resources to take action or realise no matter what the organisation does, the issue will progress along a predetermined path – the existing policy option will become the actual policy. At least the organisation is aware of coming challenges.

The adaptive change strategy does take action and reflects efforts to change. While the policy options have already begun to take shape, alternatives are offered before a policy decision is made. Managers provide and promote an alternative policy option that is friendly to the organisation. Chase uses the example of a proposed bottle bill in the US state of Virginia to address litter concerns. A bottle bill requires a deposit on all beverage bottles and reduces litter by providing people with an incentive for returning the bottles for the deposit. Beverage wholesalers dislike bottle bills because the measure complicates their operations. In one case, the beverage wholesalers proposed an alternative in the form of a roadside litter campaign that included more rubbish or trash cans. By promoting the roadside litter option, the beverage wholesalers prevented the passage of the less attractive (to them) bottle bill in Virginia.

The dynamic change strategy is truly proactive because it seeks to shape the policy options from the very start. The managers find the emerging issue then create the first policy option to be considered. The managers take control of the issue by being the ones to define what the issue is and the best way to resolve it – their policy option. In the US state of California, beverage wholesalers recognised that bottle bills were appearing in other states. They introduced a policy proposal involving litter education and anti-litter laws thereby avoiding any discussion of bottle bills. The managers used the dynamic strategy to set the parameters for the debate over the issue.

Chase felt that the decision on the change strategy option was dependent on five factors: (1) the risk created by the emerging issue; (2) the confidence managers had in their information; (3) perceived accuracy of the managers' projections; (4) the likelihood the issue will go away on its own; and (5) general direction of elements related to the issue. Two of the factors are related to managers' confidence in their own research and data collection (points 2 and 3). The other three factors are based on indicators of how likely the issue is to develop further points (4 and 5) and the effect the issue could have on the organisation (point 1). Issues management is not a precise science as each of the five factors involves subjective assessments made by managers. The goal of the issue change strategy step is a decision on how to address the issues identified in the issue analysis step.

The issue action programme step is essentially a strategic communication campaign. The managers pursue the issue change option by creating a goal, determining an objective, developing the communication strategy, assigning the necessary resources, and then developing and executing the actual messages for the communicative effort. Chase does not provide much detail about each of the elements of the issue action programme,

Mini case study 16.1
When social media helped win the 'bra war'

British woman Beckie Williams was no hardened activist. But she got really angry in mid-2008 when the clothing chain Marks and Spencer introduced a £2 surcharge for larger women's bras. She wrote to complain but got an unsatisfactory reply, and received no reply at all when she wrote again. So Ms Williams launched a Facebook page, 'Busts4Justice', to raise awareness of what she portrayed as discriminatory pricing. Within weeks the Facebook page had over 5,000 followers, while the company argued publicly that larger bras needed more material and 'additional engineering'. The Facebook followers increased to over 18,000 and the issue gained massive internet support and mainstream media coverage around the world. Ms Williams then purchased one M&S share and vowed to take the issue to the company AGM in July 2009. The company still persisted it was 'impossible for us to reduce price without cutting quality'. But they had completely misjudged the situation and misread their customers. Two days later M&S Chairman Stuart Rose said they had got it wrong and he announced an immediate withdrawal of the surcharge. The so-called 'bra war' ended in victory for the protesters and failure by M&S to manage what should have been a straightforward issue.

Explore 16.1

Critics of issue management

The modern development of issue management has seen the emergence of some outspoken critics, including some who believe it is a cloak for 'corporate spin' and gives an unfair or improper advantage to big business. These critics, from academia or journalism, include Dinan and Miller (2007), Miller and Dinan (2008), Lubbers (2002), Beder (2002, 2006) and the classic book by Stauber and Rampton (1995), *Toxic Sludge is Good For You: Lies, damn lies and the public relations industry*. What are their main criticisms? Are they mainly concerned about issue management itself or about the way it is used or misused?

Box 16.2

Where do issues come from?

One of the commonest questions in issue management is: 'Where do issues come from and how do you recognise them?' Simply maintaining a very close watch on news and current affairs is the obvious answer. As the American issue expert George McGrath (1998: 74) said: 'For most organizations, key issues will be found from reading headlines rather than tea leaves.' But there are many other sources that are obvious but are often overlooked, including:

- industry and political conferences;
- trade publications;
- industry association meetings and newsletters;
- client and customer surveys;
- industry and business allies;
- websites and information from organisations that oppose you;
- analysis by experts;
- feedback from your own staff who deal with external people.

Most of these sources are inexpensive, yet can yield priceless intelligence.

---

a point we will return to shortly. The managers then move to the final step, evaluation of the results. Managers compare the desired outcome of the policy decision to the actually policy decision.

As a process model, the Chase and Jones Model (Jones and Chase 1979) is more about what to do and not as much about how to do it. The model shows a strong influence from systems theory. This is not a criticism of the model but simply a recognition of its limits in terms of strategic communication. There is little detail about how communication is actually used to manage an issue. The issue catalyst model seeks to fill the limited discussion of strategic communication's role in issues management.

Picture 16.1 Global warming is the emblematic issue of the twenty-first century, with organisations at every level, from global to local, relying on issue management to stake out the position (*source:* Vadim Petrakov/Shutterstock)

Issue catalyst model

In 1985, Crable and Vibbert argued that the Chase and Jones model was limited in being proactive because the model waited for an issue to begin to emerge. They posited that issues managers could be even more proactive by being the ones to create the issue rather simply waiting for a trend to appear. They argued that issues arise when people attach significance to a situation. Issues can be created and do not have to emerge from trends. When the Corn Refiners Association sought to rebrand high fructose corn syrup (HFCS) as corn sugar to escape the stigma of being linked to obesity, the Sugar Association created an issue by demanding the new name be dropped. Eventually the US government agreed with the Sugar Association when the Food and Drug Administration ruled against the term corn sugar. Moreover, their model emphasised the role communication played throughout the issues management process.

Originally called the catalytic model, one of the original authors has since posited that the name issue catalyst better captures the fundamental idea behind the model. Managers can become issue catalysts by being the ones pushing for the creation and redress of the issue. The issue catalyst model has five stages: (1) potential; (2) imminent; (3) current; (4) critical; and (5) dormant (Crable and Vibbert 1985). The stages denote different saliences of issues. The issues increase in salience from the potential to the critical stage that then drops with the dormant stage. A close look at each stage will help to illustrate the way salience, stakeholder support and communication function within the model. A running example of the Alar case in the US will be used to illustrate the various stages in the issue catalyst model.

The *potential* stage is when someone or some group creates an issue by identifying a situation as important/a problem. The key communicative aspect of the potential stage is definition. Defining the issue gives issue managers some element of control (Crable and Vibbert 1985). The definition sets the parameters for the issue and helps to attract others to the issue (Dionisopolous and Crable 1988). The issue definition should be carefully constructed to help provide a successful foundation for the issues management effort. In 1989, a group called the National Resource Defense Council (NRDC) defined daminozide as a carcinogen and created the Alar issue. Alar is the brand name of a product produced by Uniroyal to allow fruit to ripen longer and was heavily used in the apple industry. Alar was the primary source of exposure to daminizide for children. Researchers found that when heated, daminozide could become a carcinogen. Alar became defined as a cancer threat to children because of the possibility daminozide could make apple sauce a cancer risk for children.

The *imminent* stage is when more stakeholders begin to accept the issue's potential. The number of people connected to the issue begins to expand. Endorsements from prominent people can help to promote an issue to the imminent stage. The key communicative aspect of the imminent stage is legitimacy (Crable and Vibbert 1985). Issue managers must convince other stakeholders that the issue is an appropriate public concern – is legitimate. Legitimacy helps to attract people to the issue and to build interest in the issue. The NRDC used a number of scientists and their research data to create legitimacy for the Alar issue. People were willing to accept that a potential cancer risk for children was something worth their attention and the issue began to spread.

The *current* stage occurs when a wide range of people are interested in the issue. The number of people interested in the issue has expanded rapidly. The current stage typically demands that the traditional and/or social media discuss the issue. The media coverage raises the salience of the issue due to the agenda-setting effect. The issue managers engage in 'agenda-stimulation' by trying to set the agenda for other stakeholders (Crable and Vibbert 1985: 10). Along with a wide audience, the current stage is marked by the emergence of policy options for addressing the issue. If an issue is a problem, the policy option is the answer. The key communicative aspect of the current stage is polarisation. Issue managers need to build support for their preferred policy option/resolution to the issue. Polarisation forces people to take sides (Crable and Vibbert 1985). Ideally issue managers prompt people to support their side by accepting their preferred policy option. Of course not everyone

---

Box 16.3

Issue catalyst model

The model has five stages:

1. Potential: efforts to define the issue
2. Imminent: efforts to legitimize the issue and increase awareness
3. Current: seek to increase significantly awareness of the issue
4. Critical: try to polarize views of the issue and win support for your side of the issue
5. Dormant: issue is considered resolved

Source: Crable, R.E. and S.L. Vibbert (1985). 'Managing issues and influencing public policy'. *Public Relations Review* 11: 3–16

will support your position so polarisation can create opposition as well. Moreover, issue managers will find others trying to influence the issue as well. The competition between the various sides in issues management becomes manifest in the current stage.

The NRDC launched a communication campaign to increase awareness of the Alar issue in February of 1989. A key element of the campaign was a segment about Alar on *60 Minutes,* a highly rated evening investigative news show in the US. The *60 Minutes* story quickly pushed Alar to the current stage. At that point, the NRDC argued that Alar should be banned from public use – the policy option was advanced. Apple growers countered that the studies were not conclusive about the link between Alar and cancer. People were being forced to choose a side, either ban Alar or allow its continued use. By defining Alar as a cancer threat to children, the NRDC had a powerful reason to support the Alar ban.

The *critical* stage indicates the time is right for a decision. People feel the need for a decision at this point, thus the issue has its greatest salience. The key communicative resource at the critical stage is identification. Issue managers need to win active support for their preferred policy option. To build support, issue managers build a sense of identification with the preferred policy option – people feel that option best captures their interests and values. Issue managers create messages that indicate how their preferred policy option reflects the identities of potential supporters. The critical stage ends with a policy decision. Keep in mind that decision might be to not take any action on the issue. Once a decision is made, an issue is considered to be in the *dormant* step. People will have lost interest once the decision is made. However, issue managers can try to restart the issue management process at any point through attempts to revive the salience of the issue (Crable and Vibbert 1985).

The NRDC kept pushing people on the cancer risk of Alar to win support for their ban on Alar. Public opinion polls and the letters to the Food and Drug Administration (FDA), the US agency responsible for food safety, overwhelmingly supported an Alar ban. Apple sales were falling as people feared for the safety of the fruit. There was pressure for the government to act even though the scientific evidence was unclear. In June of 1989, Uniroyal agreed to stop producing Alar. In November of 1989, the EPA banned Alar even though the ban announcement acknowledged the scientific evidence was vague while recognising the public concern about the product. The FDA decision moved the Alar issue to the dormant stage. There was no longer a need to discuss the Alar issue because it was removed from the market.

The issue catalyst model is about the salience of an issue and the number of people interested in the issue, two closely interrelated concepts. The movement from potential to current stages is a progression in both salience and the number of stakeholders involved with the issue. The critical step is when the issue is most salient. Issues do not automatically move from one stage to the next. An issue can fail by stagnating at any stage. The communicative skill of the issue manager is a key driver in moving an issue through the stages of the issue catalyst model towards a policy decision.

Expanding issues management beyond public policy

Although issues management is still applicable to policy decisions, there has been an expansion of the concept to include organisational decision making (e.g. Botan and Taylor 2004; Grunig and Repper 1992; Heath 2005; Jaques 2006). Robert Heath, a leading expert in issues management, documents this shift with his 2005 definition of issues management: 'a management philosophy and multidisciplinary set of strategic functions used to reduce friction and increase harmony between organizations and their stakeholders' (Heath 2005: 495). The basic elements of issues management found in the models of issues management have been applied by stakeholders in attempts to influence directly the policies and practices of organisations – to influence organisational decision making. This shift from the public to the private policy-making domains has been termed private politics by those in political science (Baron 2003). Unfortunately, the term private politics is confusing for those in public relations and strategic communication because it suggests matters managed in private versus a public discussion.

Coombs and Holladay (2018) propose the term social issues management to capture the new social issues focus emerging in issues management. Social issues management refers to efforts by firms to promote specific orientations toward social issues. Social issues management is a larger framework that would include more tactical elements such as (1) values advocacy, connect firms to positive values by praising those values (Bostdorff and Vibbert 1994); (2) organisational epideictic, take stands on controversial issues (Bigam et al. 2006), and (3) corporate social advocacy, take stands on social issues outside of the firms' CSR efforts (Dodd and Supa 2015). The key is the shift in decision making from the government to the firms. Actors seek to shape organisational behaviours by directly confronting the problematic organisational behaviour. See Mini case study 16.2.

Picture 16.2 High-profile demonstrations or media stunts to generate awareness are a standard element of many issues management strategies such as these Extinction Rebellion protestors in Madrid (*source:* Marcos del Mazo/LightRocket/Getty Images)

Mini case study 16.2
Green America

Green America was concerned that Hershey's, one of the top chocolate users in the world, was not disclosing what percentage of its cocoa supply came from countries known to allow child slave labour on cocoa plantations. Green American has used a variety of communicative efforts to force Hershey's to address the issue publicly. Green America was utilising the issue catalyst model in its social issues management effort. The non-disclosure of cocoa suppliers was defined as unacceptable and the issue was legitimised by the general global disdain for child slave labour. Green America used various internet channels and direct actions to gain wider attention for the issue (current stage) and force people to choose sides on the issue (critical stage). After three years of pushing the issue, Hershey's finally began to address the role of child slave labour in its supply chain (Coombs 2014).

Social issues management is a reversal of the business case for issues management and returns the concept to its activist roots. Managers do not apply pressure on their own or other organisations to change behaviours/influence decisions. External stakeholders are the actors most likely to initiate social issues management and seek to influence organisational decisions from the outside. Greenpeace is an excellent example of how external stakeholders engage in social issues management. Greenpeace locates a problematic corporate behaviour, conducts research and then engages in an issues management campaign that uses communication to increase issue salience and awareness. Case study 16.1 illustrates Greenpeace's use of the Issue Catalyst model.

Coombs and Holladay (2018) argue that social issues management requires an adaptation of the Issue Catalyst model that is reflective of the new digital environment. Their adaptation centres on collapsing the current and critical stages into one new stage called awareness. Awareness is premised on mobilising information and digital platforms rather than a reliance on traditional news media to spread information. Mobilising information allows people to take actions on their beliefs. For instance, telling people the time and location of a rally or how to contact managers of a firm digitally are examples of mobilising information. Issue managers now can take their messages directly to potential supporters instead of relying entirely upon the traditional news media to share information about the issue.

During the awareness stage, there is pressure on the firm to act on the issue. Managers of the firm will choose to either engage with the social issue or decline involvement. The managerial decisions are driven by assessments of stakeholder support and quiescence. Managers will engage in a social issue if they believe

Case study 16.1
Greenpeace, H&M and Detox

July of 2011 marked the beginning of Greenpeace's efforts to remove a select group of highly toxic chemicals from the fashion and garment industries. The campaign is known as Detox because Greenpeace wants corporations to detox their supply chains. The toxic chemicals are a danger to workers, people living near where the chemicals are used, and even the people wearing the clothes, especially children. Greenpeace worked with scientists to document the existence of these chemicals in the textile and garment industries and began the campaign by asking the top 13 firms in the garment industry to replace the specified toxic chemicals in the supply chain. The non-toxic alternatives are similar in price and sometimes even less expensive than the toxic chemicals. All of the 13 firms declined to detox, hence Greenpeace launched the public version of the Detox campaign which can be defined as a form of issues management. The crux of Detox is shaming firms by revealing how irresponsible the firms are by allowing harmful, toxic chemicals in their supply chains. Detox attempts to leverage organisational change by threatening reputations via perceptions of corporate social responsibility.

Within the first year, Puma, Nike, Adidas, Li Ning, Lacoste and H&M (six of the original 13 firms) all agreed to detox. The H&M case illustrates the way Greenpeace uses communication to create power to raise the salience of the detox issue for managers. H&M is a global brand that is proud of its CSR efforts. Detox posed a threat to the CSR component of H&M identity and reputation. Here is a sample Detox statement about H&M: 'There's a skeleton in H&M's closet. The fast-fashion retailer sells clothes made with chemicals which cause hazardous water pollution around the world, and the only way to stop this water pollution is to come clean and stop using such chemicals for good. As one of the largest clothing groups in the world, an H&M committed to a toxic-free future would set the trend for the rest of the fashion industry to follow' ('Will', 2011, para 1). H&M was acting irresponsibly in terms of toxins in the supply chain.

To increase the pressure on H&M management, Greenpeace used a mix on direct action (in-person) and social media messages. For direct action, Greenpeace representatives placed static stickers on the windows of H&M stores in 12 countries. The stickers had slogans such as 'Detox our Future' and 'Detox our Water'. The direct action sought to raise awareness of the issue among H&M consumers by placing the message in the stores and generating both traditional and digital media coverage of the actions. H&M has an active Facebook and Twitter account the firm uses to engage customers. As part of the Detox campaign, Greenpeace initiated a petition on Twitter about H&M and Detox. The petition collected 635,000 Twitter users and was re-tweeted over 1,200 times. Greenpeace also began posting questions to the H&M Facebook page and placing comments about Detox on the page. According to Greenpeace, the messages were designed to have people question H&M's 'reputation as a sustainability leader' (Clickers 2011, para 7).

Shortly after the Greenpeace emphasis on H&M, the firm agreed to Detox. Here is part of H&M's announcement: 'Greenpeace International is calling for zero discharge of all hazardous chemicals in the global textile supply chain. H&M shares this goal with Greenpeace; since 1995 H&M has been working practically to reduce the use and impact of hazardous chemicals using an approach based on the Precautionary Principle' ('H&M' 2011, para 1).

Think about 16.3

Visit the timeline for the Detox page for Greenpeace, the link is provide below. Review the timeline for the Detox effort. What do the past victories and length of time of the Detox issues management mean for fashion organisations that have yet to be part of this issues management effort? Can you explain the order in which Greenpeace has targeted the various fashion organisations? (Greenpeace)

Feedback

An argument can be made that organisations that make the first change in an industry can become a leader on that issue in the industry. In turn, that leadership can become a reputational asset. What does that mean for an organisation that is an initial target in social issue management effort like Detox?

Explore 16.2

Issues management in the digital age

Stakeholders frequently seek to engage organisations in change through digital channels. Organisations can learn about recent or possible issues management directed against them by visiting activist websites. Visit the Center for International Environmental Law (CIEL) blog post about nanoparticles in baby formula. There also is a link you can follow to a report on the topic by Friends of the Earth (FoE). Given that issues are often extended to other organisations in an industry, create a list of the organisations that might become a part of this issue management effort.

Explore 16.3

Issues management, especially those targeting organisational decisions, are frequently transnational. Visit the Greenpeace website. Select the 'What we do' tab and review one of the issues listed there. How has Greenpeace (1) defined the issue and (2) sought to build legitimacy for the issue? See if you can find a connection between the definition of the issue and the policy option being advocated by Greenpeace.

---

the social issue will win support among its stakeholders or promote quiescence by reassuring critics that the proper actions are being taken (Coombs and Holladay 2018). The next section elaborates on the idea of quiescence by unpacking why a social issue becomes a threat that requires efforts to reassure angry stakeholders.

An important point to consider is why the shift to social issues management. Some experts feel the shift is a result of resources. It is less expensive to engage in social issues management than in traditional issues management. Low-cost internet (digital) channels can be combined with select direct actions, such as those in the Detox case study (16.1), to create pressure for corporations to change and are less expensive and time consuming than efforts requiring traditional media attention and the public pressure necessary to influence policy decisions. The various social media channels such as blogs, micro-blogs and social networking is necessary but not sufficient to account for the popularity of social issues management. We need to look more closely at the two factors that are necessary and sufficient for social issues management to succeed: (1) a leverage point and (2) a means of leverage.

For social issues management to force firms to engage with social issues, stakeholders need some leverage points – ways to make the issue salient to the firm. If there is no salience or pressure on the firm, managers can simply ignore the external efforts to influence internal decisions. Reputation has provided the leverage point for social issues management. Managers are keenly aware of the benefits a favourable reputation can generate for a corporation (Alsop 2004; Davies et al. 2003; Fombrun and van Riel 2004). Managers spend millions of dollars cultivating and protecting favourable reputations. In short, reputation is a highly valued corporate asset. Moreover, corporate social responsibility increasingly is a significant component of corporate reputation, accounting for over 40 per cent of a corporation's reputation (Fombrun 2005). Reputation and CSR are the leverage points that make social issues management a viable option for external stakeholders. If external stakeholders can threaten to damage perceptions of CSR or reputation, leverage points exists to give salience to their issue. Essentially making other stakeholders aware of the issue can damage the corporate reputation and/or make the corporation appear irresponsible (Jones et al. 2009; Tench et al. 2012). Case study 16.1 illustrates this point. If other stakeholders become aware of the societal damage inflicted by the harmful chemicals in textile production, the CSR and reputation of the corporations using those chemicals in their supply chains is damaged. For the issue to be a threat, it must have legitimacy. If other stakeholders are unlikely to see the issue as relevant to themselves and society as a whole, managers can easily ignore the issue (Coombs and Holladay 2012).

External stakeholders have long depended on the threat of reputational damage as a source of power for influencing corporate decision making. Boycotts, for instance, work by generating negative publicity more so than through the loss of financial resources (King 2011; McDonnell and King 2013). Internet channels, including social media, are recognised as reputational concerns by corporate managers (McCorkindale and DiStaso 2015). The digital channels provide a means of leveraging corporate reputations and perceptions of CSR thereby creating power for the external stakeholders (Tench and Jones 2015). It is too simplistic to equate the digital channels' power with the effect on corporate decision making. The various digital channels provide an opportunity to cultivate stakeholder power (Coombs and Holladay 2012a). The external stakeholders must skilfully combine the channels with their communication strategies to put pressure on the corporations. Again, note how in the Detox case Greenpeace used online channels and direct action to pressure H&M to detox.

The value of digital channels as leverage is enhanced by the growth of digital naturals. Young and Åkerström (2015) coined the phrase digital naturals to denote how people of any age can be comfortable, to varying degrees, working within the digital environment. The digital naturals possess the skills to use digital channels and are comfortable using those channels. Consider how omnipresent mobile phones have become and how so many people use them to connect with the internet, making the phones an extension of their own bodies. Digital naturals add value to digital channels. Issue managers now have the skill and desire to use the digital channels to leverage corporations and there is an ever increasing number of digital naturals who can serve as a receptive audience for these digital issues management efforts (Coombs and Holladay 2016). In combination, the value of corporate reputations (a leverage point) and the potential of digital channels (means of leverage) are necessary and sufficient for the growing reliance on social issues management. However, simply engaging in social issues management is no guarantee of success for issue managers. Managers still can choose to ignore or to combat social issues management efforts. We can explore the dynamic of corporate resistance by examining how the issue catalyst and Chase and Jones models can intersect with social issues management.

The issue catalyst approach in social issues management is predominantly a tool for external stakeholders. As noted earlier, corporations are unlikely to seek to influence directly the decisions of other corporations via public politics. Once external stakeholders have initiated a social issues management effort to create change, corporate managers must decide how to respond to the potential threat. The Chase and Jones model is ideal for guiding the response to the social issues management actions. Corporate managers research the situation to determine the extent of the threat posed by the social issues management effort. This research should include an evaluation of what the proposed changes would mean for the organisation. Managers must consider at least four points: (1) determine if the corporation could benefit from the changes; (2) project how significantly the corporation could be harmed if no change is made; (3) determine the cost of the change; and (4) assess if the changes are consistent with core corporate strategy (Coombs and Holladay 2015). The managers can then decide which issue change strategy option to select. Managers may decide to do nothing (reactive), counter-argue that current practices are acceptable (reactive), or make the desired changes (dynamic). Issues always have competing sides, hence managers will have options for how they choose to respond to any issue management effort.

Box 16.4

COVID-19 as issues management

As you think about issues management, consider the importance of timing. In issues management, the earlier you are involved with the issue the better position you are in as an issue manager. In the issue catalyst model, for instance, early involvement affords the issue managers a greater opportunity to define an issue in a way favourable to their positions on the issues. More generally, early intervention is preferable in issues management. That is why scanning is so critical to issues management. The need for early action is illustrated by COVID-19. Though a public health crisis, it is also a case of issues management because there is a strong link between crises and issues. In this case, the crisis created issues that required attention (Coombs 2019). The COVID-19 pandemic became an issue that multiple governments needed to manage. Countries such as New Zealand identified and took action on the issue early in the outbreak. Others, such as the United States, were much later to take action on the issue – instead choosing to believe the issue was not that important. Early action on the COVID-19 issue saved lives while wasting time and downplaying the issue cost lives. The lesson for issue managers is that the sooner you detect or create an issue, the more likely you are to have the issue resolved in a more favourable manner for all parties involved with the issue.

The big picture for issues management

A long-time concern in issues management has been the undue influence of money. Groups with more money, it has been argued, can create greater influence on policy decisions. That is why experts such as Robert Heath (2005) have argued for responsible issues management by corporations with vast financial reserves. Generally, there is limited evidence to support that issues management has been abused by corporations. Social issues management seeks to even the playing field by allowing issue managers with fewer resources to enter into effective issues management efforts.

Even as financial costs become less of a factor, there are concerns about issues management that must be recognised. Even in social issues management, there is a need for resources such communicative skills and internet access. Many marginalised groups lack these resources and remain on the fringes of issue debates. Social issues management created change one organisation at a time rather than creating change for an entire industry as is possible with policy decisions such as regulation. Finally, social issues management contributes to the neoliberal agenda of preferring self-regulation to government regulation. The external stakeholders can agitate for change but have no means of enforcing the changes. Ultimately, corporations are self-regulating when agreeing to changes such as detox. Though not perfect, issues management provides a framework whereby various groups can seek to influence corporate behaviours and to improve society.

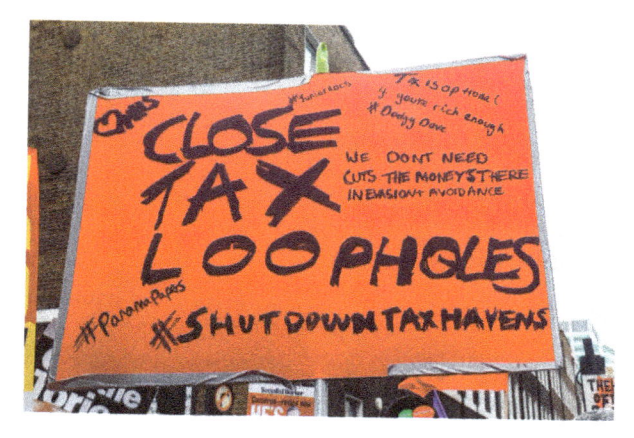

Picture 16.3 UK Uncut protested in and around several Starbucks locations in the UK. The protests drew a significant amount of media attention. (*source:* Prisma by Dukas/Universal Images Group/Getty Images)

Case study 16.2
UK Uncut and Starbucks

In 2010, a network of activist groups formed around the issue of corporate tax avoidance in the UK. UK Uncut relies heavily on direct action designed to stimulate news media coverage of the tax avoidance issue that embarrasses the corporate target. UK Uncut is using corporate reputation as a way to convince managers to pay more taxes. At the end of 2012, UK Uncut targeted Starbucks for its limited payment of taxes. On 8 December 2012, UK Uncut protested in and around a number of Starbucks locations in the UK. The protests did draw a significant amount of media attention allowing UK Uncut to explain how little taxes Starbucks has been paying on its rather large UK sales and profits. On 15 December 2012 UK Uncut moved to the digital arena. Starbucks was sponsoring the holiday ice rink at the Natural History Museum in London. As part of the sponsorship, there was a large video screen behind the ice rink. Starbucks asked people to post holiday messages on its Twitter feedback and broadcast the Tweets live on the screen. As you might guess, the Tweets were dominated by complaints by UK Uncut. To make matters worse, a filter to prevent inappropriate language from appearing on the screen failed, letting a few less-than-holiday-cheer words to appear. In response to the negative coverage in traditional and digital media, Starbucks stated it would pay more taxes in 2013 and 2014. In fact, Starbucks argued it would pay more taxes in the UK than it was legally obligated to pay.

Summary

Systems theory tells us that organisations are influenced by their environments. Issues management represent a concerted effort by management to influence the environment. Issues management began as efforts to influence policy decisions but has expanded to include efforts intended to directly shape organisational decisions. Either way, stakeholders and managers are attempting to influence the organisation's operating environment to some degree. Some efforts try to improve the operating environment while seeking to make the operating environment less negative. Strategic communication is one of the driving forces in the efforts to influence public and organisational decision making. Issues management must seek to balance the interests of all parties or risk creating a backlash if it becomes the exclusive domain of the powerful.

Issues management is intricately connected to the next chapter of crisis public relations management. Tony Jaques (2006, 2007) is the strongest advocate for the close connection between issues and crises. An issue has the potential to create a crisis for an organisation, hence issues management can be a form of crisis prevention. In addition, a crisis can bring intense public attention to an issue and precipitate an issues management effort – and create pressure for change (Coombs 2015). The interconnected nature of issues management and crisis communication management will become more evident as you read Chapter 17, 'Crisis public relations management'.

Bibliography

Alsop, R.J. (2004). *The 18 immutable laws of corporate reputation*. New York: Dow Jones & Company.

Baron, D.P. (2003). Private politics. *Journal of Economics & Management Strategy, 12*(1): pp. 31–66.

Beder, S. (2002). *Global Spin: The corporate assault on environmentalism*. Totnes, Devon: Green Books.

Beder, S. (2006). *Suiting Themselves: How corporations drive the global agenda*. London: Earthscan.

Bigam Stahley, M. and J. Boyd (2006). Winning is (n't) everything: The paradox of excellence and the challenge of organizational epideictic. *Journal of Applied Communication Research, 34*(4): pp. 311–330.

Bostdorff, D.M. and S.L. Vibbert (1994). Values advocacy: Enhancing organizational images, deflecting public criticism, and grounding future arguments. *Public Relations Review, 20*(2): pp. 141–158.

Botan, C.H. and M. Taylor (2004). Public relations: State of the field. *Journal of Communication, 54*(4): pp. 645–661.

Chase, W.H. (1984). *Issue management*. Leesburg, VA: Issue Action Publications.

CIEL https://www.ciel.org/nanoparticles-baby-formula/ [accessed 7 April 2020].

Clickers and stickers make H&M detox (2011). [online]. Available at: http://www.greenpeace.org/international/en/news/features/Clickers-and-Stickers-Make-HM-Detox/ [accessed 5 December 2019].

Conley II, J.G. (2006). Environmentalism contained: A history of corporate responses to the new environmentalism. *Ann Arbor, 1001*, pp. 48106–1346.

Coombs W.T. and S.J. Holladay (2012). Internet contagion theory 2.0: How internet communication channels empower stakeholder. In: S. Duhe, ed., *New media and public relations* (2nd edn). New York: Peter Lang, pp. 21–30.

Coombs, W.T. (2015). *Ongoing Crisis Communication: Planning, Managing, and Responding* (4th ed.). Thousand Oaks: Sage Publications.

Coombs, W.T. and S.J. Holladay (2015). CSR as crisis risk: Expanding how we conceptualize the relationship. *Corporate Communications: An International Journal, 20*(2): pp. 144–162.

Coombs, W. T. and S.J. Holladay (2010). *PR strategy and application: Managing influence*. Malden, MA: Wiley-Blackwell.

Coombs, W. T. and S.J. Holladay (2018). Social issue qua wicked problems: The role of strategic communication in social issues management. *Journal of Communication Management, 22*(1): pp. 79–95.

Coombs, W.T. (2014). *Applied Crisis Communication and Crisis Management*. Thousand Oaks: Sage Publications.

Coombs, W.T. and S.J. Holladay (2012). The paracrisis: The challenges created by publicity managing crisis prevention. *Public Relations Review, 38*(3): pp. 408–15.

Coombs, W.T. and S.J. Holladay (2016). Digital naturals and crisis communication: Significant shifts of focus. In Coombs, W.T., Falkheimer, J., Heide, M. and Young, P. (Eds.), (2016) *Strategic communication, social media and democracy: The challenge of the digital naturals* (pp. 54–62). London: Routledge.

Crable, R. E. and S.L. Vibbert (1985). Managing issues and influencing public policy. *Public Relations Review, 11*(2): pp. 3–16.

Davies, G., Chun, R., Da Silva, R.V. and S. Roper (2003). Corporate Reputation and Competitiveness. *Corporate Communications: An International Journal, 8*(2), pp. 148–149.

Detox Campaign (2011). http://www.greenpeace.org/international/en/campaigns/toxics/water/detox/intro/ accessed 20 May 2013].

Detox My Fashion (2018). [online]. Available at: https://www.greenpeace.org/international/act/detox/ [accessed 3 July 2019].

Diermeier, D. (2007). Private Politics – A Research Agenda. *The Political Economist: Newlettter of the APSA Section on Political Economy, 14*(2): 1–9.

Dinan, W. and D. Miller (eds) (2007). *Thinker, Faker, Spinner, Spy: Corporate PR and the assault on democracy*. London: Pluto Press.

Dionisopoulos, G.N. and R.E. Crable (1988). Definitional hegemony as a public relations strategy: The rhetoric of the nuclear power industry after Three Mile Island. *Communication Studies, 39*(2): pp. 134–145.

Dodd, M.D. and D. Supa (2015). Testing the Viability of Corporate Social Advocacy as a Predictor of Purchase Intention. *Communication Research Reports, 32*(4): pp. 287–293.

Edelman (2019). 2019 Edelman Trust Barometer Global Report, [online] Available at: https://www.edelman.com/sites/g/files/aatuss191/files/2019-02/2019_Edelman_Trust_Barometer_Global_Report.pdf [accessed 5 December 2019].

European Commission (2017). The EU's new conflict minerals regulations, [online]. Available at: http://trade.

ec.europa.eu/doclib/docs/2017/march/tradoc_155423.pdf [accessed 5 December 2019].

Fombrun, C.J. (2005). A world of reputation research, analysis and thinking—building corporate reputation through CSR initiatives: evolving standards. *Corporate Reputation Review, 8*(1), pp. 7–12.

Fombrun, C.J. and C.B. Van Riel (2004). *Fame & fortune: How successful companies build winning reputations.* London: FT Press.

Greenpeace (https://www.greenpeace.org/international/act/detox/) [accessed 7 April 2020].

Grunig, J.E. and F.C. Repper (1992). Strategic management, publics, and issues. In: J.E. Grunig, ed., *Excellence in public relations and communication* management. Hillsdale, NJ: Lawrence Erlbaum, pp. 117–157.

Heath, R.L. (1997). *Strategic Issues Management: Organizations and Public Policy Challenges.* Thousand Oaks, CA: Sage.

Heath, R.L. (1988). *Strategic Issues Management: How organizations influence and respond to public interests and policies.* San Francisco: Jossey-Bass.

Heath, R.L. (2005). Issues management. In: R.L. Heath, ed., *Encyclopedia of public relations* (Volume 1). Thousand Oaks, CA: Sage, pp. 460–463.

Jaques, T. (2006). Activist 'rules' and the convergence with issue management. *Journal of Communication Management, 10*(4), pp. 407–420.

Jaques, T. (2007). Issue management and crisis management: An integrated, non-linear, relational construct. *Public Relations Review, 33*(2), pp. 147–157.

Jones, B., Bowd, R. and R. Tench (2009). Corporate irresponsibility and corporate social responsibility: competing realities. *Social Responsibility Journal, 5*(3), 300–310.

Jones, B.L. and W.H. Chase (1979). Managing public policy issues. *Public Relations Review, 5*(2), pp. 3–23.

King, B.G. (2011). The tactical disruptiveness of social movements: Sources of market and mediated disruption in corporate boycotts. *Social Problems, 58*(4), pp. 491–517.

Lemert, J.B. and M.G. Aashma (1983). Extent of mobilizing information in opinion and news magazines. *Journalism and Mass Communication Quarterly, 60*(4): pp. 657–662.

Lubbers, E. (ed.) (2002). *Battling Big Business: Countering greenwash, infiltration and other forms of corporate bullying.* Totnes, Devon: Green Books.

McCorkindale, T. and M.W. DiStaso (2015). The Power of social media and its influence on corporation reputation. In: C.E. Carroll, ed., *The Handbook of Communication and Corporate Reputation.* Malden, MA: Wiley-Blackwell, pp. 497–512.

McDonnell, M.H. and B. King (2013). Keeping up appearances reputational threat and impression management after social movement boycotts. *Administrative Science Quarterly, 58*(3), pp. 387–419.

McGrath, G.B. (1998). *Issues Management: Anticipation and influence.* IABC.

Miller, D. and W. Dinan (2008). *A Century of Spin: How public relations became the cutting edge of corporate power.* London: Pluto.

Stauber, J. and S. Rampton (1995). *Toxic Sludge is Good for You: Lies, damn lies and the public relations industry.* Monroe, ME: Common Courage Press.

Tench, R. and B. Jones (2015). Social media: the Wild West of CSR communications. *Social Responsibility Journal, 11*(2), 290–305.

Tench, R., W. Sun and B. Jones. (2012) *Corporate social irresponsibility: A challenging concept Critical Studies on Corporate Responsibility, Governance and Sustainability,* Volume 4).' (2012): 3–20.

Young, P. and M. Åkerström (2015). Meet the digital naturals. In: W.T. Coombs, J. Falkheimer, M. Heide and P. Young, eds., *Strategic communication, social media and democracy: The challenge of the digital naturals.* Routledge: London, pp. 1–10.

CHAPTER 17

Tim Coombs

Crisis public relations management

Source: GUDKOV ANDREY/Shutterstock

Learning outcomes

By the end of this chapter you should be able to:
- define and describe the concepts of crisis and crisis management
- recognise the value of communication to crisis public relations management
- understand the different crisis types and how the crisis type affects crisis communication
- identify the key principles in crisis public relations management
- apply principles of crisis public relations management to actual crisis cases
- understand the effects of the internet on crisis public relations management.

Structure

- Crisis public relations management: the context
- The value of strategic communication
- Where do crises come from?
- How to prepare for a crisis?
- Communicating during a crisis
- The internet and crisis public relations management

Introduction

In October 2018 Lion Air Flight 610 crashed and 189 people died while in March 2019 Ethiopian Airlines flight 302 crashed and 157 people died. The common link between these two crises was that both involved the Boeing 737 Max, a relatively new plane that had only been flying for two years. Following the second crash, all EU countries, India, China, Japan, Canada, Indonesia, South Korea and the United States all ordered the grounding of the Boeing 737 Max. Boeing stopped delivering new planes as well as investigators carefully examining its automatic flight software called the Manoeuvring Characteristics Augmentation System (MCAS). Boeing was faced with a crisis that threatened it financially and which generated crises for many of the airlines that were using the Boeing 737 Max had to re-schedule and cancel flights due to the global groundings of the plane. In July of 2013, 63 cars carrying petroleum on a cargo train derailed in the Canadian town of Lac-Mégantic. A massive fire erupted destroying 30 buildings, requiring the evacuation of one-third of the town, and ultimately killing 47 people. The CEO of Rail World, Edward Burkhardt, became the face of the crisis response. Burkhardt failed by repeatedly communicating the wrong message and intensifying rather than reducing the harm the crisis was inflicting on his organisation. An extended example will help to illustrate the value of crisis public relations management.

In 2015, Volkswagen (VW) made headlines around the world when it was revealed many of their diesel vehicles had special software. The special software was designed to trick emission-testing machines, especially those used in the United States. The software allowed the cars to appear far less polluting than they actually were. The crisis became known as *emissiongate* or *dieselgate*. Soon other countries began investigating the vehicles in question. This included a dispute in the EU over whether or not VW should have to compensate unhappy customers of the affected vehicles. VW's initial response was to blame a few 'rogue engineers' for the problem. Stakeholders rejected that claim because they felt it was more a systemic problem at VW rather than a few bad employees. CEO Martin Winterkorn resigned and the crisis is estimated to have cost VW over 27 billion euros. The VW example reflects the dangers of ineffective crisis public relations management. By providing an ineffective response, VW prolonged the life of the crisis in the public eye by increasing media scrutiny. A more effective response could have ended media interest in the crisis much sooner.

Effective crisis public relations management protects stakeholders from harm, helps stakeholders recover from the crisis, and works to repair the financial and reputational damage a crisis can inflict on an organisation. The key difference between effective and ineffective crisis public relations management is strategic thinking. Effective crisis public relations management is built on a foundation of preparation that is informed by research. When a crisis hits, managers have practiced handling similar situations and understand what actions should help and which could hurt in their crisis situation.

Crisis public relations management is a rapidly developing field with new knowledge being added regularly. This chapter presents the key points of crisis public relations management that can help guide managers towards an effective crisis management effort.

Crisis public relations management: the context

Crisis public relations management is an applied field. Like most applied fields, understanding the field began by analysing what managers were already doing then trying to develop ways to improve on the practice. The early literature on crisis public relations management were simply lists of 'what to do' and 'what not to do' in a crisis. Box 17.1 presents a list of the common recommendations found in the early crisis writings. These lists were based upon case studies of what crisis managers had done in the past. The lists are a type of 'accepted wisdom'. Some accepted wisdom really is wisdom and some is simply urban myth. As the field matures, researchers have begun exploring crisis public relations management in a more systematic fashion to separate the wisdom from the urban myths and to begin building crisis public relations management theory. Theory improves the practice by developing and testing reasons for why certain actions are effective and others are ineffective. The accepted wisdom is replaced with evidence based on theory and empirical tests. However, wisdom is not lost in the evidence-based approach. Professionals combine research results with their own experience to fashion crisis responses. Crisis public relations management is in a transitional phase from accepted wisdom to evidence-based approaches. Researchers in stealing thunder (Arpan and Pompper 2003; Claeys 2017), Contingency Theory (e.g. Jin et al. 2007), and Situational Crisis Communication Theory (e.g. Coombs and Holladay 2001) are at the forefront of evidence-based crisis communication. The evidence-based approaches use experiments to test how people react to crises and to the crisis response strategies used in a crisis. The experiments test speculation about how people will react to a crisis or react to a crisis response strategy. Speculation is then replaced with evidence. The value of experimental research is that it

Picture 17.1 Emergency services work at the crash site near Bishoftu of Ethiopian Airlines ET302 to Nairobi (*source:* Jemal Countess/Getty Images)

can establish a cause and effect relationship between the crisis response strategies and their effects on stakeholders. Managers will know the likely effects their communicative choices will have on their stakeholders.

Box 17.1

Early crisis communication recommendations

What to do

- Speak with one voice/consistent message (Carney and Jorden 1993)
- Respond quickly (Caruba 1994)
- Be open and disclose information about the crisis (Twardy 1994)

What not to do:

- Speculate on the cause of the crisis
- Say 'no comment' (In a Crisis 1993)

Defining key concepts

We should begin the exploration of crisis public relations management by defining the key terms 'crisis' and 'crisis public relations management'. A crisis can be defined as 'the perceived violation of salient stakeholder expectations that can create negative outcomes for stakeholders and/or the organization' (Coombs 2019: 3). Crises are perceptual. If an organisation's stakeholders believe it is in a crisis, the organisation is in a crisis unless it can prove otherwise to its stakeholders. Crises violate salient stakeholder expectations for how an organisation should behave. Products should not harm customers and aeroplanes should not lose their engine power during a flight. Crises can threaten stakeholders with negative outcomes including physical harm, psychological trauma and financial loss. By violating salient expectations an organisation risks damage to its performance through loss of sales or a drop in share price. A crisis can create a range of negative outcomes beyond diminished performance including physical damage to facilities, turnover of employees, a decrease in share prices and organisational reputation, while stakeholders can suffer physical, psychological and/or economic harm. The actual damage inflicted by a crisis is determined, in part, by the effectiveness of the crisis public relations management.

To be more precise, this chapter is about organisational crises. The term crisis is very broad and often includes natural disasters and public health crises. Organisational crises have a narrower focus as indicated by the preceding definition. It is important to note that organisational crises can be sub-divided into operational crises and paracrises. Operational crises represent the origins of crisis management and crisis communication. An operational crisis is a threat that can disrupt the operation of an organisation thereby creating the risk of financial loss. A paracrisis is when an organisation manages a crisis risk in public. In other words, an organisation's stakeholders can see how the organisation is or is not managing the crisis risk (Coombs and Holladay 2012). Paracrisis have gone by other names including reputational crises and social media crises. However, both of these concepts are rather vague and create confusion rather than add clarity to crisis public relations management.

Crisis public relations management is a collection of factors that are used to address the crisis and to lessen the damage a crisis might inflict on the organisation and its stakeholders. Crisis public relations management involves interventions that occur throughout the lifecycle of a crisis. Box 17.2 outlines the commonly used three-stage crisis lifecycle. The three-stage crisis lifecycle works well for most simple crises. However, some crises are more complex and fit better with the regenerative model of crisis (Coombs 2017; 2019). The regenerative model has two stages, pre-crisis and post-crisis phases. Even though it has only two stages, the regenerative model is dynamic because crises can be reframed thereby creating new communicative demands for crisis managers. The

Box 17.2

Three-stage crisis life cycle

1. Pre-crisis: actions taken prior to occurrence of the crisis
   a. Signal detection: search for warning signs that a crisis may occur
   b. Prevention: take steps to lessen the likelihood that a crisis risk becomes a crisis
   c. Preparation: take steps to prepare for handling a crisis

2. Crisis event: a trigger event indicates a crisis has begun
   a. Crisis recognition: define the situation as a crisis
   b. Crisis containment: words and actions used to address the crisis

3. Post-crisis: actions taken after a crisis is considered to be over
   a. Learning: discover lessons from the crisis management effort
   b. Follow-up: provide any information or actions promised during the crisis
   c. Healing: address lingering psychological issues created by the crisis

(*Source*: Coombs, W. T. (2019). Ongoing crisis communication: Planning, managing, and responding, 5th ed. Los Angeles: Sage)

Box 17.3

Odwalla's 1996 Recall: an Illustration of the three-staged crisis life cycle

In 1996, US juice manufacturer Odwalla had an E. coli outbreak that made over 70 people ill and killed 16-month-old Anna Gimmestad. A review of the Odwalla case demonstrates the stages of the crisis life cycle. Odwalla sold unpasteurised juice. The idea was that the juice retained more vitamins and better taste when it was not pasteurised. However, pasteurisation is used to kill bacteria so unpasteurised juice must be carefully controlled or you have a food borne illness outbreak as Odwalla did.

There was a belief in the unpasteurised juice industry that the high acid content of juice helped to kill bacteria. To add extra protection, Odwalla used an acid wash on its fruit. A previous bacteria outbreak at another juice maker raised questions about the acid wash prior to 1996. Dave Stevenson, head of Odwalla's quality assurance, had recommended a shift to a chlorine wash. Acid wash was rated as only 8 per cent effective and the chlorine wash would have improved bacteria control. Signal detection was working. Stevenson had seen the problems in the industry and that Odwalla had had 300 reports of bacteria in juice prior to 1996. Other executives rejected Stevenson's proposal and

box 17.3 (continued)

the acid wash remained in place. Prevention was a failure because Odwalla did nothing to reduce the threat identified in signal detection. Little is known about Odwalla's state of preparation prior to the 1996 crisis (Entine 1999).

When the crisis hit, Odwalla was quick to recognise and to contain a crisis. Odwalla quickly issued a recall of its product and was among the first companies to utilise the internet as part of the crisis response. The quick action reflected crisis recognition while the recall demonstrated containment efforts. In fact, Odwalla is frequently praised in crisis case studies for its response. Unfortunately, those who praise Odwalla fail to examine how its own prevention failure helped to create the deadly recall (Coombs 2014). Odwalla did learn, as it began pasteurising its juices to kill bacteria. The internet helped providing follow-up information to stakeholders thereby keeping them informed. As part of the healing, Odwalla paid for the medical expenses of anyone who became ill from their juice (Marler 2013).

pre-crisis phase captures all factors prior to a crisis emerging. The post-crisis phase is anything after a crisis has been acknowledged. The turning point is the dynamic aspect of the model. A turning point occurs when some action or event redefines the crisis by reframing how people interpret the crisis. When a turning point occurs, previous post-communication actions by the organisation become part of the pre-crisis phase and a new post-crisis phase emerges (Coombs 2017).

The value of strategic communication

From a public relations perspective, it is important to realise a crisis creates an information vacuum. Something negative has occurred and potentially threatens an organisation and its stakeholders. People immediately want to know more about the crisis event. Who was involved? What happened? Why did it happen? What risks will it

Picture 17.2 Protest against Union Carbide following the Bhopal Chemical Plant disaster (*source:* Pallava Bagla/Corbis/Getty Images)

Think about 17.1

Every day we eat food but probably think very little about food safety. We just assume the food we eat will not make us sick. But the reality is that food recalls are common globally. Imagine a food product you eat was recalled because it posed a health risk. How would you learn about the food recall? If you did learn about the recall, would you be more likely to still eat the food product, return it for refund, or simply throw it away? What factors might shape that decision? What should the company responsible for the food product do to (1) inform you about the recall and (2) make you feel confident in consuming the food product again?

Box 17.4
Sample crisis risk score calculations

A. Airline Crash

$1 \times 10 \times 10 = 100$

Likelihood is very low

Impact on stakeholders and the organisation is very high

B. Product Recall for E. coli in beef

$5 \times 10 \times 10 = 500$

Likelihood is moderate as E. coli in beef does happen on a regular basis

Impact of stakeholders and the organisation is high because E. coli can cause death

---

create? A key to effective crisis public relations management is locating the desired information and relaying it to the interested stakeholders. The need to address the information vacuum created by a crisis places a premium on effective communication (Barton 2001). Public relations people do not simply throw information at stakeholders during a crisis. To be effective, crisis communication must be strategic. Those engaged in crisis public relations management must determine what information particular stakeholders need and the best way to deliver that information. When hazardous chemicals are released, for example, crisis communicators must determine who is at risk, if those at risk should evacuate or shelter where they are, and how best to deliver the public safety message to the targeted stakeholders.

Where do crises come from?

There is no one type of crisis that crisis public relations managers will face. There are a variety of crises and each presents its own unique demands on the public relations people attempting to manage the crisis. Situational Crisis Communication Theory (SCCT) has used empirical research to create three general categories of crises based upon evaluations of crisis responsibility (Coombs 2007). The crises in each category create similar attributions of organisational responsibility for a crisis. Crisis responsibility, stakeholder perceptions of how much an organisation is responsible for the crisis, is critical in assessing the threat posed by a crisis. Research (e.g., Coombs and Holladay 2001; Jorgensen 1996; Mowen 1980) consistently has shown that the greater the attribution of crisis responsibility, the greater the threat posed by the crisis to the organisation. Increases in crisis responsibility lead to greater reputational loss, decreases in purchase intention, decreases in supportive behaviours, and increases in likelihood to engage in negative word-of-mouth (Coombs 2007; Coombs and Holladay 2006; 2007). Box 17.4 presents the crisis categories of crisis types developed by SCCT, and distinguishes between operational and paracrises, and provides the latest modifications to the SCCT crisis types.

What should become clear by looking at the list of crises is that crises come from a variety of sources. In other words, organisations have a wide array of potential crisis risks including key stakeholders and the operation of facilities. For instance, employees can cause crises by not performing tasks properly (accidentally or purposefully), by violating laws, or by engaging in violence against co-workers. Customers can cause crises by misusing products or by protesting how an organisation behaves. Assailants can attack an organisation through product tampering, physical attacks or computer hacking. Geography can cause crises through the acts of nature that can occur at that locale such as tornadoes or floods. Products can cause crises by being manufactured improperly and harming customers. The manufacturing process can cause crises through technical failure, poor quality raw materials or the release of toxic chemicals. Potential crises can develop within the organisation and from its environment. Organisations are swimming in a sea of crisis risks. So where do crises come from? The answer is almost anywhere.

How to prepare for a crisis

Managers need to recognise that no matter how well they run the organisation a crisis can still occur. Marconi's (1992) book title sums it up best: *When Bad Things Happen to Good Companies*. Unfortunately for managers, crises are a matter of when not if. All organisations should prepare for the eventuality of a crisis. Preparing for a crisis is part prevention and part preparation.

Preventative actions

Steven Fink (1986), an influential crisis expert, argued that all crises have warning signs or what he calls 'prodomes'. The skilful crisis manager discovers the warning and takes actions to prevent the crisis from occurring. The best way to manage a crisis is to prevent one. Prevention means no stakeholders are harmed and the organisation suffers no damage. Crisis managers find warning signs by monitoring sources related to specific types of crisis risks. Typical sources to monitor for warning signs would be:

- safety data;
- consumer complaints;
- insurance audits;
- environmental audits;
- employee complaints; and
- activist activities.

Each organisation needs to design its own early warning system for crises. That involves identifying the most likely crises the organisation will have and working backwards to determine what sources of information would provide the most reliable warning signs for each crisis. The best starting point is to assemble top management from the various divisions in the organisation. This group should brainstorm all the possible crises that might befall the organisation. Once the list is created, the managers go back and assign each crisis a 'crisis risk score'. The crisis risk score is an assessment of the likelihood of the crisis occurring and the impact such a crisis would have on both stakeholders and the organisation. The managers would generate three scores:

1. crisis likelihood (L);
2. impact on stakeholders (IS); and
3. impact on the organisation (IO).

The scores would be based on a scale with '1' being unlikely or little impact and '10' being very likely and serious impact. Admittedly the scores will be rather subjective but it is a fairly effective system. The scores are then placed in the following formula: Crisis Risk Score = L × IS × OI. Box 17.4 present examples of calculating a crisis risk score.

Once all the crises have scores, the managers review the data to create a list of the most prominent crisis. The list of the most prominent crisis would serve as the foundation for creating the crisis early warning system. Managers need to determine what would be the early warning signs for each crisis and what information sources could be monitored to find those warning signs. For instance, an organisation that is at risk from industrial accidents would monitor safety data. Lapses in safety practices could indicate the potential for an industrial accident. Or an organisation that sells consumer goods would monitor consumer complaints. The consumer complaints could indicate a potential for product harm. Once a warning sign is located, actions would be taken to reduce the likelihood of the crisis occurring.

Preventative action reflects the operational crisis focus of crisis communication. Reputational risks are harder to quantify in terms of likelihood and impact than their operational counterparts. For instance, an airline can quantify likelihood and impact of a crash but find it more difficult to quantify the likelihood and impact of reputational threat such as activists posting negative comments on social media about the airline's treatment of employees. Still, managers must attempt to quantify the risks associated with reputations. One starting point is to consider the salience of the stakeholders associated with the threat and their communicative skill. Higher ratings of salience and communication skills would increase the likelihood and impact from the reputational threat (Coombs 2019; Coombs and Holladay 2015).

Value of preparation

While prevention is ideal, the reality is crises will still occur. Managers cannot locate all warning signs and preventative actions are not guaranteed to be effective. Note how the last sentence in the previous paragraph said reducing the likelihood of a crisis happening, not eliminating it. There are limits to crisis prevention. That is why organisations need to develop an insurance policy in the form of crisis preparation. Crisis preparation is built around three points:

1. a crisis management plan (CMP);
2. a crisis team; and
3. training.

Think about 17.2

Pick two organisations from two different industries. For instance, use a retail store and a university or a restaurant and coal mining company. Now create a list of potential crises each organisation might encounter. From that list, select what you feel are the top five crises an organisation in that industry should be prepared to manage. How are the lists similar and different?

Feedback

There should be some overlap in the lists because organisations share some basic crisis risks. There is a problem if the lists are exactly the same. Different industries have slightly different crisis risks. However, these slight differences can be very important when trying to identify what crises should be the most important to a particular organisation.

Box 17.5

The need to test crisis management plans

The value of testing the CMP was proven by an airport in the US. The airport was running a crisis simulation of a plane crash. The simulation involved airport personnel and emergency personnel from the community including fire, police and ambulance. When the simulation began, the emergency personnel tuned their radios to the frequency recommended in the CMP. The emergency responders found they could not talk with the airport personnel, resulting in chaos rather than coordination. The problem was that the wrong radio frequency was listed in the CMP for emergency responders. Testing the CMP discovered a serious flaw in the CMP that could have been disastrous in a real crisis.

The CMP is a rough guide for managing a crisis, not a step-by-step formula. Each crisis is a little different so the crisis team needs to adapt the CMP to the current situation. CMPs should be short and easy to use. The basic elements of a CMP are contact information (people you might need to reach during a crisis) and key reminders such as the need to document what the crisis team has done and record requests for information the crisis team received but could not answer immediately. Most CMPs are now digital and the crisis team can access them from mobile devices during a crisis. It is essential that CMPs are updated regularly, at least every six months. Personnel and procedures change in organisations. If the CMP is inaccurate, it is of little value. Box 17.5 provides an example of the need to test CMPs.

CMPs provide an organised approach to crisis management that helps to save time during a crisis. One way a CMP saves time is by making some decisions before the crisis hits. Team members will have pre-assigned tasks so they know what to do when they receive word a crisis has occurred. The Crisis Appendix is a separate set of materials that is linked to the CMP. The Crisis Appendix stores information that might be needed during a crisis, such as past safety data, and templates for messages. The templates are drafts of sample messages the organisation might use in the crisis. Essentially a template is a message with key points left blank such as the date, time and people involved. The legal department should approve the templates before the crisis. Time is saved because the complete message does not have to be written from scratch during a crisis and it has already been approved by the legal department. The templates can include news releases, Tweets, Facebook posts or blog posts.

The crisis management team are those people in the organisation that have been selected to administer the crisis response. The crisis management team is composed of personnel from a variety of departments in the organisation. The exact composition will vary according to the nature of the crisis. For instance, IT is involved when the crisis involves computer systems or the internet or human resources is included when the crisis involves personnel issues. The core of the crisis team includes: public relations, legal, operations, security, safety and quality assurance (Barton 2001).

Ideally, the crisis team begins its work by developing the CMP. However, not all crisis teams are used to create CMPs. The primary task of the crisis team is managing the crisis. The crisis team must be able to apply the CMP to a crisis – they must know how to use the CMP. If the crisis team cannot use the CMP, the CMP has no value and has failed to save time. More important than using the CMP is the ability of the crisis team to cope with factors not covered in the CMP. Remember, a CMP is a rough guide so there are many details and specifics about a crisis that the crisis team must address on their own. The CMP provides extra time by addressing the routine aspects of a crisis. Everything else must be handled by the crisis team (Barton 2001; Regester 1989; Regester and Larkin 2008).

Training is the last of the three elements of preparation but is the most critical. Without training, any

Picture 17.3 Public safety should be paramount during a crisis (*source:* CARL DE SOUZA/AFP/Getty Images)

CMP or crisis team is of unknown value. Crisis management training involves practice with handling a crisis. The crisis management team, armed with its CMP, confronts a simulated crisis. Training assesses the value of the CMP and the abilities of the crisis management team. Was the CMP useful during the training or does it require extensive revision? It is better to discover flaws in the CMP during training rather than during an actual crisis. Can the crisis team members perform their tasks effectively? Weak team members will either need additional training or may need to be replaced. Crises are time sensitive and ambiguous. Not everyone responds well to ambiguity and to time pressure. Some people should not be on crisis teams and training will indicate if the person is right for a crisis team (Coombs 2019). Again, better to learn a person is not suited for a crisis team during a simulated rather than an actual crisis.

Without training, an organisation has no idea if its CMP or crisis team is any good. Both the CMP and crisis team should be tested on a regular basis, at least once per year. Training does not have to be a complete simulation of a crisis, but can be simple such as simulated interactive exercises that test a part of the crisis management effort.

Even when crisis plans and crisis training is executed, both can become inconsequential. COVID-19 is an excellent example of how crisis preparation and planning can become meaningless if ignored by leaders. In 2019, the US ran a crisis simulation called Crimson Contagion. This exercise involved the effects of a virus arriving from China that affected the respiratory system of its victims. The debrief from the exercise found that the US was seriously unprepared for this crisis and specified much needed actions to increase preparedness. Moreover, the US government had developed a crisis plan for pandemics back in 2005. Keep in mind a crisis plan is not a step-by-step prescription of what to do but rather a set of guidance designed to aid crisis managers in decision making. We have a situation where there was a well-designed crisis plan created in advance and a failed training exercise that indicated the flaws in the current system. Yet no action was taken to correct the flaws identified by the exercise and the guidance provided by the crisis plan was ignored when COVID-19 emerged as a threat. The end result is a case where the preparation and planning for the crisis were ignored by leadership to the detriment of the stakeholders affected by the crisis.

Communicating during a crisis

Effective crisis communication is vital to a successful crisis management effort. Crisis public relations management research brings important insights to understanding what makes crisis communication effective and ineffective (Coombs 2010). Crisis communication involves managing information and managing meaning. Managing information reflects the information processing aspect of crisis communication. Crisis managers need to collect information, process it into knowledge and share it with their stakeholders. Managing meaning emphasises the strategic aspect of crisis communication. Crisis managers use crisis messages to influence how stakeholders perceive the crisis and the organisation in crisis. Managing meaning recognises that stakeholders have emotional reactions to crises (e.g. Jin and Pang 2010). The type and strength of emotions created by a crisis depend upon how people perceive the crisis. If an organisation is a victim, stakeholders are likely to feel sympathy. If the organisation is responsible for the crisis, stakeholders are likely to feel anger. Those different emotions affect how those stakeholders then perceive the organisation and behave towards that organisation (Jorgensen 1996).

The focus of crisis public relations management research has been on effective communication during the crisis event. The crisis communication research can be divided by its focus: (1) tactical and (2) strategic. The tactical focus crisis communication research examines how messages are sent during the crisis and the general characteristics of those messages. The emphasis is crisis communication as information management. The strategic focus crisis communication research examines the content of the messages sent during a crisis and the effects of those messages. The strategic focus considers the goals crisis managers are pursuing through their crisis communication.

Crisis communication: tactical focus

Early writings about crisis communication focused on the tactical aspects. Experts advise that an initial crisis response should be quick, accurate and consistent. A crisis response needs to be quick so that the organisation is part of the information used to fill the vacuum created by the crisis. Many writers note the need for the organisation to tell its side of the story (e.g. Holladay 2009). If an organisation is slow in responding, it allows other actors to define and to control the crisis (Coombs 2019). Research has confirmed the value of responding quickly. Arpan and Pompper (2003) found that an organisation suffers less reputational damage when it announces that a crisis has occurred than when someone other than the organisation makes the same announcement. They called this effect 'stealing thunder'. Additional research has further established the value stealing thunder offers as a means of protecting reputational assets during a crisis (e.g. Claeys and Cauberghe 2012).

Speed does not always fit with accuracy but crisis managers need both. If crisis messages are shown to be inaccurate, the organisation loses credibility and risks suffering additional reputational damage. We must remember that ineffective crisis communication does hurt an organisation. Part of accuracy is avoiding speculation. It is common for the news media to ask crisis managers to speculate on the cause of the crisis. A common piece of advice for crisis managers is to never speculate. If your speculation is wrong, your messages are judged as inaccurate. Inaccuracy implies that the organisation is either incompetent or hiding something from its stakeholders.

Finally, crisis messages need to be consistent. Many crisis experts talk about speaking with one voice but that phrase is often misinterpreted. It does not mean only one person speaks for the organisation during a crisis. Multiple experts may be needed to explain a crisis or a crisis can go on for days. In either situation would it be effective to have just one person speak for the organisation? Consistency is a better term. Consistency does not mean everyone using the same exact talking points. Instead, consistency means sharing information with all spokespersons so they work from a common knowledge base. You want consistency in the information your spokespersons are providing about the crisis, not consistency in phrasing of the message (Coombs 2015).

Researchers are mapping the effects of various delivery factors on the perceptions of crisis communication messages. The spokesperson delivery research has concentrated on speech rate (fast or slow) and pitch (high or low). A higher pitch is considered more sincere while a lower pitch is considered more powerful. The research finds people prefer lower pitch (more powerful) immediately after a crisis but a higher pitch (more sincere) later in the crisis (Claeys and Cauberghe 2014). In addition, researchers have found that the right pairing of pitch and speech rate matters. The post-crisis reputation of an organisation was stronger if high pitch was paired with a fast speech rate or a low pitch was paired with a slow speech rate (De Waele et al. 2017). Combined, this research proves the value of understanding the ways delivery can affect the perceptions of crisis messages.

Explore 17.1

Universities and crisis public relations management

Universities face crises just like any other organisation. Look around your university's website to see what information you can find about its preparation for crises. Do you know what you should do if particular crises occurred at your university? How did you learn about that information? What channels will your university use to inform you about a crisis? What can you do to be better prepared for a crisis at your university?

Box 17.6
Advice for crisis spokespersons

- Never say 'no comment', people hear 'I am guilty' or 'I am hiding something' when a crisis manager says 'no comment'.
- Make eye contact, avoid vocal fillers ('urhs' and 'uhms'), and avoid nervous gestures – they create the impression the spokesperson is being deceptive.
- Provide answers to the question that was asked, not the question you want to answer.
- If you do not know the answer say so and promise to deliver the necessary information when you receive it.
- Avoid using jargon because it is confusing and the spokesperson appears to be hiding something.

Sources: Carney and Jorden (1993); Feeley and de Turck (1995); Levick (2005); Mackinnon (1996); Nicholas (1995); and Pines (1985)

Box 17.7
Challenge response strategies

Refusal: Managers ignore the challenge. Hershey ignored challenges from Green America about its cocoa sourcing for over two years.

Refutation: Managers argue the challenge is factually wrong or argue the standards they are said to have violated are invalid because most of their stakeholders do not hold the violated expectations. Honey Maid Graham Crackers argued its commercial using a same-sex couple was consistent with how most stakeholders view families and refuse to end running the advertisement.

Repression: Managers seek to silence the voice of the challengers. Nestlé tried to have Greenpeace's video challenging its palm oil sourcing removed from YouTube.

Recognition/Reception: Managers acknowledge the problem noted in the challenge but make no commitment to change the behaviour. Apple recognised the problem with conflict minerals but took no actions to address the issue.

Revision: Managers make changes to their challenged behaviour but not the exact changes requested by the challengers. Nestlé chose its own method for addressing palm oil sourcing after challenges from Greenpeace.

Reform: Managers make the exact changes requested by the challengers. Nike and Adidas both engaged in reform when challenged by Greenpeace to stop using toxic chemicals in their apparel supply chain.

(*Source:* adapted from Coombs and Holladay 2015)

Crisis communication: strategic focus

Researchers have examined the strategic aspect of crisis communication by attempting to determine how crisis communication can be used most effectively to protect the organisation's reputation. The strategic crisis communication research began by trying to understand why people react favourably or unfavourably to a crisis spokesperson. Box 17.6 provides a summary of the proven advice for crisis spokespersons.

More advanced strategic crisis communication research has explored the various crisis response strategies (what an organisation says and does after a crisis hits) and how strategy choices affect the way stakeholders react to the crisis and the organisation in crisis (Coombs 2010). William Benoit (1995) was instrumental in identifying a wide range of crisis response strategies. Benoit's list of crisis response strategies was combined with works of other experts to form the crisis response strategies presented in Box 17.9. While having a list is useful, crisis managers still needed to understand when certain strategies would be more effective than others and why. Let us explore the strategic use of crisis response strategies further.

Crisis managers should start any crisis response with instructing and adjusting information. Instructing information tells stakeholders how to protect themselves physically from a crisis. Examples would be product recalls and evacuation warnings. Adjusting information helps people to cope psychologically with a crisis. This would include expressions of regret, steps taken to prevent a repeat of the crisis, and explanations of what happened during the crisis (Sturges 1994). Anxiety is the most common emotion generated by a crisis (Jin et al. 2012) and adjusting information seeks to reduce the anxiety of stakeholders during a crisis.

Public safety should be the top priority in a crisis. Failure to address public safety first is an ethical as well as a strategic failure in crisis communication.

Perceptions of crisis responsibility are critical to crisis communication. Crisis response strategies can be used to shape those perceptions. Denial strategies argue that there is no crisis, crucial in the case of a rumour, or that the organisation is uninvolved in a crisis. If there is no crisis or the organisation is not responsible for the crisis, there should be no threat to the organisation. As Benoit (1995) noted, crisis communication is only needed when there has been a crisis and the organisation is held responsible for the event. Denial should only be used when an organisation has no involvement in the crisis and can support that claim. If the organisation is later shown to be involved in the crisis, much greater damage is inflicted on the organisation than if they had not denied involvement (Ferrin et al. 2007). The dangers in using denial are evidence to support effective communication helping and ineffective communication hurting during a crisis.

Diminish strategies seek to reduce the perceptions of crisis responsibility. The organisation recognises that a crisis has occurred and they are involved to some degree with the crisis. However, communication is used in an attempt to reduce the organisation's perceived responsibility for the crisis. If the organisation had moderate responsibility for the crisis, the potential damage from the crisis is reduced. As with denial, there are limits to when diminish strategies can be used. An organisation must have a legitimate claim of limited responsibility or the diminish strategies can cause more harm than good.

At this point it is important to note that crisis communication has limits and that SCCT has boundary conditions. For SCCT, moral outrage, a specific emotion, is a boundary condition that demarks where the theory's recommendations no longer hold. Moral outrage is a distinct emotion that is created when people perceive a combination of injustice and exploitation. When a crisis contains cues that trigger moral outrage, the common short-term benefits generated by optimal crisis response strategies are lost. The common short-term benefits from optimal crisis responses include bolstering the reputation and purchase intentions while lessening the likelihood of negative word-of-mouth. Strong feelings of the moral outrage emotion preclude crisis communication strategies from achieving these benefits (Coombs and Tachkova 2019).

As noted in the discussion of crisis types, there are times when an organisation is perceived as highly responsible for the crisis and that perception is accurate.

Denial and diminish strategies would be ineffective so crisis managers must use the rebuild strategies. The rebuild strategies are compensation and apology. Organisations are perceived as clearly taking responsibility for a crisis when they use either of these two strategies. Rebuild strategies are the most appropriate response for a crisis in the preventable cluster from Box 17.8. A general piece of strategic crisis communication advice is that as perceptions of crisis responsibility increase, crisis managers should utilise strategies that are perceived to take responsibility for the crisis. There should be a match between perceived acceptance of responsibility for the crisis by the organisation and stakeholder attributions of crisis responsibility. It should be noted that crises in the 'accidental cluster' can generate strong attributions of crisis responsibility if the organisation has a history of similar crises and/or a negative prior reputation (are known to treat stakeholders badly for example) (Coombs 2007). Crisis managers should consider these two intensifying factors (crisis history and prior reputation) when selecting their crisis response strategies. These recommendations focus on operational crises but we need to consider the reputational crises as well.

Misinformation and challenges crisis types are related to paracrises. Rumours involve misinformation that indicates an organisation is involved in a crisis when there really is no connection to a crisis. Management must explain why the organisation is not involved in a crisis. During a major peanut product recall in the US, consumers mistakenly thought that various name brand peanut butters were part of the recall. The three main producers of name brand peanut butter all explained they were not part of the recall – a type of denial. In a misinformation situation, management uses denial to separate the organisation from the potential damage associated with a crisis by showing the organisation has no responsibility for the crisis or that no crisis exists.

Challenges are more complicated than misinformation because a challenge involves perceptions rather than facts. A challenge occurs when stakeholders claim that current organisational practices should be defined as irresponsible. Consider how in the 1990s the garment industry had its supply chain activities redefined as sweat shops. If stakeholders accept the redefinition, the organisation suffers reputational damage. A challenge is a reputational threat because being socially irresponsible (Jones et al. 2009; Tench et al. 2012) harms an organisation's reputation. When the challenge transpires in the digital environment, such as social media, managers are forced to

Box 17.8
Crisis types and categories from SCCT

Operational crises:
Potential to disrupt operations

Victim: minimal attributions of crisis responsibility. The organisation is considered a victim of the crisis along with the stakeholders.

- *Natural disasters:* damage from weather or 'acts of God'. An example is the 2011 tsunami and earthquakes in Japan.
- *Workplace violence:* damage from employee or former employee attacking current employees. An example is the 2001 shootings at a furniture manufacturing facility in Goshen, in USA.
- *Malevolence:* damage from outside actors attacking the organisation. An example would be the 1986 tampering of Tylenol capsules in the US.

Accidental: moderate attributions of crisis responsibility. The organisation is involved in the crisis but had limited control over the events that precipitated the crisis.

- *Technical-error accidents:* damage when technology fails creating an accident. An example would be the 2003 explosion of the West Pharmaceutical facility in Kinston, NC USA from rubber dust particles.
- *Technical-error product harm:* damage when technology fails resulting in a defective product. An example would be the 2010 HP recall of laptop batteries due to potential fire hazard from dendrite fibre build-up in the lithium batteries.

Preventable: very strong attributions of crisis responsibility. The organisation knowingly placed stakeholders at risk and/or wilfully violated laws or regulations. The preventable cluster is subdivided into three groups based upon perceptions of moral outrage. Moral outrage is a combination of injustice and exploitation (Antonetti and Maklan 2016). The three sub-clusters represent how the crisis types are likely to produce increasingly stronger perceptions of moral outrage.

1. **Human-error sub-cluster**
   Human-error accident: damage when human error causes an accident. An example is the 1999 Tosco Refinery fire in Martinez, CA USA that was a result of poor supervision of safety

   Human-error product harm: damage when human error causes a defect product. An example is the 1990 Perrier recall because of high benzene levels caused by an employee not changing a filter at the spring designed to trap the benzene

2. **Management misconduct sub-cluster**
   Organisational misdeed: damage when managers knowingly place stakeholders at risk or knowingly violate laws or regulations. An example is in 2007 melamine, which is poisonous to dogs and cats, was purposefully added to pet food so it would test with a higher protein level

3. **Scansis sub-cluster**
   A scansis is a unique situation where a crisis and a scandal fuse (Coombs et al. 2018). The hallmark of a scansis is very strong perceptions of moral outrage. The crisis is deemed to be unjust and motivated by management's desire to exploit stakeholders. The massive price increase of Mylan Pharmaceutical's EpiPen is an example of a scansis (Coombs and Tachkova 2019).

Paracrises:
Public management of crisis risks and are primarily involving reputational risks

1. **Misinformation**: stakeholders believe negative information about the organisation that is inaccurate. An example is the 2010 'report' that Pamper disposal nappies (diapers) would burn babies.

2. **Challenge**: stakeholders claim the organisation is acting irresponsibly but the organisation disagrees with that assessment. An example would be the 2005 charge by the American Family Association that Ford Motor Company was harming families by offering same-sex partner benefits and advertising in gay and lesbian publications.

3. **Faux Pas**: managers think a certain behaviour or policy is positive but some stakeholders view it as problematic or even insulting. An example is when Motrin insulted your mothers in an advertisement the company thought was funny and designed to make your mothers purchase Motrin.

Source: adapted from Coombs 2019

publicly manage the crisis risk making the situation a paracrisis (Coombs and Holladay 2012). Managers have a slightly different set of crisis response strategies to choose from when responding to a challenge/paracrisis compared to an operational crisis (Coombs and Holladay 2015). The variations in the lists of possible response strategies reflect the different foci of the operational crises and paracrises. Box 17.7 details the crisis responses that can be used during a challenge/paracrisis.

Finally, the bolster strategies are a secondary strategy that can be used in combination with denial, diminish, rebuild, or any of the challenge/paracrisis response strategies. Bolster strategies seek to create positive pieces of information to associate with an organisation in the hope of countering some of the negative information generated by the crisis. The Cadbury Chocolate case (17.1) is used to illustrate various crisis communication responses and the importance of matching the response to the level of crisis responsibility. Box 17.9 includes examples of how organisations have actually used each of the crisis response strategies.

It should be noted that the discussion of crisis communication reflects an emphasis placed on external stakeholders. Researchers have begun to emphasise the need to include employees in the discussion of crisis communication. Crisis communication plans must include the need to target employees with messages (Johansen et al. 2012). Informed employees can become ambassadors for the organisation in times of crisis by helping to explain what has happened and how the organisation is responding to the situation (Frandsen and Johansen 2011). Employees can be a vital resource that should not be ignored by managers during a crisis (Mazzei and Ravazzani 2014).

Box 17.9

Crisis response strategies

Denial strategies

Attacking the accuser:	crisis manager challenges the person or group that says a crisis exists
Denial:	crisis manager claims there is no crisis
Scapegoating:	crisis manager blames the crisis on some person or group outside of the organisation

Diminish strategies

Excusing:	crisis manager argues the organisation has minimal responsibility for the crisis
Justification:	crisis manager attempts to reduce perceptions of the seriousness of the crisis

Rebuild strategies

Compensation:	crisis manager offers money and/or gifts to people affected by the crisis
Apology:	crisis manager acknowledges responsibility of the crisis and requests forgiveness

Bolstering strategies

Ingratiation:	crisis manager praises the stakeholders
Reminding:	crisis manager informs people about the organisation's past good works
Victim:	crisis manager notes it is a victim of the crisis too

Examples of Crisis Response Strategies used in Crises

Attacking the accuser

The crisis: The news show *Dateline NBC* accused GM of selling unsafe pickup trucks.

The response: GM provided evidence that the news show was deceptive with its report of how the gas tanks on GM pickup trucks would explode. Harry Pearce of GM said: 'The 11 million households that viewed the program were never told that NBC used remotely controlled incendiary devices to try to ensure that a fire would erupt, seemingly due to the collision. We cannot allow the men and women of GM, the thousands of independent businesses that sell GM products, and the owners of these pickup trucks, to suffer the consequences of NBC's irresponsible conduct and deliberate deception' (Parrish and Nauss 1995).

Denial

The crisis: Firestone tires were associated with blowouts that caused a number of Ford Explores (an SUV) to role over.

The response: Firestone denied their tires were unsafe. Johan Lampe of Firestone said: 'Let me state categorically:

→

box 17.9 (continued)

tires supplied to Ford Motor Company and other customers, are safe, and the tires are not defective' (Bradsher 2001: C2).

Scapegoating

The crisis: The Union Carbide Bhopal explosion in India that killed thousands of people.

The response: Jackson Browning, a former safety employee at Union Carbide wrote, 'Late in 1986, Union Carbide filed a lengthy court document in India detailing the findings of its scientific and legal investigations: the cause of the disaster was undeniably sabotage. The evidence showed that an employee at the Bhopal plant had deliberately introduced water into a methyl isocyanate storage tank. Union Carbide claimed it had witnesses, evidence, and documents to prove it the explosion was sabotage by a group of workers (Weisman and Hazarika 1987).

Excusing

The crisis: People were protesting Abercrombie & Fitch's use of semi-nude photographs in its catalogues because children under 18 were bringing them to schools.

The response: Abercrombie & Fitch denies any intention to do wrong and that they could not control the misuse of their catalogues. Hampton Carney from Abercrombie & Fitch said: 'It's never been intended for anyone under 18. We're very sensitive to that matter' (Pickler 1999).

Justification

The crisis: in 2007 number of toys made in China had been recalled in the US due to lead in their paint.

The response: Carter Keithley, president of the US Toy Industry Association noted that recalls of toys due to hazardous material involved only .03 per cent of the 3 billion toys the US imported from China in 2007 (Greenlees 2008).

Compensation

The crisis: Seven people die from cyanide in Johnson & Johnson's Tylenol.

The response: In addition to a recall, Johnson & Johnson pays for psychological counselling for the families of the victims and provides other assistance (Berg and Robb 1992).

Apology

The crisis: *The News of the World*, owned by News Corp, had private investigators hack into mobile phones to get information for stories.

The response: News Corp CEO Rupert Murdoch placed advertisements in major newspaper with an apology that included the statement: '*The News of the World* was in the business of holding others to account. It failed when it came to itself. We are sorry for the serious wrongdoing that occurred. We are deeply sorry for the hurt suffered by the individuals affected. We regret not acting faster to sort things out. I realize that simply apologizing is not enough' (Ambrogi 2011).

Ingratiation

The crisis: In 2009 and 2010, Toyota recalls vehicles over problem with gas pedal and braking.

The response: Chief executive Akio Toyoda said: 'I am sincerely grateful to our dealers and suppliers who remained fully committed to providing as many cars as possible to customers, and to our employees as well as our overseas business operations for their efforts in working together so that the company will return to its normal state as soon as possible. And finally, above all, I am sincerely grateful to our customers of more than 7 million people around the world who newly purchased Toyota vehicles' (Ruddick 2010)

Reminding

The crisis: Nestlé 2010 accused of irresponsible palm oil sourcing.

The response: In a news release Nestlé stated: 'As a part of this commitment, we have accelerated the investigation of our palm oil supply chain to identify any palm oil source which does not meet our high standards for sustainability. Given our uncompromising food safety standards, we have done this in a deliberate manner as we use palm oil for food products rather than for soap or other personal care products' (Baxter 2010)

Victim

The crisis: In 1986, one person died from potassium cyanide in Johnson & Johnson's Tylenol.

The response: Johnson & Johnson noted how it was a victim of the attack as well. Johnson & Johnson CEO James Burke said: 'But we cannot control random tampering with capsules after they leave our plant' (McFadden 1986).

Source: adapted from Benoit 1995 and Coombs 2015

> **Explore 17.2**
>
> Online memorials are becoming fairly common. Most are created by individuals to remember a lost family member or friend and have nothing to do with crises. If you do a search online for memorials you are likely to find one of these individual memorials. Again, these are like plaques or memorials you find in the physical world. An example of physical memorial would be the London Bombing Memorial in Hyde Park. The 52 pillars represent each of the individuals who lost their lives in the 7 July 2005 bombings. For an example of how an organisation handles an online memorial, visit the Cantor Families Memorial. The site was created by Cantor Fitzgerald to commemorate the people the organisation lost in the September 11 attacks on the World Trade Center. By visiting these memorial sites you will gain a better appreciation of the role memorials can play in a crisis.

The limits of rationality: when crisis communication advice is ignored

The Volkswagen case presented earlier is but one example of a quality organisation responding to a crisis in an ineffective manner by selecting sub-optimal crisis response strategies. Optimal crisis response strategies are those identified and supported by research to have a positive effect on stakeholders (Claeys and Coombs 2019). Researchers have documented the willingness of crisis managers to ignore the theoretical and proven advice and to choose sub-optimal responses instead (e.g. Claeys and Opgenhaffen 2016). It is too easy to simply claim professionals do not know or understand the advice for optimal crisis response selection. A more fulfilling explanation can be found in behavioural economics.

The traditional economic theories are very rational in their approach to decision making. However, distinct patterns of anomalies do emerge in decision making that these rational models cannot explain. Behavioural economics is a mix of psychology and economics that provides possible explanations for many of these anomalies by identifying the decisional heuristics that shape the anomalies (Thaler 2015). Behavioural economics draws upon bounded rationality and prospect theory. Bounded rationality argues that people do not maximise decisions by carefully considering all options but rather satisfice by selecting decisions that work. Prospect theory argues that people feel loss much more strongly than gains and are motivated by a desire to avoid loss. Moreover, people favour immediate outcomes over those that are long term. People will satisfice in ambiguous decision situations by using heuristics (experiential self learning) rather than thoroughly evaluating the disadvantages and advantages of each decision option (Thaler 2015).

Both SCCT and stealing thunder are rational based models of crisis communication. A behavioural theory of crisis communication posits that sub-optimal crisis response are selected because crisis managers are seeking to avoid loss. The optimal crisis response in SCCT and stealing thunder both create an initial loss in favour of long-term gains (Claeys and Coombs 2019). Stealing thunder is the best example. By revealing the crisis exists, the organisation will suffer immediate loss from the crisis. Alternatively, not disclosing the crisis avoids immediate loss but risks greater future loss if or when the crisis is discovered. To avoid loss, crisis managers are likely to avoid stealing thunder and risk greater damage in the future. The lesson is that crisis managers often choose sub-optimal crisis response strategies because they are seeking to avoid immediate losses and discount the potential long-term gains of the optimal crisis response strategies (Claeys and Coombs 2019). Hence, rationality is often a limiting factor in crisis communication because heuristic approaches guided by loss avoidance are used rather than rational decision making.

The internet and crisis public relations management

If you believe the hype, the internet has revolutionised crisis public relations management rendering all previous knowledge on the subject obsolete. A word of advice, do not believe the hype. Yes, the digital world has changed crisis public relations management just as it has changed all other aspects of public relations. But we are witnessing evolution rather than a revolution. The key points are reviewed thus far and the research evidence is still valid. The question is what new challenges and opportunities does the digital environment bring to crisis public relations management? We shall explore the challenges and opportunities in this section.

Challenges

The internet is fast and has the potential to increase the transparency of an organisation by exposing previously private practices/information. The internet has changed people's perceptions of time. More specifically, people expect organisations to act much more quickly than they did in the past. As discussed earlier, organisations need to respond fast in a crisis ideally being the first one to release information about the crisis. The internet makes it more difficult for organisations to be the ones to release information about a crisis first because anyone with access to a smartphone or keyboard can post information about a crisis. Moreover, when the crisis appears online, people expect the organisation to respond in 'internet time' – very fast. A common criticism of crisis communication in the internet age is that the organisation acted too slowly. The internet has resulted in less time to formulate a crisis response and less opportunity for the organisation to be the one breaking the news about a crisis.

The pre-crisis phase of crisis management typically was not seen by most stakeholders. Even today, many internal crisis prevention activities are unseen but not for challenge and rumour crises. When stakeholders challenge the responsibility of an organisation's actions or a rumour appears, the warning signs are now public as are the organisation's efforts to prevent the crisis from developing. Let's use a challenge crisis to illustrate this point. Prior to the internet, stakeholders would challenge an organisation in private. They would contact management and explain why they were upset with how the organisation was operating. Occasionally these activist stakeholders could attract media attention but most challenges were unknown to other stakeholders (Ryan 1991). The recent development of managing crisis risks publicly has been called paracrises. As referenced earlier, a paracrisis involved managing a crisis risk publicly. In the past, most risk management was done privately but social media has made some risk management, such as challenges, open for public consumption (Coombs and Holladay 2012). It is the public nature of a challenge that makes it a reputational threat that could escalate into a reputational crisis (Coombs and Holladay 2015). Paracrises draw from the proactive nature of issues management. Issues management seeks to locate threats and opportunities that exist in an organisation's environment. Typically, issues are related to public policy concerns (Heath 2005). Paracrises broaden the scope of crisis risks by expanding beyond issues to social concerns and reputational threats (Coombs 2019).

Today, activist stakeholders take their messages to the digital environment. Other stakeholders may still miss the challenge but the challenge is public – people have the potential to see. In fact, the internet is an important tool when activist stakeholders are trying to change an organisation's behaviour (Coombs and Holladay 2009). How the organisation responds publicly to the challenge matters as well. Other stakeholders have the opportunity to watch and to evaluate both the challenge and the response. Ineffective challenge responses can change how stakeholders feel about and interact with an organisation (Coombs 2019). The once private crisis prevention activities are becoming more public. With this transparency comes greater scrutiny of crisis public relations management and increased pressure to respond effectively.

An example of the increased scrutiny of crisis public relations management is concern over worker safety in Bangladesh. On 24 April 2013, the Rana Plaza manufacturing facility in Bangladesh collapsed killing over 1,100 apparel workers and focusing work attention on the safety of apparel workers in Bangladesh. The International Labor Rights Forum (ILRF) led efforts to push apparel firms to sign the Accord on Fire and Building Safety in Bangladesh, sometimes referred to as 'the Accord'. The accord committed the firms to help improve the safety of the working environment for apparel workers in Bangladesh. H&M was quick to sign the pledge even though it did not source from Rana Plaza. Clothing retailer, H&M reinforced its commitment to CSR by committing to a responsible course of action.

We move ahead two years in our story and find the ILRF unhappy with the pace of the reform in Bangladesh – the safety improvements are being implemented far too slowly. The ILRF specifically begins to target H&M for the slow institution of the reforms. Together with a few other NGOs, the ILRF released a report that documents the failure of facilities in Bangladesh to implement fully the new safety features. Email messages and social media posts by the ILRF note how facilities in the H&M supply chain failed to meet the required changes in the agreed-upon timeframe. The ILRF claim that a majority of the deadlines for making safety renovations have not been met. The statements directly challenged H&M's commitment to the safety of its supply chain workers and accuse H&M of allowing these workers to toil in unsafe conditions – the ILRF is redefining H&M's current practices as irresponsible. Given H&M's strategic use of CSR communication to build its reputation, management had to address the charges because of the high-profile nature of the Rana Plaza tragedy. H&M argued that the report was inaccurate and that progress had been made by its suppliers in Bangladesh. When an organisation publicly commits to being socially responsible, the organisation becomes more vulnerable to attacks that question its social responsibility. Organisations that talk little about CSR are less vulnerable to such attacks. As a manager, how would you balance the risks from engaging in CSR communication against the crisis risk these messages might create? Threats posed by challenges are more difficult to assess than typical threats such as workplace safety or product defects. As a manager, how would you know when challenges to your social responsibility are a serious or an irrelevant threat? Think about what factors might affect your assessment of accusations of social irresponsibility.

Opportunities

Speed is an opportunity as well as a threat. The internet provides a number of channels a crisis communicator can use to send information rapidly to stakeholders. Many organisations prepare dark sites prior to a crisis, a site that has content but no active links to it. Each dark site is designed for a specific type of crisis and includes information stakeholders will want to know about the crisis along with templates for crisis messages. Once a crisis hits, the dark site becomes active and information is quickly sent to stakeholders. Various social media platforms (internet content created by users) including blogs, microblogs and social networking sites can be used to deliver crisis messages too. In 2019, Southwest Airlines faced flight problems when the Boeing 737 Max was grounded. Southwest Airlines leveraged its website, Facebook site, Twitter feed and its popular Nuts About Southwest blog to explain what was happening and how the changes would affect passenger travel. Southwest embraced the digital environment to provide multiple ways of reaching passengers and potential passengers about the impact of Boeing 737 Max grounding its operations.

The digital environment is invaluable for detecting potential crises. Social media platforms are a rich source of warning signs. For instance, customers might post complaints and concerns online that suggest a product defect and potential product harm crisis. When Greenpeace challenged Nestlé over unethical sourcing of palm oil in 2010, YouTube and the popular social networking site Facebook were the first places the challenge (a form of warning sign) emerged. Of course the challenge is

Case study 17.1
Cadbury chocolate recall

Cadbury is consistently the most trusted brand of chocolate in the UK. In 2006, Cadbury recalled eight of its products (over 1 million items) for salmonella contamination that caused sickness in about 40 people. This is proof that crises happen even to the best of companies. Cadbury estimates the recall cost it £20 million and resulted in a 14 per cent drop in sales for 2006 (Walsh 2011). A BrandIndex poll taken after the recall showed a sharp drop in Cadbury's reputation (Salmonellablog 2006). The lost revenue, lost sales and reputation damage reflect the negative effects a crisis can have on an organisation.

The British government determined that Cadbury's standards for assessing the risk of salmonella was unreliable and needed to be changed (Coombs 2014). Cadbury was not properly executing part of its food safety tasks. The crisis was caused by poor job performance making this at best human-error product harm crisis. Cadbury's management admitted (pleaded guilty) to breaching food and hygiene regulations. Cadbury was fined £1 million for its violations (Reuters 2007). The crisis could be considered management misconduct because there was violation of regulations. Either categorisation places the Cadbury chocolate recall in the 'preventable' crisis cluster.

Cadbury did recall the product and informed customers about the recall (instructing information). Here is a sample of Cadbury's statement following its government fine: 'Quality has always been at the heart of our business, but the process we followed in the UK in this instance has been shown to be unacceptable. We have apologised for

Picture 17.4 Cadbury recalled eight of its products (more than one million items) for salmonella contamination that caused sickness in about 40 people (*source:* AK2/E+/Getty Images)

this and do so again today. In particular, we offer our sincere regrets and apologies to anyone who was made ill as a result of this failure. We have spent over £20 million in changing our procedures to prevent this ever happening again' (Reuters 2007). The crisis response notes the corrective action taken and offers regret (adjusting information). More importantly, Cadbury's apology indicates that it accepts responsibility for the crisis. The response fits nicely with recommendations for a 'preventable' cluster crisis. Instructing and adjusting information were provided coupled with an apology (acceptance of responsibility). In 2007, Cadbury was again named the most trusted chocolate brand in Britain. Marketing analysis argued the poll results showed Cadbury had rebounded from the salmonella crisis (Rano 2008). We can argue that the crisis communication utilised by Cadbury is part of the reason its reputation was able to rebound so quickly from the crisis.

to determine which of the messages really matter and which are just background noise most stakeholders will ignore (Coombs and Holladay 2007).

The internet also provides a gauge of how people are reacting to the organisation's crisis management efforts. Crisis managers evaluate news media coverage of crises in part to determine how their crisis management efforts are being reported. The internet provides a natural environment for people to comment on the organisation's crisis management efforts.

The internet is frequently used to create online memorials for people who have passed away. The online memorials help facilitate grieving and recovering from a loss. Some crises tragically do result in the loss of life. When Ethiopian Airlines Flight 302 crashed in March of 2019, an online memorial appeared to remember the victims. The site had a simple name, 'Ethiopian Flight 302 Crash Victims (2019)'. The page noted the victims represented 35 different countries and a link was provided for people to offer condolences (Ethiopian 2019). Crisis managers need to decide how their organisation will relate to any online memorials and whether or not they should create their own online memorial.

Summary

Unfortunately, crises are a natural part of society. Organisations must accept the fact that they are not immune to crises. Effective crisis public relations management involves factors such as preventing, preparing, reacting, learning and healing. The key is preparation. If organisations think about crises and how they will respond to crises before a crisis hits, crisis public relations management will be much more effective. Being ready for a crisis improves reaction time, can save lives and allows crisis communication to be more strategic and effective. Effective crisis public relations management is good because it benefits anyone touched by a crisis.

Bibliography

Ambrogi, S. (2011). Full text of Rupert Murdoch apology in UK newspapers. [online]. Available at: https://www.reuters.com/article/us-text-murdoch-apology/full-text-of-rupert-murdoch-apology-in-uk-newspapers-idUSTRE76E48320110715 [Accessed 13 August 2011].

Antonetti, P. and S. Maklan (2016). An extended model of moral outrage at corporate social irresponsibility. *Journal of Business Ethics*, 135(3), pp. 429–444.

Arpan, L.M. and D. Pompper (2003). 'Stormy weather: Testing "stealing thunder" as a crisis communication strategy to improve communication flow between organizations and journalists'. *Public Relations Review*, 29(3), pp. 291–308.

Baxter, S. (2010). Lessons from the palm oil showdown [online]. Available at: https://www.theguardian.com/sustainable-business/palm-oil-greenpeace-social-media [Accessed 3 July 2019].

Barton, L. (2001). *Crisis in organizations II*, 2nd ed. Cincinnati, OH: College Divisions South-Western.

Benoit, W.L. (1995). *Accounts, excuses, and apologies: A theory of image restoration.* Albany: State University of New York Press.

Berg, D. and S. Robb (1992). Crisis management and the 'paradigm case.' In E.L. Toth and R.L. Heath (Eds.), *Rhetorical and critical approaches to public relations.* Hillsdale, NJ: Lawrence Erlbaum Associates, pp. 97–105.

Bradsher, K. (2001). Bridgestone disputes need for bigger Firestone recall. *The New York Times*, p, C2.

Cantor Families Memorial (http://www.cantorfamilies.com) [Accessed 7 April 2020].

Carney, A. and A. Jorden (1993). Prepare for business-related crises. *Public Relations Journal*, 49, pp. 34–35.

Caruba, A. (1994). Crisis PR: Most are unprepared. *Occupational Hazards*, 56(9), p. 85.

Claeys, A.S. (2017). Better safe than sorry: Why organizations in crisis should never hesitate to steal thunder. *Business Horizons*, 60(3), pp. 305–311.

Claeys, A.S. and V. Cauberghe (2012). Crisis response and crisis timing strategies, two sides of the same coin. *Public Relations Review*, 38(1), pp. 83–88.

Claeys, A.S. and V. Cauberghe (2014). What makes crisis response strategies work? The impact of crisis involvement and message framing. *Journal of Business Research*, 67(2), pp. 182–189.

Claeys, A.S. and M. Opgenhaffen (2016). Why practitioners do (not) apply crisis communication theory in practice. *Journal of Public Relations Research*, 28(5–6), pp. 232–247.

Claeys, A.S. and W.T. Coombs (2019). Organizational Crisis Communication: Suboptimal Crisis Response Selection Decisions and Behavioral Economics. *Communication Theory*.

Coombs, W.T. (2007). Protecting organization reputations during a crisis: The development and application of situational crisis communication theory. *Corporate Reputation Review*, 10(3), pp. 163–176.

Coombs, W.T. (2010). Parameters for Crisis Communication In: *Handbook of Crisis Communication*. W.T. Coombs and S. J. Holladay eds., Malden, MA: Blackwell Publishing.

Coombs, W.T. (2014). *Applied crisis communication and crisis management: Cases and exercises*. Thousand Oaks, CA: Sage.

Coombs, W.T. (2015). *Ongoing crisis communication: Planning, managing, and responding*, 4th edn. Los Angeles: Sage.

Coombs, W.T. (2017). Digital naturals and the rise of paracrises: The shape of modern crisis communication. In: S. Duhé (Ed.), *New media and public relations*, 3rd edn. New York: Peter Lang, pp. 281–290.

Coombs, W.T. (2019). *Ongoing crisis communication: Planning, managing, and responding*, 5th edn. Los Angeles: Sage.

Coombs, W.T. and S.J. Holladay (2001). An extended examination of the crisis situation: A fusion of the relational management and symbolic approaches. *Journal of Public Relations Research*, 13(4), pp. 321–340.

Coombs, W.T. and S.J. Holladay (2006). 'Unpacking the halo effect: Reputation and crisis management'. *Journal of Communication Management*, 10(2), pp. 123–137.

Coombs, W.T. and S.J. Holladay (2007). The negative communication dynamic: Exploring the impact of stakeholder affect on behavioural intentions. *Journal of Communication Management*, 11(4), pp. 300–312.

Coombs, W.T. and S.J. Holladay (2009). Cooperation, co-optation or capitulation: Factors shaping activist-corporate partnerships. *Ethical Space: The International Journal of Communication Ethics*, 6(2), pp. 23–29.

Coombs, W.T. and S.J. Holladay (2012). The paracrisis: The challenges created by publicly managing crisis prevention. *Public Relations Review*, 38(3), pp. 408–415.

Coombs, T. and S.J. Holladay (2015). CSR as crisis risk: expanding how we conceptualize the relationship. *Corporate Communications: An International Journal*, 20(2), pp. 144–162.

Coombs, W. T., Holladay, S.J. and E.R. Tachkova (2018). When a scandal and a crisis fuse: exploring the communicative implications of scansis. In: A. Haller, H. Michael, and M. Kraus eds., *Scandology: An interdisciplinary field*. Köln: Herbert Von Verlag, pp. 172–190.

Coombs, W.T. and E.R. Tachkova (2019). Scansis as a unique crisis type: theoretical and practical implications. *Journal of Communication Management*, 23(1), pp. 72–88.

De Waele, A., A.S. Claeys and V. Cauberghe (2017). The Impact of a Spokesperson's Visual and Vocal cues on the Public's Attitudes Towards an Organization in Crisis. In *Etmaal van de Communicatiewetenschap 2017*, Tilburg.

Entine, J. (1999). The Odwalla Affair: Reassessing Corporate Social Responsibility (1999). [online]. Available at: http://archives.jonentine.com/articles/odwalla.htm [Accessed 5 December 2019].

Ethiopian Flight 302 Crash Victims (2019).[online] Available at: http://www.legacy.com/news/celebrity-deaths/notable-deaths/article/ethiopian-airlines-flight-302-crash-victims-2019 [Accessed 5 December 2019].

Feeley, T.H. and M.A. de Turck (1995). Global cue usage in behavioral lie detection. *Communication Quarterly*, 43(4), pp. 420–430.

Ferrin, D.L., Kim, P.H., Cooper, C.D. and K. T. Dirks (2007). Silence speaks volumes: The effectiveness of reticence in comparison to apology and denial for responding to integrity- and competence-based trust violations. *Journal of Applied Psychology*, 92(4), pp. 893–908.

Fink, S. (1986). *Crisis management: Planning for the inevitable*. New York, NY: AMACOM.

Frandsen, F. and W. Johansen (2010). Crisis communication, complexity, and the cartoon affairs: A case study. In: W. T. Coombs and S. J. Holladay eds., Malden, MA: Blackwell Publishing, pp. 425–448.

Frandsen, F. and W. Johansen (2011). The study of internal crisis communication: Towards an integrative framework. *Corporate Communications: An International Journal*, 16(4), pp. 347–361.

Greenlees, D. (2008). Toy Makers Mount Drive to Salvage China's Safety Reputation. [online]. Available at: http://www.nytimes.com/2008/01/10/business/worldbusiness/10toys.html [Accessed 6 December 2019].

Harris, E. (2017). For Special-Needs Students, Custom Furniture Out of Schoolhouse Scraps. *New York Times*, [online] p.24. Available at: http://go.galegroup.com [Accessed 17 April 2019].

Heath, R.L. (2005). Issues management. In: R.L. Heath, ed., *Encyclopedia of Public Relations* (Volume 1). Thousand Oaks, CA: Sage, pp. 460–463.

Holladay, S.J. (2009). Crisis communication strategies in the media coverage of chemical accidents. *Journal of Public Relations Research*, 21 (2), pp. 208–217.

In a crisis. (1993, September). *Public Relations Journal*, 49(9), pp. 10–11.

Jin, Y. and A. Pang (2010). Future directions of crisis communication research: Emotions in crisis—The next frontier. In: W.T. Coombs & S.J. Holladay, eds., *Handbook of crisis communication*. Malden, MA: Blackwell, pp. 677–682.

Jin, Y., A. Pang and G.T. Cameron (2007). Integrated crisis mapping: Towards a public-based, emotion-driven conceptualization in crisis communication. *Sphera Publica*, 7, pp. 81–96.

Johansen, W., H.K. Aggerholmand and F. Frandsen (2012). Entering new territory: A study of internal crisis management and crisis communication in organizations. *Public Relations Review*, 38(2), pp. 270–279.

Jones, B., R. Bowd and R. Tench (2009). Corporate irresponsibility and corporate social responsibility: competing realities. *Social Responsibility Journal*, 5(3), 300–310.

Jorgensen, B.K. (1996). Components of consumer reaction to company-related mishaps: a structural equation model approach. *Advances in Consumer Research*, 23, pp. 346–351.

Levick, R. (2005, August 17). In staging responses to crises, complacency plays a big role. *PR News*, [online]. Available at: https://www.prnewsonline.com/in-staging-responses-to-crises-complacency-plays-a-big-role/ [Accessed 5 December 2019].

Mackinnon, P. (1996, July/August). When silence isn't golden. *Financial Executive*, 12(4), 45–48.

Marconi, J. (1992). *Crisis marketing: When bad things happen to good companies*. Chicago: Probus Publishing Company.

Marler, B. (2013). Another lesson earned the hard way: Odwalla E. coli outbreak 1996. [online]. Available at: https://www.marlerblog.com/legal-cases/another-lesson-learned-the-hard-way-odwalla-e-coli-outbreak-1996/ [Accessed July 3 2019].

Mazzei, A. and S. Ravazzani (2014). Internal Crisis Communication Strategies to Protect Trust Relationships A Study of Italian Companies. *International Journal of Business Communication*, 52(3), pp. 319–337.

McFadden, R. (1986). Maker of Tylenol discontinuing all over-counter capsules. *New York Times*, A-1.

Mms.com, (2015). *M&M'S Official Sustainability Report*. [online] Available at: http://www.mms.com/ [Accessed 20 April 2019].

Mowen, J.C. (1980). Further information on consumer perceptions of product recalls. *Advances in Consumer Research*, 8, pp. 519–523.

Nicholas, R. (1995). Know comment. *Marketing*, pp. 41–43.

Parrish, M. and D.W. Nauss (1995). NBC admits it rigged crash, settles GM suit. [online]. Available at: https://www.latimes.com/archives/la-xpm-1993-02-10-mn-1335-story.html [Accessed 3 July 2019].

Pickler, N. (1999). Abercrombie & Fitch agree to card young catalogue buyers (18 November 1999). Retrieved from Lexis/Nexis database 13 August 2011.

Pines, W.L. (1985, Summer). How to handle a PR crisis: Five dos and five don'ts. *Public Relations Quarterly*, 30(2), pp. 16–19.

Rano, L. (12 June 2008). Cadbury's sweet brand success despite apology. [online]. Available at: https://www.confectionerynews.com/Article/2008/06/12/Cadbury-s-sweet-brand-success-despite-apology [Accessed 5 December 2019].

Regester, M. (1989). *Crisis management: How to turns a crisis into an opportunity*. London: Hutchinson.

Regester, M. and J. Larkin (2008). *Risk issues and crisis management: A casebook of best practice* (4th edn). London: Kogan Page.

Reuters (2007) Cadbury Fined in Salmonella Case. [online]. Available at: http://uk.reuters.com/article/2007/07/16/cadbury-salmonella-idUKL1619895820070716 [Accessed 9 April 2011].

Ruddick, G. (2010). Toyota "Sincerely Grateful" as it Returns to Profit Despite Crisis. The Telegraph [online]. Available at: http://www.telegraph.co.uk/finance/newsbysector/transport/7710225/Toyota-Akio-Toyoda-sincerely-grateful-profit-recall-crisis.html [Accessed 5 December 2019].

Ryan, C. (1991). *Prime time activism: Media strategies for grassroots organizing*. Boston: South End Press.

Salomonellablog (2006) Cadbury Schweppes Reputation Suffers Following Salmonella Scare. [online]. Available at: http://www.salmonellablog.com/salmonella-watch/cadbury-schweppes-reputation-suffers-following-salmonella-scare/ [Accessed 9 April 2011].

Sturges, D.L. (1994). Communicating through crisis: A strategy for organizational survival. *Management Communication Quarterly*, 7(3): pp. 297–316.

Tench, R., W. Sun and B. Jones. (2012) *Corporate social irresponsibility: A challenging concept Critical Studies on Corporate Responsibility, Governance and Sustainability*, Volume 4). (2012): 3–20.

Thaler, R.H. (2015). *The making of behavioral economics: Misbehaving*. New York: W.W. Norton & Company.

Twardy, S.A. (1994). Attorneys and public relations professionals must work hand-in-hand when responding to an environmental investigation. *Public Relations Quarterly*, 39(2), pp. 15–6.

Walsh, F. (2011). Salmonella Outbreak Costs Cadbury £20m. *The Guardian*, [online]. Available at: http://www.guardian.co.uk/business/2006/aug/03/food.foodanddrink [Accessed 9 April 2011].

Weisman, S.R. and S. Hazarika (1987). Theory of Bhopal Sabotage is Offered. *The New York Times* [online]. Available at: http://www.nytimes.com/1987/06/23/world/theory-of-bhopal-sabotage-is-offered.html [Accessed 13 August 2011].

CHAPTER 18

Paul Willis

Public relations and the consumer

Source: Rosa Perry/EyeEm/Getty Images

Learning outcomes

By the end of this chapter you should be able to:

- understand the term 'consumer public relations'
- describe different types of consumer public relations activity
- appreciate the factors which drive successful consumer public relations campaigns
- appreciate the benefits that can be generated by a successful consumer public relations campaign
- understand some of the issues and challenges facing practice
- be aware of how the practice of consumer PR is changing.

Structure

- Public relations and marketing
- Targeting and tailoring
- PR style over substance
- Core activities
- The media landscape: continuity and change
- A shift to owned media
- Branded content
- Virtual influence
- It's going to be a bumpy ride
- Land-grab and reinvention
- New activities and practices

Introduction

Consumers are people who buy something for personal use. In the developed world we all consume incessantly, whether online, in stores, exhibitions, bars, restaurants, amusement parks and as theatre goers, music or sports fans. This chapter is intended to help people who are new to the industry understand the role public relations plays in assisting companies to promote an ever-expanding array of products and services to consumers. For a discussion of PR's role in the sale of goods and services *between* businesses, as opposed to selling direct to the consumer, see Chapter 19. At the outset it is also helpful to note that, when taken together, both chapters share a common preoccupation. As with the overview of business-to-business public relations, this chapter is concerned with how practitioners work in a marketing context to win customers and generate profits for a firm.

Considering the role of public relations in a consumer context is important given that marketing communication plays a big part in the working lives of many PR practitioners (Zerfass et al. 2008). Consumer PR is carried out in the communication departments of companies and in agencies working for private sector clients, as well as by self-employed freelancers. Some practitioners will focus exclusively on this type of work, whereas others will juggle marketing-driven campaigns alongside a host of activities involving a range of stakeholders who stretch beyond the company's customers.

To set the scene, the chapter begins by discussing PR's place in the marketing mix and its role in brand building. It then considers what consumer PR involves and the core activities it incorporates. The chapter next explores how a fast-moving media landscape challenges the ways in which organisations have traditionally sought to engage with consumers. Given PR is an applied communication discipline it is hardly surprising that its practice has been affected by the media transformation witnessed in the twenty-first century. The discussion teases out some of the issues this context generates for PR practitioners, such as a greater focus on owned media and branded content, as well as the emergence of a new generation of consumer influencers to be targeted in campaigns. It is noted how these and other developments have generated a period of considerable flux in the world of marketing. This has led to a situation in which PR practitioners and marketing professionals are claiming expertise in areas which were once regarded as the domain of other disciplines.

Given the nature of its subject, this chapter has a strong commercial focus. As one PR agency argues, the starting point for a consumer campaign can usually be summed up in a single word. The word highlighted is 'more': more sales, more enquiries, more visitors, more traffic, more listings, more customers and more money (wpragency.co.uk). This commercial reality generates both enthusiasts and critics for consumer PR. For example, some commentators argue that the increasing consumption of goods and services is economically advantageous, whereas others warn of the dangers such a focus poses to society. These and other ethical problems, including some of the specific issues generated by emerging methods of engagement, will also be investigated as the chapter unfolds.

Public relations and marketing

The world we are concerned with in this chapter is where PR interfaces with **marketing** activities, such as **advertising**, to stimulate the sale of products and services in the free market economy. Organisations have a vested interest in attracting and maintaining the support of the people who buy (or might buy) what they provide to the market. They also often have a legal and/or regulatory obligation to listen and respond to their customers (Macnamara 2015). These imperatives help to explain why the activities associated with consumer PR loom large in the working lives of so many practitioners. Although the endgame of PR activities in this context is to drive sales, its role is often more subtle than other forms of communication. By looking to change consumer attitudes towards a product or company, PR seeks to create a more favourable commercial environment for the company rather than generating outcomes that can be linked directly to an immediate increase in sales. However, it can also be a powerful sales generator.

Public relations has become a valuable part of what is known as the **'marketing mix'**, an often-quoted term that refers to the set of tools that a company has at its disposal to influence sales. The traditional formulation is popularly known as the '4Ps': product, price, place and promotion (Kotler and Keller 2016). Promotion is the area that encompasses public relations, as it is this part of the marketing equation that focuses on the content that is designed to stimulate awareness, interest and purchase. To attract interest and awareness in their products and services, companies use a combination of disciplines – including advertising, **sales promotion, direct mail** and public relations – to reach their desired audiences. When used in this way, public relations should become a planned and sustained element of the wider promotional mix, working in tandem with other marketing activities to achieve maximum impact and with the potential to meet a range of objectives, such as:

- raising a company's profile;
- redefining its image;
- helping to promote its credibility in a new or existing market;
- demonstrating empathy with a target audience;
- launching a new product or service;
- reinvigorating an existing product or service;
- stimulating trial and purchase.

It's personal

PR campaigns are often driven by the need to communicate a company's personality and set of values to consumers. If a company can communicate these qualities, it may succeed in differentiating itself from the competition. (See Think about 18.1.)

By helping to project qualities on to a company, product or service, public relations can play an active role in the world of **brand** development. It is necessary to understand the role and power of effective branding more fully to appreciate the benefits that public relations can generate within the context of a successfully executed consumer strategy.

Our societies appear to be overflowing with brands. In popular culture everything and everybody seems to be referred to as a brand: music and film stars, sportsmen, royalty, airlines, places, politicians – never mind the products that we can buy online, or which fill the shops on the high street. In one sense, everything can be legitimately called a brand because the term applies to any label that carries some meaning or association. However, for the purposes of this chapter, it is necessary to apply a more structured definition in order to fully appreciate the role that public relations can play in brand development.

Morgan (1999) defines a brand as an entity that satisfies all the following four conditions:

1. Something that has a buyer and a seller (e.g. Lady GaGa but not the Queen). Morgan also makes the distinction that 'buying and selling' does not have to be a financial transaction to be of value to both sides.

2. Something that has a differentiating name, symbol or trademark (e.g. easyJet but not aeroplanes). Moreover, it is differentiated from other similar products around it for reasons other than its name or trademark, (e.g. an iPhone rather than a smartphone).

3. Something that has positive or negative associations in consumers' minds for reasons other than its literal product characteristics (e.g. Coca-Cola but not tap-water).

4. Something that has been created, rather than is naturally occurring (e.g. the Eiffel Tower, Taj Mahal or Nou Camp, Barcelona), but not Niagara Falls or the Amazon River.

(See also Think about 18.2.)

By studying different brand definitions, such as the one put forward by Morgan, it begins to become apparent how brands can add resonance to a product or service. Successful brands offer consumers tangible and emotional benefits over other products, which consumers not only recognise but also desire, at both a conscious and subconscious level. Furthermore, great brands usually take this appeal a stage further by focusing more on emotional than rational benefits and this ultimately manifests itself in a distinct and consistent

---

Think about 18.1

Brands and their personalities

Think of five brands and the personalities they try to project.

- Do you admire these brands?
- What attracts or repels you about each brand? What qualities do they exhibit? Do any of them promote causes you feel passionate about?

Think about different brands of the same product – e.g. mobile phones or cars.

- Do they carry different personalities?
- How is that personality conveyed?

Think about 18.2

Brands

- Can you think of any other examples that fit each of Morgan's four criteria?
- How do these brands communicate with consumers?

Mini case study 18.1
The Body Shop and animal testing

The Body Shop was founded by Anita Roddick in 1976 and from the outset adopted a strong stance against the testing of cosmetic products on animals. The company has since grown into a successful international business operating in more than 60 countries and selling over 1,000 products, such as cosmetics and shampoos. Anita Roddick died in 2007 and the brand is now part owned by Natura & Co, a Brazilian global personal care cosmetics group headquartered in São Paulo. Today, The Body Shop still seeks to maintain its long-held reputation for promoting positive social change. For example, in addition to a clear statement against animal testing, its brand values include the promise to defend human rights, support community fair trade and protect the planet.

In 2018, the retailer worked with celebrities and influencers on Instagram as part of its #foreveragainstanimaltesting initiative. The campaign's aim was to collect 8 million signatures within a year to petition for a worldwide ban on animal-tested cosmetics. An integrated communication programme coordinated by the company's PR team used the support of key influencers to promote the cause, featuring websites, interactive maps and user-generated content, as well as more traditional communication material such as posters. Advocates of the campaign were also encouraged to attend rallies associated with the cause.

The campaign surpassed its aim with 8.3 million signatures gathered in just ten months. In October 2018, the company's petition was taken to the United Nations' headquarters in New York and the company is now working with individual countries interested in changing their animal testing legislation.

Picture 18.1 Cannes Lions, a five-day International Festival of Creativity, is the largest gathering in the creative marketing community (*source:* Richard Bord/Getty Images)

an attitude. Nike's 'Just Do It' slogan was first introduced in an advertising campaign in 1988 and since then, through the evocation of inspirational personal stories, has been used consistently to associate the company with customer values and desires (Yohn 2014).

The power of brands is also linked to an increasingly strong desire to express individuality through the ownership of goods and services that are perceived to be innovative, different and original. Indeed, Lewis and Bridger (2003: 12) go as far as to say that:

> *For many New Consumers the purchase of products and services has largely replaced religious faith as a source of inspiration and solace. For an even larger group, their buying decisions are driven by a deep-rooted psychological desire to enhance and develop their sense of self.*

Given the emotional capital that is invested in some, if not all, purchasing decisions, public relations can be used to demonstrate that a brand empathises with

personality running through all their marketing activities. (See Mini case study 18.1 and Think about 18.1.)

Heart versus head

It is not surprising that brand owners are increasingly turning to image and emotional marketing to win over consumers. In today's fast-paced marketplace, companies tend to copy any competitor's advantage until it is nullified, which is why emotional appeal assumes such importance and why companies such as Nike try to sell

Think about 18.3
I shop; therefore, I am?

- Is the level of consumption we see in the developed world appropriate?
- If you were a PR practitioner are there any goods and services you would not wish to promote to consumers? For example, what are your views about the promotion of e-cigarettes? How about fast food, alcohol or betting?
- What considerations shape your thinking about what you would and would not promote as a PR practitioner?

the worries, needs and aspirations of groups of people. This allows it to connect and align itself with consumers in an indirect but powerful association. From an implementation perspective, this is one of the reasons why many public relations campaigns hook into lifestyle issues and popular culture, using celebrity association, the services of psychologists, anthropologists, fashion gurus, chefs, interior designers and a range of other experts to add resonance and relevance to consumer campaigns.

Targeting and tailoring

Before discussing the various elements that can make up a consumer public relations programme, it is important to stress that the key characteristics of the target audience play an important part in defining and shaping the strategy and tactics that are deployed in a campaign. Who do we need to communicate to? How can we reach them? What are they interested in? What do we want them to do? By posing a series of simple questions it is possible to refine and sharpen the scope of the planned activity ensuring a clinical rather than a wasteful, scattergun approach to the tools and techniques that are at the practitioner's disposal (for a more detailed discussion of how to develop a PR campaign strategy see Chapter 9).

If the purpose of the campaign is to get young mothers to visit their local supermarket, a national media relations campaign might not have the same impact as activity targeted at a local newspaper. Or, if research shows that the same audience is concerned about their children walking to school, then a road safety sponsorship executed at local level and promoted through relevant social media networks may strike a chord, helping to establish a positive relationship with the store. One of public relations' great attributes is its flexibility, as campaigns can be tailored to appeal to many audiences and modified to accommodate the requirements of different delivery channels, such as the media, events or sponsorship.

PR style over substance

It is necessary to balance this picture of strategic opportunity with a note of caution linked to the role of PR in a consumer context. This warning relates to the notion of what might be termed as prioritising style over substance. In the consumer context we are concerned with, this phenomenon relates to the practice of using PR tools and techniques to obscure the fact that a product

> **Think about 18.4**
>
> Can you think of any brands that fail consistently to live up to their promise? For example, think about products you have bought recently (such as a mobile phone) and compare your experience of using it with how it was promoted.
>
> Can you identify any examples where public relations has failed to change your mind about a brand and its products/services?
>
> What about when public relations has positively helped to change your mind about a brand?

or service is flawed or problematic in some way. For example, it might be that the offer the company is providing to consumers is inferior to the competition in terms of price, range, availability or ease of use. A spectacular celebrity launch does not make such issues disappear and it is dangerous to underestimate the ability of stakeholders, such as consumers and journalists, to see through such hype.

Given this situation it is important for PR practitioners to understand the fine detail of the products they are promoting and to provide appropriate advice. The excessive promotion of a lacklustre product can be counter-productive as it might antagonise consumers and bring the organisation's credibility into question. This is also the case if the communication campaign downgrades key issues such as excessive charges and penalty clauses. Examples of this sort of practice can be found in the UK financial sector, such as among companies providing short-term loans and prepaid credit cards. (See Think about 18.4.)

PR bullshit

The requirement to promote products and services in highly competitive markets can also lead to other practices which can tarnish public relations' reputation. An example of this is when organisations promote stories in the media which have no foundation in fact or research. Ethical reflections on public relations practice usually consider issues such as propaganda, which is defined as lying as opposed to telling the truth (L'Etang 2008). What we are talking about here is not lying but a more subtle phenomenon which should also trouble those concerned with PR's reputation. Harry Frankfurt, Emeritus Professor of Philosophy at Princeton and an influential moral commentator, labels the

> **Think about 18.5**
>
> ### PR 'bullshit'
>
> Can you identify any consumer PR campaigns using news hooks that contain unsubstantiated views and opinions? Do you have a problem with this? How does it make you feel about the brand being promoted? How does it make you feel about PR practice?
>
> **Feedback**
>
> Bullshit is prevalent whenever circumstances require someone to communicate without knowing what they are communicating about. Good consumer PR should be based upon solid research.

phenomenon under discussion here as 'bullshit'. Frankfurt (2005) argues that the increase in communication in society is contributing to what he calls a 'culture of bullshit', which has become one of the most salient features of modern culture. He notes that bullshit is a form of representation that does not necessarily involve lying. While the liar and truth teller each knows what the truth is, the bullshitter is indifferent to it. The liar must remember the truth if only to ensure that it does not come out. In contrast, the bullshitter is involved in a 'kind of bluff' (Frankfurt 2005) and 'does not care whether the things he says describe reality correctly (he) just picks them up, or makes them up, to suit his purpose'. (See Think about 18.5.)

Core activities

Consumer PR campaigns have traditionally been made up of three types of activity: media relations, event management and sponsorship.

Media relations

Getting a journalist to write or talk on air about a company, product or service is still the primary objective of many consumer public relations campaigns. The persuasive power of editorial (news) is much greater than paid-for advertising. The stories and features that appear in newspapers and magazines, both in print and online, as well as on radio and television, tend to be viewed by consumers as unbiased and objective. In contrast, advertising in the same media channels relies on paid-for space and therefore lacks the same credibility as coverage that has been created by an independent third party, such as a journalist. Influencing this editorial process is a key task for the public relations practitioner. No advertisement or sales person can convince you about the virtues of a product as effectively as an independent commentator, such as a journalist, and if this opinion is then repeated to you by a friend, family member or colleague it has an even greater resonance. Indeed, most of us got to hear about Apple, Amazon and Google not through advertising but from news stories in the press, radio, TV and online, or through personal recommendation.

While the benefits of a successful media relations campaign are obvious, achieving the desired result is not so easy. As editorial coverage, by definition, cannot be bought and because someone else produces the finished article, the public relations practitioner has no direct control over it (unlike an advertisement). In addition, although there are opportunities to write straightforward product press releases that achieve positive coverage (a glance at the 'best buy' features in lifestyle magazines or an examination of the motoring press will highlight good examples of product-focused editorial), most journalists tend to shy away from commercially driven stories and are certainly not receptive to what they see as **company propaganda**.

Furthermore, to reach many consumers a company needs to be featured in the general news sections of the media rather than in specialist editorial. In this environment, media relations campaigns must incorporate an additional news hook to motivate a journalist to cover a story and this might involve independent research, a celebrity association, an anniversary, a great photograph or a new and surprising angle on a traditional theme. (See Explore 18.1.)

> **Explore 18.1**
>
> ### Media stories
>
> Take two daily newspapers – one quality paper and one popular or tabloid paper. Identify stories that you believe have been generated by an in-house public relations department or agency to promote a product or service.
>
> ### Feedback
>
> Clues to stories with a public relations source include: staged photographs accompanying the news item; results of research published on the date of the news item; anniversary of an event; book/film/CD published on the date of the news item.

Events

It is a common misconception that public relations is only concerned with the generation of positive media coverage. Open days, webinars, festivals, fashion shows, exhibitions, workshops, roadshows, conferences and AGMs are all events that can provide a company with the opportunity to interact directly with consumers, either on its home turf or out and about in the community, generating enhanced presence for the business and a forum for face-to-face, two-way communication (see Mini case study 18.2 and Think about 18.6).

Sponsorship

Whether in sport, the arts or in support of a worthy cause, sponsorship is fundamentally about third-party endorsement and as such sits neatly under the public relations umbrella. If successfully managed to maximise opportunities – and this is where advertising, digital marketing and direct mail also play a role – sponsorship can provide a powerful platform from which to increase the relevance of a company and its products among key target audiences. By harnessing the emotions, qualities and values associated with the

> **Think about 18.6**
>
> Consider the Boots mini case study and try to categorise the different aspects of the campaign into paid, owned and earned activities. What are the advantages and challenges of developing campaigns with different streams of consumer activity? Can you identify any overlaps between the highlighted activities? For example, can owned activity generate earned content?

Mini case study 18.2
The Boots Beauty Festival

Boots is a health, beauty and pharmacy retailer in the United Kingdom with over 2,500 stores. Ogilvy, the company's public relations agency, was given the task of thinking about how it could influence a greater number of 16- to 24-year-old women to consider Boots as a retail destination for their beauty needs, including makeup, cosmetics and skincare products. To meet this brief the agency focused on ideas that would help to raise awareness of Boots and its product offer with the key target audience, generate positive feelings towards the brand and improve sales of the company's core beauty products.

As part of the planning process the Boots team engaged in a programme of research which revealed a strong lifestyle link between 16- to 24-year-old women and festival attendance. Festivals are organised events featuring music, comedy, literature, film and other artistic pursuits, cultural celebrations, as well activities linked to food and drink. In the UK 14 million adults attend festivals each year with a third going to more than one event. The research further showed that 16- to 24-year-old women going to festivals search for relevant beauty trends in advance of their attendance, while also identifying that social media influencers play an important role in shaping trends and purchasing decision in this area.

Given this research Ogilvy devised the Boots Beauty Festival, an integrated influencer-led campaign designed to showcase the extent of the company's beauty products. To deliver the campaign, Ogilvy and Boots worked with influencers across a range of communication channels, such as paid (anything the company is charged money for), owned (created and managed by Boots) and earned (when other people share your content). For example, Boots partnered with leading beauty influencers to preview the latest trends that would be of interest to festival goers. A new website page was created to feature the influencers' content which, in turn, linked back to the brand's core range of products. The summer edition of Boots' own *Health & Beauty* magazine supported this editorial focus, plus tickets for a small number of consumers to attend the festival were promoted as a giveaway in another publication. The beauty editors of 20 leading media outlets also attended a press preview event which then resulted in a range of complementary and supportive content appearing before the festival took place.

On the day of the event 79 social media influencers attended (78 were unpaid) and the festival was broadcast through Facebook Live and Instagram Stories. One hundred festival-themed beauty baskets were also given to chosen influencers and journalists. Highlighting the campaign's integrated character, Facebook advertisements featuring key influencers were additionally incorporated into the activity with the specific task of increasing sales. Overall, the campaign exceeded all its key objectives, including targets related to revenue generation.

sponsorship property and perhaps providing some form of added-value experience, a business can successfully stand out in a cluttered consumer market. (See Think about 18.8 and Mini case study 18.2.)

> ### Think about 18.7
>
> ### Events
>
> - Can you think of a public relations event, like one of those listed, that you have attended in the past year?
> - What about the open day you may have attended at your current or another college or university?
> - What were the factors that made it a success or failure?

> ### Think about 18.8
>
> ### Sponsorship
>
> For a sponsorship to be truly effective, does the sponsoring company need to have an obvious link with the sponsored property (for example, Adidas and football)?
>
> Can you think of an example of a successful sponsorship where there is no obvious connection between the core activities of the business and the sponsored property, such as Mastercard and football?
>
> If you were public relations director of Coca-Cola, how would you justify its sponsorship of the Olympics? Is it about sporting performance, a lifestyle statement, credibility by association, or none of these?

Picture 18.2 The Body Shop has a long-held reputation for promoting positive social change. (*source:* Scott Barbour/Getty Images)

By discussing the different communication vehicles a practitioner has at their disposal, a consumer public relations campaign can have many dimensions, with media relations, event or sponsorship initiatives supporting one another in an integrated programme of activity.

The media landscape: continuity and change

Having set out the holy trinity of consumer PR – media relations, event management and sponsorship – it is now necessary to consider the impact of contemporary developments on this area of practice. A good place to start is with the evolution of the media landscape. It will also be helpful to look at Chapters 2 and 14, both of which explore different aspects of the modern media environment.

As discussed in the last section, media relations is the primary activity in most consumer PR campaigns. When writing the consumer PR chapter for the first edition of this book 15 years ago, the focus of this activity was on campaigns which targeted the mass media. In other words, those media outlets operating at international, national and local level (such as newspapers, magazines, radio and television stations) which have the capability to communicate to large numbers of people. This sector of the media includes brands which are recognised globally, such as the BBC, *Vogue*, CNN, *Le Figaro* and *El Pais*, as well as regional newspapers, radio stations and TV companies, which are little known beyond their own territories.

The mass media is still hugely important to PR practitioners in a marketing context. For example, a survey of practitioners revealed that seven out of ten respondents still disseminate information about an organisation, its products and services through the mass media (Zerfass et al. 2015). For many PR practitioners a well-crafted press release remains a favoured and effective form of communication in this context. When used appropriately press releases can provide a way of communicating concisely the news elements of a story (which is what the journalist is interested in) and then using this content as a platform to support a marketing objective (which is what the company is concerned with). Even those practitioners who no longer formally use a press release format will still apply its principles to frame the emails and other digital communication they send to journalists. This process can help to ensure an announcement passes the 'so what' test as far as the journalist is concerned.

Mini case study 18.3
Maximising a sponsorship: Thomas Cook Sport

Thomas Cook Sport (TCS) is the UK's leading sports tour operator, selling consumer and corporate packages to sporting events globally. One of the company's sponsorship assets is its status as Official Travel Partner to eight Premier League clubs: Arsenal, Chelsea, Everton, Leicester, Liverpool, Manchester United, Southampton and Tottenham Hotspur.

TCS tasked PR agency Hatch Communications with the job of managing its contractual rights with football clubs, maximising the sponsorship and coordinating the overall marketing strategy to promote its sport packages to fans. This included the management of the company's social media platforms to ensure a consistent and integrated approach to the campaign.

The agency's strategy and tactics were framed by several key objectives:

- to increase sales by 10 per cent;
- to develop campaigns that engage directly with a minimum of 10,000 fans in a single year;
- to deliver 15 favourable national media outcomes during the same time;
- to use this and other media coverage to drive traffic to www.thomascooksport.com;
- to use the sponsorship assets to support the Thomas Cook Children's Charity.

The agency developed a campaign that featured four key initiatives:

1. **Celebrate with TCS:** January and February is a key sales period for Thomas Cook. This is when many consumers book their summer holiday. To capitalise on this interest, Hatch created events at six partner football club stadiums. These sought to inject the vibrancy, colour and celebration of exotic holiday destinations into the football stadiums at a peak booking time.

2. **What would you do?:** To integrate TCS' social media channels with some of the more lucrative contractual rights, Hatch created the 'What would you do?' concept, whereby fans sent in entries via social media to win the chance to play on their team's home pitch. The competition received over 1,500 entries in total and included ideas such as cleaning Anfield with a toothbrush.

3. **Charity pitch days:** This provided an opportunity for the Thomas Cook Children's Charity to give underprivileged children from local schools the chance to play on the same pitch as their heroes.

4. **Player appearances:** This element of the campaign used the contractual player appearances to create branded media coverage, engage with fans via store appearances and integrate with social media and sales incentives.

Campaign results

- An annual sales increase of 30 per cent
- 85 national media hits
- 28,455 fans directly engaged through the four main campaign themes
- Traffic to the TCS website increased by 65 per cent and led to a situation in which online bookings accounted for 80 per cent of sales
- An increase in followers to TCS' Twitter feed from 1,538 to 10,284
- An increase in the company's Facebook friends from 927 to 5,713

A shift to owned media

Although the mass media is still important to consumer PR professionals the communication landscape over the last 15 years has changed considerably. While targeting the journalists who worked for these outlets would once have been the raison d'etre for most media relations activity, additional communication priorities have now emerged that generate a range of strategic issues for practitioners. For example, PR professionals increasingly predict a significant shift in emphasis away from the mass media to owned media (Zerfass et al. 2015). As illustrated in Mini case study 18.1, owned media refers to the communication channels the organisation controls, such as its own website, blogs, podcasts and apps. Companies now have the capacity to cost-effectively create content that can be instantaneously communicated to a wide range of external and internal stakeholders. This development highlights the transformation of all organisations into media organisations (Ihlen and Pallas 2014).

Organisations have long engaged in their own promotional publishing and broadcasting production in the form of corporate brochures and videos. However, the sort of distribution capacity which was once only the province of mass media outlets is now available to in-house practitioners and their agencies thanks to the development of the internet and the devices we use to download the content found online. Increasing numbers of people have access to superfast broadband and mobile network services, while the smartphone has now overtaken the laptop as the device internet users say is the most important for connecting to the internet. These technological advances have particularly increased the use of film as a method of consumer engagement. Instead of relying on the printed word or the largesse of mass media broadcast outlets, organisations can now deliver video content direct to the consumer via their website or through their own promotional social media accounts, such as YouTube, Twitter and Facebook.

This new 'owned' broadcasting capability can be used by brands to:

- launch new products and services;
- demonstrate how products work and can best be used;
- record what happened at a sponsored event;
- provide a behind-the-scenes look at a product's research and development phase;
- highlight celebrity endorsements;
- promote testimonials by experts and consumers.

From an issues management perspective video also provides a channel through which companies can quickly respond to customer service issues. Furthermore, this last point reminds us that this technology can also be used by consumers to broadcast their own views about a company and what it offers to the market. Disgruntled customers increasingly use online videos to criticise companies they believe have failed to live up to their brand promise. One early, memorable and widely quoted illustration of this was by Dave Carroll, a Canadian country and western singer. Dave could not get compensation for a broken guitar until he sung about the airline responsible for the damage in a YouTube video (see http://www.davecarrollmusic.com). His song became one of YouTube's biggest hits of the time and generated a wealth of coverage in the mass media, including CNN, the *LA Times*, *Rolling Stone* magazine and the BBC.

Branded content

The growing appetite for shared video content amongst both companies and consumers is highlighted by a couple of contemporary events. First, Facebook's introduction of its own live broadcasting service in 2016 to compete against the host of streaming apps which are now available for everyone to download. Second, the launch in the same year of the first *Brand Film Festival* in North America by *PR Week* and *Campaign* magazine. This industry awards event is designed to showcase the best videos and documentaries produced by brands and agencies in support of marketing objectives. The focus here is on what is called branded content and entertainment, terms which punctuate the conversations between consumer PR specialists, other marketing communication professionals, industry analysts and the media.

Significant investment has also been made by PR agencies seeking to position themselves as experts in branded content. For example, Weber Shandwick promotes Mediaco, its own content creation and distribution unit established to meet the opportunities generated by the shift from mass to owned media. Burson Marsteller (now known as Burson, Cohn & Wolf) similarly introduced its Creative Council to help coordinate and integrate content creation across the firm. The purported aim of both initiatives is to help clients operate more effectively as media companies in both the publishing and broadcast arenas.

One of the attributes good PR practitioners have always brought to the marketing arena is an ability to create content which people want to read, listen or watch. Therefore, journalism has – and remains – a popular recruiting ground for PR professionals. PR people understand that consumers want to be entertained and/or informed about the things that matter to them, rather than bludgeoned with seemingly random messages and images. They also have the skills to develop this content. This contemporary focus on content does, however, promise something more for PR. Firms like Weber Shandwick and Burson, Cohn & Wolf are seeking to exploit a wider business opportunity. While PR would traditionally lead on content development when it came to media relations, other forms of communication – such as videos and brochures – tended to be 'owned' by advertising agencies. Now PR professionals are trying to work in these areas as well, especially as the content required increasingly seems to suit their editorial skills. They are doing the creative work, developing concepts and then executing them (see Mini case study 18.4).

Chapter 18 Public relations and the consumer 375

Mini case study 18.4
Video killed the media star

To promote Nokia's Lumia smartphone, PR agency Cohn & Wolfe (now Burson, Cohn & Wolf) helped the company to develop an integrated marketing approach that focused on what they called content marketing and video storytelling. Instead of telling people how good the phone was they wanted to show them through a broadcast medium.

C&W created the strategy, the concept and the scripts for the video. Nokia then used the video to influence consumers in social media and at point-of-sale. The material was also used for sales training and internal communication. The campaign did include a media relations element delivered by the team. However, rather than being the centre piece of C&W's involvement, its purpose was to promote and support the video produced by the agency.

In this section on the changes to the media environment, there has yet to be an explicit focus on the impact of social media in a consumer PR context. However, the brands which forged and now dominate the social media landscape (Facebook, YouTube and Twitter) have already made an appearance. The way in which this discussion has unfolded supports a prediction Stephen Waddington (2012) made that people will eventually stop using the term 'social media' as a catch-all phrase to describe the creation and sharing of content. It will instead 'become the norm', a taken-for-granted feature of the communication landscape. Indeed, his subsequent argument that *all* media should be sociable and shareable underpins the PR industry's reconfigured preoccupation with content, as well as being a touchstone for effective practice in a consumer context.

Virtual influence

Another accepted feature of the social media world that impacts specifically on consumer PR is the emergence of a new set of influencers. Journalists have now been joined by bloggers as people whose endorsement is prized and sought by brands. While most bloggers will only receive a handful of visitors to their site, a growing number have become popular commentators on lifestyle issues, business, sport, politics and entertainment. This generates opportunities for PR professionals seeking to showcase products such as clothing, make-up, gadgets and food. For example, those working in fashion PR work hard to target influential bloggers in their sector (see songofstyle.com) given that most mention the brands they feature at the bottom of each post. However, as is the case when working with fashion journalists in the mainstream media, PR practitioners must ensure the clothes and accessories they are promoting are compatible with what is usually featured in the blog. A sure-fire way to alienate a journalist or blogger (in any sector) is failing to 'understand' their editorial focus and style. The media may be evolving but similar rules of engagement still apply.

The innovation in broadcast technology highlighted in the previous section also explains why an increasing number of blogs are no longer written journals, diaries and travelogues but are instead video broadcasts we can watch on our smartphones, tablets and laptops. These are more widely known as video blogs, video logs or vlogs. While this form of communication is enabled by a variety of open source content management systems, the most popular is the video-sharing site YouTube. From this spectacularly successful internet phenomenon has risen another new form of influencer, the YouTube Star.

This recent class of internet celebrity can command large audiences through their videos. YouTube's CEO Susan Wojcicki (2019) noted that in 2018 the number of YouTube channels having more than one million subscribers had nearly doubled. To get a better sense of the scale of this development, it is worth noting that three years previously Tubular Labs, a firm specialising in gathering data about online trends, reported there were over 17,000 YouTube channels with in excess of 100,000 subscribers and nearly 1,500 with more than 1 million (*The Guardian* 2016). In an interview with the author, Scott Guthrie, an independent consultant and expert advisor to brands wishing to work with influencers, notes that:

> This latest form of influencer marketing is no fad and is forecast to be worth almost £18 billion by 2024. It is a key development area in consumer PR and is one response to the splintering of the traditional media landscape. Brands need to be where their key audiences are and communicating through the intermediaries they listen to. Increasingly in consumer campaigns, such objectives are achieved through social media influence rather than traditional channels like newspapers, television and radio. Furthermore, working with influencers offers opportunities for brands beyond the selling of goods and service, helping them to develop engagement programmes that stretch beyond customers and clients.

In addition to general entertainment, the interests of YouTube Stars cover a wide range of lifestyle issues, from video games (Markiplier), to cooking (Ann Reardon), beauty (Jeffree Star), fashion (Jenn Im) and music (Anthony Fantano). For example, Ryan Kaji is eight years old and has amassed more than 18 million subscribers to his YouTube channel in which he reviews different toys. According to Forbes (2018) the popularity and influence of Ryan ToysReview has led to commercial partnerships with pocket.watch and Bonkers Toys to create a new range of licensed toys and books with the Ryan's World toy range first released in a partnership with Walmart, the world's largest retailer. The YouTube channel and these other activities helped Ryan and his family to generate estimated earnings of $22 million in 2018 (Forbes 2018).

The income generated by YouTube stars largely comes from brands paying to advertise on their sites, as well as paid endorsements and sponsored deals. This investment by brands is underpinned by the belief that YouTubers are not only popular but influential. In 2014 Jeetender Sehdev of the University of Southern California conducted a survey of 13- to 18-year-olds in the United States for *Variety* magazine (*Variety* 2014). This asked them to rate the 10 most popular English-language YouTubers and 10 of the most popular traditional celebrities across a range of qualities that were designed to represent 'influence'. YouTubers took the top five places in the resulting analysis, with Smosh, the Fine Bros, PewDiePie (whose channel became the first in history to exceed over 10 billion views), KSI and Ryan Higa deemed more influential than Jennifer Lawrence, Katy Perry, Paul Walker (who had recently died in a motoring accident) and other celebrities. When the survey was run again in 2015, YouTubers took the top six slots, ahead of stars including Bruno Mars and Taylor Swift (*Variety* 2015).

One of the conclusions drawn from this research is that YouTube Stars are perceived to be more engaging and authentic than mainstream celebrities. Although the latter are perceived to be the products of orchestrated image strategies, YouTubers are more likely to be viewed as 'people like me'. The author of the survey also suggests there is a technological aspect to this connection between broadcaster and audience. This form of communication started life as a format in which people would speak directly to a webcam, usually from their own home. This created a feeling of intimacy and ordinariness which many YouTube celebrities strive to maintain. An irony is that the qualities which make them so valuable to brands may be eroded by the lucrative fees they can now negotiate to promote products. While many YouTubers are transparent about their commercial endorsements, they still run the risk of producing contrived branded content which ceases to be entertaining and/or authentic. Furthermore, the Federal Trade Commission in the United States has identified several YouTubers, including PewDiePie, who received thousands of dollars to covertly promote *Middle Earth: Shadow of Mordor*, a video game produced by Warner Brothers (see Mini case study 18.5 and Think about 18.9). In 2019 the

Mini case study 18.5
YouTube and a shadowy promotion

Warner Brothers paid a marketing agency, Plaid Social Labs, to coordinate a YouTube influencer campaign to promote the launch of a new video game *Middle Earth: Shadow of Mordor*. YouTube stars, including PewDiePie, were given free access to a pre-launch version of the game, as well as cash payments. The Federal Trade Commission in the United States accused Warner Brothers of deceptive practice given its failure to inform consumers that the videos produced by the YouTube stars were part of its advertising campaign (*The Times* 14 July 2016).

The YouTube stars were instructed by the company to include a strong call to action in their videos to encourage their audience to visit the official *Shadow of Mordor* website. They were also asked to be positive about the game and to make one Facebook post or one tweet in support of the new product. All the footage supplied by the YouTubers had to be approved in advance by either Warner Brothers or Plaid Social Labs. While the YouTube stars were asked to include a sponsorship disclosure in a text box below their videos, the disclosure was often hidden from view. In addition, the YouTube stars were asked not to include disclosures within their own videos.

PewDiePie posted a seven-minute video in which he plays *Shadow of Mordor* and talks positively about the game. At the time, PewDiePie's channel on YouTube had more than 46 million subscribers and he had in excess of 8 million Twitter followers. PewDiePie does not say he was paid by Warner Brothers to play the game, or that the video had been pre-approved by the company as part of an orchestrated marketing campaign. Although text below the video said the video was sponsored by Warner Brothers this could only be accessed by clicking on a 'show more' tab. *Forbes* magazine calculated that PewDiePie earned £15.5 million in 2018.

> **Think about 18.9**
>
> In its investigation the Federal Trade Commission (FTC) concluded the videos featuring *Shadow of Mordar* produced by the YouTube Stars did not reflect the independent opinions or experiences of impartial video game enthusiasts. The FTC likened the videos to a paid sales pitch.
>
> Do you agree?
>
> Are developments in social media blurring the boundaries between paid promotion and independent analysis?
>
> What do you think is the best source of independent advice about products and services?

UK's Competition and Markets Authority took similar steps when warning more than 70 PR agencies representing a range of influencers, including pop stars Rita Ora and Ellie Goulding, to state more clearly if their clients were being paid to promote products or services online. YouTubers' status as 'people like me' could be further eroded as the distinction between them and other celebrities becomes blurred, not least because the most prominent online players are no longer flying below the radar of the mass media and have become celebrities.

It's going to be a bumpy ride

The media context in which consumer PR takes place will remain dynamic and uncertain for the next generation of professionals. Being able to cope with change and ambiguity will be a prerequisite of the job as the communication landscape continues to evolve. Gilpin and Murphy (2010) usefully conceptualised the contemporary media landscape as 'a single **complex system** that encompasses a vast range of digital, non-digital, mass and personal communication'. They highlight how it is increasingly difficult to draw neat boundaries between traditional media and digital channels, citing Qvortrup's (2006) observation that digital media 'integrate all known media into one converged multimedia system (with) an unlimited system of features'. Even traditional media, from print to broadcast, is morphing and migrating to digital formats.

These changes to the media environment not only influence the work of PR professionals. They also have a profound impact on practitioners working across the marketing mix. For example, the decline of people interacting with the traditional media has undermined the effectiveness of mass media advertising. The sort of media fragmentation discussed in this chapter means it is now difficult for marketers to harness a single communications medium to create and sustain a brand as television once did. At one time companies could reach a large slice of the public by advertising in one of a limited number of channels (for example, in the UK by advertising on the only independent channel, ITV); now they must spread their budgets over a plethora of outlets in traditional, owned and social media. Furthermore, the process of cramming more advertising into traditional media, or placing ads in new locations, both online and offline, often does nothing more than irritate consumers who are increasingly resisting mass marketing messaging, either because they are now immune to its effects, disillusioned with its intent or have simply 'tuned it out'. A key challenge for marketers is how to reach and influence the growing number of people who have become disconnected from the marketing process.

Land-grab and reinvention

This situation generates threats as well as opportunities for the PR industry. Almost a decade ago Hutton (2010: 509) warned that 'the marketing field is reinventing itself to include or subsume much or all of public relations' and 'marketing thought is evolving towards a public relations perspective to such an extent that marketing is essentially redefining itself as public relations' (2010: 515). Smith (2012) complements this analysis by highlighting how emerging digital communication technology challenges the functional boundaries between public relations and marketing.

Given the blurring of boundaries between different communication disciplines and the convergence of media channels and platforms, this development looks set to continue. McKie and Willis (2012) noted the same trend emerging in award entries to the Cannes Lions International Festival of Creativity. Cannes positions itself (www.canneslions.com) as the world's largest and most prestigious advertising awards event. Their examination of winning campaigns confirms Hutton's thesis that traditional PR skills are now so mainstream across marketing that the distinct nature of the discipline, and the ownership of many of its core activities, are under threat.

This is illustrated by the Grand Prix Winner for Creative Effectiveness in 2011 from Abbot Mead

Picture 18.3 Sponsorship is a critical income stream for an event such as the Olympics and a marketing opportunity for brands. (*source:* Scott Halleran/Getty Images)

> **Think about 18.10**
>
> **Who does consumer PR?**
>
> - Look at the latest campaigns shortlisted for the Cannes Lions and other marketing communication awards.
> - Can you neatly categorise the campaign activity that is being described? For example, is it advertising, public relations, digital marketing or a combination of several different elements?
> - What sort of agencies are behind the campaigns? Look at their websites – how do they position themselves to potential clients?

Vickers BBDO (AMVBBDO) for its client PepsiCo – the international food and drinks company whose portfolio of brands includes Walkers Crisps. To promote the snack's benefits when eaten in conjunction with a sandwich the agency planned a day of surprise events 'to make the village of Sandwich national news' (Cannes Lions 2012). Media coverage was generated using celebrities and famous sporting figures engaging in a range of community activities. This was supported by online media activity, such as films that showcased the celebrity appearances.

The campaign illustrates how tools and techniques that have traditionally been associated with public relations have been subsumed seamlessly into a wider commercial offer provided by agencies strongly associated with the advertising industry. Indeed, the Cannes Lions Festival, despite showcasing the hybrid beast of modern marketing communication, cannot entirely shake off its historic label as an advertising awards event. In the AMVBBDO award entry PepsiCo is even referred to as an advertiser, despite a campaign with all the hallmarks of classic PR execution. To muddy the water still further, Cannes Lions also introduced a separate PR Award category but the winner has repeatedly been an advertising agency rather than a PR outfit (Foster 2011). (See Think about 18.10.)

New activities and practices

At the same time as grappling with the challenge of others encroaching on its territory, the PR industry is itself working in areas which were once seen as the domain of other disciplines from across the marketing spectrum. At the same time, it is also claiming expertise in emerging communication practices. A result of these developments is that the services offered by PR agencies have increased dramatically in recent years. Alongside more traditional expertise like media relations and event planning, sit new product offers designed to attract clients, such as web design, building apps, search engine optimisation, data analysis, as well as the sort of branded content activities highlighted earlier in this chapter.

In the consumer space it is therefore becoming increasingly difficult to disentangle PR from other marketing activities. Today's consumer PR practitioners find themselves shuttling between a variety of roles and tasks which are driven by the needs of their employers and/or clients. These needs, which are shaped in turn by the demands of the market place and media environment, do not correspond neatly with traditional academic theories which are concerned with what PR practitioners should and should not do (Grunig et al. 2002). Researchers can also be slow in considering the impact of new developments and ways of working, often dismissing emerging trends as the industry's latest fads and fancies.

This climate of flux also requires PR practitioners to become integrated communicators who are comfortable coordinating and using different types of communication from across the marketing mix. However, while there is a lot of discussion about the need for greater integration in a marketing context, the European Communication Monitor (Zerfass et al. 2015) reveals that since 2011 there has been hardly any progress in this area. This represents a missed opportunity on two levels. Firstly, greater collaboration across functions and teams can enhance the efficiency and effectiveness of consumer communication campaigns. Secondly, a PR perspective can more generally enhance consumer engagement activities. For example, Macnamara (2015) warns of 'the colonization of social media by marketing departments and a resulting focus on one-way transmission of promotional messages designed to sell products and services' (p. 43). He goes on to note that 'most other marketing communication remains one-way, and true engagement with customers or other stakeholders is minimal, despite widespread claims of "customer engagement"' (p. 43). PR's foundational interest in encouraging dialogue between an organisation and is stakeholders has the potential to be an antidote to these tendencies.

Summary

This chapter has discussed the role of public relations in a consumer marketing context. The world we have explored is undergoing significant and continuing change. Although the media transformation we have witnessed in the twenty-first century has affected all aspects of PR practice, the revolution in personal communication capacity has placed consumer PR on the front line of these technological advances. The aim of the chapter has been to focus on the core tenets of consumer PR, while at the same time highlighting some of the recent developments which are shaping the work carried out by practitioners in this area.

Amidst the fog and uncertainty generated by a dynamic media landscape some things remain constant. First, the mass media is still an important channel for many practitioners. While social media can dominate the working lives of consumer PR professionals, others in the sector have not abandoned more traditional channels. What we can observe, therefore, is a mixed picture of change and innovation. Second, the ability of PR practitioners to generate third party endorsement for products and services – whether in the mass, social and owned media, or amongst established and emerging groups of influencers – is still prized highly by brand owners. Indeed, in a world where advertising is not as effective as it once was, this capability is more important than ever. Although the generation of compelling content which can inform and entertain across multiple channels is a skill claimed by others across the marketing mix, the established editorial sensibilities of PR practitioners gives them an edge. A key challenge going forward though is the requirement to think more in pictures than words, given that the ubiquity of superfast broadband and emerging 5G mobile network services allows video content to be broadcast direct to the consumer.

Just as it is helpful to view the media environment as a complex adaptive system we should also do the same when thinking of PR as a profession. Rather than a static entity, PR is a discipline which continuously responds to and changes in the context in which it operates. In a consumer context this impacts on the ways in which practitioners communicate on behalf of organisations, who they seek to target, work with and so on. It is a fluid picture as the forces which shape this context – such as the media environment – are by nature difficult to predict. Who would have thought a student (Mark Zuckerburg) working in his bedroom would quickly and dramatically change the way we communicate with each other (when the first edition of this book was published in 2006 Facebook was just two years old)? Those working as PR practitioners must continue to be agile and adaptive, as should those of us who study the discipline. Furthermore, as this chapter shows, the contemporary consumer communication landscape, while offering a wealth of opportunities for PR, also generates a range of issues relating to operational effectiveness, as well as the reputation and future identity of the PR profession.

Bibliography

Cannes Lions (2012). 'Walkers, Sandwich'. www.canneslions.com/inspiration/past_grands_prix_advert.cfm?sub.channel_id=301, accessed 12 January 2012.

Forbes (2018). 'Highest-Paid YouTube Stars 2018: Markiplier, Jake Paul, PewDiePie and More'. 3 December 2018.

Foster, S. (2011). 'Aussie ad agency Clemenger BBDO Melbourne wins Cannes PR Grand Prix'. www.moreaboutadvertising.com/2011/06/aussie-ad-agency-clemenger-bbdo-melbourne-wins-cannes-pr-grand-prix, accessed 15 July 2016.

Frankfurt, H. (2005). *On Bullshit*. Princeton, NJ: Princeton University Press.

Gilpin, D.R. and P.J. Murphy (2010). 'Implications of complexity theory for public relations: beyond crisis' in *The Sage Handbook of Public Relations*. R.L. Heath (ed.). Thousand Oaks, CA: Sage.

Grunig, L., J. Grunig and D. Dozier (2002). *Excellent Public Relations and Effective Organisations: A study of communication in three countries*. Mahwah, NJ: Lawrence Erlbaum Associates.

Hutton, J. (2010). 'Defining the relationship between public relations and marketing: public relations' most important challenge' in *The Sage Handbook of Public Relations*. R.L. Heath (ed.). Thousand Oaks, CA: Sage.

Ihlen, O. and J. Pallas (2014). 'Mediatization of corporations', in *Handbook on mediatization of communication*. K. Lundby (ed.) (pp. 423–41). Berlin: De Gruyter Mouton.

Kotler, P. and Keller, K. L. (2016). *Marketing Management*. London: Pearson.

L'Etang, J. (2008). *Public Relations: Concepts, practice and critique*. London: Sage.

Lewis, D. and D. Bridger (2003). *The Soul of the New Consumer*. London: Nicholas Brealey.

Macnamara, J. (2015). 'Creating an architecture of listening in organisations: The basis of engagement, trust, healthy democracy, social equity and business accountability'. Report. Sydney, NSW: University of Technology.

McKie, D. and P. Willis (2012). 'Renegotiating the terms of engagement: Public relations, marketing and contemporary challenges'. *Public Relations Review* 38(5): 846–52.

Morgan, A. (1999*). Eating the Big Fish: How challenger brands can compete against brand leaders*. New York, NY: John Wiley.

Qvortrup, L. (2006). 'Understanding new digital media'. *European Journal of Communication* 21(3): 345–56.

Smith, B.G. (2012). 'Communication integration: An analysis of context and conditions'. *Public Relations Review* 38(4): 600–8.

The Guardian (2016). 'Why are YouTube stars so popular?' 3 February 2016.

The Times (2016). 'YouTube star 'was paid to promote game". 14 July 2016.

Variety (2014). 'Survey: YouTube stars more popular than mainstream celebs amongst US teens'. 5 August 2014.

Variety (2015). 'Digital star popularity grows versus mainstream celebrities'. 22 July 2015.

Waddington, S. (2012). 'Introduction', in *Share This: The social media handbook for PR professionals*. S. Waddington (ed.), Chichester, West Sussex: John Wiley & Sons.

Wojcicki, S. (2019). *YouTube in 2019: Looking back and moving forward* www.youtube-creators.googleblog.com, accessed 18 June 2019.

Yohn, D.L. (2014). *What great brands do: The seven brand-building principles that separate the best from the rest*. Chichester, West Sussex: John Wiley.

Zerfass, A., A. Moreno, R. Tench, D. Verčič and P. Verhoeven (2008). 'European Communication Monitor 2008. Trends in Communication Management and Public Relations – Results and Implications'. Brussels, Leipzig: Euprera/University of Leipzig. Available at: www.communicationmonitor.eu.

Zerfass, A., D. Verčič, P. Verhoven, A. Moreno, A. and R. Tench (2015). 'European Communication Monitor 2015. Creating communication value through listening, messaging and measurement. Results of a survey in 41 countries'. Brussels: EACD/EUPRERA, Helios Media.

CHAPTER 19

Helen Gill

Business-to-business public relations

Source: Vlad61/Shutterstock

Learning outcomes

By the end of this chapter you should be able to:
- define and describe business-to-business public relations
- distinguish business-to-business public relations from consumer PR
- recognise the key role of the business and trade media in shaping perceptions
- understand the evolving role of digital and social media in business-to-business reputation and relationship building
- apply this understanding to simple, relevant, real-life scenarios
- recognise business-to-business activity through case study examples.

Structure

- Core principles of business-to-business (B2B) public relations
- B2B PR as part of the wider marketing mix
- B2B media relations
- B2B social media

Introduction

The concept of business-to-business (B2B) public relations (PR) is based on the recognition that most organisations, businesses and individual professionals sell to other businesses as well as or instead of directly to the consumer. The scope of such business transactions is enormous and incorporates products and services as diverse as aircraft and microchips, law and web design. Each sector of the marketplace has its own operating environment but the fundamental need for PR and communications activity that is aligned with business goals is a key part of the selling and relationship-building process.

The traditional focus of B2B PR has been the use of **editorial** in trade magazines as a direct method of building awareness and reputation and generating new business leads with a niche regional, national or international audience. However, as Hall (2017) points out in his book *Innovative B2B Marketing: New Models, Processes and Theories*, global business has transformed over the last decade, resulting in a need for new models for B2B interactions including embracing content and digital platforms, and using online PR to engage audiences.

Indeed, contemporary B2B PR uses the full spectrum of PR techniques as the business-to-business marketplace becomes increasingly sophisticated. An examination of entries into B2B categories in the UK Chartered Institute of Public Relations Excellence Awards and the PRCA Frontline Awards shows how PR is being successfully used to manage corporate reputations and build relationships, as well as providing vital support for sales and marketing programmes. Social media – blogging, Twitter, LinkedIn, Facebook (to a lesser extent) and other platforms – are now 'at the core of both the gathering and dissemination of news' (Brown and Waddington 2013) and are widely used by B2B PR professionals and organisations to communicate directly with target customers, clients and stakeholders.

Picture 19.1 Contemporary B2B PR uses a full spectrum of PR techniques and media (*source*: Alexandra Schuler/dpa picture alliance/Alamy Stock Photo)

Core principles of business-to-business public relations

The starting point for business-to-business (B2B) PR is a detailed understanding of the business goals, specific marketplace, the application of the products or services in question and an appreciation of the dynamics of the buying process. This reflects the traditional emphasis on supporting sales and the very real need for PR activity to present the benefits of products, services or experts.

Advocates of B2B PR as a specialism say that the depth of marketplace understanding is a point of differentiation with consumer and brand public relations (see Chapter 18), where practitioner knowledge of consumer behaviour outweighs the need for product and marketplace familiarity. Simply put, B2B PR is usually about complex messages to a niche set of publics, while consumer PR is usually about simple messages to a mass audience. Therefore, the most effective B2B PR techniques, such as expert comment and case studies, are based around demonstrating expertise and outcomes, rather than directly promoting products and services.

The characteristics of a business-to-business marketplace include:

- a relatively small number of 'buying' publics – it may even be that potential customers can be named as individuals (e.g. manufacturers of niche products such as discount toilet roll will know the specific retailers who could stock their products);
- a specific application/end user for products and services (e.g. a producer of thermal insulation boards for house building);
- defined product and service terms of technical specifications and any legal/trading restrictions (e.g. an industry trade association's Code of Practice and training courses for its members);
- purchasing decision often negotiated individually and subject to finite contract periods.

The most effective use of PR from an organisational perspective is to build a favourable reputation with key stakeholders as a thought leader. And this process is critical to B2B communications, where 'reputation' is the essential element in the buying process. No one wants to do business with an organisation or individual without a reputation, and certainly not those with a poor reputation. Thus, the PR function in a

Explore 19.1

Becoming an expert

Choose a B2B field such as commercial property law or packaging design and try to find examples of people who are 'thought leaders' in this area. How do they position themselves as an expert? What do you think/feel about them as a result?

Feedback

Examples might include a lawyer writing a blog aimed at commercial clients to help them understand how new legislation impacts on their industry, a YouTube demonstration of the application of an adhesives product for the car manufacturing market, or someone being interviewed on television news about the impact of the current economic climate on businesses and organisations in a certain sector. Their commentary will usually be a simplified explanation of a complex issue, using practical examples to bring it to life for their audience.

Think about 19.1

B2B audience characteristics

As a customer of a B2B product or service, how would you go about choosing suppliers to buy from/work with? Are your priorities the same as if you were making purchasing decisions as a consumer?

Feedback

The cheapest supplier may not always be the best option. B2B transactions are often as much about working relationships as the product/service being supplied. Questions that may be asked in the procurement process include:

- Can you provide examples and testimonials from other similar organisations that you have supplied this product/service to?
- Are you able to be flexible around our organisation/marketplace's changing needs?
- Do you share our values and ethos?
- Do you meet current legislation and best practice industry standards?

B2B organisation has the same remit as that applied in a consumer or public sector organisation – to establish and maintain mutual understanding between the organisation and its publics.

This reputation-building role will become increasingly important as external stakeholders, including customers and activist groups, start to look at the organisation behind the brand (which they can now do much more easily using digital and social media) and make purchasing decisions based on wider judgements including social responsibility considerations and corporate ethics.

Organisational leaders with an understanding of PR are using PR in two interconnected ways, regardless of the size of the operation. PR works as a promotional tool with the other marketing disciplines such as advertising and sales promotion. But PR is also being used to manage the organisational reputation at board level, with audiences beyond the marketing remit, such as shareholders, the local community, staff, suppliers and government at all levels.

B2B PR as part of the wider marketing mix

The use of PR techniques to support the marketing and sales environment is well understood and is often the motivation for appointing a PR manager or using a PR consultancy. Practitioners can demonstrate that insightful and creative PR can both indirectly and directly generate business leads, opportunities and sales. However, as corporate reputation management grows in importance, B2B PR is gaining credibility and being an overarching discipline within which other marketing communication disciplines sit. Many PR practitioners argue that they should be responsible for the communications strategy at board level and marketers should carry out tactical activities to support the strategy. Though, most in-house teams are still led by marketing directors.

In B2B PR, an understanding of the role of other marketing communication disciplines is essential, as is the timing and coordinated application of the right techniques. PR practitioners working in B2B often display an in-depth understanding of advertising, email marketing, direct mail, sales and social/digital media and of how PR can act as a unifying mechanism as part of the wider business strategy.

The marketing mix, originally defined by Borden (1964), is the combination of the major tools of

Price	Product
Cost	Product management
Profitability	New development
Value for money	Product features and benefits
Competitiveness	Branding
Incentives	Packaging
	After-sales service
Place	**Promotion**
Access to target market	Promotional mix
Channels to market	Public relations
Retailers and distributors	Advertising
Logistics	Sales promotion
	Sales management
	Direct marketing
	Social media

Table 19.1 The marketing mix (*source*: adapted from Borden 1964)

marketing, otherwise known as the 4Ps – product, price, promotion and place (see Table 19.1).

Figure 19.1 shows some of the promotional disciplines typically employed in B2B marketing. All are aimed at supporting the sales effort, and their application reflects views on the best way to reach decision makers. It is often not enough to rely on one channel, hence most promotional campaigns use a combination of techniques (known as a 'multi-channel' or 'integrated' campaign) to make up the promotion aspect of the 4Ps in the marketing mix.

Role of advertising

Advertising has the very particular job of placing a proposition in front of the target audience. The strength of advertising is in the control of message delivery. Your message is placed in front of a known audience at an agreed point in time. This precise control of the message, audience and timing can make advertising very effective and the results can usually be measured and analysed.

The very best advertisements offer a single proposition in a highly creative way.

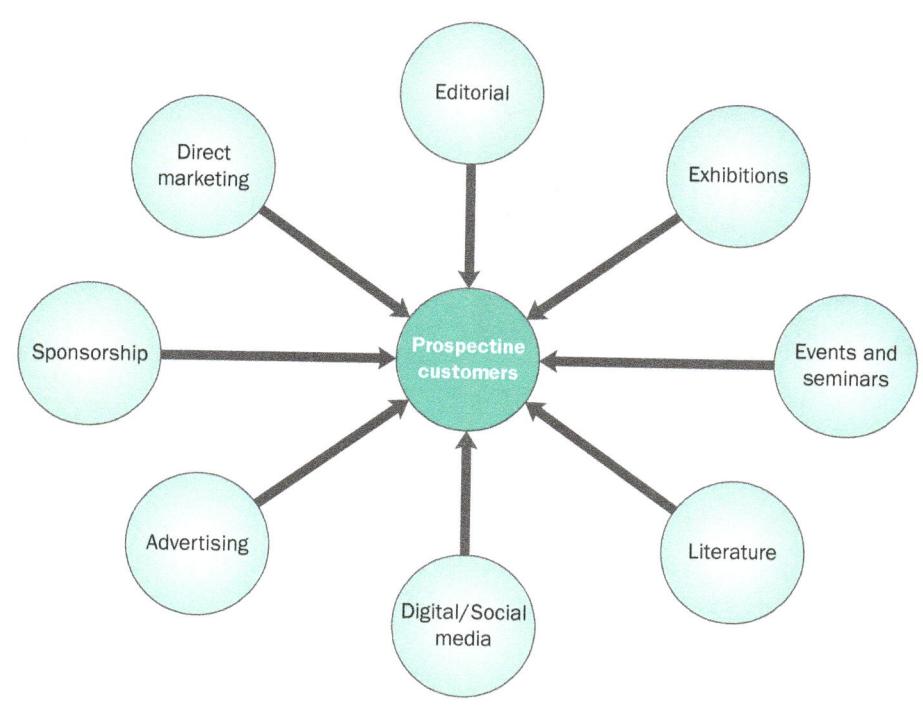

Figure 19.1 Promotional disciplines used in business-to-business (B2B) marketing

With declining readership and print sales, the importance of advertising revenue to trade magazines has increased but this doesn't mean that big advertisers can expect an editorial quid pro quo (obtain editorial coverage if they have paid for advertising space). Editorial staff cherish their independence, and this should be respected. The promise of advertising spend should not be used to influence editorial decisions. Editorial decisions should be based on the news value of content submitted in the form of press releases, comment pieces and feature articles.

Advertising has a defined role in placing repetitive messages in front of buying audiences, hence its value in B2B marketing to build long-term relationships and reputation. PR can be used in a complementary way to expand on a necessarily simple advertising message and to broaden audience reach. It is also worth noting that news value is usually enhanced if editorial is offered before an advertising campaign. Something that is already being advertised cannot really be regarded as 'news'.

However, there are instances in which paid-for advertising could be detrimental to the B2B relationship building and selling process whereby savvy customers see this as 'dumbing down' expertise or desperately seeking work, thus damaging corporate reputation (see Case study 19.1).

Role of direct marketing

Direct marketing is appropriately named as a promotional technique. The proposition is put directly to the prospective buyer, for example in an email, leaflet, brochure, or event, without an intermediary such as a distributor, agent or salesperson. This creates its major advantage in many B2B marketplaces where there are an identifiable and discrete number of buyers and/or influencers. Direct marketers traditionally worked from target lists (databases) that they either buy from a list brokerage or compile themselves with responses being tracked and measured with precision. However, General Data Protection Regulation (GDPR), which came into force in May 2018 and imposes strict rules around access to and use of customer data, has made this much more difficult and forced organisations to be less sales-lead driven, and more focused on relationship building.

Direct marketing is becoming increasingly sophisticated as a promotional technique as communication channels, message content and response rates can be tracked and refined. PR supports direct marketing by building the credibility and reputation of the organisation. It can do this by placing key messages in front of target audiences.

Case study 19.1
B2B PR as a technical sales tool: making an impact in the fintech sector

iseepr is a B2B tech PR agency established in 2005. Based in Leeds, UK, the company serves a global client base in highly specialist sectors, including fintech, payments and open banking, biometrics, secure chip technology, transport ticketing and the 'Internet of Things' (IoT).

The company was briefed to launch Silicon Valley-based open banking start-up, Token, into Europe in 2016. Since then, the agency has delivered a global media and analyst relations programme to position the firm as a revenue-generating gateway to open banking for financial institutions preparing to open their Application Programming Interfaces (APIs) in compliance with EU regulation, the Second Payment Services Directive (PSD2).

The initial objectives were to:

- generate awareness amongst banks and the wider financial services industry about the benefits of using programmable money and open banking to address a variety of payment-related challenges;
- drive Token brand awareness and recognition; and
- establish and develop relationships with key media figures and industry influencers.

Today's financial trade media are hungry for content that provides actionable insights into changes in regulation, innovations in technology and market disruption. Given Token's unique offering, the agency knew they would struggle to generate attention – the real challenge would be selecting which opportunities to accept and from which media.

The most impactful approach would be for Token to become its own publisher, creating and distributing compelling content, on its own terms, to multiple outlets. This programme encouraged syndication by the media and, as a result, delivered more coverage than working only with individual publications to provide exclusive content.

Fintech journalists and analysts are savvy, too – this isn't a media set you can bring onside with a fancy lunch and 'talking the talk'. Companies in this space have got to 'walk the walk', and while market commentary starts to build credibility, it's cemented by news stories about customer advocacy, corporate expansion and technological developments.

As such, a rolling programme of thought leadership, combined with a controlled number of exclusive articles (for the highest impact publications only), a regular flow of 'traditional' press releases, and digital content generation was created. This required agency staff to immerse themselves in Token's business and act as an extension of the internal team, rather than taking a traditional approach to the client–agency relationship.

The integrated and collaborative approach is well illustrated by a specific initiative. The agency team worked with Token's Co-founders to develop an eBook, entitled *PSD2: Hidden Revenues for Banks*, which was distributed to journalists, analysts and influencers, and was turned into thought leadership blog content for media placement, and used to underpin a targeted LinkedIn advertising campaign that was designed to attract interest in Token's offering from European banks.

In 12 months, the programme activity reached an audience of over 12,000,000, achieved 180+ coverage hits globally and attracted thousands of marketing leads, with an approximate 35 per cent conversion to qualified sales leads.

A thought leadership book provided content for journalists, analysts and influencers to attract interest in Token's offering from European banks.

Source: Erin Lovett, Senior Account Manager, iseepr

Role of sales promotion

Sales promotion techniques, such as special offers, '**bogofs**' (buy one, get one free), vouchers, redeemable gifts, competitions, etc. are well established in consumer marketing and are sometimes employed in B2B. A well-thought-through sales promotion can work and has a single objective – to increase sales. However, as with paid for advertising, it can be detrimental to corporate reputation in some sectors.

Sales promotion is very distinct from PR, but the disciplines do have much in common. When they run in tandem their effectiveness in creating sales opportunities can be enhanced. The linkage between sales

> **Think about 19.2**
>
> **B2B in action**
>
> Can you think of an exhibition/sponsorship campaign in your country or internationally that is targeted at B2B audiences?
>
> **Feedback**
>
> Think about big trade shows – for example, London Fashion Week where new fashion lines are launched to the 'trade', i.e. the people who then go on to sell them to us, the consumers. There are many other big specialist trade shows/exhibitions, such as for the automotive industry, building and even the conference/exhibition industry! To see the range of international trade exhibitions held at one site, look at the Birmingham NEC at www.thenec.co.uk.

> **Box 19.1**
>
> **Activities used in B2B public relations campaigns**
>
> Most frequently, editorial will be the lead PR tool. Other activities used in B2B PR campaigns include:
>
> - newsletters/e-newsletters;
> - literature;
> - seminars;
> - briefings;
> - conferences;
> - roadshows;
> - awards and competitions;
> - presentations;
> - sponsorship and endorsements;
> - blogging;
> - social media platforms, e.g. LinkedIn and Twitter.

promotion and PR is strong because sales promotions can offer benefits that supplement the basic product, price, place and offer.

Role of B2B public relations

B2B PR can support the other promotional disciplines and be a promotional technique. Undoubtedly, the most effective use of the promotional disciplines is shown when there is clear coordination in the planning stage. Common themes can be developed that 'work' in all channels, albeit with content and messages presented in different ways to different audiences at different times.

Creative routes can be developed jointly through '**brainstorming**', and practitioners in all the disciplines can work to a shared timetable. Cost savings will be demonstrated through minimising the time input of contributing professionals and through shared creative work (branding, design, photography, etc.).

The special role of B2B PR is in taking the proposition to a broader range of influencers using media relations and other PR techniques. Of course, PR as defined in marketing terms, as one element of the marketing mix (see Table 19.1), is a more limited concept than you will find elsewhere in this book. For a fuller discussion of PR and marketing, see Chapter 21.

The best B2B campaigns invariably use the appropriate promotional techniques in a parallel and supportive way.

B2B media relations

The business and trade media (including business newspapers, trade magazines, websites and blogs) is an important and integral part of the B2B marketplace. Examples include *The Architects' Journal*, *Building Magazine*, *PR Week*, *Dentistry News* and *Insurance Times*. The traditional use of media relations techniques in trade and specialist publications also requires a detailed understanding of the workings and requirements of these titles and their editors.

Managers and professionals tend to read the print and online titles and blogs specific to their trade or industry as part of their working lives (see Box 19.2). And it is this special linkage that attributes influence to trade and specialist magazines, websites and blogs.

Readership relates to the size of the sector and the existence or otherwise of competitive titles. Trade publications large and small are read by decision makers in their sector. The loyalty of trade press readerships creates a strong role for their titles in the B2B cycle of influence and persuasion.

This accounts for the traditional B2B PR focus on gaining editorial coverage in trade magazines.

Box 19.2

How trade publications are used by B2B professionals in the digital age

The following interview discusses how a practising real estate and banking litigation specialist uses B2B titles such as *Mortgage Finance Gazette* in her everyday working life. Christina Gill is a fully qualified Solicitor under the age of 30 who works at Top 100 UK law firm Walker Morris LLP:

Do you actively read your trade media on a regular basis?

I receive Case Law Updates in my email inbox every morning and weekly digests from legal journals such as *New Law Journal* plus real estate industry titles that my clients read such as *Estates Gazette* and *Mortgage Finance Gazette*. They combine news, case commentary from experts, and more in-depth articles and feature pieces on different practice areas and trending topics. There may also be new book reviews and profiles on individual experts, and quarterly reviews of the biggest and most important cases.

I read them all and pick out what is most relevant to me that week or save and flag articles that I think may be relevant to refer to later. I then use the insight I gain from them in my day-to-day work to advise clients on similar cases and issues.

Have you noticed trade media becoming more digitally focused in recent years?

Definitely. Even just in the five years that I've been working in a law firm we've moved from getting hard copies of journals and trade magazines to just receiving them digitally, which I prefer. The articles at the bottom of the daily Case Law Updates I receive used to be in print only so if there was something that looked interesting, I'd have to ask the firm's library to get a hard copy in but most of them can now be accessed in full via a link in the email. It means I can read things on my phone on the train on the way into work so that I'm fully up to date when I arrive at my desk.

The articles are more bite-size than they used to be, there are more pieces focused on digital trends; there is always something about digital transformation in the legal and property sectors. There's so much content out there, it's much easier to keep my finger on the pulse with filtered digital content that's tailored to my areas of work.

Can you give an example of how you've used the knowledge gained from reading and staying up to date with your trade media that has enabled you to position yourself as an expert in relevant titles?

The journals I use are quite often good to prompt an article from me commenting on something that is on the agenda, or to embellish my articles from a legal perspective. The focus on digital transformation I mentioned before has been useful for me as it's something that the Land Registry is focused on, so I've managed to get quite a few articles published about e-conveyancing where I've drawn on the insight and trends I've read about.

Reading these journals and publications also helps me understand how to identify what is different and most interesting about a topic so that it is more likely to get picked up by the journalist and helps me to write for wider audiences by stripping out some of the legal jargon and explaining things in simple terms that readers can understand. For example, I did an article on the move to electronic mortgage deeds for the *Mortgage Finance Gazette*, which is read by people from across banks and building societies who are not legally qualified. It went in the legal section, but it had to be easy for lender clients to understand, explaining what they need to be aware of and what steps they need to take to prepare for the change.

How have you positioned yourself as an expert and pitched articles like this to trade titles?

I was approached by *Mortgage Finance Gazette* to submit the article after it was published in my firm's own legal update, which a lot of journalists sign up to. It was also picked up by Lexis Nexis who asked me to adapt it into a Q&A. We publish and share a lot more content ourselves than we used to which gives the firm more profile and means it's easier to get more media coverage. Our Professional Support Lawyers and marketing team are good at drip-feeding articles as and when they're relevant so that they have the most impact. Sometimes, topics will get jumped to the front of the queue if they're being discussed in the trade media.

Journalists may also pick up articles from the firm's or my personal Twitter and LinkedIn accounts, or from our corporate website. The marketing team send us updates on our social media activity every week – what articles have been shared, which were the 'most read' etc. – which helps us to understand what topics and types of comment are the most popular.

Do you use social media personally to track what's happening in your sector?

Definitely. LinkedIn has become more and more important for keeping up to date with what's happening in my area in recent years. I now find useful articles and comment pieces daily in my LinkedIn and Twitter news feeds.

More digitally-savvy lawyers now seem to have their fingers on the pulse a lot more which helps us to advise clients and colleagues more effectively, and build our own reputations. Waiting for paper copies can result in it taking a lot longer to pick up on what's trending and means things can be missed in other sectors, but most lawyers are moving towards digital and social channels to monitor what's happening.

How does the impact of the strategic B2B media relations you do compare with other profile raising activities such as advertising?

For the kind of work, we do, adverts can help raise brand awareness, but they don't tell audiences whether we're any good or know what we're talking about. For professional services firms like ourselves, it's often more beneficial to invest our time and resources in thought leadership content. Commenting on hot topics on a regular basis keeps us front of mind with existing and potential clients and keeps reinforcing the message that we're the experts and can be trusted to advise them. It is more subtle but has a greater impact.

Quality over quantity is important; we need to be on the radar, but it is better to wait until there is something useful to say, rather than just commenting for the sake of it.

What about confidentiality issues?

Unless we have a case that's reported by the Courts in the legal media, it is difficult to go into specifics, so we need to be able to provide the journalist with just enough interesting detail without giving too much away. We also must be careful about what we say that may be detrimental to our clients. Everything is very carefully checked and approved before it goes out of the door. We don't necessarily want the big news story on the front page – we would rather get more in-depth commentary-style coverage which explains an issue.

Sometimes journalists can quite heavily edit what we provide but when you are talking about complex issues, just a small change can change or distort the meaning, which is something we must be careful about as getting the details wrong could tarnish our reputation.

Source: Interview with Solicitor Christina Gill

However, due to declining advertising revenues and increasing competition from digital and social media, the print versions of many long-established trade publications in the UK have been discontinued and those that are still in existence have fewer editorial staff on tighter deadlines, with greater pressures to contribute to selling advertising space (Dowell 2011).

Those trade publications that remain in print version tend to be the one or two key opinion-forming titles in each sector (building, health, retail, finance, etc.). These are the journals/periodicals that influence the business/sector and they are the ones organisations will look to for editorial coverage and discussion about their organisation. It's important when working in the B2B sector that you research and understand which publications, websites and blogs are key to your organisation/client organisation. It is important to note, therefore, that some publications have high 'news value' and others very low. You need to be able to discern and make use of the difference.

Business or trade media and journalists

As a PR practitioner, you will routinely find that trade press journalists have a thorough understanding of their subject area. This fact creates both an opportunity and a challenge for the practitioner. You will have an informed and potentially responsive audience. But you will need to be knowledgeable and show your competence when dealing with trade journalists. However, also remember that we all must start our careers somewhere, so you may be dealing with a **junior reporter** or a journalist who has moved recently to a title. The big media groups (such as Haymarket which owns titles as diverse as *PRWeek*, *What Car?* and *GPOnline*) have a raft of trade titles, and journalists move frequently between titles and specialist areas. They may still be learning about their new subject area, perhaps at the same time as you.

As a rule of thumb, when dealing with trade press journalists or bloggers, assume expertise. This is usually the case and it is common for editors of relatively small circulation magazines or blogs to be frequent commentators on television news programmes and in the national dailies. This is simply because such individuals do become genuine experts through their professional concentration on a subject area. For example, the editor of *The Grocer* is often used on national business broadcasts on radio and television as an expert commentator on supermarket trends and prices.

Since most trade media and journalists will also now use digital and social media to extend the reach of their content, it is necessary to adapt press releases to include 'elements a reporter would want to see before they create their own content to broadcast or transmit further' – known as a 'Social Media Release' (Steyna et al. 2010: 87).

Story ideas

The news values of trade publications obviously have a sector-specific focus, and regular reading of key magazines will readily identify the news angles adopted. Practitioners working in a B2B marketplace should be avid readers of the sector's periodicals and know which ones are most influential and credible.

News will usually be presented to the media through a press release, but other techniques of regular use to B2B PR practitioners include:

- one-to-one briefings and interviews;
- full feature articles;
- comment to be included in wider features;
- case studies;
- press conferences; and
- conferences, workshops, roundtable discussions and other events.

Some of these techniques are covered in Chapter 14, but here are some other techniques that are available to the PR practitioner.

Advertorials

The advertorial is also used frequently in B2B promotional campaigns. Advertorials are paid-for advertisements designed to look like editorial. However, journals will always indicate clearly the sponsoring company in order to differentiate from editorial. So, although advertorials may look like editorial, they do not have the credibility of news or features material written and/or edited by journalists. As advertising revenues and circulation figures decline, advertorials are becoming a key source of revenue for trade publications and journalists will

---

Think about 19.3

Typical news angles for B2B editorial

Flick through a selection of trade publications and try to identify articles that have been pitched for B2B PR purposes. What messages are they trying to convey? How is this different from more consumer-focused articles which mention consumer brands?

Feedback

Typical news angles for B2B editorial would include:

- comment on latest industry developments, innovations, trends and legislation;
- insights from major industry conferences and events;
- new senior technical and managerial appointments;
- new technology and new processes;
- new contracts;
- unusual or problem-solving contracts and applications;
- market diversification or convergence;
- partnerships, associations, mergers, takeovers;
- high-impact case studies.

---

often try and sell them as an alternative to sub-standard editorial content pitched by PR practitioners.

From the practitioner's perspective, an advertorial is often regarded as promotional material and treated much like a newsletter or a company publication.

Websites and blogs

Note must also be taken of the specialist websites which have gained common currency in most industry sectors. Many specialist and trade publications maintain their own websites to complement their printed publications. Equally, the trade associations operating in each sector often have websites. Major industry events such as conferences, seminars and exhibitions are also frequently supported by websites. Such websites are both a vital source of information for practitioners and offer an additional source of target outlets for placing product and corporate news and information.

Beyond the specific product or company-related news items, trade magazines offer a particularly good opportunity to place commentary on marketplace, technology and product developments. In-depth material available through your client company may be highly valued by the editor of trade magazines. In practice, this creates the opportunity for a client or company to be a source of authoritative industry information.

B2B social media

In his book *Engage! The complete guide for brands and businesses to build, cultivate and measure success in the new web*, Brian Solis describes social media as 'a matter of digital Darwinism that affects all forms of marketing and service' (Solis 2010: xvii). By this he means that communications are evolving with technology and that social media is more than just a 'fad' – its use has become fundamental to business. The use of social media in B2B public relations is now well established with corporate blogging being a key technique for building expertise and reputation.

While the B2B market has been much slower than the B2C (business-to-consumer) market to embrace social media, in *The B2B Social Media Book* (2012), Bodner and Cohen argue that there are five reasons

---

Explore 19.2

Finding B2B case study examples

Go into a large newsagent or magazine shop and see how many magazine/journal titles you can see that are non-consumer and are targeting the trade/specialist business-to-business marketplace. Also do a Google search for influential business websites and blogs for specific sectors. Find examples of articles that feature case study examples of a business helping another business succeed through their expertise, products and services.

Feedback

Case studies will usually appear after the main news headlines and tell a story of how a specific business problem was solved. In most cases, this will feature some sort of 'human interest' angle to bring it to life such as a testimonial from a happy customer. For confidentiality reasons (see Box 19.2) exact details of the case/customer name may not be given but a similar example will be described.

Explore 19.3 Creating business-to-business conversations online

How could you help an organisation or client get into dialogue with potential clients and customers? Search on Twitter and LinkedIn for examples of B2B organisations interacting with each other.

Feedback

B2B sales are often relationship based. B2B organisations, such as law firms, often must 'sell' the expertise of individuals within the business. Using social media such as Twitter and LinkedIn it is possible to give these individual experts a voice and the ability to engage directly with target customers. However, their complex messages need to be translated into accessible content that acts as a talking point – and can be distilled into concise statements (e.g. tweets that are no longer than 140 characters, or 500-word blogs broken down into useful points).

This is often where B2B PR practitioners can use their expertise to advise, train and create content that enables organisations and individuals to communicate and engage more effectively and strategically using social media.

The use of social media as part of B2B PR can work in conjunction with trade media relations. Many trade and business journalists now use Twitter for most of their news and feature leads, and most trade journals use social media platforms to share their content with a wider specialist audience.

Social media tools used by B2B PR practitioners include blogs, Twitter (www.twitter.com), LinkedIn (www.linkedin.com), YouTube (www.youtube.com), and to a lesser extent Facebook (www.facebook.com), Pinterest (www.pinterest.com) and Instagram (www.instagram.com). Other platforms are emerging and evolving all the time. These platforms give B2B companies and professionals the opportunity to engage directly with potential and existing customers and clients to demonstrate expertise, raise awareness, build reputation and indirectly sell their products and services.

The etiquette of social media – informality, sharing, collaboration, freedom of speech (Solis 2010) – is often at odds with the way B2B professionals are used to working. As such, there is an important role for B2B PR practitioners to advise and train colleagues and clients in adapting their communications style and techniques. In many cases, PR practitioners are responsible for managing and monitoring social media channels on behalf of B2B organisations and creating tailored content that makes their specialist areas of expertise more accessible and engaging to a wider audience.

why B2B companies are better suited to using social media to generate business:

1. Clear understanding of customers
2. Depth of subject matter expertise
3. Need for generating higher revenue with lower marketing budgets
4. Relationship-based sales
5. Already have practice using social media principles of telling business-focused stories and educating customers with content.

All five of these reasons relate to key elements of B2B PR and communications and demonstrate why B2B social media belongs within the PR discipline – as opposed to marketing, advertising or web development.

Picture 19.2 A cross-platform campaign for international stationery brand STAEDTLER drove more than £5.6 million in sales (*source*: Atmán Victor/agefotostock/Alamy Stock Photo)

Case study 19.2
Using social media to generate commercial results in the education sector

In 2012, international stationery brand STAEDTLER commissioned Welsh agency Equinox to create a fully-integrated communications model to drive sales in the education sector. STAEDTLER Teachers' Club UK – an online platform for primary school teachers to access quality teaching resources, classroom competitions and free product samples – was born.

By 2017, although the Club continued to see year-on-year growth, it was becoming more challenging to make an impact online due to ever-changing social media algorithms limiting the reach of content, increased competition from other brands investing more online, and savvy users being more selective about the content they wish to consume. The aim of the 2017–2018 campaign was to further engage the teaching community through social media, thus building brand loyalty and ultimately, driving sales.

The objectives were to:

- increase social media followers to 36,750;
- reach 200,000 social media users through original web content;
- secure 100,000 views of original multi-media content;
- attract 37,000 web sessions and 63,000 web page views;
- secure 11,000 'good quality' members by December 2018;
- secure teacher endorsements;
- develop worthwhile brand partnerships;
- contribute to education channel sales.

A social media audit and research with teachers was carried out to inform the strategy, which identified that it was more important than ever for the Club to produce highly relevant, original and shareable content to provide primary school teachers with the very best experience. As the main referral driver and hub for brand engagement, Facebook was key to Teachers' Club's success. Twitter and YouTube were secondary channels. Themes, interactivity, variety, timing and engagement were considered carefully when creating content for maximum impact.

To give the Club a fresh approach in 2017–18, as well as remaining aware of academic dates and calendar hooks to demonstrate key themes and topics, the team developed high-level brand partnerships with Penguin Schools and the presenter of Disney's Art Attack to run interactive competitions, produced enhanced content through 'Break-time Reading' (a 'Buzzfeed' for primary school teachers), and created more bespoke branded multimedia content including a 'STAEDTLER Crafty' series of how-to-videos. They also appointed a Teachers' Club Ambassador to create video content and facilitate discussions in the Club Facebook group off the back of the

2018 Facebook algorithm update favouring discussion-led content with friends and family over brand pages.

These campaign initiatives generated cross-platform content, drove membership (must register to enter), and got the STAEDTLER brand into the heart of the classroom, benefiting via brand association when teachers made stationery purchasing decisions.

All objectives set were exceeded. The campaign reached 250,000 social media users, secured 172,000 views of multi-media content, generated 14,000 new 'good quality' members and contributed to £5.6 million of sales.

Source: Cymru Wales PRide Awards 2018, winner of Best Use of Social Media

Summary

B2B PR will always concentrate on supporting the commercial performance and business goals of an organisation. The mainstay of this support has been well-placed thought leadership content via the trade media and blogs, which is read by influencers and decision makers in the buying process (the buying chain). This 'works', and there are good examples showing just how the craft skills of PR can be applied with outstanding results. This core activity is fundamental to B2B PR, and B2B practitioners can demonstrate in-depth knowledge of their client organisations, of products, services and applications, and of the mechanisms of the marketplace. The trade media landscape is developing, and online/social media is becoming an increasingly important B2B PR tool for demonstrating expertise and engaging with and selling directly to clients and customers.

The understanding that buying decisions are not solely based on promotion, price, place and product (the marketing mix: Brassington and Pettitt 2013) but also on *reputation* offers scope for PR practitioners to adopt a holistic approach to B2B communications. The concept of the influence of the 'brand' is established in consumer PR. It is now recognised that the brand – and all it stands for – is also relevant to B2B (Koporcic et al. 2018). This is an evolving area of B2B practice, with increased opportunity for creativity in supporting communications in the field.

It is also the case that buying decisions are no longer left to individuals in an organisation; their decisions may have to withstand the scrutiny of a range of internal and external stakeholders. Thus, an integrated communications strategy is essential, with consistent messages being communicated to diverse audiences.

The use of editorial and social media to support the sales environment is an essential element of most B2B PR campaigns. However, there is a fundamental difference between media relations and online engagement as a promotional technique and the comprehensive application of PR methodology to analyse trends, counsel organisational leaders and to plan and deliver reputation-building communications programmes. Media relations and social media can be used as part of the marketing mix alongside the other promotional disciplines, such as advertising and email marketing, to great effect. But the true impact of PR is seen when applied as a strategic planning tool in support of top-line corporate objectives.

An examination of award-winning B2B public relations campaigns shows a clear trend towards integrated support for sales and marketing efforts beyond media relations. Senior practitioners are imposing their professionalism on client organisations to use PR methodology to plan strategically, to integrate and unify communications around wider business goals and to build reputation with key stakeholders before the sales process is engaged. Good examples can be found on the websites of national PR organisations such as the UK's CIPR and PRCA.

Bibliography

Brown, R. and S. Waddington (2013). *Share This Too*. London: John Wiley & Sons.

Bodner, K. and J.L. Cohen (2012). *The B2B Social Media Book*. New Jersey: John Wiley & Sons.

Borden, N. (1964). 'The concept of the marketing mix'. *Journal of Advertising Research* June: 2–7.

Brassington, F. and S. Pettitt (2013). *Essentials of Marketing*. London: Pearson.

Dowell, B. (2011). 'Have trade magazines got a shelf life?' *The Guardian*. 25 April. www.guardian.co.uk/media/2011/apr/25/trade-magazines-online-only, accessed 28 August 2012.

Hall, S. (2017). *Innovative B2B Marketing: New Models, Processes and Theory*. London: Kogan Page.

Koporcic, N., M. Ivanova-Gongne, A. Nyström and J. Törnroos (2018). *Developing Insights on Branding in the B2B Context: Case Studies from Business Practice*. Emerald Publishing.

Solis, B. (2010). *Engage! The complete guide for brands and businesses to build, cultivate, and measure success in the new web*. New Jersey: John Wiley & Sons.

Steyna, P., E. Salehi-Sangari, L. Pitt, M. Parent and P. Berthond (2010). 'The Social Media Release as a public relations tool: Intentions to use among B2B bloggers'. *Public Relations Review* 36: 87–89.

Websites

Chartered Institute of Public Relations (CIPR): www.cipr.co.uk
CIPR PRide Awards: www.ciprawards.co.uk/pride
Public Relations Consultants Association (PRCA): www.prca.org.uk
Twitter: www.twitter.com
LinkedIn: www.linkedin.com
Facebook: www.facebook.com
YouTube: www.youtube.com
Pinterest: www.pinterest.com
Instagram: www.instagram.com
The NEC Birmingham www.thenec.co.uk

CHAPTER 20

Danny Moss

Public affairs

Source: HelloRF Zcool/Shutterstock

Learning outcomes

By the end of this chapter you should be able to:

- identify and critically discuss the nature, role and scope of the public affairs function and its relationship with public relations
- identify and critically review key theories, principles and their development and application in contemporary public affairs
- appreciate the value of public affairs in terms of its potential contribution to the success of organisational strategies and goals
- identify and critically review the knowledge, skills and competencies required of today's public affairs professionals
- appreciate how to apply public affairs theories/principles in practice
- evaluate your learning about public affairs and pursue further sources for investigation.

Structure

- Locating the role of public affairs within the organisation
- Defining public affairs: a confused professional identity
- The scope of public affairs
- Lobbying
- International perspectives on public affairs and lobbying
- Public affairs management

Introduction: the what and why of public affairs?

To say that we all exist in an increasingly connected world is a truism that affects not only larger corporate and small businesses, but also not-for-profit organisations, governments and transnational organisations around the world. Moreover, the notion of living in an information-rich age, fuelled by the proliferation of social and digital media means that no organisation no matter how large and powerful can afford to think it can operate in isolation and immunity from such influences. The recent (Spring 2019) international movement of schoolchildren protesting at the lack of concerted government action to tackle the threat of climate change illustrates the way social media can and has been used to mobilise public opinion and marshal large protest rallies.

Against this backdrop of increasing connectivity and social media-based information exchange, businesses around the world are facing ever greater demands for transparency about the nature of their operations and their impact on the communities in which they exist. These demands are ones that government bodies and legislators are often under considerable pressure to listen and respond to, which may then result in regulatory or legislative action that may constrain or even derail the plans and ambitions of business.

Picture 20.1 Greta Thunberg speaks at COP25 about 'Fridays For Future' movement (*source:* Pablo Blazquez Dominguez/Getty Images)

Box 20.1

The power of social media and public opinion

This current era of greater information transparency and rapid proliferation of social media has manifest itself within the business world in terms of a marked change in the way many businesses think about and relate to their stakeholders. Firstly, arguably the past two to three decades in particular, have witnessed an almost seismic change in business priorities often shifting from a narrow profit maximising, customer–supplier focal axis, towards a more pluralistic, multi-stakeholder orientation in which profitability may have to be balanced alongside other priorities affecting the longer-term sustainability of the business.

Against this backdrop, it is increasingly the case that larger corporations, in particular, will tend to have a well-established system of stakeholder monitoring, designed to keep senior management appraised of any issues/developments affecting individual or multiple stakeholders, which might, in turn, have implications for their own organisation's policies and operational tactics. Almost inevitably, the larger the business organisation the greater and more complex will be the network of those stakeholder relationships it needs to monitor and manage. Equally, it follows that when larger organisations make significant policy changes the ripple effect will be felt amongst greater numbers of related stakeholders, which will, in turn, be more likely to attract the attention of local as well perhaps national or even international governments and government bodies.

The challenge of managing what can be a quite complex array of stakeholder relationships has led many larger corporate businesses to recognise the value of having a well-organized and professional communications and public affairs function capable of handling any contingencies that may arise that might threaten the stability and reputation of the organisation (Argenti 2009; van Riel 1995). Indeed in many societies including the UK and many EU countries, regulations and legislative intervention has become a significant potential constraint on the operations and expansion plans of many businesses. The controversy surrounding attempts by the exploration company Cuadrilla to secure licences for fracking for shale gas at sites in the UK (see Mini case study 20.1) and the repeated delays caused by the objections voiced by affected communities along the planned route for the £56 billion HS2 high-speed rail link project between London and the North of England are good examples of challenge that many businesses can face when dealing with a high-profile controversial issue that has the potential to 'blow up' in the face of focal organisation.

Mini case study 20.1
The fracking controversy

One of the more controversial issues in recent years that well illustrates the potential importance of the public affairs function is the controversy that has surrounded attempts by the exploration company Cuadrilla Ltd (a subsidiary of Cuadrilla Resource Holdings Ltd (CRH)) to secure licences to explore for shale gas at a number of sites in the UK, using a process termed 'fracking', which involves shattering hard shale rocks underground to release gas using either hydraulic pressure or tiny explosions. Although fracking originated in the USA in the 1970s, interest in the use of this gas extraction technique has spreads to many other countries in recent years despite some quite intense opposition and protest almost wherever licences have been sought. The opposition to fracking has centred on fears of damage to the environment and pollution of underground water courses caused by the fracking process as well as the potential to trigger minor earthquakes; arguments that environmentalist groups such as Friends of the Earth have repeatedly emphasised in opposing fracking licences. Cuadrilla's public affairs staff fought back challenging some of the more alarmist stories circulated by opposition groups and submitting evidence of the economic benefits of energy extraction through fracking to both local authority planning committees and to the key UK government officials in Defra and the Treasury. Cuadrilla suffered a serious setback to its planned expansion in the UK in 2011, when minor earthquakes in the Fylde coast/Blackpool area in Lancashire were claimed to be caused by local fracking activity, and as a result all fracking in the UK was suspended pending detailed investigation on behalf of Defra. The fact that some four years later Cuadrilla were in a position to submit a credible proposal for two new test fracking sites in Lancashire at Little Plumpton and Roseacre Wood, arguably can be attributed in part at least to the success of its public affairs work in laying the ground for the company to submit their proposals to local planning authorities. A similar sort of regulatory and planning problem has been faced by companies seeking to expand the development of off-shore and on-land wind farms around the UK where planning applications have continued to come up against strong local and pressure group opposition which has often hampered their progress.

What these examples illustrate is that in today's society where the actions of businesses and industries are increasingly subject to public and /or official scrutiny and even regulation, public affairs can be an essential tool in enabling industries and individual organisations to ensure their voice is heard and that they obtain a 'fair hearing' in the 'court of public opinion' or perhaps more important, that key decision makers in government or other key regulatory bodies are fully aware of all sides of a case when important decisions are taken.

Picture 20.2 Global climate and anti-fracking demonstration in London (*source*: Kristian Buus/In Pictures/Getty Images)

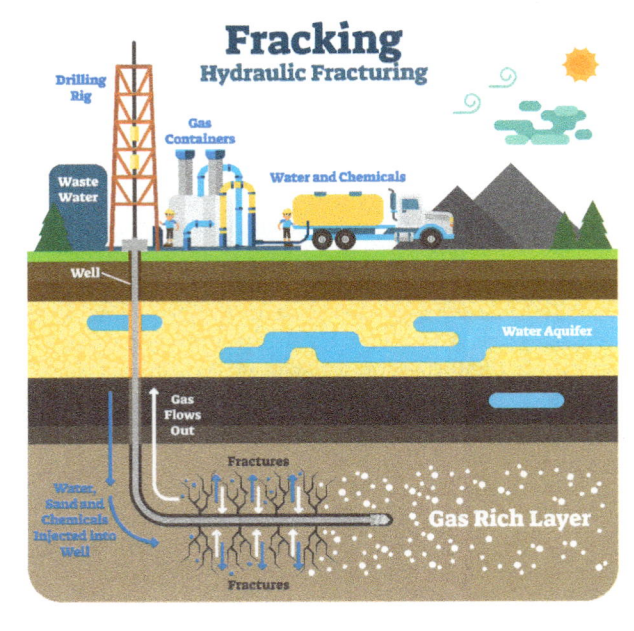

Picture 20.3 Fracking involves shattering hard shale rocks underground to release gas using either hydraulic pressure or tiny explosions. This controversial technique has been used in a number of sites across the UK (*source*: VectorMine/Shutterstock)

Locating the role of public affairs within the organisation

The above two case examples illustrate the growing pressures on businesses, particularly those businesses operating in high-profile sectors (e.g. utilities, pharmaceuticals, transport, banking etc.) or in industries or situations that are likely to bring them into potential conflict with regulators, planners, local or national interest groups and others with a vested interest in a particular issue or situation that requires careful management to advance the business's interests. The fracking issue discussed above is a perfect example of just such a scenario where Cuadrilla Ltd's ambitions to expand its exploration for shale gas in the UK has met vociferous opposition both in the local community as well as at a national level from concerned environmentalist groups. It is when businesses face strong opposition to their plans and may be struggling to have their arguments heard above the clamour of opposition that they may turn to public affairs to help get their case across to the relevant authorities. Here the corporate public affairs function can be seen to act both as the 'corporate voice' and advocate of the business's interests (Cornelissen 2008; Heath 1994; Hutton et al. 2001), while also seeking to assuage the concerns of opposing parties. This potentially difficult 'balancing act' of representing business and stakeholder interests is likely to become all the more complicated and challenging when corporations are operating across many international or global markets, and hence across a range of governmental and regulatory regimes. Thus an understanding of the role and scope of contemporary public affairs needs to be set against the particular environmental context or background in which the organisation(s) in question operate. Clearly where organisations face an increasingly politicised business environment, as is increasingly the case in most Western economies, the need for an effectively resourced public affairs function is all the more likely to be evident. Yet even here there may be quite wide variations found both in the extent to which public affairs is recognised and supported across sectors of industry or even within particular sectors, which may reflect management attitudes and prejudices towards public affairs rather than any inherent differences in the need for public affairs support between organisations or across sectors. This tendency will often be exacerbated when looking at the management of public affairs within organisations operating on an international or global scale. Here a degree of confusion about what precisely public affairs is and what expertise it requires has resulted in quite wide variations in not only who has responsibility for public affairs work within organisations, but also how it is resourced, and what expectations senior management have of what the function can realistically achieve.

Defining public affairs: a confused professional identity

Despite the significant growth of professional interest in (corporate) public affairs over the past decade or more, and a growing body of academic and professional literature about public affairs (Griffin and Dunn 2004; Hillman 2002; Showalter and Fleisher 2005), there is still considerable confusion about what public affairs is, or how it contributes to organisational success. This confusion is perhaps hardly surprising given there is still a lack of consensus among public affairs scholars and professionals themselves about the meaning of the term 'public affairs' (Fleisher and Blair 1999; McGrath et al. 2010). Nevertheless, some scholars have advanced definitions which seek to capture the essence and main characteristics of public affairs and which have gained some traction in professional and academic circles. For example, writing from a European perspective, Pedler (2002: 4) has suggested that: 'Public affairs may be defined as the management skill that *internalises* the effects of the environment in which an organisation operates and *externalises* actions to influence that environment.'

In what is still one of the more widely acknowledged explanations of public affairs, Post (1982: 30) suggests that: 'the critical role of the public affairs unit is to serve as a *window out* of the corporation, enabling management to act in the external environment, and a *window in* through which society influences corporate policy and practice.' This two-way perspective of public affairs can be seen to mirror in many ways the 'two way symmetrical' model of public relations that Grunig and his co-researchers (1992, 2002) have argued strongly represents the most effective and 'excellent' model of public relations practice. In the case of public affairs, the emphasis is ideally about balancing the organisation and external stakeholders' interests, particularly where these respective interests coalesce around issues that have some public policy dimension.

The uncertainty over how to define public affairs also extends to understanding of who and how many people work in the field of public affairs within the UK let alone worldwide. While uncertainty continues to surround the size and make-up of the public affairs sector in the UK and worldwide, a recent survey commissioned by the Public Relations Consultants Association (PRCA: www.prca.org.uk) suggested that some 86,000 people work in public relations and communications in the UK (2018). Although there was no specific breakdown of this number to indicate how many might work in public affairs, around 22 per cent of the respondents suggested that they worked in 'corporate public relations', which might arguably embrace some elements of public affairs. Of course the other caveat in interpreting such figures is that the vast majority of respondents to the PRCA database tend to be consultants and hence working in an agency setting rather than being in-house personnel. Further tangential evidence from Public Affairs Networking (www.publicaffairsnetworking.com) points to some 4,000 members across the UK and Europe. However, rather than being fixated with the question of how many people might work exclusively as public affairs professionals in the UK, it is perhaps more appropriate to return to the more pertinent question of what specifically public affairs professionals do. Given the degree of confusion that arguably still surrounds the whole area public affairs, Harris and Moss's (2001) comments expressed nearly two decades ago that the term 'public affairs' 'remains one that is surrounded by ambiguity and misunderstanding, and that public affairs remains a function in search of a clear identity' (p. 102) still appear to ring true today.

The scope of public affairs

Traditionally public affairs tends to be seen as the organisational function that focuses particularly on managing organisational relationships with government, government bodies and other political stakeholders. This notion of public affairs serving as an 'intermediary' and interpretive function between business and governments is reflected in the underlying mission of perhaps the most prominent industry association in the field of public affairs, the Washington-based *Public Affairs Council* (see Box 20.3) whose mission is to 'help the business community have a more effective voice in dealing with

Box 20.2
Public policy

Often public affairs is seen as focusing on handling and engaging on behalf of an organisation in public discourse about 'public policy' issues that might affect society and also have implications for the organisation's operations and/or future success.

The preferred definition of public policy for our purpose is:

> Public policy is a purposive and consistent course of action produced as a response to a perceived problem of a constituency, formulated by a specific political process, and adopted, implemented and enforced by a public agency.

government.' However, as its mission statement suggests, public affairs is seen to embrace a broader remit than simply government relations. Indeed, public affairs is also increasingly seen to have a broader outward-facing remit that encompasses communication and other relational activities directed towards a broader cross-section of organisational stakeholders and embracing at times a broader 'public policy' agenda (see Box 20.2). This broader 'definition' or interpretation of the remit of public affairs is illustrated in Figure 20.1.

Returning to the traditional core distinctive domain of public affairs, one relatively simple but powerful way of conceiving of where and how public affairs is likely to come to the fore and figure prominently as a key component of an organisation's communication strategy is in the form of a simplified '*business, citizens and government* Venn diagram' model (see Figure 20.2), which illustrates the overlapping spheres of interest that may exist (to a greater or lesser degree) between the three entities – business, citizens and government in any given scenario. While, of course, not all situations involving business and citizens will necessarily also involve any obvious political or public policy dimension. Indeed in the vast majority of cases, such as in normal commercial exchanges and trading relationships, or employee relationships no such political dimension will normally exist, and hence, there may be no need for specialist public affairs involvement, but in today's increasingly politicised world, even decisions and policies that might seem purely commercial can take on a 'political dimension' whether locally or centrally depending on the issues surrounding the situation. Thus, for example, where a company is one of the only major employers in a region or city, any decisions to curtail investment or even close a local plant may inevitably have significant socio-economic and political implications for that region and for the reputation of the company. In such circumstances the tripartite business–citizen–government relationship will come to the fore, and the public affairs function would be expected to play a significant part in mediating between the company and regional or central government, as well as with representative employee and local citizen groups. Mini case study 20.2 illustrates how such engagement may be needed.

Public Affairs

Broad Definitions of Public Affairs   **Narrow Definitions of Public Affairs**

Government Relations
Plus

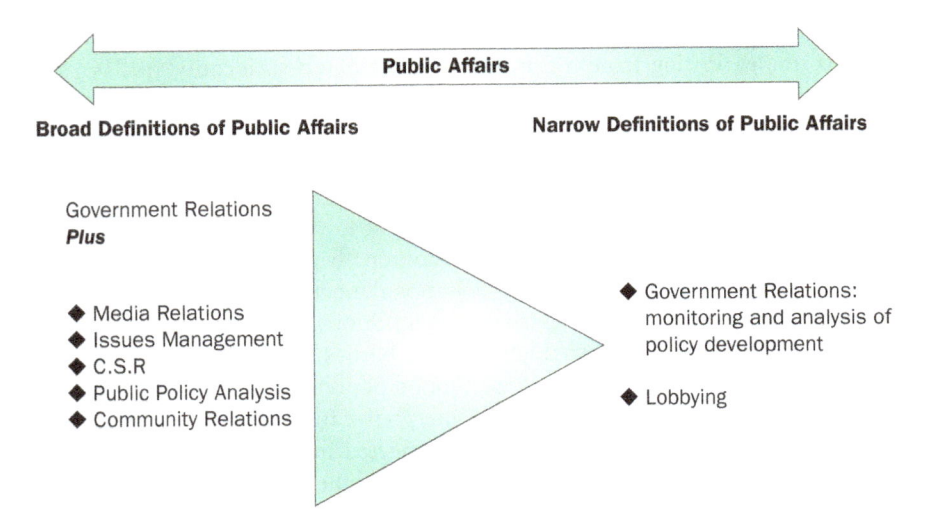

- Media Relations
- Issues Management
- C.S.R
- Public Policy Analysis
- Community Relations

- Government Relations: monitoring and analysis of policy development
- Lobbying

Figure 20.1 Broad and narrow definitions of public affairs

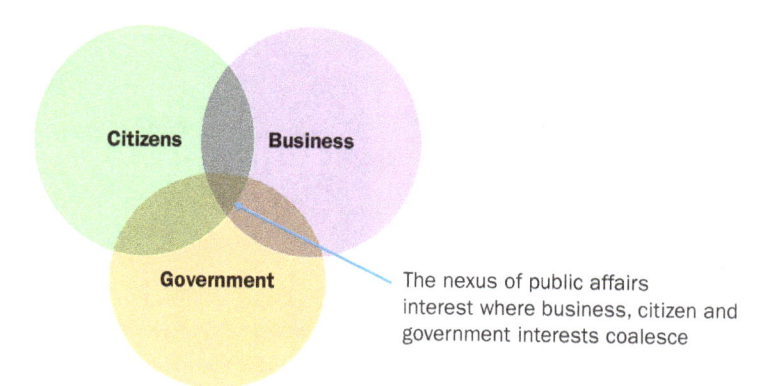

Figure 20.2 The Tripartite coalition of interests determining the role of public affairs

The nexus of public affairs interest where business, citizen and government interests coalesce

Mini case study 20.2

The broader role of public affairs: community building

The importance of aligning a company's business strategy with the local context, and with the expectations of the local communities in which it may be operating is perhaps nothing new. Indeed, most large international companies nowadays are well aware of the need to adapt to the needs of the different communities in each of the markets in which they operate if they want to have an effective, sustainable business. These principles are well illustrated in the way in which the automotive manufacturer, Renault, has sought to develop a harmonious relationship with the South American community where its plant is based – Envigado – a municipality in the Department of Antioquia in Columbia, where it is the largest employer. Renault hired a public affairs agency, Agora, to help it understand the local agendas and to build a strong and positive relationship with the local community and local authorities. Agora conducted interviews with key figures, drawn from a cross-section of local authorities, community leaders, clerical leaders, rectors of public and private schools, regional journalists and other prominent local figures to help identify a set of agendas that were then used to shape Renault's strategy for public affairs and corporate social responsibility policies and for its engagement in social and environmental initiatives to help enhance the company's position and reputation within the local community as well as internationally. Here, for Renault, public affairs embraced this extended scope including relationship building with all key stakeholder groups and key influencers within the communities where it has a significant operational presence.

Box 20.3

The Public Affairs Council (PAC)

The PAC was established in 1954 at the urging of the then President Dwight D. Eisenhower to provide unique information, training and other resources to its members to support their effective participation in government, community and public relations activities at all levels. The Council has more than 600 member companies and associations that work together towards the goal of enhancing the value and professionalism of the public affairs practice, and providing thoughtful leadership as corporate citizens. See http://pac.org/.

Reviewing the definitional question

Thus in reviewing academic and professional definitions of the (corporate) public affairs function what emerges is a broad continuum of views polarised between two dominant positions (see Figure 20.1). At one extreme lie relatively narrow politically orientated perspectives of public affairs, which treat public affairs as synonymous with 'political lobbying'. At the other extreme are interpretations of public affairs that position it as fulfilling a broader communications role, albeit focused around the nexus of politics, public policy and organisational/business concerns/issues, or as was depicted in Figure 20.2, the interface between business, citizen and government interests. What this broader perspective recognises is that public affairs will often sit alongside other communication activities and be deployed as part of an overall 'communications mix' designed to connect business or not-for-profit organisations to relevant stakeholder groups, whether they be customers, employees, suppliers, regulators or government/regulatory authorities. The specific context and situational considerations that an organisation faces at any particular time will invariably dictate the composition of the communication mix and which elements are likely to come to the fore in the particular communications strategy adopted. As far as public affairs is concerned, as illustrated earlier, its role is likely to come to the fore in cases where the organisation is dealing with scenarios involving external public policy issues, or regulatory matters that might impact on the organisation and the realisation of its goals.

Issues management

One common central element of both perspectives of the corporate public affairs function is the recognition of the central importance to public affairs of what is generally termed the 'issues management' function (Hainsworth and Meng 1988; Heath 2002). Issues management (IM) is now a widely recognised process for identifying, monitoring, analysing and ultimately containing or resolving those 'issues' that threaten the position of the organisation. IM is widely accepted as providing the underlying analysis for determining the public affairs agenda and focus for all strategic public affairs planning. Of course companies can also seek to align themselves with issues relevant to their key stakeholder groups or to society as a whole. This can often help shape public opinion on an issue or cause and have spin-off benefits to their reputation. We will examine the central importance of the issues management function and process in relation to public affairs later in the chapter, and a fuller discussion of issues management can be found in Chapter 16.

The existence of these two principal arms of public affairs – the government relations/lobbying perspective and a broader community relations/corporate reputation/ responsibility perspective – essentially frame what

Box 20.4
Defining issues management

According to Heath (2002) issues management is an anticipatory, strategic management process that helps organisations detect and respond appropriately to emerging trends or changes in the socio-political environment. 'These trends or changes may then crystallise into an "issue", which is a situation that evokes the attention and concern of influential organisational publics and stakeholders. At its best, issues management is stewardship for building, maintaining and repairing relationships with stakeholders' (Heath 2002). Also see https://www.youtube.com/watch?v=aUsiqRnTKs8

Source: Heath, R.L. (2002). 'Issues management: Its past, present and future'. Journal of Public Affairs, 2(4), 209–14

Picture 20.4 Public affairs can be used to help mobilise support for issues or charitable causes, indirectly enhancing the sponsoring organisation's reputation. (*source:* RidingMetaphor/Alamy Stock Photo)

> **Explore 20.1**
>
> **Political/regulatory influence**
>
> Consider the number of laws and bylaws that any business, charity or voluntary organisation may have to comply with or take into account when setting up operations. Think about the consequences of ignoring such legislation.

> **Think about 20.1**
>
> **Government business interaction**
>
> Taking any one industry such as automobile manufacture or construction, try putting together a list of all the key government departments whose work might affect that industry and try to build a contact list of the most important Ministers, MPs, or MEPs etc. whose support would be needed or helpful in campaigning for changes in any regulation affecting that industry.

can be seen to constitute the '*lingua franca*' of public affairs – a dialogue at both a societal and governmental level. By implication, those working in the public affairs field increasingly are required not only to be proficient communicators but to have a sound appreciation of how the political parties work, how policies are developed, how political parties may be influenced, and how campaigns are funded. Moreover, the type of issues and challenges that normally fall within the public affairs domain generally require far more complex and sophisticated solutions than those required when tackling what by comparison are generally more straightforward market-related communications campaigns (Harris and Moss 2001: 108).

Summarising what we know about public affairs

Reviewing the insights that we have presented so far drawn from academic and professional sources about what constitutes public affairs, and what role it plays in contemporary society and corporate life, the picture that emerges is in many ways similar to the betrayal of public relations as a 'boundary spanning' (BS) function. This BS role involves mediating between, on the one hand, the needs expectations and aspirations of what may be a quite diverse array of citizens and representative groups and institutions; and on the other hand, the goals and aspirations of business, focusing on how the 'touch points' and interactions between these two sets of 'actors' can be fine-tuned and balanced to their mutual benefit. However, in the case of public affairs, this business–citizen relationship is also to be viewed and managed through the 'prism' of government and government regulation, in so far as government in all its guises may or may not impinge on the interactions between the other two parties. Thus, as has been suggested, public affairs will sometimes work on a relatively narrow plane focusing primarily on government relations, working to influence and shape government engagement and/or policy in respect of the organisation's operating environment, while at other times it may adopt a much broader perspective, engaging with stakeholders concerned with a broader agenda of community relations, public policy, sustainability and corporate responsibility related issues.

In both respects, public affairs can act both **reactively** as well as **proactively**. In the latter case, scanning the external environment, analysing emerging issues that may impact on your organisation and devising appropriate strategies to help manage and resolve those issues – in short fulfilling the issues management function. Of course, not all issues can be anticipated fully and at times, public affairs may be called upon to act reactively, managing organisational responses to external challenges and threats to best protect the organisation's long-term reputation. Of course, it might be argued that much of this proactive and reactive issues management and stakeholder relations work could be just as easily labelled 'public relations' rather than public affairs. While this argument may be true to a degree, what brings this area of work into the distinctive 'orbit' of public affairs, is where the issues involved have a clear political dimension that requires the specialist knowledge and skills that public affairs professionals possess of how to work with and influence key stakeholders within the political arena. This area of various forms of government interaction and communications in its various forms, often with the aim of influencing or shaping government thinking and ultimately government policy, is generally referred to as 'lobbying'.

Lobbying

Put simply, lobbying is any action designed to influence the actions of the institutions of government. That means it covers all parts of central and local government and other public bodies both in the UK and internationally (Miller 2000: 4). In terms of its scope, therefore, lobbying can include attempts to influence legislation, regulatory and policy decisions, and negotiations on public sector contracts or grants. However, despite the increasing attention paid to, and critical scrutiny of lobbying in recent years, notably as a result of the considerable scandal surrounding the clandestine payment of MPs for their support and influence within Parliament in the UK, the process of lobbying remains an obscure practice and no definitive definition can be said to exist (Zetter 2008; Bitoni and Harris 2017).

Here it is important to distinguish between the essential *purpose* of lobbying, which does appear to be broadly understood, and the *methods or processes* used by lobbyists to achieve the desired outcome, which are generally more obscure and, in many cases, controversial. In terms of purpose, it should be stressed that lobbying is essentially a legitimate activity – a means by which various stakeholder groups can attempt to ensure that their voices are heard within government circles and the public policy arena, and hence it is important to the democratic process per se. Indeed, even where the principle of collective citizen representations to the 'governing elites' is not formally recognised, it is a right that citizens will often vociferously demand as we witnessed in the 2019 Hong Kong protests against the extradition policies that the ruling Chinese government sought to impose. While the principle of allowing the lobbying of government may be widely accepted, it is more the methods sometimes used by those seeking to lobby government on behalf of individuals, groups or various organisations or businesses that has and does continue to come under critical scrutiny.

Indeed the concern that continues to surround the practice of lobbying stems from the 'mystique' and rather 'cloak and dagger' image of the various lobbying tactics that are seen to be used to gain access to, and influence with, sections of government (see Figure 20.3). Such tactics are often portrayed as offering those with the greatest power and wealth undue influence within government circles – an accusation that has led to increasing calls for the regulation of political lobbyists. A further examination of lobbying tactics and of the regulation of lobbying is provided below.

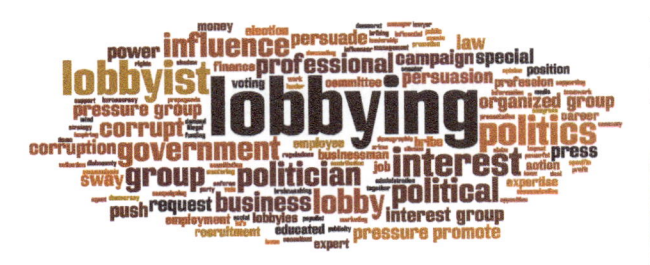

Figure 20.3 Negative perceptions of lobbying as something of a 'black art' or a questionable way of 'buying influence' with government (*source*: Boris15/Shutterstock)

Mini case study 20.3
British Gurkha Welfare Society

The British Gurkha Welfare Society (BGWS) is the largest welfare organisation supporting Gurkhas in the UK and Nepal. Founded in 2004, the BGWS has been one of the leading campaigners on issues of Gurkha welfare including settlement and pension rights.

The Gurkhas were brought fully into the public consciousness in 2009, when a high-profile media-led campaign headed by the actress Joanna Lumley overturned the policy of the then-government and secured settlement rights for Gurkhas who had retired before 1997 – thereby opening the door for these veterans to relocate to the UK. In addition to the high-profile programme of media relations, the campaign also comprised a massive grass roots programme involving hundreds of thousands of people who signed Gurkha Justice petitions, lobbied their MPs, campaigned, and attended rallies and marches.

At midday on 21 May, the then Home Secretary Jacqui Smith made the announcement to the House of Commons that the government had recognised the case advanced by the Gurkha Justice Campaign and that all ex-Gurkhas who have served more than four years in the British Army will have the right to settle in the UK if they wish. After such a long fight, with huge ups and downs, this was a superb result.

Lobbying practices

Traditionally, the general view of lobbying has been associated with mass protest and representations to government by disaffected groups; for example, Trades

Think about 20.2

What may have been the chief success factors in the Gurkhas' campaign? How important was it to have a high-profile celebrity championing the cause?

Union rallies against public sector pay cuts, or the recent junior doctors' protest and threatened strike in the UK about the new contracts that the government was proposing to bring in that would impact on junior doctors' contracts and working hours. Similarly, the British Gurkha lobbying campaign outlined above contained an element of mass rally and protest to challenge government policy. However, while such protests and rallies do undoubtedly capture public and hence government attention, their immediate effectiveness is often questionable, and their main purpose is often to generate media coverage and trigger public debate about an issue that might otherwise be lost amongst the numerous news items that circulate within the media. Moreover, the marked changes in the 'media landscape' over the past decade has forced would-be lobbyists to move away from relying on traditional media coverage to get their case heard, and instead focus on utilising increasingly pervasive social media platforms to distribute information and reach out to key influencers, often bypassing the 'traditional media' channels largely superseded by the use of an increasingly pervasive set of social media channels. While it is important not to overestimate the power of social media, there is little denying its widespread adoption and potential influence, particularly amongst the younger generations of users worldwide. In the USA, for example, the numbers of adults using at least one social media channel has grown from only 5 per cent in 2005 to over 70 per cent by 2019 with Facebook and Instagram proving the most popular channels. Perhaps the most notable impact of the growth of social media usage has been its ability to quickly disseminate information at a grassroots level and thereby help mobilise public opinion on specific issues of potential widespread concern. In recent years there have been many examples of the power of social media in helping to build popular support for particular ideas or movements, albeit to differing degrees. Barack Obama's 2008 Presidential election campaign was widely credited with having made very effective use of social media tactics (micro-blogging and Twitter) to mobilise voters in many difficult-to-reach communities. Social media was also recognised to have played a significant part in facilitating the so-called 'Arab Spring' revolutions in 2011, helping to build and sustain popular opposition to the incumbent regimes, and to keep the outside world informed of what was taking place. Similarly, as pointed to earlier, the recent Hong Kong protest movement against the Chinese government was organised primarily using social media to mobilise protesters and keep them and the world's media informed of events. What these examples illustrate is that social media allied sometimes to a traditional well-orchestrated media relations campaign has been – and continues to be – a crucial element of virtually all lobbying and broader public affairs strategies. Further insights into the growth of use of social and digital media can be found in Chapter 3.

In essence, however, lobbying is about persuasive argument, the presentation of cogent and compelling arguments to appropriate decision makers and their key advisors, whether this is in the form of one-to-one meetings, presentations to appropriate committees or in written reports/documentation or a combination of all of these different methods. These forms of direct communications with appropriate, influential decision-makers and advisors are often where much of the hard work is done in shaping or reshaping government thinking and proposals on issues or on legislation. Here the release of what might be quite sensitive information to the media relating to the issues in hand needs to be carefully handled in order not to upset what might be quite 'delicate negotiations' about the matter in hand. In essence, governments do not like to be seen to be backing down or caving in under external pressure, and hence often the lobbying strategy may involve giving government the opportunity to be seen to be engaging and responding positively to representations from industry or other bodies – 'a win-win scenario'.

Two further key principles of successful public affairs/lobbying campaigns (or for that matter any other communications campaigns) are worth highlighting:

1. **Timing is nearly always crucial**: there is a natural life cycle with all decision-making processes and especially government decision-making which will be partly determined by the particular cycle of government (when do the particular chambers of government sit, where is the incumbent government in its planned cycle of legislation, etc.). One of the keys to any successful lobbying campaign is to get the issue in question onto the government's agenda. Thus for some major issues which require a significant change in legislation or social change, there may need to be an ongoing medium- to longer-term strategy that may extend over a number of years in order to reach a position that is acceptable to all interested parties – e.g. changing the laws on the sale of tobacco products and alcohol in the UK, or animal welfare legislation relating to dog ownership and registration.

2. **Targeting is absolutely vital**: here it is essential to understand the structure and operation of the government or government bodies you are trying to influence – where does the influence lie, who are the 'power brokers' (formal and informal), who are the gatekeepers and who knows their way around

Think about 20.3

Try to construct a detailed structural 'map' of the government structures and departments that might oversee a major infrastructure project such as a new regional airport or new train line in your region of your country. Consider who would be involved in such a decision and what timescales might be involved in bringing it to fruition.

---

the system? Here authors such as Miller (2000) and Nugent (2002) offer valuable insights into the working of government in the UK and European Union. There are also a number of official and unofficial websites offering quite comprehensive information about the structure and working of government (e.g. in the UK, government websites such as www.direct.gov.uk; www.parliament.uk). Similar information sources can be found that cover government structures and government processes in countries around the world – e.g. the University of Keele's Politics Department (www.keele.ac.uk) maintains a comprehensive database of information about Governments in Latin America and information about the US government can be found from its official website, www.usa.gov/.

A legitimate activity?

Clearly a central issue with lobbying wherever it is practiced is the underlying concern that it may lead to undue and inappropriate influence on government decisions and legislation that favours the interests of one party or organisation at the expense of others and/or the 'public good'. Such concerns have been heightened in recent years as a result of a number of scandals and media exposés of corruption and illegal payment to politicians or influential officials to secure favourable decisions or contracts. The so-called 'cash for questions' scandal in the UK led to the establishment in 1994 of the *Nolan Committee on Standards in Public Life* to investigate and set out basic standard for the behaviour of MPs, Civil Servants and others holding public office – see Box 20.5 and Think about 20.4.

Building on these concerns about the conduct of civil servants and politicians when faced with perhaps a well-prepared and well-resourced lobbying strategy, guidelines have been drawn up that are intended

Box 20.5

Nolan Committee on standards in public life

Nolan principles that should govern the behaviours of all holders of public office:

- Selflessness
- Integrity
- Objectivity
- Openness
- Honesty
- Leadership

Think about 20.4

Implications for lobbyists in the UK political system

The Nolan Committee said in their first Report, 'it is the right of everyone to lobby Parliament and Ministers, and it is for public institutions to develop ways of controlling the reaction to approaches from professional lobbyists in such a way as to give due weight to their case while always taking care to consider the public interest'.

The government's approach, reflecting the approach of the Nolan Committee, is not to ban contacts between civil servants and lobbyists but to insist that wherever and whenever they take place they should be conducted in accordance with the Civil Service Code, and the principles of public life set out by the Nolan Committee. This means that civil servants can meet lobbyists, formally and informally, where this is justified by the needs of government.

---

to remind those engaged in the work of government about their primary duty to serve the state and citizens, rather than the vested interests of particular businesses or industry sectors. Guidance on acceptable lobbying activity is outlined on the parliamentary information website, www.parliament.uk

For further information about the work of the Committee on Standards in Public Life, see gov.uk

Regulation of lobbying

In June 2007, the UK government's Public Administration Select Committee (PASC) UK announced its inquiry into the lobbying industry in the UK. Following its investigations the Committee published its report, 'Lobbying: Access and influence in Whitehall', in December 2008, in which it recommended that a public register of Lobbyists be created. Despite considerable posturing and debate both amongst industry bodies such as the UK Public Affairs Council and the Chartered Institute of Public Relations (CIPR) and Public Relations Consultants Association (PRCA) limited progress was made. In 2010 then Deputy Prime Minister Nick Clegg announced that the government intended to legislate for a statutory register of lobbyists, but it took a further four years before the 'Transparency of Lobbying, Non-Party Campaigning and Trade Union Administration Act' was passed into law and a new Registrar of Consultant Lobbyist was appointed. However, because of various exclusions and a number of 'loopholes' in the legislation, many commentators have suggested that the Act has been rendered largely 'toothless'. For example, the Act specifically excludes all lobbyists working in an in-house capacity for companies. Thus it remains unclear as to how the UK government might act if the level of registrations remains persistently low. In short, control over the work of lobbyists in the UK remains relatively weak, which ironically may be something of a testament to their effectiveness in limiting controls over their role in the UK.

International perspectives on public affairs and lobbying

Reviewing the treatment of public affairs and its sub-discipline, lobbying, within a broad cross-section of academic and specialist professional literature, it is evident that until comparatively recently the vast majority of the work has focused largely on examining public affairs in either the UK or US context (see McGrath et al. 2010) as well as more recently in a wider European context (e.g. Bitoni and Harris (2017); Pedler and Van Schendelen 1994; Pedler 2002). This predominantly 'Western perspective' of public affairs has been disseminated and embraced on an international scale, at least in terms of the basic understanding of what the public affairs role should be and how it is organised and practiced. In addition to this dissemination of Western ideas via a range of literature, the Western perspective of public affairs has been spread through the expansion of Western-owned public affairs consultancies and corporate networks to other parts of the world. However, despite this apparent Western hegemony of ideas in the field of public affairs, it would be wrong to suggest that public affairs takes the same form in organisations across the world irrespective of the local economic, social and political environment. Indeed this author's own research in the field of international corporate public affairs has revealed significant variations in how public affairs is understood, organised and practiced, even across the different offices of the same global operating companies – see Think about 20.5.

It is almost certainly the case nowadays that most major international corporations have recognised the need for some form of public affairs function whether provided via an in-house team, by means of external consultants or a combination of the two. While the

Think about 20.5

Best practice concept in public affairs

The study of international public affairs completed by Moss et al. (2012) illustrates the problems of attempting to identify the characteristics of 'best practice' in any functional area. One of the organisations participating in the study had been through a major restructuring exercise, alongside a change of senior management, which had led to significant reductions in staffing across all functions including public affairs. This restructuring inevitably impacted on how the function operated both on an international global basis, as well as at each regional level as reductions in head count impacted to differing degrees across the organisation's offices. The one lesson that emerged from this study was that any attempt to achieve 'best practice' or the 'most effective practice' clearly depends on the adequacy and quality of the personnel working in the function. Where there is significant pressure on headcount and cost reduction, it may be incompatible, at least in the short term, with efforts to focus attention on defining and achieving what might constitute functional 'best practice'. Of course, in principle, staffing and cost reduction are not inconsistent with efficiencies and hence more effective practice – they may, in fact, lie at the heart of improved performance – but developing such a recognition and ingraining it into the way that the organisation and its functions operate is inevitably a challenging, and for some organisations, painful process.

underlying purpose of public affairs might be broadly understood in the same way on the international stage, how that purpose is achieved and what structures and operational tactics are used may vary quite significantly depending on an array of 'contextual variables'. Here parallels might be drawn with the research into international/global public relations practice (e.g. Sriramesh and Vercic 2009), which points to the strong influence of the 'environment context' in determining the scope and practice of public relations (public affairs) in different parts of the world. More specifically, Sriramesh and Vercic highlighted the significance of *the socio-economic, political and media environments* as constraining and influencing factors on both the historical development of public relations, as well as on contemporary practice. Arguably these same contextual variables are likely to have an equally formative influence on how public affairs has developed and is understood and practiced today. Perhaps most importantly, from a public affairs perspective, it is the political system and structures in any country/society that will very much frame and shape how far it is possible for public affairs practitioners to function in the type of conventional role that they have typically played in Western democracies. To take a somewhat extreme example, it is very difficult to see public affairs functioning in its conventional role and manner in autocratic command and control regimes such as have prevailed in North Korea or Myanmar (previously Burma). Yet public affairs practitioners have adapted and found ways to work effectively with the newly emerged states that formed after the break-up of the Soviet Union in the early 1990s, e.g. in Russia, Ukraine, etc., albeit that the nature of the political systems and climate in these newly formed states dictated that the approaches taken to corporate public affairs may be very different to those that might be adopted in most Western regimes.

Focusing on the issue of globalisation and its implications for communications/public relations practice, Wakefield (2011) suggests that the most effective approach for globally based organisations may lie in applying the principles of 'glocalisation' to all functional strategies including global communications and public affairs management. Essentially the 'glocalisation' approach attempts to apply centrally determined core strategies while also enabling locally based practitioners the freedom to adapt and tailor their public affairs approach to the local prevailing setting and priorities. This approach recognises the importance of an 'incremental' approach of gradual adaptation to circumstances, which may yield better longer-term results than an attempt to impose a standardised approach.

Indeed, in some of the more difficult political contexts around the world it is generally acknowledged that the work of the public affairs function is often critical to gaining access for companies to trade and do business in what might be quite heavily regulated or government-controlled markets. In such cases, public affairs expertise is needed to help steer the organisation through what can be very difficult and politically sensitive market channels. Further insights into working in an international context both in terms of public relations and public affairs are provided earlier in this book, notably in Chapter 6.

Public affairs management

Despite a growing base of academic and professional literature in the area of public affairs over the past decade or more (e.g. see the *Journal of Public Affairs*), which has focused on defining public affairs, and examining the role and scope and practice of public affairs; relatively little attention has been paid to the question of how the public affairs function is or should be managed, and equally, what does 'best practice' look like and how should it be achieved. Here, for example, in a study of global public affairs (see Think about 20.5) one of the underlying initial interests of organisations engaged in the research was to identify what might characterise 'best practice' in global public affairs. It soon became apparent, however, that such a quest for any *universal* principles of 'best practice' in public affairs was likely to prove elusive given marked variations between the operational environments in which different public affairs teams had to function. In effect, what emerged was that the most effective forms of practice were likely to prove situationally specific, reflecting very much the systems, values, culture and prevailing management 'worldviews' characterising each organisation/or subsidiary operating company, and thereby shaping priorities and the approach taken to public affairs. Indeed one key factor to emerge was marked variations in the quality

Explore 20.2

Conduct a search of the literature in a number of professional areas such as accountancy, medicine, engineering, etc. to identify whether and how the concept of 'best practice' is understood and what criteria, if any, have been identified to 'measure' best practice.

and experience of the personnel employed in the public affairs teams in different countries, even sometimes with the same organisation.

MACIE: a functional management framework

It is somewhat ironic that while most definitions of public relations and corporate communications or for that matter, public affairs, position these functions as essentially 'managerial' in character, talking, for example, about 'the management of communication between an organisation and its publics', or 'managing the interface between organisations and government'; few actually define the *managerial processes and responsibilities* involved in any detail. Indeed, there is a lack of any clear framework for analysing the component elements of the management process, or management stages involved in 'managing' the various forms of internal and external communication on behalf of an organisation. Indeed, as Moss (Moss et al. 2005, 2007; Moss and DeSanto 2011) has pointed out, communications/public relations scholars have generally failed to acknowledge and draw on the extensive body of management literature when discussing the management role within the function. Thus, for example, in defining the manager's role in public relations there is little recognition of the evolving debate between the 'classical' models of management as advanced by scholars such as Gulick and Urwick (1937) and Fayol (1949), which defined management in terms of a set of basic tasks or elements of management responsibility (see Box 20.6), and the subsequent behavioural critique of this classical school, which recognises the need to distinguish between management *tasks and responsibilities,* and managerial *behaviours* (Mintzberg 1973, 1990; Hales 1986). In short, distinguishing between *what* tasks or

Box 20.6

The 'classical models' of management

The classical perspective of management treats management as a logical rational activity that can be broken down into a number of discrete but related tasks. One of the best known of such models is that advanced by Gulick and Urwick (1937) which defined seven core elements of management – *planning, organising, staffing, directing, coordinating, reporting and budgeting* – which became known in management circles by the acronym 'POSDCORB'.

roles managers are responsible for carrying out, and *how* they go about performing them.

In attempting to explore the managerial dimension of public relations in more detail, Moss et al. (2000, 2005, 2007) sought to define a number of core dimensions of communication management as well as offering a strong critique of the existing definitions of the public relations manager role. Building on this work more recently, Moss and DeSanto (2011) suggested a simple yet powerful framework for exploring the key elements of the management process that arguably can be applied to all communication functions including public affairs, in terms of how key strategies and plans are put together and managed to completion. The four stages, or elements, in this management process – which arguably can be applied to most organisational settings – are designated by the acronym [C]-MACIE:

- [Communications] management analysis
- [Communications] management choice
- [Communications] management implementation
- [Communications] management evaluation

This framework adapted for public affairs purposes is illustrated in Figure 20.4. Each element or stage of the process as they relate to the area of public affairs is explained briefly in the next section of this chapter.

One significant consideration warrants mention before exploring the CMACIE framework in more detail, namely what this framework does *not* identify *explicitly* are the specific managerial *behaviours* associated with performance of key tasks at each of these stages. However, managerial *behaviour* and managerial *work* are not always so easily separated and, in fact,

Think about 20.6

What managers do

Think about what any people you know who work in a managerial type job do on a day-to-day basis. What sort of responsibilities do they have, what skills do they seem to need to demonstrate, and if you compare a number of 'managers' do they all have the same type of responsibilities? Apply this thinking to those occupying mid-level and senior posts on public relations/public affairs – do they all have the same set of responsibilities?

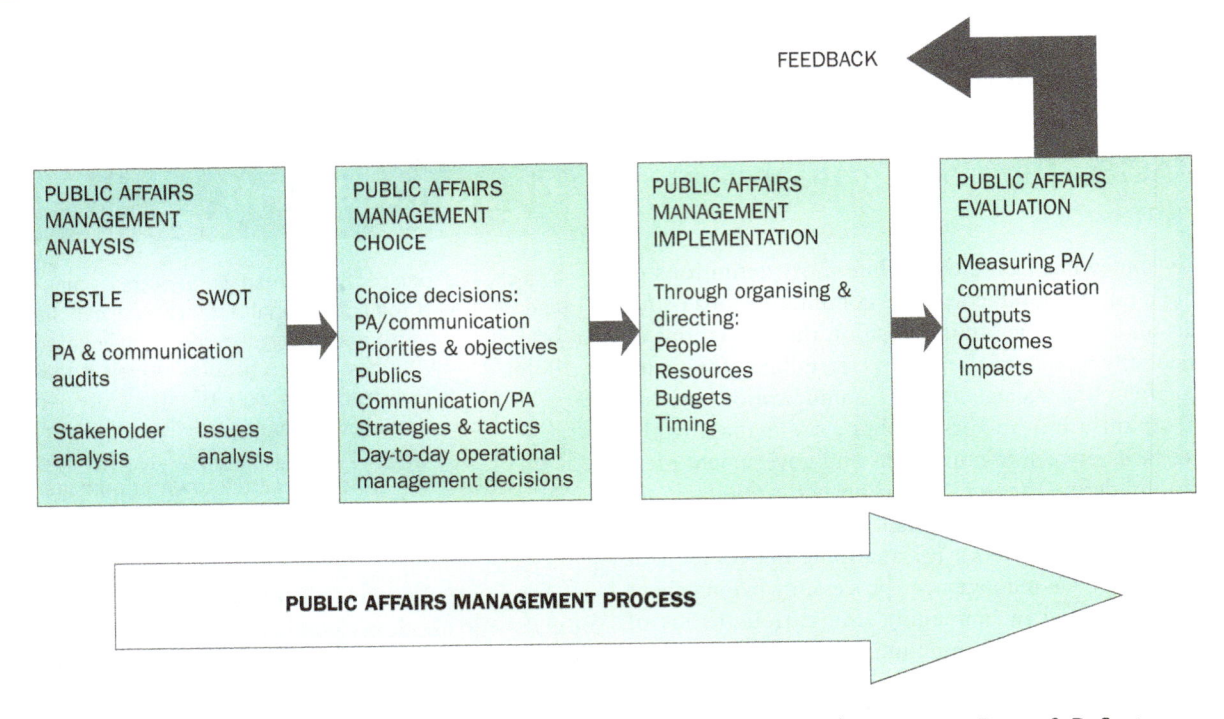

Figure 20.4 The public affairs process through the lens of the CMACIE framework (*source:* Moss, Danny & DeSanto, Barbara. (2011) Public Relations: A Managerial Perspective. SAGE, 2011)

can be seen as 'two-sides of the same coin' – representing the 'what' and the 'how' of managerial work.

Public affairs: management analysis

The first element in this framework, *communication/public affairs management analysis,* represents the essential first step in the communication management process – namely analysing the particular situation facing an organisation and determining the communication/public affairs-related issues and challenges that need to be tackled. To complete this analysis stage effectively involves:

- Ongoing scanning and careful analysis of the organisation's external and internal environments in order to identify and understand and, where possible, anticipate the forces shaping the current (and future) situation the organisation faces.
- Use of well-established scanning and analysis tools PESTLE, SWOT, etc.
- Careful audit and analysis of all key stakeholder relationships, linking these to the relevant issues and tracking their salience over time.
- Audit of all existing and past communications activity.
- Thorough issues analysis to track the origins, significance and likely impact and trajectory and potential impact of issues.

The way these analysis tools can be employed to help make sense of situations and identify priorities for action was discussed earlier in Chapter 9 and you might find it useful to revisit these sections of the book to remind yourself about these techniques at this stage.

Here, Mini case study 20.4 illustrates the importance of understanding how changes in this case in government policy might create serious issues and challenges for an organisation or whole industry's operations. This initial context analysis should not only look outward, assessing the external environment and external issues, but should also review past communications activity and internal resources and capabilities to enable the subsequent identification and choice of the most appropriate communications/public affairs strategies and tactics.

As suggested above, as well as earlier in the chapter, of the various environmental analysis techniques available, it is *issue analysis* that generally has the greatest relevance and importance for public affairs, in terms of teasing out those problematic consequences of stakeholder–organisational relationships, which in turn may

Mini case study 20.4
Turning the lights out on solar power installations

As part of its climate change strategy, the UK Government's Department of Energy and Climate Change (DECC) launched a Feed-in Tariff subsidy scheme whereby households installing solar panels to help meet their electricity consumption were able to receive a specially enhanced subsidy payment for surplus electricity generated from the solar panels that they would sell back into the local grid. The scheme generated widespread interest across the UK on the back of an extensive advertising and public relations campaign. The number of solar energy installers also expanded rapidly to meet the demand and exploit the market opportunity. Then in December 2011 the DECC announced a cut to feed-in tariff subsidies that would apply to any installation after 12 December that year. Environmental campaign group Friends of the Earth (FoE) and two solar companies – Solarcentury and HomeSun – challenged this announcement because the change was made before the end of a consultation period for the solar scheme.

The High Court then ruled in December 2011 that the change was 'legally flawed' but the DECC launched an appeal to have this ruling overturned.

The appeal leaves households who have installed solar panels after this date with no guarantee of the rate they will receive for generating energy. The change in the scheme means that the amount paid for solar panel generated electricity was reduced from 43.3p per kWh to 21p – slashing the revenue that can be earned on average by households from £1,100 to £500.

The uncertainty over the proposed change of policy with respect to the level of feed-in subsidy effectively 'torpedoed' any further growth in the household solar panel market, and threatened to bring about the demise of a number of firms that had expanded rapidly into what had promised to be a very attractive new market.

Read more: http://www.thisismoney.co.uk/money/bills/article-2082270/Government-launches-appeal-High-Court-ruling-deemed-cut-solar-panel-feed-tariff-subsidies-legally-flawed.html#ixzz1inkqMfKo

Explore 20.3

Put yourself in the position of the public affairs advisor appointed to advise the solar energy industry, and specifically solar panel installers about how they should respond to the DECC's proposed cut in fed-in tariff. What are the key issues on which to build a campaign and which stakeholder groups should the campaign engage with?

---

be shaped by environment trends and events. Indeed issues management is normally recognised as an integral part of the public affairs management framework and is crucial to its success (Hainsworth and Meng 1988; Heath 2002). Here in particular, public affairs takes the classical view of issue management that focuses on defining the key *public policy issues* that may impact on the organisation's current operations and future strategy – public policy issues being those that arise out of the nexus and interaction of business, government and citizens (see Figure 20.2). Here the issues life cycle concept is often used to help track the momentum of issues and identify their escalation towards what can be a crisis point. Further discussion of issues management process as a means of mapping and analysing issues that are relevant to any specific organisation can be found earlier in the text.

Public affairs management choice

The work of communication/public affairs analysis prepares the way for what is often seen as the core task of management, namely exercising *management choice* with respect to the appraisal and selection of alternative strategy options, or decisions about what operational actions should be undertaken. For communications/public affairs managers, these choices centre around decisions about which challenges/issues they should focus attention on, which stakeholders will need to be targeted, what communication/public affairs strategies should be adopted and what specific tactics should be used. Equally, at the communications department level, management choice may involve decisions about how to allocate responsibilities amongst staff, how resources should be utilised and what tasks should be prioritised, to name but a few of numerous 'choice decisions' that managers face every week if not every day.

Decisions particularly about the choice of alternative communications/public affairs strategies invariably involve consultation and approval of senior management. Indeed, as essentially a support function, the role of the public affairs function is to support and facilitate the achievement of the organisation's broader corporate goals and strategies, and hence communications/public affairs management decisions will normally take a lead from these higher-level decisions.

Choice tools

Choice tools or techniques are the methods that managers can draw upon to help determine the best options for the organisation to pursue. Although it is beyond the scope of this chapter to explore in detail some of the more sophisticated choice/decision-making tools available, it is worth highlighting some of the more commonly used techniques that can be used in this context. Of course, ultimately, choice decisions usually come down to a 'judgement call' by the senior professionals charged with decision-making responsibility. However, many larger organisations nowadays have access to relatively sophisticated computer systems that are capable of collecting, sifting and analysing large quantities of data, and conducting probability and risk analysis on the likely outcome of different future scenarios. Clearly, such analysis can perhaps take some of the 'guess work' out of decisions about future courses of action. However, such systems are only mathematical modelling processes, and predicting the vagaries of human behaviour and accounting for the often 'boundedly' rational behaviour of individuals and/or groups can make any such systematic reductionist approaches problematic, particularly when it comes to predicting future scenarios that depend on human actions and behaviour. Some of the more commonly used choice decision tools include:

- **Ranking methods:** alternative options are assessed against an agreed set of predetermined criteria that are identified as important to the organisation such as cost or investment considerations, and how they fit with resource capabilities, or even ethical considerations.
- **Scenario building:** the idea is to match alternative options against a range of possible future scenarios in order to assess the best fit, given alternative future situations. Of course the challenge here is to 'second guess' future developments whether they be at an industry level, or perhaps more problematically, at a societal level and how such developments might manifest themselves in terms of stakeholder behaviour.
- **Decision tree analysis:** another method of assessing alternative courses of action, but here preferred options emerge progressively by introducing requirements of preferred conditions which need to be met, such as for example, levels of acceptable risk. Here the construction of a 'decision-tree diagram' is often a usual visual aid to such decision-making.
- **Risk analysis:** an approach that often works alongside choice techniques in terms of attempts to assess the degree of hazard or adverse consequence associated with alternative courses of action, weighed against the potential rewards. Statistical 'probabilistic risk assessment' methods have been developed to try to assess the level of risk associated with specific projects, but the value and accuracy of such measures depends very much on the adequacy and accuracy of the input data – the magnitude or severity of the adverse consequences of each event, and the likelihood of occurrence of that event. Of course, the application of such probabilistic analysis is most suited to physical engineering and process projects rather than to predicting the consequences of alternative patterns of human behaviours. In the latter case, however, risk assessment can be undertaken but often based on collective judgements made by panels of experts and experienced managers from the field in question.

Public affairs management implementation

Much of the discussion of the communication/public affairs management process tends to focus on the analysis and strategic and operational decision-making (choice) stages of the process, rather than on implementation. However, how communications/public affairs departments manage the *implementation* of their policies/strategies and programmes is arguably no less important to achieving their intended outcome, since even the most well-designed strategies and programmes can fail through poorly managed implementation. It is generally recognised that the key to successful implementation of communications/public affairs policies and programmes lies in the effective management of *people* and *resources* involved in their delivery.

Arguably communications/public affairs functions and professionals have historically had a relatively poor track record in terms of many aspects of effective people management and more particularly budgetary

> **Think about 20.7**
>
> ## Public affairs accountability
>
> Perhaps one of the most controversial aspects of public affairs work relates to the expenditure on activities designed to help build and sustain key relationships with politicians, civil servants, etc. How such expenditure on corporate hospitality and other relationship-building activities is budgeted and accounted may be very difficult to assess. Moreover the professional standards and mores of doing business in the USA or UK may be very different from what is the acceptable norm in other parts of the world. Consider the challenge for public affairs when confronted with doing business in a country where effectively 'bribes' and 'under the counter' payment is treated as an acceptable part of doing business. Essentially such issues, while perhaps more relevant to a discussion of professional ethics, equally impinge on the questions of effective implementation of programmes. How would you advise your senior public affairs management team to behave faced with such a situation?

management. However, such criticisms have perhaps been much more relevant to the consultancy sector than to in-house communications/public affairs departments. Both areas of people management and budgetary/financial management are ones that have not necessarily been recognised as core areas of professional competence associated with communications/public affairs. However, with increasing investment in communications/public affairs activity notably on the part of large corporate and multinational corporations in particular, communications/public affairs functions are expected to demonstrate the same level of professionalism and accountability for the use of resources and management of people that is expected of all other corporate functions.

Public affairs evaluation

The final element of this public affairs management framework focuses on evaluation of the outcomes of the communications/public affairs function's strategies and programmes. The issue of effective evaluation has long been something of an 'Achilles heel' for all areas of communications including public affairs. However, at least in principle, evaluation should not prove an overly complicated task, but the difficulty has always been in identifying, isolating and measuring the *impact* of communications/public affairs programmes. Here the aim is to establish firstly, the extent to which the immediate programme and longer-term policy objectives have been achieved, and second, the significance of external and internal factors affecting the programme outcomes. As suggested above, organisational objectives and targets have increasingly become more diverse, reflecting the need to balance different stakeholder expectations of organisations – recognising that financial performance may have to be set against other environmental, social and even political considerations affecting an organisation's longer-term position and success. Where organisations have accepted the need for this type of 'balanced scorecard approach' (see Box 20.7) to objective and target setting (e.g. Kaplan and Norton 1992), it follows that any evaluation of performance and outcomes will need to use an appropriate set of quantitative and qualitative performance measures. While this discussion of balanced scorecards and more pluralistic organisational objectives and performance measures has focused mainly on the areas of broader corporate and business policy and strategy making, the arguments can be applied equally to the area of communications/public affairs policies and programmes. Indeed, communications/public affairs practitioners are generally seen as advocates and champions of a broader stakeholder perspective of organisational and business strategy and policy-making. Thus it is perhaps only logical to expect them to be advocates of a balanced scorecard approach to the evaluation of their work, reflecting the potentially varied range of ways in which activities can contribute to organisational success.

Thus while in principle there would appear to be broad agreement about what is required in terms of communications/public affairs evaluation; in practice, identifying appropriate measures and carrying out the evaluation of the outcomes of designated programmes has proved highly problematic, particularly in terms of isolating and measuring the specific communications/public affairs effects. Here the debates about communications evaluation have tended to crystallise around the distinction between 'process' and 'impact' measurement (Broom and Dozier 1990; Dozier 1984; Grunig and Hunt 1984; Macnamara 1992). Although this debate has focused on the evaluation of public relations programmes rather than public affairs, arguably many of the measurement techniques (both process and impact measures) can be seen to be more or less applicable to public affairs. There are, of course, some more obviously relevant impact measures, particularly where the function's goal relates to the change or modification or

Box 20.7

Balanced scorecard

According to the Balanced Score Card Institute (BSCI), a balanced scorecard is a strategic planning and management system that is used extensively in business and industry, government, as well as in non-profit organisations worldwide to align business activities to the vision and strategy of the organisation (see Figure 20.5). Here the purpose is to improve internal and external communications, and monitor the organisation's performance against strategic goals. The BSC framework adds strategic non-financial performance measures to traditional financial metrics to give managers and executives a more 'balanced' view of organisational performance. While the phrase *balanced scorecard* was coined in the early 1990s, the origins of this type of approach can be traced back to the early and mid-twentieth century including the pioneering work of General Electric on performance measurement reporting in the 1950s and the work of French process engineers in the early part of the twentieth century.

For further insight into the nature and use of the Balanced Score Card approach see the Balanced Score Card Institute: www.balancedscorecard.org

	EXPOSURE	ENGAGEMENT	INFLUENCE	IMPACT	ADVOCACY
PROGRAM METRICS	Total OTS for program content	Number of interactions with content Interaction rate Hashtag usage	Increase % association with key attributes Change in issue sentiment	New subscribers Referral traffic to website White paper downloads	Recommendation/ Total Mentions %
CHANNEL METRICS	Number of items Mentions **Reach** Impressions CPM	Post Likes Comments Shares Views RTs/1000 Followers	Net promoter % by channel	Unique visitors to website referred from each channel	Organic posts by advocates Ratings/ Reviews
BUSINESS METRICS			Purchase consideration % Likelihood to recommend % Association with brand attributes	**Sales** Repeat sales Purchase frequency Cost savings Number leads	Employee ambassadors Brand fans/ advocates

Figure 20.5 Example of the type of metrics that might be used for a 'balanced scorecard' in the communications / public affairs context

Explore 20.4

Review the public affairs campaigns that you have come across/read about over the past few months in *PR Week*, *Public affairs news* or the *Journal of Public Affairs*, etc. and identify what forms of evaluation are being used to evaluate the success of the reported campaigns.

passing of a specific piece of legislation or regulation. In such cases, any measurement of the media coverage generated can only reveal part of the story of activity directed at bringing about legislative modification or change. It is only the achievement of the legislative change itself that can be said to represent a full measure of the public affairs programme's impact/success. A fuller examination of the debates about approaches to the communications/public relations evaluation was provided earlier in Chapter 10.

Summary

Public affairs has become an increasingly important corporate/organisational function in many of today's more turbulent, increasingly globalised and politicised business environments. In this chapter we have explored how public affairs is understood and defined, highlighting the polarised nature of how public affairs tends to be viewed and understood. Traditional views of public affairs position it as essentially a specialised government relations/lobbying function, whereas public affairs has, in many cases, assumed the mantle of overseeing a broad cross section of communications related sub-functions such as issues management, community relations and CSR. However, lobbying activity in its various forms directed at government and government departments at all levels remains the day-to-day 'bread and butter' work of the public affairs function. With the internationalisation of many markets and the opening up of a number of previously closed trading areas, public affairs is playing an increasingly important role in supporting international marketing and sales strategies through its role in liaising with relevant government and regulatory bodies to help in understanding regulatory and cultural priorities in target markets, and assisting the business to adapt and comply with the needs and expectation of those targeted countries/regions. In this sense public affairs can be seen to fulfil what Post (1982) termed the 'window-out, window-in' role of public affairs. As businesses and other organisations come under increasing public and official scrutiny through both formal and informal channels (social media etc.), the need for this window-out, window-in role of public affairs arguably has never been greater. While other communications functions may also conduct similar external scanning activity, what distinguishes the work of public affairs is its ability to filter and interpret the significance of the information circulating in formal and other traditional media and social media channels through the 'tripartite lens' of the business–citizen–government prism and thereby identify the key implications that may require management attention and action. It is in this way that public affairs serves as a strategically important function to corporate business. This is particularly true for profit-related businesses but also not-for-profit organisations operating on a regional or global scale.

Bibliography

Argenti, P. (2009). *Corporate Communication: International edition*. New York: Irwin McGraw-Hill.

Bitoni, A. and P. Harris (Eds) (2017). *Lobbying in Europe: Public affairs and the lobbying industry in 28 EU countries*. London: Palgrave Macmillan.

Broom, G.M. and D.M. Dozier (1990). *Using Research in Public Relations: Applications to program management*. Englewood Cliffs, NJ, Prentice Hall.

Cornelissen, J. (2008). *Corporate Communications: A guide to theory and practice*, 2nd edn. London: Sage.

Dozier, D.M. (1984). 'Program evaluation and roles of practitioners'. *Public Relations Review*, 10(2), 13–21.

Dozier, D.M., Ed. (1992). 'The organizational roles of communicators and public relations practitioners'. in *Excellence in Public Relations and Communications Management*. Hillsdale, NJ, Lawrence Erlbaum Associates, Inc.

Fayol, H. (1949). *General and Industrial Management*. London: Pitman.

Fleisher, C.S. and N.M. Blair (1999). 'Tracing the parallel evolution of public affairs and public relations: An examination of practice, scholarship and teaching'. *Journal of Communication Management*, 3(3), 276–92.

Gov.UK Standards in Public Life (https://www.gov.uk/government/organisations/the-committee-on-standards-in-public-life) accessed 7 April 2020.

Griffin, J.J. and P. Dunn (2004). 'Corporate public affairs: Commitment, resources, and structure'. *Business & Society*, 43(2), 196–220.

Grunig, J.E. and T. Hunt (1984). *Managing Public Relations*. Orlando, Florida: Harcourt Brace Jovanovich.

Grunig, J.E. and L.A. Grunig (1992). Models of public relations and communication. *Excellence in public relations and communication management*. J. E. Grunig. Hillsdale, NJ, Lawrence Erlbaum Associates: 285–325.

Grunig, L.A. et al. (2002). *Excellent Public Relations and Effective Organisations*. Mahwah, NJ: Lawrence Erlbaum Associates.

Gulick, L. and L. Urwick (1937) (eds) *Papers on the Science of Administration*, Institute of Public Administration, New York.

Hainsworth, B. and M. Meng (1988). 'How corporations define issue management'. *Public Relations Review*, 14(4), 18–30.

Hales, C. (1986). What do managers do? A critical review of the evidence. *Journal of Management Studies*, 23(1): 88–115.

Harris, P. and D. Moss (2001). 'Editorial': In search of public affairs: A function in search of an identity'. *Journal of Public Affairs,* 1(2), 102–10.

Harris P. and C.S. Fleisher (Eds) (2016). *The Sage Handbook of International Corporate and Public Affairs.* London: Sage

Heath, R.L. (1994). *Management of Corporate Communication: From interpersonal contacts to external affairs.* Abingdon: Routledge.

Heath, R.L. (2002). 'Issues management: Its past, present and future'. *Journal of Public Affairs,* 2(4), 209–14.

Hillman, A.J. (2002). 'Public affairs, issue management and political strategy: Methodological issues that count – a different view'. *Journal of Public Affairs,* 1(4) & 2(1), 356–61.

Hutton, J.G., M.B. Goodman, J.B. Alexander and C.M. Genest (2001). 'Reputation management: the new face of corporate public relations?' *Public Relations Review,* 27(3): 247–61.

Kaplan, R. and D. Norton (1992). The balanced scorecard: Measures that drive performance. *Harvard Business Review,* 70(1), 71–79

McGrath, C., D. Moss and P. Harris (2010). 'The evolving discipline of public affairs'. *Journal of Public Affairs,* 10(4), 335–52.

MacNamara, J. (1992). Evaluation of public relations; the Achilles heel of the PR profession. *International Public Relations Review,* 15(4): 17–31.

Meznar, M.B. and D. Nigh (1995). 'Buffer or bridge? Environmental and organizational determinants of public affairs activities in American firms'. *Academy of Management Journal,* 38(4), 975–96.

Miller, C. (2000). Politico's Guide to Political Lobbying. London: Politico's Publishing.

Mintzberg, H. (1973). *The Nature of Managerial Work.* New York, Harper & Row.

Mintzberg, H. (2009). *Managing.* Harlow, FT, Prentice Hall.

Moss, D.A., G. Warnaby, et al. (2000). Public relations practitioner role enactment at the senior management level within UK companies. *Journal of Public Relations Research,* 12(4), 227–308.

Moss, D.A, A.J. Newman and B. Desanto (2005). What do Communication Managers Do? Defining and Refining the Core Elements of Management in the Public Relations/ Communications Context. *Journalism & Mass Communication Quarterly,* 82(4), pp. 873–90.

Moss, D.A., B. Desanto and A.J. Newman (2007). 'Building an understanding of the main elements of management in the communication/ public relations context: A study of U.S. practitioner practices'. *Journalism & Mass Communication Quarterly* 84(3), pp. 439–54.

Moss, D.A. and B. Desanto (Eds) (2011). *Public Relations: A managerial perspective.* London: Sage.

Nugent, N. (2010). *The Government and Politics of the European Union.* London: Palgrave Macmillan.

Pedler, P. (eds) (2002). *European Union Lobbying: Changes in the arena.* Houndmills: Palgrave.

Pedler, R. and M.P.C.M. Van Schendelen (eds) (1994). *Lobbying the European Union: companies, trade associations and issue groups.* Aldershot: Dartmouth.

Post, J. (1982). 'Public affairs: Its role'. In Nagelschmidt, J.S. (Ed.), *The Public Affairs Handbook.* New York: Amacom, 23–30.

Sriramesh, K. and D. Vercic, Eds. (2009). *The Global Public Relations Handbook: Theory, research and practice.* Mahwah, NJ: Lawrence Erlbaum Associates.

Showalter, A. and C.S. Fleisher (2005). 'The tools and techniques of public affairs'. In Harris, P. and Fleisher, C.S. (Eds), *The Handbook of Public Affairs.* London: Sage, 109–22.

van Riel, C.B.M. (1995). *Principles of Corporate Communication.* Hemel Hempstead: Prentice Hall.

Wakefield, R. (2011). Managing global public relations. *Public Relations: A managerial perspective.* D.A. Moss and B. Desanto. London, Sage: 467–85.

Watts, D. and C. Pilkington (2005). *Britain in the European Union.* Manchester: Manchester University Press.

Zetter, L. (2008). *Lobbying: The art of political persuasion.* Petersfield: Harriman House.

Websites

The Daily Telegraph: www.dailytelegraph.co.uk
The Guardian: www.guardianunlimited
Parliament www.Parliament.uk
www.food.gov.uk/news/newsarchive/2005

CHAPTER 21

Neil Kelley

Integrated marketing communications

Source: Sergey Uryadnikov/Shutterstock

Learning outcomes

By the end of this chapter you should be able to:
- understand the concept of integrated marketing communications
- evaluate the importance of integrated marketing communications
- consider a variety of different communications channels and tools in order to develop integrated marketing communications
- identify and discuss the key principles and methods used to integrate marketing communications
- review integrated marketing communications activities through case examples
- apply key principles of integrated marketing communications to real-life scenarios.

Structure

- Defining integrated marketing communications (IMC)
- The planning process
- Audiences
- Marketing communications tactics
- Touch points

Introduction

Just how many marketing messages is the average person exposed to on a daily basis? How many marketing messages do you remember from the last day – the last week? If you sat and thought about it, you'd agree that it was an awful lot. Being aware of the volume of marketing messages that people are exposed to every day is important for anyone involved in professional communications, especially as we want to be heard and not lost in the clutter and noise.

Yankelovich, an American futures and consulting organisation, published the results of their research into US advertising exposure in 2006 and estimated that the average American living in a large city would be exposed to approximately 5,000 marketing messages a day (Petrecca 2016). Since then, communication channels have significantly grown following the uptake of social media such as Facebook, Twitter, Blogs, Instagram, Pinterest, adverts on websites, sponsored online content (sometimes referred to as native advertising), affiliates and influencers. Marshall (2015) refers to research from Red Crow Marketing that estimates the average American can be exposed to anywhere between 4,00 and 10,000 marketing messages each day! Research undertaken by Scott Brinker (2016) estimates that there are over 3,500 different marketing technology platforms. Whilst a number of these relate to e-commerce, analytics and data management, over 2,000 of these are communication tools.

So, this selection of research shows that there can be an awful lot of variation in the number of marketing messages it is thought that consumers are exposed to. What communications professionals can't afford to ignore though is that there is an increasing, and rather phenomenal, number of marketing communications messages out there. Not just adverts, but brand logos, packaging, labels, websites, social media posts, videos and more.

In order to cut through this increasing volume of noise and clutter current **and**, future communications professionals need to ensure that their message stands out, that there is something in the message that reaches the audience at the right time, in the right place, with the right balance of informational and emotional content; content that has resonance, that has quality of importance and meaning. That 'something' could well be the process of planning and implementing integrated marketing communications.

From a marketing communications perspective public relations (PR) is, more often than not, classed as one of the available promotional tactics of marketing communications. This means that PR has a tactical role within integrated marketing communications, one of five communications tools that can to be integrated within a campaign. Smith and Ze Zook, (2011) refer to this particular use of PR as 'product PR' or 'marketing PR' and distinguish this from 'corporate PR' which has a more strategic focus on the company image and visibility. Other chapters throughout the book obviously deal more fulsomely with these aspects of public relations. For the purposes of this chapter, PR will be considered as 'marketing PR', a tactic used for delivering product and brand visibility.

Mini case study 21.1
Getting noticed – 'snowflake' stereotypes and 'this is belonging'

In an effort to cut through the clutter and noise associated with the sheer volume of marketing communications we are exposed to the British Army took a novel approach to engaging their target demographic – 'millennials' and Generation Z. The series of recruitment ads paid homage to the famous First World War 'Your Country Needs You' campaign. Six different posters were developed in total, to support a TV advert, and a broader campaign titled 'This is Belonging' in an effort to drive recruitment at a time when the British Army is seeing recruitment rates fall year on year.

The campaign was designed to show how the British Army sees potential in the young, as opposed to the labels given to them such as 'snowflakes', 'selfie addicts' and 'phone zombies'. It may have drawn some widespread criticism on social media, and a Scots Guardsman featured in one of the posters threatened to quit, but as a communications campaign it was successful, as it was noticed, and it got people talking.

Picture 21.1 'This is belonging' is an effort to drive recruitment at a time when the British Army is seeing recruitment rates fall year on year (*source*: Andrew Michael/Education Images/Universal Images Group/Getty Images)

As a consumer, and student of communications, you'll be familiar with lots of the other marketing communications messages – you're exposed to advertising on the television or video on demand, in magazines and on bus stops; you may be sent text messages or emails from brands you use carrying time-limited sales and deals. You'll attend events that are sponsored by brands; you'll use loyalty cards when shopping; and much, much more. All of these things will have been planned as part of a broader integrated marketing communications (IMC) strategy.

This chapter will provide clear consideration of the concept of integrated marketing communications – referred to by its acronym IMC – giving a more detailed definition; considering the strategic planning process that underpins the integration of communications; identifying the many different channels of communication that can be utilised within IMC; considering the importance of understanding audiences and discussing how communication agencies can support the process of integration.

Defining integrated marketing communications

There are many definitions of integrated marketing communications, each with their own subtle nuances and areas of focus. This section aims to shed some light on what integrated marketing communications is, as both a concept and a process. Marketing communications are defined by Dahlen et al. (2010) as being primarily concerned with engagement.

Fill and Turnbull (2016) propose engagement to be the use of communications tools to capture attention. So, when a piece of communications captures the audience's attention they engage with it, this may be for a fleeting moment, or a more substantial amount of time, perhaps days, weeks or months. Marketing communications need to engage, they need to capture attention and be actively consumed by the audience. The most effective and engaging communications are 'two-way', in that there is some form of interaction between the sender of the message and the receiver. This may be simple feedback, such as a nod of agreement during a sales pitch, to a conversation, perhaps face to face or via social media.

Fill and Turnbull (2016) also raise an interesting point that the most effective marketing communications are not always two-way. In an era of digitally enhanced marketing communications, with a variety of conversational tools that offer varying degrees of immediacy, not all audiences are looking for a two-way relationship or a conversation. One of the key factors to consider in developing effective marketing communications is that of knowing and understanding the audience.

What is IMC?

Integrated marketing communications, or IMC, is a strategic planning a process, a series of stages that any marketing or public relations professional would need to work through in order to deliver relevant communications to a defined target audience across a variety of relevant channels. Shimp (2010: 10) provides a detailed definition of IMC, stating that it is:

> ... (the) process that entails the planning, creation, integration and implementation of diverse forms of marketing communications that are delivered over time to a brand's targeted customers and prospects. The goal of IMC is ultimately to influence or directly affect the behaviour of the targeted audience. IMC considers all touch points, or courses of contact, that a customer/prospect has with the brand as potential delivery channels for messages and makes use of all communications methods that are relevant to customers/prospects.

There are a number of important points to consider within this quotation. To begin with, IMC is a **planning process** that involves a **series of important stages**. Whilst not explicitly included in Shimp's definition, there will be some form of analysis, essential for supporting effective decision-making, before moving on to develop a plan for the marketing communications tools to be brought together or integrated. Finally, the manager will move on to the implementation of

Box 21.1
What is IMC?

IMC is not just one communications tool, type or channel, it is the optimum mix of a huge variety of different communications designed to elicit desired responses from the target audience. IMC is much more than just communicating; it is a focused strategic approach. Dahlen et al. (2010) propose that IMC requires a holistic approach, with a focus on five key areas:

- brand narrative – having one 'big idea' throughout the campaign;
- a single voice – all communications used need to be coordinated;
- consistency – in voice and appearance;
- value-adding – each communications tool used works together for a cumulative effect;
- cross-media presence – delivered via media consumed and preferred by the audience.

the elements of the plan in order to influence the target audience's behaviour and then proceed with the control and measurement of performance.

A planned approach to IMC requires some work; it isn't as simple as coming up with an idea and running with it (later in the chapter we consider key planning frameworks to support the process). Successful IMC needs to be built around a 'big idea', a brand narrative, a story that engages and resonates with the target audience. It requires the development of a message that is consistently delivered across all customer 'touch points', is meaningful to that audience, and is accessible, via the audience's preferred medium at a time that is most convenient to them.

A final, and highly important, consideration for successful IMC is that the integration happens at the level of the consumer or receiver (De Pelsmacker et al. 2017). This shifts the focus of IMC from being primarily an internal process, to being customer-focused. This links back to the need for the consistency of message delivered across all customer 'touch points', and Dahlen et al. (2010) stating that there should be a consistent single voice, the experience of consuming any of these communications should be seamless from a customer perspective, so that the customer does not feel they are being they are being targeted by an organisation or that sales messages are being pushed at them.

IMC in the marketing mix

It is also important to note, from a holistic integrated marketing communications perspective, that it is not just the promotional P of the marketing mix that communicates with a target audience, but all elements of the marketing mix – product, price and place, as well as promotion, and the people, process and physical evidence elements of the extended marketing mix – have the potential to communicate, and often do.

The marketing mix of product, price, promotion and place was proposed by Jerome McCarthy in 1960, and it was further developed by Bernard Booms and Mary Bitner in 1981 to add a further 3Ps that had more relevance for services: people, process and physical evidence (Jackson 2013). As a theoretical framework it is a useful starting point for considering all the areas within which marketing, and in this context marketing communications, decisions may need to be made.

The quality and design of a product communicates something to the audience, the price can communicate quality and value, the place of consumption can communicate in similar terms, whether it's a website or

Picture 21.2 Communicating is 'with' an audience, rather than 'at' an audience. Therefore, understanding your audience is vital in order to inform effective integrated marketing communications decision-making (*source:* Rawpixel Ltd/Alamy Stock Photo)

a physical retail environment, even the logistics and delivery communicate in terms of efficiency and customer care.

The elements added to the extended marketing mix concept – people, process and physical evidence – all communicate during the delivery and consumption of a service: the person, or people, delivering the service, how customer focused the delivery of the service is and the ambience and comfort of the environment within which it's delivered.

This may seem an oversimplification, but the key point to take away here is that all of the actions of the marketer, all of the actions of a business, all of the decisions made, communicate with a wide variety of audiences and there is a need for all of the activities within both the wider marketing mix, and the narrower communications mix, to be integrated. The integration of the elements of the marketing mix works in the same way as the integration of the marketing communications mix (advertising, PR, sales promotion, personal selling and direct marketing), adding value and offering a consistent and understandable message to all audiences.

IMC is targeted

Communications are nothing without an audience. Take a moment to think about it, what might people think if they saw you talking to yourself? It is vital that the audience is considered in our approach to marketing communications, it is imperative that all the effort expended in communicating is 'with' an audience, rather than 'at' an audience (or at no one!). Therefore, understanding who the target audience is, is vital in order to inform effective integrated marketing communications decision-making.

There are many ways to define who the target audience is, based on a variety of criteria, both subjective and objective. Percy and Rosenbaum-Elliot (2016) list the subjective criteria as lifestyle, personality and values: these are key psychographic bases for segmentation. The objective criteria are listed as location, age, gender, education and income: these are the geo-demographic bases for segmentation. One further area of consideration when working to understand the target audience is behaviour. The behaviour of the target audience requires us to consider patterns of consumption in areas such as usage of the product, preference for brands and features as well as the benefits required.

Without research into the target audience, considering areas such as who they are, their needs, their communication preferences, their media consumption, their decision-making processes, their influences, valuable resources will be wasted. So, a key component of successful IMC campaigns is the identification of relevant, similar, target audiences, that would have similar, positive reactions to the marketing communications stimuli used by the communications professional. These can then be developed into customer profiles or personas, offering an informed, yet fictional, representation of different user groups within the organisation's target audience.

Explore 21.1

How do they target you?

Drawing on your experience as a consumer for one of your favourite brands, and therefore a receiver of marketing communications messages aimed at you, investigate how many different ways that brand is creating touch points for you to experience. (For more information about 'touch points' read the section later in this chapter.)

Do they advertise on television, in magazines, on the internet, via outdoor posters or screens? Do they have a web page, and are on they present on social media channels? Do they ever send anything to you by text, email or post? Do they sponsor anything? Do they get media coverage that might have resulted from sending out a press release? What else might they be doing? Consider all the different methods used to deliver the message, and consider the consistency of the message; how well do you think their IMC works and is it integrated? Does it all seem to be part of a successful IMC campaign?

Why adopt an IMC approach?

There are many benefits to be gained from adopting an IMC approach within marketing communications. De Pelsmacker et al. (2017) propose that there are two key benefits to IMC. First, achieving consistency in the marketing communications which in turn improves the effectiveness of the message; it is more meaningful and memorable and supports the desired action or reaction from the target audience. Secondly, it reaches all relevant target audiences, through all channels, so there is little wastage of resources such as time and money, making the communications more efficient. This links back to the considerations of Dahlen et al. (2010) who stated IMC needs to have consistency in its messages across all relevant touch points.

However, the consideration of all available forms of contact and message channels may not be ideal. First of all, it is incredibly time consuming to consider every single communications channel. Ubiquity, or omni-channel communications, which is the presence in all available communications channels, is as problematic as it is costly. How can all of the messages communicated via the hundreds of thousands of different media vehicles available in the UK alone be managed so that they achieve the desired result? How can the performance and contribution of these channels be assessed?

The simple answer is that they cannot. The performance and contribution of every communications channels that exists cannot possibly be measured due to the constraints of time, money and skills within an organisation. Therefore, a further key aspect of successful IMC is not through achieving ubiquity or omni-channel presence (that is having a message delivered via every possible communications channel) but a focused multi-channel approach, identifying the most relevant and most effective media channels that are consumed and/or favoured by the target audience. Identifying the right channels to use within an IMC campaign can be achieved in one of two ways. The first option is to undertake what is referred to as 'demographic matching' which is identifying the key media channels to use via secondary research into the media consumption of the target audience. The other option is to undertake what is referred to as 'direct matching' – identifying the key media channels to utilise via primary research into the media consumption of the target audience (Percy and Rosenbaum-Elliott 2016).

So, one of the main benefits of IMC is that there is consistency of message, making the same message accessible to the target audience via all the media channels used. Each marketing communications tool and medium used to deliver a consistent message supports

Mini case study 21.2
Share a Coke

In 2013 Coca-Cola ran a highly effective IMC campaign that was part of a wider, global success story. The campaign originated in Australia in 2011 and delivered some impressive results on social media, including more than 18 million media impressions (how many times the individual pieces of communications across all of the media channels were seen by the audience) and an 870 per cent increase in Facebook traffic (Grimes 2013). The big idea was built around personalised content; in total over 1,000 of the UK's most popular names were printed on to Coca-Cola labels and made available for sale.

One big idea, enabled by digital technology and improved efficiencies in printing, that was communicated via paid-for media such as TV, Out of Home and Point of Sale, owned media including packaging, social and web, and earned media as their audience shared images of the product across social media, with a key focus on Facebook and Twitter (for more information on the different types of communications tools and media considered in IMC read the section 'Marketing communications tactics' later in this chapter). This was one big global, yet localised, idea delivered through successful IMC that, according to Coca-Cola (2016), was developed from just a 151-word creative brief. The creative brief is a document often developed in conjunction between a client organisation and a communications agency, although sometimes the creative brief is developed internally, without an agency's input, often referred to as 'in-house'.

and adds value to the others in the campaign, delivering a synergistic result. Each time the same message, or elements of the same message, is consumed by the audience it adds weight and credibility to what has already been communicated, which helps to improve credibility and trust, and therefore adding value. This is highly beneficial as the audience doesn't identify the differences in these tools and media, but they are able to better understand the message, and therefore process it better, to better inform their decision-making.

The planning process

In order to deliver a successful integrated marketing communications campaign, it is essential that those individuals involved in its creation, delivery and measurement follow a logical, structured planning process. Many marketing communications scholars are advocates of this structured planning approach. Table 21.1 identifies the similarities and differences of four IMC planning frameworks in relation to the steps they

Author of IMC planning framework	Dahlen et al. (2010)	Fill and Turnbull (2016)	Hackley (2010)	De Pelsmaker et al. (2017)
Analysis	Current brand evaluation Analysis	Context analysis	Brand research Target audience	Situation analysis Target groups
Planning	Marketing communications objectives Planning Application	Communications objectives Segmentation Push-Pull-Profile Task Strategy Coordinated communications mix	Communications objectives Strategy, creative approach and media plan	Objectives Budgets Message and Creative strategies Tools, touchpoints
Implementation	Implementation	Scheduling and implementation	Action plan and tactics	
Control	Evaluation	Evaluation and control Feedback	Budget estimates	Evaluation control

Table 21.1 Comparison of selected IMC planning frameworks

propose in relation to a standard Analyse, Plan, Implement and Control (APIC) process framework proposed by Kotler et al. (2008).

It can be observed from the above comparison that there are clearly some significant similarities in the IMC planning processes proposed by different marketing communications scholars as well as some subtle differences. What can be determined is that there is a clear four-stage process that is aligned to effective IMC planning.

Analysis

The first stage requires analysis; it answers the question 'where are we now'? Fill and Turnbull (2016) refer to it as a context analysis: the analysis of factors that are relevant to the context of marketing communications. Fill and Turnbull (2016) propose that there are four key contexts that require analysis: customer, business, internal and external. Through analysis of factors present within these contexts the communications professional can identify key audiences and how they behave, communications activities of key competitors and their impact, the strengths and weaknesses of the organisation in relation to communications and branding, and finally the impact and influence of the external factors, such as political, economic, social and technological, on marketing communications (see Table 21.2).

Planning

Following the analysis stage, we move on to the planning stage. Within this stage the IMC campaign's objectives are determined, along with the strategy, creative approach, message and finally the selection of the relevant marketing communications tactics, tools and media (an overview of these different tools can be found later in the chapter, in the 'Touch points' section). This is a significant stage as it involves considerable decision-making and requires information and insight drawn from the previous analysis to inform it. This information and insight can be drawn from a variety of sources, such as consumer surveys and research reports from organisations such as Nielsen, Kantar, Mintel and Ofcom.

First are the communications objectives, developed in order to provide focus and direction, as well as being designed to deliver on broader corporate and marketing objectives that will have been set prior to the development of the IMC plan. The objectives help to answer the question 'where do we want to be' and

Context	Factors to consider
External	Political – the impact of the ruling political party on legislation, regulations and initiatives on marketing communications
	Economic – the impact of the current and future economic climate on marketing communications
	Socio-cultural – the impact of changes in social and cultural behaviour on marketing communications
	Technological – the impact of developments in technology on marketing communications
Customer	Geographic – their location
	Demographic – age, gender, income, education
	Psychographic – motivations, lifestyle, aspirations
	Behavioural – their use of the product, brand preference and patterns of consumption
Market	Competitors – focused on their communications activities
	Stakeholders – focused on relationships and their needs and wants
Internal	Resources – human, financial, material
	Current communication campaigns – strengths and weaknesses
	Corporate objectives – to be achieved
	Marketing objectives – to be achieved
	Culture – impact on decision-making and implementation
	Brand – values and desired position

Table 21.2 Key factors within the marketing communications environment

can be set using a framework such as SMART in order to offer clarity, direction and a way of measuring performance. The objectives set can be seen as specific goals as to what the IMC plan wishes to achieve, and the SMART framework supports this. SMART is a mnemonic for:

- Specific – to an audience, a brand or product;
- Measurable – to ensure that there is a metric in place to allow for control and monitoring of performance;
- Achievable – within the resources of the organisation;

- Relevant (or realistic) – based on the findings from an analysis of the marketing environment;
- Time-bound – what is to be achieved needs to have a determined time-frame in order to support measurement.

For example, a SMART objective for a university may be 'To deliver an increase in online leads of 5% from all UK A-Level students (receiving results in 2019/2020) via a four-week sponsored social media campaign for the new undergraduate PR course at the university by the 31 December 2020'.

This then leads to the determination of the communications strategy. There are a number of strategic models and frameworks that can be considered here. One key model is segmentation, targeting and positioning (or STP) and it aids any communications professional in determining exactly who the target audience(s) will be, how they will be targeted via the tactics and tools, and how the organisation, brand, product and/or message will be positioned in the market place. This will be covered in more detail later in the chapter.

Fill (Fill and Turnbull 2016) also proposes that the direction of communications need strategic consideration. He identifies three key directions that marketing communications can travel in to support positioning: push, pull and profile (Figure 21.1). Pull-positioning considers the communications tools, message and creative approach used to reach the end-user of the product or brand. Push-positioning focuses on intermediaries involved within marketing and distribution channels. Finally, profile-positioning focuses on the communications with all stakeholder groups outside of consumer and intermediaries.

With a profile strategy the focus of communications is not on the flow of products and demand but to satisfy the needs of the differing stakeholders an

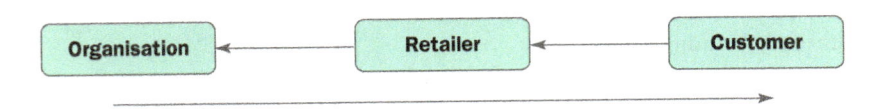

Organisation ← Retailer ← Customer

With a **pull** strategy the flow of communications goes direct from organisation to customer to create a 'pull' demand for the product.

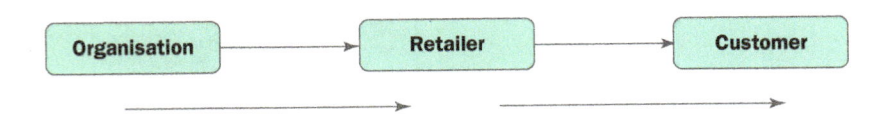

Organisation → Retailer → Customer

With a **push** strategy the flow of communications is direct to an intermediary, such as a retailer, to encourage them to 'push' the product to the customer.

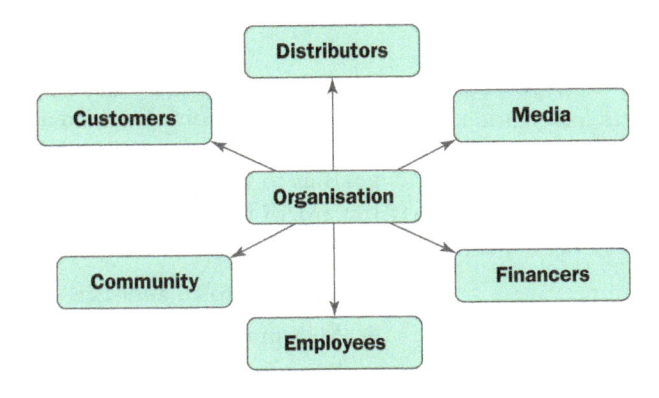

Organisation ↔ Distributors, Media, Financers, Employees, Community, Customers

A **Profile** strategy considers communications with all stakeholder groups.

Figure 21.1 Push, pull and profile strategies

organisation has. It is this communication strategy that is traditionally considered as having a corporate communications focus (Fill 2016). These three strategies are not mutually exclusive and should, in fact, be considered together, in order to maximise the effectiveness of communications, bringing in consistency and ensuring that the different media consumed by the different audiences identified across push, pull and profile strategies are identified and used.

Having determined the objectives and strategy the next stage is to decide on the marketing communications mix. As mentioned in the introduction, it is important that as a communications professional you are aware that all activities within the broader 7P marketing mix have the potential to communicate. However, within this stage of the planning process the focus is on determining an effective combination of paid, owned and earned media (Pessin and Weaver 2014): communications activities from the mix of advertising, PR, sales promotion, direct marketing and personal selling. See Table 21.3 for examples.

The mix of tools and media need to be able to successfully convey the message to the identified audience, so that the desired effect(s) specified in the communications objective(s) is(are) achieved. There is no magic formula when it comes to developing the 'right' marketing communications mix, but it is important to remember the need for consistency of the message and the brand throughout.

Implementation

Once the planning stage has been completed all of the resources necessary to effectively implement the plan can then be determined: human, financial, material, time. These will have been considered during the development of the plan to some extent, especially when determining the communications mix, but at this stage they become a reality. Project plans, or perhaps Gantt charts, are drawn up providing a schedule to support implementation and resource management. The timing of the activities is set out so that all involved in the delivery of the plan are aware of what will happen, when it will happen and who is responsible. It will also determine what material resources are needed and by when, and if there are any complex and/or critical elements to the plan that require significant focus. Project planning is also a vital tool when it comes to determining and managing the budget, as IMC campaigns can, at times, be quite expensive. For example, the Coca-Cola 'Share a Coke' global advertising budget was $4 billion in 2016 alone (Coca Cola Annual Review 2016).

Measurement and control

The final stage of the planning process is one of measurement and control. From previous stages of the IMC planning process we will now know 'where we are', we know 'where we want to be' and the strategy and tactics that set out 'how will we get there', but how do we know if we arrived at the desired outcome? Measurement and control are vital within IMC planning, as without it, there can be no learning, no feedback and ultimately no improvement.

One of the key areas to focus on when it comes to measurement is to refer back to the objectives set earlier in the planning process. If they were truly SMART then they will have two key criteria for control, a measurable outcome and a timeframe to achieve it within. Taking these criteria and relating them to the performance of the chosen communications mix is highly important in terms of measuring performance, recognising success and also learning from any mistakes. There are many well-documented examples of marketing communications campaigns that have been unsuccessful – remember Pepsi and Kendall Jenner in 2017 (the controversial advert that was accused of undermining the Black Lives Matter movement). Some have even backfired and had a negative impact on the

Media	Examples
Paid – any medium that has to be paid for by the organisation in order to communicate, often advertising	TV advertisement, print advertisement, outdoor advertisement, online advertisement, flyer, letter.
Owned – any medium possessed and controlled by the organisation	Website, corporate social media channels, vehicles, uniforms, signage.
Earned – any medium that communicates about the organisation but is not paid for or owned.	Word of mouth, customer reviews, consumer-generated content.

Table 21.3 Paid, owned and earned media

organisation's reputation and even stock market value (such as the H&M and their 'Coolest Monkey in the Jungle' gaff in 2018). What is important is that successes as well as failures within IMC campaigns are considered in order to improve future decision-making with IMC.

Benefits of following the planning process

There are many benefits proposed by authors, academics and practitioners in relation to working through a structured planning process for IMC, but there are also several barriers to successfully implementing the process and integrating marketing communications. De Pelsmacker et al. (2017) identify a range of drivers that have led to an increased need for this integrated approach. These include, but are not limited to, factors such as:

- the fragmentation of audiences and media;
- the need to be more cost-effective;
- the need for an increased impact;
- lower levels of brand differentiation;
- increased expectation of internal accountability.

It is through following the IMC planning process that these issues can be overcome; it is a strategic process that is driven by a variety of changes, both internal and external. The act of following the planning process can offer many benefits: that resources are better utilised and accounted for, relationships better managed, technology better understood and utilised and, ultimately, the delivery of a consistent and relevant series of ongoing communications to the appropriate target audience(s).

Audiences

In order for IMC to be successful, it has to be considered as a wholly strategic process. As Fill and Turnbull (2016: 177) state, a key element of successful strategy 'should be concerned with the overall direction of the programme and target audiences, the fit with marketing and corporate strategy, the key message and desired positioning the brand is to occupy in the market, and the resources necessary to deliver the position and accomplish the overall.' So, as discussed above, all of the elements of the IMC planning process considered in this chapter are part of this strategic process, and the key decision is that of the identification of the target audience(s).

It is suggested by a number of scholars (see Kotler et al. 2008; Fill and Turnbull 2016; Richardson et al. 2015) that there are three key decisions that needs to be made during this strategy stage in relation to the target audience. These are: how best to segment the market, which of those identified segments to target in a particular campaign, and, finally, how the organisation, brand and/or product is to be positioned within the communications that will form the campaign to influence the position held in the mind of the audience. These key decisions are made within what is known as the STP process – segmentation, targeting and positioning.

Segmentation

No campaign can ever be all things to all people. Even the largest mass-market campaigns will still have specific audiences, or segments, that they're designed for. Segmentation requires the target market to be broken down into groups that are discernible, accessible, measurable and profitable (Kotler et al. 2008). Details of which segment(s) a campaign needs to target is a vital part of the IMC plan as it aids decision-making in relation to the creative approach, the 'big idea' and messages, as well as ensuring that the right marketing communications tools and media are used to deliver the campaign.

Think about 21.1

Rejecting the planning process

An organisation that chooses not to follow a structured planning process for its marketing communications may face a number of issues. What do you think they might be?

Feedback

Some of the issues an organisation that doesn't plan may face include:

- a lack of direction for all employees involved;
- a lack of consistency in the brand communications which can lead to confusion;
- resources: time, financial and material, are wasted;
- no measurement of results which leads to limited learning from experience.

The key ways for communications professionals to segment their market are through the following bases:

- *Demographics:* objective characteristics of the audience such as age, gender, occupation, income, education and socio-economic status (class).
- *Geographic:* where the audience is located: local, regional, national or international.
- *Geodemographic:* synthesises information from both of the above bases to offer a more insightful set of objectives characteristics. ACORN and Mosaic are commercially available consumer classifications that use data from demographics, social factors, population and, increasingly, behavioural research.
- *Psychographic:* a more subjective classification of the audience considering their preferences with regard to their lifestyle, interests, opinions and attitudes, personality and behaviour.
- *Behavioural:* categorises the audience based on behaviour such as usage patterns, buying habits, the benefit(s) they seek and spending priorities.

Segmenting the audience by brand usage and loyalty can also be considered. Rossiter and Bellman (2005) devised a way to categorise consumers by their relationship with a brand, that still has relevance today, dividing consumers into:

- *Loyal brand users:* loyalty may come through a love of the brand or they may be loyal out of habit and inertia, but they are a highly important market segment.
- *Favourable brand switchers:* consumers who are willing to switch to, or trial, new brands (perhaps driven by sales promotions) but on the whole tend to have a favourable attitude towards the organisation's brand.
- *Other brand switchers:* another segment willing to trial new brands but have a more favourable attitude towards a competing brand rather than the organisation's brand.
- *Other brand loyals:* are loyal to a competing brand from another organisation and are less likely to switch. It can be difficult to persuade them to switch, even on a trial basis.
- *(Potential) new category users:* consumers who have just entered the market for the product category to which our brand is part. They are open to trialling a variety of brands and can respond well to offers.

Explore 21.2

Segmentation and you

Due to the volume of marketing communications we are all exposed so it is safe to assume that there are organisations out there who place you into a variety of different segments for the purpose of developing and delivering effective IMC.

What segments are you placed into by different organisations for different products? For health and beauty products you may fall into one specific market segment but for leisure activities another. Think about a special interest you might have, a hobby, sport or activity you're passionate about. What are the key themes and factors that can be identified that enable an organisation to place you into a segment? Which are subjective bases and which are objective?

Visit https://caci.co.uk/ and explore ACORN, a consumer classification tool, via the Try ACORN Now link. What segmentation bases do they use? Which segment do you fit within now? How might this change in the future?

There are other methods of segmentation: those discussed above offer some insight into some of the key approaches that can be taken. Determining which segment(s) the IMC campaign needs to be targeted towards depends on the objectives of the campaign, as well as the broader marketing and corporate objectives. It is an important stage within a set of strategic decisions informed by both secondary and primary data.

Targeting

Once the process of segmentation has been undertaken, the relevant target audience(s) can be identified in the next stage of this strategic process. It is important to select target audience(s) who can be reached through communications. Baines et al. (2013) provides a summary of what to consider when making targeting decisions. The target segment(s) chosen must be:

- *Measurable:* easy to identify and measure the response with.
- *Substantial:* provide an audience of a suitable size with which to achieve objectives.

- *Accessible:* they must consume the communications tools and media we can access.
- *Differentiable:* must have significantly different set of characteristics to justify their targeting.
- *Actionable:* the IMC campaign must be capable of actually reaching them.

Hackley (2010) states, 'get it wrong, and all the effort is wasted. If the defined audience is too narrow then opportunities for consumer engagement will be lost . . . If the target group definition is too wide, then the impact may be lost of the campaign might be scheduled on a medium which the real targets don't use'. So, this part of the targeting strategy ensures that the audiences we choose to focus on are relevant.

A further area of consideration within targeting strategy, as set out by Jobber (2010), is to consider the direction of targeting. There are four proposed directions:

- *Undifferentiated:* one communications, and marketing, mix is used for the range of relevant segments identified. This is a mass market approach.
- *Differentiated:* the communications mix is adapted for each of the different segments identified. Arguably, through effective use of data and technology in IMC, achieving differentiation is now easier, but also expected more by audiences.
- *Focused:* sometimes referred to as niche marketing. One relevant segment is identified and their needs are met better than that of the competition.
- *Customised:* the marketing, and the communications, mix are customised for a variety of diverse market segments.

This means that as well as ensuring the segments we plan to target are relevant, we also need to consider how we communicate with them and the degree to which we standardise, or customise, our message and mix.

Positioning

Positioning, ultimately, is how the consumer (or any stakeholder really) positions the organisation, brand and/or product in their mind against those of key competitors. It has a clear link to brand identity, but more specifically brand image, which is how the brand is perceived by the customer. From an IMC perspective, positioning guides how we, as communications professionals, utilise our message, tactics and media to deliver a perceived position that the organisation desires in the mind of the target audience.

Kapferer (2012) recommends four questions that should be answered in order to support effective positioning:

- A brand for what benefit? What is the brand promise, the element that makes the offering unique?
- A brand for whom? Who is this a brand for? This doesn't necessarily have to be built around geo-demographics, those objective criteria. Brands can also position based on subjective criteria, a brand for the stylish, a brand for those at the cutting edge.
- Reason? What evidence can be offered to supports the benefit?
- A brand against whom? Who are we positioning against? Within what product category are we competing?

Keller (2013) proposes something similar, based around frames of reference in relation to determining the product category the organisation, brand and/or product will compete within, the points of differentiation, what is unique about the offering, and finally points of parity, which reassure the audience that the offering is relevant to the category and builds trust. The organisation may benefit from the development of a positioning statement built around the questions posed by Kapferer and Keller, especially if what is being offered is new to market.

Successful brands will have built and maintained a successful position within their market over a substantial period of time, and consumers readily associate those brands with the communicated position. For example, Apple for innovation, design and simplicity, Virgin Atlantic for fun and glamour, Disney for family entertainment. Ouwersloot and Duncan (2008) developed a number of different criteria for consideration in order to support the development of a successful positioning strategy.

- *Category positioning:* here the brand defines, creates or owns a category. Think of Heinz and baked beans, McDonalds and American fast food, Google and search engines.
- *Unique product feature positioning:* based on a quality of feature that is genuinely unique about the brand. This could be price, quality, innovation, a particular feature or benefit.
- *Image positioning:* the position is developed through a created (or symbolic) association. This is often based on a purposefully created strong association that cannot be applied, or adopted, by competitors – think of Carlsberg and being 'probably the best lager in the world'.

Chapter 21 Integrated marketing communications

> ### Think about 21.2
> #### Positioning
>
> Apple's iPhone and Samsung's Galaxy are two very similar products, in the same product category. However, many people have a clear preference for one of these over the other. What do you think are the reasons for this, with consideration of positioning theory?
>
> #### Feedback
>
> The reasons for a preference of one smartphone brand over another may include:
>
> - the brand being positioned specifically for their age group;
> - the brand being positioned by image which is desirable to the audience;
> - the brand being positioned via a specific benefit, such as style;
> - the brand is positioned as the leader in the category and thus more recognisable.

- *Benefit positioning*: based on fulfilling a consumer need or desire. This can be tangible need, brought about by the design of the product, such as Post-It Notes, or intangible such as perfumes and fragrances and their links to desirability and sexual attraction.

Some communications professionals have taken the positioning concept further in recent years and consider the impact of everything the organisation does, how it acts and behaves, as being influential in their positioning in the minds of their audience. Graham Hales (2011), Managing Director of Interbrand UK, explained that 'organisations need to align their brand (position) with all aspects of their operations, stretching across products and services, human resources practices, corporate behaviour, environments and communications'. This is representative of truly integrated marketing communications.

Marketing communications tactics

When considering marketing communications tactics, the main area of attention in relation to theory is the marketing communications mix. This mix primarily comprises advertising, public relations, sales promotion, direct marketing and personal selling (Kotler et al. 2008; Fill and Turnbull 2016). These five tactical elements within the promotional, or communications, mix include many different channels and media, or 'tools'. When it comes to defining media there are three key types: paid, owned and earned (see Table 21.3). The increasing volume of, and accessibility to, digital media channels has meant that the focus within integration has begun to shift from a predominantly paid approach, to a more integrated effort across paid, owned and earned media channels.

Advertising

Advertising is largely thought of as the tactic that delivers mass communications via paid, or rented, media. This includes media channels such as television, radio, print, cinema, out of home (or outdoor) and online advertising. Advertising is one of the key marketing communications tactics that can be used to achieve

> ### Mini case study 21.3
> #### Targeting the TV ad – Sky AdSmart
>
> When watching commercial TV, the media buyers tend to focus on the main viewing segment of a show (or vehicle to bring in some advertising jargon) when determining which to use. However, this is beginning to change as Sky Media have recently rolled out the AdSmart service across Europe.
>
> This service provides advertisers with a never-before-offered opportunity to target individual households based on lifestyle, finance, credit, health and beauty, household composition, home ownership and vehicle ownership data. This allows a level of targeting via commercial TV shows that is only possible through the development of technology and the effective use of customer data.
>
> Sky Media claim that this helps to level the playing field in TV advertising, and can make it accessible to all organisations, as ad campaigns can now be developed by SMEs with a smaller audience and a smaller advertising budget. Success stories range from big brands in the UK such as Sainsbury's and McDonalds, to those much smaller, such as Cotswold Country Interiors and Gordale Garden and Home Centre!

mass awareness, reaching large audiences through the delivery of a message through paid-for broadcast spots and printed spaces on, or in, relevant commercial media channels. Advertising can be used to not only raise awareness of a product around its launch, but also to keep reminding the public of its existence during the year. It can also help to balance the effects of negative publicity.

Public relations

Many of the communications activities an organisation engages in can be considered to be public relations. Quite often public relations campaigns utilise owned and earned media, whereas advertising, and in association sales promotion, is predominantly delivered through paid media.

Public relations, in the form of media publicity, can be used to reinforce paid media in creating short-term awareness. A longer-term, planned approach to public relations can be used to develop stronger links with the press, and other key stakeholders, so that any potential negative coverage can be minimised. Hosting events, charity associations and building and maintaining community relations are some examples of activities that can be used to promote a positive image to a target audience. Other key public relations tools used to develop and maintain positive relations include activities such as press conferences, press releases and social media communications.

Ultimately, within the context of the marketing communications mix, public relations is considered primarily a tactical approach used to develop and maintain a positive perception of the organisation, brand and/or product in the minds of the various publics, or stakeholders, that the organisation has.

Sales promotion

Sales promotion involves offering incentives to customers in order to stimulate a desired behaviour. In the case of visiting a tourist attraction, for example, reduced price tickets might be offered on a group basis, made possible by an increase in the volume of sales. Similar offers might be made at quieter times to increase visitor numbers. Families would be less likely to visit during school time, so incentives could be offered to other groups to encourage them to visit during this period.

A sales promotion is primarily designed to increase sales at the time of the promotion and is not aimed at achieving long-term customer loyalty. However, sales promotions can be used more strategically in order to

> **Explore 21.3**
>
> ### Rewarding your loyalty
>
> Are you a member of any loyalty schemes or do you hold any loyalty cards? Have you ever used any? In the UK there are a variety of systems in place to reward the loyalty of the returning customer. O2 provide an exclusive reward system called 'Priority Moments' for their network customers. This is what is known as a 'value-adding' sales promotion, with value being added to the transaction and relationship with some more, or extra. This includes priority access to some TV shows and event tickets, as well as food-based deals and the chance to win unique experiences.
>
> But why would an organisation offer so much for free? As well as the repeat, or continued, custom that has obvious financial value, for what other reasons do organisations offer rewards for continued custom? What are the benefits an organisation can derive from this relationship?

develop more long-term relationships. Reward systems for existing customers such as the Tesco Clubcard, Nectar Card or even O2 Priority Moments are essentially sales promotions but are designed to add value over the longer term.

Organisations can use loyalty cards, or similar reward systems, to build databases of information about their customers and their preferences, in order to target promotions more effectively in future. Information can be gathered in a number of other ways, such as customer satisfaction surveys following purchases and via customer records of individual purchases. For example, car dealerships may store information for each customer on the date and nature of their last purchase, their age, social grouping and family status, in order to target those customers most likely to buy when they launch a new model or take a new vehicle when a lease is about to expire.

Direct marketing

Direct marketing is a communications tactic that is in essence advertising, as it is a paid for medium, and can offer a highly personalised form of communication. Direct marketing is a term used to describe any form of personalised, direct communications with a customer or stakeholder.

There are a number of different channels and media that can be used to directly target the recipient of the message including email, SMS, mail, telephone, TV, Video on Demand and direct selling. Ultimately, any channel through which a message and call to action can be delivered directly to the end user can be thought of as a direct marketing tool.

As technology develops, direct marketing can be used to reach target consumers based on their digital behaviour; as and when they browse, when they search, at any time and via mobile devices, in any place. It is also a beneficial tool in relation to maintaining relationships with customers and stakeholders due to the ability to personalise the message. Because of this, direct marketing is a very common supporting tactic used alongside personal selling in B2B communications and campaigns.

Personal selling

Personal selling involves the use of a sales team to promote products and services, usually on a one-to-one basis. This is more appropriate for selling in a business-to-business environment, or in the sale of services such as financial products, due to the high cost per contact. Here the product/service is complex in nature, of a high value, and needing careful explanation. The message communicated can then be personalised immediately to the buyer's need. Key Account Management (KAM) emerged out of personal selling, where the most important and/or profitable customers, clients and/or accounts are identified, and the relationship managed in order to retain the key account(s) and drive growth.

Touch points

Advertising, PR, sales promotion, direct marketing and personal selling are the five key tactics of marketing communications, those which theory tells us are five core activities through which marketers communicate, but they don't clear identify the channels, tools or media that we can use. Building on the work undertaken by Kelley (2015), Table 21.4 identifies a variety of key communications' tools that marketers can integrate in order to create multiple touch points between organisation and audience. So, tactics are the broader tools that we can use within IMC (such as advertising and PR) but tools refer to the media and channels that are present within each of the tactics.

Identified in the table are some of the tools and/or media that communications professionals can utilise to provide touch points: brand encounters, conversations or 'moments of truth'.

As mentioned already in this chapter, the emphasis when determining what communications tools and media to select is on the audience. Which of the above media does your target audience consume, which do they trust, and which do they turn to for entertainment or information? Understanding this can help create touch points that have significance and relevance. These tools and media would very rarely be used in isolation because the choice of communications tools and media need to work together to add value to each other, so that 'a synergistic effect is reached, and the resulting communications effort becomes seamless and homogenous' (De Pelsmacker et al. 2017). What's important about IMC, however, is that tools are chosen because they will work best for the organisation, the brand, the message, the target market and within the budget.

However, it's also not about using as many tactics as you possibly can. Doing this can have a negative impact

Think about 21.3

Which works best?

Select any well-known brand and consider an IMC campaign they have run recently. Take the time to consider the different tools and media used to deliver the message. Now consider the IMC of a smaller or lesser-known brand, perhaps for a company local to you or a small business that you know of (if you're struggling to find examples then you could head to marketing industry websites such as *WARC*, *The Drum* or *Campaign* to find one). Note the variation within the IMC mix, in relation to tools and media. Which do you think works best – big, bold and many – or small, subtle and few? Why have you come to this conclusion, how were you influenced by what you found considering the different campaigns? Was this because of personal preference? Are there elements within both campaigns that work well, and if so, what were they? What was the underlying message of each campaign? What did they want the receiver of the message to do?

Feedback

There is no right or wrong answer here. Different types of campaigns, and their communication's mixes, can be both successful and unsuccessful. Big, bold and many tend to be used for FMCG products, with a more mass-market appeal, whereas small and subtle campaigns are used for niche products and smaller, more specialist markets.

Broadcast advertising	Out of home advertising	Direct response advertising
■ Television ■ Radio ■ Magazine ■ Newspaper ■ Cinema ■ Product placement ■ Video on demand ■ Online (i.e. YouTube)	■ Posters ■ Billboard/banner ■ Transportation ■ Street furniture ■ Ambient ■ Digital screens ■ Guerrilla	■ Direct mail ■ Telephone ■ SMS/MMS ■ Email ■ Social media
In-store and point-of-sale advertising	**Sponsorship and events**	**Personal selling**
■ Store signage ■ In-store signage and display ■ Shopping trolley ■ In-store radio/TV ■ Packaging ■ Merchandising	■ Sport sponsorship ■ Art and festival sponsorship ■ Charity sponsorship ■ Events ■ Stunts	■ Sales team ■ Customer service ■ Demonstration ■ Presentation ■ Exhibition ■ Key account management
Sales promotions	**Online/digital**	**PR and journalism**
■ Special price offer ■ Coupon/discount ■ Samples ■ Competitions ■ Free gifts ■ Limited edition ■ Reward programs	■ Social media posts ■ Corporate website ■ Affiliates ■ Influencer ■ Reviews and ratings ■ Communities ■ Viral and buzz ■ Blogging ■ Gaming ■ SEO ■ Paid Search/Display ■ Native	■ Press release ■ Media/trade event ■ Advertorial/native ■ In-house magazine ■ Newsletters ■ Events ■ Public engagements ■ Community relations ■ Employee relations

Table 21.4 Touch points: some key IMC activities (*source:* Adapted from Keller (2013), Shimp (2010), Dahlen et al. (2010), Fill and Turnbull (2016) and Kelley (2015))

on the quality of message, and overstretch resources, especially the budget. As Nick Emmel of advertising agency Dare (Campaign 2010) said, 'It is tempting to do all these things because they are there – when a press ad would have worked just as well . . . Consumers don't always want to interact with your brand on multiple levels and sometimes a single idea communication in one channel is enough'.

The impact of technology cannot be underestimated in the development and acceptance of an IMC approach. New ways of reaching and communicating with audiences have had a significant impact on the approach communications professionals take to selecting of tools and media. Jonathan Mildenhall, CMO at Airbnb and previously Senior VP Integrated Marketing Communications at Coca-Cola, refers to the more technologically savvy audiences as being consumers in a hyper-connected world, or 'hyper-connected consumers'. There are still increasing number of communications tools and, more significantly, media available, all facilitated by technological developments. These hyper-connected consumers are more in control of what media they access, where they access it, when they access it, and the reason for accessing. This further facilitates the need for an IMC focus within all that the organisation does.

Developments in technology associated with communications, such as mobile platforms and improved connectivity, have facilitated a shift in emphasis from **promoting to** consumers to **communicating with** consumers. It has also facilitated the increased creation and consumption of consumer-generated media. Nielsen's Global Trust in Advertising Survey (2015) found that earned medium of consumer opinion posted online was trusted by 66 per cent of global consumers and drove 69 per cent to act (this could be an action such as clicking to find out more information or making a purchase). Google (Lecinski 2011) refers to these consumer opinions posted online and then read by potential customers as the 'Zero Moment of Truth'.

This has revolutionised consumer decision-making and behaviour when online. The perceived value of the (online) opinion or review, the rise of the influential celebrity blogger, the fact that the internet has changed customer's notions as to what constitutes an expert option and who customers trust (Bernhoff and Li 2011) requires more attention to be paid to how to use IMC in order to develop and maintain a two-way flow of communication with consumers.

Consumers can now be active participants within marketing communications, rather than the now obsolete view of consumers who are passive and easily influenced by marketing communication's messages. Bernhoff and Li (2011) propose that this shift in emphasis requires communications professional to at first be able to listen, before moving on to talking with their audiences, in order to deliver successful IMC.

IMC, when planned, executed and managed correctly, is a highly effective and efficient way to reach the right audiences at the right time and in a way that encourages engagement and participation with brand communications in a way that ultimately benefits both consumers and brand owners.

Case study 21.1
More than a Lidl growth

As a relatively new discount supermarket in the UK, opening in its first store in 1994, Lidl continue to face significant competition, from the big four supermarkets in the UK, from their most direct competitor, Aldi, and a growing online grocery market.

They also had to overcome a particular misconception in relation to their brand image, that higher prices equal better-quality products. With a market place worth over £100 billion a year in the UK, with all households purchasing multiple times every week, and where polygamy is the norm, Lidl needed to change perceptions and, to an extent, behaviour.

With sceptical grocery UK shoppers, assuming that cheaper prices mean lower quality, Lidl needed to find a way to address this. They also had a corporate objective of accelerating growth and a marketing objective of increasing household penetration. What followed was a four-year integrated marketing communications campaign, #LidlSurprises, increasing their share of voice in the market place and dispelling the myth of low prices equal low quality.

Picture 21.3 Lidl's four-year integrated marketing communications campaign #LidlSurprises, increased the company's share of voice in the competitive supermarket retail place and dispelled the brand's myth of low prices equal low quality (*source:* Matthew Horwood/Getty Images)

case study 21.1 (continued)

TV was at the heart of the IMC campaign, supported by out of home, cinema, digital, door drops, radio and press media, and a PR campaign that focused on pushing the quality angle to journalists and publishers. The campaign itself has won a number of awards, including the IPA Gold, at the IPA Effectiveness Awards in 2018, *Marketing Week*'s Visionary Marketer of the Year 2016 and The Drum Marketing Awards for Re-brand Strategy of the Year (to name but a few).

Changing misperceptions

The big idea behind the campaign was to shift away from short-term sales driven campaigns, and to adopt a more strategic, IMC approach to deliver a consistent message and change what people thought. How? The overall creative brief answered this with the overarching direction: 'tell people the truth about Lidl' and thus the Lidl Surprises campaign was born.

Lidl couldn't grow the market: everybody buys groceries, so customers had to come from other retailers – their competitors. Following research into the grocery market, it was found that there were no specific segments to target, that there was no supermarket that Lidl needed to attract customers away from, they needed to wage war on the market place and do so on a mass scale.

This required a national advertising campaign, but with a creative appeal that was more of a stunt. The general public were to experience and consume Lidl products in situations where quality and provenance were key drivers for purchase over price, such as farmer's markets and dining experiences at a country house and a gastro (high-quality dining) pub. The twist at the end was the big reveal; these were cheaper products from the Lidl supermarket, but the perception of quality, uninfluenced by brand image, was greeted enthusiastically.

To support this, there was a microsite that offered high-quality recipes using only Lidl products and a successful hashtag campaign, #LidlSurprises, that encouraged current customers to post about their experiences of quality with the supermarket. The hashtag element was a success, as customers using it in their social media were rewarded by seeing their posts immortalised in Lidl's Point of Sale in store, and also in their out of home posters and billboards. Allowing customers to participate in the campaign meant that the trust in the message was amplified, and perceptions began to change.

As the campaign evolved, customer participation began to play an even bigger role, and selected individuals who had expressed doubts in quality and provenance of Lidl products via social media were invited to visit the producers. Each iteration begin with a cynical or sceptical comment and ended, following their re-education, with a new brand advocate, forever changed in their perception of the brand.

The four-year campaign cost a lot, £20 million in its first year, reduced in part over the following three years, but estimated at somewhere between £70–75 million overall, but was it worth it? As a brand in a competitive marketplace trying to be heard against competitors, their share of voice increased from 6.4 to 15.5 per cent, but all this really tells us is that they spent a lot in order to be heard.

Shopper numbers grew significantly. Lidl had a 3.5 per cent market share at the start of the campaign, and a 5.1 per cent market share by the end. Lidl's annual sales grew by £2.56 billion over the four-year period that the Lidl Surprises campaign ran, from £3.27 billion in 2013 to £5.83 billion in 2017, with the investment in the campaign said to have accounted for a contribution of £627 million in 2017, and a longer-term impact on brand momentum worth 4 per cent of future growth, and not forgetting a shift in customer perceptions of the brand and associated quality.

Source: Adapted from Clouder 2018 and lidl.co.uk 2019

Summary

In this chapter we have identified and discussed the fact that IMC is a planning process. We considered that when undertaken correctly IMC can help support the successful achievement of an organisation's corporate and marketing objectives through a coordinated and synergistic marketing communication campaign. IMC should primarily be led by the audience; the media they consume, the language they respond to, content that has meaning to them, and also through the media that the consumer can now create and publish online, such as reviews and blog posts.

The key components of the IMC plan are analysis, objectives, strategy, tactics, action planning and control. It is within the tactical section that the five key areas of marketing communication are considered, advertising, PR, sales promotion, personal selling and direct marketing, and decisions made as to which of these tactics, and their related tools and media, are used in order to achievement the desired results.

Bibliography

Baines, P., C. Fill and K. Page (2013). *Essentials of Marketing.* Oxford: Oxford University Press.

Baker, M. (2014). *Marketing Strategy and Management.* London: Palgrave.

Bernhoff, J. and C. Li (2011). *Groundswell: Winning in a world transformed by social technologies.* Boston: Harvard Business School Press.

Brinker, S. (2016) *Marketing Technology Landscape Supergraphic 2016.* Chiefmartec http://chiefmartec.com/2016/03/marketing-technology-supergraphic-2016/ [Accessed 3 May 2018]

Campaign (2010). *What Next in Integration?* 3 December 2010.

CIM (2004). *You talkin' to me? – marketing communications in the age of consent.* Berkshire: Chartered Institute of Marketing.

Clouder, J. (2018) *How Lidl Grew a Lot,* WARC, available at https://www.warc.com/content/article/How_Lidl_grew_a_lot/122389 [accessed 31 May 2019]

Coca Cola Company (2016) *Annual Report Form 10-K,* available at https://www.coca-colacompany.com/content/dam/journey/us/en/private/fileassets/pdf/investors/2016-AR-10-K.pdf [accessed 25 May 2019]

Dahlen, M., F. Lange and T. Smith (2010). *Marketing Communications: A Brand Narrative Approach.* Chichester, John Wiley & Sons.

De Pelsmacker, P., M. Geuens and J. Van den Bergh (2017). *Marketing Communications: A European Perspective,* 6th edn, Harlow: Pearson Education Limited.

Fill, C. and S. Turnbull (2016). *Marketing Communications: Discovery, creation and conversations,* 7th edn, Essex: Pearson Education.

Gibson, O. (2005). Shopper's eye view of ads that pass us by. *The Guardian,* http://www.theguardian.com/media/2005/nov/19/advertising.marketingandpr [Accessed 11 January 2019].

Grimes, T. (2013). What the Share a Coke campaign can teach other brands. *The Guardian,* http://www.theguardian.com/media-network/media-network-blog/2013/jul/24/share-coke-teach-brands [Accessed 15 January 2019].

Hackley, C. (2010). *Advertising and Promotion: An integrated marketing communications approach.* London: Sage.

Hales, G. (2011). *Branding.* In: Kourdi, J. ed. *The Marketing Century.* Chichester: John Wiley & Sons, pp. 139–168.

Hepburn, M. (no date) *The Share a Coke Story,* http://www.coca-cola.co.uk/stories/history/advertising/share-a-coke/ [accessed 11 January 2018].

Hughes, G. and C. Fill (2007). 'Redefining the nature and format of the marketing communications mix.' *Marketing Review* 7(1): 45–57.

ITV, (no date), *Second Screen.* [online] Available at http://www.itvmedia.co.uk/advertising-opportunities/online-advertising/second-screen [Accessed 15 December 2018]

Jackson, N. (2013) *Promoting and Marketing Events.* London: Routledge.

Jobber, D. (2010). *Principles and Practice of Marketing.* Berkshire: McGraw Hill Education.

Kapferer, J. (2012) *The New Strategic Brand Management,* 5th edn, Kogan Page: London

Keller, K. (2013) *Strategic Brand Management: Building, measuring and managing brand equity,* 4th edn, Essex: Pearson.

Kelley, N. (2015) in N. Richardson, J. James and N. Kelley (2015) *Customer-Centric Marketing.* London, Kogan Page.

Kelley, N. (2017) *Integrated Marketing Communications.* in: Tench, R. and Yeomans, L. (2016) *Exploring Public Relations.* Harlow: Pearson Education Limited.

Kotler, P., G. Armstrong, V. Wong and J. Saunders (2008). *Principles of Marketing.* Fifth European Edition. Harlow: Prentice Hall.

Lecinski, J. (2011). *ZMOT: Winning the zero moment of truth.* Google.

Lidl Stiftung and Co., About us. Available at https://www.lidl.co.uk/en/About-Us.htm [accessed 31 May 2019].

Light, L. (2004). 'More knowledge can only lead to better ad creative'. *New Media Age,* 7 October 2004.

Marshall, A. (2015). How Many Ads do You See in One Day? available at https://www.redcrowmarketing.com/2015/09/10/many-ads-see-one-day/ [accessed 22 May 2019].

Microsoft Advertising (2011). Jonathan Mildenhall from the Coca Cola Company interviewed at AdWeek 2011 [video online] Available at https://www.youtube.com/watch?v=Wx4trKSBpvs [accessed on 15 January 2018].

Mohdin, A. (2019). UK army recruitment ads target 'snowflake' millennials, *The Guardian,* available at https://www.theguardian.com/uk-news/2019/jan/03/uk-army-recruitment-ads-target-snowflake-millennials [accessed 29 May 2019].

Ouwersloot, H. and T. Duncan (2008). *Integrated Marketing Communications*. Berkshire: McGraw Hill Education.

Percy, L. and R. Rosenbaum-Elliott (2016) *Strategic Advertising Management,* 5th edn. Oxford: Oxford University Press.

Pessin, I. and K. Weaver (2014) *Paid, Owned, Earned: Measuring POE complexity.* Admap.

Petrecca, L. (2016) *Product placement – you can't escape it.* USA Today, available at http://usatoday30.usatoday.com/money/advertising/2006-10-10-ad-nauseum-usat_x.htm [accessed 12 December 2015].

Pickton, D. and A. Broderick (2005). *Integrated Marketing Communications*. Harlow: Pearson Education Limited.

Richardson, N., J. James and N. Kelley (2015) *Customer-Centric Marketing*. London: Kogan Page.

Rossiter, J. and S. Bellman (2005). *Marketing Communications: Theory and applications*. London, Prentice Hall.

Shimp, T. (2010) *Integrated Marketing Communications in Advertising and Promotion*. USA: Cengage Learning.

Sky PLC, (2019) *About AdSmart,* available at https://www.skyadsmart.co.uk/ [accessed 30 May 2019]

Smith, P.R. and Z. Zook (2011) *Marketing Communications: Integrating Offline and Online with Social Media*. London: Kogan Page.

WARC, 2014. *Cola: Share a Coke, share your summer.* European Association of Communications Agencies Silver, Euro Effies.

CHAPTER 22
Ryan Sosna-Bowd, Ioannis Kostopoulos and Ralph Tench

Sponsorship

Source: Mariska Vermij - van Dijk/Shutterstock

Learning outcomes

By the end of this chapter you should be able to:
- define what sponsorship means
- recognise different types of sponsorship activity
- understand what these different types of sponsorship can do and how they work
- understand the types of the sponsorship and role of different audiences and parties play in the process of leveraging a sponsorship
- understand the ways by which sponsorship can be enacted and how to develop it
- critically evaluate sponsorship as an effective communication tool.

Structure

- Definitions of sponsorship
- Effective sponsorship and its impact for contemporary organisations
- Strategic planning and management of sponsorship
- Sponsorship in our digital reality
- The future of sponsorship

Introduction

Sponsorship is ever present in our society; it underpins and enables key sporting, art, societal, industrial and political events. Key shared global experiences such as the Olympics, football (soccer), rugby and music festivals. Moments such as Austrian Felix Baumgartner's world record parachute jump (in 2012 he broke the speed of sound at an estimated 1,342.8 km/h jumping from the stratosphere) down to the smallest art gallery show or local children's football team trip to a tournament are made possible by sponsorship of various forms.

The word is ubiquitously linked to financial assistance, however more appropriately it can be simply described as an exchange relationship whereby one entity (company, individual, government etc.) supports another entity (company, team, individual, league, venue, event, etc.) which controls a 'sponsorship property' via financial or value in kind (VIK) support in return for a series of 'sponsorship rights' and 'sponsorship category'. Notable examples of such relationships include Rolex's long-standing (dating back to 1978) sponsorship of Wimbledon, Coca Cola's sponsorship of the Olympic games or O2's sponsorship of 19 iconic music venues in the UK (O2 Academies).

Like other specialist areas of communication sponsorship has some key terms that are important in order to understand when talking about the practice. Box 22.1 describes some of these frequently used terms that will enable you to understand and engage in the language of sponsorship.

Picture 22.1 Austrian Felix Baumgartner and his 2012 altitude parachute jump (*source:* EDB Image Archive/Alamy Stock Photo)

Box 22.1

Key terms and definitions in sponsorship

Sponsorship property

This is a term historically used to describe the entity that can be sponsored. Typically, sponsorship properties have been:

- Awards (Man Booker prize for literature or MTV music awards globally)
- Content/programming (such as books, magazines, newspapers, television shows, programme slots, movies, music videos, YouTube, Facebook or other digital content)
- Events (political party conferences, awards, celebrations, launches, sporting games or tournaments, arts or cultural events, expeditions or record attempts and other 'firsts')
- Individuals (from adventurers, explorers, musician, writers, artists, chefs and athletes from local emerging talent to global superstars)
- Objects (buildings, planes, trains, boats, statues, object d'art)
- Organisations/groups (such as museums, art galleries, schools, universities to bands and professional associations)
- Sporting leagues (such as National Basketball League, National Football League, Premiership Football, Major League Baseball and more)
- Systems (transport [train, metro or light rail], waterways, roads, etc.)
- Teams (from mainstream to niche sports, from the grassroots of sports (local youth team) to the biggest

teams on the planet (such as Manchester United and Real Madrid football (soccer) clubs and the New York Yankees in baseball and La Lakers basketball team)
- Venues (such as stadiums and arenas)

And really anything if its 'rights' are for sale or they can be agreed. The entity that controls a sponsorship property is described as the rights holder.

Value in kind

Value in kind is 'The use of goods or services in exchange for sponsorship rights'. These goods and services can take the form of provision of physical products such as clothing, equipment or food and drink products. An example of this could be a sports nutrition's company sponsorship of a sports team such as Gatorade's sponsorship of NFL American football teams in the United States.

Service value in kind sponsorships can range from traditional consumer service sectors such as accommodation, catering or travel through to corporate services such cleaning, accounting, legal and consulting services such as PR itself. As an example most Olympic supplier or provider sponsorships are based around a required service for the Games; these include Holiday Inn's (Intercontinental Hotel Group) running the Olympic Athlete Village at the London 2012 Olympic Games or Embratel's sponsorship of the Rio 2016 Olympic Games (see website links for details).

Additionally, value-in-kind could simply be the provision of staff time to carry out roles required by an organisation such as marshalling at a sporting event like a marathon or triathlon.

Sponsorship category

Sponsorship category is a term used to describe the area of exclusivity a sponsor has with respect to sponsorship property. Categories are designed to protect both the sponsor and enable the sponsorship property 'rights holder' to sell multiple sponsorships without them being a perceived clash. For that reason, the sponsor is the only company within its product or service category associated with the sponsored entity. There are no hard or fixed categories for a sponsorship property; they tend to develop logically to match the available 'rights'. Title sponsors of a property, i.e. those with what is referred to as naming rights, tend to get both that category and their own product and service category. It is also not uncommon for a sponsor to secure multiple categories.

Rights holder

The rights holder is the individual, organisation or business that owns or has licensed the sponsorship property and its rights.

Sponsorship rights

Sponsorship rights or the 'rights' is a term used to describe what a sponsor gets in return for their financial or value in kind support of a sponsorship property. These rights are usually assigned in a legally binding contract, along with the sponsor's category or categories being defined. These may include but are not limited to:

- Naming rights: often called 'title sponsorship' rights where a sponsor has the right for the sponsorship property to be named after them. Examples include the O2 Arena in London, Allianz Arena in Munich or the Barclay's Centre in New York.
- Branding rights: the rights for a sponsor to have branding on, at or around the sponsorship property, such as branding on the pitch sides of sporting events.
- Hospitality rights: the rights for a sponsor to conduct hospitality around, at or on a sponsorship property.
- Image and name rights: the rights for a sponsor to use the sponsorship properties name or image(s) in their own communications; for example, the rights of a company such as Nike to use the images of the famous athletes they work with in their advertising, PR and marketing.
- Staff, customer and stakeholder engagement rights: these are the rights that allow the stakeholders of a sponsor to engage with the property. These could be an athlete or team providing access, coaching, insight or unique experiences for a sponsor's audiences. An example of this might be an F1 Team doing a driving experience for customers and staff of its sponsor or a Tour De France cycling team taking someone such as a key business influencer of an organisation in the team car during a stage.

Explore 22.1

With a plethora of sponsorship potential in the market, it is crucial for public relations (PR) practitioners to recognise and answer these questions. You can also think about how you would answer them for a given sponsorship you know about or are interested in:

1. Why should we sponsor?
2. What are our (corporate/organisation) goals and objectives?
3. How do potential sponsorships fit with corporate objectives?
4. What are the opportunities and what are the threats in working with the sponsorship property?
5. How will we measure our investment and its return?
6. How will we decide if we are to do it again?

There are a variety of reasons why an organisation may get involved with sponsoring and this chapter will explore many of these possibilities. Figure 22.1 identifies eight grouped reasons for an organisation to get involved in sponsorship and also identifies where some of the discussions on these topics lie outside this chapter. These reasons are:

1. To support products and services (MTV awards as a sponsorship of an annual music awards that directly supports the promotion of the music television channel). This support sometimes is through brand linkage or can be direct sales delivery. Many Olympic sponsors are able to track the direct sales increase from their involvement.

2. To build on media interest. Many events (e.g. Super bowl, NBA finals) have very high news value and therefore can generate media exposure for sponsoring organisations to reinforce, articulate or reposition the corporate identity and the brand. Sometimes it is useful to reaffirm the brand identity by sponsoring something that has positive associations for customers and other stakeholders. Other times something is required that will project an existing or new attribute to stakeholders, and in order to do this the best way is to borrow or leverage a clearly visible attribute from a third party.

3. To build goodwill. This can be done through cause-related marketing initiatives and community activity.

4. As part of an integrated campaign (to raise awareness in specific stakeholder groups ranging from customers and the media to key retailers).

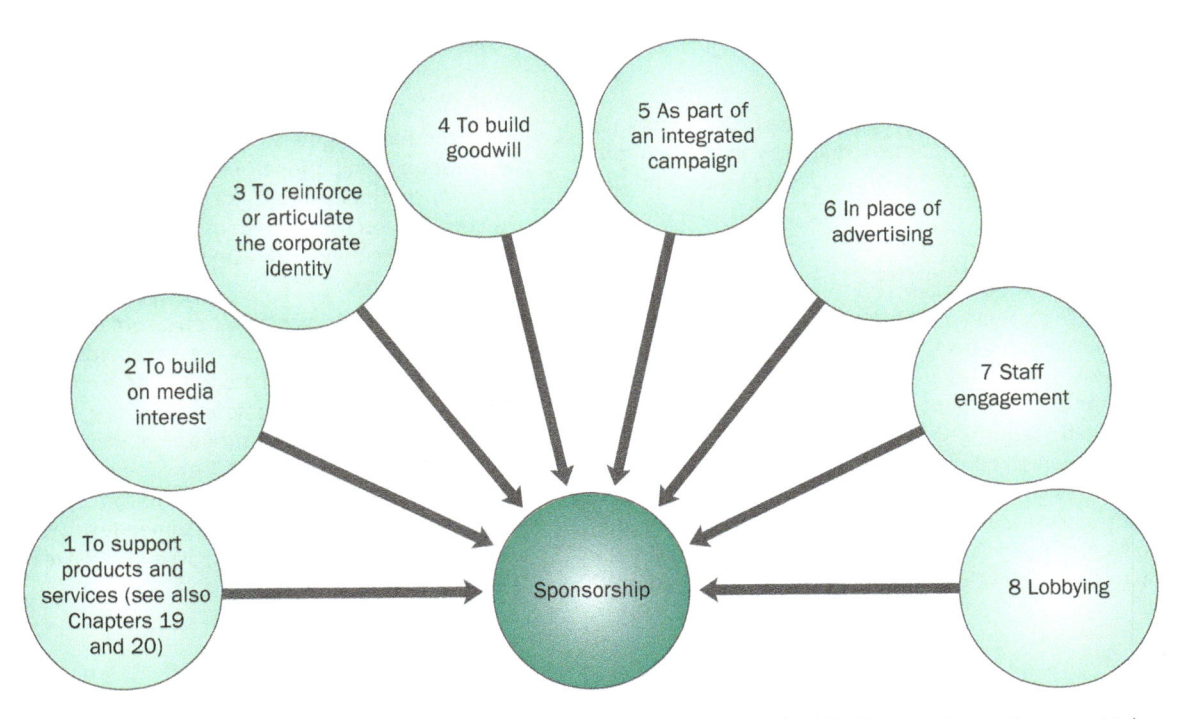

Figure 22.1 Reasons for sponsoring (*source:* Bowd, R., Sheldon, I. and Tench, R. (2013) Chapter: Sports Sponsorship)

5. In place of advertising. This is very crucial in industries where advertising is partially or fully forbidden. Tobacco companies Philip Morris International (currently with Ferrari) and British American Tobacco (currently with McLaren) both sponsor Formula 1 to get around advertising/marketing regulations in various markets.

6. Staff engagement – using sponsorships as a vehicle to build staff engagement with an organisation and brand affinity and understanding (see InterContinental Hotel Group, Case study 22.2).

7. Lobbying – sponsorship can be used as a lobbying tool either through hospitality moments that enable engagement (though as an example in some countries such as the UK, laws have been enacted to try to minimise this) or affinity through showing a mutual interest or an investment in something the organisation being lobbied is interested in or passionate about.

With the multitude of reasons for organisations to engage in sponsorship, its growth as a diverse communication tool has been exponential over the past decades. The sponsorship industry has grown from a modest $6 million in the early 1970s into a projected 65.8 billion business today, with North America, Europe and Asia being the lead markets (Statista 2019).

Industry predictions show that budgets allocated to sponsorships are expected to grow the following year. The majority of companies are expected to increase the amount of money they spend on sponsorship (33 per cent), while only 20 per cent is expected to decrease their sponsorship budget (IEG 2018).

Globally, by far the biggest sponsorship market is the North America (USA). The IEG (2003) sponsorship report estimated the market size to be about £8 billion and in 2018 this is expected to be about $24.2 billion (IEG Sponsorship Report 2018). This growing industry is fuelled not only by moderate budget increases from established sponsors but also by first-time investors. In the light of increased competition and new technologies that allow an advert-free media environment, US companies are looking into alternative promotion possibilities. As such, there has been an increasing fragmentation in the North American sponsorship market with a larger number of minor deals by small firms replacing major sponsor deals.

Definitions of sponsorship

With its huge growth and wide reasons for sponsorship engagement, it would be prudent before continuing to examine the different definitions and perspectives on sponsorship itself. Previously some of the key sponsorship lexicon, terms such as sponsorship property, sponsorship right, sponsorship category and kinds of sponsorship amongst others have been explained. Nevertheless, what exactly is a sponsorship and a sponsor have not been fully defined.

From all of this, if you were asked to explain what sponsorship is, you would probably say that it refers to any form of financial or in-kind support for a specific person, event or institution – with or without a service in return. You may also describe the term using your own experience of observing a major sporting event as an example.

Maecenatism

However, as a starting point for reflection, a historical perspective helps to shed light on the origins of the concept of sponsorship. Corporate contributions to culture, sport or social events have a long tradition, which can be traced back to Gaius C. Maecenas (70bc–8bc). As a material supporter of contemporary poets such as Horace and Virgil, his name is remembered as a generous patron of fine arts. Despite the noble image still associated with his name, the Roman diplomat and counsellor to Octavian (later Emperor Augustus) exercised patronage as a political means-end strategy. If applied to Figure 22.1 this could be interpreted as 'sponsorship as lobbying'. That is, Maecenas used the communication channel of his times publicly to praise the reign of his friend Octavian.

Nevertheless, 'Maecenatism' today stands for the altruistically motivated support of culture and communities, where the support idea and not the association with a specific patron/organisation is to the fore. In other words, where the receiver not the donor is the main purpose or focus.

Charitable donations

Closely connected to the concept of Maecenatism is the act of charitable donations. As an expression of charity it is again the altruistic (concern for other people) motive that dominates the support process. Social considerations play an important role and in its original meaning no immediate advantages such as image promotion or the representation of the donor as a 'good' citizen are being sought. Another significant aspect of charitable donations is that control is not assumed over the beneficiary or over the use of the funds. Despite this blueprint, charitable donations do present the opportunity for raising an organisation's public profile. Think, for example, about the naming of donors in TV charity shows such as Comic Relief and Sport Relief in the United Kingdom or the American TV channel PBS and its various Telethons or the financial support of political parties. (See Think about 22.2 and Explore 22.2.)

Think about 22.1

Sponsorship of events you know

Think about the main sponsor of your favourite sports personality or team and the way this sponsorship is promoted. You recognise sponsorship when you see it, don't you? On second thoughts, however, you may have come across its broader colloquial use: students might refer to their parental financial help as 'sponsoring'; interest groups donate money for political campaigns in Germany, for example political parties around the world usually have to disclose any donation of more than a certain threshold amount, in the United Kingdom this is a figure of £7500 ($12,000); and trusts support social projects (Electoral Commission 2019).

Feedback

Although these are all examples of sponsorship, they do not adequately reflect its full scope, nor do they distinguish between related concepts such as Maecenatism, charitable donations or corporate philanthropy. These ideas are now explored.

Think about 22.2

Making donations

The next time you come across a charity appeal, ask yourself what motivates you to make – or refuse – a donation.

Feedback

In the corporate world, the art of giving is not only benevolent in nature. In many cases, more tangible reasons, such as taxation laws, may drive corporate donations. Regardless of the intentions, charitable donations can be seen as a development of Maecenatism and in general describe an unidirectional, or one-way, relationship. Commercial advantages or expectations such as corporate visibility or goodwill here play a minor role, as unlike a sponsorship are not leveraged beyond what the receiver of the donation promotes it.

Explore 22.2

The bi-annual BBC television broadcast (in the United Kingdom) Comic Relief appeal is a major televised event, which reaches out to the public for donations. The appeal's 'corporate partners' include major UK brands such as Sainsbury's, BT and British Airways. Find out how companies can benefit from being associated with the charity by going to http://www.comicrelief.com

Corporate philanthropy

The dual purpose of corporate social responsibility and market orientation is reflected in the term corporate philanthropy. More than the no-profit, no-win paradigm of charity donations, corporate philanthropy embraces more directly the idea of competitive advantages (see Porter and Kramer 2002). By linking corporate giving to business-related objectives, focused charitable investments can be more strategic than unplanned, one-off donations. It allows donations to become part of a proactive communication approach aimed at commercial capitalisation. Contrary to the concepts described earlier, the spender sees to it that philanthropic activities are closely connected to the corporation (or its objectives). In return for the financial or in-kind support the corporation may publicise its efforts.

Sponsoring

'Sponsoring' is derived from the Latin word *spondere* or 'promise solemnly', hence its use as formula for prayer (*sponderis*) in a Christian context. The derivative word sponsor was used for 'godparent', which is also the original English meaning. A sponsor is defined by the Collins English Dictionary in the following ways:

1. 'a person or group that provides funds for an activity, especially
    a. a commercial organisation that pays all or part of the cost of putting on a concert, sporting event, etc.
    b. a person who donates money to a charity when the person requesting the donation has performed a specified activity as part of an organized fund-raising effort'
2. 'a person or business firm that pays the costs of a radio or television programme in return for advertising time'
3. 'a legislator who presents and supports a bill, motion, etc.'

4. *also called:* **godparent**

   a. an authorised witness who makes the required promises on behalf of a person to be baptised and thereafter assumes responsibility for his Christian upbringing

   b. a person who presents a candidate for confirmation

5. a person who undertakes responsibility for the actions, statements, obligations, etc, of another, as during a period of apprenticeship; guarantor'

(Collins English Dictionary 2019)

Alternatively, the business knowledge site, investopedia defines corporate sponsorship more specifically as: 'A form of marketing in which a corporation pays for all or some of the costs associated with a project or program in exchange for recognition. Corporations may have their logos and brand names displayed alongside that of the organisation undertaking the project or programme, with specific mention that the corporation has provided funding. Corporate sponsorships are commonly associated with non-profit groups, who generally would not be able to fund operations and activities without outside financial assistance. It is not the same as philanthropy.'

These definitions reveal three broad characteristics to sponsorship as a marketing and PR construct:

1. it entails motives for the support by the sponsor and the rights holder;
2. there is a relationship formed between spender (sponsor) and receiver (rights holder);
3. it generates publicity for the sponsor and potentially the sponsorship property or its rights holder.

In this view sponsorship brings with it a more process-orientated view that includes planning, implementing and control mechanisms (Figure 22.2). So definitions that see sponsorship as merely 'an investment in cash or kind in an activity in return for access to the exploitable commercial potential associated with this activity' do not go far enough as aforementioned (De Pelsmacker et al. 2004). Although the study of support in return for services is of interest to PR practitioners, sponsoring involves quite a bit more.

As such, one could propose a definition of organisational/corporate sponsorship that is: 'A planned organisational/corporate focused activity aimed at

> **Think about 22.3**
>
> ### Definitions of sponsorship
>
> Which of the Collins definitions of sponsoring do you think is closest to the concept discussed in this chapter?
>
> ### Feedback
>
> The first and second definitions are closest to the concept we are discussing. However, broadcasting is not the only media space that is paid for by a sponsor.

Driving by organisational/corporate goals and objectives ...

Via a	Delivered	Involving various	Manifested in various	Delivering
Planned process	**Types of sponsorship**	**Stakeholders**	**Sectors**	**Benefits**

• Analysis
• Selection/ negotiation
• Planning
• Organisation
• Execution
• Coordination
• Control
	• Financial (money)
	• In kind
	  • Product
	  • Service
	  • Know-how (e.g. human expertise)
		• Both the sponsorship property/rights holder and organisational/corporate
		• External and internal
		  • Individuals
		  • Groups
		  • Organisations
		  • Bodies
		  • Events
			• Arts
			• Broadcasting
			• Charity
			• Culture
			• Ecology/environment
			• Education
			• Industries/business/ trades
			• Sport
			• Venues and infrastructure
				• Commercial benefits
				• Revenue or operational effeciency
				• Psychological benefits
				  • Brand image and identity
				• Organisational benefits
				  • Internal or environmental

... with marketing/PR/communications strategy and activity playing an integral role in value generation through the maximisation and utilisation of sponsorship rights

Figure 22.2 What is sponsorship?

facilitating the achievement of a goal or objective that sees the provision of financial or in-kind support via a sponsorship rights holder for a sponsorship property from within a certain sector through the utilisation and leveraging of the ensuing sponsorship rights by the sponsor through marketing, PR and communications activities.'

Effective sponsorship and its impact for contemporary organisations

With this holistic viewpoint as to what sponsorship is and a clear understanding that it has grown exponentially let us now discuss why it is so popular and what sponsorship can achieve for an organisation with respect to their goals in terms of commercial, psychological or organisational benefits.

Though increasingly professional and strategic in orientation, sponsorship remains multifaceted. It reaches from high-profile media presence to the support of a local youth football club. Sponsorship can manifest in diverse societal arenas such as sport, education or arts and deliver divergent communication goals such as contact with audience (psychological benefit) or a specified market share increase (commercial benefit). Depending on the scope and importance of the investment made in the sponsorship, sponsorship can affect multiple things to achieve goals, including the following:

- passion marketing;
- image transfer;
- multiple stakeholders communications;
- direct sales;
- strategic partnerships.

Storytelling

Sponsorship is widely regarded as an inexpensive alternative to advertising. This often goes hand in hand with the common misconception that sponsorship activity is merely logo exposure. If sponsorship involved no more than brand presence, it would very likely be useless as a communication tool. After all, multimillion investments, such as Gatorade's US nine figure investment in the American NFL league or significant investment with Arsenal Football Club in the UK or FC Barcelona in Spain have to be commercially justified. This requires sponsorship to be integrated into the corporate storytelling strategy (Baker and Boyle 2009). A sponsorship needs to tell a compelling and consistent story about the brand and create audience perceptions that will enhance brand image and corporate reputation.

Image transfer

One of the main purposes of sponsorship is to affect consumers' attitudes towards, and beliefs about, a brand or corporation favourably. As attitudes can be good predictors of (consumer) behaviour and represent an overall evaluation of associations linked to an object, the formation and change of attitudes is of interest to the marketer. What makes sponsorship a unique persuasive tool is its association potential. Sponsorship generally has positive connotations among audiences. It also does not rely on elaborate cognitive information (thought) processing. Its emotional appeal makes it easy for the consumer to understand. The sponsorship entity sets the stage for inducing emotions such as joy, hope, excitement, fear, anger, etc. Marketing messages are presented in this context in the hope that consumers will experience these emotions. Research evidence suggests that it is not only the situational experience that influences behaviour, but also the overall attitude towards an event (Cooper 2003). A positive evaluation of something (event, person, team, etc.) will create positive feelings, which may then be transferred to the brand. This means that it is important to monitor opportunities carefully to ensure a good match between the sponsorship and the attitudes of the target audience.

Stakeholder approach

Beyond the function of communication with potential customers, sponsorship can aim to create additional results with other stakeholders. At the organisational level, employee motivation and identification can be supported by sponsorship activities. Research also suggests that there is a correlation between image and employment attractiveness, so that personnel marketing/recruiting might also benefit from these activities. Establishing goodwill with external groups, such as financial institutions, shareholders or investors, is an additional target variable of sponsorship. This is also true for the relationship with distributors, sales personnel and business partners (see also Chapter 19). In some cases, sponsorship activities may also be used to develop relationships with decision makers in governmental institutions. Such stakeholder relationships are often enhanced through sponsorship activities such as VIP events and corporate hospitality.

Direct sales

Beyond the ability to facilitate passion marketing, image transfer, integrated communications and stakeholder communications, sponsorship can also be a conduit to enabling direct sales. Sales not generated through the effects of a brand built through image transfer or as a result of association with one's passion but through the direct network of the sponsorship property/rights holders or its inherent power to open doors. Sponsors are usually unwilling to specifically divulge the direct results of these relationships, as it may affect their renegotiations for sponsorship renewals in a manner that may raise the cost going forward.

Taking Olympic sponsorships as an example, many of the worldwide sponsors of the Olympics, known as The Olympic Partners (TOP) and partners and suppliers of individual Organising Committees for the Olympic Games (OCOG) engage in the sponsorship for among other reasons its ability to help deliver sales. Sales derived through either selling products and services into the organisations tasked with delivering the games, other partners or via the sporting and civil infrastructure of the individual host nations as they scale up and down for each games. Additionally, sales are derived by using Olympic-themed incentive programmes to generate increased sales via the sales forces or resellers who hope to 'win' tickets through excelling in their performance beyond normal targets. For some Olympic sponsors this can create return on investment many times the value of their sponsorship in each cycle before they even start to market their relationship in traditional ways.

Direct sales are not limited to large sponsorships. As an example the hotel industry has used partnership sponsorship deals with sports bodies or events to deliver guaranteed or incremental business for decades. Mass participation sporting events (from major global marathons to regional or local runs or triathlons) often have a hotel sponsor whose motivation to sponsor is down to direct sales they can achieve. These sales are achieved as they are able to communicate directly to participants at the time of their registration to inform them of preferential rates or incentives in order to secure booking before the athlete consumers shop around. Additionally, hotel deals in sport often occur with the major leagues or governing bodies, not necessarily for the consumer

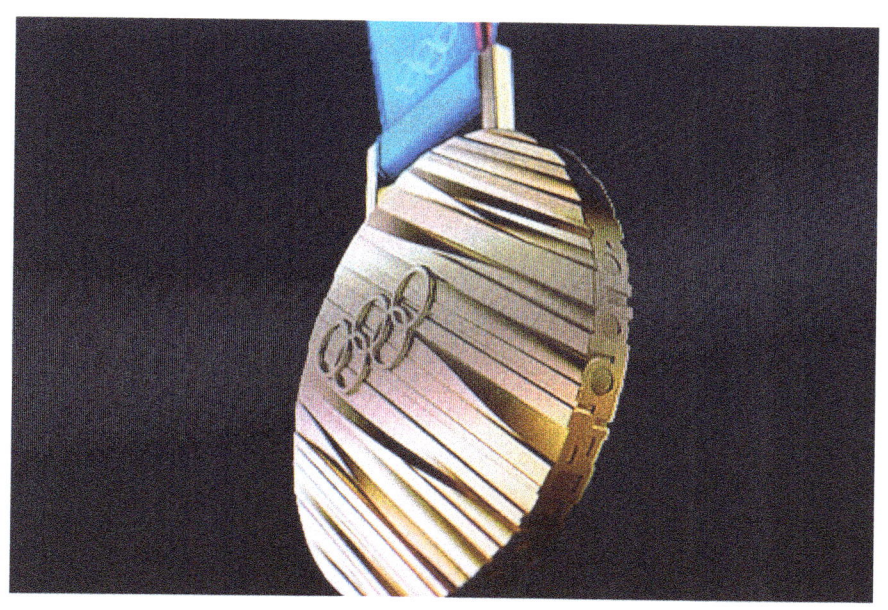

Picture 22.2 The Olympic Games every four years is one of the biggest sponsorships in the world (*source*: Vytautas Kielaitis/Shutterstock)

sales, but the sales that can be achieved via those organisation's business-to-business networks, which tend to include extensive networks of small clubs, businesses, suppliers and other sponsors. This model can also be seen to apply in the areas of arts and tourism amongst other sectors.

Strategic partnerships

Another important benefit from sponsorships for both sponsors and rights holders refers to the opportunity for the development of a long-term strategic partnership between the two parties. Specifically, when a sponsorship is successful in its initial stages, the two partners can expand the terms of their deal and develop a longer-term strategic alliance that is beneficial for both parties. Therefore, a sponsorship partnership may start as a simple sponsorship categories' dealership, but it may end up being a much deeper, more strategic collaboration between the two partners. This can include joint communication campaigns, co-branding (e.g. Red bull – GoPro, Giannis Antetokoumpo – Nike), the exchange of databases and joint ventures in large infrastructure projects. In that way, both partners can achieve synergies and fully exploit sponsorship's positive outcomes.

Social implications

As explained in Box 22.2, sponsorship is by definition associated with socially beneficial activities such as sports, charities, arts, education and many others. The main aim of sponsors is to affiliate their name with what all stakeholders perceive as the healthiest parts of society. They can then capitalise on this and improve their reputation and credibility, using various communication techniques, such as asking the sponsored entity to publicly support their brands, use their logo in advertising, promote products in a sponsored event etc.

Nevertheless, sponsorships can be valuable not only for sponsors and sponsored entities, but also for various other stakeholders, as well as the society in general. In fact, sponsorship's positive social impact is substantially stronger than the one other promotional techniques have. In some cases, this impact is longstanding and multifaceted. For instance, the Bank of America

---

Box 22.2
What can be sponsored?

- Arts (film festivals, music festivals, orchestras, galleries and exhibitions such as those sponsored by various organisations at the Guggenheim in New York or the Tate).
- Broadcasting (television programmes, series of programmes, films and content; such as in the United Kingdom Sainsbury's and BT's sponsorship of the 2012 Paralympic Broadcasts).
- Charity (events, appeals and work to social issues; such as the previously mentioned Comic Relief appeal and Red Products initiative).
- Culture (local initiatives and events; such as celebrations or festivals, e.g. New Year's Eve in Time Square in New York which in 2015 was sponsored by Planet Fitness and multiple other sponsors or winter ice rinks in United Kingdom with major outdoor rinks in London sponsored by Fortnum and Mason (Somerset House) and Swarovski (Natural History Museum)).
- Ecology/Environment (recycling and conservation programmes; such as Sky's (UK and European satellite television provider) Rain Forest Rescue Programme with the World Wildlife Fund.
- Education (for example, book series, individual academic posts, chairs, or full faculties such as in the US where corporate foundation sponsorship of business schools is common place such as the Marriott School of Management at Brigham Young University).
- Industries/business/trades (sponsorship of research initiatives, industry events, associations and awards; such as the PR Week Awards in the UK whose sponsors include major polling and services suppliers to the public relations industry).
- Sport (from athletes to teams and major tournaments and events such as big sporting events such as the Olympics with multiple sponsorship opportunities – see Mini case studies 22.1 and 22.2 for in-depth examples).
- Venues and infrastructure (from libraries and arenas, to transport infrastructure in cities; such as the Santander Bank sponsored cycle (bike) hire scheme in London or the Emirates (Airline) Air Line cable car in London).

has developed a long-standing partnership with Special Olympics, which for the 2015 Special Olympics World Games in Los Angeles was reflected to a $5 million sponsorship. This deal was also supported by hundreds of the company's employees who participated in the event as volunteers.

Sports and charities are not the only fields where sponsorships have a positive societal impact. From arts to education and from ecology to health research, sponsors are spending money in order to associate their corporate brand with positive societal activities. In arts, for example, on several occasions sponsorships constitute an imperative stream of income for artists, producers and arts events organisers. For instance, it is the money coming through sponsorships from several French corporations, such as Air France, Renault and L'Oreal that have allowed the Festival de Cannes to sustain and grow every year (www.festival-cannes.com). It's not an overstatement to say that if it had not been for sponsorship money, many art galleries, orchestras and festivals wouldn't have grown or even existed.

Determinants of sponsorship effectiveness

Sponsorship is a very promising communication practice, which however poses high risk levels. The results of a successful sponsorship can be very positive for sponsorship partners, consumers and the society in general (Becker-Olsen and Hill 2006). At the same time though an unsuccessful sponsorship can cause financial loss for the sponsor or/and negative brand effects for both partners. The success of a sponsorship is reflected on the effectiveness of a sponsorship, i.e. the degree to which it successfully fulfils its communications, marketing and sales objectives.

The factors that determine the effectiveness of a sponsorship vary according to the sector, the type of sponsorship and the objectives that have been set from both parties before the beginning of the sponsorship campaign. In general though the drivers of a sponsorship's success belong to one of the following four categories (Gwinner and Swanson 2003; Mazodier and Merunka 2012; Kim et al. 2015):

- sponsor-related factors;
- sponsee-related factors;
- combinational factors;
- target audience-related factors.

The first category includes factors related to sponsors' prior status such as reputation and brand image, as well as their strategic plan for the particular sponsorship such as the target audience identification, the size of the budget, the cohesiveness of their messages and the media exposure they will manage to get. The second category encompasses sponsee-related factors such as the sponsees' prior reputation, their current financial performance, their commitment to the sponsorship and their audience's loyalty to them. Apart from these two categories, the effectiveness of a sponsorship is also determined by variables that are linked to both parties, as the quality of their cooperation and the fit between their profiles (see Box 22.3 for details).

Finally, the success of a sponsorship is also influenced by the target audience's psychographic and behavioural characteristics, such as their general perceptions and attitude towards sponsorship – i.e. the degree to which their exposure to a sponsorship can even influence them in the first place – and their involvement with the product category, the event and the context in general (e.g. sports, arts, charity).

Audience-related factors are of paramount importance and sponsors must integrate them into their sponsorship plans. For that reason, they must collect information through market research and analyse this information in order to adjust their practices. For example, if the results of the sponsor's research show that the target audience has a negative attitude towards sponsors and the concept of sponsorship in general – a phenomenon very common in arts – the sponsor must either invest heavily in the early stages of the sponsorship in order to change this attitude or to choose a different activity to sponsor or even a different communication practice to pass their messages to the target audience.

Strategic planning and management of sponsorship

So how does an organisation arrive at its sponsorship strategy? Sponsorship involves more than the support of an event such as the FIFA World Cup™, the PGA (golf) Masters series or the local volleyball club in return for logo exposure. The activities covered in our definition highlight much of the approach, scale

> ## Box 22.3
> ## Sponsorship fit
>
> One of the major determinants of a sponsorship's success is the fit between the sponsoring organisation and the sponsored body (Becker-Olsen and Hill 2006). Sponsorship fit can be defined as the match, or congruence, of attributes between sponsoring firms and sponsored objects, as perceived by the major stakeholders (e.g. customers, participants in an event, fans, internal audiences). A sponsorship with high degree of congruence between the two parties' profile will be significantly more effective in terms of stakeholders' engagement with the sponsorship, brand results (brand image, brand equity) and financial results (Woisetschläger et al. 2010).
>
> The fit between a sponsor and a sponsored entity may emerge from a pre-existing juxtaposition of their names (natural fit), or it may be developed through marketing communications activities (created fit). The first type results in more cost-effective sponsorships, as the amount of investment needed from the sponsor is lower. On the other hand, if no natural congruence exists the sponsor must spend a significant budget on marketing communications in order to create it. This is very crucial especially in the initial stages of a sponsorship campaign.
>
> ### Sources of fit
>
> The benefits from a congruent sponsorship may originate from one or more of the following factors (Woisetschläger et al. 2010; Mazodier and Merunka 2012; Mazodier and Quester 2014):
>
> - **Functional similarity**: this occurs when the two parties operate in the same, or related, industries. For example, sports fashion brands have a natural functional fit with athletes and other sportspeople.
> - **Regional/national association**: this is a source of fit that evolves from the fact that the sponsor and the sponsored object operate or originate from the same country, region or city (e.g. Coca Cola and the 1996 Olympic Games in Atlanta).
> - **Experience similarity**: this type of similarity arises when the sponsoring and the sponsored object offer a combined experience to consumers and other stakeholders; for instance, when the fans of a football club consume the sponsor's products in the stadium.
> - **Symbolic resemblance**: this derives from the perceived similarity in symbolic characteristics, such as the shape and the colour of the logo, the brand name and other aesthetic attributes. For example, for the period 2010–2015, the two main sponsors for Ferrari's F1 cars are Santander and Marlboro – all three brands' main colours are white and red.
> - **Created concept similarity**: this is a non-natural source of fit which relates to a specific concept created from the sponsor in order to promote the sponsorship. A very indicative example is the EDF's 'Energy for the Nations' campaign, which involved a substantial sponsorship in the 2012 Olympic Games in London. During the campaign, EDF emphasised the role in 'powering the Olympics' – a concept that increased the match between EDF's profile and the Olympics.

and scope of today's sponsorship environment. It also indicates the necessary professionalism that comes with the understanding of sponsorship as part of an integrated communication and relationship strategy. In the spirit of Maecenatism, not long ago 'gut decisions' on who and what to sponsor were commonplace (this was sometimes known as 'the chairman's discretion' or 'chairman's wife syndrome', as sponsorship of one's favourite team or of the opera or society events secured grace and favour with these organisations). Despite its strategic importance and the increased professionalism of sponsorship, many decisions follow management preferences rather than calculated communication objectives. In contrast to 'gut decisions' leading to hit and miss activities, modern sponsorship thinking is planned and decisive.

Opportunity analysis, scenario planning, alternative target generation, strategy selection, budget and time horizon decisions, implementation, integration in marketing mix, communication channel coordination, evaluation and control mechanisms are all examples of a systematic and process-based view of sponsoring (see the Glossary at the end of the book for definitions of these terms). These terms also explain how sponsorship can be systematically integrated into a marketing strategy. Here the word systematic means that sponsorship should not be a question of trial and error, but should follow a management process with specified communication goals. This implies accountability and controllability, because otherwise any financial or in-kind commitment would be highly risky. As we will see later, the development of evaluation tools is, due to the nature of sponsoring, a major challenge to PR and corporate communication departments.

An organisation or corporation that takes sponsoring as a communication tool into consideration faces

Mini case study 22.1
Red Products (RED)

(RED)™ products is a unique cause-related marketing initiative. In this case, one that was initiated not by a corporate organisation, but by the supporters of a cause and specifically by U2 rock star and activist Bono and philanthropist Robert Shriver, who shared a joint desire to fight the Aids disease in Africa. The (RED)™ is licensed to companies who create red products where a portion of the profits of each sales go to a charitable partner (www.theglobalfund.org) who carries out the 'brand' mission.

Brands benefit by tapping into the consumer's desire 'to do good' and create an additional reason for their product to be chosen over a competitor (MSNBC.com 2006). This unique model has seen engagement from brands including Apple, American Express, Beats by Dr. Dre, Nike and Starbucks. For more information visit: https://red.org/about/

---

a range of challenges in planning, implementing and controlling the activities. This is the area of responsibility of sponsorship management (see Figure 22.3). There are numerous models, both academic and professional, in existence, most of which share three commonalities: international sponsorship consultancy IMG used to refer to these as the *Discover, Design* and *Delivery* phases.

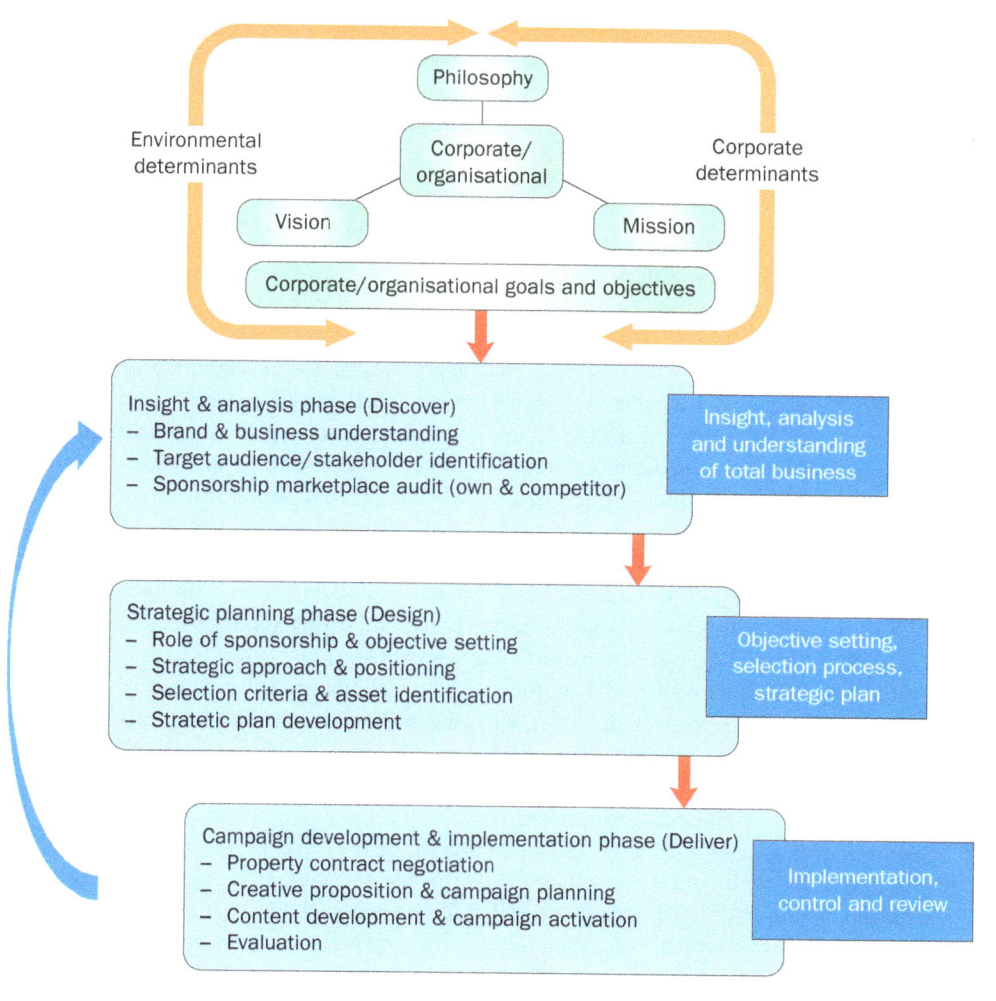

Figure 22.3 Sponsorship management as a planning process (*source*: Tench, R. and L. Yeomans (2009). Exploring Public Relations. FT Prentice Hall: London)

Strategic planning phase (discover)

Starting with the phase of analysis and prognosis, sponsorship management deals first of all with the collection and evaluation of information. It is this phase where, in coordination with other communication activities, sponsorship scenarios are developed. On the basis of target audience/stakeholder (who is key to achieving the goals and objectives?), sponsoring objectives are specified (what are the short-, medium- and long-term objectives necessary to achieve the organisational/corporate goals?), the key message is determined (what will be communicated?) and possible sponsorship activities are evaluated and pre-selected (see Meenaghan 1998; Bruhn and Homburg 2001). It is very important to note that sponsorship deals are planned and agreed a long way in advance. Ideally organisations are constantly monitoring the sponsorship environment to take advantage of upcoming opportunities.

Sponsorship programme creation phase (design)

This strategic framework with its longer-term timeframe and broad definition of the organisation's sponsoring activities ideally leads to a concrete action plan. The programme creation phase of sponsoring reflects a shorter-term timeframe, usually a financial year or cycle of a sponsorship, such as a four-year Olympic cycle. Here the strategy formulation is translated into operational and day-to-day sponsoring activities. These individual components include decisions on budget and time horizon, the fine-tuning of sponsorship programmes (e.g. selection of specific events), contractual matters and the coordination with other ongoing communication activities. In this context, special attention should be given to this organisational dimension of sponsoring. In other words, Cornwell and Maignan (2001) argue, that sponsorship activities may not, in themselves, be sufficient to achieve specific objectives for all target audiences. This is why it is important that sponsorship activities are reinforced through complementary communication activities. As these cross-marketing operations may include sales promotion, advertising or special product offers (among others) total expenditure may easily exceed the sponsorship budget. It is also important to note that the coordination of communication activities towards a common goal increasingly takes an integrative sponsorship perspective.

Implementation phase (deliver)

The process-orientated view also highlights the dual nature of sponsorship: not only does the selection of a strategic programme and its coordination need to be addressed, but also how to put this strategy into practice. It is easy to underestimate the complexity and importance of implementing sponsorship plans. Activities are as good as the weakest link in the sponsoring process and a good plan does not necessarily translate into a successful campaign. Sponsoring is sensitive to trends and sudden changes. Football teams can be relegated, events can be mismanaged, celebrities can be arrested – any of these may lead to negative publicity or inability to exercise the rights to their maximum for the sponsor.

Furthermore, a sponsorship campaign calls for the cooperation between several internal and external departments. Therefore, a manager should be involved in all phases of sponsoring and be responsible for the planning as well as the implementation. Since implementation is a key determinant of success, many specialised agencies have evolved – such as IMG; additionally, major corporations such as BMW or Microsoft have their own departments that coordinate all sponsorship activities.

The hidden fourth step – evaluation

Evaluating the effectiveness of a sponsorship is crucial. From a business perspective, the accurate evaluation of sponsorship activities provides the necessary intelligence for performance measurement, future budget and communication objectives determination and the overall communication strategy's assessment. Although imperative, the evaluation of a sponsorship's success is a very challenging process. Significant constraints during the process may derive from: the inability to separate sponsorship's contribution from the one other marketing and communications activities have, undetermined communication objectives before the sponsorship is launched, undefined competition, carry-over effects from previous marketing activities, uncontrollable media coverage (the medium is the message) and the chaotic nature of brand exposure in social media (Anderson 2003; Walliser 2003).

Although different procedures are used in the industry, there is a consensus among managers and researchers that the basis of sponsorship evaluation should be the degree to which the pre-defined objectives and KPIs have been met. For that reason, the first step for effective evaluation is the determination of specific, accurate and measurable communications and business objectives (McAlister et al. 2012). After the implementation of a sponsorship campaign, different approaches are followed. From a management point of view, the main evaluation criterion for sponsorships is the return on investment (ROI) or other relevant financial metrics. This is because, in most cases, financial and sales outcomes such as market share and sales increase will determine future strategies and budgets.

This view is however rather myopic and can lead to inaccurate results. As sponsorship is a communication practice, its influence on financial results isn't direct, but comes through the exposure that it gets in the media and the impact this exposure has on brand and reputation outcomes. For that reason, according to most contemporary evaluation models, sponsorship should be audited based on three types of measures (Anderson 2003; Walliser 2003; Crompton 2004):

- media exposure;
- brand and reputation outcomes;
- financial impact.

In order to gather the information for the measurement of a sponsorship's media exposure, managers use adapted advertising measurement tools such as contact points (verbal and visual mentions on TV), duration of radio mentions, press coverage (single column inches) and the number of mentions and linked impressions in social media. Other evaluation models suggest that managers should use recall and recognition tests to consumers, in order to identify the impact of exposure. To assess the financial return of a sponsorship several indicators exist, such as the change in the market share, sales increase (or not), sales retention and advertising cost equivalent.

Sponsorship in our digital reality

All aspects of communication have been massively influenced by the evolution of digital media. Sponsorship, as a form of business communication couldn't be an exception. The analysis of current sponsorship trends indicates that most marketing and communications practitioners focus their sponsorship-related activities in the digital environment. They have realised that consumers use social media and other digital platforms to augment the experience they receive from attending a sports event, watching a TV show or visiting an arts gallery. For example, they upload photos on Instagram and start a conversation with their friends, use hashtags to comment on something that happened in an event or watch and comment on it again on YouTube, long after it is over. At the same time, consumers now are able to enjoy traditional events from the comfort of their living room. For example, the Berliner Philharmonic Orchestra created in 2008 the now very successful Digital Concert Hall which is a website that streams the concerts of the orchestra online for registered users (www.digitalconcerthall.com), having Deutsche Bank as their main sponsor.

The new digital reality in which we all live has created a number of opportunities for sponsorship partners (Millan and Ball 2012; McDonnell and Moir 2013):

- **Digital activations** – digital technologies offer new ways of engaging audiences with brands, especially in the sports industry. Platforms and practices such as fantasy leagues, virtual events, RFID integrations and augmented reality offerings provide an excellent opportunity for sponsors seeking to influence audiences.
- **Interactivity capabilities** – utilising the new digital technologies, sponsors can offer an enhanced experience to their audiences, providing them with the opportunity to interact with them and with each other. This can be implemented not only through social media, but also through several other digital platforms such as interactive TV, virtual guides in museums, galleries and exhibitions and interactive billboards.
- **Viral effects potentiality** – when a video or photo from an event goes viral, so will the brand of the sponsor. This increases dramatically the sponsorship's visibility and therefore people's exposure to the sponsoring brand. On the other hand, this poses the danger of the sponsoring brand being associated with a negative or even offensive incident.
- **Extended period of sponsors' visibility** – video exchange platforms such as YouTube and Dailymotion allow viewers to watch advertisements and celebrities' interviews long after their original showing. In that way, the corresponding sponsoring brands gain exposure for an extended period of time, much longer than the one they have paid for.
- **Market research and feedback** – digital technologies offer an excellent platform for the collection of information on the target audiences. Through social media research, CRM data mining, virtual fingerprints and many other methods, organisations can generate knowledge on their target audiences' awareness of the sponsorship, their attitude towards it, as well as their buying behaviour in general.

Although digital platforms offer great opportunities for sponsors, they also pose several dangers. For instance, if a reputation crisis occurs for a sponsoring brand, the negative effect on the sponsor will be amplified due to the diffusion of the news online. Moreover, the use of social media and other digital platforms may make it easier for brands to carry out ambush activities.

Ambush marketing is very common in sponsorships and it becomes easier in the online environment (Weeks et al. 2017).

A new digital world

The digital environment has been used as a sponsorship activations' tool for quite a while now (Giovino 2018) and, as we discussed, the effectiveness of such activations is unquestionable. However, our new digital reality is not just another channel for brands to communicate traditional sponsorships. Nowadays sports, games, cultural events etc. sometimes exist solely in the digital world. Digital platforms, such as e-sports, e-concerts, LAN party games and many other offer opportunities for brands to exist in a new world in which brand awareness and brand relationships are developed, maintained and improved in a different way, although many of the traditional rules and norms are still applied (Summerley 2019). For example, as explained in detail in Case study 22.1 global brands such as Nike invest a lot of money in sponsoring new e-sports athletes aiming to develop brand relationship with younger audiences who are influenced significantly more by these athletes than by famous sportspeople, such as Cristiano Ronaldo and Tiger Woods.

Picture 22.3 eSports have grown exponentially, both in terms of participation and most significantly, in relation to viewership, advertisement and sponsorship (*source:* Roman Kosolapov/Shutterstock)

Case study 22.1
eSports: sponsorship in the virtual world

(prepared by Dr Konstantinos Zervas)

In recent years eSports have grown exponentially, both in terms of participation and most significantly, in relation to viewership, advertisement and sponsorship. This boom is not only driven by technological improvements (fast connections, video-streaming platforms, etc.), but primarily on the growth of competitive gaming culture and the accessibility which eSports offer to the spectators and fans. Aside from twitch, which remains the primary host of eSports events, large TV networks like ESPN and TBS have recently included live eSports events in their programmes (Keiper et al. 2017). Similarly, companies from the wider computer and gaming industry started as the primal contributors of eSports, but as viewership and participation boomed, more non-endemic companies joined in.

The market

In the first quarter of 2019 there has been a 145 per cent increase in new deals, in comparison to the last quarter of 2018, with notable brands such as Nike, Coca-Cola, AT&T, Honda, State Farm and Nissan (Hayward 2019). Nike was the latest apparel brand – following rivals Adidas and Puma into the field; signed a four-year deal with China's League of Legends Pro League and agreed to supply all squads with clothing and footwear (Fortune 2019). The company justified its decision with the following statement: 'As China becomes a new e-sports cultural center, Nike is pleased to support the next generation of athletes and establish a long-term cooperative relationship with e-sports to contribute to the future development of sports ecology' (Fortune 2019). It becomes apparent that eSports players, teams and related companies are becoming more prosperous than ever, due to this surge in sponsorship. As a result, some leading eSport players make around $1.3 million per year.

A new form of sponsorship

The above numbers and facts tell only half of the story about the sponsorship boom of eSports. Beyond these, there is another form of sponsorship developing alongside the growth of eSports, which is slightly different and more direct than the forms presented in this chapter. eSports players (and dedicated video gamers) have found a different stream of funding via the opportunities offered in social media, and more specifically YouTube and twitch. By live-streaming their games, while actively communicating with their followers they attract large numbers of subscribers paying around $5 to $25 per month (Clark 2017). For twitch users this is not just traditional entertainment, but a virtual community, where they communicate about their games, but also about their lives, politics, music, etc.

This fact makes this kind of sponsorship a more internal and direct one from the traditional form presented in this chapter. And, in addition, attracts further publicity and sponsorship deal to players within twitch. To sponsors, twitch offers a novel opportunity: access to a generation that resists traditional advertising media but is steeped in video games. Young people watch game streaming in huge numbers (twitch claims to reach half of the millennial males in the United States) and often in prodigious quantities (Clark 2017).

Case study 22.2
InterContinental Hotel Group: driving employee engagement through London 2012

Sponsorship is entered into for many reasons and increasingly companies are looking internally for the impact of their sponsorship programmes, sometimes to the exclusion of any outward facing benefits. The 2012 London Olympics was potentially a watershed for this type of sponsorship activation and certainly for IHG (InterContinental Hotel Group), who were a provider to the games through their Holiday Inn brand. IHG increased employee engagement and subsequent pride in the company (and increased productivity) – all key drivers for their sponsorship programme.

Creating unforgettable experiences for employees

Some sponsorships (in this case Olympic) deliver few opportunities for large companies to create opportunities for direct interaction for staff – ticket numbers (and similar benefits) are relatively minimal, especially as IHG were only a tier 3 partner (supplier/provider) to the 2012 Olympics.

The answer for IHG was to bring the Olympic Games to life for staff through athlete-led experiences; creating a team of 50 potential Team GB athletes (33 of which were selected for the games) through an innovative negotiation approach – delivering free hotel rooms for athletes and their coaches/family in return for their time for staff and customer engagement and PR, with top-ups for advertising and wider marketing rights.

This programme delivered:

- 37 Olympic Masterclasses covering . . .
- 20 Olympic sports involving . . .
- 62 Olympians and coaches who met . . .
- 2,500 + staff from . . .
- 77 hotels

Delivering . . . in more ways than one

Within six months employees' awareness of the sponsorship increased from 49 per cent to 73 per cent, matched by engagement levels.

The programme delivered an average Net Promotor Score (Bain and Company) of 97. . . and unexpectedly, created part-time jobs for 15 athletes within IHG. IHG were able to maximise the activity by creating parallel 'pop up' Olympic experiences for IHG Loyalty programme and Facebook followers and driving strong PR coverage: a lesson in 'sweating your assets'.

Definition: net promoter score

'The Net Promoter Score and System is defined as: Know the score.

The Net Promoter Score, or NPS®. It is based on the fundamental perspective that every company's customers can be divided into three categories: Promoters, Passives, and Detractors. By asking one simple question – How likely is it that you would recommend [your company] to a friend or colleague? – organisations can track these stakeholder groups and get a clear measure of their company's performance through the customers' eyes. Customers respond on a 0–10 point rating scale and are categorised as follows:

- Promoters (score 9–10) are loyal enthusiasts who will keep buying and refer others, fuelling growth.
- Passives (score 7–8) are satisfied but unenthusiastic customers who are vulnerable to competitive offerings.
- Detractors (score 0–6) are unhappy customers who can damage your brand and impede growth through negative word-of-mouth.
- To calculate a company's NPS, they take the percentage of customers who are Promoters and subtract the percentage who are Detractors.'

Source: Modified from www.netpromoter.com/know/

Picture 22.4 British Olympians such as former World Champion and record Tour de France stage winner, Mark Cavendish, took part in staff masterclasses as part of IHG's sponsorship to drive employee engagement (*source:* Luc Claessen/Velo/Getty Images)

Think about 22.4 — No money deals

In the IHG case study the 50 Olympic/Paralympic athletes were remunerated for their time through free hotel rooms for their personal use, or use by their friends, family and coaches, in exchange for a reasonable amount of rights.

The amount of room nights varied by athlete and was dependent on the athlete's profile (i.e. payment was commensurate with status).

This 'value in kind' (VIK) approach to sponsorship worked as the athletes received something of real use to them, something that they would normally have to pay commercial rates for, so they valued the nights at face value in exchange for their time. For IHG it meant that they were able to work with more athletes than they would have if paying cash, as they were able to benefit from the internal rate on rooms between the parent company and hotels (i.e. X dollars of room nights for IHG meant X times, say, 2 or 3 dollars' worth of athletes).

From this case example how do you think IHG managed to convince the agents who take cash commissions on deals to allow these relationships to happen?

Feedback

Agents and their companies have a similar need to the athletes, i.e. accommodation for 'business' reasons. As such IHG remunerated the agents, who normally receive a commission from athletes, with hotel room nights to a value roughly equivalent of 20 per cent of the room nights the athletes received. In order to make this attractive, IHG worked with a limited number of agents in order to maximise the benefit and incentive to allow their athletes to engage in the programme.

> **Explore 22.3**
>
> **Activating athletes at their 'level'**
>
> In the IHG case study the athletes involved in the programme existed at three predominant levels of profile: existing Olympic legends (with medals from previous games), likely medallists for 2012 (athletes who had medalled at recent world or European championships) and up and coming athletes. In most cases athletes' masterclass days involved a mix of employee, customer and media engagement.
>
> Try planning an activity schedule for each level of athlete above and think about how you might structure it.
>
> **Feedback**
>
> The higher profile the athlete, the more likely their appeal reaches beyond their sport and into the mainstream world and media. The less profiled the athlete, the more important their sport is over themselves and the more focused the media needs to be to the sport (sport specific media) or the athlete's microcosms (i.e. their local paper, etc.).

The future of sponsorship

Sponsorship is an effective communication and marketing tool that can improve brands' reputation and image, boost sales and profits and help organisations have a positive social impact. The way sponsorships are managed has changed drastically in the past few years, mostly due to the decisive transformation of the media landscape, but also due to significant shifts in consumer needs and attitudes. These changes have not gone by unnoticed by major players in communications globally. Sponsorship agencies, advertising agencies, media planning companies and research institutes have a communication expertise that they now need to extend to the sponsorship field.

The future seems bright for sponsorship and most experts predict that the amount of money spent in all types of sponsorships will keep going up. The capabilities offered by new digital technologies will extend sponsorships' visibility beyond the duration of official contracts and will enable new interactive features that will enhance consumers' engagement. Moreover, in the present saturated media landscape, where the lines between paid and earned media space are becoming blurry, sponsorship is also expected to become an effective tool for storytelling and content production. According to most experts, all these are expected to establish sponsorship as an even more attractive marketing tool, but at the same time make negotiations on sponsorship properties even more complicated.

At the same time, as societal and environmental issues will dominate the public discourse in the years to come, the debate on what should be sponsored and what shouldn't will grow, feeding therefore the discussion on what constitutes an effective sponsorship in today's society. From all of the discussions in this chapter, it becomes evident that larger and larger proportions of communication budgets are spent in sponsorships and as the need for efficiency and micro-targeting grows, it is inevitable that organisations, agencies and consultancies will need practitioners with specialised skills to develop, activate, manage and evaluate sponsorships.

Bibliography

Anderson, L. (2003). 'The sponsorship scorecard'. *B&T*, 12 December: 13–14.

Baker, B. and C. Boyle (2009). 'The timeless power of storytelling'. *Journal of Sponsorship* 3(1): 79–87.

Becker-Olsen, K.L. and R.P. Hill (2006). 'The impact of sponsor fit on brand equity the case of nonprofit service providers'. *Journal of Service Research* 9(1): 73–83.

Bruhn, M. and C. Homburg (2001). *Gabler Marketing Lexikon*. Wiesbaden: Gabler Verlag.

Clark, T. (2017) How to Get Rich Playing Video Games Online, *The New Yorker*, https://www.newyorker.com/magazine/2017/11/20/how-to-get-rich-playing-video-games-online

Collins English Dictionary (2019). Definition of Sponsorship, www.collinsdictionary.com/dictionary/english/sponsorship [Accessed 10 July 2019].

Cooper, A. (2003). 'The changing sponsorship scene'. *Admap* (144), November.

Cornwell, B. and I. Maignan (2001). 'An international review of sponsorship research'. *Journal of Advertising* 27(1): 1–21.

Crompton, J.L. (2004). Conceptualization and alternate operationalizations of the measurement of sponsorship effectiveness in sport. *Leisure studies* 23(3): 267–281.

De Pelsmacker, P., M. Geuens and J. Van den Berg (2004). 'Sponsorship' in *Marketing Communications*. Harlow: Prentice Hall.

Delaney, D. (2010). *Sponsorship Decision-making and Management: An Accounting Perspective*. Griffith University.

Do, H., E. Ko and A.G. Woodside (2015). 'Tiger Woods, Nike, and I are (not) best friends: how brand's sports sponsorship in social-media impacts brand consumer's congruity and relationship quality'. *International Journal of Advertising* 1–20.

Dozier, D.M., L.A. Grunig and J.E. Grunig (1995). *Manager's Guide to Excellence in Public Relations and Communication management*. Mahwah, NJ.: Lawrence Erlbaum.

Electoral Commission (2019) Overview of Donations to Political Parties. http://www.electoralcommission.org.uk/__data/assets/pdf_file/0014/102263/to-donations-rp.pdf [Accessed 15 July 2019].

Forbes (2018). The World's Most Valuable Esports Companies, https://www.forbes.com/sites/mikeozanian/2018/10/23/the-worlds-most-valuable-esports-companies-1/#14a35c646a6e

Fortune (2019). Nike Signs Its First Esports Sponsorship Deal, http://fortune.com/2019/02/28/nike-league-of-legends-esports-sponsorship/

Giovino, M. (2018). Aligning rights-holders' marketing assets with brand marketers' needs. *Journal of Brand Strategy* 7(2): 141–53.

Guardian (15 October 2012) Red Bull and Felix Baumgartner take sponsorship to new height http://www.guardian.co.uk/sport/blog/2012/oct/15/red-bull-felix-baumgartner-sponsorship [accessed 20 July 2016].

Gwinner, K. and S.R. Swanson (2003). 'A model of fan identification: Antecedents and sponsorship outcomes'. *Journal of Services Marketing* 17(3): 275–94.

Hayward, A. (2019) Cars, Drinks, and Clothes: Non-Endemic Sponsor Recap for Q1 2019 https://esportsobserver.com/non-endemic-sponsors-q12019/

IEG Sponsorship Report (29 May, 2012b) Following The Money: Sponsorship's Top Spenders of 2011, http://www.sponsorship.com/IEGSR/2012/05/28/Following-The-Money--Sponsorship-s-Top-Spenders-of.aspx [Accessed 15 June 2019].

IEG Sponsorship Spending Report (2015). Where the Dollars are Going and Trends for 2015. http://www.sponsorship.com/IEG/files/4e/4e525456-b2b1-4049-bd51-03d9c35ac507.pdf [Accessed 20 July 2016]. http://www.sponsorship.com/IEGSR/2015/08/03/The-Deepest-Sponsorship-Pockets-of-2014--IEG-s-Top.aspx [Accessed 15 June 2019].

IEG Sponsorship Spending Report (2016). As Sponsorship Borders Fall, Spending Rises. http://www.sponsorship.com/IEGSR/2016/01/05/As-Sponsorship-Borders-Fall,-Spending-Rises.aspx [Accessed 15 June 2019].

IEG Sponsorship Spending Report (2018). What Sponsors Want and Where Dollars Will Go. [Accessed 15 June 2019].

IFM Sports Marketing Surveys (2012). The World Sports Monitor Annual Review 2011. United Kingdom.

Investopedia.com (2012). Corporate Sponsorship www.investopedia.com/terms/c/corporate-sponsorship.asp [Accessed 20 July 2016].

Keiper, M.C., R.D. Manning, Jenny, S. Olrich, T. and C. Croft (2017). No reason to LoL at LoL: the addition of esports to intercollegiate athletic departments, *Journal for the Study of Sports and Athletes in Education* 11(2), 143–160.

Kim, Y., H.W. Lee, M.J. Magnusen and M. Kim (2015). 'Factors influencing sponsorship effectiveness: a meta-analytic review and research synthesis'. *Journal of Sport Management* 29(4).

marketingmagazine.co.uk (13 June 2012). Marketing Society Awards for Excellence 2012: Cause-related marketing www.brandrepublic.com/features/1135807/ [Accessed 15 June 2019].

Mawson, C. (2004). 'A history of the Shell county guides'. www.shellguides.freeserve.co.uk/history.htm [Accessed 15 June 2019].

Mazodier, M. and P. Quester (2014). 'The role of sponsorship fit for changing brand affect: A latent growth modeling approach'. *International Journal of Research in Marketing* 31(1): 16–29.

Mazodier, M. and D. Merunka (2012). 'Achieving brand loyalty through sponsorship: the role of fit and self-congruity'. *Journal of the Academy of Marketing Science* 40(6): 807–20.

McAlister, A.R., S.J. Kelly, M.S. Humphreys and T.B. Cornwell (2012). 'Change in a sponsorship alliance and the communication implications of spontaneous recovery'. *Journal of Advertising* 41(1): 5–16.

McDonnell, I. and M. Moir (2013). *Event Sponsorship*. Routledge.

Meenaghan, T. (1998). 'Current developments and future directions in sponsorship'. *International Journal of Advertising* 17(1): 3–28.

Measurement Matters Blog (17 July, 2012) Crisis and Social Media – A Match Made In Heaven? http://www.gorkana.com/measurement-matters/measurement-matters/brand-reputation/crisis-and-social-media-a-match-made-in-heaven/ [Accessed 24 October 2012].

Millan, A. and M. Ball (2012). 'The use of social media as a tool for consumer brands to leverage sponsorship of sporting events: a qualitative analysis'. *International Journal of Sales, Retailing and Marketing* 1(4): 27–39.

MSNBC.com (December 2nd, 2006) Retailers tap into shoppers' do-gooder spirit. www.msnbc.msn.com/id/15973282/#.UIf5MlH3B-U [Accessed 20 October 2012].

Pine, J. and J. Gilmore (1998). 'Welcome to the experience economy'. *Harvard Business Review* 76(4): 97–105.

Porter, M. and M. Kramer (2002). 'The competitive advantage of corporate philanthropy'. *Harvard Business Review* 80(12): 56–69.

Sport Business International (2010). *Sport Business In Numbers* Volume 4. London.

Statista.com (2019) Global sponsorship spending by region from 2009 to 2016 (in billion U.S. dollars). https://www.statista.com/statistics/196898/global-sponsorship-spending-by-region-since-2009/ [Accessed 15 July 2019].

Summerley, R. (2019). 'The Development of Sports: A Comparative Analysis of the Early Institutionalization of Traditional Sports and E-Sports'. *Games and Culture*, 15(1).

Tench, R. and L. Yeomans (2009). *Exploring Public Relations*. London: FT Prentice Hall.

Tench, R. and L. Yeomans (2014). *Exploring Public Relations*. London: FT Prentice Hall.

Tench, R. and L. Yeomans (2017). *Exploring Public Relations*. London: FT Prentice Hall.

Walliser, B. (2003). 'An international review of sponsorship research'. *International Journal of Advertising* 22(1): 5–40.

Weeks, C.S., P.J. O'Connor and B.A. Martin (2017). 'When ambush marketing is beneficial to sponsorship awareness: Creating sponsor distinctiveness using exclusivity and brand juxtaposition. *Journal of Marketing Management* 33(15–16): 1256–1280.

Woisetschläger, D., Eiting, A., Haselhoff, V. and M. Michaelis (2010). 'Determinants and consequences of sponsorship fit: a study of fan perceptions'. *Journal of Sponsorship* 3(2): 169–180.

Websites

Santander Cycle Hire Scheme: https://tfl.gov.uk/modes/cycling/santander-cycles
Comic Relief: www.comicrelief.com
Daily Motion: http://www.dailymotion.com
Deloitte: http://www.deloitte.co.uk/impact/2012/our-role-in-london-2012/ [Accessed 12 December 2019]
Digital Concert Hall: www.digitalconcerthall.com
Emirates Air Line: www.emiratesairline.co.uk
Festival Cannes: www.festival-cannes.com
Guggenheim: www.guggenheim.org
Gurgaon Metro: http://rapidmetrogurgaon.com/home/gallery-advertise.html [Accessed 12 December 2019]
Holiday Inn: www.holidayinn.com/hotels/gb/en/global/offers/olympics_welcome [Accessed 20 July 2016]
InterContinental Hotel Group: www.ihg.com
JP Morgan Chase & Co Sponsorships - https://www.jpmorganchase.com/corporate/Corporate-Responsibility/sponsorships.htm [Accessed 20 July 2016]
MLB: www.mlb.com
Natural History Museum Ice Rink: http://www.nhm.ac.uk/visit/exhibitions/ice-rink.html
NBA: www.nba.com
NFL: www.nfl.com
O2: www.o2.co.uk
PBS: www.pbs.org
PR Week Awards: www.prweekawards.com

websites (continued)

Red: www.red.org/about
Rugby Football Union (England Rugby Team): www.rfu.com
Sky Rainforest Rescue: https://rainforestrescue.sky.com
Somerset House Ice Rink: www.somersethouse.org.uk/ice-rink
Sports Industry Awards: www.sportindustry.biz/awards
Sports Relief: www.sportrelief.com
The O2 Arena: www.theo2.co.uk
Times Square New Year's Eve: http://www.newyearseve.nyc

CHAPTER 23

Stefania Romenti and Grazia Murtarelli

Corporate communication

Source: Barbara Brockhauser/Shutterstock

Learning outcomes

By the end of this chapter you should be able to:
- define what corporate communication is and explain key concepts associated with it
- understand the convergences and divergences among corporate communication, public relations, integrated marketing communication (IMC) and organisational communication
- contextualise the strategic role of corporate communication in the societal and organisational environments
- conceptualise 'consistency' and 'integration' as key drivers for corporate communication strategy
- understand how corporate communication can help to build and to sustain intangible values such as reputation, image, identity and legitimacy.

Structure

- Defining corporate communication in theory and practice
- The role of corporate communication in society
- The role of corporate communication in organisations
- Corporate communication and intangible assets
- Coordinating all forms of communication

Introduction

Since the second half of the twentieth century corporate communication has appealed to professionals and consultants, among whom the disciplinary area is born in the US. One of the main reasons of this evergreen appeal is the mind-set behind the concept of corporate communication, mostly focused on the management of communication processes.

Management can be conceived as planning, organising, coordinating and governing activities, tasks and resources. In fact, since in recent years the number of communication specialties has spread in private and public organisations, the need for controlling and organising of multiple activities and resources has grown. Corporate communication has undergone a profound evolution, which has increased its strategic importance in the governance and success of complex organisations.

This evolution has created the basis for the ongoing process of institutionalisation, according to which the communication role is ever more important, because it contributes to the strategic management of organisations and it increases their overall value.

The aim of this chapter is to define the terrain of practice and the conceptual domain of corporate communication, by discussing similarities as well as differences with other related concepts, such as public relations, organisational communication, integrated marketing communication and so forth.

Defining corporate communication in theory and practice

Some authors use 'corporate communication' as a generic umbrella term that covers a wide range of activities, such as for example crisis communication, public affairs and lobbying, employee relations, media relations and so on (Argenti 1996; Goodman 1994). Without providing specific definitions, these authors implicitly highlight the multifaceted and the rich nature of corporate communication. Other authors give specific definitions by stressing once one element, once another. Again, other authors evoke a need for consistency and integration among the different components of the discipline. Table 23.1 reports some definitions of corporate communication. A glance at the definitions reported in the several books written on the subject during the 1990s is enough to see that 'the academic field of corporate communication is scattered, divergent, and lacks coherence' (Belasen 2008: 3).

However, it must be stressed that there are differences among definitions, owing to the wide and interdisciplinary theoretical foundations (Box 23.1), as well as to the distinct approaches that can be applied to the area: corporate marketing/integrated marketing communication, public relations, total corporate communication, corporate communication gaps, organisational communication (Illia and Balmer 2012; Gambetti and Quigley 2012) (Table 23.2). Schultz (1993) defines Integrated Marketing Communication (IMC) as 'a concept of marketing communications planning that recognise the added value of comprehensive plan that evaluates the strategic roles of a variety of communications disciplines (i.e. advertising, direct response, sales promotion and public relations) and combines these disciplines to provide clarity, consistency and maximum communication impact' (10). Traditionally, integrated marketing communication refers more to commercial contents used by a supplier to persuade a buyer. Differently, organisational communication scholars (Jablin and Putnam 2001) focus on the activation of sense-making processes, the construction of a shared organisational reality and behaviours. Corporate communication has often been employed as a synonym of public relations (PR). But if we analyse the academic literature (Grunig and Hunt 1984; Ledingham and Bruning 2000), we can see that the attention of public relations scholars is more directed to the strategic management of relationships with key publics and influential stakeholders, both digital and offline. The differences among these disciplinary fields are increasingly blurred, but, on a broader level, what makes corporate communication distinctive compared to other related and similar concepts is the way of conceiving organisations.

In fact, the label 'corporate' derives from the Latin word 'corpus' and it stands for a 'unitarian entity', a 'whole'. Corporate communication addresses the 'one company, one voice' approach, and insists on the importance of making an organisation appear as a unique subject with a consistent narrative across different markets, audiences and brands. Traces of the potential close tie between the concepts of corporate communication and the organisation as a metaphor of unity and totality dates back at least to the pioneering work of Bernstein (1984). A corporate communication strategy should convey the unique character of the organisation (Kitchen and Schultz 2001). It implies pursuing the alignment with the corporate image among external strategic constituencies. Moreover, it requires building the antecedents of corporate image, so to involve multiple internal functions to define the corporate identity, values and culture as well as clear strategic orientations.

Definition	Source
The set of activities involved in managing and orchestrating all internal and external communications aimed at creating favourable starting points with stakeholders on which the company depends.	Van Riel and Fombrun 2007
A management function that offers a framework for the effective coordination of all internal and external communication with the overall purpose of establishing and maintaining favourable reputations with stakeholder groups upon which the organisation is dependent.	Cornelissen 2017
As a practice based on four dimensions: roles, skills and activities of practitioners; organisation of these practitioners and their work; political and cultural issues; and the communication and consumption of process and products.	Cornelissen et al. (2006)
A variety of management functions related to an organisation's internal and external communications. Depending on the organisation, corporate communication can include such traditional disciplines as public relations, investor relations, employee relations, community relations, media relations, labour relations, government relations, technical communication, training and employee development, marketing communication, management communication.	Goodman 1994
The strategic management process by which an organisation communicates with its various audiences to the mutual benefits of both and to its improved competitive advantage.	Dolphin, Fan 2000
An approach, a management philosophy that should be adopted by communication managers in order to favour the alignment and synergistic action of all communication activities carried out by firm.	Gambetti and Quigley 2012
Corporate communication transcends the areas of specialty of communication practitioners and cross-functional boundaries to harness the strategic interests of the organisation as a whole.	Belasen 2008

Table 23.1 Definitions of corporate communication

Definition	Links to corporate communication
Integrated marketing communication (IMC)	Corporate communication is seen to be part of the marketing function
Public relations (PR)	Corporate communication plays a boundary-spanning role
Total corporate communication	Corporate communication should not be merely viewed as a functional activity, but as a strategic one since whatever an organisation says and does, it communicates
Corporate communication gaps	Corporate communication's goal is to assure that no gaps exist between what an organisation does and what it says
Organizational communication	Corporate communication builds and shapes organisational sense making and behaviours

Table 23.2 Different disciplinary approaches that can be applied to the study of corporate communication

> **Box 23.1**
>
> ## Perspectives that inform corporate communication
>
> Several communication perspectives collectively constitute the construct space for corporate communication. The most significant are functionalist, interpretative and discursive/constitutive. Functionalist perspective focuses on processes and their measurement, on roles and behaviours, on the definition of goals and strategies (Argenti 1996; Van Riel 2003; Cornelissen 2017). Interpretative perspective is more related to rules, decisions, culture, symbolic processes of meanings' attribution, socially construction of reality and identity (Cheney and Christensen 2001). Finally, discursive/constitutive perspective belongs to the so-called context-centred approaches to the study of communication. More precisely, this approach goes beyond the classical functional approach to organisational communication, focused on messages, networks and channels, by focusing on the meaning-centred approach, focused on sensemaking, influence and culture (Putnam and Nicotera 2009; Cooren 2015; Weick 1995). Adopting a context-centred approach to the study and the practice of organisational communication requires a recognition of the growing interconnectedness among organisations and their stakeholders. This arises from the turbulence and complexity that affects organisational settings as well as the pervasiveness of new technology. This approach is also in line with the emerging perspectives on postmodernism, critical studies, global cultures and institutions. Following organisational communication theory, organisations are communicatively constituted because the communication (often conceptualised as discourse) is the means by which human beings coordinate actions, create relationships and constitute or maintain organisations (Christensen and Cornelissen 2011; Putnam and Nicotera 2009). As Deetz (1992) noted, communication cannot be reduced to an informational issue where meanings are assumed to be already existing, but it must be a process of meaning development and social production of perceptions, identities, social structures and affective responses.

> **Think about 23.1**
>
> When is the term 'corporate communications' used rather than 'corporate communication'?
>
> Traditionally, corporate communications implicitly draws on a 'transmission' or 'conduit' metaphor of communication. Corporate communication domain of practice primarily consists of projecting and planning contents and channels through which messages are diffused with the aim of achieving certain organisational goals. Beyond different disciplinary perspectives, the idea that the organisation should perform as an orchestra, by developing the capability of using different instruments played by different people to harmonically play the same music, is fundamental (Van Riel 2003).

The role of corporate communication in society

Communication plays its role at the increasingly more and more porous and fragile boundary between the organisation and its reference environment (White and Verčič 2001). From this viewpoint, communication exercises a function of *boundary spanning*. The fact that it has a boundary function gives corporate communication a privileged position for observing and interpreting the context in which an organisation operates, and this is considered a central theme in strategic management studies to guarantee the long-term corporate survival.

The monitoring and interpretation of the ongoing dynamics in *environmental scanning* are thus an important component of the strategic contribution of communication to the decisional processes and can be conducted at two levels: the issue and public level and the company stakeholder level (Stoffels 1994). Through such activities, communication stimulates management to formulate strategies and processes aligned with the ongoing dynamics in the company social context and with the most relevant expectations of stakeholders, rather than just limiting itself to only considering its own interests (Steyn 2003). This facilitates the progressive legitimisation of the company in its environment, which is a necessary condition to maintain its long-term 'operating licence'.

Consider examples where an organisation has failed to engage with its public or stakeholders and lost it licence to operate in a market.

Together with boundary spanning and environmental scanning activities, the aligning component of strategic communication includes bridging with and engaging stakeholders.

Case study 23.1
Barilla Centre for Food and Nutrition

The Barilla case study described in this chapter highlights how, and to what extent, communication can play a crucial role for the competitive advantage of firms by influencing the managerial processes related to the three activities mentioned earlier. For instance, the CCO proposed to set up the Barilla Centre for Food and Nutrition, devoted to research and open discussions around nutritional, health and agricultural issues. The Centre proposed a new model able to measure and to affect both consumption and manufacturing processes: the Double Pyramid Model, a tool that examines the nutritional facets of foods linked to their environmental impact (www.barillacfn.com, 2015). The model has the aim of communicating the inverse relationship between nutritionally recommended foods and their environmental impact. In other words, the healthiest foods are those with the smallest negative impact on the environment. Thanks to the BCFN, and the CCO who plays a crucial role in its life, Barilla has developed a great amount of initiatives to cultivate trust relationships with the local community, farmers, employees and every other parts of the value chain. For all these reasons, we can say that communication is able to play a strategic role in creating shared value, by aligning social needs with the development and production of Barilla products, by cultivating trust relationships with actors of the value chain and by helping and enabling local cluster development.

Source: Invernizzi, E., Romenti, S. and G. Murtarelli (2016). "Creating Shared Value through Communication: A Case Study Analysis of Barilla". In Bronn, P.S., Romenti, S., Zerfass, A. (Eds.). The management game of communication (pp. 181–201). Emerald Group Publishing Limited

Public relations scholars have traditionally identified the development of solid, lasting and symmetric relations between the organisation and its stakeholders as the strategic objective of communication (Grunig 1992; Ledingham and Bruning 2000). This role implies abandoning short-sighted management attitudes dedicated primarily to defending management's own areas of interest (*buffering*), but instead dedicating the energies to encouraging greater open-mindedness on the part of the organisation to its reference environment. Corporate communication professionals welcome *stimuli* coming from outside, and value the wealth of opinions, positions and experiences which constitute the organisational context.

Assuming an approach of this type means building bridges between the organisation and its most important stakeholders (*bridging*), as well as activating and facilitating the participation and involvement of company's members, while taking care to maintain a balance between the weight of their voices and those of the management of the organisation (Heugens et al. 2002).

Beyond bridging, stakeholder engagement means activating co-decisional processes, building partnerships and stimulating supporting behaviour from stakeholders. Activating co-decisional processes, for example through ad hoc stakeholder meetings and multi-stakeholder workshops, means incorporating stakeholders' points of view in managerial decision making. The result is shared choices that should be more aligned to meeting stakeholders' expectations. Building partnerships means working together with stakeholders to devise, plan and develop new business solutions. Stimulating supporting behaviour transforms stakeholders into real advocates for organisational projects.

The role of corporate communication in organisations

The strategic role of corporate communication inside organisations has evolved and become increasingly more important. More and more frequently, the Corporate Communication Officer (CCO) takes part in the corporate decisions of the dominant coalition.

Firstly, corporate communication enables the implementation of company decisions. The CCO contributes by following the actual decisional momentum and exercising influence on the ways in which decisions are communicated and carried out. Communication helps to govern the activities, mainly tactical in nature, which are necessary for the implementation of the decisions themselves. In fact, communication enables the decisional processes by transmitting their contents to interested parties, involving and motivating human resources, supporting the exercise of leadership, helping to plan and organise the managerial and operational activities, and making it possible to check the results obtained. Some authors define communication strategy (Argenti 1996; Van Riel and Fombrun 2007; Steyn 2003) as that which makes known, inside and outside the organisation, the decisions regarding company strategy and business objectives. According to the authors, communication helps to focus the energies of the organisation's internal and external members towards a shared goal. The enabling role coincides with the infrastructural role, traditionally attributed to communication, that is, the role of sustaining and supporting the company business. It represents a crucial component as it substantially contributes to the efficacy and quality of the results in the decisional process. This component in the communication role does not impact the content of the decision itself, but rather on the way in which the decision is carried out.

Corporate communication becomes something more than an infrastructural component of the business, when it feeds the decisional process, influencing it through reflective activities of analysis and interpretation of the internal and external context. Here the listening activity plays a different role from that of the enabling role of communication, where listening aims at aligning the communication of the decisions taken with the stakeholders' opinions and attitudes.

Context analysis conditions the formulation of the strategic options to choose from, as it widens the choice of decisional criteria because it includes the communicational ones. In other words, through reflective activity, the communicational component enters the decisional process itself and contributes to influencing its content. By carefully listening to context and understanding the expectations of the main stakeholders, the CCO can forecast the impact on them and thus contribute to making decisions in keeping with their context. The decisions of the companies that use this type of approach are more sustainable, not only from the standpoint of financing, human resources and technology as traditionally occurs in many corporations, but also from the communicational standpoint. Taking sustainable decisions from the communicational standpoint, therefore, means ensuring that the choices made are not communicated, but aligned with the expectations of the company stakeholders as well as with the public image and identity of the organisation.

The importance of the activity of dialogue between the corporation and its stakeholders within the constitutive role of communication is fundamental as it permits maintaining harmony among the respective values and helps to legitimate the organisation in the environment in which it operates (Andriof and Waddock 2017). Such dialogue may even be focused on business themes to encourage the direct involvement of certain stakeholders in decisional processes and to activate the exchange of innovative ideas.

Case study 23.2
Four dialogue strategies with stakeholders

Within the corporate communication field, increasing attention has been devoted to the relational theories and principles based on concepts such as involvement, engagement and dialogue by replacing the traditional sender-receiver model and striving for a more two-way symmetrical communication (Taylor and Kent 2014; Valentini et al. 2016). Given the major relevance attributed to cultivating relationships and a growing usage of social media, organisations are more and more required to develop dialogic strategies and competences especially within the social media context (Romenti and Murtarelli 2012; Romenti et al. 2014). Dialogue can be defined as a core process that can be used by organisations by achieving different aims. According to Romenti and Murtarelli (2012), organisations could implement four main dialogue strategies: concertative, transformative, framing and generative ones.

Concertative dialogue strategy is usually used for stimulating and facilitating consensus and agreement among participants with regards to organisational behaviours and initiatives (Innes 2004). Transformative dialogue strategy is suitable when companies call for new ideas concerning current strategies and future policies and ask for suggestions from interlocutors (Gergen et al. 2004). Framing strategy is usually used when an organisation wants to be visible and recognised as a relevant and informed actor about a specific topic or issue (Entman 1993). Finally, generative dialogue strategy is suitable when an organisation would like to stimulate the exchange of different opinions among participants in a respectful climate. By selecting each strategy, organisations need to take a decision concerning the tone of the dialogue, the type of dialogic flow and the different conversational resources to use in a dialogic process.

Case study 23.3
Ferrari as a communication-oriented company

Ferrari, the well-known auto-maker luxury company, can be defined as a communication-oriented company, since communication takes on a predominant role in guiding both the strategic and the operational decisions of the company. The re-birth of Ferrari, following a crisis, during the 1980s, is tied to the strategies put into effect by the new CEO, Luca di Montezemolo, who served as manager in the Corporate Communication department of the FIAT Group, where he reached the position of CCO. Montezemolo joined Ferrari, became President in 1991, and started a programme known as 'Formula Persona', which consisted in continuously improving innovation and creativity, centring on each employee and on what s/he could contribute. To this end, several buildings and work environments were designed to optimise the production process and emphasise individual identity and a sense of belonging of the employees. In addition, a system was designed to recognise the contributions of the employees and to implement a series of company-sponsored services, including outside services, to simplify and better employees' lives. The idea, on which the 'Formula Persona' was based, was that these measures would communicate to the employees the value the company placed on them as well as the recognition of the contribution of every person to the company's success. The results have been astonishing from the point of view of employee commitment and of the company's economic results. In the middle of the 1990s the economic bottom line turned 'from red to black' and in 1999 Ferrari started again to win the world championships non-stop up until 2008.

Source: Invernizzi, E., Romenti, S. and M. Fumagalli (2012). Identity, communication and change management in Ferrari. Corporate Communications: An International Journal, 17(4), 483–497

Picture 23.1 Ferrari's renaissance is attributed to the communication skills of CEO Luca di Montezemolo (*source:* Remo Casilli/Sintesi/Alamy Stock Photo)

A further and third strategic contribution to decision-making processes manifests itself through the participation, from the very beginning, of communication professionals in all corporate and departmental decisional processes. Or through the decisional processes that the CEO himself starts up, after considering their aims and their communicational consequences. The reasons for this important change are to be found in the progressive recognition of the relevance of the communication component in any company decision.

The presence of the director of the communication function in the executive committee has its justification in the fact that every decision must be evaluated, not only from the standpoint of necessary resources and financial impact, and, not only from the standpoint of necessary requirements and impact on human resources, but also from the standpoint of necessary communication resources and communication impact which those decisions require and imply.

Corporate communication and intangible assets

Corporate communication plays a crucial role in the process of developing intangibles, such as reputation, image and identity. Corporate communication intangibles represent the capital a company has in terms of its credibility, reliability and trustworthiness with its stakeholders (Caruana 1997; Christiansen and Vendelø 2003; Coombs and Holladay 2006) and, consequently, the degree of support the organisation has at its disposal to be legitimised as a 'good citizen' in society.

Corporate reputation crystallises the firm's ability to deliver value to its stakeholders (Fombrun et al. 2000); therefore, the quality of its reputation reflects the capacity of an organisation to satisfy the expectations of multiple categories of stakeholders (Freeman 1984). To improve reputation, communication managers should manage effectively their organisation's corporate identity (Balmer and Gray 1999; Van Riel and Fombrun 2007). Corporate identity is conceived as the backbone of reputation (Van Riel and Fombrun 2007) because it reflects managers' and employees' perceptions about the organisational core (Hatch and Schultz 1997; Davies et al. 2004). Corporate identity influences the way in which stakeholders form their judgements (Dowling 2004). On the one hand, through visible symbols (i.e. architecture, office layouts, uniforms, dress codes, language, logos) which reflect organisational self-representation (Dowling 2004) and on the other, through the expression of the deeper personality of the organisation, which is the result of the shared values and beliefs of all organisational members. Corporate identity strengthens reputation when it is unequivocal, clear and explicit, such as when it drives corporate behaviour, so reinforcing the organisation's temporal consistency in the eyes of stakeholders.

Balmer and Gray (1999: 172) state that corporate communication 'forms the nexus between an organisation's corporate identity and the coveted strategic objective of acquiring a favourable corporate reputation'.

These authors offer a broader view of corporate communication by defining three forms of it: primary, secondary and tertiary. The most interesting characteristic of this typology is that primary communication consists of organisational behaviours and their meanings transmitted to stakeholders. In other words, whatever the organisation does (for example in terms of product and services delivered, human resource policies, employees' behaviours to other stakeholders), organisational behaviours are the fundamental components of corporate reputation (Fombrun and Shanley 1990; Bromley 1993, Fombrun and Rindova 1996; Balmer 1998; Gray and Balmer 1998). Above all, behaviours and decisional processes may contribute to reinforce reputation when they are linked to ethical and sustainable principles of management, and when they are consistent with organisational core values embedded in corporate identity. The central role assigned to behaviours within the reputation management process is the reason why the most commonly used corporate reputation measurement models (i.e. Fombrun's Reputation Quotient, Financial Times' Reputational Rankings) evaluate stakeholders' perceptions of a wide range of organisational elements: product and service quality, financial performance, social responsiveness, innovation, work-environment quality and effectiveness of management. Finally, Balmer and Gray (1999) define secondary and tertiary

Explore 23.1

Purpose vs. profit

There's a change afoot within organisations that calls on the PR profession to step up to the task of helping organisations to define their purpose in a way that is meaningful to society.

It's an issue that is quickly rising up the corporate agenda. Larry Fink, CEO of BlackRock, fired a warning shot in January 2018 in his organisation's anniversary CEO letter to business leaders when he called companies to account for their societal impact.

'Purpose is not the sole pursuit of profits but the animating force for achieving them.

'Profits are in no way inconsistent with purpose – in fact, profits and purpose are inextricably linked. Profits are essential if a company is to effectively serve all of its stakeholders over time – not only shareholders, but also employees, customers, and communities.

'Similarly, when a company truly understands and expresses its purpose, it functions with the focus and strategic discipline that drive long-term profitability. Purpose unifies management, employees, and communities. It drives ethical behavior and creates an essential check on actions that go against the best interests of stakeholders.

'Purpose guides culture, provides a framework for consistent decision-making, and, ultimately, helps sustain long-term financial returns for the shareholders of your company.'

Fink's words carry the weight of the largest investment fund in the world with more than $6 trillion under management. Read his letter and consider its impact on corporate organisations and the way that they communicate with their public.

Source: A Fundamental Reshaping of Finance, Larry Fink CEO Letter, Blackrock

communication as respectively the traditional planned communication activities (i.e. advertising, visual communication, public relations) and the word-of-mouth generated by the general public and media about the organisation's activity. Consequently, scholars argue that reputation can be the result of communication carried out by the organisation both directly, through planned activities of advertising/publicity, and indirectly through daily behaviours that generate word-of-mouth communication among the general public. To enhance reputation, all the communication contents by and about an organisation should be consistent with its corporate identity over a given period (Balmer and Gray 1999; Van Riel and Fombrun 2007).

Recent researches (Doorley and Garcia 2007; Van Riel and Fombrun 2007) concur that the aim of corporate communication and public relations should concentrate on strengthening corporate reputation instead of building image, which represents only an organisation's outward appearance.

The image-building process is based on Grunig's Press-agentry Model (Grunig and Hunt 1984) where the organisation is less than truthful about its activities and the effects of its activities, and it resists establishing a dialogue with its constituencies. Already in the 1960s and 70s, Finn (1961) and Bernays (1977) were ahead of their time in pointing out the limits of the image concept. The former maintained that image is the fruit of deliberate construction, often without any real relation to true corporate identity. The latter emphasised that the term image evokes the fact that public relations deal with illusions rather than with reality. These precursors were followed, starting in the nineties, by other researchers and practitioners (Olins 1989; Invernizzi 1991; Grunig 1992) who called for abandoning the concept of image and hence the term, especially as objectives of corporate communication. In 1992 Grunig affirmed that image has many negative connotations, because it is seen as the opposite of reality, as an imitation of something. Olins (1989) attributed negative value to the concept of image, associating it with something false, the opposite of reality, and stressing its manipulative dimension.

Coordinating all forms of communication

Due to the distributed geographical responsibilities, the variety of specialisms in communication and the diversity of organisational roles, organisations are required to develop coordinating mechanisms and to stimulate cooperation among all organisational members involved in communication activities. To this regard, the SIDEC model drives the choice of a communication policy. The model stands for Strategy, Internal organisation, Internal driving forces and Communication policy (van Riel and Fombrun 2007) (see Figure 23.1). The choice of a communication policy depends on the relationships among the nature of corporate strategy, the heterogeneity of the driving forces at group and

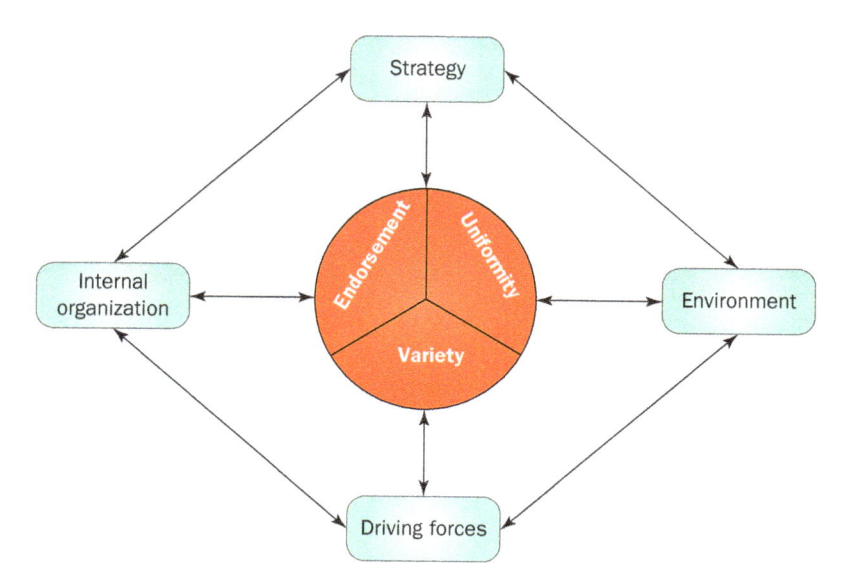

Figure 23.1 SIDEC Model (the model stands for Strategy, Internal organisation, Internal driving forces and Communication policy. Adapted from van Riel and Fombrun 2007) (*source:* Adapted from Van Riel, C.B.M. and C. Fombrun (2007). Essentials of Corporate Communication. Abingdon: Routledge)

business units' levels, the way in which internal organisation works and the nature of environments in which the organisation operates.

Company strategy should be translated into common starting points (CSPs) both at the general level and at the business units' level. CSPs are central values, which are the basis for any kinds of communication, in other words concrete statements from which central values can be consistently translated into all forms of communication. In order to coordinate diverse forms of communication, beyond CPSs, an organisation should introduce a common operational system (i.e. a general accepted approach to setting up campaigns) and select coordinating bodies (i.e. a unique department, a steering committee, ad hoc meetings).

Picture 23.2 The Sense and Simplicity campaign radically changed consumer perception of Philips and repositioned it as a leader in the health and wellbeing category (*source:* Agencja Fotograficzna Caro/Alamy Stock Photo)

Mini case study 23.1
Philips and the campaign 'Sense and simplicity'

The main goal of the Sense and Simplicity campaign was to change the existing customers' perceptions towards the company's image. Philips' strategy of using simplicity both as a design theme and a differentiator of a new brand positioning had the potential to bring good results for the company. The company's financial health deteriorated in the 1990s, partly because of a lack of focus and partly because of poor communication. In 2003, the CEO unveiled the new corporate vision and mission. He also decided to reposition the brand. In 2004, the management launched the 'Sense and Simplicity' campaign. The new brand promise was to launch high-tech able to meet customers' needs (sense) but with simple designs and easy-to-use interfaces (simplicity). Various forms of communication were used to effectively communicate the new brand promise: advertising campaign in print, TV and internet media, events, media relations, dedicated website.

Summary

This chapter helps us to understand the purpose of corporate communication (i.e. developing reputation, identity and image; maintaining legitimacy). Corporate communication helps companies to make effective and informed decision-making processes in order to meet organisational goals as well as the expectations expressed by the broader society. For this reason, organisations are required to use mechanisms for developing consistent messages and coordinated channels.

Bibliography

Andriof, J. and S. Waddock (2017). 'Unfolding stakeholder engagement'. In *Unfolding stakeholder thinking* (pp. 19–42). Routledge.

Argenti, P.A. (1996). 'Corporate communication as a discipline: toward a definition'. *Management Communication Quarterly*, 10(1), 73–97.

Balmer, J.M. (1998). 'Corporate identity and the advent of corporate marketing'. *Journal of marketing management*, 14(8), 963–996.

Balmer, J.M. and E.R. Gray (1999). 'Corporate identity and corporate communications: creating a competitive advantage'. *Corporate Communications: An International Journal, 4*(4), 171–177.

Belasen, A.T. (2008). *The theory and practice of corporate communication: A competing values perspective.* Sage Publications: Thousand Oaks, California.

Bernays, F. (1977). 'Down with image, up with reality'. *Public Relations Quarterly, 22*(1), 12–14.

Bernstein, D. (1984). *Company image and reality: A critique of corporate communications.* Taylor & Francis.

Bromley, D.B. (1993). *Reputation, image and impression management.* John Wiley & Sons.

Bruning, S.D., M. Dials and A. Shirka (2008). 'Using dialogue to build organization-public relationships, engage publics, and positively affect organizational outcomes'. *Public Relations Review 34*(1), 25–31.

Caruana, A. (1997). 'Corporate Reputation: Concept and Measurement', *Journal of Product and Brand Management, 6*(2), 109–118.

Cheney, C.G. and L.T. Christensen (2001). 'Organizational identity: linkages between internal and external organizational communication' in *The New Handbook of Organizational Communication.* F.M. Jablin and L.L. Putnam (eds). Thousand Oaks, CA: Sage.

Christiansen, J.K. and M.T. Vendelø (2003). 'The role of reputation building in international R&D project collaboration'. *Corporate Reputation Review, 5*(4), 304–329.

Christensen, L.T. and J.P. Cornelissen (2011). 'Bridging corporate and organizational communication: review, development and a look to the future'. *Management Communication Quarterly, 25*(3), 383–414.

Christensen, L.T., M. Morsing and G. Cheney (2008). *Corporate Communications: Convention, complexity and critique.* Thousand Oaks, CA: Sage.

Christensen, L.T., J. Cornelissen and A.F. Firat (2009). 'New tensions and challenges in integrated communications', *Corporate Communication: An International Journal, 14*(2), 207–219.

Coombs, T.W. and S.J. Holladay (2006). 'Unpacking the halo effect: Reputation and crisis management'. *Journal of Communication Management, 10*(2), 123–137.

Cooren, F. (2015). *Organizational Discourse: Communication and constitution.* John Wiley & Sons.

Cornelissen J. (2017). *Corporate Communication: A guide to theory and practice,* Thousand Oaks, California: Sage Publications.

Cornelissen, J., T. Van Bekkum and B. Van Ruler (2006). 'Corporate communications: a practice-based theoretical conceptualization', *Corporate Reputation Review, 9*(2), 114–133.

Davies, G., R. Chun, R.V. da Silva and S. Roper (2004). 'A corporate character scale to assess employee and customer views of organization reputation'. *Corporate reputation review, 7*(2), 125–146.

Davis, A. (2003). 'Public relations and news sources' in *News, Public Relations and Power.* S. Cottle (ed.). London: Sage.

Davis, A. and E. Seymour (2010). 'Generating forms of media capital inside and outside the political field: the strange case of David Cameron' in *Media, Culture and Society, 32*(5), 1–20.

De Bussy, N. (2010). 'Dialogue as a basis for stakeholder engagement: defining and measuring core competencies' in *The Sage Handbook of Public Relations.* R.L. Heath (ed.). Los Angeles, CA: Sage Publications.

Deephouse, D.L. and S.M. Carter (2005). 'An examination of differences between organizational legitimacy and organizational reputation', *Journal of Management Studies 42,* 329–360.

Deephouse, D.L. and M.C. Suchman (2008). 'Legitimacy in organizational institutionalism' in *The Sage Handbook of Organizational Institutionalism.* R. Greenwood, C. Oliver, K. Sahlin and R. Suddaby (eds). Thousand Oaks, CA: Sage.

Deetz, S. (1992). *Democracy in an Age of Corporate Colonization: Developments in communication and the politics of everyday life.* SUNY press.

Deetz, S. and J. Simpson (2004). 'Critical organizational dialogue: open formation and the demand of "otherness"' in *Dialogue: Theorizing difference in communication studies.* R. Anderson, L. Baxter and K. Cissna (eds). Thousand Oaks, CA: Sage.

Dolphin, R.R. and Y. Fan (2000). 'Is corporate communications a strategic function? *Management decision, 38*(2), 99–107.

Doorley, J. and F.G. Garcia (2007). 'Rumor has it: Understanding and managing rumors'. *The Public Relations Strategist,* (3), 27–31.

Dowling, G.R. (2004). 'Corporate reputations: should you compete on yours?' *California Management Review, 46*(3), 19–36.

Ehling, W.P., J. White and J.E. Grunig (1992). 'Public relations and marketing practices' in *Excellence in Public Relations and Communications Management.* J.E. Grunig (ed.). Hillsdale, NJ: Lawrence Erlbaum Associates, Inc.

Entman, R.M. (1993). 'Framing: Toward clarification of a fractured paradigm'. *Journal of communication, 43*(4), 51–58.

Finn, D. (1961). 'The price of corporate vanity'. *Harvard Business Review, 39*(4), 135–143.

Fombrun, C.J., N.A. Gardberg and J.M. Sever (2000). 'The Reputation Quotient SM: A multi-stakeholder measure of corporate reputation'. *Journal of Brand Management*, 7(4), 241–255.

Fombrun, C.J. and V. Rindova (1996). 'Who's tops and who decides? The social construction of corporate reputations'. New York University, Stern School of Business, Working Paper, 5–13.

Fombrun, C. and M. Shanley (1990). 'What's in a name? Reputation building and corporate strategy'. *Academy of Management Journal*, 33(2), 233–258.

Fombrun, C.J. and C.B. Van Riel (2004). *Fame and Fortune: How successful companies build winning reputations*. Upper Saddle River, NJ: Pearson Education.

Frankental, P. (2001). 'Corporate social responsibility – a PR invention?' *Corporate Communications: An International Journal*, 6(1), 18–23.

Freeman, R. (1984). *Strategic Management: A stakeholder approach*. Cambridge: Cambridge University Press.

Friedman, A.L. and S. Miles (2002). 'Developing stakeholder theory'. *Journal of Management Studies* 39(1): 1–22.

Gambetti, R. and S. Quigley (Eds.). (2012). *Managing Corporate Communication: A cross-cultural approach*. Macmillan International Higher Education.

Gergen, K.J., M.M. Gergen and F.J. Barrett (2004). 'Dialogue: Life and death of the organization'. Grant, D., Oswick, C., Hardy, C., Putnam, L.L. and Philips, N. (Eds.) *The Sage Handbook of Organizational Discourse*, 39–59.

Goodman, M.B. (Ed.). (1994). *Corporate Communication: Theory and practice*. SUNY Press.

Gray, E.R. and J.M. Balmer (1998). 'Managing corporate image and corporate reputation'. *Long range planning*, 31(5), 695–702.

Grunig, J.E. (ed.) (1992). *Excellence in Public Relations and Communication Management*. Hillsdale, NJ: Lawrence Erlbaum Associates, Inc.

Grunig, J.E. and T.E. Hunt (1984). *Managing Public Relations*. New York, NY: Holt, Rinehart & Winston.

Grunig, L., J.E. Grunig and D.M. Dozier (2002). *Excellent Public Relations and Effective Organizations: A study of communication management in three countries*. Abingdon: Routledge.

Habermas, J. (1973/1976). *Legitimation Crisis*. London: Heinneman.

Hatch, M.J. and M. Schultz (1997). 'Relations between organizational culture, identity and image'. *European Journal of Marketing*, 31(5/6), 356–365.

Heath, R.G. (2007). 'Rethinking community collaboration through a dialogic lens: creativity, democracy, and diversity in community organizing'. *Management Communication Quarterly* 21: 145.

Heath, R.L. (ed.) (2001). *Handbook of Public Relations*. Thousand Oaks, CA: Sage.

Heath, R., B. Pearce, J. Shotter, J. Taylor, A. Kersten, T. Zorn, J. Roper and J. Motion (2006). 'The process of dialogue: participation and legitimation', *Management Communication Quarterly* 19(3): 341–373.

Heugens, P.P., F. A. Van Den Bosch and C.B. Van Riel (2002). 'Stakeholder integration: Building mutually enforcing relationships'. *Business & Society*, 41(1), 36–60.

Hutton, J.G. (2010). 'Defining the relationship between public relations and marketing: public relations' most important challenge' in *Handbook of Public Relations*. R.L. Heath (ed.). Thousand Oaks, CA: Sage.

Hutton, J.G., M.B. Goodman, J.B. Alexander and C.M. Genest (2001). 'Reputation management: the new face of corporate public relations?' *Public Relations Review*, 27, 247–261.

Ihlen, O. (2009). 'On Bourdieu, public relations in field struggles', in *Public Relations and Social Theory*. O. Ihlen, B. Van Ruler and M. Fredriksson (eds). New York, NY: Routledge.

Illia, L. and J.M. Balmer (2012). 'Corporate communication and corporate marketing: Their nature, histories, differences and similarities'. *Corporate Communications: An International Journal*, 17(4), 415–433.

Innes, J.E. (2004). 'Consensus building: Clarifications for the critics', *Planning theory*, 3(1), 5–20.

Invernizzi, E. (1991). *Nuovi obiettivi e funzioni strategiche della comunicazione d'impresa*. L'impresa.

Invernizzi, E., S. Romenti and M. Fumagalli (2012). Identity, communication and change management in Ferrari. *Corporate Communications: An International Journal*, 17(4), 483–497.

Invernizzi, E., S. Romenti and G. Murtarelli (2016). 'Creating Shared Value through Communication: A Case Study Analysis of Barilla'. In Bronn, P.S., Romenti, S., Zerfass, A. (Eds.). *The management game of communication* (pp. 181–201). Emerald Group Publishing Limited.

Jablin, F.M. and L.L. Putnam (eds) (2001). *The New Handbook of Organizational Communication*. Thousand Oaks, CA: Sage.

Johnson, G. and K. Scholes (2002). *Exploring Corporate Strategy*, 6th edition. Harlow: Prentice Hall.

Johnson, G., R. Whittington and K. Scholes (2014). *Exploring Strategy*, 10th edition. Harlow: Prentice Hall.

Kapein, M. and R. van Tulder (2003). 'Toward effective stakeholder dialogue'. *Business and Society Review* 108(2): 203–224.

Kent, M.L. and M. Taylor (2002). 'Toward a dialogic theory of public relations'. *Public Relations Review* 28: 21–37.

Kitchen, P. and D. Schultz (eds) (2001). *Raising the Corporate Umbrella: Corporate communication in the 21st century.* London: Macmillan.

Ledingham, J.A. and S.D. Bruning (eds) (2000). *Public Relations as Relationship Management: A relational approach to the study and practice of public relations.* Mahwah, NJ: Lawrence Erlbaum Associates, Inc.

Leitch, S. and J. Motion (1999). 'Multiplicity in corporate identity strategy'. *Corporate Communications: An International Journal* 4(4): 192–200.

Leitch, S. and D. Neilson (2001). 'Bringing publics into public relations', in *Handbook of Public Relations.* R.L. Heath (ed.). Thousand Oaks, CA, London and New Delhi: Sage.

Mettzler, M.S. (2001). 'The centrality of organizational legitimacy to public relations practice' in *Handbook of Public Relations.* R.L. Heath (ed.). London: Sage.

Motion, J. and S. Leitch (2002). 'The technologies of corporate identity', *International Studies of Management and Organization* 32(3), 45–64.

OECD (2011). 'A definition of social capital measures', http://stats.oecd.org/glossary/detail.asp?ID=3560, accessed 10 September 2011.

Olins W. (1989). *Corporate Identity,* Harvard Business School Press, Boston, MA.

Pieczka, M. (2011). 'Public relations as dialogic expertise?' *Journal of Communication Management* 15(2), 108–124.

Putnam, L.L. and A.M. Nicotera (2009). *Building Theories of Organization: The constitutive role of communication.* Routledge. Riel, C.V. (1995). *Principles of Corporate Communication.* Hemel Hempstead: Prentice Hall.

Romenti, S. and G. Murtarelli (2012). 'Dialogue Strategies via social networks and Organisational Performance'. In *Conference on Corporate Communication 2012* (pp. 1–24).

Romenti, S., G. Murtarelli and C. Valentini (2014). 'Organisations' conversations in social media: applying dialogue strategies in times of crises'. *Corporate Communications: An International Journal.*

Schultz, D.E. (1993). 'Integration helps you plan communication from outside-in', *Marketing News,* 27(6), 12.

Steyn, B. (2003). 'From strategy to corporate communication strategy: a conceptualisation', *Journal of Communication Management* 8(2), 168–183.

Stoffels, J.D. (1994). *Strategic issues management: A comprehensive guide to environmental scanning.* Pergamon.

Suchman, M.C. (1992). 'Managing legitimacy: strategic and institutional approaches', *Academy of Management Review,* 20(3), 571–610.

Taylor, M. and M.L. Kent (2014). 'Dialogic engagement: Clarifying foundational concepts'. *Journal of Public Relations Research,* 26(5), 384–398.

Valentini, C., S. Romenti and D. Kruckeberg (2016). 'Language and Discourse in Social Media Relational Dynamics: A Communicative Constitution Perspective'. *International Journal of Communication,* 10.

Van Riel, C.B.M. (2003). 'Defining corporate communication', in *Corporate Communication: A strategic approach to building reputation.* P.S. Bronn and R. Wiig (eds). Oslo: Gyldendal Akademisk.

Van Riel, C.B.M. and C. Fombrun (2007). *Essentials of Corporate Communication.* Abingdon: Routledge.

Weick, K.E. (1995). *Sensemaking in organizations* (Vol. 3). Sage.

White, J. and D. Verčič (2002). 'An examination of possible obstacles to management acceptance of public relations' contribution to decision making, planning and organisation functioning', *Journal of Communication Management,* 6(2), 194–200.

PART 4

Sectoral considerations

This part of the text comprises chapters that are not conventionally included within a public relations (PR) text – yet their link to public relations seems too important for them to be left out. The discussions and debates contained within each section highlight the link to public relations, but also point out differences in worldview or approach.

The first chapter (24) contextualises the diversity of non-profit organisations and demonstrates the main differences between profit and non-profit communication by presenting strategies and instruments used with an emphasis on campaigning and fundraising. Chapter 25 explores the long-standing fascination in society with celebrity but also picks up on the newer phenomenon of the influencer and their role in the communication process. In Chapter 26 health communication is discussed with guides and insight into how to work in this substantial area of communication practice. Chapter 27 takes the reader into the dynamic and fast-changing and growing world of sports public relations and communication. Chapter 28 provides insights into a popular but often overlooked area of practice in textbooks and writing about public relations, the world of fashion public relations. Finally in this section a niche but highly relevant and rewarding field of public relations practice is explained and explored, financial public relations and working in the world of finance.

CHAPTER 24

Markus Wiesenberg

Strategic non-profit communication

Source: bearacreative/Shutterstock

Learning outcomes

By the end of this chapter you should be able to:
- contextualise the diversity of non-profit organisations
- recognise the main differences between profit and non-profit communication
- understand the different techniques that can be used in non-profit communication
- critically evaluate non-profit communication and fundraising campaigns
- understand academic critique of non-profit communication management.

Structure

- The third sector and non-profit organisations
- Strategic non-profit communication in general
- Non-profit communication management as a multi-level approach
- Marketisation of third sector organisations and its consequences for strategic non-profit communication

Introduction

Strategic non-profit communication focuses on all intended communication activities with the impetus to support and help to fulfil all non-profit goals of an independent public entity. Therefore, it covers primarily all organisations, movements and public personalities with non-profit goals that operate independently from governments, such as social movements, pressure groups and activists as well as global non-governmental organisations (NGOs), religious entities such as sects or denominations as well as charities and many more. However, there are also profit entities with a focus beyond profit, such as social entrepreneurs and businesses, as well as larger corporations with an interest in philanthropy. Finally, all non-profit entities as well as philanthropists exist because they offer services and products as well as support specific interests that neither the state and its governmental bodies (first sector) nor the market and its businesses (second sector) regulate. Therefore, this chapter explores first the third sector in general and answers the question what specific communicative challenges non-profits are facing (e.g. fundraising and donor relationship, members' interests vs. main goals, collaboration with volunteers and engagement). Secondly, it offers different case studies from diverse areas. Thirdly, it discusses critically the marketisation of the third sector and its future development in communications.

The third sector and non-profit organisations

The third sector is very diverse and overlaps with the state and business sector as well (see Figure 24.1). However, as demonstrated in Table 24.1, non-profit organisations (NPOs) perform specific functions that set them apart from the governmental and the business sector.

Before reading further, think about the differences that exist between the three sectors and between member-serving and public-serving non-profits: what are the consequences of their difference for their strategic communication? (See Think about 24.1.)

The differentiation between member- and public-serving non-profits leads to significant differences on

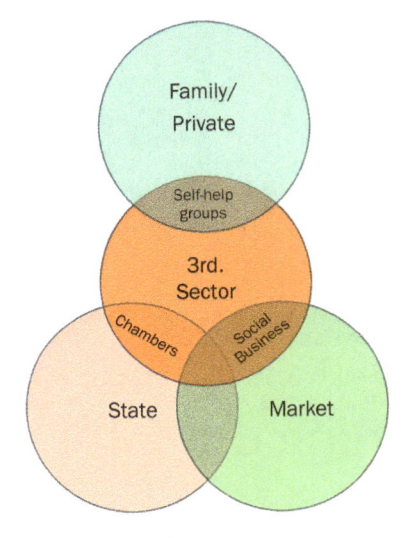

Figure 24.1 Sectors in society

Box 24.1

State, market and third sector

The third sector differs in historical background, variety and magnitude from country to country. Therefore, the different sectors are not in a perfect equilibrium as demonstrated in Figure 24.1. For instance, in Scandinavian and many European countries, the health system and the welfare system in general are provided by the government. Hence, the state takes more responsibility over the third sector. In contrast, using the United States as an example, the state takes less responsibility and the market as well as the third sector need to provide these services. Consequently, wherever the state and the market do not provide demanded services, the third sector comes into play.

NPOs and NGOs

Many textbooks do not differentiate between non-profit organisations (NPOs) and non-governmental organisations (NGOs). Baldo and Sibthorpe (1998: 64) define NGOs as 'part of civil society which is defined as the wide range of voluntary associations that occupy the broad terrain between the individual and state, and which are the primary means by which citizens can articulate their interests to both the state and to the society at large'. Moreover, empirically most organisations that are allocated to the group of NGOs have been started as social movements with a political impetus to some extent – at least the state is the reference value. They have mostly political goals and thus point out political grievances. According to Clarke (1998: 36), NGOs 'are private, non-profit, professional organisations, with a distinctive legal character, concerned with public welfare goals'.

Consequently, NGOs are a specific form of NPOs with the state and politics as a reference point. NPOs have a higher reference point to the market sector and its profit orientation. The self-interest orientation of the market and its businesses is opposed by a non-profit motivation and definition of objectives, usually labelled as 'mission'.

	Business Firm	Government Agency	Member-serving NPO (association)	Public-serving NPO (service provider)
Objective Function	Profit-maximisation	Social welfare maximisation	Member benefit maximisation	Client group benefit maximisation
Outputs	Private goods	Public/collective goods	Club goods	Collective and private goods
Distribution criteria	Exchange	Equity	Solidarity	Solidarity
Orientation	External, indiscriminate (customers)	External indiscriminate (public, citizens)	Internal, discriminate (members)	External, discriminate (targeted client groups)
Goals	Specific, clear	Complex, ambiguous	Complex, diffuse	Complex, clear
Structure	Formal	Formal	Informal	Formal
Accountability & Control	Owners/shareholders	Voters through elected officials	Members	Board
Decision-making	Hierarchical	Indirect: democratic Direct: hierarchical	Democratic	Hierarchical
Participants	Quasi-voluntary (economic needs)	Automatic/coercive	Voluntary	Voluntary/ Quasi-voluntary
Motivation	Material	Purposive	Solidaristic	Solidaristic/ Purposive
Resourcing	Commercial	Coercive (taxation)	Donative	Donative/ Commercial
Size	Large	Large	Small	Medium

Table 24.1 Ideal-typical comparison of NPOs, government agencies and businesses (*source:* adapted from Toepler and Anheier (2004: 257)) (*source:* Adapted from Toepler, S. and H.K. Anheier (2004). Organizational Theory and Nonprofit Management: An Overview. In: A. Zimmer and E. Priller, eds., Future of Civil Society, Wiesbaden, Germany: VS Verlag für Sozialwissenschaften, pp. 257)

Explore 24.1 The comparative non-profit sector project (CNP): definition and areas

About the CNP

The Johns Hopkins Comparative Non-profit Sector Project (CNP) analyses the private non-profit sector in 45 countries since 1991 (Johns Hopkins University). Have a look at the website and scroll down to find your country's specialities as well as comparative data. In the Methodology section you find beside the definition the international classification of non-profit organisations.

Defining the non-profit sector

The definition proposed by the CNP contains five key structural and operational characteristics most commonly associated with the non-profit or voluntary sector:

1. *Organised*, e.g. institutionalised to some extent
2. *Private*, e.g. institutionally separate from government

> *explore 24.1 (continued)*
>
> 3. *Non-profit-distributing*, e.g. not returning profits generated to their owners or directors
> 4. *Self-governing*, e.g. equipped to control their own activities
> 5. *Voluntary*, e.g. involving some meaningful degree of voluntary participation
>
> In most Western countries, NPOs are registered under state law as charitable or organisations with a special legal and tax status (e.g. that donations are tax deductible). The main difference between NPOs is based on their core function. Mostly, NPOs are equated with public-serving entities with the aim of maximising client group benefits (e.g. the homeless, environmentalists, opera fans). However, many NPOs are member-serving entities that pursue joint interests of their members with an internal focus (e.g. churches, sports clubs).

> **Explore 24.2**
>
> **Communication professionals working in third sector organisations**
>
> Since 2007, the European Communication Monitor (ECM) explores annually current practices and future developments of strategic communication and public relations in non-profits, governmental organisations, businesses as well as agencies. All reports are available at www.communicationmonitor.eu. Take some time and browse through the reports to explore specific empirical differences between third sector and governmental organisations as well as businesses.

> **Think about 24.1**
>
> **Member-serving vs. public-serving NPOs**
>
> 'Membership associations typically act as value guardians by primarily providing a vehicle for members to express beliefs and worldviews (e.g. religious associations) or pursue joint interests (e.g. sports and hunting clubs). Service organisations engage in the service provider and – ideally – in the vanguard roles, and interest organisations in the advocacy function. [T]hese core roles are quite frequently flanked by the pursuit of additional roles, such as membership organisations providing services for their members (or the public at large) or service organisations promulgating values (e.g. religiously-affiliated schools or hospitals) and advocating on behalf of the clientele for their services. Support organisations can pursue a variety of these roles, depending on their nature. For instance, a privately endowed foundation or fund may foster the specific values of the founding donor (value guardian), seek to fund innovation in service delivery (vanguard) or support independent policy research and analysis (advocacy).'
>
> *Source*: Toepler, S. and H.K. Anheier (2004). Organizational Theory and Nonprofit Management: An Overview. In: A. Zimmer and E. Priller, eds., Future of Civil Society, Wiesbaden, Germany: VS Verlag für Sozialwissenschaften, pp. 256

priority settings of NPOs and therefore their strategic communication. While member-serving NPOs focus on internal communication and thus membership loyalty and legitimation, public-serving NPOs prioritise external communication and are much more dependent on external legitimation – this particularly concerns non-governmental organisations (NGOs) that work for special interests in the political sphere (see for further differences Wiesenberg and Oliveira 2017). Hence, NGOs are a specification of NPOs.

Strategic non-profit communication in general

As already outlined above, there are specific preconditions for third sector organisations that have direct consequences for their planned and deliberate communication, on the strategic as well as the operative level that will be further outlined next.

Consequences for the strategic level

Member serving NPOs can plan strategically because their members are relatively stable donors (some have even a regular fee). The will and goal to attract new members differs between areas and cultures. Most member serving NPOs concentrate primarily on loyalty and long-term relationships (Pressgrove and McKeever 2016). In stark contrast, public serving NPOs are supported by diverse donors to fulfil their specific purpose and mission (e.g. fight for human rights, the environment or disaster response). Most of them are NGOs that fight in the political sphere for their purposes. Therefore, they are also dependent on emergent strategies to address their issues in the political sphere and to constantly raise money through fundraising, e.g. for a new campaign. Moreover, they concentrate more on gaining influence in the public sphere through agenda setting. This could be in the political arena using direct strategies to influence politicians, parties and parliaments or indirect through media or mobilisation strategies such as campaigns, demonstrations or petitions (Binderkrantz 2005).

What has been most challenging throughout the last decade in strategic non-profit communication is to align the overall goal(s) with the communication strategy and to demonstrate how deliberate communication contributes to the goal(s) (Tench et al. 2017: 120–123). To overcome this challenge, Zerfass and Viertmann (2017) developed a Communication Value Circle (CVC) to deduce the communication strategy

Box 24.2

Practitioner's diary: strategising communication at the Vodafone Institute

Insights from Danyal Alaybeyoglu (Head of Marketing and Campaigning) and Göran Kügler (Research Assistant) – Defining KPIs of the Communication Processes by using the Communication Value Circle (CVC)

Preconditions

As Vodafone's European Think Tank, the Vodafone Institute for Society and Communications (VFI) aims to analyse the potentials of digital technologies and their value for innovation, growth and a sustainable development of society as well as to create a platform for dialogue between politics, economics and science on the impact of digitisation on these fields of practice. As an organisation founded by the Vodafone Group, it gained a certain amount of independency; but at the same time it follows some specific strategic goals set up by the Department for External Affairs of the Group:

- Provide thought leadership on behalf of the VF Group
- Active stakeholder engagement
- Brand sophistication and visibility
- Showing positive examples for tech

Therefore, the Vodafone Institute finds itself in a special position of strategic alignment on behalf of the Vodafone Group: on the one hand, it acts as an independent organisation, examining the impact of digitisation on society, politics and economy; on the other hand it is itself a strategic tool of the Vodafone Group to position themselves as a thought leader in digitisation, artificial intelligence and new technologies in Europe and to maintain and develop their reputation. This creates a very specific legitimisation necessity of the communication activities of the VFI: it has its own communication strategy, which is aligned with the organisational strategy of the Institute; and the strategy of the institute follows the communication strategy of the Vodafone Group. Thus, in its communication controlling, the VFI has to show that its measures are creating value on behalf of the communication strategy of the Vodafone Group to legitimise the yearly budget provided by the Group.

Process

The initial point of evaluating the communication measures' outcome and connecting it to the several strategic frameworks was made by the Chairwoman of the Vodafone Institute, who inspired us to work on that topic and to create a framework for the controlling of the communication measures of the VFI and also to set up KPIs connected to the target dimensions and measures. In the very centre of the framework, we put the main goal of the communicational activities of the VFI: creating and enhancing acceptance of the digital transformation in Europe. The four mentioned objective dimensions of the department for External Affairs of the Vodafone Group were put in the first circle around the centre of the framework and were compared with the Communication Value Circle and its key strategic dimensions (dimensions of value creation through communications) and the ones which fitted the most were selected and brought into a new framework, matching the communication strategy of the VFI (see Figure 24.2).

Hence, we positioned the four key dimensions of the Vodafone Group in the middle of the circle and allocated

→

box 24.2 (continued)

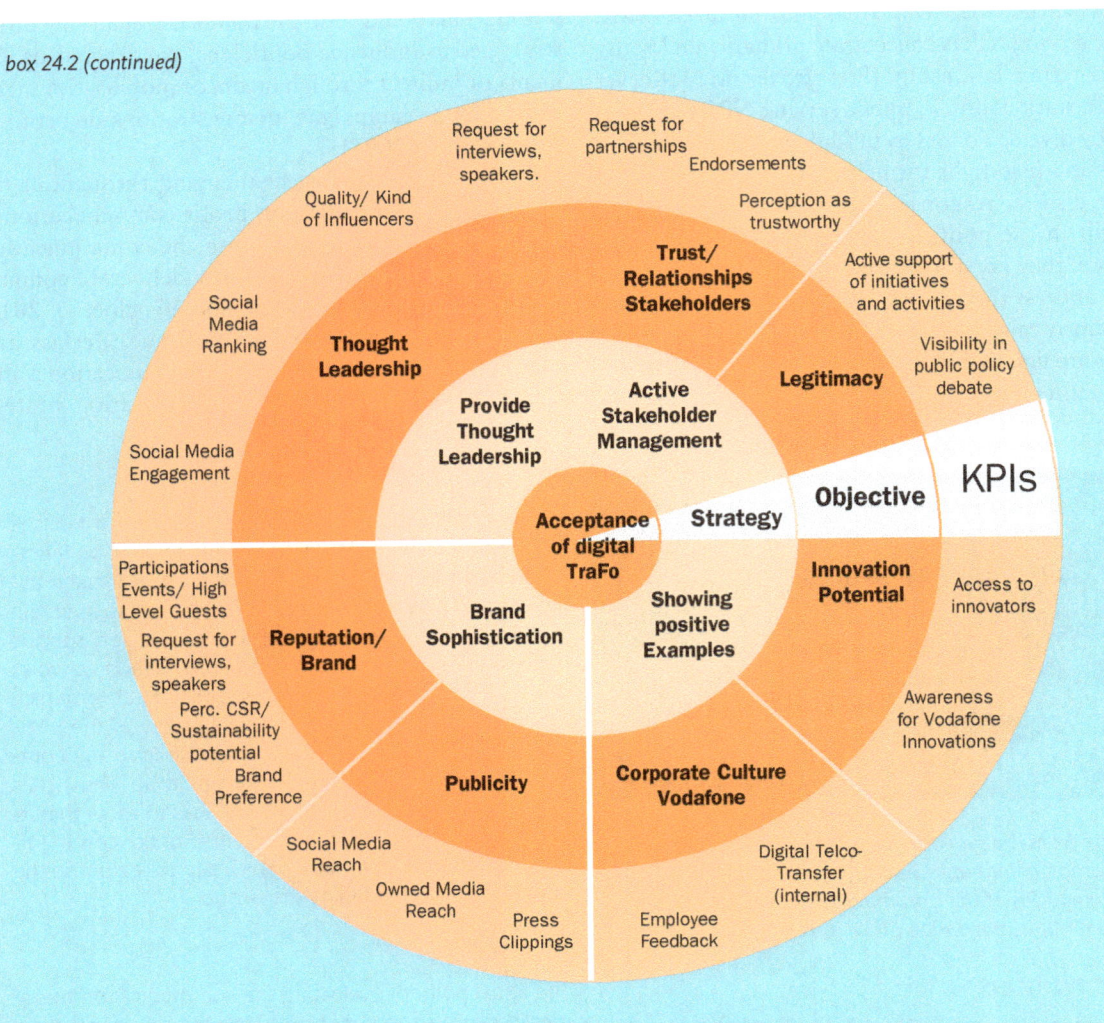

Figure 24.2 Communication value circle adapted for the Vodafone Institute (*source:* Reprinted with permission of Danyal Alaybeyoglu)

the communication objectives of the CVC to the matching dimensions in a second circle. The challenge at this point was to define the right KPIs to measure the selected goal dimensions taken out of the CVC and to choose the correct measurement procedures. Therefore, we used proposed and tested KPIs from the profit sector. Furthermore, it is necessary to mention that we went through several phases of adaption of both the communication objective dimensions (second circle) and the KPIs (third circle). Together with the Chairwomen we discussed the dimensions and how they fit with the reality of our Institute's work and the dimensions of the Vodafone Group's Communication Strategy. In the next step, we carried out the discussed changes, went again through the communication management literature and adopted theoretical and practical insights to the framework. In an early phase of the development of the framework, we also added the impact levels of the DPRG/ICV framework for communication controlling output, outcome and outflow (impact) and linked them to the various circles of our framework; in the end it seemed more logical to 'just' set up the dimensions 'Strategy', 'Objective' and 'KPIs', which is due to the more practical approach of the framework (even though we have been aware that the objectives are part of the strategy). Finally, the dimensions of the CVC and our framework were explained on an extra sheet by defining the used KPIs and explaining their very meaning for the Vodafone Institute (definition of each KPI and the way and frequency we would measure them).

Lessons learned

Defining the right set of targets and goals cannot be made in one day or just by applying a framework such as the CVC on your organisation. You have to take a closer look

> into the specific strategic goals of the company and which KPIs and measurement methods are both applicable and reasonable for your specific situation. Be prepared that the management board might not support every part of your work concerning the framework. To them, it often still seems the easiest way to just track reach and other categories on the outcome level. Although it is quite clear that to measure the real impact of communications we have to focus on the outflow and impact level to see what really happens with our stakeholders throughout our interaction with them. Communication Controlling might seem 'dry' sometimes. But once one realises what strategic potential it holds to both explain the links between the communication function and the general management with their strategy – as well as how communication creates value – the domain gets very interesting. This is true not only for your organisation, but also for you as a (future) communication practitioner, since you learn to explain what your work 'does' and how it 'contributes' to the overall organisational goals.

and goals from the overall strategy and goal(s). How this can be applied for a NPO you can read in the practitioner's diary. But first of all, become familiar with CVC and read the short article written by Zerfass and Viertmann (2016).

Regarding the European Communication Monitor 2019, communication professionals working in the third sector struggle most on the strategic level with 'building and maintaining trust' (42.8 per cent) as well as 'matching the need to address more audiences and channels with limited resources' (39.3 per cent) (Zerfass et al. 2019: 57). While the latter appears plausible, the first-mentioned challenge on *trust* needs further explanations. Trust can be considered a basic asset regarding the four most important stakeholders of NPO communication: (1) employees, (2) volunteers, (3) donors and (4) the media. NPOs depend on trust at an existential level. They can usually benefit from higher trust evaluations than other types of organisations – this results in high expectations concerning the (ethical) performances of NPOs. The following remarks demonstrate how trust in NPOs can be operationalised (see Explore 24.3 and Case study 24.1).

Explore 24.3 NPO trust map – measuring trust in the third sector

The focus of the NPO trust map was primarily media-related trust, which refers to the trust attributed to an NPO within the public sphere. The framework is based on the Corporate Trust Index (see Seiffert et al. 2011) and has been tested and modified between 2010 and 2013, conducting three waves of content analyses of crisis situations at Unicef Germany and the German committee of the WWF. Finally, the NPO Trust Map is based on five trust dimensions explicitly for NPOs:

- *Basic trust* includes publicly perceived ethical behaviour of an NPO and its members, and the amount of perceived discrepancies concerning norms and the actual ethical behaviour of the NPO.
- *Communicative action* comprises an NPO's perceived engagement in transparency and internal communication as well as media relations and public affairs (external communication).
- *Expertise* incorporates the actual project work in the field, an NPO's problem-solving skills and its perceived expert status for the work in the field.
- *Personalities* include all trust-related perceptions or evaluation of the members of an NPO.
- *Discrepancies* comprise publicly perceived contradictions of communicative action that could be differentiated into self-generated and externally generated. Contradictive behaviour often causes loss of public trust, which means that the absence of discrepancies will be measured as a positive while evaluating an NPO.

The framework has been visualised using a spider graph including a five-point scale (−2 = very negative; 0 = neutral; 2 = very positive) Figure 24.3 demonstrates an example including the most important stakeholder. All variables can be measured by using a survey as well as journalistic evaluations within the media coverage (negative, neutral or positive). The amount of perceived discrepancies is measured based on the percentage value in the media coverage (see the yellow dashed line).

→

explore 24.3 (continued)

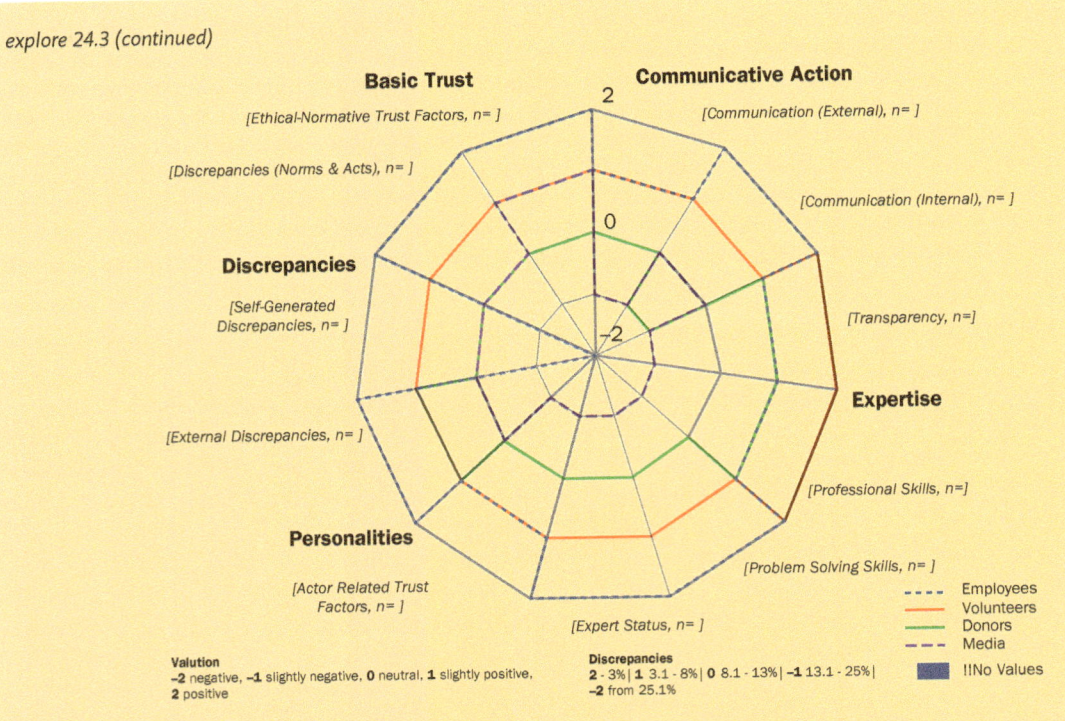

Figure 24.3 NPO Trust Map (*source:* Viertmann, C. (2015). NPO Trust Map—Measuring Trust in the Third Sector. Paper presented at BledCom Symposium 2015, Bled, July 2015)

Case study 24.1

Unicef Germany Trust Map

By the end of 2007 the United Nations Children's Fund (Unicef) in Germany had become part of a bigger donation scandal (listen to details here: dw.com). For this case, articles were collected between 1 February 2006, and 19 November 2007. With the initial article of the Frankfurter Rundschau 'Für die Kinder dieser Welt – aber nicht nur' (For the children of this world – but not only), crisis reporting began on 28 November 2007. The end of the crisis was defined as 21 February 2008 after the DZI donation seal was withdrawn (on 20 February 2008). From this day on, reporting was referred to as post-crisis and was investigated until 31 July 2008.

The Unicef Trust Map (Figure 24.4) demonstrates that the confidence levels of the pre-crisis period (see also Chapter 17) are positive. The media coverage illustrates only a minor discrepancy between talk and action. However, during the crisis period the valuations within the trust map deteriorate drastically: the confidence factors of communication and the existence of discrepancies are rated very negatively at −2. Only the professional competence – the operational action of the organisation – is described as positive (1) in the media. Topics shift at the same time and more reports are being made about the organisation, its structure and in particular its fundraising activities. In the crisis period, these are dealt with 96 times – only in four articles before the crisis and only two after the crisis.

In particular, the payment of high consultancy fees was described by the media as taboo – this also explains the high number of discrepancies between talk and action (with 49 articles at 98 per cent). The results also indicate that the articles deal with the actions of the then managing director and the CEO during the crisis. 86 per cent of the articles illustrate discrepancies between talk and action of different actors. The

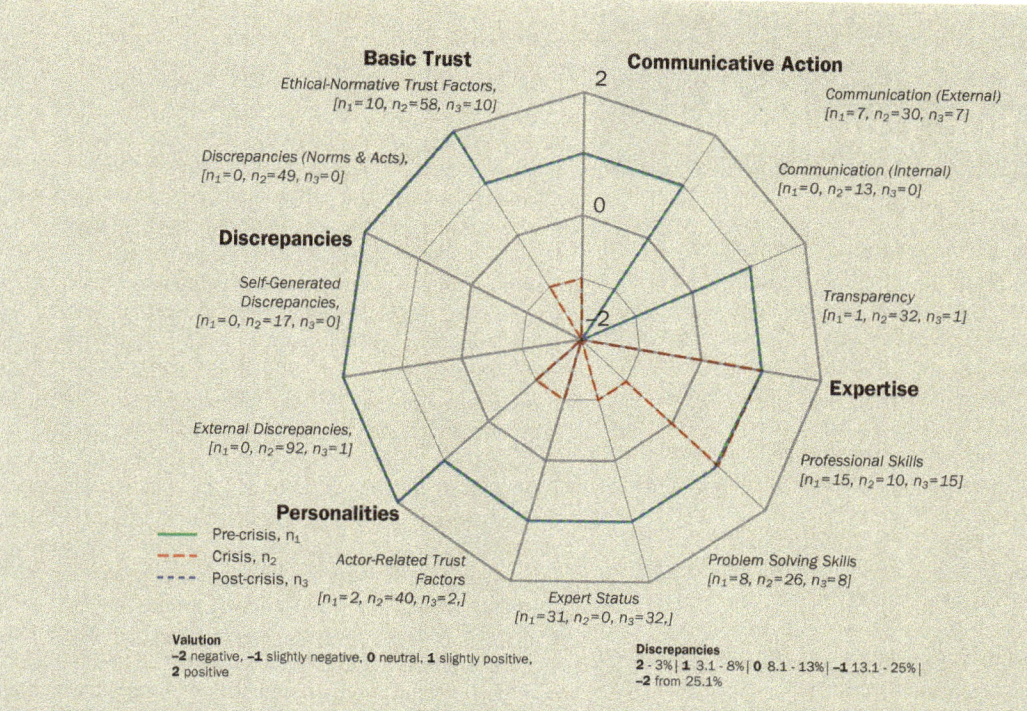

Figure 24.4 Unicef Germany Trust Map (*source:* Viertmann, C. (2015). NPO Trust Map—Measuring Trust in the Third Sector. Paper presented at BledCom Symposium 2015, Bled, July 2015)

negative assessment of actor-related confidence factors (n = 40, assessment: −1) and the high density of reporting also reflect the topic of leadership conflict. The intensity with which the crisis was dealt with in the media can be illustrated not only by the number of articles and the duration of the reporting, but also by the fact that there was increased reporting on insider knowledge and internal communication behaviour. Following the inauguration of the new managing director and the organisational adjustments (e.g. the amendment of the bylaws), Unicef was again presented as trustworthy in media reporting.

Unicef Germany was increasingly addressed in reporting in the context of its organisational goal, i.e. with self-imposed topics such as studies and campaigns for children. This is reflected, among other things, in the fact that Unicef was mentioned 32 times in its role as an expert. This also makes clear how quickly such a trust crisis can be overcome and how quickly it must be overcome by an NPO. In the course of this crisis, Unicef Germany lost more than 20,000 supporting members and donations fell by around 20 million euros. For further examples for NPO crisis communication see Schwarz and Pforr (2011) as well as Sisco (2012).

Consequences for the operational level

On the operational level, NPOs try to build strong membership and donor communities using all communication programmes and tactics online, e.g. using social media, or offline, e.g. using events or magazines. In particular, NGOs are dependent on campaigns and fundraising, but also on traditional media relations as well as blogger and influencer relations. To grasp some of the unique features of non-profit communication, we will dive deeper into guerrilla campaigns and activism as well as campaigning and fundraising (see Fact box 24.1). To get a better understanding of this singularity, one case offers an example for an offline campaign (Case study 24.2) and one offers an example for an online campaign with social media influencers (SMI) (Case study 24.3).

Fact box 24.1
(Guerrilla) Campaigns

Guerrilla can be translated with tactical resistance against an irresistible opponent. It was theoretically further developed by Mao Tse-tung and Ernesto Ché Guevara as part of warfare and war theory and got more famous in public relations with the activist movements in the post-World War II era (e.g. antinuclear, environmental or civil rights activism) (see also Heath 2018; Smith 2013). Therefore, guerrilla campaigns are planned interventions in the public sphere using the specific momentum that nobody is prepared for this intervention. It is used as well in the business sector where it is called guerrilla marketing (see, for examples, www.creativeguerrillamarketing.com). This type of campaigning can be used in a confrontational and aggressive way against an opponent (take a look more closely at some Greenpeace or Occupy campaigns) while others use campaigns in coalition, e.g. with the business and governmental sector (see for example WWF campaigns).

Fundraising

Most of the NPOs need a certain amount of yearly income to fulfil their goals according to their mission – be it member-serving or public-serving. Therefore, the ongoing financial support of donors plays a vital role for every NPO around the globe. To secure and even expand the constant cash flow, the NPO needs to be constantly fundraising because there is a specific amount of philanthropic money and different NPOs are competing for donors and their money. Especially member-serving NPOs try to build up new and long-lasting memberships with membership fees. Public-serving NPOs try to establish and maintain donor relationships. Both use controlled media tactics, direct mailings and events. Others use more interpersonal communication tactics like face-to-face conversations or personal handwritten letters. Moreover, they also use communication management for fundraising purposes (Kelly 2013). One example is Kelly's ROPES Process Model that is based on five stages (research, objectives, programming, evaluation, stewardship) (see in-depth Kelly 2012; Waters 2011). Moreover, with social media also crowdfunding becomes an important part of fundraising. Lucas (2017) demonstrates how UK NPOs use Facebook for fundraising purposes.

Case study 24.2
Activism and guerrilla campaigns: lessons learned from Urgewald

Urgewald is an environmental and human rights NGO started in 1992 in Germany addressing the underlying causes of global environmental destruction and poverty by pressuring investors who finance destructive projects in, for example, mining or weapon production. They call on international companies and banks to step back from these destructive projects and to adopt binding environmental and social standards (see Bank Track). Besides traditional forms of activism such as demonstrations, Urgewald uses guerrilla campaigns like subversive tactics.

The case demonstrated here started in 2012, when Urgewald used the annual shareholders' meeting of the second largest private bank in Germany (Commerzbank) to portray the consequences of coal mining using Mountaintop Removal.

In 2016, the NGO alienated the annual report of the bank (subvertising). Picture 24.1 shows a sporty woman (the 'face' of the bank's brand campaign) walking through a deserted dune landscape. The title 'Laufend besser' (running better) and the small note 'Geschäftsbericht 2015' (Annual Report 2015) take up the positive metaphor of movement. The picture on the left is the title page of a simple leaflet produced by Urgewald. It takes up the visual language of the right-hand title page of the annual report (subversive affirmation) and reinterprets it (alienation). One sees a human running through black coal mountains

Picture 24.1 Subvertising produced by Urgewald
(*source*: Urgewald)

from behind with a weapon on its back. The layout is almost identical to the original, only the protagonist is turned 180° and thus becomes faceless and anonymous. The headline was only supplemented. The subtitle is now 'Laufend besser?!' (running better?!): 'Die Bank und ihre Schattenseite' (the bank and its shadowy side).

This subvertising was related to the annual shareholders' meeting. In two speeches, representatives of activist organisations called on the bank's shareholders to stop climate-damaging investments and business with arms producers. The activists also link their interventions with conventional press releases.

Case study 24.3
Influencer relations at WWF Germany

Since 2015, the WWF Germany cooperates with social media influencers that are not only interested in the WWF, but also support whole-heartedly the goals of the NGO. The aim of influencer campaigns at WWF Germany are to sensitise and draw the attention of younger audiences to environmental issues. One of the first influencer campaigns aimed to draw attention to the situation in the Amazon. The campaign was triggered by the news that Brazil is planning to change its laws to open up millions of hectares of the Amazon to agriculture, mining and hydropower.

Together with the German YouTubers Simon Unge and deChangeman, two employees from WWF Germany flew with them to the Amazon to demonstrate why the Amazon should be protected. Video footage was used to bring the beauty of the Amazon and current threats to the influencer communities.

The campaign's challenges were a small budget, no contract with the influencers and no shooting schedule, so the influencers had a free hand in what they reported. The team spent in total 15 days at three stations in the Amazon. Simon Unge published seven videos that generated a total of 3.5 million views. In addition to the videos, the influencers also published material via their social media channels.

The influencer campaign was a complete success. In addition to reaching the young target group, the subscription numbers of the YouTube channel of WWF Germany doubled and the petitions page received many hits.

What are the advantages of influencer relations for NGOs? On the one hand, the creator does the work and thus the content, which fits exactly to the target group. You achieve high attention with new target groups and higher conversion rates. Challenges are posed by the loss of control that goes hand in hand with the trust placed in the influencer. Likewise, in times of the 'gold rush of influencers' and YouTuber networks, challenges arise for NGOs such as the WWF from a small budget. The most important challenge is the imbalance of expectations on both sides that needs a specific focus.

Picture 24.2 YouTuber – Unge and DeChangeman with WWF staff (*source:* WWF Germany)

Non-profit communication management as a multi-level approach

Like any business, every NPO starts on a local basis and grows over time to regional, national and international branches with more employees, processes and structures. According to our NPO definition, NPOs require some meaningful degree of voluntary participation and mostly this is manifested by membership engagement (volunteering, donations etc.). Therefore, international or even national operating NPOs are often confronted with the communicative challenge to integrate individual members and often independent local groups or clubs on the one hand and to reach their goals on the other hand (e.g. influencing the political agenda). This specific type of stakeholder management can be best described as a multi-level stakeholder approach. How this might work is theoretically described below (see Explore 24.4). Read also some practical implications written by David Therketsen (2011) and think about their consequences (Think about 24.2).

Explore 24.4 Four communication flows of NPOs' legitimation

One of the major challenges of NPOs is to maintain the balance between the members' interest (especially in member-serving NPOs) and to fulfil the NPO's mission by gaining external influence. NPOs exist qua definition because of their volunteers and individual members. Therefore, as Wiesenberg and Oliveira (2017) demonstrate (Figure 24.5), their members are the primary source of legitimation (licence to operate) of the NPO and its representatives (be it the board, the management or other leading employees). This particularly concerns member-serving NPOs, but also public-serving ones. This kind of internal legitimacy is what the authors call first communication flow. Moreover, if an unpaid member raises its voice in private or public settings in the interest of the NPO, the authors classify these action as a second communication flow (this can happen because the NPO instructed or inspired the members, e.g. through a campaign or without any knowledge and/or inspiration of the NPO). The third communication flow starts with local members that recognised something in their neighbourhood (through listening) and bring this issue or concern to the board of the NPO that starts a campaign because of this issue or concern. Finally, the fourth flow describes the communication flow of a typical campaign planned and executed by the management and staff without involving the members.

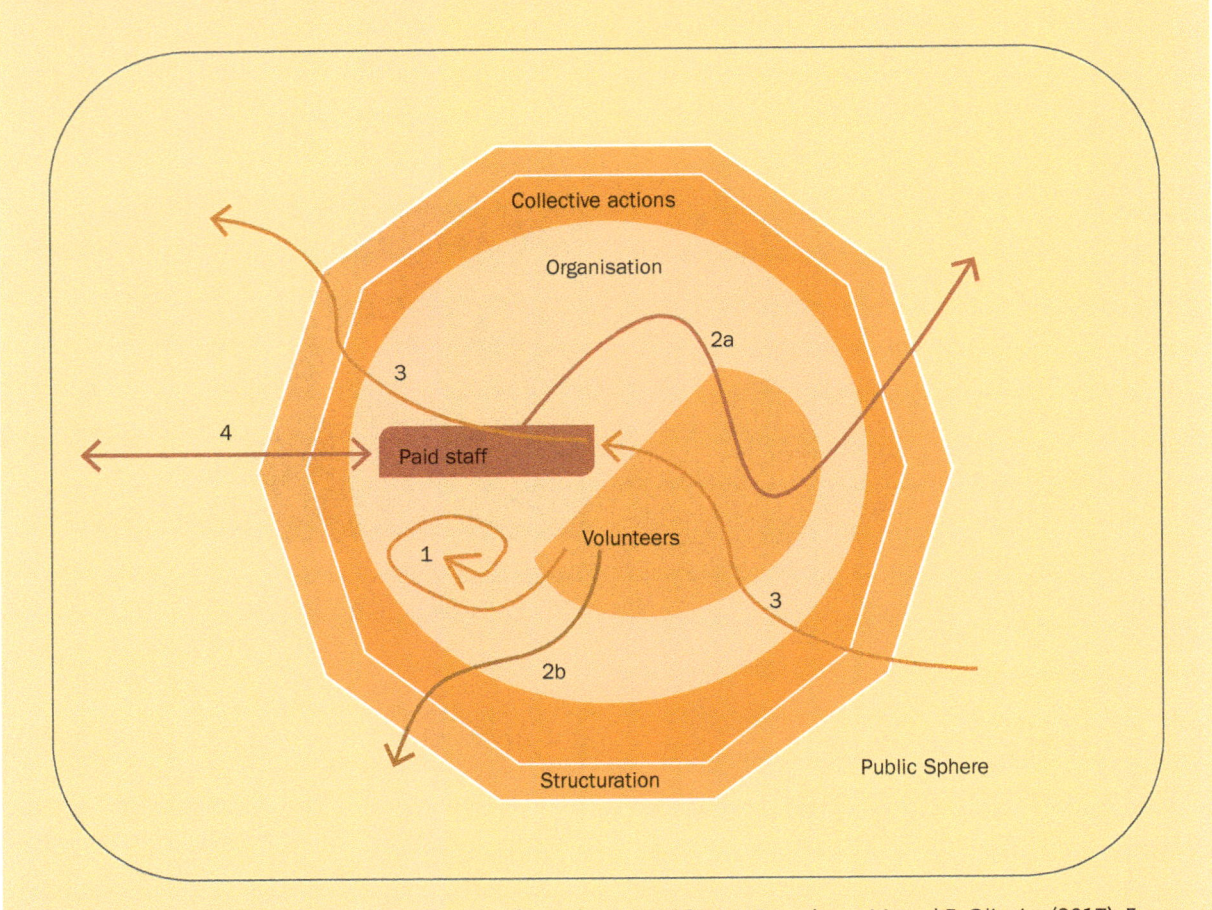

Figure 24.5 Four communication flows of NPOs (*source*: Adapted from Wiesenberg, M. and E. Oliveira (2017). From the inside out: Four communication flows of NGOs' and Churches' legitimation. In: E. Oliveira, A. Duarte Melo and G. Gonçalves, eds., Strategic communication for nonprofit organisations: Challenges and alternative approaches, Wilmington: Vernon Press, pp. 45)

> **Think about 24.2**
>
> **Engage local members and reach your international mission**
>
> International NGOs are working around the globe and at the same time they have national, regional and local branches. There are different approaches in how to deal with this kind of situation.
>
> **How to deal with this challenge?**
> International NGOs deal quite differently with such a problem. Here are three approaches describing how NGOs deal with this challenge:
>
> - Trying to control and steer volunteers on different levels facilitated by paid NGO staff.
> - Decoupling the national and international level and their goals and activities from local and regional groups' goals and activities by emulating the same vision and 'spirit'.
> - Integrating local and regional groups and their views in national and international strategies through conventions and possibilities to join national and international campaigns.

Marketisation of third sector organisations and its consequences for strategic non-profit communication

Marketisation describes the adoption of market discourse and practice (e.g. entrepreneurialism and satisfying individual clients' self-interest) in NPOs as a response to the necessity of providing sustainable solutions to social causes within a market economy (Sanders 2012). Critically, this trend can be seen as encroachment of a 'corporate ideology' that may threaten not only NPOs as single entities but also the whole third sector and its ability to create and maintain a strong civil society and social capital (Eikenberry and Kluver 2004).

NPOs especially in liberal market economies are constantly questioned on how they spend their money and what they do (licence to operate). Moreover, through marketisation, business vocabulary such as 'efficiency' and 'effectivity' have become important in the third sector too. As demonstrated with the Communication Value Circle as well as the growing importance of fundraising and donor relations, the same tendency is apparent in non-profit communication. For example, Wiesenberg (2019a) revealed in his research about membership communication, Christian denominations in Germany start centralising this communication for professionalisation purposes while local congregations at the same time suffer on resources for their local membership communication with their members (see for theoretical and practical implications also Wiesenberg 2019b).

With the so-called 'new philanthropists', donors not only want to donate money for public purposes and well-being, they also seek to gain influence for the NPO. Therefore, fundraising and donor relations have become something like investor relations as Kelly (2013) points out. Hence, donors expect some kind of revenue beyond the genuine purpose to improve society.

These are only some examples of how marketisation of the third sector can affect strategic non-profit communication. Therefore, it needs a basic understanding of the purpose, mission and goals of the specific NPO and as well as fulfilling their mission to serve either its members,

> **Box 24.3**
>
> **How to encourage donations**
>
> - Emphasise the ability to contribute (e.g. suggesting small amounts such as £1, $2 or €1).
> - Position yourself as accessible and welcome to any public donation, regardless of the amount.
> - Show the process you have used to support your targeted groups and the impact of your work.
> - Let your target groups speak about how they have benefited from the NPO's support.
> - Show how all your programmes fit together to improve the quality of life for your target groups.
> - Encourage authority figures (not necessarily celebrities) to highlight the importance of the issues you are trying to tackle.
> - Continually evaluate your programmes and make this information accessible to any of your donors.
>
> *Source:* AshraMcGrath, N. (2017). Nongovernment organisations and pressure groups. In: R. Tench and L. Yeomans, eds., Exploring Public Relations: Global Strategic Communication, 4th ed. Harlow: Pearson, pp. 482

> ### Explore 24.5
>
> **Looking at ways to donate on NPO websites**
>
> Revisit some NPO websites. Do they meet the principles outlined in Box 24.3?

> ### Think about 24.3
>
> **Communication management as market discourse and practice**
>
> The effect of marketisation on non-profit communication has so far not been investigated in depth (see for an overview Bennett 2019). *What effects do you expect on . . .*
>
> - the collaboration between unpaid members and paid staff?
> - communicating results and goals to donors?
> - future possibilities with automated communication?

the public or both. Strategic non-profit communication needs to serve these goals and mission. Management tools like the Communication Value Circle needs to be seriously taken into consideration but also adapted to the specific non-profit area – be it a foundation, a think-tank, a religious congregation or denomination.

> ### Summary
>
> Beside the governmental and the business sector, third sector organisations, groups and movements have been growing in the last century – as has non-profit communication. As some NPOs such as churches or clubs are more member centred, others like NGOs are more public centred. Therefore, on the one hand, the specific sector as well as the area have consequences for strategic non-profit communication on the strategic as well as the operative level (e.g. the specific strategic alignment of non-profit communication, the importance of campaigns and fundraising or donor relations). On the other hand, there are specific challenges for strategic non-profit communication, such as the tendency towards marketisation. Consequently, there is a need to balance the public purpose of the NPO, their own goals as well as their members. This has been exemplified by national or even international NPOs and their local branches. Strategic non-profit communication professionals need to find specific answers for their area and their NPO that cannot just be copied from the business or governmental sector, but need to fulfil the goals of the specific NPO as well as the third sector and its responsibility for the civil society.

Bibliography

Ashra-McGrath, N. (2017). Non-government organisations and pressure groups. In: R. Tench and L. Yeomans, eds., *Exploring Public Relations: Global Strategic Communication*, 4th ed. Harlow: Pearson, pp. 473–491.

Baldo, O.B. and C. Sibthorpe (1998). The sky is the limit: Electronic networking and NGOs. *South African Journal of International Affairs*, 5(2), pp. 60–79.

Bank Track (https://bit.ly/2UPK87D). Accessed 7 April 2020.

Bennett, R. (2019). *Non-profit marketing and fundraising: a research overview*. Abingdon: Routledge.

Binderkrantz, A. (2005). Interest Group Strategies: Navigating between Privileged Access and Strategies of Pressure. *Political Studies*, 53(4), pp. 694–715.

Clarke, G. (1998). Non-Governmental Organizations (NGOs) and Politics in the Developing World. *Political Studies*, 46(1), pp. 36–52.

dw.com (https:/bit.ly/2ETUlXD). Accessed 7 April 2020.

Eikenberry, A.M. and J.D. Kluver (2004). The Marketization of the Nonprofit Sector: Civil Society at Risk? *Public Administration Review*, 64(2), pp. 132–140.

European Communication Monitor (1997–2021) https:/bit.ly/2Ihgtfq. Accessed 7 April 2020

Heath, R.L. (2018). Activism. In: R.L. Heath, W. Johansen, J. Falkheimer, K. Hallahan, J. J.C. Raupp and B. Steyn, eds., *The International Encyclopedia of Strategic Communication*, Hoboken, NJ: Wiley, pp. 1–13.

Johns Hopkins University (http://ccss.jhu.edu/research-projects/comparative-nonprofit-sector-project/). Accessed 7 April 2020.

Kelly, K.S. (2012). *Effective Fund-Raising Management*. Hoboken, NJ: Taylor and Francis.

Kelly, K.S. (2013). Fundraising. In: R.L. Heath, ed., *Encyclopedia of public relations*, Los Angeles: SAGE, pp. 374–378.

Lucas, E. (2017). Reinventing the rattling tin: How UK charities use Facebook in fundraising. *International Journal of Nonprofit and Voluntary Sector Marketing*, 22(2), e1576.

Pressgrove, G.N. and B.W. McKeever (2016). Nonprofit relationship management: Extending the organization-public relationship to loyalty and behaviors. *Journal of Public Relations Research*, 28(3–4), pp. 193–211.

Sanders, M.L. (2012). Theorizing Nonprofit Organizations as Contradictory Enterprises. *Management Communication Quarterly*, 26(1), pp. 179–185.

Schwarz, A. and F. Pforr (2011). The crisis communication preparedness of nonprofit organizations: The case of German interest groups. *Public Relations Review*, 37(1), pp. 68–70.

Seiffert, J., Bentele, G. and L. Mende (2011). An explorative study on discrepancies in communication and action of German companies. *Journal of Communication Management*, 15(4), pp. 349–367.

Sisco, H.F. (2012). Nonprofit in Crisis: An Examination of the Applicability of Situational Crisis Communication Theory. *Journal of Public Relations Research*, 24(1), pp. 1–17.

Smith, M.F. (2013). Activism. In: R.L. Heath, ed., *Encyclopedia of Public Relations*, Los Angeles: Sage, pp. 6–8.

Tench, R., D. Verčič, A. Zerfass, A. Moreno and P. Verhoeven (2017). *Communication Excellence. How to develop, manage and lead exceptional communications*, Cham: Palgrave Macmillan.

Therketsen, D. (2011). Non-Profit Communication Management. In: D. Moss and B. DeSanto, eds., *Public relations: A managerial perspective*, Los Angeles: SAGE, pp. 265–279.

Toepler, S. and H.K. Anheier (2004). Organizational Theory and Nonprofit Management: An Overview. In: A. Zimmer and E. Priller, eds., *Future of Civil Society*, Wiesbaden, Germany: VS Verlag für Sozialwissenschaften, pp. 253–270.

Viertmann, C. (2015). NPO Trust Map—Measuring Trust in the Third Sector. Paper presented at BledCom Symposium 2015, Bled, July 2015.

Waters, R.D. (2011). Increasing Fundraising Efficiency Through Evaluation: Applying Communication Theory to the Nonprofit Organization— Donor Relationship. *Nonprofit and Voluntary Sector Quarterly*, 40(3), pp. 458–475.

Wiesenberg, M. (2019a). Authentic church membership communication in times of religious transformation and mediatization. *Public Relations Review* (In Press, Corrected Proof, https://doi.org/10.1016/j.pubrev.2019.101817).

Wiesenberg, M. (2019b). Beyond Organizational Centricity in Strategic Communication: Lessons Learned From Organized Religion. In: F. Frandsen, W. Johansen, R. Tench and S. Romenti, eds., *Big Ideas in Public Relations Research and Practice*. Bingley, UK: Emerald, pp. 99–114.

Wiesenberg, M. and E. Oliveira (2017). From the inside out: Four communication flows of NGOs' and Churches' legitimation. In: E. Oliveira, A. Duarte Melo and G. Gonçalves, eds., *Strategic communication for non-profit organisations: Challenges and alternative approaches*, Wilmington: Vernon Press, pp. 35–54.

Zerfass, A. and C. Viertmann (2016). The communication value circle: How communication contributes to corporate success. *Communication Director*, (2), pp. 50–53.

Zerfass, A. and C. Viertmann (2017). Creating business value through corporate communication. *Journal of Communication Management*, 21(1), pp. 68–81.

Zerfass, A., Verčič, D., Verhoeven, P., Moreno, A. and Tench, R. (2019). *European Communication Monitor 2019. Exploring trust in the profession, transparency, artificial intelligence and new content strategies. Results of a survey in 46 countries*. Brussels: EUPRERA/EACD, Quadriga Media Berlin

CHAPTER 25

Kate Fitch

Celebrities and influencers

Source: Fer Gregory/Shutterstock

Learning outcomes

By the end of this chapter you should be able to:
- define celebrity, internet celebrity, microcelebrity and influencer
- discuss celebrity culture and its relevance for contemporary public relations practice
- analyse the role of public relations in celebrity culture
- identify the rise of microcelebrities and influencers
- understand public relations practice with influencers and celebrities.

Structure

- What is celebrity?
- Celebrity and society
- Celebrity, the internet and influencers
- Celebrity and influencers in public relations practice

Introduction

Celebrity status depends on high visibility in the public arena and is generally linked with the rise of individualism, mass media and modern democracy. Celebrity offers a story of potential social mobility; it extends across diverse sectors including sport, entertainment, politics and business and draws on both growing individualism and the commodification of everyday life. Celebrities are often characterised by their ordinariness, collapsing boundaries between their public and private personas and offering insights into their 'everyday' lives.

In response to technological developments, there have been significant shifts in the kinds of work required to construct and maintain visibility and command attention. Social media has enabled shifts from the traditional celebrity who was perhaps the product of the Hollywood star machine to the rise of internet celebrities or influencers. The successful influencers model themselves on aspects of celebrity culture and work strategically using social media to construct and monetise their profile and brand.

The focus of this chapter is the promotional work associated with celebrities and influencers. Although celebrity culture has been studied primarily by media and cultural studies scholars, it has not attracted much interest among public relations scholars and, until recently, there is limited literature on the role of public relations in the production and management of celebrity or even on the now-routine work with influencers. This lack of interest may be due to the influence of the dominant paradigm in theorising about public relations, which distances contemporary public relations practice from press agentry, publicity and other promotional activity. Yet, the public relations industry is an integral part of celebrity culture and works closely with influencers as part of everyday practice; such work points to public relations' cultural intermediary role.

Media and public relations industries play a pivotal role in the construction and maintenance of celebrity status. While some celebrity publicists gain a prominent public profile, the work of many others remains hidden. This chapter acknowledges significant shifts in everyday public relations work and explores celebrity public relations and internet celebrity in order to more fully understand public relations and its societal impact and the contributions of promotional work in the growth and pervasiveness of celebrity and influence in contemporary society.

Mini case study 25.1
Museums Victoria and influencers

Influencers are not simply the domain of lifestyle public relations focusing on fashion, beauty, health and food. For example, Museums Victoria runs three Melbourne-based museums: Scienceworks, the Immigration Museum and Melbourne Museum, and influencers play an integral role in their international promotion. According to Katrina Lin (2019), Museums Victoria's Marketing and Communications Manager, Asia, several strategies help promote the museums to visitors from the Asian region. These strategies include collaborating with institutions such as the state tourism agency, Visit Victoria (their China marketing team,) and Melbourne Airport in inviting celebrities and influencers to Melbourne, offering tours and making the museums available for photo shoots and filming. Celebrities are asked to share their experiences on their social media channels. If Museums Victoria requires influencers for other promotional activity, Lin will engage them either through public relations agencies or via personal contact, drawing on her networks from her previous role in an advertising agency.

According to Lin (2019): 'Years of relationship building within the industry has helped me develop a flexible working relationship with these influencers. Before kick-starting the campaign, we map out the budget and discuss engagement approaches collaboratively to ensure the content we are making fits their followers' interest and at the same time is allied with the Museum brand. And I require tracking reports at the end of each campaign.'

Source: Katrina Lin (2019), Museums Victoria, personal correspondence

Picture 25.1 Museums Victoria in Australia worked with influencers to promote its Melbourne-based museums in China (*source:* EQRoy/Shutterstock)

What is celebrity?

Celebrities are often characterised as shallow, frivolous, superficial and manufactured yet, given their pervasiveness in everyday life and the real achievements of some individuals, who are also well known celebrities, a better understanding of what we mean by celebrity is needed. Daniel Boorstin defines celebrity as someone 'known for his well-knownness' (1962: 67); in other words, a celebrity was famous for being famous. John Hartley argues that celebrities are 'individuals who are noted for their identity in the media . . . whereby the hyper-production of images leads to some faces and bodies being more recognisable than others' (2002: 26). Graeme Turner also links celebrity to media profiles: celebrity is an 'extensive and intrusive form of public visibility . . . [and] a form of fame that is generated directly by media exposure: it is a product of the promotions and publicity industries rather than an outcome of public recognition' (2014: 86). The celebrity, then, exists primarily through their media profile and as the result of promotional activity. However, the celebrity is more than simply a media profile or the locus of fame. The celebrity maintains considerable cultural capital and is potentially a lucrative brand. Celebrity defines 'a person whose name, image, lifestyle, and opinions carry cultural and economic worth, and who are first and foremost idealised popular media constructions' (Redmond 2014: 5) and represents 'status on speed' (Kurzman et al. 2007: 363). According to Redmond:

> Celebrity matters because it exists so centrally to the way we communicate and are understood to communicate with one another in the modern world. Celebrity culture involves the transmission of power relations, is connected to identity formation and notions of shared belonging; and it circulates in commercial revenue streams and in an international context where celebrated people are seen not to be bound by national borders or geographical prisms. (2014: 3)

Much of the scholarly interest in celebrity has focused on celebrity as text, rather than on the ways in which celebrity is constructed, produced, traded and maintained. Yet celebrity culture is an important part of promotional culture that shapes cultural formation in society (Wernick 1991). This chapter, then, investigates the role of public relations in the production, maintenance and consumption of different kinds of celebrity.

Explore 25.1 — Influencers in China: key opinion leaders (KOL) and wanghong

Celebrity and internet celebrity has a greater impact on consumers in China than in any other country. There are over 20,000 influencers with more a million followers on Weibo, which enables posting words, pictures, audio clips, video clips and livestreaming (Wang 2018). Influencers known as wanghong ('internet celebrity' in Mandarin) originated in online fashion retail; they tend to be young and female. Wanghong differs from Anglocentric understandings of influencers, in that their focus is monetising audiences via retail activity and product lines rather than sponsored posts (Abidin 2018).

Wanghong is now cited as a popular and aspirational career choice. Hundreds of academies or 'incubators' have been set up to identify and train potential influencers, offer production support and content creation and even manage their careers (eMarketer 2018). Dayi Zhang started as a part-time model and is now a leading 'internet celebrity' in China with over 20 million followers and a successful business empire. One commentator referred to her as 'China's Kylie Jenner' (Ke 2019). In fact, Zhang played a pivotal role in pioneering the work of influencer incubator Ruhan (Ruhnn Holdings), by developing a large following on Weibo before launching products and online retail stores (Hallanan 2018). Today, Zhang has four online stores covering fashion, lingerie, beauty and homewares. Similarly, fashion icon Ling Ling originally developed her online profile to support her retail shop, modelling her clothes and interacting with her fans before promoting her glamorous lifestyle, involving fashion, beauty, restaurants and travel (Tsoi 2016).

Although KOL, an acronym for Key Opinion Leaders, and wanghong are often used interchangeably to describe influencers in China, KOL often have celebrity status due to their achievements in other fields and can command significant fees in exchange for social media exposure. For example, Tian Liang (who has 20 million followers on Weibo) was a champion diver who won a Gold medal at the Sydney Olympics; he retired from sport in 2007 and now works closely with brands such as Nestlé (Chernavina 2018). Often film or sports stars, KOL have a higher social and cultural status than wanghong..

> **Feedback**
>
> Assume you work for a cultural or sporting institution in your country that wants to attract more Chinese tourists to visit your venue. Challenges in China-based promotions extend to censorship of news media and the absence of Facebook and Instagram; KOL use WeChat, Weibo and other Chinese social media platforms. Research KOL or wanghong in China to shortlist five that you might consider inviting to visit your organisation. You may need to determine the sectors they work in, the demographics of their followers and identify if they have a management agency.
>
> Tip: Research internet celebrity incubator firms such as Ruhan and influencer marketing platforms such as Parklu.

Celebrity public relations

Celebrity is concerned with the creation of cultural status and, in turn, economic value (Turner 2004). The public profile of the celebrity is developed and maintained by various industries and occupations. Turner calls industries involved in the production of celebrity – and these include entertainment, image management, communication (including the media), publicity (including public relations), coaching, endorsement and legal and investment industries – 'the celebrity industries' (2004: 41). Hartley (1992) refers specifically to the media, publicity and promotional industries as 'the smiling professions' and argues they play a significant role in shaping contemporary public culture. The celebrity status of a Hollywood actor might be the result of the promotional activities of different organisational and occupational roles, including the celebrity manager, the film studio or television production company, event organisers and event publicist, magazine and newspaper editors, and sponsorship and marketing campaigns (Turner 2004). Indeed, the kinds of public relations activity involved in the promotion of celebrity status include:

> brand planning and integrated marketing strategies; maintaining brand identity and awareness; market research and evaluation; promotions; product tie-ins and endorsement opportunities; the writing and editing of press releases, articles, speeches, scripts, and publications; special event planning and organisation; issue and crisis management; press agentry; and counselling those they represent on how to handle the media and best represent themselves in the public eye. (Redmond 2014: 72)

However, there is little public relations literature on its role in producing and maintaining celebrity other than in relation to image repair strategies (Waymer et al. 2015). Ames, for example, has researched the representation of the image consultant in popular culture, particularly in relation to 'the celebrity in crisis' (2011: 90; see Box 25.4). Yet, it is not as if celebrity exists outside of promotional activity; marketing and promotional work has always been integral to the production of celebrity (Hackley and Hackley 2015). Thinking of public relations in terms of its cultural intermediary role allows an understanding of the ways in which public relations contributes to meaning-making and identity construction (L'Etang 2006). Research into the work of celebrity publicists points to their expertise in working with traditional and social media to leverage social and cultural capital for clients (see Fitch 2017; Ciszek 2020). And, as discussed later in this chapter, the internet has dramatically transformed celebrity management in that it offers new opportunities for the performance of celebrity, in terms of self-promotion and the development of microcelebrities, and increases in user-generated content and interactions with fans (Marwick and boyd 2011). Influencers, as a form of internet celebrity, are now integral to many public relations campaigns. They use internet and platforms such as Instagram and YouTube to build a direct relationship with consumers. We therefore need a stronger understanding of the role of public relations in the production, maintenance and consumption of celebrity and influence.

Celebrity and society

Globalisation is significant as it is the convergence between media, entertainment and information industries, together with the expansion of media and entertainment empires that demand celebrities. Hollywood cinema, to offer one example, has always operated globally in terms of both audience development and within transnational corporations, and is a global commodity that markets and commodifies Western culture (Turner 2004). The Disney Corporation operates in five integrated markets: 'media networks, parks and resorts, studio entertainment, consumer products and interactive media' and each of these divisions sells the idea of celebrity (Redmond 2014: 75). Globalisation therefore enables the cultural and economic power of celebrity (Turner 2004).

Celebrities are pivotal to what Rojek calls the public relations–media complex, where global public relations corporations work closely with media giants, 'dominating the market in information, opinion formation and taste' and seeking to 'shape public opinion and boost product awareness through public opinion research, press releases, press kits, photo ops, publicity stunts, talk shows, advertising and other media outlets' (2012: 22). They use it not only to increase their own economic and cultural status, but celebrity endorsement is institutionalised in the public relations–media complex in creating associations and building brands (Rojek 2012). Technological changes have transformed celebrity culture, with changing practices and new spaces for producing and creating celebrity (Marwick and boyd 2011). In addition to mainstream and tabloid media, the internet, and in particular social media, offers new opportunities for celebrities to interact with fans.

Celebrity and the media

The media and publicity industries have always played a pivotal role in the construction and maintenance of celebrity. Sectors, such as the tabloid and mass market magazines and television talk format and reality shows, as well as celebrity magazines have played increasingly significant roles in developing interest in celebrity lifestyles since the 1980s and early 1990s (Turner 2004). Boorstin (1962) characterised celebrities as a kind of anti-hero, contrasting the 'real' achievements of heroes with the manufactured ones of celebrities (see Table 25.1). He was highly critical of what he called 'pseudo-events', such as press conferences and photo opportunities that exist purely to gain media coverage. For Boorstin, the lack of authenticity associated with celebrity was part of the Hollywood factory that created and promoted stars.

More recent scholars argue that Boorstin's argument contrasting celebrities and 'real' heroes is problematic. Turner (2004) points out that Boorstin was broadly

Celebrity	Hero
Illusory	Real
Synthetic	Authentic
Pseudo events	Real achievements
Image	Accomplishment or talent

Table 25.1 Celebrity vs. hero (*source:* Adapted from Boorstin, D. J. (1962). The Image: or what happened to the American dream. Harmondsworth, Penguin)

critiquing American popular culture which he identified as increasingly inauthentic and image-driven. Yet, Boorstin fails to recognise that many 'heroes' were either experts at self-promotion or had promotional support to help them achieve hero status. Van Krieken (2012), to offer one example, argues Boorstin's distinction between heroes, such as Abraham Lincoln and Benjamin Franklin, and celebrities is unsustainable, given that he ignores the role of public relations in developing heroic status. For van Krieken, 'every celebrity lies somewhere on a spectrum of combining achievement and talent . . . and the marketing end' (2012: 7). Similarly, Hackley and Hackley (2015) point out that marketing and promotion has always been integral to celebrity and indeed a necessary part of the showmanship to create it.

Celebrity as commodity

Celebrities are commodities, 'produced, traded, and marketed by the media and publicity industries' (Turner 2004: 9). They play an important branding role, in terms of a consistent identity, across media formats and diverse markets (Turner 2004), and are themselves lucrative brands:

> Celebrities are brand names as well as cultural icons or identities: they operate as marketing tools as well as sites where the agency of the audience is clearly evident; and they represent the achievement of individualism – the triumph of the human and the familiar – as well as its commodification and commercialisation. (Turner et al. 2000: 13)

According to Redmond, 'the celebrity exists in an orgy of promotions' (2014: 9), promoting and creating a culture of consumption and individualism. Celebrity embraces neoliberalism, and effectively models identity construction in a free market in order to seek profit (Hearn 2008).

> ### Explore 25.2
>
> #### Celebrities on Instagram
>
> The top Instagrammers in the world tend to be female celebrities in the music and entertainment industries with more than 100 million followers. Although any list of leading Instagrammers is highly dynamic, in June 2019, the No. 1 Instagrammer in the world was pop star Selena Gomez who had over 135 million followers (Influencer Marketing Hub 2019). Other members of the top ten include reality TV stars Kim Kardashian (110 million) and Kylie Jenner (107 million); pop stars Beyoncé (113 million), Taylor Swift (107 million) and Ariane Grande (118 million), and footballer Cristiano Ronaldo (124 million). The audiences for celebrities on Instagram are global, with some celebrities attracting significant followers outside the US, including from Indonesia (Swift); Britain (Kardashian); Mexico (Beyoncé and Gomez) and Brazil (Grande) (Sinha-Roy 2015). Their fan bases are young, meaning that Instagram is incredibly valuable for marketers.
>
> #### Feedback
>
> Analyse the content on Instagram accounts for any of these 'top' celebrities: Taylor Swift, Kim Kardashian, Kylie Jenner, Beyoncé, Selena Gomez and Ariana Grande. What are they posting about? Do you have the impression these accounts are managed by professional communicators or are authentic in terms of being posted by the celebrity themselves and offering insights into their everyday life? Is there much engagement with fans? Can you draw conclusions about what is meant by 'performing celebrity'? To what extent do these celebrities conform to Jo Littler's (2004) markers of authenticity: intimacy, reflexivity, and 'keeping it real' (for more information, see the 'Celebrity, the internet and influencers' section).

Consuming celebrity

Writing on the television reality show, Big Brother, Annette Hill discussed audience engagement as a 'game' where the audience attempts to decipher 'the "truth" in the spectacle/performance' (2002, cited in Turner 2004: 112). Reality television is part of the history of the internet celebrity in that it enabled a 'demotic turn' by representing non-celebrities and 'ordinary' people (Khamis et al. 2017; Turner 2004). Turner suggests the audience engages in a 'sophisticated interpretative activity' that demonstrates the 'playfulness of celebrity consumption' akin to the pleasure found in reading celebrity gossip magazines (Turner 2004: 112). That is, the audience is often aware of the 'manufacturedness' in the construction of celebrity yet at the same time is a willing and knowing participant in the consumption of celebrity. With the advent of the internet, consumers and audiences are increasingly conceived of – often in terms bordering on euphoric – as active, creative, empowered and socially connected in contrast to the earlier 'perceived passivity of mass media consumers' (Jenkins 2007: 358). The active consumer is in fact a fan (Jenkins 2007). In recent scholarship on public relations, participatory communication and fandom, Hutchins and Tindall (2015) argue that whereas fandom has traditionally been understood in terms of passionate consumers of entertainment, including film, sport, TV and celebrity, there are broader implications for brands and organisations in terms of understanding engaged audiences.

Celebrity, the internet and influencers

The internet has transformed celebrity culture, offering new spaces for producing, creating and performing celebrity and for interacting with fans (Marwick and boyd 2011). Social media offers 'the illusion of "backstage", giving the impression of uncensored glimpses into the lives of the very famous' (Marwick and boyd 2011: 14). The ordinary appeal of celebrities – they are both just like us and not like us – and the intimate glimpses into their everyday lives is significant in the development of audiences and the engagement of fans. According to Littler, there are three markers of 'authenticity' for celebrities:

- presentation of emotional intimacy with the audience;
- reflexivity about being in the position of celebrity; and
- ability to reference the time before they became famous. (2004: 13).

So, the success of the celebrity brand depends on audience engagement, a self-awareness of their fame, and a narrative trajectory of the before/after of celebrity status.

Celebrity is precisely about social mobility. Alice Marwick, in her ethnographic study of the tech industry, *Status Update: Celebrity, publicity and branding in the social media age,* points out that Web 2.0 is a kind of 'imagined community' (drawing on Benedict Anderson's concept of the nation as a social construction) that appears to offer a more democratic world where anybody – potentially – can get rich. This community encompasses expectations of greater participation and user engagement, and the assumption that 'creativity and control are disseminated throughout the population rather than concentrated in the hands of a few large corporations' (2013: 7).

The 'branded self'

Alison Hearn (2008) identified promotional culture and celebrities as significant in terms of informing how individuals present themselves online. Hearn argues that reality TV participants 'function as image-entrepreneurs' in terms of the strategic choices they make, albeit within the confines for the show's format, to 'generate their own rhetorically persuasive meanings' (2008: 201, 208). Individuals construct 'branded selves' on platforms such as Facebook, recognising that their public persona is a saleable commodity, both in terms of gaining popularity and followers but also in terms of the potential for monetising such connections. Of course, the information provided also allows the media platform to sell data to advertisers and marketers. The impact of celebrity culture is evident in the construction of a branded self-identity as an 'explicitly narrativized, image-based and cynical form of labour' (Hearn 2008: 214). The celebration of individualism engendered by social media provides 'a blueprint of how to prosper in a society where status is predicated on the cultural logic of celebrity' (Marwick 2013: 7, 14).

Microcelebrities

People who become famous through social media primarily because of their ability to attract attention, rather than for any other achievements, are known as 'microcelebrities'. A microcelebrity is: 'a mind set and a collection of self-presentation practices endemic in social media, in which users strategically formulate a profile, reach out to followers, and reveal personal information to increase attention and thus improve their online status (Senft 2013)' (Marwick 2015: 138). Whereas the term originally signified the ability to attract and develop a relationship with an audience, Instagram enables a kind of attention-seeking performance that contributes to what Alice Marwick (2015) refers to as 'instafamous'. Marwick argues that the Instagram microcelebrity differs from other social media microcelebrities precisely because it is visual and image-driven; rather than demonstrating the democratic potential of the internet, the Instafamous 'tend to be conventionally good-looking, work in "cool" industries . . . and emulate the tropes and symbols of traditional celebrity culture, such as glamorous self-portraits, designer goods, or luxury cars' (2015: 139). For example, see the case study on Australian publicist Roxy Jacenko featured in Box 25.1.

Influencers and internet celebrity

Crystal Abidin (2018) argues that the influencer industry epitomises internet celebrity, in that it allows individuals to effectively monetise their visibility online. Influencers '[strategize] their content into a commercial endeavour' (Abidin 2018: 13). Abidin theorises that influencers practise a 'contrived authenticity' or 'calibrated amateurism' in that 'influencers appear less constructed, less filtered, more spontaneous, and more real, thus fostering feelings of relatability and authenticity' (2018: 92). Ironically, given the lucrativeness of the influencer industry, recent news stories suggest this 'amateurism' has led to a new kind of aesthetic where influencers aim to make their photos look terrible to highlight their lack of 'professionalism' (Lorenz 2019).

Abidin (2018) argues that scholarship on the rise of influencers are dominated by Western understandings and therefore fails to recognise diverse histories and impacts of influencers in different countries. See Explore 25.1 for a discussion of internet celebrity and influencers in China.

Box 25.1

Sweaty Betty and the Princess of Instagram

The PR Queen

Roxy Jacenko, the founder and CEO of Sweaty Betty PR (see http://www.sweatybettypr.com/), a fashion, beauty and lifestyle public relations agency and Ministry of Talent (see http://theministryoftalent.com/), a management agency for digital influencers, in Sydney, Australia, is variously referred to as a PR queen, celebrity publicist (Lewis 2014), PR powerhouse, PR guru and PR dynamo (Melocco 2014). In a recent television interview, Jacenko described herself as 'just a simple, blond PR girl' (*The Weekly* 2018). But Jacenko is no stay-behind-the-scenes publicist. She appeared on the Australian version of the TV show Celebrity Apprentice and has written three novels about a fictional Sydney-based fashion PR practitioner, Jazzy Malone. Although works of fiction, Jacenko claims the novels are 'inspired by her seven-year career in the fashion PR industry' and 'the perfect research for anyone looking to break in to the cut-throat world of fashion PR'.

Through media interviews, Jacenko tells a consistent story of her self-made success: from establishing Sweaty Betty at 24, to her success in developing a property portfolio: 'I have invested in property since the age of 21 and based on this have seen the benefits of buying, making over and then selling, then doing it all over again' (cited in Melocco 2014). We know a lot about Jacenko, or at least about a story that she has herself constructed that reveals both the ordinary along with the glamour. For example, we know about: her real estate (she bought her first property at 21); her interior design as her homes are featured in various luxury magazines; her plastic surgery (we've seen pictures of her nose job); what's in her handbag; her favourite jeans (Levis); where she gets her fake tan; and even when she is holding a garage sale to sell the designer clothes her children have grown out of (see, for example, Melocco 2014; Who's your? (n.d.)). We also know through news stories that her banker husband was found guilty in 2016 of insider trading – Jacenko instagrammed her outfits every day of the trial – and that she is estranged from her father and her sister.

The Princess of Instagram

Jacenko has established a remarkable business model based on the online persona she has developed for her young daughter, Pixie Curtis. Pixie, frequently referred to in media stories and in promotional material as 'The Princess of Instagram', charges A$500 (approximately £250) for a product-placement post on Instagram (Parnell 2015). According to Pixie's management agency, Ministry of Talent (n.d.), which is also run by Jacenko, Pixie has over 100,000 Instagram followers and 'an uncanny ability to elevate a brand simply by association, drawing mass interaction from luxury and budget-friendly products – who else wears Gucci sandals one day and CROCS the next?' The constant feed on Pixie's Instagram account ranges from an extraordinary, jet-setting lifestyle wearing designer clothes, having her hair and makeup done, flying first class, boating on the French Riviera, and launching her own accessories line (Pixie's Bows – see www.pixiespix.com.au), and staying in luxury hotels in Dubai, Paris, Tokyo and London, to the mundane such as supermarket shopping, eating ice cream and playing with her brother. In fact, the Instagram posts – which frequently become mainstream news stories – specifically contrast the extremes of trying on a couture dress and the ordinariness of supermarket shopping (albeit in pyjamas and dressing gown). With her brother Hunter, Pixie also reviews toys on their YouTube Channel.

Instakids

If celebrity, as van Krieken (2012) proposes, exists on a continuum of talent and media attention, then where does a six-year-old child sit? It is hard to argue that Pixie Curtis has become a successful commodity through her own achievements. Rather, Pixie's commercial success foregrounds the efforts of her mother, who just happens to be the successful head of a fashion and lifestyle public relations agency and a management agency for influencers. Jacenko defends herself against critics, by arguing that Pixie is simply developing – like her mother – a strong work ethic: 'Pixie is like me. I worked from a young age! [It] is all a bit of fun and cultures her to know that, if you want something in life, you need to work for it' (cited in Lewis 2014).

Sources: Fitch 2017, Lewis, M. (2014), Melocco, J. (2014), Ministry of Talent. (n.d.), Parnell, K. (2015), *The Weekly.* (2018), Who's your? (n.d.)

Picture 25.2 Roxy Jacenko is an Australian publicist who came runner up on the third season of The Celebrity Apprentice Australia (*source*: Don Arnold/Getty Images)

Think about 25.1

Instakids and Instafamous

Instagram enables a kind of attention-seeking and image-driven performance that contributes to what Alice Marwick (2015) refers to as 'instafamous'. Marwick argues that in the attention economy, people construct online identities that are underpinned by 'deregulated capitalism and entrepreneurship' and model both social mobility and aspirational consumption (2015: 10). To what extent do you think the online identities of Instakids – the children who are famous online due to the promotional efforts of their parents and/or professional communicators and marketers – conform to Marwick's notion that Instagram users model 'a neoliberal subjectivity that applies market principles to how they think about themselves, interact with others, and display their identity' (2015: 7)?

Feedback

Analyse the Instagram accounts of Australian Pixie Curtis (@pixiecurtis), Korean Breanna Youn (@officialbreannayoun), Singaporean twins Leia and Lauren Lok (@leilauren) or any Instakid with a significant following. If social media is a celebration of individualism and online identities that apply market principles, as Marwick argues, then to what extent is the identity of the child constructed around promotion and conspicuous consumption? That is, how is 'celebrity' performed and constructed through the various posts? And how do followers engage with this celebrity?

Mini case study 25.2

The Fyre Festival that wasn't

The Fyre Festival was a luxury music festival due to be held in April/May 2017 on the Bahamian island of Great Exhuma. Its spectacular failure has entered popular culture, spawning memes and two documentaries, and becoming synonymous with the superficiality and extreme consumption associated with celebrity culture.

Kendall Jenner was reportedly paid $250,000 (GB£193,000) for a single Instagram post announcing ticket sales were open (Helmore 2019). She later said of her involvement that 'I definitely do as much research as I can, but sometimes there isn't much research you can do because it's a starting brand and you kind of have to have faith in it' (*New York Times* 2019).

More than US$5 million dollars was paid to models who featured in the promotional video, including ten supermodels and influencers such as Bella Hadid, Gizele Oliveria and Emily Ratajkowski, and to influencers such as Jenner. Over 400 people were paid to promote the festival online and other influencers, such as UK beauty influencer, CC Clarke Beauty, were invited to attend the event gratis as VIPs (Soen 2019).

However, the festival never happened. The festival organiser pleaded guilty to various fraud charges and is currently serving a six-year prison term. Civil and other legal proceedings are under way and there is no doubt that the failed Fyre Festival placed influencers under scrutiny (Kleinman 2019).

Sources: Coscarelli and Ryzik (2017); Kleinman (2019); Helmore (2019); *New York Times* (2019); Soen (2019)

Celebrity and influencers in public relations practice

Celebrity practitioners

Many practitioners who work in the celebrity sector are coy about their work. Anecdotally, some prefer not to identify themselves in relation to ghostwriting social media posts on behalf of celebrity clients. Others, approached regarding a profile for an earlier version of this chapter, cited being too busy and the fact that they sign non-disclosure agreements with their clients as reasons for not participating in an interview. Reluctance to discuss the techniques of their work is perhaps not surprising – after all, it is their perceived skill or expertise that is the unique service they are able to offer celebrity clients. However, it means that the day-to-day activities and practitioner understandings of celebrity PR work are not always well documented even though some activities are highly visible across different media platforms and many practitioners outline their services on their company websites.

Betty Stewart established a public relations consultancy in Australia in 1959 that specialised in the entertainment sector. She worked in public relations for 60 years, having started her career in theatre promotion in the early 1930s, and her experiences offer some important historical insights into celebrity PR activity. In her memoir, *A Survivor in a Star Spangled World,* Stewart (2000) describes her work with visiting and local celebrities primarily as media work. Her first solo-run press conference, which was very formal, was for Gracie Fields during World War II. Stewart was aware of the need for media spectacle and photo opportunities, recruiting young women from modelling agencies to accompany clients to public events and negotiating the use of a mauve painted car with leopard skin seats for a visiting starlet. She was the National Promotion Director for the Beatles' 1964 tour of Australia, a role that included organising Paul McCartney's 22nd birthday party and negotiating an exclusive with a local newspaper in order to finance the event (Stewart 2000: 209).

Contemporary public relations agency websites point to the range of diverse activity they offer, which encompasses celebrity PR. To offer one example, Tailor Maid Communications (2019) in Sydney, Australia offer 'public relations' services in the fashion and lifestyle sectors, which include: marketing and publicity strategy, media relations, copywriting, celebrity management, celebrity affiliation and endorsement, ambassador programmes, charity alignment and both paid and unpaid influencer outreach (see http://tailormaid.com.au/). SF Celebrity Management (2019), another Australian agency, does not call their work public relations, although their website features news and social media coverage of their clients, whom they describe as 'Australia's media identities'. Their services include 'contract negotiation, endorsements, public appearances, event hosting and public speaking' as part of managing clients' 'careers and profiles' (see sfcelebritymanagement.com.au).

Box 25.2

Max Markson: Australia's agent to the stars

'I can make anyone famous' claims Max Markson, Australia's best-known celebrity publicist. It's about finding the angle. Everybody's got a story.'

He started Markson Sparks!, a public relations, events and celebrity management agency, in Sydney, Australia, in 1982. Even after 38 years in the industry, Markson remains enthusiastic about his work. When asked about what he enjoyed most, Markson identified two things. The first is 'getting stories in the paper or stories on TV. I always get a kick out of that.' The second is the bartering: 'I love the deal. And sometimes the deal takes months. So, I love that, the negotiations and see it coming to fruition.'

Aquatic shows, nightclubs and DJs

As a child, Markson used to help with his father's travelling Leon Markson Aquashow: bill posting, spotlighting and working the gate. Markson's own promotional career started in 1974 when he was still in high school in Bournemouth, England. He worked part-time in a local nightclub, initially as a spotlight operator and stage manager. He began to promote special nights with Radio 1 disc jockeys, such as Emperor Rosko and Dave Lee Travis, at the club. Markson describes 'leaving school at lunchtime to go over the road to the phone box to ring the agents in London to organise the deals.' To promote the shows, Max and a high school friend printed orange dayglo posters and persuaded shop owners to put them in

box 25.2 (continued)

windows in exchange for free tickets. They also plastered a car with the posters and drove round with a speaker. As Markson says, 'I was a real spruiker.' That first summer, they made lots of money from the holidaymakers in Bournemouth but lost much of it in the winter. He also began promoting local gigs with bands such as Hot Chocolate (famous for 'You Sexy Thing', among other hits).

After a couple years of organising and promoting DJ nights, music concerts and tours across the UK, Markson decided to take a break and holiday in Australia. He arrived in 1977 and never left. He dabbled in T-shirts and promoted diverse products such as negative ion generators and snakeheads and spiders encased in glass before running a nightclub, The Zoo, in Sydney's Kings Cross. Markson put on celebrity DJs each week: everyone and anyone from Kim Wran, Brooke Shields, Evil Knievel, George Hamilton, Dawn Fraser, Dennis Lillee, to Geoff Boycott. Markson claims it was the local hang-out for World Series cricketers and that 'every celebrity in town trying to promote a movie or record would find themselves at The Zoo' (2000: 26). Markson's publicity-grabbing stunts for the club included Belinda Green, a former Miss World, walking a tiger on a leash; she was also a regular club DJ.

Publicity versus public relations

Markson understands his role as generating revenue for his clients. Markson himself questions whether his work is public relations:

> 'I still don't think I do PR. I am a publicist. . . . . . I hark back to the old days of the circus and you sent your advance man to get publicity and get stories in the paper, on the TV and now on the internet. That's what I think my skill is. If there is any skill I have, it's an angle for a story and then making it happen and getting it the publicity.'

Markson has negotiated media coverage, endorsements and appearances for celebrities, ranging from sports champions, including athletes, cricketers, boxers, and footballers, to supermodels, actors and reality TV stars. He has also promoted visiting celebrities such as Linda Evangelista, Arnold Schwarzenegger, Pele, Kim Kardashian, and former statesmen such as Bill Clinton and Nelson Mandela. His clients include local personalities, who have gained some short-lived media fame through reality television or newsworthiness that Markson can monetise. One of his clients was infamous party boy, Corey Worthington, who as a 16-year old threw an out-of-control party, which he had advertised online, at his parent's house; Markson negotiated a now-legendary interview on commercial television and several lucrative endorsements and appearances. In fact, Markson is keen on managing (almost) anyone with a media profile and takes 20 per cent commission on any commercial sponsorships or deals (for product promotion, he charges a fee). He does not work exclusively for celebrities, but he often draws on his celebrity contacts to promote other clients. For example, he promotes his longstanding client Advanced Hair Studio, a hair replacement service, using renowned international cricketers Greg Matthews and Shane Warne. Markson is also well known for his fundraising and charity work.

'Columnists are like seagulls'

Much of the work Markson describes revolves around getting publicity for his clients. His work therefore combines product promotion, celebrity management and event management and all rely on his close relationships with journalists. In his book, *Show Me the Money!*, Markson writes: 'Columnists are like seagulls, they are always looking for a chip' (2000: 63). He describes weekly phone calls offering the media information and possible stories on clients, stating 'it's all about getting my client's name in the paper.' He has organised celebrity camel and elephant races on the beach (to promote an anti-mould product and ice cream respectively); skated up and down a bus aisle on a five-day journey from Sydney to Perth; negotiated what was then the biggest ever chequebook journalism deal for former Australian prime minister Bob Hawke and his second wife, Blanche D'Alpuget, and simultaneously represented Hazel Hawke, Hawke's first wife. From Markson's perspective, 'everyone has a story to tell' and the value often hinges on exclusivity.

Markson maintains that to be successful in celebrity PR, 'you have to have a hunger to get stories in the paper; you have to be bold; you've got to pick the phone up and make the calls; and you have to take every call.' In his book, Markson describes occasions when, in his own words, he 'stretched the truth'. Early in his career, he promoted negative ion generators and claimed Margaret Thatcher had one; when the journalist asked how he knew that, Markson replied he'd sent it to her. Similarly, promoting a New Year's Eve event in a restaurant, Markson invited celebrities, whom he described as 'all the usual suspects', and then planted 'teasers in all the columns around town'. He suggested to one newspaper columnist he was not allowed to discuss if one client would audition for Baywatch on a forthcoming US visit. He subsequently arranged for a tape of his client to be sent to the Baywatch producers. According to Markson, 'things like that I class as fun. Okay, it stretched the truth a little, but I didn't break it; it all came true and everybody was happy. My client got a heap of publicity and the journo got a story. That's the way it works' (2000: 63).

Sources: Markson, M. (2000, 2016). Interview with K. Fitch. Used with permission

Box 25.3

Beauty influencers and public relations

'I want to be 100% honest with you guys,' says Lauren Curtis (2016), one of Australia's top beauty influencers, discussing her lip injections in a video diary spanning 23 days that shows trauma and bruising to her lips and her disappointment with the experience: 'Just because you see YouTubers, or celebrities, or influencers with these procedures done, it doesn't mean it's going to be the same on you.'

Curtis, a self-taught makeup artist, created her YouTube channel in August 2011. The channel now has more than 3.5 million subscribers and Curtis manages her profile across different social media platforms. In 2019, she launched a range of pyjamas and loungewear because 'one of the biggest perks of doing what I do is the ability to work from home and being able to wear what I want (pyjamas)' (Lauren Curtis Lounge 2019).

Max Connectors (2018), self-described as 'Australia's No. 1 Influencer Agency', manages Curtis and claims that she has nearly 8 million global followers (1.4 million on Instagram; 2.2 million on Facebook; 3.6 million on YouTube and 252,000 on Twitter). Curtis's personal net worth is an estimated AUD$480,000 and her brand partnerships include global giants such as Colgate and Garnier (Eksouzian-Cavadas 2018).

Curtis discussed her relationship with the PR industry in a recent video on decluttering her makeup collection. It is part of a wider trend among beauty influencers concerned with sustainability and waste reduction (Rigby 2019). Curtis (2018) pointed to boxes and boxes of elaborately packaged PR gifts she had received gratis; she stated that although she wanted to stay on PR lists, she would not use or keep most of it. Instead, she 'asked my Australian management to not give out my PO Box details so that I can screen it first. . . . I want to reduce waste.'

Sources: Curtis (2016, 2018), Eksouzian-Cavadas (2018), Lauren Curtis Lounge (2019), MaxConnectors (2018), Rigby (2019)

Box 25.4

Celebrity and crisis: Belle Gibson, fake cancer survivor

In 2015, the life and lies of celebrity Australian food and alternative health blogger, Belle Gibson, began to unravel. Gibson had created a successful and lucrative brand, which promoted healthy eating founded on claims that Gibson had cured her terminal brain cancer through a wholesome diet and the rejection of conventional medical treatment. In addition, Gibson, who earnt more than A$1 million (approximately £500,000), maintained that a significant proportion of profits was donated to charity. Gibson, active on several social media platforms, was also lauded in mainstream media, declared 'most inspiring woman' by one magazine and awarded the 'Fun, Fearless Female' social media awarded by another. It emerged that Gibson had never been diagnosed with cancer and that the five charities Gibson allegedly donated 25 per cent of profits to, and had fundraised for, had received only small amounts, if any, money. Even Gibson's reported age proved to be a fiction. Gibson's book, *The Whole Pantry*, which had already sold well in Australia and was about to be published in the US and the UK was withdrawn by Penguin. Gibson's The Whole Pantry food and health app, which had already been purchased by 300,000 consumers, was also withdrawn from sale. In response to the media exposure, Gibson initially remained elusive. She was briefly represented pro bono by Bespoke Approach, described as an influential political lobbyist and PR firm, who arranged for Gibson to be interviewed by the iconic women's magazine *Australian Women's Weekly*. In that interview, Gibson stated that 'it's all lies . . . none of it is true'. Gibson's estranged mother was subsequently interviewed by the same magazine and although she disputed her daughter's account of her upbringing, stated that her daughter was only guilty of telling a white lie. In a later television interview, Gibson claimed that she did not lie but had been lied to herself. Gibson's social media accounts have now been deleted. At the time of writing this chapter, Gibson had not paid a A$410,000 (approximately GBP 229,000) fine for breaching consumer laws after claiming she cured her non-existent brain cancer through diet and alternative therapies (Percy 2019). Further, Penguin Publishing had to pay A$30,000 (approximately GBP 15,000) to the Victorian consumer law fund for their failure to fact check Gibson's claims.

Sources: Donnelly and Toscano (2015a, 2015b), Davey (2015), Percy, K. (2019)

Think about 25.2

The Whole Pantry and the Whole Truth

Carol Ames (2011) investigated the role of image consultant for the celebrity in crisis. Ames found that typically following a celebrity transgression, publicists issue a brief statement on behalf of the client with an apology; encourage the client to disappear briefly from public life to address 'personal' issues; manage a re-entry into public life often in association with charity work; and then – hopefully – allow the client to relaunch their successful career. If Belle Gibson was your public relations agency's client, how would you advise her as her life unravelled? In small groups, discuss the following points:

- If your client claimed to have cured themselves of cancer through healthy eating, would you seek evidence to support such claims?
- As media reporting revealed the 'celebrity self' constructed by Gibson is a fiction, what would you do?

If Gibson was not your client:

- Would you offer to take on Gibson pro bono in the face of the media storm that erupted? If so, what would you hope to achieve?

Feedback

At one point, Gibson was an extremely influential wellness blogger and campaigner. Now that she has been convicted of consumer fraud, what role did public relations and other promotional activity play in helping Gibson reach a position of influence that allowed her to peddle mistruths and potentially impact on real people in ways that could have been fatal? This example is an opportunity to reflect on whether professional communicators may have been able to expose Gibson as a fraud much earlier and what their obligations to society are.

Summary

Celebrity is pervasive in contemporary society. It has been democratised by the internet leading to the rise of the internet influencer. Public relations plays a significant cultural intermediary role in the production and representation of celebrity. Public relations is only one of the celebrity industries, but its promotional role is often marginalised within both public relations scholarship and the media and cultural scholarship that researches celebrity culture and influencers. However, studying everyday industry practices – such as the widespread use of influencers in campaigns – positions public relations within promotional culture and allows a stronger understanding of the societal impact of public relations activity, particularly in relation to commodification and capitalism. These impacts are evident in the promotional discourse and self-branding used by celebrities and influencers and emulated by consumers of celebrity and more broadly across contemporary culture.

Bibliography

Abidin, C. (2018). *Internet Celebrity: Understanding fame online*. Bingley, UK: Emerald Publishing.

Ames, C. (2011). 'Popular culture's image of the PR image consultant: The celebrity in crisis'. *The IJPC Journal*. http://ijpc.uscannenberg.org/journal/index.php/ijpcjournal/article/viewFile/28/37, accessed 24 April 2015.

Boorstin, D.J. (1962). *The Image: Or what happened to the American dream*. Harmondsworth, Penguin.

Chernavina, K. (2018, 2 July). Chinese KOL in sport, parenting, travel, skincare, health. *Hi-Com* [online]. https://www.hicom-asia.com/chinese-kol-in-sport-parenting-travel-skincare-health/ accessed 18 May 2019.

Ciszek, E. (2020). The man behind the woman: Publicity, celebrity public relations and cultural intermediation. *Public Relations Inquiry*, 9(2), 135–154.

Coscarelli, J. and M. Ryzik, (2017, 28 April). Fyre Festival, a Luxury Music Weekend, Crumbles in the Bahamas. *New York Times* [online]. https://www.nytimes.com/2017/04/28/arts/music/fyre-festival-ja-rule-bahamas.html?module=inline (accessed 5 April 2019).

Curtis, L. (2016, 9 June). My Honest Experience with Lip Injections [YouTube]. https://www.youtube.com/watch?v=H3Sw5ytyHHE (accessed 5 April 2019).

Curtis, L. (2018, November 28). Goodbye to PR packages... makeup cull. [YouTube] https://www.youtube.com/watch?v=mHeHQPX9RIA (accessed 5 April 2019).

Davey, M. (2015, 29 June). 'Belle Gibson on 60 Minutes: No remorse and the lies kept coming'. *The Guardian*. http://www.theguardian.com/tv-and-radio/2015/jun/29/belle-gibson-tells-60-minutes-she-was-the-victim-after-her-lies-were-exposed

Donnelly, B. and N. Toscano (2015a, 15 March). 'Charity money promised by "inspirational" health app developer Belle Gibson not handed over'. *The Age*. http://www.theage.com.au/digital-life/digital-life-news/charity-money-promised-by-inspirational-health-app-developer-belle-gibson-not-handed-over-20150308-13xgqk.html

Donnelly, B. and N. Toscano (2015b, 25 June). 'Belle Gibson on 60 Minutes: Don't expect an apology'. *Sydney Morning Herald*. http://www.smh.com.au/national/belle-gibson-on-60-minutes-dont-expect-an-apology-20150625-ghxjwk.html.

eMarketer. (2018, 2 August). What's the Difference Between a KOL and a Wanghong? Savvy influencer marketers in China know. https://www.emarketer.com/content/what-s-the-difference-between-a-kol-and-a-wanghong (accessed 18 May 2019).

Escobedo, J. (2017). Nearly $150K per post? What you need to know about China's Key Opinion Leaders. *Forbes* [online]. https://www.forbes.com/sites/joeescobedo/2017/05/22/key-opinion-leaders-in-china/#37faf89472ee (accessed 18 May 2019).

Eksouzian-Cavadas, E. (2018, 18 September). A definitive ranking of the highest paid beauty influencers. *Elle Australia* [online]. https://www.elle.com.au/beauty/highest-paid-beauty-bloggers-18609 (accessed 5 April 2019).

Fitch, K. (2017). Seeing 'the unseen hand': Celebrity, promotion and public relations. *Public Relations Inquiry*, 6(2), 157–169.

Google. (2014). 'Combining engaging, authentic content with smart use of the YouTube platform, Zoella keeps her fans watching and contributing' [Case Study]. https://storage.googleapis.com/think-v2-emea/docs/case_study/zoella-creator-story.pdf (accessed 30 November 2015).

Grundeberg, S. and J. Hansegard (2014, 16 June). 'YouTube's biggest draw plays games, earns $4 million a year'. *Wall Street Journal*. http://w3.salemstate.edu/~pglasser/gamer.pdf (accessed 30 November 2015).

Hackley, C. and R.A. Hackley (2015). 'Marketing and the cultural production of celebrity in the era of media convergence'. *Journal of Marketing Management* 31(5–6): 461–477.

Hallanan, L. (2018, 18 December). Alibaba-Backed Chinese Influencer Incubator Ruhan Rumored To Be Planning NASDAQ IPO. *Forbes*. https://www.forbes.com/sites/laurenhallanan/2018/12/18/alibaba-backed-chinese-influencer-incubator-ruhan-announces-plans-to-go-public/, accessed 8 August 2019.

Hartley, J. (1992). *The Politics of Pictures: The creation of the public in the age of popular media*. London: Routledge.

Hartley, J. (2002). *Communication, Cultural and Media Studies: The key concepts* (3rd edn). London: Routledge.

Hearn, A. (2008). '"Meat, mask, burden": Probing the contours of the branded "self"'. *Journal of Consumer Culture* 8(2): 197–217.

Helmore, E. (2019, 29 January). Kendall Jenner and Bella Hadid facing possible subpoenas over Fyre Festival. *The Guardian* [online]. https://www.theguardian.com/culture/2019/jan/29/kendall-jenner-bella-hadid-fyre-festival-subpoena-money (accessed 5 April 2019).

Hunt, E. (2016, 6 May). 'Belle Gibson faces legal action over 'deceptive' claims lifestyle changes could cure cancer.' *The Guardian*. http://www.theguardian.com/australia-news/2016/may/06/belle-gibson-facing-legal-action-over-deceptive-claims-lifestyle-changes-could-cure-cancer (accessed 10 May 2016).

Hutchins, A. and N. Tindall, N. (2015). '"Things that don't go together?" Considering fandom and re-thinking public relations'. *Prism* 12(10). http://www.prismjournal.org/fandom_ed.html (accessed 23 November 2015).

Hutchinson, J. (2017). *Cultural Intermediaries: Audience Participation in Media Organisations*. Cham, Switzerland: Palgrave Macmillan.

Influencer Marketing Hub (2019, 21 June). https://influencermarketinghub.com/top-instagram-influencers-in-2019/ (accessed 8 July 2019).

Jenkins, H. (2007). 'The future of fandom' in *Fandom: Identities and communities in a mediated world*. J. Gray, C. Sandvoss and C. L. Harrington (eds.). New York: New York University Press.

Ke, D. (2019). Meet the Chinese 'Kylie Jenner' Who Just Rang the Bell at Nasdaq. Medium. https://medium.com/@doriskeke/meet-the-chinese-kylie-jenner-who-rang-the-bell-at-nasdaq-f0fb28b91e0 (accessed 8 August 2019).

Khamis, S., L. Ang and R. Welling (2017). Self-branding, 'micro-celebrity' and the rise of Social Media Influencers. *Celebrity Studies*, 8(2): 191–208.

Kleinman, Z. (2019, 22 January). Has Fyre Festival burned influencers? BBC News [online]. https://www.bbc.com/news/46945662 (accessed 5 April 2019).

Kurzman, C., C. Anderson, C. Key, C. Lee, Y. Ok, M. Silver and A van Ryn (2007). 'Celebrity status'. *Sociological Theory*, 25(4), December: 347–387.

L'Etang, J. (2006). 'Public relations and sport in promotional culture'. *Public Relations Review* 32(4): 386–394.

Lauren Curtis Lounge (2019). https://laurencurtislounge.com/about/ (accessed 5 April 2019).

Lewis, M. (2014, 14 March). 'The two-year-old with a trust fund: Millionaire mum Roxy Jacenko says she has set up account for internet superstar daughter Pixie Curtis who earns $200 a post'. *Daily Mail*. http://www.dailymail.co.uk/tvshowbiz/article-2580701/Two-year-old-trust-fund-Meet-Roxy-Jacenkos-kid-Pixie-Curtis.html (accessed 29 May 2015).

Littler, J. (2004). 'Making fame ordinary: Intimacy, reflexivity and "keeping it real"'. *Mediactive* 2: 8.

Lorenz, T. (2019, 23 April). 'The Instagram Aesthetic Is Over'. *The Atlantic.* https://www.theatlantic.com/technology/archive/2019/04/influencers-are-abandoning-instagram-look/587803/ (accessed 8 July 2019).

Markson, M. (2000). *Show Me The Money! A guide to fame, fortune and business success, by Australia's agent to the stars.* Ringwood, Australia: Viking.

Markson, M. (2016, 13 May). [Personal interview with the author].

Marshall, P.D. (1997). *Celebrity and Power: Fame in contemporary culture.* Minneapolis, MN: University of Minnesota Press.

Marwick, A. (2013). *Status Update: Celebrity, publicity and branding in the social media age.* New Haven, CT: Yale University Press.

Marwick, A. (2015). 'Instafame: Luxury selfies in the attention economy'. *Public Culture,* 21(10): 137–160.

Marwick, A. and d. boyd (2011). 'To see and be seen: Celebrity practice on Twitter'. *Convergence: The International Journal of Research into New Media Technologies,* 17(2): 139–158.

MaxConnectors. (2018). https://www.maxconnectors.com.au/ (accessed 5 April 2019).

Melocco, J. (2014, 13 November). 'PR dynamo Roxy Jacenko sells glamorous Woollahra home for more than $8 million'. *Wentworth Courier.* http://www.dailytelegraph.com.au/newslocal/realestate/pr-dynamo-roxy-jacenko-sells-glamorous-woollahra-home-for-more-than-8million/story-fnq1z43j-1227120830133 (accessed 4 June 2015).

Ministry of Talent. (n.d.). 'Pixie Curtis'. Retrieved from http://theministryoftalent.com/portfolio/pixie-curtis/ (accessed 4 June 2015).

New York Times. (2019, 31 March). The Kardashians Tell All About Jordyn Woods, Fyre Festival and Being Billionaires. [online]. https://www.nytimes.com/2019/03/31/style/kardashians-tonight.html (accessed 5 April 2019).

Parnell, K. (2015, 14 June). Three year old Pixie Curtis is 'the voice of her generation'. *Sunday Style.* Retrieved from http://www.news.com.au/lifestyle/sunday-style/three-year-old-pixie-curtis-is-the-voice-of-her-generation/story-fnrmugv2-1227396868473 (accessed 16 October 2015)

Percy, K. (2019, 14 May). 'Belle Gibson questioned on spending over failure to pay $410k fine for fake cancer claims'. ABC News [online]. https://www.abc.net.au/news/2019-05-14/belle-gibson-questioned-in-federal-court-over-failure-pay-fine/11110594 (accessed 8 July 2019).

Redmond, S. (2014). *Celebrity and the Media.* Houndmills: Palgrave Macmillan.

Redmond, S. and S. Holmes (Eds.). (2007). *Stardom and Celebrity: A reader.* London: Sage.

Rigby, B. (2019, April 3). When less is more: the beauty bloggers exposing the industry's wasteful secret. *The Guardian* [online]. https://www.theguardian.com/fashion/2019/apr/03/when-less-is-more-the-beauty-bloggers-exposing-the-industrys-wasteful-secret (accessed 5 April 2019).

Rojek, C. (2001). *Celebrity.* London: Reaktion Books.

Rojek, C. (2012). *Fame Attack: The inflation of celebrity and its consequences.* London: Bloomsbury.

Selinger-Morris, S. (2015, 28 November). 'YouTube's digital darlings harness the power of print to hijack bestseller lists'. http://www.smh.com.au/entertainment/books/youtubes-digital-darlings-harness-the-power-of-print-to-hijack-bestseller-lists-20151125-gl6iwg.html (accessed 30 November 2015).

Sinha-Roy, P. (2015, 6 October). 'Taylor Swift, Kim Kardashian lead most-followed Instagram accounts'. *Reuters.* http://www.reuters.com/article/2015/10/06/us-instagram-taylorswift-idUSKCN0S012L20151006#jSUmtZWmilSpLDsV.97 (accessed 16 October 2015).

Soen, H. (2019, 17 January). The Instagram models and influencers that promoted the Fyre festival scam. *The Tab* [online]. https://thetab.com/uk/2019/01/17/fyre-festival-instagram-models-89928 (accessed 5 April 2019).

Stewart, B. (2000). *A Survivor in a Star Spangled World.* East Blaxland, Australia: Author.

Tsoi, G. (2016, 1 August). Wang Hong: China's online stars making real cash. *BBC News* [online]. https://www.bbc.com/news/world-asia-china-36802769 (accessed 18 May 2019).

Turner, G. (2004). *Understanding Celebrity*. London: Sage.

Turner, G. (2014). 'Celebrity' in *A Companion to the Australian Media*. B. Griffen-Foley (ed.). North Melbourne: Australian Scholarly Publishing.

Turner, G., F. Bonner and P.D. Marshall (2000). *Fame Games: The production of celebrity in Australia*. Melbourne: Cambridge University Press.

Van Krieken, R. (2012). *Celebrity Society*. Abingdon: Routledge.

Wang, Y. (2018, June 21). Cyber celebrity industry booms. *China Daily*. https://www.chinadaily.com.cn/a/201806/21/WS5b2b042ca3103349141dd75b.html (accessed 28 April 2020).

Waymer, D., S. VanSlette, and K. Cherry (2015). 'From Hannah Montana to naked on a wrecking ball: Miley Cyrus' issues management, and corporate celebrity debranding/rebranding efforts'. *Prism*, 12(1), http://www.prismjournal.org/homepage.html accessed 23 November 2015

Weekly, The. (2018, 5 September). Roxy Jacenko: Hard Chat. https://www.youtube.com/watch?v=-v1raI-Y1H8g (accessed 7 August 2019).

Wernick, A. (1991). *Promotional Culture: Advertising, ideology and symbolic expression*. London: Sage.

Who's your? (n.d.). 'Roxy Jacencko, Director of Sweaty Betty PR'. http://whosyour.com/interview/roxy-jacenko/ (accessed 16 October 2015).

Websites

Disrupt www.disrupt.co.uk/
Influencer Network www.influencersg.com/
Max Connectors www.maxconnectors.com.au/
Parklu www.parklu.com
Look to the Stars www.looktothestars.org/cause

CHAPTER 26

Audra Diers-Lawson and Noumaan Qureshi

Health communication

Source: Tom Tietz/123RF

Learning outcomes

By the end of this chapter you should be able to:
- define a stakeholder relationship management view of healthcare
- analyse and apply theories for persuasion to campaigns to improve health outcomes
- evaluate the opportunities for crossover between healthcare and public relations
- better understand the application of two-way symmetrical communication in healthcare.

Structure

- The high stakes of health communication require a stakeholder relationship approach
- Using persuasion theory to better understand factors affecting the 'healthcare stakeholder'
- The crossover between mass campaigns and interpersonal health communication
- Two-way symmetrical communication in healthcare

Introduction

Ben Duncan, a risk communication consultant to the World Health Organization's (WHO) Health Emergencies Programme, argues that when responding to disease outbreaks such as influenza pandemics, Ebola or Pneumonic Plague, the role of communication cannot be understated (Diers-Lawson 2020). In fact, Duncan points out that in 2017 the WHO codified a process that prioritises public outreach and communication alongside the medical response to all new disease outbreaks because it has realised that it will save lives. Beyond image and reputation management, the field of public relations serves vital roles in the global healthcare context. This chapter explores the roles that public relations can serve in modern healthcare from inside the hospital and doctor's office (Anderson and Helms 2000) out to the role that social media and health campaigns serve to improve health outcomes (Bennet and Glasgow 2009) and minimise the risks of pandemics (Guidry et al. 2017). This chapter argues that as the nature of public relations practice modernises, adopting a stakeholder relationship model helps public relations practitioners to better appreciate their role in building healthier societies. Yet, we must be cautious in understanding there is risk in the healthcare context; Duncan also points out that bad communication strategy can also cost lives (see Mini case study 26.1).

Mini case study 26.1
Bad health communication costs lives

Duncan argues that for nearly 20 years risk and crisis communication experts in the health sector have pushed to be equal members of response teams to pandemics, positioning communication as a health intervention on a par with the importance of the work done by epidemiologists and lab experts. However, communication experts also believe that bad communication could cost lives during a health emergency.

Evidence of this was illustrated during the 2014 Ebola virus outbreak in Guinea, West Africa. Because Ebola is so deadly and contagious, containment and isolation of those infected is vital to prevent an outbreak from becoming a pandemic. However, in 2014 the early public information campaign emphasised that 'Ebola kills' and 'there is no treatment for Ebola' but that if someone is ill to come to the Isolation Centres. This was counterproductive because when people experienced symptoms, they often hid them, or refused to cooperate with outbreak response teams. This accelerated the outbreak and it became the largest ever Ebola epidemic, costing over 11,000 lives. The outcome of the lessons learned have been a codification of the WHO's Emergency Response Framework providing guidance to member states on risk communication to improve the quality of the public campaigns to save lives.

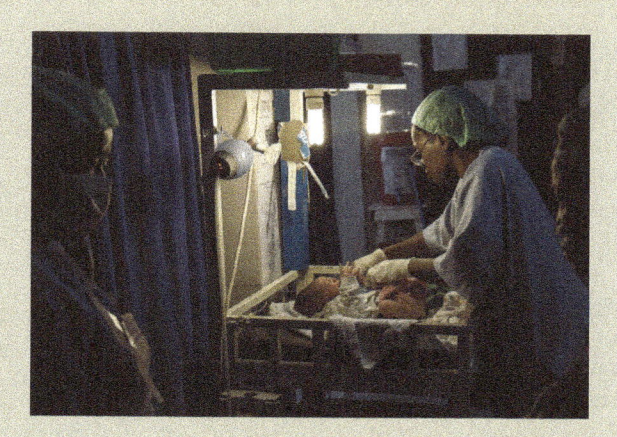

Picture 26.1 Providing medical care during disasters requires effective coordination between healthcare providers and communication experts (*source:* Lam Yik Fei/Getty Images)

The high stakes of health communication require a stakeholder relationship approach

Duncan's experiences in his work with disease outbreak and pandemics puts the potential impact that communications professionals can have into perspective – health communication when done well can save lives but when it does not match the needs of the populations affected it can not only risk being ineffective but costing lives. There are few work contexts that we, as communications professionals, have where our work can genuinely affect the course of people's lives. The health context is one of them. This means that we must be able to match the communication strategies that we develop and deploy with the specific needs of the populations we are trying reach. In short,

> **Explore 26.1**
>
> ## Thinking about your own health information needs
>
> Write down three to five health risks that you believe apply to you. This could be physical risks (e.g. allergies or injury from activities) or they could be mental health risks (e.g. anxiety or depression).
>
> For each one of them think about the last time that you heard any information about that issue. What was the source of the information and what was your reaction to that information? What impact did that information have on your own attitudes about the health risk?
>
> ### Feedback
>
> There are many different contexts in which we receive health information – from friends, entertainment-based media, advertisements, the news, and on social media. In most cases we were not looking for that information. Consider the implications of being exposed to information about health risks that you feel vulnerable to versus those you do not.

> **Explore 26.2**
>
> ## Stakeholders in the health context
>
> Stakeholders in any context represent those people or groups who can affect or be affected by an organisation. In the health context, stakeholders are tied to organisations because of health issues. For example, organisations within any health industry have stakeholders tied to them because the principle organisation mission is connected to health; however, organisations like manufacturers may have stakeholders tied to them because their work may affect the health of the surrounding communities.

the application of the public relations principles, theories and strategies discussed elsewhere in this text, that highlight the importance of communicating to specific audiences at specific times, have added importance in the context of public relations in health.

This chapter adopts a stakeholder relationship approach to discussing health communication because one of the lessons that has been learned in health communication is that it is not enough to get the message right, but the source of the message matters as well. For example, Bennett (1998) points out that trust between the communicator and the recipient is vital or the health risk message is likely to be ineffective – no matter whether the communicator is an organisation or particular healthcare provider. His research found that before a person even considers deciding whether the health risk applies to them, they will evaluate whether the source is trusted. In this context Bennett also argues that trust in health risk messages is no longer based on the expertise of the communicator (or organisation) but on a perception of openness, shared values and an overall assessment of their own susceptibility. In the 20 years since Bennett's piece was published, we argue these findings have only been magnified by the digital age. For example, in the digital age people increasingly mistrust health information unless it is delivered through interpersonal sources and credibility judgements are increasingly important to whether a piece of health information is viewed as credible (Spence et al. 2013).

In a very practical way, the credibility gap for health communicators makes the importance of a stakeholder relationship approach to health communication at the levels of the health practitioner as well as the traditional campaign even more important. We are in an era where the public demands different types of engagement; where Generations Y and Z expect all organisations to demonstrate better social responsibility, transparency and ethical decision making that is influencing not only the public relations practices, but also the organisation's core approaches to doing 'business' (Curtin et al. 2011). Public relations is even more vital to the total health communication process than at any time in the past. The stakeholder relationship model (see Diers-Lawson 2020) focuses on organisations building, maintaining and sometimes even repairing relationships with stakeholders in order to engage with them effectively and puts issues of mutual interest and impact (e.g. health) at the centre of the relationship. In a health context this has two clear implications. First, a stakeholder's attitude towards their health will affect what they expect from an organisation and how they judge that organisation. Second, similarly how an organisation performs regarding a health concern the stakeholder has will not only influence health outcomes for the stakeholders but also how readily the stakeholder engages with the organisation and its representatives (e.g. medical staff). Unlike traditional interpersonal relationships, it is important to keep in mind that stakeholder relationships are based on a stakeholder's vested interest with the health issues affecting them as well as the organisation or its representative communicating about those health issues.

Explore 26.3

Defining the stakeholder relationship model

The stakeholder relationship model identifies that organisations and stakeholders are connected together because of issues that affect both of them. Stakeholders judge organisations both based on their own connection to the issues as well as their evaluation of the organisation's performance regarding the issues.

The stakeholder relationship management model can be viewed as a recursive model (see Figure 26.1) beginning with the stakeholder's attitudes and beliefs about the state of their health and their ability to influence their health; this informs how they understand specific health issues and the types of evaluations they are likely to make about the information they receive about the issue from any organisation or healthcare practitioner. However, more than that, the stakeholder relationship model argues that their engagement with a health issue is also informed by their relationship with the organisation or practitioner communicating with them about the health issue.

The connection between stakeholders' relationships with organisations and communicating about health issues is well-established in both research and practice. For decades social campaigns designed to reduce teen and adult smoking were ineffective. Then inoculation theory was applied to the issue and was highly successful in targeting pre-teens to prevent them from starting smoking in their teens (Compton and Pfau 2009; Pfau et al. 1992). Inoculation theory introduces people to the undesirable messages (e.g. cigarette advertising at the time or peer pressure) and then provides rebuttals to those messages. However, the strategy was not nearly as successful when teens and young adults were exposed to the messaging (Pfau and Bockern 1994).

Clearly, a different approach was needed. In 1997 the four largest tobacco companies in the United States were successfully sued, in part for targeting children, teens and young adults with their advertising campaigns, and had to pay over $200 billion over 25 years. As a result, the American Legacy Foundation was created in order to try to reduce teen smoking (Apollonio and Malone 2009). The resulting campaign – the 'Truth' campaign – did something quite revolutionary, instead of targeting the health-related behaviour, the campaign targeted the tobacco industry's reputation and endeavoured to highlight that the industry's values were incongruent with those values held by young adults. The campaign emphasised 'truth' as their brand, suggesting the messages promoting cigarettes and smoking were lies and build the arguments that any messages offered by the tobacco industry were incomplete, misleading and inaccurate representations of both cigarettes and smoking. Attacking the reputation of the industry worked – following the multi-year campaign there was a significant reduction in teen and young adult smoking directly attributable to this approach (Eisenberg et al. 2004; Farrelly et al. 2005; Farrelly et al. 2002).

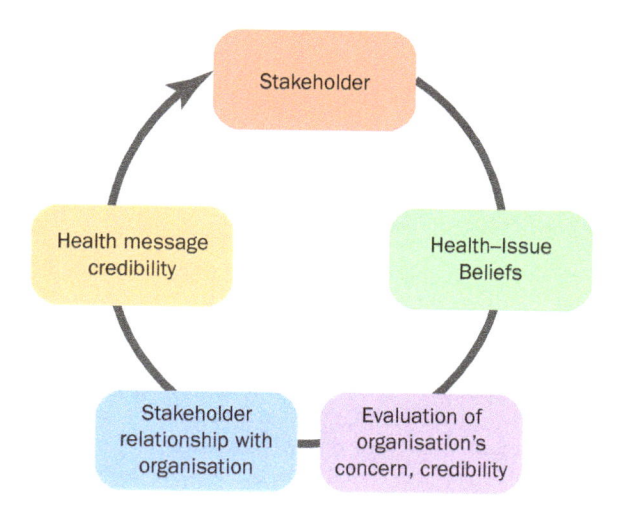

Figure 26.1 Diers-Lawson's (2020) stakeholder relationship management model applied to health communication

Explore 26.4

To boycott or not?

Think of an organisation that you are familiar with – it could be your local grocery shop, your favourite technology company, or even your favourite sports team or brand. Is there anything that would make you stop using them?

Feedback

Increasingly, people are interested in the ethics and values of organisations as a talisman of whether they want to offer their custom or patronage to those organisations. Yet, once we are already accustomed to using an organisation, we are often resistant to changing 'brands'. Thinking about your own ethical thresholds can help to better understand how people might more broadly connect to different organisations and the information they communicate.

When we consider the challenge that the lack of trust in institutions and experts diminishes the effectiveness of health communication and that health behaviours can be changed by changing an organisation's reputation, then this puts public relations squarely in the middle of what it means to do health communication in a modern, digital age. But more than that, it also means that by adopting a stakeholder relationship management perspective, the field of health communication can better interrogate the relationships between stakeholders, health issues, as well as the organisations and health practitioners communicating about those health issues with the stakeholders.

Using persuasion theory to better understand factors affecting the 'healthcare stakeholder'

Modern stakeholder research owes much of its work to the field of persuasion and in the field of communication, persuasion theories have guided health communication for years. Therefore, connecting health communication with a stakeholder perspective is about stakeholder research coming full-circle. This is the starting point for understanding a stakeholder perspective in health communication – the relationship between stakeholders and health issues. In health communication, one of the safest assumptions to make is that health issues are emotional and one of the critical components to channelling emotion into positive action is understanding how people may be triggered by different messaging from interpersonal to mass campaigns (Terblanche-Smit and Terblanch 2011). In the context of solving public health problems, amplifying the connection between the public, government and the particular health problem is often vital for the success of any effort to solve collective problems. One of the best examples of this in recent years has centred on the issue of obesity and the role that high-sugar drinks play in damaging public health. Gemma Bridge's research on the implementation of the 'sugar tax' on high-sugar beverages in the United Kingdom provides a good example of how communication campaigns can be used in tandem with policy actions to improve public health (see Box 26.1).

Moreover, the stakeholder perspective assumes that stakeholders' prior experience with issues and the

Box 26.1

Selling the sugar tax: communication lessons learned in the United Kingdom

Gemma Bridge's (Leeds Beckett University, UK) research on the successful implementation of the sugar tax in the United Kingdom (UK) provides critical transferrable lessons learned for creating successful public health campaigns.

What is the UK Soft Drink Industry Levy and why was it proposed?

Sugar sweetened beverages are one of the highest sources of sugar in the diet, especially in children (NDNS 2019; Azaïs-Braesco et al. 2017). Reflecting this, the World Health Organization (WHO) recommended

Picture 26.2 Sugary drinks are one of the highest sources of sugar in our diets, especially children's diets (*source*: Fotog/Getty Images)

the taxation of sugary drinks as a key strategy to reduce sugar consumption (WHO 2014). Since then, over 40 countries have implemented the taxation strategy with the United Kingdom adding the tax in 2018. Since the tax was introduced, many manufacturers have changed their recipes to lower the sugar in their drinks and sugar consumption from these drinks has reduced in the overall British population (Niblett et al. 2019), reflecting the same outcomes that have been achieved with the tax globally (Mitra 2019; Colchero et al. 2016; Caro et al. 2018; Alvarado et al. 2019).

Communication's vital role in implementing the sugar tax

Despite the WHO's recommendations and research supporting the use of taxes to reduce sugar consumption, the positive results are not guaranteed. Conflicts of interest between profit and social responsibility motivations within the beverage manufacturers along with the public health interests of reducing sugar consumption can function to diminish the effectiveness of the tax's objective to improve public health (Brownell and Warner 2009).

However, effective communication campaigns can improve the successful implementation of taxation strategies to reduce sugar consumption. For example, research on the implementation of the sugar tax in the UK demonstrates that with strategic and targeted advocacy the visibility of the health risks of consuming sugary drinks was improved and a greater sense of urgency for the public and policymakers to act to reduce sugar consumption was vital to the successful implementation of the tax strategy. The campaign was a multi-platform campaign targeting new and legacy media (e.g. newspapers, television, and social media) as well as formally lobbying the government (see also Chapter 20, Public affairs).

Transferrable lessons learned from the sugar tax campaign

The success of the campaign to implement the sugar tax is supported across different areas of health and public relations practice (see, e.g. Donaldson 2015) and therefore provides five transferrable lessons about creating successful public health campaigns:

1. **Build a strong evidence base.** Advocates highlighted the need to gather a strong research base in relation to the health impacts of sugar and the potential benefits of a sugar tax.

2. **Frame the issue successfully.** A frame provides a way to organise and present information in a way that is quickly recognisable for anyone who sees the information. In this way they function as a shortcut to help people understand new information quickly and easily. In this case, frames were used by advocates to draw attention to the issues and strategies that fitted with their policy preferences and emphasised the importance of societal value for individual health. They also were used to show common interests across different government departments and build cross-governmental support for the sugar tax.

3. **Develop weak ties and coalitions of actors.** Connecting with a range of actors was key to asserting influence in the policy arena and helped to develop the evidence and narrative around the urgency of acting to reduce sugar consumption in a holistic and authentic way. The different actors did not need to build enduring partnerships, but all participated together to work towards the single end. However, when different groups worked together, they were able to share evidence, resources and time to engage successfully with different media outlets. In a public policy context, this is essential to demonstrate a ground-swell of support for a policy objective and move that through to becoming law.

4. **Using consistent arguments.** The campaign for implementing the sugar tax used clear, simple and consistent arguments across actors, groups and platforms. Successfully executing a simple message strategy not only improved memorability of the message but also prevented information overload and attention fatigue.

5. **Employ policy entrepreneurs.** Nameless, faceless campaigns are often unsuccessful. The sugar tax campaign had recognisable public faces to put to the advocacy campaigns. Because these people were known to both the public and policy makers, their credibility enhanced the credibility of the campaign itself.

resulting issue-specific attitudes ultimately influences the relational quality with the organisation communicating but also how the stakeholder views the issue itself (Ki and Brown 2013). This is aligned with traditional persuasion and health communication models like the health belief model or social cognitive theory that emphasise the importance of understanding constructs such as perceived susceptibility, severity, issue beliefs and efficacy as key predictors to stimuli and situations (Diers-Lawson 2017, 2020; Diers 2012). Similarly, theories like the theory of planned behaviour assume that people typically behave sensibly and that our intentions to act (or not) are directly related to our existing attitudes, social norms and perceived situational control (Ajzen 2005). Taken together, these traditional health communication theories and stakeholder relationship approaches complement one another to help highlight the importance of stakeholder perceptions of their own control over situations and uncertainty perceptions that not only govern their reactions to issues but also towards the organisations connected to those issues (Jin et al. 2014; McDonald and Cokley 2013; Mou and Lin 2014).

While this chapter will not cover, in detail, all theories used in successful health campaigns, we will introduce three of the most widely applied theories – the theory of planned behaviour, elaboration likelihood model, and extended parallel process model – because while these theories have some common factors, their approaches to engaging stakeholders about health are all very different. This allows us to better explore how we can build from core attitudes about health care issues such as efficacy, peer pressure, demographics, threat, susceptibility and issue engagement to targeting key stakeholder attitudes about health issues to design messages – applied in both mass campaign and interpersonal contexts – to better engage with healthcare stakeholders.

(Chatzisarantis et al. 2009), and even predicting intentions to comply with food recall messages (Freberg 2013). The theory assumes that if we want to understand why people behave the way they do, we must first understand their behavioural intention (see Figure 26.2). Our intentions to act are influenced by three critical factors: attitudes, subjective norms and perceived behavioural control. In Ajzen's (2005) conceptualisation of TPB attitudes represent the combination of judgements that people make about the anticipated outcomes that enacting a behaviour will have along with whether people think the outcomes are generally positive. We can think of subjective norms as the combination of our interest in having particular individuals or groups think positively of us and our motivation to comply with other's judgements (Ajzen 2005). Finally, perceived behavioural control asks a very simple question: do we believe that we can perform a particular behaviour (i.e. self-efficacy) and a judgement about whether that behaviour will lead to desirable ends (i.e. response efficacy).

Theory of planned behaviour

In the context of health communication, the theory of planned behaviour (TPB, see Ajzen 2005) has been used in a number of different contexts such as promoting healthy eating (Povey et al. 2000; Tsorbatzoudis 2005), exercise (Payne et al. 2004), the importance of social support in the context of healthy lifestyles

Elaboration likelihood model

In the context of health communication, the elaboration likelihood model (ELM, see Petty and Cacioppo 1986), has been used to improve health outcomes across a wide variety of health issues including improving health literacy (Chiang and Jackson 2013); overcoming privacy concerns about putting health records online (Angst and Agarwal 2009); the selection of

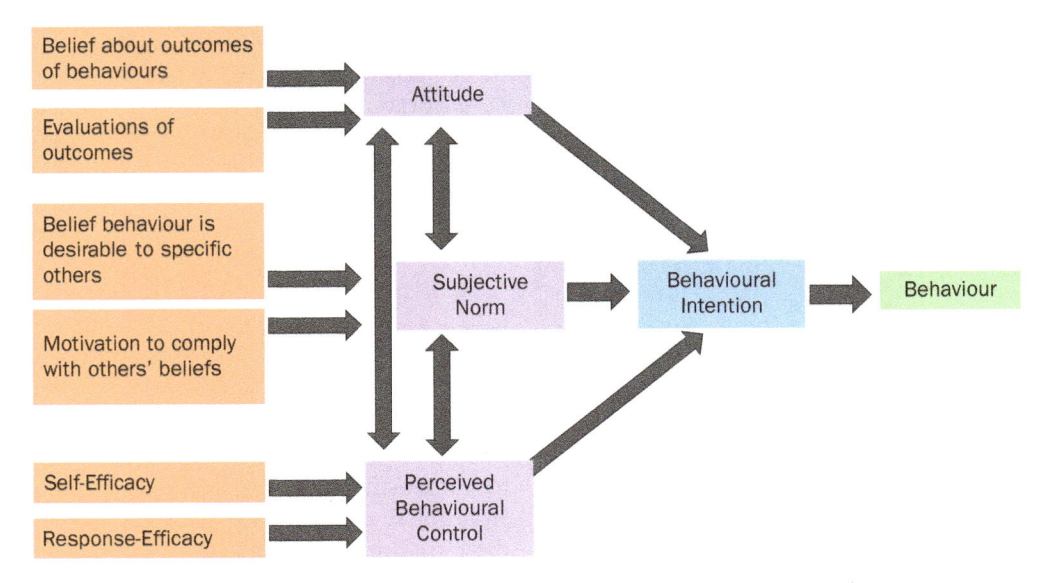

Figure 26.2 Adaptation of Ajzen's (2005) Theory of Planned Behaviour (*source:* Ajzen, I. (2005). Explaining intentions and behavior: Attitudes, personality, and behavior (Vol. 2nd). Berkshire, England: McGrawHill Education)

Think about 26.1 — Applying the theory of planned behaviour to getting a good night's sleep

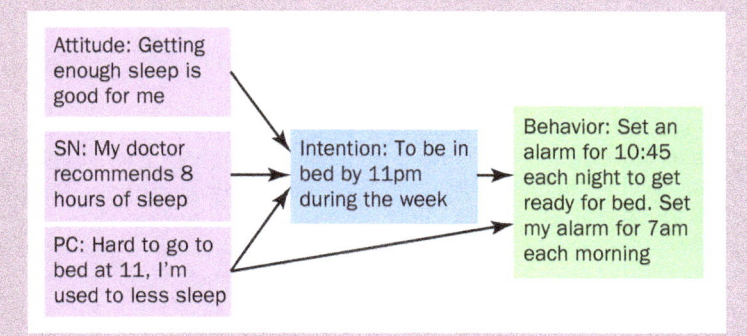

[Diagram: Attitude ("Getting enough sleep is good for me"), SN ("My doctor recommends 8 hours of sleep"), and PC ("Hard to go to bed at 11, I'm used to less sleep") → Intention ("To be in bed by 11pm during the week") → Behavior ("Set an alarm for 10:45 each night to get ready for bed. Set my alarm for 7am each morning")]

There are a lot of reasons (both good and bad) why people do not get good sleep at night. This is an application of a TPB approach to getting a good night's rest. Consider your own reaction to each of these points and then what you might need to change your behavioural intention.

Feedback

- If you reject the attitude, then consider what your attitude about a good night's sleep is – do you believe you need 8 hours' sleep? What do you define as a 'good night's sleep'? What is the benefit of getting a good night's sleep?

- If you have never discussed the importance of a good night's sleep with a doctor, then whose advice have you ever received or sought out? Did you care about that person's opinion? What kind of motivation did you have to comply with their recommendation?

- Finally, do you think you can control your ability to get a good night's sleep? Do you think that if you got a good night's sleep it would improve the following day? What factors might keep you from going to bed at a reasonable hour?

Each of these are the types of questions that the Theory of Planned Behaviour asks and that if we can diagnose across a specific population (e.g. college-aged students) what inhibits the behaviour or behavioural intention, then we have a reasonable starting point for a campaign.

---

doctors online (Cao et al. 2017); and to reducing risky health behaviours to prevent HIV (Dinoff and Kowalski 1999), smoking (Flynn et al. 2011) or drug abuse (Petty et al. 1991). ELM looks complicated (see Figure 26.3), but asks a simple question – how do people react to messages they are exposed to? If we understand the answer to that question, then we can better design messages that target how stakeholders react to health-related messages.

ELM (Petty and Cacioppo 1986) suggests that when people see a message they are either engaged by it or not. If they are highly involved with the message then

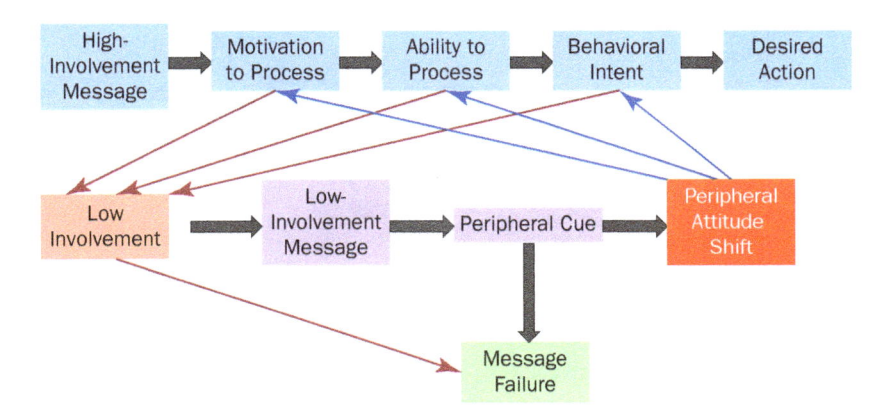

[Diagram: High-Involvement Message → Motivation to Process → Ability to Process → Behavioral Intent → Desired Action; Low Involvement → Low-Involvement Message → Peripheral Cue → Peripheral Attitude Shift; Low Involvement → Message Failure]

Figure 26.3 Adaptation of Petty and Cacioppo's (1986) elaboration likelihood model (*source:* Adapted from Petty, R. E., and Cacioppo, J. T. (1986). Message elaboration versus peripheral cues Communication and persuasion (pp. 141–172): Springer)

> **Explore 26.5**   **The next zombie apocalypse?**
>
> The United States Center for Disease Control recognised that disaster preparedness messages were not working – that most people were ignoring them, especially online. At the height of the popularity of the *Walking Dead* series and zombie stories in popular culture, they introduced a zombie apocalypse all-disaster-preparedness campaign to use humour to try to engage their audience. However, Fraustino and Ma (2015) found that while the zombie apocalypse messages resulted in significantly weaker intentions to take proactive disaster actions compared to traditional non-humorous risk messages. If you consider this within the context of ELM, would you evaluate this campaign as a failure?
>
> **Feedback**
>
> As you consider your answer to that question, consider the reason to introduce the campaign – people were simply not engaging with disaster preparedness. Consider whether the type of person that traditional non-humorous messages would appeal to compared to the type of person that would benefit from the zombie apocalypse campaign are the same or different types of health stakeholders.

they are motivated to process it and if they can understand the information, then it is likely to inform their intention to act, and thus their behaviours. However, ELM also acknowledges that not everyone is always going to be interested in or engaged with the messages they come across. This means that health communicators may have to catch their attention because they have low involvement with the message or issue. ELM is very commonly used in advertising precisely because it emphasises that communicators often have to catch their target audience's attention, especially in a crowded and chaotic message environment (Pasadeos et al. 2008). If a communicator is successful in catching their target audience's attention, then it is possible to get them into the high involvement processing route. The model also points out that one of the key reasons that people do not follow through is because they do not have the capacity to understand the information. This suggests that even if people are motivated and interested in the health issue if they do not understand the science or the information they will disengage, which is why campaigns can target health literacy using ELM to get them back on the high involvement path.

Extended parallel process model

With the previous two theories we have examined, we have learned more about the core factors that motivate our attitudes, the influence of other people in our decision-making, our sense of empowerment and our need to create engaging stakeholder-oriented messages. However, we have not effectively engaged emotion, yet this was one of our critical assumptions – that healthcare is inherently an emotive topic. In no small measure, one of the critical emotions that is triggered by health-related issues is fear or apprehension. As such, in the context of health communication, the extended parallel process model (EPPM, see Witte 1996) represents a convergence of many of the factors emerging in other theories but adding fear into understanding health communication and campaigns (see Figure 26.4). EPPM has been used successfully to

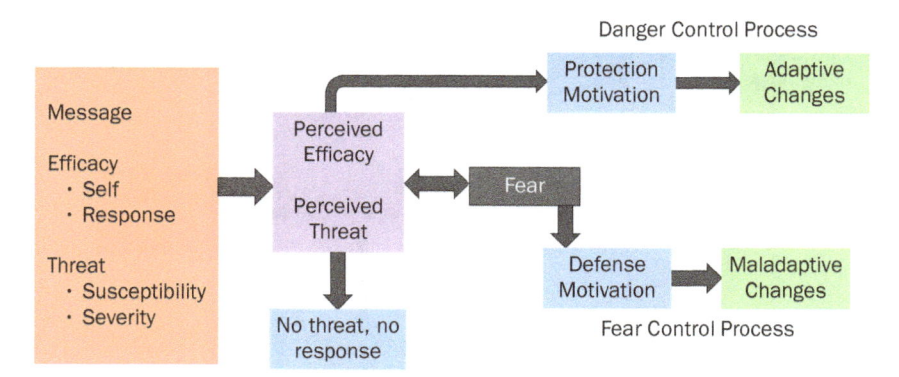

Figure 26.4 Adaptation of Witte's (1996) extended parallel process model (*source:* Adapted from Witte, K. (1996). Generating effective risk messages: How scary should your risk communication be? Communication Yearbook, 18, 229–254)

motivate behavioural changes in a variety of health contexts such as improving the use of hearing protection amongst farmers and landscape workers (Smith et al. 2008), improving mammography screening in vulnerable populations (Russell et al. 2007), and with some of the most profound results in reducing HIV/AIDS risk behaviours (Poppen and Reisen 1997; Terblanche-Smit and Terblanch 2011).

EPPM built on the health belief model (Rosenstock et al. 1988) that was developed in the 1950s by social psychologists trying to predict and design messages to improve healthy behaviours incorporating efficacy, demographics, existing attitudes along with perceptions of severity and susceptibility to the health issue in order to influence behavioural intention. Instead of focusing on social cues like TPB or whether people are interested in a message like ELM, the health belief model focused on fear and how to trigger people to act. It acknowledges that when it comes to changing health behaviours, we are often asking people to change behaviours that are a part of their routine or involve behaviours they like (e.g. eating, relaxing, and so on) and if they are not motivated to change, they probably will not. That is why the trigger is necessary and often tied to fear-based emotions.

Witte's (1996) EPPM built on the health belief model by not only refining our understanding of the influence of threat to people but also the role of strategic messaging in the process. As one of the few explicitly communication theories developed and applied in health communication, messages that people are exposed to are at the core of the model. One of Witte's key contributions was also identifying a curvilinear relationship between fear and motivations to act. What does a curvilinear relationship mean? In this case, that fear motivates people to take proactive steps to protect themselves from a negative outcome (i.e. the danger control process) resulting in adaptive changes to their behaviours, but only to a point. If people feel too afraid, instead of being motivated to act, the fear itself becomes crippling and in order to protect themselves people will take actions to reduce their fear (i.e. the fear control process) resulting in maladaptive changes to their behaviours. This suggests that while we can use fear to motivate it must be used cautiously and by understanding our stakeholder's relationship with the issue but most importantly that all behavioural change messages using fear as a motivator must include an efficacy component to ensure that the targeted stakeholder still believes they could make a productive change to lead to better health outcomes.

> **Think about 26.2**
>
> **Applying the extended parallel process model to heart disease**
>
> Consider the case of messages to reduce people's risk for heart disease through exercise. One simple message that can be used is: *20 minutes of cardiovascular exercise four times per week can significantly reduce your risk of heart disease.* Applying EPPM to this message, what kind of threat, efficacy, and fear considerations might influence whether this message is successful?
>
> **Feedback**
>
> - What about a low threat (i.e. low susceptibility) context? For example, what if someone's response were, 'Heart disease does not run in my family' or 'Many people with heart disease live normal lives'?
>
> - What about a high threat (i.e. high susceptibility), but low efficacy context? For example, if someone acknowledge that heart disease runs in their family and that it can be fatal, but also believed that exercise alone is not sufficient or that they did not have the time to exercise as recommended?
>
> - What about a high threat (i.e. high susceptibility) and high efficacy context? For example, if someone acknowledged that heart disease runs in their family and that it can be fatal, but also believed that exercise can prevent heart disease AND they have the time?
>
> Apply each of these contexts to the model to consider what additions or changes to the message might be needed in order to successfully engage each of these three types of audience more effectively.

The crossover between mass campaigns and interpersonal health communication

Another reason to adopt a stakeholder perspective in health communication focuses on an organisation's performance – that is whether an organisation or its representatives (e.g. doctors, health communicators and nurses) are meeting stakeholder expectations. The stakeholder relationship model (Diers-Lawson 2017, 2020) argues that part of an organisation's credibility on issues is determined by stakeholder evaluations of its competence, or its capacity to successfully serve the stakeholder's needs (de Fatima Oliveira 2013; Hyvärinen and Vos 2015; Sohn and Lariscy 2014).

Increasingly the lines between mass communication and interpersonal communication are being blurred as social media is being used to improve overall health outcomes for patients. For example, health organisations are increasingly using social media strategically in order to communicate about public health crises like Ebola, natural disasters or the 2020 COVID-19 pandemic (Freberg et al. 2013; Guidry et al. 2017; Sutton et al. 2015). This still represents a traditional mass campaign approach to health communication grounded in persuasion as we discussed. However, social media is allowing health organisations to learn more about the public health concerns that the public has. For example, Lazard et al. (2015) discuss the use of data mining techniques on Twitter in order to gain intelligence about public concerns about particular diseases and be able to better inform and direct information needs about health crises as they are emerging. Similarly, there have been significant efforts in the contexts of risk, disaster and health communication to use social media to help close the information gaps between agencies and people. Some of the critical findings suggest: (1) that social media can be useful in helping to close the gap in people's critical information needs about health (Sjöberg et al. 2013; Wukich and Mergel 2015); (2) improving people's preparedness for epidemics and disasters by improving risk awareness and proactive self-protection (Brynielsson et al. 2014; Dalrymple et al. 2016; Lachlan et al. 2014, Sellnow et al. 2015; Verroen et al. 2013); and (3) recommendations for using social media to build or rebuild trust in health institutions, like hospitals, in the wake of crises that shake stakeholder trust in the institutions (DiStaso et al. 2015).

However, there is a new body of research suggesting that instead of viewing social media as a tool by public health organisations to merely disseminate information and manage institutional reputations, social media can be used for direct multi-way conversations about health in order to more directly improve people's individual health outcomes (Heldman et al. 2013). For example, the National Health Service (NHS, in England and Wales) has found that that one of the critical challenges in reducing obesity is that campaigns to promote healthy eating often have limited success because people still feel isolated and unmotivated; however, creating social support networks on social media platforms provides people with ongoing support and feedback within a local area (Thomas 2009). This case supports broader findings that using social media as a tool for direct health interventions and social support provides low cost, accessible and improved approaches to better affecting public health outcomes for different publics (Bennet and Glasgow 2009; Shan et al. 2015).

Taken together, this suggests that the role for public relations practitioners is firmly grounded in the opportunities connected to mass campaigns but also applies to supporting interpersonal health communication as more of our engagement with health issues exists in a social media environment. However, one of the consistent challenges we face in a social media environment is about source credibility, sharing quality information and responding to so-called 'fake news' and scaremongering about public health concerns (Rutsaert et al. 2013). This challenge is coupled with an environment where trust in health institutions and the overall medical establishment has been eroding for decades. For example, Bruhn (2001) explains that in the health context increases in costs, problems of accessibility of healthcare and changes in the structures of health organisations have all eroded public faith in health organisations, pointing out that the disillusionment about healthcare comes from both the public and the medical practitioners alike. He also argues that medical practice has failed to provide leadership in education and disease prevention, instead focusing on diagnosing and curing disease which often fails to consider the increasing social, emotional and financial costs of illness and ignores ways to enhance total health. Further, research has found that the trust deficit in healthcare is more acute for minority populations compared to white populations, suggesting that structural inequalities in access and quality of care erodes the potential for outreach to often the most vulnerable communities (Halbert et al. 2006).

A stakeholder approach may blur the lines between mass campaign and individual health outcomes may well help to not only improve specific health outcomes for people but also heal the trust deficit that has emerged in the context of public health. For example, research suggests that the type of two-way social media engagement that provides information and support for people managing health problems also improves trust in institutions (Warren et al. 2014). Providing good information that is accessible at the stakeholder's convenience improves trust in the organisation as well as improving information seeking and sharing behaviours even amongst those with the least trust health organisations (DiStaso et al. 2015). Providing readily shareable information in social media is also vital for reaching those populations that mistrust health institutions.

Box 26.2

The American response to the 2020 COVID-19 pandemic: The deadly impact of mixed messages and 'Fake News'

The COVID-19 pandemic affected all corners of the world and as the world searched for answers as to how to contain its spread and to 'flatten the curve' to allow healthcare systems to catch up with the infection rate and ultimately mitigate the health, economic, social and political implications of the virus, one country had a distinctively different response to the crisis than others – the United States. Across platforms and organisations within the United States the response was inconsistent. One of the critical sources of misinformation about the pandemic, its spread and the overall situation was President Trump with statements that initially downplayed the risk associated with the virus, declaring in early March 2020 that the pandemic would disappear. Then, instead of following other national leaders, Trump's communication both in his daily press conferences and his Twitter account took a different approach. He focused on shifting the blame to calling it the 'Chinese Virus'; suggested that healthcare providers may have been stealing personal protective equipment (PPE), while claiming there was plenty available if states 'were nice to him'; declaring that an untested malaria treatment, 'light', and disinfectant might be effective treatments for the disease; and then fuelling protests against social distancing and 'lockdown' measures in place in different states. In many of his messages, he directly contradicted health officials, state governors, and ultimately cut American funding for the World Health Organization accusing them of bad information and colluding with China to hide the nature and origins of the pandemic. Despite the many documented examples of misinformation spread by the President during this pandemic, many of his daily press conferences involved calling media members 'fake news' or 'nasty' directly fostering mistrust in information from those outlets amongst his supporters.

In this chapter, we have discussed a practitioner's perspective (see Box 26.1) on the risks of bad health messaging costing people's lives and we have just discussed both the possibilities of using different media platforms for promoting health messages along with potential trust deficits facing healthcare organisations. The American response to the COVID-19 pandemic, lead primarily by President Trump and in combination with complementary messaging from Fox News, provides the context to evaluating the genuine risks of getting the messaging wrong during health crises. In a preliminary study and working paper presented by the Becker Friedman Institute for Economics at the University of Chicago, the authors found that in a comparison between Sean Hannity and Tucker Carlson – both Fox News presenters – that Hannity viewers were significantly less likely to follow social distancing guidelines and there were higher local rates of infection and death (Bursztyn et al. 2020). While neither host supported public health recommendations for social distancing, Hannity's content was more aligned with President Trump's rhetoric and based on early data correlates with pockets of higher infection and death.

In years to come, the differences in messaging and actions will be interrogated as will the global responses, but for now the death rates tell a very clear story (see Figure 26.5). China initiated strict measures to control and contain the virus because it was first hit and had the capacity to create and manage the outbreak. Italy was dramatically affected because it was the first European country with a severe outbreak but flattened the rate of transmissions and was able to begin to reduce social control measures. Germany and New Zealand likewise acted swiftly and communicated clear messages based on the lessons learned by the pandemic in China and Italy. The British government, like the United States, was slow to respond and there have been critiques of its decision-making. In the UK's case, the material response was the critical problem compared to the communication problem. Despite the differences in the other countries, all communicated clear messages based on emerging practice. Yet, what is also evident is that poor communication coupled with poor action has cost lives in the United States making it the country that is the most affected by COVID-19.

This section focuses on the value of the crossover between mass campaigns, interpersonal health information, and the distinctive role that public relations can play. However, COVID-19 provides a brutal reminder of the important role that good decision-making and public relations both play in managing public health crises and saving lives.

box 26.2 (continued)

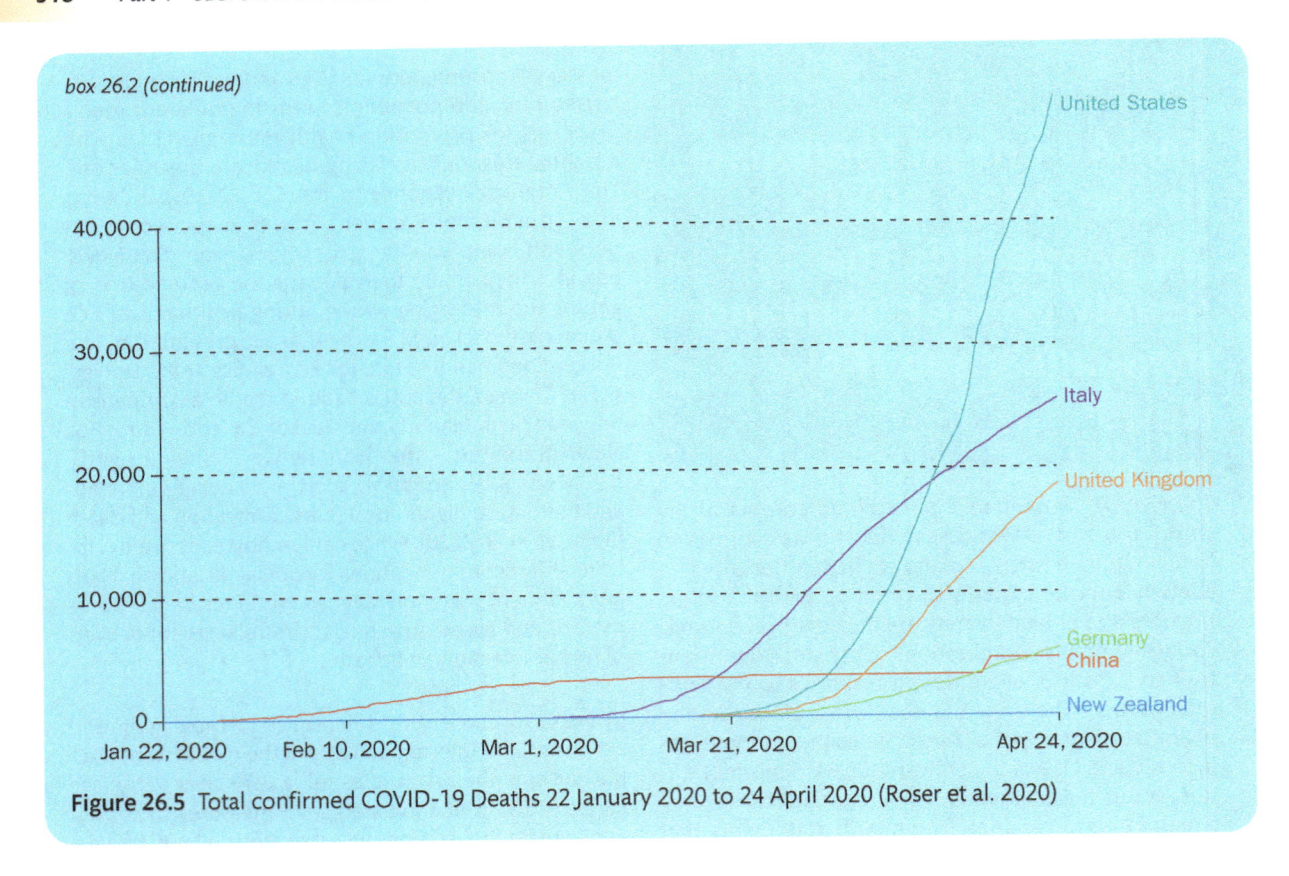

Figure 26.5 Total confirmed COVID-19 Deaths 22 January 2020 to 24 April 2020 (Roser et al. 2020)

Those populations that are the least likely to trust institutions are also most likely to seek out health information from interpersonal contacts and they actively seek out health information from people they know across different social media platforms (Spence et al. 2013). If we put it all together, the role for public relations in the transition between mass communication and individual health outcomes is clear – we are well positioned to create shareable messages, engage in two-way social media-based conversations, and develop communities of support connected to specific health issues.

Explore 26.6   The anti-vaccination debate

In the last several years, the anti-vaccination movement has gained momentum – largely because of social media. It is easier for people who believe that vaccinations can be harmful – especially to children – to find information that seems credible online. Because that information also calls into question the credibility of health institutions that were already viewed as suspect, the viability of the anti-vaccination arguments seems even more credible. Once the belief that vaccinations are harmful takes hold, it is difficult to change and is not helped by other voices online who would demonise and demean anti-vaccination advocates. As a result of the increasing movement away from immunisation, there have been substantial increases in reports of measles and other preventable diseases worldwide. The WHO provides a summary of the controversy and common misconceptions about vaccinations (see World Health Authority). How could a public relations approach – both at the campaign and individual intervention levels of engagement – be created to meaningfully engage anti-vaccination advocates? Will the COVID-19 pandemic and the disruptions to everyone's lives possibly change anti-vaccination advocates or vaccination hesitant people's perspectives on the importance of vaccinations?

Feedback

As you consider your response, be sure to think about the theories that could be helpful, the potential benefits of two-way communication, of creating shareable information, and interpersonal networks all to not only improve vaccination rates but also to improve the trust in health institutions.

Two-way symmetrical communication in healthcare

Ask a friend or colleague to describe a 'good experience' at a hospital or in any medical facility. Chances are that the description will not be positive. Amongst people who narrate a good experience, it is likely related to events like child birth or life-saving treatments. We seldom hear about the service experience of a medical institution. Yet, we will always hear about the problems and negative outcomes for hospitals. This is one of the reasons that trust in medical institutions has gone down over the decades (Bruhn 2001) and that traditional approaches to managing reputation like apology and sympathy for those affected can further damage the affected hospital (DiStaso et al. 2015). When we shift our focus from mass campaigns and even social media-based support settings for improving health outcomes to the healthcare sector in real time, then the need for a dialogic communication paradigm from the institutional level to the health care practitioner level becomes even more clear. But first, it is important to broadly understand the healthcare sector and the typical risks facing healthcare organisations.

Understanding the healthcare sector

The healthcare sector includes three parts: healthcare delivery (including hospitals), pharmaceuticals and medical technology (i.e. devices, diagnostic tools, etc.) (Cutlip et al. 2004; Porter and Teisberg 2006). Healthcare itself then can be segmented into primary, secondary and tertiary care. Primary care emphasises outpatient treatment (e.g. routine general practitioner visits), secondary care refers to hospitalisation for non-critical ailments, and tertiary care refers to specialised consultative care that includes referral from primary and/or secondary care providers but is delivered by specialists (e.g. cancer care, surgeons, and so on) working in a facility designed for those critical and specialised needs (Porter and Teisberg 2006). Most countries have a mixture of public and private healthcare systems – in some countries private systems run parallel to public ones, but in many countries these systems have some degree of mixture of public and private facilities, providers, and partnerships (Porter and Teisberg 2006).

While varying across different countries' models for healthcare, there are some long-emergent trends and challenges in healthcare and the reputation of hospitals and other healthcare facilities that are relatively universal. For example, for the last 20 years hospitals have increasingly struggled with regulations, rising operational costs, new technologies, and changing patient needs and expectations and so hospitals have found that they need help in communicating with a variety of publics in order to help meet their organisational goals as well as social expectations (Baskin et al. 1997; Bruhn 2001; DiStaso et al. 2015; Halbert et al. 2006; Hayek et al. 2014; Makarem and Al-Amin 2014). The stakeholder mix for hospitals is complex (see Figure 26.6), but this is what creates the public relations challenges for hospitals and health care facilities.

Risks in the healthcare sector

Broadly speaking there are three types of risks to most organisations: (1) those directly related to the organisation's 'business' (e.g. social policy, environmental policy, quality of products or services); (2) those related to the organisation's actions that are incompatible with the organisation's values or value proposition; and (3) those actions that are incompatible with the public's values or zeitgeist of the moment (Anthonissen 2008). Organisations within the healthcare sector face a number of specific risks or challenges including issues like accusations of medical negligence, inappropriate staff behaviour, labour actions, site risks (e.g. power failures, building suitability), biomedical waste disposal, staffing, adequate patient care access, or even conflicts arising because of patients or their friends and family (Porter and Teisberg 2006). Moreover, in the communication age digital engagement also affects doctors and healthcare facilities. For example, ratings for doctors and healthcare facilities on digital platforms are emerging as an important influence for patient decisions and care expectations – that online ratings predict underlying consumer perceived quality (Gao et al. 2015), the selection of doctors and facilities (Cao et al. 2017), and that an overwhelming majority of people are looking online for information about healthcare providers (Wallace et al. 2014).

The need for dialogue in strategy and practice

Not surprisingly, given the complex communications environment for healthcare as an industry, the opportunities and de facto requirements for two-way engagement, we argue that public relations principles already

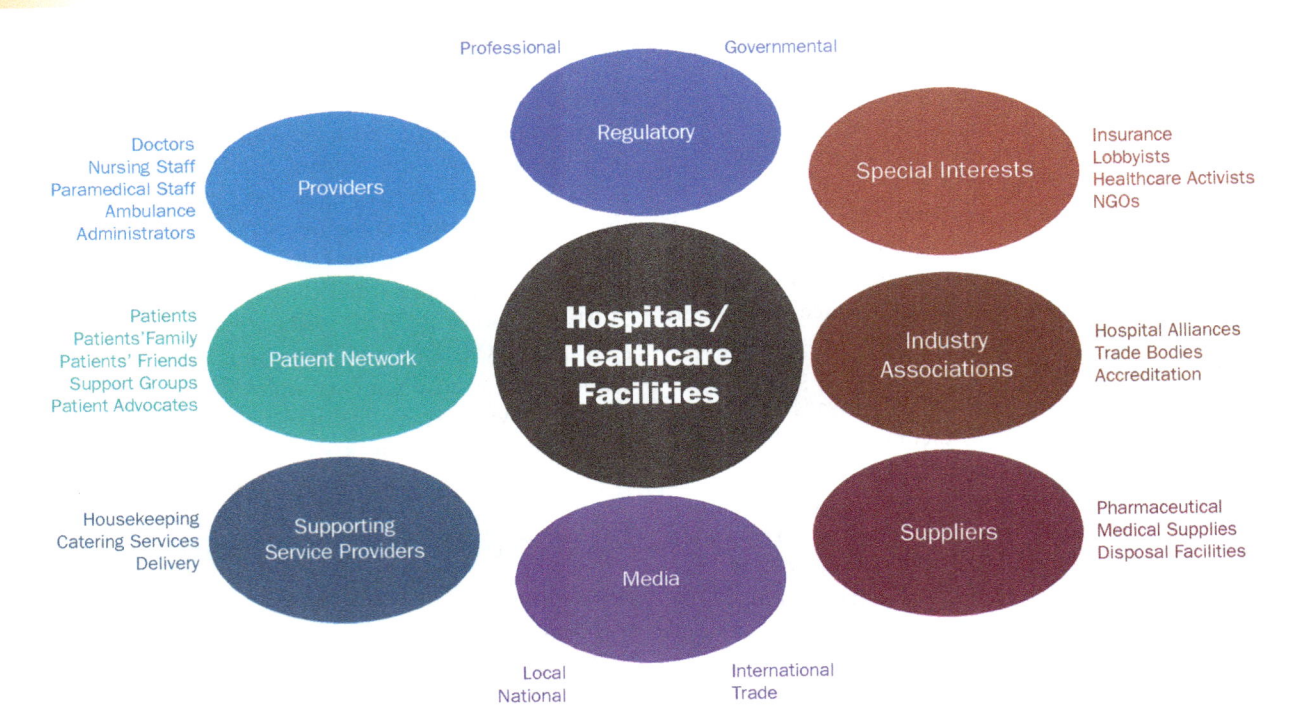

Figure 26.6 Examples of the complex stakeholder environment facing healthcare

Think about 26.3 — Considering the structure of healthcare in your country

How the healthcare industry is structured in different countries will present fundamentally different opportunities and stressors on the system based on different stakeholder needs. In the United Kingdom healthcare is devolved to the different nations in the UK – i.e. England and Wales, Scotland, and Northern Ireland all run their own version of the National Health Service (NHS). While the core principles of the NHS remain consistent across all of the UK's countries, there are also critical differences. One of the critical differences between the NHS in England and Wales compared to Scotland is how social services are integrated into the system and how that affects vulnerable populations (see Scottish Parliament Information Centre). For example, as flu season hits the UK in December and January one of the consistent challenges is a lack of beds in hospitals to accommodate all of those affected – largely the elderly and young who are most likely to suffer complications that require hospitalisation. In many cases, the elderly may be healthy enough to leave the hospital, but not able to care for themselves yet and cannot return home. In England, there is no structural mechanism to help move those elderly into temporary care homes to accommodate their needs. However, by linking social services to healthcare in Scotland, the problem is better able to be addressed because elderly patients can more readily be moved to temporary care homes, freeing up beds in hospitals.

Feedback

- Think about your own country's healthcare system. What are the structures that affect (either positively or negatively) the experiences of vulnerable populations?

- Would this connection between social services and healthcare be possible in fully privatised healthcare systems? One of the core differences in how people experience health care depends on whether the system is public or private.

Try to use your own healthcare system to identify what basic healthcare structures may improve the ease of healthcare delivery to different groups and create challenges to different groups.

play a vital role in healthcare but should play an increasing role at all levels of provision. Newsome and Hayes (2007) point out that public relations practitioners are problem finders, solvers and hopefully preventers because at the core of the work that we do is issue management and stakeholder relationship management. This has long been the argument about the core value that public relations serves organisations – that we ought to be able to build long-term strategic relationships with our publics to better enable our organisations to meet their missions (Fombrun 1996). In a healthcare context Grunig and Grunig (1991) argued that while many healthcare organisations adopted marketing models (i.e. one-way information dissemination) for communicating with their stakeholders as part of a cost-cutting measure, the resulting communication strategy would not be as successful as a communication strategy grounded in public relations theory. In a modern era of health communication, as we have noted earlier in this chapter, the principle of dialogue or two-way communication is used in social media engagement between healthcare providers and stakeholders across different platforms (Hether 2014). In fact, a US-based national survey found a strong correlation between excellence in hospital performance and those hospitals using dialogic approaches to communication with stakeholders, particularly regarding hospital management and strategic planning (Gordon and Kelly 1999).

Understanding different models for communication and public relations

While we have already discussed theories for developing persuasive messages in health contexts, we also need to discuss the broad strategic priorities and models for public relations that can emerge in organisational settings. Grunig and Hunt (1984) identified four different broad models that guide public relations programmes, strategies and tactics – press agent/publicity, public information, two-way asymmetrical model and the two-way symmetrical model. In this way, they identified two one-way and two two-way models for communication between organisations and their publics. One-way communication models focus on an organisation speaking to or at their stakeholders with little interaction and two-way communication models highlight dialogue as a critical component to the communication dynamic between organisations and stakeholders. Later, Grunig and Grunig (1991) would describe one-way communication as the core strategic approach in marketing and advertising compared to two-way communication as the core strategic approach for public relations. Similarly, Austin and Pinkleton (2015) argue that one-way flows of information and message distribution should not be considered strategic communication management because communication programmes should be designed to influence knowledge, attitudes and behaviours not simply to broadcast information. However, they point out that the two-way asymmetrical model of communication focuses on 'engineering consent' by using persuasion to influence audiences to behave as an organisation desires and represents only short-term strategy.

In the context of healthcare, therefore the two-way symmetrical model of communication is the best approach for organisations to engage their critical stakeholders (Grunig and Grunig 1991). The two-way symmetrical model is based on the principles of negotiation and dispute resolution where both the organisation and the stakeholders are viewed to be engaged in a transaction rather than an exchange. This model is commonly discussed in terms of dialogic communication and is one of the reasons that Kent and Taylor (2002) frame the concept of dialogue in public relations as both an ethical and practical approach to public relations. In viewing public relations as a dialogue between the organisation and its stakeholders, then one of the core assumptions in interactions between the two is that the relationships between organisations and stakeholders should serve both sets of interests (Kent and Taylor 2002); in fact, this view would argue that organisations exist to serve the stakeholder interests (Heath 2002).

Implications of the dialogic approach in healthcare provision

We have already seen the clear implications of a dialogic approach to healthcare in terms of mass communication, support and social media engagement. However, the value of good communication at the level of interactions between healthcare practitioners (e.g. doctors and nurses) and patients is also vital. Public relations has a role in supporting practitioners' ability to engage effectively with their patients and to help manage the practitioner/patient relationship. Consistently, research suggests that patient empowerment and improved dialogue with clinicians – no matter whether that is incorporated into shared decision-making models, routine patient/practitioner interactions or emphasising patient desires in treatment – improves health outcomes in clinical practice (Callon

Picture 26.3 Good healthcare is built on the dialogic approach between healthcare providers and their patients (*source:* Shutterstock)

et al. 2018; Castro et al. 2016; Herring et al. 2017; Polonsky et al. 2017). For example, in a study of more than 3000 people from 26 countries focusing on the influence of effective doctor/patient communication when diagnosed with type 2 diabetes, patients report that a stronger dialogue with their doctor improved their understanding of the diagnosis and led to greater patient well-being and self-care to manage their disease (Polonsky et al. 2017).

In theory, doctors in primary and secondary care settings report strong personal commitments to incorporating patient feedback into improving the quality of the care and conversations provided; however, in practice they also often express strong negative views about the credibility and competence of patient feedback in post-care surveys (Farrington et al. 2017); however, there is less known about their attitudes towards face-to-face patient feedback. Yet, in many contexts the asymmetry in information and knowledge between medical staff, patients and their families may explain the basis of breakdowns in the communication and relationships between them in healthcare settings. In extreme cases, these breakdowns in the relationships between medical professionals and their patients seem to be leading to increased violence or threats of violence worldwide with measurable changes in most countries (Ambesh 2016; Johansen et al. 2017; Kapoor 2017; Kaya et al. 2016). Box 26.3 provides a critical case to better understand some of the causes and public relations-related recommendations for addressing the types of breakdowns in dialogue between doctors, patients and their families that can lead to violence by focusing on India – where violence and threats of violence to doctors has grown to a near epidemic proportion (Ambesh 2016).

Box 26.3

The case of violence against doctors in India

Noumaan Qureshi's (University of Mumbai, India) research on violence against doctors in India points to some critical lessons learned about risk management and public relations for managing the medical professional/patient relationship.

India's healthcare services rely on both public and private systems. However, about 70 per cent of healthcare is provided by the private sector and it is expensive. In fact, in India like many countries with private healthcare systems, it is one of the principle reasons for indebtedness that often pushes people into poverty. In research on private hospitals in Mumbai, Qureshi found that there was information asymmetry with billing transparency and treatment clarity being the biggest concerns for stakeholders in the private hospitals. Moreover, the findings demonstrate that while doctors are rated as the most respected professionals, descriptions of doctors are harsh amongst people who come from lower socio-economic status reflecting the economic stressors that are placed on poorer patients seeking medical care.

As a context for the upsurge in violence against doctors in India, the core risks should be clear – there is a perfect storm of financial stress, emotional stress associated with medical care, and an apparent lack of two-way symmetrical communication between hospitals, doctors and patients or their families. Based on in-depth interviews, three clear patterns emerge – the doctors facing the brunt of the violence are younger, emergency and critical care departments are most likely to experience violence as a result of emotional shock from families, and in most incidents violence involves more than one person being present.

How can we understand these patterns? First and foremost, we have to understand that violence against doctors is not new, but the frequency has increased and legislation is ineffective in preventing it from occurring primarily because violent incidents are typically emotional outbursts and not pre-meditated attacks. Second, medical organisations lack credibility and perceptions of goodwill by public stakeholders – that is to say they have a poor reputation – which means that they do not have the credibility to deal with the issue effectively. Third, doctors are not provided training in communication as part of their regular curriculum despite their work being patient facing and involving highly emotional contexts for interacting with patients and their families. In the in-depth interviews, there was a clear lack of two-way symmetrical communication between doctors, their patients, and especially the families. For example, a consistent finding was that doctors often fail to communicate empathy for the patient and/or the situation and are, instead, often viewed as aloof for failing to engage with the families which is interpreted as condescending behaviour.

Two factors emerged as likely to diffuse emotions leading to the violent behaviour towards doctors. First, violence was less likely when families received an adequate explanation of the medical condition their loved one had and where the medical staff maintained clear lines of communication with family members. Second, doctors who were able to assess factors like attire, body language and behaviour in wards were less likely to experience violence and build better relationships with their patients.

These findings clearly suggest that violence against doctors includes both infrastructure or organisational frustrations as well as communication gaps. One of the critical questions becomes – who is the custodian of communication on behalf of the doctors? Certainly, doctors need better training in core communication competencies, but also maintaining clear lines of communication with families represents an opportunity for hospitals and medical facilities to have staff who are trained in patient and family outreach.

Summary

Herein lies both the opportunity and challenges for health communication in the twenty-first century – building better relationships between medical staff, institutions and their critical stakeholders. This is needed at the doctor or nurse/patient level, at the institutional level, and certainly at the mass communication levels of engagement. This carves out a distinctive role for the field of public relations and strategic communication along the way because we can serve as the custodians of communication on behalf of doctors, nurses and medical establishments online and face-to-face in order to not only build competency to mitigate the breakdown of relationships with stakeholders but to build better relationships with all stakeholders, but especially the patients. Taken together this means that with better communication strategy critical health outcomes can be improved, as we have seen in both social media and face-to-face contexts and risks or problems can be better managed.

Discussion in this chapter has focused on:

- the need for a stakeholder relationship approach to health communication;
- using persuasion theory to better understand factors affecting healthcare stakeholders;
- the crossover between mass campaigns and doctor or nurse/patient communication;
- the value of two-way symmetrical communication in healthcare.

Bibliography

Alvarado, M. et al. (2019). Assessing the Impact of the Barbados Sugar-Sweetened Beverage Tax on Beverage Sales: An Observational Study. *International Journal of Behavioral Nutrition and Physical Activity*, 16(1), 13.

Ajzen, I. (2005). *Explaining intentions and behavior: Attitudes, personality, and behavior* (Vol. 2nd). Berkshire, England: McGraw-Hill Education.

Ambesh, P. (2016). Violence against doctors in the Indian subcontinent: A rising bane. *Indian Heart Journal*, 68(5), 749–750.

Anderson, M.A. and L.B. Helms (2000). Talking about patients: Communication and continuity of care. *The Journal of Cardiovascular Nursing*, 14(3), 15–28.

Angst, C.M., and R. Agarwal (2009). Adoption of electronic health records in the presence of privacy concerns: The elaboration likelihood model and individual persuasion. *MIS quarterly*, 33(2), 339–370.

Anthonissen, P. (2008). *Crisis Communication: Practical PR strategies for reputation management and company survival*. London: Kogan Page Publishers.

Apollonio, D.E. and R.E. Malone (2009). Turning negative into positive: Public health mass media campaigns and negative advertising. *Health Education Research*, 24(3), 483–495.

Austin, E.W. and B.E. Pinkleton (2015). *Strategic Public Relations Management: Planning and managing effective communication campaigns*. Routledge.

Azaïs-Braesco, V. et al. (2017). A Review of Total & Added Sugar Intakes and Dietary Sources in Europe. *Nutrition Journal*, 16(1), 6.

Baskin, O. W., C.E. Aronoff and D. Lattimore (1997). *Public Relations: The profession and the practice*. McGraw-Hill Humanities, Social Sciences and World Languages.

Bennet, G. and R. Glasgow (2009). The delivery of public health interventions via the Internet: Actualizing their potential. *The Annual Review of Public Health*, 30, 273–292.

Bennett, P. (1998). *Communicating about risks to public health: Pointers to good practice*. London: Department of Health.

Brownell, K. and K. Warner (2009). 'The Perils of Ignoring History: Big Tobacco Played Dirty and Millions Died. How Similar Is Big Food?' *The Milbank Quarterly*, 87(1), 259–94.

Bruhn, J.G. (2001). *Trust and the Health of Organizations*. New York: Springer Science and Business Media.

Brynielsson, J., F. Johansson, C. Jonsson and A. Westling (2014). Emotion classification of social media posts for estimating people's reactions to communicated alert messages during crises. *Security Informatics*, 3(1), 7.

Bursztyn, L., Rao, A., Roth, C. and Yanagizawa-Drott, D. (2020). Misinformation during a pandemic. The Becker Friedman Institute for Economics at the University of Chicago. https://bfi.uchicago.edu/working-paper/2020-44/. Accessed on 24 April 2020 [Online Resource].

Callon, W., M.C. Beach, A.R. Links, C. Wasserman and E.F. Boss (2018). An expanded framework to define and measure shared decision-making in dialogue: A 'top-down' and 'bottom-up' approach. *Patient Education and Counseling*, 101(8), 1368–1377.

Caro, J. et al. (2018). Chile's 2014 Sugar-Sweetened Beverage Tax and Changes in Prices and Purchases of Sugar-Sweetened Beverages: An Observational Study in an Urban Environment. *PLoS Medicine*, 1(7).

Cao, X., Y. Liu, Z. Zhu, J. Hu and X. Chen (2017). Online selection of a physician by patients: Empirical study from elaboration likelihood perspective. *Computers in Human Behavior*, 73, 403–412.

Castro, E. M., T. Van Regenmortel, K. Vanhaecht, W. Sermeus and A. Van Hecke (2016). Patient empowerment, patient participation and patient-centeredness in hospital care: A concept analysis based on a literature review. *Patient education and counseling*, 99(12), 1923–1939.

Chatzisarantis, N. D., M.S. Hagger, C. Wang and C. Thogersen-Ntoumani (2009). The effects of social identity and perceived autonomy support on health behaviour within the theory of planned behaviour. *Current Psychology*, 28(1), 55–68.

Chiang, K. P. and A. Jackson (2013). Health literacy and its outcomes: application and extension of elaboration likelihood model. *International Journal of Healthcare Management*, 6(3), 152–157.

Colchero, M. et al. (2016). Beverage Purchases from Stores in Mexico under the Excise Tax on Sugar Sweetened Beverages: Observational Study. *BMJ* 352 (January).

Compton, J. and M. Pfau (2009). Spreading inoculation: Inoculation, resistance to influence, and word-of-mouth communication. *Communication Theory*, 19(1), 9–28.

Curtin, P.A., T. Gallicano and K. Matthews (2011). Millennials' approaches to ethical decision making: A survey of young public relations agency employees. *Public Relations Journal*, 5(2), 1–22.

Cutlip, S.M., A.H. Center, G.M. Broom and S.M. Cutlip (2004). *Effective Public Relations*. India: Pearson Education.

Dalrymple, K.E., R. Young and M. Tully (2016). 'Facts, not fear': negotiating uncertainty on social media during the 2014 Ebola crisis. *Science Communication*, 38(4), 442–467.

de Fatima Oliveira, M. (2013). Multicultural environments and their challenges to crisis communication. *Journal of Business Communication*, 50(3), 253–277.

Diers-Lawson, A. (2017). Will They Like Us When They're Angry? Antecedents and Indicators of Strong Emotional Reactions to Crises Among Stakeholders. In S.M. Croucher, B. Lewandowska-Tomaszczyk, and P. Wilson (Eds.), *Conflict, mediated message, and group dynamics* (pp. 81–136). Lanham, MD: Lexington Books.

Diers-Lawson, A. (2020). *Crisis Communication: Managing Stakeholder Relationships*. London: Routledge.

Diers, A. R. (2012). Reconstructing stakeholder relationships using 'corporate social responsibility' as a response strategy to cases of corporate irresponsibility: The case of the 2010 BP spill in the Gulf of Mexico. In R. Tench, W. Sun and B. Jones (Eds.), *Corporate*

Social Irresponsibility: A Challenging Concept (Vol. 4, pp. 177–206). United Kingdom: Emerald.

Dinoff, B.L. and R.M. Kowalski (1999). Reducing AIDS risk behavior: The combined efficacy of protection motivation theory and the elaboration likelihood model. *Journal of Social and Clinical Psychology, 18*(2), 223–239.

DiStaso, M.W., M. Vafeiadis and C. Amaral (2015). Managing a health crisis on Facebook: How the response strategies of apology, sympathy, and information influence public relations. *Public Relations Review, 41*(2), 222–231.

Donaldson, E. (2015). 'Sugar-sweetened Beverage taxation: A Case Study of Mexico'. NCD Alliance, John Hopkins Bloomberg School of Public Health. https://ncdalliance.org/sites/default/files/resource_files/Advocating_For_Sugar_Sweetened_Beverage_Taxation_0.pdf.

Eisenberg, M., C. Ringwalt, D. Driscoll, M. Vallee and G. Gullette (2004). Learning from truth: Youth participation in field marketing techniques to counter tobacco advertising. *Journal of Health Communication, 9*, 223–231.

Farrelly, M.C., K.C. Davis, M.L. Haviland, P. Messeri and C.G. Healton (2005). Evidence of a dose-response relationship between the 'truth' antismoking ads and youth smoking prevalence. *American Journal of Public Health, 95*(3), 425–431.

Farrelly, M.C., K.C. Davis, J.M. Yarsevich, M.L. Haviland, J.C. Hersey, M.E. Girlando and C.G. Healton (2002). *Getting to the truth: Assessing youths' reactions to the truth and 'Think. Don't smoke' tobacco countermarketing campaigns*. Retrieved from http://legacy.library.ucsf.edu/tid/bsp06a00/pdf

Farrington, C., J. Burt, O. Boiko, J. Campbell and M. Roland (2017). Doctors' engagements with patient experience surveys in primary and secondary care: a qualitative study. *Health Expectations, 20*(3), 385–394.

Flynn, B.S., J.K. Worden, J.Y. Bunn, S.W. Connolly and A.L. Dorwaldt (2011). Evaluation of smoking prevention television messages based on the elaboration likelihood model. *Health Education Research, 26*(6), 976–987.

Fombrun, C.J. (1996). *Reputation: Realizing Value from the Corporate Image* (Harvard Business School Press, Cambridge, MA).

Fraustino, J.D. and L. Ma (2015). CDC's Use of Social Media and Humor in a Risk Campaign—'Preparedness 101: Zombie Apocalypse'. *Journal of Applied Communication Research, 43*(2), 222–241.

Freberg, K. (2013). Using the theory of planned behavior to predict intention to comply with a food recall message. *Health communication, 28*(4), 359–365.

Freberg, K., M.J. Palenchar and S.R. Veil (2013). Managing and sharing H1N1 crisis information using social media bookmarking services. *Public Relations Review, 39*(3), 178–184.

Gao, G.G., B.N. Greenwood, R. Agarwal and J. McCullough (2015). Vocal minority and silent majority: How do online ratings reflect population perceptions of quality? *MIS quarterly, 39*(3), 565–589.

Gordon, C. G. and K.S. Kelly (1999). Public relations expertise and organizational effectiveness: A study of US hospitals. *Journal of Public Relations Research, 11*(2), 143–165.

Grunig, J.E. (1994). World view, ethics, and the two-way symmetrical model of public relations. In W. Armbrecht and U. Zabel (Eds.), *Normative Aspekte der Public Relations* (pp. 69–89). Wiesbaden: VS Verlag für Sozialwissenschaften.

Grunig, J. E. and L.A. Grunig (1991). Conceptual differences in public relations and marketing: The case of health-care organizations. *Public Relations Review, 17*(3), 257–278.

Grunig, J. E. and T.T. Hunt (1984). *Managing Public Relations*, Holt. Rinehart and Winston Inc, USA, 141.

Guidry, J., Y. Jin, C.A. Orr, M. Messner and S. Meganck (2017). Ebola on Instagram and Twitter: How health organizations address the health crisis in their social media engagement. *Public Relations Review, 43*(3), 477–486.

Halbert, C.H., K. Armstrong, O.H. Gandy and L. Shaker (2006). Racial differences in trust in health care providers. *Archives of Internal Medicine, 166*(8), 896–901.

Hayek, M., L.A. Bynum J. Smothers and W.A. Jr. Williams (2014). Managing healthcare alliance portfolios: A theory-based typology. *Journal of Applied Management and Entrepreneurship, 19*(1), 3–17.

Heath, R.L. (2002). Issues management: Its past, present, and future. *Journal of Public Affairs, 2*(2), 209–214.

Heldman, A.B., Schindelar, J. and Weaver, J. B. (2013). Social media engagement and public health communication: implications for public health organizations being truly 'social'. *Public Health Reviews, 35*(1), 13.

Herring, J., Fulford, K., Dunn, M. and Handa, A. (2017). Elbow Room for Best Practice? Montgomery, patients' values, and balanced decision-making in person-centred clinical care. *Medical Law Review, 25*(4), 582–603.

Hether, H.J. (2014). Dialogic communication in the health care context: A case study of Kaiser Permanente's social media practices. *Public Relations Review*, 40(5), 856–858.

Hyvärinen, J. and Vos, M. (2015). Developing a conceptual framework for investigating communication supporting community resilience. *Societies*, 5(3), 583–597.

Jin, Y., Liu, B. F., Anagondahalli, D. and Austin, L. (2014). Scale development for measuring publics' emotions in organizational crises. *Public Relations Review*, 40(3), 509–518.

Johansen, I.H., Baste, V., Rosta, J., Aasland, O.G. and Morken, T. (2017). Changes in prevalence of workplace violence against doctors in all medical specialties in Norway between 1993 and 2014: a repeated cross-sectional survey. *BMJ open*, 7(8), e017757.

Kapoor, M.C. (2017). Violence against the medical profession. *Journal of Anaesthesiology, Clinical Pharmacology*, 33(2), 145.

Kaya, S., Demir, I.B., Karsavuran, S., Ürek, D. and İlgün, G. (2016). Violence against doctors and nurses in hospitals in Turkey. *Journal of Forensic Nursing*, 12(1), 26–34.

Kent, M. L. and Taylor, M. (2002). Toward a dialogic theory of public relations. *Public Relations Review*, 28(1), 21–37.

Ki, E.-J. and Brown, K.A. (2013). The effects of crisis response strategies on relationship quality outcomes. *Journal of Business Communication*, 50(4), 403–420.

Lachlan, K.A., Spence, P.R. and Lin, X. (2014). Expressions of risk awareness and concern through Twitter: on the utility of using the medium as an indication of audience needs. *Computers in Human Behavior*, 35, 554–559.

Lazard, A.J., Scheinfeld, E., Bernhardt, J.M., Wilcox, G.B. and Suran, M. (2015). Detecting themes of public concern: A text mining analysis of the Centers for Disease Control and Prevention's Ebola live Twitter chat. *American Journal of Infection Control*, 43(10), 1109–1111.

Makarem, S.C. and Al-Amin, M. (2014). Beyond the service process: The effects of organizational and market factors on customer perceptions of health care services. *Journal of Service Research*, 17(4), 399–414.

McDonald, L.M. and Cokley, J. (2013). Prepare for anger, look for love: A ready reckoner for crisis scenario planners. *PRism*, 10(1), 1–11.

Mitra, N. (2019). Three Years After Soda Tax, Sugary Drink Consumption Falls Drastically in Berkeley. *Earth Island Journal*. http://www.earthisland.org/journal/index.php/articles/entry/three-years-after-soda-tax-sugary-drink-consumption-falls-drastically-in-berkeley/.

Mou, Y. and Lin, C.A. (2014). Communicating Food Safety via the Social Media The Role of Knowledge and Emotions on Risk Perception and Prevention. *Science Communication*, 36(5), 593–616.

NDNS. (2019). 'National Diet and Nutrition Survey. Years 1 to 9 of the Rolling Programme (2008/2009 – 2016/2017): Time Trend and Income Analyses'. NDNS, PHE and FSA. https://assets.publishing.service.gov.uk/government/uploads/system/uploads/attachment_data/file/772434/NDNS_UK_Y1-9_report.pdf.

Newsom, D. and Haynes, J. (2007). *Public Relations Writing: Form & style*. Cengage Learning.

Niblett, P. et al. (2019). 'Sugar Reduction: Report on Progress between 2015 and 2018', 108.

Pasadeos, Y., Phelps, J. and Edison, A. (2008). Searching for our 'own theory' in advertising: An update of research networks. *Journalism and Mass Communication Quarterly*, 85(4), 785–806.

Payne, N., Jones, F. and Harris, P.R. (2004). The role of perceived need within the theory of planned behaviour: A comparison of exercise and healthy eating. *British Journal of Health Psychology*, 9(4), 489–504.

Petty, R.E., Baker, S.M. and Gleicher, F. (1991). Attitudes and drug abuse prevention: Implications of the elaboration likelihood model of persuasion. *Persuasive Communication and Drug Abuse Prevention*, 71–90.

Petty, R.E. and Cacioppo, J.T. (1986). Message elaboration versus peripheral cues, *Communication and Persuasion* (pp. 141–172): Springer.

Pfau, M. and Bockern, S.V. (1994). The persistence of inoculation in conferring resistance to smoking initiation among adolescents: The second year. *Human Communication Research*, 20(3), 413–430.

Pfau, M., Bockern, S.V. and Kang, J.G. (1992). Use of inoculation to promote resistance to smoking initiation among adolescents. *Communications Monographs*, 59(3), 213–230.

Polonsky, W.H., Capehorn, M., Belton, A., Down, S., Gamerman, V., Nagel, F., . . . Edelman, S. (2017). Physician–patient communication at diagnosis of type 2 diabetes and its links to patient outcomes: New results from the global IntroDia® study. *Diabetes research and clinical practice*, 127, 265–274.

Poppen, P.J. and Reisen, C.A. (1997). Perception of risk and sexual self-protective behavior: A methodological critique. *AIDS Education and Prevention*, 9(4), 373–390.

Porter, M.E. and Teisberg, E.O. (2006). *Redefining Health Care: Creating value-based competition on results*: Harvard Business Press.

Povey, R., Conner, M., Sparks, P., James, R. and Shepherd, R. (2000). The theory of planned behavior and healthy eating: Examining additive and moderating effects of social influence variables. *Psychology and Health, 14*(6), 991.

Rosenstock, I.M., V.J. Strecher and M.H. Becker (1988). Social learning theory and the health belief model. *Health Education and Behavior, 15*(2), 175–183. doi:10.1177/109019818801500203

Roser, M., Ritchie, H., Ortiz-Ospina, E. and Hasell, J. (2020). Coronavirus Disease (COVID-19). Published online at OurWorldInData.org. Retrieved from: 'https://ourworldindata.org/coronavirus' on 24 April, 2020 [Online Resource].

Russell, K.M., P. Monahan, A. Wagle and V. Champion (2007). Differences in health and cultural beliefs by stage of mammography screening adoption in African American women. *Cancer: Interdisciplinary International Journal of the American Cancer Society, 109*(S2), 386–395.

Rutsaert, P., Á. Regan, Z. Pieniak, Á. McConnon, A. Moss, P. Wall and W. Verbeke (2013). The use of social media in food risk and benefit communication. *Trends in Food Science and Technology, 30*(1), 84–91.

Scottish Parliament Information Centre (http://www.parliament.scot/ResearchBriefingsAndFactsheets/S5/SB_1670_Integration_of_Health_and_Social_Care.pdf). Accessed 7 April 2020.

Sellnow, D.D., D. Lane, R.S. Littlefield, T.L. Sellnow., B. Wilson, K. Beauchamp and S. Venette (2015). A receiver-based approach to effective instructional crisis communication. *Journal of Contingencies and Crisis Management, 23*(3), 149–158.

Shan, L.C., P. Panagiotopoulos, Á. Regan, A. De Brún, J. Barnett, P. Wall and Á. McConnon (2015). Interactive Communication with the public: qualitative exploration of the use of social media by food and health organizations. *Journal of Nutrition Education and Behavior, 47*(1), 104–108.

Sjöberg, E., G.C. Barker, J. Landgren, I. Griberg, J.E. Skiby, A. Tubbin, . . . R. Knutsson (2013). Social media and its dual use in biopreparedness: Communication and visualization tools in an animal bioterrorism incident. *Biosecurity and Bioterrorism: Biodefense Strategy, Practice, and Science, 11*(S1), S264–S275.

Smith, S.W., K.D. Rosenman, M.R. Kotowski, E. Glazer, C. McFeters, N.M. Keesecker and A. Law (2008). Using the EPPM to create and evaluate the effectiveness of brochures to increase the use of hearing protection in farmers and landscape workers. *Journal of Applied Communication Research, 36*(2), 200–218.

Sohn, Y. and R.W. Lariscy (2014). Understanding reputational crisis: Definition, properties, and consequences. *Journal of Public Relations Research, 26*(1), 23–43.

Spence, P.R., K.A. Lachlan, D. Westerman and S.A. Spates (2013). Where the gates matter less: Ethnicity and perceived source credibility in social media health messages. *Howard Journal of Communications, 24*(1), 1–16.

Sutton, J., C. League, T.L. Sellnow and D.D. Sellnow (2015). Terse messaging and public health in the midst of natural disasters: The case of the Boulder floods. *Health communication, 30*(2), 135–143.

Terblanche-Smit, M. and N.S. Terblanch (2011). HIV/Aids marketing communication and the role of fear, efficacy and cultural characteristics in promoting social change. *Journal of Public Affairs, 11*(4), 279–286.

Thomas, J. (2009). Using social marketing to address obesity: The ongoing 'Liverpool's Challenge' social marketing programme. *Journal of Communication in Healthcare, 2*(3), 216–227.

Tsorbatzoudis, H. (2005). Evaluation of a planned behavior theory-based intervention programme to promote healthy eating. *Perceptual and Motor Skills, 101*(2), 587–604.

Verroen, S., Gutteling, J. M. and Vries, P. W. (2013). Enhancing Self-Protective Behavior: Efficacy Beliefs and Peer Feedback in Risk Communication. *Risk Analysis, 33*(7), 1252–1264.

Wallace, B.C., M.J. Paul, U. Sarkar, T.A. Trikalinos and M. Dredze (2014). A large-scale quantitative analysis of latent factors and sentiment in online doctor reviews. *Journal of the American Medical Informatics Association, 21*(6), 1098–1103.

Warren, A.M., A. Sulaiman and N.I. Jaafar (2014). Social media effects on fostering online civic engagement and building citizen trust and trust in institutions. *Government Information Quarterly, 31*(2), 291–301.

Witte, K. (1996). Generating effective risk messages: How scary should your risk communication be? *Communication Yearbook, 18*, 229–254.

World Health Authority (https://www.who.int/vaccine_safety/initiative/detection/immunization_misconceptions/en/). Accessed 7 April 2020

Wukich, C. and I. Mergel (2015). Closing the Citizen-Government communication gap: Content, audience, and network analysis of government tweets. *Journal of Homeland Security and Emergency Management, 12*(3), 707–735.

CHAPTER 27

Sian Rees and Iwan Williams

Sports public relations

Source: Tom Tietz/123RF

Learning outcomes

By the end of this chapter you should be able to:
- define what sports public relations means
- recognise different types of sports public relations activities
- understand the different techniques which can be used as part of sports PR programmes
- critically evaluate sports public relations campaigns
- understand academic critique of sports public relations.

Structure

- The business of sport
- Sports as brands
- Sports PR practitioners and the media
- Digital sports PR
- Promoting participation and fandom
- PR and athlete transgressions
- Sports social responsibility and ethics
- Sport as culture

Introduction

When the world's number one golfer, Tiger Woods, crashed his Cadillac Escalade into a neighbour's tree in the early hours of 25 November 2009, the ensuing media scandal, cataloguing infidelities and inappropriate behaviour, led to his indefinite withdrawal from competitive golf and the cancelling, or failure to renew, of lucrative sponsorship deals from big brands such as Gillette, AT&T and General Motors (Mahoney 2018). A decade later, Woods triumphed at the 2019 Masters at Augusta to win his first major for 11 years, amidst hugely positive media coverage charting his comeback from injury and visualising his celebrations with his children (Scrivener 2019). Woods' careful reputation recovery-management process, which has emphasised his good character (his Twitter descriptor, for example, is Father, Golfer, Entrepreneur), has led to the return of strong sponsorship alliances with brands such as Nike and TaylorMade. The dramatic fall from grace of Tiger Woods, and the subsequent resurgence of his brand, makes clear that within the world of contemporary sports, the management of news information and reputation off the field is as important as any on-field display of sporting prowess.

This chapter considers the practice of PR within the sporting world, a specialist sector of the public relations discipline, defined as: 'a managerial communication-based function designed to identify a sport organisation's key publics, evaluate its relationships with those publics, and foster desirable relationships between the sport organisation and those publics' (Stoldt et al. 2006: 2). As well as managing the media profile of sporting legends, like Tiger Woods, the sports PR function typically involves organising events, arranging sponsorships, managing fan clubs and working with traditional and digital media to raise awareness of sporting activities and ideologies (Tamir et al. 2015). This chapter considers the communications practices used by sporting organisations in their promotional endeavours, but it also explores the wider role and implications of public relations in advocating for the broader concept of sport in today's society.

The business of sport

In addition to being an activity that delivers ecstatic highs and heart-breaking lows to millions of global participants and spectators, sport has a much deeper cultural and symbolic significance. It can unite or divide communities, cities, regions and countries. It has delivered significant economic benefits to cities and countries that have hosted sporting mega-events, and the aspirational philosophy of Olympism seeks to place sport at the service of humanity.

However, in an era of professionalisation and global consumption, sport is more than a cultural signifier – it is a major contributor to national economies across the globe. In 2017, the UK sports sector contributed £9.8 billion to the UK's economy and provided jobs for 1.2 million people (DCMS 2018).

There is a lucrative interconnectivity between modern sport and commercial enterprise, including venue and team sponsorship, media broadcast rights and the attendant advertising, as well as the civic investments undertaken by countries and cities across the globe in order to attract major sporting events (Slack 2004). L'Etang (2013: 87) terms this 'sports business', which she articulates as 'commercial activities that aim to make profit, or create wealth by selling sports events, services, products and properties that can generate income through sponsorship.'

During the 2016/17 football season, the English Premiere League generated record revenues of £4.5 billion (Deloitte 2018), a year that also saw each of the 20 clubs setting their own annual revenue record. In 2011, when England put forward a bid to host the 2018 World Cup, the attempt cost the Football Association £15 million and local councils £2.1 million (House of Commons Media and Sport Committee 2011). This willingness to invest large sums in the hope of bringing a sporting mega-event to a country is indicative of how governments across the world have come to realise that such spectacles have the power to improve a nation's image on the global socio-political stage, augment its political agency and boost its economy (Grix and Lee 2013).

The communicative imperatives for governments, sporting bodies, sports organisations and sports stars are therefore complex and multi-layered. From the nuanced global public diplomacy behind a city or a nation's bid for the Olympics or other mega-sporting event, to the tactical public rehabilitation of a sporting celebrity following a professional or personal transgression, effective communications are a mandatory management function. Therefore, just as the most successful commercial non-sporting organisations recognise the need to continually invest monies and effort into maintaining brand awareness and visibility, and fostering loyalty from consumers through effective engagement tactics, those involved in sports business are aware that they must do likewise to maintain the support of fans.

Sport is a global business and the increasingly digitalised mediascape means that effective communications with a range of publics must span a variety of digital platforms – broadcast, online, social media – and the media fragmentation is unlikely to stall. While this presents challenges to the sports industry, it also offers opportunities. Organisations that can harvest and analyse consumer data from across a variety of digital platforms will be able to tailor their communications to ensure that their engagement with fans has purpose and authenticity.

The sports industry must also be cognisant of changes in fans' media consumption habits. While television remains the primary source of 'sports news' among UK adults (Ofcom 2018a), social media and the internet are rapidly catching up as preferred sources of sports news. And a separate study by Ofcom (2018b) indicates that the emerging generation of consumers (5 to 15-year-olds) is not only spending less time in front of the television, but when they do, they often use the television to watch so-called 'over-the-top' (OTT) content such as Amazon Prime Video, Netflix and Now TV in the form of audio-visual content delivered on the 'open' internet rather than over a managed internet protocol TV architecture (Ofcom 2018b). To place this in a sporting context, analysis of football viewership for the top five football leagues of England, France, Germany, Italy and Spain during the 2016–17 season by PwC (2018) showed that 'only 17 per cent of TV viewers are under the age of 35, whereas the equivalent figure for online viewers is 45 per cent'. It concludes that 'the jury is now out on understanding what the implications will be for rights holders, media partners and brands with regard to content strategy' (PwC 2018: 16).

Mini case study 27.1
esports

In a 2018 survey of world sport industry-leaders by the global accountancy firm PwC, respondents were asked which sports have the highest potential growth revenue globally. The overwhelming response was esports (PwC 2018). In January 2019, games and esports analytics company Newzoo marked 2019 as a landmark year for the esports industry, as it projected it will be the first time the global esports economy will generate revenues in excess of $US1 billion. The majority of the revenue will come from sponsorship (Pannekeet 2019).

esports at-a-glance

- Esports is competitive video gaming, where people play against each other online and at spectator events in indoor arenas, usually for cash prizes.
- Prize pools vary from a few hundred UK pounds at amateur level to $US20 million at the top global tournaments.
- Esports can be played on PCs, consoles and mobiles. There are currently around 30 different recognised competitive titles, including League of Legends, Counter-Strike: Global Offensive, Dota 2, Call of Duty.
- Depending on the game, the format can be one-to-one or team-based (three players vs. three, four players vs. four, five players vs. five and six-players vs. six).
- In the UK esports is classified as a game (like chess and bridge), although many consider esports a sport.
- Fans predominantly watch esports via online platforms such as Twitch (10m+ viewers a day) (British esports Association 2017).
- The International Olympic Committee has considered including esports as a medal event in future Olympic games.

Practitioner's diary: Svetlana Picou

Svetlana Picou is Executive Vice-President, Global and Chair, Global Olympics and Sports Industry Affairs at Weber Shandwick, one of the world's leading strategic communications and public relations firms.

Since 2003, Svetlana Picou has led Weber Shandwick's award-winning, global Olympic and Sport Industry Affairs team. She has worked on a number of global campaigns including Olympic bids for Sochi 2014, Tokyo 2020, Beijing 2022 and Los Angeles 2028. Picou has also advised sponsors, international federations, World Expo bids, and global brands looking to develop sport-focused strategies and campaigns. Hosting a global event on the scale of the Olympics is an exercise not only in public diplomacy on the world stage, it is also a manifestation of the nation's soft power, and its agency as a geo-political force. Picou agrees:

> Obviously there are different reasons for why cities or countries decide to bid to host mega events – sporting events or otherwise.
>
> Some of them want to make sure that they put a city or country on the global map; some of them want to show the influence they have on the global stage and their ability to organise mega-events is proof of that; others do it to attract and boost tourism to their cities and countries; some of them are probably looking for inward investment.

Given the scale of the investment associated with even putting together a bid to host the Olympics, what does Picou believe is the starting point in terms of developing a strategic communications strategy? She believes three perspectives need to be taken into consideration:

> The first one is the overall global context. Sports PR today very rarely happens in one market. You have to take a global perspective, and more than ever, the world is changing very rapidly. As a result, brands, sporting personalities, governing bodies and [Olympic] organising committees need to be alert to what's going on globally. Because they might come up with a great communications campaign or a great business strategy, but [it] will be off-base in three months simply because they have not taken into account certain global developments.
>
> The second one is the Olympic context. What is going on with the IOC? What does the Olympic movement stand for, what are their current priorities, what audiences are they trying to attract? Do they want to go into the developed markets where the sports industry is well-established, because that offers a certain stability? Or, do they want to go to countries where there is a huge potential for new audiences, for new engagements, for new brands to get engaged?
>
> The final consideration is the domestic appetite for placing a region into the global spotlight. The domestic context certainly matters. It's impossible to bid for an event, if you don't have public support. The decision about whether a country should bid is made by politicians, and they know they must have support for the project.

However, in addition to helping a potential host develop an understanding of a broader context, Picou sees PR and strategic communications as a crucial underpinning to a successful bid to host the Olympics. 'They are very important for any campaign because essentially it's an election campaign, and the city or country wants to be elected as the host, so communications play a very important role. You have to talk about the project. You have to talk about why you're the best city or country to win. You have to put out your vision, and communicate your strengths, because nobody else will do that. But you also have to make sure that you manage issues that come up – any issues and crisis situations – very, very carefully!'

When asked if the complexity of the stakeholder landscape associated with the bid makes client negotiations difficult, Picou's answer is diplomatic: 'It depends on the country and how they are organised, but most often there is an entity formed in each country called a Bid Committee, and that committee runs the Bid Campaign. They are supported by the City, and the Mayor plays an important role as the guarantor of the Games' delivery. In those countries where the State – through the national committees and through the Minister of Sport – is involved, because there is public money involved, the financial guarantees are put in place by the State. This is the case for the majority of countries, apart from the United States. In the United States, the Government doesn't really serve as the financial guarantor, it is run by the US Olympic Committee, and it is private money. But the entity that we most often work with directly is the Bid Committee, and supported by all the stakeholders around the Bid Committee in each country.'

Of equal importance is ensuring that any strategic communications initiative is based on research and empirical data – both in the pre-campaign planning phase, and also in the post-campaign evaluation.

> PR is not the same as it was even three or four years ago. The industry is changing, and it's critical that we look at data and analytics to inform our PR and communications strategies. The way we measure what we do, the impact we have; the issues we need to help solve are changing. Because generally, it's not about 'let's do something memorable', it's about 'what business issue do we need to solve and how can communications help solve it', and how do we measure whether we've made a difference – on people's lives, on causes, on countries winning or losing bids [for mega-events].

When asked if she is a proponent of PR as a science rather than an art in an era when brands' consumer engagement methodologies are increasingly targeted and refined, Picou's response is unequivocal. 'Absolutely! We have to base it on data, we have to always go back once we've done something to see whether it worked, we have to look at the metrics. If it didn't work, then we have to adjust it so that next time we do something it will have more impact. And this has to be the case for any brand or organisation or bid or anything else because the competition from other brands or personalities has become much more sophisticated.'

Box 27.1

Marketing the Olympic brand

- The Olympic Marketing Factfile is produced annually by the International Olympic Committee (IOC) to document its approach to communications and marketing.
- Marketing raises revenue for the IOC with US$4.15 billion raised through sponsorship and US$1 billion raised through broadcast rights for the 2013–16 period.
- Both the Summer and Winter Olympics are broadcast in 220 countries, with 3.2 billion viewers watching the Olympics in Rio 2016.
- Current Olympic sponsors are: Coca-Cola, Bridgestone, Intel, P&G, Visa, Alibaba Group, Dow, Omega, Samsung, Atos, GE, Panasonic and Toyota.
- Sponsorship provides: finance, support for event staging, training support for athletes, enhanced experiences for spectators and the creation of advertising and promotional activities.
- The IOC provides extensive media resources including: weekly press releases, photos, broadcast quality footage, twitter feeds, guidelines, reports, fact sheets and access to spokespeople.

www.olympic.org

Sports as brands

Today's sporting landscape is dominated by powerful, visible brands using sophisticated public relations techniques to great effect. According to Bouchet (2013), sports brands come in many different forms: 'classic' brands include manufacturers like Nike and retailers like JB sports; 'sports-specific' brands include famous clubs and celebrities; whilst 'certification and label' brands are federations like FIFA (Fédération Internationale de Football Association) and technical equipment such as Rossignol skis. It could be argued that sports branding is not a new twenty-first-century phenomenon. Roman gladiators, for example, were consciously branded in terms of their choice of weapon, training school affiliation and stage name (e.g. Achilles) and in more recent times there is clear evidence of the emergence of a variety of sporting leagues in the twentieth century being supported by the aggressive use of media publicity and celebrity promotion techniques (Hardy et al. 2012). The Tree of Sport Branding is a conceptual notion which visualises a progressive positioning of sport, from its identification as 'leisure' in the 1700s, through to the development of specific branded 'sport types' (rounders, cricket) in the 1800s, and then to 'sport property', in which branded leagues and clubs from 1850 onwards use branding as a tool to dominate particular sporting categories (Hardy et al. 2012).

Successful sports brands, like the National Hockey League in the USA, make use of techniques such as ownership of rules, brand associations with sporting manufacturers, and the powerful use of imagery to build a strong brand position (Hardy et al. 2012). We can see the same process today, for example the 2019 ATP Tennis tour is officially connected to Dunlop which proudly promotes itself as the 'official ball' of the tour. Dunlop promotes the relationship through Facebook and Twitter campaigns which use the hashtag #TheBallOnTour, accompanied by eye-catching still and audio-visual imagery of well-known tennis players in training and match action.

Modern sports branding is big business. Manchester United was identified by Forbes as the second most valuable sports team in the world during 2018, partly due to the £47 million shirt sponsorship deal with motoring brand Chevrolet. The attraction for these sponsors is the enthusiastic 'brand love' that sports brands can evoke, based on the effectiveness of collectivism, high visibility, high symbolic value, group affiliation and powerful identity expression they provide (Yang et al. 2018). Sports brands build enviable loyalty based on the experiential and symbolic attributes offered by teams and events (Brunello 2018) and they often rely on communications content fuelled by moments of glory, stories, symbols, mythical heroes and imaginary contests, with modern sports stars and participants depicted as modern heroes or adventurers (Bouchet et al. 2013). The drinks brand Red Bull, for example, has used its connection with adventure and motor sports such as F1 very effectively in this way. The brand is represented, not through major advertising, but through targeted digital communications, event creation and striking audio-visual content, which shows extraordinary and ordinary people engaging in a wide range of thrilling sporting moments and events, all supporting the brand idea that Red Bull 'gives you wings'.

Managing brand equity, and providing effective brand communications programmes, has become increasingly important as sport has become more commercialised (Wang and Tang 2018). For professional sports clubs, it is their star players and team successes that often form the basis of convincing and believable brand communications; however, focusing on non-product related attributes, such as the team's history, values, charitable giving and community relations can often be more fruitful in terms of encouraging fan and sponsor interaction with the brand (Maderer et al. 2018). This is easier when the location of the team is linked to its name, but can be more challenging when other brand names become involved, such as the Samsung Lions baseball team in Korea. Joint branding is quite typical in the Asia-Pacific sports industry and here, studies have shown that it is important that fans are able to identify with the sponsor brand through convincing integrated communications campaigns (Wang and Tang 2018).

Sports PR practitioners and the media

Even the most casual reader of the sports pages in the mainstream press will glean that the majority of sports journalists are generally impassioned fans of the sport they cover. The best sports journalists and columnists are able to convey to fans and readers not only the mechanics and the result of a sporting event, but also make tangible the visceral emotions and tensions of the sporting combat they witnessed at first hand. It is unsurprising that given their common interests, there have been strong professional and personal relationships between sports journalists and sports organisations' public relations practitioners (Rowe 2004). Historically, the relationship between journalists and sports organisations was friendly and collusive (Sugden and Tomlinson 2007), with sports organisations dependent on journalists to provide favourable media coverage for fans and stakeholders. In return, journalists were granted access to sports stars and officials in order to get an exclusive insider's perspective for their story, and offer fans a tantalising and (at times) titillating glimpse of their sporting heroes' lives behind the changing-room doors.

In addition to this gatekeeper role, sports organisations' media management teams also naturally provide a more normative PR function. From a journalistic perspective, these 'information subsidies' (Sherwood et al. 2017a) conform to traditional public relations activities, such as the provision of press information packs, and the facilitation of media conferences and the granting of one-to-one interviews with players to certain journalists. At sporting mega-events such as The Olympics or the World Cup, dedicated media-centres offer on-demand statistical data, pre-prepared

---

Think about 27.1

How do sports brands build authenticity?

Research focusing on the concept of authentic branding has become popular in recent years. One of the primary thinkers in this area is Michael Beverland who proposed that the ability to be authentic comes from avoiding traditional, polished, representational, top-down controlled branding and instead comes from imbuing brands with 'a warts and all humanity' (Beverland 2009: 2). Authenticity has personal meaning and is 'given' to an object by consumers based on criteria such as self-identification, creativity and sincerity (Beverland 2009: 16). Consider which sports brands you consider to be authentic and discuss how and why the brand is able to present itself authentically to brand users and maintain an authentic reputation.

Mini case study 27.2

Quiksilver: the making of an authentic brand

Created in 1969, the surf brand Quiksilver was developed by two surfers, Alan Green and John Law, who created comfortable, light surf suits, which dried quickly. The brand became recognised by the surf community as authentic and original, delivering functionality, innovation and care for surfers (Bouchet et al. 2013). It has successfully expanded into the wider lifestyle culture market benefiting from a growing fascination with lifestyle sport (L'Etang 2013). The launch of the Quiksilver Edition clothing collection in 2005 targeted non-surfers who were keen to connect themselves with the beach fashion sub-culture. The brand has 6.5 million Facebook followers, and creates a sense of brand culture through eye-catching audio-visual content of sponsored stars, customers and clothing ranges, alongside experiential opportunities linked to sponsored events such as the Quik Pro Gold Coast Surf competition in Australia and its online Young Guns Ski competition. The Quiksilver Boardrider's Foundation supports education, environment and youth related projects across Australia and, alongside events and clothing news, this helps drive significant global news coverage.

www.quiksilver.com

Picture 27.1 In the twenty-first century, sports organisations and athletes have the power to construct their own narrative across their personal digital platforms. Cristiano Ronaldo is one of football's mega stars who does this with a huge following (*source:* AFP/Getty Images)

soundbites from sports stars and management as well as daily subject-specific media-briefings (Sugden and Tomlinson 2007).

Within the context of media agenda-building theory (McCombs 2013) much academic literature has highlighted the perceived imbalance of power in the symbiotic relationship between sports journalists and their media management counterparts (Sugden and Tomlinson 2007; Hutchins and Boyle 2017; Sherwood et al. 2017a). Much of the rationale for this imbalance focuses on the increased political economy of sport, where sporting organisations are now far more cautious in exposing their multi-million pound corporate brands (and the sporting heroes who embody it), to the potentially critical scrutiny of the media.

However, another dynamic is also affecting the sports journalist–practitioner relationship. Sports organisations across the globe have invested heavily in designing and populating their websites with content that is designed to appeal to fans (Scherer and Jackson 2008), and which also offers the opportunity for sports brands to frame a narrative about the organisation in a positive way (Yanity 2013). Similarly, social media platforms such as Twitter can often give fans unprecedented glimpses into sporting icons' private lives (Pegoraro 2015), that offer fans insight without the need for incursive intrusion by the media.

In the twenty-first century, sports organisations and athletes have the power to construct their own narrative across their personal digital platforms, a change that potentially further erodes the role of journalists as suppliers of information and news to publics. Furthermore, large sporting organisations are becoming media owners (Connelly 2017; McCaskill 2018), with clubs such as Manchester United's MUTV app channelling fans onto their own subscription-based digital eco-system. It seems that digital technology is hastening the onset of a sports journalism deficit.

By conducting a series of interviews with 37 sports public relations practitioners in Australia, Sherwood et al. (2017b) analysed whether rapid advances in sports organisations' abilities to deliver their own news through their digital platforms was undercutting the primacy of 'legacy media'. While caveating their conclusions by noting that the research was based only in an Australian context, the authors state that the sports PR practitioners in question 'utilised their own platforms to communicate "sensitive" stories in which they wish to control the narrative' (2017b: 527). It appears that while the normative public relations function of facilitating journalists' access to athletes and clubs remained, they concede that the practitioners' increased ability to transmit information directly to publics would likely 'limit sports journalists' access to sources further' (2017b: 527). They conclude that their findings seem to conform to a broader trend in news distribution by public relations practitioners, citing parallels with political news distribution methodology, where journalists' access to political actors is closely managed, and politicians are increasingly adroit at shaping the news agenda through the use of social media.

Of course, it is also worth noting that any exploration of sports media relations should take into account the changing media consumption habits of audiences, and where 'legacy media' stands in the sports news consumption hierarchy. According to the annual news consumption survey by the UK Communications Regulator Ofcom (see Figure 27.1), 29 per cent of the UK population choose to consume sports news via the television, 10 per cent get their sports news from social media, a further 10 per cent cite 'other' internet' sources, 7 per cent of UK adults get information

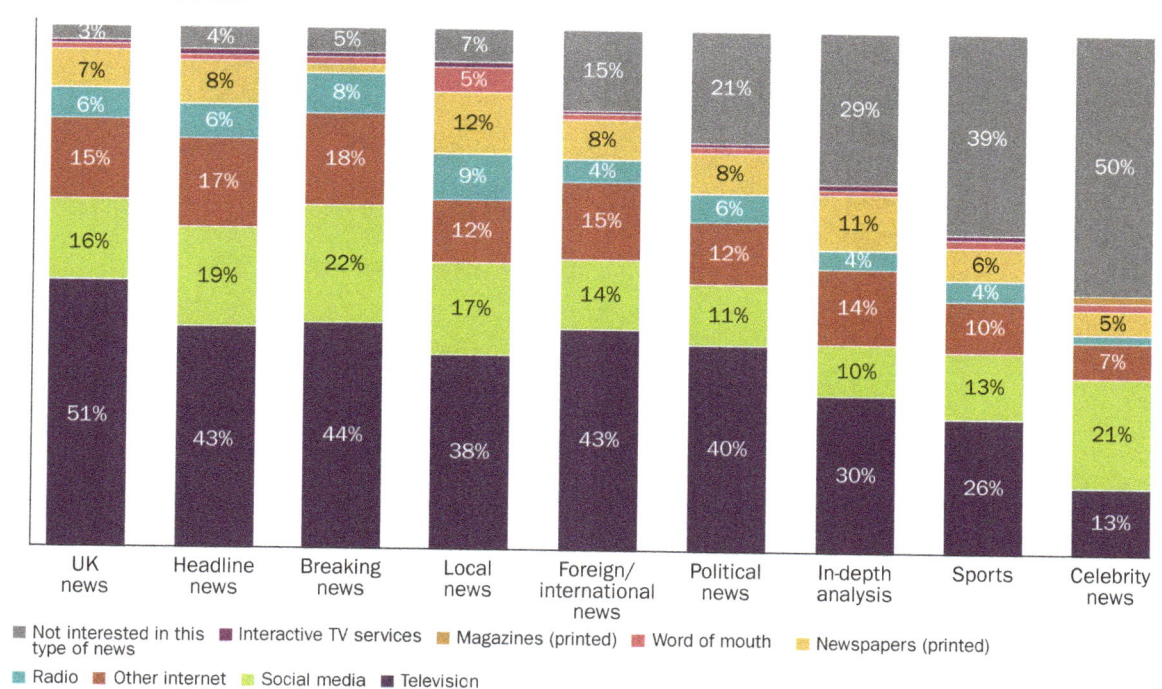

For all types of news content, TV is the most-used platform. The only exception is celebrity news, for which social media is used most often

News type	Not interested	Interactive TV	Magazines	Word of mouth	Newspapers	Radio	Other internet	Social media	Television
UK news	3%				7%	6%	15%	16%	51%
Headline news	4%				8%	6%	17%	19%	43%
Breaking news	5%					8%	18%	22%	44%
Local news	7%			5%	12%	9%	12%	17%	38%
Foreign/international news	15%				8%	4%	15%	14%	43%
Political news	21%				8%	6%	12%	11%	40%
In-depth analysis	29%				11%	4%	14%	10%	30%
Sports	39%				6%	4%	10%	13%	26%
Celebrity news	50%				5%		7%	21%	13%

Figure 27.1 Ofcom news consumption survey 2019 (*source:* Ofcom News Consumption Survey 2019. Question: D1. Where do you tend to go most often for each of the following types of news content? Base: All adults 16+ who follow news 2019 – Total = 4524)

about sports from newspapers, and 4 per cent from the radio (Ofcom 2018a). Viewed from a public relations practitioner's perspective, this is not surprising, primarily because the sports news consumption trend largely mirrors general news consumption habits – television retains its primacy, while digital and online source continue to grow to the detriment of newspapers. The exponential increase in the digital consumption of sports news arguably augers a shift in the sports PR practitioner's role, where there will be much greater emphasis on creating and curating original digital content across an organisation's digital platforms.

Digital sports PR

In just the same way that multinational businesses, retailers and consumer brands have digital networks as their individual 'centreless centre' (Hassan 2004: 10), sports organisations across the world use digital technology to connect with stakeholders, the media or fans. A dedicated website acts as the ubiquitous window into a sporting club, offering team scores, club statistics, player information as well as merchandise aimed at fans (Scholl 2015). From a public relations perspective, a well-designed, informative and content-rich website offers the opportunity for the sports organisation to bring its brand to life to a global audience (Picture 27.2). Judicious use of exclusive news, images and video interviews with players allow clubs such as Manchester United, the All Blacks and the LA Dodgers to maintain and grow allegiances with passionate followers from across the world – crucially, even during the off-season. An analysis of the websites of five of the English Premier League's top clubs (Liverpool FC, Manchester City, Tottenham Hotspur, Arsenal and Chelsea) evidences a normative industry approach to fan engagement. For example, all offer exclusive video interviews with managers and players, links to the clubs' social media accounts as well as more traditional engagement activities such as information on how to take a tour of their respective stadia.

In addition to catering to a local and national fanbase, the websites can be accessed in languages that include Chinese, Arabic and Thai as these global brands seek to establish a foothold in emerging, and potentially lucrative, foreign markets. What is evident is that behind each website is an awareness by the clubs' communications function that they must maintain a strong and sophisticated emotional engagement with fans. In an era when elite sporting icons lead very different lives to the fans who support them, and when clubs can earn millions of pounds through lucrative sponsorship deals, effective relationship marketing is crucial to develop, maintain and enhance a mutually beneficial ongoing relationship (Harwood et al. 2008) between the sports organisation and its supporters.

Picture 27.2 English Premier League football team Arsenal FC has a proactive approach to engaging and informing its fans (*source:* Julian Finney/Getty Images)

However, to address the needs of an increasingly hyper-digitalised fan-base, the execution of sports organisations' public relations and communications strategies must apply the same level of digital communications literacy to their use of social media. When used to best effect, social media platforms such as micro-blogging site Twitter, offer a two-way symmetric communications model (Grunig and Hunt 1984) that amplifies fan voices, and offers the sporting brand an opportunity to have genuine interaction with them (Stavros et al. 2014). Consequently, social media has brought a parasocial aspect to fan-athlete communications – on Twitter, followers are able to interact with their sporting hero(es) as if they were acquaintances (Pegoraro 2015). This can bring an immediacy and an authenticity to fan engagement, values that can engender fan loyalty (Pegoraro 2010). Social media offers clubs and individual athletes the ability to have a depth of engagement with fans (see Figure 27.2). There are also commercial implications. The number of followers an athlete has on Twitter is a metric of their popularity and will have a direct impact on their earning potential through sponsorship and endorsements.

Sports fans are becoming increasingly accustomed to personalised and seemingly authentic engagement with individual athletes and sporting heroes. It is therefore incumbent on sports organisations and clubs to attempt to create a similar authenticity with their audiences, given that many fans' loyalties lie with their sporting

Sport on Twitter			
Team	**Twitter account**	**Followers**	**Number of Tweets**
Real Madrid	@realmadrid	31.8m	66.1k
FC Barcelona	@FCBarcelona	29.4m	102k
NBA	@NBA	27.8m	232k
NFL	@NFL	24.4m	187k
UEFA Champions League	@ChampionsLeague	23.3m	60.1k
Premier League	@premierleague	19.3m	104k
Manchester United	@ManUtd	19.1m	53.1k
Arsenal FC	@Arsenal	14.3m	86k
FC Barcelona	@FCBarcelona_es	14m	103k
Chelsea FC	@ChelseaFC	12.6m	87.7k

(Information from Twitter, April 2019)

Figure 27.2 The most popular Twitter sports accounts (August 2019)

hero rather than with the club. When Cristiano Ronaldo left Real Madrid for Juventus in the summer of 2018, Juve gained 4.7 million new followers across their social media platforms in the two weeks following the move. In the 24 hours following the transfer announcement, Real lost 1 million Twitter followers (Gates 2018).

This is perhaps one reason why some top-flight football clubs are taking ownership of their own media. In 2017, Manchester United launched its own subscription-based app, MUTV to its 659 million fans in 165 countries (Manchester United 2017). Not only is this in answer to changes in the way fans are consuming sports events across a range of digital platforms, it also provides the club with invaluable data on its audience, thus allowing it to refine and tailor its content to individual fans' preferences. By owning, harvesting and intelligently interrogating this invaluable data, clubs are able to present personalised content to fans via the app, further augmenting the depth of connection between club and followers, with the aim of engendering ongoing brand loyalty (Connelly 2017; McCaskill 2018). Similarly, Chelsea, FC Barcelona and Bayern Munich are among 27 football clubs that joined forces in 2016 to create the digital platform Dugout (www.dugout.com), which offers fans exclusive content from the clubs. Its creation not only allows the clubs to split advertising revenues from the platform, it also takes into account a trend where fans, particularly in the increasingly important Chinese market, follow individual players and multiple clubs (Gates 2018; Connelly 2016). Dugout users can therefore customise their accounts and choose which clubs, players and influencers they follow (Connelly 2016).

The inexorable increase in the fragmented global consumption of sport across digital platforms naturally has implications for sports brands and sponsors. Having a regularly updated and content-rich website and being active on social media are currently still mandatory. But of far greater importance is an understanding of the differing cultural needs and media consumption trends of a variety of global audiences – an audience where each individual wants authentic, personal engagement with the brand.

Promoting participation and fandom

Part of the role of public relations in sport is to secure mass participation of players, fans and officials. Sports at all levels, whether professional or amateur, require sophisticated communications to help achieve this objective (L'Etang 2006a; Ruihley et al. 2016) and there is an acceptance that sport communication is now an intrinsic aspect of good sport management processes (Hambrick 2017; Rosca 2017). Ensuring that a long-term view is taken can sometimes be challenging in sports PR however, as the event-focused nature of sport lends itself to a more short-term promotional

> **Box 27.2**
>
> **Types of publics for sports PR**
>
> Whether a sports PR campaign is for a local volunteer-led league, or international professional teams, it will involve a diverse range of different publics, for example: governments, investors, leagues, clubs, teams, players, the media, officials, coaches, agents, fans/supporters, local authorities, services, sponsors and interest groups (Tamir et al. 2015).

perspective. This can lead to a focus on encouraging attendance at specific events, rather than building long-term commitment and participation (Dimitrov 2008).

Typical public relations activities to encourage participation will include the production of results announcements, events calendars, league information, player profiles and historical data all supplied via an online hub such as Facebook, Instagram or a website. Sports PR professionals and volunteers may also provide information to the news media, create and email newsletters, devise and host awards ceremonies, build partnerships with other organisations, and produce crisis communications plans and responses (Dunphy 2016; Ruihley et al. 2016). Many local groups will also be using closed social media platforms such as WhatsApp to share information, check player availability and confirm fixtures. As well as informative content, sophisticated public relations campaigns in this area will focus on persuasive messaging which highlights benefits such as the pleasure of practising a skill, the enjoyment of competition, and the sociability and networking opportunities of taking part (Kavetsos and Szymanski 2009).

Sports organisations are arguably a type of service industry, producing sporting participants, fixtures and entertainment, and in line with other service industries, they have a high level of engagement with customers who might be participants or fans (Rosca 2017). In order to facilitate consistency of communication, internal marketing and public relations programmes are important so that customer interactions are informed and reflect the sports organisation's brand values. It is important to understand that fandom is not passive consumption, but an active expression of identity which may even take on a religious nature (Tamir et al. 2015). Social media helps provide a new and enriched fan experience, enabling fans to follow leagues, teams and players as well as create and interact with content whilst watching sport either in situ or via digital platforms. This can help fuel the sense of belonging and affiliation which is at the core of fandom (Pegoraro 2015).

Crucially, the internet has provided a powerful outlet for the creativity and expertise of online fan groups and individuals, empowering them to produce millions of online interactions (comments, likes, retweets etc.) and a large amount of branded content. Enlightened sports organisations are recognising that such highly engaged fans can be active social media content producers and that pervasive user-generated content is trusted by followers even when they see traditional media as more expert in their sport (Kwak et al. 2010). Sports communications managers need to be aware of the potential this type of content brings. Appropriate strategies, such as inviting kit design ideas and creating interactive competitions, can help harness collaboration opportunities (Maderer et al. 2018: 332). Digital has also, however, empowered fan activism and disgruntled fans can quickly join together in the virtual environment to unite around club or real-world issues. In Australia, for example, the 'Footy Fans against Sexual Assault' online group waged a successful online campaign to change cultural attitudes regarding rugby stars and sexual assault incidents (Dimitrov 2008).

PR and athlete transgressions

Sport has long been an effective embodiment of nations' collective identities, and can act as a focus of glorious national pride on a global stage. However, sometimes a nation or even a global collective will focus its adoration onto one individual, who in turn becomes transformed into a team or a sport's totemic icon (Gilchrist 2005). It can be difficult to quantify the precise qualities that allow our greatest sporting heroes to achieve immortality in the eyes of the public. Their transcendence into sporting icons could be the result of a once-in-a-generation talent, dogged determination in the face of a superior opponent, an unwavering commitment to fair play or simply a telegenic charisma. But what is certain is that in the heavily mediated world

Explore 27.1

Sports PR campaign planning

Either on your own or with others, think about how to develop a PR campaign for a local competitive swimming club. Consider the need to encourage volunteering, sponsorship and participation. How will you reach out to a variety of different stakeholders? For example, you might consider how to communicate with youth influencers, parents and teachers. What kind of messages would encourage people to take part?

Mini case study 27.3
Changing perceptions of Parkour

Parkour emerged in the 1990s in Paris and was immediately seen as extreme and edgy. The UK-based organisation Parkour Generations has led a long-term initiative to change the sport's initial negative imagery, using community work and engagement as a basis for developing a more positive brand image for the sport (L'Etang 2013). The results have been impressive. Not only has parkour achieved high media visibility, for example through the opening sequence to the Casino Royale James Bond film or the 2019 Apple iPhone XR advert, but in 2017 it was officially recognised as a sport in the UK, giving it access to government funding and National Lottery funding. Parkour Earth and the World Freerunning Parkour Federation now represent the sport globally and this has been achieved through a lobbying and partnership approach. Parkour organisations have maximised the sport's strong visual potential with compelling content across social media platforms, supported by experiential events and targeted campaigns such as Parkour Generations' *SheCanTrace* initiative to shine a spotlight on the female parkour movement and inspire women to participate.

of professional sport, outstanding talent will be recognised, analysed and amplified through an intense interest by broadcast media commentators, press columnists and fan reaction on social media.

When the critical mass of media focus and fan adulation is achieved, a carefully conceived and skilfully executed ongoing public relations strategy can cement the construct and create a lucrative brand image for elite sport stars (Summers and Morgan 2008). Doing so will allow them to bolster their earnings through activities that have only tangential links to their sporting success – through endorsements, sponsorships and brand representation (Andrews and Jackson 2001). Having a high-profile star participating in a mediated event will also boost ratings and fan engagement across multiple platforms (Crawford 2004; Miah 2017) and raise the profile of the home club and the sporting code.

It is at this juncture that a sports icon becomes a 'sporting celebrity' (L'Etang 2006), and the authenticity of their sporting achievement is further enhanced by the gloss of the public articulation of their personality (Gilchrist 2005). From a story-hungry journalist's perspective, celebrities – especially ones who have currency based on exceptional sporting talent as well as the cachet of fame – are exceptionally newsworthy

(Harcup 2015), and their private lives are of as much (if not more) interest as their sporting successes. Therefore, if a story concerning a sports icon conforms to the news values of surprise, bad news and entertainment (Harcup 2001), it is journalistic gold.

The sporting mediascape is littered with the corpses of elite sports icons who have transgressed. The newsworthiness of any misdemeanour is exacerbated because these individuals have fallen from an exalted position, and in addition, as elite sports stars, fans and the public often have unrealistically high expectations of their standards of behaviour (Sassenberg 2015; Summers and Morgan 2008). Public transgressions by elite athletes come at a cost. Not only do the transgressors risk losing the respect of their teams, their peers and their fans, there is a high probability that sponsorships and endorsements may at best, not be renewed, or at worse, publicly severed. What steps, therefore, can celebrity athletes take to rebuild their public image? In a review of academic literature on athletes' responses to transgressions, Hambrick et al. (2015) cite several instances where the application of Benoit's (1997, 2000) image repair theory (see Box 27.3) was used to analyse the rhetorical effectiveness of the individual responses of fallen sporting icons.

A notable example is an analysis of the American Olympic swimmer Michael Phelps's response in 2009, when a photograph of him allegedly smoking a marijuana pipe appeared in the since-defunct British Sunday tabloid newspaper, *The News of The World* (Walsh and McAllister-Spooner 2011). The image was taken at a time when Phelps was taking a break from training after winning eight gold medals at the 2008 Beijing Olympics. The authors note that Phelps issued the following statement on the day the photograph appeared in print:

> *I engaged in behavior which was regrettable and demonstrated bad judgement. . . I acted in a youthful and inappropriate way, not in a manner that people have come to expect of me. For this I am sorry. I promise my fans and the public – it will not happen again.*

Here, Phelps uses three rhetorical strategies – mortification, bolstering and corrective action – which were deemed to be successful, as his sponsors and associated governing bodies stood by his straightforward response to what many saw as transgressive behaviour. He did not deny (nor elaborate) on his actions, but instead reinforced his successful track record as an Olympic athlete, while vowing not to repeat his mistake (Walsh and McAllister-Spooner 2011).

In their detailed analysis of Lance Armstrong's responses to doping allegations against him by the United States Anti-Doping Agency (USADA), Hambrick et al. (2015) move the debate forward by undertaking a thematic analysis of the cyclist's 859 Tweets during that period, as well as unpacking his rhetoric when he appeared on the Oprah Winfrey show in early 2013. Framed within Benoit's image repair theory, they posit that effective use of social media allows transgressive

Box 27.3

Benoit's image repair theory

Benoit's image repair theory is based on analyses of the rhetorical effectiveness of the public responses of individuals (or organisations) to real (or perceived) transgressions (Benoit 2014). In other words, did their responses improve their tarnished reputations?

The theory encompasses five broad image repair classifications, made up of 14 complementary strategies (Benoit 1997, 2000):

- **Denial** can be executed in two ways – a *'simple denial'*, where the individual denies the offending act actually took place or *'shifting blame'* where the accused points the finger of blame elsewhere.
- **Evasion of responsibility** can be manifested in four possible ways. *'Provocation'* asserts that the offending act was the result of a separate offensive act by another, and was therefore a justifiable response to that provocation. *'Defeasibility'* is based around an assertion that the accused had a lack of information or control over aspects of the situation. *'Accident'* posits that the act was a mishap, while *'good intentions'* state that the offensive act had its root in the best of intentions.
- **Reduction of offensiveness** has six associated strategies. An individual may use *'bolstering'* to remind the public of their previous achievements, and mitigate against negative feelings aroused by the offensive act. Secondly, an approach based on *'minimisation'* could seek to downplay the seriousness of the act. A third approach is *'differentiation'* where the act is compared favourably to similar, but more heinous acts. *'Transcendence'* would argue that the act was done for the greater good, and the *'attack accuser'* is self-explanatory, but aims to reduce the accuser's credibility. The final strategy is *'compensation'*, where the accused will recompense the victims.
- **Corrective action** can be taken by *'planning to solve'* the problem and/or taking positive steps to *'prevent the problem'* from reoccurring.
- **Mortification** involves the accused apologising and asking for forgiveness.

athletes to construct their own ongoing narrative directly with fans and the public, thus bypassing (or even shifting) any competing negative narrative presented in the media.

Sport social responsibility and ethics

There is a growing expectation that all organisations, including sporting ones, should demonstrate corporate social responsibility (CSR). This means fulfilling required economic and legal duties, ethical expectations and perhaps choosing to undertake voluntary philanthropic programmes (Carroll and Shabana 2010). The concept of Sport Social Responsibility (SSR) has been further developed, based on the notion that sport is unique in its nature. Sports organisations of any size specifically require public participation and community support and organisational values are usually clearly aligned with those of their fans and participants (Hopwood and Skinner 2015). There is a strong connection between social responsibility, ethics and the reputational management role of public relations, with many sports related organisations under increasing public scrutiny in relation to issues such as governance, child sexual exploitation, doping and safety from harm, such as long-term head injuries in American Football (Benson 2017) and Rugby Union. Research suggests that many professional team sports organisations now accept that SSR is necessary, not voluntary, and many use philanthropic community programmes to help boost and protect their reputations (Walzel et al. 2018). Involvement in CSR programmes can give sports teams a 'halo' effect, which positively benefits their reputations (Kim et al. 2017). In addition to this, the large following that major sports, and their stars, enjoy, means that some athletes have been able to use their fame as a tool for advocacy, highlighting specific political or social issues. For example, in 2016 ex-American Football player Colin Kaepernick refused to stand before the American flag in order to protest against racial inequality, sparking a world-wide media debate. Media stunts like this can gain significant coverage in sports media and can thus highlight political issues to a wider readership than traditional news (Schmidt 2018). The use of sporting events to gain publicity in this way is not new. In England in 1913, for example, suffragist Emily Davison died after throwing herself under the King's horse at the Epsom Derby horse race as part of a campaign to gain votes for women.

Sport has the potential to be highly effective when connected with commercial social responsibility programmes for a number of specific reasons. Sports organisations can: exert powerful influence because they are woven into society; appeal to young people; command significant media attention; have a positive health impact; and encourage social interaction

Box 27.4

Sport social responsibility in practice: categories of CSR policies in sport (Giulianotti 2015)

1. **Private philanthropy:** The Detroit Lions American Football team took a strategic approach to CSR through the development of its *Living for the City* initiative. Rather than a broad approach to charitable giving, the club focused on two themes which resonated in an authentic way with both players and the community: health and wellness; and community development. *Living for the City* was based on strong mutually beneficial partnerships with specific community organisations who helped create and deliver investment and development programmes (Heinze et al. 2014).

2. **Strategic development:** Through its Advisory Body on Sport, The Commonwealth uses a combination of international meetings and lobbying to encourage member nations to develop their own national strategies for using sport as a tool for development and peace. Commissioned research is used as a basis for sharing best practice into how the positive impact of sport at the national and Pan-Commonwealth level contributes to sustainable development, health and well-being and the building of just and inclusive societies (www.thecommonwealth.org).

3. **Developmental intervention:** The Women's Sports Foundation was set up in the United States in 1974 by US tennis legend Billie Jean King to advocate for female sport participation. It is dedicated to creating leaders by enabling access to sports for girls. Campaigns include National Girls & Women's Sports Day (6 February), grants for local sports initiatives and a sports education programme (www.womenssportsfoundation.org).

4. **Social justice campaigning:** The sporting goods manufacturer Nike was forced to adopt a strategic approach to social responsibility following a global anti-sweatshop campaign, highlighting its use of low-paid child labour overseas (Smith and Westerbeek 2007). Nike now has a *Maximum Performance Minimum Impact* policy articulated in its annual Sustainable Business Report, which details its strategies to Transform Manufacturing and Minimise Environmental Footprint (www.nike.com).

(Smith and Westerbeek 2007). CSR programmes work best when there is a good fit between the sports organisation and the CSR partner, and when that alignment is communicated effectively (Lee et al. 2018). A ten-year study of FTSE100 companies reveals a marked increase in sports-related CSR programmes. Some use corporate giving, or philanthropy, some use sponsorship of events, competitions and athletes and the biggest growth area is in personnel engagement, where employees raise money through sporting endeavours, donate their time to support sports activities, or are provided with access to facilities and equipment to take part in sport and fitness programmes (Bason and Anagnostopoulos 2015).

The sector of fitness communication has also seen significant growth (L'Etang 2006a), exemplified by a range of government education programmes, such as Michelle Obama's Let's Move! programme in America, the UK's Change4Life initiative and the New South Wales Make Healthy Normal campaign in Australia. Many organisations have developed social media sites and fitness apps, such as the Nike+ Training Club through which consumers can share fitness tips, opinions, reviews, photos and progress with their social networks instantaneously. The Strategic Fitness Communication Model recognises the uniqueness of such fitness communication, which involves dynamic content produced by and for fitness consumers, enthusiasts, professionals, brands and specialised media. It specifically recognises that communications in the sector happens at both an organisational and a personal level (Williams 2015).

Sport as culture

Sport has been connected to human culture for centuries and many contemporary sporting activities developed out of rural community activities played at local festivals (L'Etang 2006b). As a major element of society, watched by, and participated in by millions, it shapes and reflects the preferences and biases of society and is a focus for different types of human communications. Sport often takes on a political role in terms of the way it represents society, or helps to achieve social change. The promotion of high-profile male sports, and the focus on particular athletes who conform to society's expectations for example, means that there is a complex connection between sport and issues such as body shape, gender, ageism and racism (L'Etang 2013). Even US presidents use sport as part of their 'masculine' brand images, for example George Bush running and cycling, Barrack Obama playing basketball and Donald Trump connecting himself to golf (Moore and Dewberry 2012).

> **Think about 27.2**
>
> ### Co-branding in sport
>
> The co-branding of non-commercial organisations with sport is common but can sometimes be problematic, particularly when the values and aims of the organisation may be at odds with sporting or fitness objectives. There is some broad concern as to whether CSR and sport-based activities have tangible social impacts and benefits (Giulianotti 2015). McDonald's sponsors community youth football in the UK and Coca-Cola has been supporting the Olympics since 1928. Is it appropriate for these organisations to appropriate sport and sporting occasions as a propaganda tool in this way?
>
> ### Feedback
>
> You could consider whether the organisations' values match the CSR activity and what the prevailing public opinion might be towards the organisations and their activities.

Picture 27.3 Barcelona FC had a four-year partnership with UNICEF, built upon a 2 million euro annual donation (*source:* VI Images/Getty Images)

Mini case study 27.4
Barcelona Football Club Foundation – more than lip service

Barcelona FC's stated mission is to be 'More Than A Club' and to help bring about real change in the lives of disadvantaged children and youth. It does this through the Barcelona Foundation which runs education projects reaching 1.5 million children in 59 countries. The club uses its resources and star players to support a wide range of projects focusing on issues such as refugee support, anti-bullying, youth violence prevention, values education and the promotion of paediatric well-being. Social Implication is one of five key strategic objectives for the club for 2015–2021, alongside Sporting Excellence and these objectives are communicated globally via proactive media relations work and a strong social media presence. The Barcelona Foundation Facebook page has 5 million followers and is supported by a wide range of emotive audio-visual and photographic content from its wide range of global projects. Other public relations work involves the creation of high-profile partnerships, such as the club's four-year partnership with UNICEF, built upon a 2 million euro annual donation (www.fcbarcelona.com).

Over the past century, sport has evolved as a key component of mass entertainment, effectively working as an entertainment business. Globalisation and the nature of converged media have supported the development of mega-sports and mega-celebrities who have become part of everyday culture. Sporting celebrities provide media interest, which helps them attract investment, a process labelled as 'self-commodification' by L'Etang (2013). Such stars use social media and other promotional techniques to attract attention and sponsorship, often presenting themselves in ways that reflect societal assumptions about gender and behaviour. In this way public relations plays a role as a 'cultural intermediary', facilitating promotional and publicity work (L'Etang 2013).

The hosting of large-scale events such as the Olympics, or World Championships, and connections with high-profile sporting leagues, is often used to support nation-building and promote a sense of national pride and identity. It can bring credibility and boost the soft power of emerging nations as part of public diplomacy programmes, such as the investment in the Paris Saint Germain football team by the sovereign rulers of Qatar (Grix and Lee 2013; Chavanat 2017; Kolotouchkina 2018). Sports events are also used diplomatically by global organisations, such as the United Nations, to foster inter-cultural relations, or to promote diversity, such as the creation of the Paralympics or the Gay Games and in this way sport becomes a carrier for ideological meanings (L'Etang 2013). In the early 1960s Boorstin highlighted how these types of 'pseudo-events' were often created simply in order to be reported. With the power to make experience, they create their own sense of reality and often spawn other pseudo-events, such as press-conferences and experiential fan events (Boorstin 1992). Presented with reverence and ceremony, sports events such as opening and closing ceremonies, symbolically present new interpretations of culture, society and history which can boost national identities but can also, critically, marginalise those sports and sectors of society which are not presented in the same way (Dayan and Katz 1992).

The tourism power of sport is also significant. Public relations programmes often use traditional and outdoor sports (hiking, mountain-biking, river canoeing) as a motivation for visitors to travel (Van Rheenen et al. 2017), highlighting access to stunning natural environments (Hurch 2017), or use the sporting infrastructure created for mega-events to facilitate sports

Box 27.5
Researching sports PR

Critical research into sports public relations and culture covers a number of themes:

- **Sport representation**: how promotional activity adds to the dominance of major sports, but might also be appropriated to raise the profile of minority sports.
- **Stereotyping**: how public relations work contributes to cultural and gender norms.
- **The rise of promotional culture**: how mega-events create reality and how sporting celebrities contribute to a culture of self-promotion.
- **Commercialisation and sport**: the way PR has contributed to the transformation of sport from a game to a source of income.
- **Sport and politics**: the use of events such as the Olympics to promote tourism, national pride and specific socio-political ideas.

heritage tourism, celebrating past experiences such as tours of Olympic facilities in cities such as Berlin and Barcelona (Ramshaw and Gammon 2017).

The increase in health consciousness in Western societies has meant that sport has also developed as an important part of culture in its own right, whether in the form of sport viewing or participation (Tamir et al. 2015). Star athletes are now society role models and a new genre of sports entrepreneurs such as personal trainers have embraced online platforms to develop cult followings. Lifestyle sport has emerged as a significant off-shoot of this health focus and a range of postmodern non-traditional activities such as skateboarding, canyoning and BASE jumping enjoy vibrant online communities and are often targeted psychographically as part of public relations programmes (L'Etang 2006b).

Explore 27.2 — Gender, representation and bias in sport

Media representation of sport is often biased. Male sports tend to dominate coverage and this perpetuates a cycle of increased sponsorship and investment which makes it difficult for minority, lesbian, gay, bisexual, transgender and female sports to gain visibility and support. Our experience of the Olympics, for example, is shaped by what is selected, emphasised or excluded by broadcasters and journalists and stories are often racially or gender stereotypical (Billings and Brown 2015). Think about a minority sport which does not receive significant media attention. Talk to others and consider what kind of campaign or public relations activity could help the sport gain more visibility. How does the lack of coverage for the sport impact cultural expectations and norms?

Mini case study 27.5 — Sport England: This Girl Can campaign

Sport England launched its This Girl Can campaign after research revealed that fear of judgement was a primary barrier and possible cause of a significant 2 million gender gap between the number of 14- to 40-year-old men and women playing sport regularly in the UK. Now in its third phase, the 2019 campaign has a new Fit Got Real slogan and is building on the campaign's successful stakeholder activism approach, with PR work by Freud Communications. Alongside advertising, Sport England created a Supporter's Toolkit with photos, logos, templates and tips, facilitating the participation of 8000 supporters from the Football Association to small local sports clubs, charities and community groups. Strong emphasis has been given to social media with 700,000 followers across Facebook, Twitter, Instagram and YouTube sharing their tips and experiences. A ThisGirlCan mobile app enables participants to create their own poster and a significant investment in photography of real women exercising in their own way has underpinned the digital content. This Girl Can films have been viewed more than 37 million times on bespoke YouTube and Facebook channels and the campaign has encouraged the participation of 3 million women in sport and exercise to date. The VicHealth foundation in Australia is now running a local version of the campaign in Victoria, Australia.

www.thisgirlcan.co.uk

Summary

This chapter has examined the different roles undertaken by public relations practitioners working within a sporting context. It has looked at the traditional media relations functions, but it has also explored how sports communicators must have a thorough understanding of branding, marketing and digital communications practices. What becomes apparent is that the way that sports fans are consuming information is changing, with consumption across a wide variety of digital platforms becoming ever-more common, especially among younger generations. The implications for sports organisations and their public relations practitioners are significant. The expectations of a sporting organisation's global fan-base will increasingly be of authentic engagement, taking the form of exclusive, personalised content tailored to their interests.

Bibliography

Andrews, D.L. and S. Jackson (2001) *Sports stars: The cultural politics of sporting celebrity*. London: Routledge.

Bason, T. and C. Anagnostopoulos (2015) Corporate social responsibility through sport: a longitudinal study of the FTSE100 companies. *Sport, Business and Management: An International Journal*, 5(3), pp. 218–241.

Benoit, W.L. (1997) Image Repair Discourse And Crisis Communications. *Public Relations Review*, 23, pp. 177–186.

Benoit, W.L. (2000) Another visit to the theory of image restoration strategies. *Communication Quarterly*, 44, pp. 463–477.

Benoit, W.L. (2014) *Accounts, Excuses and Apologies: Image Repair Theory and Research*. New York: New York University Press.

Benson, P. (2017) Big Football: Corporate Social Responsibility and the Culture and Color of Injury in America's Most Popular Sport. *Journal of Sport and Social Issues*, 41(4), pp. 307–334.

Beverland, M. (2009) *Building Brand Authenticity: 7 Habits of Iconic Brands*. e-book: Palgrave Macmillan.

Billings, A.C. and N. Brown (2015) Understanding the Biggest Show in Media: What the Olympic Games Communicates to the World. In: P. M. Pedersen, ed., *Routledge Handbook of Sport Communication*. Abingdon: Routledge, pp. 155–164.

Boorstin, D.J. (1992) [first printed in 1961] *The Image*. New York: Vintage Books.

Bouchet, P., D. Hillairet and G. Bodet (2013) *Sport Brands*. Abingdon: Routledge.

British esports Association (2017) *The British Esports Association Who we are and what we do* [online] British esports Association. Available at https://www.britishesports.org/assets/AboutBritishEsportsPDFOCT17V22pdf. [Accessed 21 April 2019].

Brunello, A. (2018) Brand Equity in Sports Industry. *International Journal of Communication Research*, Vol. 8(1), pp. 25–30.

Carroll, A.B. and K.M. Shabana (2010) The Business Case for Corporate Social Responsibility: A review of Concepts, Research and Practice. *International Journal of Management Reviews*, 12(1), pp. 85–105.

Chavanat, N. (2017) French football, foreign investors: global sports as country branding. *Journal of Business Strategy*, 38(6), pp. 3–10.

Connelly, T. (2016) FC Barcelona, Real Madrid and 10 Premier League clubs unite to launch digital platform 'Dugout'. [online] The Drum. Available at https://www.thedrum.com/news/2016/11/28/fc-barcelona-real-madrid-and-10-premier-league-clubs-unite-launch-digital-platform [Accessed January 14 2019].

Connelly, T. (2017) A blurring of the lines: how football clubs like Manchester United are evolving into media owners. [online] The Drum. Available at https://www.thedrum.com/news/2017/05/19/blurring-the-lines-how-football-clubs-manchester-united-are-evolving-media-owners [Accessed 23 March 2019].

Crawford, G. (2004) *Consuming Sport: Fans, Sport and Culture*. Abingdon: Routledge.

Dayan, D. and E. Katz (1992) *Media Events: The live broadcasting of history*. London: Harvard University Press.

Deloitte LLP (2018) *Roar power. Annual review of football finance 2018*. [online] Deloitte. Available at https://www2.deloitte.com/uk/en/pages/sports-business-group/articles/annual-review-of-football-finance.html [Accessed 18 January 2019].

Department for Digital, Culture, Media and Sport (2018) *DCMS Sector Economic Estimates 2017 (provisional)*. [online] DCMS. Available at https://assets.publishing.service.gov.uk/government/uploads/system/uploads/attachment_data/file/759707/DCMS_Sectors_Economic_Estimates_2017__provisional__GVA.pdf [Accessed 5 January 2019].

Dimitrov, R. (2008) Gender violence, fan activism and public relations in sport: The case of "Footy Fans Against Sexual Assault". *Public Relations Review*, 34, pp. 90–98.

Dunphy, B. (2016) A Model Athletic Communications Plan. *Journal of Facility Planning, Design and Management*, 4(2), pp. 65–75.

Gates, E. (2018) The cultish lure of the modern day superstar. [online] Tifo. Available at https://www.tifo-football.com/features/the-cultish-lure-of-the-modern-day-superstar/ [Accessed 17 April 2019].

Gilchrist, D. (2005) Local heroes and global stars. In: L. Allison, ed., *The Global Politics of Sport: The role of global institutions in sport*. London: Routledge, pp.107–126.

Giulianotti, R. (2015) Corporate social responsibility in sport: critical issues and future possibilities. *Corporate Governance*, 15(2), pp. 243–248.

Grix, J. and Lee, D. (2013) Soft Power, Sports Mega-events and Emerging States: The Lure of the Politics of Attraction. *Global Society*, 27(4) pp. 521–536.

Grunig, J.E. and Hunt, T. (1984) *Managing Public Relations*. New York: Holt, Rinehart and Winston.

Hambrick, M.E. (2017) Sport communication research: A social network analysis. *Sports Management Review*, 20, pp. 170–183.

Hambrick, M.E., Frederick, E.L. and Sanderson, J. (2015) From Yellow to Blue: Exploring Lance Armstrong's Image Repair Strategies Across Traditional and Social Media. *Communication & Sport*, 3(2), pp. 196–218.

Harcup, T. (2015) *Journalism: Principles and Practice*, 3 edn. London: Sage.

Harcup, T. and O'Neill, D. (2001) What Is News? Galtung and Ruge Revisited. *Journalism Studies*, 2, pp. 261–280.

Hardy, S., Norman, B. and Sceery, S. (2012) Toward a history of sport branding. *Journal of Historical Research in Marketing*, 4(4), pp. 482–509.

Harwood, T., Garry, T. and Broderick, A. (2008) *Relationship Marketing Perspectives, Dimensions and Contexts*. London: McGraw Hill.

Hassan, R. (2004) *Media, Politics and the Network Society*. Maidenhead: Open University Press.

Heinze, K.L., Soderstrom, S. and Zdroik, J. (2014) Toward Strategic and Authentic Corporate Social Responsibility in Professional Sport; A Case Study of the Detroit Lions. *Journal of Sport Management*, 28, pp. 672–686.

Hopwood, M. and Skinner, J. (2015) Sport Communication and Social Responsibility. In: P. M. Pedersen, ed., *Routledge Handbook of Sport Communication*, Abingdon: Routledge, pp. 421–430.

House of Commons Culture, Media and Sport Committee (2011) *2018 World Cup Bid*. London: The Stationery Office Limited.

Hurych, E. (2017) Authenticity in the Perspective of Sport Tourism: Some Selected Examples. *Physical Culture and Sport: Studies and Research*, Vol. LXXIII, pp. 44–53.

Hutchins, B. and Boyle, R. (2017) A Community of Practice. *Digital Journalism*, 5(5), pp. 496–512.

Kavetsos, G. and Szymanski, S. (2009) From the Olympics to the grassroots; What will London 2012 mean for sport funding and participation in Britain? *Public Policy Research*, (Sep–Nov 2009), pp. 192–196.

Khamis, S., Ang, L. and Welling, R. (2017). Self-branding, 'micro-celebrity' and the rise of Social Media Influencers. *Celebrity Studies*, 8(2), 191–208.

Kim, J.K., Holly, K.O., Hull, K. and Choi, M. (2017) 'Double Play! Examining the Relationship Between MLB's Corporate Social Responsibility and Sport Spectators' Behavioural Intentions. *International Journal of Sport Communication*, 10, pp. 508–530.

Kolotouchkina, O. (2018) Engaging citizens in sports megaevents; the participatory strategic approach of Tokyo 2020 Olympics. *Communication & Society*, 31(4), pp. 45–58.

Kwak, D.H., Kim, Y.K. and Zimmerman, M.H. (2010) User-Versus Mainstream-Media-Generated Content: Media Source, Message Valence, and Team Identification and Sport Consumers' Response. *International Journal of Sport Communication*, Vol. 3, pp. 402–421.

Lee, S.P., Heinze, K. and Lu, L.D. (2018) Warmth, Competence, and Willingness to Donate: How Perceptions of Partner Organizations Affect Support of Corporate Social Responsibility Initiatives in Professional Sport. *Journal of Sport and Social Issues*, 42(1), pp. 23–48.

L'Etang, J. (2006a) Public Relations in Sport, Health and Tourism. In: J. L'Etang, and M. Pieczka, eds., *Public Relations: Critical Debates and Contemporary Practice*. London: Lawrence Erlbaum Associates.

L'Etang, J. (2006b) Public relations and sport in promotional culture. *Public Relations Review*, 32, pp. 386–394.

L'Etang, J. (2013) *Sports Public Relations*; London: Sage.

L'Etang, J. and Hopwood, M. (2008) Sports Public Relations. *Public Relations Review*, 34, pp. 87–89.

Maderer, D., Parganas, P. and Anagnostopoulos, C. (2018) Brand-Image Communication Through Social Media: The Case of European Professional Football Clubs. *International Journal of Sport Communication*, 11, pp. 319–338.

Mahoney, J. (2018) *Chronology of the Tiger Woods scandal*, [online] The Globe and Mail. Available at https://www.theglobeandmail.com/sports/chronology-of-the-tiger-woods-scandal/article4313560/ [Accessed 26 April 2019].

McCaskill, S. (2018) *How Manchester Unites sees digital as the key to future digital success*, [online] Forbes. Available at https://www.forbes.com/sites/stevemccaskill/2018/09/10/how-manchester-united-sees-digital-as-the-key-to-future-commercial-success/#4e8bf1cb6407 [Accessed 23 March 2019].

McCombs, M. (2013) *Setting the Agenda: The Mass Media and Public Opinion*, Hoboken: John Wiley and Sons.

Miah, A. (2017) *Sport 2.0: Transforming Sports for a Digital World*. London: MIT Press.

Moore, A.J. and Dewberry, D. (2012) The Masculine Image of Presidents As Sporting Figures: A Public Relations Perspective. *SAGE Open*, July–September 2012, pp. 1–11.

Ofcom (2018a) *News consumption in the UK: 2018* [online]. Ofcom. Available at https://www.ofcom.org.uk/__data/assets/pdf_file/0024/116529/news-consumption-2018.pdf. [Accessed 14 March 2019].

Ofcom (2018b) *Children and parents: Media use and attitudes report 2018*. [online]. Ofcom. Available at https://www.ofcom.org.uk/__data/assets/pdf_file/0024/134907/Children-and-Parents-Media-Use-and-Attitudes-2018.pdf [Accessed 27 April 2019].

Pannekeet, J. (2019) *Newzoo: Global Esports Economy Will Top $1 Billion for the First Time in 2019*. [online]. Newzoo. Available at https://newzoo.com/insights/articles/newzoo-global-esports-economy-will-top-1-billion-for-the-first-time-in-2019/ [Accessed 19 April 2019].

Pegoraro, A. (2010) Look Who's Talking – Athletes on Twitter: A Case Study. *International Journal of Sport Communication*, Vol. 3, pp. 501–514.

Pegoraro, A. (2015) Sport fandom in the digital world. In: P.M. Ederson, ed., *Routledge Handbook of Sport Communication,* Abingdon: Routledge, pp. 248–258.

PwC (2018) *Sports Industry: Lost in transition?* [online]. PwC. Available at file:///F:/Sports%20PR/Tench%20&%20Waddington/PwC%20Sports%20Survey-2018_web.pdf [Accessed 21 May 2019].

Ramshaw, G. and Gammon, S.J. (2017) Towards a critical sport heritage: implications for sport tourism. *Journal of Sport & Tourism,* 21(2), pp. 115–131.

Reenan, D.V., Cernaianu, S. and Sobry, C. (2017) Defining sport tourism: a content analysis of an evolving epistemology. *Journal of Sport & Tourism,* 21(2), pp. 75–93.

Rosca, V.I. (2017) Using Internal Marketing Communications to Improve HRM in Service-Based Sports Organizations. *Review of International Comparative Management,* 18(4), pp. 406–420.

Rowe, D. (2004) *Sport, Culture and the Media: The Unruly Trinity.* Buckingham: Open University Press.

Ruihley, B. J., Pratt, A. N., and Carpenter, T. (2016) The Role of Public Relations in College Athletics. *Journal of Applied Sport Management,* 8(1), pp. 52–74.

Sassenberg, A. (2015) Effects of sports celebrity transgressions: An exploratory study. *Sports Marketing Quarterly,* 24, pp. 78–90.

Scherer, J. and Jackson, S. (2008) Producing Allblacks.com: Cultural Intermediaries and the Policing of Electronic Spaces of Sporting Consumption. *Sociology of Sport Journal,* 25, pp. 187–205.

Schmidt, H.C. (2018) Sport Reporting in an Era of Activism: Examining the Intersection of Sport Media and Social Activism. *International Journal of Sport Communication,* 11, pp. 2–17.

Scholl, H.J. (2015) Evaluating Sports Websites From An Information Management Perspective. In P.M. Ederson, ed., *Routledge Handbook of Sport Communication,* London, Routledge, pp. 289–299.

Scrivener, P. (2019) Tiger Woods wins 2019 Masters at Augusta to claim 15th major win. [online] BBC Sport. Available at https://www.bbc.co.uk/sport/golf/47927647 [accessed 26 April 2019].

Sherwood, M., Nicholson, M. and Marjoribanks, T. (2017a) Access, Agenda Building And Information Subsidies: Media Relations In Professional Sports. *International Review for the Sociology of Sport,* 52(8), pp. 992–1007.

Sherwood, M., Nicholson, M. and Marjoribanks, T. (2017b) Controlling The Message And The Medium? *Digital Journalism,* 5(5), pp. 513–531.

Slack, T. (2004) *The Commercialisation of Sport.* London: Routledge.

Smith, A.C.T. and Westerbeek, H.M. (2007) Sports as a Vehicle for Deploying Corporate Social Responsibility. *The Journal of Corporate Citizenship,* 25, pp. 43–54.

Stavros, C., Meng, M.D., Westberg, K. and Farrelly, F. (2014) Understanding fan motivation for interacting on social media. *Sport Management Review,* 17, pp. 455–469.

Stoldt, C., Dittmore, S.W. and Branvold, S.E. (2006) *Sport Public Relations.* Champaign: Human Kinetics.

Sugden, J. and Tomlinson, A. (2007) Stories from Planet Football and Sportsworld. *Journalism Practice,* 1(1), pp. 44–61.

Summers, J. and Johnson Morgan, M. (2008) More Than Just The Media: Considering The Role Of Public Relations In The Creation Of Sporting Celebrity And The Management Of Fan Expectations. *Public Relations Review,* 34, pp. 176–182.

Tamir, I., Limor, Y.H. and Galily, Y. (2015) Sports: Faster, Higher, Stronger and Public Relations. *Human Affairs,* 25, pp. 93–109.

Turner, G. (2007) The economy of celebrity. *Stardom and celebrity: A reader,* 193–205.

Turner, G. (2010) Approaching celebrity studies. *Celebrity Studies,* 1, pp. 11–20.

Walsh, J. and McAllister-Spooner, S.M. (2011). Analysis of the image repair discourse in the Michael Phelps controversy. *Public Relations Review,* 37(2), 157–162.

Van Rheenen, D., Cernaianu, S. and Sobry, C. (2017). Defining sport tourism: A content analysis of an evolving epistemology. *Journal of Sport & Tourism,* 21(2), 75–93.

Walzel, S., Robertson, J. and Anagnostopoulos, C. (2018) Corporate Social Responsibility in Professional Team Sports Organizations: An Integrative Review. *Journal of Sport Management,* 32, pp. 511–530.

Wang, M.C. and Tang, Y. (2018) Examining the antecedents of sport team brand equity: A dual-identification perspective. *Sport Management Review,* 21, pp. 293–306.

Williams, A.S. (2015) Defining fitness communication: Conceptualising an emerging segment of the sport industry. In: P.M. Pedersen, ed., *Routledge Handbook of Sport Communication,* Abingdon: Routledge, pp. 197–207.

Yang, D., Lu, Y. and Sun, Y. (2018) Factors Influencing Chinese Consumers' Brand Love: Evidence from Sports Brand Consumption. *Social Behaviour and Personality,* 46(2), pp. 301–312.

Yanity, M. (2013) Publishing for Paydirt: A Case Study of an Athletic Department Writer. *International Journal of Sport Communication,* 6, pp. 478–479.

CHAPTER 28

Martina Topić and Mirela Polić

Fashion public relations

Source: James DeBoer/Shutterstock

Learning outcomes

By the end of this chapter you should be able to:
- understand the difference between high (haute couture) and everyday fashion (prêt-à-porter)
- understand criticism directed towards the fashion industry
- identify and discuss challenges of working in the fashion industry
- review and critique famous fashion campaigns
- analyse and apply public relations campaigning approaches to the ones in the fashion industry
- evaluate your own learning on the fashion industry and fashion public relations.

Structure

- The fashion industry: management and challenges for working in the fashion industry
- Fashion public relations
- The role of celebrities in fashion public relations
- The role of social media influencers in fashion public relations
- The role of bloggers and vloggers in fashion public relations

Introduction

In this chapter, we are discussing a niche, specialist area of business communication, fashion public relations. Since the literature in this field is scarce we are starting with an explanation of the fashion industry, and this section includes the management of fashion and some challenges when working in the fashion industry such as managing fashion, stereotypes of the fashion industry, feminist hostility towards this particular industry – which is seen as inherent to capitalism and the patriarchal oppression of women – as well as sustainability criticisms about the fashion industry.

Next the chapter will outline fashion public relations as a specialised field of public relations and we discuss some challenges and perceptions of fashion public relations practice.

We then continue with discussing main aspects of the professional fashion public relations role, such as celebrities, social media influencers, bloggers and vloggers and the influence they have on the fashion industry and public relations professionals working in fashion public relations.

We also provide a wealth of case studies with some famous campaigns from the fashion industry, which are meant to encourage the reader to further explore campaigning in this lucrative industry. The case studies are also accompanied with questions for discussion, and thus the chapter aims to encourage critical thinking about the fashion industry and the role of public relations professionals in fostering organisational goals whilst responding to a multiplicity of stakeholders and building relationships with them.

The fashion industry: management and challenges for working in the fashion industry

The management of fashion is a slightly different process than the usual management process. The reason for this can be found in fashion forecasting and the specificity of the fashion industry in successfully following trends in order to be commercially successful. In other words, the fashion industry is heavily focused on fashion trends and there is a lifecycle of each trend, which influences fashion management. Therefore, the management of fashion literature is also cyclical and characterised by 'an initial period in which the frequency of citations increases, peaks and then declines' (Clark 2004: 106), and this process may differ from country to country, thus lasting longer in some places as opposed to others (Abrahamson and Fairchild 1999; Spell 2001).

Theories of fashion focus on aesthetic, emotional well-being and our sense of gratification when purchasing fashion products, and all of this has brought to the situation that a job in the fashion industry is not taken as seriously as other positions because it is considered to be trivial (Tranberg Hansen 2004; Abrahamson 1996; Blumer 1969) and something that attracts too much excitement, conformity and mass hysteria (ibid.).

When it comes to management, the usual view is that the management of fashion is associated with the taste of its managers and senior officials (Abrahamson 1991). In addition, there is a view that 'management ideas and techniques are subject to swings in fashion in the same way that aesthetic aspects of life such as clothing styles, hair length, music tastes, furniture design, paint colours, and so forth are characterised by surges of popularity and then decline' (Clark 2004: 105). This then means that management of fashion is focused on developing mass support, because of which trends often change (Abrahamson 1996).

Some sociologists, however, argue that fashion should be studied in more detail and challenge the view of fashion as trivial because of the role of fashion in everyday life and the ability to learn social history through observation of fashion in arts, entertainment, medicine and literature (Blumer 1969). In this view, fashion can be seen as very influential and socially relevant because it can influence social movements. For example, the yellow vest movement that emerged in France in 2018 (BBC 2019) could be explained through Blumer's (1969) view because members of the French protest group have worn memorable yellow vests. While these vests are not fashionable items but road safety ones, they still provided the style and image to the protest and thus could be seen as part of the fashionable practice.

The reason fashion is connected with mass hysteria and consumerism and why it is often criticised lies in the fact that fashion is seen as a trend set by the elite groups that then spreads to non-elite groups who are trying to identify with upper classes by adopting their style, a style originally invented by the elite to set them apart from non-elite (Simmel 1904; 1957). Even though this view has been introduced in the early parts of the twentieth century it still has relevance today because we can see how elites are setting trends for the wider population. For example, in the UK, the Royal Family sets fashion trends. This particularly applies to the late Princess Diana who was a trendsetter and nowadays it applies to Kate Middleton (formally known as Princess Catherine) whose fashion sense is much praised and copied both by high-street retailers and elite and non-elite alike. Mass following of Kate Middleton's style is so big that there are even fan websites, for example 'what Kate wore' (https://whatkatewore.com/) and

Picture 28.1 The yellow vest movement that emerged could be explained through Blumer's (1969) view because members of the French protest wore memorable yellow vests. (*source:* Michel Stoupak/NurPhoto/Getty Images)

'Kate Middleton Style', the latter being the blog specifically stating its purpose is to help 'you copy Kate Middleton, The Duchess of Cambridge's style' (https://katemiddletonstyle.org/). The contribution of Kate Middleton to the British fashion industry is estimated to be so significant that the British media coined the term 'the Kate effect' due to her influence in propelling British brands Issa, Reiss and LK Bennett to global brands with major presence even in fashion centres such as New York (Thomas-Bailey and Wood 2012; Henley 2017).

In addition, Kate Middleton has helped a number of high-street brands such as Top Shop and others to increase sales at the time when the market was very slow (ibid.). Therefore, it seems that Simmel's (1904; 1957) thesis on elites setting the trend still stands; the difference is that the appeal is now global due to connectivity and globalisation, however it is still celebrities and elites that often set the trend. In addition, Simmel also emphasised that because of this trend-setting character, fashion is constantly caught up in a never-ending process of innovation, which creates a cyclical fashion process (ibid.). This is still true to a large extent, except that the digitalisation brought about bloggers and vloggers as trendsetters. Since these bloggers came from non-elite backgrounds, many saw this trend as changing the nature of influence, however popular bloggers and vloggers soon after they start receiving hits enter the elite group and start setting trends, designing their own labels or endorsing products and thus becoming versions of micro-elites themselves.

Feminist critique of the fashion industry

In addition to the challenges of stereotypes, the fashion industry has historically been one of the most criticised industries when it comes to women's rights.

Explore 28.1

Look at two blog websites that follow Kate Middleton's fashion style: https://katemiddletonstyle.org/ and https://whatkatewore.com/ to identify what Kate Middleton wore last.

Next, look for articles on the last item Kate Middleton wore in the national media in your country and then try to find press releases and social media posts from fashion companies Kate Middleton promoted. Analyse these communication documents to see how the media reacted to endorsements from public figures such as Kate Middleton.

After that, analyse the tone of articles against Simmel's observations of elite versus non-elite following of fashion. Do you see any attempt to recommend her style from the side of the media? If so, what is the tone of reporting? Which model of communication is being used here (see Chapter 8 on PR theories)? Has fashion been labelled as trivial by the media? Is there an attempt to create hysteria?

Check user comments on media reporting and see what the public in your country says and how they see this particular type of celebrity endorsement.

After all of the above, find another trend-setter from a non-elite background (e.g. a famous blogger with lots of followers) and compare their portrayal in the media. Is there a difference in reporting? Can we call media elitist? Then check public responses to these influencers.

What does this mean for PR practitioners, e.g. should they still focus on media relations and persuasive communication or move towards working more with influencers from a variety of backgrounds?

Therefore, the industry is seen as a bastion of patriarchy centred on labelling women as only interested in fashion. Thus, feminists have historically been hostile to the fashion industry, and this particularly applies to socialist feminism that sees the fashion industry as an important part of capitalism (Parkins 2006). In other words, socialist feminism speaks against 'all forms of patriarchal and sexist oppression. Such an oppositional definition posits feminism as the necessary *resistance* to patriarchal power' (Moi 1988: 5, emphasis in the original). However, patriarchal oppression is not the only reason why feminists are opposed to the fashion industry. Other reasons include the fact that majority of factory workers in the fashion industry are women, and the fashion industry is known for sweatshops, which naturally brings criticism from feminists due to the notion of the exploitation of women. In addition, many women die from chemicals and poor working conditions in textile factories, but not many in the West know details of these working conditions because factories are more often based outside the countries or regions where the products are sold, namely poor countries. In addition, the norm in the fashion industry has for a long time been to focus on white, thin and tall women and this again brings the question of equality, central to feminism (Mellicker 2016).

Nevertheless, it is one of the most admired feminist writers, Simone de Beauvoir, who is often used as a reason to criticise fashion. In her seminal work, de Beauvoir (1952) said that one is not born a woman but rather becomes one, and she has eloquently deconstructed the binary view of men as rational creatures versus women as inferior and seen through their material bodies. Therefore, many feminist scholars followed this view and criticised women's self-presentation as a cultural 'situated bodily practice' (Entwistle 2000: 11). Wolf (1991) therefore argued that there is such thing as a beauty myth which then places women's appearance at the height of her social value, and appearance is defined with thinness and youthfulness. The focus on appearance is seen as oppressing women because instead of focusing on political and social equality they are focusing on harmful and unhealthy beauty routines, which bring them no reward (Wolf 1991; Faludi 1991). Preoccupying women with appearance was seen as determined by the advertising industry dominated by men and this happened in response to the political threat of the second-wave feminism (Tyner and Ogle 2009).

However, there are some authors who have challenged this hostility towards fashion. For example, Parkins (2008) stated there is no reason not to engage with building a feminist fashion theory while Scott (2006) argued that the feminist hostility towards fashion as an oppressive control over women (with those women who engage with fashion being seen as collaborators in their own oppression) needs deconstructing because fashion has historically played a role in the women's movement. Scott (2006) therefore argues that people have decorated themselves throughout history, regardless of their gender, and that the feminist notion of fashion being unnatural is actually natural because of the history of humans engaging with decorating themselves. She sees fashion as cultural and what constitutes a natural look varies from culture to culture, thus making a feminist argument on fashion potentially futile. In addition, she argued that throughout feminist history it was always women who had more power who tried to tell other women what liberates them, and this applies to fashion as well. Parkins (2012) also emphasised that many fashion designers, even if they are men, narrate

Picture 28.2 The majority of factory workers in the fashion industry are women. The fashion industry is known for sweatshops to produce cheap, fast-fashion clothing (*source:* Frédéric Soltan/Corbis/Getty Images)

their history of women through their fashion and since fashion is so deeply tied to women it becomes problematic to trivialise it because trivialising something so inextricably linked to women may mean trivialising women as well. Nevertheless, the fashion industry is an industry where many women hold important positions and thus trivialising the industry rather than engaging in meaningful criticism of Western women not being sensitive (or feminist) enough to see suffrage of non-Western women can be seen as problematic.

Criticism of the fashion industry by environmental activists

Finally, the fashion industry has been under heavy criticism, as already mentioned, for worker exploitation and recently also for sustainability reasons. Therefore, numerous non-governmental organisations started to advocate a shift towards sustainability. For example, the *Fashion Revolution* is a group of designers, producers, makers, workers and consumers who have formed an advocacy group to promote sustainable fashion that does not make a huge environmental impact. The organisation has a manifesto and organises events to promote their views on the fashion industry (The Fashion Revolution 2019). The criticism of the fashion industry and its impact on the planet has been so vocal that, for example, in the UK, Parliament debated the fashion industry. In 2018, a Parliamentary group (Environmental Audit Committee) wrote to major UK fashion retailers asking them what action they are taking towards making their businesses sustainable, and in 2019 they released an interim report, which identifies each company and assesses them positively or negatively based on a number of factors, ranging from sustainability actions, sustainability initiatives to labour market initiatives (House of Commons 2019) (Table 28.1).

However, just like the fashion industry faces criticism and suffers from the stereotype of triviality, the situation is similar for fashion public relations, a niche field of the public relations profession discussed in the next section of this chapter.

Fashion public relations

The fashion industry is always moving and it is largely centred on modernity because it ultimately seeks to follow the trends and the time in which new products are being developed. This makes the fashion industry a challenging and dynamic sector to work in, and this then has repercussions on the role and expectations of fashion public relations practitioners.

However, as is the case with the fashion industry in general, the role of fashion public relations is not as recognised as other, more general, forms of public relations work. However, this fits well within a larger framework of public relations industry being a feminised industry in which women form the majority of the workforce but do not have the same status as men who form a minority of employees. Nevertheless, PR is seen as an industry with a gendered power structure that perpetuates the patriarchal structure (Fitch and Third 2010).

Despite the significant role that fashion plays in the global economic market and human culture, as well as a large body of literature about fashion from an anthropological, sociological and managerial standpoint, there is little academic inquiry into the speciality of fashion public relations. Namely, fashion public relations is often perceived to be 'frivolous, glamorous and primarily image management and promotion' (Cassidy and Fitch 2013a: 1), hence it is generally described as a support function of marketing. In the terms of the marketing mix, which consists of 4 Ps – product, price, place and promotion, fashion public relations is labelled as primarily a promotional activity (Sherman and Perlman 2010; Jackson and Shaw 2009) and as a communication tool used to achieve an overall marketing strategy (Jackson and Shaw 2009). This is the situation despite the fact that the fashion industry is a very lucrative industry generating high income and thus contributing to the global economy. For example, a new industry report revealed that customers are estimated to spend $1 trillion by 2020 on cross-border fashion e-commerce only (McKinsey & Company 2018).

In a study by Cassidy and Fitch (2013a), practitioners working in fashion public relations stated that fashion public relations are incorrectly considered as only centred around glamour. For example, one practitioner stated that, 'people believe PR is all about parties, air-kissing and long boozy lunches' and that even people in the personal circle of PR practitioners believe that 'it is very glamorous and they think you just teeter around in high heels and get to go to all the shows and drink champagne and that it's all quite relaxed. The reality is long hours and you are the spokesperson for an entire brand so there is a lot of pressure on you to deliver' (p. 5).

However, few authors have gone beyond the understanding of fashion public relations as a promotional activity, which brings the image of glamour. Noricks (2009) claims that the role of fashion public relations is 'to communicate information about a client's product or designs to various publics through various media channels' (p. 48), whilst Sherman and Perlman (2009) define fashion public relations as 'being in touch with the company's audiences, creating strong relationships with

1 Fashion Retailers' Responses
Table of retailers' responses

Retailer	Sustainability actions — SCAP – Sustainable Clothing Action Plan	Use of organic or sustainable cotton (e.g. BCI, Cotton 2040)	Use of recycled material in products	ZDHC – Zero Discharge of Hazardous Chemicals	In store take back scheme or textile banks	Commitment to Climate Change Risk Reporting (TCFD)	Sustainability initiatives — SAC – Sustainable Apparel Coalition	Microfibre Initiative	Make Fashion Circular	Reuse or recycling of unsold stock	Labour Market Initiatives — ACT – Action, Collaboration, Transformation	ETI – Ethical Trading Initiative	SEDEX – Supplier Ethical Data Exchange
Engaged													
ASOS	Yes	Yes	Yes	Yes	Yes	No	Yes	Yes	Yes	Yes	Yes	Yes	No
Burberry	No	Yes	Yes	Yes	Yes	Yes	Paused	Yes	Yes	Yes	No	Yes	No
Marks and Spencer Group PLC	Yes	Yes	Yes	Yes	Yes	Yes	Yes	Yes	No	Yes	No	Yes	Yes
Tesco PLC	Yes	Yes	Yes	Yes	Yes	Yes	In discussions	Yes	No	Yes	Yes	Yes	Yes
Primark Stores Ltd.	Yes	Yes	Yes	Yes	No	No	Yes	Yes	Yes	Yes	Yes	Yes	No
Moderately engaged													
Arcadia Group	Yes	Yes	No	No	Yes	No	No	Yes	No	Yes	Yes	No	No
Asda Stores Ltd.	No	No	No	No	Yes	No	Yes	Yes	No	Yes	No	Yes	Yes
Debenhams	No	Yes	Yes	No	Yes	No	No	Yes	No	Yes	Yes	Yes	No
Next PLC	Yes	Yes	Yes	Yes	No	No	No	Yes	No	Yes	Yes	Yes	No

Less engaged												
Amazon UK	No	No	No	No	No	No	No	No	No	No	No	Yes
Boohoo Group	In disscussions	No	Yes	No	No	No	No	No	Yes	No	No	Yes
JD Sports Fashion PLC	No	No	No	No	No	No	No	No	Yes	No	No	No
Missguided Ltd.	No	No	No	No	Yes	No	No	No	Yes	No	Yes	Yes
Sports Direct International PLC (See Annex 1, Note 4)	No	No	No	Yes	No	No	Yes	No	Yes	No	No	Yes
TJX Europe (TK Maxx and Home-Sense)	No	No	No	Yes	No	No	No	No	Yes	No	No	No
Kurt Geiger	×	×	×	×	×	×	×	×	×	×	×	×

Table 28.1 Sustainability in the UK's fashion industry (*source:* House of Commons (2019). Interim Report on the Sustainability of the Fashion Industry: Fifteenth Report of Session 2017–19 / Report, together with formal minutes relating to the report. London: House of Commons. Retrieved from https://publications.parliament.uk/pa/cm201719/cmselect/cmenvaud/1148/1148.pdf (5 May 2019))

> **Explore 28.2**
>
> Read the report from the British House of Commons on the fashion industry in the UK (see the reference list for a full link to access the report). Are any of your favourite brands performing unsatisfactorily in their sustainability policies? What do you think public relations departments of these companies need to do to fix this issue and gain trust from publics?
>
> Next, look at whether there is a similar report in another country (look at fashion hubs such as France and the USA or your own country). If there is no report, look at major brands from that country and compare their sustainability policies using the same criteria the UK Parliament did in the report published by the House of Commons. What is the difference between countries and brands? Is there a difference between different headquarters of the same brand? How do you think public relations professionals in each country need to respond to the sustainability challenge?

them, reaching out to the media, initiating messages that project positive images of the company' (p. xix). Cassidy and Fitch (2013a) reviewed texts with reference to 'fashion public relations' and found that the terms 'publicity' and 'promotion' were prominent along with maintaining brand image and building relationships between organisations and publics, usually through the media. Moreover, they found that in all texts 'media relations appeared to dominate understandings of fashion public relations' (Cassidy and Fitch 2013a: 3). In their study that investigated public relations in the Australian fashion industry, Cassidy and Fitch (2013a) concluded that the 'professionalization drive of public relations results in the framing of public relations as a strategic management function and, in tandem, the marginalisation of fashion public relations' (p. 10).

Media relations, celebrity endorsement and relationship management were the dominant activities of fashion public relations practitioners who perceived fashion public relations 'to be a profession where professional means working to meet the goals and objectives of their client or employer' (Cassidy and Fitch 2013a: 10). The study also revealed that all participants perceived fashion public relations to be part of the marketing mix, hence authors call for the reconceptualisation of public relations in terms of work performed and suggest that the dominant paradigm is inadequate.

Moreover, Fitch (2017) argues that 'corporatist approaches to understanding public relations as a strategic, management discipline, which continue to dominate public relations scholarships, make little sense in relations to day-to-day public relations practices' (p. 159). These claims are supported by Coombs and Holladay (2018) who state that 'public relations as a practice has been rife with both forms of innovation over the past decade as stakeholders and communication channels have transformed the landscape for the profession' (p. 382). They identified four emerging trends in modern public relations practice, theorising and research – digital channels, storytelling, stakeholder engagement and co-creation of meaning which 'contribute to the rather complex environment that presents contemporary challenges for public relations and a new mindset for public relations should be able to accommodate these trends' (Coombs and Holladay 2018: 383). This is especially true in the field of fashion public relations.

According to Coombs and Holladay (2018), digital channels 'have created new options for stakeholders and organizations to communicate with one another so public relations have to accommodate to digital channels' (p. 383). When it comes to fashion public relations, social media platforms represent one of the most utilised digital channels to reach publics, especially Facebook, Twitter, Instagram, YouTube, etc. Hence, the challenge for public relations practitioners is 'how to develop ways of engaging fashion publics in an industry where online shopping is increasingly a socially connected event and fashion publics share their wish lists and purchases with social network sites' (Cassidy and Fitch 2013: 7). Fashion public relations practitioners are not only focused on gaining media attention but as well on customer relationship building through social media platforms.

Social media channels are transforming fashion public relations by changing the way fashion designers and brands interact and engage with fashion publics. The first luxury brand that 'recognized the growing importance of digital communications and social media in order to reposition its brand as cool and trendy and increase its appeal to younger and web-savvier consumers' (Phan et al. 2011: 213) was Burberry. Burberry recognised that on social media, the customer is not only a public but an ally which additionally highlights the relationship nature of fashion public relations activity.

The second trend that Coombs and Holladay (2018) recognised as emerging in the field of public relations is the reinvigoration of storytelling. Storytelling can 'facilitate communication with stakeholders and is powerful because people are drawn to consume and generate stories' (p. 384). With the rise of social media, the new forms of stakeholders have emerged, especially in the field of fashion public relations.

Bloggers, social media influencers and celebrities influence and shape fashion public relations activities which in a large proportion include collaboration with them. Their way of storytelling affects and generates amplified eWOM which occurs when fashion public relations practitioners 'launch a campaign or in some other way encourage others to speak about a product or a company' (Kulmala et al. 2013: 21). Moreover, in order to be considered as credible and relevant as well as to build and maintain the loyalty of its publics, bloggers, social media influencers and celebrities must develop storytelling techniques that will be user-generated. They have to give good and credible information in order to increase consumers' fashion desires and to positively influence their attitude (Esteban-Santos et al. 2018).

Storytelling is closely linked to the stakeholder engagement that represents the third trend which has a long association with public relations but seems to be experiencing a renaissance (Coombs and Holladay 2018). Although both practitioners and researchers 'champion about the importance of engagement between organization and stakeholder' there are variations in the use of the term 'engagement' and a lack of consensus on the process (Taylor and Kent 2014: 384).

Conceptualisations of engagement can range from simple one-way communication, such as having stakeholders engage with (read) messages created by the organisation, to involving stakeholders in decision making. Social media platforms have changed the rules of engagement in a way that consumers and companies connect and engage through brand communities.

Consumer engagement with a virtual brand community describes the nature of participants' specific interactions and/or the interactive experiences between consumers and the brand and/or members of the community (Brodie et al. 2013). For example, Dhaoui (2014) proposes four types of consumer engagement in a Facebook brand community: 'first, endorsement of the brand and/or the values expressed in the content, e.g. liking; second, feedback or replies from users to content published by the brands; third, conversation with/among Facebook users and fourth, recommendation, i.e. passing on or sharing online content with other users' (p. 10).

eWoM and fashion public relations

When it comes to fashion public relations, one of the most important forms of consumer-brand engagement is electronic word-of-mouth (eWoM). eWoM refers to 'any positive or negative statement made by potential, actual or former customers about a product or company which is made available to a multitude of people and institutions via Internet' (Hennig-Thurau et al. 2004: 39). Consumer participation in social media brand communities may shape the perception of consumers about the brand through eWoM hence social media networks can act as a socialisation agent that facilitates eWoM.

Fourth, Botan and Taylor (2004) placed the idea of the co-creation of meaning firmly on the public relations radar and linked the concept to the social construction of reality. Co-creation of meaning is relevant to engagement processes. Co-creation involves stakeholders and organisations interpreting events or situations in a similar manner (Heath and Coombs 2006). Co-creation is often seen in fashion public relations as the win–win relationship between the bloggers, social media influencers and celebrities on the one side and the fashion brand on the other side.

Park (2015) differentiated five types of these win–win relationships – relationships established through work, fashion designers supported bloggers, social media influencers and celebrities before they gained popularity, young bloggers, social media influencers and celebrities seeking established fashion designers for help, personal friendships between the bloggers, social media influencers, celebrities and fashion designers and official requests either by the fashion designer or bloggers, social media influencers or celebrities for support. Fashion designers need to select bloggers, social media influencers and celebrities very carefully because through co-creation of meaning they influence each other. Bloggers, social media influencers and celebrities provide meaning to fashion brands through product endorsement and in a circular fashion manner, their own meaning is also created by the products they endorse (Escalas and Bettman 2015).

Fashion public relations is the field in which the synergy between owned and earned media is the most evident. Namely, fashion public relations practitioners combine owned media such as websites, blogs and social media platforms in collaboration with celebrities, social media influencers and bloggers, who endorse fashion brands through their channels, to get media coverage or eWOM – earned media.

In line with the growing relevance of social media and influencers, in subsequent sections, we will describe the role of celebrities, social media, and bloggers and vloggers in fashion public relations.

Mini case study 28.1
Inside Chanel

Paris has had the status of a fashion capital since the seventeenth century and it remains an important fashion place up to today, despite the rise of Milan, New York and London as fashion cities.

According to Steele and Major (2019), fashion is seen as part of the national culture in France, and this view originated from Louis XIV who saw fashion as a useful weapon to establish French cultural dominance. Thus, he required that all aristocrats wear appropriate fashion and France started to gain a leading status in the field of fashion. By the eighteenth century, wealthy foreigners were travelling to Paris to have their clothes made especially for them, or they were copying Paris fashion from newspapers. This is also the time when fashion started to become more expensive because the styles started to change frequently and this causes the price hike. The rise in prices raised objections in some countries and it is believed that this outrage with the price hike and constant changes in style coming from France influenced men across the European continent to embrace the English style because of its simplicity. However, this did not diminish the influence of France as a fashion capital, and this status only accelerated during the nineteenth century when the high fashion (haute couture) emerged. It was the nineteenth-century acceleration that also happened due to the fact the French government backed Paris fashion as the country's cultural product, which gave birth to the rise of fashion designers and that also further separated high fashion (haute couture) from ready-to-wear consumer fashion.

The first influential fashion designer emerged in the twentieth century (Paul Poiret) and he was soon followed by Gabrielle Coco Chanel in the 1920s. Coco redefined elegance as understatement and up to today Chanel's fashion brand is based on simplicity and the view that less is more.

Inside Chanel is a series of films and promotional materials. At the time of writing this chapter, there were 25 campaign chapters narrating the history of the company and important milestones in the development of Chanel to what it is today. The campaign, therefore, started with the film narrating the history of the company, and then it continued with narrating the relationship important company figures and some celebrities, such as Marylin Monroe, had with the company. These films, while centred personally on people important to the company, also portray business strategy and share the vision of the company. For example, Chapter 5 talks about Gabrielle Coco Chanel and this film also narrates the fashion brand the company is producing and shows to consumers that Chanel's fashion has a long tradition and continuity, especially when it comes to the iconic little black dress, main brand colours (black, white and gold), and fashion produced from the jersey, which is comfortable and convenient for everyday wear.

When the campaign is analysed in line with Chanel's history and origin, then it becomes visible that Chanel has never changed its original business purpose to respond to tacky and overdesigned clothes of the nineteenth century. The brand historically produces high fashion (haute couture) and everyday fashion (prêt-à-porter), both based on simplicity.

In 2018, Chanel revealed its earnings for the first time in the company's 108 years long history and the media assumed this was the case because of rumours of financial instability and potential takeover. According to the financial data made available to the media, in 2017, Chanel made nearly $10 billion in sales, and this cleared the doubt as to whether the company would remain independent and financially stable (Wattles 2018).

The films from the Inside Chanel can be watched at Inside Chanel.

Box 28.1

Haute couture is a term used to describe designer clothes that sets the trends and is original and exclusive. The term haute couture means high sewing or high dressmaking, and thus it is used to describe high fashion. The term is predominantly used to describe fashion for women, and haute couture is expensive due to its quality. Every haute couture piece is made according to measurements for each client and thus individually tailored in Parisian salons. For a collection to be haute couture a fashion company must have a workshop in Paris with a minimum of 15 staff members, they must design made-to-order pieces to ensure everything is tailored to an individual client. An example of haute couture is Chanel.

On the other hand, prêt-à-porter fashion is designer clothes sold ready to wear rather than to a measure. The term itself literally stands for ready to wear. While this form of fashion is not always mass-produced, it is available to many customers because the collection is made in different sizes and thus can fit everyone. The collection is not meant to fit perfectly or require a tailor.

Haute couture has collections twice a year (summer and winter season) while prêt-à-porter fashion is available twice a year, but most often in the pre-season.

Explore 28.3

Inside Chanel is a series of films portraying the history of the company and re-enforcing brand values and the brand's mission. However, these films are not the only promotional tools Chanel uses. They are also regularly launching campaigns for new products; however, as with Inside Chanel, these campaigns are never just marketing campaigns promoting a certain product. All campaigns always re-enforce the company and its long tradition and history.

As an exercise, watch Chanel's film 'The One That I Want'. This campaign was the first time Chanel had a child promoting Chanel's products and the campaign was praised as modernising the company to appeal to their female customers who now live in different circumstances.

Analyse this campaign against the Inside Chanel campaign series and discuss how this campaign fits into the Inside Chanel narrative. Also, what kind of women does this Chanel campaign appeals to? What values are being enforced in this campaign? Where do you think this campaign was promoted mostly? Which form of fashion was promoted in this campaign, haute couture or prêt-à-porter?

Picture 28.3 Haute couture is a term used to describe designer clothes that sets a trend. They are typically original and exclusive (*source:* Jun Sato/Getty Images)

Think about 28.1

Watch Chance Eau Vive campaign (https://www.youtube.com/watch?v=zhdZcBsa-dk) and discuss how this campaign fits into the wider Chanel narrative? Which form of fashion is promoted here (haute couture or prêt-à-porter)? What type of women does the campaign try to appeal to? What values are being enforced in the campaign?

The role of celebrities in fashion public relations

Turner (2014) describes celebrity as an 'extensive and intrusive form of public visibility and a form of a frame that is generated directly by media exposure' (p. 86). Social media engenders the performance of celebrity in terms of self-promotion and fan engagement. Senft (2013) defines celebrities who become famous through social media as microcelebrities who 'deploy and maintain their online identity as if it were a branded good' (p. 346).

Social media has made it possible for celebrities to provide information about themselves directly to its publics at any time and since publics are now able to connect with celebrities at any time as well, they feel like celebrities are talking to them (Kowalczyk and Pounders 2016). Moreover, publics enjoy hearing and seeing celebrities as real people and not just the aspects of their life as a celebrity. According to the study that Kowalczyk and Pounders (2016) conducted, the primary motivation to follow celebrities on social media is obtaining career information and personal information, whilst authentic posts and emotional attachment were key aspects of what consumers like about following celebrities on social media.

In the field of fashion public relations, celebrities act as the third-party endorser of the fashion product/brand and are carriers of meaning for consumers. According to Escalas and Bettman (2015) in order for the celebrity endorsement to be effective, there must be 'congruence between the celebrity image and the fashion brand image' (p. 47).

Seno and Lukas (2007) differentiate four types of celebrity endorsement – explicit ('I endorse this product'), implicit ('I use this product'), imperative ('You should buy this product') and co-presentational (merely appearing with the product). Fashion public relations practitioners mostly use the last, co-presentational endorsement in order to create a relationship between the fashion brand, celebrity and consumers.

The outcome of this process is that the co-branded product is positioned in a way that is difficult to imitate by competitors. Moreover, celebrity product endorsement is a two-way, interactive process with the celebrity and endorsed product affecting each other and the two-way communication is an essence of public relations activities. This can be seen on the example of fashion brand Nike that in 2003 spent $US1.44 billion on celebrity endorsers – basketballer Michael Jordan and the golfer Tiger Woods (Seno and Lukas 2007: 121). Celebrities attract a lot of media attention and since one of the tasks for fashion public relations practitioners is to get as much media coverage as possible, they engage celebrities to strategically position their fashion brand and get maximum press coverage.

Mini case study 28.2
Paul Smith and the celebrity culture

Paul Smith is a well-known British designer famous for his fashion brand known to combine tradition and modernity. The brand has a similar business model as the previously discussed Chanel, and thus it concentrates on 'classic with a twist' and this vision has not changed since the launch of the brand in 1970. Paul Smith stated that 'you can find inspiration in everything' and this means that his inspiration comes from everything, including high art as well as everyday life (Paul Smith 2019: n.p.). In addition, the company website states that their design is influenced by the 'dry British sense of humour: quirky but not frivolous; eccentric but not silly' (ibid.).

Over the years, Paul Smith was promoted by many celebrities including David Bowie, Led Zeppelin, The Lumineers and many other actors wore his clothes. However, Paul Smith stated in an interview with *WWD* magazine that he has never sought celebrity endorsement like many other brands do: 'We are not a pushy brand. It's not about trying to get celebrities to wear our clothes, it's the fact so many of them enjoy the clothes. Normally, they are people with character, so there's a magnet attracting them to a brand that's got character. With so many of the big financial brands, it's all about marketing and networking and association' (Medina 2018: n. p.).

In the same interview, Paul Smith also revealed that he has three people paid to do social media promotion and reply to emails whilst he and his wife do not even have a computer at home, and his wife does not own a mobile phone. Instead, he writes cards and letters to people who get in touch using this traditional method of communication (ibid.).

While the brand is originally known for men's fashion and its focus on 'classic with a twist' approach, the brand also engaged with producing women's fashion in 1998. In an interview with *the Telegraph* Paul Smith stated he likes seeing his designs on female silhouettes but that he does not want to work with celebrities like other brands do, and he does not care what others are saying, as so many brands do. In addition, he expressed criticism of celebrity brands like high-street collections of Madonna, Lily Allen and Kate Moss (Walden 2009).

'I'm not interested in all that. Those celebrity designers, they have neither the training nor the design awareness necessary in the business, which means it must be purely about ego and money. I wouldn't bring in a celebrity to work at Paul Smith in a million years. Actually, make that a trillion' (ibid.: n.p.).

Explore 28.4

When you think about the statements Paul Smith gave to the media about his views on celebrity endorsements, how did that make you feel? Do you follow social media influencers? Do you buy clothes they recommend or do you prefer to stick to your own brands you love (or no brand at all)? Do you think that Paul Smith will be able to sustain this approach as generations change and new digital generations gain more purchase power?

How do you think this personal view of celebrity culture is linked to the brand's mission?

If you were hired by the Paul Smith company to run social media and reply to emails, what would you do? How would you promote the brand on social media channels? What kind of message do you think you would create and who would be your target audience?

Think about 28.2

Paul Smith is not the only fashion designer refusing to have anything to do with celebrities and celebrity culture. Many other designers are trying to distance themselves from the celebrity label. For example, The Row brand was launched by teen stars Mary-Kate and Ashley Olsen and today this brand is worth millions and popular among many Hollywood stars. However, the brand was launched quietly in 2006 and the twins did not give an interview 'about the label for three years, which allowed it to be taken seriously and ensured that it was not seen as a "celebrity brand". By 2012, they won their first Womenswear Designer of the Year award at the CFDAs, cementing their status in American fashion' (De Klerk 2017: n.p.).

Victoria Beckham, famous for her membership in pop group Spice Girls and then marriage with the former footballer and captain of the England national team, David Beckham, also launched her designer brand quietly in 2008 'with a low-key presentation. She slowly became a fixture on the New York Fashion Week calendar and in 2011 launched her diffusion line, Victoria By Victoria Beckham. By 2014, she had opened her first bricks and mortar store on Dover Street and in 2017, she designed an affordable Victoria Beckham range for the American retailer Target' (ibid.).

Why do you think some celebrities do not want to be seen as celebrity brands? Do you think celebrities should use their status to promote their new designs? What do you think of celebrity culture?

Do you think celebrity brands are haute couture or prêt-à-porter? Would status in any of the two change (positively or negatively) if associated with celebrity status?

The role of social media influencers in fashion public relations

Social media influencers (SMIs) represent 'a new type of independent third party endorser who shape audience attitudes through blogs, tweets and the use of other social media' (Freberg et al. 2011: 90). They are individuals who have the power to affect the purchase decisions of others because of their authority, knowledge, position or relationship with their publics.

The possibilities of forging alliances with SMIs to position a brand or organisation are numerous thanks to the proliferation of social media platforms (Facebook, Twitter, Instagram, Pinterest etc.). According to Forbes (2018), Instagram was the social media platform with the highest reach for fashion influencers in 2017. When it comes to public relations, one of the most important things is earned media. Since social media influencers gain a lot of media attention, public relations practitioners tend to build and maintain relationships with SMIs in order to position their organisation/brand within the content they publish on their social media platforms in order to gain media attention.

Moreover, according to the results of the study that Cassidy and Fitch (2013) conducted in the context of Australian fashion public relations, fashion public relations practitioners perceived they 'had to engage in social media or risk getting left behind' (p. 11). They stressed the importance of having an online presence and perceived that 'social media was changing both the pace and function of public relations in a way that it is easier to achieve dialogic engagement with fashion publics' (ibid.: 14) on the one hand, but on the other hand fashion public relations practitioners are 'struggling to adapt traditional communication strategies such as employing a hierarchical top-down communication model, adapting communication for different platforms and maintaining exclusivity of new stories in a social media environment' (ibid.: 16)

Since social media influencers act as opinion leaders who set trends and influence consumers' buying decisions they are important to many organisations because they help give credibility to the message. Hence, fashion public relations practitioners need to understand the key attributes that make social media influencers credible among others and strategically compare them with mission, vision and communicational goals of their fashion organisation/brand.

Mini case study 28.3
Ted Baker's Keeping Up With the Bakers

In 2017, British fashion retailer Ted Baker started promoting its Spring/Summer 2017 collection with a film inspired by 1970s US sitcoms.

The 'Keeping Up With the Bakers' campaign narrates a story of a family in a fictional suburban neighbourhood of Tailor's Lane. The neighbours are envious and are fixated on the Baker family style. The 360-degree film is directed in pastel colours and the features of the campaign are specifically designed to appeal to users of Snapchat and Instagram.

The film is also interactive and thus users can click on clothing items featured in the film to buy individual items or the whole outfit, and they can also play games (e.g. reveal hidden content). In addition, users can join the game and become noisy neighbours in Tailor Lane and complete daily challenges. Instagram Stories then reveal winners of challenges and add new content.

This campaign was a continuation of the brand's previous campaign entitled Mission Impeccable, which was based on espionage. The campaign creators took an inspiration from James Bond and adjusted it to fashionable agents who are working to prevent a couture catastrophe. Every item of clothing used is a cinematic ad accessible through Tedbaker.com (Hobbs 2016).

The difference between the previous Mission Impeccable campaign and Keeping up with the Bakers is that 'this time around Ted Baker will also use Instagram Stories as a "gossip channel", with daily posts serving as episodic content to reveal more about different Baker family members. People are able to click through a selection of five different "TV channels" in Stories, with each showing content appropriate for the Baker's world, as well as revealing a competition winner' (Hobbs 2017: n. p.).

The campaign was highly successful with the trailer being watched 1.9 million times with 19,000 likes on its social campaign and 26,000 giveaways from in-store window engagement (Digital Training Academy 2019: n.p.).

Explore 28.5

Find other examples of successful Instagram campaigns and discuss their results against Ted Baker's results. What do you think was the reason for the success of Ted Baker's Instagram campaigning?

How do you think the success and popularity of the Instagram social network change the public relations profession? What does this change in public relations work mean for targeting and traditional public relations work?

Do you think that public relations work is more challenging since the rise of social media than it used to be? How do you think you would balance requirements of the profession and be able to maintain relationships with traditional media, as well as bloggers, vloggers, social media influencers and the wider public, which is now also well versed in social media relationship building? How would you prioritise workload?

Think about 28.3

Do you think that media relations will slowly diminish from the public relations profession in favour of digital channels? Before drawing a quick conclusion that traditional media ought to die out remember that many thought the press will lose popularity with the invention of the radio, and then the radio was predicted to die with the invention of TV, but this did not happen either and all forms of media still exist.

Speaking in terms of fashion public relations, how do you think the profession will change? In favour of more social media and digital engagement or in favour of going back towards more traditional forms of communication and relationship building?

Think how the notion of high versus everyday fashion (haute couture versus prêt-à-porter) may influence brand communication. If appointed to manage communications for a fashion brand how would you decide which form of communication to prioritise?

The role of bloggers and vloggers in fashion public relations

Esteban Santos et al. (2018) define fashion bloggers as 'one of the newest player in the fashion industry who perfectly represents the progressive democratisation of fashion and communication that we are witnessing nowadays' (p. 420). A blog connects with people on a very personal and emotional level. The personal nature of the blog discourse gives the reader a feeling of a personal conversation, not one which is being broadcast widely. In comparison to bloggers, vloggers are types of bloggers that use video as the main medium to communicate with its audience.

The emergence of fashion blogs started in 2002 with Chiara Ferragni's blog 'The Blonde Salad'. Blonde Salad turned into a global retail business with 17 million followers on Instagram which is equivalent to the population of the Netherlands. Ferragni was a fashionable Italian law student with a passion for posting photos of her personal style online and now she owns two companies worth $8 million. As a fashion vlogger, she uses her YouTube channel to produce a series of videos called 'Chiara Doing Things,' which give her fans a chance to see her life up close (Sanderson 2019).

Fashion public relations practitioners use a variety of blogger and vlogger outreach tactics to engage with their consumers. For example, in 2011, H&M launched its first fashion capsule collection designed by a fashion blogger Elin Kling called The Elin Kling collection, of which 10 per cent of the proceeds went towards Unicef.

A fashion bloggers recommendation can modify customers' attitudes towards a fashion brand, influencing how consumers perceive them (Esteban-Santos et al. 2018). Consumers consider this recommendation to be more credible since bloggers are perceived as an independent source.

In addition, in a study by Cassidy and Fitch (2013) public relations practitioners stated that working with bloggers added additional pressure to already demanding work. For example, one practitioner stated that she does not have the time to 'talk to every blogger… but we look for those that have some sort of credibility about them and we work with those directly and we have a relationship with them as we would with someone from a newspaper' (p. 15).

Credibility is a relevant concept because consumers too look at credibility. In order to investigate how consumers assess the credibility, Esteban-Santos et al. (2018) posited that it is based on three dimensions – source credibility, message credibility and site credibility. In a fashion blog, the source credibility is developed through a connection on an emotional level that creates the illusion of an interpersonal relationship between blogger and follower. Message credibility is usually measured by the numbers of visits or likes because, according to the theory of social impact, blogs become more credible when they gain popularity and several users share the same opinions about them through their comments or likes. The third aspect is site credibility and it relies on the characteristics of the platform where the blogger shares the content. In today's public relations arena, credibility is everything. Moreover, one of the key elements of excellent public relations is credibility hence fashion public relations practitioners have to take into the account the level of credibility bloggers possess in order to position fashion brand.

The credibility aspect is especially important in the context of eWOM. It is important to make a distinction between organic and amplified eWOM due to the fact that they have different impacts on credibility. Organic eWOM is a 'genuine eWOM where the blogger expresses his/her opinion without any economic support' while amplified eWOM 'occurs when the blogger is encouraged to talk about a product or a brand through a monetary or product compensation' (Kulmala et al. 2013: 21). It is critical for fashion public relations practitioners to build an environment that encourages positive eWOM communication and to constantly manage negative eWOM communication in order to prevent crisis that can damage the reputation of the fashion brand, hence the most important focus of fashion public relations is relationship building not only with bloggers but with the community which follows them in order to position the fashion brand in the desired way. They should actively monitor organic eWOM since the content bloggers distribute within organic eWOM is not controlled.

According to the study about the relationship between public relations practitioners and bloggers, Archer and Harrigan (2016) discovered that for most public relations practitioners 'the question of control and influence' (p. 72) were dominant. Namely, they expressed the desire to control the client's or organisation's message. On the other hand, for most bloggers, 'the relationship between public relations practitioners is less about dialogue and more about being given compensation/payment for any mention of brand or organisation' (Archer and Harrigan 2016: 73). This type of relationship between public relations practitioners and bloggers is the most common one in fashion public relations, which suggests that the press agentry model is coming back in the contemporary public relations scene.

Mini case study 28.4
The Blonde Salad by Chiara Ferragni

In 2009, Chiara Ferragni, a 22-year old student of International Law at the Bocconi University in Milan whose hobbies included fashion, photography, travel and posting pictures of her daily outfits on social platforms, together with her then boyfriend Riccardo Pozzoli, founded her blog 'The Blonde Salad'. Ferragni liked to mix and match different brands and styles because 'her followers always liked this because they could see how cool a cheap sweater can look when you wear it well. It was something they could really relate to'.

In autumn 2009, as part of his final year university studies, Pozzoli went to Chicago to complete a three-month-long internship and was surprised to discover that social media was already playing a significant part in the US businesses. Hence, 'one Sunday morning Ferragni and Pozzoli were having their daily Skype call and the conversation turned towards the creation of Ferragni's personal blog that the two had been discussing for a couple of months already' (Keinan et al. 2015: 3). The blog was named The Blonde Salad and it was organised around the different ingredients of the golden-haired Ferragni's salad of interests: fashion, photography, travel and lifestyle. Pozzoli bought theblondesalad.com from an American URL provider and Ferragni entered the first post on 12 October 2009.

Pozzoli advised Ferragni to post a 9 am daily entry on the blog to build loyalty among her followers (Keinan et al. 2015: 4). For many people, reading The Blonde Salad became a daily morning routine and after one month of blogging The Blonde Salad's readership grew to 30,000 daily visits. In early 2010, Ferragni received the first invitation to Milan Fashion Show and a few months later Benetton offered Ferragni the chance to act as a judge in their online talent competition for Benetton's new publicity campaign, which took Ferragni to New York on her very first business trip. In April 2010, Fiat proposed Ferragni to drive their convertible Fiat 500 for six months and sponsored a ten-day trip around Europe for both Ferragni and Pozzoli. Online fashion retailer Yoox was among the first to buy an advertisement banner on The Blonde Salad (Keinan et al. 2015: 4).

Ferragni and Pozzoli concentrated their efforts on building the international awareness of The Blonde Salad and in 2011 Ferragni was invited to all international fashion weeks. Hence, in March 2011 they founded The Blonde Salad (officially called TBS Crew S.r.l.), a company 55 per cent owned by Ferragni and 45 per cent owned by Pozzoli, and started to officially work together. At that time, The Blonde Salad reached 70,000 daily visits. Pozzoli hired Kiver, an Italian digital strategy agency, to revamp The Blonde Salad's website and create its mobile version (Keinan et al. 2015: 4). Pozzoli and Ferragni signed an exclusive agreement with Publikompass, a media company specialised in selling advertising in Italy. Dior Italy was among the first ones to contact The Blonde Salad directly to inquire about possibilities for cooperation.

At that time, many of the luxury brands had launched their e-commerce businesses and they were ready to push hard to increase their digital sale. However, some of them did not even know what a fashion blog was. Ferragni and Pozzoli were very selective when choosing the brands to work with because the stories Ferragni would tell about these brands had to reflect her own lifestyle. They started to collaborate with many different brands in various industries, and building long-term relationships was their main objective (Keinan et al. 2015: 5). One of the most successful early partnership was with Burberry. Namely, in 2012, Burberry invited Ferragni to attend two openings of their new stores in London and in Milan as well as the Burberry fashion show during the London Fashion Week. Ferragni had to choose and wear five outfits from the Burberry collection and she interviewed Burberry's art director to mark the opening of Burberry's store. All this content was posted on The Blonde Salad. One year later, Dior asked Ferragni to produce a video clip for Miss Dior perfume and invited her to participate in the Cannes Film Festival. Ferragni wrote about this on her blog and her followers 'lived the experience through the eyes of Chiara' (Keinan et al. 2015: 6). Ferragni started creating limited capsule collections. For example, in 2012 Ferragni designed underwear and a swimwear capsule collection for Yamamay, a popular underwear brand and created shoe capsule collections for Superga in Italy and Steve Madden in the US in 2013 and 2014.

As Ferragni's popularity grew, she emerged as an international celebrity and brands were willing to pay her for her presence. Pozzoli and Ferragni decided that it was time to create a dedicated team to manage Ferragni's celebrity within The Blonde Salad company. They recruited a team consisting of an accountant, a public relations professional, and a project manager, that were responsible for booking Ferragni for various events, organising magazine covers, interviews, and anything related to her image and PR (Keinan et al. 2015: 6). In the second half of 2013, Pozzoli and Ferragni noticed that The Blonde Salad's views started to slowly decline due to the growing popularity of Instagram. Ferragni started using Instagram right from the beginning and the new social media platform had a positive impact on The Blonde Salad business.

In 2013, Pozzoli and Ferragni hired Alessio Sanzogni as Communications and Editorial Manager with a view of strengthening The Blonde Salad's brand and Ferragni's image. Prior to joining The Blonde Salad, Sanzogni was an e-commerce and e-communications manager at Louis Vuitton Italy, where he worked since 2007 and, among other things, was responsible for the partnership between Louis Vuitton and The Blonde Salad (Keinan et al. 2015: 9). Pozzoli, Ferragni and Sanzogni decided to stop selling any kind of product-related editorial content and to transform the blog into a real online Ferragni's lifestyle magazine. With this strategic shift, the audience of The Blonde Salad changed significantly. Ferragni said, 'in 2011, the main followers of my blog were young girls who were inspired by what I was doing. In 2014, fashion insiders, who previously looked down on bloggers, came to read the blog' (Keinan et al. 2015: 11). In 2014, The Blonde Salad was working with luxury fashion brands like Chanel, Hermès, Louis Vuitton, Burberry, and Cartier and the priority was to build exclusive long-term partnerships with a limited number of brands.

After some time they decided to capitalise on The Blonde Salad editorial brand and build a 'shoppable experience' around it. Pozzoli explained: 'today shops need magazines to tell the stories, and magazines need shops to make money. The general trend in these industries is to merge the two' (Keinan et al. 2015: 12). The Chiara Ferragni Collection shoe line was launched and the end goal for building a strong and complete Chiara Ferragni Collection brand was to dissociate it from Chiara's celebrity. From the end of 2014 till now, The Blonde Salad and the Chiara Ferragni are managed as two brands with separate websites, social media platforms, dedicated teams, and distinct legal status.

Explore 28.6

Find other examples of popular fashion bloggers who turned their fashion blogs into successful businesses (own brand) and discuss their results in comparison to Chiara Ferragni's results. What do you think was the reason for the success of The Blonde Salad fashion blog and consequently Chiara Ferragni fashion brand?

How do you think that public relations strategy and activities have contributed to the success of the blog and the brand? How do you think business strategy and public relations strategy should be aligned to achieve expected goals? How do you think business strategy and public relations strategy were aligned in the case of The Blonde Salad fashion blog and Chiara Ferragni fashion brand?

What do you think about the separation of The Blonde Salad and Chiara Ferragni as two split brands, social media platforms and websites? What does this change in terms of followers' interaction and experience? Why do you think Chiara Ferragni wanted to distance her fashion brand from her celebrity status?

Think about 28.4

How do you think that the rise of (fashion) bloggers and (fashion) influencers are affecting and changing the public relations profession especially in the terms of relationship management, credibility and trust?

Think how fashion bloggers and fashion influencers are fitting into Grunig and Hunt's (1984) four models of public relations (press agentry, public information model, two-way asymmetrical model and two-way symmetrical model; see Chapter 8 on Public relations theories)? How do you think they affect the proposed models?

Think about the public relations strategies fashion bloggers and fashion influencers use in order to position themselves as the relevant source of information for their followers and media outlets.

Mini case study 28.5
H&M Close the Loop

H&M Close the Loop campaign is the brand's attempt to introduce sustainable shopping and to promote diversity. Therefore, they hired plus-size model Tess Holliday and Muslim model Mariah Idrissi, because of which 'the ad garnered a massively positive response for its celebration of different cultures in relation to fashion. By creating a buzz around the campaign, it ensured that its message of sustainability was heard' (Gilliland 2018: n. p.).

The campaign also encouraged consumers to recycle clothes while still looking good. This campaign was part of the commitment of the H&M brand to respond to the sustainability debate and criticism the fashion industry has been facing from sustainability advocates for its high impact on the environment.

Therefore, the 'Close the Loop' campaign encouraged consumers to 'bring a bag of used clothes and exchange it for a £5 voucher. The clothes are then either reused, or turned into new clothes, with a range of denim being the first example' (Branding Magazine 2015: n.p.).

Celebrities used in the campaign film encouraged viewers to break fashion taboos and recycle their clothes, and the film was made in locations around the world. The message of the film also stated that recycling a t-shirt saves 2,100 litres of water. The commentators stated that this was not just a campaign due to the fact that the brand invested in the denim collection called 'Close the Loop' and this sustainable agenda has been promoted by the brand for years (ibid.).

In addition, the brand launched a competition called 'Global Change Award' asking consumers to submit innovative ideas for protecting earth's resources for the competition.

But, despite the campaign achieving appraisals from marketing and public relations world, some commentators questioned the authenticity of the brand and its mission by asking 'how can fast-fashion, a business model created to bombard consumers with new apparel each week ever be sustainable? Is H&M really as green and sustainable as they seem to be, or is it just an effective marketing plan posed to cash in on the big green trend?' (Hendriksz 2015: n.p.).

However, the brand collected over 40,000 tonnes of unwanted garment since the launch of the campaign, and the strength of the campaign was that any clothes could have been brought in, not just H&M's and this enticed many customers to bring their clothes to H&M stores and obtain a voucher.

In 2017, the brand launched a new campaign with the same theme entitled 'Bring it'. The new campaign's video provided a narrative explaining the process garments go through when recycled and how recycling garments can help reduce the burden on landfills.

Explore 28.7

Explore sustainable activism directed towards the fashion industry. You can find some initiatives on this website: https://www.sustainablefashionmatterz.com

What challenges do these campaigns pose to the fashion industry? What is the challenge for a public relations professional?

If you were a public relations professional working for campaigners how would you target the fashion industry in an attempt to make the industry more sustainable?

On the other hand, if you are a public relations professional in the fashion industry, how do you think you would respond to activism?

How do you think the fashion industry could respond to criticism coming from sustainability activists? Can the fashion industry ever be sustainable?

How could public relations help the fashion industry?

Mini case study 28.6
Nasty Gal's #Girl Boss

Nasty Gal was originally launched as a brand with a mission to promote self-empowerment and this was present in their campaigns. The founder of the brand is Sophia Amoruso and the brand promoted Sophia's book (*Nasty Galaxy*) and created a separate content hub. In addition to traditional public relations content of articles on fashion and lifestyle, this content hub also had a Girl Boss radio which features a podcast where Sophia interviews various successful women. Sophia Amoruso also produced a Netflix show, Girl Boss.

Many brands have started to use podcasts to appeal to their consumers and podcasting thus presents a valuable tool in public relations practice due to the fact this form of communication enables storytelling. This, in turn, creates a better experience for brand users who can engage with content specifically linked with the brand's mission and their own values.

Sophia Amoruso originally started her business as a vintage store on eBay, and according to information released in 2016, her eBay vintage store was then turned into a company 'that generated $300 million in revenue last year and put her net worth at $280 million, according to Forbes estimates' (Ward 2016: n.p.). Her book *Nasty Galaxy* provided tips for others who want to succeed in the business world.

Nasty Gal was a major success story that grew out of a eBay vintage store to a global business with $100 million in sales in six years but then the sales started to drop 'to $85 million in 2014, and then $77 million in 2015' (Li 2017, n.p.). The company was spending a lot on marketing and advertising and spent its company assets resulting in a slowing of investment in marketing and sales began to fall in 2014, resulting in the company filing for bankruptcy in 2016.

The reason for the downturn in the brand's success, according to some analysts, was down to product quality and fast fashion from other high street bands. In addition, the brand was too specifically focused on California

case study 28.6 (continued)

cool and young girl, which was not long living due to the fact this is not attractive in the long-run around the world.

In addition, the company was centred around youth and thus the majority of staff members were young and focused too much on the creative side whilst the business side was suffering (ibid.). In addition, Sophia Amoruso became too famous and whilst she was an asset to the brand she continued to promote, she also focused on other projects such as writing a book and producing the show, which took too much of her focus from the business she was building. Because of this, employees started to complain about the lack of focus and this caused issues with employee motivation and also instigated several staff lawsuits. In 2015, Amoruso stepped down as a chief executive and remained executive chairwoman, but she resigned from this position in 2016 when the company filed for bankruptcy and when several rounds of redundancies were happening, as well as a resignation from several chief officers of the company.

Observers of the brand saw the company as one that was too personality driven i.e. linked to its founder. Amoruso's backing away from Nasty Gal as its fortunes slid also sent the wrong signal to investors or potential investors.

The company was ultimately acquired by Boohoo, which saw a potential to take over the loyal customer base and expand its global brand.

Explore 28.8

Do you agree with commentators about reasons for Nasty Gal's fall? Do you think brands should focus on a global audience rather than their local one?

Do you think the short lifespan of Nasty Gal has something to do with the brand being built on the celebrity status of its founder? Do you think that the brand's focus on everyday clothes (prêt-à-porter) has anything to do with its fall? If so, how do we explain the success of other high-street retailers?

Do you think that public relations could have helped in saving the brand from bankruptcy? If so, how?

Summary

This chapter provided a discussion on the management of fashion and some approaches to understanding what fashion is and what fashion isn't. In addition, we discussed fashion public relations and stereotypes that fashion public relations suffer from, which are linked to the general stereotype of the fashion industry as a vanity industry that does not contribute to the society in any meaningful way.

We have also provided an outline of what fashion public relations entails by discussing important aspects of the profession such as working with celebrities, bloggers, vloggers and social media influencers. We also provided some theoretical underpinning which can be helpful to both students and practitioners when analysing or working in the fashion industry (source credibility approach). In addition, we have also linked fashion with celebrity culture and through the use of examples and discussion boxes linked practice with critical thinking, thus enabling the reader to critically analyse the fashion industry and the distinctive role of a public relations professional within the industry.

We have also provided case studies from large brands that should have enabled the reader to improve understanding of how fashion industry campaigns work; specific challenges in the fashion industry (e.g. high fashion versus everyday fashion; the notion of celebrity culture and its potential impact on fashion brands); and stories of success and failure, which further demonstrate the specificity and difficulty of working in the fashion industry.

Bibliography

Abrahamson, E. and Fairchild, G. (1999). Management fashion: Lifecycles, triggers, and collective processes. *Administrative Science Quarterly* 44, 708–740.

Abrahamson, E. (1996). Management Fashion. *Academy of Management Review* 21(1), 254–285.

Abrahamson, E. (1991). Managerial fads and fashion: The diffusion and rejection of innovations. *Academy of Management Review* 16, 586–612.

Archer, C. and Harrigan, P. (2017). Show me the money: how bloggers as stakeholders are challenging theories and relationship building in public relations. *Media International Australia* 160(1), 67–77.

BBC (2019). *France yellow vest protests*. Retrieved from https://www.bbc.co.uk/news/topics/cpzg2d6re0lt/france-yellow-vest-protests (2 May 2019).

Blumer, H. (1969). Fashion: From Class Differentiation to Collective Selection. *The Sociological Quarterly* 10(3), 275–291.

Botan, C.H. and Taylor, M. (2004). Public relations: state of the field. *Journal of Communication* 54(4), 645–661.

Branding Magazine (2015). Good Campaign of the Week: H&M 'Close the Loop'. *Branding Magazine,* 13 September. Retrieved from https://www.brandingmag.com/2015/09/13/good-campaign-of-the-week-hm-close-the-loop/ (5 May 2019).

Brodie, R.J., Ilic, A., Juric, B. and Hollebeek, L. (2013). Consumer engagement in a virtual brand community: An exploratory analysis. *Journal of Business Research* 66, 105–114.

Caruso, L. (2011). Bloggers Continue To Take Over The World: Elin Kling for H&M. Retrieved from https://stylecaster.com/bloggers-continue-take-over-world-elin-kling-hm/ (accessed 17 April 2019).

Cassidy, L. and Fitch, K. (2013a). Parties, air-kissing and long boozy lunches? Public relations in the Australian fashion industry. *PRism* 10(1), 1–13. Retrieved from http://www.prismjournal.org/fileadmin/10_1/Cassidy_Fitch.pdf (accessed 17 April 2019).

Cassidy, L. and Fitch, K. (2013). Beyond the Catwalk: Fashion Public Relations and Social Media in Australia. *Asia Pacific Public Relations Journal* 14(1–2), 5–19.

Chanel The One that I Want (https://www.youtube.com/watch?v=bvVe-tGLRvo). Accessed 8 April 2020.

Clark, T. (2004). Strategy viewed from a management fashion perspective. *European Management Review* 1, 105–111.

Coombs, W.T. and Holladay, S.J. (2018). Innovation in public relation theories and practice: A transmedia narrative transportation (TNT) approach. *Journal of Communication Management* 22(4), 382–396.

De Beauvoir, S. (1952). *The Second Sex.* New York: Vintage Books.

De Klerk, A. (2017). 10 of the most successful celebrity fashion lines. *Harpers Bazaar,* 20 June. Retrieved from https://www.harpersbazaar.com/uk/fashion/what-to-wear/news/g38047/most-successful-celebrity-fashion-lines/ (5 May 2019).

Dhaoui, C. (2014). *An empirical study of luxury brand marketing effectiveness and its impact on consumer engagement on Facebook.* Retrieved from https://www.researchgate.net/publication/271936261_An_empirical_study_of_luxury_brand_marketing_effectiveness_and_its_impact_on_consumer_engagement_on_Facebook/download (18 April 2019).

Digital Training Academy (2019). *Ted Baker's new global campaign features innovative 360-degree shoppable film.* Retrieved from http://www.digitaltrainingacademy.com/casestudies/2017/04/ted_bakers_new_global_campaign_features_innovative_360degree_shoppable_film.php (5 May 2019).

Entwistle, J. (2000). Fashion and the flesh body: Dress as an embodied practice. *Fashion Theory* 4, 323–348.

Escalas, J.E. and Bettman, J.R. (2015). Managing Brand Meaning through Celebrity Endorsement. Brand Meaning Management. *Review of Marketing Research* 12, 29–52.

Esteban-Santos, L., Garcia Medina, I., Carey, L. and Bellido-Perez, E. (2018). Fashion bloggers: communication tools for the fashion industry. *Journal of Fashion Marketing and Management: An International Journal* 22(3), 420–437.

Faludi, S. (1991). *Backlash: The undeclared war against American women.* New York: Doubleday.

Fitch, K. (2017). Seeing 'the unseen hand': Celebrity, promotion and public relations. *Public Relations Inquiry* 6(2), 157–169.

Fitch, K. and Third, A. (2010). Working girls: Revisiting the gendering of public relations. *PRism* 7(4). Retrieved from http://www.prismjournal.org/fileadmin/Praxis/Files/Gender/Fitch_Third.pdf (2 May 2019).

Forbes (2018), https://www.forbes.com/sites/ryanerskine/2018/11/16/new-research-from-200-top-brands-shows-how-effective-instagram-stories-really-are/#77a5eb8022bb (accessed 22 April 2020).

Freberg, K., Graham, K., McGaughey, K. and Freberg, L.A. (2011). Who are the social media influencers? A study of public perceptions of personality. *Public Relations Review* 37, 90–92.

Gilliland, N. (2018). 10 examples of great fashion marketing campaigns. *E-consultancy blog,* 7 November. Retrieved from https://econsultancy.com/fashion-marketing-campaigns/ (5 May 2019).

Grunig, J. E. and Hunt, T. T. (1984). *Managing Public Relations.* Holt, Rinehart and Winston.

Heath, R.L. and Coombs, W.T. (2006). *Today's Public Relations.* London: SAGE.

Hendriksz, V. (2015). Is H&M really as 'green' as they seem to be? *Fashion United,* 9 October. Retrieved from https://fashionunited.uk/news/fashion/is-h-m-really-as-green-as-they-seem-to-be/2015100917940 (5 May 2019).

Henley, T. (2017). The Kate Effect: Designers open up about how the royal has impacted their business. *Hello Magazine,* 22 August. Retrieved from https://ca.hellomagazine.com/royalty/02017081638037/kate-middleton-effect-designers-talk-boost-in-business (2 May 2019).

Hennig-Thurau, T., Gwinner, K.P., Walsh, G. and Gremler, D.D. (2004). Electronic word-of-mouth via consumer-opinion platforms: what motivates consumers to articulate themselves on the internet? *Journal of Interactive Marketing* 18(1), 38–52.

Hobbs, T. (2017). Ted Baker uses Instagram for episodic storytelling in 'Keeping up with the Bakers' campaign. *Marketing Week,* 15 March. Retrieved from https://www.marketingweek.com/2017/03/15/instagram-stories-new-ted-baker-campaign (5 May 2019).

Hobbs, T. (2016). Ted Baker on why more marketers should put faith in shoppable videos. *Marketing Week,* 7 September. Retrieved from https://www.marketingweek.com/2016/09/07/ted-baker-on-why-more-marketers-should-put-their-faith-in-shoppable-videos/ (5 May 2019).

House of Commons (2019). *Interim Report on the Sustainability of the Fashion Industry: Fifteenth Report of Session 2017–19 / Report, together with formal minutes relating to the report.* London: House of Commons. Retrieved from https://publications.parliament.uk/pa/cm201719/cmselect/cmenvaud/1148/1148.pdf (5 May 2019).

Inside Chanel (http://inside.chanel.com/en/no5). Accessed 7 April 2020.

Jackson, T. and Shaw, D. (2009). *Fashion Marketing.* Basingstoke: Palgrave Macmillan.

Keinan, A., Maslauskaite, K., Crener, S. and Dessain, V. (2015). The Blonde Salad. *Harvard Business Review,* 9 January. Retrieved from https://thehighville.com/blog/wp-content/uploads/2016/03/Caso-The-Blonde-Salad.pdf (5 May 2019).

Kowalczyk, C.M. and Pounders, K.R. (2016). Transforming celebrities through social media: the role of authenticity and emotional attachment. *Journal of Product & Brand Management* 25(4), 345–356.

Kulmala, M., Mesiranta, N. and Touminen, P. (2013). Organic and amplified eWOM in consumer fashion blogs. *Journal of Fashion Marketing and Management: An International Journal* 17(1), 20–37.

Li, S. (2017). Nasty Gal, once a fashion world darling, is now bankrupt. What went wrong? *The Los Angeles Times,* 24 February. Retrieved from https://www.latimes.com/business/la-fi-nasty-gal-20170224-story.html (5 May 2019).

Loureiro, S.M.C., Costa, I. and Panchapakesan, P. (2017). A passion for fashion: The impact of social influence, vanity and exhibitionism on consumer behaviour. *International Journal of Retail & Distribution Management* 45(5), 468–484.

McKinsey & Company (2018). *The State of Fashion 2018.* Retrieved from https://cdn.businessoffashion.com/reports/The_State_of_Fashion_2018_v2.pdf (5 May 2019).

Medina, M. (2018). Paul Smith on Dressing David Bowie, Led Zeppelin and Today's Celebrities. *WWD magazine,* 12 April. Retrieved from https://wwd.com/eye/people/paul-smith-on-dressing-david-bowie-led-zeppelin-celebrities-1202647664/ (5 May 2019).

Mellicker, R. (2016). *The Feminism of Fashion.* Retrieved from https://www.huffpost.com/entry/the-feminism-of-fashion_b_9705262 (5 May 2019).

Moi, T. (1988). Feminism, Postmodernism, and Style: Recent Feminist Criticism in the United States. *Cultural Critique* 9, 3–22.

Nash, J. (2019). Exploring how social media platforms influence fashion consumer decisions in the UK retail sector. *Journal of Fashion Marketing and Management: An International Journal* 23(1), 82–103.

Noricks, C. (2009). Exploring Fashion PR. Retrieved from https://www.slideshare.net/prcouture/exploring-fashion-pr-1267609 (17 April 2019).

Park, J. (2015). Star Power in Korean Fashion: The Win-Win Relationship between Korean Celebrities and Designers. *The Journal of Design, Creative Process & the Fashion Industry* 7(1), 125–133.

Parkins, I. (2012). *Poiret, Dior and Schiaparelli: Fashion, Femininity and Modernity.* London: Berg.

Parkins, I. (2006). Building a feminist theory of fashion. *Australian Feminist Studies* 23(58), 501–515.

Parkins, I. (2008). Teaching Fashion and Feminist Theory: The Pedagogical Promise of Ambivalence. *Transformations: The Journal of Inclusive Scholarship and Pedagogy*, 18(2), 67–82.

Paul Smith (2019). *Company History*. Retrieved from https://www.paulsmith.com/uk/company-history (5 May 2019).

Phan, M., Thomas, R. and Heine, K. (2011). Social Media and Luxury Brand Management: The Case of Burberry. *Journal of Global Fashion Marketing* 2(4), 213–222.

Sanderson, R. (2019). Chiara Ferragni – the Italian influencer who built a global brand. *Financial Times*, 8 February. Retrieved from https://www.ft.com/content/9adce87c-2879-11e9-a5ab-ff8ef2b976c7 (6 May 2019).

Scott, L.M. (2006). *Fresh Lipstick: Redressing Fashion and Feminism*. London: Palgrave Macmillan.

Senft, T.M. (2013). Microcelebrity and the Branded Self. In Hartley, J., Burgess, J. and Bruns, A. (ed.) *A Companion to New Media Dynamics* (pp. 346–354). Chichester: Wiley.

Seno, D. and Lukas, B.A. (2007). The equity effect of product endorsement by celebrities: A conceptual framework from a co-branding perspective. *European Journal of Marketing* 41(1–2), 121–134.

Sherman, G. and Perlman, S. (2010). *Fashion Public Relations*. New York: Fairchild Books.

Simmel, G. (1957). Fashion. *American Journal of Sociology* 62(6), 541–558. Retrieved from http://sites.middlebury.edu/individualandthesociety/files/2010/09/Simmel.fashion.pdf (2 May 2019).

Simmel, G. (1904). Fashion. *International Quarterly* 10, 130–155. Retrieved from http://modetheorie.de/fileadmin/Texte/s/Simmel-Fashion_1904.pdf (2 May 2019).

Spell, C. (2001). Management fashions: Where do they come from: and are they old wine in a new bottle? *Journal of Management Inquiry* 10, 358–373.

Steele, V. and Major, J. S. (2019). *Paris Fashion*. Retrieved from https://fashion-history.lovetoknow.com/clothing-around-world/paris-fashion (5 May 2019).

Taylor, M. and Kent, M.L. (2014). Dialogic engagement: clarifying foundational concepts. *Journal of Public Relations Research* 26(5), 384–398.

The Fashion Revolution (2019). *Manifesto for a Fashion Revolution*. Retrieved fromhttps://www.fashionrevolution.org/manifesto/ (5 May 2019).

Thomas-Bailey, C. and Wood, Z. (2012). How the 'Duchess of Cambridge effect' is helping British fashion in US. *The Guardian*, 30 March. Retrieved from https://www.theguardian.com/uk/2012/mar/30/kate-duchess-of-cambridge-fashion-lk-bennett (2 May 2019).

Tranberg Hansen, K. (2004). The World in Dress: Anthropological Perspective on Clothing, Fashion, and Culture. *Annual Review of Anthropology* 33, 369–392.

Turner, G. (2014). *Understanding Celebrities* (2nd edition). London: SAGE.

Tyner, K.E. and Ogle, J.P. (2009). Feminist Theory of the Dressed Female Body: A Comparative Analysis and Applications for Textiles and Clothing Scholarship. *Clothing & Textiles Research* Journal 27(2), 98–121.

Walden, C. (2009). Sir Paul Smith: 'It's clothes I love, not fashion'. *The Telegraph*, 21 October. Retrieved from http://fashion.telegraph.co.uk/news-features/TMG6396170/Sir-Paul-Smith-Its-clothes-I-love-not-fashion.html (5 May 2019).

Ward, M. (2016). Multimillionaire Sophia Amoruso: 4 career lessons every young person should know. *CNBC*, 7 October. Retrieved from https://www.cnbc.com/2016/10/06/multimillionaire-sophia-amoruso-4-career-lessons-every-young-person-should-know.html?utm_content=buffer38974&utm_medium=social&utm_source=twitter.com&utm_campaign=buffer (5 May 2019).

Wattles, J. (2018). Chanel reveals earnings for the first time in its 108-year history. *CNN Business*, 22 June. Retrieved from https://money.cnn.com/2018/06/22/news/companies/chanel-revenue-earnings-financials/index.html (5 May 2019).

Wolf, N. (1991). *The Beauty Myth: How images of beauty are used against women*. Random House.

CHAPTER 29

Clea Bourne

Public relations and finance

Source: Konjushenko Vladimir/Shutterstock

Learning outcomes

By the end of this chapter you should be able to:
- identify some of the new PR challenges in global financial centres
- distinguish the range of interests represented by PR in financial markets
- understand how digital technologies are helping to communicate finance to different stakeholders
- appreciate the skills and training that are beneficial to PR practitioners in this sector.

Structure

- Public relations for global financial centres: changing contexts
- Public relations for wholesale financial markets
- Public relations for retail financial markets
- Media in financial centres
- Financial communication and social media
- Public relations and the future of finance

Introduction

Global financial markets employ thousands of public relations professionals in diverse roles. Some of these PR professionals have the most powerful, lucrative communications roles available. Despite an abundance of professional communicators working in financial markets, there are relatively few books or articles published on public relations in the world of finance, particularly in the twenty-first century (Bourne 2017). The few exceptions among academic publications focus on stock market communication, corporate governance and corporate responsibility. While these are important pursuits, they represent only a small proportion of the strategic PR programmes in global finance.

This chapter attempts to remedy this oversight by exploring the varied roles PR plays – from the apex of financial markets where PR promotes financial brands to wholesale markets, where financial professionals promote their expertise to each other; from retail markets where PR builds compelling narratives about myriad financial products and services, to grassroots PR for financial charities helping the poor and indebted.

Notwithstanding PR's contribution to building credibility in and shaping attitudes towards financial markets, financial communication is not without controversy. Many countries felt the effect of the 2008 global financial crisis, and PR was involved in promoting several of the market instruments implicated in triggering the crisis itself. In the decade following the crisis, the vital task of PR lay in publicly trumpeting news of supposed economic recovery. However, as the era of hyper-globalisation ends, the message of recovery masks economic stagnation across North Atlantic economies. According to some economic experts, the world has entered the era of de-globalisation or multi-polarisation, as world power coalesces around three centres: Europe, Asia and Americas (Credit Suisse 2015). In this multi-polarised world, economic activity is increasingly shaped by the growing importance of Asian markets on the one hand, and the North Atlantic's reaction to shifting economic geographies with trade barriers, tighter migration laws and restrictions on the free movement of labour. This complex environment is made more challenging by the speed of information on social media platforms, where financial news and opinion move more rapidly than ever before. Consequently, financial markets now require PR advisers with global, political and digital acumen, developing narratives that work across different markets, handling complex relations with different cultures and preparing for crises that happen in rapid-time via social media platforms (Bond et al. 2016).

As global economic power continues to shift, the key question for global financial centres is 'How can financial markets prosper in this new era?' Across the world's financial markets, the resounding response has been a boom in an emerging specialism known as financial technology or fintech. Signs of the fintech boom are evident in the steady stream of fintech company start-ups, and fintech product launches, all delivering financial services and transactions based on Artificial Intelligence and automation, blockchain and cloud technology. The fintech boom is also evident in the corresponding volume of so-called PR spin generated around fintech. While certain fintech innovations could prove transformative, others appear little more than dubious techno hype. Yet the fintech boom has undoubtedly sparked new and exciting forms of storytelling about everyday financial relations. Sections of this chapter will explore the role of PR in financial market storytelling (see Case study 29.1 and Explore 29.1). Meanwhile, the fintech boom has pitted traditional finance and neo-finance against each other, with PR representing both sides of the divide. PR continues to represent traditional finance, such as banks, insurers and investment companies, as they respond to the latest wave of technological disruption in financial markets. PR also eagerly represents neo-finance, including the fintech start-ups shaking up commonly held views of financial provision.

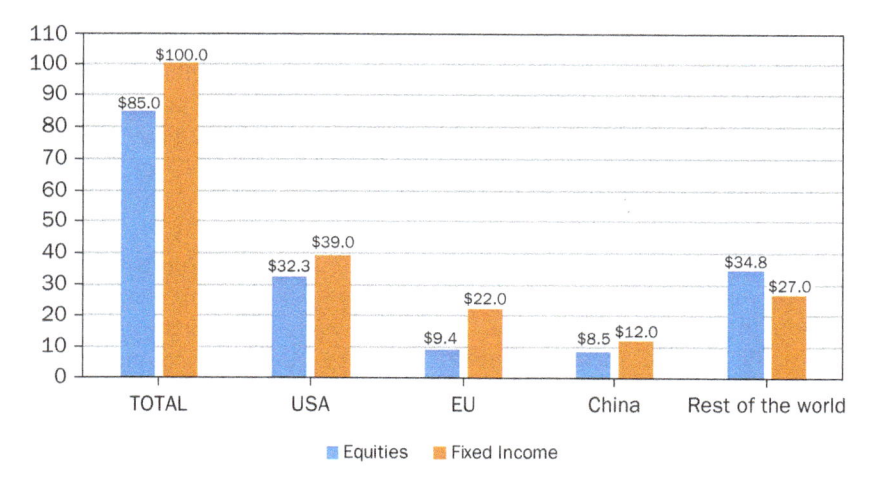

Figure 29.1 Global capital markets: equities vs. fixed income assets – in US$ trillions (Data sourced from SIFMA 2019. Graph created by author.)

> **Explore 29.1**   **Fintech public relations**
>
> ### Fintech – a growth area for the public relations industry.
>
> *Financial technology – or Fintech – companies have been around for decades.* One of the oldest fintech brands is Swift, a cooperative founded by the world's banks in 1973. Swift is a financial messaging system designed to send money instructions securely around the world from one bank to another. The first wave of fintech brands were like Swift, in that they supplied back-office services that were largely invisible to the public. PR for these fintech suppliers focused on business-to-business (B2B) communication. Today, Fintech PR has completely transformed. Many new Fintech companies are consumer-facing brands in need of business-to-consumer (B2C) campaigns, investor relations, public affairs, events management and a strong social media presence (see Figure 29.2). The Fintech industry even has its own trade bodies, and now, fintech PR firms do too. See links to two trade associations below:
>
> Innovate Finance – https://www.innovatefinance.com
>
> Global Fintech PR Network – http://globalfintechpr-network.com
>
> - Looking at both websites, what messages would you say the fintech industry is keen to promote?
> - What rationale do you think lies behind the fintech industry's storytelling strategies?
>
> | Fintech's major industry sectors ||||
> |---|---|---|---|
> | **Banking and capital markets** | **Investment management** | **Insurance** | **Real Estate** |
> | Mobile payments and authentication, neo-banks, personal loans, savings tools, etc | Robo-advisors, portfolio optimisation, financial research and analysis, etc | Claims management, customer leads, employee benefits, policy sales, reinsurance, telematics, etc | 2D/3D visual mapping, listings, property search, rental payments, home security, energy management, etc |
> | Examples ||||
> | *Klarna, Lifetise, Monzo Revolut,* | *Ellevest, Fidelity Go, Moneyfarm, Nutmeg* | *Bought By Many, Canopy, Cuvva, Lemonade* | *Hive, IMMO, Yopa, Ring* |
>
> **Figure 29.2** Fintech's major industry sectors (*source:* Author. Adapted from Deloitte, 2017)

PR for global financial centres: changing contexts

Global financial centres bring together financial infrastructure, expertise and assets in one place. For this reason, London, New York and other large financial centres have been the traditional home to financial PR, financial services PR, investor relations and other specialisms associated with PR in the world of finance. Global financial centres are more than geographic locations; they are also national and regional brands. Financial centres engage PR to build their reputation for a stable business environment, cutting-edge infrastructure and healthy capital flow, as well as accessible, networked location and cultural appeal. The more a financial centre can meet these criteria, the easier it is to attract investors, as well as financial professionals who want to live and work and there. PR for financial centres is on the rise, because there are more financial centres than ever before – 120 in total according to analysts at Z/Yen, a consultancy that ranks financial centres biannually. Greater China hosts two of the top five global financial centres (see Figure 29.3), while the Asia-Pacific region hosts eight of the top twenty financial centres.

Although there is no truly global financial authority to which financial markets report, there is an acknowledged International Financial Architecture (Vestergaard 2009). This global apparatus includes the Group of 20 most wealthy nations (G20), the World Trade Organization, and two giant international lending institutions – the International Monetary Fund (IMF) and the World Bank. From their headquarters in

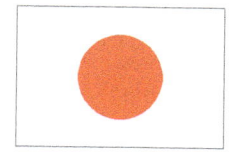

New York 1	London 2	Tokyo 3	Shanghai 4	Singapore 5
Source: charnsitr/Shutterstock	*Source:* charnsitr/Shutterstock	*Source:* Globe Turner/Shutterstock	*Source:* T. Lesia/Shutterstock	*Source:* Restimage/Shutterstock

Figure 29.3 Greater China is home to two of the top five global financial centres, according to Z/Yen (2019)

Washington DC, the IMF and World Bank both engage in PR activity to enhance their reputation as lending facilities between richer and poorer nations (Bourne 2017). Other multilateral institutions focus on lending in specific regions. These include the New Development Bank, headquartered in Shanghai; the Asian Development Bank, headquartered in Manila; and the African Development Bank, headquartered in Abidjan. These regional development banks all have PR teams, and their spokespeople are just as likely to comment on world trade and economic affairs as the IMF and the World Bank. However, the two Washington DC lenders dominate global media attention. Their deep resources produce a large, steady flow of downloadable, and increasingly, *shareable* economic and financial content, including country and sector research, market commentary and thought leadership on the global economy.

Central banks and state-run treasury departments make up a substantial layer of the International Financial Architecture. Central banks manage a nation's monetary policy (interest rates and money supply), while treasury departments manage fiscal policy (taxes and government spending). Together, central banks and treasury departments are responsible for the birth of what we now call the Debt Capital Markets, where countries, regions, municipalities and companies all go to borrow money from potential investors. At US$100 trillion, the global debt capital market is significantly larger than global stock markets, or equities capital markets (see Figure 29.1), yet debt capital-raising receives far less media attention. PR in debt capital markets may make less noise, but PR has had a presence there for decades. Early twentieth-century PR practitioner, Ivy Lee, promoted Poland, Romania, France and other countries to international lenders after World War II. When Argentina struggled to attract international investors, Lee directed the country to send a polo team to the US to promote the country's 'civilised' atmosphere to potential lenders (Kunczik 2000 citing Hiebert 1966).

Today, debt-marketing on behalf of countries and municipalities is highly professionalised. Governments

Mini case study 29.1
Central banks on social media

Central banks are 'communicators-in-chief for national economies' (Holmes 2016). Inside central banks, a larger specialist community of professionals gathers information, data, intelligence and experience from around the economy. The central bank's PR team is part of this community-of-practice, relaying resulting narratives through reports, bulletins, commentary and staged events (Holmes 2016; Smart 2006).

Much of central banking communication is dense and technical, targeting specialist financial audiences. But central banks are putting on a friendlier face, using social media to support monetary objectives, including stable prices, confidence in the currency and financial literacy.

As with all PR campaigns, social media tactics can go wrong. In 2014, the European Central Bank launched a selfie competition to highlight new 10 Euro banknotes, using the hashtag #mynew10. Despite strict rules to deter social media trolls, the competition was swiftly hijacked by a stream of selfies calling for the return of national currencies (Olaison and Taalas 2016).

It was the Bank of Jamaica that became the unexpected darling of central bank watchers in 2019. The Bank's PR team launched a campaign to build credibility in inflation targeting. Social media music videos were matched by billboards, radio jingles and television PSAs. The reggae-themed promotion may be the first central bank PR campaign ever to go viral, with one Bank of Jamaica video viewed more than 200,000 times in the first few days.

have debt management units dedicated to promoting debt issuance. Debt issuance is supported by investor relations, which includes presentations to banks, investment firms and rating agencies. PR and marketing staff in these units produce regular advertisements, public announcements, monthly bulletins, speeches, conference presentations and articles to promote new capital-raising via financial media channels (Dooner and McAlister 2013). Central banks also have sophisticated PR arrangements for promoting monetary stability and international trust in a nation's financial brand. (See Mini case study 29.1.) Financial regulators frequently have PR departments to support regulatory communication with various stakeholders across national jurisdictions. These public finance institutions operate at the apex of financial centres.

Beneath the apex are layers consisting of wholesale and retail financial markets, all engaged in PR activity targeting financial experts, companies, wealthy clients and consumers.

Every layer of activity within a financial centre is facing rapid change triggered by digital technologies. Mountains of financial data are now shared instantly across social networks. That data can be distributed, stored and easily retrieved via cloud computing. Financial data can then be rapidly mined and analysed with greater algorithmic computation power. In stock markets, super computers crunch billions of data points and execute high-frequency trades, adjusting markets in real-time. Hedge funds use Artificial Intelligence (AI) to generate trading ideas, inform investment decisions and optimise portfolios. Fund managers have drawn on AI to launch the next generation of passively managed index funds, while computerised robo-advisors help consumers select individual investment portfolios. In insurance, AI bots scour through mountains of personal data to improve calculations for products such

Box 29.1

Financial communication in East Asia

When 60 per cent of the world's index of financial centres moves from West to East in a single decade (Z/Yen 2019), it is worth exploring how global markets communication might change in the future. East Asia represents more than 1.6 billion people, and accounts for many recent financial market innovations. Asia's technology firms were far quicker to challenge traditional banks for consumer financial provision, led by trailblazers Ant Financial Services (Alipay) and Tencent in China; GO-JEK in Indonesia and Lalamove in Hong Kong. Asian financial innovation has attracted US$208 billion in international investment since 2012 (CB Insights 2019).

Governments around the region are supporting their emerging financial centres, while promoting financial services as a new growth industry. Hong Kong has always played a strategic role in modern global finance. Further to the north, Korea is developing not one but *two* financial centres – one in the Korean capital, Seoul, and another specialist centre for maritime finance and derivatives in the port city of Busan (Z/Yen 2019).

East Asia has become a key location for financial communication. While global PR firms have established offices in most Asian financial centres, these firms often bring Western approaches to Eastern media and business culture. However, specialist Asian financial PR firms are emerging.

As Asian approaches to financial communication evolve, PR professionals in financial markets will need to reflect diverse cultural attitudes to money, finance and technology, as well as the rich tapestry of languages, ethnicities, class systems, social networks, relationship-building and trust represented by Asian financial centres.

In the coming years, Asia's financial markets could be further re-shaped by a US–China trade war, the UK's Brexit from Europe, and other political realities. As Asian financial centres grapple with increasingly bearish sentiments to their domestic capital markets, the role of PR will be to press for better, more frequent communication between the rest of the world and Asia's business sector, financial institutions and its burgeoning fintech industry.

Picture 29.1 The Shanghai Stock Exchange communicates rising share prices in red and falling prices in green. The opposite is true in most Western exchanges. (*source:* Lou Linwei/Alamy Stock Photo)

as pay-as-you-go car insurance. In banking, bots manage a slew of customer enquiries on changing accounts, initiating loans and applying for mortgages. The next two sections explore the implications of some of these changes for PR in wholesale and retail financial markets.

Public relations for wholesale financial markets

Wholesale financial markets are the factory floor of global finance, where everything takes place on a large scale. Mathematicians and physicists devise complex models to forecast future financial performance. Bankers conceive large transactions or engineer new and innovative financial products. Central banks issue bank notes, monitor currency, manage inflation and act as lender-of-last-resort to other banks. Companies make a market for and trade in large blocks of company shares, in government and company loans, in commodities such as wheat, corn or soya, gold, oil or diamonds; together with derivatives of all these investments. Institutional investors manage billions in pensions and investment funds, and companies seek out insurance and reinsurance policies against potential risks and disasters. International lenders arrange large blocks of finance to assist companies with export or trade financing or help countries borrow large amounts of money. Hedge funds place multi-million bets on whether the price of just about anything will go up or down, and whether markets will stay calm or become turbulent.

While there is great demand for PR activity throughout wholesale finance, for many financial communicators, the stock market is where the action is. Stock exchanges are still perceived as the most direct connection between financial markets and the real economy, enabling ordinary citizens to own shares in familiar and exotic companies. Stock markets are an incitement to adventure and exploration, a place of myths and legends, excitement, fashion and trends (Stäheli 2008). Such drama and excitement is achieved through storytelling – precisely the sorts of narratives at which public relations excels (Westbrook 2014). PR helps transform stock market locations into themed, Disney-like environments (McGoun et al. 2003). Financial PR and investor relations specialists represent companies accessing equity capital markets for financing, via Mergers & Acquisitions (M&A), initial public offerings (IPOs) and marketing their company shares. Promoting twenty-first-century stock markets as a Disney-like environment is a greater PR challenge since the theatrical backdrop of open-outcry trading gave way to more silent electronic trading. Where possible, PR teams based within stock exchanges create stock market spectacles such as inviting celebrities and dignitaries to ring the opening bell for the day's trading. Meanwhile, external PR teams may opt to organise stunts outside the exchange to promote the flotation of a company's shares. (See Mini case study 29.2.)

In addition to representing stock exchanges and publicly listed companies, PR practitioners also act for the myriad financial institutions and professional advisory firms which help wholesale financial markets tick. Vast numbers of PR professionals represent investment banks, hedge funds, rating agencies, asset managers, private equity firms, retail banks, credit card companies, supermarket banks, insurance companies, building societies, wealth managers, stockbrokers, mortgage specialists and personal finance advisers; together with professional services firms offering financial services expertise, including law firms, accountancy firms, actuarial firms, management consultants and other intermediaries. In the largest financial centres, these roles can evolve into specialisms such as public affairs and lobbying on behalf of financial institutions and financial trade associations.

Wholesale finance is typically less regulated than consumer finance, enabling wholesale market institutions to design and market high-risk financial instruments. Some of these institutions, notably investment banks and hedge funds, developed a reputation for being shadow banks, because so much of their activity was unregulated, unreported and unseen. Shadow banks were heavily criticised for designing and mis-selling complex financial instruments which helped trigger the 2008 collapse of Lehman Brothers, the USA's fourth-largest investment bank, and the ensuing global financial crisis. The crisis kicked off a protracted debate about how to curb unconstrained risk-taking, self-interest and cowboy capitalism in wholesale financial markets (Nelson 2012; Prügl 2012). Then IMF head, Christine Lagarde, famously responded to a journalist's question, saying that 'If Lehman Brothers had been Lehman Sisters' the global financial crisis would have looked quite different. Pundits, journalists and academics advocated for greater gender diversity in wholesale finance, contending that women are more risk-averse, and more willing to uphold good corporate governance and ethics. Wholesale financial institutions embraced rising market feminism narratives proposing that a softer, gentler, capitalism could reform markets in lieu of heavy-handed regulation or radical change.

Mini case study 29.2
Fearless Girl: wholesale finance presents its softer side. . .

Following widespread critique of excessive risk-taking and toxic masculinity, wholesale financial markets have been keen to present a softer side. In 2017, State Street Global Advisors mounted its Fearless Girl campaign to coincide with International Women's Day.

The campaign featured a statue of a young girl staring down Wall Street's iconic statue of a charging bull. Fearless Girl was an instant sensation, drawing enormous crowds in New York and galvanising people across six continents. The statue was later replicated in front of the London Stock Exchange.

But State Street's efforts to promote equality for women soon backfired. Women's groups pointed to contradictions in State Street's corporate conduct, after US regulators named and shamed the investment firm for discriminating against its own female employees. State Street later became embroiled in a public spat with Fearless Girl's sculptor, Kristen Visbal, suing the artist for copyright violation after she created Fearless Girl replicas for personal sale.

Picture 29.2 The statue of Fearless Girl faces down Wall Street's statue of the Charging Bull. Both statues were installed in the wake of financial market crises (*source*: Volkan Furuncu/Anadolu Agency/Getty Images)

Throughout the 2010s, various PR campaigns sought to re-image wholesale finance, incorporating gender narratives into corporate and brand communications (see Mini case study 29.2). Financial markets also lobbied assiduously behind the scenes. The combined efforts were certainly a success in the USA, the world's largest wholesale financial market. By 2017, a newly elected administration advised US regulators and market players to swap all references to shadow banks in favour of the more benign term, market-based finance (US Treasury 2017A). The advice appears in a series of influential reports communicating new Treasury policy for financial markets. Entitled 'A Financial System that Creates Economic Opportunities', the reports were researched and co-authored by a community-of-practice within the US Treasury (Mini case study 29.1).

The Treasury co-authors included public affairs experts (see Chapter 20 for more on this PR specialism), and the reports were widely promoted by the Treasury press office. Wholesale finance returned to business-as-usual during the 2010s, and the number of hedge funds and high-risk financial instruments associated with shadow banking increased. The same series of Treasury reports also communicated the US government's support for the fast-growing fintech industry. While some of the hype around fintech might turn out to be PR spin, 3,300 fintech companies were founded in the USA between 2010 and 2017 alone (US Treasury 2017B). Fintech was not only giving US financial centres a new competitive advantage, it was helping to revive the US economy. In the first six months of 2018, the UK had four of the top 10 fintech funding

> **Think about 29.1**
>
> **Is it PR, advertising or marketing?**
>
> The Fearless Girl campaign has been presented variously as corporate social responsibility, corporate branding or a PR stunt. But the Fearless Girl statue was *also* an advertisement for State Street's new index fund. The fund is marketed as a collection of gender-diverse companies, and is listed on the NASDAQ stock exchange with the ticker symbol SHE.
>
> - Based on media coverage of Fearless Girl, would you describe the campaign as PR, advertising or marketing? Perhaps you see it as a combination of the three, in which case, where does advertising leave off and PR begin?
> - The investment vehicle known as SHE is an Exchange Traded Fund or ETF, which are fashionable products in investment communication. See if you can find press releases and media coverage about ETFs to determine why this might be.
> - Find out more about NASDAQ and how it differs from the New York Stock Exchange.

deals in Europe; the largest of these was for $250 million, raised by digital banking firm Revolut (Business Reporter 2019). (See Case study 29.1.)

Public relations for retail financial markets

Retail financial markets are the shop window of the financial world. This shop window connects ordinary people with finance in many ways – as consumers and taxpayers, savers and investors, employees and holidaymakers, and as homeowners and pensioners. The size of a country's retail financial market correlates with levels of affluence, so the narratives PR produces for retail finance often support aspirations such as buying a home, planning a family, saving for a university education, taking a dream holiday, insuring against emergencies and saving for retirement. These narratives are generally linked with bank accounts, general insurance, personal loans, mortgage loans, credit cards and more sophisticated, long-term financial products such as pensions and investments.

How we define the shop window of retail finance is changing rapidly. For one thing, that shop window was once located in a bank on the high street, or at the entrance to a comfortable advisor's office. Today, the shop window of retail financial markets is increasingly shifting to mobile phone apps. In Europe, physical bank branches are disappearing, while the number of fintech companies providing banking services has swelled to several thousand across Europe, the Middle East and Africa (Hardie and Gee 2018). In 2018, new EU rules swept in greater transparency in financial services. Known as Open Banking or PSD2, the transparency regulation permits technology companies to access banks' customer data if they have customers' permission. The regulatory change enabled consumer fintech to boom, from app-only bank accounts to digital-tracker health insurance. German digital lender Kreditech, which promotes itself as the Amazon of consumer finance, mines Facebook data voluntarily shared by customers. US company, ZestFinance, is one of many new firms providing credit-scoring services based on big data generated by consumers online (O'Dwyer 2019). UK digital-only bank, Monzo, launched in 2015 and signed more than 2 million customers by 2019 (Warren 2019). Today, many UK and European customers aggregate and see their different financial products and accounts in one place (e.g. on a single mobile phone app) for greater convenience when moving and managing money. Regulatory clarity on data-sharing is not yet mirrored throughout the world, but other markets are likely to replicate what has happened in Europe. In the largest financial centres, the fintech boom has stimulated demand for PR counsel, from product promotion and employee communication, to public affairs and crisis management. (See Case study 29.1.)

The PR profession is also compelled to learn more about new generations of retail finance customers, specifically millennials and post-millennials (also known as Generation Y and Z). An entire market research industry profits from discovering information about these younger consumers. Across many of the world's economies, the under-40s are more likely to have endured sustained austerity measures, rising income inequality, and a shift towards the so-called gig economy with its precarious working conditions. While the under-40s might be a logical target for new sales of mortgages, life insurance and income protection, many younger consumers have different priorities, including student loan payments. Changing lending conditions has meant that home ownership has been delayed for many under-40s. As a result, younger consumers are less likely to buy home insurance when they can't afford their own home, and less likely to buy life insurance, when they have fewer assets to protect (Barr et al. 2016).

Case study 29.1
Revolut

Reputation management at a challenger bank

A reputational battle is playing out across financial services as traditional financial providers get to grips with the latest wave of technological disruption, driven by next-generation fintech companies offering frictionless financial services via wearable tech and mobile phone apps.

At the centre of this reputational battle is Revolut, known in financial markets as a unicorn – one of the rare tech start-ups worth more than a billion dollars.

Launched in 2015, Revolut started out as a global travel money app, enabling customers to keep multiple currencies on one card, and transfer those currencies seamlessly via mobile phone.

Revolut's strategy was simple: charge no fees on travel money, build the largest possible customer base, then cross-sell from an expanding menu of services including insurance, cryptocurrency sales, credit card lending and pensions.

The strategy worked. In less than four years, 4.7 million customers had joined, with 12,000 new accounts signed up each day (Megaw and Bradshaw 2019). Revolut quickly became one of the world's largest challenger banks. Revolut wasn't profitable, but investors found the company's growth story captivating.

Revolut claimed its phenomenal growth had all happened 'without spending a single penny on marketing'. Yet like many start-ups, Revolut drew heavily on advertising, marketing and PR to attract investors, partners and suppliers; to recruit staff, establish market positioning, and win new customers.

Eighteen months after launch, Revolut hired a global head of communications, its first PR employee. The firm also hired PR and marketing managers across its markets in Europe. PR was expected to forge tight relationships with journalists, and be an ideas machine, constantly pitching stories to the media, as well as sourcing speaking slots at all the major tech and finance conferences across Europe. Initially, Revolut's communication was about getting the company seen and heard everywhere, needling the competition so as to attract investors' attention. The next phase was all about generating customer leads. Here PR was complemented by intensive advertising and marketing activity, including out-of-home advertising on public transport, door-to-door leaflet drops, promotional flyers posted on university campuses and promotional codes shared on social media (Mellino 2019; O'Dea 2019). As the competition with other digital banks intensified, the firm also launched its 'Revolut Pioneer' scheme, rewarding social media influencers with referral fees for getting friends and followers to sign up.

Company founder, Nikolay Storonsky, cultivated a high profile as the quintessential young tech entrepreneur, out to break things and disrupt. In media interviews and speaker slots, Storonsky adopted an adversarial stance toward traditional financial institutions, claiming that Revolut was 'tearing down financial borders and mending the broken trust'. His corporate philosophy – get shit done – was emblazoned on Revolut's London office walls in neon lights (Mellino 2019).

Then several things went wrong:

- An investigation by *The Telegraph* newspaper alleged that Revolut had disabled its automated money laundering protection system for three months.
- Several customer complaints were aired publicly, including one allegation of a delayed money transfer.
- Employee whistle-blowers cited a toxic culture of unpaid work, unachievable targets and high staff turnover.
- A spoof Valentine's Day advertising campaign was slated for shaming singles and faking data.
- The financial regulator investigated the company's compliance procedures.
- The advertising regulator investigated the company's advertising practices.
- Several senior executives resigned.

The various allegations became social media fodder, particularly among the financial community on Twitter. Revolut mounted a controversial social media defence, directing Twitter attacks on two female fintech professionals, and threatening to sue a young female journalist who posted regularly on the same platform (Bain 2019). Revolut's tactics were poorly received. Storonsky was forced to write an open letter apologising for past mistakes (Storonsky 2019). Veteran financial professionals were hired as advisers and company directors. Revolut

> further retained a financial PR firm, ostensibly to support its international expansion.
>
> So, can a fintech unicorn change its spots? Perhaps not. Months after Revolut's PR fiasco, the Careers section of the company website stated:
>
> *Banks are powerful. They owe us nothing. They watch us. They punish us for our mistakes. They have more money, more people, more connections. We are underdogs we keep learning. We innovate. Every day is a new fight. Technology is our weapon. We identify opportunities. We focus. We execute. We can create a better way to manage your money. We love the game.* (Revolut 2019)
>
> According to Revolut's head of communications: 'The communications landscape in finance is changing, because the expectations of the millennial audience are completely different. . . we want fun and fast, we want banks to speak like humans and be built around our needs. . . People are willing to put up with the hiccups along the way for a service that fits their needs' (Sims 2018).

PR practitioners representing traditional financial providers face further challenges. The under-40s have no loyalty to traditional financial brands. Younger consumers are unlikely to set foot into a bank branch, as bricks-and-mortar branches shut. Instead, they expect financial provision to be invisible and frictionless; accessible with a swipe on a phone screen. Now, many young financial consumers mix and match their financial providers, keeping a traditional bank for the primary account (to receive salaries) and a digital bank to pay bills, select investments, track monthly spending and participate in online forums (Moskvitch 2019). If trends continue, traditional finance providers could one day retreat from consumer consciousness altogether, providing their services as simple utilities to technology companies behind-the-scenes, with no need for a consumer-facing financial brand.

Media in financial centres

The media plays an important role in financial market communication, as the value of individual financial products and services are all bound up in the public's image of the financial industry. The largest, most influential financial centres support the largest pool of specialist financial media – from financial news wires, cable television and financial radio to specialist financial newspapers, magazines, websites and blogs managed by social media influencers. While national media titles have downsized in some countries, global financial media such as *CNBC, Bloomberg, Reuters, Dow Jones, The Financial Times, Wall Street Journal* and *International Business Times* have all expanded from European or North American headquarters into emerging economies of the Middle East and Asia (Chakravartty and Schiller 2010).

The financial media has always had a symbiotic if uneasy relationship with the PR profession. Global financial media plays an undeniable role in cheering on financial market activity from the side-lines. Their business model typically involves producing a constant flow of news and financial infotainment catering to market analysts, company directors, professional investors and wealthy clients. Brands such as CNBC wield substantial influence over market players; for example, helping to drive share prices up and down, or giving greater visibility to bond market trading. In the largest financial centres, PR professionals must work hard to cut through the resulting noise of proliferating corporate and financial messages. Both global and national media also support financial literacy, educating the public on relevant government and industry policy changes, as well as encouraging us to use certain financial products over others. PR professionals try to influence editorial recommendations in favour of the products and services they represent.

The uneasy symbiosis between PR and the financial media now faces new pressures, as AI and automation transform the nature and speed of financial communication, and further blur the divide between PR and the media. On the PR side, AI applications are being rapidly incorporated into various forms of PR work, including drafting, editing and disseminating financial results. On the media side, news wires now use algorithms to write articles about firms' earnings announcements. This robo-journalism synthesises and rapidly disseminates information from PR announcements and analyst reports, and market data. The resulting speed boosts the media's cheerleading effect for financial markets, since automated articles increase market trading volumes and liquidity (Chakravartty and Schiller 2010).

Within national borders, the mainstream media – national and regional newspapers, TV and radio – generally adopt a broad-spectrum approach to financial markets. Journalists working for these regional and national titles may only cover finance as part of a wider remit spanning business and the economy. Mainstream media's remit includes everything from political news, community news, sports, fashion, lifestyle and health. Few mainstream newsrooms have a dedicated financial beat. Consequently, mainstream editors will avoid in-depth financial coverage for fear of boring the audience, opting for financial stories that are entertaining, or that align with the audience's typically middle-class interests. Mainstream editors further lack time and resources to investigate new and complex financial products, market instruments or regulatory changes (Doyle 2006; Kendall 2005). When dealing with mainstream media, PR practitioners are therefore tasked with simplifying financial news, making it more interesting or controversial, frequently developing stories supporting news frames of a 'middle class in peril', with worries over pensions, high taxes, lack of job security and 'holding on by a thread' (Kendall 2005). (See Box 29.2.)

In the largest financial centres, certain mainstream media titles continue to attract volumes of financial advertising, enabling them to investigate consumer finance issues. Personal finance journalists at these mainstream titles are amongst the most influential

---

Box 29.2

Millennials and personal finance media

Gold rush or Avocado toast?

Under-40s consumers spanning two generations – millennials and post-millennials – are the next big catchment group for financial services – and for the financial media. From the outset, the mainstream media and specialist financial media adopted a different tone when addressing millennial consumers.

Specialist financial media, e.g. CNBC, *Forbes* magazine, Cheddar TV (see Explore 29.3) represent the voice of business and finance, which regard the millennial generation as a gold rush. This market voice understands there is no guarantee that millennials will choose the same financial brands their parents did, and is keen to engage with under-40s consumers, and instil an adventurous mindset to all forms of finance.

When mainstream media covers millennials and money, they adopt a very different tone. The personal finance sections of mainstream media have long represented the middle-class concerns of baby boomers who make up a large part of the audience for mainstream media (although many journalists are millennials or post-millennials themselves). The default mainstream editorial position has been to support the myth of millennials as spendthrifts who expect parental hand-outs (Cairns 2017). This millennial myth yields popular tropes, which provide excellent clickbait for struggling mainstream media titles. One common trope perpetuated by some mainstream media is the notion that millennials waste money on non-essentials such as avocado toast, instead of saving for their own home. PR has helped perpetuate this millennial myth through PR surveys, which may aim to raise *parental* awareness of financial products designed to help adult offspring.

Many under-40s consumers face genuine struggles with financial freedom. Many young consumers are poor or lead precarious financial lives, with little to spare for regular financial products. As a result, when it comes to engaging with finance, many millennials are forced to go for risky, unregulated products and expensive alternatives. (See Think about 29.3.)

Picture 29.3 Avocado on toast is a favourite of millennials to the extent that it has become a cliché (*source:* Jennifer Barrow/Alamy Stock Photo)

> **Explore 29.2**
>
> **The Panama Papers**
>
> **A complex investigation, with complex PR responses**
>
> Visit the website of the Consortium of Investigative Journalists https://www.icij.org/ and find the investigation on the Panama Papers. Get a sense of the number of countries caught up in The Panama Papers investigation. Go through some of the resulting media coverage. See if you can discern a range of PR responses mounted on behalf of politicians, public officials, companies, business directors and celebrities.

choice editors in retail financial markets. Personal finance journalists use print columns, websites, blogs, TV and radio money programmes to help consumers navigate the range of personal finance opportunities on offer. Some journalists campaign against mis-sold products, get customers to surrender flawed insurance policies or funds, or encourage consumers to avoid certain financial products and company shares altogether. Product advice is one thing, but forensic analysis of systemic market issues is a challenge even for well-resourced newsrooms. Mainstream media can only justify investigative financial reporting when the resulting story delivers big headlines and multiple story angles, attracting millions of eyeballs and click-throughs. The Panama Papers was one such story. The Panama Papers was the title given to an unprecedented investigation into the rogue offshore industry. The 2016 investigation involved cooperation between mainstream newspapers and TV channels across several countries. The depth of public outcry required PR responses from governments, monarchies, corporations and celebrities named in the cross-border investigation (see Explore 29.2).

Financial communication and social media

Social media's rapid growth and increasing influence has redrawn the borderlands of financial market communication. The avalanche of digital media outlets purporting to speak to real people now far outnumbers media outlets that only engage with the financially savvy (Bana 2016). The resulting participatory culture, in which day traders, freelance experts and consumers produce, distribute, interpret and evaluate financial news and opinion, has re-shaped many areas of financial communication. For instance, social media's participatory culture has completely transformed stock market communication, where information is speedier and noisier than ever before. Investors turn eagerly to webzines, blogs and social media influencers to interpret mass amounts of equivocal financial messages about daily stock market activity (Herrmann 2007). While investors may seek out financial blogs, social networks and news aggregators, these sites lack the investigative journalistic staff needed to hold public companies and financial institutions to account (Chakravartty and Schiller 2010). From PR's perspective, the new speed of financial information poses several concerns. First, the public increasingly expects real-time responses when communicating with financial brands. The pressure to respond quickly increases the risk of communication leaks from publicly listed companies and financial institutions, which are governed by strict rules regarding financial disclosure. A simple tweet by a company director can breach market rules. PR professionals must often act as social media gatekeepers (see Box 29.3).

Social media has added more than speed, it has made media networks more social, profoundly personalised and emotionally charged (Beckett and Deuze 2016). Financial brands have struggled with developing a relaxed, authentic social media identity, which delivers more emotional cues, gets consumers' attention and prolongs their engagement. Companies in other sectors such as sportswear, entertainment or fast food can afford to be friendly, use colloquialisms, employ humour regularly, or even be a bit risqué. PR teams find this more challenging when representing financial brands and creating financial fans. Compliance concerns can make a financial brand seem stiff and remote. And there are pitfalls in adopting a humorous approach on social media when characterising big ticket items such as mortgages, life insurance or pensions. Fintech start-ups have a clear advantage in this new environment. Where public companies and traditional financial providers might be constrained in when and what they say, fintech start-ups can be friendlier and more emotive in their PR activity.

Explore 29.3 Talking to millennials – financial TV

The rise of visual

Industry research suggests that nearly half of millennials might be more likely to trust a financial provider if that company creates useful content (Baker 2017). Today's financial communicators know that useful content increasingly means *video* content, providing 'actionable' financial advice that can be shared on social media.

Compelling stories are necessary for video content to work. However, financial brands are not acclaimed for their use of television as a medium to reach consumers. Many financial brands struggle to strike the right chord with video content in an age of participatory culture, where authenticity is valued, content is fun and relatable, and consumers expect to be the central character of the story. Meanwhile, apart from Cheddar TV in the USA few professional media outlets are dedicated to bringing financial content to millennials.

Feedback

Explore any social media platforms to which you have access such as Facebook, Instagram, Pinterest and YouTube. How many financial brands can you find with a sustained social media presence? How many of these financial brands engage in effective visual storytelling?

Despite the constraints, financial communication is undergoing a necessary shift towards more customer-friendly content in order to gain new customers, particularly millennials, who seek out more shareable content than previous generations. (See Explore 29.3.) Millennials are also more attracted to transmedia storytelling, where content relating to a story, its characters and images, can flow across different media formats. The increased focus on content requires PR to translate financial messages into persuasive storytelling through videos, slick infographics and carefully crafted social media strategies. Financial journalists are also embracing transmedia storytelling, and PR strategies must take this into account. Social media has enabled financial journalists to reach out from behind the paywalls of traditional media and adopt a different tone of voice on different platforms, while driving traffic to their original stories as published in newspapers or aired on TV and radio. The emotionally charged nature of social media plays well to journalists who enjoy campaigning on financial issues that matter to them personally. Network platforms also allow financial journalists to converse directly with PR professionals. But more often, social media allows financial journalists to divert PR gatekeepers altogether, speaking directly with financial experts, policymakers and customers, to press for answers and greater transparency.

Box 29.3

What skills and education do you need for PR in financial markets?

As with every other area of PR, financial communication requires an expanding range of new skills to complement traditional ones. Succeeding in financial communication does require some knowledge of finance. If you change careers by moving from finance into a communications role, then you may already have a financial specialism. For others, it pays to build up foundational knowledge, before moving on to specialist areas:

Start with economics *before* you move to finance: Understanding economics is a good starting point for understanding money and finance. There are a great many channels for economics information. One useful source is Rethinking Economics, an international network of students and citizens, working to 'demystify, diversify and invigorate economics' in classrooms and society. Follow them @rethinkecon on Twitter or join by visiting http://www.rethinkeconomics.org/. Good starter economics books include *Doughnut Economics* by Kate Raworth. For those working at the financial policy level, useful communications books include *Writing the Economy* by Graham Smart.

Understand financial markets: Whatever your background, you will be required to understand aspects of financial markets well, in order to explain them to your relevant stakeholders. Once you are on the job, in-house PR roles can provide training opportunities in your company's specialist field. PR agency practitioners may also have access to training budgets. In some countries, PR professional bodies have specialist financial divisions which occasionally provide training and seminars. However, it can be more productive to find specialist training providers offering financial courses tailored to the needs of non-financial professionals.

Seek out financial news: For any PR practitioner starting out in financial markets, subscriptions to global newspapers such as *The Economist, The Financial Times* and *The Wall Street Journal* are useful, as is access to television channels such as *Bloomberg, CNBC* and specialist financial programmes or other channels. Other sources are free-to-access, including the business section of *Huffington Post, TheFinanser.com* blog and webzine; as well as podcasts hosted by Fintech Insider at https://fi.11fs.com/.

Follow financial influencers: Several social media influencers specialise in finance. These include financial journalists, financial professionals and academics who research financial markets. Some influencers publish well-researched, educational insights into finance, including podcasts such as Philip Roscoe's *How to build a stock exchange*.

Keep up-to-date with financial rules and regulation: Whether you represent a life insurer, a general insurer, a bank, building society, hedge fund, investment manager, a stock broker or a listed company, PR professionals must know the appropriate rules and regulations of the market in which you operate. In addition, if you are employed in an in-house role you may be required to pass tests on anti-money laundering and anti-fraud measures, and/or to understand rules on staff share dealing before you can represent your organisation.

Consider financial qualifications: Financial literacy will be important in establishing your credibility and will help you to do financial communications well. Some PR practitioners must understand balance sheets and company accounts thoroughly. Others need to understand the basic formulae used to calculate pension products, together with bond yields and interest rates. Some financial communicators gain further credibility by earning specialist qualifications, opting to become qualified financial advisers, studying for the Certificate in Investment Management (IMC), becoming Chartered Financial Analysts (CFA) or even Chartered Management Accountants (CMA).

Public relations and the future of finance

This chapter has covered just some of the many changes taking place in the world of finance, and their implications for PR professionals and communications strategies. The fintech boom and current direction of travel, suggest that financial markets will continue to grow in importance to the world economy. This growth can have a positive impact through job creation, improved infrastructure, greater national earnings and better public access to finance. However, financial markets have a negative impact on society as well. This is evidenced by continued scandals and mis-selling of financial products and services. Such problems encompass both wholesale and retail market finance and affect nations large and small. For example, the World Bank introduced so-called pandemic bonds during the 2010s, to much acclaim. These financial instruments were designed to raise money from international investors to help developing nations face a serious outbreak of infectious disease. Shortly after, a severe attack of Ebola hit the Democratic Republic of Congo. A year after the outbreak, the World Bank's pandemic bonds had yet to pay out a penny (Allen 2019). Financial brands such as US bank, Wells Fargo, have spent years publicly apologising for deceiving US customers with fake bank accounts, unwarranted fees and unwanted products. Peer-to-peer loans and high-interest rate loans have become a growing concern internationally. Some of these high-rate loans have been likened to gambling; not only are they enticingly promoted in gamified ways, these loans trap users in a cycle of addiction to debt, which they cannot repay. In wholesale markets, investors have flocked back to the complex debt-derivatives products blamed for exacerbating the 2008 global financial crisis. Meanwhile, money-laundering scandals continue to erupt in every corner of the world. In 2018, Estonia investigated a seemingly small offence involving Swedish lender, Danske Bank, which rapidly expanded to become one of the biggest money-laundering scandals of all time, involving €200 billion of questionable money (Milne 2019).

Despite the promise of major reforms to financial markets after the 2008 global financial crisis, the culture of financial markets remains largely unchanged. This means the culture of financial communication remains unchanged too. Most financial communication focuses on elite groups of investors, entrepreneurs, company directors and policymakers. As a result, very little of the financial news and information circulated daily represents perspectives of workers, under-represented groups, and those at the margins of society (Chakravartty and Schiller 2010.)

Think about 29.2

Promoting financial market diversity to new recruits

The Investment Association (IA) is a trade body, representing a wide range of companies in the UK's savings and investment industries. In 2018, the IA launched a social media video as part of a diversity project entitled *Investment 2020 – Your Future in Finance*.

- Who are the main audiences for this social media video, and why?
- What do you think the term diversity means in the context of UK society and economy?
- How might poor diversity in the UK PR profession affect its ability to devise diversity campaigns?

For instance, stock market communication, by focusing on the 'minute-by-minute fate' of company shares, helps erase issues such as social wages. Similarly, personal finance communication focuses on those with enough income to invest, but sidelines financial planning for those with no disposable income. Changing the culture of financial markets is hardly an overnight job, but part of that change involves diversifying the make-up of those who work in financial services. This doesn't just mean highlighting the role of women in finance (e.g. Mini case study 29.2). It means recruiting a wider range of ethnic groups, socio-economic classes, and educational backgrounds into financial market jobs, including financial communication (see Think about 29.2).

Meanwhile, the rapid pace of change in financial markets, and the 2020 COVID pandemic, make it difficult to predict what the next decade of financial communication will bring. Will London's prestige as a global financial centre be eroded or fortified after Brexit, after the UK leaves the European Union? How will the fintech boom permanently alter financial markets? Will technology firms take over financial services altogether? Will PR professionals be working side by side with PR-bots to represent financial brands? (See Case study 29.2.) Will finance itself become so frictionless and invisible to the public, that the demand for PR to promote financial brands dissipates altogether?

Case study 29.2

PR-bots in financial markets?

More financial brands are incorporating AI chatbots into customer service, marketing and PR activity, as a cost-effective means of building personal, social connections with consumers. The latest generation of AI chatbot software is designed to have conversations with humans *as if the chatbot were human too*. Indeed, chatbots are envisioned to close the gap between the friendly, personalised service often promised in financial promotion, and what consumers actually get when they deal with banks, insurers and investment companies each day.

One of the most common finance bots is the robo-adviser, which guides customers through selections in their investment portfolios. Other bots act as helpdesks and support agents, automating various interactions with financial customers. These bots have the capacity to deliver the empathy and emotion that we miss out on when dealing with call centres, where humans still read from depressingly stilted scripts. Financial brands regularly use social media as a means of engaging with customers, and AI chatbots are being incorporated into public-facing communication of financial brands. As more PR and marketing departments incorporate AI tools into their daily work, the more likely we are to be talking to a chatbot in our next financial interaction.

High street banks have been early-adopters of customer service chatbots. This includes Scandinavian banks, SEB, Swedbank and Nordea Bank; along with the Bank of America and Wells Fargo in the USA. However, getting human-to-machine communication right in banking is an ongoing challenge. Swedish bank, Nordnet, incorporated Amelia, an off-the-shelf chatbot product, into its customer relations, only to discard it after underwhelming customer response. Communicating with financial customers can be much trickier than answering a balance enquiry or other queries fielded by older versions of automated software. AI chatbots are often programmed to adopt a personality and tone that supports the brand's identity.

The creators of Cleo, the personal finance chatbot, encountered serious difficulties when it programmed Cleo to chasten customers about financial management. Cleo was designed to help millennials manage and track their spending. Like many financial chatbots, Cleo adopts a feminine persona, supposedly reflecting customer preference. In addition, the brand's tone of voice is humorous and irreverent, evidenced by Cleo's strapline 'she's like your bank, if they actually cared'. As a 2019 Valentine's Day stunt, Cleo's creators introduced a savage mode, launching tough love for users' finances. Users could type 'Roast me Cleo' to the bot, to be confronted with blunt facts about money management. However, many women were appalled by the violent overtones of some of Cleo's wording. Cleo's all-female copywriting team responded quickly, but it was a warning to other financial brands that human-to-machine communication can thwart a communications strategy.

There are further ethical issues for PR professionals to consider in incorporating AI into financial communication. For instance, in stock market communication, chatbots can easily promote web links and news stories about company shares, quietly manipulating market information without investors detecting the subtle hand of PR. The plethora of apps used to manage money or offer credit-scoring should also be a concern, since these bots are collecting mountains of data on users. While current terms and conditions might wall-off customer data, what are the implications for financial customers where the chatbot gleaning their personal information isn't owned by the financial brand leading the customer interaction? What happens if the financial data gleaned by one company's chatbot is ultimately sold off to another firm?

In retail banking, PR and marketing-bots pose a trust issue, particularly where physical bank branches disappear from high streets. The problem with using bots as the new PR-friendly face of finance is that the human touch they offer is just an illusion. You think you're getting truly personalised service, when you're simply getting cheaper service. Likewise, as economic anthropologist, Brett Scott (2016) points out, a bank doesn't address itself as 'I' when issuing your monthly statements. But PR-bots will do exactly that, allowing us to think we are talking to banks in the first person, when what we are really doing is the opposite (Bourne 2018).

We could become lulled into thinking that trustworthy bots mean trustworthy banks. This would be a grave mistake as it would allow the movers-and-shakers of finance to hide behind friendly PR bot-led communication, while removing much-needed services even faster than ever.

Think about 29.3 — Debt, payday lending and living on the edge

There is a very large, hidden seam of financial markets known as fringe finance. It encompasses many unregulated companies willing to take a risk on poor or indebted consumers. Fringe finance includes companies that lend at very high rates of interest – some as high as 5,000 per cent. Getting a loan from one of these lenders can take seconds, as easy as swiping a bar on your mobile phone screen. Many of these companies have happy-sounding names, and maintain cheery PR and marketing campaigns to attract new customers. Increasingly, these companies are using AI and automation techniques such as geolocation to target students and young consumers via their phones.

- What are the ethical issues of promoting high-interest rate lending?
- How is promoting this sort of lending different from promoting a high-risk investment?
- Visit the website for the UK charity, StepChange – www.stepchange.org. Discuss the nature of the campaigning work done by the PR team within this organisation.

Summary

This chapter has provided a broad view of the different ways public relations is conducted in financial markets, on behalf of many special interests – some opposing, some overlapping. PR in the world of finance will continue to evolve and change as new financial centres emerge, and as technology and increased regulation transform financial communication. For students and researchers in the field of PR, this opens many interesting avenues for research. There is potential to analyse social media strategies in financial markets, including the increased use of visual content, as well as the use of Artificial Intelligence tools in financial communications work. Too few studies

> **summary (continued)**
>
> deconstruct the work done by PR practitioners in less visible parts of financial markets; the geographies of PR in emerging financial centres might be one interesting area for future research. Aspiring researchers might choose to uncover more hidden forms of PR activity, such as financial lobbying. It is also worth exploring how PR is used by less well-resourced organisations such as financial charities and community finance. Meanwhile, financial markets offer varied career opportunities and PR specialisms for those keen to enter the world of finance. The ever-changing nature of financial markets is undoubtedly part of its appeal for those who take up the challenge of communicating about finance and its role in shaping the way we live.

Bibliography

Allen, K. (2019) World Bank's 'pandemic bonds' under scrutiny after failing to pay out on Ebola, *Financial Times*, 21 February. https://www.ft.com/content/c3a805de-3058-11e9-ba00-0251022932c8

Bain, I. (2019) Revolt at Revolut: How the company tried to silence whistle blowers (and me), *Young Money Blog*, 1 March. https://youngmoneyblog.co.uk/revolut-whistleblowers/

Baker, D. (2017) *New Money: How top finance brands use content marketing to win in a customer-centric world*. New York: Contently.

Bana, Y. (2016) How Fintech is Challenging the Voice of Global Finance, *Translate Media*. Retrieved from: https://www.translatemedia.com/translation-blog/how-fintech-is-challenging-the-voice-of-global-finance/

Barr, C., M. Rice-Oxley and R. Jones (2016) A Hard Sell: The industries that can't get millennials buying, *The Guardian*, 18 March. https://www.theguardian.com/world/2016/mar/18/a-hard-sell-the-industries-that-cant-get-millennials-buying

Beckett, C. and M. Deuze (2016). On the role of emotion in the future of journalism. *Social Media & Society*, 1–6 July–September.

Bond, S., J. Fontanella-Khan and A. Massoudi (2016) Financial PR Spins a New Global Story, *Financial Times*, 6 May, https://www.ft.com/content/e21a373e-137e-11e6-91da-096d89bd2173

Bourne, C. (2017) *Trust, Power and Public Relations in Financial Markets*, Abingdon: Routledge.

Bourne, C. (2018) How PR-Robots are Changing the Face of Banking, *The Conversation*, 10 January. https://theconversation.com/how-pr-robots-are-changing-the-face-of-banking-89518

Business Reporter (2019) A Stellar Year for the UK Fintech Sector, *Business Reporter*, 15 March. https://www.business-reporter.co.uk/2019/03/15/a-stellar-year-for-the-uk-fintech-sector/#gsc.tab=0

Cairns, J. (2017) 'The Age of Entitlement?' In: *The Myth of the Age of Entitlement: Millennials, Austerity, and Hope*, University of Toronto Press, pp. 1–28.

CB Insights (2019) Startup Continent: The Most Well-Funded Tech Startups in Asia & the Pacific, *CB Insights*, 7 March. https://www.cbinsights.com/research/asia-startups-most-well-funded/

Chakravartty, P. and D. Schiller (2010) Neoliberal Newspeak and Digital Capitalism in Crisis, *International Journal of Communication*, 4, 670–692.

Credit Suisse (2015) Globalization or Multipolarisation – Which way is the World Heading? Credit Suisse Research, https://www.credit-suisse.com/corporate/en/articles/news-and-expertise/globalization-or-multipolarisation-which-way-is-the-world-heading-201510.html

Dooner, M. and D. McAlister (2013). Investor relations and communications: An overview of leading practices in the OECD area, *OECD Working Papers on Sovereign Borrowing and Public Debt Management*, No. 6, Paris: OECD Publishing.

Doyle, G. (2006) Financial news journalism: A post-Enron analysis of approaches towards economic and financial news production in the UK. *Journalism*, 7(4), 433–452.

Hardie and Gee (2018) FinTech Disruptors 2019, *MagnaCarta*. http://fintechdisruptors.org/wp-content/uploads/2018/12/FD2019.pdf

Herrmann, A.F. (2007) Stockholders in cyberspace: Weick's sensemaking online. *Journal of Business Communication* 44: 13–35.

Hiebert, R.E. (1966) *Courtier to the Crowd: The Story of Ivy Lee and the Development of Public Relations*, Ames: Iowa State University Press.

Holmes, D.R. (2014) *Economy of Words: Communicative Imperatives in Central Banks*, Chicago: University of Chicago Press.

Holmes, D.R. (2016) 'Public currency: Anthropological labor in central banks', *Journal of Cultural Economy*, 9 (1), pp. 5–26.

John, A. and S. Chatterjee (2019) Asia's Tech Champions Zero in on Main Street Banking, *Reuters*, 15 April. https://www.reuters.com/article/us-asia-banks-digital-analysis/asias-tech-champions-zero-in-on-main-street-banking-idUSKCN1RR017

Kendall, D. (2005) *Framing Class: Media Representations of Wealth and Poverty in America,* Plymouth: Rowland and Littlefield.

Kunczik, M. (2000). Globalization: News media, images of nations and the flow of international capital with special reference to the role of rating agencies, *IAMCR Conference,* Singapore, 17–20 July.

McGoun, E.G., M.S. Bettner, M.P. and Coyne (2007) 'Money n' motion – born to be wild', *Critical Perspectives on Accounting,* 18, pp. 343–361.

McGoun, E.G., Dunkak, W.H., Bettner, M.S. and Allen, D.E. (2003) 'Walt's Street and Wall Street: Theming, theatre, and experience in finance', *Critical Perspectives on Accounting,* 14, pp. 647–661.

Megaw, N. and T. Bradshaw (2019) Revolut Promises to Grow Up as It Seeks New Investment, *Financial Times,* 23 April. https://www.ft.com/content/6f91965c-5f8a-11e9-b285-3acd5d43599e

Mellino, E. (2019) Revolut Insiders Reveal the Human Cost of a Fintech Unicorn's Wild Rise, *Wired,* 28 February. https://www.wired.co.uk/article/revolut-trade-unions-labour-fintech-politics-storonsky

Milne, R. (2019) 'Denmark proposes tougher penalties for bankers' failings', *Financial Times,* 29 January, https://www.ft.com/content/e60cdd86-23ef-11e9-8ce6-5db4543da632

Moskvitch, K. (2019) Legacy Banks Are Fighting Back Against the Monzo Insurrection, *Wired,* 7 February. https://www.wired.co.uk/article/fintech-startups-taking-on-legacy-banks

Nelson, J. (2012) Would Women Leaders Have Prevented the Global Financial Crisis? Implications for teaching about gender, behavior, and economies, *Global Development and Environment Institute Working Paper* No. 11-03.

O'Dwyer, R. (2019) 'Cache society: Transactional records, electronic money, and cultural resistance', *Journal of Cultural Economy,* 12(2) 133–153.

Prügl, E. (2012) 'If Lehman Brothers Had Been Lehman Sisters . . . ': Gender and myth in the aftermath of the financial crisis, *International Political Sociology,* 6, 21–35.

O'Dea, S. (2019) Tired: we spend no money on marketing. Wired: we drop leaflets through doors, Micro-blog, *Twitter,* 12 April. https://twitter.com/sharonodea/status/1116626868508041216

Olaison, L. & Taalas, S. L. (2016). Game of gamification: marketing, consumer resistance and digital play (1ed.). In: Mikolaj Dymek, Peter Zackariasson (Ed.), *The business of gamification: a critical analysis* (p. 59–80). New York: Routledge.

Revolut (2019) Careers at Revolut, Revolut, https://www.revolut.com/careers

Scott, B. (2016) If you talk to bots, you're talking to their bosses. *How We Get to Next,* 26 May. Available at: https://howwegettonext.com/if-you-talk-to-bots-youre-talking-to-their-bosses-cd8e390c242f

Securities Industry and Financial Markets Association (SIFMA) (2019) *Trends in Capital Markets – 2019 Outlook,* New York/Washington: SIFMA.

Sims, M.P. (2018) Fledgling Fintechs confront PR challenge, *The Holmes Report,* 7 June. https://www.holmesreport.com/latest/article/analysis-fledgling-fintechs-confront-corporate-pr-challenge

Smart, G. (2006) *Writing the Economy: Activity, Genre and Technology in the World of Banking,* London: Equinox Publishing.

Stäheli, U. (2008). 'Watching the market': Visual representations of the financial economy in advertisements'. In Ruccio, D.F. (ed.) *Economic Representations: Academic and Everyday.* Abingdon: Routledge, pp. 242–256.

Storonsky, N. (2019) Revolut's Culture: The past, present and the future, *Revolut blog,* 4 March. https://blog.revolut.com/weve-made-mistakes-but-were-learning/

Thomson, A. and L. Camp (2018) *No Small Change: Why Financial Services Needs a New Kind of Marketing,* Wiley.

US Treasury (2017A) *A Financial System that Creates Economic Opportunities: Asset Management and Insurance,* Washington D.C.: US Department of the Treasury.

US Treasury (2017B) *A Financial System that Creates Economic Opportunities: Nonbank financials, fintech and innovation,* Washington D.C.: US Department of the Treasury.

Warren, T. (2019) Monzo and Starling are transforming UK Spending, 13 June. *The Verge.* https://www.theverge.com/2019/6/13/18663036/monzo-starling-mobile-banks-uk-report

Westbrook, I. (2014) *Strategic Financial and Investor Communication: The Stock Price Story,* Abingdon: Routledge.

Vestergaard, J. (2009) *Discipline in the Global Economy,* New York: Routledge.

Z/Yen Group. (2019) *The Global Financial Centres Index 25.* London: Z/Yen.

Z/Yen Group. (2020) *The Global Financial Centres Index 27.* London: Z/Yen.

PART 5

What next?

Finally, the last chapter takes a tentative look into the future. It asks some questions about where the discipline and the practice will go next. Through this questioning the chapter addresses some of the key issues emerging from recent research among practitioners that will be of major importance to the profession as it evolves further in an ever-changing media, business, social and political landscape.

CHAPTER 30

Ralph Tench and Stephen Waddington

Future issues for PR and strategic communication

Source: Michael Nolan/Robertharding/Alamy Stock Photo

Learning outcomes

By the end of this chapter you should be able to:
- understand the challenges and opportunities impacting the future of PR practice in the medium and long term
- discuss the impact of technology on media and PR practice and the reputation of organisations
- identify the importance of PR to modern organisations and the multi-faceted opportunities for practitioners
- understand the skills required for modern PR practice and how these are changing
- understand the changing nature of media impact of social media such as Facebook and Twitter on public discourse for good and bad
- evaluate your learning about the future of PR and investigate further sources of information and insight.

Structure

- Macro issues facing PR in society
- Challenges facing the work of practitioners
- The future of PR practice
- Management, automation and AI
- Media in pain

Introduction

The process of editing this book, now in its fifth edition, has given the authors a privileged opportunity to understand how public relations is changing. This chapter reflects on the issues covered in the book and also tries to look wider and deeper to consider the future of the profession.

There are long-standing issues such as alignment with management, measurement, talent and diversity where incremental progress is made each year. And then there are areas of practice that have moved more rapidly. The greatest of these is the shift away from media relations as the dominant means of public engagement to working across all forms of media. This trend is reflected in nearly all the chapters of this fifth edition.

The Paid, Earned, Shared and Owned (PESO) model has emerged as a planning model. PR leads with earned and owned media but also uses paid and shared media for amplification and targeting. We've lost some battles but won others. Other disciplines, notably marketing, have encroached on PR practice in areas that lead with paid media, such as influencer marketing and search engine optimisation (SEO).

Macro issues facing PR

There are two macro issues facing the industry that have been spotlighted by recent political events around the world.

First is the ease with which disinformation can be created and spread via social media which has had huge implications for public engagement and discourse in society on a range of issues from health policy debates such as the sugar tax (see Mini case study 26.1) to politics. Second, structural issues in the mainstream media as it continues to transform to digital should be a concern for all practitioners (see Chapters 2, 3 and 14). Public service broadcasting is under threat in some countries (e.g. the BBC in the UK) and is failing to pick up the shortfall.

We explore these issues, and more, in this chapter. There is a lot to consider when you think of the future of public relations and the pace of societal change so we do, unashamedly, cover a lot of ground. To help digest the themes we have organised the chapter in sections. Here are the headlines. These are some of the issues that we believe will occupy PR practitioners and scholars in the coming years – inevitably more will emerge and it is our role as scholars and academics to look out for these emerging trends and attempt to explore and understand their impact and influence not only on the discipline of public relations but on society as a whole.

Challenges facing the work of practitioners:

1. Demonstrating value and the talent paradox
2. Gender diversity in public relations is an issue as old as the industry itself
3. Representing the public that we serve
4. The mental health and wellbeing conversation is getting louder
5. Learning on the job

The future of public relations practice:

6. Tackling fake news and disinformation: an ethical issue that strikes at the heart of practice
7. Is purpose a means for organisations to rebuild trust in society?
8. Digital: investment in content and paid social, but cuts in SEO and social listening
9. Influencer relations are messy
10. The resurgence of internal communications
11. Social medvia activism: brands don't listen

Management, automation and AI:

12. Alignment with management; public relations refuses to learn
13. Public relations slow to adopt an integrated tool stack
14. Waking up to the impact of automation and AI on PR practice
15. Tell me a story

Future of media:

16. News media in pain but new formats emerge
17. Public service media is failing the public

Postscript comment: the COVID-19 Pandemic:

18. Release, recovery and reform from COVID-19

Challenges facing the work of practitioners

1. Demonstrating value and the talent paradox

Talent remains a critical challenge for the PR industry according to 'The ICCO World PR Report 2020'. At every level of the industry, and in every region of the world, there is a challenge in recruiting and retaining talent.

ICCO consists of national public relations (PR) trade associations in 55 countries. The report provides an international perspective on the challenges facing the PR business. 43 per cent of respondents reported that there is a lack of talent in PR. Almost half said that the industry failed to recruit from outside.

The issue lies in the inability of PR to achieve its value. It uses proxies as a measurement of success rather than key performance indicators that are aligned to the organisations that it serves.

Advertising value equivalent (AVE) is at the sharp end of this issue. According to 'The ICCO World PR Report', this continues to be used by almost half of respondents. Use of AVEs is reported as 16 per cent in the UK and 18 per cent in North America. It remains a dominant form of measurement in Asia Pacific (56 per cent), Africa and the Middle East (70 per cent), Latin America (74 per cent), Eastern Europe (56 per cent) and Western Europe (58 per cent).

Measurement and analytics are cited as the leading areas of investment in 2020 ahead of influencer marketing (36 per cent), content creation (34 per cent) and research (31 per cent).

Demonstrating the value of the work of PR to organisations is the profession's long-standing Achilles heel. It is its own worst enemy. AMEC is helping drive change by raising standards of evaluation all around the world. Its Integrated Evaluation Framework (see Tench et al. 2017) provides a consistent and credible approach that works for organisations of all sizes, but which can be tailored to specific use, cases and objectives.

Please refer to Chapters 9 and 10 for more information about planning and measurement for public relations campaigns.

2. Gender diversity in PR is an issue as old as the industry itself

Gender issues in the public relations industry are well documented. A study called the Velvet Ghetto commissioned by the International Association of Business Communicators (IABC) first called out the gender pay gap in the PR profession in 1986. It suggested that women see themselves as practice rather than management focused and are paid accordingly.

The issue of gender pay has continued to be explored since the IABC study with notable work by Linda Aldoory, Bettina Beurer-Zuellig, Glen M. Broom, David M. Dozier, Larissa A. Grunig and Elizabeth L. Toth and more recently from a European perspective (Fielden, Tench and Fawkes; Verhoeven and Aarts; Tench, Topic and Moreno), among others.

Other gender issues featured in a book called *Women in Public Relations – A Literature Review (1982–2019)*. This covered the glass ceiling, pay gap, lack of mentorship opportunities and stereotyped expectations of leadership style, where leadership is usually seen as a masculine trait.

The book is a multi-author project led by Dr Martina Topić, a Senior Lecturer in Public Relations at Leeds Business School. It was published by Leeds Beckett University at the Euprera Congress 2019.

Accord to Topić a possible explanation for the PR industry's lack of progress is the so-called bloke-ification in which women adopt masculine characteristics to progress faster in their career. It's a theme that Topić has been exploring in her work on women in journalism. She believes the same issues apply in advertising and PR.

Bloke-ification and masculine culture are part of patriarchal social structure, Topić argues. Offices are predominantly structured around masculine ways of working and doing things and around masculine behavioural and leadership patterns.

Gender is an issue that is researched and evaluated as a key variable in the trends for the practice community worldwide in the European Communication Monitor (and now the Global Communication Monitor with

---

Think about 30.1

A flawed measurement approach

AVE attributes an advertising value to earned media content secured by a public relations practitioner. An arbitrary multiplier is often applied, justified on the basis that editorial content has greater credibility and is valued more by consumers than advertising space. It has been used in the PR industry as a means of benchmarking earned media coverage with paid media.

Why is AVE flawed as a means of measuring the outcome of PR activity, and why is it still popular as a measurement approach?

studies in Europe, North America, Asia Pacific and Latin America) – see www.communicationmonitor.eu. Researchers can review data on gender issues each year of the ECM study since 2007 with all data available for open access for students and academic researchers.

Women in Public Relations calls on future research to investigate the hurdles that women face in their careers to address the root of the issue. It also calls for investigation into work culture and structures that have so far prevented gender equality in leadership in PR.

3. Representing the public that we serve

Like gender inequality the lack of ethnic and socio-economic diversity remains an ongoing challenge for PR (for academic discussions see Edwards 2014). It's impossible to keep coming up with creative ideas to reach and resonate with audiences who are not represented by a PR team.

Agencies are trying to improve recruitment practices or partnering with organisations such as The Taylor Bennett Foundation, a charity that exists to encourage black, Asian and minority ethnic (BAME) graduates to pursue a career in communications. BME PR Pros (https://bmeprpros.co.uk) is a UK-based community created by Elizabeth Bananuka that promotes black, Asian and ethnic minority diversity in the creative industries.

Progress is slow: 89 per cent of practitioners in the UK are white British compared with 80 per cent of the population according to the 2011 UK Census.

> **Explore 30.1**
>
> **Improving the diversity of PR**
>
> Investigate organisations such as The Taylor Bennett Foundation and BME PR Pros that are working to improve the diversity of the PR profession. How successful are they in tackling the issue and will the profession ever truly be representative of the public that it serves?

80 per cent are graduates and a third are privately educated. In 2019 they created a Schools Outreach Programme in a bid to tackle the issue. The aim is to provide practitioners with the assets and resources they need to visit schools, introduce students to PR, and drive awareness of PR as a career option. The programme is the brainchild of the PRCA's Diversity Network, led by Pema Seely and Rax Lakhani.

Each corporate PRCA member will be expected to engage with a local school each year. More than 100 members have committed to supporting the scheme.

4. The mental health and wellbeing conversation is getting louder

In 2017 Sarah Waddington (formerly Hall) and Stephen Waddington investigated the issue of mental health in PR for a #FuturePRoof report published by the PRCA. We found that mental illness in the PR profession was

Picture 30.1 The always on nature of PR can make it a stressful occupation. Crisis situations are particularly acute. (*source:* Denverdave/Shutterstock)

frequently ignored or managed as a line management or performance issue.

It's a very different situation two years on. Mental health is cited as one of the top issues impacting the profession. It is firmly on the agenda of industry bodies and progressive organisations are talking steps to address it for employees. The managers of agencies and in-house teams have recognised mental health and wellbeing as critical to retention, utilisation and good work. Bold, creative and excellent campaigns cannot be delivered by an organisation with a sick culture.

PR can be a stressful occupation. We work in an 'always on' environment, often as an intermediary between stakeholders with very different expectations. If you work in issues and crisis it can be especially acute. The 2019 CIPR State of the Profession survey reported that around a quarter of PR practitioners have taken sickness absence from work on the grounds of stress, anxiety or depression.

There's also a need for personal responsibility on the part of individuals. Good employers can support the mental health and wellbeing of employees through good management and a progressive workplace, but the organisation needs to deliver its commercial goals.

5. Learning on the job

Public relations may be a maturing professional discipline but unlike other areas of management it has yet to adopt the qualities that mark out other professions, such as formal qualifications and life-long learning. This is different in regions of the world but it is still the case in some areas of practice that practical experience counts a lot. Time served can be a typical measure of competence of PR. You'll spot seemingly random periods of time in practitioners' biographies. But not all experience is equal and when media and technology are evolving so quickly it's an out-of-date and inconsistent metric whose time has passed.

If public relations and organisational communication is to become recognised as a boardroom discipline it needs to adhere to the standards of other professional practices such as accountancy and the legal profession.

There's no barrier to entry in PR in the form of qualifications, no requirement for registration in a way that can be publicly tested and no mandatory requirement for continuing professional development (CPD). It also lacks an established community of practice as a forum for discussion and exchange of ideas between academia and practice.

This is a conversation as old as the industry itself that is slowly beginning to change thanks to the work of professional association networks such as the Global Alliance for Public Relations and Communication Management (see www.globalalliancepr.org) and in different countries (e.g. the CIPR and PRCA in the UK). This is an ongoing area of debate and research and something students of the industry and practice should explore and challenge.

Please refer to Chapter 13 for more information about professionalism in PR.

The future of PR practice

6. Tackling fake news and disinformation: an ethical issue that strikes at the heart of practice

The great hope of the web was that it would democratise the publication and sharing of information. It enabled anyone with access to the internet to publish and distribute content at no cost. The internet provided a means for people to connect and communicate with each other, irrespective of location. It disintermediated all previous forms of media, enabling anyone to become a publisher.

As traditional media has fragmented, individuals and organisations have created their own media on almost every form of social network. The web and the internet have enabled communities to form around an organisation, topic or issue. The web was the most significant shift in publishing since the invention of the printing press in the fifteenth century. The nineties and noughties were a period of huge shifts in media that continue to play out. It was also a time of incredible innovation.

This period corresponded with the rise of mobile networks and devices. You're likely to be reading this on a mobile phone or you'll have one within reach. These devices have provided the means for consumers to connect to the internet wherever and whenever.

The web has overhauled organisational communication and marketing. It has created many new forms of media for organisations to engage with their publics using paid, earned, social and owned media. Thirty years after the invention of the web we're only beginning to realise that it hasn't brought about the communication utopia that was originally envisaged.

596 Part 5 WHAT NEXT?

> **Explore 30.2**
>
> **How does a topic trend on social media?**
>
> What drives sharing of content on a social network such as Facebook and Twitter? Examine the trending topics on Twitter and the most popular posts. Can you identify any common traits that have contributed to the popularity of the topics?

7. Is purpose a means for organisations to rebuild trust in society?

Trust in organisations is at an all-time low. Seemingly every study and report points to a breakdown in the relationship between individuals and government, business, non-governmental organisations and media.

The 2019 Edelman Trust Barometer reported modest rises in trust across all areas of society, coupled with widespread disenfranchisement. It's a contradiction that Edelman suggests is contributing to a rise in activism among business leaders, employees and the public. Only one in five people believe that the system is working for them, with high levels of injustice, desire for change and lack of confidence. Fears of jobs losses, lack of skills, the rise of automation and international trade are all contributing to pessimism about the future. Edelman cites the Gilet Jaunes protests in France, India's Women's Wall for equality, and various employee protests as examples of the public taking issues into its own hands.

In 2019 Ralph Tench, working with colleagues from Germany (Zerfass and Wiesenberg) and Italy (Romenti), explored the issue of trust in communications specifically and evaluated the perceptions of different organisational stakeholders. We asked practitioners, as well as the general public, for their opinions. And it made for troubling reading. The report (#TiCS19) reveals that there are high levels of distrust in organisational spokespeople but that external experts are the most trusted advocates in the general population (see Figure 30.1). External advocates for organisations are trusted more than top executives, public relations professionals and marketers by the public (see Figure 30.2). We explored what this changing

The internet has fragmented into a series of closed networks operated by platforms including Facebook, Google, Instagram and Twitter. Each user has a different algorithm-driven experience based on the data that these platforms gather about us. Public conversation on these personal versions of the internet is corrupted by the loudest voices with the biggest budgets. Algorithms reward bullies, extremists and trolls, and can be circumvented by payment.

Finally, there's an issue of authenticity. Fake news has become a catch-all term to describe everything from nonsense to blatant manipulation. Legitimate news sources vie for attention in algorithm-driven news feeds along with disinformation and propaganda. It's a race to the bottom. Practitioners are experiencing these effects on a daily basis (Zerfass et al. 2018). Regulation is urgently required. Governments and law makers are slowly awakening to the issue but aren't moving quickly enough.

Please refer to Chapter 11 for more information about the role of PR in tackling disinformation.

High level of distrust in communication and public relations professionals in the general population

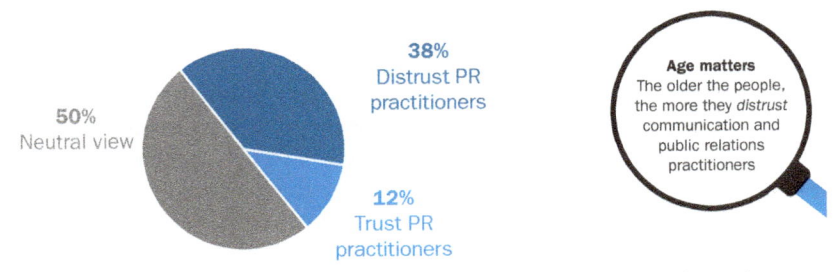

- 50% Neutral view
- 38% Distrust PR practitioners
- 12% Trust PR practitioners

Age matters
The older the people, the more they *distrust* communication and public relations practitioners

TICS19 © www.euprera.org. N = 3,130 adults aged 16-64 in Germany, Italy and the UK (representative sample). Question: How much do you trust these communicators? Item: Communication and public relations practitioners of organisations. Scale 1 (Strong distrust) - 5 (Strong trust).

Figure 30.1 High level of distrust in communication and public relations professionals in the general population (*source*: Trust in Communicators Study 2019, European Communication Monitor)

picture means for communications professionals and for the important organisational trust-building process (see Figure 30.3). The full report can be accessed at http://www.communicationmonitor.eu/2019/10/23/tics19-trust-in-communicators-study-2019/.

In 2019 purpose continued to emerge as a theme in corporate leadership as a means of reconnecting organisations with society. It's an issue that is quickly rising up the corporate agenda. Larry Fink, CEO, BlackRock, used his annual letters to business leaders in 2018 and

External experts are the most trusted advocates in the general population

#3 Other employees/members of organisations — 18%

Leaders of organisations (CEOs, board members, top executives) #5 — 12%

#1 External experts in the field (e.g. professors, consultants) — 38%

Activists and other external organisations with their own agenda #4 — 17%

#2 External supporters/fans or customers/clients of organisations — 19%

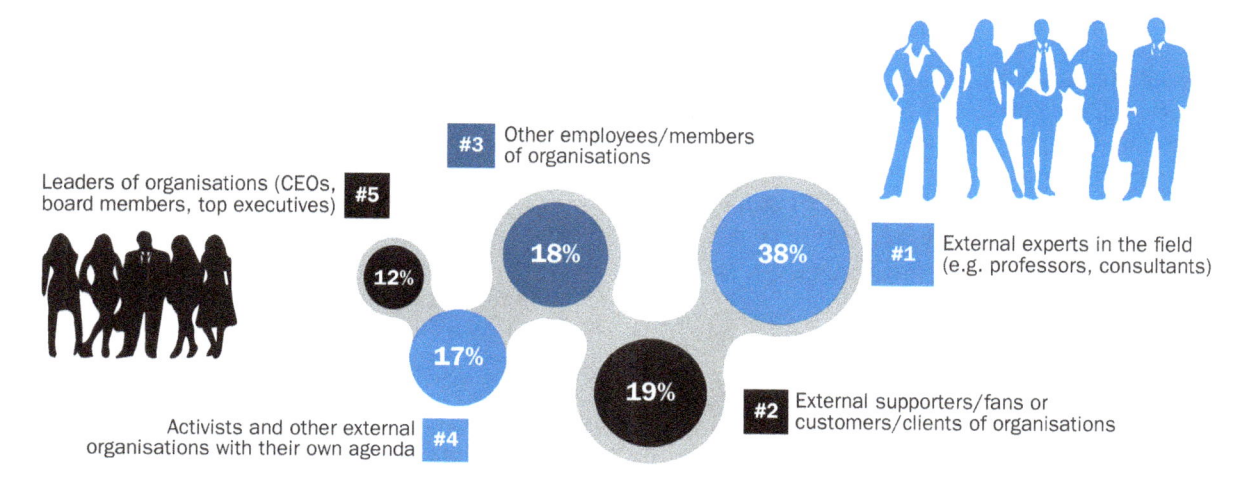

TICS19 © www.euprera.org. N = 3,130 adults aged 16-64 in Germany, Italy and the UK (representative sample). Question: The public discourse about organisations (companies, non-profits, governments, political parties, etc.) is not only shaped by journalists, but also by those who speak on behalf of an organisation. How much do you trust these communicators? Item wording see above. Scale 1 (Strong distrust) - 5(Strong trust). Percentages: Frequency based on scale points 4-5.

Figure 30.2 External experts are the most trusted advocates in the general population (*source:* Trust in Communicators Study 2019, European Communication Monitor)

Fuzzy perceptions about the general goals and essence of PR activities by the general population

Foster dialogue
One quarter agrees that PR professionals foster dialogue between organisations and those interested in their activities. **26%**

Build relationships
One third agrees that PR professionals build relationships between organisations and their stakeholders. **32%**

Manage communication
More than one third agrees that PR practitioners manage communication activities that help organisations to reach their goals. **36%**

TICS19 © www.euprera.org. N = 3,130 adults aged 16-64 in Germany, Italy and the UK (representative sample). Question: Thinking of communication and public relations professionals, how much would you agree with these statements? Items cited above. Scale 1 (Strongly disagree) - 5 (Strongly agree). Percentage: Frequency based on scale points 4-5.

Figure 30.3 Fuzzy perceptions about the general goals and essence of PR activities by the general population (*source:* Trust in Communicators Study 2019, European Communication Monitor)

2019 to call companies to account on their societal impact. Purpose is not the sole pursuit of profits but a driving force for achieving them, he said.

> *Profits are in no way inconsistent with purpose – in fact, profits and purpose are inextricably linked. Profits are essential if a company is to effectively serve all of its stakeholders over time – not only shareholders, but also employees, customers, and communities.*
>
> *Similarly, when a company truly understands and expresses its purpose, it functions with the focus and strategic discipline that drive long-term profitability. Purpose unifies management, employees and communities. It drives ethical behaviour and creates an essential check on actions that go against the best interests of stakeholders.*
>
> *Purpose guides culture, provides a framework for consistent decision-making, and, ultimately, helps sustain long-term financial returns for the shareholders of your company.*

Fink's words carry the weight of the largest investment fund in the world with more than $6 trillion under management. It's a conversation that will continue to grow louder.

Please refer to Chapters 12 and 23 for more information about corporate image, reputation and communication.

8. Digital: investment in content and paid social, but cuts in SEO and social listening

Practitioners are embracing social and owned media alongside earned as a means of engagement with an audience or public. This is the conclusion of The PRCA 2019 Digital Report.

The use of social platforms and the creation of content, notably video, are both up year-on-year. Oddly social media listening, used by practitioners as a means of planning and alerting, has fallen. However, it is also an area in which brands wanted more education, indicating that they have invested in tools that they aren't using.

Areas that have seen a reduction in budget are organic and paid social media optimisation. However, paid social media is a significant growth area. It's indicative of the fact that outside of customer service, social media engagement has largely become a paid activity.

The main reasons for brands having a social media presence are to drive awareness of what they do (86 per cent), to drive wider audience reach (71 per cent), to increase brand awareness (65 per cent), and to use it as a customer service platform (40 per cent).

61 per cent of respondents said that their PR and communications department are responsible for digital and social media content, up 4 per cent year-on-year. The most popular social media platforms amongst in-house organisations are Twitter (90 per cent), down 4 per cent year-on-year, and Facebook (81 per cent), up 9 per cent year-on-year. This is followed by LinkedIn (76 per cent), YouTube (69 per cent), and Instagram (63 per cent).

In terms of the future, technologies that practitioners are seeking to develop skills in include augmented and virtual reality (32 per cent), voice/search apps (25 per cent), and chatbots (24 per cent). Voice/search apps have taken over chatbots as one of the areas in which agencies need more education.

Also see the ECM (European Communication Monitor, www.communicationmonitor.eu) for annual trends and their reported changes. This is a study that has been recording the practice in Europe since 2007 and it's possible to track and mark the changes over time and each year issues of technology and media usage are observed and reported in the full report with data from more than 50 European countries.

9. Influencer relations is messy

In 2018, the Advertising Standards Authority (ASA) received 352 complaints about influencers. In 2019, this more than tripled to above 1,300. According to Markets and Markets (https://www.marketsandmarkets.com) the worldwide influencer market is currently estimated at £4.5 billion in 2019. The value exchange between an organisation and influencer is the driver of the relationship. It can be exclusive access to content, products and services, or financial remuneration.

The tension between earned and paid isn't only a challenge for marketing and public relations practitioners. It has also led to influencers themselves breaching advertising and trading standards law.

In the UK influencer campaigns are governed by existing ASA and Competition and Markets Authority (CMA) laws. But these laws are misunderstood. Members of the CIPR and the PRCA have to adhere to their codes of conduct.

A #FuturePRoof best practice guide published in 2019 provides practical advice on media law as well as information from advertising, marketing and PR professionals. *We're All Influencers Now* written by Scott Guthrie and Stephen Waddington, highlights best practice and addresses the need for influencer marketing governance in PR.

Please refer to Chapter 25 for more information about influencer relations.

> **Think about 30.2**
>
> ## The business of influence
>
> The common perception of influencers is individuals on Instagram or YouTube selling products and services. In fact, the market is maturing and far more nuanced. Influence is often confused with popularity. But influence is the ability to shape or change a person's opinion or behaviour.
>
> Influence is often used interchangeably with advocacy, but influence is not necessarily positive. Brands can suffer the effect of negative influencers just as much as from positive ones. Selling is only one outcome of working with influencers. What might some of the other outcomes of an influencer relations campaign be?

10. The resurgence of internal communications

Internal communications is one of the hottest areas of contemporary PR. It is enjoying significant growth. Progressive organisations have spotted the opportunity that social collaboration tools offer enterprise and are calling on internal communicators to help lead the charge along with colleagues in human resources and IT.

Forward-thinking organisations are using new technologies as a means of listening and engaging with employees. Social leaders use platforms and technology to build relationships externally with employees, customers and other stakeholders. It's a powerful form of advocacy.

Technology firms such as Microsoft with Teams and Facebook with Workplace are taking a keen interest in the market. Workplace, launched as a commercial product in 2016, applies all the learnings from the consumer product to a private enterprise environment. Most people intuitively understand how the news feed, threaded conversations and groups work, thanks to the consumer product.

Please refer to Chapter 15 for more information about internal communications and employee engagement.

11. Social media activism: brands don't listen

In 2012 Steve Earl and Stephen Waddington wrote a book called *Brand Anarchy*. It told the story of the public using social media to fight back against organisations. Any gap between a product or service and the public's expectation will become a conversation on social media.

The book holds up almost ten years on because most organisations are ineffective at using social media to listen to their customers. There are exceptions but they are limited. The most common approach to social media management is an agency or junior member armed with a monitoring tool and limited ability to feedback to operational areas of the business.

Brand shaming has become commonplace. It is almost a sport on Facebook, Instagram and Twitter. Watch out for the fed-up commuters ranting at train companies every morning or the lunchtime diners unimpressed by what's on their plate.

Most brands have learnt that the customer service or reputational impact of the occasional rogue tweet isn't worth the cost of 24/7 social media management. Twitter has recognised that brand trolling has become such an issue that it is rolling out moderation tools.

The social network will let tweeters choose from four options for individual tweets:

- Global – anyone can reply to a global tweet.
- Group – only people who you follow can reply, as well as anyone mentioned in the tweet.
- Panel – only people mentioned in the tweet can reply.
- Statement – no one can reply.

Twitter trolling is a serious issue for individuals in the public sphere. Here Twitter's moderation tool has an important application, but organisations and brands

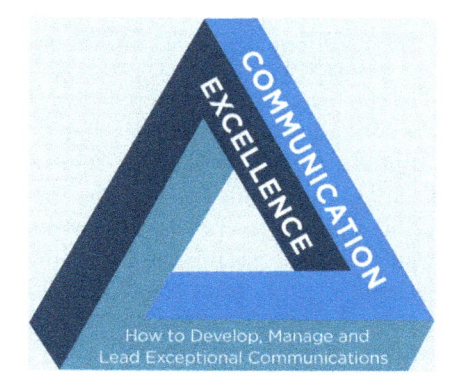

Picture 30.2 Communication Excellence: how to manage and lead excellent communications. This book summarises 10 years of studying communications in Europe by the ECM team (Tench et al. 2017) (*source:* Ralph Tench)

> **Box 30.1**
>
> ## Excellence in public relations
>
> Excellence has a specific meaning in the public relations academic literature and dates back to a ten-year research project led by Professor James Grunig that resulted in three books published between 1992 and 2002. Together with colleagues from the European Communication Monitor (ECM) team Ralph Tench has re-examined the concept and built new understanding of what good or high performing communication organisations, departments and individuals look like. This is all captured in a book *Communication Excellence: How to develop, manage and lead exceptional communications* published by Palgrave Macmillan (Tench et al. 2017). This book is the result of ten years of data and the collaboration of scholars from various European countries. It looks not only at the performance of communications teams, but at their influence within their organisations.
>
> Specifically, the authors identify three levels where excellent communications is required: at an organisational, departmental and professional level.
>
> Excellent organisations are connected to their environments and stakeholders, which requires them to be globalised, mediatised and reflective.
>
> Excellent communication departments are influential within their organisations. This means they have to be embedded, datafied and strategised.
>
> Excellent communication professionals are ambitious; this includes being sagacious, linked and solid.

would be well advised to switch it off and listen to their publics. Social media activism is only possible because brands don't listen.

Management, automation and AI

12. Alignment with management; PR refuses to learn

The drumbeat of PR as a management discipline has grown louder and louder in recent years. Practitioners seek to assert their place in the boardroom. It was cited as the second biggest challenge in the 2019 CIPR State of the Profession Survey after the changing digital landscape. However, there's a significant gap between aspiration and reality. Four per cent of senior in-house practitioners are directly responsible for the strategy of their organisation. Less than one in ten respondents in senior roles are executive members of a board.

From the 2019 survey, craft rather than technical or management skills account for the most popular skills in PR at all levels. In junior roles media relations (58 per cent) and social media relations (45 per cent) make up the top three most commonly undertaken tasks after writing. In senior roles media relations and campaigns are equal second (48 per cent).

There remains a notable difference, particularly at a senior level, between the skills that employers seek and the capabilities of practitioners. At a junior practitioner level, recruiters value technical and digital; research and evaluation; and project and account management skills. Practitioners don't identify these as strengths. At a senior level a gap exists in areas such as research, evaluation and measurement; corporate governance; and people management. PR is the profession that seemingly refuses to learn.

There's an indication that practitioners recognise their weakness. Failing to be recognised as a profession and an expanding skillset were ranked third and fourth as challenges facing the industry. The rewards are clear for practitioners with ambition and a commitment to continuous learning. Average salaries amongst full-time employees grew by almost £1,500 to £53,044 per year in 2018. Chartered Practitioners earn an average of £18,000 more per year than the average respondent, while those with a professional qualification earn an average £3,800 more.

Please refer to Chapter 7 for more information about the changing nature of skills in PR.

13. PR slow to adopt an integrated tool stack

Workflow in the PR business is typically built on point products strung together with Excel and Word documents. Meanwhile the market for technology

> ### Explore 30.3
>
> #### Practitioner PR skills
>
> Respondents to The 2019 CIPR State of the Profession survey were asked how they spend their time by selecting from a range of specific work activities. The options were developed using the Global Alliance's 'Global Body of Knowledge' framework.
>
> Senior roles – manager, head, associate director, managing director, partner
>
> 1. Copywriting and editing 50%
> 2. Media relations 48%
> 3. PR programmes/campaigns 48%
> 4. Strategic planning 46%
> 5. Crisis, issues management 45%
>
> Junior roles – intern, trainee, executive, assistant, office
>
> 1. Copywriting and editing 73%
> 2. Media relations 58%
> 3. Social media relations 45%
> 4. PR programmes/campaigns 45%
> 5. Events, conferences 41%
>
> Split the list of the top five skills between strategic and tactical activities. What do you notice, and what do you think PR practitioners need to do to improve their alignment with management?

in marketing and PR is exploding. There's seemingly a tool for every aspect of our work. It's possible to run a news desk or community management campaign from your phone using listening, content, channel and monitoring apps.

Martech: 2020 and Beyond published by BDO, WARC, and the University of Bristol, estimates that worldwide marketing technology is worth $121.5 billion. It says 22 per cent of companies are starting to embrace a platform over a suite from best in breed vendors. 48 per cent use a primary vendor along with specialist providers.

PR tools are a subset of marketing automation, characterised by a small number of platform products and a series of point solutions. Three years ago, the #PRstack project identified more than 150 different PR apps and tools.

Platforms have typically been created by acquiring and stitching together products. Cision has made more than $1 billion of acquisitions in the past five years in a bid to develop cloud-based workflow. It's the gorilla in the market. The Cision Cloud platform includes listening, influencer identification, content planning, channel distribution and measurement.

Access Intelligence built out its tool platform this year to include social media listening and audience segmentation (Pulsar) alongside influencer and journalist identification (Vuelio) and relationship management (ResponseSource). Tools to watch include answerthepublic (Google search intelligence), Brandwatch (consumer intelligence), coveragebook (automated coverage books), Newswhip (predictive news intelligence) and Traackr (influencer marketing).

14. Waking up to the impact of automation and AI on PR practice

An Office of National Statistics (ONS) report, 'The Probability of Automation in England: 2011 and 2017', published in March 2019, analysed the jobs of 20 million people in England and concluded that around 7.4 per cent or 1.5 million jobs in England are at high risk of some of their duties and tasks being automated in the future. Younger people are more likely to be in roles affected by job automation. Of those aged 20 to 24 years who are employed, 15.7 per cent were in jobs at high risk of automation.

In the PR sector AI is transforming media and workflow. The ONS report is consistent with the CIPR's analysis in this area. *Humans Still Needed,* a paper by Jean Valin published in March 2018, suggested found that 12 per cent of a PR practitioner's total skills (out of 52 skills) could be complemented or replaced by AI today, with a prediction that this could climb to 38 per cent within five years.

And then there's the issue of social (ro)bots and their influence on practice. Ralph Tench and Markus Wiesenberg (2019) published a paper identifying a lack of theoretical concepts and empirical knowledge about the perception and usage of social bots by practitioners in communication. They surveyed the attitudes towards and usage of social bots of leading European communication professionals (n = 2,247) from 49 European countries. Results indicate that leading communication professionals in Central and Western Europe as well as Scandinavia perceive highly ethical challenges, while in Southern and Eastern Europe professionals are less sceptical regarding the usage of social bots.

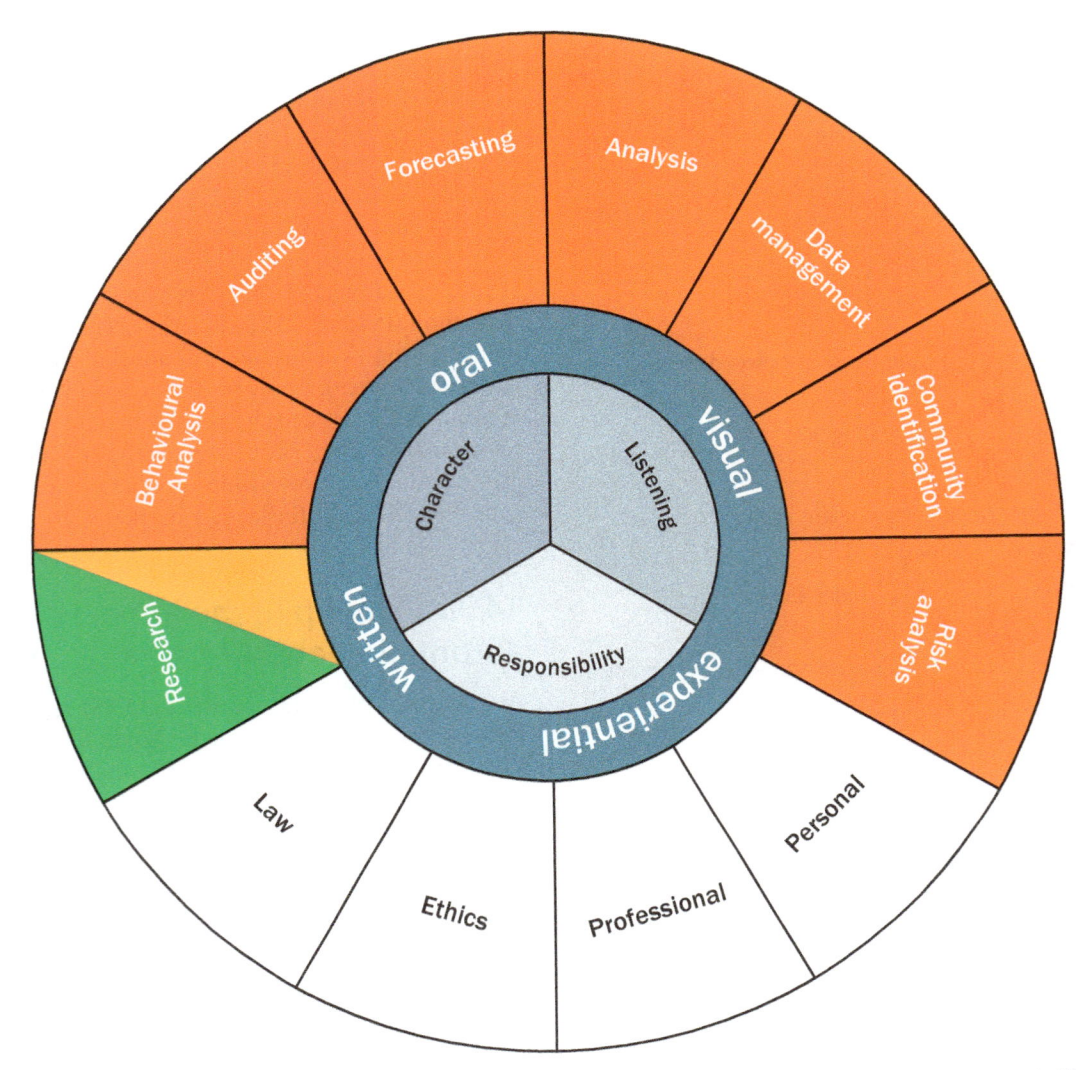

Picture 30.3 An estimate of tools capability in five years plotted against Global Alliance Capability Framework; The CIPR is grateful to Catherine Arrow Found.Chart.PR, FCIPR for allowing the use and adaptation of this graphic which is her design (*source*: CIPR)

Only 11.5 per cent (n = 257) declare their organisation uses or are making plans to use social bots for strategic communication. They are used primarily for identifying and following social networks users. This refers specifically to the usage of digital traces for strategic communication purposes, e.g. to identify topic area opinion leaders or social media influencers. However, this represents only a small minority of the sample – leading to the conclusion that only a small minority of organisations already practice what they argue is deep strategic mediatisation. Social bots are seen primarily as threat for the society and organisation that will lead to new ethical challenges.

It's not all bad news. Fundamental human traits such as empathy, trust, humour and relationship building can't be automated. AI is creating opportunities for practitioners to help organisations communicate about AI and its impact on society. Venture capital investment into the UK's AI sector has risen almost six-fold in the last five years according to TechNation. In 2018 AI companies raised almost twice the investment of counterparts in France and Germany.

Case study 30.1
Impact of AI on the professions

What is the future of a profession when a body of knowledge can be assimilated in dataset and interrogated by a machine? That's the question posed by Professor Anne Gregory in a literature review published by the CIPR called *The Effects of AI on the Professions*.

The paper is the conclusion of an 18-month project led by Professor Gregory working with Dr Swati Virmani. It raises important questions of responsibility, social impact, governance, the relevance of professions and workforce transformation. It's an abstraction of more than 170 sources. The group examined academic papers, national reports, think tank studies, research group reports, and a variety of other sources.

'The effects of AI paper shows that many other professions have a more robust approach to exploring the impact of AI. PR doesn't seem to be doing so. It's sleepwalking,' said Kerry Sheehan, chair, CIPR #AIinPR panel.

The CIPR paper suggests that AI will have a significant impact on professions, and PR specifically.

Automation of tasks

AI will render a set of professional skills redundant. Computers can assimilate knowledge faster than humans and perform repetitive tasks reliably and quickly. Media monitoring, distribution and content creation are all areas of practice that are being automated.

Marginalising minorities

AI will impact specific work groups: women, ethnic minorities, those who have lesser qualifications and undertake routine work, and entrants to the PR profession. This is a serious concern for a relatively young profession that is already struggling to get to grips with diversity.

Ethics and transparency

There are ethical issues around the nature of the power and knowledge balance for those using AI. Issues concerning the algorithms used and the lack of transparency within the black box and their inherent biases.

Changing nature of professional workforce

There will be major impacts on the professional workforce. These are the subject of advanced consideration by a number of professions. The PR is behind in tackling this issue. The IPR's Future of Work report is the only study in the repository that examines the effect of AI on the PR workforce.

The #AIinPR project raises more questions than it answers. But that's the point. It highlights the need for further work in this area.

Explore 30.4 AI and the professions

The CIPR paper, The Effects of Artificial Intelligence on the Professions, identified ten areas in which AI is impacting the professions and the nature of work.

1. The overall impact of AI, including on professional work
2. Impact on specific sectors and professions
3. Most affected and most secure groups of workers
4. AI drives people, or people driving AI
5. Ethics
6. Regulating AI
7. AI and related technologies
8. Workforce, employment, skills and education
9. Country based studies
10. Diversity and other impacts

Consider the future of PR and other professions in relation to these topics. How will it impact your career in the next decade?

15. Tell me a story

The craft of telling a story across different forms of media and engaging a public is more important than ever. It's critical to cutting through a cluttered media environment. This is the story told by Robert McKeen and Thomas Gerace in their book *Storynomics*.

In the shift to data-driven programmes there's a danger that we lose sight of creativity. Creative and content, the keys to good storytelling, are frequently overlooked elements of PR. They lie at the heart of inspiring conversations and storytelling.

The ability to communicate complex messages through compelling and relevant stories remains a fundamental value of PR. It has found its rightful place alongside advertising and creative agencies at Cannes and Eurobest and is today winning awards in its own right and as part of integrated solutions.

Media in pain

16. News media in pain but new formats emerge

More than a third (35 per cent) of the UK public claims that it avoids the news according to Reuters Institute Digital News Report 2019. The UK is suffering a collective breakdown triggered by the news media. People report that the news negatively affects their mood and they feel powerless to affect events. Trust in the news has fallen 11 per cent since 2015. Even the most trusted brands such as the BBC are perceived as biased, especially on issues such as Brexit and climate change.

Newspaper brands continue to suffer as readers shift from print to digital. Popular newspaper brands have suffered double-digit falls in print circulation year-on-year with *The Daily Star* (-18 per cent), *The Daily Mirror* (-13 per cent) and *The Daily Express* (-12 per cent) hardest hit. Broadsheet titles have also suffered significant year-on-year declines in print but are pinning their hopes on new online revenue.

Advertising-supported media has been affected by widespread job cuts including around a dozen people at digital-born *BuzzFeed*. The local and regional media has been hit hardest with the net closure of 245 local news titles in the last 13 years according to *Press Gazette* research.

This is the story that has played out over the past two decades as advertising revenues have shifted from print to online. Facebook and Google account for almost 60 per cent of the online advertising market.

Picture 30.4 Newsprint is in decline in every market around the world. Viable alternative models are a work in progress (*source*: Justasc/Shutterstock)

Good news is hard to find. Blame is directed squarely at social media platforms and the BBC. Regulation of social media platforms seems to be inevitable in response to increasing political scrutiny.

Alternative business models and content formats offer a glimmer of hope although revenues are limited despite the best efforts of the news industry.

More than a million people worldwide have voluntarily contributed to *The Guardian* in the last three years, with 650,000 currently paying to support the publication on an ongoing basis. A new slow news venture, *Tortoise*, launched in April 2019 with 2,500 paying members. It's an open model of journalism in which readers and the communities on which it reports are invited into the newsroom. *Double Down News* is an innovative news project by George Monbiot focused on the news values of people, ideas, evidence and community. Like Tortoise it engages its readers in the news-gathering process.

More publishers are getting involved in audio. *The Guardian*, *The Economist* and *The Financial Times* have launched or rebranded daily news podcasts in the last year. The BBC is investing heavily in smart speakers and AI while *The Guardian* has set up an experimental Voice Lab.

Please refer to Chapters 2 and 14 for more information about working with the media and media relations.

17. Public service media is failing the public

The audience for public service news is old and educated. Public service media in many countries is failing to provide a universal service. They are struggling to reach younger audiences and people with limited formal education. These are the findings of a report called 'Old, Educated, and Politically Diverse: The Audience of Public Service News' by the Reuters Institute for the Study of Journalism. The report draws on survey data from The Reuters' 2019 Digital News Report. It covers eight European countries: Finland, Germany, United Kingdom, Czech Republic, Spain, Italy, France and Greece.

The report finds that public service media struggles to engage with audiences online. Most of the people they reach online are already reached offline.

The BBC in the UK is a notable exception. It's the only public service media whose cross-platform reach is significantly greater (10 per cent). In most cases online adds 5 per cent or less to the audience reach. It compares online and offline news consumption by 18- to 25-year-olds. It benchmarks against rival commercial online news media, Facebook and YouTube.

Social media platforms are the primary source of news in many European countries. Herein lies a flaw in the research as public service news is also served via these platforms.

Young audiences cite Facebook as a source of news in seven out of eight countries. YouTube ranks higher in six of eight countries covered.

The report documents how public service news audiences skew towards older people. Over fifty-fives account for about half of total weekly reach, ranging from 42 per cent (Czech Republic) to 52 per cent (Germany). Public service media relies on offline news content to reach younger people. Half or more of the 18- to 24-year-old audience are reached offline only, in most countries. Public service news may be exacerbating social inequality rather than closing this gap.

The report finds that public service news is less used by those with limited formal education. In Germany, only 13 per cent of the least-educated group use the ARD and ZDF online services at least once a week. This compares with 17 per cent of the wider population. This number drops to 11 per cent for RAI in Italy, 9 per cent for RTVE in Spain, and 8 per cent for the joint PSMs' online services in France.

18. Release, recovery and reform from COVID-19

As we complete the manuscript for this book in May 2020 there are currently 4.5 billion people whose movement is restricted by some form of lockdown due to COVID-19. It's likely this situation will continue through to the summer. Thereafter there is expected to be a slow return to work, followed by a long climb out of recession.

We didn't feel we could submit the book for publication without adding a postscript on the implication of COVID-19 on public relations and management communication. This postscript reflects the current situation.

The challenge with the COVID-19 crisis is that it requires an international governmental response and there are countless unknowns.

Politicians like to throw around the word 'unprecedented', but the warning signs were there for all to see. The Severe Acute Respiratory Syndrome (SARS) and Bird Flu outbreaks at the turn of the century were both precursors of a global pandemic.

Scenario planning

The strategic role of public relations is to consider interdependent relationships, explore different scenarios and map possible outcomes. Practitioners should be working with stakeholders in their organisation to evaluate its situation.

1. The PESTLE framework (political, economic, social, technology, legal and environmental) is useful to help define a micro or macro environment.
2. Map the uncertainties related to the crisis and how these impact your organisation.
3. Explore likely outcomes and discuss the implication and pathway for each scenario.

Please refer to Chapter 9, Strategic planning and management.

So, what do we know?

We know that COVID-19 is highly contagious. People can carry the virus and infect others without exhibiting symptoms. It has an incubation rate in humans of 7 to 14 days.

We know that a vaccine will take at least 12 to 18 months to develop. It's an area of huge international effort among healthcare providers.

We know that there isn't a linear solution based on the experience of countries such as China and Singapore. These countries have released the lockdown only to revert in response to secondary waves of infection.

We know that we need to keep the reproductive number (R) below 1 to contain the virus. This means that everyone that becomes infected with the virus infects less than one other person.

This has been achieved so far by confining people to their homes. It's worked. We've passed the peak in most European countries.

However, the economic and social implications of the lockdown are brutal. The crisis has widened the socio-economic gap in society. It is clearly not a sustainable solution.

Lockdown in the UK has reduced the R number to around 0.7 according to the Institute for Global Change. The challenge is that this leaves little head room for relaxing restrictions with all other factors being equal.

The Institute for Global Change estimates that opening schools under the current conditions is estimated to increase R to 0.9. If R rises above 1 the spread of the virus will be unpredictable and potentially exponential, threatening the ability of healthcare services.

Release: protective equipment, social distancing, testing and tracing, and supported isolation

We understand the tools available to release the lockdown and the effectiveness from the response of different countries around the world. These include protective equipment; social distancing; testing and tracing; and supported isolation.

A challenge that governments face is having an open dialogue with citizens. There isn't any other topic that anyone wants to talk about; however, trust is at an all-time low.

In the US the situation is exacerbated by the tension between federal and state government. It has manifested as riots by citizens wanting to release state lockdowns and return to work.

The UK's response has been daily press conferences. It has published five tests that must be met before the lockdown is released to ensure the spread is under control.

1. Making sure the health service can cope
2. A sustained and consistent fall in the daily death rate
3. Rate of infection decreasing to manageable levels
4. Ensuring supply of tests and protective equipment can meet future demand
5. Being confident any adjustments would not risk a second peak

The tests provide an indication of the challenges faced, but we can't know whether these tests have been met without measurable objectives. Currently there is no widespread agreement about the number of people who have died from Coronavirus in England.

We've some indication of what's to come. The UK's Chief Medical Officer Professor Chris Whitty has suggested that social distancing will continue until the end of 2020.

There are a number of variables that government could use to release lockdown. These are likely to include ages, schools, sectors and geographies.

Recovery: organisational responses

Organisations have responded to the crisis in one of four ways. In each case their route out of the crisis will be different.

Box 30.2

Information seeking and government communication: information sources and credibility

Trust in government has been declining across Europe (OECD, Zerfass et al., 2019; Trust Barometer 2020). This has implications on how credible the public perceive government endorsed information and actions to be. However, during crises such as the COVID-19 pandemic, trust in government is of paramount importance as it ensures that a coordinated national response can be achieved.

To explore public trust in government communications and to identify sources of information used during the COVID-19 crisis, in the early stages of the lockdown and the crisis across Europe a group of communication researchers explored the emerging issues and implications of government communication and information sources. A large UK survey (Tench and Bridge 2020), with over 600 adults, was carried out during the early lockdown phase of the crisis in the UK, Spain and Italy (Tench et al. 2020).

Findings suggest that despite declines in usage of traditional mass media, TV and radio were key sources of information during the pandemic. Online media was also an important source of information, with Facebook and

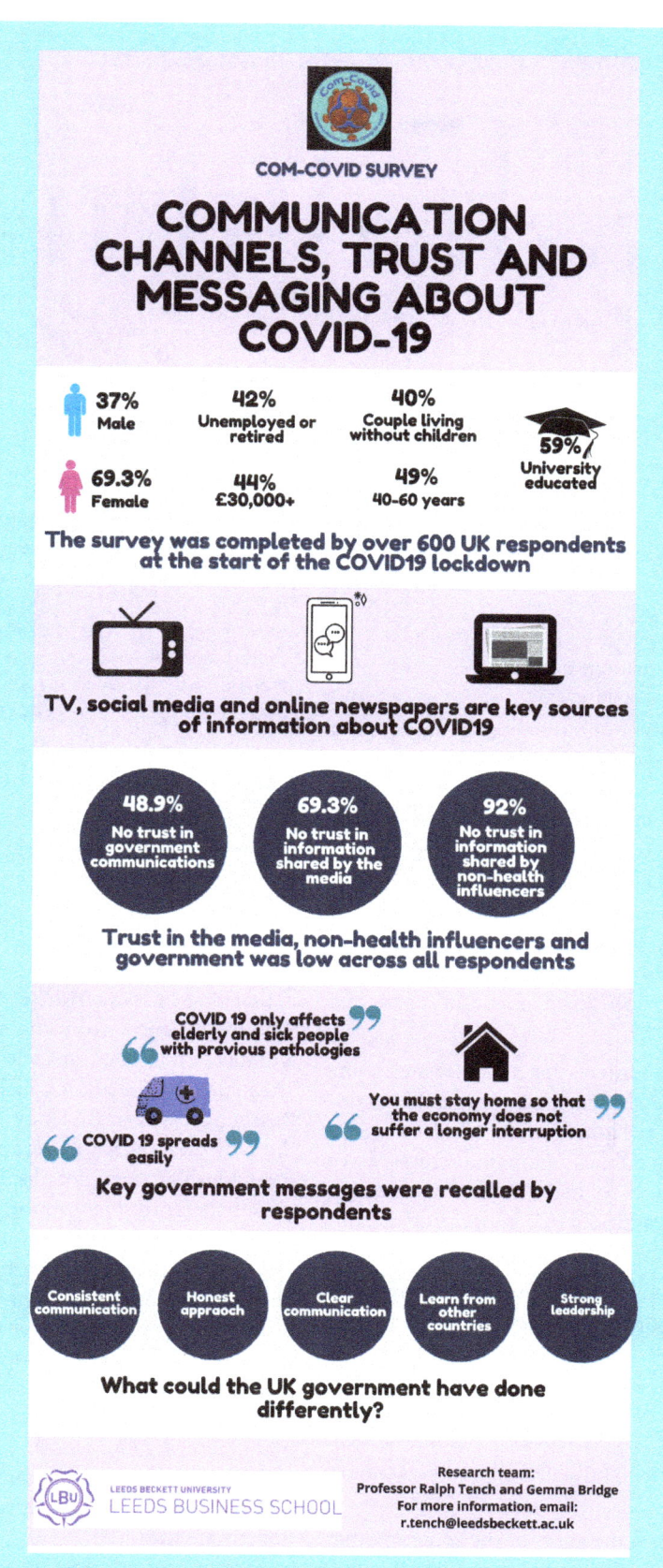

Picture 30.5 COM-COVID Communication and the COVID-19 crisis study in the UK, Italy and Spain (*source:* Tench et al. 2020)

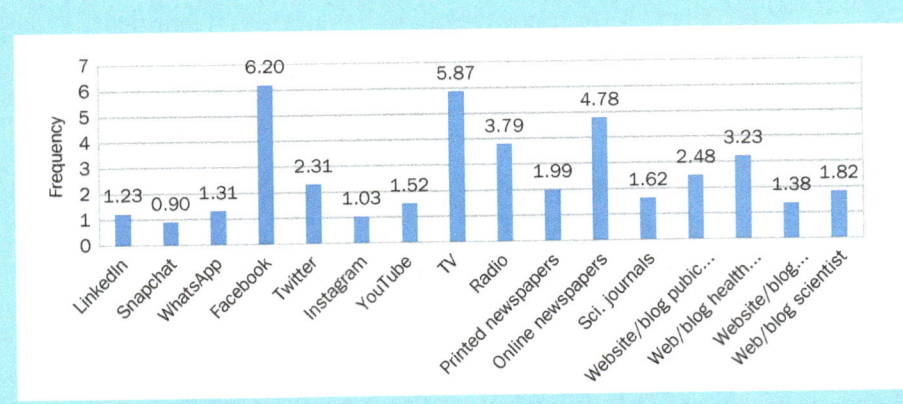

Figure 30.4 Which of the following media do you receive information from about COVID-19? (1 not at all; 7 very much)

Media	Frequency
LinkedIn	1.23
Snapchat	0.90
WhatsApp	1.31
Facebook	6.20
Twitter	2.31
Instagram	1.03
YouTube	1.52
TV	5.87
Radio	3.79
Printed newspapers	1.99
Online newspapers	4.78
Sci. journals	1.62
Website/blog public...	2.48
Web/blog health...	3.23
Website/blog...	1.38
Web/blog scientist	1.82

online newspapers also used frequently, particularly by younger people (see Figure 30.4).

Results reveal that:

- Trust in government was low, with respondents perceiving the information shared by the government to be confusing and unreliable.
- The government's response was started too late and communications generated social alarm.
- In contrast, trust in health professionals known personally and health associations such as the World Health Organization, was high.

Key messages such as the importance of social distancing and personal hygiene were retained by most respondents. However, some confusion was apparent about the causes of the pandemic and where to go for medical help.

- Protect. The lockdown has had a dramatic impact on entertainment, events, retail, travel and transport. Businesses in these markets have cut costs and sought government help in order to survive the crisis. Here the role for public relations practitioners is planning for once lockdown eases and supporting customers and staff.

- Adapting. This is an interesting area in which some organisations have shown strong leadership. Education providers have gone online, wholesalers are selling direct to the public, and manufacturers have retooled production to make safety equipment. Here the role of practitioners is supporting organisations entering new markets.

- Public information. Local government, health services and blue light services have redirected all communication to providing public information that supports the government's response to the COVID-19 crisis. Apps, social media channels and websites have been switched to providing a local context to government guidance. Practitioners have never been busier.

- Growth. There are some areas of the economy that have not only proved to be resilient but are experiencing growth through the crisis. These include supermarkets, online retail, telecom and IT providers. The challenge here is to meet new levels of demand without being opportunistic. It's a fine line to tread.

Reform: society, markets and the state

We already know from the nature of the crisis that it will have an impact on society, markets and the state. These are the areas on which we should be focusing. Resilience, self-sufficiency and safety will become the new lexicon for governments and organisations. A backlash against globalisation seems inevitable.

But there are also opportunities to create a better future. The crisis has given us a renewed appreciation of health workers, people in front line roles, and the scientific community.

In the future organisations will need to get closer to markets and demonstrate their value to society. There's been a huge wave of innovation in health and technology. The environment is benefiting from a reduction in manufacturing and travel.

Finally, we've seen humanity pull together. Communities have been strengthened through the crisis. Let's hope that continues.

So that's our glimpse into the crystal ball of the sector's future – not a complete or water-tight analysis but it may provide students and academics of the subject some ideas for areas to research or indeed find more out. We hope you find these challenges of interest and perhaps have the time or inclination through your studies to build more and new knowledge in these areas. Keep positively asking questions about what the practice currently does and think deeply about what should come next. Good luck.

Bibliography

Alvis S., Browne J., Insall L. and I. Mulheirn (2020) A Sustainable Exit Strategy: Managing Uncertainty, Minimising Harm, Institute for Global Change, April 2020.

Aldoory, L., H. Jiang, E. L. Toth and B. L. Sha (2008). Is it still just a women's issue? A study of work-life balance among men and women in public relations. *Public Relations Journal*, 2(4), 1–20.

BDO, WARC, and the University of Bristol, Martech: 2020 and Beyond (2019). Available at: https://www.bdo.co.uk/en-gb/insights/industries/technology-media-and-life-sciences/martech-2020-and-beyond [Accessed 17 January 2020].

Broom, G. M. and Dozier, D. M. (1986). Advancement for public relations models, *Public Relations Review*.

Chartered Institute of Public Relations (2019). The CIPR State of the Profession survey. Available at: https://www.cipr.co.uk/stateofpr [Accessed 17 January 2020].

Department for Digital, Culture, Media & Sport (2019), Disinformation and 'Fake News'. Available at: https://publications.parliament.uk/pa/cm201719/cmselect/cmcumeds/1791/1791.pdf [Accessed 17 January 2020].

Edelman (2019). The Edelman Trust Barometer. Available at: https://www.edelman.com/trust-barometer [Accessed 17 January 2020].

Edwards, L. (2014). *Power, Diversity and Public Relations*. Routledge.

Fielden, S.L., R. Tench and J. Fawkes (2003). Freelance communications workers in the UK: the impact of gender on well-being. *Corporate communications: an international journal*.

Gregory A. and S. Virmani (2020). *The Effects of AI on the Professions*, Chartered Institute of Public Relations. Available at: https://newsroom.cipr.co.uk/pr-is-sleepwalking-into-ai-new-cipr-aiinpr-report-finds/ [Accessed 17 January 2020].

International Association for Measurement and Evaluation of Communication (2019). Integrated Evaluation Framework. Available at: https://amecorg.com/amec-framework/ [Accessed 17 January 2020].

International Communications Consultancy Organisation (2019). The ICCO World PR Report 2020. Available at: https://iccopr.com/services/world-reports/ [Accessed 17 January 2020].

Institute of Public Relations (2019). The Future of Work. Available at: [https://instituteforpr.org/the-2019-ipr-future-of-work-study/] [Accessed 19 January 2019].

McKeen R. and Thomas G. (2018). *Storynomics: Story Driven Marketing in the Post-Advertising World*. Methuen Publishing.

OECD (2020). https://www.oecd.org/gov/trust-in-government.htm [Accessed 29 April 2020].

Office of National Statistics (2019). The Probability of Automation in England: 2011 and 2017. Available at: https://www.ons.gov.uk/employmentandlabourmarket/peopleinwork/employmentandemployeetypes/articles/theprobabilityofautomationinengland/2011and2017 [Accessed 17 January 2020].

Public Relations and Communications Association (2019). The PRCA 2019 Digital Report. Available at: https://www.flipsnack.com/PRCAUK/prca-digital-report-2019/full-view.html [Accessed 17 January 2020].

PwC, Global Artificial Intelligence Study: Exploiting the AI Revolution (2019). Available at: https://www.pwc.com/gx/en/issues/data-and-analytics/publications/artificial-intelligence-study.html [Accessed 17 January 2020].

Reuters Institute for the Study of Journalism (2019). Old, Educated, and Politically Diverse: The Audience of Public Service News. Available at: https://reutersinstitute.politics.ox.ac.uk/our-research/old-educated-and-politically-diverse-audience-public-service-news [Accessed 17 January 2020].

Reuters Institute for the Study of Journalism (2019). The Reuters' 2019 Digital News Report. Available at: http://www.digitalnewsreport.org/ [Accessed 17 January 2020].

Technation (2019). VC investment in UK Artificial Intelligence startups increases almost six-fold in five years. Available at: https://technation.io/news/venture-capital-investment-in-uk-artificial-intelligence-startups-increases-almost-six-fold-in-five-years/ [Accessed 17 January 2020].

Tench, R., M. Topić and A. Moreno (2017). Male and female communication, leadership styles and the position of women in public relations. *Interactions: Studies in Communication & Culture*, 8(2-3), 231-248.

Tench, R., D. Verčič, A. Zerfass, A. Moreno and P. Verhoeven (2017). *Communication Excellence: How to develop, manage and lead exceptional communications*. London: Palgrave Macmillan (Springer).

Topić, M. (2019). Euprera Vol. 1 No. 1 – Women in Public Relations: A Literature Review (1982–2019), Leeds Beckett University.

Trust Barometer (2020) https://cdn2.hubspot.net/hubfs/440941/Trust%20Barometer%202020/2020%20Edelman%20Trust%20Barometer%20Global%20Report.pdf?utm_campaign=Global:%20Trust%20Barometer%202020&utm_source=Website [Accessed 29 April 2020].

Valin, J. (2018). Humans Still Needed. Available at: https://cipr.co.uk/CIPR/Our_work/Policy/CIPR_Artificial_Intelligence_in_PR_panel.aspx [Accessed 17 January 2020].

Verhoeven, P., and N. Aarts (2010). How European public relations men and women perceive the impact of their professional activities. *PRism: online journal*, 7(4), 1–15.

Waddington S. and S. Earl (2012). *Brand Anarchy: Managing Corporate Reputation*. London: Bloomsbury.

Waddington S. and S. Guthrie (2019). We're All Influencers Now, #FuturePRoof. Available at: https://www.futureproofingcomms.co.uk/we-are-all-influencers-now [Accessed 17 January 2020].

Waddington S. and S. Hall (2017). Exploring the mental wellbeing of the public relations profession, #FuturePRoof. Available at: https://www.futureproofingcomms.co.uk/thelatest/2017/2/21/gd41ooq0n-ru1rsr57thsm6e5qpcx8t [Accessed 17 January 2020].

Waddington, S. (2019). Disinformation and 'Fake News', #FuturePRoof. Available at: https://www.futureproofingcomms.co.uk/thelatest/2019/8/12/disinformation-and-fake-news [Accessed 17 January 2020].

Zerfass, A., R. Tench, P. Verhoeven, D. Verčič and A. Moreno (2018). *European Communication Monitor 2018. Strategic communication and the challenges of fake news, trust, leadership, work stress and job satisfaction. Results of a survey in 48 countries*. Quadriga Media Berlin.

Zerfass, A., Wiesenberg, M., Tench, R. and Romenti, S. (2019). *Trust in communicators. How the general population trusts journalists, public relations professionals, marketeers and other communicators: A comparative study in Germany, Italy and the United Kingdom*. Brussels: EUPRERA. Retrieved from http://bit.ly/TICS19.

Glossary

Advertising A form of promotional activity that uses a totally controllable message to inform and persuade a large number of people with a single communication. The message is invariably paid for.

Advertising Value Equivalent (AVE) A very crude measure of media relations performance that is still cited and relates to a measurement of the column inches or centimetres devoted to the client or the product, and a calculation of the equivalent cost had that space been paid for as advertising.

Advertorial Bought space in a publication that is used to print an article written in the editorial style of the journal to portray a similar 'feel' of objectivity to the editorial pages.

Agenda setting (by media) Sometimes referred to as 'the ability to tell the public what issues are important', this is a theory developed by McCombs and Shaw (McCombs, M. and D. Shaw (1972). 'The agenda-setting function of the mass media'. *Public Opinion Quarterly* 36(2): 176–817) that the media direct public attention to particular issues that fit news priorities and, in doing so, influence public opinion.

Alpha The first letter of the Greek alphabet.

Alternative target generation Thinking through alternative target audiences.

Antecedents Something that has preceded, or gone before, another. Early forms of public relations, or 'proto-public relations', are antecedents.

Attitudes 'When we talk about *attitudes*, we are talking about what a person has learned in the process of becoming a member of a family, a member of a group and of society that makes him react to his social world in a consistent and characteristic way, instead of a transitory and haphazard way. We are talking about the fact that he is no longer neutral in sizing up the world around him: he is attracted or repelled, for or against, favourable or unfavourable' (Sherif, M. (1967). 'Introduction' in *Attitude, Ego-involvement, and Change*. C.W. Sherif and M. Sherif (eds). New York, NY: John Wiley & Sons).

BAME This acronym, which stands for black, Asian and minority ethnic communities, has been used extensively in the UK. However, the term is seen by some as too generalised and even patronising. In the USA there is continuing debate over the terms 'black' and 'coloured', while in Australia the term CALD (culturally and linguistically diverse) communities is used.

Belief Commitment to something, resulting from an intellectual acceptance of its validity.

Benchmark An external or previous reference point that provides a useful comparison.

Bloggers Individuals who keep a personal weblog (blog) often reflecting the personality of the author. (See **Influencers**.)

Bogof An abbreviated term used in sales promotion for selling two products for the price of one: 'buy one, get one free'.

Brainstorming When a group of colleagues get together to discuss an issue and come up with different ideas collectively.

Brand A label that seeks to add perceived value to a consumer product by generating loyalty or preference.

Brand journalism Journalism produced on behalf of a brand or 'any organisation that has contact with the public'. http://www.brand-journalism.co.uk/ (See **Content marketing** and **Native advertising**.)

Business ethics Trevino and Nelson (Trevino, L.K. and K.A. Nelson (1995). *Managing Business Ethics: Straight talk about how to do it right*. New York: Wiley & Sons) define this as 'the principles, norms and standards of conduct governing an individual or group'.

Business-to-business (B2B) The sale of a product to a manufacturer, a government body, a retailer, a not-for-profit institution – indeed any organisation or individual – for a purpose other than personal consumption.

Capitalism An economic system based on privately owned businesses producing and distributing goods, the key features of which are a free, competitive market and making a profit from the sale of goods and services.

Categorical imperative A test that can be applied to see if it conforms to the moral law. If the action could be made into a universal law, which would be regarded as acceptable if applied to everyone faced with the same situation, then it would be regarded as ethical.

Celebrity 'A person whose name, image, lifestyle, and opinions carry cultural and economic worth, and who are first and foremost idealised popular media constructions' (Redmond, S. (2014). *Celebrity and the Media*. Houndmills, Palgrave Macmillan). (See **Microcelebrity**.)

CEO Chief Executive Officer.

CESR Committee of European Regulators.

Circulation How many copies of a newspaper or magazine are distributed.

Clip counts This term comes from days when media monitoring involved physical clippings of press articles.

Company propaganda A negative term used by some journalists to describe positive statements presented by an organisation about its beliefs and practices.

Complex systems According to Gilpin and Murphy (Gilpin, D.R. and P.J. Murphy (2010). 'Implications of complexity theory for public relations: beyond crisis' in *The Sage Handbook of Public Relations*. R.L. Heath (ed.). Thousand Oaks, CA: Sage), 'complex systems' are made up of multiple interacting agents. These might be individuals, organisations or media outlets. It is the interactions between these agents that bring about fundamental changes to the system itself. The unpredictable nature of these interactions also creates a dynamic and unstable system.

Content Information and ideas created to interest a specific target audience.

Content analysis A method of quantifying the content of textual material.

Content marketing Defined by the Content Marketing Institute as 'the practice of creating relevant and compelling content in a consistent fashion to a targeted buyer, focusing on all stages of the buying process, from brand awareness through to brand evangelism'. (See **Brand journalism** and **Native advertising**.)

Convergence The process of technologies coming together from different directions. The mobile telephone is the product of the convergence between telecommunications (sending/receiving messages) and computers (processing information). Once in existence, the phone can also be used to combine (converge) further technologies – taking photographs using the mobile phone, for example.

Copy A term used generically by the communications industries to describe written text for news releases, adverts, advertorials, editorials, articles and in-house newsletter articles, etc.

Corporate culture An organisation's values and practices that underpin its operations; they can be managed to produce better business outcomes.

Corporate philanthropy An aspect of corporate citizenship – 'giving something back to the community' by improving quality of life for local communities and for employees.

CPD (continuing professional development) Acknowledgement in all professions (law, medicine, accountancy, PR, etc.) of the role of continued learning and updating throughout the career.

Cub reporter Junior or trainee reporter/journalist.

Cultural norm A pattern of behaviour that is considered acceptable and legitimate by members of society.

Culture The property of a group – a group's shared collective meaning system through which its values, attitudes, beliefs, customs and thoughts are understood. It is a product of the members' social interaction while also determining how group members communicate.

Demographics External differences between people – for example, race, age, gender, location, occupational status, group membership.

Digital divide The lack of access to information and communication is referred to as the 'digital divide'.

Direct mail Electronic and posted communications sent to individuals' text phone, email, work and home postal addresses.

Discourse Particular ways of making sense of the world, communicated, sustained and justified through language and social institutions.

Dominant coalition The group of powerful individuals within an organisation who control its direction, determining its mission and goals. It is believed that, although the decisions they make are good for the organisation's survival, their primary aim is maintaining the status quo, thereby keeping the existing dominant coalition in control. It is not a term most practitioners would recognise – in practice, terms such as 'board of directors' or 'senior management' would be used, but the inference is the same.

Downsizing The term used to describe the reduction in the number of employees working for an organisation in either full- or part-time positions.

Editorial Written text in a journal, magazine or newspaper that has been written either by a journalist/reporter or submitted by a public relations practitioner and then reviewed/edited before printing by the editor or subeditor of the publication. An 'editorial' is the opposite of 'advertising', which is bought (paid-for) space in a publication. An editorial is perceived as having greater impact because it is endorsed by the publication.

Employee engagement 'A workplace approach designed to ensure that employees are committed to their organisation's goals and values, motivated to contribute to organisational success and are able at the same time to enhance their own sense of well-being' (MacLeod, D. and N. Clarke (2009). *Engaging for Success: Enhancing performance through employee engagement.* London: Department for Business, Innovation and Skills).

Ethics Systematic frameworks that codify moral principles. The term may also be used to mean the extension of good management. (See **Morals; Values**.)

Exclusives Stories that are made available to one newspaper about issues and people (for example, an interview with Princess Diana's former butler). 'Exclusives' are often supplied by public relations consultancies on behalf of their clients.

Financial Regulation of Donations The legal requirement in the UK that any donation over £200 has to be recorded in a company's end-of-year annual report and accounts (the financial statement to shareholders).

FMCG products Products known as *FMCG* are typically those we buy from supermarkets and convenience stores – branded products from manufacturers such as Heinz, Kellogg's, Procter & Gamble – baked beans, breakfast cereals, shampoos, etc.

Formative evaluation An evaluation that takes place during a public relations programme or campaign.

Framing A term which refers to the process of presenting information or arguments to target audiences in such a way that promotes a particular interpretation (Entman, R.M. (1993). Framing: Toward clarification of a fractured paradigm. *Journal of Communication* 43(4): 51–58; Entman, R.M. (2007). 'Framing bias: Media in the distribution of power'. *Journal of Communication* 57(1): 163–73.). For example, an extremist group marching through a town centre can be framed as 'a right to free speech' or 'a threat to public safety'.

FSA Financial Services Authority.

Game theory This theory is based on observations about negotiation and compromise that demonstrate that many conflicts are based on the zero-sum principle, whereby for someone to win, their opponent has to lose. Win–win outcomes are the result of compromise and mutually satisfactory negotiation.

Heterophily The difference between speaker and audience.

Homophily The similarity between speaker and audience.

Hyper Text Mark-up Language (HTML) A programming language that allows text, graphics, photos, and even videos to be coded so that they can be viewed on any computer without the user needing to have the software in which the content was produced (unlike most text documents, graphics, spreadsheets, etc. that require the relevant application to be installed before they can be opened).

Implementation The phase where a sponsorship plan, for example, becomes a reality and is put into action.

Influencers Individuals who communicate information and ideas about brands, often through personal weblogs (blogs) and social media platforms, and have a large number of followers. (See **Bloggers**.)

Interactional see Transformational.

International communication The cultural, economic, political, social and technical analysis of communication patterns and effects across and between nation-states. It focuses on global aspects of media and communication systems and technologies.

International public relations The planned communication activity of a (multinational) organisation, government or international institution to create a positive and receptive environment through interactions in the target country, which facilitates the organisation (or government) to achieve its business (or policy) objectives without harming the interests of the host publics.

Intranets and extranets Special web sites with password restricted access to provide specialised information to internal stakeholders such as employees (referred to as intranets) and external stakeholders such as 'channel partners' – i.e. distributors and retailers (called extranets).

Interventions A term used commonly in health services and communication and some other fields to refer to planned activities designed to achieve an effect.

Listed A business whose shares are traded on a stock exchange.

Lobbying The influencing of public policy making through the private means of meeting MPs, ministers, civil servants, councillors or local government officials.

'Lurkers' Internet users who observe and monitor but do not actively contribute to discussions or content. Co-founder of the Nielsen Norman research company, Jakob Nielsen (2006), estimates that up to 90 per cent of internet users are 'lurkers' – that is, only 10 per cent are active participants in interactive environments. (Nielsen, J. (2006). 'Participation inequality: Encouraging more users to contribute'. *Jakob Nielsen's Alertbox,* 9 October. Nielsen Norman Group http://www.useit.com/alertbox/participation_inequality.html accessed 28 October 2015.)

Marketing The management process responsible for identifying, anticipating and satisfying customer requirements profitably.

Marketing mix The term used to define the four key elements of an organisation's marketing programme: product, price, place and promotion.

Marketing PR PR as a promotional tool of marketing. Content is targeted from business to the consumer (B2C) or is part of the sales process between businesses (B2B).

Media Any medium interface or channel that allows communications messages to flow between senders and receivers, in both directions.

Media effects The effects that the media has on audiences as a result of the audiences being exposed to the media and its content.

Mediatisation The process whereby the logic of the media becomes integrated into social institutions, including government and business.

Metanarrative An attempt to make sense of the larger picture, or the wider social environment. Critical theorists and postmodernists suggest organisations and individuals use metanarratives as overarching explanations of the way the world works. They believe reliance on these 'stories' can prevent closer examination of reality.

Metric A quantitative measure for evaluating public relations programmes.

Microcelebrity 'A mind set and a collection of self-presentation practices endemic in social media, in which users strategically formulate a profile, reach out to followers, and reveal personal information to increase attention and thus improve their online status (Senft 2013)' (Marwick, A. (2015). 'Instafame: Luxury selfies in the attention economy'. *Public Culture* 21(10): 137–60.). (See **Celebrity**.)

Morals Personal values or principles that guide behaviour. (See **Ethics**; **Values**.)

National Health Service (NHS) The UK National Health Service (NHS) has become the world's largest publicly funded health system. With 1.5 million staff, this complex system is also the fourth largest employer in the world.

Native advertising Content which brands directly pay for on a content distribution platform other than their own. (See **Brand journalism** and **Content marketing**.)

Neoliberal *Neoliberals* believe democracy and free-market capitalism are mutually dependent and that both are threatened by the growth of state intervention and bureaucracy (the rule of public officials in their own interests).

Non-governmental organisations (NGOs) Groups without governmental affiliation that have a particular interest in a subject: for example, charities and campaign groups.

Objective A clearly defined end-point that the public relations programme is designed to achieve.

Omega The last letter in the Greek alphabet.

Opportunity analysis The process of identifying opportunities for sponsorship.

Organisational culture The expression of attitudes within an individual organisation. This term encapsulates the values and beliefs, and patterns of behaviour and language, that are the norm for that group of people, providing a framework of meaning for the organisation.

Organisational identity The sum total of proactive, reactive and unintentional activities and messages of organisations.

OTS (Opportunities to see) The total number of times, potentially, that a public could be exposed to a message – known in the USA as 'impressions'.

Outcome The ultimate impact of public relations activity.

Output The immediate product of public relations activity.

Philanthropy Defined in the *Concise Oxford Dictionary* as 'a love of humankind; practical benevolence, especially charity on a large scale'.

Piloting Testing a questionnaire among a few people from the target population to be investigated.

Pressure group Any organised group that seeks to exert influence on government (at any level) to influence particular policies or decisions.

Proactive To control a situation, issue or crisis, rather than responding to something after it happens. (See **Reactive**.)

Psychographics Attributes relating to internal differences between personalities – e.g. anxious, approval-seeking, high self-esteem, etc.

Public diplomacy The process by which a government communicates with foreign publics in an attempt to foster an understanding of its nation's ideas and ideals, its institutions and culture, as well as its national goals and current policies.

Qualitative research A field of enquiry that aims to identify, and carry out an in-depth exploration of, phenomena such as reasons, attitudes, etc. (See **Quantitative research**.)

Quantitative research A field of enquiry that aims to quantify variables such as attitudes or behaviours and point out correlations between them. Results can be generalised, which means research that generates findings can be applied to a wider public or situation. (See **Qualitative research**.)

Reactive Responding to an issue or crisis rather than creating or controlling it: for example, a public relations activity being driven by the demands of others rather than the plans of the communicators. Sometimes communicators need to be reactive – that is, be able to respond quickly to situations. (See **Proactive**.)

Readership The actual numbers reached by written communications. Note that more people read trade journals because they are based in an office with one subscription, which is shared: for example, the *Architects' Journal* is circulated around the team in an architects' practice, often with comments on relevant or interesting features/articles.

Representative democracy A system of democracy whereby people are allowed to vote for somebody to represent them in government. In the UK, this happens at local level in council elections and at national level in the House of Commons.

Return on investment (ROI) The positive value or contribution that can be achieved by making an investment in a particular business activity. In marketing communications terms, this might include the sales resulting from specific, identifiable and measurable communications activities. For example, £5 million sales directly attributable to a direct mail campaign costing £1 million provides a £4 million return on the communication investment. Although described here in financial terms, the 'return' might also be assessed more subjectively by measuring increased brand awareness or improved corporate image resulting from a range of communications activities.

Rhetoric The study of language and how it is used to create shared meanings.

Sales promotion Short-term or temporary inducements – for example, price cuts or two-for-one offers – designed to encourage consumers to use a product or service.

Sampling Deriving a small subgroup of the research population, frequently designed to be representative.

Scenario planning Involves playing out different outcomes of a sponsorship, anticipating what could happen.

Setting the agenda see **Agenda setting**.

Social marketing The application of commercial marketing techniques to the analysis, planning, execution and evaluation of programmes designed to influence the voluntary behaviour of target audiences in order to improve their personal welfare and that of society (Andreasen, A.R. (1995) *Marketing Social Change: Changing behaviour to promote health, social development and the environment*. San Francisco CA: Jossey Bass).

Sponsorship The provision of money, services, know-how or in-kind support by corporations or organisations to individuals, groups or institutions involved in sports, charities, education or broadcasting, or in cultural and ecological activities. Activities are chosen for sponsorship based on their ability to project the right commercial and psychological message that fits in with the specific corporate goals of a sponsor.

Stakeholder Someone who has an interest (stake) in the organisation, which may be direct or indirect interest as well as active or passive, known or unknown, recognised or unrecognised.

Strategy selection Term used for selecting a sponsorship strategy.

Systems theory The theory that describes how organisations work in terms of interlocking and interdependent systems of communication, production, etc. It embraces both the internal and external environments.

Tabloids Small-format newspapers, sometimes referred to as the 'popular press', often written in a sensationalist style and containing a large number of photographs.

Terrestrial Television channels that broadcast from the UK and not via satellite. Terrestrial channels are subject to greater regulation than satellite channels.

Triple bottom-line reporting A phrase increasingly used to describe the economic, environmental and social aspects that are being defined and considered by business. These are sometimes called the three Ps – profit, plant and people.

Typology Classifying and dividing things according to 'type': for example, in a PR context, working out the key elements that distinguish one kind of PR practitioner, or activity, from another.

Upward feedback A system of communication that allows employees to feed back their views to their team leaders or line managers, and where line managers in turn feed back these views to senior management.

Vision and values The business practice of identifying an organisation's corporate vision – where it wants to go and how it wants to be perceived through its core values.

Watchdog A term used to describe a body that monitors behaviour and activities in different sections of society to protect the consumer or citizen.

Web 2.0 A term which is founded on a radical reconceptualisation of the user, from consumer of online products and information produced by companies to producer of online products and information that they share with others, including companies. (Harrison and Barthel 'Wielding new media in Web 2.0: Exploring the history of engagement with the collaborative construction of media products'. *New Media and Society* 11(1/2): 160.)

Web browsers Desktop applications that enable internet users to view HTML programmed pages hosted on Web servers. The first publicly available Web browser called WorldWideWeb was written by Berners-Lee and released in 1991. In 1992, the first widely used Web browser, Mosaic, was developed at the National Center for Supercomputing Applications (NCSA) at the University of Illinois (Urbana-Champaign)

Weblog A website in the form of a diary, containing time-stamped articles and frequently linking to sources and other sites of interest. Weblogs usually reflect the views of one person or a small group of individuals and are read generally by a limited number of people on the internet but are capable of attracting large readerships through references on other websites. Webloggers are the individuals who run weblog journals on the world wide web.

Whistleblower Someone who goes outside the normal reporting procedures to alert internal senior managers or external sources to wrongdoing, unethical behaviour or malpractice in the organisation. For example, employees who tell the public about financial mismanagement or theft inside an organisation, or government employees who leak evidence of wrongdoing such as arms sales to particular regimes, or government actions that contravene policy or legal frameworks.

Wicked problems Problems that are unstructured and difficult to define, cutting across many stakeholders (Weber, E.P. and A.M. Khademian (2008). 'Wicked problems, knowledge challenges and collaborative capacity builders in network settings'. *Public Administration Review* march/April). These characteristics require fluid problem solving, the application of many different perspectives, collaboration and long-term commitment.

Wire service A newsgathering organisation that distributes syndicated copy (information) electronically, as by teletype or the internet, usually to subscribers.

Index

Note: Page numbers in **bold** indicate Glossary entries.

4Ps 551
Access Intelligence 601
activism 180, 184, 198, 330-1, 484-5
  and the internet 358-61
  and public relations 11
  social media 100, 599-600
  see also non-governmental organisations (NGOs)
Adobe 46
advertising 4, 44, 384-5, 429-30, **611**
Advertising Value Equivalents (AVEs) 223, 593, **611**
advertorials 390, **611**
advocacy approach to PR ethics 269
AEG 8
Africa 7, 9, 12, 16, 17, 113
agencies
  for communication activities 10
  for public relations 11, 12, 13
agency 212
agenda setting (by media) 22, 27-30, 159, **611**
Agfa 8
agile planning 189
Agora 401
Airbnb 183
Airbus SAS 120-1
Alar ban 336
algorithms used to generate media content 34
Alliance for Lobbying Transparency 57
alpha **611**
alternative target generation **611**
Always #LikeAGirl campaign 76
Amazon.com 67
AMEC 593
  Integrated Evaluation Framework (IEF) 220-1
Amoruso, Sophia 565-6
Anan, Kofi 69
Ancient Greece 5
Ansoff, Igor 177
antecedents of public relations 4-9, 16-17, **611**
anti-vaccination movement 518
Apple 67, 199
Arab world, antecedents of public relations 7
Argentina 7, 113
Aristotle 269
Armstrong, Lance 539
artificial intelligence (AI) 119, 324-5, 574

impact on professions 603
Ashoka, King 6
Asia 6, 9
Associated Press (AP) 34
Association for the Measurement and Evaluation of Communications (AMEC) 202, 203
Astroturfing 239
attitudes **611**
Australia 7, 12, 114, 161
authentic company concept 250
Automation
  impact of 601-2
  of media content generation 34

B Corporation 69
Baker, Ted 560
Balanced Score Card approach 213, 414
Ball, James 53
BAME 594, **611**
Ban Bossy campaign 166
bandwagon effect 239
banks
  central 572, 573
  loss of trust in 82
Barcelona Football Club 542
Barcelona Principles 202
Barilla Centre for Food and Nutrition 463
Barnet & Reef 14
BASF 8
Baumgartner, Felix 438
Bayer 8
BBC 11, 294, 299, 301
beauty influencers 501
Beauvoir, Simone de 550
Belgium 12
beliefs **611**
Bell Pottinger 260-1
benchmarking 193, 194, **611**
Bennett, Katherine 120-1
Benoit, William 353, 354, 539
Bentele, Günter 12
Bentham, Jeremy 267
Berlin Wall, fall of (1989) 7, 8, 15
Bernardine of Siena, St 9
Bernays, Edward L. 4, 11, 16, 153

bias in sport 543
Bill and Melinda Gates Foundation 72, 181
Bio Farma-Indonesia 197-8
Bitner, Mary 420
Black, Sam 14
blog-centered crisis communication model 40
bloggers 23, 375, **611**
   in fashion public relations 561-2
blogs 390-1
bloke-ification 593
'Blonde Salad' (blog) 562-3
body language 148
Body Shop 368, 372
Boeing 345
bogof (buy one get one free) 386, **611**
Booking.com 183
Booms, Bernard 420
Boorstin, Daniel 492, 494
Boots Beauty festival 371
'bossism' in democracy 56
Botnet 240
bots 239-40
Bouazizi, Mohammed 100
boundary scanning 462
boundary spanning (BS) 403
bounded rationality 358
brainstorming 387, **611**
brand **611**
brand development 367
brand journalism 23, **611**
brand loyalty 427
brand shaming 599
brand society 245
brand switchers 427
branded content 374-5
branded self 496
branding 245, 250-4
   personal 45
brands
   consumers and 367-8
   sports as 532-3
Brazil 7, 116-17
Brexit 53, 68, 212, 234-5, 584
Bridge, Gemma 510-11
British Airways (BA) 68
British colonies 6-7, 11
British Gurkha Welfare Society 404
British Social Attitudes survey 28
Brown, Robert 5
BT 72, 74
Buddhism 6, 15
Buell, Katharine 11
Buffett, Warren 72
Bulgaria 111-12
bullet theory 212
bullshit strategy 53
Burke, James 74

Burson, Cohn & Wolfe 374, 375
Burson Marsteller 14, 374
Bursting the Bubble campaign (Australia) 161
business ethics 84-6, **611**
Business in the Community (BITC) 70
business planning model 190-202
   aims and objectives, setting 192-4
   analysis 190-2
   content 196-8
   evaluation 202
   identifying stakeholders 194-6
   resources 201-2
   review 202
   strategy 198-9
   tactics 199, 200
   time 200-1
business responses to social and economic change 68-9
business-to-business (B2B) **611**
business-to-business (B2B) public relations 381–94
   building a corporate reputation 383-4
   core principles 383-4
   in marketing mix 384-7
   media relations 387-91
   social media 382, 391-3
   trade publications 382, 385, 388-90

Cadbury 73, 81, 356, 360
campaign, definition 187
Canada 112
Cannes Lions International Festival of Creativity 377
capitalism **611-12**
Carlsberg 252-3
Carroll, Dave 374
Castells, Manuel 100
categorical imperative 86, 267, **612**
causality 216
cause-related marketing (CRM) 68, 449
celebrities 490–505
   celebrities as commodities 494
   celebrity and society 493-5
   consuming 495
   defining celebrity 492-3, **612**
   and the internet 495-8
   and the media 494
   practitioners 499
   pre-agreed stories or interviews 31
   public relations 493
   in public relations practice 499
celebrity 492-3, **612**
Central America 7
CEO **612**
CESR **612**
Chanel 556
channel preference 215
charitable donations 441-2
charities 16, 24, 152

Chartered Institute of Public Relations (CIPR) UK 16, 110, 137, 138
Chase, Howard 330, 332-4, 335
cheerleading 240
Cheney, Georges 255
China 4, 6, 9, 12, 27, 114, 572, 573
   influencers in 492-3
choice tools 412
Christensen, Lars Thoger 255
circulation 390, **612**
Cision Cloud 601
citizen journalism 23
civil servants, mediatisation 32-3
Clarke, Basil 11
Clegg, Sir Nick 235
climate change 58
clip counts **612**
closed systems organisations 150
CMACIE framework 409-14
co-branding in sport 541
Coca-Cola 73, 422, 425, 432
cocoa industry, child slave labour issue 337
codes of conduct 61
cognitive dissonance 164-5, 212
common starting points (CSPs) 468
communication managers 213
communication strategies in political realm 54-5
communication technicians 213
Communication Value Circle 488
communications
   colonial communications practices 7
   models of 148-9
   theories in PR 148-9
   trust in 118
   types of aims for 192
   see also corporate communications
communications technology, mid-twentieth century developments 15-16
community groups 24
CommunityMark 70, 71
company propaganda 370, **612**
   see also propaganda
comparative non-profit sector project (CNP) 477-8
complex systems **612**
Confédération Européenne des Relations Publique (CERP) 13
Confucianism 6, 270
consequentialism 85, 267
Consultancy Management Standard 16
consumer public relations 365–80
   branded content 374-5
   bullshit 369-70
   core activities 370-2
   developments in media 377
   effects of changes in marketing 377-8
   events 371
   and marketing 366-9
   media landscape 372

media relations 370
   new activities and practices 378-9
   prioritising style over substance 369-70
   shift to owned media 373-4
   target audience 369
   virtual influence 375-7
content **612**
content analysis 223, **612**
content marketing 294, **612**
content producers 23
context-mechanism-outcome (CM) analysis 218
contingency ethics 269
continuing professional development (CPD) 595
contra-cultures 95
convergence trend **612**
Coombs, W. Timothy 247
Co-operative Bank 73
copy (for publication) **612**
corporate branding 245, 250-4
corporate communication 459–71
   coordinating all forms of 467-8
   definitions 460-1, 462
   dialogue strategies 464
   and image formation 246
   intangible assets and 465-7
   integration and relation between 246
   role in organisations 463-5
   role in society 462-3
corporate culture 95, 97, 319, **612**
corporate identity 249-50
corporate philanthropy 72, 442, **612**
corporate scandals 67
corporate social irresponsibility (CSI) 79-80
corporate social responsibility (CSR) 69-71, 151
   business case for 73-5
   regulatory frameworks 80-2
   responsibilities to society 77-80
   responsibilities to stakeholders 75-6
   In sport 540-1
   see also corporate community involvement programmes
country profiles, origins and status of PR 111-14
Court, Hayley 271-3
Covid-19 55, 584, 605-9
   American response to 517-18
   disinformation 236
   as issues management 340
   printed newspapers and 23
CPD (continuing professional development) 122, **612**
credit crunch 68
crisis management plan (CMP) 350-1
crisis PR management 344–64
   challenge response strategies 353
   communicating during a crisis 352-8
   context 345-6
   crisis management plan (CMP) 350-1
   crisis response strategies 356-7
   crisis risk score 349

crisis PR management (*continued*)
    definitions 346-8
    early crisis communication 346
    examples 345
    and the internet 358-61
    preparation for a crisis 349-51
    three-stage crisis life cycle 347
    value of strategic communications 348
    where crises come from 348-9
crisis risk score 349
Critchlow, Julie 152
critical approaches to PR ethics 270
critical modernism 84-5
critical path analysis (CPA) 201
Cuadrilla Ltd 397, 398
cub reporters **612**
cultural context 95
cultural intermediary 542
cultural norm **612**
culturally contextualised PR practice 101
culture 185
    sports as 541-3
cultures 95, 494, **612**
    of organisations 316, 318, 319
    public relations and 96-7
    within sovereign states 96
Curtis, Lauren 501
Curtis, Pixie 498
customer loyalty 430
Cutlip, Scott 17

Daily Mail 22
dark ads 240
dashboards 229
data-gathering 324
Davies, Nick 297
De Wit's web of relational actors 181, 182
debt 585
Debt Capital Markets 573
debt-marketing 573-4
decision tree analysis 412
deep fakes 240
definitions of public relations 5
degree courses in public relations 14
deliberative democracy 53
deliberative engagement 196, 197
democracy and public relations 51–65
    communication in political realm 54-5
    consensus and conflict 60-1
    contribution to democracy 55-6
    definitions 52
    democratic concerns 56-7
    reflexivity and social change 59-60
demographics **612**
deontology 86, 267-8
dialogic theory 40
digital, sponsorship and 451-2

digital divide **612**
digital ethics 266
digital investment 598
digital media storytelling 44
digital news release 296
digital sports 535-7
direct mail 366, **612**
direct marketing 385, 430-1
discourse **612**
discourse ethics 268
disinformation 236-7
    countering 238-9
    obligations in countering 239-41
    relevance of growth of 241-2
    staying ahead of developments in use of 241
    techniques 239-40
    threat 237-8
Disney Corporation 494
distrust in communications and PR 596
dominant coalition 463, **612-13**
Dos Passos, John 11
dotcom bubble 16
Dove 34
Dowling, Grahame 246, 247
downsizing **613**
Duchene, Anne-Sophie 311
Duncan, Ben 507
Durkheim, Émile 261, 263

East India Company 6
Eastern Europe 4, 7, 8, 9
eBay 67
Ebola virus 507
echo chamber 240
economic change 68-9
economic downturns, responses of businesses 68-9
Edelman, Daniel J. 12
Edelman Trust Barometer 81, 330, 596
editorial 286, 294, 382, **613**
Editorial Services Ltd 11
education 595
education and research in PR 13, 14, 138-9
elaboration likelihood model (ELM) 155-8, 512-14
electronic word-of-mouth (eWoM) 555-7
embargoes on news stories 297
Emmel, Nick 432
Empire Marketing Board 11
employee advocacy 46
employee engagement 310-12, **613**
employee value propositions 313
employer brands 313
encoding/decoding theory 212
Enron 67, 69, 86
environment, concern for 67-8
environmental activism 330-1
    fashion industry 551
environmental scanning 462

EPISTLE analysis 178
equal opportunities 84
eSports 452-3, 530
ethical codes 59, 270-4
ethical communication 4
ethical decision-making approaches 84-6
ethical dilemmas 84, 260-1
ethical guidelines 85
ethics **613**
   approaches to PR ethics 266-70
   and business practice 84-6
   changing organisational ethics 86
   conflict between individual and corporate ethics 84
   confusion in PR 262, 263
   digital 266
   PR payments to journalists 27
   professional ethics 266-7, 268-9, 270
ethnicity 594
   language and 96
ethnography 323
Europe 7-9, 11-12
   public relations associations 138
European Commission, aims of 192
European Communication Monitor (ECM) 16, 119, 226, 593
European General Data Protection Regulation (GDPR) 47
European Parliament 58
European Public Relations Education and Research Association (EUPRERA) 13
Eurozone financial crises 68
evaluation 211-32
   application in communication 218-28
   definitions 213-15
   foundational theories 216-18
   models 219-20
   of PR programmes 202
   reason for 212-13
   reporting 228-30
   types of 215-16
event management 371
events 371
excellence approach to PR ethics 246, 269, 600
exchange theories, role of information subsidies 24-7
exclusive 297
exclusive stories 297, **613**
extended parallel process model (EPPM) 514-15
ExxonMobil 58

Facebook 22, 29, 34, 41-2, 45, 67, 235, 266, 291, 333, 338, 360, 361, 374, 375, 418, 422, 555, 599, 604
fake bots 47
fake news 53, 57, 236-7, 240, 291-2, 517-18, 595-6
   countering 238-9
   obligations in countering 239-41
   relevance of growth of 241-2
fake platform 240
fandom 537-8

fashion industry
   environmental activism 551
   feminist critique 549-51
   management of industry 548-51
fashion public relations 551-69
   bloggers and vloggers in 561-5
   eWoM and 555-7, 562
   role of celebrities 557-8
   role of social media influences in 560
fax machines 16
Fearless Girl campaign 576
feminism
   approaches to professional ethics 270
   critique, fashion industry 549-51
   and PR 154-5
Ferragni, Chiara 562-3
Ferrari 465
filter bubbles 34, 240
financial centres, global, role of PR 572-5
financial communication
   in East Asia 574
   social media and 581
financial crisis (2008) 57, 69, 583
financial institutions, loss of trust in 81-2
financial investor relations skills 126
financial markets
   media in 579-81
   role of PR in 571
financial public relations
   future of 583-4
   global financial crisis 583
   retail financial markets 577-9
   skills and education required 582-3
   wholesale financial markets 575-7
Financial Regulation of Donations **613**
financial sector, effects of lack of governance 69
financial TV 582
Fink, Steven 349
fintech (financial technology) public relations 571, 572
FIRST principles of disinformation 238-9
First World War 8, 9, 10-11
Fitzpatrick, George 12
flacks 294
Fleischman, Doris 11, 16
flooding 240
Flynn, Kyla 128-30
fmcg products **613**
Fombrun, Charles J. 248, 255
forgery 240
formative evaluation 215-16, **613**
framing 29-30, 163, 198, **613**
France 111
Franco regime in Spain 13
Frankfurt, Harry G. 53, 369-70
Friedman, Milton 73, 87
fringe finance 585
FSA **613**

Fyre Effect 47
Fyre Festival 498

game theory **613**
Gandhi, Mahatma 6
Gates, Bill 69, 72
gender
    diversity 593-4
    In sport 543
Germany 4, 7-8, 9, 11, 12, 13, 15, 111
Gibson, Belle 501
Gill, Christina 388-9
Giving Institute 7
Global Alliance for Public Relations and Communication
    Management 13, 15, 109, 595
global financial centres 572-5
global principles and specific applications 99-100
global public relations 99, 101
Global Responsible Leadership initiative 69
global village concept 100
global warming 69
globalisation 101, 179-80
glocalisation 408
Gold Papers (IPRA) 14
Google 22, 34, 67, 226, 299, 433, 604
Gore, Al 69, 88
government communications 7, 12
GREAT Britain campaign 193
Great Depression (1930s) 11
Greece 12-13
Green America 337
Greenpeace 11, 337, 338, 339, 353, 363
    Detox campaign 338
Grunig, James E. 15, 150, 245, 246, 308
    Press-agentry Model 467
guanxi (personal connections) 6
Guardian, The 22
guerrilla campaigns 484

H&M 338, 339, 359
    Close the Loop campaign 564-5
Habermas, Jürgen 268
hacks 294
Hales, Graham 429
halo effect 540
Harlow, Rex 4, 15
Hartley, John 492, 493
haute couture 556-7
health communication 506–27
    mass campaigns and interpersonal, crossover 515-18
    need for stakeholder approach 507-10
    two-way symmetric communication 519-22
    use of persuasion theory 510-15
healthcare sector 519
    dialogic approach 521-2
    need for dialogue 519-21
    risks in 519

Hearn, Alison 496
Heath, Robert L. 331, 336, 340
Hersheys 337
heterophily **613**
Hiebert, Ray 17
hierarchy of needs 312
hijacking 240240
Hill, Annette 495
Hill, John 17
Hill & Knowlton 14, 17
historical research into public relations 17
Hoechst 8
homophily **613**
Huffington Post 28
Hunt, Todd 150
Hyper Text Mark-up Language (HTML) **613**
hypodermic needle concept of communication 212

IBM 73
IBM Russia 314
ICCO 593
Iceland 274
    Rang-Tan Christmas Campaign 165
identity 246
iLobola Nge Bhubesi 289-90
image
    controversy of, 245-6
    critical point of view 255-6
    measuring corporate image 254-5
    and reputation 247-8
image repair theory 539
immigration, migration and pluralism 180
impersonator bots 239
implementation **613**
India 6, 113
    healthcare services, violence and 522-3
Indonesia 197-8
influencers 45, 47, 286-91, 598-9, **613**
    marketing 44
    marketing fraud 47
information subsidies 24-7
information technology, power of 180
information theory 149
in-house ethnography 323
injection model 212
inoculation theory 163-4, 509
Instagram 43, 45, 495, 496, 497
Institute of Public Relations (IPR) 13, 14
institutional mediatisation 32-3
integrated marketing communications (IMC) 417-36
    audiences 426-9
    benefits from the approach 421-2
    defining 419-22
    marketing communication tactics 429-31
    planning process 422-6
    role in the marketing mix 420

targeted approach 420-1
touch points 431-3
Intercontinental Hotel Group 453
intercultural knowledge 95, 102
intercultural training programme 101
internal communication 306–28, 599
  choosing effective channels 320-1
  competencies and skills required 325
  definitions 307-10
  employee engagement 307-9, 310-12, 313
  employee motivation 312-13
  evidence-based planning and evaluation 321-2
  functions of 310-12
  history of 308-9
  information gathering approaches 322-4
  leadership communication 318-19
  outcome focus 320-1
  planning 313-20
  professionalisation 325
  social media 316
International Association for Measurement and Evaluation of Communication (AMEC) 213
international communication **613**
International Communications Consultants Association (ICCO) 15
International Financial Architecture 572, 573
International History of Public Relations Conference 17
International Labor Rights Forum (LIRF) (Bangladesh) 359
International Monetary Fund (IMF) 572, 573
international public relations 14-15, 99-100, **613**
International Public Relations Associations (IPRA) 13, 14, 16
International Quality in Public Relations 16
international relations, public diplomacy 103-4
internet 288, 595-6
  and crisis PR management 358-61
Internet celebrity 496
Interpersonal communication 515-18
interpersonal relationships, importance of 6
interventions **614**
intranets **613-14**
intrinsic motivation theory 312
Ipsos MORI 28
Iraq 5
iseepr 386
Israel 16
issues management 329–43
  Chase and Jones model 332-4, 335
  Covid-19 340
  definition 402
  essence of 330-1
  expanding beyond public policy 336-40
  influence of activists 330-1
  issue catalyst mode 335-6
  models of 331-6
  origins of 330-1
  public affairs and 402-3
  and public policy making 331-
  undue influence of groups with more money 340-1
  where issues come from 334
Italy 9, 12, 13, 112

Jacenko, Roxy 496, 497
Japan 6, 12
Jaques, Tony 341
Johnson & Johnson 74
Jordan, Michael 558
Journal of Public Relations Research 17
journalism and PR
  B2B 389-90
  effects of information subsidies 24-7
  exchange between 24-7
  how PR practitioners help journalists 24
  influence of algorithms 34
  journalistic professionalism 25
  PR paying their journalists' 'expenses' 27
  range of PR information sources 22
Julius Caesar 5
junior reporter 389

Kaepernick, Colin 540
Kant, Immanuel 86, 267-8
Kellogg 81
Key Account Management (KAM) 431
Key Opinion Leaders (KOL) 492-3
Key Performance Indicators (KPIs) 213, 229
King, Sir Mervyn 69
kouhou ('widely notify', Japan) 6
Krupp (company) 8
Krupp, Alfred 8

L'Etang, Jacquie 17
Lacey, Anne-Marie 298-9
language and ethnicity 96
Laswell, Harold, communication analysis model 148-9
Latin America 7, 9, 12, 16
laundering 240
Lee, Ivy L. 10, 11, 17, 150, 291, 573
Lehman Brothers 67, 68, 69, 88
Lever's 73
Leveson Inquiry 31
Lidl 433-4
  in the UK and Croatia 87
line managers, importance of 319-20
Linear Model of Communication 149
LinkedIn 42, 43
Lion Lager 289-90
listed companies 581, 583, **614**
listening organisation 316
lobbying 55, 57, 60, 403-8, **614**
  influence of information subsidies 24
  international perspectives 407-8
  regulation of 407

local managers, communication 319-20
log frames 217
'lurkers' **614**

M&S 333
Macnamara, Jim 186
maecenatism 441
Maestre, Joaquin 13
malign rhetoric 240
management, alignment with 600
managers, local, communication 319-20
manipulation 240
Marconi Company 8
marketing 44, 366-9, **614**
marketing mix 366, **614**
   role of B2B public relations in 384-73
marketing PR 4, 8, 15, 418, **614**
marketisation 487-8
marketplace theory 269-70
Marks and Spencer 83
Markson, Max 499-500
Marshall Plan 12-13
Marwick, Alice 493, 494, 495, 496, 498
Maslow, Abraham 312
mass communication 212, 515-18
mass media 6, 284, 286, 294
Matrat, Lucien 13
McCarthy, Jerome 420
McCracken, Grant 97
McDonald's 74
MCG 128-30
McLuhan, Marshall 100
measurement 211-32
   application in communication 218-28
   definitions 213-15
   foundational theories 216-18
   qualitative methods 225, 228
   quantitative methods 224, 228
   reason for 212-13
   reporting 228-30
media **614**
   fragmentation 286-7
   as gatekeeper 286
   how PR practitioners help journalists 25
   news management strategies 26
   range of PR information sources 22
   structural relationships with PR 22-3
   sports and 533-5
media agenda resources 28
media briefings 296
media content
   analysis 216, 229-30
   automation of generation 34
media effects 27, **614**
media environments 22-3
media fragmentation 286-7
media interviews 297

media logic 32-3
media relations 15, 283–305
   agenda setting 27-9
   evaluating media coverage 296
   impact of culture on 285
   influence of information subsidies 24-7
   influencers 284, 285, 287-91
   origins and development 284-5
   power of PR practitioners 30-1
   practical 296-7
   publicity and public relations 286
   purpose of 286
   relations between PR and journalism 284-5
   as strategic management function 285
   techniques 297
   tools 296-7
   workflow steps for PR practitioners 296
media spaces, domination by elites 24-6
media systems, analysis and comparison 25
mediated democracy 53
mediatisation 31-3, **614**
mental health 594-5
message coordination strategies 26
metanarratives **614**
metrics **614**
microcelebrities 496, **614**
Microsoft 72, 599
Middle East 7, 16
Middleton, Kate, Duchess of Cambridge 548-9
Mildenhall, Jonathan 432
military recruitment 419
Mill, John Stuart 267
misappropriation 240
models of public relations 150-1
Moody-Stuart, Mark 74
morals 261, 262, **614**
Morsing, Mette 255
motivation in the workplace 313
Mouffe 60
Mr. Peanut 48
multicultural knowledge 95
multicultural public relations, key principles 102
multinational companies (MNCs) 99
Museums Victoria 491

Nally, Margaret 16
name calling 240
Nasty Gal 565-6
National Association of Local Government Officers 13
National Health Service (NHS) 516, 520, **614**
National Resource Defense Council (NRDC) 335
native advertising **614**
nature/nurture debate 95
neoliberal 498, **614**
Nessman, Karl 5
Nestlé 81, 353, 357, 361
Netflix 162

Netherlands 8-9, 12, 111
New Zealand 7, 114, 204-8
news conferences 296
news management strategies 26
news media 604
    relationship with PR 180-2
News Out of Nothing (Noon) 297
news releases 297, 299-300
news reporting, how PR practitioners help journalists 24, 25
newspapers 22, 23
Nike 38-9, 46, 81, 558
    women campaigning 167-8
NIVEA 292-3
Nolan Committee 406
non-governmental organisations (NGOs) 24, 152, 180, 182, 186, 213, **614**
    activism 152
    communication and 479
    definitions of 476-7
non-profit organisations (NPOs) 16
    communication 485-6
    definition 476-7
    donations 487
    marketisation 487-8
    member-serving vs. public-serving 478
    operational level 483
    strategic level 478-81
    third sector and 476-8
    trust map 481-2
non-verbal communication 148
normative democracy 52-3
Northern Spire Bridge 300-2
Norway 9, 32-3
nudge theory 162-3

Obama, Barack 405
objective **614**
Odwalla 347
Oeckl, Albert 14
Oliver, Jamie 152
Olympic Games
    Beijing (2008) 539
    Rio (2016) 68
    marketing 532
omega **614**
one-way communication models 149, 521
online memorials 358, 361
online persona management 34
open systems organisations 150
opportunities to see (OTS) 177, **614**
opportunity analysis **614**
Oreo 47
organisational culture 86, 97, 316, 318, 319, **614**
organisational identity **614**
organisations
    changing ethical practice 86

open and closed systems types 150
as producers of content 23
responsibilities to society 77-9
responsibilities to stakeholders 75-6
vision and values 67
OTS (opportunities to see) 177, **614**
outcomes 196, 320-1, **615**
outputs 188, **615**
outtakes 196
Oxfam 83

Page, Arthur W. 17
Panama Papers 581
Pandemic bonds 583
Parker, George 10
Parker & Lee 10
Parkour 538
parody 240
patron saints of public relations 9
Paul, St 5, 9
Peach model 70
Pearson 317-18
personal finance media 580
personal selling 431
persuasion theory 153-5, 510-15
PESO model 119, 290
PEST analysis 177-8
PETA 157
Pew Research Center 28
Phelps, Michael 539
philanthropy 71-2, **615**
Philips Sense and Simplicity campaign 468
Phillips, Robert 115
phishing 240
Picou, Svetlana 530-1
piloting **615**
Pink Sari health campaign 226-8
Plank, Betsy Ann 16
planning, implementation and impact (PII) model 219
pluralism 180
podcasts 22
poetry, importance in the Arab world 7
point and shriek 240
policy agenda resources 28
political parallelism in journalism 25
political parties, information resources 28
political public relations 54-5
politics, mediatisation 32
Porter, Michael 177
Portugal 13
power and influence 104
power shift towards PR practitioners 30-1
PR Effectiveness Yardstick 219
PR-bots 584-5
pre-agreed celebrity stories 31
press agentry 150, 284
press agents 10, 11

press conferences 293, 296, 298-9
press market, inclusiveness of 25
press releases 284, 296
pressure group **615**
priming 29
print media 22
privacy issues in social media 47
proactive 403, **615**
process evaluation 216
Proctor and Gamble 86
product PR 418
professional bodies 13, 15, 57, 59, 137, 138
professional ethics 266-7, 268-9, 270
professionalisation of public relations 13-14
professionalism 135-7
professions
    criteria for PR to be a profession 262-3
    defining 261-2
    history of 261
    models of 262
program theory evaluation (PTE) 217
programme, definition 187
programme logic models 217-18
programme theory 217
propaganda 4, 6, 11, 12, 15, 16, 17, 54, 150
    and PR ethics 270
prospect theory 358
proto-public relations 4, 5-9
Prussia 8
psychographics **615**
public affairs 55, 395–416
    CMACIE framework 409-14
    community building 401
    definitions 399, 400
    influence of information subsidies 24-6
    international perspectives 407-8
    lobbying 403–7
    management 408-14
    role within the organisation 398-9
    scope of 399-403
Public Affairs Council (PAC) (US) 401
public agenda versus other agendas 28
public attitudes surveys 28
public diplomacy 102-3, **615**
public information campaigns 12
public information model of PR 150
public opinion, influence of framing and priming 27-8
public policy, definition 400
public relations (PR)
    antecedents 5-9, 16-17
    B2B 387
    codes 59
    country profiles 111-14
    culture 97
    definitions 4-5, 110, 111-15
    democracy 56, 57
    during the Second World War 12
    excellence principles 99-100
    expansion after 1945 12-13
    expansion in the twentieth century 9–15
    global 97
    marketing communication 430
    models of PR 150-1
    origin of the term 4
    restraints on expansion 17
    springboards for expansion 16-17
    start of the practice 5
    study of how it grew 16-17
    worldwide development since mid-twentieth century 15-16
Public Relations Consultants Association 16
public relations practitioners 108–43
    case study (Kyla Flynn, MCG) 128-30
    as communicators 117-18, 120-2
    competencies 123, 130-2
    continuing professional development (CPD) 122
    disciplines that inform public relations 132-3
    education and research 138-9
    financial investor relations skills 126
    power shift towards 30-1
    professionalism 135-8
    range of PR jobs 122-3
    role of 117-18
    role of individuals 122-3
    role of theory in practice 132-3
    skills needed 124-32
    sports and 533-5
    systems theory view of the role 120-2
    trust in 118-19
    who they are 109
Public Relations Review (journal) 17
Public Relations Society of America (PRSA) 13, 59, 112
public service media 604-5
publicists 10, 11
Publicity Bureau of Boston 10
publicity stunts 284
publicity, definition 4
publics 4, 177
    segmentation 152, 195
    for sports public relations 537
    typology 150
Puerto Rico 113

qualitative methods 225, 228, **615**
quantitative methods 224, 228, **615**
quality assurance (QA) in public relations 15
quan hê (personal network) 6
Quiksilver 533

radio 22
raiding 240
Rama IV, King of Thailand 6
ranking lists of organisations 254-5
ranking methods 412

Rathenau, Werner 8
reactance 212
reactive 403, **615**
readership 385, 387, **615**
realist evaluation (RE) 218
reality television 495
recruitment advertisements 418
Red Bull 23, 285
Red Products (RED)™ 449
reflexivity 59-60
regulatory frameworks 80-3
relational harmony 6
relationship identity 246
relationship management 15, 40, 270
relationship management theory 246
relationship theories of PR 149-55
relationships, understanding 246-9
relativism in international PR 97-9
Renault 401
representative bodies 137, 138
representative democracy 52, **615**
reputation 245
   building a corporate reputation 383-4
   critical point of view 255-6
   and image 247-8
   measuring corporate reputation 254-5
   new concepts in corporate reputation 247, 248-9
   reputation commons 247, 248-9
   status 248
   stigma 248
reputation commons 247, 248-9
Reputation Institute, New York 255
reputation management 250-4
research brief preparation 323
research methods in public relations 138-9
return on investment (ROI) 230, **615**
Revolut 578-9
rhetoric 56, **615**
rhetorical theory 269
risk analysis 412
Roman empire 5
Romania 112
Rumsfeld, Donald 187
Russia 27

sales promotions 366, 386-7, 430, **615**
sampling **615**
Saro-Wiwa, Ken 75
satire 240
scenario building 412
scenario planning **615**
Second World War 12
segmentation of publics 195
segmentation, targeting and positioning (STP) model 424-5
   positioning 428-9
   segmentation 426-7
   targeting 427-8

Sehdev, Jeetender 376
Self0commodification 542
setting the agenda *see* agenda setting
Sheldrake, Philip 286
Shell 12, 74, 75, 81, 88
Shiller, Robert 69
Shilling 240
SIDEC model 467
Siemens, Werner von 8
Siemens AG 8, 98, 99
situational analysis 251, 253
situational crisis communication theory (SCCT) 40, 348-9
situational theory of PR 152-3
situationist ethics 269-70
Sky AdSmart 429
small- and medium-sized enterprises (SMEs) 67-8, 72
SMART goals 423-4, 425
SMART objectives 194, 202, 215, 218-19
Smith, Paul 558-9
Smith, William Wolf 10
Snapchat 43, 45
social change, responses of businesses 68-9
social construction of reality
   contributors to 236
   role of public relations practitioners in 235
social marketing **615**
social media 4, 604
   activism 100, 599-600
   analysis 230
   B2B 391-2
   best practices 48
   celebrity and 495
   central banks on 573
   core theories 39-40
   current state of 40
   data collection 47
   defining 39
   fake bots 47
   financial communication and 581
   future of 48
   industry 43
   influence on production of media content 22
   Influences 47
   inside organisations 316
   Internet challenge 47
   key platforms 41-3
   myths and truths 40-1
   news and 23
   opportunities for professionals 45-7
   privacy 47
   relationship building 47
   storytelling on 45-6
   traditional viewpoints 44-
   use by organisations 31
   use in B2B public relations 382, 391-2
   viral challenges 47

social media influences (SMLs) 560
social organisations 16
social trends, influence on PR 22-3
social-constructivist mediatisation 31-2
social-mediated crisis communication model 40
society, organisational responsibilities to 77-9
sock puppets 241
soft power concept 104
solar power feed-in tariff cuts 411
Solis, Brian 391
South Yorkshire Police (SYP) 271-3
Southwest Airlines 360
sovereign states 96
Soviet bloc of Eastern Europe 4, 7, 14
Soviet Union 12
Spain 13
spammer bots 239
Spinwatch 57, 60
spiral of silence 241
sponsorship 371-2, 437-58, **615**
   contemporary organisations, impact for 444-7
   definitions 441-4
   digital reality and 451-4
   fit between organisation and sponsored body 448
   future of 455
   historical perspective 441
   key terms 438-9
   strategic planning and management of 447-51
Sport England 543
Sport Social Responsibility (SSR) 540
sports public relations 528-46
   as culture 541-3
   athlete transgressions 538-40
   co-branding 541
   digital sports 535-7
   fandom 537-8
   gender, representation and bias in 543
   participation, promotion of 537-8
   practitioners and the media 533-5
   publics for 537
   researching 542
   social responsibility and ethics 540-1
   sport as business 529-30
   sports as brands 532-3
Squire, Irving 11
STAEDTLER 392-3
Stages of Change Model 160-2
stakeholder relationship model, health communication and 507-10
stakeholders 4, 75-6, 177, **616**
   identifying 194-6
   influence of 73-4
   organisational responsibilities to 75-6
Starbucks 341
state influence on the media 25
status and reputation 248
Stewart, Betty 499

Steyn, Dr Benita 185
stigma and reputation 248
story ideas 390
storytelling 555, 604
   Social media and 45-6
Strategic Fitness Communication Model 541
strategic non-profit communication 475-89
   consequences for operational level 483
   consequences for strategy level 478-81
   marketisation of third sector 487-8
   as multi-level approach 485-6
   third sector and non-profit organisations 476-8
strategic PR planning and management 175–210
   approaches to planning 189-90
   circuits of communication 183
   definition of campaign 187
   definition of programme 187
   external environment 177-84
   globalisation issues 179-80
   immigration, migration and pluralism 180
   implications of context 185-6
   importance of context 176-7
   importance of planning 187-9
   information technology 180
   internal environment 184-5
   macro environment 177-8
   news media 180-2
   PEST analysis 177-8
   power, shifts in 180
   programmes and campaigns 187
   publics 177
   scope of PR planning 189
   stakeholders 177
   strategic planning models 177
   strategic PR programmes and campaigns 187
   SWOT analysis 184
   systems approach 188-9
   task environment 182-4
strategy selection **616**
sub-cultures 95
Sugar tax 510-11
Sumeria 5
summative evaluation 216
surveys 297
sustainable business, corporate social responsibility (CSR) 69-72
Sustainable Development Goals 178, 179
Sweaty Betty 497
Swift 57
SWOT analysis 184
systematic modernism 84
systems theory 150-2, 268, **616**

tabloid press 297, **616**
tainting 241
Taiwan 6
talent 593

Tallents, Sir Stephen 11, 14
TARES test 269
Taylor Bennett Foundation 594
technological trends, influence on PR 22
technology, influence of Web 1.0 16
television, changing patterns of viewing 22-3
Tench, Ralph 596
terrestrial channels **616**
terrorism 241
Thailand 6, 9, 12, 14, 15
theories of PR 147-74
theory of change 217
Theory of Planned Behaviour 158-9, 512
Theory of Reasoned Action 158
third sector 476-8
  trust in 481
Thomas Cook Sport (TCS) 373
Thunberg, Greta 396
TikTok 45
tools, PR 601, 602
trade media 389-90
trade publications 382, 385, 388-90
training 595
Transparency International 99
Transtheoretical Model 160
triple bottom-line reporting 82, **616**
trolling 241
Trump, Donald 212, 291
trust
  in government 606-8
  loss of public trust in institutions 81-2
  rebuilding 596-8
  in third sector 481
Turner, Graeme 493, 494, 495
Twitter 42-3, 55, 418, 422, 599-600
two-step communication model 149
two-way asymmetric communication model 153
two-way asymmetrical model 521
two-way communication models 149
two-way symmetric communication model 151, 153
two-way symmetrical model 521
typology of PR 150, **616**

U2 199
Uber 183
UK Uncut 341
Unicef Germany Trust Map 482-3
Unified Evaluation Model for Public Relations 219
Unilever 85
Union Carbide 348, 357
United Kingdom 4, 8, 9, 11, 111
  after 1945 12-13
  Government Communication Service (GCS) 221-3
  government propaganda in wartime 12
  key facts about public relations in 110
  professional associations 13

United Nations Global Compact 69, 98-9
United States 4, 112-13
  Department of Defence 102
  government propaganda in wartime 12
  government public diplomacy 103
  influence after 1945 12-13
  international public relations 14-15
  models of public relations practices 9-10
  professional associations 13
  public relations research and theorisation 15
universalism in international PR 97-9
upward feedback **616**
utilitarianism 85-6, 267

value chain 186
values (corporate) 313, **616**
van Riel, Cees 249, 255
Velvet Ghetto 593
Vietnam 6
VIP facility visit, checklist for main elements 200, 201
virtue ethics 86, 268-9
vision and values of organisations 67, **616**
vloggers in fashion public relations 561-2
Vodafone 479-81
Volkswagen (VW) 345

Waddington, Stephen 286, 288
watchdog **616**
  function of the media 33
  of lobbying 57
Waugh, Paul 28
Web 1.0, the information age 16
Web 2.0, the social web **616**
Web browsers **616**
Weber, Max 8
Weber Shandwick 374
weblogs **616**
websites, B2B PR and 390-1
whistleblowers 84, 86, **616**
wicked problems **616**
Wilder, Robert 11
Williams, Beckie 333
Wilson, Kirtland 11
Winfrey, Oprah 539
wire service **616**
women in public relations 16
Woods, Tiger 529, 558
World Bank 572, 573, 583
World Trade Organization (WTO) 572
WorldCom 67, 69
WWF Germany 485

YouGov 28
Youn, Breanna 498
YouTube 42, 43, 45, 361, 374, 375-7

Zuckerberg, Mark 291

Publisher's acknowledgements

Text credits:

4 John Wiley & Sons, Inc.: Childs, H.L. (1940). An Introduction to Public Opinion. New York: John Wiley & Sons, Inc.; **4 Kogan Page Ltd:** Watson, T. and P. Noble (2014). Evaluating Public Relations: A guide to planning, research and measurement. 3rd ed. London: Kogan Page; **4 The University of Oklahoma:** Bernays, E.L. (ed.). (1955). The Engineering of Consent. Norman, OH: University of Oklahoma Press; **5 Taylor & Francis Group:** Nessman, K. (2000). The origins and development of public relations in Germany and Austria. In: D. Moss, D., Verčič, D., and Warnaby, G., eds., Perspectives on Public Relations Research. London: Routledge, pp. 211–225; **5 Dar Al Uloom:** Al-Badr, H. (2004). The Basics of Public Relations and Its Practices. Riyadh: Dar Aloloom; **5 Elsevier Inc.:** Watson, T. (2008). Creating the cult of a saint: Communication strategies in 10th century England. Public Relations Review, 34(1), pp. 19–24; **5 Merriam Webster dictionary:** Merriam Webster dictionary; **6 Springer Nature:** Hung-Baesecke, C-J.F. and Y-R.R. Chen, (2014). China. In: T. Watson, ed., Asian Perspectives on the Development of Public Relations: Other Voices. Basingstoke: Palgrave Macmillan, pp. 20–33; **6 Springer Nature:** Wu, Y-C., and Y-J. Lai (2014). Taiwan. In: T. Watson, ed., Asian Perspectives on the Development of Public Relations: Other Voices. Basingstoke: Palgrave Macmillan, pp. 114–127; **6 Springer Nature:** Tantivejakul, N. (2014). 'Thailand' in Asian Perspectives on the Development of Public Relations: Other voices, T. Watson (ed.). Basingstoke: Palgrave Macmillan; **6 Springer Nature:** Yamamura, K., S. Ikari and T. Kenmochi (2014). 'Japan' in Asian Perspectives on the Development of Public Relations: Other voices, T. Watson (ed.). Basingstoke: Palgrave Macmillan; **6 Springer Nature:** Vil'Anilam, J.V. (2014). 'India' in Asian Perspectives on the Development of Public Relations: Other voices, T. Watson (ed.). Basingstoke: Palgrave Macmillan; **6 Public Relations Institute of Australia:** Reddi, C.V.N. (1999). Notes on PR Practice in India: Emerging New Human Environment – A Challenge. Asia Pacific Public Relations Journal, 1, pp. 147–160; **7 Ministry of Higher Education:** Fakhri, S., A. Alsheekley and F. Zalzala (1980). Public Relations. Baghdad: Ministry of Higher Education and Research; **7 Springer Nature:** Badran, B.A. (2014). The Arab States of the Gulf. In: T. Watson, ed., Middle Eastern and African Perspectives on the Development of Public Relations: Other Voices. Basingstoke: Palgrave Macmillan, pp. 5–21; **7 Springer Nature:** Sheehan, M. (2014). Australia. In: T. Watson, ed., Asian Perspectives on the Development of Public Relations: Other Voices. Basingstoke: Palgrave Macmillan, pp. 5–13; **7 Springer Nature:** Galloway, C. (2014). New Zealand. In: T. Watson, ed., Asian Perspectives on the Development of Public Relations: Other Voices. Basingstoke: Palgrave Macmillan, pp. 14–19; **7, 8, 12 Springer Nature:** Bentele, G. (2015). Germany. In: T. Watson, ed., Western European Perspectives in the Development of Public Relations: Other Voices. Basingstoke: Palgrave Macmillan, pp. 44–59; **8 Lit Verlag:** Binder, E. (1983). Die Entstehung unternehmerischer Public Relations in der Bundes-republik Deutschland. Munster: Lit Verlag; **9 Springer Nature:** van Ruler, B., and A-M. Cotton (2015). Netherlands and Belgium. In: T. Watson, ed., Western European Perspectives in the Development of Public Relations: Other Voices. Basingstoke: Palgrave Macmillan, pp. 89–106; **10, 284 Colver Publishing House:** Morse, S. (1906). An Awakening in Wall Street. How the Trusts, after Years of Silence, now speak through authorized and acknowledged Press Agents. American Magazine, 62(5), pp. 457–463; **10 Elsevier Inc.:** Miller, K.S., and C.O. Bishop (2009). Understanding Ivy Lee's declaration of principles: U.S. newspaper and magazine coverage of publicity and press agentry, 1865–1904. Public Relations Review, 35(2), pp. 91–101; **10 Taylor & Francis Group:** Cutlip, S. (1994). The Unseen Power: Public Relations, a history. Hillsdale, NJ: Lawrence Erlbaum; **10 Industries Publishing Company:** Lee, I.L. (1925). Publicity. Some of the Things It is and Is Not. New York: Industries Publishing Company; **11 Spellmount:** Evans, R. (2013). From the Front Line: The Extraordinary Life of Sir Basil Clarke. Stroud: Spellmount; **12, 14 Taylor & Francis Group:** L'Etang, J. (2004). Public Relations in Britain – A History of

Professional Practice in the 20th Century. Mahwah, NJ: Lawrence Erlbaum; **12 Springer Nature:** Yamamura, K., S. Ikari and T. Kenmochi (2014). Japan. In: T. Watson, ed., Asian Perspectives on the Development of Public Relations: Other Voices. Basingstoke: Palgrave Macmillan, pp. 63–77; **12 Springer Nature:** van Ruler, B., and A-M. Cotton (2015). Netherlands and Belgium. In: T. Watson, ed., Western European Perspectives in the Development of Public Relations: Other Voices. Basingstoke: Palgrave Macmillan, pp. 89–106; **15 Houghton Mifflin Harcourt:** Grunig, J.E. and T. Hunt(1984). Managing Public Relations. New York: Holt, Rinehart & Winston; **16 Springer Nature:** Watson, T. (2015). What in the World is Public Relations? In: T. Watson, ed., Perspectives on Public Relations Historiography and Historical Theorization. Basingstoke: Palgrave Macmillan, pp. 4–19; **23 Thomson Reuters Corporation:** Nielsen, R.K. and R. Sambrook (2016). What is happening to television news? Reuters Institute for the Study of Journalism, 2016; **24 Elsevier Inc.:** Gandy, O. H. (1982). Beyond agenda setting: Information subsidies and public policy. Norwood, NJ: Ablex; **24 Elsevier Inc.:** Turk, J. V. (1985). Information subsidies and influence. Public Relations Review, 11(3), 10–25; **27 The New York Times Company:** Barboza, D. (2012). In China Press, best coverage cash can buy. New York Times, April 3, 2012. Available at: http://www.nytimes.com/2012/04/04/business/media/flattering-news-coverage-has-a-price-in-china.html; **29 American Association for the Advancement of Science:** Lazer, D. M., M. A. Baum, Y. Benkler, A. J. Berinsky, K. M. Greenhill, F. Menczer, and M. Schudson (2018). The science of fake news. Science, 359(6380), 1094–1096; **29 Oxford University Press:** Entman, R. M. (2007). Framing bias: Media in the distribution of power. Journal of communication, 57(1), 163–173; **30 The University of Manchester:** Davis, A. (2002). Public Relations Democracy: Public Relations, Politics and the Mass Media in Britain. Manchester University Press; **30 Guardian News & Media Limited:** Davies, N. (2008). 'Our Media have Become Mass Producers of Distortion'. The Guardian, February 4; **32 Taylor & Francis Group:** Hjarvard, S. (2013) The Mediatization of Culture and Society. London: Routledge; **32 John Wiley & Sons, Inc.:** Thorbjørnsrud, K., T. U. Figenschou and Ø. Ihlen, (2014). Operationalizing mediatization: A typology of mediatization in public bureaucracies. Communications: The European Journal of Communication Research, 39(1), 3–22; **33 Springer Nature:** Bentele, G. and H. Nothaft (2008). The intereffication model: Theoretical discussions and empirical research in Zerfass et al., (Eds.), Public relations research: European and international perspectives and innovations. VS: Wiesbaden (2008), pp. 33–47; **34 Penguin Random House:** Michio Kaku (2014) "The Future of the Mind: The Scientific Quest To Understand, Enhance and Empower the Mind", Penguin UK; **38 National Public Radio:** "A Blown-Out Sneaker, An Injured Superstar And A Night To Forget For Nike." NPR.org. https://www.npr.org/2019/02/21/696565989/a-blown-out-sneaker-an-injured-superstar-and-a-night-to-forget-for-nike (April 2, 2019); **39 Elsevier Inc.:** Felix, Reto; Rauschnabel, Philipp A; Hinsch, Chris (2017). "Elements of strategic social media marketing: A holistic framework". Journal of Business Research 70: 118–26. doi:10.1016/j.jbusres.2016.05.001; **39 Sage Publications:** Freberg, K. (2016). Social Media. In C. Carroll (Ed.), Encyclopaedia for Corporate Reputation. Sage Publications. Thousand Oaks, CA; **42 Pew Research Center:** "Facebook, YouTube Continue to Be the Most Widely Used Online Platforms among U.S. Adults." Pew Research Center, 9 Apr. 2019, https://www.pewresearch.org/ft_19-04-02_socialmediaplatforms_feature/; **52 Cambridge University Press:** Bennett, W. L. and Entman, R. M. (2001) 'Mediated politics: An introduction', in Bennett, W.L. & Entman, R.M. (eds.) Mediated politics: Communication in the future of democracy. Cambridge, England: Cambridge University Press, pp. 1–30; **52 Oxford University Press:** Goodin, R. E. (2009) 'The state of the discipline, the discipline of the state', in Goodin, R.E. (ed.) The Oxford handbook of political science: Oxford University Press; **52 Stanford University Press:** Held, D. (2006) Models of democracy. Stanford University Press; **53, 56 Biteback Publishing Limited:** Ball, J. (2017) Post-truth: How bullshit conquered the world. Biteback Publishing; **53 Taylor & Francis Group:** Waisbord, S. (2018) 'The elective affinity between post-truth communication and populist politics', Communication Research and Practice, 4(1), pp. 17–34; **54 Sage Publications:** Jowett, G. S. and O'Donnell, V. (2018) Propaganda and persuasion. 7 edn. London: Sage. p. 7; **54 Manchester University Press:** Taylor, P. M. (2003) Munitions of the mind: A history of propaganda from the ancient world to the present day. 3 edn. Manchester, UK: Manchester University Press; **54 Penguin Random House:** Ellul, J. (1965/1973) Propaganda: The formation of men's attitudes. Translated by: Kellen, K. & Lerner, J. New York: Vintage Books. Reprint, 1973; **54 Taylor & Francis Group:** Weaver, K., Motion, J. and Roper, J. (2006) 'From propaganda to discourse (and back again): Truth, power, the public interest and public relations', in L'Etang, J. & Pieczka,

M. (eds.) Public relations: Critical debates and contemporary practice. Mahwah, NJ: Lawrence Erlbaum, pp. 7–21; **54 Taylor & Francis Group:** Strömbäck, J. and Kiousis, S. (2019) 'Defining and mapping the field of theory and research on political public relations ', in Strömbäck, J. & Kiousis, S. (eds.) Political public relations: Principles and applications. 2 ed. New York: Routledge; **55 Sage Publications:** Harris, P. and Fleisher, C. S. (2017) 'Introduction: The continuing development of international corporate and public affairs', in Harris, P. & Fleisher, C.S. (eds.) The SAGE handbook of international corporate and public affairs. London: Sage, pp. 1–15; **55 John Wiley & Sons, Inc.:** McGrath, C. (2007) 'Framing lobbying messages: Defining and communicating political issues persuasively', Journal of Public Affairs, 7(3), pp. 269–280; **55 Taylor & Francis Group:** aylor, M., & Kent, M. L. (2014). Dialogic Engagement: Clarifying Foundational Concepts. Journal of Public Relations Research, 26(5), 384–398. doi: 10.1080/1062726x.2014.956106; **55, 60 Taylor & Francis Group:** Holtzhausen, D. R. (2012) Public relations as activism: Postmodern approaches to theory & practice. New York: Routledge; **56 Elsevier Inc.:** Heath, R. L., Waymer, D. and Palenchar, M. J. (2013) 'Is the universe of democracy, rhetoric, and public relations whole cloth or three separate galaxies?', Public Relations Review, 39(4), pp. 271–279; **57 Manchester University Press:** Davis, A. (2002) Public relations democracy: Public relations, politics and the mass media in Britain. Manchester, UK: Manchester University Press; **57 Oxford University Press:** Feintuck, M. (2004) 'The Public Interest' in regulation. New York: Oxford University Press; **57 Penguin Random House:** Dewey, J. (1935/2000) Liberalism and social action. Amherst, NY: Prometheus Books; **58 European Parliament Committees:** Hearings: Events: PETI: Committees: European Parliament. Retrieved March 25, 2019, from https://www.europarl.europa.eu/committees/en/peti/eventshearings.html?id=20190313CHE06141; **58 Exxon Mobil Corporation:** letter from Nikolaas Baeckelmans, ExxonMobil Vice President European Union Affairs; March 20, 2019; **58 Exxon Mobil Corporation:** Kimberly A. Neuendorf, Ph.D. February 22, 2018 Evaluation of the Study, "Assessing ExxonMobil's climate change communications (1977–2014)" by Geoffrey Supran and Naomi Oreskes, published in Environmental Research Letters, 2017 , https://cdn.exxonmobil.com/~/media/global/files/energy-and-environment/NeuendorfReport.pdf; **59 Taylor & Francis Group:** Ihlen, Ø., Verhoeven, P. and Fredriksson, M. (2018b) 'Conclusions on the compass, context, concepts, concerns and empirical avenues for public relations', in Ihlen, Ø. & Fredriksson, M. (eds.) Public relations and social theory: Key figures, concepts and developments. 2 ed. New York: Routledge, pp. 414–431; **59 Praxis:** Walle, M., 2003, "Commentary: What happened to public responsibility? The lack of society in public relations codes of ethics", Prism (1), http://praxis.bond.edu.au/prism/papers/commentary/paper1.pdf, accessed on 9 June 2006; **59 Taylor & Francis Group:** McKie, D. and Munshi, D. (2007) Reconfiguring public relations: Ecology, equity and enterprise. New York: Routledge; **60 Taylor & Francis Group:** Motion, J. and Leitch, S. (2015) 'Critical discourse analysis: a search for meaning and power', in L'Etang, J., McKie, D., Snow, N. & Xifra, J. (eds.) Routledge handbook of critical public relations. London: Routledge, pp. 142–150; **60 Spinwatch:** Delmar-Morgan, A. and Miller, D. (2018) The UAE lobby: Subverting British democracy? : Spinwatch/Public Interest Investigations; **60 Taylor & Francis Group:** Daymon, C. and Demetrious, K. (eds.) (2013) Gender and public relations: Critical perspectives on voice, image and identity. London: Routledge; **60 New Left Review:** Mouffe, C. (2013) Agonistics: Thinking the world politically. London: Verso Books; **61 Sage Publications:** Davidson, S. (2016) 'Public relations theory: An agonistic critique of the turns to dialogue and symmetry', Public Relations Inquiry, 5(2), pp. 145–167; **61 Procter & Gamble:** The Best Men Can Be. Retrieved from http://www.thebestmencanbe.org/; **71 BITC:** "Training Course: Community Investment Strategy - London." Business in the Community, https://www.bitc.org.uk/event/training-course-community-investment-strategy/; **72 Warren Buffet:** Quote by Warren Buffet; **72 BT Group:** BT's annual review and summary financial statement (1996/7). Retrieved 1997, from https://www.btplc.com/report/1996-97/section9.htm; **73 BUSINESSEUROPE:** European Multistakeholder Forum on CSR Report and Recommendations (2004). European Multistakeholder Forum on CSR: Final results & recommendations. Available at: http://www.corporatejustice.org/IMG/pdf/CSR_20Forum_20final_20report.pdf (Accessed 5 March 2015); **74 Mark Moody-Stuart:** Quote by Mark Moody-Stuart; **76 Procter & Gamble:** Adapted from http://www.pg.com; **77 Elsevier Inc.:** Based on Carroll, A.B. (1991). 'The pyramid of corporate social responsibility: toward the moral management of organizational stakeholders.' Business Horizons 34(4): 39–48; **78 Academy of Management Review:** Adapted Carroll, A.B. (1979). 'A Three-Dimensional Conceptual Model of Corporate Performance.'The Academy of Management Review Vol. 4, No. 4 (Oct., 1979), pp. 497–505 (9 pages); **80 Emerald Group Publishing Limited:** Jones, B; Tench, R. and Bowd, R. (2009). 'Corporate irresponsibility and corporate social responsibility: competing realities'. Social Responsibility Journal, Emerald Volume 5, No. 3 2009; **81, 98 United Nations:** The Ten Principles: UN Global Compact. Retrieved from https://www.unglobalcompact.org/what-is-gc/mission/principles; **82 Financial Trust Index:** Chicago Booth/Kellogg School Financial Trust Index Reveals Heightened Public Trust in Local Banks, Credit Unions. Retrieved from http://www.financialtrustindex.org/resultswave24.htm; **82 Edelman:** 2016 Edelman Trust Barometer. Retrieved from https://www.edelman.com/research/2016-edelman-trust-barometer; **83 Marc Bolland:** Quote by Marc Bolland; **84 John Wiley & Sons, Inc.:** Trevino, L.K. and K.A. Nelson (1995). Managing Business Ethics: Straight talk about how to do it right. New York: Wiley & Sons; **85 Unilever:** Unilever's approach Social Review 2000 to corporate social .. Retrieved 2000, from https://www.unilever.com/Images/2000-social-review-of-1999-data_tcm244-409696_en.pdf; **85 John Wiley & Sons, Inc.:** Trevino, L.K. and K.A. Nelson (1995). Managing Business Ethics: Straight talk about how to do it right. New York: Wiley & Sons. p.67; **85 Sage Publications:** Snell, R. (1997). 'Management learning perspectives on business ethics' in Management Learning. J. Burgoyne and M. Reynolds. (Eds). London: SAGE Publications; **87 Nova Southeastern University:** Topić, M. and R. Tench (2016). 'The corporate social responsibility in Lidl's communication campaigns in Croatia and the UK.' The Qualitative Report 21(2): 352; **88 Mark Hibbert:** Quote by Mark Hibbert; **88 Chris Arthur:** Quote by Chris Arthur; **89 Donna Lloyd:** Quote by Donna Lloyd; **98 Bloomberg L.P:** Catherine Hickley, Siemens Bribes Leave Von Pierer Unbowed in CEO Memoir: Books, Bloomberg L.P. Retrieved January 27, 2011; **98 United Nations:** United Nations Global Compact Annual Review 2010, Published by: United Nations; **99 Taylor & Francis Group:** Verčič, D.. L.A. Grunig and J.E. Grunig (1996). Global and specific principles of public relations: Evidence from Slovenia. In H. M. Culbertson and N. Chen (Eds.), International Public Relations: A Comparative Analysis (pp. 31–65). Mahwah, NJ: Lawrence Erlbaum Associates; **99 Taylor & Francis Group:** Verčič, D.. L.A. Grunig and J.E. Grunig (1996). Global and specific principles of public relations: Evidence from Slovenia. In H. M. Culbertson and N. Chen (Eds.), International Public Relations: A Comparative Analysis (pp. 31–65). Mahwah, NJ: Lawrence Erlbaum Associates; **100 Taylor & Francis Group:** Sriramesh, K. and D. Verčič (eds) (2009). The Global Public Relations Handbook: Theory, research, and practice, expanded and revised edition. New York, NY: Routledge; **100 Taylor & Francis Group:** Huang, Y.-H. C. (2012). Culture and Chinese public relations research. In K. Sriramesh and D. Verčič (Eds.), Culture and public relations: Links and implications (pp. 91–104). New York/London: Routledge; **101 Springer Nature:** Tench, R., D. Verčič, A. Zerfass, A. Moreno and P. Verhoeven (2017). Communication excellence: How to develop, manage and lead exceptional communications. London: Palgrave Macmillan; **101 John Wiley & Sons, Inc.:** Brislin, R.W. (2008). Intercultural communication training. In W. Donsbach (Ed.), International Encyclopedia of Communication, Vol. VI (pp. 2331–2333). Malden, MA: Blackwell; **102 Taylor & Francis Group:** Allen, M.R. and D.M.Dozier (2012). When cultures collide: Theoretical issues in global public relations. In K. Sriramesh and D. Verčič (Eds.), Culture and public relations: Links and implications (pp.). New York/London: Routledge; **103 Penguin Random House:** Pinkler, S. (2011b). The better angels of our nature: The decline of violence in history and its causes. London: Penguin; **103 United States Information Agency:** USIA (1998). United States Information Agency. Washington, DC: USIA. Retrieved on 13 June 2012 from http://dosfan.lib.uic.edu/usia/usiahome/overview.pdf; **103 U.S Department of state:** About Us – Under Secretary for Public Diplomacy and Public Affairs - United States Department of State. Retrieved from https://www.state.gov/about-us-under-secretary-for-public-diplomacy-and-public-affairs/; **103 Richard Holbrooke:** Quote by Richard Holbrooke; **104 Seven Law:** McClellan, M. (2004). Public diplomacy in the context of traditional diplomacy. Presented to Vienna Diplomatic Academy on 14 October 2004. Retrieved on 13 June 2012 from http://www.publicdiplomacy.org/45.htm; **104 Carnegie Council:** Nye, J.S. and J.J. Myers (2004). Soft power: The means to success in world politics. (Carnegie Council for Ethics in International Affairs, audio transcript.) http://www.carnegiecouncil.org/studio/multimedia/20040413/index.html; **104 Hachette Books Group:** Nye, J. (2004). Soft Power: The means to success in world politics. New York, NY: Public Affairs.(p.11); **110 Taylor & Francis Group:** Fawkes, J. (2008). 'What is public relations?' in Handbook of Public Relations, 3rd edition, A. Theaker (ed.). London: Routledge; **111 Emerald Group Publishing Limited:** Tench, R. and J. Fawkes (2005). Mind the gap – exploring attitudes to PR education between academics and employers. Paper presented at the Alan Rawel CIPR Academic Conference, University of Lincoln, March; **111 Walter de Gruyter:** van Ruler, B. and D. Verčič (eds) (2004). Public Relations and Communication Management in Europe. Berlin: de Gruter; **114 Chartered Institute of Public Relations:** Chartered Institute of Public Relations (CIPR) (2015). www.cipr.co.uk; **115 Public Relations**

Society of America: A Modern Definition of Public Relations. (2012, March 1). Retrieved from http://prdefinition.prsa.org/index.php/2012/03/01/new-definition-of-public-relations/; **116 Fabiana Gondim Mariutti:** Fabiana Gondim Mariutti; **120 Forbes Media LLC:** Pozin, I. (2014, June 6). 5 Measurements for PR ROI. Retrieved from https://www.forbes.com/sites/ilyapozin/2014/05/29/5-measurements-for-pr-roi/#494492fd77d1; **120 Sage Publications:** Pieczka, M. (2002) 'Public relations expertise deconstructed', Media, Culture and Society, 24(3), pp.301–323; **120 Katherine Bennett:** Based on interview with author and information supplied by Katherine Bennett; **123 Sage Publications:** Proctor, R.W. and A. Dutta (1995) Skill Acquisition and Human Performance. London: Sage; **125, 126 Dr. Ansgar Zerfass:** Zerfass, A., A. Moreno, R. Tench, D. Verčič and P. Verhoeven (2008) European Communication Monitor 2008. Trends in Communication Management and Public Relations – Results and Implications Brussels, Leipzig: Euprera / University of Leipzig, November 2008; **125 European Public Relations Education and Research Association:** Zerfass, A., D. Verčič, P. Verhoeven, A. Moreno and R. Tench (2012). European Communication Monitor 2012. Challenges and Competencies for Strategic Communication. Results of an Empirical Survey in 42 Countries. Brussels: EACD/EUPRERA, Helios Media; **127 Taylor & Francis Group:** Hargie, O. (2000). The Handbook of Communication Skills, 2nd edition. London: Routledge; **131 Elsevier Inc.:** Gregory, A. (2008) 'Competencies of senior communication practitioners in the UK: an initial study', Public Relations Review, 34(3), pp. 215–223; **131 Taylor & Francis Group:** Jeffrey, L.M. and M.A. Brunton (2011). 'Developing a framework for communication management competencies'. Journal of Vocational Education and Training 63(1): 57–75; **132 Springer Nature:** Szyszka, P. (1995). Öffentlichkeitsarbeit und Kompetenz: Probleme und Perspektiven künftiger Bildungsarbeit. In PR-Ausbildung in Deutschland (pp. 317–342). VS Verlag für Sozialwissenschaften; **133 University of Lincoln:** Tench, R. and J. Fawkes (2005). 'Mind the gap – exploring attitudes to PR education between academics and employers'. Paper presented at the Alan Rawel CIPR Academic Conference, University of Lincoln, March; **133 Sage Publications:** Cheney, G. and L.T. Christensen (2001). 'Public relations as contested terrain' in Handbook of Public Relations. R.L. Heath (ed.). Thousand Oaks, CA: Sage; **135 Global Alliance:** Global Alliance, Code of Ethics "GLOBAL PRINCIPLES AND CODE OF ETHICS FOR PROFESSIONAL PUBLIC RELATIONS AND COMMUNICATIONS PRACTITIONERS (GA CODE 2018)"; **135 Emerald Group Publishing Limited:** L'Etang, J. (2002). 'Public relations education in Britain: A review at the outset of the millennium and thoughts for a different research agenda'. Journal of Communication Management 7(1): 43–53; **135 Harvard Business School Publishing:** Kerr, C. (1995). The Use of the University, 4th edition. Cambridge, MA and London: Harvard University Press; **135 Emerald Group Publishing Limited:** Johansson, C. and A. Ottestig (2011). 'Communication executives in a changing world: Legitimacy beyond organizational borders'. Journal of Communications Management 15(2): 144–64; **136 Emerald Group Publishing Limited:** Valentini, C. (2010), Personalised networks of influence in public relations, Journal of communications Management, 14 (2), pp.153–166; **136 Emerald Group Publishing Limited:** Merkelson, H. (2011). 'The double-edged sword of legitimacy in Public Relations'. Journal of Communications Management 15(2): 125–43; **136 Arthur W. Page Society:** Arthur Page Society, Authentic Enterprise White Paper 2008; **136 Emerald Group Publishing Limited:** Gregory, A. (2011). 'The state of the public relations profession in the UK: A review of the first decade of the twenty-first century'. Corporate Communications: An International Journal 16(2): 89–104; **138 CIPR:** www.cipr.co.uk (CIPR); **148, 149 HarperCollins:** Lasswell, H. D. (1948). The structure and function of communication in society. In L. Bryson (Ed.), The communication of ideas (pp. 37–51). New York: Harper and Row; **150 Houghton Mifflin Harcourt:** Grunig, J.E., and Hunt, T. (1984). Managing Public Relations. New York: Holt, Rinehart and Winston; **151 Taylor & Francis Group:** Grunig, J. E. (1992). Excellence in Public Relations and Communication Management. Hillsdale: Lawrence Erlbaum Associates; **152 Center for Culture-Centered Approach to Research and Evaluation:** Kim, J-N. (2011). Public segmentation using situational theory of problem solving: Illustrating summation method and testing segmented public profiles. PRism 8(2). Retrieved from http://www.prismjournal.org/homepage.html (9 December 2015); **153 Oxford University Press:** Kim, J-N, and Grunig, J.E. (2011). Problem Solving and Communicative Action: A Situational Theory of Problem Solving. Journal of Communication 61, 120–149; **153 University of Oklahoma Press:** Bernays, E. L. (1955). The theory and practice of public relations: a resume. In - Bernays, E. L. (ed) The engineering of consent (pp. 3–25). Norman: University of Oklahoma Press; **153 W. W. Norton & Company:** Bernays, E. (1923). Crystallizing Public Opinion. New York: Boni and Liveright; **153, 154, 155, 163 Taylor & Francis Group:** Pfau, M., and Wan, H. H. (2006). Persuasion: An Intrinsic Function of Public Relations. In Botan,

C.H., and Hazleton, V. (eds) Public Relations Theories II. N. Y.: Lawrence Erlbaum Associates; **153 Lawrence Erlbaum Associates:** Grunig, L. A., & Grunig, J. E. (Eds.) (1990). Public relations research annual (Vol. 2). Hillsdale, NJ: Lawrence Erlbaum Associates, 265 pp.; **154 Common Courage Press:** Stauber, J., and Rampton, S. (1995). Toxic sludge is good for you: Lies, damn lies and the public relations industry. Monroe, Maine: Common Courage Press; **154 Ig Publishing:** Bernays, E. L. (2005[1928]). Propaganda. N. Y. Ig Publishing; **154 Taylor & Francis Group:** Miller, G. R. (1989). Persuasion and public relations: Two "ps" in a pod. In - Botan, C. H., and Hazleton, V. (eds) Public relations theory (pp. 45–66). Hillsdale, NJ: Lawrence Erlbaum Associates; **155 Oxford University Press:** Mill, J. S. (2015). On Liberty, Utilitarianism and Other Essays. Oxford: Oxford University Press; **155 Taylor & Francis Group:** Djerf-Pierre, M. (2011). The Difference Engine. Feminist Media Studies 11(1), 43–51; **155 Hachette Books Group:** Weeks, M. (2011). Philosophy in Minutes. London: Quercus; **155, 156 Association for Consumer Research:** Cacioppo, J. T., and Petty, R. E. (1984). The elaboration likelihood model of persuasion. Advances in Consumer Research 11, 673–675. Retrieved from http://acrwebsite.org/volumes/6329/volumes/v11/NA-11 (22 April 2019); **156 Changing Works:** Changing Minds (2019). The Elaboration Likelihood Model. Retrieved from http://changingminds.org/explanations/theories/elaboration_likelihood.htm (23 April 2019); **156 Oxford University Press:** Adapted from Petty, R. E. and J.T. Cacioppo, J. T. (1983). Central and peripheral routes to persuasion: Application to advertising. Advertising and Consumer Psychology, 1, 3–23. Lexington, MA: D.C. Heath and Company (pp. 3–23); **157 Businesstopia:** Maharjan, P. (2018). Elaboration Likelihood Model. Businesstopia, January 8. Retrieved from https://www.businesstopia.net/communication/elaboration-likelihood-model (24 April 2019); **157 Sage Publications:** Manca, S; Altoe, G; Wesley Schultz, P., and Fornara, F. (2019). The Persuasive Route to Sustainable Mobility: Elaboration Likelihood Model and Emotions Implicit Attitudes. Environment and Behavior. Online first. Retrieved from https://journals.sagepub.com/doi/abs/10.1177/0013916518820898 (28 April 2019); **157 Emerald Group Publishing Limited:** Kitchen, P. J; Kerr, G; Schultz, D. E; McColl, R., and Pals, H. (2014). The elaboration likelihood model: review, critique and research agenda. European Journal of Marketing 48(11/12), 2033–2050; **158 John Wiley & Sons, Inc.:** Ajzen, I. (2002). Perceived Behavioral Control, Self-Efficacy, Locus of Control, and the Theory of Planned Behaviour. Journal of Applied Social Psychology 32(4), 665–683; **158, 159 Elsevier Inc.:** Ajzen, I. (1991). The theory of planned behavior. Organizational Behavior and Human Decision Process 50, 179–211; **159 American Psychological Association:** Ajzen, I., and Fishbein, M. (2004). Editorial comment - Questions Raised by a Reasoned Action Approach: Comment on Ogden (2003). Health Psychology 23(4), 431–434; **159 Heather Hausenblas:** Hausenblas, H. A; Giacobbi, P; Cook, B; Rhodes, R. E., and Cruz, A. (2011). A prospective examination of pregnant and nonpregnant women's physical activity beliefs and behaviours. Journal of Infant and Reproductive Psychology 29, 308–319. Retrieved from https://psychology.iresearchnet.com/sports-psychology/sport-motivation/the-theory-of-planned-behavior/ (24 April 2019); **160 American Psychological Association:** Prochaska, J. O., DiClemente, C. C., & Norcross, J. C. (1992). In search of how people change: Applications to addictive behaviors. American Psychologist, 47(9), 1102–1114; **160, 161 American Psychological Association:** Prochaska, J. O; DiClemente, C. C., and Norcross, J. C. (1992). In Search of How People Change Applications to Addictive Behaviors. American Psychologist 47(9), 1102–1114; **161 John Wiley & Sons, Inc.:** Davidson, R. (1992). Prochaska and DiClemente's model of change: a case study? British Journal of Addiction 87, 821–822; **161 What's OK at Home:** WOAH (2019). The Campaign website. Retrieved from https://woah.org.au/indigo/ (23 April 2019); **162 Penguin Random House:** Thaler, R., and Sunstein C. (2009 [2008]). Nudge: Improving decisions about health, wealth and happiness. London: Penguin; **162 Penguin Random House:** Thaler, R., and Sunstein C. (2009 [2008]). Nudge: Improving decisions about health, wealth and happiness. London: Penguin cited from Benartzi, S; Beshears, J; Milkman, K.L; Sunstein, C. R; Thaler, R.H; Shankar, M; Tucker-Ray, W; Congdon, W. J., and Galing, S. (2017). Should Governments Invest More in Nudging? Psychological Science 28(8), 1041–1055; **162 Haymarket Media Group:** Maule, S. (2015). A nudge and a think – applying behavioural science in PR. PR Week, September 10. Retrieved from https://www.prweek.com/article/1363503/nudge-think-applying-behavioural-science-pr (27 April 2019); **163 Bristol University Press:** Leggett, W. (2014). The politics of behaviour change: nudge, neoliberalism and the state. Policy and Politics 42(1), 3–19; **163 Houghton Mifflin Harcourt:** Eagly, A.H., and Chaicken, S. (1993). The psychology of attitudes. Fort Worth, TX: Harcourt, Brace, and Janovich p.560; **164 Oxford University Press:** Festinger, L. (1964). Behavioral Support for Opinion Change. The Public Opinion Quarterly 28(3), 404–417; **164 American Economic Association:** Akerlof,

G. A., and Dickens, W. T. (1982).The Economic Consequences of Cognitive Dissonance. The American Economic Review 72(3), 307–319; **166 Lean In:** Ban Bossy (2019). Campaign website. Retrieved from http://banbossy.com/ (23 April 2019); **167 Semiotic Society of America:** Grow, J. M. (2006). Stories of Community: The First Ten Years of Nike Women's Advertising. Accepted version. American Journal of Semiotics 22(1-4), 165–194. Marquette University e-Publications@ Marquette Repository. Retrieved from https://epublications.marquette.edu/cgi/viewcontent.cgi?article=1022&context=comm_fac (23 April 2019); **167 Nike Inc.:** Nike (2019), Nike Tech Pack Fall 2018 Apparel. Retrieved from https://news.Nike.com/news/Nike-tech-pack-fall-2018 (23 April 2019); **167 Advertising Educational Foundation:** Grow, J. M., and Wolburg, J. M. (2006). Selling Truth: How Nike's Advertising to Women Claimed a Contested Reality Philosophy Documentation Center. Advertising and Society Review 7(2). Retrieved from: https://muse-jhu-edu.ezproxy.leedsbeckett.ac.uk/article/202976 (22 April 2019); **176 World Economic Forum:** WEF (World Economic Forum) (2019). The Global Risks Report. Edition 14. Geneva: World Economic Forum; **178 PwC:** https://www.pwc.co.uk/issues/megatrends.html and watch https://www.youtube.com/watch?v=hqthrSDHqZw; **181 Taylor & Francis Group:** Moloney, K. (2006). Rethinking Public Relations. Abingdon: Routledge; **182 Cengage Learning:** Adapted from De Wit, R. and R. Meyer (2010). Strategy: process, content, context. London: Thomson; **182 Cengage Learning:** De Wit, R. and R. Meyer (2010). Strategy: process, content, context. London: Thomson; **187 Cengage Learning:** Thompson, J., J.M. Scott and F. Martin (2017). Strategic Management: Awareness and Change, 8th edition. Andover: Cengage Learning EMEA; **188 Pearson Education:** Cutlip and Center's Effective Public Relations, 11th edition. Upper Saddle River, NJ: Prentice-Hall, Inc. (Broom & Sha, 2012); **188 Brown & Benchmark Publishers:** McElreath, M.P. (1997). Managing Systematic and Ethical Public Relations Campaigns. 2nd edition. Madison, WI: Brown and Benchmark; **189 Betteke van Ruler:** Used with permission from Betteke van Ruler; **191, 200 Kogan Page:** Gregory, A. (2015). Planning and Managing Public Relations Campaigns, 4th edition. London: Kogan Page; **192 European Commission:** TOOLKIT for the evaluation of the communication activities. (2017) Retrieved from https://ec.europa.eu/info/sites/info/files/communication-evaluation-toolkit_en.pdf; **193 Government Communication Services:** The GREAT Britain campaign - GCS - Government Communication Service. Retrieved from https://gcs.civilservice.gov.uk/case-studies/the-great-britain-campaign/; **193 Houghton Mifflin Harcourt:** Grunig, J.E. and T.E. Hunt (1984). Managing Public Relations. New York: Holt, Rinehart & Winston; **198 Sage Publications:** Cornelissen, J. (2017). Corporate Communication. London: Sage; **208 Tāmati Olsen:** Quote by Tāmati Olsen; **214 William M.K. Trochim:** Trochim, W. (2006). Evaluation research. Research methods knowledge base. [online] Available at: http://www.socialresearchmethods.net/kb/evaluation.php [Accessed 20 Feb. 2019]; **214 Taylor & Francis Group:** Owston, R. (2007). Models and methods for evaluation. In: J. Spector, D. Merrill, J. van Merriënboer and M. Driscoll, eds, Handbook of research on educational communications and technology. 3rd ed. New York, NY: Routledge, pp. 605–617; **214 Sage Publications:** Valente, T. (2001). Evaluating communication campaigns. In: R. Rice & C. Atkin, eds, Public communication campaigns. 3rd ed. Thousand Oaks, CA: Sage, pp. 105–124; **214 Taylor & Francis Group:** Rice, R. and C. Atkin (2002). Communication campaigns: Theory, design, implementation, and evaluation. In: J. Bryant & D. Zillman, eds, Media effects: Advances in theory and research. 2nd ed. Mahwah, NJ: Lawrence Erlbaum, pp. 427–451; **217 John Wiley & Sons, Inc.:** Wholey, J. (1987). Evaluability Assessment: Developing Program Theory. New Directions for Evaluation, 33, pp. 78; **217 Sage Publications:** Rossi, P., M. Lipsey and H. Freeman (2004). Evaluation: A systematic approach. 7th ed. Thousand Oaks, CA: Sage; **217 Kellogg Foundation:** Kellogg Foundation. (2004). Logic model development guide. Battle Creek, MI. [online] Available at: https://www.wkkf.org/resource-directory/resource/2006/02/wk-kellogg-foundation-logic-model-development-guide [Accessed 28 Mar. 2019]. (Original work published 1998); **218 Board of Regents of the University of Wisconsin System:** Taylor-Power, E. and E. Henert (2008). Developing a logic model: Teaching and training guide. [online] Available at: https://fyi.uwex.edu/programdevelopment/files/2016/03/lmguide-complete.pdf [Accessed 28 Mar. 2019]; **218 Kellogg Foundation:** Kellogg Foundation. (2004). Logic model development guide. Battle Creek, MI. [online] Available at: https://www.wkkf.org/resource-directory/resource/2006/02/wk-kellogg-foundation-logic-model-development-guide [Accessed 28 Mar. 2019]. (Original work published 1998); **218 Sage Publications:** Knowlton, L. and C. Phillips (2013). The logic models guidebook: Better strategies for great results. 2nd ed. Thousand Oaks, CA: Sage; **218 Sage Publications:** Atkin, C. and V. Freimuth (2013). Guidelines for formative evaluation research in campaign design. In: R. Rice and C. Atkin, eds, Public communication campaigns. 4th ed. Thousand Oaks, CA: Sage, pp. 53–68; **219 Pearson Education:** Cutlip, M., A. Center, A and G. Broom

(1985). Effective public relations (6th ed.). Englewood Cliffs, NJ: Prentice-Hall; **221 Taylor & Francis Group:** Grunig, L. J. Grunig and D. Dozier (2002). Excellent organizations and effective organizations: A study of communication management in three countries. Mahwah, NJ: Lawrence Erlbaum; **222 The Government Communication Service:** GCS (Government Communication Service). (2018). GCS evaluation framework 2.0. [online] Available at: https://gcs.civilservice.gov.uk/wp-content/uploads/2018/06/6.4565_CO_Evaluation-Framework-2.0-v11-WEB.pdf [Accessed 28 Mar. 2019]; **222 Jim Macnamara:** Macnamara, J. (2018). Evaluating public communication: Exploring new models, standards and best practice. Abingdon, UK: Routledge; **229 Crown Copyright:** Department for Transport; **230 Institute for Public Relations:** Watson, T. and A. Zerfass (2012). ROI and PR evaluation: Avoiding 'smoke and mirrors'. International Public Relations Research Conference, Miami, FL. [online] Available at: https://www.instituteforpr.org/wp-content/uploads/Watson-Zerfass-ROI-IPRRC-Miami-2012.pdf [Accessed 20 Feb. 2019]; **236 House of Commons:** House of Commons Digital, Culture, Media and Sport Committee, Disinformation and 'fake news': Final Report Eighth Report of Session 2017–19 Report, February 2019, https://www.parliament.uk/business/committees/committees-a-z/commons-select/digital-culture-media-and-sport-committee/news/fake-news-report-published-17-19/; **237 House of Commons:** House of Commons Digital, Culture, Media and Sport Committee, Disinformation and 'fake news': Final Report Eighth Report of Session 2017–19 Report, February 2019, https://www.parliament.uk/business/committees/committees-a-z/commons-select/digital-culture-media-and-sport-committee/news/fake-news-report-published-17-19/; **238 Government communication Service:** RESIST: Counter-Disinformation Toolkit, UK Government Communication Service, 2019, https://gcs.civilservice.gov.uk/wp-content/uploads/2019/03/RESIST_Toolkit.pdf; **239 Government Communication Services:** UK Government Communication Services RESIST guide, 2019; **242 Vladislav Surkov:** Quote by Vladislav Surkov; **242 Penguin Random House:** Thomas, W.I. and D.S. Thomas (1928), The child in America: Behavior problems and programs, New York: Knopf, pp: 571–572; **245 Elsevier Inc.:** Grunig, J.E. (1993). 'Image and substance: From symbolic to behavioural relationships,' Public Relations Review 19(2): 121–39; **246 Sage Publications:** Cornelissen, J. (2017). Corporate Communication: A guide to theory and practice, 5th edition. London: Sage; **246 Taylor & Francis Group:** Grunig, L, Grunig, J. E. and D. Dozier (2002). Excellent Public Relations and Effective Organizations: A Study of Communication Management in Three Countries. Mahwah, NJ: Lawrence Erlbaum; **246 Taylor & Francis Group:** Ledingham, J.A. (2003). 'Explicating relationship management as a general theory of public relations. 15(2): 181–198; **246 Taylor & Francis Group:** Frandsen, F. and W. Johansen (2015). 'Organisations, stakeholders, and intermediaries: Towards a General Theory. International Journal of Strategic Communication 9(4): 253–271; **247 Elsevier Inc.:** Dowling, G. (1986). 'Managing your corporate image', Industrial Marketing Management 15: 109–15; **247, 248 Oxford University Press:** Dowling, G. (2001). Creating Corporate Reputations: Identity, image and performance. Oxford: Oxford University Press; **247, 250 Copenhagen Business School Press:** Schultz, M. (2005). 'A cross-disciplinary perspective on corporate branding', in M. Schultz, Y.M. Antorini and F.F. Csaba (eds) Corporate Branding: Purpose, People, Process. Copenhagen: Copenhagen Business School Press; **248 Harvard Business School Publishing:** Fombrun, C.J. (1996). Reputation: Realizing value from the corporate image. Boston, MA: Harvard Business School Press; **248 Oxford University Press:** Barron, D.N. and M. Rolfe (2012). 'It ain't what you do. It's who you do it with: Distinguishing reputation and status', in M.L. Barnett and T.G. Pollock (eds). The Oxford Handbook of Corporate Reputation (pp. 160–78). Oxford: Oxford University Press; **248 Institute for Operations Research and the Management Sciences:** Devers, C.E., T. Dewett, Y. Mishina and C.A. Belsito (2009). 'A general theory of organizational stigma,' Organization Science 20(1): 154–71; **248 Springer Nature:** Barnett, M.L. and A. Hoffman (2008). 'Beyond corporate reputation: Managing reputational interdependence', Corporate Reputation Review 11(1): 1–9; **249 Pearson Education:** van Riel, C.B.M. (1995). Principles of Corporate Communication. London: Prentice Hall; **249 JAI Press:** Albert, S. and D.A. Whetten (1985). 'Organizational identity', in L.L. Cummings and M.M. Staw (eds). Research in Organizational Behavior Vol. 7 (pp. 263–95). Greenwich, Conn.: JAI Press; **250 Harvard Business School Publishing:** Gilmore, J.H. and B.J. Pine II (2007). Authenticity: What consumers really want. Boston: Harvard Business School Press; **252 Carlsberg Foundation:** J.C. Jacobsen, Carlsberg brewery was founded in 1847; **254 Harvard Business School Publishing:** Hatch, M.J. and M. Schultz (2001). 'Are the strategic stars aligned for your corporate brand? Harvard Business Review. February 2001; **255 Cambridge University Press:** Kornberger, M. (2010). Brand Society: How brands transform management and lifestyle. Cambridge: Cambridge University Press; **255 Sage Publications:** Christensen, L.T., M. Morsing and G. Cheney (2008). Corporate Communications: Convention, complexity, and critique. Los Angeles: Sage; **261 Tim Bell:** Quote by Tim Bell; **261 Public Relations Society of America:** PRSA. (2006). The Professional Bond: public relations education in the 21st century. Retrieved from New York:; **261 Pearson Education:** Gregory, A. (2009). Ethics and professionalism in public relations. In R. Tench & L. Yeomans (Eds.), Exploring Public Relations (2nd ed., pp. 273–289). Harlow, Essex: Pearson Education; **262 Sage Publications:** Sciulli, D. (2005). Continental Sociology of Professions Today: Conceptual Contributions. Current Sociology, 53(6), 915–942; **262 University of California Press:** Larson, M.S. (1977). The rise of professionalism : a sociological analysis. Berkeley ; London: University of California Press; **262, 268 Pearson Education:** Cooper, D.E. (2004). Ethics for professionals in a multicultural world. Upper Saddle River, N.J.: Prentice Hall; **262 Sage Publications:** L'Etang, J. (2008). Public relations : concepts, practice and critique. Los Angeles: SAGE; **262, 263 Sage Publications:** Sriramesh, K. and L. Hornaman (2006). Public Relations as a Profession An Analysis of Curricular Content in the United States. Journal of Creative Communications, 1(2), 155–172. Retrieved from http://crc.sagepub.com/content/1/2/155.short; **262 Elsevier Inc.:** van Ruler, B. (2005). Professionals are from Venus, scholars are from Mars. Public Relations Review, 31, 159–173; **263 Sage Publications:** Pieczka, M. and J. L'Etang (2001). Public relations and the question of professionalism. In R. L. Heath (Ed.), The Handbook of Public Relations (pp. 223–235). Thousand Oaks, CA: Sage; **263 Oxford University Press:** Cheney, G. (2010). Just a job? Communication, ethics, and professional life. Oxford; New York: Oxford University Press; **264 Anne Gregory:** Gregory, A. and Fawkes, J. (2019). A Global capability framework: Reframing public relations for a changing world. Public Relations Review. Vol. 45, No. 3, Article 101781 https://doi.org/10.1016/j.pubrev.2019.05.002; **266 Guardian News & Media Limited:** Naughton, J. (2019) Are big tech's efforts to show it cares about data ethics simply another diversion? Apr 07 2019. Guardian News & Media Limited; **266 Lucy Erickson:** Quote by Lucy Erickson; **266 Luciano Floridi:** Quote by Luciano Floridi; **268 Taylor & Francis Group:** Bowen, S.A. (2007). The extent of ethics. In E. L. Toth (Ed.), The future of excellence in public relations and communication management (pp. 275–297). Mahweh, NJ: Lawrence Erlbaum; **268 Taylor & Francis Group:** Bowen, S.A. (2008). A State of Neglect: Public Relations as 'Corporate Conscience' or Ethics Counsel. Journal of Public Relations Research, 20(3), 271–296. Retrieved from http://dx.doi.org/10.1080/10627260801962749. doi:10.1080/10627260801962749; **268 Burleson and Kline:** Burleson and Kline 1979, cited in Day et al. 2001: 408; **268 Emerald Group Publishing Limited:** Pieczka, M. (2010). Public relations as dialogic expertise? Journal of Communication Management, 15(2), 108–124; **268 Haymarket Media Group Ltd:** Bowen, S.A. (2019, 05/04/2019). PR pros can help people unite - or we can help them divide. PR Week. Retrieved from HTTPS://WWW.PRWEEK.COM/ARTICLE/1581262/PR-PROS-HELP-PEOPLE-UNITE-HELP-DIVIDE; **269 Cambridge University Press:** Oakley, J. and D. Cocking (2001). Virtue Ethics and Professional Roles. Cambridge, England: Cambridge University Press; **269 Elsevier Inc.:** Porter, L. (2010). Communicating for the good of the state: A post-symmetrical polemic on persuasion in ethical public relations. Public Relations Review, 36, 127–133; **269 University of Southern Queensland:** Harrison, K. and C. Galloway (2005). Public relations ethics: a simpler (but not simplistic) approach to the complexities. Prism, 3. Retrieved from http://www.praxis.massey.ac.nz, retrieved March 14, 2007; **269 Sage Publications:** Fitzpatrick, K. (2006). Baselines for Ethical Advocacy in the 'Marketplace of Ideas'. In K. Fitzpatrick & C. Bronstein (Eds.), Ethical Public Relations: Responsible Advocacy (pp. 1 17). Thousands Oaks, CA: Sage; **270 Taylor & Francis Group:** Holtzhausen, D. (2012). Public Relations as Activisim: Postmodern approaches to theory and practice. New York, NY: Routledge.P.33; **270 Sage Publications:** Edwards, L. (2018). Understanding public relations : theory, culture and society. Thousand Oaks, CA: Sage; **271 Telegraph Media Group Limited:** © Patrick Sawer / Telegraph Media Group Limited 2017; **272 Chartered Institute of Public Relations:** Chartered Institute of Public Relations; **272 David Crompton:** Quote by David Crompton; **272 Crown Copyright:** The Independent Police Complaints Commission; **273 Hayley Court:** Quote by Hayley Court; **274 The University of Chicago:** Abbott, A. (1983). 'Professional ethics'. The American Journal of Sociology 88(5): 855–85; **274 University of Pennsylvania Press:** Kultgen, J. (1988). Ethics and Professionalism. Philadelphia, PA: University of Philadelphia Press.P.120; **274 Hachette Books Group:** Rowson, R. (2006). Working Ethics: How to be fair in a culturally complex world. London: Jessica Kingsley Publishers.P.52; **285 Richard Pyle:** Richard Pyle, The Associated Press; **288 Adweek, LLC:** Perse, K. (2018). Why Brands Need to Prioritize Real Influencers Over the Fake Ones. AdWeek, [online]. Available at: https://www.adweek.com/brand-marketing/why-brands-need-to-prioritize-real-influencers-over-the-fake-ones/ [Accessed 12 April 2019]; **288 Stephen Waddington:** Stephen Waddington, How to do influencer marketing, March 14. Retrieved from https://wadds.co.uk/blog/2018/3/14/how-to-do-influencer-marketing; **290 Philip Trippenbach: Philip Trippenbach, Edelman UK; **290 Haymarket Media Group Ltd:** Harrington, J. (2018). Exclusive survey: what PR and marketing chiefs really think about influencer marketing. PRWeek, [online]. Available at: https://www.prweek.com/article/1491798/exclusive-survey-pr-marketing-chiefs-really-think-influencer-marketing [Accessed 12 April 2019]; **291 American Economic Association:** Alcott H. and M. Gentzkov (2017). Social Media and Fake News in the 2016 Election. Journal of Economic Perspectives, [online] Volume 31(2), pp.211–236. Available at: https://web.stanford.edu/~gentzkow/research/fake-news.pdf [Accessed 12 April 2019]; **300 Ellen Gunning:** Quoted by Ellen Gunning; **302 Chris Taylor:** Quoted by Chris Taylor; **303 Stephen Waddington:** Stephen Waddington, 'Your audience with the public'; **308 Taylor & Francis Group:** Grunig, J.E. (1992). 'Symmetrical systems of internal communication' in Excellence in Public Relations and Communication Management. J.E. Grunig (ed.). Hillsdale, NJ: Lawrence Erlbaum Associates; **308, 309 Taylor & Francis Group:** Yaxley, H. and K. Ruck (2015). 'Tracking the rise and rise of internal communication' in Exploring Internal Communication: Towards informed employee voice, 3rd edition. K. Ruck (ed.). London: Gower; **309 Kevin Ruck/Heather Yaxley:** Yaxley, H. and K. Ruck (2013). Tracking the rise and rise of internal communication from the 1980s; **309 Pearson Education:** Yeomans, L. and W. Carthew (2014). 'Internal communication' in Exploring Public Relations. 3rd edition. R. Tench and L. Yeomans (eds). Harlow: Pearson Education; **310, 315 Taylor & Francis Group:** FitzPatrick, L. (2016). Internal communication. In Theaker, A. (ed.) The Public Relations Handbook. 5th edition. Abingdon, Oxon: Routledge; **310 Emerald Group Publishing Limited:** Welch, M. (2011). 'The evolution of the employee engagement concept: Communication implications'.Corporate Communications: An International Journal 16(4): 328–46; **312 Pearson Education:** Mullins, L.J. (2013). Management and Organisational Behaviour, 10th edition. London: FT Publishing International; **313 Canongate Books:** Pink. D. (2009). Drive: The surprising truth about what motivates us. Edinburgh: Canongate Books; **316 Peter Lang Publishing** Macnamara, J. (2016). Organizational Listening: The Missing Essential in Public Communication. New York, NY: Peter Lang; **316 Taylor & Francis Group:** Lombardi, G. (2015). Social media inside a large organisation. In Ruck, K. (ed.) Exploring Internal Communication: Towards informed employee voice, 3rd edition. London: Gower; **319 John Wiley & Sons, Inc.:** Schein, E. (2010). Organizational Culture and Leadership, 4th edition. San Francisco, CA: Jossey-Bass; **319 Houghton Mifflin Harcourt:** Conrad, C. and M.S. Poole (1998). Strategic Organizational Communication: Into the twenty-first century, 4th edition. Fort Worth, TX: Harcourt Brace; **319 Emerald Group Publishing Limited:** Johansson, C., V.D. Miller and S. Hamrin (2014). Conceptualizing communicative leadership – a framework for analysing and developing leaders' communication competence. Corporate Communication: An International Journal, 19(2): 147–165; **320 Taylor & Francis Group:** FitzPatrick, L. (2008). Internal communication. In Theaker, A. (ed.) The Public Relations Handbook. London: Routledge; **330, 332 Issue Action Publications, Inc.:** Chase, W.H. (1984). Issue management. Leesburg, VA: Issue Action Publications; **331 John Wiley & Sons, Inc.:** Heath, R.L. (1988). Strategic issues management: How organizations influence and respond to public interests and policies. San Francisco: Jossey-Bass; **331 SAGE Publications:** Heath, R. L. (1997). Strategic Issues Management: Organizations and Public Policy Challenges. Thousand Oaks, CA: Sage; **333 Marks and Spencer plc:** Marks & Spencer; **334 International Association of Business Communicators:** McGrath, G.B. (1998). Issues Management: Anticipation and influence. London: IABC; **335 Elsevier Inc.:** Crable, R.E. and S.L. Vibbert (1985). 'Managing issues and influencing public policy'. Public Relations Review 11: 3–16; **336 SAGE Publications:** Heath, R.L. (2005). Issues management. In: R.L. Heath, ed., Encyclopedia of public relations (Volume 1). Thousand Oaks, CA: Sage, pp. 460–463; **338 Greenpeace International:** Will H&M make "detox" the new must have? (2011). Retrieved from http://tweetbuzz.us/entry/68200175/www.greenpeace.org/international/en/news/features/hm-detox/; **338 Greenpeace International:** Clickers and stickers make H&M detox. (2011). Retrieved from http://www.greenpeace.org/international/en/news/features/Clickers-and-Stickers-Make-HM-Detox/; **338 H&M:** H&M; **346, 347 SAGE Publications:** Coombs, W. T. (2019). Ongoing crisis communication: Planning, managing, and responding, 5th ed. Los Angeles: Sage; **356 Harry Pearce:** Harry Pearce, GM; **357 Johan Lampe:** Johan Lampe, Firestone; **357 Jackson Browning:** Jackson Browning, Union Carbide ; **357 Hampton Carney:** Hampton Carney, Abercrombie & Fitch; **357 Rupert Murdoch:** Rupert Murdoch, News Corp; **357 Akio Toyoda:** Akio Toyoda, Toyota; **357 Nestlé:** Nestlé; **357 James Burke:** James Burke, Johnson & Johnson; **360 Cadbury:** Cadbury; **367 John Wiley & Sons, Inc.:** Morgan, A. (1999). Eating the Big Fish: How challenger brands can compete against brand leaders. New York, NY: John Wiley; **368 Hachette Books Group:** Lewis, D. and D. Bridger (2003). The Soul of the New Consumer. London: Nicholas Brealey; **370 Pearson Education:** Frankfurt, H. (2005). On

Bullshit. Princeton, NJ: Princeton University Press; **375 Scott Guthrie:** Quoted by Scott Guthrie; **377 SAGE Publications:** Gilpin, D.R. and P.J. Murphy (2010). 'Implications of complexity theory for public relations: beyond crisis' in The Sage Handbook of Public Relations. R.L. Heath (ed.). Thousand Oaks, CA: Sage; **377 SAGE Publications:** Qvortrup, L. (2006). 'Understanding new digital media'. European Journal of Communi-cation 21(3): 345–56; **377 SAGE Publications:** Hutton, J. (2010). 'Defining the relationship between public relations and marketing: public relations' most important challenge' in The Sage Handbook of Public Relations. R.L. Heath (ed.). Thousand Oaks, CA: Sage; **378 Cannes Lions:** Cannes Lions (2012). 'Walkers, Sandwich'. www.canneslions.com/inspiration/past_grands_prix_advert.cfm?sub.channel_id=301 accessed 12 January 2012; **379 University of Technology Sydney:** Macnamara, J. (2015). 'Creating an architecture of listening in organisations: The basis of engagement, trust, healthy democracy, social equity and business accountabil-ity'. Report. Sydney, NSW: University of Technology; **382 John Wiley & Sons, Inc.:** Brown, R. and S. Waddington (2013). Share This Too. London: John Wiley & Sons; **384 Borden:** Adapted from Borden 1964; **388 Christina Gill:** Interview with Solicitor Christina Gill; **390 Elsevier Inc.:** Steyna, P., E. Salehi-Sangari, L. Pitt, M. Parent, and P. Berthond (2010). 'The Social Media Release as a public relations tool: Intentions to use among B2B bloggers'. Public Relations Review 36 87–89; **391, 392 John Wiley & Sons, Inc.:** Solis, B. (2010). Engage! The complete guide for brands and businesses to build, cultivate, and measure success in the new web. New Jersey: John Wiley & Sons; **399 Springer Nature:** Pedler, P. (eds) (2002) European Union lobbying : changes in the arena Houndmills : Palgrave; **399 HarperCollins:** Post, J. (1982). 'Public affairs: Its role'. In Nagelschmidt, J.S. (Ed), The Public Affairs Handbook. New York: Amacom, 23–30; **399 John Wiley & Sons, Inc.:** Harris, P. and D. Moss (2001). 'Editorial': In search of public affairs: A function in search of an identity'. Journal of Public Affairs, 1(2), 102–10; **399 Public Affairs Council:** Mission of Washington-based Public Affairs Council; **402 John Wiley & Sons, Inc.:** Heath, R.L. (2002). 'Issues management: Its past, present and future'. Journal of Public Affairs, 2(4), 209–14; **406 House of commons:** First Report of the Committee on Standards in Public Life © Parliamentary copyright 2009; **410 SAGE Publications:** Moss, Danny & DeSanto, Barbara. (2011) Public Relations: A Managerial Perspective. SAGE, 2011; **419, 432 Cengage Learning:** Shimp, T. (2010) Integrated Marketing Communications in Advertising and Promotion. USA, Cengage Learning; **419, 432 John Wiley & Sons, Inc.:** Dahlen, M., Lange, F., and T. Smith (2010). Marketing Communiciations: A Brand Narrative Approach. Chichester, John Wiley & Sons; **426, 432 Pearson Education:** Fill, C. and S. Turnbull (2016). Marketing Communications: discovery, creation and conversations. 7th Ed., Essex: Pearson Education; **427 Pearson Education:** Rossiter, J. and S. Bellman (2005). Marketing Communications: theory and applications. London, Prentice Hall; **428 SAGE Publications:** Hackley, C. (2010). Advertising and Promotion: an integrated marketing communications approach. London. Sage; **428 Penguin Random House:** Kapferer, J. (2012) The New Strategic Brand Management, 5th Edition, Kogan Page: London; **429 John Wiley & Sons, Inc.:** Hales, G. (2011). Branding In: Kourdi, J. ed. The Marketing Century Chichester, John Wiley & Sons, pp.139 – 168; **431 Springer Nature:** Ivana Bušljeta Banks, Patrick De Pelsmacker, Shintaro Okazaki (2016), Advances in Advertising Research (Vol. V): Extending the Boundaries of Advertising, Springer; **432 Pearson Education:** Adapted from Keller, K. (2013) Strategic Brand Management: building, measuring and managing brand equity, 4th edition, Essex: Pearson; **432 Pearson Education:** Kelley, N. (2017) Integrated Marketing Communications. in: Tench, R. and Yeomans, L. (2016) Exploring Public Relations. Harlow, Pearson Education Limited; **432 Nick Emmel:** Nick Emmel, Dare; **442 HarperCollins:** Collins English Dictionary 2019; **443 Investopedia:** Will Kenton (2018), Corporate Finance & Accounting, Corporate Sponsorship, Investopedia; **443 Pearson Education:** De Pelsmacker, P., Geuens, M. and J. Van den Berg (2004). 'Sponsorship' in Marketing Communications. Harlow: Prentice Hall; **452 Konstantinos Zervas:** Prepared by Dr Konstantinos Zervas; **452 Nike Inc.:** Nike; **453 Net Promoter Score:** Modified from www.netpromoter.com/know/; **460 SAGE Publications:** Belasen, A.T. (2008). The theory and practice of corporate communication: A compet-ing values perspective. Sage Publications: Thousand Oaks, California; **460 Centaur Media plc:** Schultz, D.E. (1993), "Integration helps you plan communication from outside-in", Marketing News, 27 (6), 12; **463 Emerald Group Publishing Limited:** Invernizzi, E., Romenti, S. and G. Murtarelli (2016). "Creating Shared Value through Communication: A Case Study Analysis of Barilla". In Bronn, P.S., Romenti, S., Zerfass, A. (Eds.). The management game of communication (pp. 181–201). Emerald Group Publishing Limited; **465 Emerald Group Publishing Limited:** Invernizzi, E., Romenti, S. and M. Fumagalli (2012). Identity, communication and change management in Ferrari. Corporate Communications: An International Journal, 17(4), 483–497; **466 BlackRock, Inc.:** A Fundamental Reshaping of Finance, Larry Fink CEO Letter, Blackrock; **466 Emerald Group Publishing Limited:** Balmer, J.M., and E.R. Gray (1999). "Corporate identity and corporate communications: creating a competitive advantage". Corporate Communications: An International Journal, 4(4), 171–177; **467 Taylor & Francis Group:** Van Riel, C.B.M. and C. Fombrun (2007). Essentials of Corporate Communication. Abingdon: Routledge; **476 Taylor & Francis Group:** Baldo, O. B. and C. Sibthorpe (1998). The sky is the limit: Electronic networking and NGOs. South African Journal of International Affairs, 5(2), pp. 64; **477 Sage Publications:** Clarke, G. (1998). NonGovernmental Organizations (NGOs) and Politics in the Developing World. Political Studies, 46(1), pp. 36; **477 Springer Nature:** Adapted from Toepler, S. and H.K. Anheier (2004). Organizational Theory and Nonprofit Management: An Overview. In: A. Zimmer and E. Priller, eds., Future of Civil Society, Wiesbaden, Germany: VS Verlag für Sozialwissenschaften, pp. 257; **478 Springer Nature:** Toepler, S. and H.K. Anheier (2004). Organizational Theory and Nonprofit Management: An Overview. In: A. Zimmer and E. Priller, eds., Future of Civil Society, Wiesbaden, Germany: VS Verlag für Sozialwissenschaften, pp. 256; **481 European Public Relations Education and Research Association:** Zerfass, A., Wiesenberg, M., Tench, R., & Romenti, S. (2019). Trust in communicators. How the general population trusts journalists, public relations professionals, marketeers and other communicators: A comparative study in Germany, Italy and the United Kingdom. Brussels: EUPRERA; **482 Danyal Alaybeyoglu:** Reprinted with permission of Danyal Alaybeyoglu; **482, 483 Christine Viertmann:** Viertmann, C. (2015). NPO Trust Map—Measuring Trust in the Third Sector. Paper presented at BledCom Symposium 2015, Bled, July 2015; **486 Vernon Press:** Adapted from Wiesenberg, M. and E. Oliveira (2017). From the inside out: Four communication flows of NGOs' and Churches' legitimation. In: E. Oliveira, A. Duarte Melo and G. Gonçalves, eds., Strategic communication for nonprofit organisations: Challenges and alternative approaches, Wilmington: Vernon Press, pp. 45; **487 Pearson Education:** AshraMcGrath, N. (2017). Nongovernment organisations and pressure groups. In: R. Tench and L. Yeomans, eds., Exploring Public Relations: Global Strategic Communication, 4th ed. Harlow: Pearson, pp. 482; **491 Katrina Lin:** Quoted by Katrina Lin; **492 Penguin Random House:** Boorstin, D. J. (1962). The Image: or what happened to the American dream. Harmondsworth, Penguin; **492 Taylor & Francis Group:** Hartley, J. (2002). Communication, Cultural and Media Studies: The key concepts (3rd ed.). London: Routledge; **492 Australian Scholarly Publishing:** Turner, G. (2014). 'Celebrity' in A Companion to the Australian Media. B. GriffenFoley (ed.). North Melbourne: Australian Scholarly Publishing; **492, 493, 494 Macmillan:** Redmond, S. (2014). Celebrity and the Media. Houndmills, Palgrave Macmillan; **492 John Wiley & Sons, Inc.:** Kurzman, C., C. Anderson, C. Key, C. Lee, Y. Ok, M. Silver and A van Ryn (2007). 'Celebrity status'. Sociological Theory 25(4), December: 347–387; **493, 494, 495 Sage Publications:** Turner, G. (2004). Understanding Celebrity. London, Sage; **493 Taylor & Francis Group:** Hartley, J. (1992). The Politics of Pictures: The creation of the public in the age of popular media. London: Routledge; **493 Prism:** Hutchins, A. and N. Tindall, N. (2015). '"Things that don't go together?" Considering fandom and rethinking public relations'. Prism 12(10). http://www.prismjournal.org/fandom_ed.html accessed 23 November 2015; **494 Bloomsbury Publishing Plc:** Rojek, C. (2012). Fame Attack: The inflation of celebrity and its consequences. London, Bloomsbury; **494 Taylor & Francis Group:** Van Krieken, R. (2012). Celebrity Society. Abingdon: Routledge; **494 Penguin Random House:** Adapted from Boorstin, D. J. (1962). The Image: or what happened to the American dream. Harmondsworth, Penguin; **494 Cambridge University Press:** Turner, G., Bonner, F. and P. D. Marshall (2000). Fame Games: The production of celebrity in Australia. Melbourne, Cambridge University Press; **495 New York University Press:** Jenkins, H. (2007). 'The future of fandom' in Fandom: Identities and communities in a mediated world. J. Gray, C. Sandvoss and C. L. Harrington (eds.). New York: New York University Press; **495 Sage Publications:** Marwick, A. and d. boyd (2011). 'To see and be seen: Celebrity practice on Twitter'. Convergence: The International Journal of Research into New Media Technologies 17(2): 139–158; **495 Lawrence & Wishart:** Littler, J. (2004). 'Making fame ordinary: Intimacy, reflexivity and "keeping it real"'. Mediactive 2: 8; **496 Yale University Press:** Marwick, A. (2013). Status Update: Celebrity, publicity and branding in the social media age. New Haven, Yale University Press; **496 Sage Publications:** Hearn, A. (2008). '"Meat, mask, burden": Probing the contours of the branded "self"'. Journal of Consumer Culture 8(2): 197–217; **496, 498 Duke University Press:** Marwick, A. (2015). 'Instafame: Luxury selfies in the attention economy'. Public Culture 21(10): 137–160; **496 Emerald Group Publishing Limited:** Abidin, C. (2018). Internet celebrity: Understanding fame online. Bingley, UK: Emerald Publishing; **497 Roxy Jacenko:** Roxy Jacenko; **498 Kendall Jenner:** Kendall Jenner; **499 SF Celebrity Management:** SF Celebrity Management (2019); **500 Penguin Random House:** Markson, M. (2000). Show Me The Money! A guide to fame, fortune and business success, by Australia's agent to the stars. Ringwood,

Australia: Viking; **501 Kate Fitch:** Interview with K. Fitch. Used with permission; **501 Lauren Curtis Lounge:** Lauren Curtis Lounge (2019). https://laurencurtis-lounge.com/about/ (accessed 5 April 2019); **509 Dr Audra Diers-Lawson:** Audra Diers-Lawson; **512 McGraw-Hill Education:** Ajzen, I. (2005). Explaining intentions and behavior: Attitudes, personality, and behavior (Vol. 2nd). Berkshire, England: McGrawHill Education; **513 Springer Nature:** Petty, R. E., and Cacioppo, J. T. (1986). Message elaboration versus peripheral cues Communication and persuasion (pp. 141172): Springer; **514 Taylor & Francis Group:** Adapted from Witte, K. (1996). Generating effective risk messages: How scary should your risk communication be? Communication Yearbook, 18, 229254; **518 Our World in Data:** "Roser, M., Ritchie, H., Ortiz-Ospina, E. and Hasell, J. (2020). Coronavirus Disease (COVID-19). Published online at OurWorldInData.org. Retrieved from: 'https://ourworldindata.org/coronavirus' on 24 April, 2020 [Online Resource]."; **529 Human Kinetics:** Stoldt, C., Dittmore, S. W. and Branvold, S. E. (2006) Sport public relations, Champaign: Human Kinetics; **529 Sage Publications:** L'Etang, J. (2013) Sports Public Relations; London: Sage; **530 PWC:** PwC (2018) Sports Industry: Lost in transition? [online]. PwC. Available at file:///F:/Sports%20PR/Tench%20&%20 Waddington/PwC%20Sports%20Survey-2018_web.pdf [Accessed 21 May 2019.]; **533 Springer Nature:** Beverland, M. (2009) Building Brand Authenticity: 7 Habits of Iconic Brands. e-book: Palgrave Macmillan; **534 Taylor & Francis Group:** Sherwood, M., Nicholson, M. and Marjoribanks, T. (2017b) Controlling The Message And The Medium? Digital Journalism, Vol. 5 No. 5, pp. 513–531; **535 Ofcom:** Ofcom news consumption survey 2019; **536 Twitter, Inc.:** Information from Twitter April 2019; **539 Michael Phelps:** Quoted by Michael Phelps; **548 John Wiley & Sons, Inc.:** Clark, T. (2004). Strategy viewed from a management fashion perspective. European Management Review 1, 105–111; **550 University of Minnesota Press:** Moi, T. (1988). Feminism, Postmodernism, and Style: Recent Feminist Criticism in the United States. Cultural Critique 9, 3–22; **550 Taylor & Francis Group:** Entwistle, J. (2000). Fashion and the flesh body: Dress as an embodied practice. Fashion Theory 4, 323–348; **551, 554, 560, 561 The University of Newcastle:** Cassidy, L., and Fitch, K. (2013). Beyond the Catwalk: Fashion Public Relations and Social Media in Australia. Asia Pacific Public Relations Journal 14(1-2), 5–19; **551 PR COUTURE:** Noricks, C. (2009). Exploring Fashion PR. Retrieved from https://www.slideshare.net/prcouture/exploring-fashion-pr-1267609 (17 April 2019); **551 Bloomsbury Publishing Plc:** Sherman, G., & Perlman, S. (2010). Fashion public relations. New York: Fairchild Books; **553 House of Commons:** House of Commons (2019). Interim Report on the Sustainability of the Fashion Industry: Fifteenth Report of Session 2017–19 / Report, together with formal minutes relating to the report. London: House of Commons. Retrieved from https://publications.parliament.uk/pa/cm201719/cmselect/cmenvaud/1148/1148.pdf (5 May 2019); **554 Sage Publications:** Fitch, K. (2017). Seeing 'the unseen hand': Celebrity, promotion and public relations. Public Relations Inquiry 6(2), 157–169; **554 Emerald Group Publishing Limited:** Coombs, W.T., and Holladay, S.J. (2018). Innovation in public relation theories and practice: A transmedia narrative transportation (TNT) approach. Journal of Communication Management 22(4), 382–396; **554 Taylor & Francis Group:** Phan, M; Thomas, R., and Heine, K. (2011). Social Media and Luxury Brand Management: The Case of Burberry. Journal of Global Fashion Marketing 2(4), 213–222; **555, 562 Emerald Group Publishing Limited:** Kulmala, M; Mesiranta, N., and Touminen, P. (2013). Organic and amplified eWOM in consumer fashion blogs. Journal of Fashion Marketing and Management: An International Journal 17(1), 20–37; **555 Taylor & Francis Group:** Taylor, M., and Kent, M.L. (2014). Dialogic engagement: clarifying foundational concepts. Journal of Public Relations Research 26(5), 384–398; **555 Taylor & Francis Group:** Dhaoui, C. (2014). An empirical study of luxury brand marketing effectiveness and its impact on consumer engagement on Facebook. Retrieved from https://www.researchgate.net/publication/271936261_An_empirical_study_of_luxury_brand_marketing_effectiveness_and_its_impact_on_consumer_engagement_on_Facebook/download (18 April 2019); **555 Elsevier Inc.:** Hennig-Thurau, T; Gwinner, K.P; Walsh, G., and Gremler, D. D. (2004). Electronic word-of-mouth via consumer-opinion platforms: what motivates consumers to articulate themselves on the internet? Journal of interactive marketing 18(1), 38–52; **557 Sage Publications:** Turner, G. (2014). Understanding Celebrities (2nd edition). London: SAGE; **557 John Wiley & Sons, Inc.:** Senft, T.M. (2013). Microcelebrity and the Branded Self. In - Hartley, J; Burgess, J., & Bruns, A. (ed) A Companion to New Media Dynamics (pp. 346–354). Chichester: Wiley; **558 Emerald Group Publishing Limited:** Escalas, J.E., and Bettman, J.R. (2015). Managing Brand Meaning through Celebrity Endorsement. Brand Meaning Management. Review of Marketing Research 12, 29–52; **558 Emerald Group Publishing Limited:** Seno, D., and Lukas, B.A. (2007). The equity effect of product endorsement by celebrities: A conceptual framework from a co-branding perspective. European Journal of Marketing 41(1-2), 121–134; **558 Paul**

Smith: Paul Smith (2019). Company History. Retrieved from https://www.paulsmith.com/uk/company-history (5 May 2019); **558 Paul Smith:** Paul Smith; **559 Hearst UK:** De Klerk, A. (2017). 10 of the most successful celebrity fashion lines. Harpers Bazaar, 20 June. Retrieved from https://www.harpersbazaar.com/uk/fashion/what-to-wear/news/g38047/most-successful-celebrity-fashion-lines/ (5 May 2019); **560 Elsevier Inc.:** Freberg, K; Graham, K; McGaughey, K., and Freberg, L.A. (2011). Who are the social media influencers? A study of public perceptions of personality. Public Relations Review 37, 90–92; **560 Centaur Media plc:** Hobbs, T. (2017). Ted Baker uses Instagram for episodic storytelling in 'Keeping up with the Bakers' campaign. Marketing Week, 15 March. Retrieved from https://www.marketingweek.com/2017/03/15/instagram-stories-new-ted-baker-campaign (5 May 2019); **561 Emerald Group Publishing Limited:** Esteban-Santos, L; Garcia Medina, I; Carey, L., and Bellido-Perez, E. (2018). Fashion bloggers: communication tools for the fashion industry. Journal of Fashion Marketing and Management: An International Journal 22(3), 420–437; **562 Sage Publications:** Archer, C., and Harrigan, P. (2017). Show me the money: how bloggers as stakeholders are challenging theories and relationship building in public relations. Media International Australia 160(1), 67–77; **562, 563 Harvard Business School Publishing:** Keinan, A; Maslauskaite, K; Crener, S., and Dessain, V. (2015). The Blonde Salad. Harvard Business Review, 9 January. Retrieved from https://thehighville.com/blog/wp-content/uploads/2016/03/Caso-The-Blonde-Salad.pdf (5 May 2019); **563 Chiara Ferragni:** Chiara Ferragni; **563 Riccardo Pozzoli:** Riccardo Pozzoli; **564 Centaur Media plc:** Gilliland, N. (2018). 10 examples of great fashion marketing campaigns. E-consultancy blog, 7 November. Retrieved from https://econsultancy.com/fashion-marketing-campaigns/ (5 May 2019); **564 Brandium, Inc. Ltd.:** Branding Magazine (2015). Good Campaign of the Week: H&M "Close the Loop". Branding Magazine, 13 September. Retrieved from https://www.brandingmag.com/2015/09/13/good-campaign-of-the-week-hm-close-the-loop/ (5 May 2019); **564 Fashion-United:** Hendriksz, V. (2015). Is H&M really as 'green' as they seem to be? Fashion United, 9 October. Retrieved from https://fashionunited.uk/news/fashion/is-h-m-really-as-green-as-they-seem-to-be/2015100917940 (5 May 2019); **565 CNBC LLC:** Ward, M. (2016). Multimillionaire Sophia Amoruso: 4 career lessons every young person should know. CNBC, 7 October. Retrieved from https://www.cnbc.com/2016/10/06/multimillionaire-sophia-amoruso-4-career-lessons-every-young-person-shouldknow.html?utm_content=buffer38974&utm_medium=social&utm_source=twitter.com&utm_campaign=buffer (5 May 2019); **565 Los Angeles Times:** Li, S. (2017). Nasty Gal, once a fashion world darling, is now bankrupt. What went wrong? The Los Angeles Times, 24 February. Retrieved from https://www.latimes.com/business/la-fi-nasty-gal-20170224-story.html (5 May 2019); **571 Securities Industry and Financial Markets Association:** Data sourced from SIFMA, 2019; **572 CB Information Services,Inc.:** CB Insights (2019) Global Fintech Report Q2 2019, CB Insights. https://www.cbinsights.com/research/report/fintech-trends-q2-2019/; **578 Revolut Ltd:** Revolut; **579 Revolut Ltd:** Revolut (2019) Careers at Revolut, Revolut, https://www.revolut.com/careers; **579 Chad West:** Chad West, Revolut; **580 Rowman & Littlefield:** Kendall, D. (2005) Framing Class: Media Representations of Wealth and Poverty in America, Plymouth: Rowland and Littlefield; **596, 597 Prof. Dr. Ansgar Zerfass:** Trust in Communicators Study 2019, European Communication Monitor; **598 Larry Fink:** Quoted by Larry Fink; **602 CIPR:** CIPR; **603 Kerry Sheehan:** Quoted by Kerry Sheehan.

Photo credits:

3 Shutterstock: Rafal Cichawa/Shutterstock; **8 Getty Images:** Luis Veiga/Stockbyte Unreleased/Getty Images; **11 Alamy Stock Photo:** Granger Historical Picture Archive/Alamy Stock Photo; **21 Shutterstock:** Martin Mecnarowski/Shutterstock; **24 Alamy Stock Photo:** Moviestore Collection Ltd/Alamy Stock Photo; **31 Shutterstock:** Thinglass/Shutterstock; **37 Shutterstock:** Kletr/Shutterstock; **48 Shutterstock:** James Kirkikis/Shutterstock; **51 Alamy Stock Photo:** Tim Graham/Alamy Stock Photo; **59 Alamy Stock Photo:** Yin Bogu/Xinhua/Alamy Stock Photo; **66 Shutterstock:** Volodymyr Burdiak/Shutterstock; **75 Getty Images:** PIUS UTOMI EKPEI/AFP//Getty Images; **77 Alamy Stock Photo:** Erik McGregor/Pacific Press/Alamy Stock Photo; **83 Getty Images:** Dhiraj Singh/Bloomberg/Getty Images; **89 Airbus:** Airbus; **94 Shutterstock:** Johnny Adolphson/Shutterstock; **96 Shutterstock:** PlusONE/Shutterstock; **100 Getty Images:** MOHAMMED ABED/AFP/Getty Images; **108 Shutterstock:** Mathisa/Shutterstock; **119 Ralph Tench:** Ralph Tench; **121 Alamy Stock Photo:** WENN Rights Ltd/Alamy Stock Photo; **130 Kyla Flynn:** Reprinted with permission of Kyla Flynn; **147 Alamy Stock Photo:** Reinhard Dirscherl/Alamy Stock Photo; **154 Getty Images:** Popperfoto/Getty Images; **157 Shutterstock:** marlee/Shutterstock; **166 Shutterstock:** Jklingebiel/Shutterstock; **175 Alamy Stock Photo:** Nature Picture Library/Alamy

Stock Photo; **179 Alamy Stock Photo:** White House Photo/Alamy Stock Photo; **192 Shutterstock:** sergei telegin/Shutterstock; **198 Getty Images:** Dimas Ardian/Getty Images News/Getty Images; **203 AMEC:** AMEC Integrated Framework Tutorial ; **204 Getty Images:** Torsten Blackwood/AFP/Getty Images; **211 Shutterstock:** Johan Swanepoel/Shutterstock; **212 123RF:** Steve Collender/123RF; **215 Alamy Stock Photo:** Emily Brain/Alamy Stock Photo; **220 Association for Measurement and Evaluation of Communication:** AMEC (Association for Measurement and Evaluation of Communication). (2017). AMEC integrated evaluation framework. [online] Available at: https://amecorg.com/amecframework [Accessed 28 Mar. 2019]; **227 Shutterstock:** AboliC/Shutterstock; **233 Shutterstock:** Bildagentur Zoonar GmbH. Shutterstock; **235 Getty Images:** Matt Cardy/Getty Images; **237 Getty Images:** Mladen Antonov/AFP/Getty Images; **244 Alamy Stock Photo:** Cultura RM/Alamy Stock Photo; **249 Getty Images:** Pascal George/AFP/Getty Images; **252 Alamy Stock Photo:** stuart emmerson/Alamy Stock Photo; **259 Shutterstock:** ChameleonsEye/Shutterstock; **260 Getty Images:** Andrew Cowie/AFP/Getty Images; **266 Shutterstock:** Peppinuzzo/Shutterstock; **270 Alamy Stock Photo:** Wenn Rights Ltd/Alamy Stock Photo; **283 Shutterstock:** Ruimin Wang/Shutterstock; **290 Monare Matema:** Monare Matema; **297 Shutterstock:** LightField Studios/Shutterstock; **298 Durham BID:** Durham, Durham BID and Fire&Ice InDurham!; **300 DTW:** Reprinted with permission of DTW; **306 Alamy Stock Photo:** Michael Runkel/Robertharding/Alamy Stock Photo; **313 Shutterstock:** Kapustin Igor/Shutterstock; **316 123RF:** Andriy Popov/123RF; **317 Pearson Education:** Pearson Education; **324 Shutterstock:** Metamorworks/Shutterstock; **329 Shutterstock:** Makieni/Shutterstock; **334 Shutterstock:** Vadim Petrakov/Shutterstock; **337 Getty Images:** Marcos del Mazo/LightRocket/Getty Images; **341 Getty Images:** Prisma by Dukas/Universal Images Group/Getty Images; **344 Shutterstock:** GUDKOV ANDREY/Shutterstock; **345 Getty Images:** Jemal Countess/Getty Images; **348 Getty Images:** Pallava Bagla/Corbis/Getty Images; **351 Getty Images:** CARL DE SOUZA/AFP/Getty Images; **360 Getty Images:** AK2/E+/Getty Images; **365 Getty Images:** Rosa Perry/EyeEm/Getty Images; **368 Getty Images:** Richard Bord/Getty Images; **372 Getty Images:** Scott Barbour/Getty Images; **378 Getty Images:** Scott Halleran/Getty Images; **381 Shutterstock:** Vlad61/Shutterstock; **382 Alamy Stock Photo:** Alexandra Schuler/dpa picture alliance/Alamy Stock Photo; **392 Alamy Stock Photo:** Atmán Victor/agefotostock/Alamy Stock Photo; **395 Shutterstock:** HelloRF Zcool/Shutterstock; **396 Getty Images:** Pablo Blazquez Dominguez/Getty Images; **398 Getty Images:** Kristian Buus/In Pictures/Getty Images; **398 Shutterstock:** VectorMine/Shutterstock; **402 Alamy Stock Photo:** RidingMetaphor/Alamy Stock Photo; **404 Shutterstock:** Boris15/Shutterstock; **417 Shutterstock:** Sergey Uryadnikov/Shutterstock; **418 Getty Images:** Andrew Michael/Education Images/Universal Images Group/Getty Images; **420 Alamy Stock Photo:** Rawpixel Ltd/Alamy Stock Photo; **433 Getty Images:** Matthew Horwood/Getty Images; **437 Shutterstock:** Mariska Vermij - van Dijk/Shutterstock; **438 Alamy Stock Photo:** EDB Image Archive / Alamy Stock Photo; **445 Shutterstock:** Vytautas Kielaitis/Shutterstock; **452 Shutterstock:** Roman Kosolapov/Shutterstock; **454 Getty Images:** Luc Claessen/Velo/Getty Images; **459 Shutterstock:** Barbara Brockhauser/Shutterstock; **465 Alamy Stock Photo:** Remo Casilli/Sintesi/Alamy Stock Photo; **468 Alamy Stock Photo:** Agencja Fotograficzna Caro/Alamy Stock Photo; **475 Shutterstock:** bearacreative/Shutterstock; **484 Urgewald:** Urgewald; **485 WWF Germany:** WWF Germany; **490 Shutterstock:** Fer Gregory/Shutterstock; **491 Shutterstock:** EQRoy/Shutterstock; **498 Getty Images:** Don Arnold/Getty Images; **506 123RF:** Tom Tietz/123RF; **507 Getty Images:** Lam Yik Fei/Getty Images; **510 Getty Images:** Fotog/Getty Images; **522 Shutterstock:** Shutterstock; **528 123RF:** Tom Tietz/123RF; **534 Getty Images:** AFP/Getty Images; **536 Getty Images:** Julian Finney/Getty Images; **541 Getty Images:** VI Images/Getty Images; **547 Shutterstock:** James DeBoer/Shutterstock; **549 Getty Images:** Michel Stoupak/NurPhoto/Getty Images; **550 Getty Images:** Frédéric Soltan/Corbis/Getty Images; **557 Getty Images:** Jun Sato/Getty Images; **570 Shutterstock:** Konjushenko Vladimir/Shutterstock; **573 Shutterstock:** charnsitr/Shutterstock; **573 Shutterstock:** charnsitr/Shutterstock; **573 Shutterstock:** Globe Turner/Shutterstock; **573 Shutterstock:** T. Lesia/Shutterstock; **573 Shutterstock:** Restimage/Shutterstock; **574 Alamy Stock Photo:** Lou Linwei/Alamy Stock Photo; **576 Getty Images:** Volkan Furuncu/Anadolu Agency/Getty Images; **580 Alamy Stock Photo:** Jennifer Barrow/Alamy Stock Photo; **591 Alamy Stock Photo:** Michael Nolan/Robertharding/Alamy Stock Photo; **594 Shutterstock:** Denverdave/Shutterstock; **599 Ralph Tench:** Ralph Tench; **604 Shutterstock:** Justasc/Shutterstock; **607 Ralph Tench:** Ralph Tench.